THE OFFICIAL
NASCAR 2013
PREVIEW AND PRESS GUIDE

Library and Archives Canada Cataloguing in Publication is available upon request.

Published simultaneously in the United States of America by McClelland & Stewart,
a division of Random House of Canada Limited
P.O. Box 1030, Plattsburgh, New York 12901

Library of Congress Control Number Available on Request.

Printed and bound in the United States of America

Photo Credits:
Getty Images: i-41, 50-51, 122-23, 212-15, 234-37
Courtesy of NASCAR: 42-52, 238-330
Courtesy of Tracks: 124-211
Or as noted.

McClelland & Stewart, a division of Random House of Canada Limited
One Toronto Street
Suite 300
Toronto, Ontario
M5C 2V6
www.mcclelland.com

1   2   3   4   5   16   15   14   13

NASCAR

EXECUTIVE STAFF DIRECTORY

Chairman of the Board and Chief Executive Officer	Brian Z. France
Vice Chairman/Executive Vice President	James C. France
Vice Chairwoman/Executive Vice President	Lesa France Kennedy
President	Mike Helton

Executive Vice President/Assistant Treasurer	Betty Jane France
Senior Vice President and General Counsel/Secretary	Gary Crotty
Senior Vice President of Racing Operations	Steve O'Donnell
Senior Vice President and Chief Marketing Officer	Steve Phelps
Senior Vice President and Chief Financial Officer	Todd Wilson
Senior Vice President and Chief Administrative Officer, NASCAR/Chief Executive Officer, GRAND-AM	Ed Bennett
Vice President of Brand, Consumer and Series Marketing	Kim Brink
Vice President of Racing Operations	Jim Cassidy
Vice President of Licensing and Consumer Products	Blake Davidson
Vice President of Industry Services	Jill Gregory
Vice President of Broadcasting and Production	Steve Herbst
Vice President of Public Affairs and Multicultural Development	Marcus Jadotte
Vice President of Digital Media	Marc Jenkins
Vice President and Chief Communications Officer	Brett Jewkes
Vice President and Deputy General Counsel/Assistant Secretary	Karen Leetzow
Vice President and Chief Human Resources Officer	Paula Miller
Vice President of Strategic Development	Eric Nyquist
Vice President and Chief Sales Officer	Jim O'Connell
Vice President of Competition and Racing Development	Robin Pemberton
Vice President of Finance	Doris Rumery
Vice President and Chief Accounting Officer	Susan Schandel
Vice President of Partnership Marketing	Norris Scott
Vice President of Regional and Touring Series	George Silbermann
Vice President of Entertainment Marketing and Business Development	Zane Stoddard
Vice President of Operations and Technical Production	Steve Stum

FEATURES

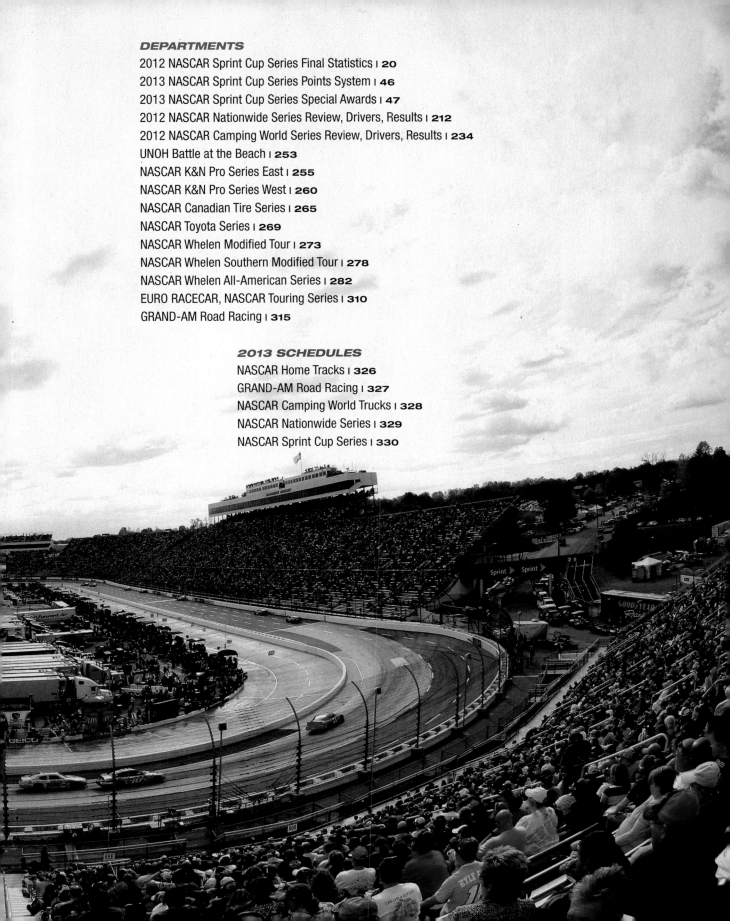

2012 NASCAR SPRINT CUP SERIES

CHAMPION

KESELOWSKI BEAT THE FAVORITES TO TAKE HOME
HIS FIRST NASCAR SPRINT CUP CHAMPIONSHIP TROPHY

BRAD

KESELOWSKI

When the 2012 NASCAR Sprint Cup Series season began in February at Daytona International Speedway, most pundits pegged reigning champion Tony Stewart, five-time champion Jimmie Johnson or another veteran to be hoisting the championship trophy 10 months later at Homestead-Miami Speedway.

Very few, if any, had penciled in the then-28-year-old Brad Keselowski as the possible victor. The season was to be only his third full season and he had only visited Victory Lane four times prior to the season.

But, they were wrong.

After 36 grueling races with plenty of ups and downs, Keselowski was able to claim his first NASCAR Sprint Cup championship and provide long-time NASCAR team owner Roger Penske his first title in the series.

"To win (the championship) for Dodge and Miller Lite and Roger Penske and all these guys who have such a great story to tell, makes it that much sweeter, so to speak," said Keselowski.

Keselowski, a third-generation driver from Rochester Hills, MI, a stone's throw away from Detroit, grew up in a racing family and learned valuable on-the-job training while working for his family's race team. His grandfather, father, uncle and brother at one point, all

suited up behind the steering wheel of a race car. However, none have experienced the amount of success the youngest Keselowski has so far in a relatively short career.

When he was 14 years old, Keselowski began racing in the Senior Honda 120 Quarter Midget division where he racked up six feature wins and five heat wins. The next year, he moved up to the Senior Honda 160 Quarter Midget division and, in just 12 starts, scored eight feature victories and eight heat wins.

His success propelled him further up the motorsports ranks, and in 2000 he moved to Factory Stock, where he won nine events and earned rookie of the year honors at two Michigan tracks – Auto City Speedway and Dixie Speedway. Over the next three years, from 2001 through 2003, Keselowski competed in limited late model and super late models events and posted five wins.

Finally, in 2004, Keselowski reached NASCAR's national series when he appeared in eight NASCAR Camping World Truck Series events for his family's race team. However, it wasn't always easy for Keselowski or his family. In 35 races over three seasons (2004–06), the youngest Keselowski posted only one top-10 finish in his family's equipment – a seventh place in the 2005 season opener at Daytona International Speedway. The first two events of the 2006 season were the last races he competed in for his family's team.

"Being a part of my family's business of racing and watching it fail, that's as low as it gets," Keselowski said. "Watching them have to sell all their assets and not even be able to get to the race track, that is as low as it gets right there. And to think that I was a part of bankrupting my family to try to pursue your own dream is

a moment where you feel so selfish and incredibly low as a human being that you don't even know how you're ever going to recover from that and those are the moments where you're challenged as a person to keep going on."

And Keselowski did just that – he kept going on.

He managed to find a ride for four more truck races during the 2006 season, and in 2007 he appeared in only three races. However, in 2006, the then-22-year-old Keselowski moved up to the NASCAR Nationwide Series to drive Keith Coleman's No. 23 Chevrolet.

Midway through the 2007 Keselowski was tabbed to drive for NASCAR Sprint Cup driver Dale Earnhardt Jr.'s JR Motorsports NASCAR Nationwide operation in the No. 88 Chevrolet. His first race driving for his new owner came in the summer of 2007 at Chicagoland. Through 14 starts for Earnhardt that season, Keselowski scored five top-10 finishes, including a sixth at Texas. His career was finally on its upward path that would eventually land him in NASCAR's premier series and hoisting the championship trophy.

Over the next four seasons, as his career in the NASCAR Nationwide and NASCAR Sprint Cup Series started to launch, Keselowski made only 12 more starts in the NASCAR Camping World Truck Series.

In 2008 and 2009 Keselowski continued to drive for Earnhardt in the NASCAR Nationwide Series and racked up a total of six victories, 33 top fives and 48 top 10s to go along with a pair of third-place finishes in the final points standings.

In 2009 Keselowski suited up for Hendrick Motorsports (seven races) and Phoenix Racing (five races) in the NASCAR Sprint Cup Series, earning the latter their first victory when he won the spring Talladega race. He appeared in the final three NASCAR Sprint Cup races that season for Penske Racing.

Keselowski left JR Motorsports's NASCAR Nationwide team prior to the start of the 2010 season to drive for Penske and their No. 22 Dodge fulltime.

As part of the deal, Keselowski would also become the full-time driver for the team's No. 12 Dodge in the NASCAR Sprint Cup Series in 2010.

In his first full year driving for Roger Penske, Keselowski won the 2010 NASCAR Nationwide championship on the strength of six wins, 26 top fives, 29 top 10s and five Coors Light Pole Awards. However, the elusive NASCAR Sprint Cup championship still fell just outside Penske's reach. In his first full season in the premier series, Keselowski only finished in the top 10 twice and finished the season ranked 25th.

Over the next two seasons in NASCAR's second-tier national series, Keselowski won a combined eight races, but was not a factor in the championship hunt either year. Shortly before the 2011 season began, NASCAR instituted a rule where drivers could only vie for one championship each year. Keselowski chose to race for the championship in the premier series – a decision that would pay off ten-fold over the course of the next two seasons.

Before the 2011 season kicked off, Keselowski was switched from the No. 12 Dodge to the famous No. 2 Dodge, popularly known as the "Blue Deuce." He had pretty big shoes to fill, because the last two drivers to pilot the Blue Deuce were, most recently, Kurt Busch and NASCAR Hall of Famer Rusty Wallace.

Keselowski didn't disappoint.

During the offseason between 2010 and 2011, Penske brought aboard crew chief Paul Wolfe to work with Keselowski and the No. 2 team. The chemistry the driver and crew chief have has drawn comparisons to five-time NASCAR Sprint Cup champion Jimmie Johnson and crew chief Chad Knaus.

Wolfe is ultimately who Keselowski wanted to work with. "I had a conversation with him in August of 2009. I told him 'Hey man, I want you to come over and crew chief this deal.' And he looked me in the eye and said, 'No, I don't want to do it,'" Keselowski said.

Keselowski had a good reason for wanting to bring Wolfe into the fold.

"He was a guy that outperformed his

resources. In this sport excellence is defined by the media and the fans as those who win," Keselowski said. "Those inside the sport, those who actually compete, define excellence as those who outperform their resources."

Eventually Wolfe came around and decided to join forces with Keselowski and Penske Racing.

The pair worked well together and found Victory Lane three times in 2011. Keselowski finished fifth in the overall points, but was determined to improve on his performance in 2012.

"I had a pretty good idea what we needed to do to win the championship at the end of last year to be quite honest," Keselowski stated. "We didn't quite execute as strongly as we needed to. We finished strong and finished fifth in the points, but that process was certainly a learning process. I think we applied some of those lessons to 2012."

Apparently, the No. 2 race team learned their lesson, and in 2012 gave Roger Penske the final jewel for his motorsport crown, having fielded championship teams in most forms of motorsports.

In addition to winning five races in 2012 (two of them in the first three races of the Chase for the NASCAR Sprint Cup), Keselowski posted career-best finishes at 12 tracks and tied his best

performances at four other tracks.

To start the 2012 Chase, Keselowski was tied with Jimmie Johnson and Tony Stewart for second with 2,009 points after winning three events during the regular season. At the first race of the Chase, at Chicagoland, Keselowski powered ahead of Jimmie Johnson to claim the victory by 3.171 seconds and the lead in the standings by three points.

Two races later, Keselowski beat Jeff Gordon to the checkered flag by 1.078 seconds. He remained out in front of Johnson by five points in the standings.

Heading into the final race at Homestead, Keselowski sat 20 points ahead of Johnson and needed a 15th-place or better finish, regardless of where Johnson finished, to capture his first NASCAR Sprint Cup championship. Although Johnson's day ended early after experiencing trouble with his rear gear, Keselowski was still determined to finish 15th, which he did, 21 spots in front of Johnson.

"I thought it was really important that we finish 15th, because we wouldn't have to hear those jabs for the foreseeable future about if things wouldn't have happened to Jimmie," Keselowski said. "That made me very proud."

That it did, as it did for his growing fan base.

2012 CHASE FOR THE NASCAR SPRINT CUP

28-YEAR-OLD BRAD KESELOWSKI CAME OUT ON TOP OF THE CHASE FOR THE NASCAR SPRINT CUP, CLINCHING HIS FIRST NASCAR SPRINT CUP SERIES TITLE

▲ The 2012 Chase for the NASCAR Sprint Cup contenders: Jimmie Johnson, Jeff Gordon, Kevin Harvick, Dale Earnhardt Jr., Martin Truex Jr., Brad Keselowski, Greg Biffle, Matt Kenseth, Clint Bowyer, Denny Hamlin, Kasey Kahne and Tony Stewart.

When the Chase for the NASCAR Sprint Cup was first introduced as NASCAR's playoff system prior to the 2004 season, everyone expected the new format to provide more drama and more close-knit racing action than ever before. Over the past nine years those expectations have been exceeded on an annual basis.

In the inaugural season of the Chase, Kurt Busch fought off a hard-charging Jimmie Johnson by only eight points, the closest finish in series history at the time. Johnson's late-season success was on full display as he visited Victory Lane four times in the new 10-race format, while Busch had only one victory.

The following year, 2005, Tony Stewart grabbed his second NASCAR Sprint Cup Series title (his first under the new format) by 35 points over Greg Biffle, despite the fact Stewart failed to cross the finish line first in any of the 10 postseason races.

In 2006 Jimmie Johnson started an incredible run of five consecutive NASCAR Sprint Cup titles to coincide with solid performances in five Chases. He found Victory Lane at Martinsville in 2006 and eventually went on to claim the title by 56 points over Matt Kenseth. In 2007 Johnson won four races in a row in the Chase to capture the championship from Jeff Gordon, who sat 77 points off the lead. In the fifth year of the Chase format, Johnson won three times in the postseason to lead Carl Edwards by 69 in the final points

▶ Dale Earnhardt Jr. was in good form to open the Chase, but missing two races saw his championship hopes end early.

standings. In 2009 the margin between Johnson and runner-up Mark Martin was the highest it's ever been under the still relatively new playoff format – 141 points. Denny Hamlin went into the last race of the 2010 season with a 15-point lead, but surrendered the advantage and lost the title to Johnson by 39 points.

Prior to the 2011 season, the points system was changed: a driver would earn 43 points for a first-place finish, the second-place finisher would earn 42 points, the third-place finisher would earn 41 points and so on all the way down to the last-place finisher receiving one point for the race. The race winner would earn an additional three points for winning the race and another bonus point for leading a lap. The driver who led the most laps during a race would earn an additional bonus point, so, in theory, a race winner could earn a maximum of 48 points. The new system was created in large part to make it easier to understand, but an added bonus was that it created even tighter points racing.

In 2011, 62 years after the NASCAR premier series' first year of competition, fans were treated to the first tie in the final points standings in NASCAR history. This was between Stewart and Edwards, with the title going to Stewart based on his five wins (all coming in the Chase) compared to Edwards' one.

The format for the Chase in 2012 remained the same as it's been since its inception in 2004, with the 36-race schedule divided into a 26-race regular season and a 10-race postseason. However, in 2011, the structure for qualifying for the 12 spots in the Chase changed slightly. Prior to 2011 the top 12 drivers in points, regardless of wins, qualified for the 12 spots after the 26th race of the season, at Richmond International Raceway. In 2011 the last two qualifying spots (11th and 12th) were turned into Wild Card spots awarded to two drivers ranked between 11th and 20th in the standings with the most victories.

Since the points disbursement for each race decreased before the 2011 season, the points allotment for the Chase qualifiers prior to the start of the Chase also changed. The 12 drivers qualified for the Chase used to have their points reset to 5,000 with an additional 10 points for each race win in the first 26 races. In 2011 NASCAR introduced a new rule resetting the points for each of the 12 Chase qualifiers to 2,000 following the Richmond race. Only the drivers in the top 10 of the Chase would receive three bonus points for each win during the first 26 races of the season, while the two Wild Card qualifiers would not receive any additional points for wins up to that point.

After posting the most victories in the regular season with four (Phoenix, Kansas, Bristol, Atlanta), Hamlin started the 2012 postseason with 2,012 points. He sat just three points ahead of Johnson, Stewart and Brad Keselowski, who all had 2,009 points and three victories apiece. Biffle, who sat atop the points standings for 14 of the 26 previous weekends, and Clint Bowyer were seeded fifth and sixth, respectively, for the start of the Chase with 2,006 points and two wins each. One win each for Dale Earnhardt Jr. and Kenseth left them seeded seventh and

eighth, respectively, with 2,003 points. Kevin Harvick and Martin Truex Jr. were the final two automatic qualifiers. Since they were winless in the regular season both of them started the Chase with 2,000 points in ninth and 10th places. The two drivers to clinch the Wild Card spots were Kasey Kahne (two wins) and Gordon (one win). Neither driver received bonus points for his wins and both started the Chase with 2,000 points.

RACE 1

As the points leader going into the Chase, Hamlin was hoping he would be able to leave Chicagoland Speedway unscathed and with his points lead intact. However, after a 16th-place finish in the GEICO 400, Hamlin left Illinois frustrated, and fourth place in the standings.

On the other hand, Keselowski shot to the top of the standings after a solid performance where he led 76 laps and beat Jimmie Johnson to the finish line by 3.171 seconds. The victory was Keselowski's fourth of the season and left him three points in front of Johnson, who started on the pole.

Seven of the Chase qualifiers finished in the top 10.

RACE 2

Still disappointed after his performance the previous week, Hamlin made a bold prediction in the week leading up to the SYLVANIA 300 at New Hampshire Motor Speedway – he would win the second race of the Chase. However, his confident forecast didn't sit well with some at Joe Gibbs Racing.

Hamlin held true to his prediction and blasted to a 2.675-second victory over Johnson after leading 193 of the 300 laps. The victory only moved Hamlin up to third in the standings but, as a result of back-to-back runner-up finishes, Johnson moved back into familiar territory – atop the standings. He held a one- point lead over Keselowski.

Seven of the Chase qualifiers finished in the top 10.

RACE 3

For the second time in three races, Keselowski found himself celebrating in Victory Lane. This time he bested Jeff Gordon by 1.078 seconds and was able to snag his fifth and final victory of the season.

Hamlin started the AAA 400 at Dover International Speedway from the pole, but after leading 39 laps he finished eighth after having to make a late pit stop. Kyle Busch was the class of the field having led 302 of the 400 laps but, like his Joe Gibbs Racing teammate, a late pit stop relegated him to a seventh-place finish.

The win moved Keselowski back into the lead over Jimmie Johnson by five points.

Six of the Chase qualifiers finished in the top 10.

RACE 4

For the majority of the Good Sam Roadside Assistance 500 at Talladega Superspeedway, the race was pretty tame – by Talladega standards. For the first 188 laps of the 189-lap race there were only four cautions that affected a total of seven drivers.

But that final turn in a long race can sometimes be a doozy. Coming out of Turn 4 and approaching the checkered flag Stewart was leading the tightly

▶ Denny Hamlin went into the 2012 Chase for the NASCAR Sprint Cup's first race as the points leader.

▼ Jimmie Johnson, in his No. 48 Lowe's Chevrolet, hoped 2012 would see him return to the championship form that saw him win five consecutive titles between 2006–10

packed field when he tried to move down the track to block Michael Waltrip. His move set off a 24-car accident that Kenseth managed to avoid to claim the victory.

Keselowski's seventh-place finish extended his lead to 14 points over Jimmie Johnson, who was caught up in the final-turn mishap and finished 17th.

Four of the Chase qualifiers finished in the top 10.

RACE 5
The Bank of America 500 at Charlotte Motor Speedway, which is the only Saturday night race in the Chase for the NASCAR Sprint Cup, featured a lot of tight racing action that included 20 lead changes among eight drivers. In the end Bowyer, who led the final 25 laps around the 1.5-mile track, staved off a hard-charging Hamlin by 0.417 seconds. It's

possible that if the race had lasted one lap longer, Hamlin's No. 11 team would have been celebrating in Victory Lane instead of Bowyer and his No. 15 crew.

Although Bowyer was the race winner, much of the discussion over the race weekend centered around Earnhardt and his decision to sit out this race and the following week's race in Kansas due to a concussion suffered at Talladega.

After an 11th-place finish, Keselowski once again saw his lead over Johnson shrink to seven points. Johnson finished third in the race, giving him four top-four finishes in the first five Chase races.

Six of the Chase qualifiers finished in the top 10.

RACE 6
At the end of the Hollywood Casino 400, Kenseth celebrated in Victory Lane at Kansas Speedway for his second win of

the 2012 Chase. The race included a track-record 14 cautions on the newly repaved surface.

After Kahne smashed the track's qualifying record by more than 10.5 mph, it was evident that the race on Sunday was going to be one fast affair. Matter of fact, all 46 drivers who attempted qualifying runs posted a faster time than the previous track record.

The two frontrunners in the standings, Keselowski and Johnson, finished eighth and ninth, respectively, in the race. However, since Johnson led at least one lap and Keselowski didn't, the pair ended up with identical point totals for the race. Therefore, Keselowski led Johnson by seven points in the standings for another week.

Eight of the Chase qualifiers finished in the top 10.

RACE 7

Finally finding Victory Lane for the first time during the 2012 Chase, Johnson used a start from the pole to catapult him to victory in the TUMS Fast Relief 500 at Martinsville Speedway. The victory gave Johnson the slightest of leads (two points) over Keselowski in the points standings. Keselowski finished sixth.

Keselowski led eight laps toward the end of the race but, after some hard side-by-side racing, Johnson passed his closest championship rival for good with 15 laps to go.

With three races left on the schedule, the championship battle had narrowed down primarily to four drivers: Johnson, Keselowski (-2), Bowyer (-26) and Kahne (-29).

The late October race marked Earnhardt's return to racing after sitting out for two weeks. He finished 21st.

Six of the Chase qualifiers finished in the top 10.

RACE 8

For the second week in a row, Johnson started on the pole and later celebrated in Victory Lane. In the AAA Texas 500 at Texas Motor Speedway, he held the point lead for 168 of the 335 laps and beat runner-up Brad Keselowski to the checkered flag by 0.808 seconds. Keselowski was out front for 75 laps.

With a 25th-place finish, Kahne was no longer part of any serious championship conversation, 58 points outside of first. Bowyer sat in third place, 29 points behind Johnson. Just two weeks earlier Johnson sat behind Keselowski by seven points, but now the tables were turned with Keselowski seven points behind Johnson.

Eight of the Chase qualifiers finished in the top 10.

RACE 9

Going into the penultimate race of the 2012 season, it appeared Johnson was

◄ Jeff Gordon (No. 24) leads Brad Keselowski (No. 2), Jimmie Johnson (No.48) and Clint Bowyer (No. 15) during the NASCAR Sprint Cup Series AdvoCare 500 at Phoenix International Raceway.

heading to another NASCAR Sprint Cup Series championship, his sixth in seven years. However, his plans were slightly derailed during the AdvoCare 500 at Phoenix International Raceway.

After blowing his front right tire and hitting the wall hard coming out of Turn 4 midrace, Jimmie Johnson had to wheel his car to garage almost ensuring that his title dreams were over. Johnson was running seventh when the tire blew, but he returned to the track and finished 32nd. He sat 20 points behind Keselowski in the standings.

In a bit of retaliation for transgressions earlier in the race, Jeff Gordon punted title-contender Clint Bowyer into the wall ending both drivers' day a bit prematurely. The early exit left Bowyer 50 points out of first place.

After 319 laps of hard-nosed racing,

Harvick claimed the checkered flag over Hamlin by 0.58 seconds. Harvick only led the final 15 circuits around the one-mile track.

Five of the Chase qualifiers finished in the top 10.

RACE 10

All Keselowski had to do to earn his first NASCAR Sprint Cup Series title was finish 15th or better in the season finale Ford EcoBoost 400 at Homestead-Miami Speedway, regardless of what second-place driver Jimmie Johnson did. And he did just that.

However, it might not have been necessary, as Johnson's day was once again marred by misfortune. On lap 224, Johnson noticed that his car wasn't handling right. So, he had to take his No. 48 Chevrolet behind the wall for the

▲ Brad Keselowski finished the Homestead-Miami race in 15th place, giving him a 39-point lead over second-place finisher Jimmie Johnson, to capture his first-ever NASCAR championship.

second week in a row, where his team discovered that a rear gear had broken. His day, and championship hunt, was officially over.

Gordon outpaced Bowyer to the finish line by 1.028 seconds for his second win of the season. The win, his first at Homestead, gave Gordon victories at every current track on the NASCAR Sprint Cup schedule except Kentucky Speedway. On the strength of his second-place finish in the race, Bowyer leapfrogged Johnson in the final points standings by one point, 39 points behind the new champion.

Six of the Chase qualifiers finished in the top 10.

2012 NASCAR SPRINT CUP SERIES
MOST POPULAR DRIVER

DALE EARNHARDT'S LEGION OF FANS STICK WITH THE DRIVER THROUGH THICK, THIN AND IN BETWEEN

The 2012 season was a "tweener" – Junior broke a four-year winless streak, led the NASCAR Sprint Cup Series points and piled up top-five and top-10 finishes in bunches. But there was disappointment as well. A concussion suffered in an accident in the fall race at Talladega Superspeedway cost Earnhardt starts in two subsequent races and ended his hopes for the NASCAR Sprint Cup championship.

His fans responded nonetheless. After 934,000 votes were counted, Dale Earnhardt Jr. was named the NASCAR/ NMPA Most Popular Driver for the 10th consecutive year. That matched Bill Elliott's record run – out of 16 Most Popular awards overall – from 1991 to 2000.

"It was an honor to hear that I won this year and am now tied with Bill for 10 in a row," Earnhardt said. "I've enjoyed this award because it's a testament to my fans. I appreciate their loyalty and dedication.

"It was great to get to Victory Lane this year for my team and for my fans. I'm looking forward to a successful 2013 and

am proud to accept this award on behalf of all the fans that voted."

The award, governed by the National Motor Sports Press Association, has been given annually since 1956 and was presented to Earnhardt in November's Champion's Week celebration during the Myers Brothers Luncheon at The Encore at Wynn in Las Vegas, NV.

After fans voted from February to September, the top-10 drivers who earned the most votes were reset to zero. Kyle Busch, Earnhardt, Carl Edwards, Jeff Gordon, Kevin Harvick, Jimmie Johnson, Kasey Kahne, Matt Kenseth, Bobby Labonte and Tony Stewart were finalists who fans voted for during the final 10 weeks of the NASCAR Sprint Cup season. The runners up, in order, were Gordon, Kahne, Stewart, Johnson, Harvick, Kyle Busch, Edwards, Kenseth and Labonte.

The greatest names in NASCAR Sprint Cup racing grace the Most Popular Driver list. The legendary Curtis Turner was the first recipient in 1956, followed by Glenn "Fireball" Roberts. NASCAR Sprint Cup champions Rex White, Joe Weatherly and

▲ Dale Earnhardt Jr. won his tenth consecutive Most Popular Driver Award in 2012.

▶ Earnhardt continues to be a fan favorite year after year.

Bobby Isaac also were honored, as was Fred Lorenzen and Darel Dieringer.

The remaining recipients are all NASCAR Hall of Fame members: Richard Petty, David Pearson, Bobby Allison, Darrell Waltrip, Glen Wood, Cale Yarborough and Dale Earnhardt.

"It is something you really don't work for, but rather it just happens," said Petty, a nine-time recipient of the award. "The Most Popular Driver Award makes the driver feel good because you're not out there to be the most popular driver; you're out there to win races. You win it at the end of the season and it's like a big bonus."

"It's the fan's voice," noted Waltrip. "They are the ones that say, 'We like this guy, we like what he does' and they vote for you. That means a lot to any of us."

It certainly means a lot to Earnhardt judging by the size of his smile upon accepting his latest award.

NASCAR SPRINT CUP SERIES MOST POPULAR DRIVER AWARD WINNERS (1956-2012)

1956	Curtis Turner		1975	Richard Petty		1994	Bill Elliott
1957	Fireball Roberts		1976	Richard Petty		1995	Bill Elliott
1958	Glen Wood		1977	Richard Petty		1996	Bill Elliott
1959	Jack Smith		1978	Richard Petty		1997	Bill Elliott
1960	Rex White		1979	David Pearson		1998	Bill Elliott
1961	Joe Weatherly		1980	Bobby Allison		1999	Bill Elliott
1962	Richard Petty		1981	Bobby Allison		2000	Bill Elliott
1963	Fred Lorenzen		1982	Bobby Allison		2001	Dale Earnhardt
1964	Richard Petty		1983	Bobby Allison		2002	Bill Elliott
1965	Fred Lorenzen		1984	Bill Elliott		2003	Dale Earnhardt Jr.
1966	Darel Dieringer		1985	Bill Elliott		2004	Dale Earnhardt Jr.
1967	Cale Yarborough		1986	Bill Elliott		2005	Dale Earnhardt Jr.
1968	Richard Petty		1987	Bill Elliott		2006	Dale Earnhardt Jr.
1969	Bobby Isaac		1988	Bill Elliott		2007	Dale Earnhardt Jr.
1970	Richard Petty		1989	Darrell Waltrip		2008	Dale Earnhardt Jr.
1971	Bobby Allison		1990	Darrell Waltrip		2009	Dale Earnhardt Jr.
1972	Bobby Allison		1991	Bill Elliott		2010	Dale Earnhardt Jr.
1973	Bobby Allison		1992	Bill Elliott		2011	Dale Earnhardt Jr.
1974	Richard Petty		1993	Bill Elliott		2012	Dale Earnhardt Jr.

2012 NASCAR SPRINT CUP SERIES
COORS LIGHT POLE AWARD WINNER

JIMMIE JOHNSON WINS THE COORS LIGHT POLE AWARD ON THE STRENGTH OF FOUR POLES IN 2012

▲ Jimmie Johnson after winning the 2012 Coors Light Pole Award during the NASCAR NMPA Myers Brothers Awards Luncheon at Encore Las Vegas.

▶ Jimmie Johnson poses with the Coors Light Pole Award after winning the pole during qualifying for the NASCAR Sprint Cup Series AAA Texas 500 at Texas Motor Speedway. He captured three others in 2012.

Writing a sentence without the words Johnson, Knaus and Coors Light Poles is difficult if not impossible. But, amazingly, the No. 48 Hendrick Motorsports Chevrolet team went without a pole in 2011 – the same season Jimmie Johnson saw his streak of five consecutive NASCAR Sprint Cup Series championships snapped. Until then, Johnson and Chad Knaus had won at least one pole in each of the California driver's full-time seasons beginning in 2002.

Johnson and Knaus started a new pole streak in 2012. It didn't give Johnson a sixth championship but – with two races remaining – provided an opportunity. Back-to-back Coors Light Poles at Martinsville and Texas during the Chase for the NASCAR Sprint Cup, from which Johnson won, put plenty of pressure on eventual champion Brad Keselowski. Just not enough. He was one of just two drivers to win from the pole in 2012. Joey Logano went pole-to-victory in June at Pocono Raceway.

Johnson won four poles overall during 2012 and won the season's Coors Light Pole Award of $100,000. He prevailed on a tie-breaker over two other four-time fast qualifiers Kasey Kahne, his HMS teammate, and Mark Martin. Johnson also won poles during the past season at Kentucky and Chicagoland.

Johnson is one of three drivers to win consecutive poles in 2012. Marcos Ambrose was the fast qualifier in June at Michigan – where he recorded a lap of 203.241 mph on the newly resurfaced two-mile layout – and over Sonoma's road course. Juan Pablo Montoya recorded back-to-back poles in August at Pocono and Watkins Glen International.

With 29 poles, Johnson ranks 23rd (with Ricky Rudd) in NASCAR Sprint Cup pole standings. He'll look for No. 30 during qualifying for the Daytona 500. He's been the fastest qualifier for the Great American Race twice, in 2002 and 2008.

Seventeen different drivers won a Coors Light Pole during the 2012 season – guaranteeing each a starting position in the February 16 Shootout at Daytona.

Martin, 54, is closing in on Harry Gant's age record of 54 years, 7 months, 17 days set August 27, 1994. He'll be old enough to eclipse Gant's age milestone at races run after mid-September. Martin is one of three active drivers with more than 50 poles sharing No. 7 on the all-time list with Bill Elliott at 55. Jeff Gordon is the active leader at 72 – third most behind Richard Petty (123) and David Pearson (113).

Seven drivers recorded multiple Coors Light Poles in 2012 – the others being Biffle, Gordon, Logano and Kyle Busch. Nine of the 12 qualifiers for the Chase won poles. Shut out were champion Keselowski, second-ranked Clint Bowyer and Kevin Harvick. There were no first-time Coors Light Pole winners during the 2012 season.

2012 NASCAR SPRINT CUP SERIES
COORS LIGHT POLE AWARDS

2012 COORS LIGHT POLE AWARD WINNERS

Driver	Poles		Driver	Poles
Jimmie Johnson	4		Joey Logano	2
Kasey Kahne	4		Juan Pablo Montoya	2
Mark Martin	4		AJ Allmendinger	1
Greg Biffle	3		Aric Almirola	1
Denny Hamlin	3		Dale Earnhardt Jr.	1
Marcos Ambrose	2		Carl Edwards	1
Kyle Busch	2		Matt Kenseth	1
Jeff Gordon	2		Tony Stewart	1
			Martin Truex Jr.	1

NASCAR SPRINT CUP SERIES 2012 COORS LIGHT POLE AWARDS

Date	Event	Location	Pole Winner	Speed (Time)	Fin.Pos.
2/27	Daytona 500	Daytona	Carl Edwards	194.738 mph (46.216 sec.)	8
3/4	Subway Fresh Fit 500	Phoenix	Mark Martin	136.815 mph (26.313 sec.)	9
3/11	KOBALT Tools 400	Las Vegas	Kasey Kahne	190.456 mph (28.353 sec.)	19
3/18	Food City 500	Bristol	Greg Biffle	125.215 mph (15.324 sec.)	13
3/25	Auto Club 400	Auto Club	Denny Hamlin	186.403 mph (38.626 sec.)	11
4/1	Goody's Fast Relief 500	Martinsville	Kasey Kahne	97.128 mph (19.496 sec.)	38
4/14	Samsung Mobile 500	Texas	Martin Truex Jr.	190.369 mph (28.366 sec.)	6
4/22	STP 400	Kansas	AJ Allmendinger	175.993 mph (30.683 sec.)	32
4/28	Capital City 400 Presented by Virginia Is for Lovers	Richmond	Mark Martin	128.327 mph (21.040 sec.)	8
5/6	Aaron's 499	Talladega	Jeff Gordon	191.623 mph (49.973 sec.)	33
5/12	Bojangles' Southern 500	Darlington	Greg Biffle	180.257 mph (27.281 sec.)	12
5/27	Coca-Cola 600	Charlotte	Aric Almirola	192.94 mph (27.988 sec.)	16
6/3	FedEx 400 Benefiting Autism Speaks	Dover	Mark Martin	158.297 mph (22.742 sec.)	14
6/10	Pocono 400 Presented by #NASCAR	Pocono	Joey Logano	179.598 mph (50.112 sec.)	1
6/17	Quicken Loans 400	Michigan	Marcos Ambrose	203.241 mph (35.426 sec.)	9
6/24	Toyota/Save Mart 350	Sonoma	Marcos Ambrose	95.262 mph (75.203 sec.)	8
6/30	Quaker State 400	Kentucky	Jimmie Johnson	181.818 mph (29.700 sec.)	6
7/7	Coke Zero 400 Powered by Coca-Cola	Daytona	Matt Kenseth	192.386 mph (46.781 sec.)	3
7/15	LENOX Industrial Tools 301	Loudon	Kyle Busch	133.417 mph (28.548 sec.)	16
7/29	Crown Royal Presents the Curtiss Shaver 400 at the Brickyard Powered by Big Machine Records	Indianapolis	Denny Hamlin	182.763 mph (49.244 sec.)	6
8/5	Pennsylvania 400	Pocono	Juan Pablo Montoya	176.043 mph (51.124 sec.)	20
8/12	Finger Lakes 355 at The Glen	Watkins Glen	Juan Pablo Montoya	127.02 mph (69.438 sec.)	33
8/19	Pure Michigan 400	Michigan	Mark Martin	199.706 mph (36.053 sec.)	35
8/25	IRWIN Tools Night Race	Bristol	None due to inclement weather		
9/2	AdvoCare 500	Atlanta	Tony Stewart	186.121 mph (29.787 sec.)	22
9/8	Federated Auto Parts 400	Richmond	Dale Earnhardt Jr.	127.023 mph (21.256 sec.)	14
9/16	GEICO 400	Chicago	Jimmie Johnson	182.865 mph (29.530 sec.)	2
9/23	SYLVANIA 300	Loudon	Jeff Gordon	134.911 mph (28.232 sec.)	3
9/30	AAA 400	Dover	Denny Hamlin	159.299 mph (22.599 sec.)	8
10/7	Good Sam Roadside Assistance 500	Talladega	Kasey Kahne	191.455 mph (50.017 sec.)	12
10/13	Bank of America 500	Charlotte	Greg Biffle	193.708 mph (27.877 sec.)	4
10/21	Hollywood Casino 400	Kansas	Kasey Kahne	191.36 mph (28.219 sec.)	4
10/28	TUMS Fast Relief 500	Martinsville	Jimmie Johnson	97.598 mph (19.402 sec.)	1
11/4	AAA Texas 500	Texas	Jimmie Johnson	191.076 mph (28.261 sec.)	1
11/11	AdvoCare 500	Phoenix	Kyle Busch	138.766 mph (25.943 sec.)	3
11/18	Ford EcoBoost 400	Homestead	Joey Logano	176.056 mph (30.672 sec.)	14

2012 NASCAR SPRINT CUP SERIES
MANUFACTURERS' CHAMPIONSHIP

CHEVROLET CONTINUES ITS DOMINANCE OF THE NASCAR SPRINT CUP SERIES MANUFACTURERS' AWARD IN 2012

The 2012 NASCAR Sprint Cup Manufacturers' Championship was Chevrolet's 36th, and their 32nd since 1972. The icing on the cake: the automaker scored its milestone 700th NASCAR Sprint Cup Series victory when five-time champion Jimmie Johnson won at Texas Motor Speedway on November 4. Chevrolet's first win, by Fonty Flock at Columbia (SC) Speedway, came on March 26, 1955.

"The unparalleled dedication and tireless effort of all our Team Chevy members have made this important achievement possible," said Jim Campbell, the car maker's U.S. vice president performance vehicles and motorsports.

Chevrolet's all-time win total stands at 702 entering the 2013 Daytona 500 – 90 more victories than Ford. Toyota, which first raced in the series in 2007, has won 49 times. Chevrolet won 15 races in 2012 NASCAR Sprint Cup competition claiming the Manufacturers' Championship by a 249 to 213 point count over Toyota, which went to Victory Lane 10 times. The 2013 season marked Chevrolet's 12th consecutive season with 10 or more wins. Ford ranked third with 174 points and six wins followed by Dodge's 156 points and five victories. Chevrolet teams made up half of the 12-driver Chase for the NASCAR Sprint Cup. Johnson, who finished third, was the highest ranked in final 2013 points.

Chevrolet's major race victories in 2012 included the Coca-Cola 600 (Kasey Kahne), The Brickyard 400 at Indianapolis Motor Speedway (Johnson) and Bojangles' Southern 500 at historic Darlington Raceway (Johnson). Johnson's Southern 500 victory marked the 200th win for Hendrick Motorsports – all coming in Chevrolets.

▲ Jimmie Johnson helped Chevrolet win the Manufacturers Award with a win at Indianapolis in his No. 48 Lowe's Chevrolet.

Chevrolet drivers also won 14 Coors Light Poles with Johnson one of only two drivers able to win from a pole start – which he did in back-to-back weeks at Martinsville and Texas during the Chase for the NASCAR Sprint Cup.

Ford captured the Daytona 500 for the second consecutive year with Matt Kenseth winning the Great American Race for the second time. Kenseth's Roush Fenway Racing Ford was the dominant car on the schedule's superspeedways also winning Talladega's fall race after finishing third in the spring. Kenseth finished third in Daytona's Coke Zero 400.

Toyota won both Richmond races. Clint Bowyer, whose Michael Waltrip Racing qualified for the Chase for the first time, won for Toyota at Sonoma Raceway (CA), road course – a first for the brand since 2008.

Although last among the season's series auto makers, Dodge carried Brad Keselowski to his first NASCAR Sprint Cup championship. Penske Racing was the only full-time team to campaign a Dodge in 2012. Penske's title broke a seven-year run of champions driving a Chevrolet.

In 2013 NASCAR Sprint Cup Manufacturers' Championship points are determined on a 9–6–4 basis – in other words, the highest-finishing make earns nine points, the second-highest earns six and third-highest four. Furthermore, only the first car across the finish line for each manufacturer is eligible for points. For example, even if the first three cars are the same make, only the first-place car is awarded points. Simply put, it's a race within a race.

NASCAR SPRINT CUP SERIES
WINS BY MANUFACTURER
(1949–2012)

Year	Chevrolet	Dodge	Ford	Toyota	Pontiac	Olds-mobile	Plymouth	Mercury	Hudson	Buick	Chrysler	Jaguar	AMC	Lincoln	Stude-baker	Nash	Races
1949	0	0	0	0	0	5	1	0	0	0	0	0	0	2	0	0	8
1950	0	0	1	0	0	10	4	2	0	0	0	0	0	2	0	0	19
1951	0	0	0	0	0	20	2	2	12	0	1	0	0	0	3	0	41
1952	0	0	0	0	0	3	3	0	27	0	1	0	0	0	0	1	34
1953	0	6	0	0	0	9	0	0	22	0	0	0	0	0	0	0	37
1954	0	1	0	0	0	11	0	0	17	0	7	1	0	0	0	0	37
1955	2	1	2	0	0	10	0	0	1	2	27	0	0	0	0	0	45
1956	3	11	14	0	0	1	0	5	0	0	22	0	0	0	0	0	56
1957	21	0	26	0	2	4	0	0	0	0	0	0	0	0	0	0	53
1958	25	0	16	0	3	7	0	0	0	0	0	0	0	0	0	0	51
1959	16	0	16	0	1	4	7	0	0	0	0	0	0	0	0	0	44
1960	13	1	15	0	7	0	8	0	0	0	0	0	0	0	0	0	44
1961	11	0	7	0	30	0	3	0	0	0	1	0	0	0	0	0	52
1962	14	0	6	0	22	0	11	0	0	0	0	0	0	0	0	0	53
1963	8	0	23	0	5	0	18	1	0	0	0	0	0	0	0	0	55
1964	1	14	30	0	0	0	12	5	0	0	0	0	0	0	0	0	62
1965	0	2	48	0	0	0	4	1	0	0	0	0	0	0	0	0	55
1966	3	18	10	0	0	0	16	2	0	0	0	0	0	0	0	0	49
1967	3	5	10	0	0	0	31	0	0	0	0	0	0	0	0	0	49
1968	1	5	20	0	0	0	16	7	0	0	0	0	0	0	0	0	49
1969	0	22	26	0	0	0	2	4	0	0	0	0	0	0	0	0	54
1970	0	17	6	0	0	0	21	4	0	0	0	0	0	0	0	0	48
1971	3	8	0	0	0	0	22	11	0	0	0	0	0	0	0	0	48
1972	10	5	0	0	0	0	7	9	0	0	0	0	0	0	0	0	31
1973	7	8	0	0	0	0	1	11	0	0	0	0	1	0	0	0	28
1974	12	0	0	0	0	0	0	7	0	0	0	0	1	0	0	0	30
1975	6	14	4	0	0	0	0	3	0	0	0	0	3	0	0	0	30
1976	13	6	1	0	0	0	0	10	0	0	0	0	0	0	0	0	30
1977	21	7	0	0	0	0	0	2	0	0	0	0	0	0	0	0	30
1978	10	0	5	0	0	11	0	4	0	0	0	0	0	0	0	0	30
1979	18	0	5	0	0	5	0	3	0	0	0	0	0	0	0	0	31
1980	22	0	3	0	0	3	0	3	0	0	0	0	0	0	0	0	31
1981	1	0	7	0	1	0	0	0	0	22	0	0	0	0	0	0	31
1982	3	0	2	0	0	0	0	0	0	25	0	0	0	0	0	0	30
1983	15	0	4	0	5	0	0	0	0	6	0	0	0	0	0	0	30
1984	21	0	4	0	3	0	0	0	0	2	0	0	0	0	0	0	30
1985	14	0	14	0	0	0	0	0	0	0	0	0	0	0	0	0	28
1986	18	0	5	0	2	1	0	0	0	3	0	0	0	0	0	0	29
1987	15	0	11	0	2	0	0	0	0	1	0	0	0	0	0	0	29
1988	8	0	9	0	8	2	0	0	0	2	0	0	0	0	0	0	29
1989	13	0	8	0	6	1	0	0	0	1	0	0	0	0	0	0	29
1990	13	0	11	0	3	1	0	0	0	1	0	0	0	0	0	0	29
1991	11	0	10	0	3	0	5	0	0	0	0	0	0	0	0	0	29
1992	8	0	16	0	3	0	2	0	0	0	0	0	0	0	0	0	29
1993	9	0	10	0	11	0	0	0	0	0	0	0	0	0	0	0	30
1994	11	0	20	0	0	0	0	0	0	0	0	0	0	0	0	0	31
1995	21	0	8	0	2	0	0	0	0	0	0	0	0	0	0	0	31
1996	17	0	13	0	1	0	0	0	0	0	0	0	0	0	0	0	31
1997	11	0	19	0	2	0	0	0	0	0	0	0	0	0	0	0	32
1998	16	0	15	0	2	0	0	0	0	0	0	0	0	0	0	0	33
1999	12	0	13	0	9	0	0	0	0	0	0	0	0	0	0	0	34
2000	9	0	14	0	11	0	0	0	0	0	0	0	0	0	0	0	34
2001	16	4	11	0	5	0	0	0	0	0	0	0	0	0	0	0	36
2002	10	7	14	0	5	0	0	0	0	0	0	0	0	0	0	0	36
2003	19	9	7	0	1	0	0	0	0	0	0	0	0	0	0	0	36
2004	22	4	10	0	0	0	0	0	0	0	0	0	0	0	0	0	36
2005	17	3	16	0	0	0	0	0	0	0	0	0	0	0	0	0	36
2006	23	7	6	0	0	0	0	0	0	0	0	0	0	0	0	0	36
2007	26	3	7	0	0	0	0	0	0	0	0	0	0	0	0	0	36
2008	11	4	11	10	0	0	0	0	0	0	0	0	0	0	0	0	36
2009	18	4	3	11	0	0	0	0	0	0	0	0	0	0	0	0	36
2010	18	2	4	12	0	0	0	0	0	0	0	0	0	0	0	0	36
2011	18	5	7	6	0	0	0	0	0	0	0	0	0	0	0	0	36
2012	15	5	6	10	0	0	0	0	0	0	0	0	0	0	0	0	36
Total	702	218	612	49	155	115	189	96	79	65	59	1	5	4	3	1	2354

2012 NASCAR SPRINT CUP SERIES
SPRINT UNLIMITED

THE SPRINT UNLIMITED RETURNS TO ITS ROOTS IN 2013

What was good before should be even better now. The Sprint Unlimited, which has signaled the start of a new NASCAR Sprint Cup Series season since 1979, returns to its roots this year. The field for the 35th running of the event will consist of 2012 Coors Light Pole winners and past event winners who have attempted to qualify for at least one race during the 2012 season. Eligibility for the non-points race mirror those from 1979–2008 and puts greater emphasis on each weekend's NASCAR Sprint Cup Series Coors Light Pole qualifying session.

Last year's race saw Kyle Busch pass defending event champion Tony Stewart in the 2.5-mile track's tri-oval. The margin of victory was 0.013 seconds – the closest in event history.

The race will continue to be 75 laps (187.5 miles) and consist of two segments of 25 and 50 laps. Both green and yellow-flag laps will count. Between segments there is a 10-minute pit stop at which time teams can pit to change tires, add fuel and make normal chassis adjustments. Starting positions are determined by a blind draw.

Sixteen different drivers qualified for the 35th Sprint Unlimited through time trials held at last year's schedule of 36 races. Four past winners will be added to create a 20-car starting field. Every winner from 1999 forward – excepting the retired Daytona 500 winner and past NASCAR Sprint Cup champion Dale Jarrett – are qualified for the race.

Three competitors each won four Coors Light Poles in 2012. Kasey Kahne punched his ticket in the season's third race at Las Vegas. Jimmie Johnson (2005) and Mark Martin (1999) are previous event winners. Busch, Stewart (2001–02, 2010), Jeff Gordon (1994, 1997), Denny Hamlin (2006) and Dale Earnhardt Jr. (2003) are former winners who also scored poles last season.

Drivers who qualified solely on the basis of a 2012 Coors Light Pole are Greg Biffle, Joey Logano, Marcos Ambrose, Juan Pablo Montoya, Matt Kenseth, Martin Truex Jr., Carl Edwards and AJ Allmendinger. Logano and Kenseth, will be making their 2013 debut in new rides. Logano will be behind the wheel of the No. 22 Penske Racing Ford while Kenseth is set to drive the No. 20 Joe Gibbs Racing Toyota.

Kevin Harvick goes into the race as a past winner. Also qualified via Sprint Unlimited winner status are Ken Schrader (1989–90), Bill Elliott (1987) and Terry Labonte (1985).

2012 NASCAR SPRINT CUP SERIES
NASCAR SPRINT ALL-STAR RACE

JIMMIE JOHNSON WINS THE NON-POINTS EVENT UNDER ITS NEW FORMAT

2012's NASCAR Sprint All-Star Race defined the championship in microcosm. Jimmie Johnson won the 28th running of the non-points lead-in to the Coca-Cola 600 at Charlotte Motor Speedway. He beat Brad Keselowski by 0.841 second. Six months later, in South Florida, the pair went head to head again – this time for the NASCAR Sprint Cup title. Advantage: Keselowski.

Interestingly, the NASCAR Sprint All-Star Race was one of few missing pieces in Keselowski's season. He'll get another opportunity to win the $1 million prize on May 18, 2013.

The race, first run in 1985 and won by NASCAR Hall of Famer Darrell Waltrip, includes race-winning drivers and car owners from the 2012–13 NASCAR Sprint Cup seasons, NASCAR Sprint Cup champions from the past 10 years

(2003–2012) who are active drivers and have competed in at least one series event during the 2012–13 season, and past winners of the NASCAR Sprint All-Star Race from the past 10 years (2003–2012). Additionally, two drivers can qualify for the premier event by finishing first and second, respectively, after two, 20-lap segments in the Sprint Showdown. Finally, one driver joins the event by winning the NASCAR Sprint Fan Vote.

Last year's "transfers" were Dale Earnhardt Jr. and AJ Allmendinger. Former champion Bobby Labonte won the fan vote.

The 2012 race was comprised of five segments, with the first four segments consisting of 20 laps, and the fifth and final segment being a 10-lap dash. The segment winners were guaranteed track position for the 10-lap segment.

The NASCAR Sprint Pit Crew Challenge, at Time Warner Cable Arena in Charlotte two nights before the NASCAR Sprint All-Star Race, is directly linked to the event, as the finishing order in the pit-crew competition determines the selection order of pit stalls for the race. Johnson's No. 48 Hendrick Motorsports Chevrolet team, overseen by crew chief Chad Knaus, won last year's Pit Crew Challenge ahead of the No. 11 Joe Gibbs Racing Toyota of Denny Hamlin/Darian Grubb and No. 17 Roush Fenway Racing Ford of Matt Kenseth/Jimmy Fennig.

Any "tweaks" in format for the 2013 race will be announced.

Earnhardt, non-exempt in 2012, regained his NASCAR Sprint All-Star Race spot by winning last June at Michigan International Speedway. Also eligible with a 2012 victory (at Pocono in June) is Joey Logano. Logano will

drive for Penske Racing in 2013 – with the No. 22 team that won the NASCAR Sprint All-Star Race in 2010 with Kurt Busch.

Among drivers who'll have to race their way into the NASCAR Sprint All-Star Race are Sunoco Rookie of the Year contenders Ricky Stenhouse Jr., the two-time reigning NASCAR Nationwide Series champion and Danica Patrick.

Earnhardt Ganassi Racing with Felix Sabates teammates Jamie McMurray and Juan Pablo Montoya also are not yet eligible. McMurray came up one position short of qualifying in last year's Sprint Showdown. Martin Truex Jr. is last year's only Chase qualifier without a confirmed spot in the NASCAR Sprint All-Star Race.

PAST WINNERS

2012	Jimmie Johnson
2011	Carl Edwards
2010	Kurt Busch
2009	Tony Stewart
2008	Kasey Kahne
2007	Kevin Harvick
2006	Jimmie Johnson
2005	Mark Martin
2004	Matt Kenseth
2003	Jimmie Johnson
2002	Ryan Newman
2001	Jeff Gordon
2000	Dale Earnhardt Jr.
1999	Terry Labonte
1998	Mark Martin
1997	Jeff Gordon
1996	Michael Waltrip
1995	Jeff Gordon
1994	Geoff Bodine
1993	Dale Earnhardt
1992	Davey Allison
1991	Davey Allison
1990	Dale Earnhardt
1989	Rusty Wallace
1988	Terry Labonte
1987	Dale Earnhardt
1986*	Bill Elliott
1985	Darrell Waltrip

*Held at Atlanta Motor Speedway

NASCAR SPRINT CUP SERIES
CHAMPIONS AND LEADERS (1949-2012)

1949 **Red Byron** **842.5**
Lee Petty 725
Bob Flock 704
Bill Blair 567.5
Fonty Flock 554.5
Curtis Turner 430
Ray Erickson 422
Tim Flock 421
Glenn Dunaway 384
Frank Mundy 375

1950 **Bill Rexford** **1959**
Fireball Roberts 1848.5
Lee Petty 1590
Lloyd Moore 1398
Curtis Turner 1375.5
Johnny Mantz 1282
Chuck Mahoney 1217.5
Dick Linder 1121
Jim Florian 801
Bill Blair 766

1951 **Herb Thomas** **4208.5**
Fonty Flock 4062.25
Tim Flock 3722.5
Lee Petty 2392.25
Frank Mundy 1963.5
Buddy Shuman 1368.75
James Taylor 1214
Dick Rathmann 1040
Bill Snowden 1009.25
Joe Eubanks 1005.5

1952 **Tim Flock** **6858.5**
Herb Thomas 6752.5
Lee Petty 6498.5
Fonty Flock 5183.5
Dick Rathmann 3952.25
Bill Blair 3449
Joe Eubanks 3090.5
Ray Duhigg 2986.5
Don Thomas 2574
Buddy Shuman 2483

1953 **Herb Thomas** **8460**
Lee Petty 7814
Dick Rathmann 7362
Buck Baker 6713
Fonty Flock 6174
Tim Flock 5011
Jim Paschal 4211
Joe Eubanks 3603
Jimmy Lewallen 3508
Curtis Turner 3508

1954 **Lee Petty** **8649**
Herb Thomas 8366
Buck Baker 6893
Dick Rathmann 6760
Joe Eubanks 5467
Hershel McGriff 5137
Jim Paschal 3903
Jimmy Lewallen 3233
Curtis Turner 2994
Ralph Ligouri 2955

1955 **Tim Flock** **9596**
Buck Baker 9088
Lee Petty 7194
Bob Welborn 5460
Herb Thomas 5186
Junior Johnson 4810
Eddy Skinner 4652
Jim Paschal 4572
Jimmy Lewallen 4360
Fonty Flock 4266

1956 **Buck Baker** **9272**
Herb Thomas 8586
Al Thompson 8328
Lee Petty 8324
Jim Paschal 7878
Bill Myers 6920
Fireball Roberts 5794
Ralph Moody 5548
Tim Flock 5062
Marvin Panch 4680

1957 **Buck Baker** **10716**
Marvin Panch 9956
Al Thompson 8580
Lee Petty 8528
Jack Smith 8464
Fireball Roberts 8268
Johnny Allen 7068
L.D. Austin 6532
Bob King 5740
Jim Paschal 5136

1958 **Lee Petty** **12232**
Buck Baker 11586
Al Thompson 8792
Lloyd Rollins 8124
Jack Smith 7666
L.D. Austin 6972
Rex White 6552
Junior Johnson 6380
Ed Pagan 4910
Jim Reed 4762

1959 **Lee Petty** **11792**
Cotton Owens 9962
Al Thompson 7684
Herman Beam 7396
Buck Baker 7170
Tom Pistone 7050
L.D. Austin 6519
Jack Smith 6150
Jim Reed 7714
Rex White 5526

1960 **Rex White** **21164**
Richard Petty 17228
Bobby Johns 14964
Buck Baker 14674
Ned Jarrett 14660
Lee Petty 14510
Junior Johnson 9932
Emanuel Zervakis 9720
Jim Paschal 8968
Banjo Matthews 8458

1961 **Ned Jarrett** **27272**
Rex White 26442
Emanuel Zervakis 22312
Joe Weatherly 17894
Fireball Roberts 17600
Junior Johnson 17178
Jack Smith 15186
Richard Petty 14984
Jim Paschal 13922
Buck Baker 13746

1962 **Joe Weatherly** **30836**
Richard Petty 28440
Ned Jarrett 25336
Jack Smith 22870
Rex White 19424
Jim Paschal 18128
Fred Lorenzen 17554
Fireball Roberts 16380
Marvin Panch 15138
David Pearson 14404

1963 **Joe Weatherly** **33398**
Richard Petty 31170
Fred Lorenzen 29684
Ned Jarrett 27214
Fireball Roberts 22642
Jim Pardue 22228
Darel Dieringer 21418
David Pearson 21156
Rex White 20976
Tiny Lund 19624

1964 **Richard Petty** **40252**
Ned Jarrett 34950
David Pearson 32146
Billy Wade 28474
Jim Pardue 26570
Curtis Crider 25606
Jim Paschal 25450
Larry Thomas 22950
Buck Baker 22366
Marvin Panch 21480

1965 **Ned Jarrett** **38824**
Dick Hutcherson 35790
Darel Dieringer 24696
G.C. Spencer 24314
Marvin Panch 22798
Bob Derrington 21394
J.T. Putney 20928
Neil Castles 20848
Buddy Baker 20672
Cale Yarborough 20192

1966 **David Pearson** **35638**
James Hylton 33688
Richard Petty 22952
Henley Gray 22468
Paul Goldsmith 22078
Wendell Scott 21702
John Sears 21432
J.T. Putney 21208
Neil Castles 20446
Bobby Allison 19910

1967 **Richard Petty** **42472**
James Hylton 36444
Dick Hutcherson 33658
Bobby Allison 30812
John Sears 29078
Jim Paschal 27624
David Pearson 26302
Neil Castles 23218
Elmo Langley 22286
Wendell Scott 20700

1968 **David Pearson** **3499**
Bobby Isaac 3373
Richard Petty 3123
Clyde Lynn 3041
John Sears 3017
Elmo Langley 2823
James Hylton 2719
Jabe Thomas 2687
Wendell Scott 2685
Roy Tyner 2504

1969 **David Pearson** **4170**
Richard Petty 3813
James Hylton 3750
Neil Castles 3530
Elmo Langley 3383
Bobby Isaac 3301
John Sears 3166
Jabe Thomas 3103
Wendell Scott 3015
Cecil Gordon 3002

1970 **Bobby Isaac** **3911**
Bobby Allison 3860
James Hylton 3788
Richard Petty 3447
Neil Castles 3158
Elmo Langley 3154
Jabe Thomas 3120
Benny Parsons 2993
Dave Marcis 2820
Frank Warren 2697

1971 **Richard Petty** **4435**
James Hylton 4071
Cecil Gordon 3677
Bobby Allison 3636
Elmo Langley 3356
Jabe Thomas 3200
Bill Champion 3058
Frank Warren 2886
J.D. McDuffie 2862
Walter Ballard 2633

1972 **Richard Petty** **8701.4**
Bobby Allison 8573.5
James Hylton 8158.7
Cecil Gordon 7326.05
Benny Parsons 6844.15
Walter Ballard 6781.45
Elmo Langley 6656.25
John Sears 6298.5
Dean Dalton 6295.05
Ben Arnold 6179

1973 **Benny Parsons** **7173.8**
Cale Yarborough 7106.65
Cecil Gordon 7046.8
James Hylton 6972.75
Richard Petty 6877.95
Buddy Baker 6327.6
Bobby Allison 6272.3
Walter Ballard 5955.7
Elmo Langley 5826.85
J.D. McDuffie 5743.9

1974 **Richard Petty** **5037.75**
Cale Yarborough 4470.3
David Pearson 2389.25
Bobby Allison 2019.195
Benny Parsons 1591.5
Dave Marcis 1378.2
Buddy Baker 1016.88
Earl Ross 1009.47
Cecil Gordon 1000.65
David Sisco 956.2

1975 **Richard Petty** **4783**
Dave Marcis 4061
James Hylton 3914
Benny Parsons 3820
Richard Childress 3818
Cecil Gordon 3702
Darrell Waltrip 3462
Elmo Langley 3399
Cale Yarborough 3295
Richard Brooks 3182

1976 **Cale Yarborough** **4644**
Richard Petty 4449
Benny Parsons 4304
Bobby Allison 4097
Lennie Pond 3930
Dave Marcis 3875
Buddy Baker 3745
Darrell Waltrip 3505
David Pearson 3483
Richard Brooks 3447

1977 Cale Yarborough — 5000
Richard Petty	4614
Benny Parsons	4570
Darrell Waltrip	4498
Buddy Baker	3961
Richard Brooks	3742
James Hylton	3476
Bobby Allison	3467
Richard Childress	3463
Cecil Gordon	3294

1978 Cale Yarborough — 4841
Bobby Allison	4367
Darrell Waltrip	4362
Benny Parsons	4350
Dave Marcis	4335
Richard Petty	3949
Lennie Pond	3794
Dick Brooks	3769
Buddy Arrington	3626
Richard Childress	3566

1979 Richard Petty — 4830
Darrell Waltrip	4819
Bobby Allison	4633
Cale Yarborough	4604
Benny Parsons	4256
Joe Millikan	4014
Dale Earnhardt	3749
Richard Childress	3735
Ricky Rudd	3642
Terry Labonte	3615

1980 Dale Earnhardt — 4661
Cale Yarborough	4642
Benny Parsons	4278
Richard Petty	4255
Darrell Waltrip	4239
Bobby Allison	4019
Jody Ridley	3972
Terry Labonte	3766
Dave Marcis	3745
Richard Childress	3742

1981 Darrell Waltrip — 4880
Bobby Allison	4827
Harry Gant	4210
Terry Labonte	4052
Jody Ridley	4002
Ricky Rudd	3988
Dale Earnhardt	3975
Richard Petty	3880
Dave Marcis	3507
Benny Parsons	3449

1982 Darrell Waltrip — 4489
Bobby Allison	4417
Terry Labonte	4211
Harry Gant	3877
Richard Petty	3814
Dave Marcis	3666
Buddy Arrington	3642
Ron Bouchard	3545
Ricky Rudd	3537
Morgan Shepherd	3451

1983 Bobby Allison — 4667
Darrell Waltrip	4620
Bill Elliott	3279
Richard Petty	4042
Terry Labonte	4004
Neil Bonnett	3842
Harry Gant	3790
Dale Earnhardt	3732
Ricky Rudd	3693
Tim Richmond	3612

1984 Terry Labonte — 4508
Harry Gant	4443
Bill Elliott	4377
Dale Earnhardt	4265
Darrell Waltrip	4230
Bobby Allison	4094
Ricky Rudd	3918
Neil Bonnett	3802
Geoff Bodine	3734
Richard Petty	3643

1985 Darrell Waltrip — 4292
Bill Eilliott	4191
Harry Gant	4033
Neil Bonnett	3902
Geoff Bodine	3862
Ricky Rudd	3857
Terry Labonte	3683
Dale Earnhardt	3561
Kyle Petty	3528
Lake Speed	3507

1986 Dale Earnhardt — 4468
Darrell Waltrip	4180
Tim Richmond	4174
Bill Elliott	3844
Ricky Rudd	3823
Rusty Wallace	3762
Bobby Allison	3698
Geoff Bodine	3678
Bobby Hillin	3546
Kyle Petty	3537

1987 Dale Earnhardt — 4696
Bill Elliott	4207
Terry Labonte	4007
Darrell Waltrip	3911
Rusty Wallace	3818
Ricky Rudd	3742
Kyle Petty	3737
Richard Petty	3708
Bobby Allison	3530
Ken Schrader	3405

1988 Bill Elliott — 4488
Rusty Wallace	4464
Dale Earnhardt	4256
Terry Labonte	4007
Ken Schrader	3858
Geoff Bodine	3799
Darrell Waltrip	3764
Davey Allison	3631
Phil Parsons	3630
Sterling Marlin	3621

1989 Rusty Wallace — 4176
Dale Earnhardt	4164
Mark Martin	4053
Darrell Waltrip	3971
Ken Schrader	3786
Bill Elliott	3774
Harry Gant	3610
Ricky Rudd	3608
Geoff Bodine	3600
Terry Labonte	3569

1990 Dale Earnhardt — 4430
Mark Martin	4404
Geoff Bodine	4017
Bill Elliott	3999
Morgan Shepherd	3689
Rusty Wallace	3676
Ricky Rudd	3601
Alan Kulwicki	3599
Ernie Irvan	3593
Ken Schrader	3572

1991 Dale Earnhardt — 4287
Ricky Rudd	4092
Davey Allison	4088
Harry Gant	3985
Ernie Irvan	3925
Mark Martin	3914
Sterling Marlin	3839
Darrell Waltrip	3711
Ken Schrader	3690
Rusty Wallace	3582

1992 Alan Kulwicki — 4078
Bill Elliott	4068
Davey Allison	4015
Harry Gant	3955
Kyle Petty	3945
Mark Martin	3887
Ricky Rudd	3735
Terry Labonte	3674
Darrell Waltrip	3659
Sterling Marlin	3603

1993 Dale Earnhardt — 4526
Rusty Wallace	4446
Mark Martin	4150
Dale Jarrett	4000
Kyle Petty	3860
Ernie Irvan	3834
Morgan Shepherd	3807
Bill Elliott	3774
Ken Schrader	3715
Ricky Rudd	3644

1994 Dale Earnhardt — 4694
Mark Martin	4250
Rusty Wallace	4207
Ken Schrader	4060
Ricky Rudd	4050
Morgan Shepherd	4029
Terry Labonte	3876
Jeff Gordon	3776
Darrell Waltrip	3688
Bill Elliott	3617

1995 Jeff Gordon — 4614
Dale Earnhardt	4580
Sterling Marlin	4361
Mark Martin	4320
Rusty Wallace	4240
Terry Labonte	4146
Ted Musgrave	3949
Bill Elliott	3746
Ricky Rudd	3734
Bobby Labonte	3718

1996 Terry Labonte — 4657
Jeff Gordon	4620
Dale Jarrett	4568
Dale Earnhardt	4327
Mark Martin	4278
Ricky Rudd	3845
Rusty Wallace	3717
Sterling Marlin	3682
Bobby Hamilton	3639
Ernie Irvan	3632

1997 Jeff Gordon — 4710
Dale Jarrett	4696
Mark Martin	4681
Jeff Burton	4285
Dale Earnhardt	4216
Terry Labonte	4177
Bobby Labonte	4101
Bill Elliott	3836
Rusty Wallace	3598
Ken Schrader	3576

1998 Jeff Gordon — 5328
Mark Martin	4964
Dale Jarrett	4619
Rusty Wallace	4501
Jeff Burton	4415
Bobby Labonte	4180
Jeremy Mayfield	4157
Dale Earnhardt	3928
Terry Labonte	3901
Bobby Hamilton	3786

1999 Dale Jarrett — 5262
Bobby Labonte	5061
Mark Martin	4943
Tony Stewart	4774
Jeff Burton	4733
Jeff Gordon	4620
Dale Earnhardt	4492
Rusty Wallace	4155
Ward Burton	4062
Mike Skinner	4003

2000 Bobby Labonte — 5130
Dale Earnhardt	4865
Jeff Burton	4836
Dale Jarrett	4684
Ricky Rudd	4575
Tony Stewart	4570
Rusty Wallace	4544
Mark Martin	4410
Jeff Gordon	4361
Ward Burton	4152

2001 Jeff Gordon — 5112
Tony Stewart	4763
Sterling Marlin	4741
Ricky Rudd	4706
Dale Jarrett	4612
Bobby Labonte	4561
Rusty Wallace	4481
Dale Earnhardt Jr.	4460
Kevin Harvick	4406
Jeff Burton	4394

2002 Tony Stewart — 4800
Mark Martin	4762
Kurt Busch	4641
Jeff Gordon	4607
Jimmie Johnson	4600
Ryan Newman	4593
Rusty Wallace	4574
Matt Kenseth	4432
Dale Jarrett	4415
Ricky Rudd	4323

2003 Matt Kenseth — 5022
Jimmie Johnson	4932
Dale Earnhardt Jr.	4815
Jeff Gordon	4785
Kevin Harvick	4770
Ryan Newman	4711
Tony Stewart	4549
Bobby Labonte	4377
Bill Elliott	4303
Terry Labonte	4162

2004 Kurt Busch — 6506
Jimmie Johnson	6498
Jeff Gordon	6490
Mark Martin	6399
Dale Earnhardt Jr.	6368
Tony Stewart	6326
Ryan Newman	6180
Matt Kenseth	6069
Elliott Sadler	6024
Jeremy Mayfield	6000

2005 Tony Stewart — 6533
Greg Biffle	6498
Carl Edwards	6498
Mark Martin	6428
Jimmie Johnson	6406
Ryan Newman	6359
Matt Kenseth	6352
Rusty Wallace	6140
Jeremy Mayfield	6073
Kurt Busch	5974

2006 Jimmie Johnson — 6475
Matt Kenseth	6419
Denny Hamlin	6407
Kevin Harvick	6397
Dale Earnhardt Jr.	6328
Jeff Gordon	6256
Jeff Burton	6228
Kasey Kahne	6183
Mark Martin	6168
Kyle Busch	6027

2007 Jimmie Johnson — 6723
Jeff Gordon	6646
Clint Bowyer	6377
Matt Kenseth	6298
Kyle Busch	6293
Tony Stewart	6242
Kurt Busch	6231
Jeff Burton	6231
Carl Edwards	6222
Kevin Harvick	6199

2008 Jimmie Johnson — 6684
Carl Edwards	6615
Greg Biffle	6467
Kevin Harvick	6408
Clint Bowyer	6381
Jeff Burton	6335
Jeff Gordon	6316
Denny Hamlin	6214
Tony Stewart	6202
Kyle Busch	6186

2009 Jimmie Johnson — 6652
Mark Martin	6511
Jeff Gordon	6473
Kurt Busch	6446
Denny Hamlin	6335
Tony Stewart	6309
Greg Biffle	6292
Juan Pablo Montoya	6252
Ryan Newman	6175
Kasey Kahne	6128

2010 Jimmie Johnson — 6622
Denny Hamlin	6583
Kevin Harvick	6581
Carl Edwards	6393
Matt Kenseth	6294
Greg Biffle	6247
Tony Stewart	6221
Kyle Busch	6182
Jeff Gordon	6176
Clint Bowyer	6155

2011 Tony Stewart — 2403
Carl Edwards	2403
Kevin Harvick	2345
Matt Kenseth	2330
Brad Keselowski	2319
Jimmie Johnson	2304
Dale Earnhardt Jr.	2290
Jeff Gordon	2287
Denny Hamlin	2284
Ryan Newman	2284

2012 Brad Keselowski — 2400
Clint Bowyer	2361
Jimmie Johnson	2360
Kasey Kahne	2345
Greg Biffle	2332
Denny Hamlin	2329
Matt Kenseth	2324
Kevin Harvick	2321
Tony Stewart	2311
Jeff Gordon	2303

2012 NASCAR SPRINT CUP SERIES
FINAL DRIVER POINTS

Pos.	Driver	Points	Starts	Wins	Top 5	Top 10
1	Brad Keselowski	2400	36	5	13	23
2	Clint Bowyer	2361	36	3	10	23
3	Jimmie Johnson	2360	36	5	18	24
4	Kasey Kahne	2345	36	2	12	19
5	Greg Biffle	2332	36	2	12	21
6	Denny Hamlin	2329	36	5	14	17
7	Matt Kenseth	2324	36	3	13	19
8	Kevin Harvick	2321	36	1	5	14
9	Tony Stewart	2311	36	3	12	16
10	Jeff Gordon	2303	36	2	11	18
11	Martin Truex Jr.	2299	36	0	7	19
12	Dale Earnhardt Jr.	2245	34	1	10	20
13	Kyle Busch	1133	36	1	13	20
14	Ryan Newman	1051	36	1	6	14
15	Carl Edwards	1030	36	0	3	13
16	Paul Menard	1006	36	0	1	9
17	Joey Logano	965	36	1	2	12
18	Marcos Ambrose	950	36	1	3	8
19	Jeff Burton	883	36	0	2	6
20	Aric Almirola	868	36	0	1	4
21	Jamie McMurray	868	36	0	0	3
22	Juan Pablo Montoya	810	36	0	0	2
23	Bobby Labonte	772	36	0	0	2
24	Regan Smith	747	34	0	1	4
25	Kurt Busch	735	35	0	1	5
26	Mark Martin	701	24	0	4	10
27	Travis Kvapil	638	35	0	0	1
28	David Ragan	622	36	0	1	2
29	Casey Mears	612	36	0	0	0
30	David Gilliland	605	36	0	0	0
31	Landon Cassill	598	36	0	0	0
32	AJ Allmendinger	453	21	0	1	3
33	Dave Blaney	417	34	0	0	0
34	David Reutimann	373	25	0	0	0
35	Brian Vickers	250	8	0	3	5
36	David Stremme	236	28	0	0	0
37	Michael McDowell	187	30	0	0	0
38	J.J. Yeley	166	24	0	0	0
39	Josh Wise	147	30	0	0	0
40	Ken Schrader	146	13	0	0	0
41	Stephen Leicht	126	15	0	0	0
42	Scott Speed	124	17	0	0	0
43	Michael Waltrip	94	4	0	0	1
44	Terry Labonte	94	4	0	0	0
45	Tony Raines	71	7	0	0	0
46	Scott Riggs	56	20	0	0	0
47	Brendan Gaughan	50	4	0	0	0
48	Boris Said	34	2	0	0	0
49	Bill Elliott	14	2	0	0	0
50	Hermie Sadler	13	1	0	0	0
51	Mike Olsen	11	1	0	0	0
52	Robby Gordon	11	3	0	0	0
53	Mike Skinner	10	4	0	0	0
54	Kelly Bires	9	3	0	0	0
55	Tomy Drissi	6	1	0	0	0
56	Stacy Compton	5	1	0	0	0
57	David Mayhew	4	1	0	0	0
58	Patrick Long	2	1	0	0	0
59	Sam Horninsh Jr. (i)	0	20	0	1	1
60	Trevor Bayne (i)	0	16	0	0	2
61	Ricky Stenhouse Jr. (i)	0	4	0	0	0
62	Danica Patrick (i)	0	10	0	0	0
63	Timmy Hill (i)	0	5	0	0	0
64	Mike Bliss (i)	0	19	0	0	0
65	Austin Dillon (i)	0	1	0	0	0
66	Robert Richardson Jr. (i)	0	2	0	0	0
67	Elliott Sadler (i)	0	1	0	0	0
68	Joe Nemechek (i)	0	31	0	0	0
69	Reed Sorenson (i)	0	19	0	0	0
70	T.J. Bell (i)	0	5	0	0	0
71	Jason Leffler (i)	0	5	0	0	0
72	Jason White (i)	0	1	0	0	0
73	Cole Whitt (i)	0	5	0	0	0
74	Chris Cook (i)	0	2	0	0	0
75	Kenny Wallace (i)	0	0	0	0	0
76	Mike Wallace (i)	0	0	0	0	0
77	Jeff Green (i)	0	0	0	0	0
78	Tim Andrews (i)	0	0	0	0	0
79	Brian Simo	0	0	0	0	0
80	Mark Green	0	0	0	0	0

(i) = Ineligible for driver points in this series

2012 NASCAR SPRINT CUP SERIES
FINAL OWNER POINTS

Pos.	Car	Owner	Points	Starts	Wins	Top 5	Top 10	Qualifying Attempts
1	2	Roger Penske	2400	36	5	13	23	36
2	15	Rob Kauffman	2361	36	3	10	23	36
3	48	Jeff Gordon	2360	36	5	18	24	36
4	5	Linda Hendrick	2345	36	2	12	19	36
5	16	Jack Roush	2332	36	2	12	21	36
6	11	J D Gibbs	2329	36	5	14	17	36
7	17	John Henry	2324	36	3	13	19	36
8	29	Richard Childress	2321	36	1	5	14	36
9	14	Margaret Haas	2311	36	3	12	16	36
10	24	Rick Hendrick	2303	36	2	11	18	36
11	56	Michael Waltrip	2299	36	0	7	19	36
12	88	Rick Hendrick	2288	36	1	10	21	36
13	18	Joe Gibbs	1133	36	1	13	20	36
14	39	Tony Stewart	1051	36	1	6	14	36
15	55	Bill Jenkins	1045	36	0	7	16	36
16	99	Jack Roush	1030	36	0	3	13	36
17	27	Richard Childress	1006	36	0	1	9	36
18	20	Joe Gibbs	965	36	1	2	12	36
19	9	Richard Petty	950	36	1	3	8	36
20	31	Richard Childress	883	36	0	2	6	36
21	22	Walter Czarnecki	869	36	0	2	4	36
22	43	Richard Petty	868	36	0	1	4	36
23	1	Felix Sabates	868	36	0	0	3	36
24	78	Barney Visser	848	36	0	1	6	36
25	42	Chip Ganassi	810	36	0	0	2	36
26	47	Tad Geschickter	772	36	0	0	2	36
27	51	James Finch	667	36	0	1	2	36
28	93	Thomas Ueberall	664	36	0	0	1	36
29	34	Bob Jenkins	622	36	0	1	2	36
30	13	Bob Germain	612	36	0	0	0	36
31	38	Brad Jenkins	605	36	0	0	0	36
32	83	Thomas Ueberall	598	36	0	0	0	36
33	10	Tommy Baldwin	519	36	0	0	0	36
34	32	Frank Stoddard Jr.	493	36	0	0	0	36
35	36	Allan Heinke	427	36	0	0	0	36
36	21	Glen Wood	346	16	0	0	2	16
37	33	Richard Childress	253	26	0	0	0	36
38	30	Kevin Buckler	238	29	0	0	0	36
39	98	Mike Curb	199	33	0	0	0	36
40	26	Jerry Freeze	172	31	0	0	0	36
41	87	Andrea Nemechek	154	31	0	0	0	36
42	249	Jay Robinson	150	17	0	0	0	25
43	195	Bob Leavine	121	15	0	0	0	16
44	23	Robert Richardson Sr.	82	22	0	0	0	31
45	119	Randy Humphrey	72	21	0	0	0	29
46	6	John Henry	46	3	0	0	0	3
47	37	Larry Gunselman	30	9	0	0	0	20
48	132	Frank Stoddard Jr.	27	1	0	0	0	1
49	12	Roger Penske	26	1	0	0	0	1
50	74	Vickie Compton	22	7	0	0	0	11
51	191	Mark Smith	20	11	0	0	0	15
52	179	Archie St Hilaire	14	6	0	0	0	11
53	7	Robby Gordon	11	3	0	0	0	5
54	97	Andrea Nemechek	9	2	0	0	0	3
55	50	Steve Turner	7	1	0	0	0	1
56	144	Johnathan Cohen	4	1	0	0	0	1
57	52	Kelly Owen	3	1	0	0	0	3
58	173	Scott Gunderson	0	1	0	0	0	2
59	109	Brack Maggard	0	0	0	0	0	1
60	140	Michael Hillman	0	0	0	0	0	1
61	0	Steven Scharr	0	0	0	0	0	1

DRIVER VICTORIES (THREE OR MORE WINS) (1949-2012)

Richard Petty	200	Bobby Isaac	37	Davey Allison	19	Tim Richmond	13	Dave Marcis	5	Glen Wood	4
David Pearson	105	Fireball Roberts	33	Buddy Baker	19	Donnie Allison	10	Jeremy Mayfield	5	Bill Blair	3
Jeff Gordon	87	Dale Jarrett	32	Dale Earnhardt Jr.	19	Sterling Marlin	10	Ralph Moody	5	Robby Gordon	3
Bobby Allison	84	Rex White	28	Carl Edwards	19	Paul Goldsmith	9	Lloyd Dane	4	Dick Linder	3
Darrell Waltrip	84	Fred Lorenzen	26	Fonty Flock	19	Brad Keselowski	9	Bob Flock	4	Frank Mundy	3
Cale Yarborough	83	Jim Paschal	25	Kevin Harvick	19	Cotton Owens	9	Charlie Glotzbach	4	Elliott Sadler	3
Dale Earnhardt	76	Joe Weatherly	25	Greg Biffle	18	Bob Welborn	9	Eddie Gray	4	Gwyn Staley	3
Jimmie Johnson	60	Kurt Busch	24	Geoff Bodine	18	Clint Bowyer	8	Bobby Hamilton	4	
Rusty Wallace	55	Kyle Busch	24	Neil Bonnett	18	Kyle Petty	8	Pete Hamilton	4	
Lee Petty	54	Matt Kenseth	24	Harry Gant	18	Darel Dieringer	7	Parnelli Jones	4	
Ned Jarrett	50	Ricky Rudd	23	Marvin Panch	17	A.J. Foyt	7	Hershel McGriff	4	
Junior Johnson	50	Denny Hamlin	22	Curtis Turner	17	Jim Reed	7	Joe Nemechek	4	
Herb Thomas	48	Terry Labonte	22	Ryan Newman	16	Marshall Teague	7	Eddie Pagan	4	
Tony Stewart	47	Jeff Burton	21	Ernie Irvan	15	Jamie McMurray	6	Ken Schrader	4	
Buck Baker	46	Bobby Labonte	21	Dick Hutcherson	14	Ward Burton	5	Morgan Shepherd	4	
Bill Elliott	44	Benny Parsons	21	Kasey Kahne	14	Dan Gurney	5	Nelson Stacy	4	
Mark Martin	40	Jack Smith	21	LeeRoy Yarbrough	14	Alan Kulwicki	5	Billy Wade	4	
Tim Flock	39	Speedy Thompson	20	Dick Rathmann	13	Tiny Lund	5	Michael Waltrip	4	

2012 NASCAR SPRINT CUP SERIES
FINAL BOX SCORES

Points Pos.	Car No.	Driver	Avg. Start	Avg. Mid Race	Avg. Finish	Avg. Pos.	Pass Diff.	Green Passes	Green Times Passed	Quality Passes	% of Quality Passes	No. of Fastest Laps	Laps in Top 15	% of Laps in Top 15	Laps Led	% of Laps Led	Total Laps	Driver Rating	Pts.
1	2	Brad Keselowski	16.2	10.5	10.1	11.2	119	3676	3557	2201	59.9	538	8059	77.2	735	7.0	10328	99.0	2400
2	15	Clint Bowyer	12.8	11.9	10.9	11.8	103	2850	2747	1618	56.8	342	8006	76.7	388	3.7	10271	96.5	2361
3	48	Jimmie Johnson	10.6	8.8	11.2	9.2	250	2390	2140	1572	65.8	1171	8813	84.4	1744	16.7	9924	109.5	2360
4	5	Kasey Kahne	8.8	11.6	13.1	12.6	64	3035	2971	1840	60.6	696	7626	73.0	282	2.7	9919	96.3	2345
5	16	Greg Biffle	9.9	10.2	10.2	10.3	56	2989	2933	1912	64.0	355	7759	74.3	721	6.9	10397	99.5	2332
6	11	Denny Hamlin	11.9	11.7	12.8	10.7	39	2515	2476	1415	56.3	801	7721	73.9	1226	11.7	10274	100.9	2329
7	17	Matt Kenseth	13.3	8.1	11.1	10.4	136	2958	2822	1923	65.0	357	7857	75.2	480	4.6	10367	99.9	2324
8	29	Kevin Harvick	14.6	11.6	12.1	12.9	175	3276	3101	1547	47.2	269	7362	70.5	256	2.5	10398	91.0	2321
9	14	Tony Stewart	18.3	14.8	13.6	15.4	175	3113	2938	1508	48.4	264	5340	51.1	420	4.0	10195	86.1	2311
10	24	Jeff Gordon	12.9	11.3	14.1	11.4	132	3037	2905	1986	65.4	658	8017	76.8	568	5.4	10006	98.0	2303
11	56	Martin Truex Jr.	12.1	12.6	12.1	12.0	-12	3036	3048	1671	55.0	367	8001	76.6	434	4.2	10100	95.6	2299
12	88	Dale Earnhardt Jr.	15.4	12.1	10.9	11.6	91	3173	3082	1879	59.2	331	7248	73.7	358	3.6	9817	95.9	2245
13	18	Kyle Busch	10.2	12.0	13.3	11.2	105	3023	2918	1993	65.9	635	7642	73.2	1436	13.8	9844	101.5	1133
14	39	Ryan Newman	10.9	15.4	15.0	15.8	-229	2652	2881	1280	48.3	78	5633	53.9	39	.4	9767	82.0	1051
15	99	Carl Edwards	14.5	15.4	15.6	15.5	-58	2835	2893	1443	50.9	225	5865	56.2	254	2.4	9968	84.2	1030
16	27	Paul Menard	16.2	17.8	15.5	17.3	-73	3328	3401	1325	39.8	78	4098	39.2	26	.2	10406	78.0	1006
17	20	Joey Logano	11.9	17.2	17.4	16.7	-171	3023	3194	1267	41.9	149	5165	49.5	190	1.8	10224	79.4	965
18	9	Marcos Ambrose	14.3	17.0	17.9	16.9	-101	3619	3720	1818	50.2	177	4036	38.7	74	.7	10198	79.9	950
19	31	Jeff Burton	23.1	20.6	19.6	19.6	-16	3487	3503	1204	34.5	89	3174	30.4	38	.4	10139	72.3	883
20	43	Aric Almirola	16.2	19.4	20.0	19.1	-214	3603	3817	1559	43.3	132	3681	35.3	78	.7	10045	73.6	868
21	1	Jamie McMurray	21.3	19.9	20.1	19.4	-3	3649	3652	1504	41.2	91	2661	25.5	58	.6	10206	73.0	868
22	42	Juan Pablo Montoya	23.3	20.6	21.7	21.5	-39	3260	3299	988	30.3	98	2324	22.3	22	.2	10079	67.4	810
23	47	Bobby Labonte	26.6	24.6	22.6	24.9	-140	2436	2576	295	12.1	49	987	9.5	1	.0	10071	59.7	772
24	51	Regan Smith	18.2	22.3	22.1	21.8	-124	2664	2788	681	25.6	48	1716	17.9	2	.0	8819	67.1	747
25	78	Kurt Busch	22.2	20.3	23.2	20.9	13	3002	2989	1234	41.1	174	2738	26.6	19	.2	9738	71.0	735
26	55	Mark Martin	9.1	12.4	15.2	11.8	-157	1905	2062	1079	56.6	182	5251	77.1	197	2.9	6590	93.2	701
27	93	Travis Kvapil	36.6	28.0	25.7	28.7	84	2499	2415	275	11.0	46	204	2.0	13	.1	9604	51.0	638
28	34	David Ragan	29.9	29.1	27.0	29.0	-183	2498	2681	409	16.4	42	237	2.3	13	.1	9685	49.2	622
29	13	Casey Mears	26.4	28.0	27.2	27.3	-35	2767	2802	731	26.4	63	523	5.0	41	.4	8616	54.5	612
30	38	David Gilliland	33.8	28.5	27.3	29.0	-120	2355	2475	385	16.3	60	243	2.3	5	.0	9503	49.8	605
31	83	Landon Cassill	29.0	29.5	27.5	28.5	-104	2613	2717	435	16.6	61	226	2.2	5	.0	9593	51.8	598
32	51	AJ Allmendinger	16.3	22.4	22.6	20.0	-31	1803	1834	733	40.7	112	2423	37.5	99	1.5	5816	74.5	453
33	36	Dave Blaney	35.2	32.4	31.8	31.9	-9	2062	2071	394	19.1	40	215	2.1	7	.1	6607	44.9	417
34	10	David Reutimann	31.9	29.2	29.1	28.7	-77	1966	2043	328	16.7	26	137	1.9	0	.0	6132	52.1	373
35	55	Brian Vickers	16.0	14.5	13.3	15.3	11	387	376	179	46.3	99	1791	63.6	158	5.6	2726	89.1	250

Points Pos.	Car No.	Driver	Avg. Start	Avg. Mid Race	Avg. Finish	Avg. Pos.	Pass Diff.	Green Passes	Green Times Passed	Quality Passes	% of Quality Passes	No. of Fastest Laps	Laps in Top 15	% of Laps in Top 15	Laps Led	% of Laps Led	Total Laps	Driver Rating	Pts.
36	30	David Stremme	32.6	34.8	35.6	34.9	-120	1059	1179	186	17.6	53	66	.8	0	.0	3612	37.5	236
37	98	Michael McDowell	29.1	38.1	37.8	37.2	-189	827	1016	61	7.4	14	31	.3	1	.0	3001	36.8	187
38	37	J.J. Yeley	37.2	37.4	37.1	37.5	-5	388	393	4	1.0	4	4	.1	1	.0	3134	33.5	166
39	26	Josh Wise	33.2	39.1	39.1	39.0	-160	314	474	15	4.8	14	6	.1	3	.0	1590	32.0	147
40	32	Ken Schrader	39.5	34.3	32.8	34.6	-65	217	282	0	.0	9	2	.0	0	.0	3660	36.2	146
41	33	Stephen Leicht	39.1	36.3	35.6	36.7	37	172	135	0	.0	13	0	.0	0	.0	2067	32.6	126
42	95	Scott Speed	30.6	37.6	36.7	37.1	27	294	267	16	5.4	16	20	.4	0	.0	1411	37.5	124
43	55	Michael Waltrip	21.8	23.5	20.8	21.3	-22	934	956	540	57.8	16	243	30.0	21	2.6	804	70.9	94
44	32	Terry Labonte	34.0	28.3	20.8	26.8	-39	632	671	51	8.1	21	39	5.2	3	.4	694	55.3	94
45	36	Tony Raines	41.4	35.1	33.9	35.6	-49	171	220	6	3.5	6	17	1.1	0	.0	771	35.5	71
46	23	Scott Riggs	36.6	41.1	41.2	40.8	-136	84	220	0	.0	3	4	.1	0	.0	511	30.9	56
47	33	Brendan Gaughan	33.0	34.8	31.5	33.3	-61	62	123	2	3.2	0	79	6.5	0	.0	1057	42.7	50
48	32	Boris Said	26.5	28.0	27.0	28.3	3	76	73	1	1.3	1	9	.5	0	.0	200	49.2	34
49	50	Bill Elliott	21.0	28.0	37.0	28.0	-27	183	210	55	30.1	2	63	17.8	0	.0	160	51.1	14
50	33	Hermie Sadler	41.0	33.0	31.0	34.0	-14	24	38	0	.0	0	0	.0	0	.0	505	33.8	13
51	32	Mike Olsen	42.0	33.0	33.0	34.2	1	9	8	0	.0	0	0	.0	0	.0	289	34.8	11
52	7	Robby Gordon	30.0	37.3	40.3	37.5	-8	76	84	0	.0	4	1	.2	0	.0	131	35.6	11
53	98	Mike Skinner	40.0	40.8	40.8	40.3	20	28	8	0	.0	0	1	.1	0	.0	82	32.4	10
54	79	Kelly Bires	41.0	41.0	41.0	40.9	4	12	8	0	.0	0	0	.0	0	.0	67	30.6	9
55	10	Tomy Drissi	41.0	37.0	38.0	37.1	2	16	14	0	.0	0	0	.0	0	.0	78	31.6	6
56	74	Stacy Compton	39.0	38.0	39.0	37.8	1	5	4	0	.0	0	1	.6	0	.0	24	35.4	5
57	98	David Mayhew	33.0	40.0	40.0	38.3	0	5	5	0	.0	0	0	.0	0	.0	25	36.5	4
58	30	Patrick Long	43.0	42.0	42.0	42.0	1	1	0	0	.0	0	0	.0	0	.0	2	32.4	2
59	22	Sam Hornish Jr.	16.8	17.0	19.4	17.8	36	1955	1919	805	41.2	74	2304	40.5	16	.3	5448	75.7	0
60	21	Trevor Bayne	17.7	21.7	22.5	22.6	-137	2523	2660	1096	43.4	47	591	14.4	9	.2	3852	64.9	0
61	6	Ricky Stenhouse Jr.	23.5	23.8	26.5	25.3	-18	306	324	37	12.1	7	194	16.1	0	.0	946	62.2	0
62	10	Danica Patrick	36.1	28.3	28.3	30.6	-19	476	495	16	3.4	8	21	.6	0	.0	3115	46.3	0
63	32	Timmy Hill	40.0	35.6	34.2	35.8	-45	158	203	6	3.8	2	2	.1	0	.0	811	34.6	0
64	19	Mike Bliss	35.5	39.6	39.5	39.5	-87	142	229	0	.0	1	3	.1	1	.0	831	32.7	0
65	33	Austin Dillon	22.0	15.0	24.0	21.9	-7	56	63	9	16.1	0	23	11.5	0	.0	198	65.1	0
66	23	Robert Richardson Jr.	41.0	35.5	31.0	31.8	-13	264	277	0	.0	20	0	.0	0	.0	362	39.7	0
67	33	Elliott Sadler	10.0	26.0	27.0	24.1	-29	151	180	45	29.8	0	35	17.3	0	.0	196	53.1	0
68	87	Joe Nemechek	37.0	39.0	39.0	38.8	-84	263	347	1	.4	5	4	.0	0	.0	1507	31.8	0
69	91	Reed Sorenson	38.3	39.7	39.2	39.8	-58	206	264	0	.0	3	0	.0	0	.0	1749	31.1	0
70	32	T.J. Bell	40.6	33.6	31.4	33.9	9	162	153	2	1.2	2	0	.0	0	.0	1468	35.9	0
71	91	Jason Leffler	37.4	38.6	37.8	38.4	4	30	26	0	.0	5	0	.0	0	.0	560	33.3	0
72	32	Jason White	41.0	31.0	31.0	32.6	-2	29	31	0	.0	1	0	.0	0	.0	81	36.8	0
73	33	Cole Whitt	37.4	39.4	39.4	39.6	-24	108	132	18	16.7	0	6	.4	0	.0	183	30.6	0
74	19	Chris Cook	38.5	41.5	41.5	41.2	4	6	2	0	.0	0	0	.0	0	.0	18	30.4	0

2013 NASCAR SPRINT CUP SERIES
SEASON PREVIEW

NASCAR UNVEILS GEN-6 RACE CAR TO KICK OFF THE 2013 SEASON

For the NASCAR Sprint Cup Series, 2013 represents a whole new ballgame, beginning with the race cars themselves. The Chevrolets, Fords and Toyotas the teams off-load from their haulers when Speedweeks and the signature Daytona 500 arrive in mid-February will more closely resemble their highway brethren than the vehicles raced since 2007.

In the 2013 season, NASCAR debuts the sixth generation – in shorthand, Gen-6 – of NASCAR's premier series race car. Teams and manufacturers have put countless hours toward designing and testing the new cars to enhance competition. The new body designs

– the Chevrolet SS, Ford Fusion and Toyota Camry – mark a return to the roots of the sport, where competitors turned street cars into race cars. Each manufacturer will now run unique panels to better represent the cars on the road. The cars feature longer noses and shorter tails to better mimic cars on the street. The driver's last name will appear on the windshield and the sponsor logo on the roof.

"Everything is recognizable, instantly recognizable," said Dale Earnhardt Jr. "You don't have to think about the driver and the team itself to associate with a manufacturer. You look at the car and you can see it instantly. That is a great

Dale Earnhardt Jr. driving the new Gen-6 race car during December testing at Charlotte Motor Speedway.

feeling for me. I can appreciate the cars for that fact."

His crew chief, Steve Letarte, agreed.

"This car is the perfect example of technology helping our sport. I think we now have three makes out here that my little boy at nine years old can tell the difference between the Chevy and the Ford," said Letarte during a recent pre-season test. "I think that is the goal – that anybody can walk through the

Brad Keselowski and Penske Racing look to win consecutive championships in 2013.

parking lot and see a Chevy, a Ford and a Toyota and know that they are different.

"If you're into racing you want to watch cool cars go around the track. I think the simple fact is in 2013 we have cooler cars."

Chances are fans will see it the same way, rekindling an affinity for brand as well as driver – a love affair with a favorite kind of car that fueled the sport's popularity through its formative years. Beauty, however, may prove to be more than skin deep.

The Gen-6 car is designed to rely more on mechanical grip than aero grip – and should provide greater likelihood of side-by-side racing, particularly on intermediate tracks. With weight reduced by 150 pounds from the 2012 models, NASCAR believes lap speeds will be similar to those of previous seasons. The Gen-6 cars are built on an existing chassis that incorporates continually evolving driver safety initiatives. A new roll bar component has been added for 2013.

This year's schedule, featuring racing on short tracks, road courses, intermediate tracks and superspeedways, is virtually identical to those of recent seasons:

- The Sprint Unlimited, with the elite field now comprised of 2012 Coors Light Pole winners and former event winners, opens the year in a non-points format on February 16.
- The 55th annual Daytona 500 follows on February 24, kicking off the regular season of 26 races.
- The non-points NASCAR Sprint All-Star Race will be held May 18 at Charlotte Motor Speedway.
- The 10th Chase for the NASCAR Sprint Cup begins September 15 at Chicagoland Speedway featuring the top 10 in regular season driver points standings – plus two Wild Card qualifiers – through the previous

week's event at Richmond International Raceway.

- The 2013 season ends November 17 at Homestead-Miami Speedway.

Only one driver – Jimmie Johnson – has been able to win consecutive championships since Jeff Gordon in 1997–98. Reigning NASCAR Sprint Cup Series champion Brad Keselowski hopes to join Johnson, who occupied the top spot in the standings five straight seasons from 2006–2010. It won't be easy.

With the Gen-6 car, every team starts from scratch. And for Keselowski and Penske Racing, the No. 2 car that comes to Daytona will be a Ford – not his championship-winning Dodge. The 28-year-old Michigan driver believes his team, which obviously flies under the radar no longer, can repeat if they avoid a post-championship malaise.

"It's really tough for any

championship team to be able to keep all of the people motivated because you've achieved a goal," said Keselowski, a five-time winner in 2012. "I think everybody starts out their career wanting to be a champion and wanting to be the best and that keeps you motivated. But once you get that, it's easy to lose your motivation and we have to find ways to motivate ourselves."

The switch to Ford, which owner Roger Penske campaigned successfully

Jimmie Johnson hopes that 2013 sees him return to championship form in order to capture his sixth NASCAR Sprint Cup Series championship.

for many years, just might be the key to keeping the No. 2 team, led by Paul Wolfe, fired up in the new year.

"It gives us something to prove all over again, that we can continue to be successful no matter what the manufacturer or no matter what the circumstance is and I think that's very healthy," he said.

Keselowski gets a new teammate – Joey Logano – in 2013. Logano, who won't celebrate his 23rd birthday until May 24, spent his entire NASCAR Sprint Cup career of 147 races with Joe Gibbs Racing. He won twice, most recently at Pocono Raceway last June.

Keselowski calls his young protege a superstar in the making that will significantly strengthen Penske Racing.

"I think Joey is an elite talent in this sport and if we can work together we can both be better," he said.

Two-time and reigning Daytona 500 winner Matt Kenseth moves from Roush Fenway Racing, where he won the 2003 NASCAR Sprint Cup title, to the No. 20 JGR Toyota formerly helmed by Logano. Steady defines the Wisconsin native, although the word doesn't do Kenseth justice. Since his debut with Jack Roush in 1999, Kenseth has won 24 times and finished among the top five in the standings on five occasions. He led last year's regular season points seven times and posted three victories including two in the Chase.

Kenseth's presence – and veteran's persona – might be just what Joe Gibbs

Jeff Gordon, whose last title came in 2001, looks to end his championship drought in 2013.

Racing needs to win a fourth NASCAR Sprint Cup championship. Denny Hamlin put a disappointing 2011 season behind him with five victories last season. Kyle Busch, whose only NASCAR victory of 2012 was in Richmond's spring race, figures to recreate the form that produced more than 100 national series wins in just eight seasons.

Nobody does NASCAR Sprint Cup championships better than Hendrick Motorsports – or has more frequent title contenders or race winners. Johnson takes his third crack at championship

No. 6; Gordon his fifth. Both of HMS' other drivers, Earnhardt Jr. and Kasey Kahne, also made last year's Chase and are heavy favorites to again be part of the series' elite 12 when the post season rolls around in September. The quartet combined for 10 wins in 2012 – or more than a quarter of the 36 points-paying races.

Johnson and his No. 48 Chevrolet SS team, led by Chad Knaus, have never missed a Chase – the only driver to qualify in all nine seasons under the format. He's also got at least two victories in each of his 11 seasons as a full-time NASCAR Sprint Cup competitor and 60 overall – second only to Gordon among active drivers. It's no stretch to suggest No. 65 isn't out of the question in 2013.

Gordon has been stuck on four titles

for more than a decade but has finished outside the top 10 just once since 1994. A victory in last year's Homestead-Miami finale – a week after an infamous brawl-igniting crash in Phoenix – suggests there's plenty of wins left in Gordon's tank. He's won 87 times.

Earnhardt erased a four-year winless streak in 2012. That euphoria was tempered by the concussion that cost him two Chase starts. The driver of the No. 88 Chevrolet so far likes the handling characteristics of the Gen-6 car. Perhaps it will better suit Earnhardt's style – like the predecessor of the fifth generation car in which Junior scored 17 victories.

Kahne, the Hendrick newcomer, suffered a rocky start that forced him to qualify for the Chase as a Wild Card. The former open-wheel star more than made

Clint Bowyer wants to improve his second-place 2012 finish and capture his first series championship in 2013.

it up at the end, ranking fourth in points with two victories. With six top-10 finishes during the Chase, Kahne definitely possesses championship potential in 2013.

With a second-place points finish in his first season with Michael Waltrip Racing, what will Clint Bowyer do for an encore? You don't have to think twice to guess Bowyer's answer – and who's to argue? Bowyer keyed MWR's rise to title contention in 2012 and, along with teammate Martin Truex Jr., bids to duplicate the success that previously had

eluded Waltrip's Toyotas. Except for two accidents – Talladega and Phoenix – we might be referring to the Kansan as "reigning champion." Each of his other eight Chase finishes was 10th or better, including a second in the season finale.

Roush Fenway Racing looks for its third NASCAR Sprint Cup title in 2013 missing one of the two drivers – Kenseth – who finished highest in last year's standings. Greg Biffle led the points during the regular season, winning twice at Texas and Michigan. He ranked fifth at season's end.

The mystery of Carl Edwards' fall from championship contention remains largely unsolved despite a variety of personnel tweaks during a winless and Chase-less season. Will it be the Edwards of 2012 or will the driver who

battled Tony Stewart to a points deadlock in 2011 emerge? Time will tell.

Ah, Stewart. Thwarted in his bid for a fourth championship, the owner-driver must rectify the hit-and-miss performance that similarly plagued teammate Ryan Newman, who missed the Chase. Stewart won three times but posted 12 finishes of 20th or worse.

Wholesale changes are in store at Richard Childress Racing where only Kevin Harvick qualified for the Chase and, despite his Phoenix victory in November, considered 2012 a lost year. The bright spot at RCR is the continuing progress of Paul Menard, who posted career bests in overall finish (16th) and top 10s (nine).

There's plenty of room for improvement for other returning drivers and teams. Richard Petty Motorsports again showed flashes of competitiveness – Marcos Ambrose winning at Watkins Glen for a second straight year and Aric Almirola qualifying fifth or better eight times.

Single-car Furniture Row Racing will field Kurt Busch, who joined the team with six races remaining in 2012. The 2004 champion finished the season with back-to-back-to-back top 10s – a first for the Denver-based team.

Earnhardt Ganassi Racing with Felix Sabates likely opens the year with incremental goals. Jamie McMurray and Juan Pablo Montoya, 21st and 22nd in the standings respectively, combined for zero top-five finishes in the past season.

The NASCAR Sprint Cup Series will have a conversation-starting Sunoco Rookie of the Year battle. Two-time

NASCAR Nationwide Series champion Ricky Stenhouse Jr. steps into the No. 17 Roush Fenway Racing Ford vacated by Kenseth. The 25-year-old Olive Branch, MS, competitor was the 2010 NASCAR Nationwide Series' rookie of the year.

Stenhouse's freshman rival is Danica Patrick, the first female competitor projected to run a full NASCAR Sprint Cup Series schedule. Patrick ran the complete NASCAR Nationwide Series campaign in 2012 finishing 10th in points – the highest ever ranking by a female competitor in a NASCAR national series. Patrick, the first female to win a major closed-course race at Motegi, Japan, in the IndyCar Series, became NASCAR's highest finishing driver of her sex with a NASCAR Nationwide Series fourth place at Las Vegas Motor Speedway in 2011. She was the series'

Most Popular Driver in 2012. The 30-year-old native of Roscoe, IL, who currently resides in Phoenix, ran 10 NASCAR Sprint Cup races a year ago, with a best finish of 17th at Phoenix, with her 2013 crew chief Tony Gibson calling the shots. Patrick will team with Stewart and Newman at Stewart-Haas Racing.

Kenseth is the most recent NASCAR Sprint Cup Series rookie of the year (2000) to later win a series championship. Stewart (1999) and Gordon (1993) also won both titles among active competitors.

Danica Patrick begins racing fulltime in the NASCAR Sprint Cup Series in 2013 and hopes to capture Sunoco Rookie of the Year honors, or more.

2013 NASCAR NATIONWIDE SERIES

SEASON

PREVIEW

NEW CARS. NEW TRACK. NEW DRIVER LINEUPS. THAT, IN A NUTSHELL, DESCRIBES THE NASCAR NATIONWIDE SERIES IN 2013, WHICH IS DUE TO CELEBRATE A MILESTONE, 1,000TH RACE IN SEPTEMBER AT RICHMOND INTERNATIONAL RACEWAY.

The 2013 schedule of 33 races begins February 23 at Daytona International Speedway and concludes in Florida at Homestead-Miami Speedway on November 16.

Chevrolet, the defending winner at Daytona, debuts a new model this year – the 2013 Camaro. The reigning Bill France Performance Award winner – manufacturer championship bragging rights – is looking for a signature 375th victory in the season opener, by far the most by any nameplate.

The Camaro is the latest muscle-type model to join the NASCAR Nationwide Series, competing alongside Ford's Mustang. Ford, which enters the season with 196 wins, is likely to reach 200 victories. Camaro vs. Mustang recalls a golden era of racing in the 1960s and 70s and is sure to ramp up fan interest.

Toyota's Camry, however, will not merely be a bystander, having won the owner's championship with Joe Gibbs Racing in 2012 and in four of the past seven seasons.

NASCAR Nationwide teams will visit all of last year's short tracks and speedways plus return to Road America, the popular four-mile, 14-turn road course in Wisconsin, and famed Watkins Glen International in New York alongside the NASCAR Sprint Cup Series in August. This year also marks the second race at the Indianapolis Motor Speedway.

The series makes its first appearance in Ohio on August 17, at the Mid-Ohio Sports Car Course. Mid-Ohio, a 2.4-mile, 15-turn road course in Lexington, sits between Columbus, home of series sponsor Nationwide Insurance, and Cleveland. Mid-Ohio is a historic road course built in 1962 and has hosted most of America's top racing series. Its 2013 schedule includes visits

Trevor Bayne replaces 2012 NASCAR Nationwide Series champion Ricky Stenhouse Jr. in the No. 6 Ford for the 2013 season.

by the Rolex GRAND-AM Road Racing Series as well as the American Le Mans Series, two circuits due to merge under NASCAR's banner in 2014.

Odds favor there being a new NASCAR Nationwide Series champion in 2013. Only one former titlist, Brian Vickers, is expected to compete fulltime this year.

Ricky Stenhouse Jr., back-to-back titleholder in 2011–12, won a promotion to the NASCAR Sprint Cup Series where he'll run for Sunoco Rookie of the Year against former NASCAR Nationwide rival Danica Patrick. Stenhouse joins two former NASCAR Nationwide Series champions, Greg Biffle and Carl Edwards, at Roush Fenway Racing – thus making 2013 a year of opportunity for several dozen championship aspirants.

Chief among them is Trevor Bayne, the 2011 Daytona 500 winner and former Stenhouse teammate at RFR. Bayne, who "inherits" the No. 6 Ford, mounted a championship effort two years ago that was abbreviated by illness. Bayne won once, at Texas Motor Speedway. He'll do double-duty on a partial basis as the NASCAR Sprint Cup driver of the No. 21 Wood Brothers Ford. Roush Fenway Racing is just one stop on the roster of driver movement as the new season unfolds.

Perhaps the greatest change comes at Joe Gibbs Racing, the current owner champion, who brings Vickers back into the series in its Toyotas. Vickers hopped into JGR's No. 20 Toyota in the penultimate race at Phoenix and finished second to then-teammate Joey Logano. Vickers won three times in capturing the 2003 championship while driving for Hendrick Motorsports.

He's not the only newcomer at JGR. Elliott Sadler, who unsuccessfully dueled Stenhouse during the past two seasons, leaves Richard Childress Racing for a

Elliot Sadler put together a great 2012 campaign with Richard Childress Racing, but hopes a switch to Joe Gibbs Racing will help him capture his first championship.

full-time slot in the Gibbs organization. Sadler, a NASCAR Sprint Cup veteran, did everything but win a championship at RCR, finishing second in each of the last two campaigns. Last year's loss was particularly bitter as the Virginian led the standings 25 times over the 33-race season. He won four times in 2012 – his first victories in the series since 1998.

JGR is expected to run a third Toyota shared by its NASCAR Sprint Cup roster of Kyle Busch, Denny Hamlin and newcomer Matt Kenseth. Logano won a series-high nine times in a part-time role in 2012.

RCR boasts one returnee – the owner's grandson, Austin Dillon, the 2012 Sunoco Rookie of the Year – and Brian Scott. A third Camaro will see a rotation of NASCAR Sprint Cup drivers including 2001 NASCAR Nationwide champion Kevin Harvick. Brendan Gaughan, one of RCR's full-time NASCAR Camping World Truck Series drivers, will see action as well. Dillon fell

just short in his bid to become the first to win overall and rookie championships in the same season, ultimately finishing third. With a pair of wins – both at Kentucky – and a series-leading 27 top-10 finishes, the 23-year-old (in April) can't be discounted as a title contender.

Scott compiled a creditable 11 top 10s in JGR equipment in 2012. He posted a pair of top fives – a third at Dover, where he won a NASCAR Camping World Truck race, and fourth at Auto Club Speedway in Southern California.

JR Motorsports with Hendrick Motorsports could be the dark horse championship contender that really wouldn't surprise. Regan Smith becomes the organization's full-time driver – a move that was celebrated by Smith's victory in last year's Homestead finale.

Similarly, 2012's fourth- and fifth-place finishers – Penske Racing's Sam Hornish Jr. and Richard Petty Motorsports' Michael Annett – should contend for victories. Hornish didn't win in 2012 but piled up top-five (10) and top-10 (22) performances and was especially solid after taking over Penske's No. 22 NASCAR Sprint Cup car at mid-season. His No. 12 Ford will be

joined on a limited basis by the No. 22 driven by Logano and reigning NASCAR Sprint Cup and 2010 NASCAR Nationwide Series champion Brad Keselowski among others.

Annett will compete in his fifth full season but his second in Petty's No. 43 Ford. He continues to pursue his first victory.

Kyle Busch Motorsports, which spent its first season with a rotation of drivers including Richmond winner Kurt Busch, expects to have a full-time,

points-eligible campaigner in the seat of its No. 54 Toyota.

Turner Motorsports won three times in 2012 and finished among the top 10 in owner points will likely compete for the championship with multiple Camaro entries.

Austin Dillon won the Sunoco Rookie of the Year Award and came close to being the NASCAR Nationwide Series champion in 2012.

SEASON PREVIEW

ROAD RACING RETURNS. A DIRT RACE AT ONE OF AMERICA'S BEST KNOWN TRACKS. YOUNG GUNS BATTLING SEASONED VETERANS. A CHAMPIONSHIP BATTLE LIKELY AS CLOSE AS A YEAR AGO WHEN FIVE DRIVERS MATHEMATICALLY HAD TITLE HOPES ENTERING THE FINAL RACE. THE NASCAR CAMPING WORLD TRUCK SERIES' 22-RACE 19TH SEASON HAS SOMETHING FOR EVERYONE IN 2013.

Daytona International Speedway hosts the traditional season opener on February 22 with the series due to run its 450th race at Pocono Raceway on August 3. Homestead-Miami Speedway closes the year on November 15.

In between?

Action and plenty of it.

And, for the first time, on an international stage, NASCAR Camping World trucks return to road racing. The last road race was in 2000 at Watkins Glen International. Left- and right-turn competition is restored to the schedule on Labor Day weekend at Canadian Tire Motorsport Park in Bowmanville, Ontario, near Toronto. The 2.459-mile, 10-turn road course has hosted the NASCAR Canadian Tire Series since 2007. The September 1 event will be a learning experience for most competitors. Not for four-time series champion Ron Hornaday Jr., who won road-course events at three circuits in the 1990s: Watkins Glen, Sonoma and Heartland Park Topeka.

You could say trucks, created as on- and off-highway workhorses, will return to their roots on July 24 when the series visits Eldora Speedway in Rossburg, Ohio. The .5-mile dirt track is owned by three-time NASCAR Sprint Cup Series champion Tony Stewart. Sophomore competitor Ty Dillon, a frequent dirt-track racer – and winner – when not in his No. 3 Richard Childress Racing Chevrolet, may well be the driver to beat in the Ohio inaugural.

Stewart's event is one of two Wednesday night affairs joining the popular Bristol Motor Speedway's August 21 mid-week race.

2012 NASCAR Camping World Truck Series' runner-up Timothy Peters looks to capture a championship in 2013.

Youth being served was a key storyline in 2012 when James Buescher became the series' second-youngest champion at age 22 and four of the top five competitors in final standings had yet to celebrate their 25th birthdays.

Drivers could get even younger this season. NASCAR has reduced its minimum age requirement to 16 years for competition on tracks measuring 1.1 miles in length or less and road courses. The previous minimum age was 18. The move is likely to attract rising stars from the NASCAR K&N Pro Series East and West to selected events such as Martinsville, Bristol, Iowa, Phoenix, Eldora, Rockingham and Canadian Tire Motorsports Park.

Buescher is returning to the series in 2013 to defend his championship. His Turner Motorsports Chevrolet team, the reigning owner's champion, will also be in the thick of the action with third-year driver Miguel Paludo and Jeb Burton, son of former Daytona 500 winner Ward Burton.

Steve Turner's organization will make its 200th start at Daytona.

The runner-up in 2012, Timothy Peters, returns with an equally strong Red Horse Racing – a team that won with four different drivers in 2012. Peters is by far the most experienced of last year's championship contenders. He won for the fourth consecutive season and enjoyed a career-high points finish. Peters has finished second, fifth, sixth and eighth in the standings since joining the organization jointly owned by Tom DeLoach and Jeff Hammond.

Red Horse hired Parker Kligerman at mid-season – a move that cemented the Connecticut driver's bid for a top-five championship finish.

Ty Dillon (speaking with grandfather Richard Childress) is looking to turn a 2012 Sunoco Rookie of the Year win into a 2013 championship.

After 13 seasons racing in the NASCAR Camping World Truck Series, Matt Crafton is set to make his 300th start in 2013.

Dillon came within a few laps of becoming the series' first overall champion and Sunoco Rookie of the Year. He settled for a fourth-place finish, his title bid derailed at Homestead by a late accident with NASCAR Next9 competitor and NASCAR K&N Pro Series East champion Kyle Larson. Dillon will attempt to duplicate his older brother Austin Dillon's exploits – a championship in his post-rookie season. He won a single race a year ago.

Larson, who recorded top-10 finishes in three consecutive starts (including second at Phoenix) figures to have some role in the series going forward.

The coming year is one of change at Richard Childress Racing. Former rookie of the year Joey Coulter, who finished third in points and won at Pocono – one of a record nine first-time winners – leaves the organization for Kyle Busch Motorsports.

Dillon will have a veteran teammate in Brendan Gaughan, who's due to make his 200th series start May 17 at Charlotte Motor Speedway. Gaughan's last full season was 2011, when he finished 12th with Germain Racing. He drove RCR trucks and cars in limited roles in all three NASCAR national series a year ago with a best NCWTS finish of second (Chicagoland) among four top-five finishes. Tim George Jr. also will be part of the RCR contingent.

Coulter, meanwhile, has a huge opportunity with the KBM Toyota organization. He is the team's first full-time competitor. KBM fielded multiple drivers in 2012 – Kyle and Kurt Busch among them – with Denny Hamlin winning the fall Martinsville race. Coulter, 22, was both fast and consistent a year ago with a victory among eight top-five and 15 top-10 finishes.

Hornaday hopes to regain his winning ways in 2013. He returns to the No. 9 Chevrolet owned by Joe Denette, who merged his operation with NTS Motorsports and Bob Newberry during the winter. Hornaday, the series' all-time winner (51) will be competing in his 14th full season with contender Brennan Newberry as teammate. NTS also will field a third truck.

Thorsport Racing begins its 18th season in the series returning veterans Matt Crafton and Johnny Sauter. The longtime Chevrolet team switched to Toyota a year ago and didn't hit its stride until after mid-season. Crafton finished sixth in the standings while Sauter, a two-time winner, ranked ninth.

Crafton's 13th season – all consecutive – ranks No. 2 only to Hornaday. He'll make his 300th start on May 31 at Dover International Speedway. His last of two wins came at Iowa in 2011. Sauter, the 2009 rookie of the year, has victories in each of the past four seasons and six overall. He swept both Texas races a year ago.

Ron Hornaday Jr. enters his 14th full-time season in 2013 as the all-time race winner (51) in the NASCAR Camping World Truck Series.

2013 NASCAR HOME TRACKS
SEASON PREVIEW

THE FUTURE OF NASCAR CONTINUES TO TAKE ROOT IN THE NASCAR HOME TRACKS SERIES

THE SOUL OF NASCAR

Covering eight series and encompassing thousands of competitors, NASCAR Home Tracks is also the grassroots foundation and the proving ground for the future stars of NASCAR.

It's where neighborhood racers compete in a street stock that was worked on amongst friends on weeknight gatherings in small garages, and where future NASCAR Sprint Cup Series stars are cutting their teeth before they're old enough to graduate from high school.

From Radford, VA, to Spain, from Las Vegas and Monterrey to Barrie and Stafford, the footprint of the NASCAR Home Tracks stretches across North America and Europe. The variety of vehicles covers just as much ground: From the open-wheel Modifieds of the northeast to stock cars at LeMans, from Late Models on dirt in the Midwest and asphalt in the West and Southeast.

Together, they all have one thing in common: They are NASCAR.

SOLID FOUNDATION: NASCAR WHELEN ALL-AMERICAN SERIES

It all starts in the NASCAR Whelen All-American Series, which is comprised of more than 50 NASCAR-sanctioned short tracks across the United States and Canada.

The tracks come in all shapes and sizes, and races are held on dirt and asphalt, and the drivers range in experience from the novice just learning to race to the long-time veteran whose made a name and carved out a niche on

the local circuit.

Lee Pulliam, the 2012 NASCAR Whelen All-American Series Division I national champion, is the quintessential NASCAR short-track story. He didn't start racing until he was 16, when he and his father went in together on a Limited Sportsman car.

An all-volunteer crew helped power Pulliam to the top of the series, a year after he finished third.

"They stuck with me through the ups and downs, supported me and kept me motivated," said the 24-year-old Semora, NC, driver after collecting 22 wins in the asphalt Late Model divisions at four tracks throughout the southeast. "We couldn't have contended for this championship without every single person on the team. They worked tirelessly. They'd change shocks and springs. They'd do anything I asked on a moment's notice. They deserve this championship."

A national championship is awarded, along with U.S. state and Canadian province championships, rookies of the year and track championships. A driver's best 18 NASCAR results count toward their states and national point totals, and the champions are decided on overall points total.

In the NASCAR Whelen All-American Series, many drivers race as a weekend hobby on their hometown tracks, while others use the series as a spring board to the next rungs of the NASCAR ladder.

Larry Phillips (five) and Philip Morris (four) have won multiple NASCAR national championships, while Nebraska's Joe Kosiski holds the record with 17 track titles.

Greg Biffle, Clint Bowyer, Jeff Burton, Dale Earnhardt Jr., Carl Edwards and Denny Hamlin all began their careers in this series.

In 2011 NASCAR lowered the minimum age to 14 to run in all NASCAR Whelen All-American Series sanctioned track events, further cementing the series' status as the foundation for drivers looking to make their way up the NASCAR ladder. NASCAR also implemented the Finalist Division recognition

program to spotlight the accomplishments of drivers outside of the Division I at their respective tracks.

K&N PRO SERIES PROVIDING THE SPORT'S NEXT STARS
The future of NASCAR was on full display in 2012 as records fell to young drivers in the NASCAR K&N Pro Series.

Dylan Kwasniewski, 17, of Las Vegas, became the youngest champion in the 59-year history of the NASCAR K&N Pro Series West. His title run came a year after he set series marks as the youngest pole winner and race winner.

He was joined as champion by 20-year-old Kyle Larson, an open-wheel prodigy who made a successful transition to stock cars. The Elk Grove, CA, driver delivered the first NASCAR touring series championship to Rev Racing and the NASCAR Drive for Diversity initiative. An Earnhardt Ganassi Racing development driver, Larson nearly scored his first NASCAR Camping World Truck Series victory at Phoenix for Turner Motorsports.

Kwasniewski and Larson were members of the 2012 Next9 class, an industry initiative designed to spotlight the rising stars of the sport in the NASCAR K&N Pro Series. Also included were Corey LaJoie, who scored an East series-high five wins; Chase Elliott, son of NASCAR legend Bill Elliott, who won his first NASCAR race in May and also became the youngest pole winner in East history; and Drive for Diversity graduate Darrell Wallace Jr., who captured a NASCAR Nationwide Series pole at Dover.

The NASCAR K&N Pro Series is the top step of the NASCAR regional touring series ladder and serves as the jumping off point for competitors looking to break through to the three national series.

They run a competitive mixture of short tracks, NASCAR national series companion events and road courses. The race cars are similar to the chassis previously used in the NASCAR Sprint Cup and NASCAR Nationwide Series.

For NASCAR K&N Pro Series teams, new cost-saving technology makes this division a cost-effective driver development program.

An optional "spec" engine was introduced in 2006. It is designed to be powerful and durable, yet is made from a precisely-specified set of components that help to keep engine costs down. A composite body, molded from synthetic materials, is also available as an alternative to expensive sheet metal bodies. These items help teams control costs while providing them the opportunity to advance from their hometown short tracks to the next level.

The minimum age for the touring series is 15, allowing for the NASCAR K&N Pro Series to become a proving ground for drivers signed by NASCAR Sprint Cup Series teams to development deals.

Many of today's top drivers established their careers in the NASCAR K&N Pro Series, including Trevor Bayne, Austin and Ty Dillon, Kevin Harvick, Joey Logano, Martin Truex Jr. and Ryan Truex.

OPEN-WHEEL COMPETITION A FAN FAVORITE
.003 seconds.

That was the margin of victory for Mike Stefanik in the summer NASCAR Whelen Modified Tour race at New Hampshire Motor Speedway. Incredibly, it was the *second* closest finish in series history.

It's this type of close competition that is the hallmark of the NASCAR Modifieds, whose roots stretch back to the very first NASCAR race on Daytona Beach in 1948.

Many of the early NASCAR race cars were "modified" and the division evolved from there. In the 1970s and early 80s, the late Richie Evans of Rome, NY, barnstormed his way to nine NASCAR Modified championships. He was recognized for his historic accomplishments with election into the NASCAR

Hall of Fame in 2012.

The modern version of the NASCAR Whelen Modified Tour was born in 1985 and continues to be one of the most popular forms of racing in the northeast, competing at some of the most historic NASCAR tracks in the region. Today's Modifieds are easily recognizable by their low chassis, wide tires, lack of fenders and their nerf bars.

Doug Coby of Milford, CT, spent the first 10 years of his Modified career bouncing between full-time and part-time rides. He was always competing for wins but until 2012 had come up short. It all came together this past season, as he rolled to five victories and his first NASCAR championship. He became the fifth different tour champion in the last six years.

The NASCAR Whelen Southern Modified Tour competes with the same cars and rules packages as its northeast brethren. The tour races in North Carolina and Virginia, with an annual combination race with the NASCAR

Whelen Modifiied Tour at Bristol Motor Speedway.

George Brunnhoelzl III, a transplanted Long Island-native, has made North Carolina – and the NASCAR Whelen Southern Modified Tour his home. He moved atop the record books in 2012 in the tour with his 17th career victory en route to capturing his third tour championship.

INTERNATIONAL DEVELOPMENT SPURS NASCAR GROWTH

NASCAR's international presence grew in 2012 with the addition of a sanction for the EURO RACECAR, NASCAR Touring Series.

The series joined the NASCAR Canadian Tire Series presented by Mobil 1 and Mexico's NASCAR Toyota Series as the cornerstones of NASCAR's international growth.

D.J. Kennington earned his second NASCAR Canadian Tire Series title in three years, while Jorge Goeters won his

second Mexico championship and first under the NASCAR banner. Both series have been sanctioned by NASCAR since 2007, offering opportunities for Canada's and Mexico's top teams and drivers to showcase their talents in the NASCAR system.

The NASCAR Canadian Tire Series, which features cars similar to those used on the former CASCAR Super Series, operates throughout Canada with a schedule from May to October.

The NASCAR Toyota Series features cars similar to those used in Late Model classes at short tracks in the U.S., with fiberglass composite bodies and spec engines. The EURO RACECAR, NASCAR Touring Series also closely resemble a short-track Late Model.

Spain's Ander Vilarino won the first NASCAR championship in Europe, and American Ben Kennedy – the great-grandson of NASCAR founder Bill France Sr. – made history by winning the first NASCAR oval points race in Tours, France.

2013 NASCAR SPRINT CUP SERIES
POINTS SYSTEM

THE POINTS SYSTEM, REVAMPED PRIOR TO THE 2011 SEASON, MAKES IT EASIER TO TRACK POINTS

The NASCAR Sprint Cup Series has used several points systems since its inception in 1949. NASCAR designed the current system, which has built-in incentives that reward teams for winning and leading laps, prior to the start of the 2011 season. NASCAR implemented a system that distributed points in one-point increments. For example, a race winner would earn 43 points, while the second-place finisher would earn 42 points, the third-place finisher 41 points and so on. NASCAR switched to this simpler scoring model so it would be easier to track and score finishes.

The only way a driver can receive bonus points is to lead a race. One bonus point is awarded to any driver who leads at least one lap. An additional point is awarded to the driver who leads the most laps during each event. The race winner earns an additional three points for winning the event for a maximum 48 points per race if the winner also led the most laps.

Prior to the 2011 season, NASCAR introduced a new rule where each driver has to designate one national series in which he or she will compete for the championship. A driver who chooses to run for the NASCAR Sprint Cup Series championship can still compete in the NASCAR Nationwide or NASCAR Camping World Truck Series, but will receive zero points for their finish, regardless of whether they win or not. For example, in 2012, NASCAR Sprint Cup Series regular Joey Logano competed in 22 NASCAR Nationwide races winning nine of them. Because Logano had selected the NASCAR Sprint Cup Series as his home series, his nine victories in the NASCAR Nationwide Series netted him zero points.

Before the first race of the Chase for the NASCAR Sprint Cup, the top 10 drivers in the points standings and the two Wild-Card qualifiers will have their points reset to 2,000. The drivers in the top 10 will receive an additional three points for each win during the first 26 races of the season. The two Wild-Card drivers will not receive points for any victory during the first 26 races, regardless of how many races they might have won. Points earned during the final 10 races will be accrued the same as if it were one of the first 26 races.

NASCAR Sprint Cup Series points are awarded to the starting driver of each car, regardless of who is driving at the finish. The starting driver must take the green flag and complete at least one lap before turning the car over to a relief driver. Any qualified NASCAR Sprint Cup Series driver may drive in relief. In some cases, a driver without a scheduled ride for a particular race may make practice laps in anticipation of driving in relief for someone during the race. Other times, starters who have fallen out of an event may make themselves available to take over another car if needed.

In cases where two or more drivers have the same number of points at the end of the first 26 races and season, the number of wins during the season is used to break the tie. Successive tiebreakers are the number of second-place finishes, third-place finishes and so on until the tie is broken.

Owner points are distributed in the same manner as driver points except that the owner receives points based on the performance of the car, regardless of who is driving it. For example, the owner of a winning car would receive 43 points for the first-place finish, three points for winning the race and an additional point for leading at least one lap for a total of 47 points. If that particular car happened to lead the most laps during the race, an additional point would be awarded, and the owner would receive 48 points.

Owner points standings are used to determine starting lineups when qualifying is canceled, starting positions when identical qualifying times are posted, preference for provisional starting spots and the distribution of NASCAR plan money.

SPECIAL AWARDS

IN EACH NASCAR SPRINT CUP SERIES RACE, DRIVERS COMPETE FOR PRIZE MONEY AND SPECIAL AWARDS PROVIDED BY MANY CONTINGENCY SPONSORS. THE FOLLOWING IS A SUMMARY OF EACH SPECIAL AWARD FOR THE 2013 SEASON.

3M LAP LEADER

3M Lap Leader award goes to the eligible driver who leads the most laps in an event. In the event of a tie, the highest finishing eligible driver will win the award.
  2012 Winner – Jimmie Johnson

AMERICAN ETHANOL GREEN FLAG RESTART

American Ethanol Green Flag Restart award goes to the eligible driver who records the fastest average speed on restarts during an event and finishes the race on the lead lap. In the event of a tie, the highest finishing eligible driver will win the award.
  2012 Winner – Jimmie Johnson

COORS LIGHT POLE

Coors Light Pole award goes to the driver with the fastest qualifying time eligible to participate under the Manufacturer Prize Money Conditions.
  2012 Winner – Jimmie Johnson

FREESCALE WIDE OPEN

Freescale Wide Open award goes to the eligible driver that is the most aggressive during the final 20% of the race, measured by having the throttle "wide open" the greatest amount of time, who finishes in the Top 5. Points will be awarded on a 5-4-3-2-1 basis, with the winner receiving 5, second place 4, etc.

    2012 Winner – Matt Kenseth

GOODYEAR TIRE & RUBBER COMPANY

Goodyear Tire & Rubber Company Award is presented to the 2013 NASCAR Sprint Cup Series champion.

    2012 Winner – Brad Keselowski

MAHLE CLEVITE ENGINE BUILDER OF THE RACE

MAHLE Clevite Engine Builder of the Race award goes to the eligible engine builder who accumulates the greatest number of MAHLE Clevite points during the Event. Points will be awarded based on qualifying position (1st – 5 points, 2nd – 3 points, 3rd – 1 point) and finishing position (1st – 15 points, 2nd – 14 points, 3rd, 13 points, etc. 15th – 1 point). Bonus points will be awarded to the team that leads the most laps in the Event (5 points). In the event an engine builder prepares engines for more than one team, the points will be accrued by the team and may not be combined. In the event of a tie, the engine builder of the team with the highest finishing position in the Event will receive the award. To be eligible for this award the engine builder's team must run the decal.

    2012 Winner – Shane Parsnow, Hendrick Motorsports No. 48 Team

MECHANIX WEAR MOST VALUABLE PIT CREW

The season is divided into four quarters. Eligible crew chiefs cast a vote each quarter for the pit crew they think has been the most valuable. The four quarterly winners are voted on by eligible crew chiefs at Homestead to determine a year-end winner.

    2012 Winner – Michael Waltrip Racing No. 56 Team

MOBIL 1 DRIVER OF THE RACE

Mobil 1 Driver of the Race award goes to the highest finishing eligible driver.

    2012 Winner – Denny Hamlin

MOOG STEERING & SUSPENSION PROBLEM SOLVER OF THE RACE

Moog Steering & Suspension Problem Solver of the Race award goes to the crew chief that improves the most from the first half of the race to the second half of the race utilizing the 40 best lap times (10 best lap times for road course events).

    2012 Winner – Steve Addington, Crew Chief for Tony Stewart

SUNOCO DIAMOND PERFORMANCE

Sunoco Diamond Performance Award is presented to the 2013 NASCAR Sprint Cup Series champion.

    2012 Winner – Brad Keselowski

SUNOCO ROOKIE OF THE RACE

Sunoco Rookie of the Race award goes to the highest finishing eligible 2013 NASCAR Sprint Cup Series Rookie of the Year Candidate.

    2012 Winner – Stephen Leicht

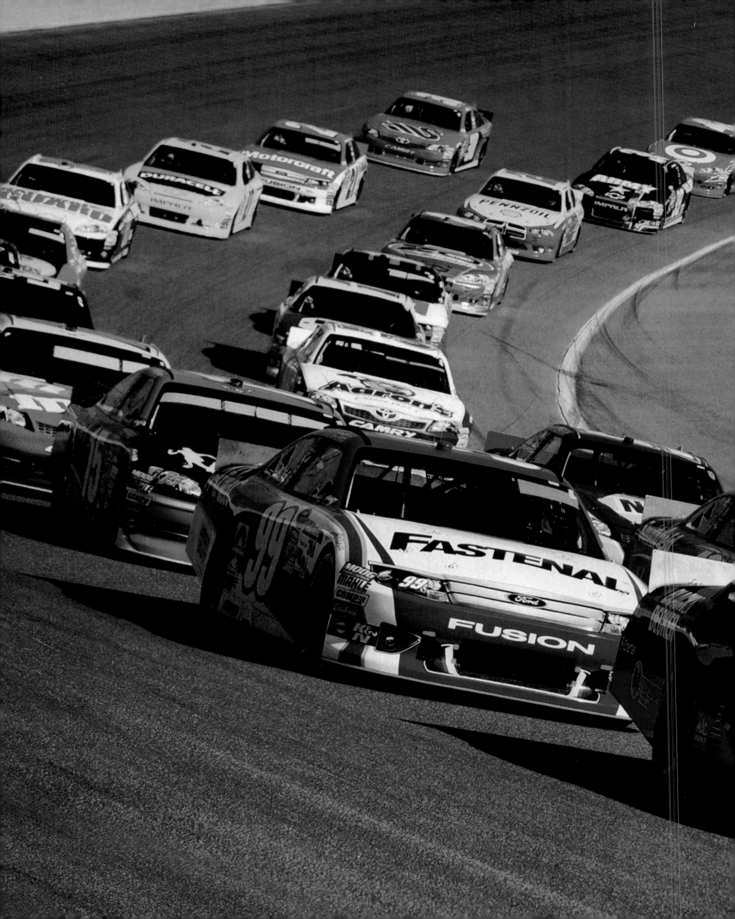

2013 NASCAR SPRINT CUP SERIES
DRIVERS

AJ Allmendinger	52	Denny Hamlin	78	Juan Pablo Montoya	104
Aric Almirola	54	Kevin Harvick	80	Ryan Newman	106
Marcos Ambrose	56	Jimmie Johnson	82	Danica Patrick	108
Greg Biffle	58	Kasey Kahne	84	David Ragan	110
Dave Blaney	60	Matt Kenseth	86	Ricky Stenhouse Jr.	112
Clint Bowyer	62	Brad Keselowski	88	Tony Stewart	114
Jeff Burton	64	Travis Kvapil	90	David Stremme	116
Kurt Busch	66	Bobby Labonte	92	Martin Truex Jr.	118
Kyle Busch	68	Joey Logano	94	J.J Yeley	120
Dale Earnhardt Jr.	70	Mark Martin	96		
Carl Edwards	72	Jamie McMurray	98		
David Gilliland	74	Casey Mears	100		
Jeff Gordon	76	Paul Menard	102		

AJ ALLMENDINGER

AJ ALLMENDINGER NO. 51 PHOENIX RACING CHEVROLET

Birth Date: **December 16, 1981** • Hometown: **Los Gatos, CA** • Twitter: **@AJDinger**

Photo courtesy of AJ Allmendinger; CIA Stock Photography, Inc.

51

Phoenix Racing
Chevrolet

After a rocky 2012 season, AJ Allmendinger is hoping to use 2013 as a springboard to better things. In the first 17 races of 2012 he posted three top-10 finishes with a career-best finish of second in the Goody's Fast Relief 500 at Martinsville Speedway. However, during the July Daytona race weekend, it was announced that Allmendinger had failed a drug test. He was promptly suspended from on-track action until he completed a recovery program and was let go by his team, Penske Racing. Upon completing NASCAR's Road to Recovery program, Allmendinger signed on to drive for Phoenix Racing in four races, never finishing better than 24th.

Allmendinger's best statistical season was 2011; he finished 15th in the final points standings with one top-five and 10 top-10 finishes. He made his first NASCAR Sprint Cup Series start in the March 2007 race at Bristol Motor Speedway for Red Bull Racing. Allmendinger has limited experience in the NASCAR Nationwide and NASCAR Camping World Truck Series with only eight and 13 starts, respectively. In only his second start in the truck series, Allmendinger placed fifth at Talladega. In 2004, he was the first American to win the Autosport International Rookie of the Year. That year he also won the Rookie of the Year Award in the Champ Car World Series. Two years later, he finished third in the series on the strength of five wins and one pole.

Photo not available at press time

NASCAR SPRINT CUP SERIES
CAREER RECORD (Through 2012)

Year	Races	Wins	Top 5	Top 10	Poles	Points Standing
2007	17	0	0	0	0	43rd
2008	27	0	0	2	0	36th
2009	36	0	1	6	0	24th
2010	36	0	2	8	1	19th
2011	36	0	1	10	0	15th
2012	21	0	1	3	1	32nd

Best Race Finish: 2nd (1 time)
Best Points Finish: 15th (2011)

Photo not available at press time

**2013
Car Owner**
James Finch

Photo not available at press time

**2013
Crew Chief**
Nick Harrison

NASCAR SPRINT CUP SERIES 2012 RACE-BY-RACE RESULTS

RACE	EVENT	LOCATION	START	FINISH	PTS.	STATUS	POS.
1	Daytona 500	Daytona	15	34	10	Running	31
2	Subway Fresh Fit 500	Phoenix	15	18	36	Running	26
3	KOBALT Tools 400	Las Vegas	14	37	44	Running	30
4	Food City 500	Bristol	2	17	72	Running	26
5	Auto Club 400	Fontana	25	15	101	Running	26
6	Goody's Fast Relief 500	Martinsville	27	2	143	Running	20
7	Samsung Mobile 500	Texas	12	15	172	Running	19
8	STP 400	Kansas	1	32	185	Running	23
9	Capital City 400 Presented by Virginia Is for Lovers	Richmond	4	16	213	Running	21
10	Aaron's 499	Talladega	2	15	242	Running	20
11	Bojangles' Southern 500	Darlington	16	33	253	Running	22
12	Coca-Cola 600	Charlotte	11	33	264	Running	24
13	FedEx 400 Benefiting Autism Speaks	Dover	23	16	292	Running	23
14	Pocono 400 Presented by #NASCAR	Pocono	19	31	305	Accident	25
15	Quicken Loans 400	Michigan	20	19	330	Running	24
16	Toyota/Save Mart 350	Sonoma	17	9	365	Running	23
17	Quaker State 400	Kentucky	16	9	400	Running	23
18	Coke Zero 400 Powered by Coca-Cola	Daytona	DNE		400		23
19	Lenox Industrial Tools 301	New Hampshire	DNE		400		24
20	Crown Royal Presents the Curtiss Shaver 400 at the Brickyard Powered by Big Machine Records	Indianapolis	DNE		400		25
21	Pennsylvania 400	Pocono	DNE		400		27
22	Finger Lakes 355 at The Glen	Watkins Glen	DNE		400		28
23	Pure Michigan 400	Michigan	DNE		400		29
24	IRWIN Tools Night Race	Bristol	DNE		400		30
25	AdvoCare 500	Atlanta	DNE		400		31
26	Federated Auto Parts 400	Richmond	DNE		400		32
27	GEICO 400	Chicagoland	DNE		400		32
28	SYLVANIA 300	New Hampshire	DNE		400		32
29	AAA 400	Dover	DNE		400		32
30	Good Sam Roadside Assistance 500	Talladega	DNE		400		32
31	Bank of America 500	Charlotte	38	24	420	Running	32
32	Hollywood Casino 400	Kansas	13	35	429	Accident	32
33	TUMS Fast Relief 500	Martinsville	26	28	445	Running	32
34	AAA Texas 500	Texas	26	36	453	Accident	32
35	AdvoCare 500	Phoenix	DNE		453		32
36	Ford EcoBoost 400	Homestead-Miami	DNE		453		32

ARIC ALMIROLA

Birth Date: March 14, 1984 • Hometown: **Tampa, FL** • Twitter: **@Aric_Almirola**

Photos courtesy of Richard Petty Motorsports

43

**Richard Petty
Motorsports Ford**

With a finish of 20th in the final points standings, Aric Almirola had his best year in the NASCAR Sprint Cup Series in 2012. For the first time in his career Almirola raced a complete schedule in the series, posting one top-five finish (a fourth in the October Martinsville race) and four top 10s. He also grabbed the pole (the only one of his NASCAR Sprint Cup career) for the Coca-Cola 600 over Memorial Day Weekend at Charlotte Motor Speedway.

Almirola made his first start in the series in the March 2007 UAW-Daimler Chrysler 400 at Las Vegas Motor Speedway. After starting 31st, he finished 41st. His best points finish prior to 2012 was in 2008 when he finished 42nd, but only competed in 12 of 36 races. In 73 races in the NASCAR Nationwide Series, Almirola has one victory (Milwaukee Mile in 2007). In 2011 he finished fourth overall in the NASCAR Nationwide final standings behind the wheel of the JR Motorsports-owned No. 88 Chevrolet. In the NASCAR Camping World Truck Series, Almirola captured two checkered flags (Dover and Michigan) during the 2010 season and finished runner-up to Todd Bodine in the championship standings. He debuted as a member of Joe Gibbs Racing's diversity program in 2004, racing late models at Ace Speedway in Altamahaw, NC. Almirola won rookie of the year titles in two modified divisions in 2000 – Florida Modified and the Southern Automobile Racing Association. He began racing go-karts at the age of eight.

NASCAR SPRINT CUP SERIES
CAREER RECORD (Through 2012)

Year	Races	Wins	Top 5	Top 10	Poles	Points Standing
2007	6	0	0	0	0	52nd
2008	12	0	0	1	0	42nd
2009	8	0	0	0	0	46th
2010	9	0	1	1	0	48th
2012	36	0	1	4	1	20th

Best Race Finish: 4th (2 times)
Best Points Finish: 20th (2012)

**2013
Car Owner
Richard
Petty**

**2013
Crew Chief
Todd Parrott**

NASCAR SPRINT CUP SERIES 2012 RACE-BY-RACE RESULTS

RACE	EVENT	LOCATION	START	FINISH	PTS.	STATUS	POS.
1	Daytona 500	Daytona	27	33	11	Accident	30
2	Subway Fresh Fit 500	Phoenix	18	12	43	Running	21
3	KOBALT Tools 400	Las Vegas	27	24	63	Running	23
4	Food City 500	Bristol	7	19	88	Running	22
5	Auto Club 400	Fontana	28	25	107	Running	21
6	Goody's Fast Relief 500	Martinsville	19	8	144	Running	19
7	Samsung Mobile 500	Texas	23	22	166	Running	22
8	STP 400	Kansas	26	23	187	Running	20
9	Capital City 400 Presented by Virginia Is for Lovers	Richmond	11	26	205	Running	24
10	Aaron's 499	Talladega	4	12	237	Running	22
11	Bojangles' Southern 500	Darlington	13	19	262	Running	21
12	Coca-Cola 600	Charlotte	1	16	291	Running	19
13	FedEx 400 Benefiting Autism Speaks	Dover	12	6	329	Running	17
14	Pocono 400 Presented by #NASCAR	Pocono	29	28	345	Running	20
15	Quicken Loans 400	Michigan	15	17	372	Running	22
16	Toyota/Save Mart 350	Sonoma	30	28	388	Running	21
17	Quaker State 400	Kentucky	13	26	406	Running	22
18	Coke Zero 400 Powered by Coca-Cola	Daytona	17	19	431	Running	22
19	Lenox Industrial Tools 301	New Hampshire	23	28	447	Running	22
20	Crown Royal Presents the Curtiss Shaver 400 at the Brickyard Powered by Big Machine Records	Indianapolis	4	19	472	Running	22
21	Pennsylvania 400	Pocono	13	18	498	Running	22
22	Finger Lakes 355 at The Glen	Watkins Glen	29	18	524	Running	21
23	Pure Michigan 400	Michigan	41	20	548	Running	21
24	IRWIN Tools Night Race	Bristol	5	35	557	Accident	22
25	AdvoCare 500	Atlanta	13	32	569	Running	22
26	Federated Auto Parts 400	Richmond	18	26	587	Running	22
27	GEICO 400	Chicagoland	2	17	615	Running	22
28	SYLVANIA 300	New Hampshire	19	23	636	Running	22
29	AAA 400	Dover	21	19	661	Running	22
30	Good Sam Roadside Assistance 500	Talladega	18	19	686	Running	21
31	Bank of America 500	Charlotte	17	12	718	Running	21
32	Hollywood Casino 400	Kansas	5	29	734	Accident	21
33	TUMS Fast Relief 500	Martinsville	10	4	774	Running	21
34	AAA Texas 500	Texas	14	15	803	Running	21
35	AdvoCare 500	Phoenix	5	16	831	Running	21
36	Ford EcoBoost 400	Homestead-Miami	5	7	868	Running	20

MARCOS AMBROSE

Birth Date: **September 1, 1976** • Hometown: **Launceston, Tasmania, Australia** • Twitter: **@MarcosAmbrose**

Photos courtesy of Richard Petty Motorsports

Stanley Ford

Marcos Ambrose tied his career-best final points standings finish in the NASCAR Sprint Cup Series with an 18th-place finish in 2012, matching his performance in 2009. For the second year in a row, Ambrose showcased his road-course talents by winning the mid-August race at Watkins Glen International in upstate New York. In the 2011 event, the Australian driver was ahead of Brad Keselowski when the Heluva Good! Sour Cream Dips at The Glen ended under caution. In 2012 Ambrose was again out in front of Brad Keselowski to win the Finger Lakes 355 at The Glen by 0.571 seconds. He posted career highs in average starting position (14.3) and average finishing position (17.9) while finishing on the lead lap in 18 of the 36 races in 2012. Ambrose also captured his first two Coors Light Pole Awards in the premier series. The Richard Petty Motorsports driver will return in 2013 in the No. 9 Ford.

Ambrose made his first start behind the wheel of the famed Wood Brothers Racing No. 21 Ford in the 2008 Sonoma race where he started seventh but finished second-to-last due to transmission problems. In 75 starts in the NASCAR Nationwide Series, Ambrose has four victories, three of them coming at Watkins Glen in back-to-back-to-back seasons (2008–2010). His last NASCAR Nationwide victory came in 2011 at Montreal's Circuit Gilles Villeneuve. He also appeared in 22 NASCAR Camping World Truck Series races. Prior to winning 27 races and consecutive titles (2003–2004) in V8 Supercar, Ambrose won four Tasmanian Junior karting titles.

NASCAR SPRINT CUP SERIES
CAREER RECORD (Through 2012)

Year	Races	Wins	Top 5	Top 10	Poles	Points Standing
2008	11	0	1	1	0	45th
2009	36	0	4	7	0	18th
2010	36	0	2	5	0	26th
2011	36	1	5	12	0	19th
2012	36	1	3	8	2	18th

Best Race Finish: 1st (2 times)
Best Points Finish: 18th (2009, 2012)

**2013
Car Owner
Richard
Petty**

**2013
Crew Chief
Drew
Blickensderfer**

NASCAR SPRINT CUP SERIES 2012 RACE-BY-RACE RESULTS

RACE	EVENT	LOCATION	START	FINISH	PTS.	STATUS	POS.
1	Daytona 500	Daytona	7	13	31	Running	13
2	Subway Fresh Fit 500	Phoenix	14	32	43	Engine	22
3	KOBALT Tools 400	Las Vegas	15	13	74	Running	19
4	Food City 500	Bristol	12	36	82	Running	24
5	Auto Club 400	Fontana	29	21	105	Running	24
6	Goody's Fast Relief 500	Martinsville	12	15	134	Running	23
7	Samsung Mobile 500	Texas	7	20	159	Running	24
8	STP 400	Kansas	28	16	187	Running	21
9	Capital City 400 Presented by Virginia Is for Lovers	Richmond	14	22	209	Running	22
10	Aaron's 499	Talladega	3	14	239	Running	21
11	Bojangles' Southern 500	Darlington	28	9	274	Running	18
12	Coca-Cola 600	Charlotte	2	32	287	Running	20
13	FedEx 400 Benefiting Autism Speaks	Dover	21	10	321	Running	19
14	Pocono 400 Presented by #NASCAR	Pocono	9	13	352	Running	17
15	Quicken Loans 400	Michigan	1	9	388	Running	17
16	Toyota/Save Mart 350	Sonoma	1	8	425	Running	16
17	Quaker State 400	Kentucky	12	13	456	Running	17
18	Coke Zero 400 Powered by Coca-Cola	Daytona	10	30	470	Accident	19
19	Lenox Industrial Tools 301	New Hampshire	20	19	495	Running	18
20	Crown Royal Presents the Curtiss Shaver 400 at the Brickyard Powered by Big Machine Records	Indianapolis	23	20	519	Running	18
21	Pennsylvania 400	Pocono	5	10	553	Running	18
22	Finger Lakes 355 at The Glen	Watkins Glen	5	1	600	Running	17
23	Pure Michigan 400	Michigan	8	5	639	Running	17
24	IRWIN Tools Night Race	Bristol	9	5	679	Running	16
25	AdvoCare 500	Atlanta	10	17	706	Running	16
26	Federated Auto Parts 400	Richmond	22	15	735	Running	15
27	GEICO 400	Chicagoland	17	27	752	Running	17
28	SYLVANIA 300	New Hampshire	21	24	772	Running	17
29	AAA 400	Dover	27	18	798	Running	17
30	Good Sam Roadside Assistance 500	Talladega	20	27	816	Accident	17
31	Bank of America 500	Charlotte	18	33	828	Running	18
32	Hollywood Casino 400	Kansas	18	12	860	Running	17
33	TUMS Fast Relief 500	Martinsville	33	24	880	Running	18
34	AAA Texas 500	Texas	15	32	893	Accident	18
35	AdvoCare 500	Phoenix	17	18	918	Running	18
36	Ford EcoBoost 400	Homestead-Miami	2	13	950	Running	18

GREG BIFFLE

Birth Date: December 23, 1969 • Hometown: **Vancouver, WA** • Twitter: **@gbiffle**

Photos courtesy of Roush Fenway Racing

16

3M Ford

In 2013 Greg Biffle will once again be behind the wheel of the No. 16 Ford for Roush Fenway Racing. In 2012 he was running at the end of all 36 races (for the first time in his career) and finished on the lead lap in 32 of them. Biffle finished fifth in the final points standings after leading the standings for several weeks early in the season. He had career bests in average starting position (9.9) and average finishing position (10.2), and tied his career best in poles (three) and top-10 finishes (21). His two victories (Texas in April and Michigan in August) give him a total of 18 victories in the series, which leaves him tied for 43rd in career wins with three other drivers. His best finish in the premier series was in 2005 when he finished second to Tony Stewart on the strength of six wins and 15 top fives, both career highs.

Biffle has excelled at every level of NASCAR's national series and is one of only two drivers to win both the NASCAR Nationwide (2002) and NASCAR Camping World Truck Series (2000) championships. He was also named the Rookie of the Year for both series – in 1998 and 2001. His 20 wins in NASCAR Nationwide and 16 wins in the truck series give him 54 combined national series wins, good for 16th on the all-time combined wins list, tied with Lee Petty. From 1994–97 Biffle competed in the NASCAR Whelen All-American Series, earning late-model track championships at Tri City Raceway (WA) and Portland (OR) Speedway.

NASCAR SPRINT CUP SERIES
CAREER RECORD (Through 2012)

Year	Races	Wins	Top 5	Top 10	Poles	Points Standing
2002	7	0	0	0	0	48th
2003	35	1	3	6	0	20th
2004	36	2	4	8	1	17th
2005	36	6	15	21	0	2nd
2006	36	2	8	15	2	13th
2007	36	1	5	11	1	14th
2008	36	2	12	17	2	3rd
2009	36	0	10	16	0	7th
2010	36	2	9	19	0	6th
2011	36	0	3	10	3	16th
2012	36	2	12	21	3	5th

Best Race Finish: 1st (18 times)
Best Points Finish: 2nd (2005)

2013 Car Owner
Jack Roush, John Henry

2013 Crew Chief
Matt Puccia

NASCAR SPRINT CUP SERIES 2012 RACE-BY-RACE RESULTS

RACE	EVENT	LOCATION	START	FINISH	PTS.	STATUS	POS.
1	Daytona 500	Daytona	2	3	42	Running	3
2	Subway Fresh Fit 500	Phoenix	7	3	83	Running	2
3	KOBALT Tools 400	Las Vegas	9	3	125	Running	1
4	Food City 500	Bristol	1	13	157	Running	1
5	Auto Club 400	Fontana	4	6	195	Running	1
6	Goody's Fast Relief 500	Martinsville	26	13	226	Running	1
7	Samsung Mobile 500	Texas	3	1	273	Running	1
8	STP 400	Kansas	17	5	312	Running	1
9	Capital City 400 Presented by Virginia Is for Lovers	Richmond	28	18	338	Running	1
10	Aaron's 499	Talladega	6	5	378	Running	1
11	Bojangles' Southern 500	Darlington	1	12	411	Running	1
12	Coca-Cola 600	Charlotte	4	4	453	Running	1
13	FedEx 400 Benefiting Autism Speaks	Dover	7	11	486	Running	1
14	Pocono 400 Presented by #NASCAR	Pocono	13	24	507	Running	3
15	Quicken Loans 400	Michigan	3	4	548	Running	3
16	Toyota/Save Mart 350	Sonoma	4	7	585	Running	2
17	Quaker State 400	Kentucky	11	21	608	Running	4
18	Coke Zero 400 Powered by Coca-Cola	Daytona	4	21	632	Running	3
19	Lenox Industrial Tools 301	New Hampshire	11	9	667	Running	3
20	Crown Royal Presents the Curtiss Shaver 400 at the Brickyard Powered by Big Machine Records	Indianapolis	5	3	709	Running	3
21	Pennsylvania 400	Pocono	12	15	738	Running	3
22	Finger Lakes 355 at The Glen	Watkins Glen	15	6	776	Running	2
23	Pure Michigan 400	Michigan	13	1	823	Running	1
24	IRWIN Tools Night Race	Bristol	3	19	849	Running	1
25	AdvoCare 500	Atlanta	2	15	879	Running	1
26	Federated Auto Parts 400	Richmond	23	9	2006	Running	5
27	GEICO 400	Chicagoland	22	13	2037	Running	8
28	SYLVANIA 300	New Hampshire	13	18	2063	Running	9
29	AAA 400	Dover	6	16	2091	Running	11
30	Good Sam Roadside Assistance 500	Talladega	5	6	2130	Running	9
31	Bank of America 500	Charlotte	1	4	2171	Running	6
32	Hollywood Casino 400	Kansas	11	27	2188	Running	11
33	TUMS Fast Relief 500	Martinsville	30	10	2222	Running	9
34	AAA Texas 500	Texas	2	10	2256	Running	9
35	AdvoCare 500	Phoenix	20	7	2293	Running	7
36	Ford EcoBoost 400	Homestead-Miami	13	5	2332	Running	5

DAVE BLANEY

Birth Date: **October 24, 1962** • Hometown: **Hartford, OH** • Twitter: **@Dave_Blaney**

Photo courtesy of Tommy Baldwin Racing

7

Accell/SealWrap Chevrolet

Dave Blaney only led seven laps during the 2012 season; however, six of them came during the Daytona 500. Matter of fact, he was leading the race under caution when Juan Pablo Montoya infamously crashed into the jet dryer circling the track and caused the race to be red flagged on lap 161. Four laps after the race was restarted, Blaney gave up the lead to eventual race winner Matt Kenseth. The only other lap Blaney led in 2012 came in June's Michigan race. He finished on the lead lap just three times and was 33rd in the final points standings in 2012.

Blaney's first race in the NASCAR Sprint Cup Series came in 1992 at Rockingham Speedway (NC) in the No. 80 Pontiac owned by Stan Hover. After placing 31st in the race, it would be seven years before he entered another NASCAR premier series race – piloting the Bill Davis Racing No. 93 Pontiac at Michigan in 1999. As of the end of the 2012 season, Blaney had racked up 431 starts with no visits to Victory Lane.

In 1999 he finished seventh in the NASCAR Nationwide Series standings, posting five top fives, 12 top 10s and four poles in 31 starts. He scored his only national series win in NASCAR Nationwide in 2006. After winning the 1995 World of Outlaws championship and being named the Sprint Car Driver of the Year, Blaney finished runner-up on the circuit the following two years. Before that, Blaney won the Eastern World Sprint Car championship in 1988.

Photo not available at press time

NASCAR SPRINT CUP SERIES
CAREER RECORD (Through 2012)

Year	Races	Wins	Top 5	Top 10	Poles	Points Standing
1992	1	0	0	0	0	80th
1999	5	0	0	0	0	51st
2000	33	0	0	2	0	31st
2001	36	0	0	6	0	22nd
2002	36	0	0	5	0	19th
2003	36	0	1	4	1	28th
2004	16	0	0	0	0	38th
2005	36	0	0	2	0	26th
2006	36	0	1	2	0	26th
2007	33	0	1	4	1	31st
2008	35	0	0	2	0	30th
2009	30	0	0	0	0	41st
2010	29	0	0	0	0	37th
2011	35	0	1	1	0	32nd
2012	34	0	0	0	0	33rd

Best RAce Finish: 3rd (3 times)
Best Points Finish: 19th (2002)

2013 Car Owner
Tommy Baldwin

2013 Crew Chief
Tommy Baldwin

NASCAR SPRINT CUP SERIES 2012 RACE-BY-RACE RESULTS

RACE	EVENT	LOCATION	START	FINISH	PTS.	STATUS	POS.
1	Daytona 500	Daytona	24	15	30	Running	15
2	Subway Fresh Fit 500	Phoenix	23	23	51	Running	16
3	KOBALT Tools 400	Las Vegas	38	29	66	Running	21
4	Food City 500	Bristol	35	34	76	Running	25
5	Auto Club 400	Fontana	34	33	87	Running	28
6	Goody's Fast Relief 500	Martinsville	42	34	97	Brakes	29
7	Samsung Mobile 500	Texas	41	37	104	Vibration	32
8	STP 400	Kansas	33	37	111	Vibration	32
9	Capital City 400 Presented by Virginia Is for Lovers	Richmond	17	29	126	Running	32
10	Aaron's 499	Talladega	38	30	140	Accident	33
11	Bojangles' Southern 500	Darlington	34	27	157	Running	32
12	Coca-Cola 600	Charlotte	36	40	161	Engine	34
13	FedEx 400 Benefiting Autism Speaks	Dover	41	32	173	Accident	34
14	Pocono 400 Presented by #NASCAR	Pocono	42	25	192	Running	33
15	Quicken Loans 400	Michigan	36	25	212	Running	34
16	Toyota/Save Mart 350	Sonoma	32	37	219	Suspension	33
17	Quaker State 400	Kentucky	42	35	228	Engine	34
18	Coke Zero 400 Powered by Coca-Cola	Daytona	33	22	250	Running	34
19	Lenox Industrial Tools 301	New Hampshire	35	39	255	Brakes	34
20	Crown Royal Presents the Curtiss Shaver 400 at the Brickyard Powered by Big Machine Records	Indianapolis	32	23	276	Running	34
21	Pennsylvania 400	Pocono	DNE		276		34
22	Finger Lakes 355 at The Glen	Watkins Glen	31	36	284	Suspension	34
23	Pure Michigan 400	Michigan	42	38	290	Vibration	34
24	IRWIN Tools Night Race	Bristol	25	26	308	Accident	34
25	AdvoCare 500	Atlanta	22	25	327	Running	33
26	Federated Auto Parts 400	Richmond	33	33	338	Running	33
27	GEICO 400	Chicagoland	42	33	349	Engine	33
28	SYLVANIA 300	New Hampshire	DNE		349		33
29	AAA 400	Dover	43	41	352	Overheating	33
30	Good Sam Roadside Assistance 500	Talladega	39	29	367	Accident	33
31	Bank of America 500	Charlotte	42	43	368	Transmission	33
32	Hollywood Casino 400	Kansas	41	39	373	Brakes	33
33	TUMS Fast Relief 500	Martinsville	37	35	382	Brakes	33
34	AAA Texas 500	Texas	40	39	387	Brakes	33
35	AdvoCare 500	Phoenix	42	26	405	Running	33
36	Ford EcoBoost 400	Homestead-Miami	31	32	417	Running	33

CLINT BOWYER

Birth Date: May 30, 1979 • Hometown: **Emporia, KS** • Twitter: **@ClintBowyer**

Photo courtesy of Michael Waltrip Racing

15

Five-Hour Energy Toyota

Everything could have turned out differently for Clint Bowyer if he had decided not take a strange phone call in 2003 that ultimately changed his life. Bowyer was at work at a car dealer's body shop in his hometown of Emporia, KS, when the legendary car owner Richard Childress called. The driver, thinking it was a joke, almost didn't take the call. It turned out that Childress had seen Bowyer compete in an ARCA race in Nashville and wanted him as a driver.

Bowyer made his first start for Childress in 2005, placing 22nd at Phoenix. However, after six full seasons with Richard Childress Racing, during which he scored five victories, in 2012 Bowyer raced for Michael Waltrip Racing – a season in which he posted career bests in points finish (second), wins (three), top fives (10), top 10s (23), average starting position (12.8) and average finishing position (10.9). Heading into the season finale at Homestead, Bowyer sat fourth in the points standings, 52 points outside of first. However, after finishing second in the final race, Bowyer jumped Jimmie Johnson and Kasey Kahne to finish second in the final standings. His three victories in 2012 came at Sonoma, Richmond (September race) and Charlotte (October race).

In 2008, Bowyer won the NASCAR Nationwide Series championship after winning one race and posting 14 top fives and 29 top 10s (both career highs in the series for Bowyer). He has eight wins in the NASCAR Nationwide and three wins in the NASCAR Camping World Truck Series.

Photo courtesy of NASCAR The Game. www.NASCARTheGame.com

NASCAR SPRINT CUP SERIES
CAREER RECORD (Through 2012)

Year	Races	Wins	Top 5	Top 10	Poles	Points Standing
2005	1	0	0	0	0	69th
2006	36	0	4	11	0	17th
2007	36	1	5	17	2	3rd
2008	36	1	7	17	0	5th
2009	36	0	4	16	0	15th
2010	36	2	7	18	0	10th
2011	36	1	4	16	0	13th
2012	36	3	10	23	0	2nd

Best Race Finish: 1st (8 times)
Best Points Finish: 2nd (2012)

2013
Car Owner
Michael Waltrip, Rob Kauffman

2013
Crew Chief
Brian Pattie

NASCAR SPRINT CUP SERIES 2012 RACE-BY-RACE RESULTS

RACE	EVENT	LOCATION	START	FINISH	PTS.	STATUS	POS.
1	Daytona 500	Daytona	30	11	33	Running	11
2	Subway Fresh Fit 500	Phoenix	16	30	47	Running	17
3	KOBALT Tools 400	Las Vegas	5	6	86	Running	15
4	Food City 500	Bristol	16	4	126	Running	8
5	Auto Club 400	Fontana	11	13	157	Running	8
6	Goody's Fast Relief 500	Martinsville	4	10	192	Running	9
7	Samsung Mobile 500	Texas	18	17	219	Running	10
8	STP 400	Kansas	8	36	227	Engine	11
9	Capital City 400 Presented by Virginia Is for Lovers	Richmond	23	7	264	Running	12
10	Aaron's 499	Talladega	24	6	302	Running	10
11	Bojangles' Southern 500	Darlington	26	11	335	Running	11
12	Coca-Cola 600	Charlotte	5	13	366	Running	12
13	FedEx 400 Benefiting Autism Speaks	Dover	4	5	405	Running	10
14	Pocono 400 Presented by #NASCAR	Pocono	16	6	443	Running	9
15	Quicken Loans 400	Michigan	13	7	481	Running	9
16	Toyota/Save Mart 350	Sonoma	6	1	529	Running	7
17	Quaker State 400	Kentucky	6	16	557	Running	7
18	Coke Zero 400 Powered by Coca-Cola	Daytona	29	29	572	Accident	10
19	Lenox Industrial Tools 301	New Hampshire	5	3	614	Running	9
20	Crown Royal Presents the Curtiss Shaver 400 at the Brickyard Powered by Big Machine Records	Indianapolis	33	15	643	Running	10
21	Pennsylvania 400	Pocono	19	8	679	Running	10
22	Finger Lakes 355 at The Glen	Watkins Glen	8	4	719	Running	7
23	Pure Michigan 400	Michigan	12	7	757	Running	7
24	IRWIN Tools Night Race	Bristol	23	7	794	Running	6
25	AdvoCare 500	Atlanta	30	27	811	Running	8
26	Federated Auto Parts 400	Richmond	4	1	2006	Running	6
27	GEICO 400	Chicagoland	9	10	2041	Running	6
28	SYLVANIA 300	New Hampshire	12	4	2081	Running	6
29	AAA 400	Dover	2	9	2117	Running	4
30	Good Sam Roadside Assistance 500	Talladega	3	23	2139	Accident	5
31	Bank of America 500	Charlotte	4	1	2186	Running	4
32	Hollywood Casino 400	Kansas	3	6	2225	Running	4
33	TUMS Fast Relief 500	Martinsville	8	5	2265	Running	3
34	AAA Texas 500	Texas	4	6	2303	Running	3
35	AdvoCare 500	Phoenix	16	28	2319	Accident	4
36	Ford EcoBoost 400	Homestead-Miami	6	2	2361	Running	2

JEFF BURTON

Birth Date: **June 29, 1967** • Hometown: **South Boston, VA** • Twitter: **@RCR31JeffBurton**

Photo courtesy of Richard Childress Racing

31

Caterpillar/Cheerios Chevrolet

After 21 wins and 20 years in NASCAR's premier series, Jeff Burton has the experience and know-how to break his 149-race winless streak in 2013. His last victory came in Charlotte at the sixth-to-last race of 2008. Hopefully, a win in the upcoming season would launch him into the 2013 10-race Chase for the NASCAR Sprint Cup. Burton missed the post season in both of the last two years finishing 19th in 2012 and 20th in 2011. His best performance in 2012 was in the July Daytona race where he finished second to Tony Stewart. At the helm of the Richard Childress Racing No. 31 Chevrolet, Jeff Burton grabbed two top-five and six top-10 finishes. Burton came to RCR in the middle of the 2004 season from Jack Roush's outfit. His best season (1999) in the NASCAR Sprint Cup Series came in his fourth season with Roush. In 1999, Burton posted six wins, 18 top fives and 23 top 10s, and finished fifth in the final points standings. The next year Burton posted his best points finish – third.

His series debut came at New Hampshire in his only start of 1993, where he finished 37th after qualifying sixth. In 2007 Burton won five of 19 NASCAR Nationwide Series starts with 17 top-10 finishes as he and teammate Scott Wimmer won the series' owners' championship for Richard Childress Racing. In 306 NASCAR Nationwide starts, Burton has 27 wins. In 1998 Burton won seven NASCAR weekly series races at South Boston (VA) Speedway and was voted the track's most popular driver.

Photo courtesy of NASCAR The Game. www.NASCARTheGame.com

NASCAR SPRINT CUP SERIES
CAREER RECORD (Through 2012)

Year	Races	Wins	Top 5	Top 10	Poles	Points Standing
1993	1	0	0	0	0	83rd
1994	30	0	2	3	0	24th
1995	29	0	1	2	0	32nd
1996	30	0	6	12	1	13th
1997	32	3	13	18	0	4th
1998	33	2	18	23	0	5th
1999	34	6	18	23	0	5th
2000	34	4	15	22	1	3rd
2001	36	2	8	16	0	10th
2002	36	0	5	14	0	12th
2003	36	0	3	11	0	12th
2004	36	0	2	6	0	18th
2005	36	0	3	6	0	18th
2006	36	1	7	20	4	7th
2007	36	1	9	18	0	8th
2008	36	2	7	18	0	6th
2009	36	0	5	10	0	17th
2010	36	0	6	15	0	12th
2011	36	0	2	5	0	20th
2012	36	0	2	6	0	19th

Best Race Finish: 1st (21 times)
Best Points Finish: 3rd (2000)

2013 Car Owner
Richard Childress

2013 Crew Chief
Luke Lambert

NASCAR SPRINT CUP SERIES 2012 RACE-BY-RACE RESULTS

RACE	EVENT	LOCATION	START	FINISH	PTS.	STATUS	POS.
1	Daytona 500	Daytona	9	5	40	Running	5
2	Subway Fresh Fit 500	Phoenix	11	33	52	Engine	13
3	KOBALT Tools 400	Las Vegas	22	14	82	Running	16
4	Food City 500	Bristol	33	6	120	Running	12
5	Auto Club 400	Fontana	19	22	142	Running	15
6	Goody's Fast Relief 500	Martinsville	18	22	164	Running	15
7	Samsung Mobile 500	Texas	24	29	179	Running	16
8	STP 400	Kansas	12	22	201	Running	17
9	Capital City 400 Presented by Virginia Is for Lovers	Richmond	30	31	214	Running	20
10	Aaron's 499	Talladega	29	10	249	Running	18
11	Bojangles' Southern 500	Darlington	10	18	275	Running	17
12	Coca-Cola 600	Charlotte	22	19	300	Running	17
13	FedEx 400 Benefiting Autism Speaks	Dover	15	22	322	Engine	18
14	Pocono 400 Presented by #NASCAR	Pocono	20	15	351	Running	18
15	Quicken Loans 400	Michigan	33	21	375	Running	21
16	Toyota/Save Mart 350	Sonoma	35	11	408	Running	19
17	Quaker State 400	Kentucky	29	24	428	Running	20
18	Coke Zero 400 Powered by Coca-Cola	Daytona	20	2	470	Running	18
19	Lenox Industrial Tools 301	New Hampshire	25	21	493	Running	19
20	Crown Royal Presents the Curtiss Shaver 400 at the Brickyard Powered by Big Machine Records	Indianapolis	21	32	505	Running	20
21	Pennsylvania 400	Pocono	23	22	527	Running	20
22	Finger Lakes 355 at The Glen	Watkins Glen	28	30	541	Running	19
23	Pure Michigan 400	Michigan	32	19	566	Running	20
24	IRWIN Tools Night Race	Bristol	6	33	577	Running	20
25	AdvoCare 500	Atlanta	26	12	609	Running	20
26	Federated Auto Parts 400	Richmond	20	6	647	Running	19
27	GEICO 400	Chicagoland	32	24	667	Running	19
28	SYLVANIA 300	New Hampshire	11	15	696	Running	19
29	AAA 400	Dover	39	27	713	Running	19
30	Good Sam Roadside Assistance 500	Talladega	26	10	748	Running	19
31	Bank of America 500	Charlotte	39	28	764	Running	19
32	Hollywood Casino 400	Kansas	20	28	780	Running	19
33	TUMS Fast Relief 500	Martinsville	4	22	802	Running	19
34	AAA Texas 500	Texas	22	19	827	Running	19
35	AdvoCare 500	Phoenix	33	13	858	Running	19
36	Ford EcoBoost 400	Homestead -Miami	33	19	883	Running	19

KURT BUSCH

Birth Date: **August 4, 1978** • Hometown: **Las Vegas, NV** • Twitter: **@KurtBusch**

Photo courtesy of Furniture Row Racing

78

Furniture Row Chevrolet

Kurt Busch has just as much talent as any driver in the NASCAR Sprint Cup Series, as evidenced by his four perfect Driver Ratings (150.0) and 24 victories. The 2004 series champion changed teams midway through the 2012 season, jumping from the No. 51 Chevrolet of Phoenix Racing to the No. 78 Chevrolet of Furniture Row Racing after the fall Talladega race. He returns to Barney Visser's Furniture Row Racing team in 2013 having posted three top-10 finishes over the last six races of 2012. Prior to switching teams, Busch had a third-place finish at Sonoma and a ninth-place finish at Auto Club. Before the 2012 season even began, Busch and Roger Penske of Penske Racing, his team for six seasons, came to a mutual agreement to go their separate ways. In 216 races with Penske, Busch visited Victory Lane 10 times. Prior to joining Penske Racing for the start of the 2006 season, Busch spent his first six seasons in the series with Roush Fenway Racing.

In 2004 Busch won the championship on the strength of three wins, 10 top fives and 21 top 10s. However, a year later his owner Jack Roush suspended Busch for the final two races of 2005, which ultimately led to him signing with Penske.

Photo courtesy of NASCAR The Game. www.NASCARTheGame.com

NASCAR SPRINT CUP SERIES
CAREER RECORD *(Through 2012)*

Year	Races	Wins	Top 5	Top 10	Poles	Points Standing
2000	7	0	0	0	0	48th
2001	35	0	3	6	1	27th
2002	36	4	12	20	1	3rd
2003	36	4	9	14	0	11th
2004	36	3	10	21	1	1st
2005	34	3	9	18	0	10th
2006	36	1	7	12	6	16th
2007	36	2	6	14	1	7th
2008	36	1	5	10	0	18th
2009	36	2	10	21	0	4th
2010	36	2	9	17	2	11th
2011	36	2	8	16	3	11th
2012	35	0	1	5	0	25th

Best Race Finish: 1st (24 times)
Best Points Finish: 1st (2004)

**2013
Car Owner**
Barney
Visser

**2013
Crew Chief**
Todd Berrier

NASCAR SPRINT CUP SERIES 2012 RACE-BY-RACE RESULTS

RACE	EVENT	LOCATION	START	FINISH	PTS.	STATUS	POS.
1	Daytona 500	Daytona	28	39	5	Running	34
2	Subway Fresh Fit 500	Phoenix	19	15	35	Running	27
3	KOBALT Tools 400	Las Vegas	12	35	44	Accident	29
4	Food City 500	Bristol	27	18	70	Running	27
5	Auto Club 400	Fontana	23	9	105	Running	23
6	Goody's Fast Relief 500	Martinsville	40	33	116	Running	26
7	Samsung Mobile 500	Texas	27	13	147	Running	26
8	STP 400	Kansas	14	17	174	Running	25
9	Capital City 400 Presented by Virginia Is for Lovers	Richmond	13	28	190	Running	26
10	Aaron's 499	Talladega	33	20	215	Running	25
11	Bojangles' Southern 500	Darlington	25	21	238	Running	25
12	Coca-Cola 600	Charlotte	42	27	255	Running	25
13	FedEx 400 Benefiting Autism Speaks	Dover	9	24	275	Engine	26
14	Pocono 400 Presented by #NASCAR	Pocono	DNE		275		27
15	Quicken Loans 400	Michigan	26	30	289	Running	27
16	Toyota/Save Mart 350	Sonoma	8	3	331	Running	27
17	Quaker State 400	Kentucky	14	19	356	Running	24
18	Coke Zero 400 Powered by Coca-Cola	Daytona	35	35	365	Running	25
19	Lenox Industrial Tools 301	New Hampshire	14	24	386	Running	25
20	Crown Royal Presents the Curtiss Shaver 400 at the Brickyard Powered by Big Machine Records	Indianapolis	13	36	394	Engine	26
21	Pennsylvania 400	Pocono	6	30	409	Accident	25
22	Finger Lakes 355 at The Glen	Watkins Glen	27	31	422	Running	25
23	Pure Michigan 400	Michigan	26	30	436	Accident	25
24	IRWIN Tools Night Race	Bristol	20	28	452	Running	25
25	AdvoCare 500	Atlanta	16	13	483	Running	25
26	Federated Auto Parts 400	Richmond	30	28	499	Running	25
27	GEICO 400	Chicagoland	30	32	511	Running	26
28	SYLVANIA 300	New Hampshire	23	25	530	Running	25
29	AAA 400	Dover	28	23	551	Running	26
30	Good Sam Roadside Assistance 500	Talladega	29	39	557	Parked	26
31	Bank of America 500	Charlotte	21	21	580	Running	26
32	Hollywood Casino 400	Kansas	29	25	599	Running	26
33	TUMS Fast Relief 500	Martinsville	19	15	628	Running	25
34	AAA Texas 500	Texas	18	8	664	Running	25
35	AdvoCare 500	Phoenix	6	8	700	Running	25
36	Ford EcoBoost 400	Homestead -Miami	26	9	735	Running	25

KYLE BUSCH

Birth Date: May 2, 1985 • Hometown: **Las Vegas, NV** • Twitter: **@KyleBusch**

Photos courtesy of Joe Gibbs Racing

18

M&M's/Interstate Batteries Toyota

Perhaps one of the most talented drivers in NASCAR, Kyle Busch is third all-time on the combined national series wins list with 105 total victories (24 in NASCAR Sprint Cup, 51 in NASCAR Nationwide and 30 in NASCAR Camping World Truck Series), trailing only Richard Petty and David Pearson. It's almost a given that the younger of the Busch brothers will surpass Pearson on this list during the 2013 season. He currently sits one win behind Pearson and needs only two more wins to move into sole possession of second place. His only victory of the 2012 season (in any of the three national series) came in Richmond's spring race in the premier series. His victory extended his streak of eight consecutive seasons in the NASCAR Sprint Cup Series in which he won at least one race. He finished 13th in the points standings, one position outside the Chase for the NASCAR Sprint Cup. In 2008 he scored a series-high eight victories, but because of a lackluster performance during NASCAR's playoff only came away with a 10th-place finish.

While Busch was able to extend his streak of seasons with at least one win in the premier series, another streak came to a crashing halt – eight consecutive seasons of posting at least one victory in the NASCAR Nationwide Series which began in 2004. However, his 51 victories in the series is a record – two more than Mark Martin. His 30 wins in the truck series is second behind Ron Hornaday Jr.

NASCAR SPRINT CUP SERIES
CAREER RECORD (Through 2012)

Year	Races	Wins	Top 5	Top 10	Poles	Points Standing
2004	6	0	0	0	0	52nd
2005	36	2	9	13	1	20th
2006	36	1	10	18	1	10th
2007	36	1	11	20	0	5th
2008	36	8	17	21	2	10th
2009	36	4	9	13	1	13th
2010	36	3	10	18	2	8th
2011	35	4	14	18	1	12th
2012	36	1	13	20	2	13th

Best Race Finish: 1st (24 times)
Best Points Finish: 5th (2007)

2013
Car Owner
Joe Gibbs

2013
Crew Chief
Dave Rogers

NASCAR SPRINT CUP SERIES 2012 RACE-BY-RACE RESULTS

RACE	EVENT	LOCATION	START	FINISH	PTS.	STATUS	POS.
1	Daytona 500	Daytona	14	17	27	Running	17
2	Subway Fresh Fit 500	Phoenix	12	6	66	Running	9
3	KOBALT Tools 400	Las Vegas	2	23	87	Running	12
4	Food City 500	Bristol	13	32	99	Running	16
5	Auto Club 400	Fontana	2	2	143	Running	14
6	Goody's Fast Relief 500	Martinsville	8	36	151	Running	16
7	Samsung Mobile 500	Texas	17	11	184	Running	14
8	STP 400	Kansas	25	10	218	Running	13
9	Capital City 400 Presented by Virginia Is for Lovers	Richmond	5	1	265	Running	11
10	Aaron's 499	Talladega	21	2	308	Running	9
11	Bojangles' Southern 500	Darlington	5	4	349	Running	9
12	Coca-Cola 600	Charlotte	17	3	391	Running	8
13	FedEx 400 Benefiting Autism Speaks	Dover	8	29	406	Engine	9
14	Pocono 400 Presented by #NASCAR	Pocono	4	30	420	Engine	12
15	Quicken Loans 400	Michigan	34	32	432	Running	12
16	Toyota/Save Mart 350	Sonoma	7	17	459	Running	12
17	Quaker State 400	Kentucky	2	10	495	Running	12
18	Coke Zero 400 Powered by Coca-Cola	Daytona	22	24	516	Running	12
19	Lenox Industrial Tools 301	New Hampshire	1	16	545	Running	13
20	Crown Royal Presents the Curtiss Shaver 400 at the Brickyard Powered by Big Machine Records	Indianapolis	7	2	588	Running	11
21	Pennsylvania 400	Pocono	20	33	599	Accident	15
22	Finger Lakes 355 at The Glen	Watkins Glen	2	7	638	Running	14
23	Pure Michigan 400	Michigan	23	13	668	Running	14
24	IRWIN Tools Night Race	Bristol	10	6	707	Running	13
25	AdvoCare 500	Atlanta	3	6	746	Running	12
26	Federated Auto Parts 400	Richmond	15	16	774	Running	13
27	GEICO 400	Chicagoland	21	4	814	Running	13
28	SYLVANIA 300	New Hampshire	2	28	831	Running	13
29	AAA 400	Dover	5	7	870	Running	13
30	Good Sam Roadside Assistance 500	Talladega	13	3	912	Running	13
31	Bank of America 500	Charlotte	8	5	951	Running	13
32	Hollywood Casino 400	Kansas	4	31	964	Accident	13
33	TUMS Fast Relief 500	Martinsville	3	2	1006	Running	13
34	AAA Texas 500	Texas	3	3	1048	Running	13
35	AdvoCare 500	Phoenix	1	3	1091	Running	13
36	Ford EcoBoost 400	Homestead-Miami	8	4	1133	Running	13

DALE EARNHARDT JR.

Birth Date: **October 10, 1974** • Hometown: **Kannapolis, NC**

Photo courtesy of Hendrick Motorsports/JRMotorsports

National Guard Chevrolet

The 2012 season marked the 10th consecutive year that Dale Earnhardt Jr. walked away with the Most Popular Driver Award during the awards ceremonies in Las Vegas at the end of the season. He is second to only Bill Elliott, who won 16, in the number of Most Popular Driver Awards. Earnhardt gave members of Junior Nation reason to celebrate after winning Michigan's Quicken Loans 400 almost four years to the day after his last victory in the series. Not only did Earnhardt win a race in 2012, he performed consistently throughout the season and led the standings after two races. In a testament to his remarkable start to the season, he finished on the lead lap in the first 20 races before finishing 18 laps off the lead at Pocono in the 21st race. He easily made the Chase for the NASCAR Sprint Cup and was 12th in the final standings. However, the driver with 19 career wins in the series might have finished a couple spots higher if he hadn't sat out the Charlotte and Kansas October races with a concussion. In the 34 races Earnhardt did compete in, he was running at the finish in all of them and had a career-best average finishing position of 10.9.

Earnhardt was the fourth driver to win back-to-back championships in the NASCAR Nationwide Series (1998 and 1999), and has 23 career wins in the series, including an emotional win in the 2010 July Daytona race at the wheel of the No. 3 Wrangler Chevrolet.

NASCAR SPRINT CUP SERIES
CAREER RECORD (Through 2012)

Year	Races	Wins	Top 5	Top 10	Poles	Points Standing
1999	5	0	0	1	0	48th
2000	34	2	3	5	2	16th
2001	36	3	9	15	2	8th
2002	36	2	11	16	2	11th
2003	36	2	13	21	0	3rd
2004	36	6	16	21	0	5th
2005	36	1	7	13	0	19th
2006	36	1	10	17	0	5th
2007	36	0	7	12	1	16th
2008	36	1	10	16	1	12th
2009	36	0	2	5	0	25th
2010	36	0	3	8	1	21st
2011	36	0	4	12	1	7th
2012	34	1	10	20	1	12th

Best Race Finish: 1st (19 times)
Best Points Finish: 3rd (2003)

2013 Car Owner
Rick Hendrick

2013 Crew Chief
Steve Letarte

NASCAR SPRINT CUP SERIES 2012 RACE-BY-RACE RESULTS

RACE	EVENT	LOCATION	START	FINISH	PTS.	STATUS	POS.
1	Daytona 500	Daytona	5	2	42	Running	2
2	Subway Fresh Fit 500	Phoenix	29	14	72	Running	5
3	KOBALT Tools 400	Las Vegas	4	10	107	Running	4
4	Food City 500	Bristol	18	15	137	Running	6
5	Auto Club 400	Fontana	14	3	178	Running	3
6	Goody's Fast Relief 500	Martinsville	14	3	220	Running	2
7	Samsung Mobile 500	Texas	16	10	254	Running	3
8	STP 400	Kansas	7	7	291	Running	4
9	Capital City 400 Presented by Virginia Is for Lovers	Richmond	10	2	333	Running	2
10	Aaron's 499	Talladega	18	9	369	Running	3
11	Bojangles' Southern 500	Darlington	24	17	397	Running	3
12	Coca-Cola 600	Charlotte	12	6	435	Running	4
13	FedEx 400 Benefiting Autism Speaks	Dover	17	4	476	Running	3
14	Pocono 400 Presented by #NASCAR	Pocono	8	8	513	Running	2
15	Quicken Loans 400	Michigan	17	1	561	Running	2
16	Toyota/Save Mart 350	Sonoma	19	23	582	Running	3
17	Quaker State 400	Kentucky	7	4	622	Running	2
18	Coke Zero 400 Powered by Coca-Cola	Daytona	24	15	651	Running	2
19	Lenox Industrial Tools 301	New Hampshire	9	4	691	Running	2
20	Crown Royal Presents the Curtiss Shaver 400 at the Brickyard Powered by Big Machine Records	Indianapolis	20	4	731	Running	1
21	Pennsylvania 400	Pocono	8	32	744	Running	1
22	Finger Lakes 355 at The Glen	Watkins Glen	16	28	760	Running	4
23	Pure Michigan 400	Michigan	22	4	801	Running	3
24	IRWIN Tools Night Race	Bristol	16	12	834	Running	3
25	AdvoCare 500	Atlanta	35	7	871	Running	2
26	Federated Auto Parts 400	Richmond	1	14	2003	Running	7
27	GEICO 400	Chicagoland	4	8	2039	Running	7
28	SYLVANIA 300	New Hampshire	14	13	2070	Running	7
29	AAA 400	Dover	25	11	2103	Running	7
30	Good Sam Roadside Assistance 500	Talladega	12	20	2128	Running	11
31	Bank of America 500	Charlotte	DNE		2128		12
32	Hollywood Casino 400	Kansas	DNE		2128		12
33	TUMS Fast Relief 500	Martinsville	20	21	2151	Running	12
34	AAA Texas 500	Texas	19	7	2188	Running	12
35	AdvoCare 500	Phoenix	23	21	2211	Running	12
36	Ford EcoBoost 400	Homestead-Miami	16	10	2245	Running	12

CARL EDWARDS

Birth Date: **August 15, 1979** • Hometown: **Columbia, MO**

Photo courtesy of Roush Fenway Racing

99

Fastenal/Aflac/UPS/Subway/ Kellogg's/Geek Squad Ford

After coming closer to winning a NASCAR Sprint Cup Series title in 2011 than any other runner-up in NASCAR history by losing a tiebreaker to Tony Stewart, Carl Edwards entered the 2012 season prepared to make a serious run at his first championship in NASCAR's premier series. Things didn't go according to plan for Edwards and his No. 99 Roush Fenway Racing Ford team. Edwards failed to reach Victory Lane in 2012 and had career lows in top fives (3), top 10s (13) and average finishing position (15.6). He also placed 15th in the final points standings, his lowest since 2004 (37th) when he only competed in 13 events. Statistically, Edwards' best season was 2008 when he won a series-high nine races, but finished second in the standings to Jimmie Johnson. That season, Edwards posted 19 top fives and 27 top 10s along with a 9.5 average finishing position.

Edwards won seven races in the NASCAR Nationwide Series in 2008. In 2007 he captured the NASCAR Nation-wide Series title after winning four times. He was also runner-up in the NASCAR Nationwide final standings four times (2006, 2008–2010). Although he wasn't driver points-eligible for the NASCAR Nationwide title in 2011, he won the owners' championship for Roush Fenway Racing. Edwards also won the Rookie of the Year in the NASCAR Camping World Truck and NASCAR Nationwide Series in 2003 and 2005, respectively. In 2007, he won the Prelude to the Dream charity dirt late model event at Eldora Speedway.

Photo courtesy of NASCAR The Game. www.NASCARTheGame.com

NASCAR SPRINT CUP SERIES
CAREER RECORDS (Through 2012)

Year	Races	Wins	Top 5	Top 10	Poles	Points Standings
2004	13	0	1	5	0	37th
2005	36	4	13	18	2	3rd
2006	36	0	10	20	0	12th
2007	36	3	11	15	1	9th
2008	36	9	19	27	1	2nd
2009	36	0	7	14	0	11th
2010	36	2	9	19	3	4th
2011	36	1	19	26	3	2nd
2012	36	0	3	13	1	15th

Best Career Finish: 1st (19 times)
Best Points Finish: 2nd (2008, 2011)

2013 Car Owner
Jack Roush, John Henry

2013 Crew Chief
Jimmy Fennig

NASCAR SPRINT CUP SERIES 2012 RACE-BY-RACE RESULTS

RACE	EVENT	LOCATION	START	FINISH	PTS.	STATUS	POS.
1	Daytona 500	Daytona	1	8	36	Running	8
2	Subway Fresh Fit 500	Phoenix	24	17	63	Running	10
3	KOBALT Tools 400	Las Vegas	21	5	102	Running	6
4	Food City 500	Bristol	8	39	107	Running	15
5	Auto Club 400	Fontana	12	5	146	Running	12
6	Goody's Fast Relief 500	Martinsville	28	11	179	Running	11
7	Samsung Mobile 500	Texas	20	8	215	Running	11
8	STP 400	Kansas	21	9	251	Running	9
9	Capital City 400 Presented by Virginia Is for Lovers	Richmond	2	10	287	Running	9
10	Aaron's 499	Talladega	7	31	300	Accident	11
11	Bojangles' Southern 500	Darlington	7	7	337	Running	10
12	Coca-Cola 600	Charlotte	28	9	372	Running	10
13	FedEx 400 Benefiting Autism Speaks	Dover	19	26	390	Running	12
14	Pocono 400 Presented by #NASCAR	Pocono	2	11	423	Running	11
15	Quicken Loans 400	Michigan	42	11	456	Running	11
16	Toyota/Save Mart 350	Sonoma	11	21	479	Running	11
17	Quaker State 400	Kentucky	25	20	503	Running	11
18	Coke Zero 400 Powered by Coca-Cola	Daytona	12	6	541	Running	11
19	Lenox Industrial Tools 301	New Hampshire	21	18	567	Running	11
20	Crown Royal Presents the Curtiss Shaver 400 at the Brickyard Powered by Big Machine Records	Indianapolis	2	29	582	Running	12
21	Pennsylvania 400	Pocono	17	7	619	Running	12
22	Finger Lakes 355 at The Glen	Watkins Glen	18	14	650	Running	12
23	Pure Michigan 400	Michigan	2	6	689	Running	12
24	IRWIN Tools Night Race	Bristol	27	22	712	Running	12
25	AdvoCare 500	Atlanta	12	36	720	Engine	14
26	Federated Auto Parts 400	Richmond	16	17	747	Running	14
27	GEICO 400	Chicagoland	5	19	772	Running	15
28	SYLVANIA 300	New Hampshire	5	19	797	Running	15
29	AAA 400	Dover	15	5	836	Running	14
30	Good Sam Roadside Assistance 500	Talladega	7	36	844	Running	15
31	Bank of America 500	Charlotte	19	7	881	Running	15
32	Hollywood Casino 400	Kansas	17	14	911	Running	14
33	TUMS Fast Relief 500	Martinsville	23	18	937	Running	14
34	AAA Texas 500	Texas	9	16	965	Running	15
35	AdvoCare 500	Phoenix	13	11	998	Running	15
36	Ford EcoBoost 400	Homestead-Miami	4	12	1030	Running	15

DAVID GILLILAND

Birth Date: **April 1, 1976** • Hometown: **Riverside, CA** • Twitter: **@DGilliland2010**

Photos courtesy of Front Row Motorsports

**Front Row
Motorsports Ford**

As of the beginning of the 2013 season, David Gilliland's best finish is a second-place effort at Sonoma Raceway in 2008. In 36 races in 2012, Gilliland was running at the finish in 32 of them. His best finish of the season was 13th in the April Talladega race. He posted five top-20 finishes, three of them consecutively (Watkins Glen, Michigan and Bristol), and led at least one lap in four different races (Pocono and Michigan in June, Daytona in July and Kansas in October). He placed 30th in the points standings and posted his best average finishing position (27.3) in four seasons.

In the NASCAR Nationwide Series, Gilliland scored a dramatic victory at Kentucky Speedway in 2006 in only his seventh career start. In three starts in the NASCAR Camping World Truck Series, Gilliland's best performance is a sixth-place finish at Charlotte in 2009.

Gilliland began his career in the NASCAR K&N Pro Series West where he served as crew chief for his father Butch Gilliland's team that won the 1997 series championship. The younger Gilliland made his first stock car race start in 1998 on dirt at Perris Auto Speedway (CA), winning two of his first seven starts. In 1999, at Perris, Gilliland won nine stock car division features. In 2001 he started competing in the NASCAR Southwest Tour and won in only his fourth start. The following year he won five times. In 2004 and 2005 he raced fulltime in the NASCAR K&N Pro Series West and won the Rookie of the Year in 2004.

DAVID GILLILAND NO. 38 FRONT ROW MOTORSPORTS FORD

NASCAR SPRINT CUP SERIES
CAREER RECORD *(Through 2012)*

Year	Races	Wins	Top 5	Top 10	Poles	Points Standing
2006	15	0	0	0	1	42nd
2007	36	0	1	2	1	28th
2008	36	0	1	2	0	27th
2009	31	0	0	0	0	37th
2010	32	0	0	0	0	32nd
2011	36	0	1	2	0	30th
2012	36	0	0	0	0	30th

Best Race Finish: 2nd (1 time)
Best Points Finish: 27th (2008)

**2013
Car Owner**
Bob Jenkins

Photo not available at press time

**2013
Crew Chief**
Frank Kerr

NASCAR SPRINT CUP SERIES 2012 *RACE-BY-RACE RESULTS*

RACE	EVENT	LOCATION	START	FINISH	PTS.	STATUS	POS.
1	Daytona 500	Daytona	33	23	21	Running	22
2	Subway Fresh Fit 500	Phoenix	36	28	37	Running	25
3	KOBALT Tools 400	Las Vegas	34	33	48	Running	27
4	Food City 500	Bristol	26	26	66	Running	29
5	Auto Club 400	Fontana	41	30	80	Running	30
6	Goody's Fast Relief 500	Martinsville	38	28	96	Running	30
7	Samsung Mobile 500	Texas	35	31	109	Running	30
8	STP 400	Kansas	22	27	126	Running	29
9	Capital City 400 Presented by Virginia Is for Lovers	Richmond	41	36	134	Running	30
10	Aaron's 499	Talladega	26	13	165	Running	30
11	Bojangles' Southern 500	Darlington	36	25	184	Running	30
12	Coca-Cola 600	Charlotte	39	26	202	Running	29
13	FedEx 400 Benefiting Autism Speaks	Dover	30	40	206	Accident	30
14	Pocono 400 Presented by #NASCAR	Pocono	36	23	228	Running	30
15	Quicken Loans 400	Michigan	35	27	246	Running	30
16	Toyota/Save Mart 350	Sonoma	27	26	264	Running	30
17	Quaker State 400	Kentucky	40	28	280	Running	30
18	Coke Zero 400 Powered by Coca-Cola	Daytona	32	31	294	Accident	30
19	Lenox Industrial Tools 301	New Hampshire	39	27	311	Running	30
20	Crown Royal Presents the Curtiss Shaver 400 at the Brickyard Powered by Big Machine Records	Indianapolis	31	27	328	Running	30
21	Pennsylvania 400	Pocono	26	21	351	Running	30
22	Finger Lakes 355 at The Glen	Watkins Glen	34	20	375	Running	30
23	Pure Michigan 400	Michigan	36	18	401	Running	28
24	IRWIN Tools Night Race	Bristol	18	20	425	Running	27
25	AdvoCare 500	Atlanta	29	31	438	Running	27
26	Federated Auto Parts 400	Richmond	35	31	451	Running	28
27	GEICO 400	Chicagoland	40	28	467	Running	28
28	SYLVANIA 300	New Hampshire	37	32	479	Running	27
29	AAA 400	Dover	42	32	491	Running	28
30	Good Sam Roadside Assistance 500	Talladega	32	15	520	Running	28
31	Bank of America 500	Charlotte	36	23	541	Running	27
32	Hollywood Casino 400	Kansas	38	23	563	Running	28
33	TUMS Fast Relief 500	Martinsville	35	30	577	Running	28
34	AAA Texas 500	Texas	30	35	586	Engine	29
35	AdvoCare 500	Phoenix	31	36	594	Accident	30
36	Ford EcoBoost 400	Homestead-Miami	40	33	605	Running	30

NASCAR SPRINT CUP SERIES DRIVERS | 75

JEFF GORDON®

Birth Date: **August 4, 1971** • Hometown: **Pittsboro, IN** • Twitter: **@JeffGordonWeb**

©2013 HGJ Licensing, LLC.

24

AARP/Drive to End Hunger Chevrolet

Jeff Gordon headed into the 2012 season with 85 career victories, the third-most in the NASCAR Sprint Cup Series and the lead among active drivers. He used victories at the August Pocono race and the season finale at Homestead to add to this stat. For the majority of the regular season (the first 26 races of the season), Gordon sat outside the Chase for the NASCAR Sprint Cup looking in. It wasn't until a second-place finish at Richmond in the 26th race of the season, the race that sets the contenders for the Chase, that Jeff Gordon saw top 12 in points. After a second-place finish in the October Talladega race, Gordon rose to sixth in the points – the closest he would ever get to the top of the standings. He got back up to sixth three races later after Martinsville, but finished the season in 10th.

Gordon made his debut in the series in the final race of the 1992 season, which was also Richard Petty's final race. Twenty-one years and 87 victories later, Gordon has cemented his place among the greatest legends of NASCAR with four NASCAR Sprint Cup titles (1995, 1997, 1998, 2001). He was the runner-up in the final standings in 1996 and 2007. After winning at Homestead in 2012, Gordon has won at least once at every track on the current NASCAR Sprint Cup schedule with the exception of Kentucky Speedway, which has hosted just two series events.

NASCAR SPRINT CUP SERIES
CAREER RECORD *(Through 2012)*

Year	Races	Wins	Top 5	Top 10	Poles	Points Standing
1992	1	0	0	0	0	81st
1993	30	0	7	11	1	14th
1994	31	2	7	14	1	1st
1995	31	7	17	23	8	1st
1996	31	10	21	24	5	2nd
1997	32	10	22	23	1	1st
1998	33	13	26	28	7	1st
1999	34	7	18	21	7	6th
2000	34	3	11	22	3	9th
2001	36	6	18	24	6	1st
2002	36	3	13	20	3	5th
2003	36	3	15	20	4	4th
2004	36	5	16	25	6	3rd
2005	36	4	8	14	2	11th
2006	36	2	14	18	2	6th
2007	36	6	21	30	7	2nd
2008	36	0	13	19	4	7th
2009	36	1	16	25	1	3rd
2010	36	0	11	17	1	9th
2011	36	3	13	18	1	8th
2012	36	2	11	18	2	10th

Best Race Finish: 1st (87 times)
Best Points Finish: 1st (1995, 1997, 1998, 2001)

2013 Car Owner
Rick Hendrick

2013 Crew Chief
Alan Gustafson

NASCAR SPRINT CUP SERIES 2012 RACE-BY-RACE RESULTS

RACE	EVENT	LOCATION	START	FINISH	PTS.	STATUS	POS.
1	Daytona 500	Daytona	16	40	5	Engine	35
2	Subway Fresh Fit 500	Phoenix	30	8	42	Running	23
3	KOBALT Tools 400	Las Vegas	16	12	75	Running	18
4	Food City 500	Bristol	4	35	85	Running	23
5	Auto Club 400	Fontana	21	26	104	Running	25
6	Goody's Fast Relief 500	Martinsville	9	14	136	Running	21
7	Samsung Mobile 500	Texas	34	4	177	Running	17
8	STP 400	Kansas	20	21	200	Running	18
9	Capital City 400 Presented by Virginia Is for Lovers	Richmond	6	23	221	Running	17
10	Aaron's 499	Talladega	1	33	232	Accident	23
11	Bojangles' Southern 500	Darlington	12	35	241	Running	24
12	Coca-Cola 600	Charlotte	23	7	279	Running	22
13	FedEx 400 Benefiting Autism Speaks	Dover	14	13	311	Running	21
14	Pocono 400 Presented by #NASCAR	Pocono	12	19	336	Running	22
15	Quicken Loans 400	Michigan	28	6	375	Running	20
16	Toyota/Save Mart 350	Sonoma	2	6	414	Running	18
17	Quaker State 400	Kentucky	9	5	453	Running	18
18	Coke Zero 400 Powered by Coca-Cola	Daytona	5	12	485	Running	17
19	Lenox Industrial Tools 301	New Hampshire	8	6	524	Running	17
20	Crown Royal Presents the Curtiss Shaver 400 at the Brickyard Powered by Big Machine Records	Indianapolis	9	5	564	Running	15
21	Pennsylvania 400	Pocono	27	1	611	Running	13
22	Finger Lakes 355 at The Glen	Watkins Glen	12	21	634	Running	15
23	Pure Michigan 400	Michigan	11	28	650	Engine	15
24	IRWIN Tools Night Race	Bristol	11	3	691	Running	14
25	AdvoCare 500	Atlanta	5	2	734	Running	13
26	Federated Auto Parts 400	Richmond	2	2	2000	Running	12
27	GEICO 400	Chicagoland	19	35	2009	Accident	12
28	SYLVANIA 300	New Hampshire	1	3	2051	Running	12
29	AAA 400	Dover	7	2	2094	Running	10
30	Good Sam Roadside Assistance 500	Talladega	6	2	2137	Running	6
31	Bank of America 500	Charlotte	13	18	2164	Running	9
32	Hollywood Casino 400	Kansas	19	10	2199	Running	8
33	TUMS Fast Relief 500	Martinsville	11	7	2237	Running	6
34	AAA Texas 500	Texas	16	14	2256	Running	10
35	AdvoCare 500	Phoenix	11	30	2256	Accident	11
36	Ford EcoBoost 400	Homestead-Miami	15	1	2303	Running	10

DENNY HAMLIN

Birth Date: **November 18, 1980** • Hometown: **Chesterfield, VA** • Twitter: **@DennyHamlin**

Driver photo courtesy of Action Sports Photography; other photos courtesy of Joe Gibbs Racing

11

FedEx Toyota

Denny Hamlin tied eventual NASCAR Sprint Cup Series champion Brad Keselowski and five-time champion Jimmie Johnson with five victories during the 2012 season. Hamlin won four times during the regular season – Phoenix, Kansas, Bristol and Atlanta – and started the postseason as the top seed. However, his most impressive victory came in the second round of the Chase for the NASCAR Sprint Cup. Disappointed by his performance in the opening Chase race at Chicagoland, Hamlin called his own shot and predicted a return to Victory Lane the following weekend at New Hampshire. The weekend didn't start off on the right foot after qualifying 32nd, but that didn't deter the Virginia native. He quickly shot to the front and led 193 of the 300 laps to win the race. However, due to three finishes of 20th or worse in the Chase, Hamlin finished the season ranked sixth.

Hamlin's best season came in 2010 where he had a series-high eight wins and led Johnson by 15 points going into the last race of the season. However, a 14th-place finish in the final race compared to Johnson's second-place finish gave the latter the title by 39 points. Hamlin has at least one victory in seven consecutive seasons dating back to the 2006 campaign, when he swept the two Pocono events and won the Rookie of the Year award. In addition to his 22 victories in the premier series, Hamlin has 11 and two wins in the NASCAR Nationwide and NASCAR Camping World Truck Series, respectively.

NASCAR SPRINT CUP SERIES
CAREER RECORD (Through 2012)

Year	Races	Wins	Top 5	Top 10	Poles	Points Standing
2005	7	0	0	3	1	41st
2006	36	2	8	20	3	3rd
2007	36	1	12	18	1	12th
2008	36	1	12	18	1	8th
2009	36	4	15	20	1	5th
2010	36	8	14	18	2	2nd
2011	36	1	5	14	0	9th
2012	36	5	14	17	3	6th

Best Race Finish: 1st (22 times)

Best Points Finish: 2nd (2010)

**2013
Car Owner**
Joe Gibbs

**2013
Crew Chief**
Darian
Grubb

NASCAR SPRINT CUP SERIES 2012 RACE-BY-RACE RESULTS

RACE	EVENT	LOCATION	START	FINISH	PTS.	STATUS	POS.
1	Daytona 500	Daytona	31	4	42	Running	4
2	Subway Fresh Fit 500	Phoenix	13	1	89	Running	1
3	KOBALT Tools 400	Las Vegas	17	20	113	Running	3
4	Food City 500	Bristol	20	20	137	Running	5
5	Auto Club 400	Fontana	1	11	171	Running	7
6	Goody's Fast Relief 500	Martinsville	3	6	210	Running	7
7	Samsung Mobile 500	Texas	13	12	242	Running	6
8	STP 400	Kansas	4	1	289	Running	5
9	Capital City 400 Presented by Virginia Is for Lovers	Richmond	7	4	329	Running	3
10	Aaron's 499	Talladega	22	23	351	Running	4
11	Bojangles' Southern 500	Darlington	8	2	394	Running	4
12	Coca-Cola 600	Charlotte	8	2	437	Running	3
13	FedEx 400 Benefiting Autism Speaks	Dover	10	18	464	Running	4
14	Pocono 400 Presented by #NASCAR	Pocono	5	5	504	Running	4
15	Quicken Loans 400	Michigan	11	34	514	Accident	5
16	Toyota/Save Mart 350	Sonoma	16	35	523	Suspension	8
17	Quaker State 400	Kentucky	3	3	565	Running	5
18	Coke Zero 400 Powered by Coca-Cola	Daytona	23	25	584	Running	7
19	Lenox Industrial Tools 301	New Hampshire	3	2	628	Running	5
20	Crown Royal Presents the Curtiss Shaver 400 at the Brickyard Powered by Big Machine Records	Indianapolis	1	6	667	Running	5
21	Pennsylvania 400	Pocono	2	29	683	Accident	8
22	Finger Lakes 355 at The Glen	Watkins Glen	23	34	693	Engine	10
23	Pure Michigan 400	Michigan	21	11	727	Running	10
24	IRWIN Tools Night Race	Bristol	8	1	774	Running	8
25	AdvoCare 500	Atlanta	7	1	822	Running	7
26	Federated Auto Parts 400	Richmond	7	18	2012	Running	1
27	GEICO 400	Chicagoland	8	16	2041	Running	4
28	SYLVANIA 300	New Hampshire	32	1	2089	Running	3
29	AAA 400	Dover	1	8	2126	Running	3
30	Good Sam Roadside Assistance 500	Talladega	23	14	2156	Running	3
31	Bank of America 500	Charlotte	9	2	2199	Running	3
32	Hollywood Casino 400	Kansas	9	13	2230	Running	3
33	TUMS Fast Relief 500	Martinsville	5	33	2242	Running	5
34	AAA Texas 500	Texas	12	20	2266	Running	6
35	AdvoCare 500	Phoenix	3	2	2309	Running	5
36	Ford EcoBoost 400	Homestead-Miami	41	24	2329	Running	6

KEVIN HARVICK

Birth Date: **December 8, 1975** • Hometown: **Bakersfield, CA** • Twitter: **@KevinHarvick**

Photo courtesy of Richard Childress Racing

29

Budweiser/Jimmy John's/ Rheem Chevrolet

After back-to-back third-place finishes in the final points standings in 2010 and 2011, Kevin Harvick and his team were expecting even greater success in 2012. Harvick started the season consistently and stayed in the top 10 for the first 32 races. However, a 32nd-place finish at Martinsville in the seventh race of the Chase for the NASCAR Sprint Cup dropped him to 11th in the standings. Harvick would scratch his way back to eighth place in the standings after winning the penultimate race at Phoenix two races later, but that's where he would end the season. The Phoenix win was his only checkered flag in 2012. He posted five top fives and 14 top 10s, both far off from the career highs of 16 and 26, respectively, he set in 2010. Harvick has 19 career wins in the NASCAR Sprint Cup Series with five of them coming during the 2006 season. In 2001 he was named the Rookie of the Year in NASCAR's premier series.

On the strength of five and nine victories, Harvick was crowned the NASCAR Nationwide Series champion in 2001 and 2006. He ranks third in career wins in NASCAR Nationwide competition with 39 victories, behind only Kyle Busch and Mark Martin. In the NASCAR Camping World Truck Series, Harvick has visited Victory Lane 14 times for a total of 72 triumphs between the three national series – 10th best on the all-time combined wins list. Along with his wife, DeLana, Kevin won the owners' championship in the truck series in 2007, 2009 and 2011.

Photo courtesy of NASCAR The Game. www.NASCARTheGame.com

NASCAR SPRINT CUP SERIES
CAREER RECORD *(Through 2012)*

Year	Races	Wins	Top 5	Top 10	Poles	Points Standing
2001	35	2	6	16	0	9th
2002	35	1	5	8	1	21st
2003	36	1	11	18	1	5th
2004	36	0	5	14	0	14th
2005	36	1	3	10	2	14th
2006	36	5	15	20	1	4th
2007	36	1	4	15	0	10th
2008	36	0	7	19	0	4th
2009	36	0	5	9	0	19th
2010	36	3	16	26	0	3rd
2011	36	4	9	19	0	3rd
2012	36	1	5	14	0	8th

Best Race Finish: 1st (19 times)
Best Points Finish: 3rd (2010, 2011)

**2013
Car Owner
Richard
Childress**

**2013
Crew Chief
Gil Martin**

NASCAR SPRINT CUP SERIES 2012 RACE-BY-RACE RESULTS

RACE	EVENT	LOCATION	START	FINISH	PTS.	STATUS	POS.
1	Daytona 500	Daytona	13	7	37	Running	7
2	Subway Fresh Fit 500	Phoenix	8	2	81	Running	3
3	KOBALT Tools 400	Las Vegas	3	11	115	Running	2
4	Food City 500	Bristol	14	11	148	Running	2
5	Auto Club 400	Fontana	7	4	188	Running	2
6	Goody's Fast Relief 500	Martinsville	2	19	214	Running	5
7	Samsung Mobile 500	Texas	15	9	249	Running	5
8	STP 400	Kansas	2	6	287	Running	6
9	Capital City 400 Presented by Virginia Is for Lovers	Richmond	3	19	313	Running	7
10	Aaron's 499	Talladega	20	25	333	Accident	5
11	Bojangles' Southern 500	Darlington	23	16	361	Running	8
12	Coca-Cola 600	Charlotte	14	8	398	Running	7
13	FedEx 400 Benefiting Autism Speaks	Dover	6	2	440	Running	7
14	Pocono 400 Presented by #NASCAR	Pocono	21	14	470	Running	6
15	Quicken Loans 400	Michigan	2	10	504	Running	6
16	Toyota/Save Mart 350	Sonoma	26	16	532	Running	6
17	Quaker State 400	Kentucky	4	11	565	Running	6
18	Coke Zero 400 Powered by Coca-Cola	Daytona	11	23	586	Running	6
19	Lenox Industrial Tools 301	New Hampshire	12	8	622	Running	6
20	Crown Royal Presents the Curtiss Shaver 400 at the Brickyard Powered by Big Machine Records	Indianapolis	27	13	653	Running	6
21	Pennsylvania 400	Pocono	21	16	681	Running	9
22	Finger Lakes 355 at The Glen	Watkins Glen	19	15	710	Running	9
23	Pure Michigan 400	Michigan	20	16	738	Running	8
24	IRWIN Tools Night Race	Bristol	13	15	767	Running	9
25	AdvoCare 500	Atlanta	24	5	807	Running	9
26	Federated Auto Parts 400	Richmond	13	10	2000	Running	9
27	GEICO 400	Chicagoland	35	12	2032	Running	10
28	SYLVANIA 300	New Hampshire	16	11	2065	Running	8
29	AAA 400	Dover	13	13	2096	Running	9
30	Good Sam Roadside Assistance 500	Talladega	21	11	2130	Running	10
31	Bank of America 500	Charlotte	11	16	2158	Running	10
32	Hollywood Casino 400	Kansas	10	11	2191	Running	10
33	TUMS Fast Relief 500	Martinsville	13	32	2203	Engine	11
34	AAA Texas 500	Texas	23	9	2238	Running	11
35	AdvoCare 500	Phoenix	19	1	2285	Running	8
36	Ford EcoBoost 400	Homestead-Miami	23	8	2321	Running	8

JIMMIE JOHNSON®

Birth Date: **September 17, 1975** • Hometown: **El Cajon, CA** • Twitter: **@JimmieJohnson**

©2013 HGJ Licensing, LLC.

48
Lowe's® Chevrolet

After two consecutive seasons in which the five-time NASCAR Sprint Cup Series champion Jimmie Johnson was not the one celebrating on the championship stage after the season finale at Homestead-Miami Speedway, everyone has to be on high alert that he's itching to get back there, and 2013 could be the year. Although he hasn't been the one holding the championship trophy the past two seasons, it's not like he's had bad years. In 2012, he tied eventual champion Brad Keselowski and Denny Hamlin for the most victories (5) and tied his career-best for top-10 finishes with 24. He entered the second-to-last race with the lead in the points standings; however, due to issues in that race and the finale that relegated him to 32nd- and 36th-place finishes, Johnson fell to third in the overall standings by the time the final checkered flag had fallen on the season. The year before Johnson finished with two wins and a sixth-place finish in the standings. Although these performances were solid, they weren't what Johnson ultimately set out to achieve at the beginning of each of those seasons. So, you have to imagine that Johnson and his long-time crew-chief Chad Knaus will approach the 2013 season with a renewed vigor.

Johnson has posted multiple wins in 11 straight seasons going back to 2002, his first full-time season in NASCAR Sprint Cup racing. Johnson saves his best performances for late in the season, as he has 22 victories in only 90 Chase for the NASCAR Sprint Cup events.

Photo courtesy of NASCAR The Game. www.NASCARTheGame.com

NASCAR SPRINT CUP SERIES
CAREER RECORD (Through 2012)

Year	Races	Wins	Top 5	Top 10	Poles	Points Standing
2001	3	0	0	0	0	52nd
2002	36	3	6	21	4	4th
2003	36	3	14	20	2	2nd
2004	36	8	20	23	1	2nd
2005	36	4	13	22	1	5th
2006	36	5	13	24	1	1st
2007	36	10	20	24	4	1st
2008	36	7	15	22	6	1st
2009	36	7	16	24	4	1st
2010	36	6	17	23	2	1st
2011	36	2	14	21	0	6th
2012	36	5	18	24	4	3rd

Best Race Finish: 1st (60 times)
Best Points Finish: 1st (2006–10)

2013
Car Owner
Rick Hendrick

2013
Crew Chief
Chad Knaus

NASCAR SPRINT CUP SERIES 2012 RACE-BY-RACE RESULTS

RACE	EVENT	LOCATION	START	FINISH	PTS.	STATUS	POS.
1	Daytona 500	Daytona	8	42	2	Accident	37
2	Subway Fresh Fit 500	Phoenix	4	4	43	Running	20
3	KOBALT Tools 400	Las Vegas	6	2	86	Running	13
4	Food City 500	Bristol	22	9	121	Running	11
5	Auto Club 400	Fontana	10	10	156	Running	9
6	Goody's Fast Relief 500	Martinsville	22	12	189	Running	10
7	Samsung Mobile 500	Texas	10	2	233	Running	8
8	STP 400	Kansas	15	3	275	Running	7
9	Capital City 400 Presented by Virginia Is for Lovers	Richmond	27	6	314	Running	6
10	Aaron's 499	Talladega	19	35	324	Engine	8
11	Bojangles' Southern 500	Darlington	2	1	372	Running	5
12	Coca-Cola 600	Charlotte	3	11	405	Running	5
13	FedEx 400 Benefiting Autism Speaks	Dover	2	1	453	Running	5
14	Pocono 400 Presented by #NASCAR	Pocono	24	4	493	Running	5
15	Quicken Loans 400	Michigan	10	5	532	Running	4
16	Toyota/Save Mart 350	Sonoma	3	5	571	Running	4
17	Quaker State 400	Kentucky	1	6	610	Running	3
18	Coke Zero 400 Powered by Coca-Cola	Daytona	16	36	618	Accident	4
19	Lenox Industrial Tools 301	New Hampshire	7	7	656	Running	4
20	Crown Royal Presents the Curtiss Shaver 400 at the Brickyard Powered by Big Machine Records	Indianapolis	6	1	704	Running	4
21	Pennsylvania 400	Pocono	10	14	736	Running	4
22	Finger Lakes 355 at The Glen	Watkins Glen	3	3	777	Running	1
23	Pure Michigan 400	Michigan	3	27	795	Engine	4
24	IRWIN Tools Night Race	Bristol	37	2	838	Running	2
25	AdvoCare 500	Atlanta	8	34	848	Accident	4
26	Federated Auto Parts 400	Richmond	5	13	2009	Running	2
27	GEICO 400	Chicagoland	1	2	2053	Running	2
28	SYLVANIA 300	New Hampshire	20	2	2096	Running	1
29	AAA 400	Dover	11	4	2137	Running	2
30	Good Sam Roadside Assistance 500	Talladega	17	17	2165	Running	2
31	Bank of America 500	Charlotte	5	3	2207	Running	2
32	Hollywood Casino 400	Kansas	7	9	2243	Running	2
33	TUMS Fast Relief 500	Martinsville	1	1	2291	Running	1
34	AAA Texas 500	Texas	1	1	2339	Running	1
35	AdvoCare 500	Phoenix	24	32	2351	Running	2
36	Ford EcoBoost 400	Homestead-Miami	10	36	2360	Rear Gear	3

KASEY KAHNE ®

Birth Date: **April 10, 1980** • Hometown: **Enumclaw, WA** • Twitter: **@kaseykahne**

©2013 HGJ Licensing, LLC.

5

Farmers Insurance Chevrolet

Kasey Kahne's first year driving for Rick Hendrick and the powerhouse team of Hendrick Motorsports provided Kahne with a career year. Although he finished with two victories, four less than his career-high six victories in 2006, Kahne posted his best points finish (4th), average starting position (8.8) and average finishing position (13.1), as well as tying his career-best in top-10 finishes (19). When Kahne moved over to Hendrick after the 2011 season, his long-time crew chief Kenny Francis joined him and the move paid off. In the longest race of the season, the Coca-Cola 600 at Charlotte, Kahne led 96 of the 400 laps for his first victory in Hendrick Motorsports equipment. Two months later, Kahne led a hard-charging Denny Hamlin and Clint Bowyer to the finish line at New Hampshire Motor Speedway in the LENOX Industrial Tools 301. In nine full seasons in the NASCAR Sprint Cup Series, Kahne has 14 trips to Victory Lane. In 2008, Kahne became the first driver to be voted into the NASCAR Sprint All-Star Race and win the event. The very next week he won the Coca-Cola 600. In 2004 Kahne was named the NASCAR Sprint Cup Rookie of the Year after finishing 13th in the points standings.

In the NASCAR Nationwide Series, Kahne has seven career victories. In the NASCAR Camping World Truck Series, Kahne has won four of the five races he's entered for a winning percentage of 80 percent. In 2000 Kahne won the USAC National Midget Series title.

Photo courtesy of NASCAR The Game. www.NASCARTheGame.com

NASCAR SPRINT CUP SERIES
CAREER RECORD *(Through 2012)*

Year	Races	Wins	Top 5	Top 10	Poles	Points Standing
2004	36	0	13	14	4	13th
2005	36	1	5	8	2	23rd
2006	36	6	12	19	6	8th
2007	36	0	1	8	2	19th
2008	36	2	4	14	2	14th
2009	36	2	7	14	0	10th
2010	36	0	7	10	4	20th
2011	36	1	8	15	2	14th
2012	36	2	12	19	4	4th

Best Race Finish: 1st (14 times)
Best Points Finish: 4th (2012)

2013 Car Owner
Rick Hendrick

2013 Crew Chief
Kenny Francis

NASCAR SPRINT CUP SERIES 2012 RACE-BY-RACE RESULTS

RACE	EVENT	LOCATION	START	FINISH	PTS.	STATUS	POS.
1	Daytona 500	Daytona	20	29	15	Accident	26
2	Subway Fresh Fit 500	Phoenix	10	34	25	Running	33
3	KOBALT Tools 400	Las Vegas	1	19	50	Running	26
4	Food City 500	Bristol	10	37	57	Running	32
5	Auto Club 400	Fontana	5	14	87	Running	27
6	Goody's Fast Relief 500	Martinsville	1	38	93	Engine	31
7	Samsung Mobile 500	Texas	5	7	130	Running	27
8	STP 400	Kansas	9	8	166	Running	26
9	Capital City 400 Presented by Virginia Is for Lovers	Richmond	9	5	205	Running	23
10	Aaron's 499	Talladega	5	4	246	Running	19
11	Bojangles' Southern 500	Darlington	3	8	283	Running	16
12	Coca-Cola 600	Charlotte	7	1	330	Running	15
13	FedEx 400 Benefiting Autism Speaks	Dover	13	9	365	Running	14
14	Pocono 400 Presented by #NASCAR	Pocono	10	29	380	Accident	16
15	Quicken Loans 400	Michigan	4	33	391	Accident	16
16	Toyota/Save Mart 350	Sonoma	15	14	421	Running	17
17	Quaker State 400	Kentucky	19	2	463	Running	14
18	Coke Zero 400 Powered by Coca-Cola	Daytona	3	7	500	Running	16
19	Lenox Industrial Tools 301	New Hampshire	2	1	547	Running	12
20	Crown Royal Presents the Curtiss Shaver 400 at the Brickyard Powered by Big Machine Records	Indianapolis	15	12	579	Running	13
21	Pennsylvania 400	Pocono	4	2	622	Running	11
22	Finger Lakes 355 at The Glen	Watkins Glen	20	13	653	Running	11
23	Pure Michigan 400	Michigan	5	3	694	Running	11
24	IRWIN Tools Night Race	Bristol	12	9	730	Running	11
25	AdvoCare 500	Atlanta	11	23	751	Running	11
26	Federated Auto Parts 400	Richmond	21	12	2000	Running	11
27	GEICO 400	Chicagoland	6	3	2041	Running	5
28	SYLVANIA 300	New Hampshire	6	5	2081	Running	5
29	AAA 400	Dover	9	15	2110	Running	6
30	Good Sam Roadside Assistance 500	Talladega	1	12	2143	Running	4
31	Bank of America 500	Charlotte	10	8	2179	Running	5
32	Hollywood Casino 400	Kansas	1	4	2220	Running	5
33	TUMS Fast Relief 500	Martinsville	15	3	2262	Running	4
34	AAA Texas 500	Texas	13	25	2281	Running	4
35	AdvoCare 500	Phoenix	4	4	2321	Running	3
36	Ford EcoBoost 400	Homestead-Miami	12	21	2345	Running	4

MATT KENSETH

Birth Date: **March 10, 1972** • Hometown: **Cambridge, WA** • Twitter: **@Matt_Kenseth17**

Photos courtesy of Autostock

20

Home Depot/Dollar General Toyota

Coming off a solid season in which he scored three victories, including the first-ever Monday night live showing of the Daytona 500, Matt Kenseth takes his talents to Joe Gibbs Racing and the No. 20 Toyota. In 471 of 472 of his previous starts in the NASCAR Sprint Cup Series, Kenseth has been behind the wheel of the Roush Fenway Racing No. 17 Ford. In addition to his victory in the Great American Race, Kenseth celebrated in Victory Lane in the Chase races at Talladega and Kansas. After winning the Daytona 500 Kenseth led the points standings, but dropped to fourth the following week at Phoenix. He would later regain the top position in the standings after the first Pocono race and hold it for six consecutive weeks. However, after a 35th-place finish at Indianapolis, Kenseth dropped from the lead for good. He finished the season seventh.

Kenseth was named the NASCAR Sprint Cup Series Rookie of the Year in 2000 over Dale Earnhardt Jr. after winning one race and finishing 14th in the standings. On the strength of 25 top-10 finishes in the 2003 season, and only one victory, Kenseth claimed his only NASCAR Sprint Cup championship by 90 points over Jimmie Johnson. He won his first Daytona 500 in 2009. His 24 career wins in the series ties him for 26th overall with brothers Kurt and Kyle Busch. In two complete seasons and parts of 14 other seasons, Kenseth has accumulated 26 victories in the NASCAR Nationwide Series.

NASCAR SPRINT CUP SERIES
CAREER RECORD (Through 2012)

Year	Races	Wins	Top 5	Top 10	Poles	Points Standing
1998	1	0	0	1	0	56th
1999	5	0	1	1	0	49th
2000	34	1	4	11	0	14th
2001	36	0	4	9	0	13th
2002	36	5	11	19	1	9th
2003	36	1	11	25	0	1st
2004	36	2	8	16	0	8th
2005	36	1	12	17	2	7th
2006	36	4	15	21	0	2nd
2007	36	2	13	22	0	4th
2008	36	0	9	20	0	11th
2009	36	2	7	12	1	14th
2010	36	0	6	15	0	5th
2011	36	3	12	20	3	4th
2012	36	3	13	19	1	7th

Best Race Finish: 1st (24 times)
Best Points Finish: 1st (2003)

**2013
Car Owner
Joe Gibbs**

**2013
Crew Chief
Jason
Ratcliff**

NASCAR SPRINT CUP SERIES 2012 RACE-BY-RACE RESULTS

RACE	EVENT	LOCATION	START	FINISH	PTS.	STATUS	POS.
1	Daytona 500	Daytona	4	1	47	Running	1
2	Subway Fresh Fit 500	Phoenix	26	13	79	Running	4
3	KOBALT Tools 400	Las Vegas	11	22	102	Running	5
4	Food City 500	Bristol	21	2	145	Running	3
5	Auto Club 400	Fontana	15	16	173	Running	6
6	Goody's Fast Relief 500	Martinsville	21	4	214	Running	4
7	Samsung Mobile 500	Texas	2	5	254	Running	2
8	STP 400	Kansas	18	4	295	Running	3
9	Capital City 400 Presented by Virginia Is for Lovers	Richmond	24	11	328	Running	4
10	Aaron's 499	Talladega	10	3	371	Running	2
11	Bojangles' Southern 500	Darlington	19	6	409	Running	2
12	Coca-Cola 600	Charlotte	20	10	443	Running	2
13	FedEx 400 Benefiting Autism Speaks	Dover	5	3	485	Running	2
14	Pocono 400 Presented by #NASCAR	Pocono	14	7	523	Running	1
15	Quicken Loans 400	Michigan	6	3	565	Running	1
16	Toyota/Save Mart 350	Sonoma	9	13	596	Running	1
17	Quaker State 400	Kentucky	20	7	633	Running	1
18	Coke Zero 400 Powered by Coca-Cola	Daytona	1	3	676	Running	1
19	Lenox Industrial Tools 301	New Hampshire	27	13	707	Running	1
20	Crown Royal Presents the Curtiss Shaver 400 at the Brickyard Powered by Big Machine Records	Indianapolis	10	35	717	Accident	2
21	Pennsylvania 400	Pocono	7	23	739	Running	2
22	Finger Lakes 355 at The Glen	Watkins Glen	24	8	775	Running	3
23	Pure Michigan 400	Michigan	4	17	803	Running	2
24	IRWIN Tools Night Race	Bristol	17	25	823	Running	4
25	AdvoCare 500	Atlanta	4	9	858	Running	3
26	Federated Auto Parts 400	Richmond	17	5	2003	Running	8
27	GEICO 400	Chicagoland	3	18	2030	Running	11
28	SYLVANIA 300	New Hampshire	25	14	2061	Running	11
29	AAA 400	Dover	12	35	2070	Running	12
30	Good Sam Roadside Assistance 500	Talladega	15	1	2117	Running	12
31	Bank of America 500	Charlotte	7	14	2147	Running	11
32	Hollywood Casino 400	Kansas	12	1	2195	Running	9
33	TUMS Fast Relief 500	Martinsville	6	14	2226	Running	8
34	AAA Texas 500	Texas	10	4	2267	Running	5
35	AdvoCare 500	Phoenix	22	14	2297	Running	6
36	Ford EcoBoost 400	Homestead-Miami	11	18	2324	Running	7

BRAD KESELOWSKI

Birth Date: February 12, 1984 • Hometown: **Rochester Hills, MI** • Twitter: **@keselowski**

Photos courtesy of Penske Racing

2
Miller Lite Ford

After a disappointing start to the 2012 season (two 32nd-place finishes and a fifth-place finish in the first three races), Brad Keselowski rebounded at Bristol to win the fourth race of the season by leading 232 of the 500 laps. That spring boarded the 28-year-old driver to four more victories and his first championship in the NASCAR Sprint Cup Series, as well as the first for his owner, Roger Penske, who has been running teams in NASCAR's premier series since 1972. By season's end, the Michigan native stood atop the standings by 39 points over Clint Bowyer and 40 points in front of Jimmie Johnson. He also captured the checkered flag at Talladega, Kentucky, Chicagoland and Dover. However, the most impressive stat throughout his championship season was the number of tracks at which he posted or tied career-best finishes; by the end of the season he had posted career-best finishes at 12 different tracks while tying his career best at four others.

Keselowski became only the second driver to win both a NASCAR Sprint Cup and NASCAR Nationwide Series title, which he won in 2010, giving Penske his first NASCAR national series championship. The other driver to accomplish this was Bobby Labonte, who won the NASCAR Nationwide title in 1991 and followed that up with a NASCAR Sprint Cup title nine years later, in 2000.

NASCAR SPRINT CUP SERIES
CAREER RECORD (Through 2012)

Year	Races	Wins	Top 5	Top 10	Poles	Points Standing
2008	2	0	0	0	0	57th
2009	15	1	1	4	0	38th
2010	36	0	0	2	1	25th
2011	36	3	10	14	1	5th
2012	36	5	13	23	0	1st

Best Race Finish: 1st (9 times)
Best Points Finish: 1st (2012)

**2013
Car Owner
Roger
Penske**

**2013
Crew Chief
Paul Wolfe**

NASCAR SPRINT CUP SERIES 2012 RACE-BY-RACE RESULTS

RACE	EVENT	LOCATION	START	FINISH	PTS.	STATUS	POS.
1	Daytona 500	Daytona	23	32	12	Accident	29
2	Subway Fresh Fit 500	Phoenix	28	5	52	Running	12
3	KOBALT Tools 400	Las Vegas	20	32	65	Running	22
4	Food City 500	Bristol	5	1	113	Running	14
5	Auto Club 400	Fontana	17	18	139	Running	16
6	Goody's Fast Relief 500	Martinsville	7	9	175	Running	12
7	Samsung Mobile 500	Texas	8	36	183	Running	15
8	STP 400	Kansas	11	11	217	Running	15
9	Capital City 400 Presented by Virginia Is for Lovers	Richmond	16	9	252	Running	13
10	Aaron's 499	Talladega	13	1	299	Running	12
11	Bojangles' Southern 500	Darlington	15	15	328	Running	12
12	Coca-Cola 600	Charlotte	24	5	368	Running	11
13	FedEx 400 Benefiting Autism Speaks	Dover	16	12	400	Running	11
14	Pocono 400 Presented by #NASCAR	Pocono	31	18	426	Running	10
15	Quicken Loans 400	Michigan	25	13	458	Running	10
16	Toyota/Save Mart 350	Sonoma	13	12	490	Running	10
17	Quaker State 400	Kentucky	8	1	537	Running	10
18	Coke Zero 400 Powered by Coca-Cola	Daytona	9	8	573	Running	9
19	Lenox Industrial Tools 301	New Hampshire	22	5	613	Running	10
20	Crown Royal Presents the Curtiss Shaver 400 at the Brickyard Powered by Big Machine Records	Indianapolis	22	9	649	Running	9
21	Pennsylvania 400	Pocono	31	4	690	Running	7
22	Finger Lakes 355 at The Glen	Watkins Glen	4	2	733	Running	5
23	Pure Michigan 400	Michigan	19	2	776	Running	5
24	IRWIN Tools Night Race	Bristol	2	30	790	Running	7
25	AdvoCare 500	Atlanta	21	3	831	Running	6
26	Federated Auto Parts 400	Richmond	10	7	2009	Running	4
27	GEICO 400	Chicagoland	13	1	2056	Running	1
28	SYLVANIA 300	New Hampshire	15	6	2095	Running	2
29	AAA 400	Dover	10	1	2142	Running	1
30	Good Sam Roadside Assistance 500	Talladega	22	7	2179	Running	1
31	Bank of America 500	Charlotte	20	11	2214	Running	1
32	Hollywood Casino 400	Kansas	25	8	2250	Running	1
33	TUMS Fast Relief 500	Martinsville	32	6	2289	Running	2
34	AAA Texas 500	Texas	8	2	2332	Running	2
35	AdvoCare 500	Phoenix	14	6	2371	Running	1
36	Ford EcoBoost 400	Homestead-Miami	3	15	2400	Running	1

TRAVIS KVAPIL

Birth Date: March 1, 1976 • **Hometown:** Janesville, WI • Twitter: @traviskvapil

Photos courtesy of BK Racing

93
**Burger King
Toyota**

Travis Kvapil joined BK Racing for the 2012 season, their first year competing in the NASCAR Sprint Cup Series. He gave the team a solid anchor as a steady, if not spectacular, qualifier who could be counted on to show up at the finish when it counted. The former NASCAR Camping World Truck Series champion's average finish was 10.9 positions better than his average start and included nine top-20 performances in the 35 races he piloted the No. 93 Toyota. Kvapil led eight races and recorded a best finish of eighth in the fall race at Talladega. He finished 27th in points – his best performance since 2008 – in a season that saw him compete in his 200th NASCAR Sprint Cup Series race. He expects to improve considerably in 2013 as the organization matures.

The 36-year-old Kvapil, an unabashed Green Bay Packer fan, was a star on NASCAR's regional late-model circuit before moving to the NASCAR Camping World Truck Series in 2001. In his first season, Kvapil won rookie of the year and, two years later, captured the series championship (2003). He also gave Toyota its first NASCAR national series victory at Michigan in 2004.

Kvapil made his NASCAR Sprint Cup debut with Penske Racing in 2004. Prior to joining BK Racing, Kvapil drove for Cal Wells; Yates Racing, where he logged his best finish to date – a sixth at Talladega in 2008; and Front Row Motorsports. The 2.66-mile Talladega Superspeedway is the site of Kvapil's only Coors Light Pole, which came in the fall of 2008.

NASCAR SPRINT CUP SERIES
CAREER RECORD (Through 2012)

Year	Races	Wins	Top 5	Top 10	Poles	Points Standing
2004	3	0	0	0	0	63rd
2005	36	0	0	2	0	33rd
2006	31	0	0	0	0	36th
2008	36	0	0	4	1	23rd
2009	6	0	0	0	0	49th
2010	34	0	0	0	0	33rd
2011	29	0	0	0	0	56th
2012	35	0	0	1	0	27th

Best Race Finish: 6th (1 time)
Best Points Finish: 23rd (2008)

2013 Car Owner
Ron Devine, Wayne Press

2013 Crew Chief
Todd Anderson

NASCAR SPRINT CUP SERIES 2012 RACE-BY-RACE RESULTS

RACE	EVENT	LOCATION	START	FINISH	PTS.	STATUS	POS.
1	Daytona 500	Daytona	DNE				
2	Subway Fresh Fit 500	Phoenix	41	19	25	Running	32
3	KOBALT Tools 400	Las Vegas	37	39	30	Engine	35
4	Food City 500	Bristol	34	27	47	Running	35
5	Auto Club 400	Fontana	40	29	62	Running	33
6	Goody's Fast Relief 500	Martinsville	34	27	79	Running	33
7	Samsung Mobile 500	Texas	37	38	85	Engine	34
8	STP 400	Kansas	35	25	104	Running	33
9	Capital City 400 Presented by Virginia Is for Lovers	Richmond	29	30	119	Running	34
10	Aaron's 499	Talladega	41	16	148	Running	32
11	Bojangles' Southern 500	Darlington	33	32	148	Running	34
12	Coca-Cola 600	Charlotte	37	29	163	Running	33
13	FedEx 400 Benefiting Autism Speaks	Dover	42	23	184	Running	33
14	Pocono 400 Presented by #NASCAR	Pocono	37	26	202	Running	32
15	Quicken Loans 400	Michigan	39	26	220	Running	31
16	Toyota/Save Mart 350	Sonoma	39	36	228	Running	31
17	Quaker State 400	Kentucky	34	17	256	Running	31
18	Coke Zero 400 Powered by Coca-Cola	Daytona	40	16	284	Running	31
19	Lenox Industrial Tools 301	New Hampshire	30	30	298	Running	31
20	Crown Royal Presents the Curtiss Shaver 400 at the Brickyard Powered by Big Machine Records	Indianapolis	30	37	305	Accident	31
21	Pennsylvania 400	Pocono	37	25	324	Running	31
22	Finger Lakes 355 at The Glen	Watkins Glen	42	24	344	Running	31
23	Pure Michigan 400	Michigan	30	15	373	Running	31
24	IRWIN Tools Night Race	Bristol	41	18	399	Running	31
25	AdvoCare 500	Atlanta	41	26	417	Running	30
26	Federated Auto Parts 400	Richmond	32	27	434	Running	30
27	GEICO 400	Chicagoland	38	31	447	Running	30
28	SYLVANIA 300	New Hampshire	33	31	460	Running	30
29	AAA 400	Dover	33	29	475	Running	30
30	Good Sam Roadside Assistance 500	Talladega	36	8	512	Running	29
31	Bank of America 500	Charlotte	41	25	531	Running	29
32	Hollywood Casino 400	Kansas	31	17	559	Running	29
33	TUMS Fast Relief 500	Martinsville	41	31	573	Running	29
34	AAA Texas 500	Texas	38	23	595	Running	28
35	AdvoCare 500	Phoenix	39	20	620	Running	27
36	Ford EcoBoost 400	Homestead-Miami	38	26	638	Running	27

BOBBY LABONTE

Birth Date: **May 8, 1964** • Hometown: **Corpus Christi, TX** • Twitter: **@Bobby_Labonte**

Photo courtesy of JTG Daugherty Racing

47

Kingsford/Clorox/Scott/ Bush's Beans Toyota

After having celebrated his 20th season as a full-time NASCAR Sprint Cup Series competitor, Texan Bobby Labonte shows no signs of slowing down. He returns to JTG/ Daugherty Racing in 2013 for a third campaign with the organization jointly owned by Tad and Jodi Geschickter and former NBA all-star and current ESPN analyst Brad Daugherty. The single-car team made significant strides in 2012 as Labonte climbed to 23rd in points – an improvement of six places over the previous year. Labonte, the 2000 NASCAR Sprint Cup champion, posted a pair of top-10 finishes, coming in ninth in Martinsville's fall race and 10th in July's Coke Zero 400 at Daytona. The team ended the season with five top-20 finishes during the Chase for the NASCAR Sprint Cup, including a 14th-place finish at Dover. This was a significant improvement over the six finishes of 21st or worse in the year's 10 opening events.

Until Brad Keselowski won the 2012 championship, Labonte was the only competitor holding both NASCAR Sprint Cup and NASCAR Nationwide Series titles. He won the latter championship in 1991, the same season he made his first NASCAR Sprint Cup start. Labonte, whose elder brother Terry is a two-time NASCAR Sprint Cup champion, has 21 first-place finishes in the series, the most recent coming in 2003 at Homestead. With 688 consecutive starts, Labonte ranks second among active drivers (to Jeff Gordon's 689) and fourth all-time. The majority of Labonte's NASCAR Sprint Cup career – 11 seasons – was spent with Joe Gibbs Racing, a tenure that ended after the 2005 season. He finished among the top 10 in points seven times in JGR equipment.

Photo courtesy of NASCAR The Game. www.NASCARTheGame.com

NASCAR SPRINT CUP SERIES
CAREER RECORD (Through 2012)

Year	Races	Wins	Top 5	Top 10	Poles	Points Standing
1991	2	0	0	0	0	66th
1993	30	0	0	6	1	19th
1994	31	0	1	2	0	21st
1995	31	3	7	14	2	10th
1996	31	1	5	14	4	11th
1997	32	1	9	18	3	7th
1998	33	2	11	18	3	6th
1999	34	5	23	26	5	2nd
2000	34	4	19	24	2	1st
2001	36	2	9	20	1	6th
2002	36	1	5	7	0	16th
2003	36	2	12	17	4	8th
2004	36	0	5	11	1	12th
2005	36	0	4	7	0	24th
2006	36	0	3	8	0	21st
2007	36	0	0	3	0	18th
2008	36	0	1	2	0	21st
2009	36	0	0	2	0	30th
2010	36	0	0	0	0	31st
2011	36	0	1	2	0	29th
2012	36	0	0	2	0	23rd

Best Race Finish: 1st (21 times)
Best Points Finish: 1st (2000)

2013 Car Owner
Tad and Jodi Geschickter, Brad Daugherty

2013 Crew Chief
Brian Burns

NASCAR SPRINT CUP SERIES 2012 RACE-BY-RACE RESULTS

RACE	EVENT	LOCATION	START	FINISH	PTS.	STATUS	POS.
1	Daytona 500	Daytona	32	14	30	Running	14
2	Subway Fresh Fit 500	Phoenix	17	16	58	Running	11
3	KOBALT Tools 400	Las Vegas	24	26	76	Running	17
4	Food City 500	Bristol	36	28	92	Running	21
5	Auto Club 400	Fontana	26	28	108	Running	20
6	Goody's Fast Relief 500	Martinsville	16	17	135	Running	22
7	Samsung Mobile 500	Texas	30	27	152	Running	25
8	STP 400	Kansas	30	35	161	Engine	27
9	Capital City 400 Presented by Virginia Is for Lovers	Richmond	19	17	188	Running	27
10	Aaron's 499	Talladega	42	21	211	Running	26
11	Bojangles' Southern 500	Darlington	22	29	226	Running	27
12	Coca-Cola 600	Charlotte	26	28	242	Running	27
13	FedEx 400 Benefiting Autism Speaks	Dover	22	20	266	Running	27
14	Pocono 400 Presented by #NASCAR	Pocono	27	22	288	Running	26
15	Quicken Loans 400	Michigan	31	16	316	Running	26
16	Toyota/Save Mart 350	Sonoma	18	24	336	Running	26
17	Quaker State 400	Kentucky	28	27	353	Running	25
18	Coke Zero 400 Powered by Coca-Cola	Daytona	41	10	387	Running	24
19	Lenox Industrial Tools 301	New Hampshire	18	23	408	Running	23
20	Crown Royal Presents the Curtiss Shaver 400 at the Brickyard Powered by Big Machine Records	Indianapolis	29	26	427	Running	23
21	Pennsylvania 400	Pocono	39	27	444	Running	23
22	Finger Lakes 355 at The Glen	Watkins Glen	26	27	461	Running	24
23	Pure Michigan 400	Michigan	28	22	483	Running	24
24	IRWIN Tools Night Race	Bristol	36	14	513	Running	24
25	AdvoCare 500	Atlanta	25	19	538	Running	24
26	Federated Auto Parts 400	Richmond	29	25	557	Running	24
27	GEICO 400	Chicagoland	23	26	575	Running	24
28	SYLVANIA 300	New Hampshire	17	20	599	Running	24
29	AAA 400	Dover	16	14	629	Running	24
30	Good Sam Roadside Assistance 500	Talladega	40	18	655	Running	24
31	Bank of America 500	Charlotte	15	32	667	Running	24
32	Hollywood Casino 400	Kansas	22	33	678	Accident	24
33	TUMS Fast Relief 500	Martinsville	18	9	713	Running	24
34	AAA Texas 500	Texas	29	33	724	Running	23
35	AdvoCare 500	Phoenix	30	15	753	Running	23
36	Ford EcoBoost 400	Homestead-Miami	32	25	772	Running	23

JOEY LOGANO

Birth Date: **May 24, 1990** • Hometown: **Middletown, CT** • Twitter: **@JLogano**

Photos courtesy of Penske Racing

22

Shell/Pennzoil Ford

At age 22 Joey Logano remains the youngest full-time NASCAR Sprint Cup Series competitor as well as the youngest series pole and race winners (both feats accomplished at 19 years). Logano, however, faces a new challenge in 2013 as he moves from Joe Gibbs Racing to Penske Racing's No. 22 Ford and becomes teammate to reigning champion Brad Keselowski. The Connecticut driver made his series debut as an 18-year-old at New Hampshire in 2008. In four full seasons with JGR, Logano has collected two victories – New Hampshire in 2009 and Pocono in 2012 – and finished a standings-best 16th in 2010. He ranked 17th in 2012 with one win, two Coors Light Poles (Pocono and Homestead), two top-five and 12 top-10 finishes. Logano led three races, including Bristol's second event in which he paced 139 laps and finished eighth. The poles qualify Logano for the season-opening Sprint Unlimited while his second career victory makes him eligible for the 2013 NASCAR Sprint All-Star Race at Charlotte.

Age – or lack thereof – has never been an obstacle for Logano. He was seven years old when he began competing in quarter midget cars; he was the first NASCAR K&N Pro Series East joint champion/rookie of the year; and, until recently, was the touring series' youngest winner (age 16). Logano won the first of his 18 NASCAR Nationwide Series races in just his third start (Kentucky in 2008). He led all NASCAR Nationwide winners in 2012 with nine victories and led Joe Gibbs Racing to the Owner's Championship.

NASCAR SPRINT CUP SERIES
CAREER RECORD (Through 2012)

Year	Races	Wins	Top 5	Top 10	Poles	Points Standing
2008	3	0	0	0	0	63rd
2009	36	1	3	7	0	20th
2010	36	0	7	16	1	16th
2011	36	0	4	6	2	24th
2012	36	1	2	12	2	17th

Best Race Finish: 1st (2 times)
Best Points Finish: 16th (2010)

2013
Car Owner
Roger
Penske

2013
Crew Chief
Todd
Gordon

NASCAR SPRINT CUP SERIES 2012 *RACE-BY-RACE RESULTS*

RACE	EVENT	LOCATION	START	FINISH	PTS.	STATUS	POS.
1	Daytona 500	Daytona	12	9	36	Running	9
2	Subway Fresh Fit 500	Phoenix	9	10	70	Running	8
3	KOBALT Tools 400	Las Vegas	8	16	98	Running	9
4	Food City 500	Bristol	9	16	126	Running	9
5	Auto Club 400	Fontana	8	24	146	Running	13
6	Goody's Fast Relief 500	Martinsville	10	23	167	Running	13
7	Samsung Mobile 500	Texas	14	19	192	Running	13
8	STP 400	Kansas	3	15	221	Running	12
9	Capital City 400 Presented by Virginia Is for Lovers	Richmond	18	24	241	Running	15
10	Aaron's 499	Talladega	30	26	259	Accident	15
11	Bojangles' Southern 500	Darlington	21	10	293	Running	15
12	Coca-Cola 600	Charlotte	19	23	314	Running	16
13	FedEx 400 Benefiting Autism Speaks	Dover	11	8	350	Running	16
14	Pocono 400 Presented by #NASCAR	Pocono	1	1	398	Running	15
15	Quicken Loans 400	Michigan	9	35	407	Accident	15
16	Toyota/Save Mart 350	Sonoma	14	10	441	Running	15
17	Quaker State 400	Kentucky	18	22	463	Running	16
18	Coke Zero 400 Powered by Coca-Cola	Daytona	19	4	503	Running	14
19	Lenox Industrial Tools 301	New Hampshire	16	14	533	Running	16
20	Crown Royal Presents the Curtiss Shaver 400 at the Brickyard Powered by Big Machine Records	Indianapolis	3	33	544	Running	17
21	Pennsylvania 400	Pocono	14	13	575	Running	17
22	Finger Lakes 355 at The Glen	Watkins Glen	14	32	587	Running	18
23	Pure Michigan 400	Michigan	16	31	600	Running	18
24	IRWIN Tools Night Race	Bristol	4	8	638	Running	18
25	AdvoCare 500	Atlanta	9	18	664	Running	18
26	Federated Auto Parts 400	Richmond	8	30	678	Running	18
27	GEICO 400	Chicagoland	10	7	715	Running	18
28	SYLVANIA 300	New Hampshire	18	8	751	Running	18
29	AAA 400	Dover	14	10	785	Running	18
30	Good Sam Roadside Assistance 500	Talladega	14	32	797	Running	18
31	Bank of America 500	Charlotte	12	9	832	Running	17
32	Hollywood Casino 400	Kansas	8	19	857	Running	18
33	TUMS Fast Relief 500	Martinsville	14	16	885	Running	17
34	AAA Texas 500	Texas	6	11	918	Running	17
35	AdvoCare 500	Phoenix	15	27	935	Accident	17
36	Ford EcoBoost 400	Homestead-Miami	1	14	965	Running	17

MARK MARTIN

Birth Date: **January 9, 1959** • Hometown: **Batesville, AR** • Twitter: **@55markmartin**

55

Aaron's Dream Machine Toyota

Despite competing just 24 times in the 2012 season, Mark Martin came within a few points of finishing among the top 25. His four top-five finishes included a second at Pocono and thirds at Texas, Richmond and Dover. He won Michigan's Coors Light Pole in August and led the majority of the first 64 laps before being eliminated in a multi-car accident. Martin, who'll again share Michael Waltrip Racing's No. 55 Toyota with Waltrip and Brian Vickers in 2013, won four Coors Light Poles in 2012 to reach 55 all-time poles won.

Martin, an Arkansas native, has won 40 points-paying races during a NASCAR Sprint Cup Series career that began in 1981. His best season was in 1998, when he won seven times in a Ford owned by Jack Roush. He was selected by owner Roush as his first driver when Roush created his NASCAR Sprint Cup team in 1988. Martin won the NASCAR Sprint All-Star Race in 1998 and 2005, as well as the Shootout at Daytona in 1999. He finished second in NASCAR Sprint Cup standings on five occasions, most recently in 2009 at the age of 50. Martin ranked among the top 10 in points for 12 consecutive seasons between 1989 and 2000. His 448 top 10s rank second all-time and first among active drivers. He likewise ranks among the top 10 in top-five finishes (470), second to Jeff Gordon among active. Martin is one of the few competitors to have won races in all three NASCAR national series. His 49 NASCAR Nationwide Series wins rank second all-time.

Photo courtesy of Michael Waltrip Racing

NASCAR SPRINT CUP SERIES
CAREER RECORD (Through 2012)

Year	Races	Wins	Top 5	Top 10	Poles	Points Standing
1981	5	0	1	2	2	42nd
1982	30	0	2	8	0	14th
1983	16	0	1	3	0	30th
1986	5	0	0	0	0	48th
1987	1	0	0	0	0	102nd
1988	29	0	3	10	1	15th
1989	29	1	14	18	6	3rd
1990	29	3	16	23	3	2nd
1991	29	1	14	17	5	6th
1992	29	2	10	17	1	6th
1993	30	5	12	19	5	3rd
1994	31	2	15	20	1	2nd
1995	31	4	13	22	4	4th
1996	31	0	14	23	4	5th
1997	32	4	16	24	3	3rd
1998	33	7	22	26	3	2nd
1999	34	2	19	26	1	3rd
2000	34	1	13	20	0	8th
2001	36	0	3	15	2	12th
2002	36	1	12	22	0	2nd
2003	36	0	5	10	0	17th
2004	36	1	10	15	0	4th
2005	36	1	12	19	0	4th
2006	36	0	7	15	0	9th
2007	24	0	5	11	0	27th
2008	24	0	4	11	0	28th
2009	36	5	14	21	7	2nd
2010	36	0	7	11	1	13th
2011	36	0	2	10	2	22nd
2012	24	0	4	10	4	26th

Best Race Finish: 1st (40 times)

Best Points Finish: 2nd (1990, 1994, 1998, 2002, 2009)

2013 Car Owner
Michael Waltrip, Rob Kauffman

2013 Crew Chief
Rodney Childers

MARK MARTIN NO. 55 AARON'S DREAM MACHINE TOYOTA

NASCAR SPRINT CUP SERIES 2012 RACE-BY-RACE RESULTS

RACE	EVENT	LOCATION	START	FINISH	PTS.	STATUS	POS.
1	Daytona 500	Daytona	22	10	35	Running	10
2	Subway Fresh Fit 500	Phoenix	1	9	71	Running	7
3	KOBALT Tools 400	Las Vegas	13	18	97	Running	10
4	Food City 500	Bristol	DNE		97		17
5	Auto Club 400	Fontana	3	12	129	Running	17
6	Goody's Fast Relief 500	Martinsville	DNE		129		25
7	Samsung Mobile 500	Texas	4	3	170	Running	20
8	STP 400	Kansas	5	33	181	Engine	24
9	Capital City 400 Presented by Virginia Is for Lovers	Richmond	1	8	218	Running	19
10	Aaron's 499	Talladega	DNE		218		24
11	Bojangles' Southern 500	Darlington	18	20	242	Running	23
12	Coca-Cola 600	Charlotte	6	34	252	Engine	26
13	FedEx 400 Benefiting Autism Speaks	Dover	1	14	283	Running	24
14	Pocono 400 Presented by #NASCAR	Pocono	6	2	326	Running	23
15	Quicken Loans 400	Michigan	14	29	341	Engine	23
16	Toyota/Save Mart 350	Sonoma	DNE		341		24
17	Quaker State 400	Kentucky	DNE		341		27
18	Coke Zero 400 Powered by Coca-Cola	Daytona	DNE		341		28
19	Lenox Industrial Tools 301	New Hampshire	DNE		341		28
20	Crown Royal Presents the Curtiss Shaver 400 at the Brickyard Powered by Big Machine Records	Indianapolis	19	11	374	Running	27
21	Pennsylvania 400	Pocono	18	12	406	Running	26
22	Finger Lakes 355 at The Glen	Watkins Glen	DNE		406		26
23	Pure Michigan 400	Michigan	1	35	417	Accident	26
24	IRWIN Tools Night Race	Bristol	DNE		417		28
25	AdvoCare 500	Atlanta	6	10	451	Running	26
26	Federated Auto Parts 400	Richmond	6	3	492	Running	26
27	GEICO 400	Chicagoland	15	14	522	Running	25
28	SYLVANIA 300	New Hampshire	DNE		522		26
29	AAA 400	Dover	26	3	563	Running	25
30	Good Sam Roadside Assistance 500	Talladega	DNE		563		25
31	Bank of America 500	Charlotte	2	6	602	Running	25
32	Hollywood Casino 400	Kansas	2	24	623	Running	25
33	TUMS Fast Relief 500	Martinsville	DNE		623		26
34	AAA Texas 500	Texas	11	29	638	Accident	26
35	AdvoCare 500	Phoenix	10	10	673	Running	26
36	Ford EcoBoost 400	Homestead-Miami	9	16	701	Running	26

JAMIE McMURRAY

Birth Date: **June 3, 1976** • Hometown: **Joplin, MO** • Twitter: **@JamieMcMurray**

Photo courtesy of Earnhardt Ganassi Racing with Felix Sabates

1

McDonald's Chevrolet

Jamie McMurray returns to the No. 1 Chevrolet hoping to replicate the success he had in the 2010 season. That was a year which saw him post victories at three of the circuit's most iconic tracks, Daytona, Indianapolis and Charlotte, and come within two spots of making the Chase for the NASCAR Sprint Cup. The 2012 season, in which McMurray failed to post a top-five finish for the first time since making his NASCAR Sprint Cup Series debut in 2002, is one to be forgotten. Neither McMurray nor his Earnhardt Ganassi Racing with Felix Sabates teammate Juan Pablo Montoya were able to crack the top 20 in points – although the Missouri native's 21st-place ranking was a step up from 27th in 2011. The 36-year-old McMurray got off to a rough start in 2012, finishing 31st and 37th at Daytona and Phoenix, but rebounded with consecutive top-10 finishes at Las Vegas and Bristol. The latter success was transitory. Just one top 10 – a 10th-place finish at Pocono in June – filled out the remainder of McMurray's dance card.

The former U.S. and world go-kart champion has won at all rungs of the NASCAR ladder, beginning with a NASCAR Whelen All-American Series track title in 1997. He moved to the NASCAR Camping World Truck Series, winning at Martinsville in 2004, and became the NASCAR Nationwide Series' 100th different winner in 2002 at Atlanta. McMurray has driven for two teams in the NASCAR Sprint Cup Series, twice with his current organization and with Roush Fenway Racing from 2006–2009.

Photo courtesy of NASCAR The Game. www.NASCARTheGame.com

NASCAR SPRINT CUP SERIES
CAREER RECORD (Through 2012)

Year	Races	Wins	Top 5	Top 10	Poles	Points Standing
2002	6	1	1	2	0	46th
2003	36	0	5	13	1	13th
2004	36	0	9	23	0	11th
2005	36	0	4	10	1	12th
2006	36	0	3	7	0	25th
2007	36	1	3	9	1	17th
2008	36	0	4	11	0	16th
2009	36	1	1	5	0	22nd
2010	36	3	9	12	4	14th
2011	36	0	2	4	1	27th
2012	36	0	0	3	0	21st

Best Race Finish: 1st (6 times)
Best Points Finish: 11th (2004)

2013 Car Owner
Chip Ganassi, Felix Sabates, Teresa Earnhardt

2013 Crew Chief
Kevin "Bono" Manion

NASCAR SPRINT CUP SERIES 2012 RACE-BY-RACE RESULTS

RACE	EVENT	LOCATION	START	FINISH	PTS.	STATUS	POS.
1	Daytona 500	Daytona	19	31	13	Accident	28
2	Subway Fresh Fit 500	Phoenix	21	37	21	Engine	37
3	KOBALT Tools 400	Las Vegas	19	8	57	Running	25
4	Food City 500	Bristol	17	7	94	Running	19
5	Auto Club 400	Fontana	16	32	106	Running	22
6	Goody's Fast Relief 500	Martinsville	20	20	130	Running	24
7	Samsung Mobile 500	Texas	9	14	160	Running	23
8	STP 400	Kansas	36	14	190	Running	19
9	Capital City 400 Presented by Virginia Is for Lovers	Richmond	37	14	220	Running	18
10	Aaron's 499	Talladega	23	11	253	Running	16
11	Bojangles' Southern 500	Darlington	11	34	263	Running	20
12	Coca-Cola 600	Charlotte	31	21	286	Running	21
13	FedEx 400 Benefiting Autism Speaks	Dover	24	19	311	Running	22
14	Pocono 400 Presented by #NASCAR	Pocono	11	10	346	Running	19
15	Quicken Loans 400	Michigan	19	14	377	Running	18
16	Toyota/Save Mart 350	Sonoma	25	19	402	Running	20
17	Quaker State 400	Kentucky	17	15	431	Running	19
18	Coke Zero 400 Powered by Coca-Cola	Daytona	30	13	462	Running	20
19	Lenox Industrial Tools 301	New Hampshire	28	20	486	Running	20
20	Crown Royal Presents the Curtiss Shaver 400 at the Brickyard Powered by Big Machine Records	Indianapolis	16	22	508	Running	19
21	Pennsylvania 400	Pocono	16	17	536	Running	19
22	Finger Lakes 355 at The Glen	Watkins Glen	10	39	541	Accident	20
23	Pure Michigan 400	Michigan	24	14	571	Running	19
24	IRWIN Tools Night Race	Bristol	26	17	598	Running	19
25	AdvoCare 500	Atlanta	20	24	618	Running	19
26	Federated Auto Parts 400	Richmond	26	22	640	Running	20
27	GEICO 400	Chicagoland	12	21	664	Running	20
28	SYLVANIA 300	New Hampshire	29	26	682	Running	20
29	AAA 400	Dover	20	24	702	Running	20
30	Good Sam Roadside Assistance 500	Talladega	24	34	714	Accident	20
31	Bank of America 500	Charlotte	30	17	741	Running	20
32	Hollywood Casino 400	Kansas	21	15	770	Running	20
33	TUMS Fast Relief 500	Martinsville	24	17	797	Running	20
34	AAA Texas 500	Texas	24	18	823	Running	20
35	AdvoCare 500	Phoenix	18	23	844	Running	20
36	Ford EcoBoost 400	Homestead-Miami	14	20	868	Running	21

CASEY MEARS

Birth Date: **March 12, 1978** • Hometown: **Bakersfield, CA**

Photos courtesy of Germain Racing

GEICO Ford

Casey Mears and the No. 13 Germain Racing team made progress in 2012, gaining two spots in the final points, from 31st to 29th, and adding four points to his season-long Driver Rating (50.4 to 54.5). The team kicked off their first season with Ford by starting on the outside of the first row for the second Budweiser Duel during the 2012 Daytona Speedweeks. Road racing being the great equalizer, Mears had his best performances at Sonoma and Watkins Glen, finishing 15th and 16th, respectively. He also recorded lead-lap efforts at Talladega in the spring, Daytona in July, Texas in November and Kentucky. Mears led 10 laps during the October Talladega race where he was in position to win before a last-lap accident ended his day. He sat on the pole for the August Bristol race after posting the fastest speed in practice. Mears and his team are proud of what they accomplished last year and hope to improve and have stronger performances and better luck in 2013.

During prior stints with Earnhardt Ganassi Racing with Felix Sabates, and with Hendrick Motorsports, Mears challenged for a spot in the Chase for the NASCAR Sprint Cup, finishing 14th and 15th in points in 2006–07. The Bakersfield, California, native has won in all disciplines of motorsport, including the Rolex GRAND-AM Sports Car Series where he became the first full-time NASCAR driver to score an overall win in the Rolex 24 at Daytona (2006).

NASCAR SPRINT CUP SERIES
CAREER RECORD (Through 2012)

Year	Races	Wins	Top 5	Top 10	Poles	Points Standing
2003	36	0	0	0	0	35th
2004	36	0	1	9	2	22nd
2005	36	0	3	9	0	22nd
2006	36	0	2	8	0	14th
2007	36	1	5	10	1	15th
2008	36	0	1	6	0	20th
2009	36	0	0	4	0	21st
2010	21	0	0	0	0	36th
2011	35	0	0	0	0	31st
2012	36	0	0	0	0	29th

Best Race Finish: 1st (1 time)
Best Points Finish: 14th (2006)

2013 Car Owner
Steve Germain

2013 Crew Chief
Robert "Bootie" Barker

NASCAR SPRINT CUP SERIES 2012 RACE-BY-RACE RESULTS

RACE	EVENT	LOCATION	START	FINISH	PTS.	STATUS	POS.
1	Daytona 500	Daytona	36	25	19	Running	24
2	Subway Fresh Fit 500	Phoenix	31	39	24	Accident	34
3	KOBALT Tools 400	Las Vegas	32	27	41	Running	31
4	Food City 500	Bristol	24	25	60	Running	31
5	Auto Club 400	Fontana	33	23	81	Running	29
6	Goody's Fast Relief 500	Martinsville	25	25	100	Running	27
7	Samsung Mobile 500	Texas	22	25	119	Running	28
8	STP 400	Kansas	40	26	137	Running	28
9	Capital City 400 Presented by Virginia Is for Lovers	Richmond	26	21	160	Running	28
10	Aaron's 499	Talladega	25	18	187	Running	28
11	Bojangles' Southern 500	Darlington	31	22	209	Running	28
12	Coca-Cola 600	Charlotte	25	22	231	Running	28
13	FedEx 400 Benefiting Autism Speaks	Dover	40	41	234	Accident	28
14	Pocono 400 Presented by #NASCAR	Pocono	26	35	243	Brakes	28
15	Quicken Loans 400	Michigan	24	20	267	Running	28
16	Toyota/Save Mart 350	Sonoma	20	15	296	Running	28
17	Quaker State 400	Kentucky	21	18	323	Running	28
18	Coke Zero 400 Powered by Coca-Cola	Daytona	7	18	350	Running	27
19	Lenox Industrial Tools 301	New Hampshire	33	36	358	Vibration	27
20	Crown Royal Presents the Curtiss Shaver 400 at the Brickyard Powered by Big Machine Records	Indianapolis	25	34	368	Running	28
21	Pennsylvania 400	Pocono	29	35	377	Brakes	28
22	Finger Lakes 355 at The Glen	Watkins Glen	30	16	405	Running	27
23	Pure Michigan 400	Michigan	29	37	412	Vibration	27
24	IRWIN Tools Night Race	Bristol	1	21	436	Running	26
25	AdvoCare 500	Atlanta	19	33	447	Engine	27
26	Federated Auto Parts 400	Richmond	42	29	462	Running	27
27	GEICO 400	Chicagoland	27	36	470	Accident	27
28	SYLVANIA 300	New Hampshire	30	36	479	Vibration	28
29	AAA 400	Dover	30	31	492	Running	27
30	Good Sam Roadside Assistance 500	Talladega	19	26	511	Accident	30
31	Bank of America 500	Charlotte	27	29	526	Running	30
32	Hollywood Casino 400	Kansas	28	37	533	Accident	30
33	TUMS Fast Relief 500	Martinsville	22	25	552	Running	30
34	AAA Texas 500	Texas	20	21	575	Running	30
35	AdvoCare 500	Phoenix	25	22	597	Running	29
36	Ford EcoBoost 400	Homestead-Miami	28	29	612	Running	29

PAUL MENARD

Birth Date: **August 21, 1980** • Hometown: **Eau Claire, WI**

Photo courtesy of Richard Childress Racing

Menards Chevrolet

Flip a coin as to which season was more successful for the 32-year-old Paul Menard: 2011, when he won the Brickyard 400 at Indianapolis, or 2012, when the Wisconsin native finished 16th in points and recorded nine top-10 finishes, both career bests. Menard would just as soon settle that argument in 2013, his seventh full season in the NASCAR Sprint Cup series, by taking the next step: returning his No. 27 Richard Childress Racing Chevrolet to Victory Lane and qualifying for the Chase for the NASCAR Sprint Cup. In 2012, he opened the season with a sixth in the Daytona 500 and closed equally strong with a ninth-place performance in Phoenix's fall event. He finished among the top five just once, but that third – in October's Chase race at Kansas Speedway – proves the foundation exists to build greater success on in 2013. Menard finished on the lead lap 24 times and led four races.

After winning races on both ovals and road courses in NASCAR regional touring series, the one-time ice racer made his debut in the NASCAR Sprint Cup Series in 2003, driving for ESPN analyst Andy Petree. Menard spent 2005–06 in the NASCAR Nationwide Series, winning at The Milwaukee Mile and twice finishing sixth in the points standings. Prior to joining RCR, Menard competed for Dale Earnhardt Inc. – where he recorded his first top-five finish in 2008 (Talladega) – and Doug Yates.

Photo courtesy of NASCAR The Game. www.NASCARTheGame.com

NASCAR SPRINT CUP SERIES
CAREER RECORD (Through 2012)

Year	Races	Wins	Top 5	Top 10	Poles	Points Standing
2003	1	0	0	0	0	66th
2005	1	0	0	0	0	71st
2006	7	0	0	1	0	45th
2007	30	0	0	0	0	34th
2008	36	0	1	1	1	26th
2009	36	0	0	0	0	31st
2010	36	0	1	6	0	23rd
2011	36	1	4	8	0	17th
2012	36	0	1	9	0	16th

Best Race Finish: 1st (1 time)
Best Points Finish: 16th (2012)

2013 Car Owner
Richard Childress

2013 Crew Chief
Richard "Slugger" Labbe

NASCAR SPRINT CUP SERIES 2012 RACE-BY-RACE RESULTS

RACE	EVENT	LOCATION	START	FINISH	PTS.	STATUS	POS.
1	Daytona 500	Daytona	37	6	39	Running	6
2	Subway Fresh Fit 500	Phoenix	20	31	52	Running	14
3	KOBALT Tools 400	Las Vegas	26	7	89	Running	11
4	Food City 500	Bristol	11	10	123	Running	10
5	Auto Club 400	Fontana	27	19	148	Running	11
6	Goody's Fast Relief 500	Martinsville	11	26	166	Running	14
7	Samsung Mobile 500	Texas	11	18	192	Running	12
8	STP 400	Kansas	19	18	218	Running	14
9	Capital City 400 Presented by Virginia Is for Lovers	Richmond	31	13	249	Running	14
10	Aaron's 499	Talladega	17	17	277	Running	14
11	Bojangles' Southern 500	Darlington	14	13	308	Running	13
12	Coca-Cola 600	Charlotte	9	15	337	Running	14
13	FedEx 400 Benefiting Autism Speaks	Dover	20	17	364	Running	15
14	Pocono 400 Presented by #NASCAR	Pocono	3	9	399	Running	13
15	Quicken Loans 400	Michigan	18	22	421	Running	14
16	Toyota/Save Mart 350	Sonoma	23	20	445	Running	14
17	Quaker State 400	Kentucky	15	12	477	Running	13
18	Coke Zero 400 Powered by Coca-Cola	Daytona	13	14	507	Running	13
19	Lenox Industrial Tools 301	New Hampshire	13	17	534	Running	15
20	Crown Royal Presents the Curtiss Shaver 400 at the Brickyard Powered by Big Machine Records	Indianapolis	8	14	564	Running	16
21	Pennsylvania 400	Pocono	3	11	597	Running	16
22	Finger Lakes 355 at The Glen	Watkins Glen	22	12	629	Running	16
23	Pure Michigan 400	Michigan	10	9	640	Running	16
24	IRWIN Tools Night Race	Bristol	7	10	674	Running	17
25	AdvoCare 500	Atlanta	18	8	710	Running	15
26	Federated Auto Parts 400	Richmond	25	23	731	Running	17
27	GEICO 400	Chicagoland	11	15	760	Running	16
28	SYLVANIA 300	New Hampshire	7	12	792	Running	16
29	AAA 400	Dover	19	22	814	Running	16
30	Good Sam Roadside Assistance 500	Talladega	16	28	830	Accident	16
31	Bank of America 500	Charlotte	24	27	847	Running	16
32	Hollywood Casino 400	Kansas	14	3	889	Running	16
33	TUMS Fast Relief 500	Martinsville	9	12	921	Running	16
34	AAA Texas 500	Texas	27	27	938	Running	16
35	AdvoCare 500	Phoenix	7	9	973	Running	16
36	Ford EcoBoost 400	Homestead-Miami	18	11	1006	Running	16

JUAN PABLO MONTOYA

Birth Date: **September 20, 1975** • Hometown: **Bogota, Columbia** • Twitter: **@jpmontoya**

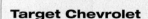

42
Target Chevrolet

Photos courtesy of Earnhardt Ganassi Racing with Felix Sabates

Juan Pablo Montoya enters his seventh full NASCAR Sprint Cup Series season bidding to regain the momentum that carried him to the Chase for the NASCAR Sprint Cup and an eighth-place finish in 2009. The driver of the No. 42 Earnhardt Ganassi Racing with Felix Sabates Chevrolet has the attitude that there's only way one to go: up. The six-season Formula One veteran and Indianapolis 500 winner failed to post a top-five finish for the first time in six NASCAR seasons in 2012. Eighth-place finishes in Bristol's spring race and at Michigan in June stood as highlights in Montoya's effectively lost campaign, one that mirrored teammate Jamie McMurray's year. Montoya finished 22nd in the standings, one spot behind McMurray. He did win a pair of Coors Light Poles – back to back at Pocono and Watkins Glen – which qualified him for February's Sprint Unlimited. All of his NASCAR Sprint Cup starts have come in Ganassi and Earnhardt Ganassi cars.

Montoya has two first-place finishes – at Sonoma in 2007 and Watkins Glen in 2010. The 2009 season remains Montoya's best with seven top-five and 18 top-10 finishes plus a pair of poles. Montoya made his NASCAR Sprint Cup debut in 2006 after a decorated open-wheel career that included seven wins, 30 podium finishes and 13 poles in Formula One competition. He won the 2000 Indianapolis 500 in his first trip to the Speedway a year after Montoya claimed both CART championship and rookie of the year award.

NASCAR SPRINT CUP SERIES
CAREER RECORD (Through 2012)

Year	Races	Wins	Top 5	Top 10	Poles	Points Standing
2006	1	0	0	0	0	69th
2007	36	1	3	6	0	20th
2008	36	0	2	3	0	25th
2009	36	0	7	18	2	8th
2010	36	1	6	14	3	17th
2011	36	0	2	8	2	21st
2012	36	0	0	2	2	22nd

Best Race Finish: 1st (2 times)

Best Points Finish: 8th (2009)

2013
Car Owner
Chip Ganassi,
Felix Sabates,
Teresa
Earnhardt

2013
Crew Chief
Chris Heroy

NASCAR SPRINT CUP SERIES 2012 RACE-BY-RACE RESULTS

RACE	EVENT	LOCATION	START	FINISH	PTS.	STATUS	POS.
1	Daytona 500	Daytona	35	36	8	Accident	32
2	Subway Fresh Fit 500	Phoenix	5	11	41	Running	24
3	KOBALT Tools 400	Las Vegas	29	25	60	Running	24
4	Food City 500	Bristol	30	8	96	Running	18
5	Auto Club 400	Fontana	24	17	123	Running	18
6	Goody's Fast Relief 500	Martinsville	32	21	146	Running	17
7	Samsung Mobile 500	Texas	25	16	174	Running	18
8	STP 400	Kansas	39	12	207	Running	16
9	Capital City 400 Presented by Virginia Is for Lovers	Richmond	20	12	239	Running	16
10	Aaron's 499	Talladega	12	32	252	Accident	17
11	Bojangles' Southern 500	Darlington	27	24	272	Running	19
12	Coca-Cola 600	Charlotte	29	20	296	Running	18
13	FedEx 400 Benefiting Autism Speaks	Dover	31	28	312	Running	20
14	Pocono 400 Presented by #NASCAR	Pocono	17	17	340	Running	21
15	Quicken Loans 400	Michigan	21	8	377	Running	19
16	Toyota/Save Mart 350	Sonoma	12	34	387	Running	22
17	Quaker State 400	Kentucky	31	14	417	Running	21
18	Coke Zero 400 Powered by Coca-Cola	Daytona	14	28	433	Accident	21
19	Lenox Industrial Tools 301	New Hampshire	31	25	452	Running	21
20	Crown Royal Presents the Curtiss Shaver 400 at the Brickyard Powered by Big Machine Records	Indianapolis	12	21	475	Running	21
21	Pennsylvania 400	Pocono	1	20	500	Running	21
22	Finger Lakes 355 at The Glen	Watkins Glen	1	33	512	Accident	22
23	Pure Michigan 400	Michigan	25	26	530	Running	22
24	IRWIN Tools Night Race	Bristol	28	13	561	Running	21
25	AdvoCare 500	Atlanta	33	21	584	Running	21
26	Federated Auto Parts 400	Richmond	24	20	608	Running	21
27	GEICO 400	Chicagoland	28	23	629	Running	21
28	SYLVANIA 300	New Hampshire	24	22	651	Running	21
29	AAA 400	Dover	35	26	669	Running	21
30	Good Sam Roadside Assistance 500	Talladega	27	38	675	Engine	22
31	Bank of America 500	Charlotte	22	19	700	Running	22
32	Hollywood Casino 400	Kansas	24	16	728	Running	22
33	TUMS Fast Relief 500	Martinsville	25	20	752	Running	22
34	AAA Texas 500	Texas	25	34	762	Running	22
35	AdvoCare 500	Phoenix	21	12	794	Running	22
36	Ford EcoBoost 400	Homestead-Miami	21	28	810	Running	22

RYAN NEWMAN

Birth Date: **December 8, 1977** • Hometown: **South Bend, IN** • Twitter: **@RyanNewman39**

Photos courtesy of Stewart-Haas Racing

39

Quicken Loans Chevrolet

Reunited with crew chief Matt Borland in the waning weeks of an up-and-down season, Ryan Newman ended his 2012 campaign on a high note by finishing third at Homestead. One finish may not equate to championship form, but there's little doubt that Newman, Borland and the No. 39 Stewart-Haas Racing Chevrolet team have the tools to be contenders and more in the 2013 season. Not that 2012 was a total loss, Newman won his 16th career race at Martinsville in the spring and was in the mix for a Chase for the NASCAR Sprint Cup wild card berth all the way to Richmond's regular season finale. He ultimately ranked 14th with six top-five and 14 top-10 finishes. The 2012 season saw Newman's 11-season-long Coors Light Pole streak end as he attempted without success to fashion his 50th career pole. Newman came close, qualifying second at Daytona in July and Talladega in the fall.

A member of the Quarter Midget Hall of Fame — Newman began racing the cars at age four — and a former USAC Silver Coors Light Silver Bullet Series champion (1999), he made several ARCA appearances with a victory at Pocono. Newman made his NASCAR Sprint Cup debut with Penske Racing in 2000. In nine seasons with Penske Racing, he won 13 times and added 43 poles, earning the nickname "Rocketman." After four top-10 championship finishes, Newman moved to Stewart-Haas Racing in 2009 where he's won three times and qualified for the Chase twice in four seasons. Newman holds a Bachelor of Science degree in Vehicle Structure Engineering from Purdue University.

NASCAR SPRINT CUP SERIES
CAREER RECORD (Through 2012)

Year	Races	Wins	Top 5	Top 10	Poles	Points Standing
2000	1	0	0	0	0	70th
2001	7	0	2	2	1	49th
2002	36	1	14	22	6	7th
2003	36	8	17	22	11	6th
2004	36	2	11	14	9	7th
2005	36	1	8	16	8	6th
2006	36	0	2	7	2	18th
2007	36	0	7	15	5	13th
2008	36	1	2	8	1	17th
2009	36	0	5	15	2	9th
2010	36	1	4	14	1	15th
2011	36	1	9	17	3	10th
2012	36	1	6	14	0	14th

Best Race Finish: 1st (16 times)
Best Points Finish: 6th (2003, 2005)

2013 Team Owner
Tony Stewart, Gene Haas

2013 Crew Chief
Matt Borland

NASCAR SPRINT CUP SERIES 2012 RACE-BY-RACE RESULTS

RACE	EVENT	LOCATION	START	FINISH	PTS.	STATUS	POS.
1	Daytona 500	Daytona	18	21	23	Running	20
2	Subway Fresh Fit 500	Phoenix	6	21	46	Running	18
3	KOBALT Tools 400	Las Vegas	18	4	86	Running	14
4	Food City 500	Bristol	3	12	118	Running	13
5	Auto Club 400	Fontana	6	7	155	Running	10
6	Goody's Fast Relief 500	Martinsville	5	1	202	Running	8
7	Samsung Mobile 500	Texas	6	21	225	Running	9
8	STP 400	Kansas	13	20	249	Running	10
9	Capital City 400 Presented by Virginia Is for Lovers	Richmond	12	15	278	Running	10
10	Aaron's 499	Talladega	14	36	286	Engine	13
11	Bojangles' Southern 500	Darlington	4	23	307	Running	14
12	Coca-Cola 600	Charlotte	16	14	337	Running	13
13	FedEx 400 Benefiting Autism Speaks	Dover	3	15	366	Running	13
14	Pocono 400 Presented by #NASCAR	Pocono	18	12	398	Running	14
15	Quicken Loans 400	Michigan	5	15	427	Running	13
16	Toyota/Save Mart 350	Sonoma	10	18	453	Running	13
17	Quaker State 400	Kentucky	5	34	463	Engine	15
18	Coke Zero 400 Powered by Coca-Cola	Daytona	2	5	502	Running	15
19	Lenox Industrial Tools 301	New Hampshire	6	10	536	Running	14
20	Crown Royal Presents the Curtiss Shaver 400 at the Brickyard Powered by Big Machine Records	Indianapolis	11	7	573	Running	14
21	Pennsylvania 400	Pocono	9	6	611	Running	14
22	Finger Lakes 355 at The Glen	Watkins Glen	6	11	644	Running	13
23	Pure Michigan 400	Michigan	15	8	680	Running	13
24	IRWIN Tools Night Race	Bristol	19	36	688	Accident	15
25	AdvoCare 500	Atlanta	17	35	697	Accident	17
26	Federated Auto Parts 400	Richmond	14	8	734	Running	16
27	GEICO 400	Chicagoland	20	5	773	Running	14
28	SYLVANIA 300	New Hampshire	8	10	807	Running	14
29	AAA 400	Dover	8	21	830	Running	15
30	Good Sam Roadside Assistance 500	Talladega	2	9	865	Running	14
31	Bank of America 500	Charlotte	3	20	889	Running	14
32	Hollywood Casino 400	Kansas	6	30	903	Accident	15
33	TUMS Fast Relief 500	Martinsville	17	11	936	Running	15
34	AAA Texas 500	Texas	36	12	969	Running	14
35	AdvoCare 500	Phoenix	12	5	1009	Running	14
36	Ford EcoBoost 400	Homestead-Miami	19	3	1051	Running	14

DANICA PATRICK

Birth Date: **March 25, 1982** • Hometown: **Roscoe, IL** • Twitter: **@DanicaPatrick**

Photos courtesy of Stewart-Haas Racing

10

GoDaddy.com Chevrolet

After setting numerous records as a female competitor in NASCAR national series racing, Danica Patrick moves fulltime to the NASCAR Sprint Cup Series in 2013 driving the No. 10 Stewart-Haas Racing Chevrolet. In addition to her NASCAR Nationwide Series schedule, Patrick competed in 10 Sprint Cup Series events during the 2012 season at some of the most challenging tracks on the schedule. She posted her best finish of the season – 17th – in her last start at Phoenix in November. Patrick also recorded top-25 finishes at Texas, where she finished on the lead lap, and Chicagoland.

In her first full NASCAR Nationwide season, Patrick became the first female driver to record a top-10 (10th) championship finish. She logged four top 10s, the best an eighth at Texas in the spring. Her first career Coors Light Pole came in the 2012 season's opening race at Daytona. In 2011 Patrick recorded the highest national race finish by a female driver – fourth at Las Vegas.

Like many in this era, Patrick began her competitive career in karting, winning several regional and national championships, before moving to England where she competed in various open-wheel series. She became the first female to win a Formula Atlantic pole (at Portland in 2003) before moving to the IndyCar Series. Patrick started and finished fourth in the 2005 Indianapolis 500 and bettered that performance with a third in 2009. She became the first woman to win a major closed-course auto race, the 2008 IndyCar event at Japan's Twin Ring Motegi.

NASCAR SPRINT CUP SERIES
CAREER RECORD (Through 2012)

Year	Races	Wins	Top 5	Top 10	Poles	Points Standing
2012	10	0	0	0	0	n/a

Best Race Finish: 17th (1 time)
Best Points Finish: n/a

2013 Team Owner
Tony Stewart, Gene Haas

2013 Crew Chief
Tony Gibson

NASCAR SPRINT CUP SERIES 2012 RACE-BY-RACE RESULTS

RACE	EVENT	LOCATION	START	FINISH	PTS.	STATUS	POS.
1	Daytona 500	Daytona	29	38	0	Running	0
2	Subway Fresh Fit 500	Phoenix	DNE		0		0
3	KOBALT Tools 400	Las Vegas	DNE		0		0
4	Food City 500	Bristol	DNE		0		0
5	Auto Club 400	Fontana	DNE		0		0
6	Goody's Fast Relief 500	Martinsville	DNE		0		0
7	Samsung Mobile 500	Texas	DNE		0		0
8	STP 400	Kansas	DNE		0		0
9	Capital City 400 Presented by Virginia Is for Lovers	Richmond	DNE		0		0
10	Aaron's 499	Talladega	DNE		0		0
11	Bojangles' Southern 500	Darlington	38	31	0	Running	0
12	Coca-Cola 600	Charlotte	40	30	0	Running	0
13	FedEx 400 Benefiting Autism Speaks	Dover	DNE		0		0
14	Pocono 400 Presented by #NASCAR	Pocono	DNE		0		0
15	Quicken Loans 400	Michigan	DNE		0		0
16	Toyota/Save Mart 350	Sonoma	DNE		0		0
17	Quaker State 400	Kentucky	DNE		0		0
18	Coke Zero 400 Powered by Coca-Cola	Daytona	DNE		0		0
19	Lenox Industrial Tools 301	New Hampshire	DNE		0		0
20	Crown Royal Presents the Curtiss Shaver 400 at the Brickyard Powered by Big Machine Records	Indianapolis	DNE		0		0
21	Pennsylvania 400	Pocono	DNE		0		0
22	Finger Lakes 355 at The Glen	Watkins Glen	DNE		0		0
23	Pure Michigan 400	Michigan	DNE		0		0
24	IRWIN Tools Night Race	Bristol	43	29	0	Accident	0
25	AdvoCare 500	Atlanta	23	29	0	Running	0
26	Federated Auto Parts 400	Richmond	DNE		0		0
27	GEICO 400	Chicagoland	41	25	0	Running	0
28	SYLVANIA 300	New Hampshire	DNE		0		0
29	AAA 400	Dover	38	28	0	Running	0
30	Good Sam Roadside Assistance 500	Talladega	DNE		0		0
31	Bank of America 500	Charlotte	DNE		0		0
32	Hollywood Casino 400	Kansas	40	32	0	Accident	0
33	TUMS Fast Relief 500	Martinsville	DNE		0		0
34	AAA Texas 500	Texas	32	24	0	Running	0
35	AdvoCare 500	Phoenix	37	17	0	Running	0
36	Ford EcoBoost 400	Homestead-Miami	DNE		0		0

DAVID RAGAN

Birth Date: **December 24, 1985** • Hometown: **Unadilla, GA** • Twitter: **@David_Ragan**

34

Peanut Patch Ford

Photos courtesy of
Front Row Motorsports

After five full seasons at Roush Fenway Racing, David Ragan moved to Front Row Motorsports in 2012 and finished 28th in final points standings. Ragan's best finishes came at Talladega, where he finished fourth in the superspeedway's fall race and had a seventh-place performance in the spring. Ragan's No. 34 Ford qualified for all 36 races, leading at least one lap in nine of them. He also competed in the Shootout at Daytona and the NASCAR Sprint All-Star Race.

Ragan made his NASCAR Sprint Cup Series debut at Dover in 2006, finishing 42nd. He previously competed in the NASCAR Dash compact car series, ARCA and the NASCAR Camping World Truck Series, where his best finish was a fifth at Kentucky in 2006. Ragan ultimately drove for Roush Fenway Racing in 182 NASCAR Sprint Cup races, winning the 2011 Coke Zero 400 at Daytona. Ragan's best season came in 2008 when he posted six top-five and 14 top-10 finishes and ranked 13th in final points. He has two career Coors Light poles, captured at Texas and Indianapolis, both in the 2011 season. The Georgia native, son of retired NASCAR Sprint Cup driver Ken Ragan, also has placed first twice in the NASCAR Nationwide Series, those wins coming at Bristol and Talladega in 2009. He owns a Ford dealership in Perry, Georgia, and competes in late-model cars when his schedule allows.

NASCAR SPRINT CUP SERIES
CAREER RECORD (Through 2012)

Year	Races	Wins	Top 5	Top 10	Poles	Points Standing
2006	2	0	0	0	0	63rd
2007	36	0	2	3	0	23rd
2008	36	0	6	14	0	13th
2009	36	0	0	2	0	27th
2010	36	0	0	3	0	24th
2011	36	1	4	8	2	23rd
2012	36	0	1	2	0	28th

Best Race Finish: 1st (1 time)

Best Points Finish: 13th (2008)

2013 Car Owner
Bob Jenkins

2013 Crew Chief
Jay Guy

NASCAR SPRINT CUP SERIES 2012 RACE-BY-RACE RESULTS

RACE	EVENT	LOCATION	START	FINISH	PTS.	STATUS	POS.
1	Daytona 500	Daytona	25	43	1	Accident	38
2	Subway Fresh Fit 500	Phoenix	34	25	21	Running	36
3	KOBALT Tools 400	Las Vegas	35	21	45	Running	28
4	Food City 500	Bristol	31	23	66	Running	28
5	Auto Club 400	Fontana	38	31	79	Running	31
6	Goody's Fast Relief 500	Martinsville	21	24	99	Running	28
7	Samsung Mobile 500	Texas	21	35	109	Running	29
8	STP 400	Kansas	27	30	123	Running	30
9	Capital City 400 Presented by Virginia Is for Lovers	Richmond	38	32	135	Running	29
10	Aaron's 499	Talladega	32	7	172	Running	29
11	Bojangles' Southern 500	Darlington	37	28	188	Running	29
12	Coca-Cola 600	Charlotte	30	35	198	Engine	30
13	FedEx 400 Benefiting Autism Speaks	Dover	28	21	222	Running	29
14	Pocono 400 Presented by #NASCAR	Pocono	34	27	240	Running	29
15	Quicken Loans 400	Michigan	38	23	261	Running	29
16	Toyota/Save Mart 350	Sonoma	29	27	278	Running	29
17	Quaker State 400	Kentucky	33	29	293	Running	29
18	Coke Zero 400 Powered by Coca-Cola	Daytona	27	26	312	Accident	29
19	Lenox Industrial Tools 301	New Hampshire	19	34	322	Engine	29
20	Crown Royal Presents the Curtiss Shaver 400 at the Brickyard Powered by Big Machine Records	Indianapolis	36	28	338	Running	29
21	Pennsylvania 400	Pocono	32	28	354	Running	29
22	Finger Lakes 355 at The Glen	Watkins Glen	32	22	376	Running	29
23	Pure Michigan 400	Michigan	37	23	397	Running	30
24	IRWIN Tools Night Race	Bristol	24	32	409	Running	29
25	AdvoCare 500	Atlanta	14	28	425	Running	29
26	Federated Auto Parts 400	Richmond	27	32	437	Running	29
27	GEICO 400	Chicagoland	37	22	460	Running	29
28	SYLVANIA 300	New Hampshire	26	29	475	Running	29
29	AAA 400	Dover	31	30	489	Running	29
30	Good Sam Roadside Assistance 500	Talladega	25	4	530	Running	27
31	Bank of America 500	Charlotte	25	34	540	Running	28
32	Hollywood Casino 400	Kansas	37	20	564	Running	27
33	TUMS Fast Relief 500	Martinsville	16	26	582	Running	27
34	AAA Texas 500	Texas	33	28	598	Running	27
35	AdvoCare 500	Phoenix	29	33	609	Accident	28
36	Ford EcoBoost 400	Homestead-Miami	34	31	622	Running	28

RICKY STENHOUSE JR.

Birth Date: **October 2, 1987** • Hometown: **Olive Branch, MS** • Twitter: **@StenhouseJr**

17

Best Buy/Zest/Fifth Third Bank Ford

With Ricky Stenhouse Jr.'s move to the NASCAR Sprint Cup Series in 2013, Roush Fenway Racing will boast three NASCAR Nationwide Series champions in its trio of Ford Fusions. Stenhouse, who last year became just the sixth driver to win consecutive titles in the NASCAR Nationwide Series, joins Greg Biffle and Carl Edwards in the formidable lineup. Stenhouse moves into the No. 17 Ford vacated by 2003 NASCAR Sprint Cup champion Matt Kenseth. Stenhouse warmed up for his rookie campaign with four starts in NASCAR's premier series in 2012 and had a best finish of 12th at Dover. The Mississippi native made his series debut in relief of 2011 Daytona 500 winner Trevor Bayne and drove the fabled No. 21 Wood Brothers Ford to an 11th-place finish in the 2011 Coca-Cola 600 at Charlotte.

Stenhouse began his career in karts at the age of six and graduated to sprint cars in 2003. He won two sprint car and five midget races for three-time NASCAR champion Tony Stewart's USAC team in 2007. After winning twice in ARCA, Stenhouse caught the eye of owner Jack Roush. Stenhouse won NASCAR Nationwide Series Sunoco Rookie of the Year honors in 2010 and the overall championship the following year, a year which saw him win both Iowa races. Last year was a breakout performance as Stenhouse drove his No. 6 Ford to six victories and finished in the top five and top 10 19 and 26 times, respectively.

Photo courtesy of Roush Fenway Racing

Photo courtesy of NASCAR The Game. www.NASCARTheGame.com

NASCAR SPRINT CUP SERIES
CAREER RECORD (Through 2012)

Year	Races	Wins	Top 5	Top 10	Poles	Points Standing
2011	1	0	0	0	0	n/a
2012	4	0	0	0	0	n/a

Best Race Finish: 11th (1 time)
Best Points Finish: n/a

2013
Car Owner
Jack Roush,
John Henry

2013
Crew Chief
Scott
Graves

NASCAR SPRINT CUP SERIES 2012 RACE-BY-RACE RESULTS

RACE	EVENT	LOCATION	START	FINISH	PTS.	STATUS	POS.
1	Daytona 500	Daytona	21	20	0	Running	0
2	Subway Fresh Fit 500	Phoenix	DNE		0		0
3	KOBALT Tools 400	Las Vegas	DNE		0		0
4	Food City 500	Bristol	DNE		0		0
5	Auto Club 400	Fontana	DNE		0		0
6	Goody's Fast Relief 500	Martinsville	DNE		0		0
7	Samsung Mobile 500	Texas	DNE		0		0
8	STP 400	Kansas	DNE		0		0
9	Capital City 400 Presented by Virginia Is for Lovers	Richmond	DNE		0		0
10	Aaron's 499	Talladega	DNE		0		0
11	Bojangles' Southern 500	Darlington	DNE		0		0
12	Coca-Cola 600	Charlotte	DNE		0		0
13	FedEx 400 Benefiting Autism Speaks	Dover	DNE		0		0
14	Pocono 400 Presented by #NASCAR	Pocono	DNE		0		0
15	Quicken Loans 400	Michigan	DNE		0		0
16	Toyota/Save Mart 350	Sonoma	DNE		0		0
17	Quaker State 400	Kentucky	DNE		0		0
18	Coke Zero 400 Powered by Coca-Cola	Daytona	DNE		0		0
19	Lenox Industrial Tools 301	New Hampshire	DNE		0		0
20	Crown Royal Presents the Curtiss Shaver 400 at the Brickyard Powered by Big Machine Records	Indianapolis	DNE		0		0
21	Pennsylvania 400	Pocono	DNE		0		0
22	Finger Lakes 355 at The Glen	Watkins Glen	DNE		0		0
23	Pure Michigan 400	Michigan	DNE		0		0
24	IRWIN Tools Night Race	Bristol	DNE		0		0
25	AdvoCare 500	Atlanta	DNE		0		0
26	Federated Auto Parts 400	Richmond	DNE		0		0
27	GEICO 400	Chicagoland	DNE		0		0
28	SYLVANIA 300	New Hampshire	DNE		0		0
29	AAA 400	Dover	17	12	0	Running	0
30	Good Sam Roadside Assistance 500	Talladega	DNE		0		0
31	Bank of America 500	Charlotte	29	35	0	Engine	0
32	Hollywood Casino 400	Kansas	DNE		0		0
33	TUMS Fast Relief 500	Martinsville	DNE		0		0
34	AAA Texas 500	Texas	DNE		0		0
35	AdvoCare 500	Phoenix	DNE		0		0
36	Ford EcoBoost 400	Homestead-Miami	27	39	0	Accident	0

TONY STEWART

Birth Date: **May 20, 1971** • Hometown: **Columbus, IN**

Photos courtesy of Stewart-Haas Racing

14

Bass Pro Shops/Mobil 1 Chevrolet

"Good, but not great" describes Tony Stewart's 14th season. The three-time champion won three times and qualified for his eighth Chase for the NASCAR Sprint Cup in 2012. Stewart, who won five of 10 Chase races and the title in 2011, saw that magic vanish with the turning of the calendar. Despite entering the post season with a No. 3 seeding, the veteran from Columbus, Indiana, was unable to match momentum and results. Three finishes outside the top 10 in the final four races left Stewart ninth in points – matching his second worst series ranking. Not to worry, as Stewart returns in 2013 willing and able to pursue championship No. 4, a plateau only four competitors have reached. Among Stewart's goals for the 2013 season is to capture his 50th NASCAR Sprint Cup Series victory. He won for the 47th time in Daytona's Coke Zero 400 in 2012 and has won three or more times in 10 different seasons. Only two active drivers – Jeff Gordon and Jimmie Johnson – have reached the half-century mark.

One of 23 drivers to win races in all three NASCAR national series, Stewart is an IndyCar champion as well as the first to sweep championships in USAC's midget, sprint and Silver Crown divisions in the same season (1995). He was the Indianapolis 500 rookie of the year in 1996 after winning the pole and leading the first 44 laps. Stewart also won the 2006 International Race of Champions title. In 2011 Stewart became the first owner-driver to win the NASCAR Sprint Cup title since Alan Kulwicki nearly two decades earlier.

TONY STEWART NO. 14 BASS PRO SHOPS/ MOBIL 1 CHEVROLET

NASCAR SPRINT CUP SERIES
CAREER RECORD (Through 2012)

Year	Races	Wins	Top 5	Top 10	Poles	Points Standing
1999	34	3	12	21	2	4th
2000	34	6	12	23	2	6th
2001	36	3	15	22	0	2nd
2002	36	3	15	21	2	1st
2003	36	2	12	18	1	7th
2004	36	2	10	19	0	6th
2005	36	5	17	25	3	1st
2006	36	5	15	19	0	11th
2007	36	3	11	23	0	6th
2008	36	1	10	16	0	9th
2009	36	4	15	23	0	6th
2010	36	2	9	17	2	7th
2011	36	5	9	19	1	1st
2012	36	3	12	16	1	9th

Best Race Finish: 1st (47 times)
Best Points Finish: 1st (2002, 2005, 2011)

2013 Team Owner
Tony Stewart, Gene Haas

2013 Crew Chief
Steve Addington

NASCAR SPRINT CUP SERIES 2012 RACE-BY-RACE RESULTS

RACE	EVENT	LOCATION	START	FINISH	PTS.	STATUS	POS.
1	Daytona 500	Daytona	3	16	29	Running	16
2	Subway Fresh Fit 500	Phoenix	2	22	52	Running	15
3	KOBALT Tools 400	Las Vegas	7	1	100	Running	7
4	Food City 500	Bristol	23	14	130	Running	7
5	Auto Club 400	Fontana	9	1	177	Running	4
6	Goody's Fast Relief 500	Martinsville	15	7	214	Running	3
7	Samsung Mobile 500	Texas	29	24	234	Running	7
8	STP 400	Kansas	23	13	265	Running	8
9	Capital City 400 Presented by Virginia Is for Lovers	Richmond	22	3	307	Running	8
10	Aaron's 499	Talladega	8	24	328	Running	7
11	Bojangles' Southern 500	Darlington	17	3	369	Running	7
12	Coca-Cola 600	Charlotte	21	25	388	Running	9
13	FedEx 400 Benefiting Autism Speaks	Dover	29	25	407	Running	8
14	Pocono 400 Presented by #NASCAR	Pocono	22	3	448	Running	8
15	Quicken Loans 400	Michigan	8	2	491	Running	8
16	Toyota/Save Mart 350	Sonoma	24	2	533	Running	5
17	Quaker State 400	Kentucky	22	32	545	Running	9
18	Coke Zero 400 Powered by Coca-Cola	Daytona	42	1	586	Running	5
19	Lenox Industrial Tools 301	New Hampshire	10	12	618	Running	7
20	Crown Royal Presents the Curtiss Shaver 400 at the Brickyard Powered by Big Machine Records	Indianapolis	28	10	652	Running	8
21	Pennsylvania 400	Pocono	28	5	691	Running	6
22	Finger Lakes 355 at The Glen	Watkins Glen	7	19	716	Running	8
23	Pure Michigan 400	Michigan	14	32	728	Engine	9
24	IRWIN Tools Night Race	Bristol	21	27	746	Running	10
25	AdvoCare 500	Atlanta	1	22	769	Running	10
26	Federated Auto Parts 400	Richmond	28	4	2009	Running	3
27	GEICO 400	Chicagoland	29	6	2048	Running	3
28	SYLVANIA 300	New Hampshire	3	7	2086	Running	4
29	AAA 400	Dover	24	20	2110	Running	5
30	Good Sam Roadside Assistance 500	Talladega	4	22	2133	Accident	7
31	Bank of America 500	Charlotte	32	13	2164	Running	8
32	Hollywood Casino 400	Kansas	33	5	2203	Running	7
33	TUMS Fast Relief 500	Martinsville	7	27	2220	Running	10
34	AAA Texas 500	Texas	21	5	2259	Running	7
35	AdvoCare 500	Phoenix	9	19	2284	Running	9
36	Ford EcoBoost 400	Homestead-Miami	35	17	2311	Running	9

DAVID STREMME

Birth Date: **June 19, 1977** • Hometown: **South Bend, IN** • Twitter: **@DavidStremme**

**Swan Energy
Toyota**

Photo not available at press time

With his fourth different owner in as many seasons, David Stremme hopes potential becomes success in 2013. The Indiana native completed only five of the 28 races in which he competed for Inception Motorsports in 2012, finishing on the lead lap just once (Indianapolis). With the No. 30 Toyota team sold to oil and gas entrepreneur Brandon Davis – and renamed Swan Racing – Stremme is looking for more than a 36th-place championship finish in the new year. The former NASCAR Nationwide Series rookie of the year has found the opportunities fleeting at the NASCAR Sprint Cup Series level. He made his first NASCAR Sprint Cup start in 2005 at Chicagoland. His best season, 2007, found him finishing 24th overall with three top 10s driving for Chip Ganassi. The year's highlight was an eighth-place finish in the spring race at Talladega.

Stremme began racing at age 15 and moved through local and regional stock car classes before winning three ARCA races, the first coming in 2003. He posted a victory at Michigan in 2006 in a car owned by NASCAR Hall of Famer Rusty Wallace. After winning 2003 NASCAR Nationwide Series Sunoco Rookie of the Year honors, Stremme finished ranked ninth the following season in cars owned by Todd Braun and former NFL quarterback Terry Bradshaw. In nearly 150 starts, Stremme's best NASCAR Nationwide finish is second, which he achieved three times, at Milwaukee (2004), Talladega and Nashville (both in 2008).

Photo courtesy of NASCAR The Game. www.NASCARTheGame.com

NASCAR SPRINT CUP SERIES
CAREER RECORD (Through 2012)

Year	Races	Wins	Top 5	Top 10	Poles	Points Standing
2005	4	0	0	0	0	57th
2006	34	0	0	0	0	33rd
2007	36	0	0	3	0	24th
2008	1	0	0	0	0	66th
2009	33	0	0	0	0	32nd
2010	11	0	0	0	0	46th
2011	18	0	0	0	0	41st
2012	28	0	0	0	0	36th

Best Race Finish: 8th (1 time)
Best Points Finish: 27th (2007)

Photo not available at press time

2013 Car Owner
Brandon Davis

2013 Crew Chief
Tony Eury Jr.

NASCAR SPRINT CUP SERIES 2012 RACE-BY-RACE RESULTS

RACE	EVENT	LOCATION	START	FINISH	PTS.	STATUS	POS.
1	Daytona 500	Daytona	42	37	7	Engine	33
2	Subway Fresh Fit 500	Phoenix	43	29	22	Running	35
3	KOBALT Tools 400	Las Vegas	43	28	38	Running	34
4	Food City 500	Bristol	28	38	44	Accident	36
5	Auto Club 400	Fontana	20	39	49	Rear Gear	36
6	Goody's Fast Relief 500	Martinsville	39	30	63	Running	36
7	Samsung Mobile 500	Texas	DNQ		63		36
8	STP 400	Kansas	24	38	69	Overheating	36
9	Capital City 400 Presented by Virginia Is for Lovers	Richmond	34	37	76	Brakes	35
10	Aaron's 499	Talladega	27	39	81	Transmission	35
11	Bojangles' Southern 500	Darlington	32	39	86	Overheating	35
12	Coca-Cola 600	Charlotte	35	38	92	Rear Gear	35
13	FedEx 400 Benefiting Autism Speaks	Dover	32	33	103	Overheating	35
14	Pocono 400 Presented by #NASCAR	Pocono	DNQ		103		35
15	Quicken Loans 400	Michigan	DNQ		103		36
16	Toyota/Save Mart 350	Sonoma	DNE		103		37
17	Quaker State 400	Kentucky	32	36	111	Vibration	36
18	Coke Zero 400 Powered by Coca-Cola	Daytona	26	39	116	Rear Gear	36
19	Lenox Industrial Tools 301	New Hampshire	40	35	125	Vibration	36
20	Crown Royal Presents the Curtiss Shaver 400 at the Brickyard Powered by Big Machine Records	Indianapolis	26	24	145	Running	35
21	Pennsylvania 400	Pocono	36	34	155	Transmission	35
22	Finger Lakes 355 at The Glen	Watkins Glen	DNE		155		35
23	Pure Michigan 400	Michigan	31	34	165	Electrical	35
24	IRWIN Tools Night Race	Bristol	31	37	172	Rear Gear	36
25	AdvoCare 500	Atlanta	31	39	177	Suspension	36
26	Federated Auto Parts 400	Richmond	31	37	184	Brakes	35
27	GEICO 400	Chicagoland	31	39	189	Transmission	35
28	SYLVANIA 300	New Hampshire	43	35	198	Transmission	36
29	AAA 400	Dover	DNQ		198		36
30	Good Sam Roadside Assistance 500	Talladega	30	33	209	Running	36
31	Bank of America 500	Charlotte	31	37	216	Rear Gear	35
32	Hollywood Casino 400	Kansas	DNQ		216		35
33	TUMS Fast Relief 500	Martinsville	40	40	220	Accident	36
34	AAA Texas 500	Texas	DNQ		220		36
35	AdvoCare 500	Phoenix	32	34	230	Brakes	36
36	Ford EcoBoost 400	Homestead-Miami	22	38	236	Electrical	36

MARTIN TRUEX JR.

Birth Date: **June 29, 1980** • Hometown: **Mayetta, NJ** • Twitter: **@martintruexjr56**

Photo courtesy of Michael Waltrip Racing

NAPA AUTO PARTS
Toyota

For Martin Truex Jr. 2012 was all about the journey – not necessarily the destination. In retrospect, at least statistically, a ranking of 11th is hardly earth shaking, even though Truex matched his best championship finish, achieved in 2007 when he was with Dale Earnhardt Inc. Truex also had finishes of 18th and 22nd with four top fives in two previous seasons with Michael Waltrip Racing. Realistically, no one expected either Truex or his team to even qualify for the Chase for the NASCAR Sprint Cup in 2012. Yet he made it, as did Truex's stable mate, Clint Bowyer – who was a serious championship contender until being wrecked at Phoenix. Truex ranked outside the top 10 only once during the regular season – when he finished 12th in the Daytona 500. The New Jersey native reached second in points with a runner-up finish (leading 173 laps) in the spring Kansas race, one of seven top-five and 19 top-10 finishes. Truex also finished second in Kansas Speedway's Chase race and posted thirds at Bristol and Pocono. Truex, whose only series victory came more than five years ago at Dover, hopes to erase a 200-plus race winless streak in 2013. With last year's Chase berth a foundation, both Truex and MWR figure to be serious championship contenders in the coming season.

Truex followed father Martin Truex, a NASCAR K&N Pro Series East campaigner, into racing. He's one of six drivers to win consecutive NASCAR Nationwide Series championships (2004 and 2005). His younger brother, Ryan, competes in the NASCAR Nationwide and NASCAR Camping World Truck Series.

Photo courtesy of NASCAR The Game. www.NASCARTheGame.com

NASCAR SPRINT CUP SERIES
CAREER RECORD (Through 2012)

Year	Races	Wins	Top 5	Top 10	Poles	Points Standing
2004	2	0	0	0	0	70th
2005	7	0	0	1	0	47th
2006	36	0	2	5	0	19th
2007	36	1	7	14	1	11th
2008	36	0	3	11	0	15th
2009	36	0	1	6	3	23rd
2010	36	0	1	7	1	22nd
2011	36	0	3	12	1	18th
2012	36	0	7	19	1	11th

Best Race Finish: 1st (1 time)
Best Points Finish: 11th (2007, 2012)

2013 Car Owner
Michael Waltrip, Robert Kauffman

2013 Crew Chief
Chad Johnston

NASCAR SPRINT CUP SERIES 2012 RACE-BY-RACE RESULTS

RACE	EVENT	LOCATION	START	FINISH	PTS.	STATUS	POS.
1	Daytona 500	Daytona	26	12	33	Running	12
2	Subway Fresh Fit 500	Phoenix	25	7	71	Running	6
3	KOBALT Tools 400	Las Vegas	10	17	98	Running	8
4	Food City 500	Bristol	15	3	139	Running	4
5	Auto Club 400	Fontana	13	8	175	Running	5
6	Goody's Fast Relief 500	Martinsville	13	5	214	Running	6
7	Samsung Mobile 500	Texas	1	6	253	Running	4
8	STP 400	Kansas	6	2	297	Running	2
9	Capital City 400 Presented by Virginia Is for Lovers	Richmond	8	25	316	Running	5
10	Aaron's 499	Talladega	15	28	332	Accident	6
11	Bojangles' Southern 500	Darlington	6	5	372	Running	6
12	Coca-Cola 600	Charlotte	15	12	404	Running	6
13	FedEx 400 Benefiting Autism Speaks	Dover	18	7	441	Running	6
14	Pocono 400 Presented by #NASCAR	Pocono	23	20	465	Running	7
15	Quicken Loans 400	Michigan	16	12	497	Running	7
16	Toyota/Save Mart 350	Sonoma	5	22	520	Running	9
17	Quaker State 400	Kentucky	10	8	556	Running	8
18	Coke Zero 400 Powered by Coca-Cola	Daytona	18	17	584	Running	8
19	Lenox Industrial Tools 301	New Hampshire	4	11	617	Running	8
20	Crown Royal Presents the Curtiss Shaver 400 at the Brickyard Powered by Big Machine Records	Indianapolis	17	8	653	Running	7
21	Pennsylvania 400	Pocono	15	3	694	Running	5
22	Finger Lakes 355 at The Glen	Watkins Glen	9	10	728	Running	6
23	Pure Michigan 400	Michigan	7	10	763	Running	6
24	IRWIN Tools Night Race	Bristol	15	11	797	Running	5
25	AdvoCare 500	Atlanta	28	4	838	Running	5
26	Federated Auto Parts 400	Richmond	9	21	2000	Running	10
27	GEICO 400	Chicagoland	18	9	2035	Running	9
28	SYLVANIA 300	New Hampshire	9	17	2062	Running	10
29	AAA 400	Dover	3	6	2100	Running	8
30	Good Sam Roadside Assistance 500	Talladega	9	13	2131	Running	8
31	Bank of America 500	Charlotte	6	10	2165	Running	7
32	Hollywood Casino 400	Kansas	16	2	2207	Running	6
33	TUMS Fast Relief 500	Martinsville	12	23	2228	Running	7
34	AAA Texas 500	Texas	5	13	2259	Running	8
35	AdvoCare 500	Phoenix	2	43	2260	Engine	10
36	Ford EcoBoost 400	Homestead-Miami	7	6	2299	Running	11

J.J. YELEY

Birth Date: **October 5, 1976** • Hometown: **Phoenix, AZ** • Twitter: **@JJYeley1**

Photo courtesy of Tommy Baldwin Racing

36

Golden Corral Chevrolet

Having not completed a full schedule of races in the NASCAR Sprint Cup Series since 2007, J.J. Yeley looks to compete in as many races as possible in 2013. After splitting time between Robinson-Blakeney Racing, Tommy Baldwin Racing and Max Q Motorsports in 2012, he finds himself as the full-time driver of the No. 36 Golden Corral Chevrolet. Yeley competed in 24 races in 2012 and had his best finish of 26th in his first event of the season – at Phoenix in March. In the 14 races he appeared in for Robinson-Blakeney Racing, Yeley completed 97 percent of the laps in races which he finished. Yeley's best season came in 2007 when he finished a career-best 21st in the final points standings. That year he piloted the Joe Gibbs Racing No. 18 Chevrolet to the first of his two career top-five finishes with a second-place finish in the Coca-Cola 600 at Charlotte Motor Speedway, where he also led a lap. That season he also captured his only Coors Light Pole Award, in the June Michigan race. Yeley finished on the lead lap in 18 races.

Outside of the NASCAR Sprint Cup Series, Yeley had 13 top-five finishes in the NASCAR Nationwide Series. In 13 starts in the NASCAR Camping World Truck Series he had one top-10 finish (2010 season-opening event at Daytona). Yeley was the 2013 United States Auto Club Triple Crown (Silver Crown, Sprint, Midget) champion. In addition, he won the 2002 USAC Silver Crown and the 2001 USAC sprint car championship.

Photo not available at press time

NASCAR SPRINT CUP SERIES
CAREER RECORD (Through 2012)

Year	Races	Wins	Top 5	Top 10	Poles	Point Standing
2004	2	0	0	0	0	69th
2005	4	0	0	0	0	56th
2006	36	0	0	3	0	29th
2007	36	0	1	3	1	21st
2008	17	0	1	1	0	41st
2010	17	0	0	0	0	44th
2011	31	0	0	0	0	35th
2012	24	0	0	0	0	38th

Best Career Finish: 2nd (1 time)
Best Points Finish: 21st (2007)

**2013
Car Owner
Bob Jenkins**

Photo not available at press time

**2013
Crew Chief
TBA**

NASCAR SPRINT CUP SERIES 2012 RACE-BY-RACE RESULTS

RACE #	EVENT	LOCATION	START	FINISH	PTS.	STATUS	POS.
1	Daytona 500	Daytona	DNQ		0		
2	Subway Fresh Fit 500	Phoenix	35	26	18	Running	38
3	KOBALT Tools 400	Las Vegas	36	43	19	Engine	40
4	Food City 500	Bristol	40	30	33	Running	39
5	Auto Club 400	Fontana	36	35	42	Running	37
6	Goody's Fast Relief 500	Martinsville	43	37	49	Brakes	38
7	Samsung Mobile 500	Texas	36	33	60	Running	37
8	STP 400	Kansas	31	31	73	Running	35
9	Capital City 400 Presented by Virginia Is for Lovers	Richmond	DNQ		73		36
10	Aaron's 499	Talladega	DNQ		73		36
11	Bojangles' Southern 500	Darlington	43	37	80	Clutch	36
12	Coca-Cola 600	Charlotte	DNQ		80		36
13	FedEx 400 Benefiting Autism Speaks	Dover	34	34	90	Overheating	36
14	Pocono 400 Presented by #NASCAR	Pocono	32	36	98	Accident	36
15	Quicken Loans 400	Michigan	43	37	106	Brakes	35
16	Toyota/Save Mart 350	Sonoma	38	33	117	Running	35
17	Quaker State 400	Kentucky	DNQ		117		35
18	Coke Zero 400 Powered by Coca-Cola	Daytona	43	40	121	Overheating	35
19	Lenox Industrial Tools 301	New Hampshire	38	43	122	Engine	37
20	Crown Royal Presents the Curtiss Shaver 400 at the Brickyard Powered by Big Machine Records	Indianapolis	41	39	127	Transmission	37
21	Pennsylvania 400	Pocono	35	40	131	Brakes	37
22	Finger Lakes 355 at The Glen	Watkins Glen	37	40	135	Brakes	37
23	Pure Michigan 400	Michigan	DNQ		135		37
24	IRWIN Tools Night Race	Bristol	DNQ		135		37
25	AdvoCare 500	Atlanta	43	41	138	Brakes	37
26	Federated Auto Parts 400	Richmond	DNQ		138		37
27	GEICO 400	Chicagoland	DNQ		138		37
28	SYLVANIA 300	New Hampshire	40	41	141	Brakes	37
29	AAA 400	Dover	40	34	151	Running	37
30	Good Sam Roadside Assistance 500	Talladega	DNE		151		38
31	Bank of America 500	Charlotte	35	42	153	Brakes	38
32	Hollywood Casino 400	Kansas	27	42	155	Vibration	38
33	TUMS Fast Relief 500	Martinsville	DNQ		155		38
34	AAA Texas 500	Texas	28	42	157	Overheating	38
35	AdvoCare 500	Phoenix	DNQ		157		38
36	Ford EcoBoost 400	Homestead -Miami	39	35	166	Running	38

NASCAR RACING 2013 HOST TRACKS

NASCAR PREVIEW AND PRESS GUIDE 2013

ATLANTA MOTOR SPEEDWAY

ATLANTA MOTOR SPEEDWAY®

1500 Highway 19 & 41 South, Hampton, GA 30228 • **Tickets:** 1-866-GO-NASCAR or 1-877-9-AMS-TIX • **Web site:** www.atlantamotorspeedway.com
Facebook: www.facebook.com/atlmotorspeedway • **Twitter:** @amsupdates

(side) ATLANTA MOTOR SPEEDWAY

NASCAR

CONFIGURATION
Distance: 1.54 miles
Banking: 24 degrees in turns,
5 degrees on straights

TRACK RECORDS
Qualifying Records
Geoff Bodine,
197.478 mph (28.074 sec.),
Set November 15, 1997

Race Record
Bobby Labonte, 159.904 mph,
Set November 16, 1997

2013 TRACK LAYOUT

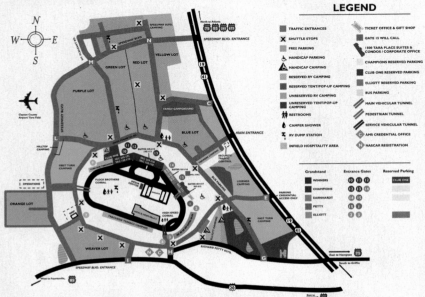

LEGEND

■	TRAFFIC ENTRANCES		TICKET OFFICE & GIFT SHOP
X	SHUTTLE STOPS		GATE 15 WILL CALL
	FREE PARKING		1500 TARA PLACE SUITES & CONDOS / CORPORATE OFFICE
	HANDICAP PARKING		CHAMPIONS RESERVED PARKING
▲	HANDICAP CAMPING		CLUB ONE RESERVED PARKING
	RESERVED RV CAMPING		ELLIOTT RESERVED PARKING
	RESERVED TENT/POP-UP CAMPING		BUS PARKING
	UNRESERVED RV CAMPING		MAIN VEHICULAR TUNNEL
	UNRESERVED TENT/POP-UP CAMPING		PEDESTRIAN TUNNEL
	RESTROOMS		SERVICE VEHICULAR TUNNEL
	CAMPER SHOWER		AMS CREDENTIAL OFFICE
	RV DUMP STATION		NASCAR REGISTRATION
	INFIELD HOSPITALITY AREA		

Grandstand	Entrance Gates	Reserved Parking
WINNERS	10 11 12	CLUB ONE
CHAMPIONS	13 14	
EARNHARDT	14 15	
PETTY	16 1	
ELLIOTT	2 3	

2013 SCHEDULE
August 31: NASCAR Nationwide Series
September 1: NASCAR Sprint Cup Series

TRACK OFFICIALS

Ed Clark *President*

PR CONTACTS
Marcy Scott *Director of Marketing & Promotion*

VISITOR INFORMATION
County Chamber of Commerce
(770) 957-5786 – **www.henrycounty.com**

DIRECTIONS
From the south: Take I-75 north to exit 218 (GA Hwy. 20).
Travel on Hwy. 20 for approx. 11 miles to track. *From the north:* Take I-75 south to exit 235 and continue on US Hwys. 19 and 41 for 15 miles. Track will be on the right.

ATLANTA MOTOR SPEEDWAY
ADVOCARE 500
OFFICIAL RACE RESULTS: RACE #25 – SEPTEMBER 2, 2012

NASCAR SPRINT CUP SERIES RACE RESULTS

Fin Pos	Str Pos	Car No	Driver	Team	Laps	Points	Bonus Points	Status
1	7	11	Denny Hamlin	Sport Clips Toyota	327	48	5	Running
2	5	24	Jeff Gordon	DuPont Chevrolet	327	43	1	Running
3	21	2	Brad Keselowski	Miller Lite Dodge	327	41	0	Running
4	28	56	Martin Truex Jr.	NAPA Shocks Toyota	327	41	1	Running
5	24	29	Kevin Harvick	Rheem Chevrolet	327	40	1	Running
6	3	18	Kyle Busch	Wrigley/Doublemint Toyota	327	39	1	Running
7	35	88	Dale Earnhardt Jr.	National Guard/Diet Mountain Dew Chev.	327	37	0	Running
8	18	27	Paul Menard	Quaker State/Menards Chevrolet	327	36	0	Running
9	4	17	Matt Kenseth	Ford EcoBoost Ford	327	35	0	Running
10	6	55	Mark Martin	Aaron's Dream Machine Toyota	327	34	0	Running
11	15	22	Sam Hornish Jr. (i)	Shell Pennzoil Dodge	327	0	0	Running
12	26	31	Jeff Burton	Caterpillar Chevrolet	327	32	0	Running
13	16	51	Kurt Busch	Hendrickcars.com Chevrolet	327	31	0	Running
14	27	78	Regan Smith	Furniture Row/Farm American Chevrolet	327	30	0	Running
15	2	16	Greg Biffle	3M/Manheim Auctions Ford	327	30	1	Running
16	32	21	Trevor Bayne (i)	Good Sam/Camping World Ford	327	0	0	Running
17	10	9	Marcos Ambrose	DeWalt Ford	327	27	0	Running
18	9	20	Joey Logano	The Home Depot Toyota	327	26	0	Running
19	25	47	Bobby Labonte	Kingsford Toyota	327	25	0	Running
20	40	83	Landon Cassill	Burger King Toyota	326	24	0	Running
21	33	42	Juan Pablo Montoya	Target Chevrolet	326	23	0	Running
22	1	14	Tony Stewart	Office Depot/Mobil 1 Chevrolet	326	23	1	Running
23	11	5	Kasey Kahne	Hendrickcars.com Chevrolet	325	21	0	Running
24	20	1	Jamie McMurray	Bass Pro Shops/Tracker Boats Chevrolet	325	20	0	Running
25	22	36	Dave Blaney	Tommy Baldwin Racing Chevrolet	324	19	0	Running
26	41	93	Travis Kvapil	Dr. Pepper/Burger King Toyota	324	18	0	Running
27	30	15	Clint Bowyer	5-hour Energy Toyota	324	17	0	Running
28	14	34	David Ragan	Glory Foods Ford	323	16	0	Running
29	23	10	Danica Patrick (i)	GoDaddy.com Chevrolet	321	0	0	Running
30	42	32	T.J. Bell (i)	Greensmoke Ford	319	0	0	Running
31	29	38	David Gilliland	House - Autry Ford	298	13	0	Running
32	13	43	Aric Almirola	AdvoCare Ford	297	12	0	Running
33	19	13	Casey Mears	GEICO Ford	291	11	0	Engine
34	8	48	Jimmie Johnson	Lowe's/Kobalt Tools Chevrolet	269	10	0	Accident
35	17	39	Ryan Newman	ARMY Medicine Chevrolet	268	9	0	Accident
36	12	99	Carl Edwards	Subway Ford	264	8	0	Engine
37	36	95	Scott Speed	Jordan Truck Sales Ford	196	7	0	Suspension
38	34	49	Jason Leffler (i)	Robinson-Blakeney Racing Toyota	77	0	0	Vibration
39	31	30	David Stremme	Inception Motorsports Toyota	54	5	0	Suspension
40	39	23	Scott Riggs	North Texas Pipe Chevrolet	43	4	0	Vibration
41	43	37	J.J. Yeley	MaxQworkforce.com Chevrolet	32	3	0	Brakes
42	38	91	Reed Sorenson (i)	Plinker Tactical Toyota	24	0	0	Overheating
43	37	87	Joe Nemechek (i)	AM/FM Energy Wood & Pellet Stoves Toyota	22	0	0	Rear Gear

Sunoco Rookie of the Year Contender. Bonus Points: includes winner, lap leader & most laps led points. (i) = Ineligible for driver points in this series. Failed to qualify: (4) #98 Michael McDowell; #26 Josh Wise; #33 Stephen Leicht; #19 Mike Bliss.

Race Comments: Before an estimated crowd of 90,300, Denny Hamlin won the ADVOCARE 500, his 21st NASCAR Sprint Cup Series victory. To start the race, prior to the green flag the following car dropped to the rear of the field: #15 (engine change).

RACE STATISTICS

TIME OF RACE: 3 hours, 32 minutes, 45 seconds
AVERAGE SPEED: 142.02 mph
MARGIN OF VICTORY: 0.378 secs.
COORS LIGHT POLE AWARD: Tony Stewart (186.121 mph. 29.787 secs.)
3M LAP LEADER: Denny Hamlin (105 Laps)
AMERICAN ETHANOL GREEN FLAG RESTART AWARD: Denny Hamlin
DIRECTV CREW CHIEF OF THE RACE: Denny Hamlin (crew chief Darian Grubb)
MAHLE CLEVITE ENGINE BUILDER OF THE RACE: Toyota Racing Development (TRD) (#11)

MOBIL 1 OIL DRIVER OF THE RACE: Denny Hamlin
MOOG STEERING AND SUSPENSION PROBLEM SOLVER OF THE RACE: Martin Truex Jr. (crew chief Chad Johnston, 0.229 seconds)
NASCAR SPRINT CUP LEADER BONUS: No winner: rolls over to $30,000 at next event++
USG IMPROVING THE FINISH: Dale Earnhardt Jr. (28 places)
CAUTION FLAGS: 6 cautions for 31 laps. [Beneficiary in Brackets] 40–43 (Oil On The Track [95]); 131–134 (Debris Backstretch [27]); 243–247 (Car #42 Accident Turn 1 [27]); 266–269 (Oil On The Track [None]);

271–279 (Car #48, 22, 39 Accident Backstretch [None]); 321–325 (Car #1 Accident Frontstretch [51]).
LAP LEADERS: 18 lead changes among 7 drivers. Stewart–pole, Biffle 1, Stewart 2–9, J. Gordon 10–15, Ky. Busch 16–34, Hamlin 35–40, Ky. Busch 41–81, Hamlin 82, Harvick 83–84, Ky. Busch 85–90, Hamlin 91–134, Harvick 135–173, Hamlin 174–176, Harvick 177–215, Hamlin 216–221, Harvick 222–242, Hamlin 243–281, Truex Jr. 282–321, Hamlin 322–327.

++Rollover money awarded at year's end, amount not included in race winnings.

POINT LEADERS
(After 25 Races)

1	GREG BIFFLE	879
2	Dale Earnhardt Jr.	871
3	Matt Kenseth	858
4	Jimmie Johnson	848
5	Martin Truex Jr.	838
6	Brad Keselowski	831
7	Denny Hamlin	822
8	Clint Bowyer	811
9	Kevin Harvick	807
10	Tony Stewart	769
11	Kasey Kahne	751
12	Kyle Busch	746

ATLANTA MOTOR SPEEDWAY

ALL TIME LEADERS AND PAST WINNERS

TOP 20 ACTIVE NASCAR SPRINT CUP SERIES DRIVERS (MINIMUM 2 STARTS)

Driver	Races	Wins	Top 5s	Top 10s	Poles	Total Laps	Laps Led	Avg. Start	Avg. Finish
Jimmie Johnson	21	3	11	13	0	6674	440	8.6	11.1
Tony Stewart	26	3	10	15	1	8201	974	15.3	11.7
Jeff Gordon	39	5	16	25	2	11,674	1,280	12.3	11.9
Dale Earnhardt Jr.	25	1	8	11	2	8034	632	16.2	12.5
Matt Kenseth	24	0	8	14	0	7407	253	21.6	12.7
AJ Allmendinger	7	0	0	2	0	2298	1	27.9	14.4
Carl Edwards	15	3	8	10	0	4582	345	10.3	15.1
Greg Biffle	18	0	3	9	1	5670	291	12.5	16.0
Denny Hamlin	13	1	2	5	1	4063	314	13.4	16.2
Terry Labonte	55	0	10	24	1	15,893	245	17.1	16.3
Brian Vickers	15	0	1	7	0	4488	8	16.2	16.4
Jeff Burton	35	0	8	14	0	10,705	104	25.3	16.5
Kyle Busch	15	1	3	4	0	4610	385	11.6	16.9
Kurt Busch	22	3	4	9	0	6471	665	15.5	17.2
Mark Martin	52	2	14	24	2	14,806	929	10.4	17.2
Juan Pablo Montoya	10	0	3	4	0	3201	34	16.2	17.3
Brad Keselowski	4	0	1	2	0	1298	2	22.8	17.5
Clint Bowyer	12	0	0	5	0	3835	66	16.0	18.2
Bobby Labonte	38	6	12	13	2	11,016	959	18.0	18.4
Ryan Newman	20	0	1	6	7	6310	172	7.1	18.4

KOBALT TOOLS 500

Year	Driver	Car	Average Speed
1960	Bobby Johns	60 Pontiac	108.408
1961	Bob Burdick	61 Pontiac	123.920
1962	Fred Lorenzen	62 Ford	101.983
1963	Fred Lorenzen	63 Ford	130.580
1964	Fred Lorenzen	64 Ford	132.959
1965	Marvin Panch	65 Ford	129.410
1966	Jim Hurtubise	66 Plymouth	131.266
1967	Cale Yarborough	67 Ford	131.238
1968	Cale Yarborough	68 Mercury	125.564
1969	Cale Yarborough	69 Mercury	132.191
1970	Bobby Allison	69 Dodge	139.554
1971	A.J. Foyt	71 Mercury	131.375
1972	Bobby Allison	72 Chevrolet	128.214
1973	David Pearson	71 Mercury	139.351
1974	Cale Yarborough	74 Chevrolet	136.910
1975	Richard Petty	Dodge	133.496
1976	David Pearson	Mercury	128.904
1977	Richard Petty	Dodge	144.093
1978	Bobby Allison	Ford	142.520
1979	Buddy Baker	Oldsmobile	135.136
1980	Dale Earnhardt	Chevrolet	134.808
1981	Cale Yarborough	Buick	133.619
1982	Darrell Waltrip	Buick	124.824
1983	Cale Yarborough	Chevrolet	137.643
1984	Benny Parsons	Chevrolet	144.945
1985	Bill Elliott	Ford	140.273
1986	Morgan Shepherd	Buick	132.126
1987	Ricky Rudd	Ford	133.689
1988	Dale Earnhardt	Chevrolet	137.588
1989	Darrell Waltrip	Chevrolet	139.684
1990	Dale Earnhardt	Chevrolet	156.849
1991	Ken Schrader	Chevrolet	140.470
1992	Bill Elliott	Ford	147.746
1993	Morgan Shepherd	Ford	150.442
1994	Ernie Irvan	Ford	146.136
1995	Jeff Gordon	Chevrolet	150.115
1996	Dale Earnhardt	Chevrolet	161.298
1997	Dale Jarrett	Ford	132.731
1998	Bobby Labonte	Pontiac	139.501
1999	Jeff Gordon	Chevrolet	143.284
2000	Dale Earnhardt	Chevrolet	131.759
2001	Kevin Harvick	Chevrolet	143.273
2002	Tony Stewart	Pontiac	148.443
2003	Bobby Labonte	Chevrolet	146.048
2004	Dale Earnhardt Jr.	Chevrolet	158.679
2005	Carl Edwards	Ford	143.478
2006	Kasey Kahne	Dodge	144.098
2007	Jimmie Johnson	Chevrolet	152.915
2008	Kyle Busch	Toyota	140.975
2009	Kurt Busch	Dodge	127.573
2010	Kurt Busch	Dodge	131.294

ADVOCARE 500

Year	Driver	Car	Average Speed
1960	Fireball Roberts	60 Pontiac	112.652
1961	David Pearson	61 Pontiac	125.230
1962	Rex White	62 Chevrolet	124.896
1963	Junior Johnson	63 Chevrolet	121.139
1964	Ned Jarrett	64 Ford	112.535
1965	Marvin Panch	65 Ford	110.120
1966	Richard Petty	66 Plymouth	130.244
1967	Dick Hutcherson	67 Ford	132.286
1968	LeeRoy Yarbrough	68 Mercury	127.068
1969	LeeRoy Yarbrough	69 Ford	133.001
1970	Richard Petty	70 Plymouth	142.712
1971	Richard Petty	71 Plymouth	129.061
1972	Bobby Allison	72 Chevrolet	131.295
1973	David Pearson	71 Mercury	130.211
1974	Richard Petty	74 Dodge	131.651
1975	Buddy Baker	Ford	130.900
1976	Dave Marcis	Dodge	127.396
1977	Darrell Waltrip	Chevrolet	110.052
1978	Donnie Allison	Chevrolet	124.312
1979	Neil Bonnett	Mercury	140.120
1980	Cale Yarborough	Chevrolet	131.190
1981	Neil Bonnett	Ford	130.391
1982	Bobby Allison	Buick	130.884
1983	Neil Bonnett	Chevrolet	137.643
1984	Dale Earnhardt	Chevrolet	134.610
1985	Bill Elliott	Ford	139.597
1986	Dale Earnhardt	Chevrolet	152.523
1987	Bill Elliott	Ford	139.047
1988	Rusty Wallace	Pontiac	129.024
1989	Dale Earnhardt	Chevrolet	140.229
1990	Morgan Shepherd	Ford	140.911
1991	Mark Martin	Ford	137.968
1992	Bill Elliott	Ford	133.322
1993	Rusty Wallace	Pontiac	125.221
1994	Mark Martin	Ford	148.982
1995	Dale Earnhardt	Chevrolet	163.633
1996	Bobby Labonte	Chevrolet	134.661
1997	Bobby Labonte	Pontiac	159.904
1998	Jeff Gordon	Chevrolet	114.915
1999	Bobby Labonte	Pontiac	137.932
2000	Jerry Nadeau	Chevrolet	141.296
2001	Bobby Labonte	Pontiac	151.756
2002	Kurt Busch	Ford	127.519
2003	Jeff Gordon	Chevrolet	127.769
2004	Jimmie Johnson	Chevrolet	145.847
2005	Carl Edwards	Ford	146.834
2006	Tony Stewart	Chevrolet	143.421
2007	Jimmie Johnson	Chevrolet	135.260
2008	Carl Edwards	Ford	134.272
2009	Kasey Kahne	Dodge	134.033
2010	Tony Stewart	Chevrolet	129.041
2011	Jeff Gordon	Chevrolet	124.623
2012	Denny Hamlin	Toyota	142.020

ATLANTA MOTOR SPEEDWAY

AUTO CLUB SPEEDWAY

9300 Cherry Ave. Fontana, CA 92335 • **Tickets:** 1-866-GO-NASCAR or 1-800-944-7223 • **Web site:** www.autoclubspeedway.com
Facebook: www.facebook.com/AutoClubSpeedway • **Twitter:** @ACSupdates

NASCAR

CONFIGURATION
Distance: 2 miles
Banking: 14 degrees in turns,
11 degrees on frontstretch,
3 degrees on backstretch

TRACK RECORDS
Qualifying Records
Kyle Busch, 188.245 mph
(38.248 sec.), Set February 25,
2005

Race Record
Tony Stewart, 160.166 mph,
Set March 25, 2012

AUTO CLUB SPEEDWAY

2013 TRACK LAYOUT

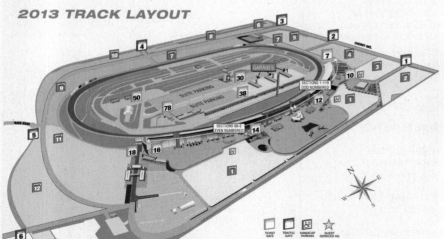

TICKET GATE TRAFFIC GATE HANDICAP PARKING GUEST SERVICES HQ

2013 SCHEDULE
March 23: NASCAR Nationwide Series
March 24: NASCAR Sprint Cup Series

TRACK OFFICIALS

Gillian Zucker *President*

PR CONTACTS
David Talley *Director of Communications*

VISITOR INFORMATION
Fontana Chamber of Commerce
(909) 822-4433 – www.fontanachamber.org

DIRECTIONS
From I-10: East of Los Angeles, exit Cherry Ave. and head
north. Speedway is located on Cherry Ave. *From I-15 North:*
Exit 4th Street, east to Cherry Ave. and head north.

AUTO CLUB 400
OFFICIAL RACE RESULTS: RACE #5 – MARCH 25, 2012

NASCAR SPRINT CUP SERIES RACE RESULTS

Fin Pos	Str Pos	Car No	Series Driver	Team	Laps	Points	Bonus Points	Status
1	9	14	Tony Stewart	Office Depot/Mobil 1 Chevrolet	129	47	4	Running
2	2	18	Kyle Busch	Interstate Batteries Toyota	129	44	2	Running
3	14	88	Dale Earnhardt Jr.	Diet Mountain Dew/National Guard Chev.	129	41	0	Running
4	7	29	Kevin Harvick	Jimmy John's Chevrolet	129	40	0	Running
5	12	99	Carl Edwards	Subway Ford	129	39	0	Running
6	4	16	Greg Biffle	3M Ford	129	38	0	Running
7	6	39	Ryan Newman	U.S. ARMY Chevrolet	129	37	0	Running
8	13	56	Martin Truex Jr.	NAPA Auto Parts Toyota	129	36	0	Running
9	23	51	Kurt Busch	Phoenix Construction Services Inc. Chev.	129	35	0	Running
10	10	48	Jimmie Johnson	Lowe's/Jimmie Johnson Foundation Chev.	129	35	1	Running
11	1	11	Denny Hamlin	FedEx Express Toyota	129	34	1	Running
12	3	55	Mark Martin	Aaron's Toyota	129	32	0	Running
13	11	15	Clint Bowyer	5-hour Energy Toyota	129	31	0	Running
14	5	5	Kasey Kahne	Quaker State Chevrolet	129	30	0	Running
15	25	22	AJ Allmendinger	Southern California AAA Dodge	129	29	0	Running
16	15	17	Matt Kenseth	Ford EcoBoost Ford	129	28	0	Running
17	24	42	Juan Pablo Montoya	Target Chevrolet	128	27	0	Running
18	17	2	Brad Keselowski	Miller Lite Dodge	128	26	0	Running
19	27	27	Paul Menard	Menards/CertainTeed Chevrolet	128	25	0	Running
20	22	78	Regan Smith	Furniture Row/Farm American Chevrolet	128	24	0	Running
21	29	9	Marcos Ambrose	DeWalt Ford	128	23	0	Running
22	19	31	Jeff Burton	Caterpillar Chevrolet	128	22	0	Running
23	33	13	Casey Mears	GEICO Ford	128	21	0	Running
24	8	20	Joey Logano	Dollar General Toyota	128	20	0	Running
25	28	43	Aric Almirola	Medallion Financial Ford	128	19	0	Running
26	21	24	Jeff Gordon	Drive to End Hunger Chevrolet	128	19	1	Running
27	18	10	David Reutimann	Accell Construction Chevrolet	127	17	0	Running
28	26	47	Bobby Labonte	Charter Toyota	127	16	0	Running
29	40	93	Travis Kvapil	Burger King/Dr. Pepper Toyota	127	15	0	Running
30	41	38	David Gilliland	1-800 LoanMart Ford	127	14	0	Running
31	38	34	David Ragan	Front Row Motorsports Ford	127	13	0	Running
32	16	1	Jamie McMurray	Bass Pro Shops/Allstate Chevrolet	126	12	0	Running
33	34	36	Dave Blaney	Tommy Baldwin Racing Chevrolet	126	11	0	Running
34	42	32	Ken Schrader	US Chrome/1 Less Than 2 Ltd. Ford	125	10	0	Running
35	36	49	J.J. Yeley	America Israel Racing Chevrolet	125	9	0	Running
36	31	83	Landon Cassill	Burger King/Dr. Pepper Toyota	124	8	0	Running
37	30	26	Josh Wise #	MDS Ford	51	7	0	Vibration
38	32	98	Michael McDowell	Curb Records Ford	40	6	0	Vibration
39	20	30	David Stremme	@TheNascarFans Toyota	36	5	0	Rear Gear
40	39	19	Mike Bliss (i)	Ironclad Toyota	18	0	0	Transmission
41	35	23	Scott Riggs	North TX Pipe Chevrolet	17	3	0	Vibration
42	43	74	Reed Sorenson (i)	Turn One Racing Chevrolet	6	0	0	Vibration
43	37	33	Brendan Gaughan	South Point Casino Chevrolet	1	1	0	Engine

 # Sunoco Rookie of the Year Contender. Bonus Points: includes winner, lap leader & most laps led points. (i) = Ineligible for driver points in this series. Failed to qualify: (3) #7 Robby Gordon; #87 Joe Nemechek; #37 Timmy Hill.

RACE COMMENTS: Before an estimated crowd of 90,000, Tony Stewart won the Auto Club 400, his 46th NASCAR Sprint Cup Series victory. Prior to the green flag, the following car dropped to the rear of the field for the reason indicated: #30 (transmission change).

RACE STATISTICS

TIME OF RACE: 1 hour, 36 minutes, 39 seconds
AVERAGE SPEED: 160.166 mph
MARGIN OF VICTORY: Under Caution
COORS LIGHT POLE AWARD: Denny Hamlin (186.403 mph. 38.626 secs.)
3M LAP LEADER: Kyle Busch (80 Laps)
AMERICAN ETHANOL GREEN FLAG RESTART AWARD: No winner, rolls over to the year-end award winner
DIRECTV CREW CHIEF OF THE RACE: Kyle Busch (crew chief Dave Rogers)
FREESCALE "WIDE OPEN": Carl Edwards
MAHLE CLEVITE ENGINE BUILDER OF THE

RACE: Toyota Racing Development (TRD) (#18)
MOBIL 1 OIL DRIVER OF THE RACE: Tony Stewart
MOOG STEERING AND SUSPENSION PROBLEM SOLVER OF THE RACE: Kurt Busch (crew chief Nicholas Harrison, 0.069 seconds)
NASCAR SPRINT CUP LEADER BONUS: No winner: rolls over to $40,000 at next event++
USG IMPROVING THE FINISH: Kurt Busch (14 places)
CAUTION FLAGS: 1 cautions for 5 laps. [Beneficiary in Brackets] 125–129 (Rain {Red Flag After Lap 129} [22]).

LAP LEADERS: 9 lead changes among 5 drivers. Hamlin 1, Ky. Busch 2–67, Hamlin 68, J. Gordon 69, Johnson 70, Ky. Busch 71–84, Stewart 85–104, Johnson 105, J. Gordon 106–107, Stewart 108–129.

++Rollover money awarded at year's end, amount not included in race winnings.

POINT LEADERS
(After 5 Races)

1	GREG BIFFLE	195
2	Kevin Harvick	188
3	Dale Earnhardt Jr.	178
4	Tony Stewart	177
5	Martin Truex Jr.	175
6	Matt Kenseth	173
7	Denny Hamlin	171
8	Clint Bowyer	157
9	Jimmie Johnson	156
10	Ryan Newman	155
11	Paul Menard	148
12	Carl Edwards	146

AUTO CLUB SPEEDWAY

TOP 20 ACTIVE NASCAR SPRINT CUP SERIES DRIVERS (MINIMUM 2 STARTS)

Driver	Races	Wins	Top 5s	Top 10s	Poles	Total Laps	Laps Led	Avg. Start	Avg. Finish
Jimmie Johnson	18	5	12	14	1	4284	851	9.1	5.4
Carl Edwards	15	1	7	12	1	3518	121	18.5	8.7
Matt Kenseth	20	3	8	13	0	4782	497	20.4	10.3
Clint Bowyer	12	0	2	7	0	2778	45	14.3	10.8
Kyle Busch	15	1	6	10	1	3486	474	11.7	11.3
Jeff Gordon	23	3	10	11	2	5486	622	12.9	11.8
Kurt Busch	19	1	4	9	3	4530	231	15.2	12.7
Tony Stewart	21	2	6	12	0	4871	314	14.8	13.5
Mark Martin	21	1	6	10	0	4890	324	12.7	13.6
Kasey Kahne	16	1	4	9	1	3545	268	10.3	14.9
Kevin Harvick	19	1	4	9	0	4463	60	18.1	15.5
Brian Vickers	14	0	1	5	2	3435	54	15.2	16.1
Jeff Burton	23	0	6	7	0	5509	127	18.5	17.1
Greg Biffle	18	1	4	6	0	4035	297	14.0	17.2
Joey Logano	6	0	1	1	0	1277	0	13.3	17.5
Ryan Newman	18	0	4	7	1	3904	19	13.9	17.6
Jamie McMurray	17	0	3	5	2	3872	57	19.8	17.8
Denny Hamlin	12	0	1	4	2	2570	73	13.2	18.5
David Ragan	10	0	0	1	0	2269	1	23.9	18.7
Juan Pablo Montoya	10	0	1	2	1	2163	118	14.5	19.1

AUTO CLUB 400

Year	Driver	Car	Average Speed
1997	Jeff Gordon	Chevrolet	155.012
1998	Mark Martin	Ford	140.020
1999	Jeff Gordon	Chevrolet	150.276
2000	Jeremy Mayfield	Ford	149.378
2001	Rusty Wallace	Ford	143.118
2002	Jimmie Johnson	Chevrolet	150.088
2003	Kurt Busch	Ford	140.111
2004	Jeff Gordon	Chevrolet	137.268
2005	Greg Biffle	Ford	139.697
2006	Matt Kenseth	Ford	147.852
2007	Matt Kenseth	Ford	138.451
2008	Carl Edwards	Ford	132.704
2009	Matt Kenseth	Ford	135.839
2010	Jimmie Johnson	Chevrolet	141.911
2011	Kevin Harvick	Chevrolet	150.849
2012	Tony Stewart	Chevrolet	160.166

PEPSI MAX 400

Year	Driver	Car	Average Speed
2004	Elliott Sadler	Ford	128.324
2005	Kyle Busch	Chevrolet	136.356
2006	Kasey Kahne	Dodge	144.462
2007	Jimmie Johnson	Chevrolet	131.502
2008	Jimmie Johnson	Chevrolet	138.857
2009	Jimmie Johnson	Chevrolet	143.908
2010	Tony Stewart	Chevrolet	131.953

BRISTOL MOTOR SPEEDWAY

Bristol
Motor Speedway

151 Speedway Blvd. Bristol, TN 37620 • **Tickets:** 1-866-GO-NASCAR or 1-423-BRISTOL • **Web site:** www.bristolmotorspeedway.com
Facebook: www.facebook.com/bristolmotorspeedway • **Twitter:** @BMSupdates

NASCAR®

CONFIGURATION
Distance: .533 mile
Banking: 24 to 28 degrees
in turns, 5 to 9 degrees on
frontstretch, 4 to 8 degrees
on backstretch

TRACK RECORDS
Qualifying Records
**Ryan Newman, 128.709 mph
(14.908 sec.), Set March 21,
2003**

Race Record
**Charlie Glotzbach, 101.074 mph,
Set July 11, 1971**

2013 TRACK LAYOUT

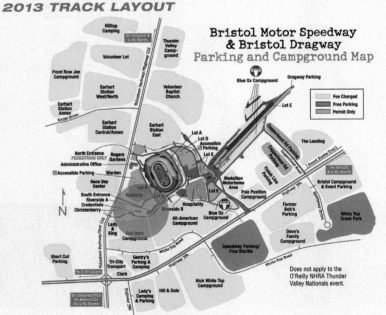

Bristol Motor Speedway
& Bristol Dragway
Parking and Campground Map

Fee Charged
Free Parking
Permit Only

Does not apply to the
O'Reilly NHRA Thunder
Valley Nationals event.

2013 SCHEDULE
March 16: NASCAR Nationwide Series
March 17: NASCAR Sprint Cup Series;
August 21: NASCAR Camping World Truck Series
August 23: NASCAR Nationwide Series
August 24: NASCAR Sprint Cup Series

TRACK OFFICIALS

Jerry Caldwell *General Manager*

PR CONTACTS
Lori Worley *Senior Director of Communications*

VISITOR INFORMATION
Bristol Chamber of Commerce
(423) 989-4850 – **www.bristolchamber.org**

DIRECTIONS
From the south: Exit I-81 at I-81 to 11E; or at Tennessee exit 69 and take Hwy. 394 to 11E South. *From the north:* Exit I-81 at Virginia exit 3 and take 11E south; or at Virginia exit 17 and take VA 75 south, TN 44 south, to US 421 north, to TN 394 south. Speedway is located on Hwy. 11, on south side of Bristol.

FOOD CITY 500
OFFICIAL RACE RESULTS: RACE #4 – MARCH 18, 2012

NASCAR SPRINT CUP SERIES RACE RESULTS

Fin Pos	Str Pos	Car No	Series Driver	Team	Laps	Points	Bonus Points	Status
1	5	2	Brad Keselowski	Miller Lite Dodge	500	48	5	Running
2	21	17	Matt Kenseth	Best Buy Ford	500	43	1	Running
3	15	56	Martin Truex Jr.	NAPA Auto Parts Toyota	500	41	0	Running
4	16	15	Clint Bowyer	5-hour Energy Toyota	500	40	0	Running
5	25	55	Brian Vickers	Aaron's Toyota	500	40	1	Running
6	33	31	Jeff Burton	BB&T Chevrolet	500	38	0	Running
7	17	1	Jamie McMurray	McDonald's Chevrolet	500	37	0	Running
8	30	42	Juan Pablo Montoya	Target Chevrolet	500	36	0	Running
9	22	48	Jimmie Johnson	Lowe's/Kobalt Tools Chevrolet	500	35	0	Running
10	11	27	Paul Menard	Menards/MOEN Chevrolet	500	34	0	Running
11	14	29	Kevin Harvick	Budweiser Chevrolet	500	33	0	Running
12	3	39	Ryan Newman	Quicken Loans Chevrolet	500	32	0	Running
13	1	16	Greg Biffle	811/3M Ford	500	32	1	Running
14	23	14	Tony Stewart	Office Depot/Mobil 1 Chevrolet	500	30	0	Running
15	18	88	Dale Earnhardt Jr.	National Guard/Diet Mountain Dew Chev.	500	30	1	Running
16	9	20	Joey Logano	The Home Depot Toyota	498	28	0	Running
17	2	22	AJ Allmendinger	Shell Pennzoil Dodge	498	28	1	Running
18	27	51	Kurt Busch	Hendrickcars.com Chevrolet	498	26	0	Running
19	7	43	Aric Almirola	Charter Communications Ford	498	25	0	Running
20	20	11	Denny Hamlin	FedEx Ground Toyota	498	24	0	Running
21	19	10	David Reutimann	TRADEBANK Chevrolet	497	23	0	Running
22	32	33	Brendan Gaughan	South Point Hotel & Casino Chevrolet	496	22	0	Running
23	31	34	David Ragan	Long John Silver's Ford	496	21	0	Running
24	6	78	Regan Smith	Furniture Row Racing/CSX Play It Safe Chev.	496	20	0	Running
25	24	13	Casey Mears	GEICO Ford	496	19	0	Running
26	26	38	David Gilliland	Taco Bell Ford	496	18	0	Running
27	34	93	Travis Kvapil	Burger King/Dr. Pepper Toyota	496	17	0	Running
28	36	47	Bobby Labonte	Clorox/Scott Products Toyota	495	16	0	Running
29	29	83	Landon Cassill	Burger King/Dr. Pepper Toyota	495	15	0	Running
30	40	49	J.J. Yeley	JPO Absorbents Toyota	493	14	0	Running
31	39	98	Michael McDowell	K-LOVE - Let It Start With Me Ford	492	13	0	Running
32	13	18	Kyle Busch	Wrigley Doublemint Toyota	423	12	0	Running
33	42	32	Ken Schrader	We Drive Sales - TMone.com Ford	420	11	0	Running
34	35	36	Dave Blaney	Seal Wrap/Widow Wax Chevrolet	417	10	0	Running
35	4	24	Jeff Gordon	Drive to End Hunger Chevrolet	395	10	1	Running
36	12	9	Marcos Ambrose	MAC Tools Ford	389	8	0	Running
37	10	5	Kasey Kahne	Farmers Insurance Chevrolet	366	7	0	Running
38	28	30	David Stremme	Food Country USA/Inception Motorsports Toyota	334	6	0	Accident
39	8	99	Carl Edwards	Kellogg's/Cheez-It Ford	245	5	0	Running
40	41	87	Joe Nemechek (i)	AM/FM Energy Wood & Pellet Stoves Toyota	57	0	0	Brakes
41	43	23	Scott Riggs	North Texas Pipe Chevrolet	26	3	0	Vibration
42	38	74	Reed Sorenson (i)	Carnegie Hotel/Turn One Racing Chevrolet	17	0	0	Vibration
43	37	26	Josh Wise #	Morristown Drivers Service Ford	16	1	0	Spindle

Sunoco Rookie of the Year Contender. Bonus Points: includes winner, lap leader & most laps led points. (i) = Ineligible for driver points in this series . Failed to qualify: (1) #37 Timmy Hill.

RACE COMMENTS: Before an estimated crowd of 102,000, Brad Keselowski won the Food City 500, his fifth NASCAR Sprint Cup Series victory. To start the race, prior to the green flag the following cars dropped to the rear of the field for the reasons indicated: #30, 36 (transmission change).

RACE STATISTICS

TIME OF RACE: 2 hours, 51 minutes, 52 seconds
AVERAGE SPEED: 93.037 mph
MARGIN OF VICTORY: 0.714 seconds
COORS LIGHT POLE AWARD: Greg Biffle (125.215 mph. 15.324 secs.)
3M LAP LEADER: Brad Keselowski (232 Laps)
AMERICAN ETHANOL GREEN FLAG RESTART AWARD: Brad Keselowski
DIRECTV CREW CHIEF OF THE RACE: Greg Biffle (crew chief Matt Puccia)
MAHLE CLEVITE ENGINE BUILDER OF THE RACE: Penske Engines (#2)

MOBIL 1 OIL DRIVER OF THE RACE: Martin Truex Jr.
MOOG STEERING AND SUSPENSION PROBLEM SOLVER OF THE RACE: Matt Kenseth (crew chief Jimmy Fennig, -0.087 seconds)
NASCAR SPRINT CUP LEADER BONUS: No winner: rolls over to $30,000 at next event++
USG IMPROVING THE FINISH: Jeff Burton (27 places)
CAUTION FLAGS: 5 cautions for 49 laps. [Beneficiary in Brackets] 25–46 (Car #2, 5, 9, 18, 29, 78, 99 Accident Turn 1 [23]); 117–121 (Car #32 Accident Turn 2 [36]); 341–346 (Car #30 Accident Turn 4 [14]);

361–371 (Car #24 Accident Turn 3 [39]); 479–483 (Car #14 Accident Turn 3 [39]).
LAP LEADERS: 13 lead changes among 7 drivers. Biffle 1–41, Allmendinger 42–95, Vickers 96–116, Earnhardt Jr. 117, Vickers 118–216, Keselowski 217–254, Kenseth 255–256, J. Gordon 257, Vickers 258–262, Keselowski 263–341, Earnhardt Jr. 342, Keselowski 343–346, Kenseth 347–389, Keselowski 390–500.

++Rollover money awarded at year's end, amount not included in race winnings.

POINT LEADERS
(After 4 Races)

1	GREG BIFFLE	157
2	Kevin Harvick	148
3	Matt Kenseth	145
4	Martin Truex Jr.	139
5	Denny Hamlin	137
6	Dale Earnhardt Jr.	137
7	Tony Stewart	130
8	Clint Bowyer	126
9	Joey Logano	126
10	Paul Menard	123
11	Jeff Burton	120
12	Ryan Newman	118

IRWIN TOOLS NIGHT RACE
OFFICIAL RACE RESULTS: RACE #24 – AUGUST 25, 2012

BRISTOL MOTOR SPEEDWAY

NASCAR SPRINT CUP SERIES RACE RESULTS

Fin Pos	Str Pos	Car No	Series Driver	Team	Laps	Points	Bonus Points	Status
1	8	11	Denny Hamlin	FedEx Ground Toyota	500	47	4	Running
2	37	48	Jimmie Johnson	Lowe's Dover White Chevrolet	500	43	1	Running
3	11	24	Jeff Gordon	FarmVille/Drive to End Hunger Chevrolet	500	41	0	Running
4	22	55	Brian Vickers	MyClassicGarage.com Toyota	500	41	1	Running
5	9	9	Marcos Ambrose	DeWalt Ford	500	40	1	Running
6	10	18	Kyle Busch	M&M's Toyota	500	38	0	Running
7	23	15	Clint Bowyer	5-hour Energy Toyota	500	37	0	Running
8	4	20	Joey Logano	Dollar General Toyota	500	38	2	Running
9	12	5	Kasey Kahne	Hendrickcars.com Chevrolet	500	36	1	Running
10	7	27	Paul Menard	Menards/Schrock Chevrolet	500	34	0	Running
11	15	56	Martin Truex Jr.	NAPA Auto Parts Toyota	500	34	1	Running
12	16	88	Dale Earnhardt Jr.	Diet Mountain Dew/National Guard Chevrolet	500	33	1	Running
13	28	42	Juan Pablo Montoya	Target Chevrolet	500	31	0	Running
14	36	47	Bobby Labonte	Bush's Beans Toyota	500	30	0	Running
15	13	29	Kevin Harvick	Rheem Chevrolet	500	29	0	Running
16	14	78	Regan Smith	Furniture Row/Farm American Chevrolet	500	28	0	Running
17	26	1	Jamie McMurray	Bass Pro Shops/Allstate Chevrolet	500	27	0	Running
18	41	93	Travis Kvapil	Burger King/Dr. Pepper Toyota	500	26	0	Running
19	3	16	Greg Biffle	3M/Bondo Ford	500	26	0	Running
20	18	38	David Gilliland	Taco Bell Ford	500	24	0	Running
21	1	13	Casey Mears	GEICO Ford	499	24	1	Running
22	27	99	Carl Edwards	Fastenal Ford	496	23	1	Running
23	30	98	Michael McDowell	K-LOVE/Curb Records Ford	496	21	0	Running
24	33	83	Landon Cassill	Burger King/Dr. Pepper Toyota	490	20	0	Running
25	17	17	Matt Kenseth	Valvoline NextGen Ford	486	20	1	Running
26	25	36	Dave Blaney	Seal Wrap Chevrolet	476	18	0	Accident
27	21	14	Tony Stewart	Mobil 1/Office Depot Chevrolet	471	18	1	Running
28	20	51	Kurt Busch	Phoenix Construction Chevrolet	440	16	0	Running
29	43	10	Danica Patrick (i)	Go Daddy Racing Chevrolet	434	0	0	Accident
30	2	2	Brad Keselowski	Miller Lite Dodge	434	14	0	Running
31	39	49	Jason Leffler (i)	America Israel Racing Toyota	417	0	0	Running
32	24	34	David Ragan	Glory Foods Ford	409	12	0	Running
33	6	31	Jeff Burton	Caterpillar Chevrolet	360	11	0	Running
34	29	22	Sam Hornish Jr. (i)	Shell Pennzoil Dodge	343	0	0	Running
35	5	43	Aric Almirola	Goody's Ford	235	9	0	Accident
36	19	39	Ryan Newman	Outback Steakhouse Chevrolet	189	8	0	Accident
37	31	30	David Stremme	Inception Motorsports Toyota	159	7	0	Rear Gear
38	32	26	Josh Wise #	MDS Transport Ford	150	6	0	Brakes
39	40	87	Joe Nemechek (i)	AM/FM Energy/AC General Toyota	130	0	0	Electrical
40	38	33	Stephen Leicht #	LittleJoesAuto.com Chevrolet	56	4	0	Fuel Pressure
41	35	23	Scott Riggs	North Texas Pipe Chevrolet	20	3	0	Brakes
42	42	32	Ken Schrader	Federated Auto Parts Ford	9	2	0	Accident
43	34	19	Mike Bliss (i)	Plinker Tactical Toyota	6	0	0	Power Steering

Sunoco Rookie of the Year Contender. Bonus Points: includes winner, lap leader & most laps led points. (i) = Ineligible for driver points in this series. Failed to qualify: (4) #95 Scott Speed; #79 Kelly Bires; #91 Reed Sorenson; #37 J.J. Yeley.

RACE COMMENTS: Before an estimated crowd of 145,000, Denny Hamlin won the Irwin Tools Night Race, his 20th NASCAR Sprint Cup Series victory. There were no cars that dropped to the rear of the field prior to the green flag.

RACE STATISTICS

TIME OF RACE: 3 hours, 9 minutes, 27 seconds
AVERAGE SPEED: 84.402 mph
MARGIN OF VICTORY: 1.103 second(s)
COORS LIGHT POLE AWARD: None - due to inclement weather
3M LAP LEADER: Joey Logano (139 Laps)
AMERICAN ETHANOL GREEN FLAG RESTART AWARD: Joey Logano
DIRECTV CREW CHIEF OF THE RACE: Denny Hamlin (crew chief Darian Grubb)
FREESCALE "WIDE OPEN": Brian Vickers
MAHLE CLEVITE ENGINE BUILDER OF THE RACE: Toyota Racing Development (TRD) (#11)
MOBIL 1 OIL DRIVER OF THE RACE: Denny Hamlin
MOOG STEERING AND SUSPENSION

PROBLEM SOLVER OF THE RACE: Jimmie Johnson (crew chief Chad Knaus, 0.215 seconds)
NASCAR SPRINT CUP LEADER BONUS: No winner: rolls over to $20,000 at next event++
SUNOCO ROOKIE OF THE RACE: Josh Wise
USG IMPROVING THE FINISH: Jimmie Johnson (35 places)
CAUTION FLAGS: 13 cautions for 87 laps. [Beneficiary in Brackets] 11–17 (Car #32, 49 Accident Frontstretch [None]); 83–89 (Debris In Turn 2 [98]); 123–129 (Car #22, 34 Accident Turn 4 [17]); 149–158 (Car #34 Spin Turn 4 [14]); 192–199 (Car #42, 39, 31 Accident Turn 4 [5]); 225–230 (Car #43, 38 Accident Turn 1 [10]); 272–276 (Car #2, 47 Accident Backstretch [55]); 323–328 (Car #78, 51 Accident Frontstretch [55]); 334–339 (Car #14, 17 Accident Frontstretch [78]); 347–352 (Car #36 Accident Turn 1 [78]); 415–419 (Car #13 Accident Turns 1 & 2 [10]); 424–429 (Debris In Turn 1 [13]); 436–443 (Car #10, 78 Accident Frontstretch [98]).
LAP LEADERS: 22 lead changes among 13 drivers. Mears 1–26, Logano 27–84, Hamlin 85, Logano 86–107, Kahne 108–149, Logano 150–192, Earnhardt Jr. 193–205, Hamlin 206–226, Biffle 227–253, Kenseth 254–272, Johnson 273–324, Hamlin 325, Kenseth 326–331, Stewart 332, Logano 333–348, Ambrose 349, Biffle 350-363, Truex Jr. 364–407, Hamlin 408–415, Edwards 416–443, Vickers 444, Edwards 445–461, Hamlin 462–500.

++Rollover money awarded at year's end, amount not included in race winnings.

POINT LEADERS
(After 24 Races)

1	GREG BIFFLE	849
2	Jimmie Johnson	838
3	Dale Earnhardt Jr.	834
4	Matt Kenseth	823
5	Martin Truex Jr.	797
6	Clint Bowyer	794
7	Brad Keselowski	790
8	Denny Hamlin	774
9	Kevin Harvick	767
10	Tony Stewart	746
11	Kasey Kahne	730
12	Carl Edwards	712

TOP 20 ACTIVE NASCAR SPRINT CUP SERIES DRIVERS (MINIMUM 2 STARTS)

Driver	Races	Wins	Top 5s	Top 10s	Poles	Total Laps	Laps Led	Avg. Start	Avg. Finish
Kyle Busch	16	5	7	11	0	7810	1,375	19.3	10.3
Dale Earnhardt Jr.	26	1	7	12	0	12,865	758	21.3	11.8
Jeff Gordon	40	5	16	22	5	19,126	2,647	6.8	11.9
Matt Kenseth	26	2	10	17	1	12,711	922	17.0	12.1
Greg Biffle	20	0	6	11	1	9830	438	12.9	12.2
Kevin Harvick	24	1	9	12	0	11,790	427	17.8	12.5
Terry Labonte	57	2	19	33	1	25,530	808	14.6	13.1
Brad Keselowski	6	2	2	2	0	2933	347	14.8	13.7
Mark Martin	46	2	16	23	9	21,488	1,199	10.3	13.7
Kurt Busch	24	5	6	13	1	11,359	840	19.2	13.8
Jimmie Johnson	22	1	7	13	1	10,764	789	15.9	14.0
Carl Edwards	17	2	4	7	2	8084	345	18.4	14.4
Denny Hamlin	14	1	4	7	0	6681	352	20.6	14.8
Marcos Ambrose	8	0	2	4	0	3839	1	14.4	16.5
Bill Elliott	44	1	6	14	1	20,095	464	17.5	16.8
Clint Bowyer	14	0	4	7	0	6433	82	20.1	17.0
Jamie McMurray	20	0	3	8	0	9753	21	16.9	17.1
Ryan Newman	22	0	1	12	3	10,254	112	9.5	17.4
Tony Stewart	28	1	6	8	1	13,480	1,355	15.1	17.6
Juan Pablo Montoya	12	0	0	3	0	5996	29	20.7	17.8

FOOD CITY 500

Year	Driver	Car	Average Speed
1961	Jack Smith	61 Pontiac	68.370
1962	Bobby Johns	62 Pontiac	73.320
1963	Fireball Roberts	63 Ford	76.910
1964	Fred Lorenzen	64 Ford	72.196
1965	Junior Johnson	65 Ford	74.938
1966	Dick Hutcherson	66 Ford	69.952
1967	David Pearson	67 Dodge	75.930
1968	David Pearson	68 Ford	77.247
1969	Bobby Allison	69 Dodge	81.455
1970	Donnie Allison	69 Ford	87.543
1971	David Pearson	71 Ford	91.704
1972	Bobby Allison	72 Chevrolet	92.826
1973	Cale Yarborough	73 Chevrolet	88.952
1974	Cale Yarborough	74 Chevrolet	64.533
1975	Richard Petty	Dodge	97.053
1976	Cale Yarborough	Chevrolet	87.377
1977	Cale Yarborough	Chevrolet	100.989
1978	Darrell Waltrip	Chevrolet	92.401
1979	Dale Earnhardt	Chevrolet	91.033
1980	Dale Earnhardt	Chevrolet	96.977
1981	Darrell Waltrip	Buick	89.530
1982	Darrell Waltrip	Buick	94.025
1983	Darrell Waltrip	Chevrolet	93.445
1984	Darrell Waltrip	Chevrolet	93.967
1985	Dale Earnhardt	Chevrolet	81.790
1986	Rusty Wallace	Pontiac	89.747
1987	Dale Earnhardt	Chevrolet	75.621
1988	Bill Elliott	Ford	83.115
1989	Rusty Wallace	Pontiac	76.034
1990	Davey Allison	Ford	87.258
1991	Rusty Wallace	Pontiac	72.809
1992	Alan Kulwicki	Ford	86.316
1993	Rusty Wallace	Pontiac	84.730
1994	Dale Earnhardt	Chevrolet	89.647
1995	Jeff Gordon	Chevrolet	92.011
1996	Jeff Gordon	Chevrolet	91.308
1997	Jeff Gordon	Chevrolet	75.035
1998	Jeff Gordon	Chevrolet	82.850
1999	Rusty Wallace	Ford	93.363
2000	Rusty Wallace	Ford	88.018
2001	Elliott Sadler	Ford	86.949
2002	Kurt Busch	Ford	82.281
2003	Kurt Busch	Ford	76.185
2004	Kurt Busch	Ford	82.607
2005	Kevin Harvick	Chevrolet	77.496
2006	Kurt Busch	Dodge	79.427
2007	Kyle Busch	Chevrolet	81.969
2008	Jeff Burton	Chevrolet	89.775
2009	Kyle Busch	Toyota	92.139
2010	Jimmie Johnson	Chevrolet	79.618
2011	Kyle Busch	Toyota	91.941
2012	Brad Keselowski	Dodge	93.037

IRWIN TOOLS NIGHT RACE

Year	Driver	Car	Average Speed
1961	Joe Weatherly	61 Pontiac	72.450
1962	Jim Paschal	62 Plymouth	75.280
1963	Fred Lorenzen	63 Ford	74.844
1964	Fred Lorenzen	64 Ford	78.044
1965	Ned Jarrett	65 Ford	61.826
1966	Paul Goldsmith	66 Plymouth	77.963
1967	Richard Petty	67 Plymouth	78.705
1968	David Pearson	68 Ford	76.310
1969	David Pearson	69 Ford	79.737
1970	Bobby Allison	69 Dodge	84.880
1971	Charlie Glotzbach	71 Chevrolet	101.074
1972	Bobby Allison	72 Chevrolet	92.735
1973	Benny Parsons	73 Chevrolet	91.342
1974	Cale Yarborough	74 Chevrolet	75.430
1975	Richard Petty	Dodge	97.016
1976	Cale Yarborough	Chevrolet	99.175
1977	Cale Yarborough	Chevrolet	79.726
1978	Cale Yarborough	Oldsmobile	88.628
1979	Darrell Waltrip	Chevrolet	91.493
1980	Cale Yarborough	Chevrolet	86.973
1981	Darrell Waltrip	Buick	84.723
1982	Darrell Waltrip	Buick	94.318
1983	Darrell Waltrip	Chevrolet	89.430
1984	Terry Labonte	Chevrolet	85.365
1985	Dale Earnhardt	Chevrolet	81.388
1986	Darrell Waltrip	Chevrolet	86.934
1987	Dale Earnhardt	Chevrolet	90.373
1988	Dale Earnhardt	Chevrolet	78.775
1989	Darrell Waltrip	Chevrolet	85.554
1990	Ernie Irvan	Chevrolet	91.782
1991	Alan Kulwicki	Ford	82.028
1992	Darrell Waltrip	Chevrolet	91.198
1993	Mark Martin	Ford	88.172
1994	Rusty Wallace	Ford	91.363
1995	Terry Labonte	Chevrolet	81.979
1996	Rusty Wallace	Ford	91.267
1997	Dale Jarrett	Ford	80.013
1998	Mark Martin	Ford	86.949
1999	Dale Earnhardt	Chevrolet	91.276
2000	Rusty Wallace	Ford	85.394
2001	Tony Stewart	Pontiac	85.106
2002	Jeff Gordon	Chevrolet	77.097
2003	Kurt Busch	Ford	77.421
2004	Dale Earnhardt Jr.	Chevrolet	88.538
2005	Matt Kenseth	Ford	84.678
2006	Matt Kenseth	Ford	90.025
2007	Carl Edwards	Ford	89.006
2008	Carl Edwards	Ford	91.581
2009	Kyle Busch	Toyota	84.820
2010	Kyle Busch	Toyota	99.071
2011	Brad Keselowski	Dodge	96.753
2012	Denny Hamlin	Toyota	84.402

BRISTOL MOTOR SPEEDWAY

CANADIAN TIRE MOTORSPORT PARK

3233 Concession Road 10, Bowman, ON L1C 3K6 • **Tickets:** 1-866-GO-NASCAR or 1-800-866-1072 • **Web site:** www.canadiantiremotorsportpark.com
Facebook: www.facebook.com/CanadianTireMotorsportPark • **Twitter:** @CTMPOfficial

NASCAR

CONFIGURATION
Distance: 2.459 miles
No. of Turns: 10

TRACK RECORDS
Qualifying Records
NA

Race Record
NA

2013 TRACK LAYOUT

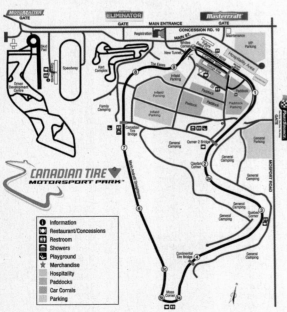

Legend:
- ℹ Information
- Restaurant/Concessions
- Restroom
- Showers
- Playground
- ★ Merchandise
- Hospitality
- Paddocks
- Car Corrals
- Parking

2013 SCHEDULE
September 1 – NASCAR Camping World Truck Series

TRACK OFFICIALS

Myles Brandt *President*

PR CONTACTS
Ryan Chalmers *Communications and Promotions Manager*

VISITOR INFORMATION
Tourism Clarington
(855) 779-1923 – **www.clarington-tourism.ca**

DIRECTIONS
From Toronto and points west: Take Highway 401 East to Highway 57 Bowmanville (exit 431). Follow Highway 57 north to Durham Road 20 and turn right (east). Continue on Durham Road 20 to Concession Road 10 and turn right. Mosport is on the right hand side of Concession Road 10. From Kingston and points east: Take Highway 401 West to Highway 57 Bowmanville (exit 431). Follow Highway 57 north to Durham Road 20 and turn right (east). Continue on Durham Road 20 to Concession Road 10 and turn right. Canadian Tire Motorsport Park is on the right hand side of Concession Road 10.
From Barrie and points north: Take Highway 400 South to Highway 401 East. Take Highway 401 West to Highway 57 Bowmanville (exit 431). Follow Highway 57 north to Durham Road 20 and turn right (east). Continue on Durham Road 20 to Concession Road 10 and turn right. Canadian Tire Motorsport Park is on the right hand side of Concession Road 10.

CHARLOTTE MOTOR SPEEDWAY

5555 Concord Parkway South Concord, NC 28027 • **Tickets:** 1-866-GO-NASCAR or 1-800-455-FANS • **Web site:** www.charlottemotorspeedway.com
Facebook: www.facebook.com/CharlotteMotorSpeedway • **Twitter:** @CLTMotorSpdwy

CHARLOTTE MOTOR SPEEDWAY

NASCAR

CONFIGURATION
Distance: 1.5 miles
Banking: 24 degrees in corners,
5 degrees on straights

TRACK RECORDS
Qualifying Records
Greg Biffle, 193.708 mph (27.877
sec.), Set October 11, 2012

Race Record
500 Miles – Jeff Gordon, 160.306
mph, Set October 11, 1999; 600
Miles – Kasey Kahne, 155.687
mph, Set May 27, 2012

2013 TRACK LAYOUT

[Track layout map]

2013 SCHEDULE
May 17: NASCAR Camping World Truck Series
May 18: NASCAR Sprint Cup Series (non-points event)
May 25: NASCAR Nationwide Series
May 26: NASCAR Sprint Cup Series
October 11: NASCAR Nationwide Series
October 12: NASCAR Sprint Cup Series

TRACK OFFICIALS

Marcus Smith *President and
General Manager*

PR CONTACTS
Scott Cooper *Vice President of Communications*

VISITOR INFORMATION
Visit Charlotte (800) 722-1994/(704) 334-2282
www.charlottesgotalot.com
Cabarrus County Convention & Visitors Bureau
(800) 848-3740/(704) 782-4340 – **www.visitcabarrus.com**

DIRECTIONS
From I-85 north of Charlotte: take exit 49 (Bruton Smith Blvd.).
Charlotte Motor Speedway is located on Concord Park South.

COCA-COLA 600
OFFICIAL RACE RESULTS: RACE #12 – MAY 27, 2012

NASCAR SPRINT CUP SERIES RACE RESULTS

Fin Pos	Str Pos	Car No	Series Driver	Team	Laps	Points	Bonus Points	Status
1	7	5	Kasey Kahne	Quaker State Chevrolet	400	47	4	Running
2	8	11	Denny Hamlin	FedEx Ground Toyota	400	43	1	Running
3	17	18	Kyle Busch	M&M's Red-White-Blue Toyota	400	42	1	Running
4	4	16	Greg Biffle	Fastenal Ford	400	42	2	Running
5	24	2	Brad Keselowski	Miller Lite Dodge	400	40	1	Running
6	12	88	Dale Earnhardt Jr.	Nat'l Guard-An American Salute/Diet Mtn. Dew Chev	400	38	0	Running
7	23	24	Jeff Gordon	Drive to End Hunger Chevrolet	400	38	1	Running
8	14	29	Kevin Harvick	Budweiser Folds of Honor Chevrolet	400	37	1	Running
9	28	99	Carl Edwards	Fastenal Ford	400	35	0	Running
10	20	17	Matt Kenseth	Fastenal Ford	399	34	0	Running
11	3	48	Jimmie Johnson	Lowe's Patriotic Chevrolet	399	33	0	Running
12	15	56	Martin Truex Jr.	NAPA Auto Parts Toyota	399	32	0	Running
13	5	15	Clint Bowyer	5-hour Energy Toyota	398	31	0	Running
14	16	39	Ryan Newman	U.S. ARMY Chevrolet	398	30	0	Running
15	9	27	Paul Menard	Menards/Serta Chevrolet	398	29	0	Running
16	1	43	Aric Almirola	U.S. Air Force Ford	398	29	1	Running
17	10	78	Regan Smith	Furniture Row Chevrolet	398	27	0	Running
18	18	83	Landon Cassill	Burger King Real Fruit Smoothies Toyota	398	27	1	Running
19	22	31	Jeff Burton	Wheaties Chevrolet	398	25	0	Running
20	29	42	Juan Pablo Montoya	Target Chevrolet	398	24	0	Running
21	31	1	Jamie McMurray	Bass Pro Shops/Arctic Cat Chevrolet	397	23	0	Running
22	25	13	Casey Mears	GEICO Ford	397	22	0	Running
23	19	20	Joey Logano	Dollar General Toyota	397	21	0	Running
24	13	21	Trevor Bayne (i)	Motorcraft/Quick Lane Tire & Auto Ctr. Ford	397	0	0	Running
25	21	14	Tony Stewart	Office Depot/Mobil 1 Chevrolet	397	19	0	Running
26	39	38	David Gilliland	Mod Space Ford	397	18	0	Running
27	42	51	Kurt Busch	Phoenix Construction Services Inc. Chevrolet	396	17	0	Running
28	26	47	Bobby Labonte	Kingsford Charcoal Toyota	396	16	0	Running
29	37	93	Travis Kvapil	Dr. Pepper Toyota	395	15	0	Running
30	40	10	Danica Patrick (i)	GoDaddy.com Chevrolet	395	0	0	Running
31	41	32	T.J. Bell (i)	Green Smoke Ford	390	0	0	Running
32	2	9	Marcos Ambrose	DeWalt Ford	367	13	1	Running
33	11	22	AJ Allmendinger	Shell Pennzoil Dodge	361	11	0	Running
34	6	55	Mark Martin	Aaron's Armed Forces Foundation Toyota	338	10	0	Engine
35	30	34	David Ragan	Al's Liners/Scorpion Coatings Ford	281	10	1	Engine
36	32	98	Michael McDowell	Presbyterian Healthcare Ford	228	8	0	Engine
37	38	95	Scott Speed	Jordan Truck Sales Ford	136	7	0	Fuel Pump
38	35	30	David Stremme	Inception Motorsports Toyota	86	6	0	Rear Gear
39	34	33	Stephen Leicht #	Little Joe's Autos/Precon Chevrolet	74	5	0	Vibration
40	36	36	Dave Blaney	SealWrap Chevrolet	54	4	0	Engine
41	43	87	Joe Nemechek (i)	AM/FM Energy/SWM Toyota	47	0	0	Vibration
42	27	74	Cole Whitt (i)	Turn One Racing Chevrolet	33	0	0	Vibration
43	33	26	Josh Wise #	MDS Transport Ford	15	1	0	Vibration

Sunoco Rookie of the Year Contender. Bonus Points: includes winner, lap leader & most laps led points. (i) = Ineligible for driver points in this series. Failed to qualify: (4) #19 Mike Bliss; #73 David Reutimann; #49 J.J. Yeley; #23 Scott Riggs.

RACE COMMENTS: Before an estimated crowd of 140,000, Kasey Kahne won the Coca-Cola 600, his 13th NASCAR Sprint Cup Series victory. Prior to the green flag, the following car dropped to the rear of the field for the reason indicated: #51 (back-up car).

RACE STATISTICS

TIME OF RACE: 3 hours, 51 minutes, 14 seconds
AVERAGE SPEED: 155.687 mph
MARGIN OF VICTORY: 4.295 seconds
FASTEST QUALIFIER: Aric Almirola (192.94 mph. 27.988 secs.)
3M LAP LEADER: Greg Biffle (204 Laps)
AMERICAN ETHANOL GREEN FLAG RESTART AWARD: Kyle Busch
DIRECTV CREW CHIEF OF THE RACE: Greg Biffle (crew chief Matt Puccia)
MAHLE CLEVITE ENGINE BUILDER OF THE RACE: Roush Yates Engines (#16)
MOBIL 1 OIL DRIVER OF THE RACE: Denny Hamlin
MOOG STEERING AND SUSPENSION PROBLEM SOLVER OF THE RACE: Dale Earnhardt Jr. (crew chief Steve Letarte, 0.150 seconds.)
NASCAR SPRINT CUP LEADER BONUS: No winner: rolls over to $60,000 at next event++
USG IMPROVING THE FINISH: Carl Edwards (19 places)
CAUTION FLAGS: 5 cautions for 23 laps. [Beneficiary in Brackets] 113–117 (Debris Backstretch [42]); 135–138 (Debris Turn 1 [14]); 171–174 (Car #93 Accident Turn 4 [24]); 179–182 (Debris Turn 3 [99]); 320–325 (Debris Turn 1 [55]).

LAP LEADERS: 31 lead changes among 11 drivers. Almirola–pole, Ambrose 1–2, Almirola 3–5, Ambrose 6–8, Biffle 9–14, Ambrose 15–22, Biffle 23–113, Ambrose 114–120, Ky. Busch 121–124, Biffle 125–134, J. Gordon 135–138, Ky. Busch 139–171, Ragan 172, Ky. Busch 173–190, Biffle 191–219, Kahne 220–221, Biffle 222, Cassill 223, Biffle 224–280, Kahne 281–307, Hamlin 308, Biffle 309–315, Kahne 316, Biffle 317, Kahne 318, Biffle 319–320, Hamlin 321–332, Ambrose 333–353, Keselowski 354, Harvick 355, J. Gordon 356, Kahne 357–400.

++Rollover money awarded at year's end, amount not included in race winnings.

POINT LEADERS
(After 12 Races)

1	GREG BIFFLE	453
2	Matt Kenseth	443
3	Denny Hamlin	437
4	Dale Earnhardt Jr.	435
5	Jimmie Johnson	405
6	Martin Truex Jr.	404
7	Kevin Harvick	398
8	Kyle Busch	391
9	Tony Stewart	388
10	Carl Edwards	372
11	Brad Keselowski	368
12	Clint Bowyer	366

CHARLOTTE MOTOR SPEEDWAY

BANK OF AMERICA 500
OFFICIAL RACE RESULTS: RACE #31 – OCTOBER 13, 2012

NASCAR SPRINT CUP SERIES RACE RESULTS

Fin Pos	Str Pos	Car No	Series Driver	Team	Laps	Points	Bonus Points	Status
1	4	15	Clint Bowyer	5-hour Energy/Avon Foun. for Women Toyota	334	47	4	Running
2	9	11	Denny Hamlin	FedEx Ground Toyota	334	43	1	Running
3	5	48	Jimmie Johnson	Mylowes Chevrolet	334	42	1	Running
4	1	16	Greg Biffle	3M/IDG Ford	334	41	1	Running
5	8	18	Kyle Busch	M&M's Toyota	334	39	0	Running
6	2	55	Mark Martin	Aaron's Dream Machine Toyota	334	39	1	Running
7	19	99	Carl Edwards	Kellogg's Ford	333	37	0	Running
8	10	5	Kasey Kahne	Time Warner Cable Chevrolet	333	36	0	Running
9	12	20	Joey Logano	The Home Depot Toyota	333	35	0	Running
10	6	56	Martin Truex Jr.	NAPA Auto Parts Toyota	333	34	0	Running
11	20	2	Brad Keselowski	Miller Lite Dodge	333	35	2	Running
12	17	43	Aric Almirola	Smithfield Ford	333	32	0	Running
13	32	14	Tony Stewart	Mobil 1/Office Depot Chevrolet	333	31	0	Running
14	7	17	Matt Kenseth	Best Buy Ford	333	30	0	Running
15	14	22	Sam Hornish Jr. (i)	Shell Pennzoil Dodge	333	0	0	Running
16	11	29	Kevin Harvick	Jimmy John's Chevrolet	333	28	0	Running
17	30	1	Jamie McMurray	McDonald's Chevrolet	333	27	0	Running
18	13	24	Jeff Gordon	Drive to End Hunger Chevrolet	332	27	1	Running
19	22	42	Juan Pablo Montoya	Target/Kellogg's Chevrolet	332	25	0	Running
20	3	39	Ryan Newman	Quicken Loans Chevrolet	332	24	0	Running
21	21	78	Kurt Busch	Furniture Row/Farm American Chevrolet	332	23	0	Running
22	16	21	Trevor Bayne (i)	Good Sam/Camping World Ford	332	0	0	Running
23	36	38	David Gilliland	Glory Foods Ford	331	21	0	Running
24	38	51	AJ Allmendinger	Phoenix Construction Chevrolet	330	20	0	Running
25	41	93	Travis Kvapil	Dr Pepper Toyota	330	19	0	Running
26	37	83	Landon Cassill	Burger King Toyota	329	18	0	Running
27	24	27	Paul Menard	Menards/Pittsburgh Paints Chevrolet	328	17	0	Running
28	39	31	Jeff Burton	Caterpillar Chevrolet	327	16	0	Running
29	27	13	Casey Mears	GEICO Ford	327	15	0	Running
30	34	10	David Reutimann	TBR/TMone.com Chevrolet	327	14	0	Running
31	33	98	Michael McDowell	K-Love/Curb Records Ford	326	13	0	Running
32	15	47	Bobby Labonte	Scott Brand Toyota	324	12	0	Running
33	18	9	Marcos Ambrose	Stanley Ford	303	12	1	Running
34	25	34	David Ragan	Glory Foods Ford	287	10	0	Running
35	29	6	Ricky Stenhouse Jr. (i)	Best Buy Ford	190	0	0	Engine
36	40	32	Timmy Hill (i)	U.S. Chrome Ford	182	0	0	Engine
37	31	30	David Stremme	Inception Motorsports Toyota	62	7	0	Rear Gear
38	26	88	Regan Smith	AMP Energy/National Guard Chevrolet	61	6	0	Engine
39	28	19	Mike Bliss (i)	Plinker Tactical Toyota	53	0	0	Rear Gear
40	23	95	Scott Speed	B&D Electrical Ford	50	4	0	Vibration
41	43	91	Reed Sorenson (i)	Aquaria USA Toyota	32	0	0	Vibration
42	35	37	J.J. Yeley	MaxQWorkForce.com Chevrolet	30	2	0	Brakes
43	42	36	Dave Blaney	Tommy Baldwin Racing Chevrolet	25	1	0	Transmission

Sunoco Rookie of the Year Contender. Bonus Points: includes winner, lap leader & most laps led points. (i) = Ineligible for driver points in this series. Failed to qualify: (4) #87 Joe Nemechek; #26 Josh Wise; #23 Scott Riggs; #33 Cole Whitt.

RACE COMMENTS: Before an estimated crowd of 100,000, Clint Bowyer won the Bank of America 500, his eighth NASCAR Sprint Cup Series victory. Prior to the green flag, the following cars dropped to the rear of the field for the reason indicated: #31, 39, 42, 91 (engine change); #38, 93 (transmission change).

RACE STATISTICS

TIME OF RACE: 3 hours, 14 minutes, 1 seconds
AVERAGE SPEED: 154.935 mph
MARGIN OF VICTORY: 0.417 seconds
COORS LIGHT POLE AWARD: Greg Biffle (193.708 mph. 27.877 secs.)
3M LAP LEADER: Brad Keselowski (139 Laps)
AMERICAN ETHANOL GREEN FLAG RESTART AWARD: Greg Biffle
DIRECTV CREW CHIEF OF THE RACE: Clint Bowyer (crew chief Brian Pattie)
FREESCALE "WIDE OPEN": Greg Biffle
MAHLE CLEVITE ENGINE BUILDER OF THE RACE: Roush Yates Engines (#16)

MOBIL 1 OIL DRIVER OF THE RACE: Denny Hamlin
MOOG STEERING AND SUSPENSION PROBLEM SOLVER OF THE RACE: Clint Bowyer (crew chief Chad Norris, 0.000 seconds)
NASCAR SPRINT CUP LEADER BONUS: No winner: rolls over to $30,000 at next event++
USG IMPROVING THE FINISH: Tony Stewart (19 places)
CAUTION FLAGS: 5 cautions for 23 laps. [Beneficiary in Brackets] 12–15 (Car #17 Spinout (Turn 4) [None]); 17–21 (Car #31, 34 Accident (Frontstretch) [95]); 37–41 (Car #27 Spinout (Turn 4) [None]); 168–172

(Debris (Turn 1) [22]); 224–227 (Debris (Frontstretch) [17]).
LAP LEADERS: 20 lead changes among 8 drivers. Biffle 1–2, Martin 3–4, Biffle 5–37, Keselowski 38–41, Ambrose 42–43, Keselowski 44–71, Johnson 72–83, J. Gordon 84–85, Keselowski 86–97, Johnson 98–134, Hamlin 135–167, Keselowski 168, Johnson 169–172, Biffle 173–179, Keselowski 180–220, Bowyer 221–222, Keselowski 223–275, Bowyer 276–277, Hamlin 278–280, Biffle 281–309, Bowyer 310–334.

++Rollover money awarded at year's end, amount not included in race winnings.

POINT LEADERS
(After 31 Races)

1	**BRAD KESELOWSKI**	2214
2	Jimmie Johnson	2207
3	Denny Hamlin	2199
4	Clint Bowyer	2186
5	Kasey Kahne	2179
6	Greg Biffle	2171
7	Martin Truex Jr.	2165
8	Tony Stewart	2164
9	Jeff Gordon	2164
10	Kevin Harvick	2158
11	Matt Kenseth	2147
12	Dale Earnhardt Jr.	2128

CHARLOTTE MOTOR SPEEDWAY

TOP 20 ACTIVE NASCAR SPRINT CUP SERIES DRIVERS (MINIMUM 2 STARTS)

Driver	Races	Wins	Top 5s	Top 10s	Poles	Total Laps	Laps Led	Avg. Start	Avg. Finish
Joey Logano	8	0	2	5	0	2761	3	14.5	10.1
Jimmie Johnson	23	6	11	15	3	7865	1,439	7.3	11.4
Carl Edwards	16	0	5	10	0	5652	98	18.3	12.0
Kasey Kahne	18	4	7	10	0	6237	807	10.5	12.4
Aric Almirola	2	0	0	0	1	731	3	9.0	14.0
Tony Stewart	28	1	6	12	1	9567	695	15.8	14.0
Denny Hamlin	15	0	3	8	0	5094	159	14.1	14.1
Matt Kenseth	27	2	7	14	0	9038	455	17.8	14.2
Kyle Busch	18	0	8	11	1	5987	793	15.0	15.3
Bobby Labonte	40	2	12	17	3	13,410	807	15.7	15.5
Jeff Gordon	40	5	16	21	8	13,314	679	10.5	15.7
Brad Keselowski	7	0	1	1	1	2534	149	21.0	15.7
Jeff Burton	38	3	8	15	0	12,909	435	23.1	15.9
Greg Biffle	20	0	5	8	1	6389	437	18.4	16.4
Clint Bowyer	14	1	2	4	0	4924	115	16.9	16.4
Mark Martin	56	4	18	24	2	18,025	1,185	10.4	16.6
David Reutimann	11	1	2	5	0	3746	9	21.3	17.1
Jamie McMurray	21	2	5	8	0	6912	238	23.1	17.6
Bill Elliott	62	2	11	22	4	19,539	1,337	16.0	17.9
Kevin Harvick	24	1	2	7	0	8286	6	18.9	18.0

COCA-COLA 600

Year	Driver	Car	Average Speed
1960	Joe Lee Johnson	60 Chevrolet	107.735
1961	David Pearson	61 Pontiac	111.633
1962	Nelson Stacy	62 Ford	125.552
1963	Fred Lorenzen	63 Ford	132.418
1964	Jim Paschal	64 Plymouth	125.772
1965	Fred Lorenzen	65 Ford	121.772
1966	Marvin Panch	65 Plymouth	135.042
1967	Jim Paschal	67 Plymouth	135.832
1968	Buddy Baker	68 Dodge	104.207
1969	LeeRoy Yarbrough	69 Mercury	134.361
1970	Donnie Allison	69 Ford	129.680
1971	Bobby Allison	69 Mercury	140.442
1972	Buddy Baker	72 Dodge	142.255
1973	Buddy Baker	73 Dodge	134.890
1974	David Pearson	73 Mercury	135.720
1975	Richard Petty	Dodge	145.327
1976	David Pearson	Mercury	137.352
1977	Richard Petty	Dodge	137.676
1978	Darrell Waltrip	Chevrolet	138.355
1979	Darrell Waltrip	Chevrolet	136.674
1980	Benny Parsons	Chevrolet	119.265
1981	Bobby Allison	Buick	129.326
1982	Neil Bonnett	Ford	130.058
1983	Neil Bonnett	Chevrolet	140.707
1984	Bobby Allison	Buick	129.233
1985	Darrell Waltrip	Chevrolet	141.807
1986	Dale Earnhardt	Chevrolet	140.406
1987	Kyle Petty	Ford	131.483
1988	Darrell Waltrip	Chevrolet	124.460
1989	Darrell Waltrip	Chevrolet	144.077
1990	Rusty Wallace	Pontiac	137.650
1991	Davey Allison	Ford	138.951
1992	Dale Earnhardt	Chevrolet	132.980
1993	Dale Earnhardt	Chevrolet	145.504
1994	Jeff Gordon	Chevrolet	139.445
1995	Bobby Labonte	Chevrolet	151.952
1996	Dale Jarrett	Ford	147.581
1997	Jeff Gordon	Chevrolet	136.745
1998	Jeff Gordon	Chevrolet	136.424
1999	Jeff Burton	Ford	151.367
2000	Matt Kenseth	Ford	142.640
2001	Jeff Burton	Ford	138.107
2002	Mark Martin	Ford	137.729
2003	Jimmie Johnson	Chevrolet	126.198
2004	Jimmie Johnson	Chevrolet	142.763
2005	Jimmie Johnson	Chevrolet	114.698
2006	Kasey Kahne	Dodge	128.840
2007	Casey Mears	Chevrolet	130.222
2008	Kasey Kahne	Dodge	135.772
2009	David Reutimann	Toyota	120.899
2010	Kurt Busch	Dodge	144.966
2011	Kevin Harvick	Chevrolet	132.414
2012	Kasey Kahne	Chevrolet	155.687

BANK OF AMERICA 500

Year	Driver	Car	Average Speed
1960	Speedy Thompson	60 Ford	112.760
1961	Joe Weatherly	61 Pontiac	119.800
1962	Junior Johnson	62 Pontiac	132.085
1963	Junior Johnson	63 Chevrolet	132.105
1964	Fred Lorenzen	64 Ford	134.559
1965	Fred Lorenzen	65 Ford	119.118
1966	*LeeRoy Yarbrough	66 Dodge	130.743
1967	Buddy Baker	67 Dodge	130.317
1968	Charlie Glotzbach	68 Dodge	135.324
1969	Donnie Allison	69 Ford	131.271
1970	LeeRoy Yarbrough	69 Mercury	123.246
1971	Bobby Allison	69 Mercury	126.140
1972	Bobby Allison	71 Chevrolet	133.234
1973	Cale Yarborough	73 Chevrolet	145.240
1974	David Pearson	73 Mercury	119.912
1975	Richard Petty	Dodge	132.209
1976	Donnie Allison	Chevrolet	141.226
1977	Benny Parsons	Chevrolet	142.780
1978	Bobby Allison	Ford	141.826
1979	Cale Yarborough	Chevrolet	134.266
1980	Dale Earnhardt	Chevrolet	135.243
1981	Darrell Waltrip	Buick	117.483
1982	Harry Gant	Buick	137.208
1983	Richard Petty	Pontiac	139.998
1984	Bill Elliott	Ford	146.861
1985	Cale Yarborough	Ford	136.761
1986	Dale Earnhardt	Chevrolet	132.403
1987	Bill Elliott	Ford	128.443
1988	Rusty Wallace	Pontiac	130.677
1989	Ken Schrader	Chevrolet	149.863
1990	Davey Allison	Ford	137.428
1991	Geoff Bodine	Ford	138.984
1992	Mark Martin	Ford	153.537
1993	Ernie Irvan	Ford	154.537
1994	Dale Jarrett	Chevrolet	145.922
1995	Mark Martin	Ford	145.358
1996	Terry Labonte	Chevrolet	143.143
1997	Dale Jarrett	Ford	144.323
1998	Mark Martin	Ford	123.188
1999	Jeff Gordon	Chevrolet	160.306
2000	Bobby Labonte	Pontiac	133.630
2001	Sterling Marlin	Dodge	139.006
2002	Jamie McMurray	Dodge	141.481
2003	Tony Stewart	Chevrolet	142.871
2004	Jimmie Johnson	Chevrolet	130.214
2005	Jimmie Johnson	Chevrolet	120.334
2006	Kasey Kahne	Dodge	132.142
2007	Jeff Gordon	Chevrolet	125.868
2008	Jeff Burton	Chevrolet	133.699
2009	Jimmie Johnson	Chevrolet	137.658
2010	Jamie McMurray	Chevrolet	140.391
2011	Matt Kenseth	Ford	146.194
2012	Clint Bowyer	Toyota	154.935

*Race changed from 400 to 500 miles.

CHARLOTTE MOTOR SPEEDWAY

CHICAGOLAND SPEEDWAY

500 Speedway Blvd., Joliet, IL 60433 • **Tickets:** 1-866-GO-NASCAR or 1-888-629-RACE • **Web site:** www.chicagolandspeedway.com
Facebook: www.facebook.com/ChicagolandSpeedway • **Twitter:** @ChicagolndSpdwy

CONFIGURATION

Distance: 1.5 miles
Banking: 18 degrees in turns,
11 degrees on tri-oval, 5 degrees
on backstretch

TRACK RECORDS

Qualifying Records
Jimmie Johnson, 188.147 mph
(28.701 sec.), Set July 8, 2005

Race Record
David Reutimann, 145.138 mph,
Set July 10, 2010

© Edward Corra/Chicagoland Speedway

2013 SCHEDULE
July 21: NASCAR Nationwide Series
September 13: NASCAR Camping World Truck Series
September 14: NASCAR Nationwide Series
September 15: NASCAR Sprint Cup Series

TRACK OFFICIALS

Scott Paddock *President*

PR CONTACTS
Nichole Meager *Senior Manager, Communications*
Patrick Kenny *Communications Coordinator*

VISITOR INFORMATION
Heritage Corridor CVB (800) 926-2262
www.heritagecorridorcvb.com

DIRECTIONS
I-55 SB: S on I-55 to I-80 (exit 250A). E on I-80 to Illinois Hwy.
53 (exit 132A). S on Hwy. 53 to track. *I-55 NB*: N on I-55 to River
Road (exit 241). Left on River Rd. then E to Hwy. 53 and go N to
Schweitzer Road, then to track. *I-80 WB*: W on I-80 to Hwy. 30
(exit 137). Left on Hwy. 30 to Gouger Road, then South to
Laraway Road. Right on Laraway to track. *I-57 WB*: W on I-57 to
Wilmington (exit 327). W on Wilmington to Hwy. 45. N on Hwy. 45
to Hwy. 52. N on Hwy. 52 to Schweitzer Road then to track.

2013 TRACK LAYOUT

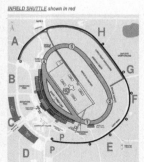

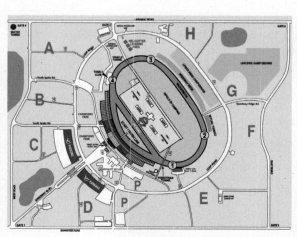

GEICO 400

OFFICIAL RACE RESULTS: RACE #27 – SEPTEMBER 16, 2012

NASCAR SPRINT CUP SERIES RACE RESULTS

Fin Pos	Str Pos	Car No	Series Driver	Team	Laps	Points	Bonus Points	Status
1	13	2	Brad Keselowski	Miller Lite Dodge	267	47	4	Running
2	1	48	Jimmie Johnson	Lowe's/Kobalt Tools Chevrolet	267	44	2	Running
3	6	5	Kasey Kahne	Farmers Insurance Chevrolet	267	41	0	Running
4	21	18	Kyle Busch	Wrigley Toyota	267	40	0	Running
5	20	39	Ryan Newman	Gene Haas Foun. Workshops For Warriors Chev.	267	39	0	Running
6	29	14	Tony Stewart	Office Depot/Mobil 1 Chevrolet	267	39	1	Running
7	10	20	Joey Logano	Dollar General Toyota	267	37	0	Running
8	4	88	Dale Earnhardt Jr.	AMP Energy/7-Eleven/National Guard Chev.	267	36	0	Running
9	18	56	Martin Truex Jr	NAPA Auto Parts Toyota	267	35	0	Running
10	9	15	Clint Bowyer	5-hour Energy Toyota	267	35	1	Running
11	16	22	Sam Hornish Jr. (i)	Shell Pennzoil Dodge	267	0	0	Running
12	35	29	Kevin Harvick	Budweiser Chevrolet	267	32	0	Running
13	22	16	Greg Biffle	Scotch Blue Ford	267	31	0	Running
14	15	55	Mark Martin	LG Partner of the Year/Aaron's Toyota	267	30	0	Running
15	11	27	Paul Menard	Menards/Libman Chevrolet	267	29	0	Running
16	8	11	Denny Hamlin	FedEx Ground Toyota	267	29	1	Running
17	2	43	Aric Almirola	Farmland Ford	266	28	1	Running
18	3	17	Matt Kenseth	Best Buy Ford	266	27	1	Running
19	5	99	Carl Edwards	Fastenal Ford	266	25	0	Running
20	14	21	Trevor Bayne (i)	Good Sam/Camping World Ford	266	0	0	Running
21	12	1	Jamie McMurray	McDonald's Chevrolet	266	24	1	Running
22	37	34	David Ragan	Distraction.gov Ford	266	23	1	Running
23	28	42	Juan Pablo Montoya	Target Chevrolet	265	21	0	Running
24	32	31	Jeff Burton	Caterpillar Chevrolet	265	20	0	Running
25	41	10	Danica Patrick (i)	GoDaddy.com Chevrolet	265	0	0	Running
26	23	47	Bobby Labonte	Bubba Burger Toyota	264	18	0	Running
27	17	9	Marcos Ambrose	Stanley Ford	263	17	0	Running
28	40	38	David Gilliland	1800LoanMart Ford	263	16	0	Running
29	26	83	Landon Cassill	Burger King Toyota	262	15	0	Running
30	39	32	T.J. Bell (i)	U.S. Chrome Ford	261	0	0	Running
31	38	93	Travis Kvapil	Burger King/Dr. Pepper Toyota	259	13	0	Running
32	30	51	Kurt Busch	Phoenix Construction Chevrolet	245	12	0	Running
33	42	36	Dave Blaney	Tommy Baldwin Racing Chevrolet	199	11	0	Engine
34	7	78	Regan Smith	Furniture Row Racing/Farm American Chev.	197	10	0	Engine
35	19	24	Jeff Gordon	DuPont Chevrolet	190	9	0	Accident
36	27	13	Casey Mears	GEICO Ford	146	8	0	Accident
37	36	33	Cole Whitt (i)	LittleJoesAutos.com Chevrolet	70	0	0	Fuel Pressure
38	43	26	Josh Wise #	MDS Transport Ford	66	6	0	Vibration
39	31	30	David Stremme	Inception Motorsports Toyota	60	5	0	Transmission
40	33	87	Joe Nemechek (i)	AM/FM Energy Wood & Pellet Stoves Toyota	52	0	0	Vibration
41	25	95	Scott Speed	JTS Ford	49	3	0	Suspension
42	34	19	Mike Bliss (i)	Plinker Tactical Toyota	41	0	0	Brakes
43	24	98	Michael McDowell	Phil Parson Racing Ford	38	1	0	Rear Gear

Sunoco Rookie of the Year Contender. Bonus Points: includes winner, lap leader & most laps led points. (i) = Ineligible for driver points in this series. Failed to qualify: (4) #23 Scott Riggs; #91 Reed Sorenson; #37 J.J. Yeley; #49 Jason Leffler.

RACE COMMENTS: Before an estimated crowd of 65,000, Brad Keselowski won the Geico 400, his eighth NASCAR Sprint Cup Series victory. Prior to the green flag, the following car dropped to the rear of the field for the reason indicated: #88 (engine change).

RACE STATISTICS

TIME OF RACE: 2 hours, 47 minutes, 37 seconds

AVERAGE SPEED: 143.363 mph

MARGIN OF VICTORY: 3.171 seconds

COORS LIGHT POLE AWARD: Jimmie Johnson (182.865 mph. 29.530 secs.)

3M LAP LEADER: Jimmie Johnson (173 Laps)

AMERICAN ETHANOL GREEN FLAG RESTART AWARD: Jimmie Johnson

DIRECTV CREW CHIEF OF THE RACE: Joey Logano (crew chief Jason Ratcliff)

FREESCALE "WIDE OPEN": Ryan Newman

MAHLE CLEVITE ENGINE BUILDER OF THE

RACE: Hendrick Engines (#48)

MOBIL 1 OIL DRIVER OF THE RACE: Kyle Busch

MOOG STEERING AND SUSPENSION PROBLEM SOLVER OF THE RACE: Ryan Newman (crew chief Tony Gibson, -0.538 seconds)

NASCAR SPRINT CUP LEADER BONUS: Brad Keselowski ($40,000 ++)

USG IMPROVING THE FINISH: Tony Stewart (23 places)

CAUTION FLAGS: 4 cautions for 23 laps. [Beneficiary in Brackets] 67–71 (Debris [31]); 102–105 (Debris [22]); 150–157 (Car #13 Accident Turn 2 [34]); 189–194 (Car #24 Accident Turn 1 [1]).

LAP LEADERS: 16 lead changes among 9 drivers. Johnson–pole, Almirola 1–3, Johnson 4–45, Keselowski 46, Kenseth 47–48, Johnson 49–102, Keselowski 103–150, Johnson 151–189, Ragan 190–191, Johnson 192–228, Keselowski 229, Hamlin 230, Stewart 231–233, Bowyer 234–239, McMurray 240, Ragan 241, Keselowski 242–267.

++Rollover money awarded at year's end, amount not included in race winnings.

POINT LEADERS
(After 27 Races)

1	**BRAD KESELOWSKI**	2056
2	Jimmie Johnson	2053
3	Tony Stewart	2048
4	Denny Hamlin	2041
5	Kasey Kahne	2041
6	Clint Bowyer	2041
7	Dale Earnhardt Jr.	2039
8	Greg Biffle	2037
9	Martin Truex Jr.	2035
10	Kevin Harvick	2032
11	Matt Kenseth	2030
12	Jeff Gordon	2009

CHICAGOLAND SPEEDWAY

TOP 20 ACTIVE NASCAR SPRINT CUP SERIES DRIVERS (MINIMUM 2 STARTS)

Driver	Races	Wins	Top 5s	Top 10s	Poles	Total Laps	Laps Led	Avg. Start	Avg. Finish
Tony Stewart	12	3	8	10	1	3196	434	17.7	8.5
Jimmie Johnson	11	0	6	9	2	2894	537	7.5	9.3
Brian Vickers	6	0	1	3	1	1605	12	5.8	9.5
Clint Bowyer	7	0	1	6	0	1872	8	15.0	10.1
Kevin Harvick	12	2	6	7	0	3190	282	18.8	10.5
Jeff Gordon	12	1	6	7	1	3110	134	12.1	12.1
Mark Martin	12	1	1	5	0	3204	239	15.5	12.6
Matt Kenseth	12	0	2	4	1	3203	348	17.1	12.8
Kyle Busch	8	1	3	3	0	2128	174	15.4	13.4
Brad Keselowski	4	1	2	2	0	1065	80	19.5	14.0
Dale Earnhardt Jr.	12	1	3	5	0	3145	121	17.0	14.3
Ryan Newman	11	1	3	7	1	2831	181	10.2	14.9
Joey Logano	4	0	0	1	0	1067	0	15.5	15.0
Juan Pablo Montoya	6	0	0	1	0	1600	1	20.8	16.0
Carl Edwards	8	0	3	3	0	2040	56	14.6	16.6
AJ Allmendinger	4	0	0	0	0	1066	0	22.5	16.8
Martin Truex Jr.	7	0	0	2	0	1816	28	16.7	16.9
David Ragan	6	0	0	1	0	1597	3	23.5	17.2
Greg Biffle	10	0	1	1	0	2625	77	15.7	18.2
Kurt Busch	12	0	0	6	0	2924	67	21.2	18.3

GEICO 400

Year	Driver	Car	Average Speed
2001	Kevin Harvick	Chevrolet	121.200
2002	Kevin Harvick	Chevrolet	136.832
2003	Ryan Newman	Dodge	134.059
2004	Tony Stewart	Chevrolet	129.507
2005	Dale Earnhardt Jr.	Chevrolet	127.638
2006	Jeff Gordon	Chevrolet	132.077
2007	Tony Stewart	Chevrolet	134.258
2008	Kyle Busch	Toyota	133.996
2009	Mark Martin	Chevrolet	133.810
2010	David Reutimann	Toyota	145.138
2011	Tony Stewart	Chevrolet	143.306
2012	Brad Keselowski	Dodge	143.363

DARLINGTON RACEWAY

DARLINGTON
too tough to tame ®

1301 Harry Byrd Hwy. Darlington, SC 29540 • **Tickets:** 1-866-GO-NASCAR or 1-866-459-RACE • **Web site:** www.darlingtonraceway.com
Facebook: http://www.facebook.com/DarlingtonRaceway • **Twitter:** @TooToughToTame

DARLINGTON RACEWAY

///// NASCAR®

CONFIGURATION
Distance: 1.366 miles
Banking: 25 degrees in turns 1 &
2, 23 degrees in turns 3 & 4, 6
degrees on straights

TRACK RECORDS
Qualifying Records
**Kasey Kahne, 181.254 mph
(27.131 sec.), Set May 6, 2011**

Race Record
**Kyle Busch, 140.350 mph,
Set May 10, 2008**

2013 TRACK LAYOUT

DARLINGTON
too tough to tame

2013 SCHEDULE
May 10: NASCAR Nationwide Series
May 11: NASCAR Sprint Cup Series

TRACK OFFICIALS

Chris Browning *President*

PR CONTACTS
Dennis Worden *Director, Public Relations*

VISITOR INFORMATION
Darlington County Tourism (888) 427-8720/(843) 339-9511
www.darlingtoncounty.org

DIRECTIONS
From I-95: Take Hwy. 52 to Darlington. *From I-20:* Take 401
East to Darlington. Track is on Hwy. 151-34, two miles west
of Darlington.

BOJANGLES' SOUTHERN 500

OFFICIAL RACE RESULTS: RACE #11 – MAY 12, 2012

NASCAR SPRINT CUP SERIES RACE RESULTS

Fin Pos	Str Pos	Car No	Series Driver	Team	Laps	Points	Bonus Points	Status
1	2	48	Jimmie Johnson	Lowe's/Kobalt Tools Chevrolet	368	48	5	Running
2	8	11	Denny Hamlin	Sport Clips Toyota	368	43	1	Running
3	17	14	Tony Stewart	Office Depot/MOBIL 1 Chevrolet	368	41	0	Running
4	5	18	Kyle Busch	Wrigley Doublemint Toyota	368	41	1	Running
5	6	56	Martin Truex Jr.	NAPA Auto Parts Toyota	368	40	1	Running
6	19	17	Matt Kenseth	Zest Ford	368	38	0	Running
7	7	99	Carl Edwards	Ford EcoBoost Fusion Ford	368	37	0	Running
8	3	5	Kasey Kahne	Rockwell Tools Chevrolet	368	37	1	Running
9	28	9	Marcos Ambrose	DeWalt Ford	368	35	0	Running
10	21	20	Joey Logano	The Home Depot Toyota	368	34	0	Running
11	26	15	Clint Bowyer	5-hour Energy Toyota	368	33	0	Running
12	1	16	Greg Biffle	3M/OH/ES Ford	368	33	1	Running
13	14	27	Paul Menard	Menards/Pittsburgh Paints Chevrolet	368	31	0	Running
14	9	78	Regan Smith	Furniture Row/CSX Play it Safe Chevrolet	368	30	0	Running
15	15	2	Brad Keselowski	Miller Lite Dodge	368	29	0	Running
16	23	29	Kevin Harvick	Budweiser Chevrolet	368	28	0	Running
17	24	88	Dale Earnhardt Jr.	Diet Mountain Dew/National Guard Chev.	368	28	1	Running
18	10	31	Jeff Burton	BB&T Chevrolet	368	26	0	Running
19	13	43	Aric Almirola	Gravely Mower Ford	368	25	0	Running
20	18	55	Mark Martin	Aaron's Dream Machine Toyota	368	24	0	Running
21	25	51	Kurt Busch	Phoenix Construction Services Chevrolet	368	23	0	Running
22	31	13	Casey Mears	GEICO Ford	367	22	0	Running
23	4	39	Ryan Newman	WIX Chevrolet	367	21	0	Running
24	27	42	Juan Pablo Montoya	Target Chevrolet	366	20	0	Running
25	36	38	David Gilliland	A&W All American Food Ford	366	19	0	Running
26	20	83	Landon Cassill	Burger King/Dr. Pepper Toyota	366	19	1	Running
27	34	36	Dave Blaney	SealWrap.com Chevrolet	365	17	0	Running
28	37	34	David Ragan	Peanut Patch/Margaret Holmes Ford	364	16	0	Running
29	22	47	Bobby Labonte	Scott Products Toyota	364	15	0	Running
30	42	32	Reed Sorenson (i)	Southern Pride Trucking Ford	363	0	0	Running
31	38	10	Danica Patrick (i)	GoDaddy.com Chevrolet	362	0	0	Running
32	33	73	Travis Kvapil	Burger King/Dr. Pepper Toyota	362	0	0	Running
33	16	22	AJ Allmendinger	Shell Pennzoil Dodge	357	11	0	Running
34	11	1	Jamie McMurray	Bass Pro Shops/Allstate Chevrolet	345	10	0	Running
35	12	24	Jeff Gordon	Drive to End Hunger/AARP Chevrolet	339	9	0	Running
36	41	93	David Reutimann	Burger King/Dr. Pepper Toyota	314	8	0	Running
37	43	49	J.J. Yeley	America Israel Racing/JPO Absorbents Toyota	132	7	0	Clutch
38	39	74	Cole Whitt (i)	Turn One Racing Chevrolet	35	0	0	Vibration
39	32	30	David Stremme	Inception Motorsports Toyota	32	5	0	Overheating
40	40	87	Joe Nemechek (i)	AM/FM Energy Wood & Pellet Stoves Toyota	27	0	0	Power Steering
41	35	52	Mike Skinner (i)	CrusaderStaffing.com Toyota	20	0	0	Electrical
42	29	79	Scott Speed	Team Kyle/KOMA Unwind Ford	20	2	0	Overheating
43	30	26	Josh Wise #	Morristown Drivers Service Ford	19	1	0	Vibration

Sunoco Rookie of the Year Contender. Bonus Points: includes winner, lap leader & most laps led points. (i) = Ineligible for driver points in this series. Failed to qualify: (4) #23 Scott Riggs; #98 Michael McDowell; #33 Stephen Leicht; #19 Mike Bliss.

RACE COMMENTS: Before an estimated crowd of 63,000, Jimmie Johnson won the Bojangles' Southern 500, his 56th NASCAR Sprint Cup Series victory. Prior to the green flag, no cars dropped to the rear of the field.

RACE STATISTICS

TIME OF RACE: 3 hours, 45 minutes, 25 seconds
AVERAGE SPEED: 133.802 mph
MARGIN OF VICTORY: 0.781 seconds
COORS LIGHT POLE AWARD: Greg Biffle (180.257 mph. 27.281 secs.)
3M LAP LEADER: Jimmie Johnson (134 Laps)
AMERICAN ETHANOL GREEN FLAG RESTART AWARD: Jimmie Johnson
DIRECTV CREW CHIEF OF THE RACE: Kyle Busch (crew chief Dave Rogers)
FREESCALE "WIDE OPEN": Martin Truex Jr.
MAHLE CLEVITE ENGINE BUILDER OF THE RACE: Hendrick Engines (#48)

MOBIL 1 OIL DRIVER OF THE RACE: Denny Hamlin
MOOG STEERING AND SUSPENSION PROBLEM SOLVER OF THE RACE: Tony Stewart (crew chief Steve Addington, 0.323 seconds)
NASCAR SPRINT CUP LEADER BONUS: No winner: rolls over to $50,000 at next event++
USG IMPROVING THE FINISH: Marcos Ambrose (19 places)
CAUTION FLAGS: 8 cautions for 38 laps. [Beneficiary in Brackets] 173–179 (Debris [15]); 195–199 (Debris [39]); 231–235 (Debris [88]); 299–303 (Car #47 Spin [1]); 308–311 (Car #78 Spin [31]); 317–319 (Car #1, 22 Accident Turn 4 [9]); 331–334 (Car #32 Spin [2]); 362–366 (Car #39, 51 Accident Turn 2 [55]).

LAP LEADERS: 22 lead changes among 8 drivers. Biffle 1–48, Kahne 49, Johnson 50, Cassill 51, Ky. Busch 52–72, Biffle 73–98, Hamlin 99–100, Johnson 101–172, Ky. Busch 173, Johnson 174–179, Ky. Busch 180–188, Johnson 189–194, Ky. Busch 195, Hamlin 196–199, Kahne 200–231, Hamlin 232–280, Earnhardt Jr. 281, Truex Jr. 282–298, Hamlin 299, Truex Jr. 300–307, Johnson 308–312, Ky. Busch 313–324, Johnson 325–368.

++Rollover money awarded at year's end, amount not included in race winnings.

POINT LEADERS
(After 11 Races)

1	GREG BIFFLE	411
2	Matt Kenseth	409
3	Dale Earnhardt Jr.	397
4	Denny Hamlin	394
5	Jimmie Johnson	372
6	Martin Truex Jr.	372
7	Tony Stewart	369
8	Kevin Harvick	361
9	Kyle Busch	349
10	Carl Edwards	337
11	Clint Bowyer	335
12	Brad Keselowski	328

ALL TIME LEADERS AND PAST WINNERS

TOP 20 ACTIVE NASCAR SPRINT CUP SERIES DRIVERS (MINIMUM 2 STARTS)

Driver	Races	Wins	Top 5s	Top 10s	Poles	Total Laps	Laps Led	Avg. Start	Avg. Finish
Denny Hamlin	7	1	3	6	0	2573	354	10.7	5.9
Jimmie Johnson	14	3	7	10	0	4733	543	12.5	9.1
Brad Keselowski	4	0	1	2	0	1472	0	16.3	9.3
Bill Elliott	52	5	22	35	5	17,477	980	11.0	9.4
Martin Truex Jr.	7	0	1	3	0	2572	98	24.3	11.3
Jeff Gordon	32	7	18	21	3	9983	1,720	6.7	11.8
Tony Stewart	20	0	4	11	0	6567	20	17.1	11.8
Jeff Burton	30	2	8	16	0	9578	817	20.7	12.3
Mark Martin	46	2	17	26	2	15,221	801	13.3	12.4
Ryan Newman	14	0	7	9	1	4804	325	7.9	12.4
Carl Edwards	9	0	3	6	0	3171	94	15.8	13.1
Kasey Kahne	10	0	3	4	4	3599	328	8.4	13.9
Greg Biffle	12	2	2	5	2	4126	713	9.5	14.0
Dale Earnhardt Jr.	18	0	3	7	0	6100	171	17.3	15.3
Kyle Busch	8	1	2	4	0	2849	323	18.6	15.5
Jamie McMurray	12	0	3	5	1	4093	163	14.0	16.1
Bobby Labonte	32	1	5	11	1	10,081	131	16.1	16.3
Regan Smith	5	1	1	1	0	1835	11	21.8	16.4
Terry Labonte	54	2	11	20	0	16,175	81	18.1	17.0
Kurt Busch	16	0	2	5	1	5441	183	13.1	17.4

BOJANGLES' SOUTHERN 500

Year	Driver	Car	Average Speed
1950	Johnny Mantz	50 Plymouth	76.260
1951	Herb Thomas	51 Hudson	76.900
1952	Fonty Flock	52 Oldsmobile	74.510
1953	Buck Baker	53 Oldsmobile	92.780
1954	Herb Thomas	54 Hudson	94.930
1955	Herb Thomas	55 Chevrolet	93.281
1956	Curtis Turner	56 Ford	95.067
1957	Speedy Thompson	57 Chevrolet	100.094
1958	Fireball Roberts	57 Chevrolet	102.590
1959	Jim Reed	57 Chevrolet	111.840
1960	Buck Baker	60 Pontiac	105.901
1961	Nelson Stacy	61 Ford	117.787
1962	Larry Frank	62 Ford	117.965
1963	Fireball Roberts	63 Ford	129.784
1964	Buck Baker	64 Dodge	117.757
1965	Ned Jarrett	65 Ford	115.924
1966	Darel Dieringer	66 Mercury	114.830
1967	Richard Petty	67 Plymouth	130.423
1968	Cale Yarborough	68 Mercury	126.132
1969	LeeRoy Yarbrough	69 Ford	105.612
1970	Buddy Baker	69 Dodge	128.817
1971	Bobby Allison	69 Mercury	131.398
1972	Bobby Allison	71 Chevrolet	128.124
1973	Cale Yarborough	73 Chevrolet	134.033
1974	Cale Yarborough	74 Chevrolet	111.075
1975	Bobby Allison	Matador	116.825
1976	David Pearson	Mercury	120.534
1977	David Pearson	Mercury	106.797
1978	Cale Yarborough	Oldsmobile	116.828
1979	David Pearson	Chevrolet	126.259
1980	Terry Labonte	Chevrolet	115.210
1981	Neil Bonnett	Ford	126.410
1982	Cale Yarborough	Buick	115.224
1983	Bobby Allison	Buick	123.343
1984	Harry Gant	Chevrolet	128.270
1985	Bill Elliott	Ford	121.254
1986	Tim Richmond	Chevrolet	121.068
1987	Dale Earnhardt	Chevrolet	115.520
1988	Bill Elliott	Ford	128.297
1989	Dale Earnhardt	Chevrolet	135.462
1990	Dale Earnhardt	Chevrolet	123.141
1991	Harry Gant	Oldsmobile	133.508
1992	Darrell Waltrip	Chevrolet	129.114
1993	Mark Martin	Ford	137.932
1994	Bill Elliott	Ford	127.952
1995	Jeff Gordon	Chevrolet	121.231
1996	Jeff Gordon	Chevrolet	135.757
1997	Jeff Gordon	Chevrolet	121.149
1998	Jeff Gordon	Chevrolet	139.031
1999	Jeff Burton	Ford	107.816
2000	Bobby Labonte	Pontiac	108.273
2001	Ward Burton	Dodge	122.773
2002	Jeff Gordon	Chevrolet	118.617
2003	Terry Labonte	Chevrolet	120.744
2004	Jimmie Johnson	Chevrolet	125.044
2009	Mark Martin	Chevrolet	119.687
2010	Denny Hamlin	Toyota	126.605
2011	Regan Smith	Chevrolet	129.678
2012	Jimmie Johnson	Chevrolet	133.802

DODGE CHALLENGER 500

Year	Driver	Car	Average Speed
1957	Fireball Roberts	57 Ford	107.940
1958	Curtis Turner	58 Ford	109.624
1959	Fireball Roberts	59 Chevrolet	115.380
1960	Joe Weatherly	60 Pontiac	102.260
1961	Fred Lorenzen	61 Ford	119.520
1962	Nelson Stacy	62 Ford	117.429
1963	Joe Weatherly	63 Pontiac	122.745
1964	Fred Lorenzen	64 Ford	130.013
1965	Junior Johnson	65 Ford	111.849
1966	*Richard Petty	66 Plymouth	131.993
1967	Richard Petty	67 Plymouth	125.738
1968	David Pearson	68 Ford	132.699
1969	LeeRoy Yarbrough	69 Mercury	131.572
1970	David Pearson	69 Ford	129.668
1971	Buddy Baker	71 Dodge	130.678
1972	David Pearson	71 Mercury	124.406
1973	**David Pearson	71 Mercury	122.655
1974	David Pearson	73 Mercury	117.543
1975	Bobby Allison	Matador	117.597
1976	David Pearson	Mercury	122.973
1977	Darrell Waltrip	Chevrolet	128.817
1978	Benny Parsons	Chevrolet	127.544
1979	Darrell Waltrip	Chevrolet	121.721
1980	David Pearson	Chevrolet	112.397
1981	Darrell Waltrip	Buick	126.703
1982	Dale Earnhardt	Ford	123.554
1983	Harry Gant	Buick	130.406
1984	Darrell Waltrip	Chevrolet	119.925
1985	Bill Elliott	Ford	126.295
1986	Dale Earnhardt	Chevrolet	128.994
1987	Dale Earnhardt	Chevrolet	122.540
1988	Lake Speed	Oldsmobile	131.284
1989	Harry Gant	Oldsmobile	115.475
1990	Dale Earnhardt	Chevrolet	124.073
1991	Ricky Rudd	Chevrolet	135.594
1992	Bill Elliott	Ford	139.364
1993	Dale Earnhardt	Chevrolet	139.958
1994	***Dale Earnhardt	Chevrolet	132.432
1995	Sterling Marlin	Chevrolet	111.392
1996	Jeff Gordon	Chevrolet	124.792
1997	Dale Jarrett	Ford	121.162
1998	Dale Jarrett	Ford	127.962
1999	Jeff Burton	Ford	121.294
2000	Ward Burton	Pontiac	128.076
2001	Dale Jarrett	Ford	126.557
2002	Sterling Marlin	Dodge	126.070
2003	Ricky Craven	Pontiac	126.214
2004	Jimmie Johnson	Chevrolet	114.001
2005	****Greg Biffle	Ford	123.031
2006	Greg Biffle	Ford	135.127
2007	Jeff Gordon	Chevrolet	124.372
2008	Kyle Busch	Toyota	140.350

*Race changed from 300 to 400 miles.
**Race changed from 400 to 500 miles.
***Race changed from 500 to 400 miles.
****Race changed from 400 to 500 miles.

DARLINGTON RACEWAY

DAYTONA

DAYTONA
INTERNATIONAL SPEEDWAY

INTERNATIONAL SPEEDWAY

1801 W. Int'l Speedway Blvd., Daytona Beach, FL 32114 • **Tickets:** 1-866-GO-NASCAR or 1-800-PITSHOP • **Web site:** www.daytonainternationalspeedway.com
Facebook: www.facebook.com/DaytonaInternationalSpeedway • **Twitter:** @DISupdates

CONFIGURATION
Distance: 2.5 miles
Banking: 31 degrees in turns,
18 degrees on tri-oval, 3 degrees
on straights

TRACK RECORDS
Qualifying Records
Bill Elliott, 210.364 mph (42.783
sec.), Set February 9, 1987

Race Record
400 Miles – Bobby Allison,
173.473 mph, Set July 4, 1980;
500 Miles – Buddy Baker, 177.602
mph, Set February 17, 1980

2013 TRACK LAYOUT

2013 SCHEDULE
February 16: NASCAR Sprint Cup Series (non-points event)
February 21: NASCAR Sprint Cup Series (non-points event)
February 22: NASCAR Camping World Truck Series
February 23: NASCAR Nationwide Series
February 24: NASCAR Sprint Cup Series
July 5: NASCAR Nationwide Series
July 6: NASCAR Sprint Cup Series

TRACK OFFICIALS

Joie Chitwood *President*

PR CONTACTS
Lenny Santiago *Senior Director of Public Relations*
Andrew Booth *Senior Manager of Media Relations*

VISITOR INFORMATION
Daytona Regional Chamber of Commerce (386) 255-0981
www.daytonachamber.com

DIRECTIONS
Located approximately one mile east of I-95 on West Int'l
Speedway Blvd. (US 92).

NASCAR SPRINT CUP SERIES RACE RESULTS

Fin Pos	Str Pos	Car No	Series Driver	Team	Laps	Points	Bonus Points	Status
1	4	17	Matt Kenseth	Best Buy Ford	202	47	4	Running
2	5	88	Dale Earnhardt Jr.	Diet Mountain Dew/National Guard Chev.	202	42	0	Running
3	2	16	Greg Biffle	3M Ford	202	42	1	Running
4	31	11	Denny Hamlin	FedEx Express Toyota	202	42	2	Running
5	9	31	Jeff Burton	Caterpillar Chevrolet	202	40	1	Running
6	37	27	Paul Menard	Menards/Peak Chevrolet	202	39	1	Running
7	13	29	Kevin Harvick	Budweiser Chevrolet	202	37	0	Running
8	1	99	Carl Edwards	Fastenal Ford	202	36	0	Running
9	12	20	Joey Logano	The Home Depot Toyota	202	36	1	Running
10	22	55	Mark Martin	Aaron's Toyota	202	33	0	Running
11	30	15	Clint Bowyer	5-hour Energy Toyota	202	33	0	Running
12	26	56	Martin Truex Jr.	NAPA Auto Parts Toyota	202	33	1	Running
13	7	9	Marcos Ambrose	Stanley Ford	202	31	0	Running
14	32	47	Bobby Labonte	Kroger Toyota	202	30	0	Running
15	24	36	Dave Blaney	Ollie's Bargain Outlet Chevrolet	202	30	1	Running
16	3	14	Tony Stewart	Office Depot/Mobil 1 Chevrolet	202	29	1	Running
17	14	18	Kyle Busch	M&M's Brown Toyota	202	27	0	Running
18	43	32	Terry Labonte	C&J Energy Ford	202	27	1	Running
19	41	26	Tony Raines	Front Row Motorsports Ford	202	25	0	Running
20	21	6	Ricky Stenhouse Jr. (i)	Ford EcoBoost Ford	202	0	0	Running
21	18	39	Ryan Newman	U.S. Army/Quicken Loans Chevrolet	202	23	0	Running
22	39	83	Landon Cassill	Burger King Toyota	202	22	0	Running
23	33	38	David Gilliland	MHP/Power Pak Pudding Ford	201	21	0	Running
24	6	78	Regan Smith	Furniture Row/CSX Play It Safe Chevrolet	200	21	1	Running
25	36	13	Casey Mears	GEICO Ford	199	19	0	Running
26	38	93	David Reutimann	Burger King Toyota	196	18	0	Accident
27	10	33	Elliott Sadler (i)	General Mills/Kroger Chevrolet	196	0	0	Running
28	34	87	Joe Nemechek (i)	AM FM Energy Wood & Pellet Stoves Toyota	194	0	0	Running
29	20	5	Kasey Kahne	Farmers Insurance Chevrolet	189	15	0	Accident
30	11	98	Michael McDowell	K-LOVE/Curb Records Ford	189	14	0	Running
31	19	1	Jamie McMurray	Bass Pro Shops/Tracker Boats Chevrolet	188	13	0	Accident
32	23	2	Brad Keselowski	Miller Lite Dodge	187	12	0	Accident
33	27	43	Aric Almirola	Smithfield Helping Hungry Homes Ford	187	11	0	Accident
34	15	22	AJ Allmendinger	Shell Pennzoil Dodge	177	10	0	Running
35	40	21	Trevor Bayne (i)	Motorcraft/Quick Lane Tire & Auto Center Ford	164	0	0	Running
36	35	42	Juan Pablo Montoya	Target Chevrolet	159	8	0	Accident
37	42	30	David Stremme	Inception Motorsports Chevrolet	156	7	0	Engine
38	29	10	Danica Patrick (i)	GoDaddy.com Chevrolet	138	0	0	Running
39	28	51	Kurt Busch	Hendrickcars.com Chevrolet	113	5	0	Running
40	16	24	Jeff Gordon	Drive to End Hunger Chevrolet	81	5	1	Engine
41	17	7	Robby Gordon	MAPEI/Menards/SPEED Energy Dodge	25	3	0	Engine
42	8	48	Jimmie Johnson	Lowe's Chevrolet	1	2	0	Accident
43	25	34	David Ragan	Scorpion Truck Bedliners Ford	1	1	0	Accident

Sunoco Rookie of the Year Contender. Bonus Points: includes winner, lap leader & most laps led points. (i) = Ineligible for driver points in this series. Failed to qualify (6): #40 Michael Waltrip; #23 Robert Richardson; #97 Bill Elliott; #37 Mike Wallace; #49 J.J. Yeley.

RACE COMMENTS: Before an estimated crowd of 140,000 (originally estimated at 180,000), Matt Kenseth won the Daytona 500, his 22nd NASCAR Sprint Cup Series victory and second Daytona 500 win. To start the race, prior to the green flag the following cars dropped to the rear of the field for the reasons indicated: #27, 42, 10, 38 (backup car); #51 (engine change). The event was originally scheduled for Feb. 26.

RACE STATISTICS

TIME OF RACE: 3 hours, 36 minutes, 2 seconds
AVERAGE SPEED: 140.256 mph
MARGIN OF VICTORY: 0.21 seconds
COORS LIGHT POLE AWARD: Carl Edwards (194.738 mph, 46.216 secs.)
3M LAP LEADER AWARD: Denny Hamlin (57 Laps)
AMERICAN ETHANOL GREEN FLAG RESTART AWARD: Bobby Labonte
DIRECTV CREW CHIEF OF THE RACE: Jimmy Fennig (crew chief for Matt Kenseth)
FREESCALE "WIDE OPEN" AWARD: Jeff Burton
MAHLE CLEVITE ENGINE BUILDER OF THE RACE: Toyota Racing Development (TRD) (No. 11)

MOBIL 1 OIL DRIVER OF THE RACE: Denny Hamlin
MOOG STEERING AND SUSPENSION PROBLEM SOLVER OF THE RACE: Richard Labbe (crew chief for Paul Menard, 0.169 seconds)
NASCAR SPRINT CUP LEADER BONUS: No winner
SUNOCO ROOKIE OF THE RACE: No rookies
USG IMPROVING THE FINISH AWARD: Denny Hamlin (27 places)
CAUTION FLAGS: 10 cautions for 42 laps. [Beneficiary in Brackets] 3–7 (Car #10, 21, 33, 34, 48, 51 Accident Frontstretch [None]); 14–16 (Car #39 Spin Turn 2 [None]); 65–67 (Debris [83]); 82–85 (Oil on Track [26]); 89–91 (Car #9, 32 Accident Tri-Oval [39]); 130–132 (Car #15 Stopped on Track [39]); 158–166 (Car

#30 Spin Turn 3 [Red Flag: Lap 161, 2.05:29] [47]); 179–182 (Car #6, 9, 13, 43 Accident Frontstretch [15]); 189–193 (Car #1, 2,5, 14, 43, 78, 99 Accident Frontstretch [15]); 198–200 (Car #6, 14, 18, 20, 36, 38, 39, 93 Accident Frontstretch [9]).
LAP LEADERS: 25 lead changes among 13 drivers. Edwards–pole, Biffle 1–9, Smith 10–11, Biffle 12–14, Menard 15–16, Hamlin 17–40, Burton 41–57, j. Gordon 58, Stewart 59–60, Burton 61–67, Biffle 68–76, Truex Jr. 77–81, Biffle 82, T. Labonte 83–85, Biffle 86–99, Truex Jr. 100–101, Hamlin 102–129, Biffle 130, Martin 131–132, Biffle 133–138, Hamlin 139–143, Logano 144–145, Kenseth 146–157, Biffle 158, Blaney 159–164, Kenseth 165–202.

POINT LEADERS
(After 1 Race)

1	MATT KENSETH	47
2	Dale Earnhardt Jr.	42
3	Greg Biffle	42
4	Denny Hamlin	42
5	Jeff Burton	40
6	Paul Menard	39
7	Kevin Harvick	37
8	Carl Edwards	36
9	Joey Logano	36
10	Mark Martin	35
11	Clint Bowyer	33
12	Martin Truex Jr.	33

COKE ZERO 400 POWERED BY COCA-COLA
OFFICIAL RACE RESULTS: RACE #18 – JULY 7, 2012

NASCAR SPRINT CUP SERIES RACE RESULTS

Fin Pos	Str Pos	Car No	Series Driver	Team	Laps	Points	Bonus Points	Status
1	42	14	Tony Stewart	MOBIL 1/Office Depot Chevrolet	160	47	4	Running
2	20	31	Jeff Burton	Wheaties Chevrolet	160	42	0	Running
3	1	17	Matt Kenseth	Zest Ford	160	43	2	Running
4	19	20	Joey Logano	Dollar General Toyota	160	40	0	Running
5	2	39	Ryan Newman	Aspen Dental Chevrolet	160	39	0	Running
6	12	99	Carl Edwards	Subway Ford	160	38	0	Running
7	3	5	Kasey Kahne	HendrickCars.com Chevrolet	160	37	0	Running
8	9	2	Brad Keselowski	Miller Lite Dodge	160	36	0	Running
9	28	55	Michael Waltrip	Aaron's Dream Machine Toyota	160	35	0	Running
10	41	47	Bobby Labonte	Kingsford Charcoal Toyota	160	34	0	Running
11	39	10	David Reutimann	CarportEmpire.com/TMone.com Call Ctrs Chev	160	33	0	Running
12	5	24	Jeff Gordon	PepsiMax Chevrolet	160	32	0	Running
13	30	1	Jamie McMurray	Bass Pro Shops/NRA Museum Chevrolet	160	31	0	Running
14	13	27	Paul Menard	Quaker State/Menards Chevrolet	160	30	0	Running
15	24	88	Dale Earnhardt Jr.	Nat'l Guard-An American Salute/Diet Mtn Dew Chev	160	29	0	Running
16	40	93	Travis Kvapil	Burger King/Dr. Pepper Toyota	160	28	0	Running
17	18	56	Martin Truex Jr.	NAPA Batteries Toyota	160	28	1	Running
18	7	13	Casey Mears	GEICO Ford	160	27	1	Running
19	17	43	Aric Almirola	U.S. Air Force Ford	160	25	0	Running
20	34	32	Terry Labonte	C & J Energy Services Ford	160	24	0	Running
21	4	16	Greg Biffle	3M Ford	160	24	1	Running
22	33	36	Dave Blaney	Golden Corral Chevrolet	160	22	0	Running
23	11	29	Kevin Harvick	Budweiser Folds of Honor Chevrolet	159	21	0	Running
24	22	18	Kyle Busch	Interstate Batteries Toyota	159	21	1	Running
25	23	11	Denny Hamlin	FedEx Office Toyota	156	19	0	Running
26	27	34	David Ragan	MHP 8-hour Alert Ford	154	19	1	Accident
27	15	21	Trevor Bayne (i)	Motorcraft/Quick Lane Tire & Auto Center Ford	152	0	0	Accident
28	14	42	Juan Pablo Montoya	Target Chevrolet	152	16	0	Accident
29	29	15	Clint Bowyer	5-hour Energy Toyota	152	15	0	Accident
30	10	9	Marcos Ambrose	DeWalt Ford	152	14	0	Accident
31	32	38	David Gilliland	Glory Foods Ford	152	14	1	Accident
32	38	83	Landon Cassill	Burger King/Dr. Pepper Toyota	151	12	0	Running
33	8	22	Sam Hornish Jr. (i)	Shell Pennzoil Dodge	149	0	0	Running
34	25	78	Regan Smith	Furniture Row/Farm American Chevrolet	133	10	0	Running
35	35	51	Kurt Busch	Phoenix Construction Services Chevrolet	132	9	0	Running
36	16	48	Jimmie Johnson	Lowe's Chevrolet	123	8	0	Accident
37	6	50	Bill Elliott	Walmart Chevrolet	123	7	0	Accident
38	31	26	Josh Wise #	MDS Transport Ford	47	7	1	Transmission
39	26	30	David Stremme	Stock Car Steel and Aluminum Toyota	25	5	0	Rear Gear
40	43	49	J.J. Yeley	Robinson-Blakeney Racing Toyota	16	4	0	Overheating
41	36	87	Joe Nemechek (i)	AM/FM Energy Wood & Pellet Stoves Toyota	10	0	0	Overheating
42	37	33	Stephen Leicht #	LittleJoesAutos.com Chevrolet	4	2	0	Overheating
43	21	98	Michael McDowell	Phil Parsons Racing Ford	3	1	0	Overheating

Sunoco Rookie of the Year Contender. Bonus Points: includes winner, lap leader & most laps led points. (i) = Ineligible for driver points in this series. Failed to qualify: (1) #23 Robert Richardson.

RACE COMMENTS: Before an estimated crowd of 115,000, Tony Stewart won the Coke Zero 400 Powered by Coca-Cola, his 47th NASCAR Sprint Cup Series victory. Prior to the green flag, the following cars dropped to the rear of the field for the reasons indicated: #9 (unapproved adjustments); #22, 98 (driver change).

RACE STATISITCS

TIME OF RACE: 2 hours, 32 minutes, 14 seconds
AVERAGE SPEED: 157.653 mph
MARGIN OF VICTORY: Under Caution
COORS LIGHT POLE AWARD: Matt Kenseth (192.386 mph. 46.781 secs.)
3M LAP LEADER: Matt Kenseth (89 Laps)
AMERICAN ETHANOL GREEN FLAG RESTART AWARD: Joey Logano
DIRECTV CREW CHIEF OF THE RACE: Matt Kenseth (crew chief Jimmy Fennig)
MAHLE CLEVITE ENGINE BUILDER OF THE RACE: Roush Yates Engines (#17)
MOBIL 1 OIL DRIVER OF THE RACE: Tony Stewart
MOOG STEERING AND SUSPENSION PROBLEM SOLVER OF THE RACE: Tony Stewart (crew chief Steve Addington, -0.047 seconds)
NASCAR SPRINT CUP LEADER BONUS: No winner: rolls over to $120,000 at next event++
USG IMPROVING THE FINISH: Tony Stewart (41 places)
CAUTION FLAGS: 6 cautions for 23 laps. [Beneficiary in Brackets] 82–85 (Car #22 Accident Backstretch [32]); 92–95 (Car #21, 47, 51, 43, 11, 42 Accident Turn 2 [36]); 125–130 (Car #48, 24, 55, 20, 50, 78, 56 Accident Turn 4 [47]); 146–148 (Car #2 Spin Turn 2 [83]); 154–158 (Car #11, 42, 21, 9, 15, 24, 18, 10, 36, 38, 13, 27, 34, 56 Accident Tri-Oval [83]); 160 (Car #29, 43, 16, 36, 18, 34, 5, 93, 88, 78, 99, 17, 27, 32, 1 Accident Turn 4 [None]).
LAP LEADERS: 12 lead changes among 9 drivers. Kenseth 1–41, Ragan 42, Wise 43–45, Truex Jr. 46–47, Biffle 48–82, Mears 83, Kenseth 84–123, Ky. Busch 124–126, Gilliland 127, Ky. Busch 128–130, Stewart 131–151, Kenseth 152–159, Stewart 160.

++Rollover money awarded at year's end, amount not included in race winnings.

POINT LEADERS
(After 18 Races)

1	MATT KENSETH	676
2	Dale Earnhardt Jr.	651
3	Greg Biffle	632
4	Jimmie Johnson	618
5	Tony Stewart	592
6	Kevin Harvick	586
7	Denny Hamlin	584
8	Martin Truex Jr.	584
9	Brad Keselowski	573
10	Clint Bowyer	572
11	Carl Edwards	541
12	Kyle Busch	516

DAYTONA INTERNATIONAL SPEEDWAY

TOP 20 ACTIVE NASCAR SPRINT CUP SERIES DRIVERS (MINIMUM 2 STARTS)

Driver	Races	Wins	Top 5s	Top 10s	Poles	Total Laps	Laps Led	Avg. Start	Avg. Finish
Dale Earnhardt Jr.	26	2	9	14	1	4431	396	10.8	14.5
Kevin Harvick	23	2	5	10	1	3768	178	15.8	15.4
Terry Labonte	59	0	11	26	0	9742	158	20.6	15.4
Clint Bowyer	14	0	2	6	0	2496	149	19.6	15.8
Bill Elliott	60	4	15	24	5	9913	617	17.2	16.0
Jeff Gordon	40	6	12	19	3	6667	590	10.5	16.1
Tony Stewart	28	4	8	13	1	4559	665	11.6	16.1
Matt Kenseth	26	2	6	13	1	4229	222	19.9	16.2
Carl Edwards	16	0	4	8	1	2707	4	16.3	16.6
Paul Menard	11	0	0	3	1	1933	37	22.6	17.0
Jeff Burton	38	1	9	11	1	6258	145	20.5	17.1
Kasey Kahne	18	0	2	7	0	3050	28	21.3	17.3
Ken Schrader	45	0	7	22	3	7059	298	18.0	17.3
Elliott Sadler	25	0	4	9	0	4276	58	24.9	17.9
Kurt Busch	24	0	10	12	0	3949	239	21.1	18.0
Kyle Busch	16	1	5	6	0	2714	281	14.2	18.0
Mark Martin	54	0	9	19	3	8396	273	15.0	18.2
David Ragan	12	1	3	4	0	1854	25	23.2	18.4
Joey Logano	8	0	2	3	0	1333	3	21.0	18.8
Jimmie Johnson	22	1	6	9	2	3536	60	9.6	19.0

DAYTONA 500

Year	Driver	Car	Average Speed
1959	Lee Petty	59 Oldsmobile	135.521
1960	Junior Johnson	59 Chevrolet	124.740
1961	Marvin Panch	60 Pontiac	149.601
1962	Fireball Roberts	62 Pontiac	152.529
1963	Tiny Lund	63 Ford	151.566
1964	Richard Petty	64 Plymouth	154.334
1965	Fred Lorenzen	65 Ford	141.539
1966	Richard Petty	66 Plymouth	160.627
1967	Mario Andretti	67 Ford	146.926
1968	Cale Yarborough	68 Mercury	143.251
1969	LeeRoy Yarbrough	69 Ford	157.950
1970	Pete Hamilton	70 Plymouth	149.601
1971	Richard Petty	71 Plymouth	144.462
1972	A.J. Foyt	71 Mercury	161.550
1973	Richard Petty	73 Dodge	157.205
1974	Richard Petty	74 Dodge	140.894
1975	Benny Parsons	Chevrolet	153.649
1976	David Pearson	Mercury	152.181
1977	Cale Yarborough	Chevrolet	153.218
1978	Bobby Allison	Ford	159.730
1979	Richard Petty	Oldsmobile	143.977
1980	Buddy Baker	Oldsmobile	177.602
1981	Richard Petty	Buick	169.651
1982	Bobby Allison	Buick	153.991
1983	Cale Yarborough	Pontiac	155.979
1984	Cale Yarborough	Chevrolet	150.994
1985	Bill Elliott	Ford	172.265
1986	Geoff Bodine	Chevrolet	148.124
1987	Bill Elliott	Ford	176.263
1988	Bobby Allison	Buick	137.531
1989	Darrell Waltrip	Chevrolet	148.466
1990	Derrike Cope	Chevrolet	165.761
1991	Ernie Irvan	Chevrolet	148.148
1992	Davey Allison	Ford	168.256
1993	Dale Jarrett	Chevrolet	154.972
1994	Sterling Marlin	Chevrolet	156.931
1995	Sterling Marlin	Chevrolet	141.710
1996	Dale Jarrett	Ford	154.308
1997	Jeff Gordon	Chevrolet	148.295
1998	Dale Earnhardt	Chevrolet	172.712
1999	Jeff Gordon	Chevrolet	161.551
2000	Dale Jarrett	Ford	155.669
2001	Michael Waltrip	Chevrolet	161.783
2002	Ward Burton	Dodge	142.971
2003	Michael Waltrip	Chevrolet	133.870
2004	Dale Earnhardt Jr.	Chevrolet	156.345
2005	Jeff Gordon	Chevrolet	135.173
2006	Jimmie Johnson	Chevrolet	142.667
2007	Kevin Harvick	Chevrolet	149.335
2008	Ryan Newman	Dodge	152.672
2009	Matt Kenseth	Ford	132.816
2010	Jamie McMurray	Chevrolet	137.284
2011	Trevor Bayne	Ford	130.326
2012	Matt Kenseth	Ford	140.256

COKE ZERO 400 POWERED BY COCA-COLA

Year	Driver	Car	Average Speed
1959	Fireball Roberts	59 Pontiac	140.581
1960	Jack Smith	60 Pontiac	146.842
1961	David Pearson	61 Pontiac	154.294
1962	Fireball Roberts	62 Pontiac	153.688
1963	*Fireball Roberts	63 Ford	150.927
1964	A.J. Foyt	64 Dodge	151.451
1965	A.J. Foyt	65 Ford	150.046
1966	Sam McQuagg	66 Dodge	153.813
1967	Cale Yarborough	67 Ford	143.583
1968	Cale Yarborough	68 Mercury	167.247
1969	LeeRoy Yarbrough	69 Ford	160.875
1970	Donnie Allison	69 Ford	162.235
1971	Bobby Isaac	71 Dodge	161.947
1972	David Pearson	71 Mercury	160.821
1973	David Pearson	71 Mercury	158.468
1974	David Pearson	73 Mercury	138.301
1975	Richard Petty	Dodge	158.381
1976	Cale Yarborough	Chevrolet	160.966
1977	Richard Petty	Dodge	142.716
1978	David Pearson	Mercury	154.340
1979	Neil Bonnett	Mercury	172.890
1980	Bobby Allison	Mercury	173.473
1981	Cale Yarborough	Buick	142.588
1982	Bobby Allison	Buick	163.099
1983	Buddy Baker	Ford	167.442
1984	Richard Petty	Pontiac	171.204
1985	Greg Sacks	Chevrolet	158.730
1986	Tim Richmond	Chevrolet	131.916
1987	Bobby Allison	Buick	161.074
1988	Bill Elliott	Ford	163.302
1989	Davey Allison	Ford	132.207
1990	Dale Earnhardt	Chevrolet	160.894
1991	Bill Elliott	Ford	159.116
1992	Ernie Irvan	Chevrolet	170.457
1993	Dale Earnhardt	Chevrolet	151.755
1994	Jimmy Spencer	Ford	155.558
1995	Jeff Gordon	Chevrolet	166.976
1996	Sterling Marlin	Chevrolet	161.602
1997	John Andretti	Ford	157.791
1998	Jeff Gordon	Chevrolet	144.549
1999	Dale Jarrett	Ford	169.213
2000	Jeff Burton	Ford	148.576
2001	Dale Earnhardt Jr.	Chevrolet	157.601
2002	Michael Waltrip	Chevrolet	135.952
2003	Greg Biffle	Ford	166.109
2004	Jeff Gordon	Chevrolet	145.117
2005	Tony Stewart	Chevrolet	145.161
2006	Tony Stewart	Chevrolet	153.143
2007	Jamie McMurray	Ford	138.983
2008	Kyle Busch	Toyota	138.554
2009	Tony Stewart	Chevrolet	142.461
2010	Kevin Harvick	Chevrolet	135.843
2011	David Ragan	Ford	159.491
2012	Tony Stewart	Chevrolet	157.653

*Race changed from 250 to 400 miles.

GATORADE DUELS

Year	Driver	Car	Average Speed
1959	Lloyd "Shorty" Rollins	Ford	129.500
	Bob Wellborn	Chevrolet	143.198
1960	Fireball Roberts	Pontiac	137.614
	Jack Smith	Pontiac	146.520
1961	Fireball Roberts	Pontiac	133.037
	Joe Weatherly	Pontiac	152.671
1962	Fireball Roberts	Pontiac	156.999
	Joe Weatherly	Pontiac	145.395
1963	Junior Johnson	Chevrolet	164.083
	Johnny Rutherford	Chevrolet	162.969
1964	Junior Johnson	Dodge	170.777
	Bobby Isaac	Dodge	169.811
1965	Darel Dieringer	Mercury	165.669
	Junior Johnson	Ford	111.076
1966	Paul Goldsmith	Plymouth	167.988
	Earl Balmer	Dodge	153.257
1967	LeeRoy Yarbrough	Dodge	163.934
	Fred Lorenzen	Ford	174.583
1969*	David Pearson	Ford	152.181
	Bobby Isaac	Dodge	151.668
1970	Cale Yarborough	Mercury	183.295
	Charle Glotzbach	Dodge	147.734
1971	Pete Hamilton	Plymouth	175.029
	David Pearson	Mercury	168.728
1972	Bobby Isaac	Dodge	127.118
	Bobby Allison	Chevrolet	178.217
1973	Buddy Baker	Dodge	173.611
	Coo Coo Marlin	Chevrolet	157.177
1974	Bobby Isaac	Chevrolet	123.212
	Cale Yarborough	Chevrolet	129.724
1975	Bobby Isaac	Matador	156.685
	David Pearson	Mercury	156.958
1976	Dave Marcis	Dodge	119.458
	Darrell Waltrip	Chevrolet	156.250
1977	Richard Petty	Dodge	179.856
	Cale Yarborough	Chevrolet	171.429
1978	A.J. Foyt	Buick	123.018
	Darrell Waltrip	Chevrolet	169.683
1979	Buddy Baker	Oldsmobile	167.598
	Darrell Waltrip	Oldsmobile	153.009
1980	Neil Bonnett	Mercury	138.249
	Donnie Allison	Oldsmobile	165.441
1981	Bobby Allsion	Pontiac	150.125
	Darrell Waltrip	Buick	152.905
1982	Cale Yarborough	Buick	135.298
	Buddy Baker	Buick	144.509
1983	Dale Earnhardt	Ford	157.746
	Neil Bonnett	Chevrolet	122.183
1984	Cale Yarborough	Chevrolet	129.459
	Bobby Allison	Chevrolet	139.578
1985	Bill Elliott	Ford	179.784
	Cale Yarborough	Ford	155.387
1986	Bill Elliott	Ford	153.636
	Dale Earnhardt	Chevrolet	153.270
1987	Ken Schrader	Chevrolet	130.397
	Benny Parsons	Chevrolet	182.778
1988	Bobby Allison	Buick	130.960
	Darrell Waltrip	Chevrolet	133.889
1989	Ken Schrader	Chevrolet	147.203
	Terry Labonte	Ford	189.554
1990	Geoff Bodine	Ford	187.110
	Dale Earnhardt	Chevrolet	157.123
1991	Davey Allison	Ford	165.380
	Dale Earnhardt	Chevrolet	156.972
1992	Dale Earnhardt	Chevrolet	116.430
	Bill Elliott	Ford	169.811
1993	Jeff Gordon	Chevrolet	153.270
	Dale Earnhardt	Chevrolet	157.288
1994	Ernie Irvan	Ford	156.304
	Dale Earnhardt	Chevrolet	146.771
1995	Sterling Marlin	Chevrolet	150.050
	Dale Earnhardt	Chevrolet	131.887
1996	Dale Earnhardt	Chevrolet	143.039
	Ernie Irvan	Ford	186.027
1997	Dale Jarrett	Ford	166.113
	Dale Earnhardt	Chevrolet	162.749
1998	Sterling Marlin	Chevrolet	139.925
	Dale Earnhard	Chevrolet	147.203
1999	Bobby Labonte	Pontiac	163.517
	Dale Earnhardt	Chevrolet	155.280
2000	Bill Elliott	Ford	188.758
	Ricky Rudd	Ford	188.048
2001	Sterling Marlin	Dodge	147.493
	Mike Skinner	Chevrolet	162.338
2002	Jeff Gordon	Chevrolet	183.674
	Michael Waltrip	Chevrolet	131.965
2003	Robby Gordon	Chevrolet	181.159
	Dale Earnhardt Jr.	Chevrolet	180.868
2004	Dale Earnhardt Jr.	Chevrolet	156.087
	Elliott Sadler	Ford	182.334
2005**	Michael Waltrip	Chevrolet	140.442
	Tony Stewart	Chevrolet	140.625
2006	Elliott Sadler	Ford	146.490
	Jeff Gordon	Chevrolet	113.491
2007	Tony Stewart	Chevrolet	154.950
	Jeff Gordon	Chevrolet	160.810
2008	Dale Earnhardt Jr.	Chevrolet	128.428
	Denny Hamlin	Toyota	139.463
2009	Jeff Gordon	Chevrolet	157.251
	Kyle Busch	Toyota	146.461
2010	Jimmie Johnson	Chevrolet	174.644
	Kasey Kahne	Ford	159.794
2011	Kurt Busch	Dodge	136.571
	Jeff Burton	Chevrolet	159.104
2012	Tony Stewart	Chevrolet	194.175
	Matt Kenseth	Ford	

*Race changed from 100 to 125 miles.
**Race changed from 125 to 150 miles.

DOVER INTERNATIONAL SPEEDWAY

1131 N. Dupont Hwy., Dover, DE 19901 • **Tickets:** 1-866-GO-NASCAR or 1-800-441-RACE • **Web site:** www.doverspeedway.com
Facebook: www.facebook.com/DoverInternationalSpeedway • **Twitter:** @MonsterMile

CONFIGURATION

Distance: 1 mile
Banking: 24 degrees in turns, 9 degrees on straights

TRACK RECORDS

Qualifying Records
Jeremy Mayfield, 161.522 mph (22.288 sec.), Set June 4, 2004

Race Record
Mark Martin, 132.719 mph, Set September 21, 1997

2013 TRACK LAYOUT

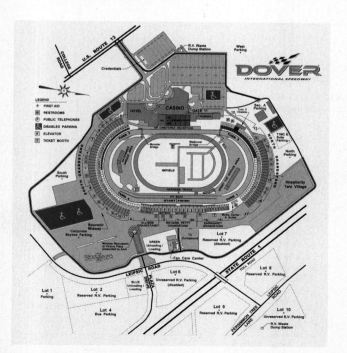

2013 SCHEDULE
May 31: NASCAR Camping World Truck Series
June 1: NASCAR Nationwide Series
June 2: NASCAR Sprint Cup Series
September 28: NASCAR Nationwide Series
September 29: NASCAR Sprint Cup Series

TRACK OFFICIALS

Denis McGlynn *President & CEO*

PR CONTACTS
Gary Camp *Senior Director of Communications*

VISITOR INFORMATION
Central Delaware Chamber of Commerce (302) 734-7513
www.cdcc.net

DIRECTIONS
From NJ/NY: NJ Turnpike South, across Delaware Mem. Bridge to US 13 South. *From Philadelphia*: I-95 S to I-495 S to US 13 S (exit 1). *From Baltimore/Washington*: US 50/301 E across Bay Bridge, follow to MD 302 E. Right on MD 454 at Templeville, which becomes DE 8 at state line and leads to Dover. Left on US 13 in Dover. Track on right (East) of US 13

FEDEX 400 BENEFITING AUTISM SPEAKS
OFFICIAL RACE RESULTS: RACE #13 – JUNE 3, 2012

NASCAR SPRINT CUP SERIES RACE RESULTS

Fin Pos	Str Pos	Car No	Series Driver	Team	Laps	Points	Bonus Points	Status
1	2	48	Jimmie Johnson	Lowe's Medagascar Chevrolet	400	48	5	Running
2	6	29	Kevin Harvick	Jimmy John's Chevrolet	400	42	0	Running
3	5	17	Matt Kenseth	Best Buy Ford	400	42	1	Running
4	17	88	Dale Earnhardt Jr.	AMP Energy/Diet Mtn. Dew/Nat'l Guard Chev	400	41	1	Running
5	4	15	Clint Bowyer	5-hour Energy Toyota	400	39	0	Running
6	12	43	Aric Almirola	Jani-King/Smithfield Ford	400	38	0	Running
7	18	56	Martin Truex Jr.	NAPA Auto Parts Toyota	400	37	0	Running
8	11	20	Joey Logano	The Home Depot Toyota	400	36	0	Running
9	13	5	Kasey Kahne	Hendrickcars.com Chevrolet	400	35	0	Running
10	21	9	Marcos Ambrose	Stanley Ford	400	34	0	Running
11	7	16	Greg Biffle	3M/Heiling (EMD) Ford	400	33	0	Running
12	16	2	Brad Keselowski	Miller Lite Dodge	400	32	0	Running
13	14	24	Jeff Gordon	DuPont Chevrolet	400	32	1	Running
14	1	55	Mark Martin	Aaron's Dream Machine Toyota	400	31	1	Running
15	3	39	Ryan Newman	Quicken Loans Chevrolet	400	29	0	Running
16	23	22	AJ Allmendinger	Shell Pennzoil Dodge	400	28	0	Running
17	20	27	Paul Menard	Menards/Pittsburgh Paints Chevrolet	400	27	0	Running
18	10	11	Denny Hamlin	FedEx Freight/Autism Speaks Toyota	400	27	1	Running
19	24	1	Jamie McMurray	Bass Pro Shops/Allstate Chevrolet	400	25	0	Running
20	22	47	Bobby Labonte	Scott Products Toyota	399	24	0	Running
21	28	34	David Ragan	MHP/8 hour Alert Ford	398	24	1	Running
22	15	31	Jeff Burton	BB&T Chevrolet	364	22	0	Engine
23	42	93	Travis Kvapil	Burger King/Dr. Pepper Toyota	348	21	0	Running
24	9	51	Kurt Busch	Phoenix Construction Services Chevrolet	338	20	0	Engine
25	29	14	Tony Stewart	MOBIL 1/Office Depot Chevrolet	331	19	0	Running
26	19	99	Carl Edwards	SUBWAY Ford	318	18	0	Running
27	26	78	Regan Smith	Furniture Row/CSX Play it Safe Chevrolet	306	17	0	Running
28	31	42	Juan Pablo Montoya	Target Chevrolet	296	16	0	Engine
29	8	18	Kyle Busch	M&M's Toyota	202	15	0	Accident
30	38	32	Reed Sorenson (i)	FAS Lane Racing Ford	124	0	0	Engine
31	39	10	David Reutimann	Tommy Baldwin Racing Chevrolet	110	13	0	Accident
32	41	36	Dave Blaney	Tommy Baldwin Racing Chevrolet	65	12	0	Accident
33	32	30	David Stremme	Inception Motorsports Toyota	63	11	0	Overheating
34	34	49	J.J. Yeley	America Israel Racing/JPO Absorbents Toyota	41	10	0	Overheating
35	37	33	Stephen Leicht #	LittleJoesAutos.com Chevrolet	29	9	0	Accident
36	36	19	Mike Bliss (i)	Humphrey Smith Racing Toyota	23	0	0	Steering
37	43	23	Scott Riggs	North Texas Pipe Chevrolet	21	7	0	Vibration
38	27	83	Landon Cassill	Burger King/Dr. Pepper Toyota	9	6	0	Accident
39	35	87	Joe Nemechek (i)	AM/FM Energy Wood & Pellet Stoves Toyota	9	0	0	Accident
40	30	38	David Gilliland	Autism Speaks Ford	9	4	0	Accident
41	40	13	Casey Mears	GEICO Ford	8	3	0	Accident
42	33	98	Michael McDowell	Phil Parsons Racing Ford	8	2	0	Accident
43	25	79	Scott Speed	Team Kyle/Koma Unwind Ford	8	1	0	Accident

Sunoco Rookie of the Year Contender. Bonus Points: includes winner, lap leader & most laps led points. (i) = Ineligible for driver points in this series. Failed to qualify: (2) #26 Josh Wise; #74 Cole Whitt.

RACE COMMENTS: Before an estimated crowd of 85,000, Jimmie Johnson won the FedEx 400 benefiting Autism Speaks, his 57th NASCAR Sprint Cup Series victory. Prior to the green flag, no cars dropped to the rear of the field.

RACE STATISTICS

TIME OF RACE: 3 hours, 15 minutes, 23 seconds
AVERAGE SPEED: 122.835 mph
MARGIN OF VICTORY: 2.55 seconds
COORS LIGHT POLE AWARD: Mark Martin (158.297 mph. 22.742 secs.)
3M LAP LEADER: Jimmie Johnson (289 Laps)
AMERICAN ETHANOL GREEN FLAG RESTART AWARD: Jimmie Johnson
DIRECTV CREW CHIEF OF THE RACE: Kevin Harvick (crew chief Shane Wilson)
FREESCALE "WIDE OPEN": Kevin Harvick
MAHLE CLEVITE ENGINE BUILDER OF THE RACE: Hendrick Engines (#48)

MOBIL 1 OIL DRIVER OF THE RACE: Kevin Harvick
MOOG STEERING AND SUSPENSION PROBLEM SOLVER OF THE RACE: Martin Truex Jr. (crew chief Chad Johnston, -0.009 seconds)
NASCAR SPRINT CUP LEADER BONUS: No winner: rolls over to $70,000 at next event++
SUNOCO ROOKIE OF THE RACE: Stephen Leicht
USG IMPROVING THE FINISH: Travis Kvapil (19 places)
CAUTION FLAGS: 7 cautions for 32 laps. [Beneficiary in Brackets] 10–12 (Car #13,14, 32, 33, 36, 38, 42, 78, 79, 83, 93, 98 Accident Backstretch [Red Flag 19 Min 54 Sec] [None]); 112–116 (Oil On The Track [22]); 165–168 (Car #99 Accident Turn 2 [9]); 227–231 (Debris Frontstretch [27]); 341–344 (Debris Turn 3 [1]); 347–352 (Oil On The Track [39]); 365–369 (Oil On The Track [11]).

LAP LEADERS: 17 lead changes among 7 drivers. Martin-pole, Johnson 1–6, Martin 7–29, Johnson 30–60, Martin 61–70, Kenseth 71, Ragan 72–74, Martin 75–84, Johnson 85–210, J. Gordon 211–227, Johnson 228, J. Gordon 229–244, Johnson 245–293, Kenseth 294, Earnhardt Jr. 295, Hamlin 296–297, J. Gordon 298–324, Johnson 325–400.

++Rollover money awarded at year's end, amount not included in race winnings.

POINT LEADERS
(After 13 Races)

1	GREG BIFFLE	486
2	Matt Kenseth	485
3	Dale Earnhardt Jr.	476
4	Denny Hamlin	464
5	Jimmie Johnson	453
6	Martin Truex Jr.	441
7	Kevin Harvick	440
8	Tony Stewart	407
9	Kyle Busch	406
10	Clint Bowyer	405
11	Brad Keselowski	400
12	Carl Edwards	390

AAA 400
OFFICIAL RACE RESULTS: RACE #29 – SEPTEMBER 30, 2012

NASCAR SPRINT CUP SERIES RACE RESULTS

Fin Pos	Str Pos	Car No	Series Driver	Team	Laps	Points	Bonus Points	Status
1	10	2	Brad Keselowski	Miller Lite Dodge	400	47	4	Running
2	7	24	Jeff Gordon	Drive to End Hunger Chevrolet	400	43	1	Running
3	26	55	Mark Martin	Aaron's 2000th Store - Bronx, NY Toyota	400	41	0	Running
4	11	48	Jimmie Johnson	Lowe's/Kobalt Tools Chevrolet	400	41	1	Running
5	15	99	Carl Edwards	Fastenal Ford	400	39	0	Running
6	3	56	Martin Truex Jr.	NAPA Auto Parts Toyota	400	38	0	Running
7	5	18	Kyle Busch	Interstate Batteries Toyota	399	39	2	Running
8	1	11	Denny Hamlin	FedEx Office Toyota	399	37	1	Running
9	2	15	Clint Bowyer	5-hour Energy Toyota	399	36	1	Running
10	14	20	Joey Logano	The Home Depot Toyota	399	34	0	Running
11	25	88	Dale Earnhardt Jr.	National Guard/Diet Mountain Dew Chev.	398	33	0	Running
12	17	6	Ricky Stenhouse Jr. (i)	Cargill Ford	397	0	0	Running
13	13	29	Kevin Harvick	Budweiser Chevrolet	397	31	0	Running
14	16	47	Bobby Labonte	Kingsford Charcoal Toyota	397	30	0	Running
15	9	5	Kasey Kahne	Farmers Insurance Chevrolet	397	29	0	Running
16	6	16	Greg Biffle	Scotch-Brite Ford	397	28	0	Running
17	18	78	Regan Smith	Furniture Row/Farm American Chevrolet	397	27	0	Running
18	27	9	Marcos Ambrose	DeWalt Ford	397	26	0	Running
19	21	43	Aric Almirola	Super 8 Ford	397	25	0	Running
20	24	14	Tony Stewart	Office Depot/Mobil 1 Chevrolet	397	24	0	Running
21	8	39	Ryan Newman	U.S. ARMY Chevrolet	397	23	0	Running
22	19	27	Paul Menard	Menards/CertainTeed Chevrolet	396	22	0	Running
23	28	51	Kurt Busch	Phoenix Construction Chevrolet	395	21	0	Running
24	20	1	Jamie McMurray	McDonald's Chevrolet	394	20	0	Running
25	4	22	Sam Hornish Jr. (i)	Shell Pennzoil Dodge	393	0	0	Running
26	35	42	Juan Pablo Montoya	Target Chevrolet	393	18	0	Running
27	39	31	Jeff Burton	Caterpillar Chevrolet	393	17	0	Running
28	38	10	Danica Patrick (i)	GoDaddy.com Chevrolet	393	0	0	Running
29	33	93	Travis Kvapil	Burger King Toyota	392	15	0	Running
30	31	34	David Ragan	Long John Silver's Ford	392	14	0	Running
31	30	13	Casey Mears	GEICO Ford	391	13	0	Running
32	42	38	David Gilliland	Taco Bell Ford	391	12	0	Running
33	41	32	T.J. Bell (i)	Green Smoke Ford	390	0	0	Running
34	40	36	J.J. Yeley	Drive Sober, Arrive Alive DE Chevrolet	388	10	0	Running
35	12	17	Matt Kenseth	Ford EcoBoost Ford	371	9	0	Running
36	22	83	Landon Cassill	Burger King Toyota	354	8	0	Running
37	23	26	Josh Wise #	MDS Transport Ford	92	7	0	Vibration
38	32	98	Michael McDowell	Phil Parsons Racing Ford	51	6	0	Suspension
39	37	87	Joe Nemechek (i)	AM/FM Energy Wood & Pellet Stoves Toyota	48	0	0	Electrical
40	34	95	Scott Speed	Jordan Truck Sales Ford	32	4	0	Suspension
41	43	37	Dave Blaney	MaxQWorkforce.com Chevrolet	29	3	0	Overheating
42	36	23	Scott Riggs	North Texas Pipe Chevrolet	26	2	0	Brakes
43	29	91	Reed Sorenson (i)	Plinker Tactical Toyota	18	0	0	Brakes

Sunoco Rookie of the Year Contender. Bonus Points: includes winner, lap leader & most laps led points. (i) = Ineligible for driver points in this series. Failed to qualify: (5) #30 David Stremme; #19 Mike Bliss; #49 Jason Leffler; #33 Cole Whitt; #79 Kelly Bires.

RACE COMMENTS: Before an estimated crowd of 85,000, Brad Keselowski won the AAA 400, his ninth NASCAR Sprint Cup Series victory. Prior to the green flag, the following car dropped to the rear of the field for the reason indicated: #38 (transmission change).

RACE STATISTICS

TIME OF RACE: 3 hours, 11 minutes, 53 seconds
AVERAGE SPEED: 125.076 mph
MARGIN OF VICTORY: 1.078 seconds
COORS LIGHT POLE AWARD: Denny Hamlin (159.299 mph. 22.599 secs.)
3M LAP LEADER: Kyle Busch (302 Laps)
AMERICAN ETHANOL GREEN FLAG RESTART AWARD: Jimmie Johnson
DIRECTV CREW CHIEF OF THE RACE: Martin Truex Jr. (crew chief Chad Johnston)
FREESCALE "WIDE OPEN": Brad Keselowski

MAHLE CLEVITE ENGINE BUILDER OF THE RACE: Penske Engines (#2)
MOBIL 1 OIL DRIVER OF THE RACE: Kyle Busch
MOOG STEERING AND SUSPENSION PROBLEM SOLVER OF THE RACE: Carl Edwards (crew chief Chad Norris, 0.053 seconds)
NASCAR SPRINT CUP LEADER BONUS: Brad Keselowski ($20,000 ++)
USG IMPROVING THE FINISH: Mark Martin (23 places)
CAUTION FLAGS: 5 cautions for 28 laps. [Beneficiary in Brackets] 70–76 (Debris [47]); 180–184 (Debris [99]); 247–252

(Debris [5]); 310–315 (Debris From #17 [55]); 318–321 (Car #17 Accident Turn 4 [56]).
LAP LEADERS: 11 lead changes among 6 drivers. Hamlin 1–34, Ky. Busch 35–145, J. Gordon 146, Bowyer 147, Keselowski 148–151, Ky. Busch 152–180, Hamlin 181–184, Ky. Busch 185–311, Johnson 312–354, Ky. Busch 355–389, Hamlin 390, Keselowski 391–400.

++Rollover money awarded at year's end, amount not included in race winnings.

POINT LEADERS
(After 29 Races)

1	BRAD KESELOWSKI	2142
2	Jimmie Johnson	2137
3	Denny Hamlin	2126
4	Clint Bowyer	2117
5	Tony Stewart	2110
6	Kasey Kahne	2110
7	Dale Earnhardt Jr.	2103
8	Martin Truex Jr.	2100
9	Kevin Harvick	2096
10	Jeff Gordon	2094
11	Greg Biffle	2091
12	Matt Kenseth	2070

DOVER INTERNATIONAL SPEEDWAY

ALL TIME LEADERS AND PAST WINNERS

TOP 20 ACTIVE NASCAR SPRINT CUP SERIES DRIVERS (MINIMUM 2 STARTS)

Driver	Races	Wins	Top 5s	Top 10s	Poles	Total Laps	Laps Led	Avg. Start	Avg. Finish
Carl Edwards	17	1	8	12	0	6717	532	15.0	8.3
Jimmie Johnson	22	7	11	16	3	8619	2,318	9.7	8.6
Jeff Gordon	40	4	15	22	4	15,984	2,292	11.6	12.0
Ryan Newman	22	3	6	11	4	8752	842	9.5	12.1
Mark Martin	53	4	24	32	5	21,321	1,769	12.3	12.3
Greg Biffle	21	2	6	10	1	8345	463	11.7	12.4
Aric Almirola	2	0	0	1	0	797	0	16.5	12.5
Matt Kenseth	28	2	13	18	1	10,895	746	16.1	12.6
Clint Bowyer	14	0	1	7	0	5575	34	17.6	13.2
Tony Stewart	28	2	10	15	0	10,744	1,072	20.5	13.7
Kyle Busch	16	2	7	10	0	5626	750	12.4	13.9
Brad Keselowski	6	1	1	1	0	2396	16	16.8	14.3
Bill Elliott	43	4	12	19	3	18,910	2,050	11.1	14.4
Martin Truex Jr.	14	1	1	6	2	5426	225	14.4	15.6
Jeff Burton	38	1	8	15	0	14,237	136	24.8	15.7
Kevin Harvick	24	0	3	10	0	9461	144	20.3	15.9
Terry Labonte	52	0	8	16	2	21,896	443	17.2	16.8
Dale Earnhardt Jr.	26	1	5	8	0	10,305	368	15.2	17.2
Marcos Ambrose	9	0	1	3	0	3413	0	22.6	18.0
Bobby Labonte	41	1	11	14	3	15,504	148	16.8	18.0

DOVER 400

Year	Driver	Car	Average Speed
1969	Richard Petty	69 Ford	115.772
1970	Richard Petty	70 Plymouth	112.103
1971	*Bobby Allison	71 Ford	123.119
1972	Bobby Allison	72 Chevrolet	118.663
1973	David Pearson	71 Mercury	119.745
1974	Cale Yarborough	74 Chevrolet	119.990
1975	David Pearson	Mercury	100.820
1976	Benny Parsons	Chevrolet	115.436
1977	Cale Yarborough	Chevrolet	123.237
1978	David Pearson	Mercury	114.664
1979	Neil Bonnett	Mercury	111.269
1980	Bobby Allison	Ford	113.866
1981	Jody Ridley	Ford	116.595
1982	Bobby Allison	Chevrolet	120.136
1983	Bobby Allison	Buick	114.847
1984	Richard Petty	Pontiac	118.717
1985	Bill Elliott	Ford	123.094
1986	Geoff Bodine	Chevrolet	115.009
1987	Davey Allison	Ford	112.958
1988	Bill Elliott	Ford	118.726
1989	Dale Earnhardt	Chevrolet	121.670
1990	Derrike Cope	Chevrolet	123.960
1991	Ken Schrader	Chevrolet	120.152
1992	Harry Gant	Oldsmobile	109.456
1993	Dale Earnhardt	Chevrolet	105.600
1994	Rusty Wallace	Ford	102.529
1995	Kyle Petty	Pontiac	119.880
1996	Jeff Gordon	Chevrolet	122.741
1997	Ricky Rudd	Ford	114.635
1998	**Dale Jarrett	Ford	119.522
1999	Bobby Labonte	Pontiac	120.603
2000	Tony Stewart	Pontiac	109.514
2001	Jeff Gordon	Chevrolet	120.361
2002	Jimmie Johnson	Chevrolet	117.551
2003	Ryan Newman	Dodge	106.896
2004	Mark Martin	Ford	97.042
2005	Greg Biffle	Ford	122.626
2006	Matt Kenseth	Ford	109.865
2007	Martin Truex Jr.	Chevrolet	118.959
2008	Kyle Busch	Toyota	121.171
2009	Jimmie Johnson	Chevrolet	115.237
2010	Kyle Busch	Toyota	128.790
2011	Matt Kenseth	Ford	125.578
2012	Jimmie Johnson	Chevrolet	122.835

*Race changed from 300 to 500 miles.
*Race changed from 500 to 400 miles.

AAA 400

Year	Driver	Car	Average Speed
1971	Richard Petty	71 Plymouth	123.245
1972	David Pearson	71 Mercury	120.506
1973	David Pearson	71 Mercury	112.852
1974	Richard Petty	74 Dodge	113.640
1975	Richard Petty	Dodge	113.372
1976	Cale Yarborough	Chevrolet	115.740
1977	Benny Parsons	Chevrolet	114.708
1978	Bobby Allison	Ford	119.323
1979	Richard Petty	Chevrolet	114.366
1980	Darrell Waltrip	Chevrolet	116.024
1981	Neil Bonnett	Ford	119.561
1982	Darrell Waltrip	Buick	107.642
1983	Bobby Allison	Buick	116.077
1984	Harry Gant	Chevrolet	111.856
1985	Harry Gant	Chevrolet	120.538
1986	Ricky Rudd	Ford	114.329
1987	Ricky Rudd	Ford	124.706
1988	Bill Elliott	Ford	109.349
1989	Dale Earnhardt	Chevrolet	122.909
1990	Bill Elliott	Ford	125.945
1991	Harry Gant	Oldsmobile	110.179
1992	Ricky Rudd	Chevrolet	115.289
1993	Rusty Wallace	Pontiac	100.334
1994	Rusty Wallace	Ford	112.556
1995	Jeff Gordon	Chevrolet	124.740
1996	Jeff Gordon	Chevrolet	105.646
1997	*Mark Martin	Ford	132.719
1998	Mark Martin	Ford	113.834
1999	Mark Martin	Ford	127.434
2000	Tony Stewart	Pontiac	115.191
2001	Dale Earnhardt Jr.	Chevrolet	101.559
2002	Jimmie Johnson	Chevrolet	120.805
2003	Ryan Newman	Dodge	108.802
2004	Ryan Newman	Dodge	119.067
2005	Jimmie Johnson	Chevrolet	115.054
2006	Jeff Burton	Chevrolet	111.966
2007	Carl Edwards	Ford	101.846
2008	Greg Biffle	Ford	114.168
2009	Jimmie Johnson	Chevrolet	118.704
2010	Jimmie Johnson	Chevrolet	131.543
2011	Kurt Busch	Dodge	119.413
2012	Brad Keselowski	Dodge	125.076

*Race changed from 500 to 400 miles.

DOVER INTERNATIONAL SPEEDWAY

ELDORA SPEEDWAY

13929 State Route 118, New Weston, OH 45348 • **Tickets:** 1-866-GO-NASCAR or 937-338-3815 • **Web site:** www.EldoraSpeedway.com
Facebook: www.facebook.com/eldoraspeedway • **Twitter:** @EldoraSpeedway

//// NASCAR®

CONFIGURATION
Distance: .5 mile
Banking: 24 degrees in turns, 8 degrees on straights

TRACK RECORDS
Qualifying Records
NA

Race Record
NA

2013 TRACK LAYOUT

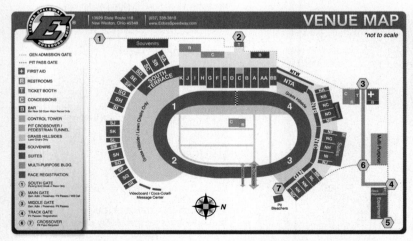

2013 SCHEDULE
July 24 – NASCAR Camping World Truck Series

TRACK OFFICIALS

Tony Stewart *President*

PR CONTACTS
Roger Slack *Promoter & General Manager*

VISITOR INFORMATION
Darke County Visitors Bureau
(800) 504-2995 – **www.visitdarkecounty.org**

DIRECTIONS
From Toledo/Detroit: South on I-75 to Wapakoneta, west on US 33, continue west on St Route 29 to Celina, south on US 127 to North Star, turn right at traffic light, continue to Eldora Speedway. *From Fort Wayne:* South on US 33 into Ohio, south on US 127 to North Star, turn right at traffic light, continue to Eldora Speedway. *From Dayton/Cincinnati:* North on I-75 to I-70, west on I-70 to exit 24, north on St Route 49 to Greenville, north on US 127 to North Star, turn left at traffic light, continue to Eldora Speedway. *From Indianapolis:* East on I-70 to Ohio exit 10, north on US 127 to North Star, turn left at traffic light, continue to Eldora Speedway. *From Columbus:* West on I-70 to exit 24, North on St Route 49 to Greenville, north on US 127 to North Star, turn left at traffic light, continue to Eldora Speedway.

HOMESTEAD-MIAMI SPEEDWAY

HOMESTEADMIAMI SPEEDWAY®

One Speedway Blvd., Homestead, FL 33035 • **Tickets:** 1-866-GO-NASCAR or 1-866-409-RACE • **Web site:** www.HomesteadMiamiSpeedway.com
Facebook: www.facebook.com/HomesteadMiamiSpeedway • **Twitter:** @HomesteadMiami

NASCAR

CONFIGURATION
Distance: 1.5 miles
Banking: 18 to 20 degrees in turns, 4 degrees on straights

TRACK RECORDS
Qualifying Records
Jamie McMurray, 181.111 mph (29.816 sec.), Set November 14, 2003

Race Record
Jeff Gordon, 142.245 mph, Set November 18, 2012

2013 TRACK LAYOUT

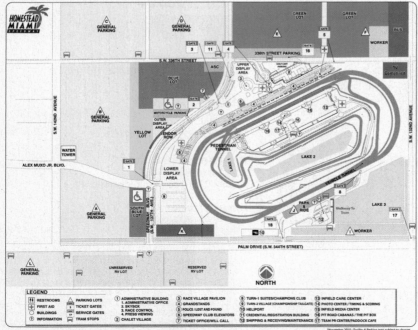

2013 SCHEDULE
November 15: NASCAR Camping World Truck Series
November 16: NASCAR Nationwide Series
November 17: NASCAR Sprint Cup Series

TRACK OFFICIALS

Matthew Becherer *President*

PR CONTACTS
George Stieren *Manager, Media Relations*

VISITOR INFORMATION
The Greater Homestead/Florida City Chamber of Commerce
(305) 247-2332 – www.chamberinaction.com
Greater Miami Convention & Visitors Bureau
(800) 933-8448/(305) 539-3000

DIRECTIONS
Via Florida's Turnpike: Exit 6/Speedway Blvd./SW 137th Ave.; south 5 miles to the Speedway; follow signs to rear tunnel entrance (Gate 18). *Via US 1:* Take Palm Dr. east 4 miles to the Speedway; follow signs to rear tunnel infield entrance (Gate 18).

FORD ECOBOOST 400
OFFICIAL RACE RESULTS: RACE #36 - NOVEMBER 18, 2012

NASCAR SPRINT CUP SERIES OFFICIAL RACE RESULTS

Fin Pos	Str Pos	Car No	Driver	Team	Laps	Points	Bonus Points	Status
1	15	24	Jeff Gordon	DuPont 20 Years Celebratory Chevrolet	267	47	4	Running
2	6	15	Clint Bowyer	5-hour Energy Toyota	267	42	0	Running
3	19	39	Ryan Newman	U.S. ARMY Chevrolet	267	42	1	Running
4	8	18	Kyle Busch	M&M's Toyota	267	42	2	Running
5	13	16	Greg Biffle	3M/SP Richards Ford	267	39	0	Running
6	7	56	Martin Truex Jr.	NAPA Auto Parts Toyota	267	39	1	Running
7	5	43	Aric Almirola	Smithfield Ford	267	37	0	Running
8	23	29	Kevin Harvick	Budweiser Chevrolet	267	36	0	Running
9	26	78	Kurt Busch	Furniture Row Chevrolet	267	35	0	Running
10	16	88	Dale Earnhardt Jr.	National Guard/Diet Mountain Dew Chev.	267	34	0	Running
11	18	27	Paul Menard	Menards/Duracell Chevrolet	267	33	0	Running
12	4	99	Carl Edwards	Fastenal Ford	267	32	0	Running
13	2	9	Marcos Ambrose	Black & Decker Ford	267	32	1	Running
14	1	20	Joey Logano	Home Depot/redbeacon.com Toyota	267	30	1	Running
15	3	2	Brad Keselowski	Miller Lite Dodge	266	29	0	Running
16	9	55	Mark Martin	Aaron's Dream Machine Toyota	266	28	0	Running
17	35	14	Tony Stewart	Office Depot/Mobil 1 Chevrolet	266	27	0	Running
18	11	17	Matt Kenseth	Best Buy Ford	266	27	1	Running
19	33	31	Jeff Burton	Caterpillar Chevrolet	266	25	0	Running
20	14	1	Jamie McMurray	Bass Pro Shops/Tracker Boats Chevrolet	266	24	0	Running
21	12	5	Kasey Kahne	Farmers Insurance Chevrolet	266	24	1	Running
22	17	22	Sam Hornish Jr. (i)	Shell Pennzoil Dodge	266	0	0	Running
23	20	21	Trevor Bayne (i)	Motorcraft/Quick Lane Tire & Auto Center Ford	266	0	0	Running
24	41	11	Denny Hamlin	FedEx Express Toyota	266	20	0	Running
25	32	47	Bobby Labonte	Clorox Toyota	265	19	0	Running
26	38	93	Travis Kvapil	Dr. Pepper Toyota	265	18	0	Running
27	30	83	Landon Cassill	Burger King Toyota	265	17	0	Running
28	21	42	Juan Pablo Montoya	Target Chevrolet	264	16	0	Running
29	28	13	Casey Mears	GEICO Ford	264	15	0	Running
30	24	51	Regan Smith	Phoenix Construction Chevrolet	264	14	0	Running
31	34	34	David Ragan	Ford	263	13	0	Running
32	31	36	Dave Blaney	Florida Lottery Chevrolet	263	12	0	Running
33	40	38	David Gilliland	Long John Silver's Ford	262	11	0	Running
34	37	10	David Reutimann	TMone in Iowa City, IA/Spearfish Chevrolet	261	10	0	Running
35	39	37	J.J. Yeley	C&C Audio Video & Appliance, Inc. Chevrolet	261	9	0	Running
36	10	48	Jimmie Johnson	Lowe's Chevrolet	224	9	1	Rear Gear
37	42	32	Ken Schrader	Federated Auto Parts Ford	219	7	0	Engine
38	22	30	David Stremme	Swan Racing Toyota	183	6	0	Electrical
39	27	6	Ricky Stenhouse Jr. (i)	Fifth Third Ford	157	0	0	Accident
40	36	26	Josh Wise #	MDS Transport Ford	38	4	0	Vibration
41	25	98	Michael McDowell	Phil Parsons Racing Ford	34	3	0	Overheating
42	43	23	Scott Riggs	North Texas Pipe Chevrolet	23	2	0	Vibration
43	29	19	Mike Bliss (i)	Plinker Tactical Toyota	16	0	0	Electrical

Sunoco Rookie of the Year Contender. Bonus Points: includes winner, lap leader & most laps led points. (i) = Ineligible for driver points in this series. Failed to qualify: (4) #79 Reed Sorenson; #33 Stephen Leicht; #91 Jason Leffler; #87 Joe Nemechek.

RACE COMMENTS: Before an estimated crowd of 76,000, Jeff Gordon won the Ford EcoBoost 400, his 87th NASCAR Sprint Cup Series victory. Prior to the green flag, the following cars dropped to the rear for the reason indicated: #11, 16, 20, 51 (backup car).

RACE STATISTICS

TIME OF RACE: 2 hours, 48 minutes, 56 seconds
AVERAGE SPEED: 142.245 mph
MARGIN OF VICTORY: 1.028 second
COORS LIGHT POLE AWARD: Joey Logano (176.056 mph. 30.672 secs.)
3M LAP LEADER: Kyle Busch (191 Laps)
AMERICAN ETHANOL GREEN FLAG RESTART AWARD: Kyle Busch
DIRECTV CREW CHIEF OF THE RACE: Clint Bowyer (crew chief Brian Pattie)
FREESCALE "WIDE OPEN": Ryan Newman
MAHLE CLEVITE ENGINE BUILDER OF THE

RACE: Toyota Racing Development (#18)
MOBIL 1 OIL DRIVER OF THE RACE: Ryan Newman
MOOG STEERING AND SUSPENSION PROBLEM SOLVER OF THE RACE: Greg Biffle (crew chief Matt Puccia, 0.294 seconds)
NASCAR SPRINT CUP LEADER BONUS: Jimmie Johnson ($20,000)
USG IMPROVING THE FINISH: Tony Stewart (18 places)
CAUTION FLAGS: 3 cautions for 17 laps. [Beneficiary in Brackets] 79-83 (Debris [16]); 144-148 (Debris [31]); 155-161 (Car #6 Accident Turn 3 [47]).

LAP LEADERS: 19 lead changes among 8 drivers. Logano-pole, Ambrose 1-14, Ky. Busch 15-49, Newman 50, Ky. Busch 51-116, Truex Jr. 117-127, Johnson 128, Kenseth 129-130, Newman 131-132, Ky. Busch 133-144, Johnson 145-157, Kahne 158-161, Ky. Busch 162-165, Kahne 166, Ky. Busch 167-199, Kahne 200-201, Johnson 202-212, J. Gordon 213, Ky. Busch 214-254, J. Gordon 255-267.

++Rollover money awarded at year's end, amount not included in race winnings.

POINT LEADERS
(After 36 Races)

1	BRAD KESELOWSKI	2400
2	Clint Bowyer	2361
3	Jimmie Johnson	2360
4	Kasey Kahne	2345
5	Greg Biffle	2332
6	Denny Hamlin	2329
7	Matt Kenseth	2324
8	Kevin Harvick	2321
9	Tony Stewart	2311
10	Jeff Gordon	2303
11	Martin Truex Jr.	2299
12	Dale Earnhardt Jr.	2245

ALL TIME LEADERS AND PAST WINNERS

TOP 20 ACTIVE NASCAR SPRINT CUP SERIES DRIVERS (MINIMUM 2 STARTS)

Driver	Races	Wins	Top 5s	Top 10s	Poles	Total Laps	Laps Led	Avg. Start	Avg. Finish
Carl Edwards	9	2	5	7	2	2408	560	11.0	6.0
Kevin Harvick	12	0	5	10	0	3208	128	14.7	7.9
Martin Truex Jr.	8	0	2	6	0	2121	108	16.0	9.9
AJ Allmendinger	4	0	1	2	0	1068	0	18.3	10.3
Jeff Gordon	14	1	7	11	0	3671	83	15.8	10.6
Tony Stewart	14	3	4	7	0	3739	450	15.9	11.9
Clint Bowyer	7	0	2	4	0	1845	1	15.1	12.1
Denny Hamlin	8	1	3	4	0	2132	91	32.3	12.5
Mark Martin	13	0	4	5	0	3449	30	15.7	13.5
Greg Biffle	11	3	4	5	0	2794	175	16.1	14.4
Aric Almirola	3	0	1	2	0	799	0	23.0	15.3
Jimmie Johnson	12	0	4	7	2	3017	99	16.6	15.3
Kasey Kahne	9	0	1	4	2	2326	107	7.8	15.4
Jeff Burton	14	0	4	6	0	3677	29	21.8	15.7
Bill Elliott	10	1	1	3	1	2662	248	20.0	15.8
Jamie McMurray	11	0	1	3	1	2921	1	15.4	16.5
Ryan Newman	11	0	1	4	0	2787	143	12.2	17.0
Matt Kenseth	13	1	3	5	0	3187	305	18.9	17.6
Brad Keselowski	5	0	0	0	0	1332	11	16.8	19.2
Kurt Busch	12	1	4	5	2	2720	92	15.6	19.8

FORD 400

Year	Driver	Car	Average Speed
1999	Tony Stewart	Pontiac	140.335
2000	Tony Stewart	Pontiac	127.480
2001	Bill Elliott	Dodge	117.449
2002	Kurt Busch	Ford	116.462
2003	Bobby Labonte	Chevrolet	116.868
2004	Greg Biffle	Ford	105.623
2005	Greg Biffle	Ford	131.431
2006	Greg Biffle	Ford	125.375
2007	Matt Kenseth	Ford	131.888
2008	Carl Edwards	Ford	129.472
2009	Denny Hamlin	Toyota	126.986
2010	Carl Edwards	Ford	126.585
2011	Tony Stewart	Chevrolet	114.976
2012	Jeff Gordon	Chevrolet	142.245

INDIANAPOLIS MOTOR SPEEDWAY

4790 W. 16th Street Indianapolis, IN 46222 • **Tickets:** 1-866-GO-NASCAR or 1-800-822-INDY • **Web site:** www.indianapolismotorspeedway.com
Facebook: www.facebook.com/IndianapolisMotorSpeedway • **Twitter:** @IMS

CONFIGURATION
Distance: 2.5 miles
Banking: 9 degrees in turns,
0 degrees on straights

TRACK RECORDS
Qualifying Records
**Casey Mears, 186.293 mph
(48.311 sec.), Set August 7, 2004**

Race Record
**Bobby Labonte, 155.912,
Set August 5, 2000**

2013 TRACK LAYOUT

2013 SCHEDULE
July 27: NASCAR Nationwide Series
July 28: NASCAR Sprint Cup Series

TRACK OFFICIALS

Jeff Belskus *President*

PR CONTACTS
Doug Boles *Vice President, Communications*
Tim Sullivan *Media Center Manager*

VISITOR INFORMATION
Visit Indy (317)262-3000
www.visitindy.com

DIRECTIONS
From downtown: Take Meridian St. north to 16th St., turn left on 16th and go 4.3 miles. Track is on right.
From Indianapolis International Airport: Follow signs to Interstate 70 East, take I-70 East to I-465 North, to exit 16A/ Crawfordsville Road. The track is two miles east on the left.

INDIANAPOLIS MOTOR SPEEDWAY | **157**

CROWN ROYAL PRESENTS THE CURTISS SHAVER 400 AT THE BRICKYARD

OFFICIAL RACE RESULTS: RACE #20 – JULY 29, 2012

NASCAR SPRINT CUP SERIES RACE RESULTS

Fin Pos	Str Pos	Car No	Series Driver	Team	Laps	Points	Bonus Points	Status
1	6	48	Jimmie Johnson	Lowe's/Kobalt Tools Chevrolet	160	48	5	Running
2	7	18	Kyle Busch	M&M's Toyota	160	43	1	Running
3	5	16	Greg Biffle	3M Ford	160	42	1	Running
4	20	88	Dale Earnhardt Jr.	AMP Energy/National Guard Chevrolet	160	40	0	Running
5	9	24	Jeff Gordon	Drive to End Hunger Chevrolet	160	40	1	Running
6	1	11	Denny Hamlin	FedEx Express Toyota	160	39	1	Running
7	11	39	Ryan Newman	Quicken Loans Chevrolet	160	37	0	Running
8	17	56	Martin Truex Jr.	NAPA Auto Parts Toyota	160	36	0	Running
9	22	2	Brad Keselowski	Miller Lite Dodge	160	36	1	Running
10	28	14	Tony Stewart	Mobil 1/Office Depot Chevrolet	160	34	0	Running
11	19	55	Mark Martin	Aaron's Dream Machine Toyota	160	33	0	Running
12	15	5	Kasey Kahne	Farmers Insurance Chevrolet	160	32	0	Running
13	27	29	Kevin Harvick	Jimmy John's Chevrolet	160	31	0	Running
14	8	27	Paul Menard	Menards/Nibco Chevrolet	160	30	0	Running
15	33	15	Clint Bowyer	5-hour Energy Toyota	160	29	0	Running
16	24	22	Sam Hornish Jr. (i)	Shell Pennzoil Dodge	160	0	0	Running
17	18	21	Trevor Bayne (i)	Motorcraft/Quick Lane Tire & Auto Center Ford	160	0	0	Running
18	14	78	Regan Smith	Furniture Row/Farm American Chevrolet	160	26	0	Running
19	4	43	Aric Almirola	Eckrich Ford	160	25	0	Running
20	23	9	Marcos Ambrose	DeWalt Ford	160	24	0	Running
21	12	42	Juan Pablo Montoya	Target Chevrolet	160	23	0	Running
22	16	1	Jamie McMurray	Bass Pro Shops/Tracker Chevrolet	160	22	0	Running
23	32	36	Dave Blaney	SealWrap Chevrolet	160	21	0	Running
24	26	30	David Stremme	Inception Motorsports Toyota	160	20	0	Running
25	38	83	Landon Cassill	Burger King Toyota	160	20	1	Running
26	29	47	Bobby Labonte	Scott Products Toyota	160	19	1	Running
27	31	38	David Gilliland	Big Machine Records Ford	160	17	0	Running
28	36	34	David Ragan	Scorpion Coatings/Al's Liners Ford	160	16	0	Running
29	2	99	Carl Edwards	Fastenal Ford	156	15	0	Running
30	42	32	Ken Schrader	Special Operations For America.org Ford	156	14	0	Running
31	37	33	Stephen Leicht #	LittleJoesAuto.com Chevrolet	154	13	0	Running
32	21	31	Jeff Burton	Rain-X Chevrolet	151	12	0	Running
33	3	20	Joey Logano	Dollar General Toyota	144	11	0	Running
34	25	13	Casey Mears	GEICO Ford	137	10	0	Running
35	10	17	Matt Kenseth	Fifth Third Bank Ford	132	10	1	Accident
36	13	51	Kurt Busch	Hendrickcars.com Chevrolet	126	8	0	Engine
37	30	93	Travis Kvapil	Burger King Toyota	40	7	0	Accident
38	34	95	Scott Speed	Leavine Family Racing Ford	23	6	0	Brakes
39	41	10	J.J. Yeley	Tommy Baldwin Racing Chevrolet	20	5	0	Transmission
40	35	26	Josh Wise #	Taco Bell Chevrolet	19	4	0	Brakes
41	40	23	Scott Riggs	North Texas Pipe Chevrolet	14	3	0	Rear Gear
42	39	79	Mike Skinner	Koma Unwind Ford	11	2	0	Rear Gear
43	43	19	Mike Bliss (i)	Humphrey-Smith Racing LLC Toyota	5	0	0	Engine

Sunoco Rookie of the Year Contender. Bonus Points: includes winner, lap leader & most laps led points. (i) = Ineligible for driver points in this series. Failed to qualify: (3) #91 Reed Sorenson; #87 Joe Nemechek; #98 Michael McDowell.

RACE COMMENTS: Before an estimated crowd of 125,000, Jimmie Johnson won the Crown Royal Presents the Curtis Shaver 400 at The Brickyard, his 58th NASCAR Sprint Cup Series victory. To start the race, prior to the green flag no cars dropped to the rear of the field.

RACE STATISTICS

TIME OF RACE: 2 hours, 54 minutes, 19 seconds
AVERAGE SPEED: 137.68 mph
MARGIN OF VICTORY: 4.758 seconds
COORS LIGHT POLE AWARD: Denny Hamlin (182.763 mph. 49.244 secs.)
3M LAP LEADER: Jimmie Johnson (99 Laps)
AMERICAN ETHANOL GREEN FLAG RESTART AWARD: Jimmie Johnson
DIRECTV CREW CHIEF OF THE RACE: Denny Hamlin (crew chief Darian Grubb)
FREESCALE "WIDE OPEN": Greg Biffle
MAHLE CLEVITE ENGINE BUILDER OF THE

RACE: Hendrick Engines (#48)
MOBIL 1 OIL DRIVER OF THE RACE: Kyle Busch
MOOG STEERING AND SUSPENSION PROBLEM SOLVER OF THE RACE: Dale Earnhardt Jr. (crew chief Steve Letarte, 0.345 seconds)
NASCAR SPRINT CUP LEADER BONUS: No winner: rolls over to $140,000 at next event++
SUNOCO ROOKIE OF THE RACE: Stephen Leicht
USG IMPROVING THE FINISH: Tony Stewart (18 places)
CAUTION FLAGS: 5 cautions for 25 laps. [Beneficiary in Brackets] 42–45 (Car #93

Accident Turn 2 [83]); 48–51 (Car #15 Accident Turn 2 [13]); 95–100 (Car #13 Accident Turn 2 [83]); 126–129 (Debris Backstretch [36]); 134–140 (Car #17, 20, 21, 47 Accident Turn 1 [34]).
LAP LEADERS: 17 lead changes among 9 drivers. Hamlin 1–26, Ky. Busch 27–28, Johnson 29–41, Hamlin 42, Keselowski 43–45, Johnson 46–71, J. Gordon 72, Kenseth 73, B. Labonte 74, Cassill 75, Keselowski 76–89, Johnson 90–95, Keselowski 96–100, Johnson 101–125, Ky. Busch 126, Cassill 127, Biffle 128–131, Johnson 132–160.

++Rollover money awarded at year's end, amount not included in race winnings.

POINT LEADERS
(After 20 Races)

1	DALE EARNHARDT JR.	731
2	Matt Kenseth	717
3	Greg Biffle	709
4	Jimmie Johnson	704
5	Denny Hamlin	667
6	Kevin Harvick	653
7	Martin Truex Jr.	653
8	Tony Stewart	652
9	Brad Keselowski	649
10	Clint Bowyer	643
11	Kyle Busch	588
12	Carl Edwards	582

INDIANAPOLIS MOTOR SPEEDWAY

TOP 20 ACTIVE NASCAR SPRINT CUP SERIES DRIVERS (MINIMUM 2 STARTS)

Driver	Races	Wins	Top 5s	Top 10s	Poles	Total Laps	Laps Led	Avg. Start	Avg. Finish
Tony Stewart	14	2	6	10	1	2241	227	16.7	8.2
Jeff Gordon	19	4	11	15	3	2919	477	12.4	8.8
Kevin Harvick	12	1	4	7	1	1909	92	15.6	10.3
Kyle Busch	8	0	2	6	0	1232	42	21.1	11.8
Greg Biffle	10	0	3	6	0	1601	53	15.3	12.1
Clint Bowyer	7	0	2	2	0	1120	2	20.4	12.3
Brad Keselowski	3	0	0	2	0	480	39	12.7	12.3
Bill Elliott	16	1	5	9	0	2558	157	14.7	12.4
Mark Martin	19	0	6	11	1	2876	67	12.2	12.8
Carl Edwards	8	0	1	3	0	1276	5	22.0	13.3
Jamie McMurray	10	1	3	5	0	1580	43	15.4	14.0
Kasey Kahne	9	0	2	4	0	1319	88	8.7	15.4
Matt Kenseth	13	0	5	7	0	1878	39	19.7	15.8
Denny Hamlin	7	0	1	3	1	1103	53	13.4	16.7
Jimmie Johnson	11	4	4	5	1	1571	229	13.5	16.8
AJ Allmendinger	4	0	0	1	0	640	4	20.3	17.0
Bobby Labonte	19	1	4	5	0	2960	31	22.3	17.5
Ken Schrader	14	0	0	2	0	2234	5	22.3	18.1
Brian Vickers	7	0	2	2	0	1051	19	17.1	18.9
Ryan Newman	12	0	1	2	0	1771	14	7.9	19.1

CROWN ROYAL PRESENTS THE "YOUR HERO'S NAME" 400 AT THE BRICKYARD

Year	Driver	Car	Average Speed
1994	Jeff Gordon	Chevrolet	131.977
1995	Dale Earnhardt	Chevrolet	155.206
1996	Dale Jarrett	Ford	139.508
1997	Ricky Rudd	Ford	130.814
1998	Jeff Gordon	Chevrolet	126.772
1999	Dale Jarrett	Ford	148.194
2000	Bobby Labonte	Pontiac	155.912
2001	Jeff Gordon	Chevrolet	130.790
2002	Bill Elliott	Dodge	125.033
2003	Kevin Harvick	Chevrolet	134.554
2004	Jeff Gordon	Chevrolet	115.037
2005	Tony Stewart	Chevrolet	118.782
2006	Jimmie Johnson	Chevrolet	137.182
2007	Tony Stewart	Chevrolet	117.379
2008	Jimmie Johnson	Chevrolet	115.117
2009	Jimmie Johnson	Chevrolet	145.882
2010	Jamie McMurray	Chevrolet	136.054
2011	Paul Menard	Chevrolet	140.762
2012	Jimmie Johnson	Chevrolet	137.680

IOWA SPEEDWAY

America's Place To Race™

3333 Rusty Wallace Drive, Newton, IA 50208 • **Tickets:** 1-866-GO-NASCAR or 1-866-787-8946 • **Web site:** www.iowaspeedway.com
Facebook: www.facebook.com/Iowa-Speedway • **Twitter:** @iowaspeedway.com

//// NASCAR®

CONFIGURATION
Distance: 875 mile
Banking: 12 to 14 degrees in turns, 10
degrees on frontstretch,
4 degrees on backstretch

TRACK RECORDS

Qualifying Records
NASCAR Nationwide Series: Elliott
Sadler, 135.141 mph (23.309 sec.),
Set August 4, 2012; NASCAR Camping
World Truck Series: Parker Kligerman,
137.507 mph (22.908 sec.), Set September 15, 2012

Race Record
NASCAR Nationwide Series: Elliott
Sadler, 115.622 mph, Set August 4,
2012; NASCAR Camping World Truck
Series: Mike Skinner, 99.181 mph,
September 5, 2009

2013 TRACK LAYOUT

2013 SCHEDULE
June 8: NASCAR Nationwide Series
July 13: NASCAR Camping World Truck Series
August 3: NASCAR Nationwide Series
September 8: NASCAR Camping World Truck Series

TRACK OFFICIALS

Doug Fritz *CEO*

PR CONTACTS
Craig Armstrong *Director of Communications*

VISITOR INFORMATION
Chamber of Commerce
(641) 792-5545 – **www.experiencenewton.com**

DIRECTIONS
Take Exit 168 off I-80 in Newton, IA. 30 miles east of Des
Moines, 80 miles west of Iowa City.

KANSAS SPEEDWAY

400 Speedway Blvd., Kansas City, KS 66111 • **Tickets:** 1-866-GO-NASCAR or 1-866-460-RACE • **Web site:** www.kansasspeedway.com
Facebook: www.facebook.com/KansasSpeedway • **Twitter:** @kansasspeedway

NASCAR

CONFIGURATION
Distance: 1.5 miles
Banking: 17 to 20 degrees in turns,
10 degrees on frontstretch,
5 degrees on backstretch

TRACK RECORDS
Qualifying Records
**Kasey Kahne, 191.360 mph
(28.219 sec.),
Set October 19, 2012**

Race Record
**Denny Hamlin, 144.122 mph,
Set April 22, 2012**

2013 SCHEDULE
April 20: NASCAR Camping World Truck Series
April 21: NASCAR Sprint Cup Series
October 5: NASCAR Nationwide Series
October 6: NASCAR Sprint Cup Series

TRACK OFFICIALS

Pat Warren *President*

PR CONTACTS
Kelly Hale *Director of Public Relations*

VISITOR INFORMATION
Kansas City, Kansas Convention & Visitors Bureau
(800) 264-1563/(913) 321-5800 – **www.visitkansascityks.com**
Kansas City Convention & Visitors Association
(800) 767-7700/(816) 221-5242 – **www.visitkc.com**
Hotel & Lodging Association of Greater Kansas City
(816) 421-3646 – **www.kansascitylodging.org**

DIRECTIONS
From the North: I-435 South to Parallel Parkway East (heading away from track). Turn right onto 98th Street to France Family Drive. Turn right onto France Family Drive. *From the South:* I-435 North to Parallel Parkway East (heading away from track). Turn right onto 98th Street to France Family Drive. *From the East:* I-70 West to I-435 North. North to Parallel Parkway East (heading away from track). Turn right onto 98th Street to France Family Drive. Turn right onto France Family Drive. *From the West:* I-70 East to I-435 North to Parallel East (heading away from track). Turn right onto 98th Street to France Family Driver. Turn right onto France Family Drive.

2013 TRACK LAYOUT

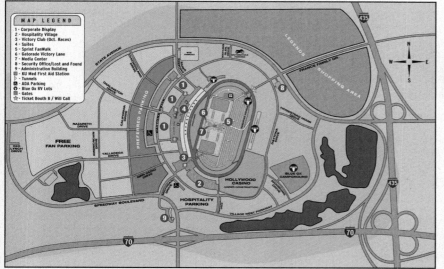

NASCAR SPRINT CUP SERIES RACE RESULTS

Fin Pos	Str Pos	Car No	Series Driver	Team	Laps	Points	Bonus Points	Status
1	4	11	Denny Hamlin	FedEx Ground Toyota	267	47	4	Running
2	6	56	Martin Truex Jr.	NAPA Auto Parts Toyota	267	44	2	Running
3	15	48	Jimmie Johnson	Lowe's Chevrolet	267	42	1	Running
4	18	17	Matt Kenseth	Ford EcoBoost Ford	267	41	1	Running
5	16	16	Greg Biffle	3M Novec 1230 Ford	267	39	0	Running
6	2	29	Kevin Harvick	Rheem Chevrolet	267	38	0	Running
7	7	88	Dale Earnhardt Jr.	Diet Mountain Dew/National Guard Chev.	267	37	0	Running
8	9	5	Kasey Kahne	Farmers Insurance Chevrolet	267	36	0	Running
9	21	99	Carl Edwards	Aflac Ford	267	36	1	Running
10	25	18	Kyle Busch	M&M's Toyota	267	34	0	Running
11	11	2	Brad Keselowski	Miller Lite Dodge	267	34	1	Running
12	39	42	Juan Pablo Montoya	Target Chevrolet	267	33	1	Running
13	23	14	Tony Stewart	Office Depot/Mobil 1 Chevrolet	267	31	0	Running
14	36	1	Jamie McMurray	McDonald's Chevrolet	266	30	0	Running
15	3	20	Joey Logano	The Home Depot Toyota	266	29	0	Running
16	28	9	Marcos Ambrose	DeWalt Ford	266	28	0	Running
17	14	51	Kurt Busch	Phoenix Construction Services, Inc. Chev.	266	27	0	Running
18	19	27	Paul Menard	Menards/Zecol Chevrolet	266	26	0	Running
19	10	12	Sam Hornish Jr. (i)	SKF Dodge	266	0	0	Running
20	13	39	Ryan Newman	Haas Automation Chevrolet	265	24	0	Running
21	20	24	Jeff Gordon	Drive to End Hunger Chevrolet	264	23	0	Running
22	12	31	Jeff Burton	Caterpillar Chevrolet	264	22	0	Running
23	26	43	Aric Almirola	STP Ford	264	21	0	Running
24	29	78	Regan Smith	Furniture Row/Farm American Chevrolet	263	20	0	Running
25	35	93	Travis Kvapil	Burger King Real Fruit Smoothies Toyota	263	19	0	Running
26	40	13	Casey Mears	GEICO Ford	263	18	0	Running
27	22	38	David Gilliland	Front Row Motorsports Ford	263	17	0	Running
28	42	32	Reed Sorenson (i)	@TMone We Drive Sales/FAS Lane Ford	263	0	0	Running
29	16	10	David Reutimann	Accell Construction Chevrolet	262	15	0	Running
30	27	34	David Ragan	Barrett-Jackson Ford	262	14	0	Running
31	31	49	J.J. Yeley	JPO Absorbents Toyota	261	13	0	Running
32	1	22	AJ Allmendinger	AAA Dodge	257	13	1	Running
33	5	55	Mark Martin	Aaron's Dream Machine Toyota	255	11	0	Running
34	32	83	Landon Cassill	Burger King Real Fruit Smoothies Toyota	214	10	0	Running
35	30	47	Bobby Labonte	Reese Towpower Toyota	132	9	0	Engine
36	8	15	Clint Bowyer	5-hour Energy Toyota	125	8	0	Engine
37	33	36	Dave Blaney	Tommy Baldwin Racing Chevrolet	82	7	0	Vibration
38	24	30	David Stremme	Inception Motorsports Toyota	80	6	0	Overheating
39	38	26	Josh Wise #	Morristown Driver's Service Ford	65	5	0	Rear Gear
40	37	98	Michael McDowell	Curb Records Ford	58	4	0	Overheating
41	41	87	Joe Nemechek (i)	AM/FM Energy Wood & Pellet Stoves Toyota	47	0	0	Vibration
42	43	19	Mike Bliss (i)	Humphrey Smith Racing LLC Toyota	27	0	0	Brakes
43	34	23	Scott Riggs	North TX Pipe Chevrolet	18	1	0	Rear Gear

Sunoco Rookie of the Year Contender. Bonus Points: includes winner, lap leader & most laps led points. (i) = Ineligible for driver points in this series. Failed to qualify: (3) #79 Tim Andrews; #33 Jeff Green; #74 Tony Raines.

RACE COMMENTS: Before an estimated crowd of 75,000, Denny Hamlin won the STP 400, his 19th NASCAR Sprint Cup Series victory. Prior to the green flag, the following car dropped to the rear of the field for the reason indicated: #20 (engine change).

RACE STATISTICS

TIME OF RACE: 2 hours, 46 minutes, 44 seconds
AVERAGE SPEED: 144.122 mph
MARGIN OF VICTORY: 0.7 seconds
COORS LIGHT POLE AWARD: AJ Allmendinger (175.993 mph. 30.683 secs.)
3M LAP LEADER: Martin Truex Jr. (173 Laps)
AMERICAN ETHANOL GREEN FLAG RESTART AWARD: Martin Truex Jr.
DIRECTV CREW CHIEF OF THE RACE: Denny Hamlin (crew chief Darian Grubb)
FREESCALE "WIDE OPEN": Greg Biffle
MAHLE CLEVITE ENGINE BUILDER OF THE

RACE: Toyota Racing Development (TRD) (#56)
MOBIL 1 OIL DRIVER OF THE RACE: Denny Hamlin
MOOG STEERING AND SUSPENSION PROBLEM SOLVER OF THE RACE: Jimmie Johnson (crew chief Chad Knaus, 0.117 seconds)
NASCAR SPRINT CUP LEADER BONUS: No winner: rolls over to $20,000 at next event++
USG IMPROVING THE FINISH: Juan Pablo Montoya (27 places)
CAUTION FLAGS: 3 cautions for 18 laps. [Beneficiary in Brackets] 53–56 (Car #15 Spins Turn 4 [10]); 133–141 (Debris

Backstretch [27]); 188–192 (Debris Turns 3 And 4 [20]).
LAP LEADERS: 14 lead changes among 9 drivers. Allmendinger 1–44, Hamlin 45, Edwards 46, Truex Jr. 47–91, Johnson 92–93, Kenseth 94, Montoya 95–96, Truex Jr. 97–177, Kenseth 178, Keselowski 179–180, Truex Jr. 181–223, Montoya 224–225, Hornish Jr. 226–232, Truex Jr. 233–236, Hamlin 237–267.

++Rollover money awarded at year's end, amount not included in race winnings.

POINT LEADERS
(After 8 Races)

1	GREG BIFFLE	312
2	Martin Truex Jr.	297
3	Matt Kenseth	295
4	Dale Earnhardt Jr.	291
5	Denny Hamlin	289
6	Kevin Harvick	287
7	Jimmie Johnson	275
8	Tony Stewart	265
9	Carl Edwards	251
10	Ryan Newman	249
11	Clint Bowyer	227
12	Joey Logano	221

HOLLYWOOD CASINO 400

OFFICIAL RACE RESULTS: RACE #32 – OCTOBER 21, 2012

NASCAR SPRINT CUP SERIES RACE RESULTS

Fin Pos	Str Pos	Car No	Series Driver	Team	Laps	Points	Bonus Points	Status
1	12	17	Matt Kenseth	Zest Ford	267	48	5	Running
2	16	56	Martin Truex Jr.	NAPA Auto Parts Toyota	267	42	0	Running
3	14	27	Paul Menard	Menards/CertainTeed Insulation Chevrolet	267	42	1	Running
4	1	5	Kasey Kahne	Farmers Insurance Chevrolet	267	41	1	Running
5	33	14	Tony Stewart	Office Depot/Mobil 1 Chevrolet	267	39	0	Running
6	3	15	Clint Bowyer	5-hour Energy/Avon Foun. for Women Toyota	267	39	1	Running
7	39	88	Regan Smith	National Guard/Diet Mountain Dew Chev.	267	37	0	Running
8	25	2	Brad Keselowski	Miller Lite Dodge	267	36	0	Running
9	7	48	Jimmie Johnson	Lowe's Chevrolet	267	36	1	Running
10	19	24	Jeff Gordon	DuPont Chevrolet	267	35	1	Running
11	10	29	Kevin Harvick	Budweiser Chevrolet	267	33	0	Running
12	18	9	Marcos Ambrose	Black & Decker Ford	267	32	0	Running
13	9	11	Denny Hamlin	FedEx Freight Toyota	267	31	0	Running
14	17	99	Carl Edwards	Fastenal Ford	267	30	0	Running
15	21	1	Jamie McMurray	Bass Pro Shops/Arctic Cat Chevrolet	267	29	0	Running
16	24	42	Juan Pablo Montoya	Taylor Swift/Target Chevrolet	267	28	0	Running
17	31	93	Travis Kvapil	Burger King/Dr. Pepper Toyota	267	28	1	Running
18	26	83	Landon Cassill	Burger King Toyota	267	26	0	Running
19	8	20	Joey Logano	Dollar General Toyota	267	25	0	Running
20	37	34	David Ragan	Client One Securities LLC Ford	267	24	0	Running
21	32	21	Trevor Bayne (i)	Motorcraft/Quick Lane Tire & Auto Center Ford	267	0	0	Running
22	42	32	Timmy Hill (i)	Southern Pride Trucking/U.S. Chrome Ford	267	0	0	Running
23	38	38	David Gilliland	Long John Silver's Ford	266	22	1	Running
24	2	55	Mark Martin	Aaron's Dream Machine Toyota	266	21	1	Running
25	29	78	Kurt Busch	Furniture Row/Farm American Chevrolet	265	19	0	Running
26	15	22	Sam Hornish Jr. (i)	Shell Pennzoil Dodge	234	0	0	Accident
27	11	16	Greg Biffle	3M/Sherwin-Williams Ford	227	17	0	Running
28	20	31	Jeff Burton	Caterpillar Chevrolet	214	16	0	Running
29	5	43	Aric Almirola	Farmland Ford	212	16	1	Accident
30	6	39	Ryan Newman	Code 3 Associates Chevrolet	188	14	0	Accident
31	4	18	Kyle Busch	M&M's Halloween Toyota	181	13	0	Accident
32	40	10	Danica Patrick (i)	GoDaddy Racing Chevrolet	154	0	0	Accident
33	22	47	Bobby Labonte	Kingsford Charcoal Toyota	140	11	0	Accident
34	35	95	Scott Speed	B&D Electrical Ford	77	10	0	Electrical
35	13	51	AJ Allmendinger	Phoenix Construction Chevrolet	69	9	0	Accident
36	30	19	Mike Bliss (i)	Plinker Tactical/Crowne Plaza Toyota	47	0	0	Vibration
37	28	13	Casey Mears	GEICO Ford	29	7	0	Accident
38	43	79	Kelly Bires	Bestway Disposal/Re-Load.biz Ford	28	6	0	Rear Gear
39	41	36	Dave Blaney	TBR/TMone Chevrolet	25	5	0	Brakes
40	36	87	Joe Nemechek (i)	AM/FM Energy Wood & Pellet Stoves Toyota	22	0	0	Rear Gear
41	34	91	Reed Sorenson (i)	Plinker Tactical/Crowne Plaza Toyota	18	0	0	Overheating
42	27	37	J.J. Yeley	MaxQWorkForce.com Chevrolet	11	2	0	Vibration
43	23	98	Michael McDowell	K-Love/Curb Records Ford	7	1	0	Vibration

Sunoco Rookie of the Year Contender. Bonus Points: includes winner, lap leader & most laps led points. (i) = Ineligible for driver points in this series. Failed to qualify: (3) #33 Cole Whitt; #30 David Stremme; #26 Josh Wise.

RACE COMMENTS: Before an estimated crowd of 78,000, Matt Kenseth won the Hollywood Casino 400, his 24th NASCAR Sprint Cup Series victory. Prior to the green flag, the following cars dropped to the rear of the field for the reason indicated: #10, 31 (engine change).

RACE STATISTICS

TIME OF RACE: 3 hours, 28 minutes, 48 seconds
AVERAGE SPEED: 115.086 mph
MARGIN OF VICTORY: 0.495 seconds
COORS LIGHT POLE AWARD: Kasey Kahne (191.36 mph. 28.219 secs.)
3M LAP LEADER: Matt Kenseth (78 Laps)
AMERICAN ETHANOL GREEN FLAG RESTART AWARD: Matt Kenseth
DIRECTV CREW CHIEF OF THE RACE: Clint Bowyer (crew chief Brian Pattie)
MAHLE CLEVITE ENGINE BUILDER OF THE RACE: Roush Yates Engines (#17)
MOBIL 1 OIL DRIVER OF THE RACE: Tony Stewart

MOOG STEERING AND SUSPENSION PROBLEM SOLVER OF THE RACE: Tony Stewart (crew chief Steve Addington, 0.372 seconds)
NASCAR SPRINT CUP LEADER BONUS: No winner: rolls over to $40,000 at next event++
USG IMPROVING THE FINISH: Regan Smith (32 places)
CAUTION FLAGS: 14 cautions for 66 laps. [Beneficiary in Brackets] 32–36 (Debris [95]); 41–44 (Car #18 Spin Turn 4 [None]); 72–76 (Car #51 Accident Turn 3 [38]); 84–86 (Car #14, 31 Accident Turn 4 [None]); 123–127 (Debris [34]); 137–141 (Car #48 Accident Turn 4 [83]); 143–146 (Car #47 Accident Turn 3 [None]); 156–162 (Car #10, 83 Accident Turn 2 [1]); 166–168 (Car #14 Spin Backstretch [42]); 170–172 (Car #9, 21 Accident Turn 3 [32]); 176–180 (Car #16 Accident Turn 4 [43]); 183–188 (Car #18, 22, 39, 78 Accident Turn 4 [9]); 215–222 (Car #43 Accident Turn 4 [55]); 237–239 (Car #22 Accident Turn 1 [34]).
LAP LEADERS: 16 lead changes among 10 drivers. Kahne–pole, Martin 1–6, Almirola 7–33, Gilliland 34, Almirola 35–73, Kvapil 74, Johnson 75–118, Almirola 119–121, Bowyer 122–123, J. Gordon 124, Bowyer 125–127, Kenseth 128–156, J. Gordon 157, Martin 158–211, Menard 212–217, Kahne 218, Kenseth 219–267.

++Rollover money awarded at year's end, amount not included in race winnings.

POINT LEADERS
(After 32 Races)

1	BRAD KESELOWSKI	2250
2	Jimmie Johnson	2243
3	Denny Hamlin	2230
4	Clint Bowyer	2225
5	Kasey Kahne	2220
6	Martin Truex Jr.	2207
7	Tony Stewart	2203
8	Jeff Gordon	2199
9	Matt Kenseth	2195
10	Kevin Harvick	2191
11	Greg Biffle	2188
12	Dale Earnhardt Jr.	2128

TOP 20 ACTIVE NASCAR SPRINT CUP SERIES DRIVERS (MINIMUM 2 STARTS)

Driver	Races	Wins	Top 5s	Top 10s	Poles	Total Laps	Laps Led	Avg. Start	Avg. Finish
Jimmie Johnson	13	2	5	11	3	3390	547	10.6	8.0
Greg Biffle	13	2	7	9	1	3186	346	15.2	9.5
Brad Keselowski	6	1	2	3	0	1606	17	17.0	9.8
Carl Edwards	11	0	4	8	0	2856	72	18.5	10.8
Jeff Gordon	14	2	8	10	0	3646	208	11.6	11.0
Tony Stewart	14	2	6	9	0	3643	152	18.1	11.7
Kevin Harvick	14	0	1	6	0	3576	83	19.9	12.9
Clint Bowyer	8	0	1	4	0	2207	48	15.2	14.0
Denny Hamlin	10	1	3	3	0	2614	68	13.6	14.0
Kasey Kahne	11	0	2	5	3	2832	78	11.0	15.0
Mark Martin	14	1	2	5	1	3654	212	16.4	15.3
Matt Kenseth	14	1	5	8	1	3472	316	13.7	15.8
Dale Earnhardt Jr.	13	0	1	6	1	3342	81	13.5	16.5
Brian Vickers	7	0	0	1	0	1814	0	12.3	17.9
Paul Menard	8	0	1	2	0	2079	17	12.4	18.0
Kurt Busch	14	0	0	3	1	3532	239	18.2	18.1
Ryan Newman	14	1	3	4	0	3457	120	14.2	18.4
Juan Pablo Montoya	8	0	1	1	0	2079	15	22.9	18.6
Bill Elliott	7	0	2	2	0	1732	151	12.7	18.9
Jamie McMurray	12	0	0	2	0	3007	26	20.8	19.8

STP 400

Year	Driver	Car	Average Speed
2011	Brad Keselowski	Dodge	137.184
2012	Denny Hamlin	Toyota	144.122

HOLLYWOOD CASINO 400

Year	Driver	Car	Average Speed
2001	Jeff Gordon	Chevrolet	110.576
2002	Jeff Gordon	Chevrolet	119.394
2003	Ryan Newman	Dodge	121.630
2004	Joe Nemechek	Chevrolet	128.058
2005	Mark Martin	Ford	137.774
2006	Tony Stewart	Chevrolet	121.753
2007	Greg Biffle	Ford	104.981
2008	Jimmie Johnson	Chevrolet	133.549
2009	Tony Stewart	Chevrolet	137.144
2010	Greg Biffle	Ford	138.077
2011	Jimmie Johnson	Chevrolet	137.181
2012	Matt Kenseth	Ford	115.086

TOP 20 ACTIVE NASCAR SPRINT CUP SERIES DRIVERS (MINIMUM 2 STARTS)

Driver	Races	Wins	Top 5s	Top 10s	Poles	Total Laps	Laps Led	Avg. Start	Avg. Finish
Brad Keselowski	2	1	1	2	0	534	147	7.0	4.0
Jimmie Johnson	2	0	1	2	1	534	21	3.0	4.5
Kyle Busch	2	1	1	2	0	534	243	1.5	5.5
Matt Kenseth	2	0	0	2	0	534	0	16.5	6.5
Denny Hamlin	2	0	1	1	0	534	63	14.5	7.0
Jeff Gordon	2	0	1	2	0	534	0	11.5	7.5
Kasey Kahne	2	0	1	1	0	534	1	11.5	7.5
Carl Edwards	2	0	1	1	0	533	0	16.0	12.5
David Reutimann	2	0	1	1	0	533	7	27.5	12.5
Martin Truex Jr.	2	0	0	1	0	534	1	13.0	13.0
Kevin Harvick	2	0	0	0	0	534	0	11.5	13.5
Kurt Busch	2	0	0	1	0	534	41	8.5	14.0
Juan Pablo Montoya	2	0	0	0	0	534	0	16.5	14.5
Marcos Ambrose	2	0	0	0	0	534	0	11.5	16.5
Dale Earnhardt Jr.	2	0	1	1	0	532	0	18.0	17.0
Joey Logano	2	0	0	0	0	533	0	16.5	18.0
Paul Menard	2	0	0	0	0	533	0	12.5	18.0
AJ Allmendinger	2	0	0	1	0	532	0	19.5	18.5
David Ragan	2	0	0	1	0	530	3	20.5	18.5
Ryan Newman	2	0	1	1	0	475	0	11.5	19.0

QUAKER STATE 400

Year	Driver	Car	Average Speed
2011	Kyle Busch	Toyota	137.314
2012	Brad Keselowski	Dodge	145.607

LAS VEGAS MOTOR SPEEDWAY

7000 Las Vegas Blvd. North Las Vegas, NV 89115 • **Tickets:** 1-866-GO-NASCAR or 1-800-644-4444 • **Web site:** www.lvms.com
Facebook: www.facebook.com/lasvegasmotorspeedway • **Twitter:** @LVMotorSpeedway

NASCAR®

CONFIGURATION
Distance: 1.5 miles
Banking: 20 degrees in turns,
9 degrees on straights

TRACK RECORDS
Qualifying Records
Kasey Kahne, 190.456 mph
(28.353 sec.), Set March 9, 2012

Race Record
Mark Martin, 146.554 mph,
Set March 1, 1998

2013 TRACK LAYOUT

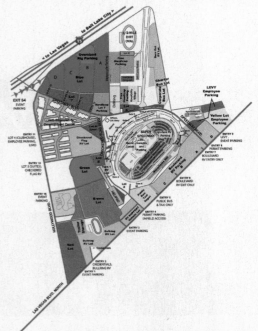

2013 SCHEDULE
March 9: NASCAR Nationwide Series
March 10: NASCAR Sprint Cup Series
September 28: NASCAR Camping World Truck Series

TRACK OFFICIALS

Chris Powell *President*

PR CONTACTS
Jeff Motley *Vice President of Public Relations*

VISITOR INFORMATION
Las Vegas Convention and Visitors Authority
(702) 892-0711 – **www.lvcva.com**

DIRECTIONS
From Las Vegas: take I-15 North to Speedway (exit 54).

NASCAR SPRINT CUP SERIES RACE RESULTS

Fin Pos	Str Pos	Car No	Series Driver	Team	Laps	Points	Bonus Points	Status
1	7	14	Tony Stewart	Mobil 1/Office Depot Chevrolet	267	48	5	Running
2	6	48	Jimmie Johnson	Lowe's/Kobalt Tools Chevrolet	267	43	1	Running
3	9	16	Greg Biffle	3M/Meguiars Ford	267	42	1	Running
4	18	39	Ryan Newman	Quicken Loans Chevrolet	267	40	0	Running
5	21	99	Carl Edwards	Aflac Ford	267	39	0	Running
6	5	15	Clint Bowyer	5-hour Energy Toyota	267	39	1	Running
7	26	27	Paul Menard	Menards/Schrock Chevrolet	267	37	0	Running
8	19	1	Jamie McMurray	McDonald's Chevrolet	267	36	0	Running
9	25	21	Trevor Bayne (i)	Motorcraft/Quick Lane Tire & Auto Center Ford	267	0	0	Running
10	4	88	Dale Earnhardt Jr.	National Guard/Diet Mountain Dew Chev.	267	35	1	Running
11	3	29	Kevin Harvick	Budweiser Chevrolet	267	34	1	Running
12	16	24	Jeff Gordon	DuPont 20 Years Chevrolet	267	33	1	Running
13	15	9	Marcos Ambrose	DeWalt Ford	267	31	0	Running
14	22	31	Jeff Burton	Caterpillar Chevrolet	267	30	0	Running
15	28	78	Regan Smith	Furniture Row/Farm American Chevrolet	267	29	0	Running
16	8	20	Joey Logano	Dollar General Toyota	267	28	0	Running
17	10	56	Martin Truex Jr.	NAPA Auto Parts Toyota	267	27	0	Running
18	13	55	Mark Martin	Aaron's Toyota	267	26	0	Running
19	1	5	Kasey Kahne	Farmers Insurance Chevrolet	267	25	0	Running
20	17	11	Denny Hamlin	FedEx Freight Toyota	267	24	0	Running
21	35	34	David Ragan	Front Row Motorsports Ford	267	24	1	Running
22	11	17	Matt Kenseth	Zest Ford	267	23	1	Running
23	2	18	Kyle Busch	M&M's Brown Toyota	266	21	0	Running
24	27	43	Aric Almirola	Richard Petty Fantasy Racing Camp Ford	266	20	0	Running
25	29	42	Juan Pablo Montoya	Clorox Chevrolet	264	19	0	Running
26	24	47	Bobby Labonte	Kingsford/Bush's Beans Toyota	264	18	0	Running
27	32	13	Casey Mears	GEICO Ford	264	17	0	Running
28	43	30	David Stremme	Inception Motorsports Toyota	263	16	0	Running
29	38	36	Dave Blaney	Ollie's Bargain Outlet Chevrolet	263	15	0	Running
30	41	32	Ken Schrader	Federated Auto Parts Ford	263	14	0	Running
31	31	10	David Reutimann	Accell Construction Chevrolet	261	13	0	Running
32	20	2	Brad Keselowski	Miller Lite Dodge	259	13	1	Running
33	34	38	David Gilliland	Front Row Motorsports Ford	258	11	0	Running
34	23	33	Brendan Gaughan	South Point Casino Chevrolet	252	10	0	Running
35	12	51	Kurt Busch	Tag Heuer Eyewear Chevrolet	251	9	0	Accident
36	30	83	Landon Cassill	Burger King Toyota	240	8	0	Engine
37	14	22	AJ Allmendinger	Pennzoil Dodge	238	8	1	Running
38	39	98	Michael McDowell	Phil Parsons Racing Ford	147	6	0	Rear Gear
39	37	93	Travis Kvapil	Burger King Toyota	123	5	0	Engine
40	33	26	Josh Wise #	1-800-Loan Mart Ford	64	4	0	Brakes
41	40	87	Joe Nemechek (i)	AM/FM Energy Wood & Pellet Stoves Toyota	44	0	0	Vibration
42	42	37	Timmy Hill #	Poynt.com Ford	42	2	0	Accident
43	36	49	J.J. Yeley	America Israel Racing Toyota	39	1	0	Engine

Sunoco Rookie of the Year Contender. Bonus Points: includes winner, lap leader & most laps led points. (i) = Ineligible for driver points in this series. Failed to qualify: (2) #23 Scott Riggs; #7 Robby Gordon.

RACE COMMENTS: Before an estimated crowd of 150,000, Tony Stewart won the Kobalt Tools 400, his 45th NASCAR Sprint Cup Series victory and first at Las Vegas Motor Speedway. To start the race, prior to the green flag the following cars dropped to the rear of the field for the reasons indicated: #18, 48 (backup cars), #42 (engine change), #78 (transmission change).

RACE STATISTICS

TIME OF RACE: 2 hours, 54 minutes, 44 seconds
AVERAGE SPEED: 137.524 mph
MARGIN OF VICTORY: 0.461 seconds
COORS LIGHT POLE AWARD: Kasey Kahne (190.456 mph. 28.353 secs.)
3M LAP LEADER: Tony Stewart (127 Laps)
AMERICAN ETHANOL GREEN FLAG RESTART AWARD: Tony Stewart
DIRECTV CREW CHIEF OF THE RACE: Tony Stewart (crew chief Steve Addington)
FREESCALE "WIDE OPEN": Greg Biffle
MAHLE CLEVITE ENGINE BUILDER OF THE RACE: Hendrick Engines (#14)

MOBIL 1 OIL DRIVER OF THE RACE: Tony Stewart
MOOG STEERING AND SUSPENSION PROBLEM SOLVER OF THE RACE: Jamie McMurray (crew chief Kevin Manion, 0.302 seconds)
NASCAR SPRINT CUP LEADER BONUS: No winner: rolls over to $20,000 at next event++
SUNOCO ROOKIE OF THE RACE: Josh Wise
USG IMPROVING THE FINISH: Carl Edwards (16 places)
CAUTION FLAGS: 8 cautions for 33 laps. [Beneficiary in Brackets] 46–49 (Car #37 Accident Turn 2 [34]); 74–77 (Car #10 Accident Turn 4 [51]); 128–133 (Fluid [11]); 206–209 (Debris [21]); 230–233 (Debris [31]); 246–250 (Fluid [20]); 256–258 (Car #51 Accident Backstretch [34]); 261–263 (Debris [43]).
LAP LEADERS: 16 lead changes among 11 drivers. Kahne–pole, Earnhardt Jr. 1–43, Harvick 44–45, Biffle 46, Earnhardt Jr. 47–73, Biffle 74, Ragan 75, Harvick 76–77, Kenseth 78–98, Johnson 99–133, Stewart 134–175, Keselowski 176, Allmendinger 177, J. Gordon 178–179, Stewart 180–230, Bowyer 231–233, Stewart 234–267.

++Rollover money awarded at year's end, amount not included in race winnings

POINT LEADERS
(After 3 Races)

1	GREG BIFFLE	125
2	Kevin Harvick	115
3	Denny Hamlin	113
4	Dale Earnhardt Jr.	107
5	Matt Kenseth	102
6	Carl Edwards	102
7	Tony Stewart	100
8	Martin Truex Jr.	98
9	Joey Logano	98
10	Mark Martin	97
11	Paul Menard	89
12	Kyle Busch	87

LAS VEGAS MOTOR SPEEDWAY

TOP 20 ACTIVE NASCAR SPRINT CUP SERIES DRIVERS (MINIMUM 2 STARTS)

Driver	Races	Wins	Top 5s	Top 10s	Poles	Total Laps	Laps Led	Avg. Start	Avg. Finish
Jimmie Johnson	11	4	5	6	0	2955	355	14.4	9.8
Carl Edwards	8	2	3	4	0	2157	160	13.5	10.3
Jeff Burton	15	2	5	8	0	3827	280	19.1	10.9
Matt Kenseth	13	2	5	6	1	3093	471	17.2	12.5
Marcos Ambrose	4	0	1	1	0	1085	1	13.5	12.8
Denny Hamlin	7	0	1	4	0	1889	0	22.1	12.9
Tony Stewart	14	1	6	9	0	3395	482	14.2	12.9
Kevin Harvick	12	0	3	4	0	3220	58	22.2	13.0
Greg Biffle	9	0	2	6	1	2176	115	9.0	13.4
Mark Martin	15	1	6	10	0	3566	259	13.0	13.5
Trevor Bayne	2	0	0	1	0	534	0	20.5	14.5
Joey Logano	4	0	0	1	0	1085	1	10.0	14.5
Jeff Gordon	15	1	6	7	0	3752	457	13.9	14.7
Kasey Kahne	9	0	2	4	3	2295	58	12.0	15.3
Clint Bowyer	7	0	1	3	0	1860	17	20.0	15.7
Kyle Busch	9	1	3	4	2	2007	113	6.4	15.9
Dale Earnhardt Jr.	13	0	2	6	0	3045	232	21.8	16.3
Ryan Newman	12	0	3	6	1	3028	98	12.2	16.4
Bill Elliott	8	0	1	3	0	1915	11	21.6	17.0
Martin Truex Jr.	7	0	0	1	0	1886	5	21.4	17.4

KOBALT TOOLS 400

Year	Driver	Car	Average Speed
1998	Mark Martin	Ford	146.554
1999	Jeff Burton	Ford	137.537
2000	Jeff Burton	Ford	119.982
2001	Jeff Gordon	Chevrolet	135.546
2002	Sterling Marlin	Dodge	136.754
2003	Matt Kenseth	Ford	132.934
2004	Matt Kenseth	Ford	128.790
2005	Jimmie Johnson	Chevrolet	121.038
2006	Jimmie Johnson	Chevrolet	133.358
2007	Jimmie Johnson	Chevrolet	128.183
2008	Carl Edwards	Ford	127.729
2009	Kyle Busch	Toyota	119.515
2010	Jimmie Johnson	Chevrolet	141.450
2011	Carl Edwards	Ford	135.508
2012	Tony Stewart	Chevrolet	137.524

LAS VEGAS MOTOR SPEEDWAY

MARTINSVILLE SPEEDWAY

340 Speedway Road, Ridgeway, VA 24148 • **Tickets:** 1-866-GO-NASCAR or 1-877-RACE-TIX • **Web site:** www.martinsvillespeedway.com
Facebook: www.facebook.com/MartinsvilleSpeedway • **Twitter:** @MartinsvilleSwy

NASCAR

CONFIGURATION
Distance: .526 mile
Banking: 12 degrees in turns,
0 degrees on straights

TRACK RECORDS
Qualifying Records
Tony Stewart, 98.083 mph
(19.306 sec.),
Set October 21, 2005

Race Record
Jeff Gordon, 82.223 mph,
Set September 22, 1996

2013 SCHEDULE
April 6: NASCAR Camping World Truck Series
April 7: NASCAR Sprint Cup Series
October 26: NASCAR Camping World Truck Series
October 27: NASCAR Sprint Cup Series

2013 TRACK LAYOUT

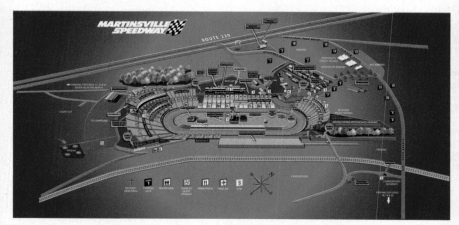

TRACK OFFICIALS

Clay Campbell *President*

PR CONTACTS
Mike Smith *Director, Public Relations*

VISITOR INFORMATION
Martinsville Henry County Chamber of Commerce
(276) 632-6401 – **www.martinsville.com**

DIRECTIONS
On US Highway 220 South: two miles south of Martinsville,
VA halfway between Roanoke, VA and Greensboro, NC

GOODY'S FAST RELIEF 500

OFFICIAL RACE RESULTS: RACE #6 – APRIL 1, 2012

NASCAR SPRINT CUP SERIES RACE RESULTS

Fin Pos	Str Pos	Car No	Series Driver	Team	Laps	Points	Bonus Points	Status
1	5	39	Ryan Newman	Outback Steakhouse Chevrolet	515	47	4	Running
2	27	22	AJ Allmendinger	Shell Pennzoil Dodge	515	42	0	Running
3	14	88	Dale Earnhardt Jr.	AMP Energy/Diet Mtn. Dew/Nat'l Guard Chev.	515	42	1	Running
4	21	17	Matt Kenseth	Stephen Siller Tunnel to Towers/Gary Sinise Foun. Ford	515	41	1	Running
5	13	56	Martin Truex Jr.	NAPA Auto Parts Toyota	515	39	0	Running
6	3	11	Denny Hamlin	FedEx Freight Toyota	515	39	1	Running
7	15	14	Tony Stewart	Office Depot/Mobil 1 Chevrolet	515	37	0	Running
8	19	43	Aric Almirola	Smithfield Helping Hungry Homes Ford	515	37	1	Running
9	7	2	Brad Keselowski	Miller Lite Dodge	515	36	1	Running
10	4	15	Clint Bowyer	5-hour Energy Toyota	515	35	1	Running
11	28	99	Carl Edwards	Fastenal Ford	515	33	0	Running
12	22	48	Jimmie Johnson	myLowes Chevrolet	515	33	1	Running
13	26	16	Greg Biffle	3M Ford	514	31	0	Running
14	9	24	Jeff Gordon	Drive to End Hunger Chevrolet	514	32	2	Running
15	12	9	Marcos Ambrose	DeWalt Ford	513	29	0	Running
16	17	78	Regan Smith	Furniture Row Racing/CSX Play It Safe Chevr.	513	28	0	Running
17	16	47	Bobby Labonte	Bush's Best Beans Toyota	513	27	0	Running
18	6	55	Brian Vickers	RKMotorsCharlotte.com/Aaron's Toyota	513	26	0	Running
19	2	29	Kevin Harvick	Budweiser is Back Chevrolet	513	26	1	Running
20	20	1	Jamie McMurray	Belkin Chevrolet	513	24	0	Running
21	32	42	Juan Pablo Montoya	Target Chevrolet	512	23	0	Running
22	18	31	Jeff Burton	BB&T Chevrolet	512	22	0	Running
23	10	20	Joey Logano	The Home Depot Toyota	511	21	0	Running
24	24	34	David Ragan	Front Row Motorsports Ford	511	20	0	Running
25	25	13	Casey Mears	GEICO Ford	511	19	0	Running
26	11	27	Paul Menard	Menards/LIBMAN Chevrolet	510	18	0	Running
27	34	93	Travis Kvapil	Burger King/Dr. Pepper Toyota	510	17	0	Running
28	38	38	David Gilliland	Long John Silver's Ford	509	16	0	Running
29	31	83	Landon Cassill	Burger King/Dr. Pepper Toyota	507	15	0	Running
30	39	30	David Stremme	Inception Motorsports Toyota	506	14	0	Running
31	41	33	Hermie Sadler	Anderson's Pure Maple Syrup Chevrolet	505	13	0	Running
32	36	32	Ken Schrader	Federated Auto Parts Ford	503	12	0	Running
33	40	51	Kurt Busch	Phoenix Construction Services Chevrolet	497	11	0	Running
34	42	36	Dave Blaney	Ollie's Bargain Outlet Chevrolet	439	10	0	Brakes
35	29	10	David Reutimann	Accell Construction Chevrolet	436	9	0	Engine
36	8	18	Kyle Busch	M&M's Toyota	435	8	0	Running
37	43	49	J.J. Yeley	America Israel Racing/JPO Absorbents Toyota	359	7	0	Brakes
38	1	5	Kasey Kahne	Hendrickcars.com Chevrolet	256	6	0	Engine
39	37	87	Joe Nemechek (i)	AM/FM Energy Wood & Pellet Stoves Toyota	74	0	0	Brakes
40	23	98	Michael McDowell	Curb Records Ford	60	4	0	Brakes
41	30	26	Josh Wise #	Morristown Drivers Service Ford	49	3	0	Brakes
42	33	23	Scott Riggs	North Texas Pipe Chevrolet	30	2	0	Brakes
43	35	74	Reed Sorenson (i)	Turn One Racing Chevrolet	25	0	0	Brakes

Sunoco Rookie of the Year Contender. Bonus Points: includes winner, lap leader & most laps led points. (i) = Ineligible for driver points in this series. Failed to qualify: (3) #52 Scott Speed; #19 Mike Bliss; #37 Tony Raines.

RACE COMMENTS: Before an estimated crowd of 63,000, Ryan Newman won the Goody's Fast Relief 500, his 16th NASCAR Sprint Cup Series victory and first at Martinsville Speedway.

RACE STATISITCS

TIME OF RACE: 3 hours, 26 minutes, 12 seconds
AVERAGE SPEED: 78.823 mph
MARGIN OF VICTORY: 0.342 seconds
COORS LIGHT POLE AWARD: Kasey Kahne (97.128 mph. 19.496 secs.)
3M LAP LEADER: Jeff Gordon (328 Laps)
AMERICAN ETHANOL GREEN FLAG RESTART AWARD: Dale Earnhardt Jr.
DIRECTV CREW CHIEF OF THE RACE: Ryan Newman (crew chief Tony Gibson)
FREESCALE "WIDE OPEN": AJ Allmendinger
MAHLE CLEVITE ENGINE BUILDER OF THE RACE: Hendrick Engines (#39)

MOBIL 1 OIL DRIVER OF THE RACE: Ryan Newman
MOOG STEERING AND SUSPENSION PROBLEM SOLVER OF THE RACE: Matt Kenseth (crew chief Jimmy Fennig, 0.059 seconds)
NASCAR SPRINT CUP LEADER BONUS: No winner: rolls over to $50,000 at next event++
USG IMPROVING THE FINISH: Matt Kenseth (17 places)
CAUTION FLAGS: 7 cautions for 56 laps. [Beneficiary in Brackets] 99–104 (Car #18 Accident Turn 3 [27]); 246–254 (Car #36 Accident Turn 2 [22]); 265–270 (Car #42, 32 Accident Backstretch [39]); 316–328 (Car #5 Blown Engine Backstretch [16]); 362–368 (Car #93 Spin Turn 2 [99]); 498–503 (Car #10 Stalled Frontstretch [14]); 505–513 (Car #15, 24, 48 Accident Turns 1 & 2 [99]).
LAP LEADERS: 18 lead changes among 10 drivers. Kahne–pole, Harvick 1–21, J. Gordon 22–99, Keselowski 100, J. Gordon 101–228, Earnhardt Jr. 229–231, J. Gordon 232, Hamlin 233, Bowyer 234–235, Kenseth 236, Almirola 237–239, J. Gordon 240–322, Keselowski 323, J. Gordon 324–355, Johnson 356–362, Hamlin 363–392, Johnson 393–496, J. Gordon 497–503, Newman 504–515.

++Rollover money awarded at year's end, amount not included in race winnings.

POINT LEADERS
(After 6 Races)

1	GREG BIFFLE	226
2	Dale Earnhardt Jr.	220
3	Tony Stewart	214
4	Matt Kenseth	214
5	Kevin Harvick	214
6	Martin Truex Jr.	214
7	Denny Hamlin	210
8	Ryan Newman	202
9	Clint Bowyer	192
10	Jimmie Johnson	189
11	Carl Edwards	179
12	Brad Keselowski	175

MARTINSVILLE SPEEDWAY

TUMS FAST RELIEF 500

OFFICIAL RACE RESULTS: RACE #33 – OCTOBER 28, 2012

NASCAR SPRINT CUP SERIES RACE RESULTS

Fin Pos	Str Pos	Car No	Series Driver	Team	Laps	Points	Bonus Points	Status
1	1	48	Jimmie Johnson	Lowe's Chevrolet	500	48	5	Running
2	3	18	Kyle Busch	M&M's Halloween Toyota	500	42	0	Running
3	15	5	Kasey Kahne	Hendrickcars.com Chevrolet	500	42	1	Running
4	10	43	Aric Almirola	Gwaltney Ford	500	40	0	Running
5	8	15	Clint Bowyer	5-hour Energy Benefitting Avon Foun. for Women Toyota	500	40	1	Running
6	32	2	Brad Keselowski	Miller Lite Dodge	500	39	1	Running
7	11	24	Jeff Gordon	Pepsi MAX Chevrolet	500	38	1	Running
8	2	55	Brian Vickers	MyClassicGarage.com Toyota	500	37	1	Running
9	18	47	Bobby Labonte	Pine-Sol Toyota	500	35	0	Running
10	30	16	Greg Biffle	3M Ford	500	34	0	Running
11	17	39	Ryan Newman	Quicken Loans Chevrolet	500	33	0	Running
12	9	27	Paul Menard	Zecol/Menards Chevrolet	500	32	0	Running
13	27	22	Sam Hornish Jr. (i)	Shell Pennzoil Dodge	500	0	0	Running
14	6	17	Matt Kenseth	Ford EcoBoost Ford	500	31	1	Running
15	19	78	Kurt Busch	Furniture Row/Farm American Chevrolet	500	29	0	Running
16	14	20	Joey Logano	The Home Depot/redbeacon.com Toyota	500	28	0	Running
17	24	1	Jamie McMurray	McDonald's Chevrolet	500	27	0	Running
18	23	99	Carl Edwards	Geek Squad Ford	500	26	0	Running
19	34	83	Landon Cassill	Burger King/Dr Pepper Toyota	500	25	0	Running
20	25	42	Juan Pablo Montoya	Target Chevrolet	500	24	0	Running
21	20	88	Dale Earnhardt Jr.	Diet Mtn. Dew/Nat'l Guard/AMP Energy Chev.	500	23	0	Running
22	4	31	Jeff Burton	Odyssey Battery/EnerSys Chevrolet	499	22	0	Running
23	12	56	Martin Truex Jr.	NAPA Auto Parts Toyota	499	21	0	Running
24	33	9	Marcos Ambrose	Black & Decker Ford	499	20	0	Running
25	22	13	Casey Mears	GEICO Ford	499	19	0	Running
26	16	34	David Ragan	Where's Waldo? Ford	499	18	0	Running
27	7	14	Tony Stewart	Office Depot/Mobil 1 Chevrolet	498	17	0	Running
28	26	51	AJ Allmendinger	Phoenix Construction Chevrolet	498	16	0	Running
29	28	32	Ken Schrader	Southern Pride Trucking/U.S. Chrome Ford	495	15	0	Running
30	35	38	David Gilliland	Long John Silver's Ford	494	14	0	Running
31	41	93	Travis Kvapil	Burger King/Dr Pepper Toyota	492	14	1	Running
32	13	29	Kevin Harvick	Rheem Chasing the Cure Chevrolet	473	12	0	Engine
33	5	11	Denny Hamlin	FedEx Express Toyota	466	12	1	Running
34	42	33	Stephen Leicht #	LittleJoesAutos.com Chevrolet	253	10	0	Brakes
35	37	36	Dave Blaney	MOHAWK Northeast/TMone Call Center Chev.	193	9	0	Brakes
36	29	10	David Reutimann	@TMone Drive Sales Fast Chevrolet	185	8	0	Overheating
37	43	95	Scott Speed	Jordan Truck Sales Ford	116	7	0	Suspension
38	31	26	Josh Wise #	MDS Transport Ford	85	6	0	Brakes
39	21	98	Michael McDowell	Phil Parsons Racing Ford	61	5	0	Brakes
40	40	30	David Stremme	Inception Motorsports Toyota	46	4	0	Accident
41	38	87	Joe Nemechek (i)	AM/FM Energy Wood & Pellet Stoves Toyota	35	0	0	Brakes
42	36	23	Scott Riggs	North Texas Pipe Chevrolet	22	2	0	Overheating
43	39	91	Reed Sorenson (i)	Plinker Tactical Chevrolet	19	0	0	Overheating

Sunoco Rookie of the Year Contender. Bonus Points: includes winner, lap leader & most laps led points. (i) = Ineligible for driver points in this series. Failed to qualify: (2) #19 Mike Bliss; #37 J.J. Yeley.

RACE COMMENTS: Before an estimated crowd of 60,000, Jimmie Johnson won the TUMS Fast Relief 500, his 59th NASCAR Sprint Cup Series victory. Prior to the green flag, no cars dropped to the rear.

RACE STATISTICS

TIME OF RACE: 3 hours, 23 minutes, 9 seconds
AVERAGE SPEED: 77.677 mph
MARGIN OF VICTORY: 0.479 seconds
COORS LIGHT POLE AWARD: Jimmie Johnson (97.598 mph. 19.402 secs.)
3M LAP LEADER: Jimmie Johnson (193 Laps)
AMERICAN ETHANOL GREEN FLAG RESTART AWARD: Jimmie Johnson
DIRECTV CREW CHIEF OF THE RACE: Kyle Busch (crew chief Dave Rogers)
FREESCALE "WIDE OPEN": Kyle Busch
MAHLE CLEVITE ENGINE BUILDER OF THE RACE: Hendrick Engines (#48)
MOBIL 1 OIL DRIVER OF THE RACE: Kyle Busch
MOOG STEERING AND SUSPENSION

PROBLEM SOLVER OF THE RACE: Brad Keselowski (crew chief Paul Wolfe, 0.159 seconds)
NASCAR SPRINT CUP LEADER BONUS: Jimmie Johnson ($40,000 ++)
SUNOCO ROOKIE OF THE RACE: Stephen Leicht
USG IMPROVING THE FINISH: Greg Biffle (20 places)
CAUTION FLAGS: 11 cautions for 64 laps. [Beneficiary in Brackets] 46–51 (Car #30 Accident Turn 1 [38]); 98–103 (Car #38 Accident Turn 3 [10]); 129–136 (Car #93 Spin Turn 2 [83]); 151–155 (Car #18 Spin Turn 4 [93]); 200–204 (Car #9 Spin Turn 2 [None]); 213–218 (Car #9, 93 Accident Turn 2 [34]); 230–234 (Car #78 Spin Turn 4 [93]); 393–399 (Car #11 Stopped On The Track [47]); 440–445 (Car #48, 42, 93, 14

Accident Turn 2 [78]); 476–481 (Oil On The Track [27]); 492–495 (Car #88, 99 Accident Turn 2 [42]).
LAP LEADERS: 22 lead changes among 9 drivers. Johnson 1–47, Kvapil 48, Johnson 49–67, J. Gordon 68–98, Johnson 99–106, J. Gordon 107–146, Vickers 147–164, Hamlin 165–170, Johnson 171–182, Bowyer 183–200, Johnson 201–204, J. Gordon 205–225, Bowyer 226–234, Johnson 235–237, Bowyer 238–349, Hamlin 350–355, Vickers 356–364, Kenseth 365, Kahne 366–377, Bowyer 378–392, Johnson 393–477, Keselowski 478–485, Johnson 486–500.

++Rollover money awarded at year's end, amount not included in race winnings.

POINT LEADERS
(After 33 Races)

1	JIMMIE JOHNSON	2291
2	Brad Keselowski	2289
3	Clint Bowyer	2265
4	Kasey Kahne	2262
5	Denny Hamlin	2242
6	Jeff Gordon	2237
7	Martin Truex Jr.	2228
8	Matt Kenseth	2226
9	Greg Biffle	2222
10	Tony Stewart	2220
11	Kevin Harvick	2203
12	Dale Earnhardt Jr.	2151

MARTINSVILLE SPEEDWAY

TOP 20 ACTIVE NASCAR SPRINT CUP SERIES DRIVERS (MINIMUM 2 STARTS)

Driver	Races	Wins	Top 5s	Top 10s	Poles	Total Laps	Laps Led	Avg. Start	Avg. Finish
Jimmie Johnson	22	7	15	19	2	10,980	1,981	11.9	5.5
Jeff Gordon	40	7	25	32	7	19,769	3,515	7.2	7.1
Denny Hamlin	15	4	9	12	2	7307	1,139	10.9	8.2
Brad Keselowski	6	0	0	3	0	3021	10	19.8	12.2
Dale Earnhardt Jr.	26	0	10	14	0	12,879	868	13.7	13.0
Mark Martin	48	2	12	25	3	22,572	344	14.0	13.3
Ryan Newman	22	1	7	11	3	10,673	194	9.0	13.6
Tony Stewart	28	3	9	15	3	13,492	1,208	13.0	13.7
Clint Bowyer	14	0	2	8	0	6889	247	16.4	14.0
Terry Labonte	53	0	12	27	1	23,802	508	16.7	14.0
Jeff Burton	37	1	10	16	0	17,346	940	17.1	15.0
Joey Logano	8	0	1	2	0	4015	0	16.3	15.3
Juan Pablo Montoya	12	0	2	3	0	5918	46	22.4	15.7
Matt Kenseth	26	0	3	8	0	12,901	73	21.7	15.9
Carl Edwards	17	0	1	5	0	8351	31	18.1	16.1
Kevin Harvick	23	1	3	10	0	11,236	363	13.3	16.7
Kyle Busch	16	0	7	8	0	7684	397	13.9	16.8
Bill Elliott	45	0	3	14	0	20,510	241	15.8	17.0
Jamie McMurray	20	0	1	10	1	9378	117	15.3	17.0
Bobby Labonte	40	1	6	14	1	18,591	320	18.6	18.4

VIRGINIA 500

Year	Driver	Car	Average Speed
1950	Curtis Turner	Oldsmobile	N/A
1951	Curtis Turner	Oldsmobile	N/A
1952	Dick Rathmann	Hudson	42.862
1953	Lee Petty	Dodge	N/A
1954	Jim Paschal	Oldsmobile	46.153
1955	Tim Flock	Chrysler	52.554
1956	Buck Baker	Dodge	66.103
1957	Buck Baker	Chevrolet	57.318
1958	Bob Welborn	Chevrolet	64.910
1959	Lee Petty	57 Oldsmobile	59.440
1960	Richard Petty	60 Plymouth	63.940
1961	Fred Lorenzen	61 Ford	68.370
1962	Richard Petty	62 Plymouth	66.430
1963	Richard Petty	63 Plymouth	64.823
1964	Fred Lorenzen	64 Ford	70.098
1965	Fred Lorenzen	65 Ford	66.765
1966	Jim Paschal	66 Plymouth	69.156
1967	Richard Petty	67 Plymouth	67.446
1968	Cale Yarborough	68 Mercury	66.686
1969	Richard Petty	69 Ford	64.405
1970	Bobby Isaac	69 Dodge	68.512
1971	Richard Petty	71 Plymouth	77.707
1972	Richard Petty	72 Plymouth	72.657
1973	David Pearson	71 Mercury	70.251
1974	Cale Yarborough	73 Chevrolet	69.936
1975	Richard Petty	Dodge	69.282
1976	Darrell Waltrip	Chevrolet	71.759
1977	Cale Yarborough	Chevrolet	77.405
1978	Darrell Waltrip	Chevrolet	77.971
1979	Richard Petty	Chevrolet	76.562
1980	Darrell Waltrip	Chevrolet	69.049
1981	Morgan Shepherd	Pontiac	75.019
1982	Harry Gant	Buick	75.073
1983	Darrell Waltrip	Chevrolet	66.460
1984	Geoff Bodine	Chevrolet	73.264
1985	Harry Gant	Chevrolet	73.022
1986	Ricky Rudd	Ford	76.882
1987	Dale Earnhardt	Chevrolet	72.808
1988	Dale Earnhardt	Chevrolet	74.740
1989	Darrell Waltrip	Chevrolet	79.025
1990	Geoff Bodine	Ford	77.423
1991	Dale Earnhardt	Chevrolet	75.139
1992	Mark Martin	Ford	78.086
1993	Rusty Wallace	Pontiac	79.078
1994	Rusty Wallace	Ford	76.700
1995	Rusty Wallace	Ford	72.145
1996	Jeff Gordon	Chevrolet	82.223
1997	Jeff Gordon	Chevrolet	70.347
1998	Bobby Hamilton	Chevrolet	70.709
1999	John Andretti	Pontiac	75.653
2000	Mark Martin	Ford	71.161
2001	Dale Jarrett	Ford	70.799
2002	Bobby Labonte	Pontiac	73.951
2003	Jeff Gordon	Chevrolet	75.557
2004	Rusty Wallace	Dodge	68.169
2005	Jeff Gordon	Chevrolet	72.099
2006	Tony Stewart	Chevrolet	72.741
2007	Jimmie Johnson	Chevrolet	70.258
2008	Denny Hamlin	Toyota	73.613
2009	Jimmie Johnson	Chevrolet	75.938
2010	Denny Hamlin	Toyota	73.180
2011	Kevin Harvick	Chevrolet	74.195
2012	Ryan Newman	Chevrolet	78.823

GOODY'S RELIEF 500

Year	Driver	Car	Average Speed
1949	Red Byron	Oldsmobile	N/A
1950	Herb Thomas	Plymouth	N/A
1951	Frank Mundy	Oldsmobile	N/A
1952	Herb Thomas	Hudson	47.556
1953	Jim Paschal	Dodge	56.013
1954	Lee Petty	Chrysler	44.547
1955	Speedy Thompson	Chrysler	N/A
1956	Jack Smith	Dodge	61.136
1957	Bob Welborn	Chevrolet	63.025
1958	Fireball Roberts	Chevrolet	64.344
1959	Rex White	Chevrolet	60.500
1960	Rex White	60 Chevrolet	60.440
1961	Joe Weatherly	61 Pontiac	62.590
1962	Nelson Stacy	62 Ford	66.870
1963	Fred Lorenzen	63 Ford	67.486
1964	Fred Lorenzen	64 Ford	67.320
1965	Junior Johnson	65 Ford	67.056
1966	Fred Lorenzen	66 Ford	69.177
1967	Richard Petty	67 Plymouth	69.606
1968	Richard Petty	68 Plymouth	65.808
1969	Richard Petty	69 Ford	63.127
1970	Richard Petty	70 Plymouth	72.159
1971	Bobby Isaac	71 Dodge	73.681
1972	Richard Petty	72 Plymouth	69.989
1973	Richard Petty	73 Dodge	68.831
1974	Earl Ross	72 Chevrolet	66.232
1975	Dave Marcis	Dodge	75.800
1976	Cale Yarborough	Chevrolet	75.370
1977	Cale Yarborough	Chevrolet	73.447
1978	Cale Yarborough	Oldsmobile	79.336
1979	Buddy Baker	Chevrolet	75.119
1980	Dale Earnhardt	Chevrolet	69.654
1981	Darrell Waltrip	Buick	70.089
1982	Darrell Waltrip	Buick	71.315
1983	Ricky Rudd	Chevrolet	76.134
1984	Darrell Waltrip	Chevrolet	75.532
1985	Dale Earnhardt	Chevrolet	70.694
1986	Rusty Wallace	Pontiac	73.191
1987	Darrell Waltrip	Chevrolet	76.410
1988	Darrell Waltrip	Chevrolet	74.988
1989	Darrell Waltrip	Chevrolet	76.571
1990	Geoff Bodine	Ford	76.386
1991	Harry Gant	Oldsmobile	74.535
1992	Geoff Bodine	Ford	75.424
1993	Ernie Irvan	Ford	74.101
1994	Rusty Wallace	Ford	77.139
1995	Dale Earnhardt	Chevrolet	73.946
1996	Rusty Wallace	Ford	81.410
1997	Jeff Burton	Ford	73.072
1998	Ricky Rudd	Ford	73.350
1999	Jeff Gordon	Chevrolet	72.347
2000	Tony Stewart	Pontiac	73.859
2001	Ricky Craven	Ford	75.750
2002	Kurt Busch	Ford	74.651
2003	Jeff Gordon	Chevrolet	67.658
2004	Jimmie Johnson	Chevrolet	66.103
2005	Jeff Gordon	Chevrolet	69.695
2006	Jimmie Johnson	Chevrolet	70.446
2007	Jimmie Johnson	Chevrolet	66.608
2008	Jimmie Johnson	Chevrolet	75.931
2009	Denny Hamlin	Toyota	73.633
2010	Denny Hamlin	Toyota	71.619
2011	Tony Stewart	Chevrolet	68.648
2012	Jimmie Johnson	Chevrolet	77.677

MARTINSVILLE SPEEDWAY

MICHIGAN INTERNATIONAL SPEEDWAY

MICHIGAN INTERNATIONAL SPEEDWAY
It's your speed.

12626 US Hwy., 12 Brooklyn, MI 49230 • **Tickets:** 1-866-GO-NASCAR or 1-800-354-1010 • **Web site:** www.MISpeedway.com
Facebook: www.facebook.com/MISpeedway • **Twitter:** @MISpeedway

//// NASCAR®

CONFIGURATION

Distance: 2 miles
Banking: 18 degrees in turns,
12 degrees on frontstretch,
5 degrees on backstretch

TRACK RECORDS

Qualifying Records
Marcos Ambrose, 203.241 mph
(35.426 sec.), Set June 16, 2012

Race Record
Dale Jarrett, 173.977 mph,
Set June 13, 1999

2013 TRACK LAYOUT

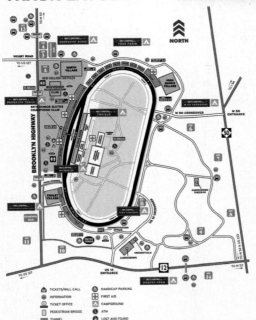

2013 SCHEDULE
June 15: NASCAR Nationwide Series
June 16: NASCAR Sprint Cup Series
August 17: NASCAR Camping World Truck Series
August 18: NASCAR Sprint Cup Series

TRACK OFFICIALS

Rodger Curtis *President*

PR CONTACTS
Sammie Lukaskiewicz *Senior Director of Communications*

VISITOR INFORMATION
Brooklyn-Irish Hills Chamber of Commerce
(517) 592-8907 – **www.brooklynmi.com**

DIRECTIONS
From Detroit: go west on I-94 to Hwy. 12. Take Hwy. 12 West
(exit 181A). Track is located one mile west of Hwy. 12 and
M-50.

QUICKEN LOANS 400

OFFICIAL RACE RESULTS: RACE #15 – JUNE 17, 2012

NASCAR SPRINT CUP SERIES RACE RESULTS

Fin Pos	Str Pos	Car No	Series Driver	Team	Laps	Points	Bonus Points	Status
1	17	88	Dale Earnhardt Jr.	Diet Mtn Dew/The Dark Knight Rises/Natl Guard Chev	200	48	5	Running
2	8	14	Tony Stewart	Office Depot/Mobil 1 Chevrolet	200	43	1	Running
3	6	17	Matt Kenseth	Ford EcoBoost Ford	200	42	1	Running
4	3	16	Greg Biffle	3M/Salute Ford	200	41	1	Running
5	10	48	Jimmie Johnson	Lowe's Chevrolet	200	39	0	Running
6	28	24	Jeff Gordon	DuPont Chevrolet	200	39	1	Running
7	13	15	Clint Bowyer	5-hour Energy Toyota	200	38	1	Running
8	21	42	Juan Pablo Montoya	Target Chevrolet	200	37	1	Running
9	1	9	Marcos Ambrose	Stanley Ford	200	36	1	Running
10	2	29	Kevin Harvick	Budweiser Folds of Honor Chevrolet	200	34	0	Running
11	42	99	Carl Edwards	Fastenal Ford	200	33	0	Running
12	16	56	Martin Truex Jr.	NAPA Auto Parts Toyota	200	32	0	Running
13	25	2	Brad Keselowski	Miller Lite Dodge	200	32	1	Running
14	19	1	Jamie McMurray	McDonald's Chevrolet	200	31	1	Running
15	5	39	Ryan Newman	US ARMY Chevrolet	199	29	0	Running
16	31	47	Bobby Labonte	Charter Toyota	199	28	0	Running
17	15	43	Aric Almirola	Medallion Ford	199	27	0	Running
18	32	83	Landon Cassill	Burger King Toyota	199	26	0	Running
19	20	22	AJ Allmendinger	Shell Pennzoil Dodge	199	25	0	Running
20	24	13	Casey Mears	Valvoline NEXTGEN Ford	199	24	0	Running
21	33	31	Jeff Burton	Caterpillar Chevrolet	199	24	1	Running
22	18	27	Paul Menard	Menards/Duracell Chevrolet	199	22	0	Running
23	38	34	David Ragan	Front Row Motorsports Ford	199	21	0	Running
24	22	33	Austin Dillon (i)	American Ethanol Chevrolet	198	0	0	Running
25	36	36	Dave Blaney	SealWrap Chevrolet	198	20	1	Running
26	39	93	Travis Kvapil	Burger King Toyota	197	18	0	Running
27	35	38	David Gilliland	Long John Silver's Ford	197	18	1	Running
28	12	78	Regan Smith	Furniture Row Chevrolet	197	16	0	Running
29	14	55	Mark Martin	Aaron's Dream Machine Toyota	195	15	0	Engine
30	26	51	Kurt Busch	Phoenix Construction Services, Inc. Chevrolet	194	14	0	Running
31	40	32	Ken Schrader	Federated Auto Parts Ford	193	13	0	Running
32	34	18	Kyle Busch	Snickers Toyota	157	12	0	Running
33	4	5	Kasey Kahne	Farmers Insurance Chevrolet	151	11	0	Accident
34	11	11	Denny Hamlin	FedEx Office Toyota	132	10	0	Accident
35	9	20	Joey Logano	The Home Depot Toyota	125	9	0	Accident
36	41	10	Tony Raines	Tommy Baldwin Racing Chevrolet	68	8	0	Vibration
37	43	49	J.J. Yeley	America Israel Racing/JPO Absorbents Toyota	67	8	1	Brakes
38	27	98	Michael McDowell	Presbyterian Healthcare Ford	41	6	0	Vibration
39	29	19	Mike Bliss (i)	Humphrey Smith Racing, LLC Toyota	35	0	0	Overheating
40	37	87	Joe Nemechek (i)	AM/FM Energy Wood & Pellet Stoves Toyota	32	0	0	Vibration
41	23	23	Scott Riggs	North TX Pipe Chevrolet	27	3	0	Power Steering
42	30	26	Josh Wise #	MDS Transport Ford	9	2	0	Engine
43	7	21	Trevor Bayne (i)	Motorcraft/Quick Lane Tire & Auto Center Ford	7	0	0	Engine

Sunoco Rookie of the Year Contender. Bonus Points: includes winner, lap leader & most laps led points. (i) = Ineligible for driver points in this series. Failed to qualify: (2) #30 David Stremme; #74 Stacy Compton.

RACE COMMENTS: Before an estimated crowd of 82,000, Dale Earnhardt Jr. won the Quicken Loans 400, his 19th NASCAR Sprint Cup Series victory. Prior to the green flag, the following cars dropped to the rear of the field for the reasons indicated: #39, 48 (engine change).

RACE STATISTICS

TIME OF RACE: 2 hours, 52 minutes, 29 seconds
AVERAGE SPEED: 139.144 mph
MARGIN OF VICTORY: 5.393 seconds
COORS LIGHT POLE AWARD: Marcos Ambrose (203.241 mph, 35.426 secs.)
3M LAP LEADER: Dale Earnhardt Jr. (95 Laps)
AMERICAN ETHANOL GREEN FLAG RESTART AWARD: Greg Biffle
DIRECTV CREW CHIEF OF THE RACE: Greg Biffle (crew chief Matt Puccia)
FREESCALE "WIDE OPEN": Matt Kenseth
MAHLE CLEVITE ENGINE BUILDER OF THE RACE: Hendrick Engines (#88)

MOBIL 1 OIL DRIVER OF THE RACE: Tony Stewart
MOOG STEERING AND SUSPENSION PROBLEM SOLVER OF THE RACE: Jimmie Johnson (crew chief Chad Knaus, 0.345 seconds)
NASCAR SPRINT CUP LEADER BONUS: No winner: rolls over to $90,000 at next event++
USG IMPROVING THE FINISH: Carl Edwards (31 places)
CAUTION FLAGS: 8 cautions for 39 laps. [Beneficiary in Brackets] 3–4 (Car #38, 51 Accident Turn 2 [None]); 11–16 (Oil On Track From #26 [None]); 27–30 (Competition [None]); 52–55 (Competition [10]); 82–86 (Debris [51]); 121–125 (Car

#51 Spin Turn 2 [55]); 127–132 (Car #5, 20, 38 Accident Backstretch [None]); 134–140 (Car #11, 39 Accident Turn 4 [22]).
LAP LEADERS: 23 lead changes among 14 drivers. Ambrose 1–5, Biffle 6–26, Ambrose 27–31, Kenseth 32–48, Ambrose 49–52, Yeley 53, Biffle 54–68, Ambrose 69, Earnhardt Jr. 70–82, Blaney 83, Gilliland 84, Earnhardt Jr. 85–86, Stewart 87–104, Earnhardt Jr. 105–117, J. Gordon 118, Montoya 119–122, J. Gordon 123–125, Earnhardt Jr. 126–162, Biffle 163–164, Bowyer 165, McMurray 166, Keselowski 167–169, Burton 170, Earnhardt Jr. 171–200.

++Rollover money awarded at year's end, amount not included in race winnings.

POINT LEADERS
(After 15 Races)

1	MATT KENSETH	565
2	Dale Earnhardt Jr.	561
3	Greg Biffle	548
4	Jimmie Johnson	532
5	Denny Hamlin	514
6	Kevin Harvick	504
7	Martin Truex Jr.	497
8	Tony Stewart	491
9	Clint Bowyer	481
10	Brad Keselowski	458
11	Carl Edwards	456
12	Kyle Busch	432

PURE MICHIGAN 400
OFFICIAL RACE RESULTS: RACE #23 – AUGUST 19, 2012

NASCAR SPRINT CUP SERIES RACE RESULTS

Fin Pos	Str Pos	Car No	Driver	Team	Laps	Points	Bonus Points	Status
1	13	16	Greg Biffle	3M Ford	201	47	4	Running
2	19	2	Brad Keselowski	Miller Lite Dodge	201	43	1	Running
3	5	5	Kasey Kahne	Farmers Insurance Chevrolet	201	41	0	Running
4	22	88	Dale Earnhardt Jr.	National Guard/Diet Mountain Dew Chevrolet	201	41	1	Running
5	8	9	Marcos Ambrose	Stanley Ford	201	39	0	Running
6	2	99	Carl Edwards	Geek Squad Ford	201	39	1	Running
7	12	15	Clint Bowyer	5-hour Energy Toyota	201	38	1	Running
8	15	39	Ryan Newman	WIX Chevrolet	201	36	0	Running
9	10	27	Paul Menard	Menards/Pittsburgh Paints Chevrolet	201	36	1	Running
10	7	56	Martin Truex Jr.	NAPA Auto Parts Toyota	201	35	1	Running
11	21	11	Denny Hamlin	FedEx Office Toyota	201	34	1	Running
12	17	22	Sam Hornish Jr. (i)	Shell Pennzoil Dodge	201	0	0	Running
13	23	18	Kyle Busch	Interstate Batteries Toyota	201	31	0	Running
14	24	1	Jamie McMurray	Bass Pro Shops/Mercury Chevrolet	201	30	0	Running
15	30	93	Travis Kvapil	Burger King/Dr. Pepper Toyota	201	29	0	Running
16	20	29	Kevin Harvick	Jimmy John's Chevrolet	201	28	0	Running
17	4	17	Matt Kenseth	Fifth Third Bank Ford	201	28	1	Running
18	36	38	David Gilliland	Taco Bell Ford	201	26	0	Running
19	32	31	Jeff Burton	Wheaties Chevrolet	201	25	0	Running
20	41	43	Aric Almirola	Eckrich Ford	201	24	0	Running
21	39	10	David Reutimann	TMone.com Chevrolet	200	23	0	Running
22	28	47	Bobby Labonte	Clorox Toyota	199	22	0	Running
23	37	34	David Ragan	Long John Silver's Ford	199	21	0	Running
24	6	21	Trevor Bayne (i)	Motorcraft/Quick Lane Tire & Auto Center Ford	199	0	0	Running
25	9	83	Landon Cassill	Burger King/Dr. Pepper Toyota	198	20	1	Running
26	25	42	Juan Pablo Montoya	Target Chevrolet	197	18	0	Running
27	3	48	Jimmie Johnson	Lowe's Chevrolet	195	18	1	Engine
28	11	24	Jeff Gordon	Drive to End Hunger/AARP Chevrolet	167	16	0	Engine
29	18	78	Regan Smith	Furniture Row/Farm American Chevrolet	154	15	0	Running
30	26	51	Kurt Busch	Hendrickcars.com Chevrolet	135	14	0	Accident
31	16	20	Joey Logano	The Home Depot Toyota	132	13	0	Running
32	14	14	Tony Stewart	MOBIL 1/Office Depot Chevrolet	109	12	0	Engine
33	40	32	T.J. Bell (i)	Southern Pride Trucking/U.S. Chrome Ford	108	0	0	Transmission
34	31	30	David Stremme	Inception Motorsports Toyota	72	10	0	Electrical
35	1	55	Mark Martin	Aaron's Dream Machine Toyota	64	11	2	Accident
36	35	87	Joe Nemechek (i)	AM/FM Energy Wood & Pellet Stoves Toyota	38	0	0	Rear Gear
37	29	13	Casey Mears	GEICO Ford	36	7	0	Vibration
38	42	36	Dave Blaney	Tommy Baldwin Racing Chevrolet	34	6	0	Vibration
39	43	98	Mike Skinner	Phil Parsons Racing Ford	25	5	0	Electrical
40	34	26	Josh Wise #	MDS Transport Ford	21	4	0	Suspension
41	38	23	Scott Riggs	North Texas Pipe Chevrolet	20	3	0	Suspension
42	27	91	Reed Sorenson (i)	Plinker Tactical Toyota	15	0	0	Overheating
43	33	19	Jason Leffler (i)	Plinker Tactical Ford	14	0	0	Fuel Pressure

Sunoco Rookie of the Year Contender. Bonus Points: includes winner, lap leader & most laps led points. (i) = Ineligible for driver points in this series. Failed to qualify: (2) #33 Stephen Leicht; #37 J.J. Yeley.

RACE COMMENTS: Before an estimated crowd of 83,000, Greg Biffle won the Pure Michigan 400, his 18th NASCAR Sprint Cup Series victory. Prior to the green flag, the following cars dropped to the rear of the field for the reasons indicated: #43, 88 (back-up car); #22 (driver change); #48 (engine change).

RACE STATISTICS

TIME OF RACE: 2 hours, 46 minutes, 44 seconds
AVERAGE SPEED: 144.662 mph
MARGIN OF VICTORY: 0.416 seconds
COORS LIGHT POLE AWARD: Mark Martin (199.706 mph. 36.053 secs.)
3M LAP LEADER: Mark Martin (54 Laps)
AMERICAN ETHANOL GREEN FLAG RESTART AWARD: Martin Truex Jr.
DIRECTV CREW CHIEF OF THE RACE: Carl Edwards (crew chief Chad Norris)
FREESCALE "WIDE OPEN": Greg Biffle
MAHLE CLEVITE ENGINE BUILDER OF THE RACE: Roush Yates Engines (#16)
MOBIL 1 OIL DRIVER OF THE RACE: Clint Bowyer

MOOG STEERING AND SUSPENSION PROBLEM SOLVER OF THE RACE: Dale Earnhardt Jr. (crew chief Steve Letarte, 0.364 seconds)
NASCAR SPRINT CUP LEADER BONUS: Greg Biffle ($160,000 ++)
USG IMPROVING THE FINISH: Aric Almirola (21 places)
CAUTION FLAGS: 8 cautions for 35 laps. [Beneficiary in Brackets] 7–9 (Car #38 Spin Turn 4 [None]); 65–73 (Car #5, 42, 47, 55 Accident Turn 4 [34]); 77–80 (Car #9, 78 Accident Turn 4 [93]); 90–92 (Car #20 Accident Turn 3 [10]); 137–140 (Car #51 Accident Turn 3 [38]); 144–147 (Debris [1]); 182–186 (Car #21 Accident Turn 1 [43]);

197–199 (Oil On Track From #48 [38]).
LAP LEADERS: 26 lead changes among 13 drivers. Martin 1–35, Keselowski 36–38, Johnson 39–42, Hornish Jr. 43–45, Martin 46–64, Kenseth 65–69, Truex Jr. 70, Bowyer 71–89, Truex Jr. 90–100, Biffle 101–110, Hornish Jr. 111–112, Menard 113, Earnhardt Jr. 114–123, Johnson 124–125, Keselowski 126–128, Biffle 129–137, Earnhardt Jr. 138–152, Johnson 153–165, Keselowski 166–168, Edwards 169, Hornish Jr. 170–173, Hamlin 174, Menard 175–181, Cassill 182, Keselowski 183–190, Johnson 191–194, Biffle 195–201.

++Rollover money awarded at year's end, amount not included in race winnings.

POINT LEADERS
(After 23 Races)

1	GREG BIFFLE	823
2	Matt Kenseth	803
3	Dale Earnhardt Jr.	801
4	Jimmie Johnson	795
5	Brad Keselowski	776
6	Martin Truex Jr.	763
7	Clint Bowyer	757
8	Kevin Harvick	738
9	Tony Stewart	728
10	Denny Hamlin	727
11	Kasey Kahne	694
12	Carl Edwards	689

MICHIGAN INTERNATIONAL SPEEDWAY

TOP 20 ACTIVE NASCAR SPRINT CUP SERIES DRIVERS (MINIMUM 2 STARTS)

Driver	Races	Wins	Top 5s	Top 10s	Poles	Total Laps	Laps Led	Avg. Start	Avg. Finish
Carl Edwards	17	2	9	13	0	3310	275	21.1	8.2
Matt Kenseth	27	2	12	17	0	5172	284	18.3	9.6
Jeff Gordon	40	2	18	25	5	7592	954	11.1	11.7
Greg Biffle	20	3	9	12	1	3930	517	13.3	11.8
Tony Stewart	28	1	11	19	0	5162	224	19.4	11.9
Denny Hamlin	14	2	5	7	0	2649	149	14.5	13.6
Mark Martin	54	5	18	31	1	9886	965	11.7	14.0
Bill Elliott	61	7	17	29	6	11,212	1,004	11.0	14.6
Dale Earnhardt Jr.	27	2	6	10	2	5252	293	15.0	14.8
Kevin Harvick	24	1	3	8	0	4660	149	18.1	14.8
Brian Vickers	14	1	2	8	3	2631	95	10.9	14.9
Jimmie Johnson	22	0	4	9	0	4209	565	9.2	15.2
Kasey Kahne	18	1	7	8	2	3445	49	11.2	15.7
Kyle Busch	16	1	3	5	0	2909	169	15.0	16.4
Jeff Burton	38	0	4	9	2	7151	76	19.6	16.6
Martin Truex Jr.	14	0	2	4	0	2729	71	13.4	16.6
Clint Bowyer	14	0	0	6	0	2690	27	18.4	16.7
Bobby Labonte	41	3	9	16	4	7411	241	16.1	17.0
Ryan Newman	23	2	5	7	1	4278	97	11.4	17.7
David Ragan	12	0	1	2	0	2403	12	24.4	18.2

MICHIGAN 400

Year	Driver	Car	Average Speed
1969	Cale Yarborough	69 Mercury	139.254
1970	*Cale Yarborough	69 Mercury	138.302
1971	Bobby Allison	69 Mercury	149.567
1972	David Pearson	71 Mercury	146.639
1973	David Pearson	71 Mercury	153.485
1974	Richard Petty	74 Dodge	127.098
1975	David Pearson	Mercury	131.398
1976	David Pearson	Mercury	141.148
1977	Cale Yarborough	Chevrolet	135.033
1978	Cale Yarborough	Oldsmobile	149.563
1979	Buddy Baker	Chevrolet	135.798
1980	Benny Parsons	Chevrolet	131.808
1981	Bobby Allison	Buick	130.589
1982	Cale Yarborough	Buick	118.101
1983	Cale Yarborough	Chevrolet	138.728
1984	Bill Elliott	Ford	134.705
1985	Bill Elliott	Ford	144.724
1986	Bill Elliott	Ford	138.851
1987	Dale Earnhardt	Chevrolet	148.454
1988	Rusty Wallace	Pontiac	153.551
1989	Bill Elliott	Ford	139.023
1990	Dale Earnhardt	Chevrolet	150.219
1991	Davey Allison	Ford	160.912
1992	Davey Allison	Ford	152.672
1993	Ricky Rudd	Chevrolet	148.484
1994	Rusty Wallace	Ford	125.022
1995	Bobby Labonte	Chevrolet	134.141
1996	Rusty Wallace	Ford	166.033
1997	Ernie Irvan	Ford	153.338
1998	Mark Martin	Ford	158.695
1999	Dale Jarrett	Ford	173.997
2000	Tony Stewart	Pontiac	143.926
2001	Jeff Gordon	Chevrolet	134.203
2002	Matt Kenseth	Ford	154.822
2003	Kurt Busch	Ford	131.219
2004	Ryan Newman	Dodge	139.292
2005	Greg Biffle	Ford	150.596
2006	Kasey Kahne	Dodge	118.788
2007	Carl Edwards	Ford	148.072
2008	Dale Earnhardt Jr.	Chevrolet	145.375
2009	Mark Martin	Chevrolet	155.491
2010	Denny Hamlin	Toyota	156.386
2011	Denny Hamlin	Toyota	153.029
2012	Dale Earnhardt Jr.	Chevrolet	139.144

*Race changed to 400 miles.

PURE MICHIGAN 400

Year	Driver	Car	Average Speed
1969	David Pearson	69 Ford	115.508
1970	*Charlie Glotzbach	69 Dodge	147.571
1971	Bobby Allison	69 Mercury	149.862
1972	David Pearson	71 Mercury	134.416
1974	David Pearson	73 Mercury	133.045
1975	Richard Petty	74 Dodge	107.583
1976	David Pearson	Mercury	140.078
1977	Darrell Waltrip	Chevrolet	137.944
1978	David Pearson	Mercury	129.566
1979	Richard Petty	Chevrolet	130.376
1980	Cale Yarborough	Chevrolet	145.352
1981	Richard Petty	Buick	123.457
1982	Bobby Allison	Buick	136.454
1983	Cale Yarborough	Chevrolet	147.511
1984	Darrell Waltrip	Chevrolet	153.863
1985	Bill Elliott	Ford	137.430
1986	Bill Elliott	Ford	135.376
1987	Bill Elliott	Ford	138.648
1988	Davey Allison	Ford	156.863
1989	Rusty Wallace	Pontiac	157.704
1990	Mark Martin	Ford	138.822
1991	Dale Jarrett	Ford	142.972
1992	Harry Gant	Oldsmobile	146.056
1993	Mark Martin	Ford	144.564
1994	Geoff Bodine	Ford	139.914
1995	Bobby Labonte	Chevrolet	157.739
1996	Dale Jarrett	Ford	139.792
1997	Mark Martin	Ford	126.883
1998	Jeff Gordon	Chevrolet	151.995
1999	Bobby Labonte	Pontiac	144.332
2000	Rusty Wallace	Ford	132.597
2001	Sterling Marlin	Dodge	140.513
2002	Dale Jarrett	Ford	140.556
2003	Ryan Newman	Dodge	127.310
2004	Greg Biffle	Ford	139.063
2005	Jeremy Mayfield	Dodge	141.551
2006	Matt Kenseth	Ford	135.097
2007	Kurt Busch	Dodge	117.012
2008	Carl Edwards	Ford	140.351
2009	Brian Vickers	Toyota	131.531
2010	Kevin Harvick	Chevrolet	144.029
2011	Kyle Busch	Toyota	150.898
2012	Greg Biffle	Ford	144.662

*Race changed to 400 miles.

MICHIGAN INTERNATIONAL SPEEDWAY

MID-OHIO
SPORTS CAR COURSE

MID-OHIO SPORTS CAR COURSE

7721 Steam Corners Road, Lexington, OH 44904 • **Tickets:** 1-866-GO-NASCAR or 1-800-MIDOHIO • **Web site:** www.midohio.com
Facebook: www.facebook.com/MidOhioSportsCarCourse • **Twitter:** @FollowMidOhio

CONFIGURATION
Distance: 2.258 miles
Number of Turns: 13

TRACK RECORDS
Qualifying Records
NA

Race Record
NA

2013 TRACK LAYOUT

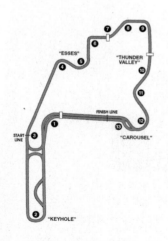

2013 SCHEDULE
August 17: NASCAR Nationwide Series

TRACK OFFICIALS

Craig Rust *President*

PR CONTACTS
Jesse Ghiorzi *Marketing & Communications Manager*

VISITOR INFORMATION
Lexington Business & Growth Association
(419) 884-1119 – **www.lexington-oh.com**

DIRECTIONS
From the North: Take I-71 South to exit 165. Turn right at State Route 97 West. Turn left at East Main Street/US-42 and continue to follow East Main/US-97. Turn left at Lexington Steam Corners Road. Mid-Ohio is two miles ahead on the right. *From the South:* Take I-71 North to exit 151. Turn right off the ramp and follow State Route 95 East for two miles. Turn left on State Route 314 North and drive 15 miles. Turn right on Lexington Steam Corners Road. Mid-Ohio is one mile ahead on the left. *From the East:* Take US-30 West to I-71 South. Take I-71 South to exit 165. Turn right at State Route 97 West. Turn left at East Main Street/US-42 and continue to follow East Main. Turn left at Lexington Steam Corners Road. Mid-Ohio is two miles ahead on the right. *From the West:* Take US-30 East to the Fourth Street Exit. Turn right on Fourth Street then right at State Route 314 South. Turn left on Lexington Steam Corners Road. Mid-Ohio is two miles ahead on the right.

NEW HAMPSHIRE MOTOR SPEEDWAY

1122 Route 106 North Loudon, NH 03307 • **Tickets:** 1-866-GO-NASCAR or 1-603-783-4931
Web site: www.nhms.com • **Facebook:** www.facebook.com/nhmotorspeedway • **Twitter:** @NHMS

NEW HAMPSHIRE MOTOR SPEEDWAY

NASCAR

CONFIGURATION
Distance: 1.058 miles
Banking: Variable banking at 2 & 7 degrees

TRACK RECORDS
Qualifying Records
Ryan Newman, 135.232 mph
(28.165 sec.), Set July 15, 2011

Race Record
Jeff Burton, 117.134 mph,
Set July 13, 1997

2013 TRACK LAYOUT

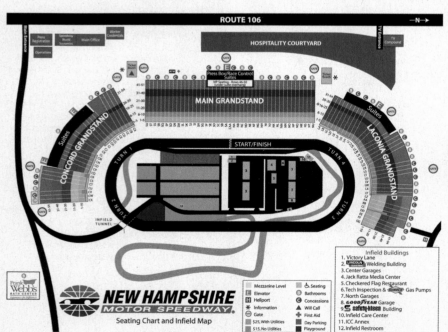

NEW HAMPSHIRE
MOTOR SPEEDWAY
Seating Chart and Infield Map

Infield Buildings
1. Victory Lane
2. LINCOLN Welding Building
3. Center Garages
4. Jack Ratta Media Center
5. Checkered Flag Restaurant
6. Tech Inspection & Gas Pumps
7. North Garages
8. GOODYEAR Garage
9. safety-kleen Building
10. Infield Care Center
11. ICC Annex
12. Infield Restroom

Mezzanine Level
Elevator
Heliport
Information
Gate
$25, With Utilities
$15, No Utilities

Seating
Bathrooms
Concessions
Will Call
First Aid
Day Parking
Playground

2013 SCHEDULE
July 13: NASCAR Nationwide Series
July 14: NASCAR Sprint Cup Series
September 22: NASCAR Sprint Cup Series

TRACK OFFICIALS

Jerry Gappens *President*

PR CONTACTS
Kristen Costa *Director of Communications*

VISITOR INFORMATION
Greater Concord Chamber of Commerce
(603) 224-2508 – www.concordnhchamber.com

DIRECTIONS
From the south: Take Interstate 93 to Exit 15E, Interstate 393. Take Exit 3. Turn left onto Route 106 North. NHMS will be 9 miles north on the right. *From the North*: Take I-93 to the Tilton Exit 20 to Route 140 through Belmont to Route 106 South. Follow Route 106 South to the Speedway which is approximately 7 miles on the left.

LENOX INDUSTRIAL TOOLS 301

OFFICIAL RACE RESULTS: RACE #19 – JULY 15, 2012

 NASCAR Sprint CUP SERIES

NASCAR SPRINT CUP SERIES RACE RESULTS

Fin Pos	Str Pos	Car No	Series Driver	Team	Laps	Points	Bonus Points	Status
1	2	5	Kasey Kahne	Farmers Insurance Chevrolet	301	47	4	Running
2	3	11	Denny Hamlin	FedEx Freight Toyota	301	44	2	Running
3	5	15	Clint Bowyer	5-hour Energy Toyota	301	42	1	Running
4	9	88	Dale Earnhardt Jr.	National Guard/Diet Mountain Dew Chevrolet	301	40	0	Running
5	22	2	Brad Keselowski	Miller Lite Dodge	301	40	1	Running
6	8	24	Jeff Gordon	DuPont Chevrolet	301	39	1	Running
7	7	48	Jimmie Johnson	Lowe's Chevrolet	301	38	1	Running
8	12	29	Kevin Harvick	Rheem Chevrolet	301	36	0	Running
9	11	16	Greg Biffle	3M/WB Mason/Post-it Ford	301	35	0	Running
10	6	39	Ryan Newman	ARMY ROTC Chevrolet	301	34	0	Running
11	4	56	Martin Truex Jr.	NAPA Auto Parts Toyota	301	33	0	Running
12	10	14	Tony Stewart	MOBIL 1/Office Depot Chevrolet	301	32	0	Running
13	27	17	Matt Kenseth	NESN Ford	301	31	0	Running
14	16	20	Joey Logano	The Home Depot Toyota	301	30	0	Running
15	15	55	Brian Vickers	MyClassicGarage.com/Aaron's Toyota	301	29	0	Running
16	1	18	Kyle Busch	Interstate Batteries Toyota	301	29	1	Running
17	13	27	Paul Menard	Menards/Duracell Chevrolet	301	27	0	Running
18	21	99	Carl Edwards	Fastenal/LENOX Ford	301	26	0	Running
19	20	9	Marcos Ambrose	DeWalt Ford	301	25	0	Running
20	28	1	Jamie McMurray	Bass Pro Shops/Allstate Chevrolet	300	24	0	Running
21	25	31	Jeff Burton	Caterpillar Chevrolet	300	23	0	Running
22	24	22	Sam Hornish Jr. (i)	Shell Pennzoil/AAA Dodge	300	0	0	Running
23	18	47	Bobby Labonte	Luke & Associates Toyota	300	21	0	Running
24	14	51	Kurt Busch	Phoenix Construction Services Chevrolet	299	21	1	Running
25	31	42	Juan Pablo Montoya	Degree Chevrolet	299	19	0	Running
26	17	78	Regan Smith	Furniture Row/Farm American Chevrolet	298	18	0	Running
27	39	38	David Gilliland	Taco Bell Ford	298	17	0	Running
28	23	43	Aric Almirola	Medallion Financial Ford	298	16	0	Running
29	29	83	Landon Cassill	Burger King/Dr. Pepper Toyota	297	15	0	Running
30	30	93	Travis Kvapil	Burger King/Dr. Pepper Toyota	297	14	0	Running
31	37	32	Ken Schrader	Federated Auto Parts Ford	294	13	0	Running
32	43	33	Stephen Leicht #	LittleJoesAutos.com Chevrolet	293	12	0	Running
33	26	10	David Reutimann	Mohawk Northeast Chevrolet	229	11	0	Engine
34	19	34	David Ragan	Front Row Motorsports Ford	139	10	0	Engine
35	40	30	David Stremme	Inception Motorsports Toyota	101	9	0	Vibration
36	33	13	Casey Mears	GEICO Ford	91	8	0	Vibration
37	32	26	Josh Wise #	MDS Transport Ford	82	7	0	Brakes
38	34	87	Joe Nemechek (i)	AM/FM Energy Wood & Pellet Stoves Toyota	71	0	0	Brakes
39	35	36	Dave Blaney	Tommy Baldwin Racing Chevrolet	68	5	0	Brakes
40	36	98	Michael McDowell	Phil Parsons Racing Ford	63	4	0	Vibration
41	41	23	Scott Riggs	North Texas Pipe Chevrolet	32	3	0	Vibration
42	42	79	Kelly Bires	Team Kyle/Bestway Disposal Ford	19	2	0	Brakes
43	38	49	J.J. Yeley	Robinson-Blakely Racing Toyota	4	1	0	Engine

Sunoco Rookie of the Year Contender. Bonus Points: includes winner, lap leader & most laps led points. (i) = Ineligible for driver points in this series. Failed to qualify: (1) #19 Mike Bliss.

RACE COMMENTS: Before an estimated crowd of 95,000, Kasey Kahne won the LENOX Industrial Tools 301, his 14th NASCAR Sprint Cup Series victory.

RACE STATISTICS

TIME OF RACE: 2 hours, 44 minutes, 24 seconds

AVERAGE SPEED: 116.226 mph

MARGIN OF VICTORY: 2.738 seconds

COORS LIGHT POLE AWARD: Kyle Busch (133.417 mph. 28.548 secs.)

3M LAP LEADER: Denny Hamlin (150 Laps)

AMERICAN ETHANOL GREEN FLAG RESTART AWARD: Kasey Kahne

DIRECTV CREW CHIEF OF THE RACE: Denny Hamlin (crew chief Darian Grubb)

FREESCALE "WIDE OPEN": Denny Hamlin

MAHLE CLEVITE ENGINE BUILDER OF THE RACE: Toyota Racing Development

(TRD) (#11)

MOBIL 1 OIL DRIVER OF THE RACE: Denny Hamlin

MOOG STEERING AND SUSPENSION PROBLEM SOLVER OF THE RACE: Clint Bowyer (crew chief Brian Pattie, 0.129 seconds)

NASCAR SPRINT CUP LEADER BONUS: No winner: rolls over to $130,000 at next event++

SUNOCO ROOKIE OF THE RACE: Stephen Leicht

USG IMPROVING THE FINISH: Matt Kenseth (14 places)

CAUTION FLAGS: 3 cautions for 15 laps. [Beneficiary in Brackets] 90–93 (Debris [47]); 191–196 (Debris [27]); 235–239 (Oil On Track From #10 [48]).

LAP LEADERS: 16 lead changes among 8 drivers. Ky. Busch 1–66, Hamlin 67, J. Gordon 68, Johnson 69, Ku. Busch 70–71, Hamlin 72–89, J. Gordon 90–93, Hamlin 94–153, Johnson 154, Keselowski 155–156, Ky. Busch 157, Hamlin 158–190, Keselowski 191, Ky. Busch 192–196, Hamlin 197–234, Bowyer 235, Kahne 236–301.

++Rollover money awarded at year's end, amount not included in race winnings.

POINT LEADERS
(After 19 Races)

1	MATT KENSETH	707
2	Dale Earnhardt Jr.	691
3	Greg Biffle	667
4	Jimmie Johnson	656
5	Denny Hamlin	628
6	Kevin Harvick	622
7	Tony Stewart	618
8	Martin Truex Jr.	617
9	Clint Bowyer	614
10	Brad Keselowski	613
11	Carl Edwards	567
12	Kasey Kahne	547

SYLVANIA 300

OFFICIAL RACE RESULTS: RACE #28– SEPTEMBER 23, 2012

NASCAR SPRINT CUP SERIES RACE RESULTS

Fin Pos	Str Pos	Car No	Series Driver	Team	Laps	Points	Bonus Points	Status
1	32	11	Denny Hamlin	FedEx Freight Toyota	300	48	5	Running
2	20	48	Jimmie Johnson	Lowe's Chevrolet	300	43	1	Running
3	1	24	Jeff Gordon	Drive to End Hunger Chevrolet	300	42	1	Running
4	12	15	Clint Bowyer	5-hour Energy Toyota	300	40	0	Running
5	6	5	Kasey Kahne	Farmers Insurance Chevrolet	300	40	1	Running
6	15	2	Brad Keselowski	Miller Lite Dodge	300	39	1	Running
7	3	14	Tony Stewart	Mobil 1/Office Depot Chevrolet	300	38	1	Running
8	18	20	Joey Logano	The Home Depot Toyota	300	36	0	Running
9	4	55	Brian Vickers	Freightline Jet Edge Toyota	300	36	1	Running
10	8	39	Ryan Newman	Aspen Dental Chevrolet	300	34	0	Running
11	16	29	Kevin Harvick	Budweiser Chevrolet	300	33	0	Running
12	7	27	Paul Menard	Sylvania/Menards Chevrolet	300	32	0	Running
13	14	88	Dale Earnhardt Jr.	AMP Energy/Diet Mtn. Dew/Nat'l Guard Chev.	300	31	0	Running
14	25	17	Matt Kenseth	Zest Ford	300	31	1	Running
15	11	31	Jeff Burton	Wheaties Chevrolet	300	29	0	Running
16	22	78	Regan Smith	Furniture Row/Farm American Chevrolet	300	28	0	Running
17	9	56	Martin Truex Jr.	NAPA Auto Parts Toyota	300	27	0	Running
18	13	16	Greg Biffle	3M/GE Appliances Ford	300	26	0	Running
19	5	99	Carl Edwards	Aflac Ford	300	25	0	Running
20	17	47	Bobby Labonte	Bush's Beans Toyota	299	24	0	Running
21	10	22	Sam Hornish Jr. (i)	Shell Pennzoil Dodge	299	0	0	Running
22	24	42	Juan Pablo Montoya	Energizer Chevrolet	299	22	0	Running
23	19	43	Aric Almirola	Trim Fit Ford	298	21	0	Running
24	21	9	Marcos Ambrose	Stanley Ford	298	20	0	Running
25	23	51	Kurt Busch	Phoenix Construction Chevrolet	298	19	0	Running
26	29	1	Jamie McMurray	LiftMaster Chevrolet	298	18	0	Running
27	28	83	Landon Cassill	Burger King/Dr. Pepper Toyota	298	17	0	Running
28	2	18	Kyle Busch	M&M's Toyota	298	17	1	Running
29	26	34	David Ragan	Shriner's Hospital for Children Ford	297	15	0	Running
30	34	10	David Reutimann	Tommy Baldwin Racing Chevrolet	296	14	0	Running
31	33	93	Travis Kvapil	Burger King/Dr. Pepper Toyota	296	13	0	Running
32	37	38	David Gilliland	Taco Bell Ford	296	12	0	Running
33	42	32	Mike Olsen	North Country Ford	289	11	0	Running
34	39	33	Stephen Leicht #	LittleJoesAutos.com Chevrolet	151	10	0	Brakes
35	43	30	David Stremme	Inception Motorsports Toyota	145	9	0	Transmission
36	30	13	Casey Mears	GEICO Ford	100	9	1	Vibration
37	31	98	Michael McDowell	Phil Parsons Racing Ford	97	7	0	Vibration
38	27	95	Scott Speed	Jordan Truck Sales Ford	88	6	0	Suspension
39	36	87	Joe Nemechek (i)	AM/FM Energy Wood Stoves/Genny Light Toyota	78	0	0	Brakes
40	41	36	Tony Raines	Tommy Baldwin Racing Chevrolet	68	4	0	Rear Gear
41	40	37	J.J. Yeley	MAXQWorkForce.com Chevrolet	29	3	0	Brakes
42	35	91	Reed Sorenson (i)	Plinker Tactical Chevrolet	21	0	0	Brakes
43	38	79	Kelly Bires	BBI/Bestway Ford	20	1	0	Brakes

Sunoco Rookie of the Year Contender. Bonus Points: includes winner, lap leader & most laps led points. (i) = Ineligible for driver points in this series. Failed to qualify: (4) #23 Scott Riggs; #49 Jason Leffler; #19 Jeff Green; 26 Josh Wise.

RACE COMMENTS: Before an estimated crowd of 98,000, Denny Hamlin won the SYLVANIA 300, his 22nd NASCAR Sprint Cup Series victory. Prior to the green flag, the following cars dropped to the rear of the field for the reasons indicated: #22 (driver change) and #55 (engine change).

RACE STATISTICS

TIME OF RACE: 2 hours, 43 minutes, 2 seconds
AVERAGE SPEED: 116.81 mph
MARGIN OF VICTORY: 2.675 seconds
COORS LIGHT POLE AWARD: Jeff Gordon (134.911 mph. 28.232 secs.)
3M LAP LEADER: Denny Hamlin (193 Laps)
AMERICAN ETHANOL GREEN FLAG RESTART AWARD: Denny Hamlin
DIRECTV CREW CHIEF OF THE RACE: Tony Stewart (crew chief Steve Addington)
FREESCALE "WIDE OPEN": Clint Bowyer
MAHLE CLEVITE ENGINE BUILDER OF THE

RACE: Toyota Racing Development (TRD) (#11)
MOBIL 1 OIL DRIVER OF THE RACE: Denny Hamlin
MOOG STEERING AND SUSPENSION PROBLEM SOLVER OF THE RACE: Brian Vickers (crew chief Rodney Childers, 0.298 seconds)
NASCAR SPRINT CUP LEADER BONUS: No winner: rolls over to $20,000 at next event++
SUNOCO ROOKIE OF THE RACE: Stephen Leicht
USG IMPROVING THE FINISH: Denny Hamlin (31 places)
CAUTION FLAGS: 4 cautions for 17 laps.

[Beneficiary in Brackets] 42–45 (Competition [98]); 130–133 (Debris Turn 3 [47]); 179–183 (Debris Turn 1 [22]); 274–277 (Debris Turn 2 [99]).
LAP LEADERS: 17 lead changes among 10 drivers. J. Gordon 1–3, Stewart 4–41, J. Gordon 42, Mears 43, J. Gordon 44–45, Ky. Busch 46–93, Hamlin 94–107, Kahne 108, Johnson 109, Kenseth 110, Keselowski 111–112, Hamlin 113–179, Vickers 180–184, Hamlin 185–244, Johnson 245, J. Gordon 246, Keselowski 247–248, Hamlin 249–300.

++Rollover money awarded at year's end, amount not included in race winnings.

POINT LEADERS

(After 28 Races)

1	JIMMIE JOHNSON	2096
2	Brad Keselowski	2095
3	Denny Hamlin	2089
4	Tony Stewart	2086
5	Kasey Kahne	2081
6	Clint Bowyer	2081
7	Dale Earnhardt Jr.	2070
8	Kevin Harvick	2065
9	Greg Biffle	2063
10	Martin Truex Jr.	2062
11	Matt Kenseth	2061
12	Jeff Gordon	2051

TOP 20 ACTIVE NASCAR SPRINT CUP SERIES DRIVERS (MINIMUM 2 STARTS)

Driver	Races	Wins	Top 5s	Top 10s	Poles	Total Laps	Laps Led	Avg. Start	Avg. Finish
Denny Hamlin	14	2	7	10	0	4166	417	13.6	7.9
Jimmie Johnson	22	3	8	15	0	6407	321	11.1	9.5
Jeff Gordon	36	3	16	21	4	10,456	1,316	9.9	10.5
Tony Stewart	28	3	14	17	1	7825	1,218	11.3	11.4
Mark Martin	30	1	9	14	2	8840	514	15.3	12.5
Ryan Newman	22	3	6	15	6	6389	720	8.0	12.7
Kevin Harvick	24	1	5	12	1	7021	319	14.1	13.7
Jeff Burton	36	4	8	13	0	10,091	783	19.4	13.8
Matt Kenseth	26	0	5	12	0	7571	89	21.1	14.0
Brad Keselowski	7	0	2	4	1	2030	10	15.6	14.0
Carl Edwards	17	0	2	3	0	5065	70	15.2	14.5
Kurt Busch	24	3	7	11	0	6750	438	13.0	14.8
Martin Truex Jr.	14	0	3	5	0	4068	50	11.6	14.9
Clint Bowyer	14	2	4	6	1	4157	475	12.6	15.1
Joey Logano	9	1	2	4	0	2629	15	23.7	15.3
Dale Earnhardt Jr.	27	0	7	11	0	7483	351	16.4	16.1
Kasey Kahne	18	1	3	8	0	4930	274	12.9	16.2
Greg Biffle	21	1	5	8	0	5947	86	15.5	16.3
Kyle Busch	16	1	4	6	1	4652	345	12.1	16.7
Bobby Labonte	36	0	5	11	1	10,240	72	16.1	16.9

NEW HAMPSHIRE 300

Year	Driver	Car	Average Speed
1993	Rusty Wallace	Pontiac	105.947
1994	Ricky Rudd	Ford	87.599
1995	Jeff Gordon	Chevrolet	107.029
1996	Ernie Irvan	Ford	98.930
1997	Jeff Burton	Ford	117.134
1998	Jeff Burton	Ford	102.996
1999	Jeff Burton	Ford	101.876
2000	Tony Stewart	Pontiac	103.145
2001	Dale Jarrett	Ford	102.131
2002	Ward Burton	Dodge	92.342
2003	Jimmie Johnson	Chevrolet	96.924
2004	Kurt Busch	Ford	97.862
2005	Tony Stewart	Chevrolet	102.608
2006	Kyle Busch	Chevrolet	101.384
2007	Denny Hamlin	Chevrolet	108.215
2008	Kurt Busch	Dodge	106.719
2009	Joey Logano	Toyota	97.497
2010	Jimmie Johnson	Chevrolet	113.308
2011	Ryan Newman	Chevrolet	104.100
2012	Kasey Kahne	Chevrolet	116.226

SYLVANIA 300

Year	Driver	Car	Average Speed
1997	Jeff Gordon	Chevrolet	100.364
1998	Jeff Gordon	Chevrolet	112.078
1999	Joe Nemechek	Chevrolet	100.673
2000	Jeff Burton	Ford	102.003
2001	Robby Gordon	Chevrolet	103.594
2002	Ryan Newman	Ford	105.081
2003	Jimmie Johnson	Chevrolet	106.580
2004	Kurt Busch	Ford	109.753
2005	Ryan Newman	Dodge	95.891
2006	Kevin Harvick	Chevrolet	102.195
2007	Clint Bowyer	Chevrolet	110.475
2008	Greg Biffle	Ford	105.468
2009	Mark Martin	Chevrolet	100.753
2010	Clint Bowyer	Chevrolet	106.769
2011	Tony Stewart	Chevrolet	116.679
2012	Denny Hamlin	Toyota	116.810

PHOENIX INTERNATIONAL RACEWAY

7602 S. Avondale Blvd., Avondale, AZ 85323 • **Tickets:** 1-866-GO-NASCAR or 1-866-408-7223 • **Web site:** www.phoenixraceway.com
Facebook: www.facebook.com/PhoenixRaceway • **Twitter:** @PhoenixRaceway

NASCAR

CONFIGURATION
Distance: 1 mile
**Banking: 11 degrees in Turns
1 & 2, 9 degrees in Turns 3 & 4,
3 degrees on frontstretch,
9 degrees on backstretch**

TRACK RECORDS
Qualifying Records
**Kyle Busch, 138.766 mph
(25.943 sec.),
Set November 9, 2012**

Race Record
**Tony Stewart, 118.132 mph,
Set November 7, 1999**

2013 TRACK LAYOUT

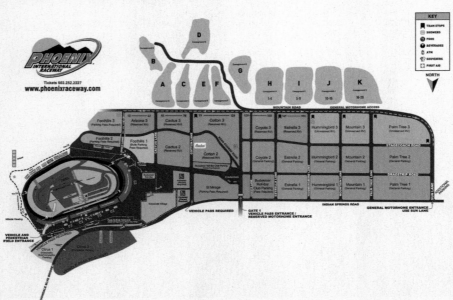

2013 SCHEDULE
March 2: NASCAR Nationwide Series
March 3: NASCAR Sprint Cup Series
November 8: NASCAR Camping World Truck Series
November 9: NASCAR Nationwide Series
November 10: NASCAR Sprint Cup Series

TRACK OFFICIALS

Bryan Sperber *President*

PR CONTACTS
Jennifer Jepson *Manager of Communications*
David Alvarez *Manager of Communications*

VISITOR INFORMATION
Greater Phoenix Chamber of Commerce
(602) 495-2195 – www.phoenixchamber.com

DIRECTIONS
From downtown and Sky Harbor Airport: I-10 West to any of
four exits: 99th Ave., Avondale Blvd., Litchfield Rd. or Estrella
Pkwy. Follow exits south for six miles. All surface roads are
well marked. Track is on left, one mile beyond Avondale Blvd.
and Southern Ave. intersection. Credential office is located at
Gate 1 intersection of Indian Springs Rd. and El Mirage Rd.

SUBWAY FRESH FIT 500
OFFICIAL RACE RESULTS: RACE #2 – MARCH 4, 2012

NASCAR SPRINT CUP SERIES RACE RESULTS

Fin Pos	Str Pos	Car No	Driver	Team	Laps	Points	Bonus Points	Status
1	13	11	Denny Hamlin	FedEx Office Toyota	312	47	4	Running
2	8	29	Kevin Harvick	Rheem Chevrolet	312	44	2	Running
3	7	16	Greg Biffle	3MWraps.com Ford	312	41	0	Running
4	4	48	Jimmie Johnson	Lowe's/Kobalt Tools Chevrolet	312	41	1	Running
5	28	2	Brad Keselowski	Miller Lite Dodge	312	40	1	Running
6	12	18	Kyle Busch	M&M's Brown Toyota	312	39	1	Running
7	25	56	Martin Truex Jr.	NAPA Filters Toyota	312	38	1	Running
8	30	24	Jeff Gordon	Drive to End Hunger Chevrolet	312	37	1	Running
9	1	55	Mark Martin	Aaron's Toyota	312	36	1	Running
10	9	20	Joey Logano	The Home Depot Toyota	312	34	0	Running
11	5	42	Juan Pablo Montoya	Target Chevrolet	312	33	0	Running
12	18	43	Aric Almirola	Smithfield/Allez Cuisine Ford	312	32	0	Running
13	26	17	Matt Kenseth	Best Buy Ford	312	32	1	Running
14	29	88	Dale Earnhardt Jr.	National Guard/Diet Mountain Dew Chev.	312	30	0	Running
15	19	51	Kurt Busch	Phoenix Construction Services Chevrolet	312	30	1	Running
16	17	47	Bobby Labonte	Kingsford/Scotts Toyota	312	28	0	Running
17	24	99	Carl Edwards	SUBWAY Ford	312	27	0	Running
18	15	22	AJ Allmendinger	Shell Pennzoil Dodge	311	26	0	Running
19	41	93	Travis Kvapil	Burger King/Dr. Pepper Toyota	311	25	0	Running
20	3	78	Regan Smith	Furniture Row Racing/Farm American Chev.	311	24	0	Running
21	6	39	Ryan Newman	WIX Filters Chevrolet	310	23	0	Running
22	2	14	Tony Stewart	Office Depot/Mobil 1 Chevrolet	310	23	1	Running
23	23	36	Dave Blaney	Ollie's Bargain Outlet Chevrolet	309	21	0	Running
24	42	32	Mike Bliss (i)	Southern Pride Trucking/U.S. Chrome Ford	309	0	0	Running
25	34	34	David Ragan	Barrett-Jackson Ford	309	20	1	Running
26	35	49	J.J. Yeley	America Israel Racing Toyota	309	18	0	Running
27	40	33	Brendan Gaughan	South Point Hotel & Casino Chevrolet	308	17	0	Running
28	36	38	David Gilliland	Rick Santorum for President Ford	308	16	0	Running
29	43	30	David Stremme	Inception Motorsports Toyota	306	15	0	Running
30	16	15	Clint Bowyer	5-hour Energy Toyota	306	14	0	Running
31	20	27	Paul Menard	Menards/Tarkett Chevrolet	303	13	0	Running
32	14	9	Marcos Ambrose	Stanley Ford	295	12	0	Engine
33	11	31	Jeff Burton	Wheaties Chevrolet	291	12	1	Engine
34	10	5	Kasey Kahne	Farmers Insurance Chevrolet	274	10	0	Running
35	22	83	Landon Cassill	Burger King/Dr. Pepper Toyota	272	9	0	Running
36	32	10	David Reutimann	Accell Construction Chevrolet	248	8	0	Engine
37	21	1	Jamie McMurray	Bass Pro Shops/Tracker Boats Chevrolet	212	8	1	Engine
38	33	26	Josh Wise #	Morristown Drivers Service Ford	110	6	0	Vibration
39	31	13	Casey Mears	GEICO Ford	109	5	0	Accident
40	38	87	Joe Nemechek (i)	AM/FM Energy Wood & Pellet Stoves Toyota	62	0	0	Brakes
41	39	7	Robby Gordon	SPEED Energy/Bashas' Dodge	33	3	0	Brakes
42	27	23	Scott Riggs	North Texas Pipe Chevrolet	29	2	0	Brakes
43	37	98	Michael McDowell	Curb Records Ford	8	1	0	Brakes

Sunoco Rookie of the Year Contender. Bonus Points: includes winner, lap leader & most laps led points. (i) = Ineligible for driver points in this series. Failed to qualify: (1) #37 Timmy Hill.

RACE COMMENTS: Before an estimated crowd of 76,000, Denny Hamlin won the Subway Fresh Fit 500, his 18th NASCAR Sprint Cup Series victory and first at Phoenix International Raceway.

RACE STATISTICS

TIME OF RACE: 2 hours, 50 minutes, 35 seconds
AVERAGE SPEED: 110.085 mph
MARGIN OF VICTORY: 7.315 seconds
COORS LIGHT POLE AWARD: Mark Martin (136.815 mph. 26.313 secs.)
3M LAP LEADER: Kevin Harvick (88 Laps)
AMERICAN ETHANOL GREEN FLAG RESTART AWARD: Kevin Harvick
DIRECTV CREW CHIEF OF THE RACE: Kevin Harvick (crew chief Shane Wilson)
FREESCALE "WIDE OPEN": Denny Hamlin
MAHLE CLEVITE ENGINE BUILDER OF THE RACE: Earnhardt-Childress Racing Engines (#29)

MOBIL 1 OIL DRIVER OF THE RACE: Denny Hamlin
MOOG STEERING AND SUSPENSION PROBLEM SOLVER OF THE RACE: Martin Truex Jr. (crew chief Chad Johnston, 0.230 seconds)
NASCAR SPRINT CUP LEADER BONUS: Denny Hamlin ($20,000 ++)
SUNOCO ROOKIE OF THE RACE: Josh Wise
USG IMPROVING THE FINISH: Jeff Gordon (22 places)
CAUTION FLAGS: 7 cautions for 37 laps. [Beneficiary in Brackets] 17–20 (Debris On Track [None]); 60–64 (Debris On Track [49]); 112–117 (Car #13 Accident Turn 2 [36]); 134–140 (Car #1,22,27 Accident Frontstretch [93]); 229–233 (Debris On Track [42]); 248–253 (Fluid On Track [47]); 257–260 (Car #39,99 Accident Turn 3 [93]).
LAP LEADERS: 25 lead changes among 15 drivers. Martin 1, Stewart 2–10, Johnson 11–16, Harvick 17–59, Johnson 60, Bliss 61, Ragan 62, Johnson 63–64, Ku. Busch 65–66, Johnson 67–112, Ky. Busch 113–140, Harvick 141–144, Ky. Busch 145–168, Harvick 169–183, Keselowski 184–186, Hamlin 187, J. Gordon 188, Kenseth 189, Burton 190–196, Truex Jr. 197–206, McMurray 207, Harvick 208–228, Hamlin 229, Truex Jr. 230–248, Harvick 249–253, Hamlin 254–312.

++Rollover money awarded at year's end, amount not included in race winnings.

POINT LEADERS
(After 2 Races)

1	**DENNY HAMLIN**	89
2	Greg Biffle	83
3	Kevin Harvick	81
4	Matt Kenseth	79
5	Dale Earnhardt Jr.	72
6	Martin Truex Jr.	71
7	Mark Martin	71
8	Joey Logano	70
9	Kyle Busch	66
10	Carl Edwards	63
11	Bobby Labonte	58
12	Brad Keselowski	52

PHOENIX INTERNATIONAL RACEWAY

ADVOCARE 500
OFFICIAL RACE RESULTS: RACE #35 - NOVEMBER 11, 2012

PHOENIX INTERNATIONAL RACEWAY

NASCAR SPRINT CUP SERIES RACE RESULTS

Fin Pos	Str Pos	Car No	Series Driver	Team	Laps	Points	Bonus Points	Status
1	19	29	Kevin Harvick	Budweiser Chevrolet	319	47	4	Running
2	3	11	Denny Hamlin	FedEx Ground Toyota	319	43	1	Running
3	1	18	Kyle Busch	M&M's Toyota	319	43	2	Running
4	4	5	Kasey Kahne	Farmers Insurance Chevrolet	319	40	0	Running
5	12	39	Ryan Newman	Quicken Loans/U.S. Army Chevrolet	319	40	1	Running
6	14	2	Brad Keselowski	Miller Lite Dodge	319	39	1	Running
7	20	16	Greg Biffle	Filtrete Ford	319	37	0	Running
8	6	78	Kurt Busch	Furniture Row/Farm American Chevrolet	319	36	0	Running
9	7	27	Paul Menard	Rheem/Menards Chevrolet	319	35	0	Running
10	10	55	Mark Martin	Aaron's Dream Machine Toyota	319	35	1	Running
11	13	99	Carl Edwards	Fastenal Ford	319	33	0	Running
12	21	42	Juan Pablo Montoya	Target Chevrolet	319	32	0	Running
13	33	31	Jeff Burton	Caterpillar Chevrolet	319	31	0	Running
14	22	17	Matt Kenseth	Ford EcoBoost Ford	319	30	0	Running
15	30	47	Bobby Labonte	Vektor Vodka Toyota	319	29	0	Running
16	5	43	Aric Almirola	Farmland Ford	319	28	0	Running
17	37	10	Danica Patrick (i)	GoDaddy Racing Chevrolet	318	0	0	Running
18	17	9	Marcos Ambrose	Black & Decker Ford	318	26	0	Running
19	9	14	Tony Stewart	MOBIL 1/Office Depot Chevrolet	318	25	0	Running
20	39	93	Travis Kvapil	Burger King/Dr Pepper Toyota	318	25	1	Running
21	23	88	Dale Earnhardt Jr.	Diet Mtn. Dew/AMP Energy/Nat'l Guard Chev.	317	23	0	Running
22	25	13	Casey Mears	GEICO Ford	317	22	0	Running
23	18	1	Jamie McMurray	Bass Pro Shops/Allstate Chevrolet	317	21	0	Running
24	8	51	Regan Smith	Phoenix Construction Chevrolet	316	20	0	Running
25	27	83	Landon Cassill	Burger King/Dr. Pepper Toyota	316	19	0	Running
26	42	36	Dave Blaney	Accell Construction Chevrolet	316	18	0	Running
27	15	20	Joey Logano	Dollar General Toyota	312	17	0	Accident
28	16	15	Clint Bowyer	5-hour Energy Toyota	312	16	0	Accident
29	41	32	Timmy Hill (i)	U.S. Chrome/TMone Ford	312	0	0	Running
30	11	24	Jeff Gordon	DuPont Chevrolet	309	14	0	Accident
31	26	22	Sam Hornish Jr. (i)	Shell Pennzoil Dodge	299	0	0	Accident
32	24	48	Jimmie Johnson	Lowe's/Kobalt Tools Chevrolet	281	12	0	Running
33	29	34	David Ragan	Barrett Jackson Ford	280	11	0	Accident
34	32	30	David Stremme	Inception Motorsports Toyota	86	10	0	Brakes
35	35	33	Stephen Leicht #	LittleJoesAutos.com Chevrolet	74	9	0	Rear Gear
36	31	38	David Gilliland	Loan Mart Ford	50	8	0	Accident
37	38	26	Josh Wise #	MDS Transport Ford	50	7	0	Brakes
38	28	98	Michael McDowell	Phil Parson Racing Ford	36	6	0	Brakes
39	43	87	Joe Nemechek (i)	AM/FM Energy Stoves/aloft hotel tempe Toyota	30	0	0	Brakes
40	34	44	David Reutimann	No Label Ford	28	4	0	Vibration
41	36	19	Mike Bliss (i)	Plinker Tactical/Value Place Toyota	15	0	0	Accident
42	40	91	Jason Leffler (i)	Plinker Tactical/Value Place Chevrolet	10	0	0	Brakes
43	2	56	Martin Truex Jr.	NAPA Auto Parts Toyota	10	1	0	Engine

Sunoco Rookie of the Year Contender. Bonus Points: includes winner, lap leader & most laps led points. (i) = Ineligible for driver points in this series. Failed to qualify: (1) #37 J.J. Yeley.

RACE COMMENTS: Before an estimated attendance of 87,000, Kevin Harvick won the AdvoCare 500, his 19th NASCAR Sprint Cup Series victory. Prior to the green flag, the following cars dropped to the rear for the reasons indicated: #31 (backup car).

RACE STATISTICS

TIME OF RACE: 2 hours, 52 minutes, 9 seconds
AVERAGE SPEED: 111.182 mph
MARGIN OF VICTORY: 0.58 second
COORS LIGHT POLE AWARD: Kyle Busch (138.766 mph. 25.943 secs.)
3M LAP LEADER: Kyle Busch (237 Laps)
AMERICAN ETHANOL GREEN FLAG RESTART AWARD: Kyle Busch
DIRECTV CREW CHIEF OF THE RACE: Kyle Busch (crew chief Dave Rogers)
MAHLE CLEVITE ENGINE BUILDER OF THE RACE: Toyota Racing Development (#18)
MOBIL 1 OIL DRIVER OF THE RACE: Kevin Harvick

MOOG STEERING AND SUSPENSION PROBLEM SOLVER OF THE RACE: Kevin Harvick (crew chief Gil Martin, 0.226 seconds)
NASCAR SPRINT CUP LEADER BONUS: No winner: rolls over to $20,000 at next event++
USG IMPROVING THE FINISH: Jeff Burton (20 places)
CAUTION FLAGS: 8 cautions for 38 laps. [Beneficiary in Brackets] 18–20 (Car #19 Accident Turn 3 [None]); 53–59 (Car #38 Accident Turn 4 [30]); 168–173 (Debris [99]); 236–241 (Car #48 Accident Turn 4 [78]); 274–277 (Car #34 Accident Turn 4 [16]); 282–284 (Car #14 Spin Turn 2 [10]); 302–304 (Car #22 Accident Turn 3 [47]);

312–317 (Car #15,20,24,43 Accident Turn 4 {Red Flag 14 Min 58 Sec After Lap 312} [None]).
LAP LEADERS: 11 lead changes among 7 drivers. Ky. Busch 1–53, Kvapil 54–57, Martin 58–59, Ky. Busch 60–117, Hamlin 118–128, Keselowski 129–133, Hamlin 134–168, Newman 169–173, Ky. Busch 174–232, Keselowski 233–237, Ky. Busch 238–304, Harvick 305–319.

++Rollover money awarded at year's end, amount not included in race winnings.

POINT LEADERS
(After 35 Races)

1	BRAD KESELOWSKI	2371
2	Jimmie Johnson	2351
3	Kasey Kahne	2321
4	Clint Bowyer	2319
5	Denny Hamlin	2309
6	Matt Kenseth	2297
7	Greg Biffle	2293
8	Kevin Harvick	2285
9	Tony Stewart	2284
10	Jeff Gordon	2281
11	Martin Truex Jr.	2260
12	Dale Earnhardt Jr.	2211

TOP 20 ACTIVE NASCAR SPRINT CUP SERIES DRIVERS (MINIMUM 2 STARTS)

Driver	Races	Wins	Top 5s	Top 10s	Poles	Total Laps	Laps Led	Avg. Start	Avg. Finish
Jimmie Johnson	19	4	12	15	1	5966	931	13.0	6.7
Mark Martin	32	2	12	21	2	9849	836	12.0	9.1
Denny Hamlin	15	1	7	8	1	4729	399	12.8	10.3
Jeff Gordon	28	2	10	19	3	8573	389	11.1	11.5
Tony Stewart	22	1	8	11	0	6927	555	13.3	12.1
Carl Edwards	17	1	6	10	3	5091	228	11.8	12.5
Jeff Burton	27	2	7	13	0	8373	222	23.8	12.8
Kevin Harvick	20	3	6	10	0	6296	420	19.1	12.9
Kurt Busch	20	1	4	11	0	6299	750	13.1	13.3
Kyle Busch	16	1	3	10	2	4868	509	13.6	13.3
Greg Biffle	18	0	5	7	0	5544	349	14.2	13.7
Terry Labonte	19	1	4	5	0	5426	177	24.5	15.3
Juan Pablo Montoya	12	0	1	2	0	3811	104	20.3	16.1
AJ Allmendinger	8	0	0	2	1	2559	17	11.1	16.3
Marcos Ambrose	9	0	0	1	0	2862	0	16.4	16.7
Joey Logano	8	0	1	3	0	2460	0	16.1	17.0
Martin Truex Jr.	14	0	1	5	1	3844	101	11.3	17.1
Clint Bowyer	15	0	2	5	0	4679	21	19.3	17.7
Matt Kenseth	21	1	5	8	1	6066	212	20.7	17.7
Ryan Newman	21	1	8	8	4	6139	176	12.5	18.0

SUBWAY FRESH FIT 500

Year	Driver	Car	Average Speed
2005	Kurt Busch	Ford	102.707
2006	Kevin Harvick	Chevrolet	107.063
2007	Jeff Gordon	Chevrolet	107.710
2008	Jeff Gordon	Chevrolet	103.292
2009	Mark Martin	Chevrolet	108.042
2010	Ryan Newman	Chevrolet	99.372
2011	Jeff Gordon	Chevrolet	102.961
2012	Denny Hamlin	Toyota	110.085

KOBALT TOOLS 500

Year	Driver	Car	Average Speed
1988	Alan Kulwicki	Ford	90.457
1989	Bill Elliott	Ford	105.683
1990	Dale Earnhardt	Chevrolet	96.786
1991	Davey Allison	Ford	95.746
1992	Davey Allison	Ford	103.885
1993	Mark Martin	Ford	100.375
1994	Terry Labonte	Chevrolet	107.463
1995	Ricky Rudd	Ford	102.128
1996	Bobby Hamilton	Pontiac	109.709
1997	Dale Jarrett	Ford	110.824
1998	Rusty Wallace	Ford	108.211
1999	Tony Stewart	Pontiac	118.132
2000	Jeff Burton	Ford	105.041
2001	Jeff Burton	Ford	102.613
2002	Matt Kenseth	Ford	113.857
2003	Dale Earnhardt Jr.	Chevrolet	93.984
2004	Dale Earnhardt Jr.	Chevrolet	94.848
2005	Kyle Busch	Chevrolet	102.641
2006	Kevin Harvick	Chevrolet	96.131
2007	Jimmie Johnson	Chevrolet	102.989
2008	Jimmie Johnson	Chevrolet	97.804
2009	Jimmie Johnson	Chevrolet	110.486
2010	Carl Edwards	Ford	110.758
2011	Kasey Kahne	Toyota	112.918
2012	Kevin Harvick	Chevrolet	111.182

POCONO RACEWAY

Pocono Raceway
THE TRICKY TRIANGLE

1234 Long Pond Road, Long Pond, PA 18334 • **Tickets:** 1-866-GO-NASCAR or 1-800-RACEWAY • **Web site:** www.poconoraceway.com
Facebook: www.facebook.com/poconoraceway • **Twitter:** @poconoraceway

NASCAR

CONFIGURATION
Distance: 2.5 miles
Banking: 14 degrees in Turn 1,
8 degrees in Turn 2,
6 degrees in Turn 3

TRACK RECORDS
Qualifying Records
Joey Logano, 179.598 mph
(50.112 sec.), Set June 9, 2012

Race Record
Jeff Gordon, 145.384 mph,
Set June 12, 2011

2013 TRACK LAYOUT

2013 SCHEDULE
June 9: NASCAR Sprint Cup Series
August 3: NASCAR Camping World Truck Series
August 4: NASCAR Sprint Cup Series

TRACK OFFICIALS

Brandon Igdalsky
President & CEO

PR CONTACTS
Bob Pleban *Vice President of Communications*
Kevin Heaney *Manager of Interactive Marketing,*
Community Relations

VISITOR INFORMATION
Pocono Mountains Visitors Bureau
(800) POCONOS or (800) 762-6667 – www.800poconos.com

DIRECTIONS
Located on Route 115, three miles south of Interstate 80 at
exit 284 in Northeastern Pennsylvania.

POCONO 400 PRESENTED BY #NASCAR

OFFICIAL RACE RESULTS: RACE #14 – JUNE 10, 2012

NASCAR SPRINT CUP SERIES RACE RESULTS

Fin Pos	Str Pos	Car No	Driver	Team	Laps	Points	Bonus Points	Status
1	1	20	Joey Logano	The Home Depot Toyota	160	48	5	Running
2	6	55	Mark Martin	Aaron's Dream Machine Toyota	160	43	1	Running
3	22	14	Tony Stewart	MOBIL 1/Office Depot Chevrolet	160	41	0	Running
4	24	48	Jimmie Johnson	Lowe's/Kobalt Tools Chevrolet	160	40	0	Running
5	5	11	Denny Hamlin	FedEx Express Toyota	160	40	1	Running
6	16	15	Clint Bowyer	5-hour Energy Toyota	160	38	0	Running
7	14	17	Matt Kenseth	Ford EcoBoost Fusion Ford	160	38	1	Running
8	8	88	Dale Earnhardt Jr.	National Guard/Diet Mtn. Dew Chevrolet	160	37	1	Running
9	3	27	Paul Menard	Menards/Sylvania Chevrolet	160	35	0	Running
10	11	1	Jamie McMurray	Banana Boat Chevrolet	160	35	1	Running
11	2	99	Carl Edwards	Kellogg's/Cheez-It Ford	160	33	0	Running
12	18	39	Ryan Newman	HAAS Automation Chevrolet	160	32	0	Running
13	9	9	Marcos Ambrose	DeWalt Ford	160	31	0	Running
14	21	29	Kevin Harvick	Rheem Chevrolet	160	30	0	Running
15	20	31	Jeff Burton	The Armed Forces Foundation Chevrolet	160	29	0	Running
16	7	78	Regan Smith	Furniture Row Chevrolet	160	28	0	Running
17	17	42	Juan Pablo Montoya	Target Chevrolet	160	28	1	Running
18	31	2	Brad Keselowski	Miller Lite Dodge	160	26	0	Running
19	12	24	Jeff Gordon	DuPont Chevrolet	160	25	0	Running
20	23	56	Martin Truex Jr.	NAPA Auto Parts Toyota	160	24	0	Running
21	25	51	David Reutimann	Phoenix Construction Services Chevrolet	160	23	0	Running
22	27	47	Bobby Labonte	Bubba Burgers Toyota	160	22	0	Running
23	36	38	David Gilliland	ModSpace Motorsports Ford	160	22	1	Running
24	13	16	Greg Biffle	3M/Rite Aid/NextCare Ford	160	21	1	Running
25	42	10	Dave Blaney	Tommy Baldwin Racing Chevrolet	159	19	0	Running
26	37	93	Travis Kvapil	Burger King/Dr. Pepper Toyota	159	18	0	Running
27	34	34	David Ragan	Taco Bell Ford	159	18	1	Running
28	29	43	Aric Almirola	Transportation Impact Ford	158	16	0	Running
29	10	5	Kasey Kahne	Farmers Insurance Chevrolet	139	15	0	Accident
30	4	18	Kyle Busch	M&M's Toyota	76	14	0	Engine
31	19	22	AJ Allmendinger	Shell Pennzoil Dodge	64	13	0	Accident
32	40	36	Tony Raines	SealWrap.com Chevrolet	47	12	0	Accident
33	43	33	Stephen Leicht #	LittleJoesAutos.com Chevrolet	39	11	0	Brakes
34	30	98	Michael McDowell	Presbyterian Healthcare Ford	37	10	0	Rear Gear
35	26	13	Casey Mears	GEICO Ford	36	9	0	Brakes
36	32	49	J.J. Yeley	America Israel Racing/JPO Absorbents Toyota	33	8	0	Accident
37	33	87	Joe Nemechek (i)	AM/FM Energy Wood & Pellet Stoves Toyota	30	0	0	Brakes
38	28	19	Mike Bliss (i)	Humphrey Smith Racing Toyota	26	0	0	Brakes
39	39	74	Stacy Compton	Turn One Racing/Country Suites Chevrolet	24	5	0	Transmission
40	38	23	Scott Riggs	North Texas Pipe Chevrolet	19	4	0	Overheating
41	41	32	Reed Sorenson (i)	Herr Foods/Hero Energy Shot Ford	12	0	0	Accident
42	35	26	Josh Wise #	MDS Transport Ford	12	2	0	Brakes
43	15	83	Landon Cassill	Burger King - Real Fruit Smoothies Toyota	1	1	0	Accident

Sunoco Rookie of the Year Contender. Bonus Points: includes winner, lap leader & most laps led points. (i) = Ineligible for driver points in this series. Failed to qualify: (1) #30 David Stremme.

RACE COMMENTS: Before an estimated crowd of 100,000, Joey Logano won the Pocono 400 presented by #NASCAR, his second NASCAR Sprint Cup Series victory. Prior to the green flag, no cars dropped to the rear of the field.

RACE STATISTICS

TIME OF RACE: 3 hours, 3 minutes, 12 seconds
AVERAGE SPEED: 131.004 mph
MARGIN OF VICTORY: 0.997 seconds
COORS LIGHT POLE AWARD: Joey Logano (179.598 mph. 50.112 secs.)
3M LAP LEADER: Joey Logano (49 Laps)
AMERICAN ETHANOL GREEN FLAG RESTART AWARD: Joey Logano
DIRECTV CREW CHIEF OF THE RACE: Joey Logano (crew chief Jason Ratcliff)
MAHLE CLEVITE ENGINE BUILDER OF THE RACE: Toyota Racing Development (TRD) (#20)

MOBIL 1 OIL DRIVER OF THE RACE: Joey Logano
MOOG STEERING AND SUSPENSION PROBLEM SOLVER OF THE RACE: Tony Stewart (crew chief Steve Addington, 0.540 seconds)
NASCAR SPRINT CUP LEADER BONUS: No winner: rolls over to $80,000 at next event++
USG IMPROVING THE FINISH: Jimmie Johnson (20 places)
CAUTION FLAGS: 7 cautions for 35 laps. [Beneficiary in Brackets] 3–5 (Car #83, 56, 22 Accident Turn 3 [None]); 15–20 (Car #32, 36, 49 Accident Turn 3 [22]); 67–71 (Car #22 Accident Turn 2 [10]); 75–82 (Debris Turn 1 [None]); 125–128 (Debris Short Chute [38]); 138–143 (Car #5 Accident Turn 2 [51]); 150–152 (Debris Turn 2 [2]).
LAP LEADERS: 19 lead changes among 10 drivers. Logano 1–16, McMurray 17–22, Hamlin 23–31, McMurray 32, Earnhardt Jr. 33–43, Kenseth 44, Biffle 45–46, Ragan 47, Hamlin 48–59, Earnhardt Jr. 60–67, McMurray 68–74, Biffle 75–91, Kenseth 92–101, Logano 102–103, Montoya 104–106, Gilliland 107–108, Earnhardt Jr. 109–125, Logano 126–152, Martin 153–156, Logano 157–160.

++Rollover money awarded at year's end, amount not included in race winnings.

POINT LEADERS
(After 14 Races)

1	MATT KENSETH	523
2	Dale Earnhardt Jr.	513
3	Greg Biffle	507
4	Denny Hamlin	504
5	Jimmie Johnson	493
6	Kevin Harvick	470
7	Martin Truex Jr.	465
8	Tony Stewart	448
9	Clint Bowyer	443
10	Brad Keselowski	426
11	Carl Edwards	423
12	Kyle Busch	420

PENNSYLVANIA 400
OFFICIAL RACE RESULTS: RACE #21 – AUGUST 5, 2012

NASCAR SPRINT CUP SERIES RACE RESULTS

Fin Pos	Str Pos	Car No	Series Driver	Team	Laps	Points	Bonus Points	Status
1	27	24	Jeff Gordon	Drive to End Hunger Chevrolet	98	47	4	Running
2	4	5	Kasey Kahne	Farmers Insurance Chevrolet	98	43	1	Running
3	15	56	Martin Truex Jr.	NAPA Auto Parts Toyota	98	41	0	Running
4	31	2	Brad Keselowski	Miller Lite Dodge	98	41	1	Running
5	28	14	Tony Stewart	Office Depot Back to School Chevrolet	98	39	0	Running
6	9	39	Ryan Newman	HAAS Automation/Quicken Loans Chevrolet	98	38	0	Running
7	17	99	Carl Edwards	Fastenal Ford	98	37	0	Running
8	19	15	Clint Bowyer	5-hour Energy Toyota	98	36	0	Running
9	11	78	Regan Smith	Furniture Row/Farm American Chevrolet	98	35	0	Running
10	5	9	Marcos Ambrose	Stanley Ford	98	34	0	Running
11	3	27	Paul Menard	Menards/Serta Chevrolet	98	33	0	Running
12	18	55	Mark Martin	Aaron's Dream Machine Toyota	98	32	0	Running
13	14	20	Joey Logano	The Home Depot Toyota	98	31	0	Running
14	10	48	Jimmie Johnson	Lowe's Chevrolet	98	32	2	Running
15	12	16	Greg Biffle	3M Ford	98	29	0	Running
16	21	29	Kevin Harvick	Budweiser Chevrolet	98	28	0	Running
17	16	1	Jamie McMurray	Bass Pro Shops/Allstate Chevrolet	98	28	1	Running
18	13	43	Aric Almirola	Automotive Lift Institute Ford	98	26	0	Running
19	25	22	Sam Hornish Jr. (i)	Shell Pennzoil Dodge	98	0	0	Running
20	1	42	Juan Pablo Montoya	Target Chevrolet	98	25	1	Running
21	26	38	David Gilliland	ModSpace Motorsports Ford	98	23	0	Running
22	23	31	Jeff Burton	Enersys/Odyssey Battery Chevrolet	98	22	0	Running
23	7	17	Matt Kenseth	Zest Ford	98	22	1	Running
24	24	10	David Reutimann	TMone.com Chevrolet	97	20	0	Running
25	37	93	Travis Kvapil	Burger King/Dr. Pepper Toyota	97	19	0	Running
26	22	83	Landon Cassill	Burger King/Dr. Pepper Toyota	97	18	0	Running
27	39	47	Bobby Labonte	Scott Products Toyota	96	17	0	Running
28	32	34	David Ragan	Taco Bell Ford	96	16	0	Running
29	2	11	Denny Hamlin	FedEx Ground Toyota	90	16	1	Accident
30	6	51	Kurt Busch	Phoenix Construction Services Chevrolet	84	15	1	Accident
31	41	32	Jason White (i)	Zaxby's Ford	81	0	0	Transmission
32	8	88	Dale Earnhardt Jr.	Diet Mtn. Dew/AMP Energy/Nat'l Guard Chev	80	13	1	Running
33	20	18	Kyle Busch	M&M's Toyota	74	11	0	Accident
34	36	30	David Stremme	Inception Motorsports Toyota	43	10	0	Transmission
35	29	13	Casey Mears	GEICO Ford	40	9	0	Brakes
36	38	87	Joe Nemechek (i)	AM/FM Energy Wood & Pellet Stoves Toyota	37	0	0	Brakes
37	34	26	Josh Wise #	MDS Transport Ford	34	7	0	Brakes
38	42	36	Tony Raines	@Tmone/CRM Hiring Veterans Chevrolet	31	6	0	Fuel Pump
39	30	19	Mike Bliss (i)	Plinker Tactical Toyota	29	0	0	Overheating
40	35	37	J.J. Yeley	Max Q Motorsports Chevrolet	27	4	0	Brakes
41	43	98	Mike Skinner	TRAQM.com Ford	26	3	0	Rear Gear
42	40	91	Reed Sorenson (i)	Plinker Tactical Toyota	10	0	0	Brakes
43	33	23	Scott Riggs	North Texas Pipe Chevrolet	9	1	0	Brakes

Sunoco Rookie of the Year Contender. Bonus Points: includes winner, lap leader & most laps led points. (i) = Ineligible for driver points in this series. Failed to qualify: (1) #33 Stephen Leicht.

RACE COMMENTS: Before an estimated crowd of 85,000, Jeff Gordon won the Pennsylvania 400, his 86th NASCAR Sprint Cup Series victory. Prior to the green flag, the following car dropped to the rear of the field for the reason indicated: #36 (engine change).

RACE STATISTICS

TIME OF RACE: 1 hours, 45 minutes, 34 seconds
AVERAGE SPEED: 139.249 mph
MARGIN OF VICTORY: Under Caution
COORS LIGHT POLE AWARD: Juan Pablo Montoya (176.043 mph. 51.124 secs.)
3M LAP LEADER: Jimmie Johnson (44 Laps)
AMERICAN ETHANOL GREEN FLAG RESTART AWARD: Juan Pablo Montoya
DIRECTV CREW CHIEF OF THE RACE: Paul Menard (crew chief Richard Labbe)
FREESCALE "WIDE OPEN": Martin Truex Jr.
MAHLE CLEVITE ENGINE BUILDER OF THE RACE: Hendrick Engines (#24)
MOBIL 1 OIL DRIVER OF THE RACE: Martin Truex Jr.
MOOG STEERING AND SUSPENSION PROBLEM SOLVER OF THE RACE: Martin Truex Jr. (crew chief Chad Johnston, -2.264 seconds)
NASCAR SPRINT CUP LEADER BONUS: No winner: rolls over to $150,000 at next event++
USG IMPROVING THE FINISH: Jeff Gordon (26 places)
CAUTION FLAGS: 3 cautions for 14 laps. [Beneficiary in Brackets] 20–22 (Car #18 Accident Turn 1 [None]); 87–90 (Car #51 Accident Turn 2 [42]); 92–98 (Car #11, 16, 17, 31, 48 Accident Turn 1 [38]).

LAP LEADERS: 13 lead changes among 10 drivers. Montoya 1–7, Hamlin 8–10, Earnhardt Jr. 11–20, McMurray 21–23, Keselowski 24–31, Earnhardt Jr. 32–38, Johnson 39–46, Kenseth 47, Kahne 48, Ku. Busch 49–51, Johnson 52–75, Kenseth 76–78, Johnson 79–90, J. Gordon 91–98.

++Rollover money awarded at year's end, amount not included in race winnings.

POINT LEADERS
(After 21 Races)

1	DALE EARNHARDT JR.	744
2	Matt Kenseth	739
3	Greg Biffle	738
4	Jimmie Johnson	736
5	Martin Truex Jr.	694
6	Tony Stewart	691
7	Brad Keselowski	690
8	Denny Hamlin	683
9	Kevin Harvick	681
10	Clint Bowyer	679
11	Kasey Kahne	622
12	Carl Edwards	619

POCONO RACEWAY

ALL TIME LEADERS AND PAST WINNERS

TOP 20 ACTIVE NASCAR SPRINT CUP SERIES DRIVERS (MINIMUM 2 STARTS)

Driver	Races	Wins	Top 5s	Top 10s	Poles	Total Laps	Laps Led	Avg. Start	Avg. Finish
Jimmie Johnson	22	2	9	15	2	4138	562	9.3	9.0
Jeff Gordon	40	6	18	28	2	7437	965	11.4	10.2
Denny Hamlin	14	4	8	9	2	2538	663	5.6	10.7
Mark Martin	52	0	20	34	3	9490	448	9.3	11.1
Tony Stewart	28	2	11	20	2	5198	156	12.4	11.3
Ryan Newman	22	1	7	10	2	4097	163	9.8	12.4
Carl Edwards	16	2	5	8	0	2826	212	19.0	13.2
Kevin Harvick	24	0	5	8	0	4368	5	19.8	14.1
Matt Kenseth	26	0	3	10	0	4896	54	18.5	14.3
Brad Keselowski	6	1	2	2	0	1062	27	19.5	14.5
Martin Truex Jr.	14	0	2	5	0	2567	4	18.6	14.8
Clint Bowyer	14	0	1	7	0	2517	91	19.7	15.1
Kurt Busch	23	2	9	12	1	4155	449	11.3	16.1
Jeff Burton	38	0	7	17	0	7117	104	18.1	16.2
Terry Labonte	54	2	7	21	1	9884	162	18.3	16.5
Brian Vickers	14	0	4	5	0	2528	159	12.0	16.6
Kasey Kahne	18	1	4	6	2	3345	151	8.7	16.8
Bill Elliott	48	5	14	22	5	8524	429	13.3	17.1
Dale Earnhardt Jr.	26	0	5	9	1	4796	151	15.0	17.3
Joey Logano	8	1	1	1	2	1462	93	13.3	17.4

POCONO 400

Year	Driver	Car	Average Speed
1982	Bobby Allison	Buick	113.579
1983	Bobby Allison	Buick	128.636
1984	Cale Yarborough	Chevrolet	138.164
1985	Bill Elliott	Ford	138.974
1986	Tim Richmond	Chevrolet	113.279
1987	Tim Richmond	Chevrolet	122.166
1988	Geoff Bodine	Chevrolet	126.147
1989	Terry Labonte	Ford	131.320
1990	Harry Gant	Oldsmobile	120.600
1991	Darrell Waltrip	Chevrolet	122.666
1992	Alan Kulwicki	Ford	144.023
1993	Kyle Petty	Pontiac	138.005
1994	Rusty Wallace	Ford	128.801
1995	Terry Labonte	Chevrolet	137.720
1996	Jeff Gordon	Chevrolet	139.104
1997	Jeff Gordon	Chevrolet	139.828
1998	Jeremy Mayfield	Ford	117.809
1999	Bobby Labonte	Pontiac	118.898
2000	Jeremy Mayfield	Ford	139.741
2001	Ricky Rudd	Ford	134.389
2002	Dale Jarrett	Ford	143.426
2003	Tony Stewart	Chevrolet	134.892
2004	Jimmie Johnson	Chevrolet	112.129
2005	Carl Edwards	Ford	129.177
2006	Denny Hamlin	Chevrolet	131.656
2007	Jeff Gordon	Chevrolet	136.887
2008	Kasey Kahne	Dodge	125.209
2009	Tony Stewart	Chevrolet	138.515
2010	Denny Hamlin	Toyota	136.303
2011	Jeff Gordon	Chevrolet	145.384
2012	Joey Logano*	Toyota	131.004

*Race changed to 400 miles.

PENNSYLVANIA 400

Year	Driver	Car	Average Speed
1974	Richard Petty	74 Dodge	115.593
1975	David Pearson	Mercury	111.179
1976	Richard Petty	Dodge	115.875
1977	Benny Parsons	Chevrolet	128.379
1978	Darrell Waltrip	Chevrolet	142.540
1979	Cale Yarborough	Chevrolet	115.207
1980	Neil Bonnett	Mercury	124.395
1981	Darrell Waltrip	Buick	119.111
1982	Bobby Allison	Buick	115.496
1983	Tim Richmond	Pontiac	114.818
1984	Harry Gant	Chevrolet	121.351
1985	Bill Elliott	Ford	134.008
1986	Tim Richmond	Chevrolet	124.218
1987	Dale Earnhardt	Chevrolet	121.745
1988	Bill Elliott	Ford	122.866
1989	Bill Elliott	Ford	117.847
1990	Geoff Bodine	Ford	124.007
1991	Rusty Wallace	Pontiac	115.459
1992	Darrell Waltrip	Chevrolet	134.058
1993	Dale Earnhardt	Chevrolet	133.343
1994	Geoff Bodine	Ford	136.075
1995	Dale Jarrett	Ford	134.038
1996	Rusty Wallace	Ford	144.892
1997	Dale Jarrett	Ford	142.068
1998	Jeff Gordon	Chevrolet	134.660
1999	Bobby Labonte	Pontiac	116.982
2000	Rusty Wallace	Ford	130.662
2001	Bobby Labonte	Pontiac	134.590
2002	Bill Elliott	Dodge	125.809
2003	Ryan Newman	Dodge	127.705
2004	Jimmie Johnson	Chevrolet	126.271
2005	Kurt Busch	Ford	125.283
2006	Denny Hamlin	Chevrolet	132.626
2007	Kurt Busch	Dodge	131.627
2008	Carl Edwards	Ford	130.567
2009	Denny Hamlin	Toyota	126.396
2010	Greg Biffle	Ford	132.246
2011	Brad Keselowski	Dodge	137.878
2012	Jeff Gordon	Chevrolet	139.249

*Race changed to 400 miles.

POCONO RACEWAY

RICHMOND INTERNATIONAL RACEWAY

600 E. Laburnum Ave., Richmond, VA 23222 • **Tickets:** 1-866-GO-NASCAR or 1-866-455-RACE • **Web site:** www.rir.com
Facebook: www.facebook.com/RichmondInternationalRaceway • **Twitter:** @RIRInsider

RICHMOND INTERNATIONAL RACEWAY

CONFIGURATION

Distance: 0.75 miles
Banking: 14 degrees in turns,
8 degrees on frontstretch,
2 degrees on backstretch

TRACK RECORDS

Qualifying Records
Brian Vickers, 129.983 mph
(20.772 sec.), Set May 14, 2004

Race Record
Dale Jarrett, 109.047 mph,
Set September 6, 1997

2013 TRACK LAYOUT

2013 SCHEDULE

April 26: NASCAR Nationwide Series
April 27: NASCAR Sprint Cup Series
September 6: NASCAR Nationwide Series
September 7: NASCAR Sprint Cup Series

TRACK OFFICIALS

Dennis Bickmeier *President*

PR CONTACTS

Aimee Turner *Director of Public Relations*

VISITOR INFORMATION

Richmond Metropolitan Convention and Visitors Bureau
(800) 370-9004/(888) RICHMOND – www.visitrichmondva.com

DIRECTIONS

Richmond International Raceway is located northwest of the
city of Richmond in Henrico County near the intersection of
East/West I-64, North/South I-95, and East/West I-295.

CAPITAL CITY 400 PRESENTED BY VIRGINIA IS FOR LOVERS

OFFICIAL RACE RESULTS: RACE #9 – APRIL 28, 2012

NASCAR SPRINT CUP SERIES RACE RESULTS

Fin Pos	Str Pos	Car No	Series Driver	Team	Laps	Points	Bonus Points	Status
1	5	18	Kyle Busch	M&M's Brown Toyota	400	47	4	Running
2	10	88	Dale Earnhardt Jr.	National Guard/Diet Mountain Dew Chev.	400	42	0	Running
3	22	14	Tony Stewart	MOBIL 1/Office Depot Chevrolet	400	42	1	Running
4	7	11	Denny Hamlin	FedEx Freight Toyota	400	40	0	Running
5	9	5	Kasey Kahne	Farmers Insurance Chevrolet	400	39	0	Running
6	27	48	Jimmie Johnson	Lowe's Chevrolet	400	39	1	Running
7	23	15	Clint Bowyer	5-hour Energy Toyota	400	37	0	Running
8	1	55	Mark Martin	Aaron's Dream Machine Toyota	400	37	1	Running
9	16	2	Brad Keselowski	Miller Lite Dodge	400	35	0	Running
10	2	99	Carl Edwards	Ford EcoBoost Ford	400	36	2	Running
11	24	17	Matt Kenseth	Ford EcoBoost Ford	400	33	0	Running
12	20	42	Juan Pablo Montoya	Target Chevrolet	400	32	0	Running
13	31	27	Paul Menard	Menards/NIBCO Chevrolet	400	31	0	Running
14	37	1	Jamie McMurray	McDonald's Chevrolet	400	30	0	Running
15	12	39	Ryan Newman	Army Reserve Chevrolet	400	29	0	Running
16	4	22	AJ Allmendinger	Shell Pennzoil Dodge	400	28	0	Running
17	19	47	Bobby Labonte	Bush's Beans Toyota	400	27	0	Running
18	28	16	Greg Biffle	3M/GKAS Ford	400	26	0	Running
19	3	29	Kevin Harvick	Jimmy John's Chevrolet	400	26	1	Running
20	21	83	Landon Cassill	Burger King/Dr. Pepper Toyota	399	24	0	Running
21	26	13	Casey Mears	GEICO Ford	399	23	0	Running
22	14	9	Marcos Ambrose	Stanley Ford	399	22	0	Running
23	6	24	Jeff Gordon	DuPont Chevrolet	399	21	0	Running
24	18	20	Joey Logano	The Home Depot Toyota	399	20	0	Running
25	8	56	Martin Truex Jr.	NAPA Brakes Toyota	399	19	0	Running
26	11	43	Aric Almirola	Smithfield Helping Hungry Homes Ford	398	18	0	Running
27	15	78	Regan Smith	Furniture Row Racing/Farm American Chev.	398	17	0	Running
28	13	51	Kurt Busch	Phoenix Construction Services Chevrolet	397	16	0	Running
29	17	36	Dave Blaney	SealWrap.com Chevrolet	397	15	0	Running
30	29	93	Travis Kvapil	Burger King/Dr. Pepper Toyota	397	15	1	Running
31	30	31	Jeff Burton	BB&T Chevrolet	396	13	0	Running
32	38	34	David Ragan	Front Row Motorsports Ford	394	12	0	Running
33	33	10	David Reutimann	Tommy Baldwin Racing Chevrolet	394	11	0	Running
34	42	32	Reed Sorenson (i)	Virginia Faith & Freedom Coalition Ford	392	0	0	Running
35	40	33	Stephen Leicht	LittleJoesAutos.com/Link-Belt Chevrolet	391	9	0	Running
36	41	38	David Gilliland	Long John Silver's Ford	355	8	0	Running
37	34	30	David Stremme	Inception Motorsports Toyota	139	7	0	Brakes
38	32	26	Josh Wise #	Morristown Drivers Service Ford	127	6	0	Accident
39	25	98	Michael McDowell	Curb Records Ford	67	5	0	Brakes
40	43	74	Cole Whitt (i)	Turn One Racing Chevrolet	29	0	0	Vibration
41	35	87	Joe Nemechek (i)	AM/FM Energy Wood & Pellet Stoves Toyota	28	0	0	Brakes
42	39	19	Mike Bliss (i)	Humphrey Smith Racing Toyota	23	0	0	Rear Gear
43	36	95	Scott Speed	TWD Drywall Ford	19	1	0	Electrical

Sunoco Rookie of the Year Contender. Bonus Points: includes winner, lap leader & most laps led points. (i) = Ineligible for driver points in this series. Failed to qualify: (2) #23 Scott Riggs; #49 J.J. Yeley.

RACE COMMENTS: Before an estimated crowd of 88,000, Kyle Busch won the Capital City 400 Presented by Virginia is for Lovers, his 24th NASCAR Sprint Cup Series victory. Prior to the green flag, no cars dropped to the rear of the field.

RACE STATISTICS

TIME OF RACE: 2 hours, 51 minutes, 6 seconds
AVERAGE SPEED: 105.202 mph
MARGIN OF VICTORY: 1.095 seconds
COORS LIGHT POLE AWARD: Mark Martin (128.327 mph. 21.040 secs.)
3M LAP LEADER: Carl Edwards (206 Laps)
AMERICAN ETHANOL GREEN FLAG RESTART AWARD: Carl Edwards
DIRECTV CREW CHIEF OF THE RACE: Kyle Busch (crew chief Dave Rogers)
FREESCALE "WIDE OPEN": Tony Stewart
MAHLE CLEVITE ENGINE BUILDER OF THE RACE: Toyota Racing Development (TRD) (#18)
MOBIL 1 OIL DRIVER OF THE RACE: Kyle Busch
MOOG STEERING AND SUSPENSION PROBLEM SOLVER OF THE RACE: Clint Bowyer (crew chief Brian Pattie, 0.270 seconds)
NASCAR SPRINT CUP LEADER BONUS: No winner: rolls over to $30,000 at next event++
USG IMPROVING THE FINISH: Jamie McMurray (23 places)
CAUTION FLAGS: 5 cautions for 31 laps. [Beneficiary in Brackets] 52–56 (Competition [36]); 118–122 (Car #51 Spin Frontstretch [20]); 228–236 (Debris [83]); 311–318 (Debris [18]); 388–391 (Debris [99]).
LAP LEADERS: 14 lead changes among 7 drivers. Martin 1–29, Edwards 30–53, Kvapil 54, Edwards 55–200, Stewart 201–205, Edwards 206, Harvick 207–219, Edwards 220–250, Stewart 251–285, Ky. Busch 286–304, Stewart 305–309, Johnson 310, Edwards 311–314, Stewart 315–387, Ky. Busch 388–400.

++Rollover money awarded at year's end, amount not included in race winnings.

POINT LEADERS
(After 9 Races)

1	GREG BIFFLE	338
2	Dale Earnhardt Jr.	333
3	Denny Hamlin	329
4	Matt Kenseth	328
5	Martin Truex Jr.	316
6	Jimmie Johnson	314
7	Kevin Harvick	313
8	Tony Stewart	307
9	Carl Edwards	287
10	Ryan Newman	278
11	Kyle Busch	265
12	Clint Bowyer	264

RICHMOND INTERNATIONAL RACEWAY

FEDERATED AUTO PARTS 400
OFFICIAL RACE RESULTS: RACE #26 – SEPTEMBER 8, 2012

NASCAR SPRINT CUP SERIES RACE RESULTS

Fin Pos	Str Pos	Car No	Series Driver	Team	Laps	Points	Bonus Points	Status
1	4	15	Clint Bowyer	5-hour Energy Toyota	400	47	4	Running
2	2	24	Jeff Gordon	Drive to End Hunger Chevrolet	400	43	1	Running
3	6	55	Mark Martin	Aaron's Dream Machine Toyota	400	41	0	Running
4	28	14	Tony Stewart	Office Depot/Mobil 1 Chevrolet	400	41	1	Running
5	17	17	Matt Kenseth	Best Buy Ford	400	39	0	Running
6	20	31	Jeff Burton	Caterpillar Chevrolet	400	38	0	Running
7	10	2	Brad Keselowski	Miller Lite Dodge	400	37	0	Running
8	14	39	Ryan Newman	Quicken Loans Chevrolet	400	37	1	Running
9	23	16	Greg Biffle	3M/Owens & Minor Ford	400	35	0	Running
10	13	29	Kevin Harvick	Budweiser Chevrolet	400	34	0	Running
11	11	22	Sam Hornish Jr. (i)	Shell Pennzoil Dodge	400	0	0	Running
12	21	5	Kasey Kahne	Quaker State Chevrolet	399	33	1	Running
13	5	48	Jimmie Johnson	Lowe's Chevrolet	399	32	1	Running
14	1	88	Dale Earnhardt Jr.	Diet Mountain Dew/National Guard Chev.	399	31	1	Running
15	22	9	Marcos Ambrose	MAC Tools Ford	399	29	0	Running
16	15	18	Kyle Busch	M&M's Toyota	399	28	0	Running
17	16	99	Carl Edwards	Kellogg's Ford	399	27	0	Running
18	7	11	Denny Hamlin	FedEx Express Toyota	399	28	2	Running
19	12	83	Landon Cassill	Burger King Toyota	399	25	0	Running
20	24	42	Juan Pablo Montoya	Target Chevrolet	399	24	0	Running
21	9	56	Martin Truex Jr.	NAPA Auto Parts Toyota	399	24	1	Running
22	26	1	Jamie McMurray	Bass Pro Shops/Allstate Chevrolet	398	22	0	Running
23	25	27	Paul Menard	Menards/Moen Chevrolet	398	21	0	Running
24	3	78	Regan Smith	Furniture Row/Farm American Chevrolet	398	20	0	Running
25	29	47	Bobby Labonte	Bush's Beans Toyota	397	19	0	Running
26	18	43	Aric Almirola	Smithfield Ford	397	18	0	Running
27	32	93	Travis Kvapil	Burger King/Dr. Pepper Toyota	397	17	0	Running
28	30	51	Kurt Busch	Phoenix Construction Chevrolet	396	16	0	Running
29	42	13	Casey Mears	GEICO Ford	396	15	0	Running
30	8	20	Joey Logano	The Home Depot Toyota	396	14	0	Running
31	35	38	David Gilliland	Mossy Oak/Pursuit Channel Ford	395	13	0	Running
32	27	34	David Ragan	Taco Bell Ford	395	12	0	Running
33	33	36	Dave Blaney	Tommy Baldwin Racing Chevrolet	395	11	0	Running
34	37	10	David Reutimann	No.10 Inc. 5000-@TMone 6-peat Chevrolet	393	10	0	Running
35	39	32	Ken Schrader	Federated Auto Parts Ford	393	9	0	Running
36	36	33	Stephen Leicht #	Special Ops OPSEC Chevrolet	390	8	0	Running
37	31	30	David Stremme	Inception Motorsports Chevrolet	127	7	0	Brakes
38	34	87	Joe Nemechek (i)	AM/FM Energy Wood & Pellet Stoves Toyota	90	0	0	Brakes
39	38	23	Scott Riggs	North Texas Pipe Chevrolet	78	5	0	Brakes
40	40	19	Mike Bliss (i)	Plinker Tactical Toyota	70	0	0	Wheel Bearing
41	19	98	Michael McDowell	Phil Parsons Racing Ford	63	4	1	Brakes
42	41	26	Josh Wise #	MDS Transport Ford	57	2	0	Brakes
43	43	91	Reed Sorenson (i)	Plinker Tactical Chevrolet	57	0	0	Power Steering

 # Sunoco Rookie of the Year Contender. Bonus Points: includes winner, lap leader & most laps led points. (i) = Ineligible for driver points in this series. Failed to qualify: (2) #37 J.J. Yeley; #0 Mark Green.

Race Comments: Before an estimated crowd of 89,000, Clint Bowyer won the Federated Auto Parts 400, his seventh NASCAR Sprint Cup Series victory.

RACE STATISITICS

TIME OF RACE: 2 hours, 59 minutes, 58 seconds
AVERAGE SPEED: 100.019 mph
MARGIN OF VICTORY: 1.198 seconds
COORS LIGHT POLE AWARD: Dale Earnhardt Jr. (127.023 mph. 21.256 secs.)
3M LAP LEADER: Denny Hamlin (202 Laps)
AMERICAN ETHANOL GREEN FLAG RESTART AWARD: Kevin Harvick
DIRECTV CREW CHIEF OF THE RACE: Clint Bowyer (crew chief Brian Pattie)
FREESCALE "WIDE OPEN": Tony Stewart
MAHLE CLEVITE ENGINE BUILDER OF THE RACE: Hendrick Engines (#24)

MOBIL 1 OIL DRIVER OF THE RACE: Clint Bowyer
MOOG STEERING AND SUSPENSION PROBLEM SOLVER OF THE RACE: Tony Stewart (crew chief Steve Addington, 0.059 seconds)
NASCAR SPRINT CUP LEADER BONUS: No winner: rolls over to $40,000 at next event++
SUNOCO ROOKIE OF THE RACE: Stephen Leicht
USG IMPROVING THE FINISH: Tony Stewart (24 places)
CAUTION FLAGS: 6 cautions for 41 laps. [Beneficiary in Brackets] 1–6 (Competition [None]); 47–50 (Competition [87]); 53–56 (Car #34 Accident Frontstretch [38]); 139–155 (Precipitation [Red Flag: Lap 152; 51:45] [39]); 236–239 (Car #15 Spin Frontstretch [31]); 277–282 (Precipitation [24]).
LAP LEADERS: 17 lead changes among 10 drivers. Earnhardt Jr. 1–6, J. Gordon 7–8, Earnhardt Jr. 9–47, McDowell 48, Earnhardt Jr. 49–58, Hamlin 59–84, Earnhardt Jr. 85–93, Hamlin 94–155, Earnhardt Jr. 156–158, Hamlin 159–231, Johnson 232–233, Hamlin 234–241, Truex Jr. 242–284, Hamlin 249–281, Kahne 282–284, Stewart 285–299, Newman 300–312, Bowyer 313–400.

++Rollover money awarded at year's end, amount not included in race winnings.

POINT LEADERS
(After 26 Races)

1	**DENNY HAMLIN**	2012
2	Jimmie Johnson	2009
3	Tony Stewart	2009
4	Brad Keselowski	2009
5	Greg Biffle	2006
6	Clint Bowyer	2006
7	Dale Earnhardt Jr.	2003
8	Matt Kenseth	2003
9	Kevin Harvick	2000
10	Martin Truex Jr.	2000
11	Kasey Kahne	2000
12	Jeff Gordon	2000

RICHMOND INTERNATIONAL RACEWAY

TOP 20 ACTIVE NASCAR SPRINT CUP SERIES DRIVERS (MINIMUM 2 STARTS)

Driver	Races	Wins	Top 5s	Top 10s	Poles	Total Laps	Laps Led	Avg. Start	Avg. Finish
Kyle Busch	16	4	12	13	1	6409	891	12.7	5.4
Denny Hamlin	14	2	7	9	2	5605	1,390	9.6	8.1
Clint Bowyer	14	2	2	8	0	5609	163	14.1	9.6
Tony Stewart	28	3	11	19	0	11,021	950	17.7	10.4
Ryan Newman	22	1	5	13	1	8682	450	11.3	11.6
Kevin Harvick	24	2	6	15	1	9486	942	16.5	11.7
Mark Martin	54	1	18	30	5	20,854	449	9.7	11.9
Dale Earnhardt Jr.	27	3	9	11	1	10,707	494	15.9	13.9
Jeff Gordon	40	2	16	25	5	14,856	1,415	7.9	14.4
Terry Labonte	56	3	13	28	2	19,628	663	15.6	14.6
Carl Edwards	17	0	3	8	1	6587	442	11.7	14.9
Jeff Burton	37	2	9	16	1	13,977	942	15.2	15.0
Marcos Ambrose	8	0	1	2	0	3194	0	21.8	16.0
Bill Elliott	46	1	8	15	3	17,352	492	17.4	16.2
Greg Biffle	21	0	2	6	1	8188	77	18.0	16.3
Jimmie Johnson	22	3	5	8	2	8297	417	12.0	16.5
Matt Kenseth	26	1	4	10	0	10,158	223	21.6	16.5
Ken Schrader	47	0	3	12	1	18,263	42	18.3	17.2
Kasey Kahne	18	1	4	7	1	6756	281	13.2	18.0
Kurt Busch	24	1	4	7	0	9380	348	20.3	18.3

TOYOTA OWNERS 400

Year	Driver	Car	Average Speed
1953	Lee Petty	Dodge	45.535
1955	Tim Flock	Chrysler	54.298
1956	Buck Baker	Dodge	56.232
1957	Paul Goldsmith	Ford	62.445
1959	Tom Pistone	59 Thunderbird	56.860
1960	Lee Petty	60 Plymouth	62.250
1961	Richard Petty	60 Plymouth	62.460
1962	Rex White	61 Chevrolet	51.360
1963	Joe Weatherly	63 Pontiac	58.624
1964	David Pearson	64 Dodge	58.660
1965	Junior Johnson	65 Ford	61.416
1966	David Pearson	64 Dodge	66.539
1967	Richard Petty	67 Plymouth	65.982
1968	David Pearson	68 Ford	65.217
1969	David Pearson	69 Ford	73.752
1970	James Hylton	70 Plymouth	82.044
1971	Richard Petty	70 Plymouth	79.836
1972	Richard Petty	72 Plymouth	76.258
1973	Richard Petty	73 Dodge	74.764
1974	Bobby Allison	74 Chevrolet	80.095
1975	Richard Petty	Dodge	74.913
1976	*Dave Marcis	Dodge	72.792
1977	Cale Yarborough	Chevrolet	73.084
1978	Benny Parsons	Chevrolet	80.304
1979	Cale Yarborough	Oldsmobile	83.608
1980	Darrell Waltrip	Chevrolet	67.703
1981	Darrell Waltrip	Buick	76.570
1982	Dave Marcis	Chevrolet	72.914
1983	Bobby Allison	Buick	79.584
1984	Ricky Rudd	Ford	76.736
1985	Dale Earnhardt	Chevrolet	67.945
1986	Kyle Petty	Ford	71.078
1987	Dale Earnhardt	Chevrolet	81.520
1988	Neil Bonnett	Chevrolet	66.401
1989	Rusty Wallace	Pontiac	89.619
1990	Mark Martin	Ford	92.158
1991	Dale Earnhardt	Chevrolet	105.397
1992	Bill Elliott	Ford	104.378
1993	Davey Allison	Ford	107.709
1994	Ernie Irvan	Ford	98.334
1995	Terry Labonte	Chevrolet	106.425
1996	Jeff Gordon	Chevrolet	102.750
1997	Rusty Wallace	Ford	108.499
1998	Terry Labonte	Chevrolet	97.044
1999	Dale Jarrett	Ford	100.102
2000	Dale Earnhardt Jr.	Chevrolet	99.374
2001	Tony Stewart	Pontiac	95.872
2002	Tony Stewart	Pontiac	86.824
2003	Joe Nemechek	Chevrolet	86.783
2004	Dale Earnhardt Jr.	Chevrolet	98.253
2005	Kasey Kahne	Dodge	100.316
2006	Dale Earnhardt Jr.	Chevrolet	97.061
2007	Jimmie Johnson	Chevrolet	91.270
2008	Clint Bowyer	Chevrolet	95.786
2009	Kyle Busch	Toyota	90.627
2010	Kyle Busch	Toyota	99.567
2011	Kyle Busch	Toyota	95.280
2012	Kyle Busch	Toyota	105.202

*Race changed from 500 to 400 miles.

FEDERATED AUTO PARTS 400

Year	Driver	Car	Average Speed
1958	Speedy Thompson	Chevrolet	57.878
1959	Cotton Owens	59 Thunderbird	60.380
1960	Speedy Thompson	60 Ford	63.740
1961	Joe Weatherly	61 Pontiac	61.680
1962	Joe Weatherly	62 Pontiac	64.980
1963	Ned Jarrett	63 Ford	66.339
1964	Cotton Owens	64 Dodge	61.955
1965	David Pearson	65 Dodge	60.983
1966	David Pearson	65 Dodge	62.886
1967	Richard Petty	67 Plymouth	57.631
1968	Richard Petty	68 Plymouth	85.659
1969	Bobby Allison	69 Dodge	76.388
1970	Richard Petty	70 Plymouth	81.476
1971	Richard Petty	71 Plymouth	80.025
1972	Richard Petty	72 Plymouth	75.899
1973	Richard Petty	73 Dodge	63.198
1974	Richard Petty	74 Dodge	64.430
1975	Darrell Waltrip	Chevrolet	81.886
1976	*Cale Yarborough	Chevrolet	77.993
1977	Neil Bonnett	Dodge	80.644
1978	Darrell Waltrip	Chevrolet	79.568
1979	Bobby Allison	Ford	80.604
1980	Bobby Allison	Ford	79.722
1981	Benny Parsons	Ford	69.998
1982	Bobby Allison	Chevrolet	82.800
1983	Bobby Allison	Buick	79.381
1984	Darrell Waltrip	Chevrolet	74.780
1985	Darrell Waltrip	Chevrolet	72.508
1986	Tim Richmond	Chevrolet	70.161
1987	Dale Earnhardt	Chevrolet	67.074
1988	Davey Allison	Ford	95.770
1989	Rusty Wallace	Pontiac	88.380
1990	Dale Earnhardt	Chevrolet	95.567
1991	Harry Gant	Oldsmobile	101.361
1992	Rusty Wallace	Pontiac	104.661
1993	Rusty Wallace	Pontiac	99.917
1994	Terry Labonte	Chevrolet	104.156
1995	Rusty Wallace	Ford	104.459
1996	Ernie Irvan	Ford	105.469
1997	Dale Jarrett	Ford	109.047
1998	Jeff Burton	Ford	91.985
1999	Tony Stewart	Pontiac	104.006
2000	Jeff Gordon	Chevrolet	99.871
2001	Ricky Rudd	Ford	95.146
2002	Matt Kenseth	Ford	94.787
2003	Ryan Newman	Dodge	94.945
2004	Jeremy Mayfield	Dodge	98.946
2005	Kurt Busch	Ford	98.567
2006	Kevin Harvick	Chevrolet	101.342
2007	Jimmie Johnson	Chevrolet	91.813
2008	Jimmie Johnson	Chevrolet	92.680
2009	Denny Hamlin	Toyota	96.601
2010	Denny Hamlin	Toyota	104.096
2011	Kevin Harvick	Chevrolet	89.910
2012	Clint Bowyer	Toyota	100.019

*Race changed from 500 to 400 miles.

ROAD AMERICA

N7390 State Highway 67, Plymouth, WI 53073 • **Tickets:** 1-866-GO-NASCAR or 1-800-365-7223 • **Web site:** www.roadamerica.com
Facebook: www.facebook.com/RoadAmerica • **Twitter:** @roadamerica

NASCAR

CONFIGURATION
Distance: 4 miles
Number of Turns: 14

TRACK RECORDS
Qualifying Records
Nelson Piquet, 109.516 mph
(133.065 sec.),
Set June 23, 2012

Race Record
Nelson Piquet, 85.171 mph, Set
June 23, 2012

2013 TRACK LAYOUT

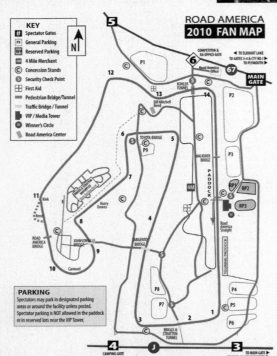

ROAD AMERICA
2010 FAN MAP

KEY
- **#** Spectator Gates
- **PF** General Parking
- **RPF** Reserved Parking
- **4M** 4 Mile Merchant
- **C** Concession Stands
- **S** Security Check Point
- **First Aid**
- Pedestrian Bridge/Tunnel
- Traffic Bridge / Tunnel
- VIP / Media Tower
- **W** Winner's Circle
- Road America Center

PARKING
Spectators may park in designated parking areas or around the facility unless posted. Spectator parking is NOT allowed in the paddock or in reserved lots near the VIP Tower.

2013 SCHEDULE
June 22: NASCAR Nationwide Series

TRACK OFFICIALS

George Bruggenthies *President*

PR CONTACTS
John Ewert *Communications Director*

VISITOR INFORMATION
Plymouth Wisconsin Chamber of Commerce
(920) 893-0079/(888) 693-8263
www.plymouthwisconsin.com

DIRECTIONS
From Chicago and Milwaukee's Mitchell Airport: I-94 North to I-43 North to WI Hwy 57 North (Plymouth) Left on County J, right on Hwy 67 to track. Track will be on your left. *From West/Madison:* Hwy 23 East to Hwy 67 North, left on Hwy 67 to track. Track will be on left. *From North/Green Bay airport:* I-43 South to Hwy 23 West, exit Hwy 67 North to track. Track will be on left.

ROCKINGHAM SPEEDWAY

2152 North U.S. Highway 1, Rockingham, NC 28379 • **Tickets:** 1-866-GO-NASCAR • **Web site:** www.rockinghamspeedway.com
Facebook: www.facebook.com/RockinghamSpeed • **Twitter:** @RockinghamSpeed

CONFIGURATION

Distance: 1 mile

**Banking: 22 degrees in turns 1 &
2, 25 degrees in turns 3 & 4,
8 degrees on straights**

TRACK RECORDS

Qualifying Records

**Nelson Piquet Jr., 144.387 mph
(24.933 sec.), Set April 15, 2012**

Race Record

**Kasey Kahne, 107.239 mph, Set
April 15, 2012**

2013 TRACK LAYOUT

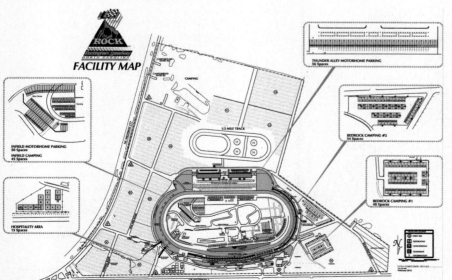

FACILITY MAP

2013 SCHEDULE
April 14: NASCAR Camping World Truck Series

TRACK OFFICIALS
Andy Hillenburg *President*

PR CONTACTS
Andy Cagle *Public Relations Director*

VISITOR INFORMATION
Richmond County Chamber of Commerce
(910) 895-9058 – **www.richmondcountychamber.com**

DIRECTIONS
US Highway 1 North, 10 miles north of Rockingham, NC
and approximately 20 miles south of Southern Pines, NC.

SONOMA RACEWAY

SONOMA RACEWAY
THINK OUTSIDE THE OVAL

Highways 37 & 121 Sonoma, CA 95476 • **Tickets:** 1-866-GO-NASCAR or 1-800-870-RACE • **Web site:** www.racesonoma.com
Facebook: www.facebook.com/racesonoma • **Twitter:** @RaceSonoma

NASCAR

CONFIGURATION
Distance: 1.99 miles
Banking: NA

TRACK RECORDS
Qualifying Records
Marcos Ambrose, 95.262 mph
(75.203 sec.), Set June 22, 2012

Race Record
Clint Bowyer, 81.007 mph,
Set June 24, 2012

2013 TRACK LAYOUT

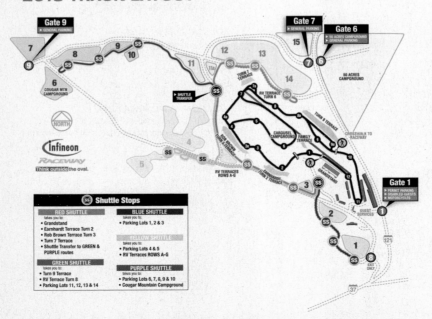

Shuttle Stops

RED SHUTTLE
takes you to:
• Grandstand
• Earnhardt Terrace Turn 2
• Rob Brown Terrace Turn 3
• Turn 7 Terrace
• Shuttle Transfer to GREEN & PURPLE routes

GREEN SHUTTLE
takes you to:
• Turn 9 Terrace
• RV Terrace Turn 8
• Parking Lots 11, 12, 13 & 14

BLUE SHUTTLE
takes you to:
• Parking Lots 1, 2 & 3

YELLOW SHUTTLE
takes you to:
• Parking Lots 4 & 5
• RV Terraces ROWS A-G

PURPLE SHUTTLE
takes you to:
• Parking Lots 6, 7, 8, 9 & 10
• Cougar Mountain Campground

2013 SCHEDULE
June 23: NASCAR Sprint Cup Series

TRACK OFFICIALS

Steve Page *President & General Manager*

PR CONTACTS
Diana Brennan *Director, Community & Media Relations*

VISITOR INFORMATION
Sonoma Valley Chamber of Commerce
(707) 996-1033 – **www.sonomachamber.org**
Sonoma Valley Visitors Bureau
(866) 996-1090/(707) 996-1090 – **www.sonomavalley.com**

DIRECTIONS
From San Francisco: Take Hwy. 101 north across Golden Gate Bridge. Take Hwy. 37 east. Turn left at Highway 121 and track is on left side. *From Sacramento:* Take I-80 west to Highway 37 west toward Novato. Follow Highway 37 until you come to Highway 121. Make a right. Entrance to the track is on your left at Gate 1.

TOYOTA/SAVE MART 350
OFFICIAL RACE RESULTS: RACE #16 – JUNE 24, 2012

NASCAR SPRINT CUP SERIES RACE RESULTS

Fin Pos	Str Pos	Car No	Series Driver	Team	Laps	Points	Bonus Points	Status
1	6	15	Clint Bowyer	5-hour Energy Toyota	112	48	5	Running
2	24	14	Tony Stewart	Office Depot/MOBIL 1 Chevrolet	112	42	0	Running
3	8	51	Kurt Busch	Phoenix Construction Services Chevrolet	112	42	1	Running
4	21	55	Brian Vickers	RKMotorsCharlotte.com Toyota	112	40	0	Running
5	3	48	Jimmie Johnson	Lowe's Chevrolet	112	39	0	Running
6	2	24	Jeff Gordon	Drive to End Hunger Chevrolet	112	39	1	Running
7	4	16	Greg Biffle	3M/US Stationary Ford	112	37	0	Running
8	1	9	Marcos Ambrose	Stanley Ford	112	37	1	Running
9	17	22	AJ Allmendinger	Shell Pennzoil Dodge	112	35	0	Running
10	14	20	Joey Logano	The Home Depot Toyota	112	34	0	Running
11	35	31	Jeff Burton	Wheaties Chevrolet	112	33	0	Running
12	13	2	Brad Keselowski	Miller Lite Dodge	112	32	0	Running
13	9	17	Matt Kenseth	Ford EcoBoost Ford	112	31	0	Running
14	15	5	Kasey Kahne	Farmers Insurance Chevrolet	112	30	0	Running
15	20	13	Casey Mears	GEICO Ford	112	29	0	Running
16	26	29	Kevin Harvick	Rheem Chevrolet	112	28	0	Running
17	7	18	Kyle Busch	M&M's Toyota	112	27	0	Running
18	10	39	Ryan Newman	Quicken Loans/Children's Tumor Foun. Chevrolet	112	26	0	Running
19	25	1	Jamie McMurray	McDonald's Chevrolet	112	25	0	Running
20	23	27	Paul Menard	Menards/Moen Chevrolet	112	24	0	Running
21	11	99	Carl Edwards	Aflac Ford	112	23	0	Running
22	5	56	Martin Truex Jr.	NAPA Auto Parts Toyota	112	23	1	Running
23	19	88	Dale Earnhardt Jr.	Diet Mountain Dew/National Guard/7-Eleven Chevrolet	112	21	0	Running
24	18	47	Bobby Labonte	Clorox Toyota	111	20	0	Running
25	22	95	Scott Speed	Leavine Family Racing Ford	111	19	0	Running
26	27	38	David Gilliland	1-800-LoanMart Ford	111	18	0	Running
27	29	34	David Ragan	Green 1 High Performance Green Ford	111	17	0	Running
28	30	43	Aric Almirola	Medallion Ford	110	16	0	Running
29	28	32	Boris Said	HendrickCars.com Ford	110	15	0	Running
30	40	26	Josh Wise #	MDS Transport Ford	110	14	0	Running
31	42	83	Landon Cassill	Burger King/Dr. Pepper Toyota	110	13	0	Running
32	31	78	Regan Smith	Furniture Row/Farm American Chevrolet	109	12	0	Running
33	38	49	J.J. Yeley	America Israel Racing/JPO Absorbents Toyota	107	11	0	Running
34	12	42	Juan Pablo Montoya	Target Chevrolet	107	10	0	Running
35	16	11	Denny Hamlin	FedEx Ground Toyota	98	9	0	Suspension
36	39	93	Travis Kvapil	Burger King/Dr. Pepper Toyota	92	8	0	Running
37	32	36	Dave Blaney	Tommy Baldwin Racing Chevrolet	84	7	0	Suspension
38	41	10	Tomy Drissi	Ice Age Continental Drift Chevrolet	78	6	0	Accident
39	34	7	Robby Gordon	MAPEI/Save Mart Supermarkets Dodge	73	5	0	Steering
40	33	98	David Mayhew	Phil Parsons Racing Ford	25	4	0	Brakes
41	43	33	Stephen Leicht #	LittleJoesAutos.com Chevrolet	22	3	0	Brakes
42	37	19	Chris Cook	Humphrey Smith Racing Toyota	13	2	0	Brakes
43	36	87	Joe Nemechek (i)	AM/FM Energy Wood & Pellet Stoves Toyota	1	0	0	Engine

Sunoco Rookie of the Year Contender. Bonus Points: includes winner, lap leader & most laps led points. (i) = Ineligible for driver points in this series. Failed to qualify: (1) #30 Brian Simo.

RACE COMMENTS: Before an estimated crowd of 91,000, Clint Bowyer won the Toyota/Save Mart 350, his sixth NASCAR Sprint Cup Series victory. Prior to the green flag, the following cars dropped to the rear of the field for the reasons indicated: #33 (engine change), #38 (missed drivers meeting).

RACE STATISTICS

TIME OF RACE: 2 hours, 39 minutes, 55 seconds
AVERAGE SPEED: 83.624 mph
MARGIN OF VICTORY: 0.829 seconds
COORS LIGHT POLE AWARD: Marcos Ambrose (95.262 mph. 75.203 secs.)
3M LAP LEADER: Clint Bowyer (71 Laps)
AMERICAN ETHANOL GREEN FLAG RESTART AWARD: Clint Bowyer
DIRECTV CREW CHIEF OF THE RACE: Clint Bowyer (crew chief Brian Pattie)
FREESCALE "WIDE OPEN": Tony Stewart
MAHLE CLEVITE ENGINE BUILDER OF

THE RACE: Toyota Racing Development (TRD) (#15)
MOBIL 1 OIL DRIVER OF THE RACE: Clint Bowyer
MOOG STEERING AND SUSPENSION PROBLEM SOLVER OF THE RACE: Brian Vickers (crew chief Rodney Childers, 0.328 seconds)
NASCAR SPRINT CUP LEADER BONUS: No winner: rolls over to $100,000 at next event++
SUNOCO ROOKIE OF THE RACE: Josh Wise
USG IMPROVING THE FINISH: Jeff Burton (24 places)
CAUTION FLAGS: 2 cautions for 7 laps.

[Beneficiary in Brackets] 83–86 (Car #10 Accident Turn 8 [29]); 108–110 (Car #18,27 Spin Turn 7 [39]).
LAP LEADERS: 8 lead changes among 5 drivers. Ambrose 1–11, J. Gordon 12–24, Bowyer 25–33, Ku. Busch 34, Truex Jr. 35–47, Bowyer 48–70, Ku. Busch 71, Truex Jr. 72–73, Bowyer 74–112.

++Rollover money awarded at year's end, amount not included in race winnings.

POINT LEADERS
(After 16 Races)

1	MATT KENSETH	596
2	Greg Biffle	585
3	Dale Earnhardt Jr.	582
4	Jimmie Johnson	571
5	Tony Stewart	533
6	Kevin Harvick	532
7	Clint Bowyer	529
8	Denny Hamlin	523
9	Martin Truex Jr.	520
10	Brad Keselowski	490
11	Carl Edwards	479
12	Kyle Busch	459

SONOMA RACEWAY

TOP 20 ACTIVE NASCAR SPRINT CUP SERIES DRIVERS (MINIMUM 2 STARTS)

Driver	Races	Wins	Top 5s	Top 10s	Poles	Total Laps	Laps Led	Avg. Start	Avg. Finish
Jeff Gordon	20	5	12	16	5	2013	450	7.4	8.6
Clint Bowyer	7	1	4	5	0	777	73	17.1	9.7
Tony Stewart	14	2	5	9	1	1531	82	11.1	10.9
Mark Martin	21	1	7	13	1	1975	161	10.0	11.9
Marcos Ambrose	5	0	2	4	1	528	46	5.0	12.8
Ryan Newman	11	0	2	5	0	1217	11	10.9	12.9
Juan Pablo Montoya	6	1	1	4	0	662	9	18.8	13.2
Jimmie Johnson	11	1	4	6	0	1210	85	16.0	13.8
Greg Biffle	10	0	2	4	0	1103	9	16.4	14.9
Elliott Sadler	12	0	0	5	0	1310	4	23.7	15.4
AJ Allmendinger	5	0	0	2	0	554	0	19.0	15.8
Kevin Harvick	12	0	3	4	0	1328	10	16.7	16.1
Michael Waltrip	19	0	1	7	0	1770	7	20.8	16.4
Bill Elliott	15	0	3	5	0	1347	28	13.2	16.5
Kurt Busch	12	1	5	5	1	1312	139	10.3	17.0
Joey Logano	4	0	0	2	1	443	5	11.8	17.0
Carl Edwards	8	0	1	3	0	884	14	19.6	17.1
Jamie McMurray	10	0	1	1	1	1106	30	15.0	17.1
Kyle Busch	8	1	1	2	0	840	88	17.6	18.6
Brad Keselowski	3	0	0	1	0	324	0	21.3	19.0
Casey Mears	9	0	1	2	0	995	5	29.0	19.7

TOYOTA/SAVE MART 350

Year	Driver	Car	Average Speed
1989	Ricky Rudd	Buick	76.088
1990	Rusty Wallace	Pontiac	69.245
1991	Davey Allison	Ford	72.970
1992	Ernie Irvan	Chevrolet	81.413
1993	Geoff Bodine	Ford	77.013
1994	Ernie Irvan	Ford	77.458
1995	Dale Earnhardt	Chevrolet	70.681
1996	Rusty Wallace	Ford	77.673
1997	Mark Martin	Ford	75.788
1998	Jeff Gordon	Chevrolet	72.387
1999	Jeff Gordon	Chevrolet	70.378
2000	Jeff Gordon	Chevrolet	78.789
2001	Tony Stewart	Pontiac	75.889
2002	Ricky Rudd	Ford	81.007
2003	Robby Gordon	Chevrolet	73.821
2004	Jeff Gordon	Chevrolet	77.456
2005	Tony Stewart	Chevrolet	72.845
2006	Jeff Gordon	Chevrolet	73.953
2007	Juan Pablo Montoya	Dodge	74.547
2008	Kyle Busch	Toyota	76.445
2009	Kasey Kahne	Dodge	71.012
2010	Jimmie Johnson	Chevrolet	74.357
2011	Kurt Busch	Dodge	75.411
2012	Clint Bowyer	Toyota	83.624

TALLADEGA SUPERSPEEDWAY

3366 Speedway Blvd., Talladega, AL 35160 • **Tickets:** 1-866-GO-NASCAR or 1-877-GO2-DEGA • **Web site:** www.talladegasuperspeedway.com
Facebook: www.facebook.com/TalladegaSuperspeedway • **Twitter:** @TalladegaSuperS

NASCAR

CONFIGURATION
Distance: 2.66 miles
Banking: 33 degrees in turns,
16.5 degrees on frontstretch,
2 degrees on backstretch

TRACK RECORDS
Qualifying Records
Bill Elliott, 212.809 mph (44.998
sec.), Set April 30, 1987

Race Record
Mark Martin, 188.354 mph,
Set May 10, 1997

2013 TRACK LAYOUT

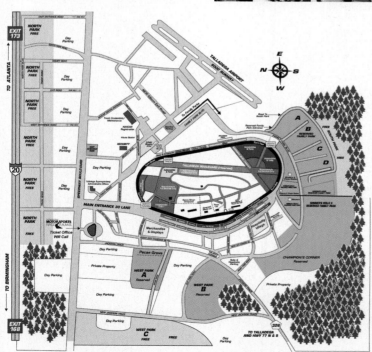

2013 SCHEDULE
May 4: NASCAR Nationwide Series
May 5: NASCAR Sprint Cup Series
October 19: NASCAR Camping World Truck Series
October 20: NASCAR Sprint Cup Series

TRACK OFFICIALS

Grant Lynch *President*

PR CONTACTS
Andrew Smith *Senior Manager of Public and Community Relations*

VISITOR INFORMATION
Greater Talladega/Lincoln Area Chamber of Commerce
(256) 362-9075 – **www.talladegachamber.com**

DIRECTIONS
From Atlanta: Take I-20 west to exit 173. *From Birmingham:* Take I-20 east to exit 168.

AARON'S 499

OFFICIAL RACE RESULTS: RACE #10 – MAY 6, 2012

NASCAR SPRINT CUP SERIES RACE RESULTS

Fin Pos	Str Pos	Car No	Series Driver	Team	Laps	Points	Bonus Points	Status
1	13	2	Brad Keselowski	Miller Lite Dodge	194	47	4	Running
2	21	18	Kyle Busch	M&M's Toyota	194	43	1	Running
3	10	17	Matt Kenseth	Best Buy Ford	194	43	2	Running
4	5	5	Kasey Kahne	Farmers Insurance Chevrolet	194	41	1	Running
5	6	16	Greg Biffle	3M/O'Reilly Auto Parts Ford	194	40	1	Running
6	24	15	Clint Bowyer	Aaron's/Alabama National Championship Toyota	194	38	0	Running
7	32	34	David Ragan	Front Row Motorsports Ford	194	37	0	Running
8	11	21	Trevor Bayne (i)	Motorcraft/Quick Lane Tire & Auto Center Ford	194	0	0	Running
9	18	88	Dale Earnhardt Jr.	National Guard/Diet Mountain Dew Chevrolet	194	36	1	Running
10	29	31	Jeff Burton	Caterpillar Chevrolet	194	35	1	Running
11	23	1	Jamie McMurray	Bass Pro Shops/Tracker Boats Chevrolet	194	33	0	Running
12	4	43	Aric Almirola	VeriFone Sail Ford	194	32	0	Running
13	26	38	David Gilliland	Taco Bell Ford	194	31	0	Running
14	3	9	Marcos Ambrose	Stanley Ford	194	30	0	Running
15	2	22	AJ Allmendinger	Shell Pennzoil/AAA Dodge	194	29	0	Running
16	41	93	Travis Kvapil	Burger King/Dr. Pepper Toyota	194	29	1	Running
17	17	27	Paul Menard	Menards/Turtle Wax Chevrolet	194	28	1	Running
18	25	13	Casey Mears	GEICO Ford	194	27	1	Running
19	9	55	Michael Waltrip	Aaron's Color Your Way Toyota	194	26	1	Running
20	33	51	Kurt Busch	Phoenix Construction Services Inc. Chevrolet	193	25	1	Running
21	42	47	Bobby Labonte	Bush's Beans Toyota	192	23	0	Running
22	34	10	David Reutimann	Tommy Baldwin Racing Chevrolet	192	22	0	Running
23	22	11	Denny Hamlin	FedEx Express Toyota	192	22	1	Running
24	8	14	Tony Stewart	Office Depot/Mobil 1 Chevrolet	190	21	1	Running
25	20	29	Kevin Harvick	Rheem Chevrolet	184	20	1	Accident
26	30	20	Joey Logano	Dollar General Toyota	184	18	0	Accident
27	39	23	Robert Richardson (i)	North TX Pipe Toyota	182	0	0	Accident
28	15	56	Martin Truex Jr.	NAPA Auto Parts Toyota	166	16	0	Accident
29	28	32	Terry Labonte	C&J Energy Ford	143	15	0	Accident
30	38	36	Dave Blaney	Golden Corral Chevrolet	142	14	0	Accident
31	7	99	Carl Edwards	Fastenal Ford	142	13	0	Accident
32	12	42	Juan Pablo Montoya	Target/Kraft Chevrolet	142	13	1	Accident
33	1	24	Jeff Gordon	DuPont Chevrolet	142	11	0	Accident
34	40	83	Landon Cassill	Burger King/Dr. Pepper Toyota	141	10	0	Accident
35	19	48	Jimmie Johnson	Lowe's Chevrolet	61	10	1	Engine
36	14	39	Ryan Newman	Bass Pro Shops/Tracker Boats Chevrolet	42	8	0	Engine
37	36	97	Bill Elliott	NEMCO Motorsports Toyota	37	7	0	Electrical
38	43	33	Tony Raines	Little Joe's Autos Chevrolet	32	6	0	Engine
39	27	30	David Stremme	Stock Car Steel and Aluminum Toyota	30	5	0	Transmission
40	31	78	Regan Smith	Furniture Row Chevrolet	15	4	0	Engine
41	37	87	Joe Nemechek (i)	AM/FM Energy Wood & Pellet Stoves Toyota	7	0	0	Vibration
42	16	26	Josh Wise #	Morristown Driver's Service Ford	5	2	0	Rear Gear
43	35	98	Michael McDowell	Curb Records Ford	2	1	0	Vibration

Sunoco Rookie of the Year Contender. Bonus Points: includes winner, lap leader & most laps led points. (i) = Ineligible for driver points in this series. Failed to qualify: (1) #49 J.J. Yeley.

RACE COMMENTS: Before an estimated crowd of 108,500, Brad Keselowski won the Aaron's 499, his sixth NASCAR Sprint Cup Series victory. Prior to the green flag, the following cars dropped to the rear of the field for the reason indicated: #38, 93 (adjustments outside impound).

RACE STATISTICS

TIME OF RACE: 3 hours, 13 minutes, 17 seconds
AVERAGE SPEED: 160.192 mph
MARGIN OF VICTORY: 0.304 seconds
COORS LIGHT POLE AWARD: Jeff Gordon (191.623 mph. 49.973 secs.)
3M LAP LEADER: Matt Kenseth (73 Laps)
AMERICAN ETHANOL GREEN FLAG RESTART AWARD: Travis Kvapil
DIRECTV CREW CHIEF OF THE RACE: Greg Biffle (crew chief Matt Puccia)
MAHLE CLEVITE ENGINE BUILDER OF THE RACE: Roush Yates Engines (#17)
MOBIL 1 OIL DRIVER OF THE RACE: Kyle Busch

MOOG STEERING AND SUSPENSION PROBLEM SOLVER OF THE RACE: Dale Earnhardt Jr. (crew chief Steve Letarte, 0.039 seconds)
NASCAR SPRINT CUP LEADER BONUS: No winner: rolls over to $40,000 at next event++
USG IMPROVING THE FINISH: David Ragan (25 places)
CAUTION FLAGS: 5 cautions for 24 laps. [Beneficiary in Brackets] 17–20 (Oil On Track From #78 [None]); 144–150 (Car #20, 24, 32, 36, 42, 43, 56, 83, 99 Accident Turn 3 [11]); 177–179 (Car #9, 13, 21 Accident Turn 2 [29]); 182–184 (Car #2, 51 Accident Frontstretch [38]); 186–192 (Car #11, 14, 16, 20, 22, 23, 27, 29, 55 Accident Turn 1 [93]).
LAP LEADERS: 33 lead changes among 17 drivers. Stewart 1–16, Menard 17, Kvapil 18, Kenseth 19–24, Waltrip 25–45, Johnson 46–50, Kenseth 51–59, Burton 60–61, Earnhardt Jr. 62–71, Kenseth 72–86, Kahne 87–94, Montoya 95, Kahne 96–98, Montoya 99–100, Biffle 101, Harvick 102, Menard 103–104, Biffle 105–111, Burton 112, Biffle 113–119, Ku. Busch 120–121, Kenseth 122–133, Ku. Busch 134–135, Kenseth 136–142, Ky. Busch 143, Menard 144–150, Keselowski 151–158, Hamlin 159–161, Mears 162–163, Hamlin 164–166, Kenseth 167–174, Hamlin 175–176, Kenseth 177–192, Keselowski 193–194.

++Rollover money awarded at year's end, amount not included in race winnings.

POINT LEADERS

(After 10 Races)

1	GREG BIFFLE	378
2	Matt Kenseth	371
3	Dale Earnhardt Jr.	369
4	Denny Hamlin	351
5	Kevin Harvick	333
6	Martin Truex Jr.	332
7	Tony Stewart	328
8	Jimmie Johnson	324
9	Kyle Busch	308
10	Clint Bowyer	302
11	Carl Edwards	300
12	Brad Keselowski	299

TALLADEGA SUPERSPEEDWAY

GOOD SAM ROADSIDE ASSISTANCE 500

OFFICIAL RACE RESULTS: RACE #30 – OCTOBER 7, 2012

NASCAR SPRINT CUP SERIES RACE RESULTS

Fin Pos	Str Pos	Car No	Series Driver	Team	Laps	Points	Bonus Points	Status
1	15	17	Matt Kenseth	Ford EcoBoost/Nat'l Breast Cancer Foun. Ford	189	47	4	Running
2	6	24	Jeff Gordon	Drive to End Hunger Chevrolet	189	43	1	Running
3	13	18	Kyle Busch	M&M's Toyota	189	42	1	Running
4	25	34	David Ragan	MHP-8 hour Alert Ford	189	41	1	Running
5	28	78	Regan Smith	Furniture Row/Farm American Chevrolet	189	39	0	Running
6	5	16	Greg Biffle	3M/National Breast Cancer Foundation Ford	189	39	1	Running
7	22	2	Brad Keselowski	Miller Lite Dodge	189	37	0	Running
8	36	93	Travis Kvapil	Burger King/Dr. Pepper Toyota	189	37	1	Running
9	2	39	Ryan Newman	U.S. Army Chevrolet	189	35	0	Running
10	26	31	Jeff Burton	Caterpillar/DriveCat.com Chevrolet	189	35	1	Running
11	21	29	Kevin Harvick	Budweiser Chevrolet	189	34	1	Running
12	1	5	Kasey Kahne	Hendrickcars.com Chevrolet	189	33	1	Running
13	9	56	Martin Truex Jr.	NAPA Auto Parts Toyota	189	31	0	Running
14	23	11	Denny Hamlin	FedEx Freight Toyota	189	30	0	Running
15	32	38	David Gilliland	Peanut Patch Boiled Peanuts/M. Holmes Ford	189	29	0	Running
16	31	32	Terry Labonte	C&J Energy Services Ford	189	28	0	Running
17	17	48	Jimmie Johnson	Lowe's Chevrolet	189	28	1	Running
18	40	47	Bobby Labonte	Scott/Kingsford/Bush Beans Toyota	189	26	0	Running
19	18	43	Aric Almirola	Gwaltney Ford	189	25	0	Running
20	12	88	Dale Earnhardt Jr.	Diet Mountain Dew Paint 88/Nat'l Guard Chev.	189	25	1	Running
21	8	21	Trevor Bayne (i)	Motorcraft/Quick Lane/Warriors in Pink Ford	189	0	0	Running
22	4	14	Tony Stewart	Mobil 1/Office Depot Chevrolet	188	23	1	Accident
23	3	15	Clint Bowyer	5-hour Energy/Avon Foun for Women Toyota	188	22	1	Accident
24	10	22	Sam Hornish Jr. (i)	SKF Dodge	188	0	0	Accident
25	11	55	Michael Waltrip	Charlie Loudermilk Aaron's Dream Machine Toyota	188	19	0	Accident
26	19	13	Casey Mears	GEICO Ford	188	19	1	Accident
27	20	9	Marcos Ambrose	DeWalt Ford	188	18	1	Accident
28	16	27	Paul Menard	Certain Teed Insulation/Menards Chevrolet	188	16	0	Accident
29	39	36	Dave Blaney	Golden Corral Chevrolet	188	15	0	Accident
30	38	83	Landon Cassill	Burger King/Dr. Pepper Toyota	188	14	0	Running
31	34	98	Michael McDowell	K-LOVE/Curb Records Ford	188	13	0	Running
32	14	20	Joey Logano	The Home Depot Toyota	187	12	0	Running
33	30	30	David Stremme	SwanEnergyInc.com Toyota	187	11	0	Running
34	24	1	Jamie McMurray	Bass Pro Shops/Allstate Chevrolet	184	12	2	Accident
35	43	23	Robert Richardson (i)	North Texas Pipe Toyota	180	0	0	Accident
36	7	99	Carl Edwards	Subway Ford	179	8	0	Running
37	41	10	David Reutimann	CVP@Tmone.com Chevrolet	162	7	0	Engine
38	27	42	Juan Pablo Montoya	Target/Gillette Chevrolet	156	6	0	Engine
39	29	51	Kurt Busch	Phoenix Construction Chevrolet	98	6	1	Parked
40	42	33	Cole Whitt (i)	LittleJoesAutos.com Chevrolet	16	0	0	Accident
41	37	87	Joe Nemechek (i)	AM/FM Energy Wood & Pellet Stoves Toyota	12	0	0	Vibration
42	35	97	Timmy Hill (i)	AM/FM Energy Wood Stoves/SWM Toyota	8	0	0	Electrical
43	33	26	Josh Wise #	MDS Transport Ford	5	1	0	Overheating

Sunoco Rookie of the Year Contender. Bonus Points: includes winner, lap leader & most laps led points. (i) = Ineligible for driver points in this series. Failed to qualify: n/a.

RACE COMMENTS: Before an estimated crowd of 88,000, Matt Kenseth won the Good Sam Roadside Assistance 500, his 23rd NASCAR Sprint Cup Series victory. Prior to the green flag, the following car dropped to the rear of the field for the reason indicated: #36 (unapproved adjustments during impound).

RACE STATISTICS

TIME OF RACE: 2 hours, 56 minutes, 12 seconds
AVERAGE SPEED: 171.194 mph
MARGIN OF VICTORY: Under Caution
COORS LIGHT POLE AWARD: Kasey Kahne (191.455 mph. 50.017 secs.)
3M LAP LEADER: Jamie McMurray (38 Laps)
AMERICAN ETHANOL GREEN FLAG RESTART AWARD: Matt Kenseth
DIRECTV CREW CHIEF OF THE RACE: Greg Biffle (crew chief Matt Puccia)
FREESCALE "WIDE OPEN": Matt Kenseth
MAHLE CLEVITE ENGINE BUILDER OF THE RACE: Roush Yates Engines (#17)
MOBIL 1 OIL DRIVER OF THE RACE: Kyle Busch
MOOG STEERING AND SUSPENSION

PROBLEM SOLVER OF THE RACE: Greg Biffle (crew chief Matt Puccia, 0.079 seconds)
NASCAR SPRINT CUP LEADER BONUS: No winner: rolls over to $20,000 at next event++
USG IMPROVING THE FINISH: Travis Kvapil (28 places)
CAUTION FLAGS: 5 cautions for 17 laps. [Beneficiary in Brackets] 18–21 (Car #13, 20, 33, 99 Accident Turn 3 [None]); 100–103 (Car #1, 51 Accident Turn 2 [21]); 140–143 (Debris Backstretch [18]); 184–187 (Car #1 Spin Frontstretch [36]); 189 (Car #88, 29, 11, 47, 32, 48, 5, 43, 36, 78, 55, 13, 2, 15, 34, 27, 9, 56, 38, 18, 22, 31, 16, 93, 14 Accident Turn 4 [None]).
LAP LEADERS: 54 lead changes among 18 drivers. Kahne 1–7, Bowyer 8, Kahne 9–10, Bayne 11, Bowyer 12, Earnhardt Jr. 13–14, Ky. Busch 15–17, Harvick 18, Kvapil 19, Ky. Busch 20–22, Kenseth 23–32, Earnhardt Jr. 33–40,

Kenseth 41, Earnhardt Jr. 42–49, Mears 50, Burton 51–52, Bayne 53–56, Mears 57–61, Johnson 62–71, J. Gordon 72–78, McMurray 79–89, Ku. Busch 90–93, Kenseth 94–96, Ku. Busch 97–98, Burton 99, Johnson 100, Ragan 101, Ambrose 102–103, Kenseth 104–108, Harvick 109–116, McMurray 117–118, Kenseth 119–126, Biffle 127, Kenseth 128–131, McMurray 132–139, Kvapil 140–141, Mears 142–143, Biffle 144–145, Harvick 146–147, Biffle 148–151, McMurray 152, Biffle 153–155, McMurray 156–160, Biffle 161, McMurray 162, Biffle 163–167, McMurray 168, Harvick 169, McMurray 170, Kenseth 171, Mears 172–173, McMurray 174–181, Bowyer 182–187, Stewart 188, Kenseth 189.

++Rollover money awarded at year's end, amount not included in race winnings.

POINT LEADERS
(After 30 Races)

1	BRAD KESELOWSKI	2179
2	Jimmie Johnson	2165
3	Denny Hamlin	2156
4	Kasey Kahne	2143
5	Clint Bowyer	2139
6	Jeff Gordon	2137
7	Tony Stewart	2133
8	Martin Truex Jr.	2131
9	Greg Biffle	2130
10	Kevin Harvick	2130
11	Dale Earnhardt Jr.	2128
12	Matt Kenseth	2117

TALLADEGA SUPERSPEEDWAY

TOP 20 ACTIVE NASCAR SPRINT CUP SERIES DRIVERS (MINIMUM 2 STARTS)

Driver	Races	Wins	Top 5s	Top 10s	Poles	Total Laps	Laps Led	Avg. Start	Avg. Finish
Brendan Gaughan	2	0	1	1	0	376	7	23.0	8.5
Brad Keselowski	8	2	3	6	0	1480	31	18.9	12.3
Dale Earnhardt Jr.	26	5	9	13	0	4546	737	15.6	15.0
Kevin Harvick	24	1	6	10	1	4446	155	22.0	15.4
Bill Elliott	57	2	10	22	8	9594	526	14.2	15.7
Tony Stewart	28	1	9	13	0	5179	317	16.5	15.8
Mark Martin	48	2	11	24	3	8097	328	13.7	15.9
David Ragan	12	0	3	5	0	2143	27	19.8	16.0
Clint Bowyer	14	2	4	7	0	2245	96	18.7	16.1
Kurt Busch	24	0	6	13	0	4302	143	20.8	16.1
Jeff Gordon	40	6	15	19	3	6849	839	11.5	16.4
Jimmie Johnson	22	2	5	9	1	3906	234	10.2	17.7
Travis Kvapil	10	0	0	2	1	1882	17	22.1	17.8
Denny Hamlin	14	0	3	5	0	2511	204	19.0	17.9
Jeff Burton	38	0	5	16	0	6467	153	24.5	18.0
Matt Kenseth	26	1	5	8	0	4631	294	21.4	18.0
Joey Logano	8	0	2	4	0	1502	24	24.3	18.1
Terry Labonte	57	2	14	23	1	8947	362	17.3	18.5
Bobby Labonte	40	1	6	13	1	7143	154	21.4	18.9
Scott Speed	4	0	1	1	0	766	1	23.8	19.0

AARON'S 499

Year	Driver	Car	Average Speed
1970	Pete Hamilton	70 Plymouth	152.321
1971	Donnie Allison	69 Mercury	147.419
1972	David Pearson	71 Mercury	134.400
1973	David Pearson	71 Mercury	131.956
1974	David Pearson	73 Mercury	130.220
1975	Buddy Baker	Ford	144.948
1976	Buddy Baker	Ford	169.887
1977	Darrell Waltrip	Chevrolet	164.877
1978	Cale Yarborough	Oldsmobile	159.699
1979	Bobby Allison	Ford	154.770
1980	Buddy Baker	Oldsmobile	170.481
1981	Bobby Allison	Buick	149.376
1982	Darrell Waltrip	Buick	156.697
1983	Richard Petty	Pontiac	153.936
1984	Cale Yarborough	Chevrolet	172.988
1985	Bill Elliott	Ford	186.288
1986	Bobby Allison	Buick	157.698
1987	Davey Allison	Ford	154.228
1988	Phil Parsons	Oldsmobile	156.547
1989	Davey Allison	Ford	155.869
1990	Dale Earnhardt	Chevrolet	159.571
1991	Harry Gant	Oldsmobile	165.620
1992	Davey Allison	Ford	167.609
1993	Ernie Irvan	Chevrolet	155.412
1994	Dale Earnhardt	Chevrolet	157.478
1995	Mark Martin	Ford	178.902
1996	Sterling Marlin	Chevrolet	149.999
1997	Mark Martin	Ford	188.354
1998	Bobby Labonte	Pontiac	142.428
1999	Dale Earnhardt	Chevrolet	163.395
2000	Jeff Gordon	Chevrolet	161.157
2001	Bobby Hamilton	Chevrolet	184.003
2002	Dale Earnhardt Jr.	Chevrolet	159.022
2003	Dale Earnhardt Jr.	Chevrolet	144.625
2004	Jeff Gordon	Chevrolet	129.396
2005	Jeff Gordon	Chevrolet	146.904
2006	Jimmie Johnson	Chevrolet	142.880
2007	Jeff Gordon	Chevrolet	154.167
2008	Kyle Busch	Toyota	157.409
2009	Brad Keselowski	Chevrolet	147.565
2010	Kevin Harvick	Chevrolet	150.590
2011	Jimmie Johnson	Chevrolet	156.261
2012	Brad Keselowski	Dodge	160.192

CAMPING WORLD 500

Year	Driver	Car	Average Speed
1969	Richard Brickhouse	69 Dodge	153.778
1970	Pete Hamilton	70 Plymouth	158.517
1971	Bobby Allison	69 Mercury	145.945
1972	James Hylton	71 Mercury	148.728
1973	Dick Brooks	72 Plymouth	145.454
1974	Richard Petty	74 Dodge	148.637
1975	Buddy Baker	Ford	130.892
1976	Dave Marcis	Dodge	157.547
1977	Donnie Allison	Chevrolet	162.524
1978	Lennie Pond	Oldsmobile	174.700
1979	Darrell Waltrip	Oldsmobile	161.229
1980	Neil Bonnett	Mercury	166.894
1981	Ron Bouchard	Buick	156.737
1982	Darrell Waltrip	Buick	168.157
1983	Dale Earnhardt	Ford	170.611
1984	Dale Earnhardt	Chevrolet	155.485
1985	Cale Yarborough	Ford	148.772
1986	Bobby Hillin	Buick	151.552
1987	Bill Elliott	Ford	171.293
1988	Ken Schrader	Chevrolet	154.505
1989	Terry Labonte	Ford	157.354
1990	Dale Earnhardt	Chevrolet	174.430
1991	Dale Earnhardt	Chevrolet	147.383
1992	Ernie Irvan	Chevrolet	176.309
1993	Dale Earnhardt	Chevrolet	153.858
1994	Jimmy Spencer	Ford	163.217
1995	Sterling Marlin	Chevrolet	173.188
1996	Jeff Gordon	Chevrolet	133.387
1997	Terry Labonte	Chevrolet	156.601
1998	Dale Jarrett	Ford	159.318
1999	Dale Earnhardt	Chevrolet	166.632
2000	Dale Earnhardt	Chevrolet	165.681
2001	Dale Earnhardt Jr.	Chevrolet	164.185
2002	Dale Earnhardt Jr.	Chevrolet	183.665
2003	Michael Waltrip	Chevrolet	156.045
2004	Dale Earnhardt Jr.	Chevrolet	156.929
2005	Dale Jarrett	Ford	143.818
2006	Brian Vickers	Chevrolet	157.602
2007	Jeff Gordon	Chevrolet	143.438
2008	Tony Stewart	Toyota	140.281
2009	Jamie McMurray	Ford	157.213
2010	Clint Bowyer	Chevrolet	163.618
2011	Clint Bowyer	Chevrolet	143.404
2012	Matt Kenseth	Ford	171.194

TALLADEGA SUPERSPEEDWAY

TEXAS MOTOR SPEEDWAY

TEXAS MOTOR SPEEDWAY®

The Great American Speedway!®

3601 Highway 114, Ft. Worth, TX 76177 • **Tickets:** 1-866-GO-NASCAR or 1-817-215-8500 • **Web site:** www.texasmotorspeedway.com
Facebook: www.facebook.com/texasmotorspeedway • **Twitter:** @TXMotorSpeedway

//// NASCAR®

CONFIGURATION
Distance: 1.5 miles
Banking: 24 degrees in turns,
5 degrees on dogleg,
5 degrees on backstretch

TRACK RECORDS
Qualifying Records
Brian Vickers, 196.235 mph
(27.518 sec.),
Set November 3, 2006

Race Record
Tony Stewart, 152.705 mph,
Set November 6, 2011

2013 TRACK LAYOUT

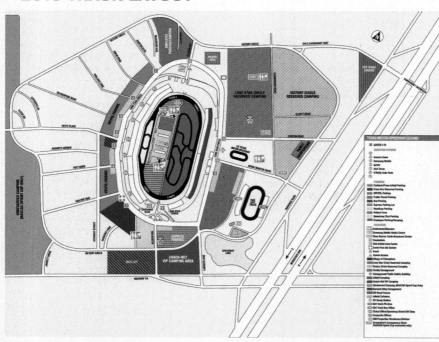

2013 SCHEDULE
April 12: NASCAR Nationwide Series
April 13: NASCAR Sprint Cup Series
June 7: NASCAR Camping World Truck Series
November 1: NASCAR Camping World Truck Series
November 2: NASCAR Nationwide Series
November 3: NASCAR Sprint Cup Series

TRACK OFFICIALS

Eddie Gossage *President*

PR CONTACT
Mike Zizzo *Vice President of Media Relations*

VISITOR INFORMATION
Fort Worth Convention & Visitors Bureau
(800) 433-5747 – **www.fortworth.com**

DIRECTIONS
Take I-35W north of downtown Ft. Worth to Hwy. 114. From
DFW Airport, take north exit, go west on Hwy 114 to track.

SAMSUNG MOBILE 500
OFFICIAL RACE RESULTS RACE #7 – APRIL 14, 2012

NASCAR SPRINT CUP SERIES RACE RESULTS

Fin Pos	Str Pos	Car No	Series Driver	Team	Laps	Points	Bonus Points	Status
1	3	16	Greg Biffle	Filtrete Ford	334	47	4	Running
2	10	48	Jimmie Johnson	Lowe's/Kobalt Tools Chevrolet	334	44	2	Running
3	4	55	Mark Martin	Aaron's Best of the Best Toyota	334	41	0	Running
4	34	24	Jeff Gordon	DuPont Chevrolet	334	41	1	Running
5	2	17	Matt Kenseth	Best Buy Ford	334	40	1	Running
6	1	56	Martin Truex Jr.	NAPA Auto Parts Toyota	334	39	1	Running
7	5	5	Kasey Kahne	Farmers Insurance Chevrolet	334	37	0	Running
8	20	99	Carl Edwards	Fastenal Ford	334	36	0	Running
9	15	29	Kevin Harvick	Budweiser Chevrolet	334	35	0	Running
10	16	88	Dale Earnhardt Jr.	Diet Mountain Dew/National Guard Chev.	334	34	0	Running
11	17	18	Kyle Busch	Interstate Batteries Toyota	334	33	0	Running
12	13	11	Denny Hamlin	FedEx Office/March of Dimes Toyota	334	32	0	Running
13	27	51	Kurt Busch	Phoenix Construction Services, Inc. Chev.	333	31	0	Running
14	9	1	Jamie McMurray	Bass Pro Shops/Tracker Boats Chevrolet	333	30	0	Running
15	12	22	AJ Allmendinger	Shell Pennzoil Dodge	333	29	0	Running
16	25	42	Juan Pablo Montoya	Target Chevrolet	333	28	0	Running
17	18	15	Clint Bowyer	5-hour Energy Toyota	333	27	0	Running
18	11	27	Paul Menard	Quaker State/Menards Chevrolet	333	26	0	Running
19	14	20	Joey Logano	Dollar General Toyota	333	25	0	Running
20	7	9	Marcos Ambrose	Stanley Ford	333	25	1	Running
21	6	39	Ryan Newman	US ARMY Chevrolet	332	23	0	Running
22	23	43	Aric Almirola	Smithfield Ford	332	22	0	Running
23	26	78	Regan Smith	Furniture Row/Farm American Chevrolet	332	21	0	Running
24	29	14	Tony Stewart	Mobil 1 Adv'd Fuel Economy/Office Depot Chev	332	20	0	Running
25	22	13	Casey Mears	GEICO Ford	331	19	0	Running
26	31	10	David Reutimann	Accell Construction Chevrolet	331	18	0	Running
27	30	47	Bobby Labonte	Bush's Beans/Tom Thumb Toyota	330	17	0	Running
28	19	21	Trevor Bayne (i)	Motorcraft/Quick Lane Tire & Auto Center Ford	330	0	0	Running
29	24	31	Jeff Burton	Caterpillar Chevrolet	330	15	0	Running
30	28	83	Landon Cassill	Burger King/Dr. Pepper Toyota	330	14	0	Running
31	35	38	David Gilliland	Mod Space Ford	328	13	0	Running
32	39	32	Reed Sorenson (i)	JaniKing Ford	327	0	0	Running
33	36	49	J.J. Yeley	JPO Absorbents Toyota	325	11	0	Running
34	42	33	Tony Raines	Precon Marine Chevrolet	323	10	0	Running
35	21	34	David Ragan	Scorpion Truck Bed Liners Ford	313	10	1	Running
36	8	2	Brad Keselowski	Miller Lite Dodge	312	8	0	Running
37	41	36	Dave Blaney	Jimmie Johnson's Anything With An Engine Chev	228	7	0	Vibration
38	37	93	Travis Kvapil	Dr. Pepper Toyota	114	6	0	Engine
39	32	26	Josh Wise #	Morristown Driver's Service Ford	66	5	0	Vibration
40	43	19	Mike Bliss (i)	Humphrey Smith Racing, LLC Toyota	38	0	0	Brakes
41	33	98	Michael McDowell	Curb Records Ford	36	3	0	Vibration
42	40	23	Scott Riggs	North TX Pipe/Embassy Suites Chevrolet	25	2	0	Vibration
43	38	95	Scott Speed	TWD Drywall Ford	13	1	0	Overheating

Sunoco Rookie of the Year Contender. Bonus Points: includes winner, lap leader & most laps led points.(i) = Ineligible for driver points in this series. Failed to qualify: (3) #30 David Stremme; #87 Joe Nemechek; #74 Stacy Compton.

RACE COMMENTS: Before an estimated crowd of 159,200, Greg Biffle won the Samsung Mobile 500, his 17th NASCAR Sprint Cup Series victory.

RACE STATISTICS

TIME OF RACE: 3 hours, 7 minutes, 12 seconds
AVERAGE SPEED: 160.577 mph
MARGIN OF VICTORY: 3.235 seconds
COORS LIGHT POLE AWARD: Martin Truex Jr. (190.369 mph. 28.366 secs.)
3M LAP LEADER: Jimmie Johnson (156 Laps)
AMERICAN ETHANOL GREEN FLAG RESTART AWARD: Greg Biffle
DIRECTV CREW CHIEF OF THE RACE: Greg Biffle (crew chief Matt Puccia)
FREESCALE "WIDE OPEN": Matt Kenseth
MAHLE CLEVITE ENGINE BUILDER OF THE

RACE: Hendrick Engines (#48)
MOBIL 1 OIL DRIVER OF THE RACE: Mark Martin
MOOG STEERING AND SUSPENSION PROBLEM SOLVER OF THE RACE: Jeff Gordon (crew chief Alan Gustafson, -0.183 seconds)
NASCAR SPRINT CUP LEADER BONUS: Greg Biffle ($50,000 ++)
USG IMPROVING THE FINISH: Jeff Gordon (30 places)
CAUTION FLAGS: 2 cautions for 10 laps. [Beneficiary in Brackets] 68–71 (Debris [34]); 95–100 (Debris [10]).
LAP LEADERS: 18 lead changes among 7 drivers. Truex Jr. 1–31, Biffle 32–45, Kenseth 46, Ambrose 47, Biffle 48–68, Truex Jr. 69–71, Biffle 72–81, Kenseth 82–95, Biffle 96, Ragan 97, Truex Jr. 98–100, Biffle 101–112, Johnson 113–146, Biffle 147, Truex Jr. 148–179, Johnson 180–282, J. Gordon 283–284, Johnson 285–303, Biffle 304–334.

++Rollover money awarded at year's end, amount not included in race winnings.

POINT LEADERS
(After 7 Races)

1	GREG BIFFLE	273
2	Matt Kenseth	254
3	Dale Earnhardt Jr.	254
4	Martin Truex Jr.	253
5	Kevin Harvick	249
6	Denny Hamlin	242
7	Tony Stewart	234
8	Jimmie Johnson	233
9	Ryan Newman	225
10	Clint Bowyer	219
11	Carl Edwards	215
12	Paul Menard	192

TEXAS MOTOR SPEEDWAY

AAA TEXAS 500
OFFICIAL RACE RESULTS: RACE #34 – NOVEMBER 4, 2012

NASCAR SPRINT CUP SERIES RACE RESULTS

Fin Pos	Str Pos	Car No	Series Driver	Team	Laps	Points	Bonus Points	Status
1	1	48	Jimmie Johnson	Lowe's Chevrolet	335	48	5	Running
2	8	2	Brad Keselowski	Miller Lite Dodge	335	43	1	Running
3	3	18	Kyle Busch	Snickers Toyota	335	42	1	Running
4	10	17	Matt Kenseth	Ford EcoBoost Ford	335	41	1	Running
5	21	14	Tony Stewart	Office Depot/Mobil 1 Chevrolet	335	39	0	Running
6	4	15	Clint Bowyer	5-hour Energy Toyota	335	38	0	Running
7	19	88	Dale Earnhardt Jr.	National Guard/Diet Mountain Dew Chev.	335	37	0	Running
8	18	78	Kurt Busch	Furniture Row Chevrolet	335	36	0	Running
9	23	29	Kevin Harvick	Rheem/Budweiser Chevrolet	335	35	0	Running
10	2	16	Greg Biffle	3M Ford	335	34	0	Running
11	6	20	Joey Logano	Home Depot/redbeacon.com Toyota	335	33	0	Running
12	36	39	Ryan Newman	Quicken Loans Chevrolet	335	33	1	Running
13	5	56	Martin Truex Jr.	Carlyle Tools by NAPA Toyota	335	31	0	Running
14	16	24	Jeff Gordon	Drive to End Hunger Chevrolet	335	30	0	Running
15	14	43	Aric Almirola	Farmland Ford	335	29	0	Running
16	9	99	Carl Edwards	Aflac Ford	335	28	0	Running
17	17	22	Sam Hornish Jr. (i)	Shell Pennzoil Dodge	335	0	0	Running
18	24	1	Jamie McMurray	McDonald's Chevrolet	335	26	0	Running
19	22	31	Jeff Burton	Caterpillar Chevrolet	335	25	0	Running
20	12	11	Denny Hamlin	FedEx Office Toyota	335	24	0	Running
21	20	13	Casey Mears	GEICO Ford	335	23	0	Running
22	7	21	Trevor Bayne (i)	Motorcraft/Quick Lane Tire & Auto Center Ford	335	0	0	Running
23	38	93	Travis Kvapil	Dr. Pepper Toyota	335	22	1	Running
24	32	10	Danica Patrick (i)	GoDaddy.com Chevrolet	335	0	0	Running
25	13	5	Kasey Kahne	Hendrickcars.com/Great Clips Chevrolet	334	19	0	Running
26	41	83	Landon Cassill	Burger King Toyota	333	18	0	Running
27	27	27	Paul Menard	Quaker State/Menards Chevrolet	332	17	0	Running
28	33	34	David Ragan	CertainTeed/31-W Ford	331	16	0	Running
29	11	55	Mark Martin	Aaron's Dream Machine Toyota	329	15	0	Accident
30	31	95	Scott Speed	B&D Electrical/TWD Ford	328	14	0	Running
31	42	32	Ken Schrader	Federated Auto Parts Ford	328	13	0	Running
32	15	9	Marcos Ambrose	Mac Tools Ford	310	12	0	Accident
33	29	47	Bobby Labonte	Wounded Warrior Project Toyota	284	11	0	Running
34	25	42	Juan Pablo Montoya	Huggies Chevrolet	279	10	0	Running
35	30	38	David Gilliland	Long John Silver's Ford	225	9	0	Engine
36	26	51	AJ Allmendinger	Phoenix Construction Chevrolet	107	8	0	Accident
37	35	26	Josh Wise #	MDS Transport Ford	41	7	0	Vibration
38	37	98	Michael McDowell	Phil Parsons Racing Ford	37	6	0	Overheating
39	40	36	Dave Blaney	Tommy Baldwin Racing Chevrolet	37	5	0	Brakes
40	43	87	Joe Nemechek (i)	AM/FM Energy Wood & Pellet Stoves Toyota	33	0	0	Vibration
41	34	19	Mike Bliss (i)	Plinker Tactical/MCM Elegante Toyota	32	0	0	Brakes
42	28	37	J.J. Yeley	MaxQWorkForce.com Chevrolet	10	2	0	Overheating
43	39	91	Reed Sorenson	Plinker Tactical/MCM Elegante Toyota	6	0	0	Electrical

Sunoco Rookie of the Year Contender. Bonus Points: includes winner, lap leader & most laps led points. (i) = Ineligible for driver points in this series. Failed to qualify: (3) #33 Stephen Leicht; #79 Kelly Bires; #30 David Stremme.

RACE COMMENTS: Before an estimated crowd of 146,000, Jimmie Johnson won the AAA Texas 500, his 60th NASCAR Sprint Cup Series victory.

RACE STATISTICS

TIME OF RACE: 3 hours, 41 minutes, 30 seconds
AVERAGE SPEED: 136.117 mph
MARGIN OF VICTORY: 0.808 seconds
COORS LIGHT POLE AWARD: Jimmie Johnson (191.076 mph. 28.261 secs.)
3M LAP LEADER: Jimmie Johnson (168 Laps)
AMERICAN ETHANOL GREEN FLAG RESTART AWARD: Jimmie Johnson
DIRECTV CREW CHIEF OF THE RACE: Kyle Busch (crew chief Dave Rogers)
FREESCALE "WIDE OPEN": Matt Kenseth
MAHLE CLEVITE ENGINE BUILDER OF THE RACE: Hendrick Engines (#48)

MOBIL 1 OIL DRIVER OF THE RACE: Kyle Busch
MOOG STEERING AND SUSPENSION PROBLEM SOLVER OF THE RACE: Matt Kenseth (crew chief Jimmy Fennig, 0.448 seconds)
NASCAR SPRINT CUP LEADER BONUS: Jimmie Johnson ($10,000 ++)
USG IMPROVING THE FINISH: Ryan Newman (24 places)
CAUTION FLAGS: 9 cautions for 49 laps. [Beneficiary in Brackets] 101–104 (Debris [22]); 110–118 (Car #51 Accident Frontstretch [None]); 120–128 (42, 47, 21 Accident Frontstretch [31]); 186–190 (Debris [1]); 224–227 (Debris [21]); 276–280 (Debris [21]); 311–315 (Car #9

Accident Turn 1 [31]); 322–326 (Debris [31]); 331–333 (Car #55, 99 Accident Frontstretch [13]).
LAP LEADERS: 20 lead changes among 7 drivers. Johnson 1–48, Newman 49–50, Johnson 51–101, Newman 102–105, Keselowski 106–118, Johnson 119–165, Ky. Busch 166, Kenseth 167, Bayne 168–171, Kvapil 172, Johnson 173–190, Ky. Busch 191–223, Keselowski 224, Ky. Busch 225–235, Keselowski 236–276, Ky. Busch 277–311, Johnson 312, Keselowski 313–326, Johnson 327, Keselowski 328–333, Johnson 334–335.

++Rollover money awarded at year's end, amount not included in race winnings.

POINT LEADERS
(After 34 Races)

1	JIMMIE JOHNSON	2339
2	Brad Keselowski	2332
3	Clint Bowyer	2303
4	Kasey Kahne	2281
5	Matt Kenseth	2267
6	Jeff Gordon	2267
7	Denny Hamlin	2266
8	Tony Stewart	2259
9	Martin Truex Jr.	2259
10	Greg Biffle	2256
11	Kevin Harvick	2238
12	Dale Earnhardt Jr.	2188

TEXAS MOTOR SPEEDWAY

TOP 20 ACTIVE NASCAR SPRINT CUP SERIES DRIVERS (MINIMUM 2 STARTS)

Driver	Races	Wins	Top 5s	Top 10s	Poles	Total Laps	Laps Led	Avg. Start	Avg. Finish
Matt Kenseth	21	2	12	15	0	6973	772	15.8	8.3
Jimmie Johnson	19	2	9	14	1	6153	443	8.8	9.3
Denny Hamlin	15	2	5	8	0	5008	131	17.0	10.9
Kevin Harvick	20	0	3	10	0	6677	5	20.8	12.5
Tony Stewart	22	2	6	12	1	7255	727	18.2	12.7
Clint Bowyer	14	0	3	8	0	4662	84	12.7	12.8
Dale Earnhardt Jr.	21	1	3	12	2	6829	448	11.8	13.6
Mark Martin	24	1	8	13	0	7569	208	15.1	13.9
Kyle Busch	16	0	5	6	0	4935	521	14.4	14.0
Kurt Busch	20	1	3	12	0	6567	235	16.4	14.1
Carl Edwards	16	3	5	7	0	5097	493	14.4	15.1
Greg Biffle	18	2	7	11	1	5668	732	11.2	15.9
Martin Truex Jr.	15	0	1	7	2	4742	89	17.2	15.9
Jeff Gordon	24	1	8	11	2	7197	584	12.5	16.1
Jeff Burton	24	2	3	9	0	7662	180	24.9	17.0
Jamie McMurray	18	0	3	6	0	5803	70	24.8	17.8
Casey Mears	17	0	2	4	0	5638	39	25.0	18.7
Kasey Kahne	17	1	4	5	1	5412	218	11.8	19.2
Terry Labonte	12	1	2	5	1	3639	231	25.5	19.3
Marcos Ambrose	9	0	0	1	0	2859	2	17.7	19.4

TEXAS 500

Year	Driver	Car	Average Speed
1997	Jeff Burton	Ford	125.111
1998	Mark Martin	Ford	136.771
1999	Terry Labonte	Chevrolet	144.276
2000	Dale Earnhardt Jr.	Chevrolet	131.152
2001	Dale Jarrett	Ford	141.804
2002	Matt Kenseth	Ford	142.453
2003	Ryan Newman	Dodge	134.517
2004	Elliott Sadler	Ford	138.845
2005	Greg Biffle	Ford	130.055
2006	Kasey Kahne	Dodge	137.943
2007	Jeff Burton	Chevrolet	143.359
2008	Carl Edwards	Ford	144.814
2009	Jeff Gordon	Chevrolet	146.372
2010	Denny Hamlin	Toyota	146.230
2011	Matt Kenseth	Ford	149.231
2012	Greg Biffle	Ford	160.577

AAA TEXAS 500

Year	Driver	Car	Average Speed
2005	Carl Edwards	Ford	151.055
2006	Tony Stewart	Chevrolet	134.891
2007	Jimmie Johnson	Chevrolet	131.219
2008	Carl Edwards	Ford	144.219
2009	Kurt Busch	Dodge	147.137
2010	Denny Hamlin	Toyota	140.456
2011	Tony Stewart	Chevrolet	152.705
2012	Jimmie Johnson	Chevrolet	136.117

TEXAS MOTOR SPEEDWAY

WATKINS GLEN INTERNATIONAL

2790 County Route 16 Watkins Glen, NY 14891 • **Tickets:** 1-866-GO-NASCAR or 1-866-461-RACE • **Web site:** www.theglen.com
Facebook: www.facebook.com/WatkinsGlenInternational • **Twitter:** @WGI

NASCAR

CONFIGURATION
Distance: 2.45 miles
Banking: N/A

TRACK RECORDS
Qualifying Records
Juan Pablo Montoya, 127.020
mph (69.438 sec.),
Set August 11, 2012

Race Record
Mark Martin, 103.030 mph,
Set August 13, 1995

2013 TRACK LAYOUT

Watkins Glen International
Facility Map - NASCAR

LEGEND
- McDonald's Kid's Zone
- Shower
- Food Concession
- ATM
- Pedestrian Crossover
- Restroom
- Information Booth
- Hospitality Area
- Handicap Parking
- Unreserved Camping
- Town Hall
- Medical Building

2013 SCHEDULE
August 10: NASCAR Nationwide Series
August 11: NASCAR Sprint Cup Series

TRACK OFFICIALS

Michael Printup *President*

PR CONTACTS
Elizabeth Mayer *Public Relations Manager*

VISITOR INFORMATION
Watkins Glen Area Chamber of Commerce
(607) 535-4300 – www.watkinsglenchamber.com

DIRECTIONS
Located five miles SW of Watkins Glen. *From Elmira-Corning Reg. Airport:* turn right on Sing Sing Road. Left at Chambers Road for 4.7 miles and straight onto Catlin Hill Road. Left at stop sign on Moreland/Beaver Dams Road, then right onto Russell Hill, then left onto Route 414. Right on Bronson Hill Road, then bear right to gate 2.

FINGER LAKES 355 AT THE GLEN

OFFICIAL RACE RESULTS: RACE #22 – AUGUST 12, 2012

NASCAR SPRINT CUP SERIES RACE RESULTS

Fin Pos	Str Pos	Car No	Series Driver	Team	Laps	Points	Bonus Points	Status
1	5	9	Marcos Ambrose	Stanley Ford	90	47	4	Running
2	4	2	Brad Keselowski	Miller Lite Dodge	90	43	1	Running
3	3	48	Jimmie Johnson	Lowe's Cortez Silver Chevrolet	90	41	0	Running
4	8	15	Clint Bowyer	5-hour Energy Toyota	90	40	0	Running
5	17	22	Sam Hornish Jr. (i)	Shell Pennzoil Dodge	90	0	0	Running
6	15	16	Greg Biffle	3M Ford	90	38	0	Running
7	2	18	Kyle Busch	M&M's Toyota	90	39	2	Running
8	24	17	Matt Kenseth	Ford EcoBoost Ford	90	36	0	Running
9	13	78	Regan Smith	Furniture Row/Farm American Chevrolet	90	35	0	Running
10	9	56	Martin Truex Jr.	NAPA Auto Parts Toyota	90	34	0	Running
11	6	39	Ryan Newman	U.S. ARMY Chevrolet	90	33	0	Running
12	22	27	Paul Menard	Menards/Rheem Chevrolet	90	32	0	Running
13	20	5	Kasey Kahne	Farmers Insurance Chevrolet	90	31	0	Running
14	18	99	Carl Edwards	Fastenal Ford	90	31	1	Running
15	19	29	Kevin Harvick	Budweiser Chevrolet	90	29	0	Running
16	30	13	Casey Mears	GEICO Ford	90	28	0	Running
17	21	95	Scott Speed	TWD Ford	90	27	0	Running
18	29	43	Aric Almirola	Smithfield Ford	90	26	0	Running
19	7	14	Tony Stewart	Office Depot/Mobil 1 Chevrolet	90	25	0	Running
20	34	38	David Gilliland	Mod Space Ford	90	24	0	Running
21	12	24	Jeff Gordon	Drive to End Hunger Chevrolet	90	23	0	Running
22	32	34	David Ragan	Scorpion Coatings/Al's Liners Ford	90	22	0	Running
23	35	83	Landon Cassill	Burger King/Dr. Pepper Toyota	90	21	0	Running
24	42	93	Travis Kvapil	Burger King/Dr. Pepper Toyota	90	20	0	Running
25	25	32	Boris Said	Hendrickcars.com Ford	90	19	0	Running
26	39	33	Stephen Leicht #	LittleJoesAuto.com Chevrolet	90	18	0	Running
27	26	47	Bobby Labonte	Miller Welders/Freightliner Toyota	90	17	0	Running
28	16	88	Dale Earnhardt Jr.	National Guard/Diet Mountain Dew Chevrolet	89	16	0	Running
29	36	87	Joe Nemechek (i)	Genny Light/AM/FM Energy Toyota	88	0	0	Running
30	28	31	Jeff Burton	Caterpillar Chevrolet	84	14	0	Running
31	27	51	Kurt Busch	Phoenix Construction Services Inc. Chevrolet	81	13	0	Running
32	14	20	Joey Logano	The Home Depot Toyota	71	12	0	Running
33	1	42	Juan Pablo Montoya	Target Chevrolet	63	12	1	Accident
34	23	11	Denny Hamlin	FedEx Freight Toyota	57	10	0	Engine
35	41	49	Jason Leffler (i)	America Israel Racing Toyota	42	0	0	Engine
36	31	36	Dave Blaney	Tommy Baldwin Racing Chevrolet	41	8	0	Suspension
37	11	98	Michael McDowell	TRAQM Ford	30	7	0	Rear Gear
38	38	26	Josh Wise #	MDS Transport Ford	25	6	0	Electrical
39	10	1	Jamie McMurray	McDonald's Chevrolet	24	5	0	Accident
40	37	10	J.J. Yeley	Tommy Baldwin Racing Chevrolet	15	4	0	Brakes
41	40	19	Chris Cook	Plinker Tactical Toyota	5	3	0	Brakes
42	43	30	Patrick Long	Inception Motorsports Toyota	2	2	0	Brakes
43	33	55	Brian Vickers	MyClassicGarage.com Toyota	0	1	0	Engine

Sunoco Rookie of the Year Contender. Bonus Points: includes winner, lap leader & most laps led points. (i) = Ineligible for driver points in this series. Failed to qualify: n/a.

RACE COMMENTS: Before an estimated crowd of 90,000, Marcos Ambrose won the Finger Lakes 355, his second NASCAR Sprint Cup Series victory. Prior to the green flag, the following car dropped to the rear of the field for the reason indicated: #93 (back-up car).

RACE STATISTICS

TIME OF RACE: 2 hours, 14 minutes, 48 seconds
AVERAGE SPEED: 98.145 mph
MARGIN OF VICTORY: 0.571 seconds
COORS LIGHT POLE AWARD: Juan Pablo Montoya (127.02 mph. 69.438 secs.)
3M LAP LEADER: Kyle Busch (43 Laps)
AMERICAN ETHANOL GREEN FLAG RESTART AWARD: Brad Keselowski
DIRECTV CREW CHIEF OF THE RACE: Marcos Ambrose (crew chief Todd Parrott)
FREESCALE "WIDE OPEN": Sam Hornish Jr.
MAHLE CLEVITE ENGINE BUILDER OF THE RACE: Toyota Racing Development

(TRD) (#18)
MOBIL 1 OIL DRIVER OF THE RACE: Clint Bowyer
MOOG STEERING AND SUSPENSION PROBLEM SOLVER OF THE RACE: Greg Biffle (crew chief Matt Puccia, 0.519 seconds)
NASCAR SPRINT CUP LEADER BONUS: No winner: rolls over to $160,000 at next event++
SUNOCO ROOKIE OF THE RACE: Stephen Leicht
USG IMPROVING THE FINISH: Travis Kvapil (18 places)
CAUTION FLAGS: 4 cautions for 13 laps. [Beneficiary in Brackets] 27–29 (Car #1

Accident Turn 4 [95]); 59–61 (Oil On Backstretch From #11 [38]); 65–68 (Oil On Backstretch From #49 [33]); 72–74 (Car #14 Accident Frontstretch [33]).
LAP LEADERS: 10 lead changes among 5 drivers. Montoya-pole, Ky. Busch 1–26, Montoya 27, Keselowski 28–38, Ambrose 39–45, Keselowski 46–56, Ky. Busch 57–58, Edwards 59, Keselowski 60–74, Ky. Busch 75–89, Ambrose 90.

++Rollover money awarded at year's end, amount not included in race winnings.

POINT LEADERS
(After 22 Races)

1	JIMMIE JOHNSON	777
2	Greg Biffle	776
3	Matt Kenseth	775
4	Dale Earnhardt Jr.	760
5	Brad Keselowski	733
6	Martin Truex Jr.	728
7	Clint Bowyer	719
8	Tony Stewart	716
9	Kevin Harvick	710
10	Denny Hamlin	693
11	Kasey Kahne	653
12	Carl Edwards	650

NASCAR NATIONWIDE SERIES CAREER VICTORIES (1982 THRU 2012)

Driver	Victories	Driver	Victories	Driver	Victories	Driver	Victories
Kyle Busch	51	Tony Stewart	10	L.D. Ottinger	3	Neil Bonnett	1
Mark Martin	49	David Green	9	Steve Park	3	James Buescher	1
Kevin Harvick	39	Jimmy Hensley	9	Johnny Sauter	3	Ronald Cooper	1
Carl Edwards	38	Rick Mast	9	Brian Vickers	3	Derrike Cope	1
Jack Ingram	31	Elliott Sadler	9	Mike Alexander	2	Bobby Dotter	1
Jeff Burton	27	Kenny Wallace	9	Bobby Allison	2	Bill Elliott	1
Matt Kenseth	26	Clint Bowyer	8	Casey Atwood	2	Jeff Fuller	1
Tommy Houston	24	Jamie McMurray	8	Mike Bliss	2	David Gilliland	1
Dale Earnhardt Jr.	23	Ricky Stenhouse Jr.	8	Ron Bouchard	2	Robby Gordon	1
Sam Ard	22	Kasey Kahne	7	Austin Dillon	2	Bobby Hamilton	1
Tommy Ellis	22	Ryan Newman	7	Bobby Hillin Jr.	2	Sam Hornish Jr.	1
Dale Earnhardt	21	Geoff Bodine	6	Buckshot Jones	2	Jimmie Johnson	1
Harry Gant	21	Butch Lindley	6	Jason Leffler	2	Justin Labonte	1
Greg Biffle	20	Chad Little	6	Kevin Lepage	2	Stephen Leicht	1
Brad Keselowski	20	Mike McLaughlin	6	Sterling Marlin	2	Tracy Leslie	1
Joey Logano	18	Rob Moroso	6	Butch Miller	2	Dick McCabe	1
Jeff Green	16	Scott Wimmer	6	Hank Parker Jr.	2	Casey Mears	1
Joe Nemechek	16	Brett Bodine	5	Phil Parsons	2	Paul Menard	1
Todd Bodine	15	Kurt Busch	5	David Ragan	2	Juan Pablo Montoya	1
Randy LaJoie	15	Jeff Gordon	5	Tim Richmond	2	David Pearson	1
Larry Pearson	15	Bobby Hamilton Jr.	5	Johnny Rumley	2	Nelson Piquet Jr.	1
Morgan Shepherd	15	Marcos Ambrose	4	Hermie Sadler	2	Larry Pollard	1
Martin Truex Jr.	13	Ward Burton	4	Elton Sawyer	2	David Reutimann	1
Darrell Waltrip	13	Ricky Craven	4	Ken Schrader	2	Ricky Rudd	1
Jimmy Spencer	12	Tim Fedewa	4	Dennis Setzer	2	Joe Ruttman	1
Chuck Bown	11	Ron Fellows	4	Ronnie Silver	2	Greg Sacks	1
Steve Grissom	11	Ron Hornaday Jr.	4	Dick Trickle	2	Boris Said	1
Denny Hamlin	11	Jeff Purvis	4	Rick Wilson	2	Andy Santerre	1
Dale Jarrett	11	Scott Riggs	4	Aric Almirola	1	John Settlemyre	1
Terry Labonte	11	Reed Sorenson	4	Jamie Aube	1	Mike Skinner	1
Michael Waltrip	11	Mike Wallace	4	Trevor Bayne	1	Jack Sprague	1
Jason Keller	10	Justin Allgaier	3	Ed Berrier	1	Brad Teague	1
Bobby Labonte	10	Johnny Benson	3	Joe Bessey	1		
Robert Pressley	10	Ernie Irvan	3	Dave Blaney	1		

NASCAR LATE MODEL SPORTSMAN DIVISION CHAMPIONS (1950-1981)

PRIOR TO THE CREATION OF THE NASCAR NATIONWIDE SERIES

Year	Champion	Year	Champion	Year	Champion
1950	Mike Klapak*	1962	Rene Charland	1974	Jack Ingram
1951	Mike Klapak	1963	Rene Charland	1975	L.D. Ottinger
1952	Mike Klapak	1964	Rene Charland	1976	L.D. Ottinger
1953	Johnny Roberts	1965	Rene Charland	1977	Butch Lindley
1954	Danny Graves	1966	Don MacTavish	1978	Butch Lindley
1955	Billy Myers	1967	Pete Hamilton	1979	Gene Glover
1956	Ralph Earnhardt	1968	Joe Thurman**	1980	Morgan Shepherd
1957	Ned Jarrett	1969	Red Farmer	1981	Tommy Ellis
1958	Ned Jarrett	1970	Red Farmer		
1959	Rick Henderson	1971	Red Farmer		
1960	Bill Wimble	1972	Jack Ingram		
1961	Dick Nephew	1973	Jack Ingram		

*division called NASCAR Sportsman from 1950-1967;
**division name changed to NASCAR Late Model Sportsman in 1968

NASCAR NATIONWIDE SERIES FINAL 2012 OWNER POINTS STANDINGS

Pos.	Car	Owner	Points	Starts	Wins	Top 5	Top 10	Qualifying Attempts
1	18	Joe Gibbs	1274	33	7	22	28	33
2	6	Jack Roush	1251	33	6	19	26	33
3	2	DeLana Harvick	1228	33	4	15	24	33
4	3	Morgan Shepherd	1227	33	2	16	27	33
5	33	DeLana Harvick	1182	33	2	16	24	33
6	22	Roger Penske	1149	33	3	13	23	33
7	12	Roger Penske	1146	33	0	10	22	33
8	54	Kyle Busch	1122	33	1	15	22	33
9	43	Sandra Turner	1082	33	0	6	17	33
10	31	Sandra Turner	1076	33	1	6	19	33
11	30	Harry Scott Jr.	1007	33	2	3	12	33
12	88	Dale Earnhardt Jr.	994	33	0	4	14	33
13	38	Steve Turner	956	33	0	3	11	33
14	44	Mark Smith	866	33	0	0	1	33
15	11	J.D. Gibbs	853	33	0	2	11	33
16	87	Andrea Nemechek	841	33	0	0	1	33
17	7	Kelley Earnhardt-Miller	838	33	0	0	4	33
18	199	Robby Benton	768	33	0	0	3	33
19	01	Johnny Davis	749	33	0	0	1	33
20	19	Mark Smith	746	33	0	0	1	33
21	51	Tony Clements	725	33	0	1	3	33
22	81	Gina MacDonald	715	33	0	0	0	33
23	20	Joe Gibbs	710	21	2	4	13	21
24	14	Mark Smith	662	33	0	0	0	33
25	4	Rusty Wallace	603	33	0	0	1	33
26	40	Curtis Key Sr.	601	33	0	0	0	33
27	70	Mary Louise Miller	596	32	0	0	0	33
28	124	Jason Sciavicco	593	33	0	0	0	33
29	23	Robert Richardson Sr.	568	33	0	0	1	33
30	41	Rick Ware	560	33	0	0	0	33
31	39	Archie St Hilaire	544	32	0	0	0	33
32	108	Randy Hill	436	28	0	0	0	33
33	52	Jimmy Means	338	9	0	0	0	9
34	60	Jack Roush	318	8	1	2	5	8
35	5	Rick Hendrick	306	24	1	6	6	27
36	50	Rusty Wallace	288	21	0	0	0	31
37	89	Morgan Shepherd	239	25	0	0	1	28
38	15	Rick Ware	228	33	0	0	0	33
39	10	Mark Smith	182	8	0	0	2	8
40	136	Beth Baldwin	175	7	0	0	1	7
41	198	Fred Biagi	173	4	0	1	3	4
42	1	James Finch	133	8	1	1	1	8
43	27	Steve Meehan	125	31	0	0	1	33
44	42	Curtis Key Sr.	121	22	0	0	0	27
45	174	Mike Harmon	120	31	0	0	0	33
46	46	Curtis Key Sr.	112	9	0	0	0	9
47	86	Scott Deware	103	15	0	0	0	18
48	175	Rick Ware	92	30	0	0	0	33
49	47	Curtis Key Sr.	89	11	0	0	0	12
50	171	Rick Ware	74	2	0	0	1	2
51	21	Richard Childress	64	3	0	0	1	3
52	275	Kenny Habul	62	3	0	0	0	3
53	8	Scott Lagasse	62	11	0	0	0	13
55	100	Mike Ruch	59	7	0	0	0	7
54	28	Jay Robinson	59	3	0	0	0	3
56	159	Bob Kelley	55	4	0	0	0	4
57	117	Adrian Berryhill	50	2	0	0	0	4
58	113	Jennifer Jo Cobb	30	2	0	0	0	3
59	126	John Young	29	1	0	0	0	1
60	82	Pat MacDonald	25	1	0	0	0	3
61	73	Gary Keller	20	2	0	0	0	2
62	97	Andrea Nemechek	19	2	0	0	0	2
63	153	Robert Torriere	17	1	0	0	0	1
64	32	Steve Turner	16	4	0	0	0	4
65	191	Mark Smith	13	2	0	0	0	5
67	172	James Carter	10	1	0	0	0	1
66	03	Robert Richardson Sr.	10	1	0	0	0	1
68	109	Robby Benton	0	1	0	1	1	1
69	176	Ray Hackett	0	0	0	0	0	1

NASCAR NATIONWIDE SERIES FINAL 2012 DRIVER POINTS STANDINGS

Pos.	Driver	Points	Starts	Wins	Top 5	Top 10
1	Ricky Stenhouse Jr.	1251	33	6	19	26
2	Elliott Sadler	1228	33	4	15	24
3	Austin Dillon	1227	33	2	16	27
4	Sam Hornish Jr.	1146	33	0	10	22
5	Michael Annett	1082	33	0	6	17
6	Justin Allgaier	1076	33	1	6	19
7	Cole Whitt	994	33	0	4	14
8	Mike Bliss	902	33	0	0	1
9	Brian Scott	853	33	0	2	11
10	Danica Patrick	838	33	0	0	4
11	Joe Nemechek	816	32	0	0	1
12	Mike Wallace	749	33	0	0	1
13	Jason Bowles	715	33	0	0	0
14	Jeremy Clements	701	33	0	0	2
15	Tayler Malsam	609	26	0	0	1
16	Eric McClure	559	28	0	0	0
17	Erik Darnell	558	31	0	0	0
18	Brad Sweet	469	18	0	0	2
19	Timmy Hill	452	28	0	0	2
20	Johanna Long	428	21	0	0	0
21	Danny Efland	327	18	0	0	0
22	Kenny Wallace	311	14	0	1	3
23	Ryan Truex	298	11	0	1	4
24	Jamie Dick	282	14	0	0	0
25	T.J. Bell	258	22	0	0	0
26	Jeff Green	256	32	0	0	0
27	Josh Richards	256	14	0	0	0
28	Robert Richardson Jr.	248	16	0	0	0
29	Morgan Shepherd	239	21	0	0	0
30	Joey Gase	236	18	0	0	0
31	Blake Koch	230	23	0	0	0
32	Trevor Bayne	208	6	0	1	3
33	Travis Pastrana	204	9	0	0	0
34	Benny Gordon	198	11	0	0	0
35	Kevin Lepage	175	20	0	0	0
36	Darrell Wallace Jr.	139	4	0	0	3
37	Casey Roderick	136	8	0	0	0
38	Kyle Fowler	127	7	0	0	0
39	Reed Sorenson	124	6	0	0	0
40	Daryl Harr	123	8	0	0	0
41	Ron Fellows	120	3	0	3	3
42	Tim Schendel	113	11	0	0	0
43	Jeffrey Earnhardt	112	6	0	0	0
44	Chase Miller	107	29	0	0	0
45	Mike Harmon	106	19	0	0	0
46	Alex Bowman	100	4	0	0	0
47	Tim Andrews	100	11	0	0	0
48	Dexter Stacey	90	7	0	0	0
49	Jacques Villeneuve	82	2	0	1	2
50	John Blankenship	66	4	0	0	0
51	Brad Teague	65	4	0	0	0
52	Derek White	64	4	0	0	0
53	Tanner Berryhill	64	5	0	0	0
54	Steve Arpin	62	2	0	0	1
55	Kenny Habul	62	3	0	0	0
56	Scott Lagasse Jr.	62	3	0	0	0
57	Matt Frahm	61	6	0	0	0
58	Kevin Swindell	59	2	0	0	1
59	Alex Kennedy	56	3	0	0	0
60	Victor Gonzalez Jr.	55	2	0	0	0
61	Kyle Kelley	55	3	0	0	0
62	Matthew Carter	54	7	0	0	0
63	Derrike Cope	49	3	0	0	0
64	Carl Long	48	9	0	0	0
65	Hal Martin	47	3	0	0	0
66	Max Papis	41	1	0	1	1
67	Drew Herring	41	1	0	1	1
68	Juan Carlos Blum	40	3	0	0	0
69	Scott Saunders	38	3	0	0	0
70	Billy Johnson	36	1	0	0	1
71	Brett Moffitt	35	1	0	0	1
72	Steve Wallace	33	1	0	0	0
73	John Young	29	2	0	0	0
74	Andrew Ranger	28	2	0	0	0
75	David Green	27	3	0	0	0
76	Angela Cope	25	3	0	0	0
77	Alex Tagliani	23	1	0	0	0
78	Fain Skinner	23	2	0	0	0
79	Matt DiBenedetto	21	7	0	0	0
80	Tim Connolly	19	1	0	0	0
81	Charles Lewandoski	19	5	0	0	0
82	Amber Cope	18	1	0	0	0
83	Matthew Bell	18	2	0	0	0
84	Bill Prietzel	17	1	0	0	0
85	Eric Curran	17	2	0	0	0
86	Tim Bainey Jr.	16	1	0	0	0
87	Jamie Mosley	15	1	0	0	0
88	Patrick Carpentier	15	1	0	0	0
89	Stanton Barrett	15	1	0	0	0
90	Noel Dowler	12	1	0	0	0
91	Bobby Santos III	11	1	0	0	0
92	Nur Ali	11	1	0	0	0
93	John Jackson	10	2	0	0	0
94	Michael Guerity	9	2	0	0	0
95	Alex Popow	6	1	0	0	0
96	Louis-Philippe Dumoulin	6	1	0	0	0
97	Chris Cook	5	2	0	0	0
98	Ryan Ellis	5	1	0	0	0
99	Joey Logano	0	22	9	12	17
100	Brad Keselowsk	0	21	3	11	14
101	Kevin Harvick	0	13	2	9	10
102	Kurt Busch	0	15	2	7	11
103	James Buescher	0	20	1	2	8
104	Nelson Piquet Jr.	0	2	1	1	1
105	Carl Edwards	0	1	1	1	1
106	Regan Smith	0	1	1	1	1
107	Kyle Busch	0	22	0	9	14
108	Denny Hamlin	0	12	0	8	9
109	Paul Menard	0	7	0	3	6
110	Kasey Kahne	0	15	0	3	9
111	Michael McDowell	0	6	0	2	5
112	Ryan Blaney	0	13	0	1	7
113	Mark Martin	0	1	0	1	1
114	Brian Vickers	0	1	0	1	1
115	Brendan Gaughan	0	10	0	3	5
116	Ty Dillon	0	3	0	1	3
117	Dale Earnhardt Jr.	0	4	0	2	2
118	David Ragan	0	2	0	0	1
119	Parker Kligerman	0	3	0	0	2
120	Jason Leffler	0	2	0	0	1
121	Tony Stewart	0	1	0	0	1
122	Jamie McMurray	0	1	0	0	1
123	Joey Coulter	0	2	0	0	1
124	Miguel Paludo	0	2	0	0	0
125	Josh Wise	0	26	0	0	0
126	John Wes Townley	0	5	0	0	0
127	Ryan Newman	0	1	0	0	0
128	Bryan Silas	0	1	0	0	0
129	Paulie Harraka	0	2	0	0	0
130	Jennifer Jo Cobb	0	2	0	0	0
131	Kelly Bires	0	2	0	0	0
132	Tony Raines	0	11	0	0	0
133	David Starr	0	6	0	0	0
134	J.J. Yeley	0	14	0	0	0
135	Dakoda Armstrong	0	1	0	0	0
136	Justin Jennings	0	2	0	0	0
137	Clint Bowyer	0	1	0	0	0
138	Scott Riggs	0	14	0	0	0
139	Rick Crawford	0	1	0	0	0
140	Scott Speed	0	11	0	0	0
141	Dusty Davis	0	1	0	0	0
142	Stephen Leicht	0	5	0	0	0
143	Johnny Sauter	0	1	0	0	0

NASCAR NATIONWIDE SERIES 2012 SPECIAL AWARDS

COORS LIGHT POLE AWARD WINNER

JOEY LOGANO

Year	Driver	Poles	Year	Driver	Poles
1982	Sam Ard	7	1998	Dale Earnhardt Jr.	3
1983	Sam Ard	10	1999	Jeff Green	4
1984	Sam Ard	7	2000	Jeff Green	7
1985	J. Hensley/T. Houston	4	2001	Ryan Newman	6
1986	Brett Bodine	8	2002	Greg Biffle	5
1987	Mark Martin	6	2003	Kevin Harvick	5
1988	Larry Pearson	5	2004	Martin Truex Jr.	7
1989	Rob Moroso	6	2005	Carl Edwards	4
1990	C. Bown/J. Hensley	4	2006	Denny Hamlin	6
1991	Chuck Bown	5	2007	Denny Hamlin	5
1992	Jeff Gordon	11	2008	Carl Edwards	4
1993	Ward Burton	4	2009	Carl Edwards	7
1994	David Green	9	2010	Joey Logano	8
1995	David Green	4	2011	Carl Edwards	6
1996	David Green	4	2012	Joey Logano	6
1997	Elliott Sadler	4			

MOST POPULAR DRIVER

DANICA PATRICK

Past Winners (1982 thru 2012)		Past Winners (1982 thru 2012)	
1982	Jack Ingram	1998	Buckshot Jones
1983	Sam Ard	1999	Dale Earnhardt Jr.
1984	Sam Ard	2000	Ron Hornaday
1985	Jimmy Hensley	2001	Kevin Harvick
1986	Brett Bodine	2002	Greg Biffle
1987	Jimmy Hensley	2003	Scott Riggs
1988	Larry Pearson	2004	Martin Truex Jr.
1989	Rob Moroso	2005	Martin Truex Jr.
1990	Bobby Labonte	2006	Kenny Wallace
1991	Kenny Wallace	2007	Carl Edwards
1992	Joe Nemechek	2008	Brad Keselowski
1993	Joe Nemechek	2009	Brad Keselowski
1994	Kenny Wallace	2010	Brad Keselowski
1995	Chad Little	2011	Elliott Sadler
1996	David Green	2012	Danica Patrick
1997	Mike McLaughlin		

NASCAR NATIONWIDE SERIES CHAMPIONS AND LEADERS (1982 THRU 2012)

1982

Jack Ingram	4495
Sam Ard	4446
Tommy Ellis	3873
Tommy Houston	3827
Phil Parsons	3783
Dale Jarrett	3332
Pete Silva	2349
Jimmy Lawson	2106
Bob Shreeves	1928
Butch Lindley	1581

1983

Sam Ard	5454
Jack Ingram	5367
Tommy Houston	4933
Tommy Ellis	4929
Dale Jarrett	4837
Ronnie Silver	4058
Pete Silva	3945
Jimmy Hensley	3716
Eddie Falk	3617
Jeff Hensley	3444

1984

Sam Ard	4552
Jack Ingram	4126
Tommy Houston	4070
Dale Jarrett	4014
Ronnie Silver	3398
Joe Thurman	3221
Charlie Luck	3172
L.D. Ottinger	3069
Jeff Hensley	3032
Bob Shreeves	2869

1985

Jack Ingram	4106
Jimmy Hensley	4077
Larry Pearson	3951
Tommy Houston	3936
Dale Jarrett	3774
L.D. Ottinger	3732
Rick Mast	3589
Ronnie Silver	3425
Larry Pollard	3197
Eddie Falk	3044

1986

Larry Pearson	4551
Brett Bodine	4531
Jack Ingram	4301
Dale Jarrett	4261
L.D. Ottinger	4153
Tommy Houston	4121
Ronnie Silver	3967
Jimmy Hensley	3950
Charlie Luck	3847
Larry Pollard	3726

1987

Larry Pearson	3999
Jimmy Hensley	3617
Brett Bodine	3611
Jack Ingram	3598
Mike Alexander	3497
Dale Jarrett	3444
Brad Teague	3391
Mark Martin	3349
Rick Mast	3319
L.D. Ottinger	3318

1988

Tommy Ellis	4310
Rob Moroso	4071
Mike Alexander	4053
Larry Pearson	4050
Tommy Houston	4042
Jimmy Hensley	3904
Jimmy Spencer	3839
Rick Mast	3809
L.D. Ottinger	3732
Jack Ottinger	3610

1989

Rob Moroso	4001
Tommy Houston	3946
Tommy Ellis	3945
L.D. Ottinger	3916
Jack Ingram	3802
Kenny Wallace	3750
Rick Mast	3558
Ronald Cooper	3554
Chuck Bown	3349
Tom Peck	3171

1990

Chuck Bown	4372
Jimmy Hensley	4172
Steve Grissom	3982
Bobby Labonte	3977
Tom Peck	3868
Tommy Ellis	3829
Kenny Wallace	3829
L.D. Ottinger	3693
Tommy Houston	3667
Rick Mast	3617

1991

Bobby Labonte	4264
Kenny Wallace	4190
Robert Pressley	3929
Chuck Bown	3922
Jimmy Hensley	3916
Joe Nemechek	3902
Todd Bodine	3825
Tommy Houston	3777
Tom Peck	3746
Steve Grissom	3689

1992

Joe Nemechek	4275
Bobby Labonte	4272
Todd Bodine	4212
Jeff Gordon	4053
Robert Pressley	3988
Kenny Wallace	3966
Butch Miller	3725
Ward Burton	3648
Jeb Burton	3609
Tommy Houston	3599

1993

Steve Grissom	3846
Ricky Craven	3593
David Green	3584
Chuck Bown	3532
Joe Nemechek	3443
Ward Burton	3413
Bobby Dotter	3406
Robert Pressley	3389
Todd Bodine	3387
Hermie Sadler	3362

1994

David Green	3725
Ricky Craven	3679
Chad Little	3662
Kenny Wallace	3554
Hermie Sadler	3466
Johnny Benson	3303
Bobby Dotter	3299
Larry Pearson	3277
Dennis Setzer	3273
Tim Fedewa	3125

1995

Johnny Benson	3688
Chad Little	3284
Mike McLaughlin	3273
Jason Keller	3211
Jeff Green	3182
Larry Pearson	3029
Tim Fedewa	3022
Phil Parsons	2985
Elton Sawyer	2952
Jeff Fuller	2845

1996

Randy LaJoie	3714
David Green	3685
Todd Bodine	3064
Jeff Green	3059
Chad Little	2984
Jason Keller	2900
Jeff Purvis	2894
Kevin Lepage	2870
Phil Parsons	2854
Mike McLaughlin	2853

1997

Randy LaJoie	4381
Todd Bodine	4115
Steve Park	4080
Mike McLaughlin	3614
Elliott Sadler	3534
Phil Parsons	3523
Buckshot Jones	3437
Elton Sawyer	3419
Tim Fedewa	3398
Hermie Sadler	3340

1998

Dale Earnhardt Jr.	4469
Matt Kenseth	4421
Mike McLaughlin	4045
Randy LaJoie	3543
Elton Sawyer	3533
Phil Parsons	3525
Tim Fedewa	3515
Elliott Sadler	3470
Buckshot Jones	3453
Hermie Sadler	3340

1999

Dale Earnhardt Jr.	4647
Jeff Green	4367
Matt Kenseth	4327
Todd Bodine	4029
Elton Sawyer	3891
Jeff Purvis	3658
Dave Blaney	3582
Jason Keller	3537
Mike McLaughlin	3478
Randy LaJoie	3379

2000

Jeff Green	5005
Jason Keller	4389
Kevin Harvick	4113
Todd Bodine	4075
Ron Hornaday	3870
Elton Sawyer	3776
Randy LaJoie	3670
Casey Atwood	3404
David Green	3316
Jimmie Johnson	3264

2001

Kevin Harvick	4813
Jeff Green	4689
Jason Keller	4637
Greg Biffle	4509
Elton Sawyer	4100
Tony Raines	3975
Mike McLaughlin	3962
Jimmie Johnson	3871
Chad Little	3846
Kenny Wallace	3799

2002

Greg Biffle	4919
Jason Keller	4655
Scott Wimmer	4488
Mike McLaughlin	4253
Jack Sprague	4206
Jamie McMurray	4147
Kenny Wallace	4078
Bobby Hamilton Jr.	4058
Stacy Compton	4042
Scott Riggs	4023

2003

Brian Vickers	4637
David A. Green	4623
Ron Hornaday	4591
Bobby Hamilton Jr.	4588
Jason Keller	4528
Scott Riggs	4462
Kasey Kahne	4104
Johnny Sauter	4098
Scott Wimmer	4059
Mike Bliss	3932

2004

Martin Truex Jr.	5173
Kyle Busch	4943
Greg Biffle	4568
Ron Hornaday Jr.	4258
Mike Bliss	4115
Jason Keller	4088
David A. Green	4082
Ashton Lewis	3892
Kenny Wallace	3851
David Stremme	3738

2005

Martin Truex Jr.	4937
Clint Bowyer	4869
Carl Edwards	4601
Reed Sorenson	4453
Denny Hamlin	4143
Paul Menard	4101
Kenny Wallace	4068
David A. Green	3908
Jason Keller	3866
Greg Biffle	3865

2006

Kevin Harvick	5648
Carl Edwards	4824
Clint Bowyer	4683
Denny Hamlin	4667
J.J. Yeley	4487
Paul Menard	4075
Kyle Busch	3921
Johnny Sauter	3794
Greg Biffle	3789
Reed Sorenson	3670

2007

Carl Edwards	4805
David Reutimann	4187
Jason Leffler	3996
Kevin Harvick	3993
David Ragan	3739
Bobby Hamilton Jr.	3667
Stephen Leicht	3603
Marcos Ambrose	3477
Greg Biffle	3466
Matt Kenseth	3451

2008

Clint Bowyer	5132
Carl Edwards	5111
Brad Keselowski	4794
David Ragan	4525
Mike Bliss	4518
Kyle Busch	4461
David Reutimann	4388
Mike Wallace	4128
Jason Leffler	4086
Marcos Ambrose	3991

2009

Kyle Busch	5682
Carl Edwards	5472
Brad Keselowski	5364
Jason Leffler	4540
Mike Bliss	4075
Justin Allgaier	4049
Steve Wallace	4007
Jason Keller	3960
Brendan Gaughan	3914
Michael Annett	3598

2010

Brad Keselowski	5639
Carl Edwards	5194
Kyle Busch	4934
Justin Allgaier	4679
Paul Menard	4467
Kevin Harvick	4389
Trevor Bayne	4041
Joey Logano	4038
Jason Leffler	3941
Steve Wallace	3940

2011

Ricky Stenhouse Jr.	1222
Elliott Sadler	1177
Justin Allgaier	1105
Aric Almirola	1095
Reed Sorenson	1062
Jason Leffler	1028
Kenny Wallace	963
Brian Scott	947
Michael Annett	944
Steve Wallace	921

2012

Ricky Stenhouse Jr.	1251
Elliott Sadler	1228
Austin Dillon	1227
Sam Hornish Jr.	1146
Michael Annett	1082
Justin Allgaier	1076
Cole Whitt	994
Mike Bliss	902
Brian Scott	853
Danica Patrick	838

NASCAR NATIONWIDE SERIES
2013 DRIVERS

JUSTIN ALLGAIER

Birth Date:	June 6, 1986
Hometown:	Riverton, IL
Team:	No. 31 Turner Scott Motorsports Chevrolet

CAREER RECORD

Year	Starts	Wins	Top 5	Top 10	Points Standing
2008	4	0	0	0	72
2009	35	0	3	12	6
2010	35	1	8	20	4
2011	34	1	6	17	3
2012	33	1	6	19	6

Best Finish: 1st — 3 times
Most Recent: 2012 NAPA Auto Parts 200 Presented by Dodge (Montreal)

MICHAEL ANNETT

Birth Date:	June 23, 1986
Hometown:	Des Moines, IA
Team:	No. 43 Richard Petty Motorsports Ford

CAREER RECORD

Year	Starts	Wins	Top 5	Top 10	Points Standing
2008	1	0	0	0	138
2009	35	0	0	4	10
2010	35	0	0	2	13
2011	34	0	0	7	9
2012	33	0	6	17	5

Best Finish: 3rd — 2 times
Most Recent: 2012 OneMain Financial 200 (Dover)

TREVOR BAYNE

Birth Date:	February 19, 1991
Hometown:	Knoxville, TN
Team:	No. 6 Roush Fenway Racing Ford

CAREER RECORD

Year	Starts	Wins	Top 5	Top 10	Points Standing
2009	15	0	0	2	32
2010	35	0	6	11	7
2011	29	1	5	14	11
2012	6	0	1	3	32

Best Finish: 1st — 1 time
Most Recent: 2011 O'Reilly Auto Parts Challenge (Texas)

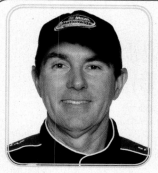

MIKE BLISS

Birth Date:	April 5, 1965
Hometown:	Milwaukie, OR
Team:	TBA

CAREER RECORD

Year	Starts	Wins	Top 5	Top 10	Points Standing
1998	2	0	0	1	71
1999	3	0	0	0	84
2000	1	0	0	0	100
2001	1	0	0	0	142
2003	34	0	8	14	10
2004	34	1	6	14	5
2005	1	0	0	0	129
2006	8	0	0	0	62
2007	24	0	3	8	21
2008	35	0	3	15	5
2009	35	1	7	15	5
2010	34	0	2	4	15
2011	34	0	0	1	12
2012	33	0	0	1	8

Best Finish: 1st — 2 times; Most Recent: 2009 CARQUEST Auto Parts 300 (Charlotte)

JASON BOWLES

Birth Date: November 4, 1982
Hometown: Ontario, CA
Team: No. 81 MacDonald Motorsports Toyota

CAREER RECORD

Year	Starts	Wins	Top 5	Top 10	Points Standing
2009	1	0	0	0	139
2010	1	0	0	0	118
2011	3	0	0	0	61
2012	33	0	0	0	13

Best Finish: 13th — 1 time
Most Recent: 2011 NAPA Auto Parts 200 Presented by Dodge (Montreal)

JEREMY CLEMENTS

Birth Date: January 16, 1985
Hometown: Spartanburg, SC
Team: No. 51 Jeremy Clements Racing Chevrolet

CAREER RECORD

Year	Starts	Wins	Top 5	Top 10	Points Standing
2003	1	0	0	0	137
2007	5	0	0	0	87
2008	2	0	0	0	102
2009	12	0	0	0	50
2010	16	0	0	1	34
2011	34	0	0	0	15
2012	33	0	0	2	14

Best Finish: 10th — 3 times
Most Recent: 2012 Indiana 250 (Indianapolis)

AUSTIN DILLON

Birth Date: April 27, 1990
Hometown: Clemmons, NC
Team: No. 3 Richard Childress Racing Chevrolet

CAREER RECORD

Year	Starts	Wins	Top 5	Top 10	Points Standing
2008	2	0	1	1	85
2009	4	0	0	0	80
2010	1	0	0	0	119
2011	4	0	1	3	107
2012	33	2	16	27	3

Best Finish: 1st — 2 times
Most Recent: 2012 Kentucky 300 (Kentucky)

SAM HORNISH JR.

Birth Date: July 2, 1979
Hometown: Defiance, OH
Team: No. 12 Penske Racing Ford

CAREER RECORD

Year	Starts	Wins	Top 5	Top 10	Points Standing
2006	2	0	0	0	117
2007	9	0	0	0	68
2008	8	0	0	0	51
2010	1	0	0	0	114
2011	13	1	2	6	23
2012	33	0	10	22	4

Best Finish: 1st — 1 time
Most Recent: 2011 WYPALL 200 (Phoenix)

NASCAR NATIONWIDE SERIES

PARKER KLIGERMAN

Birth Date: **August 8, 1990**
Hometown: **Westport, CT**
Team: **No. 77 Kyle Busch Motorsports Toyota**

CAREER RECORD

Year	Starts	Wins	Top 5	Top 10	Points Standing
2009	2	0	0	0	95
2010	12	0	0	2	39
2011	1	0	0	1	115
2012	3	0	0	2	119

Best Finish: 7th — 1 time
Most Recent: 2012 STP 300 (Chicagoland)

SCOTT LAGASSE JR.

Birth Date: **January 31, 1981**
Hometown: **St. Augustine, FL**
Team: **No. 8 Team SLR Chevrolet**

CAREER RECORD

Year	Starts	Wins	Top 5	Top 10	Points Standing
2005	5	0	0	0	81
2007	2	0	0	0	123
2008	7	0	0	0	59
2009	21	0	0	4	21
2010	14	0	0	1	37
2012	3	0	0	0	56

Best Finish: 8th — 2 times
Most Recent: 2010 Bashas' Supermarkets 200 (Phoenix)

JOHANNA LONG

Birth Date: **May 26, 1992**
Hometown: **Pensacola, FL**
Team: **No. 70 ML Motorsports Chevrolet**

CAREER RECORD

Year	Starts	Wins	Top 5	Top 10	Points Standing
2012	21	0	0	0	20

Best Finish: 12th — 2 times
Most Recent: 2012 Kentucky 300 (Kentucky)

TRAVIS PASTRANA

Birth Date: **October 8, 1983**
Hometown: **Annapolis, MD**
Team: **No. 60 Roush Fenway Racing Ford**

CAREER RECORD

Year	Starts	Wins	Top 5	Top 10	Points Standing
2012	9	0	0	0	33

Best Finish: 13th — 1 time
Most Recent: 2012 Indiana 250 (Indianapolis)

NASCAR NATIONWIDE SERIES

NASCAR Nationwide SERIES

ELLIOTT SADLER

Birth Date: **April 30, 1975**
Hometown: **Emporia, VA**
Team: **No. 11 Joe Gibbs Racing Toyota**

CAREER RECORD

Year	Starts	Wins	Top 5	Top 10	Points Standing
1995	2	0	0	1	70
1996	13	0	1	3	35
1997	30	3	6	10	5
1998	31	2	5	10	8
1999	15	0	1	3	36
2000	3	0	0	0	80
2003	1	0	0	0	144
2005	16	0	5	9	25
2006	7	0	0	0	63
2007	2	0	0	0	101
2008	4	0	0	0	71
2009	1	0	0	0	126
2010	5	0	1	2	62
2011	34	0	12	24	2
2012	33	4	15	24	2

Best Finish: 1st — 9 times
Most Recent: 2012 U.S. Cellular Presented by Enlist Weed Control System (Iowa)

BRIAN SCOTT

Birth Date: **January 12, 1988**
Hometown: **Boise, ID**
Team: **No. 2 Richard Childress Racing Chevrolet**

CAREER RECORD

Year	Starts	Wins	Top 5	Top 10	Points Standing
2009	7	0	0	0	64
2010	35	0	1	5	14
2011	34	0	2	7	8
2012	33	0	2	11	9

Best Finish: 3rd — 3 times
Most Recent: 2012 5-Hour Energy 200 (Dover)

REGAN SMITH

Birth Date: **September 23, 1983**
Hometown: **Cato, NY**
Team: **No. 7 JR Motorsports Chevrolet**

CAREER RECORD

Year	Starts	Wins	Top 5	Top 10	Points Standing
2002	1	0	0	0	118
2003	18	0	0	0	38
2004	10	0	0	0	45
2005	21	0	0	0	33
2006	35	0	0	1	20
2007	17	0	3	5	31
2012	1	1	1	1	106

Best Finish: 1st — 1 time
Most Recent: 2012 Ford EcoBoost 300 (Homestead)

BRIAN VICKERS

Birth Date: **October 24, 1983**
Hometown: **Thomasville, NC**
Team: **No. 20 Joe Gibbs Racing Toyota**

CAREER RECORD

Year	Starts	Wins	Top 5	Top 10	Points Standing
2001	4	0	0	0	72
2002	21	0	0	1	33
2003	34	3	13	21	1
2005	6	0	1	2	60
2006	8	0	2	4	42
2007	7	0	0	3	53
2008	12	0	6	8	36
2009	17	0	7	12	20
2010	5	0	2	5	56
2011	3	0	0	3	111
2012	1	0	1	1	114

Best Finish: 1st — 3 times
Most Recent: 2003 Stacker 200 Presented by YJ Stinger (Dover)

NASCAR Nationwide Series

NASCAR NATIONWIDE SERIES
2012 RESULTS

1 DRIVE4COPD 300
February 25, 2012 — Daytona International Speedway — 300 Miles – 120 Laps

Fin	Str	No	Driver	Team	Laps	Status	Fin	Str	No	Driver	Team	Laps	Status
1	15	30	James Buescher	FOE Chevrolet	120	Running	23	27	87	Joe Nemechek	D.A.B. Constructors Toyota	116	Accident
2	9	22	Brad Keselowski	Discount Tire Dodge	120	Running	24	39	50	T.J. Bell	Eastbound & Down Chevrolet	115	Accident
3	3	2	Elliott Sadler	OneMain Financial Chevrolet	120	Running	25	36	51	Jeremy Clements	Kevin Whitaker Chevrolet/92.5 WESC Chevrolet	115	Running
4	8	88	Cole Whitt #	Hellmann's Chevrolet	120	Running	26	23	27	David Ragan	CertainTeed/Mercury Ford	113	Accident
5	5	3	Austin Dillon #	AdvoCare Chevrolet	120	Running	27	16	43	Michael Annett	Pilot/Flying J Ford	113	Accident
6	25	19	Tayler Malsam	G-Oil Toyota	120	Running	28	28	01	Mike Wallace	G&K Services Chevrolet	112	Running
7	29	15	Timmy Hill	Poynt.com Ford	120	Running	29	35	39	Joey Gase #	Go Green Racing/JoeyGase.com Ford	108	Running
8	7	33	Tony Stewart	Oreo/Ritz Chevrolet	120	Running	30	26	99	Kenny Wallace	Family Farmers Toyota	104	Accident
9	11	38	Kasey Kahne	Great Clips Chevrolet	120	Running	31	18	36	Ryan Truex	Grime Boss Chevrolet	104	Accident
10	14	1	Kurt Busch	Hendrickcars.com Chevrolet	120	Running	32	17	18	Denny Hamlin	Z-Line Designs Toyota	103	Accident
11	2	60	Trevor Bayne	RFR 25th Ford	120	Running	33	12	31	Justin Allgaier	Brandt Chevrolet	103	Accident
12	33	24	Benny Gordon	Kentucky Antler Co. & VFI Toyota	120	Running	34	42	52	Reed Sorenson	Better Business Bureau Chevrolet	103	Accident
13	41	4	Danny Efland	Danny Efland Racing Chevrolet	120	Running	35	34	23	Robert Richardson	North Texas Pipe Chevrolet	103	Accident
14	37	40	Josh Wise	Curtis Key Plumbing Chevrolet	120	Running	36	32	08	Casey Roderick #	Randy Hill Racing Ford	103	Accident
15	4	5	Dale Earnhardt Jr.	TaxSlayer.com Chevrolet	120	Running	37	19	11	Brian Scott	Dollar General Toyota	96	Running
16	22	20	Joey Logano	GameStop Toyota	120	Running	38	1	7	Danica Patrick	GoDaddy.com Chevrolet	72	Running
17	31	41	Blake Koch	Rise Up and Register Ford	120	Running	39	13	44	Mike Bliss	TriStar Motorsports Toyota	59	Accident
18	24	54	Kyle Busch	Monster Energy Toyota	119	Accident	40	38	28	J.J. Yeley	JPO Absorbents Chevrolet	43	Engine
19	10	6	Ricky Stenhouse Jr.	Kellogg's Pop Tarts Ford	119	Accident	41	40	81	Jason Bowles #	American Majority Dodge	28	Engine
20	6	12	Sam Hornish Jr.	Alliance Truck Parts Dodge	119	Running	42	30	97	Johnny Sauter	AM FM Wood & Pellet Stoves Toyota	14	Electrical
21	21	70	Johanna Long #	Foretravel Chevrolet	119	Running	43	43	10	Jeff Green	TriStar Motorsports Toyota	3	Vibration
22	20	14	Eric McClure	Hefty/Reynolds Wrap Toyota	118	Running				# Sunoco Rookie of the Year Contender.			

RACE COMMENTS: Before an estimated crowd of 82,000, James Buescher won the DRIVE4COPD 300, his first NASCAR Nationwide Series victory. To start the race, prior to the green flag the following cars dropped to the rear of the field for the reasons indicated: #27, 28 (missing drivers meeting), #97 (adjustments during impound).

TIME OF RACE: 2 hours, 18 minutes, 51 seconds — **AVERAGE SPEED:** 129.636 mph — **MARGIN OF VICTORY:** Under Caution — **COORS LIGHT POLE AWARD:** Danica Patrick (182.741 mph. 49.250 secs.) — **CAUTION FLAGS:** 8 cautions for 35 laps — **LAP LEADERS:** 38 lead changes among 16 drivers. Patrick 1–2, Bayne 3, Sadler 4, Stewart 5–8, Kahne 9–12, Hamlin 13, Bayne 14–15, Hornish Jr. 16–20, Bliss 21–25, Earnhardt Jr. 26, Bliss 27, Ku. Busch 28–29, Earnhardt Jr. 30–32, Ku. Busch 33–36, Stewart 37–43, Ku. Busch 44–48, Earnhardt Jr. 49–50, Hamlin 51–53, Ku. Busch 54–64, Sadler 65–66, Earnhardt Jr. 67, Sadler 68–72, Ky. Busch 73, Ku. Busch 74–76, Richardson 77, Nemechek 78–79, Hornish Jr. 80–81, Ku. Busch 82, Stewart 83–88, Ky. Busch 89, Hamlin 90, Earnhardt Jr. 91, Stewart 92–94, Hill 95–98, Wallace 99, Hamlin 100–101, Stewart 102–103, Ku. Busch 104–119, Buescher 120.

NASCAR NATIONWIDE SERIES

2 BASHAS' SUPERMARKETS 200

March 3, 2012 — Phoenix International Raceway — 200 Laps – 200 Miles

Fin	Str	No	Driver	Team	Laps	Status
1	8	2	Elliott Sadler	OneMain Financial Chevrolet	200	Running
2	7	22	Brad Keselowski	Discount Tire Dodge	200	Running
3	2	6	Ricky Stenhouse Jr.	Roush Fenway Racing/25 Years Ford	200	Running
4	9	3	Austin Dillon #	AdvoCare Chevrolet	200	Running
5	12	33	Kevin Harvick	South Point Casino & Hotel Chevrolet	200	Running
6	6	12	Sam Hornish Jr.	Alliance Truck Parts Dodge	200	Running
7	5	60	Trevor Bayne	Ford EcoBoost Ford	200	Running
8	10	20	Joey Logano	Dollar General Toyota	200	Running
9	1	18	Denny Hamlin	GameStop/MASS3 Effect Toyota	200	Running
10	21	43	Michael Annett	Pilot/Flying J Ford	200	Running
11	14	54	Kyle Busch	Monster Energy Toyota	200	Running
12	25	30	James Buescher	ABF U-Pack Moving Chevrolet	200	Running
13	17	88	Cole Whitt #	TaxSlayer.com Chevrolet	200	Running
14	11	11	Brian Scott	Dollar General Toyota	200	Running
15	13	31	Justin Allgaier	Brandt Chevrolet	200	Running
16	19	44	Mike Bliss	TriStar Motorsports Toyota	200	Running
17	22	08	Casey Roderick #	RandyHillRacing.com Ford	200	Running
18	4	38	Kasey Kahne	Great Clips Chevrolet	198	Running
19	18	81	Jason Bowles #	American Majority Dodge	197	Running
20	24	19	Tayler Malsam	G-Oil Toyota	197	Running
21	30	7	Danica Patrick	GoDaddy.com Chevrolet	197	Running
22	28	51	Jeremy Clements	Clements Automotive Chevrolet	197	Running
23	32	23	Jamie Dick	Viva Auto Group Chevrolet	196	Running
24	15	87	Joe Nemechek	AM/FM Energy Wood & Pellet Stoves Toyota	195	Throttle
25	31	39	Joey Gase #	Go Green Racing/JoeyGase.com Ford	195	Running
26	36	40	Erik Darnell	Curtis Key Plumbing Chevrolet	194	Running
27	39	24	Benny Gordon	VSI Racing Chevrolet	194	Running
28	37	14	Eric McClure	Hefty/Reynolds Wrap Toyota	193	Running
29	41	50	T.J. Bell	TPT/GulfcoastLossPrevention/Liberty Chev.	189	Running
30	38	52	Tim Schendel	Mathews Solocam Archery Chevrolet	189	Running
31	34	41	Blake Koch	RiseUpandRegister.com Ford	166	Running
32	23	01	Mike Wallace	G&K Services Chevrolet	162	Wheel Bearing
33	40	4	Daryl Harr	Danny Efland Racing Chevrolet	149	Running
34	42	70	Charles Lewandoski	ML Motorsports Chevrolet	115	Brakes
35	35	28	David Green	Robinson-Blakeney Racing Dodge	109	Vibration
36	3	99	Kenny Wallace	RAB Racing with Brack Maggard Toyota	102	Accident
37	16	27	J.J. Yeley	GCMI Ford	25	Vibration
38	29	89	Morgan Shepherd	goodinfo.com/Hyland's Chevrolet	17	Fuel Pressure
39	43	74	Mike Harmon	Coma Unwind/American Heros Chevrolet	8	Fly Wheel
40	33	42	Josh Wise	Curtis Key Plumbing Chevrolet	7	Electrical
41	26	46	Chase Miller	Curtis Key Plumbing Chevrolet	6	Electrical
42	20	47	Scott Speed	Curtis Key Plumbing Chevrolet	3	Electrical
43	27	10	Jeff Green	TriStar Motorsports Toyota	3	Vibration

Sunoco Rookie of the Year Contender.

RACE COMMENTS: Before an estimated crowd of 36,000, Elliott Sadler won the Bashas' Supermarket 200, his sixth NASCAR Nationwide Series victory. To start the race, prior to the green flag the following cars dropped to the rear of the field for the reasons indicated: #74 (adjustments outside impound).

TIME OF RACE: 1 hour, 43 minutes, 10 seconds — AVERAGE SPEED: 116.317 mph — MARGIN OF VICTORY: 0.259 seconds — COORS LIGHT POLE AWARD: Denny Hamlin (132.979 mph. 27.072 secs.) — CAUTION FLAGS: 3 cautions for 15 laps — LAP LEADERS: 8 lead changes among 5 drivers. Hamlin 1–4, Bayne 5–8, Hamlin 9–52, Harvick 53–105, Hamlin 106–110, Harvick 111–164, Hamlin 165–167, Keselowski 168–174, Sadler 175–200.

3 SAM'S TOWN 300

March 10, 2012 — Las Vegas Motor Speedway — 200 Laps – 300 Miles

Fin	Str	No	Driver	Team	Laps	Status
1	6	6	Ricky Stenhouse Jr.	EcoBoost Ford	200	Running
2	7	18	Mark Martin	Interstate Batteries Toyota	200	Running
3	1	2	Elliott Sadler	OneMain Financial Chevrolet	200	Running
4	14	60	Trevor Bayne	Roush-Fenway Racing Ford	200	Running
5	9	33	Brendan Gaughan	South Point Hotel & Casino Chevrolet	200	Running
6	22	88	Cole Whitt #	TaxSlayer.com Chevrolet	200	Running
7	3	3	Austin Dillon #	American Ethanol Chevrolet	200	Running
8	8	31	Justin Allgaier	Brandt Chevrolet	200	Running
9	13	12	Sam Hornish Jr.	Alliance Truck Parts Dodge	200	Running
10	2	38	Kasey Kahne	Great Clips Chevrolet	200	Running
11	18	99	Kenny Wallace	RAB Racing with Brack Maggard Toyota	200	Running
12	12	7	Danica Patrick	GoDaddy.com Chevrolet	200	Running
13	21	43	Michael Annett	Pilot/Flying J Ford	200	Running
14	11	30	James Buescher	Turner Motorsports Chevrolet	200	Running
15	19	44	Mike Bliss	TriStar Motorsports Toyota	200	Running
16	17	19	Tayler Malsam	G-Oil Toyota	200	Running
17	24	01	Mike Wallace	The Gun Store/G&K Services Chevrolet	198	Running
18	32	41	Blake Koch	Poynt.com Ford	198	Running
19	15	70	Johanna Long #	Foretravel/Race Fuel Energy Chevrolet	198	Running
20	31	87	Joe Nemechek	AM/FM Energy Wood & Pellet Stoves Toyota	198	Running
21	25	51	Jeremy Clements	Clements Automotive Chevrolet	197	Running
22	43	89	Morgan Shepherd	goodinfo.com/Hyland's Chevrolet	197	Running
23	5	22	Brad Keselowski	Discount Tire Dodge	196	Running
24	40	23	Robert Richardson	NTX Pipe/Riviera Hotel Chevrolet	196	Running
25	27	14	Eric McClure	Hefty Black Out/Reynolds Wrap Toyota	196	Running
26	42	4	Daryl Harr	iWorld Chevrolet	194	Running
27	10	81	Jason Bowles #	American Majority Toyota	188	Running
28	16	08	Kyle Fowler	RandyHillRacing.com Ford	165	Oil Cooler
29	35	52	Tim Schendel	All Sports Tailgating Chevrolet	164	Running
30	29	24	Benny Gordon	Revita Anti-Aging/VSI Chevrolet	146	Running
31	38	50	T.J. Bell	Turbine Powered Technology Chevrolet	140	Engine
32	36	28	Derrike Cope	JPO Abosorbents Dodge	137	Electrical
33	20	54	Kyle Busch	Monster Energy Toyota	127	Running
34	4	11	Brian Scott	Dollar General Toyota	94	Accident
35	34	40	Erik Darnell	Curtis Key Plumbing Chevrolet	91	Fly Wheel
36	37	13	Jennifer Jo Cobb	Glen Lerner Dodge	72	Steering
37	30	39	Joey Gase #	Go Green Racing Ford	41	Accident
38	23	27	J.J. Yeley	GCMI Ford	39	Oil Pump
39	33	46	Chase Miller	Curtis Key Plumbing Chevrolet	6	Electrical
40	28	10	Jeff Green	TriStar Motorsports Toyota	4	Vibration
41	39	42	Josh Wise	Curtis Key Plumbing Chevrolet	4	Electrical
42	26	47	Scott Speed	Curtis Key Plumbing Chevrolet	3	Vibration
43	41	74	Mike Harmon	Koma Unwind Relaxation Drink Chevrolet	3	Vibration

Sunoco Rookie of the Year Contender.

RACE COMMENTS: Before an estimated crowd of 70,000, Ricky Stenhouse Jr. won the Sam's Town 300, his third NASCAR Nationwide Series victory.

TIME OF RACE: 2 hours, 21 minutes, 46 seconds — AVERAGE SPEED: 129.969 mph — MARGIN OF VICTORY: 5.904 seconds — COORS LIGHT POLE AWARD: Elliott Sadler (181.366 mph. 29.774 secs.) — CAUTION FLAGS: 7 cautions for 32 laps — LAP LEADERS: 8 lead changes among 8 drivers. Sadler 1–26, Yeley 27–28, Kahne 29–47, Scott 48–52, Kahne 53–73, Keselowski 74–100, Wallace 101, Martin 102–145, Stenhouse Jr. 146–200.

4 FORD ECOBOOST 300

March 17, 2012 — Bristol Motor Speedway — 300 Laps – 159.9 Miles

Fin	Str	No	Driver	Team	Laps	Status
1	4	2	Elliott Sadler	OneMain Financial Chevrolet	300	Running
2	12	38	Kasey Kahne	Great Clips Chevrolet	300	Running
3	7	22	Brad Keselowski	Discount Tire Dodge	300	Running
4	1	18	Joey Logano	GameStop/Turtle Beach Toyota	300	Running
5	16	5	Dale Earnhardt Jr.	TaxSlayer.com Chevrolet	300	Running
6	3	6	Ricky Stenhouse Jr.	Cargill/Blackwell Angus Ford	300	Running
7	10	31	Justin Allgaier	Brandt Chevrolet	300	Running
8	2	60	Trevor Bayne	yourracecar.com/Crawdads Classics Ford	300	Running
9	6	33	Kevin Harvick	Armour Chevrolet	300	Running
10	15	20	Ryan Truex	Grime Boss Toyota	300	Running
11	21	43	Michael Annett	Pilot/Flying J Ford	300	Running
12	9	3	Austin Dillon #	AdvoCare Chevrolet	300	Running
13	23	12	Sam Hornish Jr.	Alliance Truck Parts Dodge	300	Running
14	11	30	James Buescher	Turner Motorsports Chevrolet	299	Running
15	13	44	Mike Bliss	BanditChippers.com Toyota	299	Running
16	14	88	Cole Whitt	Hendrickcars.com Chevrolet	299	Running
17	8	54	Kyle Busch	Monster Energy Toyota	299	Running
18	18	19	Tayler Malsam	G-Oil Toyota	298	Running
19	27	7	Danica Patrick	GoDaddy.com Chevrolet	298	Running
20	25	51	Jeremy Clements	goodinfo.com/Mahle Chevrolet	297	Running
21	29	40	Erik Darnell	Curtis Key Plumbing Chevrolet	297	Running
22	36	23	Jamie Dick	Viva Auto Group Chevrolet	296	Running
23	37	01	Mike Wallace	G&K Services Chevrolet	296	Running
24	31	24	Benny Gordon	Kentucky Antler Co./VSI/eye79.com Chev.	294	Running
25	34	81	Jason Bowles #	American Majority Dodge	293	Running
26	32	15	Jeffrey Earnhardt	Sam's Club Ford	293	Running
27	40	14	Eric McClure	Hefty/Reynolds Wrap Toyota	292	Running
28	20	08	Kyle Fowler	RandyHillRacing.com Ford	292	Running
29	24	70	Johanna Long #	Foretravel Motorcoach Chevrolet	291	Running
30	30	87	Joe Nemechek	AM/FM Energy Wood & Pellet Stoves Toyota	291	Running
31	42	28	Kevin Lepage	JPO Absorbents Chevrolet	284	Running
32	41	4	Brad Teague	Food Country USA Chevrolet	284	Running
33	17	99	Kenny Wallace	Mac Tools Toyota	201	Engine
34	33	50	T.J. Bell	TPT Chevrolet	186	Accident
35	5	11	Brian Scott	Dollar General Toyota	183	Clutch
36	38	39	Joey Gase #	Go Green Racing/JoeyGase.com Ford	123	Handling
37	39	52	Tim Schendel	Metro Ministries Chevrolet	119	Suspension
38	19	41	Blake Koch	RiseUpandRegister.com Ford	117	Engine
39	43	27	J.J. Yeley	GCMI Ford	15	Brakes
40	26	46	Chase Miller	Curtis Key Plumbing Chevrolet	7	Brakes
41	22	47	Scott Speed	Curtis Key Plumbing Chevrolet	6	Vibration
42	28	10	Jeff Green	TriStar Motorsports Toyota	3	Vibration
43	35	42	Josh Wise	Curtis Key Plumbing Chevrolet	3	Electrical

Sunoco Rookie of the Year Contender.

RACE COMMENTS: Before an estimated crowd of 55,000, Elliott Sadler won the Ford EcoBoost 300, his seventh NASCAR Nationwide Series victory and second at Bristol Motor Speedway. To start the race, prior to the green flag the following cars dropped to the rear of the field for the reasons indicated: #14 (missed driver introductions).

TIME OF RACE: 1 hour, 41 minutes, 16 seconds — AVERAGE SPEED: 94.74 mph — MARGIN OF VICTORY: 1.159 seconds — COORS LIGHT POLE AWARD: Joey Logano (124.21 mph. 15.448 secs.) — CAUTION FLAGS: 4 cautions for 30 laps — LAP LEADERS: 5 lead changes among 5 drivers. Logano 1–66, K. Busch 67–106, Logano 107–159, Bayne 160–223, Stenhouse Jr. 224–264, Sadler 265–300.

5 ROYAL PURPLE 300

March 24, 2012 — Auto Club Speedway — 150 Laps – 300 Miles

Fin	Str	Car	Driver	Team	Laps	Status
1	1	18	Joey Logano	Translux Toyota	150	Running
2	10	6	Ricky Stenhouse Jr.	Roush Fenway Racing Ford	150	Running
3	3	22	Brad Keselowski	America's Tire Dodge	150	Running
4	7	11	Brian Scott	Dollar General Toyota	150	Running
5	4	3	Austin Dillon #	AdvoCare Chevrolet	150	Running
6	14	38	Brad Sweet #	Great Clips Chevrolet	150	Running
7	6	99	Kenny Wallace	RAB Racing with Brack Maggard Toyota	150	Running
8	15	54	Kyle Busch	Monster Energy Toyota	150	Running
9	5	2	Elliott Sadler	Pierre Drive Thru Chevrolet	150	Running
10	8	33	Brendan Gaughan	South Point Casino Chevrolet	150	Running
11	16	43	Michael Annett	Pilot/Flying J Ford	150	Running
12	17	30	James Buescher	Deft Finishes Chevrolet	150	Running
13	11	12	Sam Hornish Jr.	Alliance Truck Parts Dodge	150	Running
14	9	60	Trevor Bayne	Ford EcoBoost Ford	150	Running
15	13	81	Jason Bowles #	American Majority Toyota	150	Running
16	22	19	Tayler Malsam	G-Oil Toyota	150	Running
17	18	44	Mike Bliss	Bandit Chippers Toyota	150	Running
18	19	01	Mike Wallace	Global Barter Corp. Chevrolet	150	Running
19	20	87	Joe Nemechek	AM/FM Energy Wood & Pellet Stoves Toyota	149	Running
20	28	51	Jeremy Clements	Clements Automotive Chevrolet	148	Running
21	35	23	Robert Richardson	North TX Pipe Chevrolet	148	Running
22	33	24	Benny Gordon	Kentucky Antler Company/VSI Chevrolet	148	Running
23	32	39	Joey Gase #	Go Green Racing Ford	148	Running
24	31	40	Erik Darnell	Curtis Key Plumbing Chevrolet	147	Running
25	24	41	Blake Koch	Rise Up and Register Chevrolet	147	Running
26	25	14	Eric McClure	Hefty/Reynolds Wrap Toyota	146	Running
27	27	50	T.J. Bell	TPT/apex Construction Chevrolet	145	Running
28	39	4	Daryl Harr	iWorld Chevrolet	145	Running
29	34	52	Tim Schendel	Metro Ministries Chevrolet	145	Running
30	12	88	Cole Whitt	TaxSlayer.com Chevrolet	142	Accident
31	40	70	David Green	ML Motorsports Dodge	139	Suspension
32	2	31	Justin Allgaier	Brandt Chevrolet	112	Engine
33	38	28	Kevin Lepage	Robinson-Blackeney Racing Chevrolet	82	Rear Gear
34	37	89	Morgan Shepherd	Shepherd Ventures Racing Chevrolet	66	Engine
35	21	7	Danica Patrick	GoDaddy.com Chevrolet	63	Engine
36	29	08	Tim Andrews	Randy Hill Racing Ford	22	Vibration
37	43	15	Scott Riggs	Rick Ware Racing Chevrolet	9	Rear Gear
38	36	46	Chase Miller	Curtis Key Plumbing Chevrolet	8	Vibration
39	30	42	Josh Wise	Curtis Key Plumbing Chevrolet	6	Electrical
40	41	74	Mike Harmon	Koma Unwind Chevrolet	5	Rear End
41	23	47	Scott Speed	Curtis Key Plumbing Chevrolet	4	Vibration
42	42	72	John Jackson	Crash Claims R US Toyota	3	Fuel Pump
43	26	10	Jeff Green	TriStar Motorsports Toyota	2	Vibration

Sunoco Rookie of the Year Contender.

RACE COMMENTS: Before an estimated crowd of 40,000, Joey Logano won the Royal Purple 300, his 10th NASCAR Nationwide Series victory. Prior to the green flag, the following cars dropped to the rear of the field for the reason indicated: #70 (missing drivers meeting); #54 (missing driver introductions).

TIME OF RACE: 2 hours, 6 minutes, 28 seconds — AVERAGE SPEED: 142.33 mph — MARGIN OF VICTORY: 1.066 seconds — COORS LIGHT POLE AWARD: Joey Logano (178.984 mph. 40.227 secs.) — CAUTION FLAGS: 4 cautions for 18 laps — LAP LEADERS: 15 lead changes among 7 drivers. Logano 1–26, Keselowski 27–59, Logano 60–62, Sadler 63–64, Logano 65–68, Allgaier 69, Logano 70–77, Allgaier 78, Logano 79–101, Stenhouse Jr. 102, Logano 103–111, K. Busch 112–124, Keselowski 125–128, Logano 129–135, Bayne 136–138, Logano 139–150.

6 O'REILLY AUTO PARTS 300

April 13, 2012 — Texas Motor Speedway — 200 Laps – 300 Miles

Fin	Str	Car	Driver	Team	Laps	Status
1	3	6	Ricky Stenhouse Jr.	Pure Michigan Ford	200	Running
2	1	33	Paul Menard	Menards/Rheem Chevrolet	200	Running
3	8	38	Kasey Kahne	Great Clips Chevrolet	200	Running
4	2	18	Denny Hamlin	SportClips Toyota	200	Running
5	4	3	Austin Dillon #	American Ethanol Chevrolet	200	Running
6	30	27	David Ragan	Mercury Ford	200	Running
7	16	31	Justin Allgaier	Brandt Chevrolet	200	Running
8	17	7	Danica Patrick	GoDaddy.com Chevrolet	200	Running
9	18	43	Michael Annett	Pilot/Flying J Ford	200	Running
10	9	30	Steve Arpin	Mike's On The Rocks Chevrolet	200	Running
11	14	12	Sam Hornish Jr.	Wurth Dodge	200	Running
12	5	2	Elliott Sadler	OneMain Financial Chevrolet	200	Running
13	7	88	Cole Whitt #	TaxSlayer.com Chevrolet	200	Running
14	20	5	Dale Earnhardt Jr.	Degree Chevrolet	200	Running
15	12	20	Joey Logano	GameStop/Batman 2 DC Super Heroes Toyota	200	Running
16	10	44	Mike Bliss	TriStar Motorsports Toyota	199	Running
17	33	87	Joe Nemechek	SWM International Toyota	199	Running
18	23	81	Jason Bowles #	American Majority Toyota	199	Running
19	24	01	Mike Wallace	G&K Services Chevrolet	198	Running
20	15	70	Johanna Long #	Foretravel Chevrolet	197	Running
21	21	08	Kyle Fowler	Randy Hill Racing Ford	196	Running
22	31	39	Kelly Bires	Fenton Motors Ford	196	Running
23	27	40	Erik Darnell	TheMotorsportsGroup.com Chevrolet	196	Running
24	42	14	Eric McClure	Hefty/Reynolds Wrap Toyota	192	Running
25	28	19	Tayler Malsam	G-Oil Toyota	192	Running
26	40	50	T.J. Bell	Gulf Coast Software Chevrolet	192	Running
27	38	52	Tim Schendel	Metro Ministries Chevrolet	192	Running
28	26	41	Timmy Hill	Poynt.com Ford	191	Running
29	37	51	Jeremy Clements	US Petroleum Consulting Chevrolet	188	Running
30	6	54	Kurt Busch	Monster Energy Toyota	187	Overheating
31	25	4	Danny Efland	Danny Efland Racing Chevrolet	187	Running
32	19	99	Ryan Truex	Grime Boss Toyota	182	Engine
33	41	24	Benny Gordon	Silestone/Dillon Manufacturing Chevrolet	175	Running
34	39	23	Robert Richardson	Tia Rosa/Embassy Suites Chevrolet	169	Running
35	13	22	Brad Keselowski	Discount Tire Dodge	159	Running
36	29	15	Blake Koch	Rick Ware Racing Chevrolet	92	Accident
37	11	11	Brian Scott	Dollar General Toyota	61	Engine
38	34	75	Scott Riggs	RWR Chevrolet	9	Rear Gear
39	36	46	Chase Miller	Key Motorsports Chevrolet	8	Vibration
40	32	42	Josh Wise	Key Motorsports Chevrolet	7	Electrical
41	35	47	Scott Speed	Key Motorsports Chevrolet	7	Fuel Pump
42	43	74	Kevin Lepage	Koma Unwind Chevrolet	4	Ignition
43	22	10	Jeff Green	TriStar Motorsports Toyota	3	Vibration

Sunoco Rookie of the Year Contender.

RACE COMMENTS: Before an estimated crowd of 73,600, Ricky Stenhouse Jr. won the O'Reilly Auto Parts 300, his fourth NASCAR Nationwide Series victory. Prior to the green flag, the following cars dropped to the rear of the field for the reason indicated: #47, 75 (missing drivers meeting; missing driver introductions).

TIME OF RACE: 2 hours, 22 minutes, 31 seconds — AVERAGE SPEED: 126.301 mph — MARGIN OF VICTORY: 1.434 seconds — COORS LIGHT POLE AWARD: Paul Menard (181.714 mph. 29.717 secs.) — CAUTION FLAGS: 5 cautions for 33 laps — LAP LEADERS: 14 lead changes among 7 drivers. Menard 1–3, Stenhouse Jr. 4–48, Menard 49–52, Kahne 53, Menard 54–94, Hamlin 95–103, Sadler 104–107, Menard 108–146, Hamlin 147–148, Ragan 149–150, Menard 151–163, Dillon 164–176, Stenhouse Jr. 177–194, Hamlin 195, Stenhouse Jr. 196–200.

7 VIRGINIA 529 COLLEGE SAVINGS 250

April 27, 2012 — Richmond International Raceway — 250 Laps – 187.5 Miles

Fin	Str	Car	Driver	Team	Laps	Status
1	10	54	Kurt Busch	Monster Energy Toyota	250	Running
2	2	18	Denny Hamlin	Z-Line Designs Toyota	250	Running
3	1	33	Kevin Harvick	Fast Fixin' Chevrolet	250	Running
4	6	6	Ricky Stenhouse Jr.	Cargill/Blackwell Angus Ford	250	Running
5	12	12	Sam Hornish Jr.	Wurth Dodge	250	Running
6	7	2	Elliott Sadler	OneMain Financial Chevrolet	250	Running
7	8	36	Ryan Blaney	SealWrap Chevrolet	250	Running
8	19	43	Michael Annett	Pilot/Flying J Ford	250	Running
9	3	3	Austin Dillon #	AdvoCare Chevrolet	250	Running
10	5	38	Kasey Kahne	Great Clips Chevrolet	250	Running
11	11	4	Steve Wallace	LoanMax Ford	250	Running
12	21	30	James Buescher	AccuDoc Solutions Chevrolet	249	Running
13	17	87	Joe Nemechek	AM/FM Energy Wood & Pellet Stoves Toyota	249	Running
14	15	11	Brian Scott	Dollar General Toyota	249	Running
15	13	31	Justin Allgaier	Brandt Chevrolet	249	Running
16	9	22	Brad Keselowski	Discount Tire/SKF Dodge	249	Running
17	20	44	Mike Bliss	BanditChippers.com Toyota	249	Running
18	14	20	Joey Logano	Dollar General Toyota	249	Running
19	4	88	Cole Whitt #	TaxSlayer Chevrolet	248	Running
20	24	70	Johanna Long #	Foretravel Motorcoach/Grand Springs Chev.	248	Running
21	16	7	Danica Patrick	GoDaddy.com Chevrolet	248	Running
22	25	99	Travis Pastrana	boostmobile Toyota	248	Running
23	18	08	Casey Roderick #	West Virginia Miners Ford	247	Running
24	26	01	Mike Wallace	JD Motorsports Chevrolet	247	Running
25	27	19	Tayler Malsam	G-Oil/NOYS Toyota	246	Running
26	33	41	Timmy Hill	Poynt.com Ford	245	Running
27	40	52	Kevin Lepage	Victory Precision Valves Chevrolet	245	Running
28	43	50	T.J. Bell	Gulf Coast Loss Prevention Chevrolet	244	Running
29	31	24	Tanner Berryhill	NewGulfResources/DillonManufacturing Chev.	244	Running
30	28	81	Jason Bowles #	American Majority Toyota	243	Running
31	34	14	Eric McClure	Hefty/Reynolds Wrap Toyota	243	Running
32	38	39	Matt Frahm	New Lifestyle Diet/Maui Jim Sunglasses Ford	243	Running
33	29	51	Jeremy Clements	Clements Automotive Chevrolet	229	Running
34	37	23	Robert Richardson	North Texas Pipe Chevrolet	162	Running
35	30	40	Erik Darnell	TheMotorsportsGroup.com Chevrolet	145	Clutch
36	32	89	Morgan Shepherd	Racing with Jesus Chevrolet	90	Handling
37	22	17	J.J. Yeley	AmeriCashAdvance.com Toyota	66	Accident
38	23	42	Josh Wise	Curtis Key Plumbing Chevrolet	12	Suspension
39	42	75	Blake Koch	Rick Ware Racing Chevrolet	10	Vibration
40	36	47	Scott Speed	Curtis Key Plumbing Chevrolet	9	Electrical
41	39	74	Mike Harmon	Koma Unwind Chevrolet	7	Rear Gear
42	35	46	Chase Miller	Curtis Key Plumbing Chevrolet	7	Clutch
43	41	10	Jeff Green	TriStar Motorsports Toyota	3	Vibration

Sunoco Rookie of the Year Contender.

RACE COMMENTS: Before an estimated crowd of 42,000 Kurt Busch won the Virginia 529 College Savings 250, his fourth NASCAR Nationwide Series victory. Prior to the green flag, the following car dropped to the rear of the field for the reason indicated: #47 (missing drivers meeting).

TIME OF RACE: 1 hour, 48 minutes, 6 seconds — AVERAGE SPEED: 104.07 mph — MARGIN OF VICTORY: 0.062 seconds — COORS LIGHT POLE AWARD: Kevin Harvick (124.625 mph. 21.665 secs.) — CAUTION FLAGS: 3 cautions for 20 laps — LAP LEADERS: 13 lead changes among 6 drivers. Harvick–pole, Hamlin 1, Harvick 2–70, Shepherd 71–73, Harvick 74–76, K. Busch 77–79, Harvick 80–117, Hamlin 118, Harvick 119–166, K. Busch 167–202, Hamlin 203–206, Annett 207–208, Logano 209–221, K. Busch 222–250.

8 AARON'S 312

May 5, 2012 — Talladega Superspeedway — 117 Laps – 311.22 Miles

Fin	Str	Car	Driver	Team	Laps	Status
1	4	18	Joey Logano	GameStop/Max Payne 3 Toyota	122	Running
2	12	54	Kyle Busch	Monster Energy Toyota	122	Running
3	2	6	Ricky Stenhouse Jr.	Cargill/Blackwell Angus Ford	122	Running
4	11	88	Cole Whitt	TaxSlayer.com Chevrolet	122	Running
5	33	5	Dale Earnhardt Jr.	Hellmann's Chevrolet	122	Running
6	31	1	Kurt Busch	HendrickCars.com Chevrolet	122	Running
7	7	30	James Buescher	Accudoc Chevrolet	122	Running
8	13	31	Justin Allgaier	Brandt Chevrolet	122	Running
9	20	99	Kenny Wallace	American Ethanol Toyota	122	Running
10	1	2	Elliott Sadler	OneMain Financial Chevrolet	122	Running
11	18	20	Ryan Truex	Grime Boss Toyota	122	Running
12	8	12	Sam Hornish Jr.	Alliance Dodge	122	Running
13	17	7	Danica Patrick	GoDaddy.com Chevrolet	122	Running
14	27	40	Erik Darnell	TheMotorsportsGroup.com Chevrolet	122	Running
15	26	24	John Wes Townley	Toyota Save in May Sales Event Toyota	122	Running
16	23	4	Danny Efland	JDMotorsports.com Chevrolet	122	Running
17	5	3	Austin Dillon #	AdvoCare Chevrolet	122	Running
18	15	44	Mike Bliss	TriStar Motorsports Toyota	122	Running
19	16	87	Joe Nemechek	AM/FM Energy Wood & Pellet Stoves Toyota	122	Running
20	9	22	Brad Keselowski	Discount Tire Dodge	121	Running
21	28	41	Timmy Hill	Poynt.com/Shania Kidscan Ford	117	Running
22	3	33	Kevin Harvick	Armour Chevrolet	116	Accident
23	10	43	Michael Annett	Pilot/Flying J Ford	116	Accident
24	14	19	Tayler Malsam	G-Oil Toyota	116	Accident
25	43	15	Jeffrey Earnhardt	Fastwax.com Ford	116	Accident
26	34	23	Robert Richardson	North TX Pipe Chevrolet	116	Accident
27	29	14	Eric McClure	Hefty/Reynolds Wrap Toyota	116	Accident
28	19	01	Mike Wallace	Restaurant.com Chevrolet	113	Accident
29	21	51	Jeremy Clements	Clements Automotive Chevrolet	113	Running
30	36	39	Josh Richards	Joy Ford	85	Fuel Pump
31	35	50	T.J. Bell	Gulfcoast Loss Prevention Chevrolet	82	Running
32	30	08	Tim Andrews	Randy Hill Racing Ford	64	Overheating
33	6	38	Brad Sweet #	Great Clips Chevrolet	62	Accident
34	25	81	Jason Bowles #	American Majority Toyota	32	Accident
35	38	89	Morgan Shepherd	Shepherd Racing Ventures Chevrolet	29	Accident
36	22	11	Brian Scott	Dollar General Toyota	29	Accident
37	24	70	Johanna Long #	Foretravel Chevrolet	18	Overheating
38	42	74	Mike Harmon	Koma Unwind Chevrolet	12	Vibration
39	32	10	Jeff Green	TriStar Motorsports Toyota	9	Vibration
40	40	42	Josh Wise	Key Motorsports Chevrolet	9	Electrical
41	39	46	Chase Miller	Key Motorsports Chevrolet	8	Vibration
42	41	47	Scott Speed	Key Motorsports Chevrolet	2	Ignition
43	37	52	Kevin Lepage	TTTR Racing Engines Chevrolet	1	Clutch

Sunoco Rookie of the Year Contender.

RACE COMMENTS: Before an estimated crowd of 66,000, Joey Logano won the Aaron's 312, his 11th NASCAR Nationwide Series victory. Prior to the green flag, the following car dropped to the rear of the field for the reason indicated: #50 (adjustments outside impound).

TIME OF RACE: 2 hours, 22 minutes, 54 seconds — AVERAGE SPEED: 136.258 mph — MARGIN OF VICTORY: 0.034 seconds — COORS LIGHT POLE AWARD: None - due to inclement weather — CAUTION FLAGS: 7 cautions for 27 laps — LAP LEADERS: 37 lead changes among 18 drivers. Sadler 1–4, Harvick 5, Dillon 6–7, Buescher 8–13, Ku. Busch 14, Logano 15, Sadler 16–17, Ky. Busch 18, Buescher 19–21, Stenhouse Jr. 22, Andrews 23, Ky. Busch 24–25, Earnhardt Jr. 26, Logano 27–30, Earnhardt Jr. 31–34, Logano 35–41, Bliss 42–43, Logano 44–46, Earnhardt Jr. 47–51, Nemechek 52, Wallace 53, Earnhardt Jr. 54–63, Harvick 64–65, Dillon 66–67, Whitt 68–70, Wallace 71, Earnhardt Jr. 72, Sadler 73–74, Truex 75, Earnhardt Jr. 76–77, Patrick 78, Earnhardt Jr. 79–80, Harvick 81–82, Hornish Jr. 83–84, Harvick 85–87, Logano 88, Ky. Busch 89–121, Logano 122.

9 VFW SPORT CLIPS HELP A HERO 200

May 11, 2012 — Darlington Raceway — 147 Laps – 200.8 Miles

Fin	Str	Car	Driver	Team	Laps	Status
1	5	20	Joey Logano	Dollar General Toyota	151	Running
2	2	18	Denny Hamlin	SportClips Toyota	151	Running
3	13	22	Brad Keselowski	Snap-on Dodge	151	Running
4	8	12	Sam Hornish Jr.	Alliance Truck Parts Dodge	151	Running
5	3	3	Austin Dillon #	AdvoCare Chevrolet	151	Running
6	1	6	Ricky Stenhouse Jr.	Cargill Beef Ford	151	Running
7	7	11	Brian Scott	Dollar General Toyota	151	Running
8	4	54	Kurt Busch	Monster Energy Toyota	151	Running
9	14	30	James Buescher	AccuDoc Solutions Chevrolet	151	Running
10	40	88	Cole Whitt	TaxSlayer.com Chevrolet	151	Running
11	16	87	Joe Nemechek	SWMTX.com Toyota	151	Running
12	15	7	Danica Patrick	GoDaddy.com Chevrolet	151	Running
13	10	31	Justin Allgaier	Brandt Chevrolet	151	Running
14	22	43	Michael Annett	Pilot/Flying J Ford	151	Running
15	12	44	Mike Bliss	TriStar Motorsports Toyota	151	Running
16	31	41	Timmy Hill	Poynt.com Ford	151	Running
17	25	99	Travis Pastrana	boostmobile Toyota	151	Running
18	9	38	Kasey Kahne	Great Clips Chevrolet	151	Running
19	26	14	Jeff Green	Hefty/Reynolds Wrap Toyota	149	Running
20	36	4	Danny Efland	EMS Speak/Trade Bank Chevrolet	148	Running
21	32	81	Jason Bowles #	American Majority Toyota	148	Running
22	37	89	Morgan Shepherd	Racing with Jesus Chevrolet	147	Running
23	28	23	Jamie Dick	Viva Auto Group Chevrolet	144	Running
24	6	2	Elliott Sadler	OneMain Financial Chevrolet	143	Accident
25	19	39	Josh Richards	NSWKids.com Ford	143	Running
26	11	33	Brendan Gaughan	South Point Hotel & Casino Chevrolet	138	Accident
27	42	70	Derrike Cope	ML Motorsports Dodge	138	Running
28	41	08	Matt Frahm	Maui Jim/New Life Diets Ford	125	Engine
29	20	40	Erik Darnell	TheMotorsportsGroup.com Chevrolet	91	Clutch
30	21	01	Mike Wallace	Restaurant.com Chevrolet	81	Running
31	30	19	Tayler Malsam	G-Oil/NOYS/Ryobi Toyota	60	Transmission
32	18	50	T.J. Bell	Twin Oaks Services Chevrolet	44	Accident
33	23	51	Jeremy Clements	Clements Automotive Chevrolet	42	Running
34	35	15	Blake Koch	CapitalPlasticSurgery.com Chevrolet	29	Electrical
35	43	52	Kevin Lepage	Second Chance Race Parts Chevrolet	25	Engine
36	34	10	Tony Raines	TriStar Motorsports Toyota	14	Vibration
37	39	74	Mike Harmon	Koma Unwind Chevrolet	10	Brakes
38	38	75	Scott Riggs	RWR Chevrolet	7	Vibration
39	24	42	Josh Wise	Curtis Key Plumbing Chevrolet	7	Electrical
40	27	24	Casey Roderick #	West Virginia Miners/Linda K, Epling Chev.	3	Accident
41	29	46	Chase Miller	Curtis Key Plumbing Chevrolet	2	Accident
42	33	47	Scott Speed	Curtis Key Plumbing Chevrolet	2	Clutch
43	17	36	Ryan Blaney	SealWrap.com/Advance Auto Parts Chev.	1	Accident

Sunoco Rookie of the Year Contender.

RACE COMMENTS: Before an estimated crowd of 23,000, Joey Logano won the VFW Sport Clips Help a Hero 200, his 12th NASCAR Nationwide Series victory. Prior to the green flag, the following cars dropped to the rear of the field for the reason indicated: #42 (missing drivers meeting), #88 (backup car), #74, 99 (adjustments outside impound).

TIME OF RACE: 1 hour, 50 minutes, 29 seconds — AVERAGE SPEED: 112.017 mph — MARGIN OF VICTORY: 0.255 seconds — COORS LIGHT POLE AWARD: Ricky Stenhouse Jr. (173.546 mph. 28.336 secs.) — CAUTION FLAGS: 6 cautions for 32 laps — LAP LEADERS: 13 lead changes among 7 drivers. Stenhouse Jr. 1–18, Hamlin 19–41, Logano 42, Hamlin 43–50, K. Busch 51–52, Hamlin 53–90, K. Busch 91, Logano 92, Gaughan 93, Allgaier 94–101, Hamlin 102–128, Sadler 129–142, Hamlin 143–149, Logano 150–151.

10 PIONEER HI-BRED 250

May 20, 2012 — Iowa Speedway — 250 Laps – 218.75 Miles

Fin	Str	Car	Driver	Team	Laps	Status
1	3	6	Ricky Stenhouse Jr.	Cargill Ford	250	Running
2	1	2	Elliott Sadler	OneMain Financial Chevrolet	250	Running
3	4	18	Michael McDowell	Pizza Ranch Toyota	250	Running
4	6	3	Austin Dillon #	AdvoCare Chevrolet	250	Running
5	31	54	Kurt Busch	Monster Energy Toyota	250	Running
6	5	31	Justin Allgaier	Brandt Chevrolet	250	Running
7	12	88	Cole Whitt #	DewCrew.com Chevrolet	250	Running
8	10	22	Parker Kligerman	Discount Tire Dodge	250	Running
9	8	20	Darrell Wallace Jr.	Dollar General Toyota	250	Running
10	13	33	Brendan Gaughan	South Point Chevrolet	250	Running
11	7	11	Brian Scott	Dollar General Toyota	250	Running
12	2	12	Sam Hornish Jr.	Detroit Genuine Parts Dodge	250	Running
13	20	38	Brad Sweet #	Great Clips Chevrolet	250	Running
14	18	43	Michael Annett	Pilot/Flying J Ford	249	Running
15	23	44	Mike Bliss	TriStar Motorsports Toyota	249	Running
16	11	30	Steve Arpin	Mike's Hard Lemonade Chevrolet	249	Running
17	24	81	Jason Bowles #	American Majority Toyota	248	Running
18	33	40	Erik Darnell	TheMotorsportsGroup.com Chevrolet	248	Running
19	25	87	Joe Nemechek	AM/FM Energy Wood & Pellet Stoves Toyota	247	Running
20	14	24	Casey Roderick #	West Virginia Miners Baseball Chevrolet	247	Running
21	26	01	Mike Wallace	Restaurant.com Chevrolet	247	Running
22	19	70	Johanna Long #	Foretravel Chevrolet	246	Running
23	17	51	Jeremy Clements	Clements Automotive Chevrolet	245	Running
24	29	23	Jamie Dick	Viva Auto Group Chevrolet	244	Running
25	21	41	Timmy Hill	Poynt.com Ford	244	Running
26	15	99	Travis Pastrana	boost mobile Toyota	228	Running
27	27	50	T.J. Bell	Twin Oaks/Beaver Bail Bonds Chevrolet	214	Alternator
28	36	4	Daryl Harr	iWorld Chevrolet	207	Engine
29	16	19	Tayler Malsam	Iron Horse Jeans/G-Oil Toyota	179	Accident
30	9	7	Danica Patrick	GoDaddy.com Chevrolet	113	Accident
31	28	89	Morgan Shepherd	MorganShepherd.com Chevrolet	87	Handling
32	22	14	Jeff Green	Hefty/Reynolds Wrap Toyota	70	Accident
33	34	52	Joey Gaseb #	Pauliewood.com Chevrolet	50	Engine
34	32	39	Josh Richards	NSW Kids Ford	48	Engine
35	42	74	Mike Harmon	Koma Unwind Chevrolet	12	Ignition
36	41	72	John Jackson	Crash Claims R Us Toyota	7	Vibration
37	37	08	Tim Andrews	Randy Hill Racing Ford	6	Vibration
38	40	42	Matt Frahm	Curtis Key Plumbing Chevrolet	5	Vibration
39	43	75	Michael Guerity	RWR Chevrolet	4	Brakes
40	38	15	Blake Koch	Capital Plastic Surgery Chevrolet	3	Vibration
41	30	10	Kevin Lepage	TriStar Motorsports Toyota	3	Vibration
42	39	47	Tim Schendel	Curtis Key Plumbing Chevrolet	3	Overheating
43	35	46	Chase Miller	Curtis Key Plumbing Chevrolet	2	Handling

Sunoco Rookie of the Year Contender.

RACE COMMENTS: Before an estimated crowd of 34,000, Ricky Stenhouse Jr. won the Pioneer Hi-Bred 250, his fifth NASCAR Nationwide Series victory. To start the race, prior to the green flag the following cars dropped to the rear of the field for the reasons indicated: #44, 54, 87 (Driver Change).

TIME OF RACE: 2 hours, 2 minutes, 29 seconds — AVERAGE SPEED: 107.157 mph — MARGIN OF VICTORY: 1.465 seconds — COORS LIGHT POLE AWARD: Elliott Sadler (133.911 mph. 23.523 secs.) — CAUTION FLAGS: 4 cautions for 27 laps — LAP LEADERS: 9 lead changes among 6 drivers. Sadler–pole, Hornish Jr. 1–30, Stenhouse Jr. 31–83, Allgaier 84–86, Stenhouse Jr. 87–115, Whitt 116–119, Sadler 120–121, Stenhouse Jr. 122–188, K. Busch 189–190, Stenhouse Jr. 191–250.

11 HISTORY 300

May 26, 2012 — Charlotte Motor Speedway — 200 Laps – 300 Miles

Fin	Str	Car	Driver	Team	Laps	Status
1	10	22	Brad Keselowski	Discount Tire Dodge	200	Running
2	13	18	Denny Hamlin	SportClips Toyota	200	Running
3	12	54	Kyle Busch	Monster Energy Toyota	200	Running
4	7	33	Kevin Harvick	Hunt Brothers Pizza Chevrolet	200	Running
5	6	2	Elliott Sadler	OneMain Financial Chevrolet	200	Running
6	1	20	Joey Logano	GameStop/Hitman Absolution Toyota	200	Running
7	8	30	James Buescher	ABF Chevrolet	200	Running
8	16	31	Justin Allgaier	Brandt Chevrolet	200	Running
9	5	12	Sam Hornish Jr.	Alliance Truck Parts Dodge	200	Running
10	21	21	Joey Coulter	Sherwin Williams Chevrolet	200	Running
11	2	3	Austin Dillon #	Bass Pro Shops/NWTF Chevrolet	200	Running
12	20	44	Mike Bliss	TriStar Motorsports Toyota	200	Running
13	3	7	Danica Patrick	GoDaddy.com Chevrolet	200	Running
14	22	43	Michael Annett	Pilot/Flying J Ford	200	Running
15	19	01	Mike Wallace	Restaurant.com Chevrolet	200	Running
16	23	98	Reed Sorenson	Carroll Shelby Motors Ford	200	Running
17	14	38	Kasey Kahne	Great Clips Chevrolet	200	Running
18	25	51	Jeremy Clements	Clements Automotive Chevrolet	199	Running
19	24	41	Timmy Hill	Poynt.com Ford	199	Running
20	28	19	Tayler Malsam	G-Oil Toyota	198	Running
21	34	24	Casey Roderick #	West Virginia Miners Baseball Chevrolet	198	Running
22	26	70	Johanna Long #	Wish For Our Heroes Chevrolet	198	Running
23	31	08	Kyle Fowler	Randy Hill Racing Ford	196	Running
24	42	99	Travis Pastrana	boost mobile Toyota	195	Running
25	36	52	Joey Gase #	Pauliewood.com Chevrolet	193	Running
26	4	6	Ricky Stenhouse Jr.	Ford EcoBoost Ford	179	Running
27	37	40	Erik Darnell	Strutmasters, LLC Chevrolet	176	Accident
28	11	88	Cole Whitt #	Ingersoll Rand Chevrolet	167	Running
29	29	87	Joe Nemechek	GBCAM/FM Energy/SWM Toyota	157	Running
30	39	50	T.J. Bell	Liberty Tire Recycling Chevrolet	151	Handling
31	9	11	Brian Scott	Dollar General Toyota	146	Accident
32	18	14	Jeff Green	Hefty/Reynolds Wrap Toyota	141	Drive Shaft
33	15	81	Jason Bowles #	American Majority Toyota	137	Accident
34	17	39	Josh Richards	NSW Kids Ford	134	Accident
35	32	4	Danny Efland	Tradebank/Doug Herbert Performance Parts Chev.	103	Brake
36	35	00	Angela Cope	Highland Wealth Advisors/Luichiny Shoes Chev.	51	Engine
37	43	89	Morgan Shepherd	Shepherd Racing Ventures Chevrolet	39	Electrical
38	40	74	Mike Harmon	Koma Unwind Chevrolet	30	Overheating
39	41	23	Robert Richardson	North TX Pipe Chevrolet	13	Engine
40	38	46	Chase Miller	Curtis Key Plumbing Chevrolet	10	Ignition
41	27	42	Josh Wise	Curtis Key Plumbing Chevrolet	8	Ignition
42	30	47	Scott Speed	Curtis Key Plumbing Chevrolet	5	Electrical
43	33	10	Kevin Lepage	TriStar Motorsports Toyota	3	Vibration

Sunoco Rookie of the Year Contender.

RACE COMMENTS: Before an estimated crowd of 45,000, Brad Keselowski won the History 300, his 18th NASCAR Nationwide Series victory.

TIME OF RACE: 2 hours, 25 minutes, 51 seconds — AVERAGE SPEED: 123.414 mph — MARGIN OF VICTORY: 0.838 seconds — COORS LIGHT POLE AWARD: Joey Logano (179.063 mph. 30.157 secs.) — CAUTION FLAGS: 7 cautions for 38 laps — LAP LEADERS: 12 lead changes among 7 drivers. Logano 1–21, Harvick 22–54, Bowles 55, Harvick 56–58, Kahne 59–67, Harvick 68–110, Logano 111, Allgaier 112, Wallace 113–114, Harvick 115–127, Logano 128–131, Kahne 132–133, Keselowski 134–200.

12 5-HOUR ENERGY 200

June 2, 2012 — Dover International Speedway — 200 Laps – 200 Miles

Fin	Str	Car	Driver	Team	Laps	Status
1	2	18	Joey Logano	Dollar General Toyota	200	Running
2	1	20	Ryan Truex	Grime Boss Toyota	200	Running
3	5	11	Brian Scott	Dollar General Toyota	200	Running
4	9	54	Kurt Busch	Monster Energy Toyota	200	Running
5	7	31	Justin Allgaier	Brandt Chevrolet	200	Running
6	11	3	Austin Dillon #	American Ethanol/New Holland Chevrolet	200	Running
7	6	2	Elliott Sadler	OneMain Financial Chevrolet	200	Running
8	3	33	Ty Dillon	South Point Hotel & Casino Chevrolet	200	Running
9	14	30	James Buescher	AccuDoc Solutions Chevrolet	200	Running
10	15	51	Jeremy Clements	Clements Automotive Chevrolet	199	Running
11	23	43	Michael Annett	Pilot/Flying J Ford	199	Running
12	12	22	Parker Kligerman	Snap-on Dodge	199	Running
13	10	12	Sam Hornish Jr.	Wurth Dodge	199	Running
14	19	88	Cole Whitt	Clean Coal/AmericasPower.org Chevrolet	199	Running
15	30	81	Jason Bowles #	American Majority Toyota	198	Running
16	20	19	Tayler Malsam	G-Oil/Ryobi Toyota	198	Running
17	28	14	Jeff Green	Hefty/Reynolds Wrap Toyota	198	Running
18	27	01	Mike Wallace	G&K Services Chevrolet	198	Running
19	21	87	Joe Nemechek	AM/FM Energy Wood & Pellet Stoves Toyota	197	Running
20	13	99	John Wes Townley	Barberitos Toyota	197	Running
21	34	23	Jamie Dick	Viva Auto Group Chevrolet	194	Running
22	18	39	Josh Richards	NSWKids.com Ford	194	Running
23	22	38	Brad Sweet #	Great Clips Chevrolet	193	Running
24	32	50	T.J. Bell	Liberty Tire Recycling Chevrolet	193	Running
25	40	4	Brad Teague	TradeBank Chevrolet	190	Running
26	36	52	Joey Gase #	Pauliewood.com Chevrolet	189	Running
27	29	40	Erik Darnell	TheMotorsportsGroup.com Chevrolet	179	Running
28	41	24	Tim Bainey Jr.	Del Grosso/Window World Chevrolet	144	Accident
29	35	89	Morgan Shepherd	Racing with Jesus Chevrolet	144	Transmission
30	17	7	Danica Patrick	GoDaddy.com Chevrolet	133	Accident
31	26	41	Timmy Hill	Poynt.com Ford	120	Accident
32	4	6	Ricky Stenhouse Jr.	Cargill Beef Ford	119	Running
33	8	44	Mike Bliss	TriStar Motorsports Toyota	36	Electrical
34	39	74	Mike Harmon	Koma Unwind Relaxation Drink Chevrolet	14	Vibration
35	37	71	Matt Carter	RWR/Lilly Trucking Chevrolet	11	Electrical
36	38	75	Scott Riggs	RWR/Lilly Trucking Chevrolet	10	Suspension
37	24	42	Josh Wise	Curtis Key Plumbing Chevrolet	5	Ignition
38	16	47	Scott Speed	Curtis Key Plumbing Chevrolet	4	Vibration
39	25	10	Kevin Lepage	TriStar Motorsports Toyota	4	Vibration
40	31	08	Tim Andrews	Randy Hill Racing Ford	2	Accident
41	42	15	Blake Koch	RWR Chevrolet	2	Brakes
42	33	46	Matt DiBenedetto	TheMotorsportsGroup.com Chevrolet	2	Electrical

Sunoco Rookie of the Year Contender.

RACE COMMENTS: Before an estimated crowd of 28,000, Joey Logano won the 5-Hour Energy 200, his 13th NASCAR Nationwide Series victory. Prior to the green flag, the following car dropped to the rear of the field for the reason indicated: #88 (unapproved adjustments during impound).

TIME OF RACE: 1 hour, 48 minutes, 36 seconds — AVERAGE SPEED: 110.497 mph — MARGIN OF VICTORY: 1.526 seconds — COORS LITE POLE AWARD: Ryan Truex (154.746 mph. 23.264 secs.) — CAUTION FLAGS: 6 cautions for 27 laps — LAP LEADERS: 5 lead changes among 3 drivers. Truex–pole, Logano 1–42, Allgaier 43–45, Logano 46–151, Truex 152–194, Logano 195–200.

13 ALLIANCE TRUCK PARTS 250

June 16, 2012 — Michigan International Speedway — 125 Laps – 250 Miles

Fin	Str	Car	Driver	Team	Laps	Status
1	3	18	Joey Logano	Dollar General Toyota	125	Running
2	4	30	James Buescher	Amway/Gaddes Foundation Chevrolet	125	Running
3	15	54	Kurt Busch	Monster Energy Toyota	125	Running
4	2	88	Cole Whitt #	Clean Coal Chevrolet	125	Running
5	1	3	Austin Dillon #	AdvoCare Chevrolet	125	Running
6	11	12	Sam Hornish Jr.	Alliance Truck Parts Dodge	125	Running
7	13	20	Michael McDowell	Pizza Ranch Toyota	125	Running
8	7	33	Paul Menard	Menards/Rheem Chevrolet	125	Running
9	17	11	Brian Scott	Dollar General Toyota	125	Running
10	9	22	Brad Keselowski	Discount Tire Dodge	125	Running
11	6	2	Elliott Sadler	OneMain Financial Chevrolet	125	Running
12	18	43	Michael Annett	Pilot/Flying J Ford	125	Running
13	16	44	Mike Bliss	Bandit Chippers Toyota	125	Running
14	8	31	Justin Allgaier	Brandt Chevrolet	125	Running
15	23	87	Joe Nemechek	AM/FM Energy Wood & Pellet Stoves Toyota	125	Running
16	14	70	Johanna Long #	Foretravel Chevrolet	125	Running
17	22	14	Jeff Green	Hefty/Reynolds Wrap Toyota	125	Running
18	5	7	Danica Patrick	GoDaddy.com/KickstartAmerica.US Chev.	125	Running
19	19	81	Jason Bowles #	American Majority Toyota	124	Running
20	30	01	Mike Wallace	Tradebank/Carl Ent Chevrolet	124	Running
21	28	19	Tayler Malsam	G-Oil/Ryobi Toyota	124	Running
22	27	40	Erik Darnell	TheMotorsportsGroup.com Chevrolet	124	Running
23	36	08	Tony Raines	Black Cat Fireworks Ford	124	Running
24	12	38	Brad Sweet #	Great Clips Chevrolet	123	Running
25	20	6	Ricky Stenhouse Jr.	Roush-Fenway Racing Ford	123	Running
26	32	41	Timmy Hill	Poynt.com Ford	123	Running
27	33	4	Danny Efland	TradeBank Chevrolet	122	Running
28	37	24	Angela Cope	Dillon Manufacturing/United Mobile Auctions Chev.	119	Running
29	21	23	Jamie Dick	Viva Auto Group Chevrolet	116	Accident
30	24	39	Josh Richards	NSW Kids Ford	116	Accident
31	31	51	Jeremy Clements	Diamond Pistons Chevrolet	76	Engine
32	35	50	T.J. Bell	Hantz Bank/Gulf Coast loss Prevention Chev.	56	Engine
33	39	89	Morgan Shepherd	MorganShepherd.com Chevrolet	42	Handling
34	10	99	Kenny Wallace	Family Farmers Toyota	32	Engine
35	42	52	Tim Schendel	Victory Precision Valves Chevrolet	15	Overheating
36	34	15	Blake Koch	RWR Chevrolet	12	Vibration
37	38	75	Scott Riggs	RWR Chevrolet	11	Engine
38	29	46	Chase Miller	Curtis Key Plumbing Chevrolet	9	Overheating
39	26	42	Josh Wise	Curtis Key Plumbing Chevrolet	8	Engine
40	41	71	Michael Guerity	RWR Chevrolet	6	Vibration
41	40	47	Matt DiBenedetto	Curtis Key Plumbing Chevrolet	5	Vibration
42	25	10	Kevin Lepage	TriStar Motorsports Toyota	4	Vibration
43	43	74	Mike Harmon	Koma Unwind Chevrolet	1	Vibration

Sunoco Rookie of the Year Contender.

RACE COMMENTS: Before an estimated crowd of 32,000, Joey Logano won the Alliance Truck Parts 200, his 14th NASCAR Nationwide Series victory. Prior to the green flag, the following cars dropped to the rear of the field for the reasons indicated: #8 and 74 (missing drivers meeting).

TIME OF RACE: 1 hour, 52 minutes, 48 seconds — AVERAGE SPEED:132.979 mph — MARGIN OF VICTORY: 0.208 seconds — COORS LIGHT POLE AWARD: Austin Dillon (190.375 mph. 37.820 secs.) — CAUTION FLAGS: 7 cautions for 26 laps — LAP LEADERS: 14 lead changes among 10 drivers. Dillon 1–4, Whitt 5–13, Dillon 14–20, Logano 21–27, Clements 28, Hornish Jr. 29–49, Menard 50–57, Buescher 58–59, Menard 60–88, Whitt 89, Patrick 90, Hornish Jr. 91–94, Allgaier 95–98, Sadler 99–101, Logano 102–125.

14 SARGENTO 200

June 23, 2012 — Road America — 50 Laps – 202.4 Miles

Fin	Str	Car	Driver	Team	Laps	Status
1	1	30	Nelson Piquet Jr.	Qualcomm/Autotrac Chevrolet	50	Running
2	2	18	Michael McDowell	Pizza Ranch Toyota	50	Running
3	3	5	Ron Fellows	AER Manufacturing Chevrolet	50	Running
4	5	33	Max Papis	Menards/Rheem Chevrolet	50	Running
5	8	12	Sam Hornish Jr.	Alliance Truck Parts Dodge	50	Running
6	4	22	Jacques Villeneuve	Discount Tire Dodge	50	Running
7	6	11	Brian Scott	Dollar General Toyota	50	Running
8	22	54	Kurt Busch	Monster Energy Toyota	50	Running
9	14	88	Cole Whitt #	VooDoo Ride Chevrolet	50	Running
10	7	31	Justin Allgaier	Brandt Chevrolet	50	Running
11	11	6	Ricky Stenhouse Jr.	Ford EcoBoost Ford	50	Running
12	10	7	Danica Patrick	GoDaddy.com Chevrolet	50	Running
13	19	44	Mike Bliss	Mark Smith Toyota	50	Running
14	15	81	Jason Bowles #	American Majority Toyota	50	Running
15	13	2	Elliott Sadler	Charter Chevrolet	50	Running
16	20	75	Kenny Habul	SunEnergy 1 Racing Toyota	50	Running
17	17	99	Victor Gonzalez Jr.	Delta Commercial/IMCA Toyota	50	Running
18	23	3	Austin Dillon #	AdvoCare Chevrolet	50	Running
19	28	01	Mike Wallace	G&K Services Chevrolet	50	Running
20	16	38	Brad Sweet #	Great Clips Chevrolet	50	Running
21	29	14	Eric McClure	Hefty/Reynolds Wrap Toyota	50	Running
22	25	41	Timmy Hill	Poynt.com Ford	50	Running
23	33	40	Erik Darnell	SheboyganAuto.com Chevrolet	50	Running
24	37	70	Tony Raines	Country Inn & Suites Dodge	50	Running
25	26	51	Jeremy Clements	Clements Automotive Chevrolet	50	Running
26	12	43	Michael Annett	Pilot/Flying J Ford	48	Running
27	36	23	Bill Prietzel	R3 Motorsports Chevrolet	48	Running
28	27	26	John Young	Eklekt Technologies Group Dodge	47	Out of Fuel
29	9	32	Miguel Paludo	Duroline Brakes Chevrolet	47	Running
30	24	19	Tayler Malsam	G-Oil/Ryobi Toyota	46	Running
31	32	39	Josh Richards	NSW Kids Ford	41	Running
32	34	24	Casey Roderick #	West Virginia Miners Baseball Chevrolet	40	Running
33	18	87	Alex Kennedy	Global Barter/St.Baldrick's Toyota	38	Running
34	42	4	Matthew Bell	Extreme Bidder Chevrolet	36	Running
35	21	59	Kyle Kelley	Jamison Eng./UPR.com Chevrolet	29	Engine
36	41	89	Morgan Shepherd	Schneider Electric Chevrolet	26	Handling
37	43	50	T.J. Bell	Beaver Bail Bonds Chevrolet	24	Rear End
38	40	08	Matt Frahm	Randy Hill Racing Ford	14	Brakes
39	35	52	Ryan Ellis	Cobblestone Inn Chevrolet	4	Ignition
40	39	46	Chase Miller	TheMotorsportsGroup.com Chevrolet	4	Brakes
41	31	47	Matt DiBenedetto	Curtis Key Plumbing Chevrolet	3	Overheating
42	38	42	Tim Schendel	SheboyganAuto.com Chevrolet	3	Vibration
43	30	10	Jeff Green	TriStar Motorsports Toyota	2	Vibration

Sunoco Rookie of the Year Contender.

RACE COMMENTS: Before an estimated crowd of 56,000, Nelson Piquet Jr. won the Sargento 200, his first NASCAR Nationwide Series victory. To start the race, prior to the green flag the following cars dropped to the rear of the field for the reasons indicated: #4, 10, 24, 51, 54 (unapproved adjustments).

TIME OF RACE: 2 hours, 22 minutes, 35 seconds — AVERAGE SPEED: 85.171 mph — MARGIN OF VICTORY: 2.258 seconds — COORS LIGHT POLE AWARD: Nelson Piquet Jr. (109.516 mph. 133.065 secs.) — CAUTION FLAGS: 5 cautions for 8 laps — LAP LEADERS: 9 lead changes among 8 drivers. Piquet Jr. 1–2, McDowell 3–4, Fellows 5–8, Scott 9–13, McDowell 14–15, Papis 16, Paludo 17–20, Villeneuve 21–30, Hornish Jr. 31–33, Piquet Jr. 34–50.

15 FEED THE CHILDREN 300

June 29, 2012 — Kentucky Speedway — 200 Laps – 300 Miles

Fin	Str	Car	Driver	Team	Laps	Status
1	1	3	Austin Dillon #	Bass Pro Shops Chevrolet	200	Running
2	8	54	Kurt Busch	Monster Energy Toyota	200	Running
3	2	33	Kevin Harvick	Hunt Brothers Pizza Chevrolet	200	Running
4	9	43	Michael Annett	Pilot/Flying J Ford	200	Running
5	7	31	Justin Allgaier	Brandt Chevrolet	200	Running
6	4	12	Sam Hornish Jr.	Wurth Dodge	200	Running
7	3	22	Brad Keselowski	Discount Tire Dodge	200	Running
8	5	6	Ricky Stenhouse Jr.	Sam's Club/Cargill Ford	200	Running
9	12	2	Elliott Sadler	OneMain Financial Chevrolet	199	Running
10	13	30	James Buescher	Fresh from Florida Gulf Seafood Chevrolet	199	Running
11	26	99	Kenny Wallace	American Ethanol/Family Farmers Toyota	198	Running
12	11	7	Danica Patrick	GoDaddy.com Chevrolet	198	Running
13	25	98	Reed Sorenson	Shelby Engine Co. Ford	198	Running
14	10	88	Cole Whitt #	Degree Men Chevrolet	198	Running
15	14	36	Ryan Blaney	SealWrap Chevrolet	198	Running
16	20	38	Brad Sweet #	Great Clips Chevrolet	198	Running
17	17	44	Mike Bliss	TriStar Motorsports Toyota	197	Running
18	24	87	Joe Nemechek	AM/FM Energy Wood & Pellet Stoves Toyota	197	Running
19	42	70	Johanna Long #	Keen Parts Chevrolet	196	Running
20	18	39	Josh Richards	Joy Ford	196	Running
21	21	51	Jeremy Clements	Clements Automotive Chevrolet	196	Running
22	19	81	Jason Bowles #	American Majority Toyota	195	Running
23	33	19	Tayler Malsam	G-Oil/Ryobi Toyota	195	Running
24	16	23	Jamie Dick	Viva Auto Group Chevrolet	195	Running
25	35	40	Erik Darnell	TheMotorsportsGroup.com Chevrolet	193	Running
26	40	14	Eric McClure	Hefty/Reynolds Wrap Toyota	193	Running
27	37	50	T.J. Bell	Beaver Bail Bonds Chevrolet	192	Running
28	23	17	Tanner Berryhill	New Gulf Resources/Excel Therapy Specialists Toyota	192	Running
29	41	24	Jamie Mosley	Telmate Chevrolet	182	Running
30	15	11	Brian Scott	Dollar General Toyota	176	Engine
31	34	01	Mike Wallace	G&K Services Chevrolet	143	Accident
32	30	41	Timmy Hill	Poynt.com Ford	141	Rear Gear
33	6	18	Denny Hamlin	Dollar General Toyota	132	Engine
34	27	4	Danny Efland	TradeBank Chevrolet	103	Ignition
35	36	89	Morgan Shepherd	A+ Building Services Chevrolet	48	Fuel Pressure
36	39	52	Kevin Lepage	Metro Ministries Chevrolet	32	Wheel Bearing
37	29	74	Scott Riggs	Koma Unwind Chevrolet	11	Ignition
38	32	08	Tim Andrews	Randy Hill Racing Ford	10	Rear Gear
39	31	46	Chase Miller	TheMotorsportsGroup.com Chevrolet	6	Ignition
40	38	42	Josh Wise	Curtis Key Plumbing Chevrolet	5	Vibration
41	43	15	Blake Koch	RWR Chevrolet	5	Engine
42	28	10	Jeff Green	TriStar Motorsports Toyota	4	Vibration
43	22	47	Scott Speed	Curtis Key Plumbing Chevrolet	2	Engine

Sunoco Rookie of the Year Contender.

RACE COMMENTS: Before an estimated crowd of 30,000, Austin Dillon won the Feed The Children 300, his first NASCAR Nationwide Series victory. To start the race, prior to the green flag the following car dropped to the rear of the field for the reasons indicated: #24 (adjustments during impound).

TIME OF RACE: 1 hour, 58 minutes, 42 seconds — AVERAGE SPEED: 151.643 mph — MARGIN OF VICTORY: 9.828 seconds — COORS LIGHT POLE AWARD: Austin Dillon (172.199 mph. 31.359 secs.) — CAUTION FLAGS: 2 cautions for 12 laps — LAP LEADERS: 7 lead changes among 4 drivers. Dillon 1–81, Stenhouse Jr. 82, Annett 83, Allgaier 84–86, Dillon 87–141, Annett 142–143, Allgaier 144, Dillon 145–200.

16 SUBWAY JALAPENO 250 *powered by* COCA-COLA

July 6, 2012 — Daytona International Speedway — 100 Laps – 250 Miles

Fin	Str	Car	Driver	Team	Laps	Status
1	5	1	Kurt Busch	HendrickCars.com Chevrolet	101	Running
2	1	6	Ricky Stenhouse Jr.	NOS Energy Drink Ford	101	Running
3	17	43	Michael Annett	Pilot/Flying J Ford	101	Running
4	42	3	Austin Dillon #	Bass Pro Shops/NRA Museum Chevrolet	101	Running
5	8	18	Joey Logano	SportClips Toyota	101	Running
6	13	2	Elliott Sadler	OneMain Financial Chevrolet	101	Running
7	21	31	Justin Allgaier	Brandt Chevrolet	101	Running
8	15	44	Mike Bliss	BanditChippers.com Toyota	101	Running
9	37	41	Timmy Hill	Poynt.com Chevrolet	101	Running
10	16	12	Sam Hornish Jr.	Wurth Dodge	101	Running
11	33	51	Jeremy Clements	Curry's Roofing/USS James E.Williams DDG 95 Chev.	101	Running
12	11	70	Johanna Long #	WishForOurHeroes.org Chevrolet	101	Running
13	28	4	Danny Efland	TradeBank Chevrolet	101	Running
14	29	81	Jason Bowles #	American Majority Toyota	101	Running
15	22	19	Tayler Malsam	G-Oil/Noah's Light Foundation Toyota	101	Running
16	27	39	Josh Richards	Joy Ford	101	Running
17	34	23	Robert Richardson	North Texas Pipe Chevrolet	101	Running
18	26	14	Eric McClure	Hefty/Reynolds Wrap Toyota	101	Running
19	31	82	Blake Koch	SilverSaver.com Dodge	101	Running
20	32	08	Bryan Silas	Randy Hill Racing Ford	100	Running
21	41	40	Erik Darnell	Curtis Key Plumbing Chevrolet	99	Running
22	25	87	Joe Nemechek	AM/FM Energy/D.A.B./TSA Toyota	97	Running
23	20	54	Kyle Busch	Monster Energy Toyota	94	Running
24	19	38	Brad Sweet #	Great Clips Chevrolet	93	Running
25	18	99	John Wes Townley	Barberitos Toyota	89	Running
26	12	20	Clint Bowyer	Dollar General Toyota	86	Running
27	24	24	Casey Roderick #	West Virginia Miners Baseball Toyota	84	Running
28	4	33	Kevin Harvick	Rheem/Menards Chevrolet	84	Accident
29	2	88	Cole Whitt	Degree MEN/Winn-Dixie Chevrolet	83	Running
30	30	15	Jeffrey Earnhardt	TobaccoFreeFlorida.com/Nuts Off Ford	82	Accident
31	3	7	Danica Patrick	GoDaddy.com/NASCAR Unites-An American Salute Chev.	82	Accident
32	9	11	Brian Scott	Dollar General Toyota	82	Running
33	10	36	Bobby Santos	Tommy Baldwin Racing Chevrolet	80	Accident
34	14	30	James Buescher	Ron Jon Surf Shop/Quiksilver Chevrolet	71	Accident
35	6	22	Brad Keselowski	Discount Tire Dodge	66	Accident
36	7	01	Mike Wallace	G&K Services Chevrolet	65	Accident
37	40	52	Joey Gase #	My Three Sons Vending Chevrolet	5	Overheating
38	36	74	Mike Harmon	Koma Unwind Relaxation Drink Chevrolet	31	Overheating
39	35	50	T.J. Bell	Hantz Bank/Gulfcoast Loss Prevention Chev.	22	Engine
40	43	46	Chase Miller	TheMotorsportsGroup.com Chevrolet	5	Vibration
41	39	42	Josh Wise	Curtis Key Plumbing Chevrolet	4	Transmission
42	38	47	Stephen Leicht	Curtis Key Plumbing Chevrolet	3	Overheating
43	23	10	Jeff Green	TriStar Motorsports Toyota	3	Overheating

Sunoco Rookie of the Year Contender.

RACE COMMENTS: Before an estimated crowd of 50,000, Kurt Busch won the Subway Jalapeno 250, his fifth NASCAR Nationwide Series victory. Prior to the green flag, the following car dropped to the rear of the field for the reasons indicated: #12 (engine change).

TIME OF RACE: 1 hour, 54 minutes, 44 seconds — AVERAGE SPEED: 132.045 mph — MARGIN OF VICTORY: 0.054 seconds — COORS LIGHT POLE AWARD: Ricky Stenhouse Jr. (177.253 mph. 50.775 secs.) — CAUTION FLAGS: 6 cautions for 24 laps — LAP LEADERS: 41 lead changes among 16 drivers. Stenhouse Jr.–pole, Whitt 1–3, Bowyer 4, Keselowski 5, Sadler 6, Ku. Busch 7, Logano 8, Clements 9, Hornish Jr. 10–14, Logano 15, Ku. Busch 16–17, Patrick 18–22, Ku. Busch 23–30, Wallace 31, Nemechek 32–33, Ky. Busch 34–36, Ku. Busch 37–42, Patrick 43–45, Nemechek 46–48, Logano 49–52, Keselowski 53, Logano 54–55, Patrick 56, Wallace 57–58, Patrick 59–62, Buescher 63, Harvick 64–65, Allgaier 66–67, Patrick 68, Allgaier 69–72, Logano 73–75, Dillon 76, Ku. Busch 77–81, Sadler 82–89, Hornish Jr. 90, Dillon 91, Sadler 92, Dillon 93–95, Allgaier 96, Dillon 97–99, Logano 100, Ku. Busch 101.

17 F.W. WEBB 200

July 14, 2012 — New Hampshire Motor Speedway — 200 Laps – 211.6 Miles

Fin	Str	Car	Driver	Team	Laps	Status
1	1	22	Brad Keselowski	Snap-on Dodge	200	Running
2	4	33	Kevin Harvick	Barber Foods Chevrolet	200	Running
3	12	3	Austin Dillon #	AdvoCare Chevrolet	200	Running
4	6	12	Sam Hornish Jr.	Alliance Truck Parts Dodge	200	Running
5	3	6	Ricky Stenhouse Jr.	Cargill Beef Ford	200	Running
6	2	38	Kasey Kahne	Great Clips Chevrolet	200	Running
7	7	2	Elliott Sadler	OneMain Financial Chevrolet	200	Running
8	13	31	Justin Allgaier	Brandt Chevrolet	200	Running
9	9	30	Jamie McMurray	LiftMaster Chevrolet	200	Running
10	11	18	Ryan Truex	Grime Boss Toyota	200	Running
11	14	43	Michael Annett	Pilot/Flying J Ford	200	Running
12	8	11	Brian Scott	Dollar General Toyota	200	Running
13	15	44	Mike Bliss	TriStar Motorsports Toyota	200	Running
14	18	7	Danica Patrick	GoDaddy.com Chevrolet	200	Running
15	27	01	Mike Wallace	Team Fox Chevrolet	200	Running
16	16	81	Jason Bowles #	American Majority Toyota	199	Running
17	25	51	Jeremy Clements	Phoenix Automotive Cores Chevrolet	199	Running
18	10	88	Cole Whitt #	TaxSlayer.com Chevrolet	199	Running
19	19	87	Joe Nemechek	Wildco Petroleum Equipment Sales Toyota	197	Running
20	22	19	Tayler Malsam	G-Oil/Ryobi Toyota	196	Running
21	28	41	Timmy Hill	Poynt.com Ford	196	Running
22	37	14	Eric McClure	Hefty/Reynolds Wrap Toyota	196	Running
23	33	70	Tony Raines	ML Motorsports Chevrolet	196	Running
24	32	39	Josh Richards	NSWKids.com Ford	194	Running
25	21	08	Matt Frahm	Harvey Building Products/Maui Jim Ford	194	Running
26	42	24	Amber Cope	Maxelence/Luichiny Chevrolet	167	Running
27	40	52	Joey Gase #	BBB.org/Chamber of Commerce Chevrolet	130	Vibration
28	5	54	Kyle Busch	Monster Energy Toyota	21	Fuel Pressure
29	36	4	Danny Efland	TradeBank Chevrolet	116	Accident
30	17	23	Jamie Dick	Viva Auto Group Chevrolet	79	Sway Bar
31	20	99	Travis Pastrana	Boost Mobile Toyota	77	Accident
32	34	89	Morgan Shepherd	PPG/Racing with Jesus Chevrolet	47	Handling
33	30	86	Kevin Lepage	Deware Racing Group Ford	19	Wheel Bearing
34	29	71	Scott Riggs	Poynt.com Ford	9	Ignition
35	38	50	T.J. Bell	CrashClaimsR.Us Toyota	6	Brakes
36	43	74	Mike Harmon	Koma Unwind Relaxation Drink Chevrolet	6	Overheating
37	39	75	Matt Carter	RWR Chevrolet	5	Vibration
38	35	46	Chase Miller	TheMotorsportsGroup.com Chevrolet	5	Brakes
39	41	15	Charles Lewandoski	RWR Chevrolet	4	Brakes
40	26	40	Erik Darnell	Curtis Key Plumbing Chevrolet	3	Engine
41	24	42	Josh Wise	Curtis Key Plumbing Chevrolet	3	Rear Gear
42	31	47	Stephen Leicht	Curtis Key Plumbing Chevrolet	3	Transmission
43	23	10	Jeff Green	TriStar Motorsports Toyota	2	Vibration

Sunoco Rookie of the Year Contender.

RACE COMMENTS: Before an estimated crowd of 42,000, Brad Keselowski won the F.W. Webb 200, his 19th NASCAR Nationwide Series victory. Prior to the green flag, the following car dropped to the rear of the field for the reasons indicated: #24 (missed drivers meeting; unapproved adjustments after impound).

TIME OF RACE: 1 hour, 58 minutes, 46 seconds — AVERAGE SPEED: 106.899 mph — MARGIN OF VICTORY: 0.717 seconds — COORS LIGHT POLE AWARD: Brad Keselowski (131.035 mph. 29.067 secs.) — CAUTION FLAGS: 4 cautions for 23 laps — LAP LEADERS: 7 lead changes among 5 drivers. Keselowski 1–38, Kahne 39–81, Dillon 82, Keselowski 83–123, Bowles 124, Keselowski 125–154, Harvick 155–178, Keselowski 179–200.

18 STP 300

July 22, 2012 — Chicagoland Speedway — 200 Laps – 300 Miles

Fin	Str	Car	Driver	Team	Laps	Status
1	15	2	Elliott Sadler	Hunt Brothers Pizza Chevrolet	201	Running
2	1	6	Ricky Stenhouse Jr.	Rancher's Reserve/Dominick's/Cargill Ford	201	Running
3	16	31	Justin Allgaier	Brandt Chevrolet	201	Running
4	11	09	Kenny Wallace	Family Farmers Toyota	201	Running
5	14	43	Michael Annett	Pilot/Flying J Ford	201	Running
6	2	3	Austin Dillon #	AdvoCare Chevrolet	201	Running
7	5	22	Parker Kligerman	Discount Tire Dodge	201	Running
8	3	12	Sam Hornish Jr.	Alliance Truck Parts Dodge	201	Running
9	8	88	Cole Whitt #	TaxSlayer.com Chevrolet	201	Running
10	9	18	Ryan Truex	Grime Boss Toyota	201	Running
11	6	11	Brian Scott	Dollar General Toyota	201	Running
12	7	44	Mike Bliss	TriStar Motorsports Toyota	201	Running
13	22	87	Joe Nemechek	AM/FM Energy Wood & Pellet Stoves Toyota	201	Running
14	13	7	Danica Patrick	GoDaddy.com Chevrolet	201	Running
15	18	30	James Buescher	Fresh from Florida Gulf Seafood Chevrolet	200	Running
16	24	01	Mike Wallace	Gerber Collision & Glass Chevrolet	200	Running
17	32	99	Travis Pastrana	boost mobile Toyota	200	Running
18	25	41	Timmy Hill	Poynt.com Ford	200	Running
19	21	38	Brad Sweet #	Great Clips Chevrolet	200	Running
20	28	39	Josh Richards	NSWKids.com Ford	199	Running
21	12	70	Johanna Long #	Foretravel Motorcoach Chevrolet	199	Running
22	27	51	Jeremy Clements	Phoenix Automotive Cores/USS James E. Williams Chev.	199	Running
23	17	81	Jason Bowles #	American Majority Toyota	198	Running
24	19	14	Eric McClure	Hefty/Reynolds Wrap Toyota	198	Running
25	30	19	Tayler Malsam	G-Oil/Noah's Light Foundation Toyota	197	Running
26	35	17	Tanner Berryhill	New Gulf Resources Toyota	194	Running
27	4	54	Kyle Busch	Monster Energy Toyota	193	Accident
28	10	33	Brendan Gaughan	Rheem/Menards Chevrolet	192	Accident
29	20	23	Jamie Dick	Viva Auto Group Chevrolet	192	Running
30	26	40	Erik Darnell	Curtis Key Plumbing Chevrolet	179	Running
31	36	24	Benny Gordon	SR2 Motorsports Chevrolet	60	Transmission
32	33	4	Danny Efland	TradeBank Chevrolet	47	Engine
33	37	52	Tim Schendel	Metro Ministries Chevrolet	28	Engine
34	41	89	Morgan Shepherd	Racing with Jesus/Hyland's Leg Cramps Chevrolet	19	Handling
35	40	71	Matt Carter	RWR/Lilly Trucking Chevrolet	18	Handling
36	29	42	Blake Koch	Curtis Key Plumbing Chevrolet	14	Ignition
37	39	08	Tim Andrews	Randy Hill Racing Ford	13	Rear Gear
38	38	50	T.J. Bell	Beaver Bail Bonds Chevrolet	13	Vibration
39	42	74	Mike Harmon	Koma Unwind Relaxation Drink Chevrolet	12	Overheating
40	34	46	Chase Miller	TheMotorsportsGroup.com Chevrolet	11	Vibration
41	31	47	Stephen Leicht	Curtis Key Plumbing Chevrolet	6	Clutch
42	43	15	Carl Long	RWR/Lilly Trucking Chevrolet	4	Overheating
43	23	10	Jeff Green	TriStar Motorsports Toyota	4	Vibration

Sunoco Rookie of the Year Contender.

RACE COMMENTS: Before an estimated crowd of 25,000, Elliott Sadler won the STP 300, his eighth NASCAR Nationwide Series victory.

TIME OF RACE: 2 hours, 18 minutes, 10 seconds — AVERAGE SPEED: 130.929 mph — MARGIN OF VICTORY: 0.331 seconds — COORS LIGHT POLE AWARD: Ricky Stenhouse Jr. (176.916 mph. 30.523 secs.) — CAUTION FLAGS: 5 cautions for 25 laps — LAP LEADERS: 13 lead changes among 8 drivers. Stenhouse Jr.–pole, Hornish Jr. 1–6, Stenhouse Jr. 7–48, Dillon 49, Whitt 50–51, Bliss 52–55, Stenhouse Jr. 56–59, Hornish Jr. 60–75, Stenhouse Jr. 76–107, Annett 108, Stenhouse Jr. 109–165, Sadler 166–168, Allgaier 169, Sadler 170–201.

19 INDIANA 250

July 28, 2012 — Indianapolis Motor Speedway — 100 Laps – 250 Miles

Fin	Str	Car	Driver	Team	Laps	Status
1	8	22	Brad Keselowski	Discount Tire Dodge	100	Running
2	13	12	Sam Hornish Jr.	Alliance Truck Parts Dodge	100	Running
3	3	51	Ty Dillon	Wesco Chevrolet	100	Running
4	4	18	Denny Hamlin	SportClips Toyota	100	Running
5	7	3	Austin Dillon #	AdvoCare Chevrolet	100	Running
6	21	43	Michael Annett	Pilot/Flying J/M&M's Snack Mix Ford	100	Running
7	6	20	Joey Logano	GameStop/Damage Inc. Toyota	100	Running
8	9	33	Paul Menard	Menards/Rheem Chevrolet	100	Running
9	10	6	Ricky Stenhouse Jr.	Sam's Club/Cargill Ford	100	Running
10	16	4	Jeremy Clements	TradeBank Chevrolet	100	Running
11	12	44	Mike Bliss	Bandit Chippers Toyota	100	Running
12	14	31	Justin Allgaier	Brandt/PT&E Chevrolet	100	Running
13	19	99	Travis Pastrana	Boost Mobile Toyota	100	Running
14	15	11	Brian Scott	Dollar General Toyota	100	Running
15	5	2	Elliott Sadler	OneMain Financial Chevrolet	100	Running
16	24	81	Jason Bowles #	American Majority Toyota	100	Running
17	40	88	Cole Whitt #	TaxSlayer.com Chevrolet	100	Running
18	28	87	Joe Nemechek	AM/FM Energy Wood & Pellet Stoves Toyota	100	Running
19	26	24	Kenny Wallace	Family Farmers Toyota	100	Running
20	23	01	Mike Wallace	G&K Services Chevrolet	100	Running
21	39	39	Jeffrey Earnhardt	FastWax.com Chevrolet	100	Running
22	2	54	Kyle Busch	Monster Energy Toyota	100	Running
23	37	41	Timmy Hill	RWR Ford	100	Running
24	34	14	Eric McClure	Hefty/Reynolds Wrap Toyota	100	Running
25	1	38	Kasey Kahne	Great Clips Chevrolet	99	Running
26	25	30	James Buescher	ABF Chevrolet	99	Running
27	11	36	Ryan Blaney	SealWrap Chevrolet	99	Running
28	41	52	Tim Schendel	Better Business Bureau Chevrolet	99	Running
29	22	19	Tayler Malsam	G-Oil/Noah's Light Foundation Toyota	99	Running
30	17	70	Johanna Long #	KeenParts.com/Riley Chevrolet	90	Running
31	42	23	Robert Richardson	North Texas Pipe Chevrolet	79	Running
32	29	08	Kyle Fowler	Randy Hill Racing Ford	72	Engine
33	27	98	Reed Sorenson	Shelby Engine Co. Ford	49	Accident
34	18	1	Kurt Busch	HendrickCars.com Chevrolet	41	Electrical
35	20	7	Danica Patrick	GoDaddy.com Chevrolet	38	Accident
36	35	10	Jeff Green	TriStar Motorsports Toyota	23	Vibration
37	38	15	Scott Riggs	RWR Ford	18	Rear Gear
38	33	40	Erik Darnell	Key Motorsports Chevrolet	17	Engine
39	43	50	T.J. Bell	Beaver Bail Bonds Chevrolet	10	Overheating
40	36	86	Kevin Lepage	Deware Racing Group Ford	8	Drive Shaft
41	30	46	Chase Miller	The Motorsports Group Chevrolet	6	Vibration
42	31	42	Josh Wise	Key Motorsports Chevrolet	4	Electrical
43	32	47	Stephen Leicht	Key Motorsports Chevrolet	0	Engine

Sunoco Rookie of the Year Contender.

RACE COMMENTS: Before an estimated crowd of 40,000, Brad Keselowski won the Indiana 250, his 20th NASCAR Nationwide Series victory.

TIME OF RACE: 1 hour, 59 minutes, 0 seconds — AVERAGE SPEED: 126.05 mph — MARGIN OF VICTORY: 3.304 seconds — COORS LIGHT POLE AWARD: Kasey Kahne (176.284 mph. 51.054 secs.) — CAUTION FLAGS: 5 cautions for 24 laps — LAP LEADERS: 9 lead changes among 6 drivers. Kahne–pole, Ky. Busch 1–17, Green 18, Hamlin 19–22, Keselowski 23–26, Ky. Busch 27–36, Kahne 37–40, Ky. Busch 41–64, Hornish Jr. 65–71, Keselowski 72–100.

20 U.S. CELLULAR 250 *presented by* ENLIST WEED CONTROL SYSTEM

August 4, 2012 — IOWA SPEEDWAY — 250 Laps – 218.75 Miles

Fin	Str	Car	Driver	Team	Laps	Status
1	1	2	Elliott Sadler	OneMain Financial Chevrolet	250	Running
2	5	31	Justin Allgaier	Brandt Chevrolet	250	Running
3	7	12	Sam Hornish Jr.	Wurth Dodge	250	Running
4	17	43	Michael Annett	Northland Oil Ford	250	Running
5	11	6	Ricky Stenhouse Jr.	Fastenal Ford	250	Running
6	8	18	Michael McDowell	Pizza Ranch Toyota	250	Running
7	2	20	Darrell Wallace Jr.	Z-Line Designs Toyota	250	Running
8	4	30	Jason Leffler	AccuDoc Solutions Chevrolet	250	Running
9	10	99	Brett Moffitt	Toyota Care Toyota	250	Running
10	13	22	Ryan Blaney	Discount Tire Dodge	250	Running
11	18	7	Danica Patrick	GoDaddy.com Chevrolet	250	Running
12	16	38	Brad Sweet #	Great Clips Chevrolet	250	Running
13	14	70	Johanna Long #	Foretravel Chevrolet	250	Running
14	6	33	Brendan Gaughan	Menards/Rheem Chevrolet	250	Running
15	3	3	Austin Dillon #	American Ethanol Chevrolet	249	Running
16	20	87	Joe Nemechek	AM/FM Energy Wood & Pellet Stoves Toyota	249	Running
17	15	54	Kurt Busch	Monster Energy Toyota	249	Running
18	9	11	Brian Scott	Dollar General Toyota	249	Running
19	12	88	Cole Whitt #	Clean Coal Chevrolet	249	Running
20	21	10	Mike Bliss	TriStar MotorsportsToyota	248	Running
21	24	51	Jeremy Clements	USS James E. Williams DDG 95 Chevrolet	247	Running
22	23	19	Tayler Malsam	G-Oil/Noah's Light Foundation Toyota	247	Running
23	26	44	John Blankenship	Coal Chevrolet	245	Running
24	19	23	Jamie Dick	Viva Auto Group Chevrolet	244	Running
25	32	01	Mike Wallace	G&K Services Chevrolet	244	Running
26	34	52	Justin Jennings	BBB/Cline Tools/LG Seeds Chevrolet	243	Running
27	28	40	Erik Darnell	Key Motorsports Chevrolet	242	Running
28	36	24	Scott Saunders	inox/Standout Wraps Chevrolet	240	Running
29	22	81	Jason Bowles #	American Majority Toyota	238	Running
30	42	41	Timmy Hill	Poynt.com Ford	233	Engine
31	33	14	Eric McClure	Hefty/Reynolds Wrap Toyota	231	Fuel Pump
32	25	39	Joey Gase #	Go Green Racing Ford	216	Running
33	41	4	Daryl Harr	iWorld Chevrolet	176	Running
34	29	08	Josh Richards	Randy Hill Racing Ford	32	Brakes
35	39	89	Morgan Shepherd	Hyland's Leg Cramps Chevrolet	24	Brakes
36	37	50	T.J. Bell	Beaver Bail Bonds Chevrolet	20	Electrical
37	40	74	Mike Harmon	Koma Unwind Chevrolet	19	Power Steering
38	35	71	Carl Long	Lilly Trucking Chevrolet	16	Transmission
39	38	42	Tim Schendel	Key Motorsports Chevrolet	15	Fuel Pump
40	43	15	Dusty Davis	RWR Chevrolet	12	Carburetor
41	30	47	Matt DiBenedetto	Curtis Key Plumbing Chevrolet	6	Vibration
42	31	46	Chase Miller	The Motorsports Group Chevrolet	4	Brakes
43	27	91	Jeff Green	TriStar Motorsports Toyota	4	Vibration

Sunoco Rookie of the Year Contender.

RACE COMMENTS: Before an estimated crowd of 50,000, Elliott Sadler won the U.S. Cellular 250 presented by the Enlist Weed Control System at Iowa Speedway, his 9th NASCAR Nationwide Series victory.

TIME OF RACE: 1 hour, 53 minutes, 31 seconds — AVERAGE SPEED: 115.622 mph — MARGIN OF VICTORY: 0.649 seconds — COORS LIGHT POLE AWARD: Elliott Sadler (135.141 mph. 23.309 secs.) — CAUTION FLAGS: 3 cautions for 16 laps — LAP LEADERS: 6 lead changes among 4 drivers. Sadler–pole, Wallace Jr. 1–36, Dillon 37–56, Sadler 57–58, Dillon 59–91, Allgaier 92–192, Sadler 193–250.

21 ZIPPO 200

August 11, 2012 — Watkins Glen International — 82 Laps – 200.9 Miles

Fin	Str	Car	Driver	Team	Laps	Status
1	2	60	Carl Edwards	Subway Ford	82	Running
2	4	22	Brad Keselowski	SKF/Discount Tire Dodge	82	Running
3	1	12	Sam Hornish Jr.	PPG Dodge	82	Running
4	10	6	Ricky Stenhouse Jr.	Ford EcoBoost Ford	82	Running
5	15	5	Ron Fellows	Canadian Tire Chevrolet	82	Running
6	5	54	Kyle Busch	Monster Energy Toyota	82	Running
7	11	38	Kasey Kahne	Great Clips Chevrolet	82	Running
8	3	33	Paul Menard	Menards/Rheem Chevrolet	82	Running
9	8	31	Justin Allgaier	Brandt Chevrolet	82	Running
10	9	11	Brian Scott	Dollar General Toyota	82	Running
11	19	43	Michael Annett	Pilot/Flying J Ford	82	Running
12	7	2	Elliott Sadler	Charter Chevrolet	82	Running
13	14	30	Miguel Paludo	Duroline Chevrolet	82	Running
14	20	44	Mike Bliss	TriStar Motorsports Toyota	82	Running
15	13	20	Ryan Truex	Grime Boss Toyota	82	Running
16	16	99	Victor Gonzalez Jr.	Delta Commercial/IMCA Toyota	82	Running
17	27	81	Jason Bowles #	American Majority Toyota	82	Running
18	28	01	Mike Wallace	JD Motorsports Chevrolet	82	Running
19	21	51	Jeremy Clements	USS James E Williams DDG 95 Chevrolet	82	Running
20	34	75	Kenny Habul	SunEnergy 1 Racing, LLC Toyota	82	Running
21	24	59	Kyle Kelley	Jamison Eng./UPR.com Chevrolet	82	Running
22	6	18	Joey Logano	GameStop/BuyMyTronics.com Toyota	82	Running
23	30	3	Austin Dillon #	AdvoCare Chevrolet	82	Running
24	12	88	Cole Whitt #	TaxSlayer.com Chevrolet	81	Running
25	39	24	Tim Connolly	M. Connolly Endowment for Lung Cancer Research Chev.	81	Running
26	40	14	Eric McClure	Hefty/Reynolds Wrap Toyota	77	Running
27	26	97	Joe Nemechek	AM/FM Energy Wood & Pellet Stoves Toyota	55	Engine
28	41	70	Tony Raines	ML Motorsports Dodge	45	Vibration
29	25	87	Alex Kennedy	Global Barter Corporation/Dream Factory Toyota	37	Accident
30	38	4	Daryl Harr	iWorld Chevrolet	33	Running
31	31	40	J.J. Yeley	Key Motorsports Chevrolet	27	Electrical
32	42	23	Dexter Stacey	R3 Motorsports Chevrolet	25	Handling
33	43	89	Morgan Shepherd	Hyland's Leg Cramps Chevrolet	23	Brakes
34	35	53	Eric Curran	Whelen/Michael J. Fox Foundation Dodge	18	Electrical
35	29	41	Timmy Hill	Lilly Trucking Ford	14	Alternator
36	37	39	Matthew Bell	Global Barter Corporation Ford	11	Accident
37	32	15	Chris Cook	Lilly Trucking Chevrolet	8	Overheating
38	17	19	Alex Popow	G-Oil/Noah's Light Foundation Toyota	5	Accident
39	18	42	Josh Wise	Key Motorsports Chevrolet	3	Vibration
40	33	10	Jeff Green	TriStar Motorsports Toyota	3	Vibration
41	36	46	Matt DiBenedetto	The Motorsports Group Chevrolet	2	Brakes
42	22	47	Stephen Leicht	Curtis Key Plumbing Chevrolet	2	Brakes
43	23	7	Danica Patrick	GoDaddy.com Chevrolet	2	Accident

Sunoco Rookie of the Year Contender.

RACE COMMENTS: Before an estimated crowd of 40,000, Carl Edwards won the ZIPPO 200, his 38th NASCAR Nationwide Series victory. Prior to the green flag, the following cars dropped to the rear of the field for the reasons indicated: #15, 53 (missing drivers meeting); #54 (unapproved adjustments during the impound).

TIME OF RACE: 2 hours, 12 minutes, 19 seconds — AVERAGE SPEED: 91.1 mph — MARGIN OF VICTORY: 1.13 seconds — COORS LIGHT POLE AWARD: Sam Hornish Jr. (122.454 mph. 72.027 secs.) — CAUTION FLAGS: 5 cautions for 15 laps — LAP LEADERS: 13 lead changes among 9 drivers. Hornish Jr. 1–11, Keselowski 12–19, Hornish Jr. 20–23, Kennedy 24–28, Keselowski 29–50, K. Busch 51, Truex 52–53, Paludo 54–57, Allgaier 58, Clements 59, Keselowski 60–72, Edwards 73–75, Keselowski 76, Edwards 77–82.

22 NAPA AUTO PARTS 200 presented by DODGE

August 18, 2012 — Circuit Gilles Villeneuve — 74 Laps – 200.466 Miles

Fin	Str	No	Driver	Team	Laps	Status
1	15	31	Justin Allgaier	Brandt Chevrolet	81	Running
2	2	12	Sam Hornish Jr.	Alliance Truck Parts Dodge	81	Running
3	3	22	Jacques Villeneuve	Dodge Dodge	81	Running
4	17	2	Elliott Sadler	OneMain Financial Chevrolet	81	Running
5	8	5	Ron Fellows	Canadian Tire Chevrolet	81	Running
6	6	18	Michael McDowell	FedEx Express Toyota	81	Running
7	22	01	Mike Wallace	TradeBank Chevrolet	81	Running
8	9	60	Billy Johnson	Roush Fenway 25 Winning Years Ford	81	Running
9	19	3	Austin Dillon #	AdvoCare Chevrolet	81	Running
10	5	54	Kyle Busch	Monster Energy Toyota	81	Running
11	11	33	Brendan Gaughan	South Point Hotel & Casino Chevrolet	81	Running
12	16	6	Ricky Stenhouse Jr.	Ford EcoBoost Ford	81	Running
13	23	44	Mike Bliss	TriStar Motorsports Chevrolet	81	Running
14	32	19	Tayler Malsam	G-Oil/Noah's Light Foundation Toyota	81	Running
15	20	87	Alex Kennedy	Global Barter Corporation/Dream Factory Toyota	81	Running
16	34	40	Erik Darnell	Key Motorsports Chevrolet	81	Running
17	36	39	Tim Andrews	Go Green Racing Ford	81	Running
18	42	24	Derek White	SR2 Motorsports Chevrolet	81	Running
19	41	14	Eric McClure	Hefty/Reynolds Wrap Toyota	81	Running
20	21	38	Brad Sweet #	Great Clips Chevrolet	81	Running
21	27	59	Kyle Kelley	Jamison Eng./UPR.com Chevrolet	81	Running
22	1	30	Alex Tagliani	Oasis/Motegi Racing Chevrolet	81	Running
23	31	4	Daryl Harr	Danny Efland Racing Chevrolet	81	Running
24	10	11	Brian Scott	Dollar General Toyota	81	Running
25	26	51	Jeremy Clements	USS James E Williams DDG 95 Chevrolet	81	Running
26	18	81	Jason Bowles #	American Majority Toyota	77	Brakes
27	4	7	Danica Patrick	GoDaddy.com Chevrolet	75	Running
28	33	43	Michael Annett	Pilot/Flying J Ford	73	Running
29	13	99	Patrick Carpentier	NAPA Auto Parts Toyota	69	Running
30	39	70	Joe Nemechek	ML Motorsports Dodge	62	Radiator
31	37	26	John Young	Eklekt Technologies Group Dodge	59	Drive Train
32	12	27	Andrew Ranger	Dodge Dodge	57	Suspension
33	7	88	Cole Whitt #	TaxSlayer.com Chevrolet	54	Engine
34	28	75	Kenny Habul	SunEnergy 1 Racing, LLC Toyota	46	Accident
35	38	23	Dexter Stacey	North Texas Pipe Chevrolet	30	Accident
36	29	41	Timmy Hill	Lilly Trucking Ford	21	Transmission
37	14	53	Eric Curran	Whelen/Team Fox Dodge	15	Transmission
38	35	08	Louis-Philippe Dumoulin	Randy Hill Racing Ford	14	Suspension
39	24	15	Chris Cook	Lilly Trucking Chevrolet	6	Brakes
40	43	47	Matt DiBenedetto	Curtis Key Plumbing Chevrolet	6	Overheating
41	30	42	Blake Koch	Key Motorsports Chevrolet	5	Brakes
42	40	46	Chase Miller	The Motorsports Group Chevrolet	4	Brakes
43	25	10	Jeff Green	TriStar Motorsports Toyota	2	Vibration

Sunoco Rookie of the Year Contender.

RACE COMMENTS: Before an estimated crowd of 60,000, Justin Allgaier won the NAPA Auto Parts 200 presented by Dodge, his third NASCAR Nationwide Series victory. To start the race, prior to the green flag the following cars dropped to the rear of the field: #75 (back-up car), #41, 43, 24, 47 (adjustments during impound), #70, 54 (driver change), #01 (engine change).

TIME OF RACE: 3 hours, 7 minutes, 58 seconds — AVERAGE SPEED: 70.043 mph — MARGIN OF VICTORY: 0.353 seconds — COORS LIGHT POLE AWARD: Alex Tagliani (96.688 mph. 100.865 secs.) — CAUTION FLAGS: 8 cautions for 22 laps — LAP LEADERS: 12 lead changes among 6 drivers. Tagliani 1–2, Hornish Jr. 3, Tagliani 4–5, Hornish Jr. 6–7, Villeneuve 8–19, Hornish Jr. 20, Patrick 21–40, Villeneuve 41–45, Sadler 46–51, Villeneuve 52–63, Tagliani 64–66, Villeneuve 67–80, Allgaier 81.

23 FOOD CITY 250

August 24, 2012 — Bristol Motor Speedway — 250 Laps – 133.25 Miles

Fin	Str	No	Driver	Team	Laps	Status
1	2	18	Joey Logano	Dollar General Toyota	250	Running
2	5	6	Ricky Stenhouse Jr.	NOS Ford	250	Running
3	10	54	Kyle Busch	Monster Energy Toyota	250	Running
4	4	3	Austin Dillon #	American Ethanol Chevrolet	250	Running
5	7	2	Elliott Sadler	OneMain Financial Chevrolet	250	Running
6	19	88	Cole Whitt #	Spy Optic Chevrolet	250	Running
7	12	36	Ryan Blaney	SealWrap Chevrolet	250	Running
8	18	43	Michael Annett	Pilot/Flying J Ford	250	Running
9	34	7	Danica Patrick	GoDaddy.com Chevrolet	250	Running
10	9	12	Sam Hornish Jr.	Detroit Genuine Parts Dodge	250	Running
11	16	87	Joe Nemechek	AM/FM Energy Wood & Pellet Stoves/AC General Toyota	250	Running
12	23	19	Tayler Malsam	G-Oil/Noah's Light Foundation Toyota	250	Running
13	14	44	Mike Bliss	Bandit Chippers Toyota	250	Running
14	15	38	Kasey Kahne	Great Clips Chevrolet	250	Running
15	13	33	Kevin Harvick	Hunt Brothers Pizza Chevrolet	250	Running
16	1	60	Trevor Bayne	Yourracecar.com Ford	250	Running
17	33	01	Mike Wallace	Tradebank Chevrolet	247	Running
18	26	81	Jason Bowles #	American Majority Dodge	247	Running
19	27	39	Josh Richards	Joy Global Ford	247	Running
20	30	86	Kevin Lepage	Qello Ford	247	Running
21	11	30	Nelson Piquet Jr.	Autotrac/Qualcomm Chevrolet	246	Running
22	38	24	Benny Gordon	Big Timber/Horizon Entertainment Toyota	246	Running
23	20	99	John Wes Townley	Zaxby's Toyota	246	Running
24	42	23	Robert Richardson	North Texas Pipe Chevrolet	246	Running
25	28	15	Timmy Hill	Lilly Trucking Chevrolet	245	Running
26	41	4	Brad Teague	SCAG Commercial Mowers Chevrolet	245	Running
27	39	14	Eric McClure	Hefty/Reynolds Wrap Toyota	244	Running
28	36	41	Fain Skinner	Carport Empire Ford	244	Running
29	29	70	Johanna Long #	Foretravel Chevrolet	244	Running
30	6	31	Justin Allgaier	Brandt Chevrolet	242	Running
31	32	52	Joey Gase #	Jimco Windows Chevrolet	239	Running
32	8	22	Brad Keselowski	Discount Tire Dodge	226	Running
33	21	51	Jeremy Clements	stjude.org Chevrolet	213	Running
34	3	11	Brian Scott	Dollar General Toyota	198	Clutch
35	22	40	Erik Darnell	The Motorsports Group Chevrolet	173	Electrical
36	40	74	Rick Crawford	Koma Unwind Chevrolet	55	Overheating
37	43	71	Carl Long	Lilly Trucking Chevrolet	27	Oil Pressure
38	25	75	Scott Riggs	Lilly Trucking Chevrolet	20	Electrical
39	37	50	David Starr	Make Motorsports Chevrolet	19	Engine
40	24	42	Josh Wise	Curtis Key Plumbing Chevrolet	14	Electrical
41	35	08	Tim Andrews	Randy Hill Racing Ford	11	Brakes
42	17	10	Jeff Green	TriStar Motorsports Toyota	6	Vibration
43	31	46	Chase Miller	The Motorsports Group Chevrolet	2	Ignition

Sunoco Rookie of the Year Contender.

RACE COMMENTS: Before an estimated crowd of 85,000, Joey Logano won the Food City 250, his 15th NASCAR Nationwide Series victory. Prior to the green flag, the following car dropped to the rear of the field for the reasons indicated: #87 (missed drivers meeting).

TIME OF RACE: 1 hour, 44 minutes, 26 seconds — AVERAGE SPEED: 76.556 mph — MARGIN OF VICTORY: 0.503 seconds — COORS LIGHT POLE AWARD: Trevor Bayne (121.19 mph. 15.833 secs.) — CAUTION FLAGS: 9 cautions for 59 laps — LAP LEADERS: 7 lead changes among 4 drivers. Bayne–pole, Logano 1–35, Sadler 36–46, Stenhouse Jr. 47–105, Logano 106–116, Stenhouse Jr. 117, Harvick 118–215, Logano 216–250.

24 NRA AMERICAN WARRIOR 300

September 1, 2012 — Atlanta Motor Speedway — 195 Laps – 300.3 Miles

Fin	Str	No	Driver	Team	Laps	Status
1	2	6	Ricky Stenhouse Jr.	Cargill Beef Ford	195	Running
2	8	22	Brad Keselowski	Discount Tire Dodge	195	Running
3	3	33	Kevin Harvick	Bad Boy Buggies Chevrolet	195	Running
4	7	2	Elliott Sadler	OneMain Financial Chevrolet	195	Running
5	13	31	Justin Allgaier	Brandt Chevrolet	195	Running
6	9	3	Austin Dillon #	AdvoCare Chevrolet	195	Running
7	1	54	Kyle Busch	Monster Energy Toyota	195	Running
8	12	88	Cole Whitt #	NASCAR Bashers Chevrolet	195	Running
9	6	12	Sam Hornish Jr.	Alliance Truck Parts Dodge	195	Running
10	14	43	Michael Annett	Old Wisconsin/Pilot/Flying J Ford	195	Running
11	15	11	Brian Scott	Dollar General Toyota	193	Running
12	5	18	Denny Hamlin	Z-Line Designs Toyota	193	Running
13	17	7	Danica Patrick	GoDaddy.com Chevrolet	193	Running
14	18	87	Joe Nemechek	AM/FM Energy Wood & Pellet Stoves Toyota	193	Running
15	25	51	Jeremy Clements	Phoenix Group Metals/stjude.org Chevrolet	191	Running
16	20	81	Jason Bowles #	theRANDOMact.org Toyota	191	Running
17	27	01	Mike Wallace	G&K Services Chevrolet	191	Running
18	38	19	Tayler Malsam	G-Oil Toyota	189	Running
19	36	4	Danny Efland	Tradebank Chevrolet	187	Running
20	28	40	Erik Darnell	Park 'N Fly Chevrolet	187	Running
21	30	14	Eric McClure	Hefty/Reynolds Wrap Toyota	187	Running
22	10	44	Mike Bliss	BanditChippers.com Toyota	186	Accident
23	23	30	James Buescher	Central Wire Chevrolet	185	Accident
24	35	24	Benny Gordon	American Childhood Cancer Organization Toyota	184	Running
25	24	08	Kyle Fowler	Commercial Disposal/Techniweld Ford	183	Accident
26	16	99	Travis Pastrana	Boost Mobile Toyota	173	Running
27	19	50	David Starr	Liberty Tire Recycling Chevrolet	130	Engine
28	4	38	Kasey Kahne	Great Clips Chevrolet	128	Accident
29	40	70	Tony Raines	Tidal Wave Response Chevrolet	105	Brakes
30	26	39	Matt Carter	RIMZ One/Go Green Racing Ford	101	Ignition
31	41	23	Robert Richardson	North Texas Pipe Chevrolet	68	Accident
32	11	98	Reed Sorenson	Carroll Shelby Engines Ford	63	Accident
33	33	15	Timmy Hill	CarportEmpire.com Ford	42	Electrical
34	37	89	Morgan Shepherd	Hyland's Leg Cramps/Racing with Jesus Chevrolet	35	Handling
35	21	10	Jeff Green	TriStar MotorsportsToyota	25	Vibration
36	22	00	Blake Koch	Ruch Motorsports Chevrolet	14	Ignition
37	42	41	Fain Skinner	CarportEmpire.com Ford	8	Engine
38	31	46	Chase Miller	TheMotorsportsGroup.com Chevrolet	7	Vibration
39	39	74	Mike Harmon	Koma Unwind Relaxation Drink Chevrolet	6	Overheating
40	29	42	Josh Wise	Curtis Key Plumbing Chevrolet	5	Electrical
41	32	71	Carl Long	RWR/Lilly Trucking Chevrolet	4	Fuel Pressure
42	34	47	J.J. Yeley	Curtis Key Plumbing Chevrolet	3	Overheating
43	43	52	Joey Gase #	Metro Ministries Chevrolet	2	Accident

Sunoco Rookie of the Year Contender.

RACE COMMENTS: Before an estimated crowd of 47,700, Ricky Stenhouse Jr.won the NRA American Warrior 300, his sixth NASCAR Nationwide Series victory.

TIME OF RACE: 2 hours, 32 minutes, 51 seconds — AVERAGE SPEED: 117.88 mph — MARGIN OF VICTORY: 0.157 seconds — COORS LIGHT POLE AWARD: Kyle Busch (176.28 mph. 31.450 secs.) — CAUTION FLAGS: 8 cautions for 43 laps — LAP LEADERS: 9 lead changes among 6 drivers. K. Busch 1–2, Stenhouse Jr. 3–17, Harvick 18–49, Hornish Jr. 50, Harvick 51–120, Pastrana 121–126, Harvick 127–170, Allgaier 171–183, Harvick 184–194, Stenhouse Jr. 195.

25 VIRGINIA 529 COLLEGE SAVINGS 250

September 7, 2012 — Richmond International Raceway — 250 Laps – 187.5 Miles

Fin	Str	No	Driver	Team	Laps	Status
1	3	33	Kevin Harvick	Armour Chevrolet	250	Running
2	1	6	Ricky Stenhouse Jr.	Ford EcoBoost Ford	250	Running
3	17	54	Kurt Busch	Monster Energy Toyota	250	Running
4	6	18	Denny Hamlin	SportClips Toyota	250	Running
5	13	43	Michael Annett	Pilot/Flying J Ford	250	Running
6	2	3	Austin Dillon #	AdvoCare Chevrolet	250	Running
7	11	51	Ty Dillon	Wesco Chevrolet	250	Running
8	14	87	Joe Nemechek	AM/FM Energy Wood & Pellet Stoves Toyota	250	Running
9	27	22	Ryan Blaney	Snap-On Dodge	250	Running
10	20	20	Darrell Wallace Jr.	Dollar General Toyota	250	Running
11	15	30	James Buescher	ABF Chevrolet	250	Running
12	12	2	Elliott Sadler	OneMain Financial Chevrolet	250	Running
13	10	31	Justin Allgaier	Brandt Chevrolet	250	Running
14	19	88	Cole Whitt #	Hellmann's Chevrolet	250	Running
15	9	44	Mike Bliss	TriStar Motorsports Toyota	250	Running
16	33	99	Ryan Truex	Toyota Care Toyota	250	Running
17	5	60	Travis Pastrana	Ford EcoBoost Ford	250	Running
18	28	40	Erik Darnell	Key Motorsports Chevrolet	250	Running
19	30	19	Tayler Malsam	G-Oil Toyota	250	Running
20	23	38	Brad Sweet #	Great Clips Chevrolet	250	Running
21	31	01	Mike Wallace	JD Motorsports Chevrolet	250	Running
22	39	23	Robert Richardson	North Texas Pipe Chevrolet	250	Running
23	21	81	Jason Bowles #	@THERANDOMACTORG/ITEX.NET Dodge	250	Running
24	22	4	Jeremy Clements	stjude.org Chevrolet	249	Running
25	26	08	Paulie Harraka	Randy Hill Racing Ford	249	Running
26	41	14	Eric McClure	Hefty/Reynolds Wrap Toyota	249	Running
27	40	39	Dexter Stacey	MaddiesPlaceRocks.com Ford	248	Running
28	7	11	Brian Scott	Dollar General Toyota	246	Running
29	24	7	Danica Patrick	GoDaddy.com Chevrolet	218	Running
30	4	12	Sam Hornish Jr.	Alliance Truck Parts Dodge	162	Running
31	32	41	Timmy Hill	Lilly Trucking CDL Driver Search Ford	153	Accident
32	8	70	Johanna Long #	KeenParts.com Chevrolet	109	Accident
33	35	86	Kevin Lepage	Qello Corp/Trivette Trucking Ford	51	Power Steering
34	42	24	Derek White	OCR Gaz Bar Toyota	45	Battery
35	34	17	Tanner Berryhill	Race City Steel/Nationalcashlenders.com Toyota	35	Accident
36	37	75	Scott Riggs	RWR Chevrolet	28	Overheating
37	43	00	Blake Koch	Ruch Motorsports Chevrolet	18	Brakes
38	38	71	Carl Long	Rick Ware Racing Chevrolet	15	Rear Gear
39	36	15	Matt Carter	Rick Ware Racing Chevrolet	11	Clutch
40	29	42	Josh Wise	Key Motorsports Chevrolet	7	Brakes
41	25	47	J.J. Yeley	Curtis Key Plumbing Chevrolet	7	Brakes
42	16	46	Chase Miller	The Motorsports Group Chevrolet	6	Overheating
43	18	10	Jeff Green	TriStar Motorsports Toyota	3	Vibration

Sunoco Rookie of the Year Contender.

RACE COMMENTS: Before an estimated crowd of 38,000, Kevin Harvick won the Virginia 529 College Savings 250, his 38th NASCAR Nationwide Series victory.

TIME OF RACE: 2 hours, 2 minutes, 39 seconds — AVERAGE SPEED: 91.724 mph — MARGIN OF VICTORY: 1.944 seconds — COORS LIGHT POLE AWARD: Ricky Stenhouse Jr. (122.822 mph. 21.983 secs.) — CAUTION FLAGS: 7 cautions for 45 laps — LAP LEADERS: 8 lead changes among 6 drivers. Stenhouse Jr.–pole, Dillon 1–14, Stenhouse Jr. 15–70, Harvick 71–187, Wallace 188–189, Buescher 190–192, Stenhouse Jr. 193–201, K. Busch 202–226, Harvick 227–250.

26 DOLLAR GENERAL 300 *powered by* COCA-COLA

September 15, 2012 — Chicagoland Speedway — 200 Laps – 300 Miles

Fin	Str	No	Driver	Team	Laps	Status
1	3	6	Ricky Stenhouse Jr.	Blue Bird Ford	200	Running
2	6	54	Kyle Busch	Monster Energy Toyota	200	Running
3	2	3	Austin Dillon #	American Ethanol Chevrolet	200	Running
4	16	22	Brad Keselowski	Discount Tire Dodge	200	Running
5	7	33	Paul Menard	Menards/Rheem Chevrolet	200	Running
6	4	12	Sam Hornish Jr.	AVIS Dodge	200	Running
7	8	43	Michael Annett	Pilot/Flying J Ford	200	Running
8	5	2	Elliott Sadler	OneMain Financial Chevrolet	200	Running
9	1	18	Joey Logano	Dollar General Toyota	200	Running
10	42	11	Brian Scott	Dollar General Toyota	200	Running
11	10	31	Justin Allgaier	Brandt Chevrolet	200	Running
12	12	7	Danica Patrick	GoDaddy.com Chevrolet	200	Running
13	9	44	Mike Bliss	BanditChippers.com Toyota	200	Running
14	13	88	Cole Whitt #	Degree Men Chevrolet	200	Running
15	18	38	Brad Sweet #	Great Clips Chevrolet	199	Running
16	25	87	Joe Nemechek	AM/FM Energy Wood & Pellet Stoves Toyota	199	Running
17	20	30	Alex Bowman	Allegiant Chevrolet	199	Running
18	19	19	Tayler Malsam	G-Oil Toyota	198	Running
19	21	01	Mike Wallace	G&K Services Chevrolet	198	Running
20	11	99	Kenny Wallace	Family Farmers Toyota	196	Running
21	17	70	Johanna Long #	Foretravel Chevrolet	196	Running
22	34	40	Erik Darnell	Curtis Key Plumbing Chevrolet	195	Running
23	22	23	Jamie Dick	Viva Auto Group Chevrolet	195	Running
24	24	39	Dexter Stacey	Maddies Place Ford	194	Running
25	30	14	Eric McClure	Hefty/Reynolds Wrap Toyota	194	Running
26	37	41	Juan Carlos Blum	VMP Nutrition/The New Miami Subs Chevrolet	193	Running
27	35	4	Danny Efland	Tradebank Chevrolet	192	Running
28	15	81	Jason Bowles #	25Hill.com Now on DVD Toyota	153	Engine
29	14	24	Benny Gordon	O.C.R. Gaz Bar/Affichage.CO Toyota	122	Suspension
30	31	51	Jeremy Clements	USS James E Williams DDG 95 Chevrolet	68	Oil Leak
31	27	10	Jeff Green	TriStar Motorsports Toyota	30	Vibration
32	39	89	Morgan Shepherd	Victory In Jesus Chevrolet	30	Engine
33	36	15	Timmy Hill	Carport Empire Ford	28	Vibration
34	38	28	Tony Raines	Robinson-Blakeney Racing Chevrolet	26	Electrical
35	40	52	Joey Gase #	Competition Transmission Chevrolet	23	Handling
36	29	00	Blake Koch	O.C.R. Gaz Bar Toyota	19	Vibration
37	33	71	Scott Riggs	Lilly Trucking Chevrolet	19	Ignition
38	32	75	Matt Carter	Lilly Trucking Chevrolet	15	Rear Gear
39	41	74	Mike Harmon	Koma Unwind Chevrolet	12	Overheating
40	28	47	J.J. Yeley	Curtis Key Plumbing Chevrolet	11	Vibration
41	23	42	Josh Wise	Key Motorsports Chevrolet	10	Electrical
42	26	46	Chase Miller	The Motorsports Group Chevrolet	9	Overheating
43	43	08	Tim Andrews	Randy Hill Racing Ford	9	Ignition

Sunoco Rookie of the Year Contender.

RACE COMMENTS: Before an estimated crowd of 34,000, Ricky Stenhouse Jr. won the Dollar General 300 powered by Coca-Cola, his seventh NASCAR Nationwide Series victory. Prior to the green flag, the following cars dropped to the rear of the field for the reasons indicated: #71 (missing drivers meeting).

TIME OF RACE: 2 hours, 10 minutes, 5 seconds — AVERAGE SPEED: 138.373 mph — MARGIN OF VICTORY: 2.402 seconds — COORS LIGHT POLE AWARD: Joey Logano (178.012 mph. 30.335 secs.) — CAUTION FLAGS: 5 cautions for 20 laps — LAP LEADERS: 17 lead changes among 9 drivers. Logano 1–7, Hornish Jr. 8, Logano 9–59, Dillon 60, K. Busch 61–62, Dillon 63, K. Busch 64–69, Dillon 70–95, Stenhouse Jr. 96, Annett 97, Allgaier 98–100, Nemechek 101, Dillon 102–125, Logano 126–134, K. Busch 135–168, Sadler 169–171, K. Busch 172–179, Stenhouse Jr. 180–200.

27 KENTUCKY 300

September 22, 2012 — Kentucky Speedway — 200 Laps – 300 Miles

Fin	Str	No	Driver	Team	Laps	Status
1	1	3	Austin Dillon #	AdvoCare Chevrolet	200	Running
2	3	12	Sam Hornish Jr.	Alliance Truck Parts Dodge	200	Running
3	6	33	Brendan Gaughan	South Point Chevrolet	200	Running
4	4	18	Drew Herring	SportClips Toyota	200	Running
5	8	2	Elliott Sadler	OneMain Financial Chevrolet	200	Running
6	15	88	Cole Whitt #	Clean Coal Chevrolet	200	Running
7	5	43	Michael Annett	Pilot/Flying J Ford	200	Running
8	10	31	Justin Allgaier	Brandt Chevrolet	200	Running
9	20	22	Ryan Blaney	Discount Tire Dodge	200	Running
10	13	38	Brad Sweet #	Great Clips Chevrolet	200	Running
11	7	11	Brian Scott	Dollar General Toyota	199	Running
12	12	70	Johanna Long #	Keen Parts Chevrolet	199	Running
13	19	30	James Buescher	Fraternal Order of Eagles Chevrolet	199	Running
14	11	7	Danica Patrick	GoDaddy.com Chevrolet	198	Running
15	18	51	Jeremy Clements	All South Electrical Constructors, Inc. Chevrolet	198	Running
16	23	81	Jason Bowles #	Thrush and Son/HI Technologies Toyota	197	Running
17	2	6	Ricky Stenhouse Jr.	EcoBoost Ford	197	Running
18	17	44	Mike Bliss	BanditChippers.com Toyota	197	Running
19	16	23	Jamie Dick	Viva Auto Group Chevrolet	196	Running
20	22	01	Mike Wallace	G&K Services Chevrolet	196	Running
21	27	39	Josh Richards	Joy Ford	196	Running
22	24	14	Eric McClure	Hefty/Reynolds Wrap Toyota	196	Running
23	33	19	Tayler Malsam	G-Oil Toyota	195	Running
24	30	40	Erik Darnell	Curtis Key Plumbing Chevrolet	194	Running
25	9	99	Alex Bowman	Penserra Securities/Allegiant Air Toyota	194	Running
26	21	8	Scott Lagasse Jr.	HybridLight/BSA Chevrolet	187	Running
27	32	87	Joe Nemechek	AM/FM Energy Wood & Pellet Stoves Toyota	143	Engine
28	14	54	Kurt Busch	Monster Energy Toyota	128	Rear Gear
29	40	41	Timmy Hill	RWR Ford	104	Handling
30	25	4	Danny Efland	Tradebank Chevrolet	81	Engine
31	42	89	Morgan Shepherd	Victory In Jesus Chevrolet	55	Handling
32	29	24	Benny Gordon	O.C.R. Gaz Bar/Snappy Tomato Pizza Toyota	52	Vibration
33	36	50	David Starr	Gulf Coast Loss Prevention Chevrolet	47	Rear Gear
34	34	86	Kevin Lepage	DT Trivette Trucking Ford	46	Vibration
35	37	52	Joey Gase #	Metro Ministries Chevrolet	38	Clutch
36	43	08	Mike Harmon	Randy Hill Racing Ford	22	Vibration
37	41	15	Carl Long	Lilly Trucking Chevrolet	16	Overheating
38	38	00	Tanner Berryhill	O.C.R. Gaz Bar Toyota	15	Rear Gear
39	26	46	Chase Miller	The Motorsports Group Chevrolet	13	Vibration
40	39	75	Matt Carter	Lilly Trucking Chevrolet	13	Transmission
41	31	47	Matt DiBenedetto	Curtis Key Plumbing Chevrolet	10	Vibration
42	35	42	Matt Frahm	Key Motorsports Chevrolet	6	Brakes
43	28	10	Charles Lewandoski	TriStar Motorsports Toyota	4	Vibration

Sunoco Rookie of the Year Contender.

RACE COMMENTS: Before an estimated crowd of 23,000, Austin Dillon won the Kentucky 300, his second NASCAR Nationwide Series victory. Prior to the green flag, the following car dropped to the rear of the field for the reason indicated: #54 (driver change).

TIME OF RACE: 2 hours, 10 minutes, 55 seconds — AVERAGE SPEED: 137.492 mph — MARGIN OF VICTORY: 1.059 seconds — COORS LIGHT POLE AWARD: Austin Dillon (177.264 mph. 30.463 secs.) — CAUTION FLAGS: 6 cautions for 26 laps — LAP LEADERS: 11 lead changes among 7 drivers. Dillon–pole, Stenhouse Jr. 1–32, Lepage 33, Dillon 34–43, Hornish Jr. 44–46, Sadler 47–87, Dillon 88–92, Sadler 93–144, Hornish Jr. 145–146, Herring 147–148, Annett 149–150, Dillon 151–200

28 ONEMAIN FINANCIAL 200

September 29, 2012 — Dover International Speedway — 200 Laps – 200 Miles

Fin	Str	No	Driver	Team	Laps	Status
1	3	18	Joey Logano	SportClips Toyota	200	Running
2	10	33	Paul Menard	Menards/Rheem Chevrolet	200	Running
3	12	43	Michael Annett	Pilot/Flying J Ford	200	Running
4	4	2	Elliott Sadler	OneMain Financial Chevrolet	200	Running
5	7	54	Kyle Busch	Monster Energy Toyota	200	Running
6	13	88	Cole Whitt #	TaxSlayer.com Chevrolet	200	Running
7	38	11	Brian Scott	Dollar General Toyota	200	Running
8	5	38	Kasey Kahne	Great Clips Chevrolet	200	Running
9	6	6	Ricky Stenhouse Jr.	Cargill/Rancher's Reserve Ford	200	Running
10	9	3	Austin Dillon #	AdvoCare Chevrolet	200	Running
11	15	19	Mike Bliss	Bandit Chippers Toyota	200	Running
12	1	20	Darrell Wallace Jr.	Freightliner Toyota	200	Running
13	8	22	Ryan Blaney	Discount Tire Dodge	200	Running
14	11	99	Ryan Truex	SeaWatch International/Grime Boss Toyota	200	Running
15	21	44	Jeff Green	G-Oil Toyota	200	Running
16	25	7	Danica Patrick	GoDaddy.com Chevrolet	200	Running
17	24	87	Joe Nemechek	AM/FM Energy Wood & Pellet Stoves Toyota	200	Running
18	14	12	Sam Hornish Jr.	Alliance Truck Parts Dodge	199	Running
19	16	30	Alex Bowman	Allegiant Air Chevrolet	198	Running
20	23	81	Jason Bowles #	SupportMilitary.org Dodge	198	Running
21	29	01	Mike Wallace	HelpJD01.com Chevrolet	197	Running
22	18	24	Blake Koch	Wings To Go Toyota	197	Running
23	34	27	J.J. Yeley	Drive Sober, Arrive Alive DE Ford	197	Running
24	33	41	Timmy Hill	Lilly Trucking Ford	197	Running
25	31	23	Jamie Dick	Viva Auto Group Chevrolet	197	Running
26	37	14	Eric McClure	Hefty/Reynolds Wrap Toyota	197	Running
27	27	51	Jeremy Clements	stjude.org/Clements Automotive Chevrolet	194	Running
28	41	4	Brad Teague	Danny Efland Racing Chevrolet	193	Running
29	39	39	Tim Andrews	Go Green Racing Ford	174	Oil Leak
30	2	31	Justin Allgaier	Brandt Chevrolet	164	Running
31	30	40	Erik Darnell	Key Motorsports Chevrolet	148	Running
32	35	52	Justin Jennings	Jimmy Means Racing Chevrolet	108	Suspension
33	42	70	Tony Raines	ML Motorsports Dodge	53	Engine
34	17	86	Kevin Lepage	Qello Corp Ford	35	Axle
35	40	08	Danny Efland	Randy Hill Racing Ford	14	Overheating
36	43	75	Scott Riggs	Rick Ware Racing Chevrolet	14	Suspension
37	32	71	Carl Long	Rick Ware Racing Ford	12	Handling
38	26	46	Chase Miller	The Motorsports Group Chevrolet	9	Handling
39	20	42	Josh Wise	Key Motorsports Chevrolet	6	Electrical
40	19	00	Michael McDowell	O.C.R. Gaz Bar Toyota	6	Rear End
41	36	47	T.J. Bell	Curtis Key Plumbing Chevrolet	6	Vibration
42	28	15	Kelly Bires	Rick Ware Racing Chevrolet	4	Brakes
43	22	10	Charles Lewandoski	TriStar Motorsports Toyota	3	Vibration

Sunoco Rookie of the Year Contender.

RACE COMMENTS: Before an estimated crowd of 29,000, Joey Logano won the OneMain Financial 200, his 16th NASCAR Nationwide Series victory. Prior to the green flag, the following car dropped to the rear of the field for the reason indicated: #15 (missed drivers meeting).

TIME OF RACE: 1 hours, 37 minutes, 0 seconds — AVERAGE SPEED: 123.711 mph — MARGIN OF VICTORY: 0.876 seconds — COORS POLE AWARD: Darrell Wallace Jr. (155.905 mph. 23.091 secs.) — CAUTION FLAGS: 3 cautions for 15 laps — LAP LEADERS: 4 lead changes among 3 drivers. Wallace Jr.–pole, Allgaier 1–13, Logano 14–47, Kahne 48–50, Logano 51–200.

29 DOLLAR GENERAL 300

October 12, 2012 — Charlotte Motor Speedway — 200 Laps – 300 Miles

Fin	Str	No	Driver	Team	Laps	Status
1	3	20	Joey Logano	GameStop/Call Of Duty Black Ops II Toyota	200	Running
2	5	33	Kevin Harvick	Menards/Rheem Chevrolet	200	Running
3	1	2	Elliott Sadler	OneMain Financial Chevrolet	200	Running
4	6	54	Kyle Busch	Monster Energy Toyota	200	Running
5	8	18	Denny Hamlin	Dollar General Toyota	200	Running
6	2	3	Austin Dillon #	Bass Pro Shops/Tracker Boats Chevrolet	200	Running
7	4	6	Ricky Stenhouse Jr.	Cargill Ford	200	Running
8	7	11	Brian Scott	Dollar General Toyota	200	Running
9	18	30	James Buescher	AccuDoc/Great Clips Chevrolet	200	Running
10	13	43	Michael Annett	Cheez-it/Pilot/Flying J Ford	200	Running
11	11	7	Danica Patrick	GoDaddy.com/Chevrolet	199	Running
12	29	98	Reed Sorenson	Carroll Shelby Motors Ford	199	Running
13	19	88	Cole Whitt #	Hellmann's Chevrolet	199	Running
14	22	36	Ryan Blaney	SealWrap Chevrolet	198	Running
15	15	38	Brad Sweet #	Great Clips Chevrolet	198	Running
16	27	44	Jeff Green	G-Oil Toyota	198	Running
17	33	87	Joe Nemechek	HostGator.com Toyota	198	Running
18	9	22	Brad Keselowski	Discount Tire Dodge	198	Running
19	17	51	Jeremy Clements	USSJamesEWilliamsDDG95/Flounder Chev.	198	Running
20	41	23	Robert Richardson	BrysonsFuel.org Chevrolet	196	Running
21	38	40	Erik Darnell	Curtis Key Plumbing Chevrolet	196	Running
22	25	14	Eric McClure	Hefty/Reynolds Wrap Toyota	195	Running
23	40	01	Mike Wallace	Smith Transport Chevrolet	195	Running
24	21	08	Kyle Fowler	Speedway Children's Charity/reload.biz Ford	195	Running
25	26	24	David Starr	Striping Technologies Inc./Hwy 55 Toyota	195	Running
26	24	86	Kevin Lepage	Kengor Metals Ford	195	Running
27	28	39	Jeffrey Earnhardt	Uponor Ford	194	Running
28	20	81	Jason Bowles #	Thrush & Son/HI-Technologies Toyota	194	Running
29	23	15	Stanton Barrett	FAIRGirls.org Ford	193	Running
30	42	70	Tony Raines	Nice Fries Chevrolet	193	Running
31	39	4	Danny Efland	Tradebank Chevrolet	191	Running
32	12	99	John Wes Townley	Zaxby's Toyota	186	Running
33	32	41	Timmy Hill	Lilly Trucking Ford	176	Running
34	16	31	Justin Allgaier	Brandt Foundation Chevrolet	166	Running
35	10	12	Sam Hornish Jr.	Wurth Dodge	104	Running
36	14	19	Mike Bliss	G-Oil Toyota	79	Accident
37	34	46	Chase Miller	The Motorsports Group Chevrolet	19	Ignition
38	30	47	J.J. Yeley	Curtis Key Plumbing Chevrolet	18	Vibration
39	43	74	David Green	Applebee's Chevrolet	16	Rear Gear
40	37	75	Scott Riggs	RWR Chevrolet	14	Suspension
41	31	42	Josh Wise	Key Motorsports Chevrolet	14	Clutch
42	36	10	Charles Lewandoski	TriStar Motorsports Toyota	12	Vibration
43	35	00	Angela Cope	Highland Wealth Advisors/Hwy 55 Toyota	0	Accident

Sunoco Rookie of the Year Contender.

RACE COMMENTS: Before an estimated crowd of 40,000, Joey Logano won the Dollar General 300, his 17th NASCAR Nationwide Series victory. Prior to the green flag, the following car dropped to the rear of the field for the reason indicated: #74 (missed drivers meeting).

TIME OF RACE: 2 hours, 10 minutes, 7 seconds — AVERAGE SPEED: 138.337 mph — MARGIN OF VICTORY: 2.76 seconds — COORS LIGHT POLE AWARD: Elliott Sadler (184.237 mph. 29.310 secs.) — CAUTION FLAGS: 5 cautions for 25 laps — LAP LEADERS: 21 lead changes among 9 drivers. Sadler 1–15, Stenhouse Jr. 16–42, Harvick 43, Stenhouse Jr. 44–50, Harvick 51–53, Keselowski 54, Logano 55–58, Nemechek 59–60, Harvick 61–71, Keselowski 72–84, Hamlin 85–87, Logano 88, Hamlin 89–95, Logano 96–99, Keselowski 100–133, Logano 134–154, Harvick 155–161, Logano 162–185, Keselowski 186–189, K. Busch 190–191, Scott 192, Logano 193–200.

30 KANSAS LOTTERY 300
October 20, 2012 — Kansas Speedway — 200 Laps – 300 Miles

Fin	Str	No	Driver	Team	Laps	Status
1	10	6	Ricky Stenhouse Jr.	Cargill/Sam's Club Ford	206	Running
2	2	3	Austin Dillon #	AdvoCare Chevrolet	206	Running
3	1	18	Joey Logano	GameStop/Need For Speed Most Wanted Toyota	206	Running
4	7	2	Elliott Sadler	OneMain Financial Chevrolet	206	Running
5	8	88	Cole Whitt #	Clean Coal Chevrolet	206	Running
6	6	54	Kyle Busch	Monster Energy Toyota	206	Running
7	21	31	Justin Allgaier	Brandt Chevrolet	206	Running
8	14	43	Michael Annett	EFS Ford	206	Running
9	12	12	Sam Hornish Jr.	Alliance Truck Parts Dodge	206	Running
10	13	7	Danica Patrick	Tissot/GoDaddy.com Chevrolet	206	Running
11	27	22	Ryan Blaney	Discount Tire Dodge	206	Running
12	22	87	Joe Nemechek	AM/FM Energy Wood & Pellet Stoves Toyota	206	Running
13	23	19	Mike Bliss	Bandit Chippers/Crowne Plaza Toyota	206	Running
14	37	4	Danny Efland	Tradebank Chevrolet	206	Running
15	15	14	Eric McClure	Hefty/Reynolds Wrap/Crowne Plaza Toyota	205	Running
16	5	33	Paul Menard	Menards/Rheem Chevrolet	204	Fuel
17	39	40	Erik Darnell	Curtis Key Plumbing Chevrolet	204	Running
18	4	99	Kenny Wallace	American Ethanol Toyota	203	Fuel
19	32	52	Joey Gase #	www.BBB.org Chevrolet	202	Running
20	24	81	Jason Bowles #	SupportMilitary.org Dodge	201	Running
21	29	01	Mike Wallace	HelpJD01.com Chevrolet	200	Running
22	33	13	Jennifer Jo Cobb	Mark One Electric Chevrolet	200	Running
23	26	38	Brad Sweet #	Great Clips Chevrolet	199	Engine
24	19	8	Scott Lagasse Jr.	Hybrid Light/BSA Chevrolet	197	Accident
25	16	44	Hal Martin	American Custom Yachts/Crowne Plaza Toyota	182	Accident
26	3	11	Brian Scott	Dollar General Toyota	177	Running
27	42	39	Dexter Stacey	Maddie's Place Ford	165	Running
28	17	30	James Buescher	Great Clips Chevrolet	155	Engine
29	40	24	Derek White	O.C.R. Gaz Bar Toyota	130	Accident
30	31	28	Tony Raines	Jay Robinson Inc. Chevrolet	123	Vibration
31	9	70	Johanna Long #	Foretravel Chevrolet	109	Accident
32	43	89	Morgan Shepherd	Hyland's Leg Cramps Chevrolet	75	Rear Gear
33	41	41	Nur Ali	RWR Chevrolet	68	Accident
34	30	08	Scott Saunders	Broo Premium Australian Beer Ford	31	Accident
35	11	51	Jeremy Clements	St. Jude/USS James E. Williams DDG 95 Chevrolet	24	Water Pump
36	25	00	Blake Koch	Ruch Motorsports Toyota	24	Ignition
37	36	75	Carl Long	RWR Chevrolet	23	Overheating
38	34	71	Timmy Hill	RWR Ford	14	Engine
39	35	23	Robert Richardson	North Texas Pipe Chevrolet	14	Clutch
40	28	47	J.J. Yeley	Curtis Key Plumbing Chevrolet	9	Vibration
41	38	74	Mike Harmon	Koma Unwind Chevrolet	8	Rear Gear
42	18	10	Jeff Green	TriStar Motorsports/Crowne Plaza Toyota	4	Vibration
43	20	46	Chase Miller	The Motorsports Group Chevrolet	4	Ignition

Sunoco Rookie of the Year Contender.

RACE COMMENTS: Before an estimated crowd of 63,000, Ricky Stenhouse Jr. won the Kansas Lottery 300, his eighth NASCAR Nationwide Series victory. Prior to the green flag, the following car dropped to the rear of the field for the reason indicated: #01 (adjustments outside impound).

TIME OF RACE: 2 hours, 46 minutes, 8 seconds — AVERAGE SPEED: 111.597 mph — MARGIN OF VICTORY: 0.288 seconds — COORS LIGHT POLE AWARD: Joey Logano (182.914 mph. 29.522 secs.) — CAUTION FLAGS: 12 cautions for 50 laps — LAP LEADERS: 14 lead changes among 6 drivers. Logano 1–34, Stenhouse Jr. 35–37, Menard 38–44, Stenhouse Jr. 45–53, Menard 54–58, Stenhouse Jr. 59–70, Menard 71–112, Dillon 113–117, Menard 118–139, Allgaier 140–142, Menard 143–175, K. Busch 176–183, Menard 184, K. Busch 185–205, Stenhouse Jr. 206.

31 O'REILLY AUTO PARTS CHALLENGE
November 3, 2012 — Texas Motor Speedway — 200 Laps – 300 Miles

Fin	Str	No	Driver	Team	Laps	Status
1	3	33	Kevin Harvick	OneMain Financial Chevrolet	200	Running
2	19	22	Ryan Blaney	Discount Tire Dodge	200	Running
3	1	54	Kyle Busch	Monster Energy Toyota	200	Running
4	5	6	Ricky Stenhouse Jr.	NOS Ford	200	Running
5	9	18	Denny Hamlin	Z-Line Designs Toyota	200	Running
6	4	3	Austin Dillon #	AdvoCare Chevrolet	200	Running
7	14	12	Sam Hornish Jr.	Alliance Truck Parts Dodge	200	Running
8	17	31	Justin Allgaier	Brandt Chevrolet	200	Running
9	20	98	Kevin Swindell	Carroll Shelby Motors Ford	200	Running
10	7	20	Joey Logano	GameStop/NASCAR The Game Toyota	200	Running
11	2	2	Elliott Sadler	OneMain Financial Chevrolet	200	Running
12	6	88	Cole Whitt #	NASCAR Bashers Chevrolet	200	Running
13	15	38	Brad Sweet #	Great Clips Chevrolet	200	Running
14	8	7	Danica Patrick	SEGA Sonic the Hedgehog/GoDaddy.com Chevrolet	200	Running
15	10	99	Kenny Wallace	Toyota Toyota	200	Running
16	13	51	Jeremy Clements	Kelly-Moore Paints/stjude.org Chevrolet	200	Running
17	18	43	Michael Annett	Pilot/Flying J Ford	200	Running
18	16	10	Mike Bliss	Bandit Chippers/Radisson Toyota	200	Running
19	12	30	Ryan Newman	Great Clips Chevrolet	199	Running
20	23	87	Joe Nemechek	SWM Toyota	199	Running
21	22	14	Eric McClure	Hefty/Reynolds Wrap/Radisson Toyota	199	Running
22	11	11	Brian Scott	Dollar General Toyota	198	Running
23	24	24	David Starr	Chasco Toyota	198	Running
24	27	01	Mike Wallace	G&K Services Chevrolet	198	Running
25	39	40	Erik Darnell	Key Motorsports Chevrolet	198	Running
26	26	44	John Blankenship	Coal Save the Country Chevrolet	197	Running
27	40	23	Robert Richardson	Tia Rosa Chevrolet	197	Running
28	42	4	Danny Efland	Tradebank/Shaug Construction Chevrolet	194	Running
29	41	41	Juan Carlos Blum	VMP Nutrition/Momentis/34 Technologies Chevrolet	194	Running
30	34	19	Hal Martin	American Custom Yachts/US Forensics/Radisson Toyota	192	Running
31	33	52	Joey Gase #	www.BBB.org Chevrolet	191	Running
32	36	08	Scott Saunders	Broo Premium Australian Beer Ford	191	Running
33	30	81	Jason Bowles #	Undauntedmovie.com Toyota	175	Running
34	32	03	Scott Riggs	Wollbros Chevrolet	154	Rear Gear
35	38	39	Tim Andrews	United Supermarkets Ford	105	Electrical
36	21	70	Johanna Long #	Foretravel Chevrolet	56	Transmission
37	31	91	Jeff Green	TriStar Motorsports/Radisson Toyota	30	Vibration
38	25	00	Blake Koch	Ruch Motorsports Toyota	23	Rear Gear
39	35	75	Timmy Hill	RWR Ford	22	Vibration
40	37	86	Kevin Lepage	Qello Ford	20	Transmission
41	29	47	J.J. Yeley	Curtis Key Plumbing Chevrolet	7	Brakes
42	28	42	Josh Wise	Chevrolet	6	Electrical
43	43	50	T.J. Bell	Gulf Coast Loss Prevention Chevrolet	1	Engine

Sunoco Rookie of the Year Contender.

RACE COMMENTS: Before an estimated crowd of 68,500, Kevin Harvick won the O'Reilly Auto Parts Challenge, his 39th NASCAR Nationwide Series victory. Prior to the green flag, the following cars dropped to the rear for the reasons indicated: #75 (driver change).

TIME OF RACE: 2 hours, 6 minutes, 50 seconds — AVERAGE SPEED: 141.919 mph — MARGIN OF VICTORY: 1.628 seconds — COORS LIGHT POLE AWARD: Kyle Busch (183.051 mph. 29.500 secs.) — CAUTION FLAGS: 5 cautions for 22 laps — LAP LEADERS: 11 lead changes among 5 drivers. K. Busch 1–63, Harvick 64–89, K. Busch 90, Harvick 91, Sadler 92, Harvick 93–143, Dillon 144, Harvick 145–156, Hamlin 157–162, Harvick 163–181, K. Busch 182, Harvick 183–200.

32 GREAT CLIPS 200
November 10, 2012 — Phoenix International Raceway — 200 Laps – 200 Miles

Fin	Str	No	Driver	Team	Laps	Status
1	1	18	Joey Logano	GameStop/Epic Mickey2 Toyota	204	Running
2	5	20	Brian Vickers	Dollar General Toyota	204	Running
3	8	6	Ricky Stenhouse Jr.	Valvoline NextGen Ford	204	Running
4	2	54	Kyle Busch	Monster Energy Toyota	204	Running
5	7	38	Kasey Kahne	Great Clips Chevrolet	204	Running
6	3	3	Austin Dillon #	AdvoCare Chevrolet	204	Running
7	17	43	Michael Annett	Pilot/Flying J Ford	204	Running
8	10	11	Brian Scott	Dollar General Toyota	204	Running
9	6	22	Brad Keselowski	Discount Tire Dodge	204	Running
10	14	7	Danica Patrick	GoDaddy.com Chevrolet	204	Running
11	12	31	Justin Allgaier	Brandt Chevrolet	204	Running
12	9	30	Jason Leffler	FOE Chevrolet	204	Running
13	15	19	Mike Bliss	BanditChippers.com/Embassy Suites Toyota	204	Running
14	4	12	Sam Hornish Jr.	Alliance Truck Parts Dodge	204	Running
15	22	99	Alex Bowman	Port of Tucson/Levin Financial Toyota	204	Running
16	20	87	Joe Nemechek	AM/FM Energy Wood & Pellet Stoves Toyota	204	Running
17	27	81	Jason Bowles #	MacDonald Motorsport Toyota	204	Running
18	36	23	Jamie Dick	Vivi Auto Group Chevrolet	204	Running
19	34	01	Mike Wallace	DSTP Motorsports Chevrolet	204	Running
20	18	14	Eric McClure	Hefty/Reynolds Wrap/Embassy Suites Toyota	204	Running
21	23	08	Paulie Harraka	MC-10 Ford	203	Running
22	16	2	Elliott Sadler	OneMain Financial Chevrolet	203	Running
23	19	10	Jeff Green	G-Oil/Embassy Suites Toyota	201	Running
24	33	73	Derrike Cope	MaxElence MVP/Dobson Inn Chevrolet	200	Running
25	39	44	John Blankenship	Coal Save the Country Chevrolet	200	Running
26	11	33	Brendan Gaughan	South Point Hotel & Casino Chevrolet	199	Accident
27	42	70	Timmy Hill	Tweaker Energy Shot Chevrolet	199	Running
28	38	4	Daryl Harr	iWorld Chevrolet	199	Running
29	13	88	Cole Whitt #	Takagi Chevrolet	198	Accident
30	37	39	Dexter Stacey	Maddies Place Ford	197	Running
31	41	24	Derek White	OCR Gazbar Toyota	188	Running
32	40	41	Noel Dowler	Prairie Tech/Apollo Ford	182	Accident
33	21	51	Jeremy Clements	Phoenix Group Metals/stjude.org Chevrolet	86	Oil Pump
34	26	86	Kevin Lepage	Qello/Kenger Metals Ford	39	Axle
35	32	89	Morgan Shepherd	Hyland's Leg Cramps Chevrolet	20	Engine
36	43	74	Mike Harmon	Koma Unwind Relaxation Drink Chevrolet	18	Overheating
37	25	40	Erik Darnell	TheMotorsportsGroup.com Chevrolet	18	Ignition
38	28	47	J.J. Yeley	Curtis Key Plumbing Chevrolet	17	Rear Gear
39	24	00	Blake Koch	CHASCO Toyota	17	Brakes
40	29	42	Josh Wise	Curtis Key Plumbing Chevrolet	15	Electrical
41	35	15	Carl Long	RWR/Lilly Trucking Ford	12	Brakes
42	30	46	Chase Miller	Curtis Key Plumbing Chevrolet	8	Brakes
43	31	91	Tony Raines	TriStar Motorsports/Embassy Suites Toyota	5	Vibration

Sunoco Rookie of the Year Contender.

RACE COMMENTS: Before an estimated crowd of 42,000 Joey Logano won the Great Clips 200, his 18th NASCAR Nationwide Series victory. Prior to the green flag, the following cars dropped to the rear for the reasons indicated: #01 (adjustments outside impound),#2 (backup car), #15,70 (driver changes).

TIME OF RACE: 2 hours, 4 minutes, 48 seconds — AVERAGE SPEED: 98.077 mph — MARGIN OF VICTORY: 0.668 seconds — COORS LIGHT POLE AWARD: Joey Logano (132.621 mph. 27.145 secs.) — CAUTION FLAGS: 10 cautions for 40 laps — LAP LEADERS: 6 lead changes among 4 drivers. Logano 1–71, Stenhouse Jr 72–74, Logano 75–121, Keselowski 122–153, Logano 154–197, Vickers 198, Logano 199–204.

33 FORD ECOBOOST 300
November 17, 2012 — Homestead-Miami Speedway — 200 Laps – 300 Miles

Fin	Str	No	Driver	Team	Laps	Status
1	10	5	Regan Smith	Hendrickcars.com Chevrolet	200	Running
2	1	54	Kyle Busch	Monster Energy Toyota	200	Running
3	16	33	Brendan Gaughan	South Point Chevrolet	200	Running
4	11	12	Sam Hornish Jr.	Alliance Truck Parts Dodge	200	Running
5	3	3	Austin Dillon #	Bass Pro Shops/Tracker Boats Chevrolet	200	Running
6	4	6	Ricky Stenhouse Jr.	Cargill Ford	200	Running
7	7	11	Brian Scott	Dollar General Toyota	200	Running
8	20	22	Ryan Blaney	Discount Tire Dodge	200	Running
9	2	2	Elliott Sadler	OneMain Financial Chevrolet	200	Running
10	8	88	Cole Whitt #	TaxSlayer.com/Gator Bowl Chevrolet	200	Running
11	6	31	Justin Allgaier	Brandt Chevrolet	200	Running
12	32	43	Michael Annett	Pilot/Flying J Ford	200	Running
13	14	7	Danica Patrick	GoDaddy.com Chevrolet	200	Running
14	15	21	Joey Coulter	Darrell Gwynn Foundation Chevrolet	200	Running
15	17	99	Kenny Wallace	Toyota Toyota	200	Running
16	5	18	Joey Logano	GameStop/Afterglow Toyota	200	Running
17	18	38	Brad Sweet #	Great Clips Chevrolet	200	Running
18	25	87	Joe Nemechek	AM/FM Energy Wood & Pellet Stoves Toyota	200	Running
19	24	10	Mike Bliss	G-Oil Toyota	200	Running
20	13	8	Scott Lagasse Jr.	Hybrid Light/BSA Chevrolet	199	Running
21	22	98	Kevin Swindell	Carroll Shelby Motors Ford	199	Running
22	23	51	Jeremy Clements	St.Jude/USS James E Williams DDG 95 Chevrolet	199	Running
23	31	08	Jeffrey Earnhardt	Tobacco Free Florida Ford	198	Running
24	28	24	David Starr	Headrush Toyota	198	Running
25	19	30	Dakoda Armstrong	flalottery.com Chevrolet	197	Running
26	34	01	Mike Wallace	G&K Services Chevrolet	197	Running
27	30	14	Eric McClure	Hefty/Reynolds Wrap Toyota	196	Running
28	21	27	Andrew Ranger	GCMI Ford	195	Running
29	35	81	Jason Bowles #	Thrush & Sons Toyota	195	Running
30	26	19	Hal Martin	American Custom Yachts/US Forensics Toyota	195	Running
31	42	4	Danny Efland	Tradebank Chevrolet	193	Running
32	33	52	Joey Gase #	BBB/My Three Sons Vending Chevrolet	190	Running
33	41	23	Robert Richardson	North Texas Pipe Chevrolet	188	Running
34	37	70	Johanna Long #	Foretravel Chevrolet	177	Accident
35	38	40	Erik Darnell	Chevrolet	147	Engine
36	27	44	John Blankenship	Coal Save the Country Chevrolet	92	Accident
37	39	41	Juan Carlos Blum	Key Motorsports Chevrolet	92	Engine
38	12	20	Ryan Truex	Grime Boss Toyota	66	Accident
39	9	00	Blake Koch	teamboom Toyota	40	Fuel Pump
40	43	91	Jeff Green	Bandit Chippers Toyota	17	Vibration
41	29	46	Chase Miller	The Motorsports Group Chevrolet	6	Vibration
42	36	42	Josh Wise	Chevrolet	6	Overheating
43	40	39	Dexter Stacey	Maddies Place Ford	0	Engine

Sunoco Rookie of the Year Contender.

RACE COMMENTS: Before an estimated crowd of 40,000, Regan Smith won the Ford EcoBoost 300, his first NASCAR Nationwide Series victory.

TIME OF RACE: 2 hours, 19 minutes, 44 seconds — AVERAGE SPEED: 128.817 mph — MARGIN OF VICTORY: 1.375 seconds — COORS LIGHT POLE AWARD: Kyle Busch (167.984 mph. 32.146 secs.) — CAUTION FLAGS: 5 cautions for 24 laps — LAP LEADERS: 13 lead changes among 10 drivers. K. Busch 1–49, Logano 50, K. Busch 51–67, Sadler 68–70, K. Busch 71–93, Smith 94–95, Patrick 96–99, Hornish Jr. 100–105, Dillon 106–148, Stenhouse Jr. 149–150, Wallace 151–152, Dillon 153–175, Swindell 176–178, Smith 179–200.

NASCAR
CAMPING WORLD TRUCK SERIES

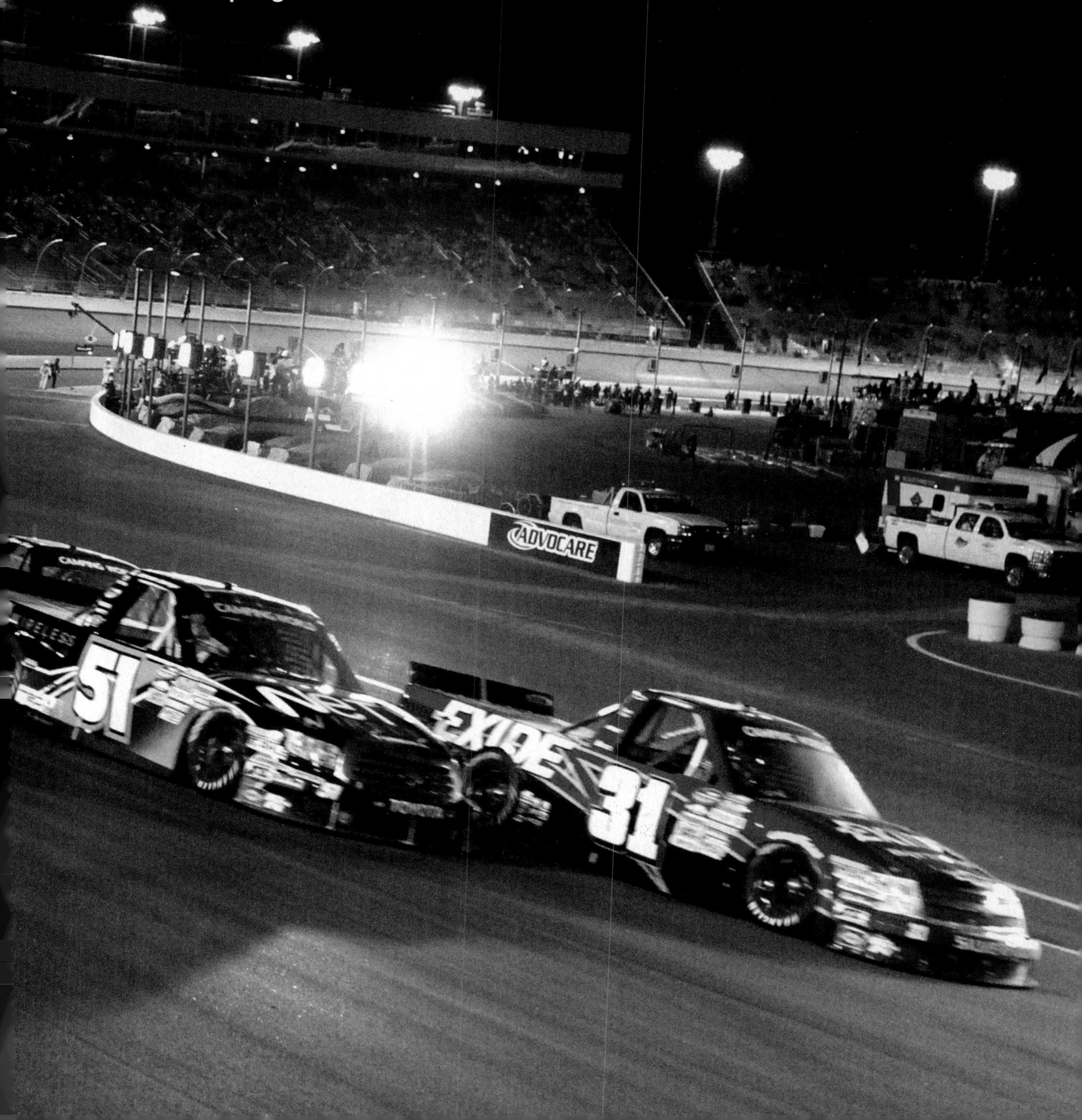
ADVOCARE
51
EXIDE
31

NASCAR CAMPING WORLD TRUCK SERIES
2012 SEASON REVIEW

JAMES BUESCHER PUT TOGETHER A CHAMPIONSHIP SEASON THAT PROVES ONCE AGAIN THE YOUTH MOVEMENT IN THE NASCAR CAMPING WORLD TRUCK SERIES IS HERE TO STAY.

For seven consecutive seasons, from 2004 through 2010, the man who raised the NASCAR Camping World Truck Series championship trophy at season's end had already celebrated his 40th birthday. But in 2011, Austin Dillon became the series' youngest champion at the age of 21 years, 6 months and 22 days.

The 2012 season continued the youth movement as James Buescher won the title at the age of 22 years, 7 months and 21 days – the second-youngest champion in series history. Buescher battled Austin's younger brother, Ty, throughout the 2012 campaign. Ty Dillon, 20 years of age, finished fourth in the series. In fact,

four of the top five final points finishers – Buescher, Dillon, Joey Coulter and Parker Kligerman – have yet to turn 23. The youth movement continues.

As is always the case in the NASCAR Camping World Truck Series, there were some outstanding performances and spectacular highlights that took place during 2012 NASCAR Camping World Truck season. The following is a look back at some of those standout performers and memorable races.

Buescher became the first Texan to win the NASCAR Camping World Truck Series championship. All four of his wins, a series-high, came at 1.5-mile venues. The 2012 season was one of redemption for

Buescher, in 2011, he had failed to qualify at Phoenix, the second race of the season. Though finishing that season third in points, the Phoenix setback spoiled a campaign that otherwise saw Buescher chip in one championship-worthy performance after another. This season, however, he started all 22 races, and was stationed in the top five in the points standings after 20 of them.

Timothy Peters, the oldest member of the final top five at only 32 years of age, was the picture of consistency during the 2012 season. Peters, who finished second in the championship points and never fell out of the top three, tallied two wins, 10 top fives and 16 top 10s. His personal

2012 NASCAR CAMPING WORLD TRUCK SERIES CHAMPION

JAMES BUESCHER

Birth Date:	**March 26, 1990**
Hometown:	**Plano, TX**
Truck Owner:	**Turner Motorsports**
Crew Chief:	**Michael Shelton**
Team:	**No. 31 Chevrolet**

Year	Stats	Wins	Top 5	Top 10	Point Standings
2008	1	0	0	0	82nd
2009	25	0	1	3	14th
2010	22	0	6	10	11th
2011	24	0	10	19	3rd
2012	22	4	10	14	1st
Career	**94**	**4**	**27**	**46**	

Best Finish: 1st — 4 times
Most Recent: 2012 Kentucky 201 (Kentucky)

highlight of the 2012 season came at Bristol Motor Speedway, where he turned in one of the most dominating performances in the last 15 years. There, he led all 204 laps, becoming the first driver to lead every single lap in a truck series event since Ron Hornaday Jr. did it in 1997.

For his rookie season, Ty Dillon stepped into a truck owned by his grandfather, Richard Childress, that had won the championship with his brother Austin driving the previous season, and was sporting one NASCAR's most iconic numbers – the No. 3. So, it would have been understandable if there were some rookie jitters. There weren't any. He opened up the season with nine consecutive top-10 finishes, and eventually took the points lead after race No. 15. He nabbed his first series win – at Atlanta – and threatened to become the first driver in series history to win the Sunoco Rookie of the Year and the championship in the same season. He came close, but a late-race wreck in the season finale crushed any hopes of a title. Still, he easily won rookie honors.

Few handled adversity with the type of determination that Parker Kligerman

showed in 2012. After losing his ride with Brad Keselowski Racing midseason, Tom DeLoach offered Kligerman a job at his Red Horse Racing organization. Kligerman made DeLoach look smart, scoring eight top 10s in 11 starts, including his first win (Talladega) and a fifth-place points finish.

Justin Lofton personified the "sophomore slump" phenomenon in 2011. After a solid 2010 rookie season, Lofton failed to score a single top five in 2011. There was little reason to believe he'd be a factor in 2012. He shrugged off those beliefs, big time. Driving for Eddie Sharp Racing, Lofton captured his first series win at Charlotte and finished eighth in points, scoring a career-high 13 top 10s. At Chicagoland Speedway, Lofton also captured his first Keystone Light Pole Award.

The championship-winning team, Turner Motorsports, won a series-high seven races in 2012, with three different drivers. Champion James Buescher won four, Nelson Piquet Jr. won two and NASCAR Sprint Cup Series star Kasey

Kahne won the inaugural series race at Rockingham Speedway. Team owner Steve Turner accomplished all of that after coming into the 2012 season without a single victory to his credit.

Although a driver from Red Horse Racing didn't win the championship, the team has plenty of reason to hold their heads high. Actually, there are four good reasons: Timothy Peters, Parker Kligerman, John King and Todd Bodine. All four drivers won at least one race for owner Tom DeLoach. That's never happened in the 18-year history of the series. Better yet, the team had two legitimate championship threats in Peters and Kligerman, who finished second and fifth, respectively.

Iowa Speedway has quickly developed the reputation of providing unmatched entertainment and drama when hosting NASCAR national series' events. The American Ethanol 200 in September was no different. The race was a battle of young guns, as Parker Kligerman and

Ryan Blaney proved to be the class of the field. Kligerman led the most laps, but his hopes for a first win were dashed after a late race spin. Blaney went on to became the youngest winner in series history at 18 years, 8 months and 15 days in only his third career race.

Five drivers entered the season finale, the Ford EcoBoost 200 at Homestead-Miami Speedway, with a mathematical chance at winning the championship. Buescher ended the night as champion – but it was far from a sure thing throughout the race. Ty Dillon posed the biggest threat, but his hopes evaporated after colliding with NASCAR Drive for Diversity product Kyle Larson for the lead with less than 10 laps remaining. Larson led the most laps in the event, with Cale Gale capturing his first series victory. Gale became the 16th different winner and ninth different first-time winner of the season, both series records.

NASCAR CAMPING WORLD TRUCK SERIES CHAMPION JAMES BUESCHER'S 2012 SEASON RECORD

Date	Event Name	Speedway	Start	Finish	Status
2/24	NextEra Energy Resources 250	Daytona International Speedway	3	17	Running
3/31	Kroger 250	Martinsville Speedway	9	3	Running
4/15	Good Sam Roadside Assistance 200	Rockingham Speedway	16	2	Running
4/21	SFP 250	Kansas Speedway	6	1	Running
5/18	North Carolina Education Lottery 200	Charlotte Motor Speedway	10	22	Running
6/1	Lucas Oil 200	Dover International Speedway	15	7	Running
6/8	WinStar World Casino 400	Texas Motor Speedway	4	15	Running
6/28	UNOH 225	Kentucky Speedway	3	1	Running
7/14	American Ethanol 200	Iowa Speedway	4	30	Accident
7/21	American Ethanol 225	Chicagoland Speedway	11	1	Running
8/4	Pocono Mountains 125	Pocono Raceway	5	2	Running
8/18	VFW 200	Michigan International Speedway	8	5	Running
8/22	UNOH 200	Bristol Motor Speedway	28	7	Running
8/31	Jeff Foxworthy's Grit Chips 200	Atlanta Motor Speedway	3	3	Running
9/15	American Ethanol 200 Presented by Hy-Vee	Iowa Speedway	5	17	Running
9/21	Kentucky 201	Kentucky Speedway	8	1	Running
9/29	Smith's 350	Las Vegas Motor Speedway	15	6	Running
10/6	Fred's 250 Powered by Coca-Cola	Talladega Superspeedway	3	3	Running
10/27	Kroger 200	Martinsville Speedway	10	6	Running
11/2	WinStar World Casino 350	Texas Motor Speedway	2	11	Running
11/9	Lucas Oil 150	Phoenix International Raceway	9	17	Running
11/16	Ford EcoBoost 200	Homestead-Miami Speedway	17	13	Running

NASCAR CAMPING WORLD TRUCK SERIES FINAL 2012 DRIVER POINTS STANDINGS

Pos.	Driver	Points	Starts	Wins	Top 5	Top 10	Pos.	Driver	Points	Starts	Wins	Top 5	Top 10
1	James Buescher	808	22	4	10	14	56	Todd Peck	42	2	0	0	0
2	Timothy Peters	802	22	2	10	16	57	Scott Stenzel	41	2	0	0	0
3	Joey Coulter	789	22	1	8	15	58	Wes Burton	37	2	0	0	0
4	Ty Dillon	784	22	1	7	17	59	Ward Burton	36	1	0	0	1
5	Parker Kligerman	778	22	1	8	15	60	Ryan Lynch	29	2	0	0	0
6	Matt Crafton	759	22	0	8	14	61	Ryan Reed	27	1	0	0	0
7	Nelson Piquet Jr.	747	22	2	9	15	62	Ryan Hackett	27	1	0	0	0
8	Justin Lofton	710	22	1	4	13	63	Brandon McReynolds	26	1	0	0	0
9	Johnny Sauter	678	22	2	6	9	64	Brandon Knupp	26	4	0	0	0
10	Miguel Paludo	668	22	0	1	5	65	Peyton Sellers	24	1	0	0	0
11	Jason White	635	22	0	2	5	66	Mario Gosselin	23	1	0	0	0
12	Cale Gale	634	22	1	3	8	67	Wayne Edwards	20	1	0	0	0
13	Ron Hornaday Jr.	591	22	0	2	6	68	Sean Corr	19	1	0	0	0
14	Todd Bodine	574	22	1	5	7	69	Benjamin Reynolds	18	1	0	0	0
15	Ryan Sieg	531	22	0	0	1	70	Brian Weber	18	1	0	0	0
16	John Wes Townley	521	21	0	0	2	71	Brent Raymer	18	1	0	0	0
17	Ross Chastain	502	22	0	1	4	72	August Grill	17	1	0	0	0
18	Bryan Silas	471	22	0	0	0	73	TJ Duke	13	1	0	0	0
19	David Starr	423	16	0	0	1	74	Caleb Roark	12	1	0	0	0
20	Dakoda Armstrong	370	15	0	1	1	75	Todd Shafer	12	1	0	0	0
21	Norm Benning	346	17	0	0	0	76	Adam Edwards	11	1	0	0	0
22	Tim George Jr.	298	12	0	0	1	77	Kevin Harvick	0	3	1	2	2
23	Jason Leffler	294	10	0	1	6	78	Brian Scott	0	5	1	2	3
24	Max Gresham	291	13	0	0	0	79	Denny Hamlin	0	2	1	2	2
25	Chris Fontaine	271	15	0	0	1	80	Kasey Kahne	0	1	1	1	1
26	Ryan Blaney	258	9	1	2	5	81	Brad Keselowski	0	6	0	3	4
27	Jennifer Jo Cobb	248	15	0	0	0	82	Kyle Busch	0	3	0	3	3
28	Paulie Harraka	223	11	0	0	0	83	Brendan Gaughan	0	8	0	4	4
29	Jeff Agnew	204	11	0	0	0	84	Travis Kvapil	0	1	0	1	1
30	Caleb Holman	183	8	0	0	0	85	Aric Almirola	0	3	0	1	2
31	Brennan Newberry	182	10	0	0	0	86	Scott Riggs	0	6	0	1	1
32	Chris Jones	170	15	0	0	0	87	Kurt Busch	0	3	0	0	3
33	John King	169	7	1	1	2	88	Drew Herring	0	1	0	0	1
34	Clay Greenfield	164	9	0	0	1	89	David Mayhew	0	5	0	0	1
35	Kyle Larson	134	4	0	1	3	90	Ryan Truex	0	2	0	0	1
36	Jeb Burton	133	5	0	0	1	91	Cole Whitt	0	1	0	0	0
37	Jake Crum	128	6	0	0	0	92	Travis Pastrana	0	1	0	0	0
38	Dennis Setzer	124	14	0	0	0	93	Josh Richards	0	1	0	0	0
39	Johnny Chapman	119	10	0	0	0	94	David Reutimann	0	3	0	0	0
40	German Quiroga	101	4	0	0	1	95	Brandon Miller	0	1	0	0	0
41	Rick Crawford	96	5	0	0	0	96	Kyle Martel	0	1	0	0	0
42	Chad McCumbee	92	5	0	0	0	97	Mike Harmon	0	4	0	0	0
43	Jeff Choquette	83	3	0	0	1	98	Stephen Leicht	0	4	0	0	0
44	Chris Cockrum	78	4	0	0	0	99	Donnie Neuenberger	0	1	0	0	0
45	Tyler Young	75	4	0	0	0	100	Blake Koch	0	5	0	0	0
46	Grant Enfinger	73	3	0	0	0	101	Mike Skinner	0	1	0	0	0
47	C E Falk III	53	3	0	0	0	102	T.J. Bell	0	2	0	0	0
48	Dusty Davis	52	3	0	0	0	103	Josh Wise	0	1	0	0	0
49	Travis Miller	51	4	0	0	0	104	Jeff Green	0	1	0	0	0
50	BJ McLeod Jr.	50	4	0	0	0	105	Tim Andrews	0	0	0	0	0
51	Chris Lafferty	48	5	0	0	0	106	Tyler Tanner	0	0	0	0	0
52	Justin Jennings	45	2	0	0	0	107	Natalie Sather	0	0	0	0	0
53	Russ Dugger	44	3	0	0	0	108	Derek White	0	0	0	0	0
54	Matt Merrell	43	2	0	0	0							
55	JR Fitzpatrick	42	2	0	0	0							

NASCAR CAMPING WORLD TRUCK SERIES DRIVER VICTORIES (1995 THRU 2012)

Driver	Victories	Driver	Victories	Driver	Victories	Driver	Victories
Ron Hornaday Jr.	51	Timothy Peters	5	Ron Fellows	2	Bobby Labonte	1
Kyle Busch	30	Scott Riggs	5	Denny Hamlin	2	Terry Labonte	1
Mike Skinner	28	Mike Wallace	5	Jimmy Hensley	2	Jason Leffler	1
Jack Sprague	28	James Buescher	4	Kenny Irwin Jr.	2	Donny Lia	1
Todd Bodine	22	Kurt Busch	4	Nelson Piquet Jr.	2	Justin Lofton	1
Dennis Setzer	18	Rick Carelli	4	Robert Pressley	2	Jamie McMurray	1
Ted Musgrave	17	Austin Dillon	4	Brian Scott	2	Butch Miller	1
Greg Biffle	16	Kasey Kahne	4	Tony Stewart	2	Ryan Newman	1
Johnny Benson	14	Tony Raines	4	Randy Tolsma	2	Steve Park	1
Kevin Harvick	14	Jay Sauter	4	Jon Wood	2	Bryan Reffner	1
Mike Bliss	13	David Starr	4	Ryan Blaney	1	David Reutimann	1
Joe Ruttman	13	Rich Bickle	3	Colin Braun	1	Elliott Sadler	1
Bobby Hamilton	10	Clint Bowyer	3	Joey Coulter	1	Boris Said	1
Travis Kvapil	9	Andy Houston	3	Ricky Craven	1	Ken Schrader	1
Brendan Gaughan	8	Dave Rezendes	3	Ty Dillon	1	Scott Speed	1
Mark Martin	7	Aric Almirola	2	Ricky Hendrick	1	Jimmy Spencer	1
Terry Cook	6	Chad Chaffin	2	Shane Hmiel	1	Michael Waltrip	1
Carl Edwards	6	Stacy Compton	2	Bob Keselowski	1	Brandon Whitt	1
Johnny Sauter	6	Matt Crafton	2	John King	1		
Rick Crawford	5	Erik Darnell	2	Parker Kligerman	1		

NASCAR CAMPING WORLD TRUCK SERIES 2012 SPECIAL AWARDS

KEYSTONE LIGHT POLE AWARD WINNERS

NELSON PIQUET JR.

Year	Driver	Poles
1995	Mike Skinner	10
1996	Mike Skinner	5
1997	Mike Bliss	6
1998	Mike Bliss	4
1999	Stacy Compton	6
2000	Joe Ruttman	8
2001	Jack Sprague	7
2002	Jason Leffler	8
2003	Ted Musgrave	4
2004	Jack Sprague	6
2005	Mike Skinner	6
2006	Mike Skinner	8
2007	Mike Skinner	11
2008	Ron Hornaday Jr.	5
2009	Colin Braun	5
2010	Austin Dillon	7
2011	Austin Dillon	5
2012	Nelson Piquet Jr.	4

MOST POPULAR DRIVER

NELSON PIQUET JR.

Past Winners (1995 thru 2012)

1995	Butch Miller
1996	Jimmy Hensley
1997	Ron Hornaday
1998	Stacy Compton
1999	Dennis Setzer
2000	Greg Biffle
2001	Joe Ruttman
2002	David Starr
2003	Brendan Gaughan
2004	Steve Park
2005	Ron Hornaday Jr.
2006	Johnny Benson
2007	Johnny Benson
2008	Johnny Benson
2009	Ricky Carmichael
2010	Narain Karthikeyan
2011	Austin Dillon
2012	Nelson Piquet Jr.

NASCAR CAMPING WORLD TRUCK SERIES FINAL 2012 OWNER POINTS STANDINGS

Pos.	Car	Owner	Points	Starts	Wins	Top 5	Top 10	Qualifying Attempts
1	31	Steve Turner	808	22	4	10	14	22
2	17	Tom Deloach	802	22	2	10	16	22
3	22	Richard Childress	789	22	1	8	15	22
4	3	Richard Childress	784	22	1	7	17	22
5	18	Kyle Busch	764	22	1	7	17	22
6	88	Rhonda Thorson	759	22	0	8	14	22
7	30	Steve Turner	747	22	2	9	15	22
8	29	Brad Keselowski	730	22	1	4	12	22
9	6	Eddie Sharp	710	22	1	4	13	22
10	13	Mike Curb	678	22	2	6	9	22
11	2	DeLana Harvick	673	22	1	6	7	22
12	32	Steve Turner	668	22	0	1	5	22
13	23	Steve Urvan	635	22	0	2	5	22
14	33	DeLana Harvick	634	22	1	3	8	22
15	9	Joe Denette	591	22	0	2	6	22
16	11	Tom Deloach	574	22	1	5	7	22
17	09	Robby Benton	561	22	0	1	3	22
19	39	Susan Bates	530	22	0	0	1	22
18	7	Tom Deloach	530	16	2	7	10	16
20	08	Bobby Dotter	517	22	0	1	4	22
21	99	Stacy Compton	471	22	0	0	0	22
22	27	Michael Hillman	469	22	0	0	3	22
23	5	David Dollar	425	20	0	1	2	20
24	81	Billy Ballew	423	16	0	0	1	16
25	98	Duke Thorson	386	15	0	1	1	15
26	84	Chris Fontaine	368	20	0	0	1	22
27	57	Norm Benning	346	17	0	0	0	22
28	07	Ken Smith	326	21	0	0	0	22
29	93	Pam Sieg	319	21	0	0	0	22
30	119	Brad Keselowski	280	9	0	3	4	9
31	10	Jennifer Jo Cobb	238	14	0	0	0	22
32	4	Steve Turner	237	8	1	2	4	8
33	275	Charles Henderson	183	8	0	0	0	9
34	214	Bob Newberry	182	11	0	0	0	12
35	92	Ricky Benton	178	7	0	1	1	8
36	24	Bob Germain	162	8	0	0	0	8
37	8	DeLana Harvick	150	7	0	0	0	7
38	151	Kyle Busch	148	5	1	1	2	5
39	168	Bill Alger	144	7	0	0	1	9
40	165	Michael Mittler	106	5	0	0	0	8
41	38	Pam Sieg	105	14	0	0	0	18
42	60	Stacy Compton	102	6	0	0	0	6
43	101	Sabrina Crum	102	5	0	0	0	5
44	297	Gary Adrian	83	3	0	0	1	3
45	174	Mike Harmon	82	9	0	0	0	15
46	202	Randy Young	75	4	0	0	0	4
47	0	Jennifer Jo Cobb	70	10	0	0	0	14
48	73	Ron Crosby	67	3	0	0	0	3
49	220	George Bragg	63	3	0	0	0	3
50	15	Steve Acor	54	3	0	0	0	4
51	170	Edward Asbury	49	3	0	0	0	3
52	135	Kevin Cywinski	43	2	0	0	0	2
53	51	Billy Ballew	34	1	0	0	1	1
54	186	Michael Greenfield	30	3	0	0	0	3
55	176	Ray Hackett	27	1	0	0	0	2
57	175	Kevin Dargie	21	2	0	0	0	2
56	28	Jim Rosenblum	21	1	0	0	0	5
58	282	John Corr	19	1	0	0	0	2
59	147	Donald Reynolds	18	1	0	0	0	3
60	196	Michael Peck	16	1	0	0	0	3
61	261	Samuel Pearce	16	1	0	0	0	1
62	1	Rick Ware	15	1	0	0	0	1
63	225	Michael Hillman	14	7	0	0	0	7
64	112	Michelle Gosselin	11	1	0	0	0	1
65	200	Rick Lind	10	1	0	0	0	1
67	137	Rod Sieg	0	2	0	0	0	3
66	159	William Martel	0	1	0	0	0	1
68	136	Mike Allgaier	0	0	0	0	0	2
69	183	Chris Fontaine	0	0	0	0	0	2
70	150	Tracy Lowe	0	0	0	0	0	2

NASCAR CAMPING WORLD TRUCK SERIES CHAMPIONS AND LEADERS (1995 THRU 2012)

1995
Mike Skinner 3224
Joe Ruttman 3098
Ron Hornaday 2986
Butch Miller 2812
Jack Sprague 2740
Rick Carelli 2683
Bill Sedgwick 2681
Mike Bliss 2636
Scott Lagasse 2470
Tobey Butler 2358

1996
Ron Hornaday 3831
Jack Sprague 3778
Mike Skinner 3771
Joe Ruttman 3275
Mike Bliss 3190
Dave Rezendes 3179
Butch Miller 3126
Jimmy Hensley 3029
Bryan Reffner 2961
Rick Carelli 2953

1997
Jack Sprague 3969
Rich Bickle 3737
Joe Ruttman 3736
Mike Bliss 3611
Ron Hornaday 3574
Jay Sauter 3467
Rick Carelli 3461
Jimmy Hensley 3385
Chuck Bown 3320
Kenny Irwin 3220

1998
Ron Hornaday 4072
Jack Sprague 4069
Joe Ruttman 3874
Jay Sauter 3672
Tony Raines 3596
Jimmy Hensley 3570
Stacy Compton 3542
Greg Biffle 3276
Ron Barfield 3227
Mike Bliss 3216

1999
Jack Sprague 3747
Greg Biffle 3739
Dennis Setzer 3639
Stacy Compton 3623
Jay Sauter 3543
Mike Wallace 3494
Ron Hornaday 3488
Andy Houston 3359
Mike Bliss 3294
Jimmy Hensley 3280

2000
Greg Biffle 3826
Kurt Busch 3596
Andy Houston 3566
Mike Wallace 3450
Jack Sprague 3316
Joe Ruttman 3278
Dennis Setzer 3214
Randy Tolsma 3157
Bryan Reffner 3153
Steve Grissom 3113

2001
Jack Sprague 3670
Ted Musgrave 3597
Joe Ruttman 3570
Travis Kvapil 3547
Scott Riggs 3526
Ricky Hendrick 3412
Terry Cook 3327
Rick Crawford 3320
Dennis Setzer 3306
Coy Gibbs 2875

2002
Mike Bliss 3359
Rick Crawford 3313
Ted Musgrave 3308
Jason Leffler 3156
David Starr 3144
Dennis Setzer 3132
Robert Pressley 3097
Terry Cook 3070
Travis Kvapil 3039
Coy Gibbs 3010

2003
Travis Kvapil 3837
Dennis Setzer 3828
Ted Musgrave 3819
Brendan Gaughan 3797
Jon Wood 3659
Bobby Hamilton 3627
Rick Crawford 3578
Carl Edwards 3416
Terry Cook 3212
Chad Chaffin 3143

2004
Bobby Hamilton 3624
Dennis Setzer 3578
Ted Musgrave 3554
Carl Edwards 3493
Matt Crafton 3379
David Starr 3298
Jack Sprague 3167
Travis Kvapil 3152
Steve Park 3138
Chad Chaffin 3122

2005
Ted Musgrave 3535
Dennis Setzer 3480
Todd Bodine 3462
Ron Hornaday Jr. 3369
Mike Skinner 3273
Bobby Hamilton 3164
David Starr 3148
Jack Sprague 3137
Matt Crafton 3095
Johnny Benson 3076

2006
Todd Bodine 3666
Johnny Benson 3539
David Reutimann 3530
David Starr 3355
Jack Sprague 3328
Ted Musgrave 3314
Ron Hornaday Jr. 3313
Terry Cook 3265
Rick Crawford 3252
Mike Skiner 3219

2007
Ron Hornaday Jr. 3982
Mike Skinner 3928
Johnny Benson 3557
Todd Bodine 3525
Rick Crawford 3523
Travis Kvapil 3511
Ted Musgrave 3183
Matt Crafton 3060
Jack Sprague 3001
David Starr 2921

2008
Johnny Benson 3725
Ron Hornaday Jr. 3718
Todd Bodine 3621
Erik Darnell 3412
Matt Crafton 3392
Mike Skinner 3363
Rick Crawford 3315
Dennis Setzer 3197
Jack Sprague 3125
Terry Cook 3072

2009
Ron Hornaday Jr. 3959
Matt Crafton 3772
Mike Skinner 3602
Todd Bodine 3432
Colin Braun 3338
Johnny Sauter 3331
Brian Scott 3307
Timothy Peters 3289
David Starr 3271
Rick Crawford 3161

2010
Todd Bodine 3937
Aric Almirola 3730
Johnny Sauter 3676
Matt Crafton 3547
Austin Dillon 3379
Timothy Peters 3343
Ron Hornaday Jr. 3310
Mike Skinner 3256
David Starr 3170
Jason White 2979

2011
Austin Dillon 888
Johnny Sauter 882
James Buescher 859
Ron Hornaday Jr. 838
Timothy Peters 832
Todd Bodine 803
Joey Coulter 796
Matt Crafton 785
Cole Whitt 764
Nelson Piquet Jr. 752

2012
James Buescher 808
Timothy Peters 802
Joey Coulter 789
Ty Dillon 784
Parker Kligerman 778
Matt Crafton 759
Nelson Piquet Jr. 747
Justin Lofton 710
Johnny Sauter 678
Miquel Paludo 668

RYAN BLANEY

Birth Date: **December 31, 1993**
Hometown: **High Point, NC**
Team: **No. 29 Brad Keselowski Racing Ram**

CAREER RECORD

Year	Starts	Wins	Top 5	Top 10	Points Standing
2012	9	1	2	5	26

Best Finish: 1st — 1 time
Most Recent: 2012 American Ethanol 200 Presented by Hy-Vee (Iowa)

JAMES BUESCHER

Birth Date: **March 26, 1990**
Hometown: **Plano, TX**
Team: **No. 31 Turner Scott Motorsports Chevrolet**

CAREER RECORD

Year	Starts	Wins	Top 5	Top 10	Points Standing
2008	1	0	0	0	82
2009	25	0	1	3	14
2010	22	0	6	10	11
2011	24	0	10	19	3
2012	22	4	10	14	1

Best Finish: 1st — 4 times
Most Recent: 2012 Kentucky 201 (Kentucky)

JEB BURTON

Birth Date: **August 6, 1992**
Hometown: **Halifax, VA**
Team: **No. 4 Turner Scott Motorsports Chevrolet**

CAREER RECORD

Year	Starts	Wins	Top 5	Top 10	Points Standing
2012	5	0	0	1	35

Best Finish: 8th — 1 time
Most Recent: 2012 North Carolina Education Lottery 200 (Charlotte)

JOEY COULTER

Birth Date: **June 8, 1990**
Hometown: **Miami Springs, FL**
Team: **No. 18 Kyle Busch Motorsports Toyota**

CAREER RECORD

Year	Starts	Wins	Top 5	Top 10	Points Standing
2011	25	0	5	13	7
2012	22	1	8	15	3

Best Finish: 1st — 1 time
Most Recent: 2012 Pennsylvania Mountains 125 (Pocono)

NASCAR CAMPING WORLD TRUCK SERIES

MATT CRAFTON

Birth Date: June 11, 1976
Hometown: Tulare, CA
Team: No. 88 ThorSport Racing Toyota

CAREER RECORD

Year	Starts	Wins	Top 5	Top 10	Points Standing
2000	1	0	0	1	76
2001	24	0	0	11	12
2002	22	0	0	6	15
2003	25	0	0	11	11
2004	25	0	6	17	5
2005	25	0	2	10	9
2006	25	0	4	10	14
2007	25	0	1	10	8
2008	25	1	9	12	5
2009	25	0	11	21	2
2010	25	0	10	20	4
2011	25	1	5	13	8
2012	22	0	8	14	6

Best Finish: 1st — 2 times
Most Recent: 2011 Coca-Cola Presented by Hy-Vee (Iowa)

TY DILLON

Birth Date: February 27, 1992
Hometown: Lewisville, NC
Team: No. 3 Richard Childress Racing Chevrolet

CAREER RECORD

Year	Starts	Wins	Top 5	Top 10	Points Standing
2011	3	0	1	2	39
2012	22	1	7	17	4

Best Finish: 1st — 1 time
Most Recent: 2012 Jeff Foxworthy's Grit Chips 200 (Atlanta)

BRENDAN GAUGHAN

Birth Date: July 10, 1975
Hometown: Las Vegas, NV
Team: No. 62 Richard Childress Racing Chevrolet

CAREER RECORD

Year	Starts	Wins	Top 5	Top 10	Points Standing
1997	1	0	0	0	101
1998	2	0	0	0	77
1999	2	0	0	0	71
2000	5	0	0	0	40
2001	7	0	2	3	31
2002	22	2	5	9	11
2003	25	6	14	18	4
2005	23	0	2	7	19
2006	25	0	4	5	15
2007	25	0	3	8	11
2008	25	0	2	5	15
2011	25	0	1	8	12
2012	8	0	4	4	83

Best Finish: 1st — 8 times
Most Recent: 2003 Silverado 350 (Texas)

MAX GRESHAM

Birth Date: April 30, 1993
Hometown: Griffin, GA
Team: No. 8 Eddie Sharp Racing Chevrolet

CAREER RECORD

Year	Starts	Wins	Top 5	Top 10	Points Standing
2011	3	0	0	0	54
2012	13	0	0	0	24

Best Finish: 11th — 1 time
Most Recent: 2012 Kroger 200 (Martinsville)

NASCAR CAMPING WORLD TRUCK SERIES

NASCAR CAMPING WORLD TRUCK SERIES

RON
HORNADAY JR.

Birth Date: **June 20, 1958**
Hometown: **Palmdale, CA**
Team: **No. 9 NTS Motorsports Chevrolet**

CAREER RECORD

Year	Starts	Wins	Top 5	Top 10	Points Standing
1995	20	6	10	14	3
1996	24	4	18	23	1
1997	26	7	13	17	5
1998	27	6	16	22	1
1999	25	2	7	16	7
2002	2	1	1	1	53
2004	1	0	0	0	85
2005	25	1	7	13	4
2006	25	2	8	12	7
2007	25	4	13	22	1
2008	25	6	14	18	2
2009	25	6	15	20	1
2010	25	2	11	13	7
2011	25	4	13	17	4
2012	22	0	2	6	13

Best Finish: 1st — 51 times
Most Recent: 2011 Smith's 350 (Las Vegas)

KYLE
LARSON

Birth Date: **July 31, 1992**
Hometown: **Elk Grove, CA**
Team: **TBA**

CAREER RECORD

Year	Starts	Wins	Top 5	Top 10	Points Standing
2012	4	1	1	3	35

Best Finish: 2nd — 1 time
Most Recent: 2012 Lucas Oil 150 (Phoenix)

BRENNAN
NEWBERRY

Birth Date: **February 9, 1990**
Hometown: **Bakersfield, CA**
Team: **No. 14 NTS Motorsports Chevrolet**

CAREER RECORD

Year	Starts	Wins	Top 5	Top 10	Points Standing
2012	10	0	0	0	31

Best Finish: 19th — 1 time
Most Recent: 2012 VFW 200 (Michigan)

MIGUEL
PALUDO

Birth Date: **July 26, 1983**
Hometown: **Nova Prata, Brazil**
Team: **No. 32 Turner Scott Motorsports Chevrolet**

CAREER RECORD

Year	Starts	Wins	Top 5	Top 10	Points Standing
2010	4	0	0	2	53
2011	25	0	3	7	17
2012	22	0	1	5	10

Best Finish: 3rd — 1 time
Most Recent: 2011 VFW 200 (Michigan)

TIMOTHY PETERS

Birth Date: **August 29, 1980**
Hometown: **Providence, NC**
Team: **No. 17 Red Horse Racing Toyota**

CAREER RECORD

Year	Starts	Wins	Top 5	Top 10	Points Standing
2005	16	0	0	2	28
2006	17	0	0	1	27
2007	2	0	0	1	74
2008	8	0	0	1	36
2009	25	1	5	13	8
2010	25	1	5	16	6
2011	25	1	7	12	5
2012	22	2	10	16	2

Best Finish: 1st —5 times
Most Recent: 2012 UNOH 200 (Bristol)

NELSON PIQUET JR.

Birth Date: **July 25, 1985**
Hometown: **Brasilia, Brazil**
Team: **No. 30 Turner Motorsports Chevrolet**

CAREER RECORD

Year	Starts	Wins	Top 5	Top 10	Points Standing
2010	5	0	0	3	44
2011	25	0	6	10	10
2012	22	2	9	15	7

Best Finish: 1st — 2 times
Most Recent: 2012 Smith's 350 (Las Vegas)

JOHNNY SAUTER

Birth Date: **May 1, 1978**
Hometown: **Necedah, WI**
Team: **No. 13 ThorSport Racing Toyota**

CAREER RECORD

Year	Starts	Wins	Top 5	Top 10	Points Standing
2003	3	0	0	1	69
2004	2	0	1	1	54
2005	3	0	0	0	59
2006	2	0	0	0	57
2008	1	0	0	0	87
2009	25	1	7	13	6
2010	25	1	14	16	3
2011	25	2	11	16	2
2012	22	2	6	9	9

Best Finish: 1st — 6 times
Most Recent: 2012 WinStar World Casino 350 (Texas)

JOHN WES TOWNLEY

Birth Date: **December 31, 1989**
Hometown: **Watkinsville, GA**
Team: **No. 7 Red Horse Racing Toyota**

CAREER RECORD

Year	Starts	Wins	Top 5	Top 10	Points Standing
2008	7	0	0	0	39
2012	21	0	0	2	16

Best Finish: 8th — 1 time
Most Recent: 2012 Pennsylvania 125 (Pocono)

NASCAR CAMPING WORLD TRUCK SERIES

NASCAR CAMPING WORLD TRUCK SERIES
2012 RESULTS

1 NEXTERA ENERGY RESOURCES 250
February 24, 2012 — Daytona International Speedway — 100 Laps – 250 Miles

Fin	Str	Car	Driver	Team	Laps	Status
1	23	7	John King #	Red Horse Racing Toyota	109	Running
2	27	17	Timothy Peters	Tire Kingdom/Service Central Toyota	109	Running
3	15	6	Justin Lofton	CollegeComplete.com Chevrolet	109	Running
4	19	09	Travis Kvapil	Toyota Parts & Service Toyota	109	Running
5	8	23	Jason White	GunBroker.com Ford	109	Running
6	10	11	Todd Bodine	Good Sam Toyota	109	Running
7	22	84	Chris Fontaine	Glenden Enterprises/Ultra-Fit Toyota	109	Running
8	25	27	Ward Burton	State Water Heaters Chevrolet	109	Running
9	4	3	Ty Dillon #	Bass Pro Shops/Tracker Boats Chevrolet	109	Running
10	26	68	Clay Greenfield	Dawn Stanfill Foundation RAM	109	Running
11	28	29	Parker Kligerman	Cooper Standard RAM	109	Running
12	21	82	Grant Enfinger	BRG Motorsports Ford	109	Running
13	16	15	Dusty Davis #	Thunderexhaust.com Toyota	109	Running
14	12	9	Ron Hornaday Jr.	Anderson's Maple Syrup Chevrolet	109	Running
15	33	39	Ryan Sieg	Pull-A-Part LLC Chevrolet	109	Running
16	35	93	Chris Cockrum	Advanced Comm. Group/Accu-Tech Chev.	109	Running
17	3	31	James Buescher	AccuDoc Solutions Chevrolet	109	Running
18	9	22	Joey Coulter	Mama Lucia Meatballs Chevrolet	108	Running
19	14	5	Paulie Harraka #	Wauters Motorsports Ford	105	Running
20	11	2	Brendan Gaughan	South Point Hotel & Casino Chevrolet	104	Accident
21	17	81	David Starr	Zachry Toyota	104	Accident
22	2	30	Nelson Piquet Jr.	Autotrac/Qualcomm Chevrolet	104	Accident
23	30	88	Matt Crafton	Menards/Ideal Door Toyota	104	Accident
24	20	13	Johnny Sauter	Hot Honeys Toyota	104	Accident
25	36	73	Rick Crawford	Superseal/Trans Pecos Trucking Chevrolet	101	Accident
26	29	24	Max Gresham #	Made In USA Chevrolet	100	Accident
27	5	19	Brad Keselowski	Twitter Ram	99	Accident
28	24	08	Ross Chastain #	Nat'l Watermelon Assn & Promo.Board Toyota	94	Accident
29	32	99	Bryan Silas	Rockingham Speedway Ford	93	Accident
30	1	32	Miguel Paludo	Duroline Brakes & Components Chevrolet	83	Accident
31	34	07	TJ Duke III	Maco/Duke Masonry Chevrolet	62	Accident
32	7	33	Cale Gale #	Rheem Chevrolet	61	Accident
33	13	8	Mike Skinner	Paytas Home Chevrolet	61	Accident
34	31	60	J.R. Fitzpatrick	Equipment Express Chevrolet	61	Accident
35	18	98	Dakoda Armstrong #	Ever Fi Toyota	33	Accident
36	6	18	Jason Leffler	Dollar General Toyota	17	Accident

Sunoco Rookie of the Year Contender.

RACE COMMENTS: Before an estimated crowd of 57,000, John King won the NextEra Energy Resources 250, his first NASCAR Camping World Truck Series victory. To start the race, prior to the green flag the following trucks dropped to the rear of the field for the reasons indicated: #81 (pitting before pit road is open), #29 (adjustments outside the impound procedure).

TIME OF RACE: 2 hours, 17 minutes, 13 seconds — AVERAGE SPEED: 119.169 mph — MARGIN OF VICTORY: Under Caution — KEYSTONE LIGHT POLE AWARD: Miguel Paludo (181.514 mph. 49.583 secs.) — CAUTION FLAGS: 9 cautions for 37 laps — LAP LEADERS: 11 lead changes among 8 drivers. Paludo 1–20, Silas 21, Paludo 22–43, Chastain 44, Paludo 45–46, Buescher 47–54, Paludo 55–66, Buescher 67–68, Piquet Jr. 69–83, White 84–99, Sauter 100–103, King 104–109.

2 KROGER 250
March 31, 2012 — Martinsville Speedway — 250 Laps – 131.5 Miles

Fin	Str	Car	Driver	Team	Laps	Status
1	1	2	Kevin Harvick	Tide/Kroger Chevrolet	250	Running
2	2	3	Ty Dillon #	Bass Pro Shops/Tracker Boats Chevrolet	250	Running
3	9	31	James Buescher	AccuDoc Solutions Chevrolet	250	Running
4	6	6	Justin Lofton	CollegeComplete.com Chevrolet	250	Running
5	3	17	Timothy Peters	NTB Service Central Toyota	250	Running
6	16	30	Nelson Piquet Jr.	AutoTrac/Qualcomm Chevrolet	250	Running
7	17	08	Ross Chastain #	Watermelon.org Toyota	250	Running
8	12	18	Jason Leffler	Dollar General/Kangaroo Express Toyota	250	Running
9	32	7	John King #	Red Horse Racing Toyota	250	Running
10	22	23	Jason White	GunBroker.com Ford	250	Running
11	15	29	Parker Kligerman	Cooper Standard RAM	250	Running
12	20	60	J.R. Fitzpatrick	Equipment Express Chevrolet	250	Running
13	7	27	Jeb Burton	State Water Heaters Chevrolet	250	Running
14	27	81	David Starr	Zachry Toyota	250	Running
15	4	33	Cale Gale #	Rheem Chevrolet	250	Running
16	5	9	Ron Hornaday Jr.	Anderson's Maple Syrup/AMFMEnergy.com Chev.	250	Running
17	14	32	Miguel Paludo	Duroline Brakes Chevrolet	250	Running
18	31	07	Jake Crum	Bandit Chippers Chevrolet	249	Running
19	26	24	Max Gresham #	Made in USA/PledgeforUSA.com Chevrolet	249	Running
20	25	32	David Reutimann	FleetHQ.com/BTS Tire/Smith Paving Chev.	249	Running
21	36	98	Dakoda Armstrong #	EverFi.com Toyota	248	Running
22	18	5	Paulie Harraka #	MC10 Ford F-150 Ford	248	Running
23	30	09	John Wes Townley #	RAB Racing Toyota	248	Running
24	11	88	Matt Crafton	Menards/Ideal Doors Chevrolet	246	Running
25	13	11	Todd Bodine	Red Horse Racing Toyota	246	Running
26	33	99	Bryan Silas #	Rockingham Speedway Ford	244	Running
27	35	93	Chris Cockrum	RSS Racing/Advanced Comms. Group Chev.	241	Running
28	19	14	Brennan Newberry	Ironclad Performance Wear Chevrolet	234	Accident
29	8	13	Johnny Sauter	Hot Honeys/Curb Records Toyota	231	Running
30	21	22	Joey Coulter	Steak-umm/Kroger Chevrolet	228	Running
31	29	68	Clay Greenfield	@claygreenfield/Performance Automotive RAM	151	Suspension
32	28	39	Ryan Sieg	Pull-A-Part Used Auto Parts Chevrolet	148	Oil Line
33	24	15	Dusty Davis #	thunderexhaust.com Toyota	104	Rear Gear
34	34	8	Jennifer Jo Cobb	Driven2Honor.org RAM	95	Suspension
35	10	70	Jeff Agnew	Clarence's Steak House Chevrolet	90	Accident
36	23	74	Rick Crawford	Koma Unwind Chevrolet	6	Brakes

Sunoco Rookie of the Year Contender.

RACE COMMENTS: Before an estimated attendance of 20,000, Kevin Harvick won the Kroger 250, his 14th NASCAR Camping World Truck Series victory and third at Martinsville Speedway.

TIME OF RACE: 1 hour, 51 minutes, 31 seconds — AVERAGE SPEED: 70.752 mph — MARGIN OF VICTORY: 0.953 seconds — KEYSTONE LIGHT POLE AWARD: Kevin Harvick (95.665 mph. 19.794 secs.) — CAUTION FLAGS: 7 cautions for 49 laps — LAP LEADERS: 2 lead changes among 2 drivers. Harvick 1–3, Dillon 4–5, Harvick 6–250.

3 GOOD SAM ROADSIDE ASSISTANCE 200

April 15, 2012 — Rockingham Speedway — 200 Laps – 200 Miles

Fin	Str	Car	Driver	Team	Laps	Status
1	5	4	Kasey Kahne	Rockwell Tools Chevrolet	200	Running
2	16	31	James Buescher	Koike.com Chevrolet	200	Running
3	8	88	Matt Crafton	Menards/Ideal Door Toyota	200	Running
4	10	13	Johnny Sauter	Hot Honeys/Curb Records Toyota	200	Running
5	3	17	Timothy Peters	Strutmasters.com Toyota	200	Running
6	17	22	Joey Coulter	Strutmasters.com/RCR Chevrolet	200	Running
7	1	30	Nelson Piquet Jr.	Qualcomm/AutoTrac Chevrolet	200	Running
8	12	3	Ty Dillon #	Bass Pro Shops/Tracker Boats Chevrolet	200	Running
9	6	29	Parker Kligerman	Draw-Tite/Mopar Ram	200	Running
10	19	6	Justin Lofton	CollegeComplete.com Chevrolet	200	Running
11	27	27	Jeb Burton #	State Water Heaters Chevrolet	200	Running
12	22	9	Ron Hornaday Jr.	Joe Denette Motorsports Chevrolet	200	Running
13	21	81	David Starr	Zachry Toyota	200	Running
14	11	98	Dakoda Armstrong #	EverFi.com Toyota	199	Running
15	23	32	Miguel Paludo	Duroline Brakes Chevrolet	198	Running
16	29	2	Tim George Jr.	Applebee's Chevrolet	198	Running
17	13	33	Cale Gale #	Rheem Chevrolet	197	Running
18	15	24	Max Gresham #	Made in USA Brand Chevrolet	197	Running
19	18	92	David Reutimann	FleetHQ.com/BTS Tire/QMI Chevrolet	197	Running
20	20	09	John Wes Townley #	RAB Racing Toyota	197	Running
21	24	75	Caleb Holman #	Food Country USA/Wise Snack Foods Chev.	197	Running
22	32	39	Ryan Sieg	RSS Racing Chevrolet	197	Running
23	30	14	Brennan Newberry	Ironclad Performance Wear Chevrolet	197	Running
24	28	23	Jason White	GunBroker.com Ford	196	Running
25	14	08	Ross Chastain #	Florida Watermelon Association Toyota	196	Running
26	2	5	Paulie Harraka #	Send a Soldier to the Rock/Wauters Mtrsprts Ford	195	Running
27	36	70	Jeff Agnew	Team 7 Motorsports Chevrolet	195	Running
28	26	02	Tyler Young #	Young's Building Systems Chevrolet	193	Running
29	33	93	Chris Cockrum	RSS Racing/Advanced Communications Chevrolet	193	Running
30	35	57	Norm Benning	Ladybug Cleaning/G.L. Hubbard & Sons Chev.	189	Running
31	7	11	Todd Bodine	Toyota Care Toyota	135	Running
32	31	99	Bryan Silas #	Rockingham Speedway Ford	119	Accident
33	25	7	John King #	Consol Energy Toyota	56	Accident
34	4	18	Jason Leffler	Dollar General Toyota	19	Engine
35	34	07	Johnny Chapman	ASI Limited Toyota	13	Clutch
36	9	60	Grant Enfinger	Turn One Racing Chevrolet	12	Transmission

Sunoco Rookie of the Year Contender.

RACE COMMENTS: Before an estimated crowd of 27,500, Kasey Kahne won the Good Sam Roadside Assistance 200, his fourth NASCAR Camping World Truck Series victory. To start the race, prior to the green flag the following trucks dropped to the rear of the field for the reasons indicated: #60 (adjustments outside impound), #4, 92 (driver change).

TIME OF RACE: 1 hour, 51 minutes, 54 seconds — AVERAGE SPEED: 107.239 mph — MARGIN OF VICTORY: 1.478 seconds — KEYSTONE LIGHT POLE AWARD: Nelson Piquet Jr. (144.387 mph. 24.933 secs.) — CAUTION FLAGS: 4 cautions for 25 laps — LAP LEADERS: 7 lead changes among 4 drivers. Piquet Jr. 1–67, Crafton 68–82, Piquet Jr. 83–108, Crafton 109, Piquet Jr. 110–123, Peters 124–130, Crafton 131–154, Kahne 155–200.

4 SFP 250

April 21, 2012 — Kansas Speedway — 167 Laps – 250.5 Miles

Fin	Str	Car	Driver	Team	Laps	Status
1	6	31	James Buescher	Progenex Chevrolet	167	Running
2	10	17	Timothy Peters	Red Horse Racing Toyota	167	Running
3	12	19	Brad Keselowski	Brad Keselowski's Checkered Flag Foun. Ram	167	Running
4	8	30	Nelson Piquet Jr.	Qualcomm/Autotrac Chevrolet	167	Running
5	9	11	Todd Bodine	Toyota Care Toyota	167	Running
6	16	9	Ron Hornaday Jr.	Joe Denette Motorsports Chevrolet	167	Running
7	3	6	Justin Lofton	CollegeComplete.com Chevrolet	167	Running
8	11	29	Parker Kligerman	Reese Towpower Ram	167	Running
9	5	3	Ty Dillon #	Bass Pro Shops/Ram Chevrolet	167	Running
10	13	32	Miguel Paludo	Duroline Brakes Chevrolet	167	Running
11	15	33	Cale Gale #	Rheem Chevrolet	167	Running
12	17	88	Matt Crafton	Menards/Jeld-Wen Toyota	167	Running
13	19	7	John King #	CONSOL Energy Toyota	167	Running
14	7	22	Joey Coulter	Husky Liners Chevrolet	166	Running
15	20	98	Dakoda Armstrong #	EverFi.com Toyota	166	Running
16	18	09	John Wes Townley #	RAB Racing Toyota	166	Running
17	1	2	Tim George Jr.	Applebee's Chevrolet	166	Running
18	2	18	Jason Leffler	Shore Lodge Toyota	165	Running
19	4	23	Jason White	GunBroker.com Ford	164	Running
20	31	84	Chris Fontaine	Glenden Enterprises Chevrolet	164	Running
21	29	99	Bryan Silas #	Rockingham Speedway Ford	164	Running
22	23	24	Max Gresham #	In USA Brand Chevrolet	163	Running
23	32	65	Scott Stenzel	Making the Driver Chevrolet	163	Running
24	14	13	Johnny Sauter	Hot Honeys/Curb Records Toyota	162	Running
25	36	10	Jennifer Jo Cobb	Mark One Electric Ram	160	Running
26	34	93	Chris Cockrum	Advanced Communications Group Chevrolet	159	Running
27	27	5	Paulie Harraka #	Wauters Motorsports Ford	158	Running
28	35	57	Norm Benning	G.L. Hubbard & Sons, Inc./Ash Group Chevrolet	155	Running
29	30	39	Ryan Sieg	S&W Services Chevrolet	128	Rear Gear
30	28	60	Chad McCumbee	Turn One Racing Chevrolet	54	Fuel Pump
31	22	81	David Starr	AdvoCare Toyota	41	Accident
32	26	14	Brennan Newberry	Ironclad Performance Wear Chevrolet	40	Accident
33	21	12	Russ Dugger	JPO Absorbents Chevrolet	39	Accident
34	24	08	Ross Chastain #	Florida Watermelon Association Toyota	17	Engine
35	33	07	Chris Jones	ASI Limited Toyota	14	Rear End
36	25	27	Jeb Burton #	State Water Heaters Chevrolet	2	Accident

Sunoco Rookie of the Year Contender.

RACE COMMENTS: Before an estimated crowd of 40,000, James Buescher won the SFP 250, his first NASCAR Camping World Truck Series victory. Prior to the green flag, the following truck dropped to the rear of the field for the reason indicated: #12 (unapproved adjustments).

TIME OF RACE: 2 hours, 4 minutes, 6 seconds — AVERAGE SPEED: 121.112 mph — MARGIN OF VICTORY: 5.32 seconds — KEYSTONE LIGHT POLE AWARD: Tim George Jr. (172.436 mph. 31.316 secs.) — CAUTION FLAGS: 5 cautions for 28 laps — LAP LEADERS: 16 lead changes among 8 drivers. George Jr.–pole, Leffler 1–5, White 6–33, Buescher 34–36, White 37, McCumbee 38, Bodine 39–40, Buescher 41–96, Hornaday Jr. 97–99, Buescher 100–104, Keselowski 105–121, Buescher 122–149, Hornaday Jr. 150, Bodine 151–153, Armstrong 154, Keselowski 155–156, Buescher 157–167.

5 NORTH CAROLINA EDUCATION LOTTERY 200

May 18, 2012 — Charlotte Motor Speedway — 134 Laps – 201 Miles

Fin	Str	Car	Driver	Team	Laps	Status
1	2	6	Justin Lofton	CollegeComplete.com Chevrolet	134	Running
2	9	19	Brad Keselowski	Cooper Standard Ram	134	Running
3	17	11	Todd Bodine	Toyota Care Toyota	134	Running
4	5	18	Jason Leffler	Dollar General Toyota	134	Running
5	15	9	Ron Hornaday Jr.	Joe Denette Motorsports Chevrolet	134	Running
6	7	23	Jason White	JW Demolition/GunBroker.com Ford	134	Running
7	3	22	Joey Coulter	RCR Chevrolet	134	Running
8	21	27	Jeb Burton #	State Water Heaters Chevrolet	134	Running
9	4	17	Timothy Peters	Tire Kingdom Toyota	134	Running
10	1	3	Ty Dillon #	Bass Pro Shops/Allstate Chevrolet	134	Running
11	14	29	Parker Kligerman	Draw-Tite/MOPAR RAM	134	Running
12	11	2	Brendan Gaughan	Southpoint Hotel & Casino Chevrolet	134	Running
13	24	98	Dakoda Armstrong #	EverFi.com Toyota	134	Running
14	12	32	Miguel Paludo	Duroline Brakes Chevrolet	134	Running
15	6	88	Matt Crafton	Menards/Fisher Nuts Toyota	134	Running
16	22	09	John Wes Townley #	Toyota Save in May Sales Event Toyota	134	Running
17	34	81	David Starr	Build Your Future/Zachry Toyota	134	Running
18	31	92	David Reutimann	FleetHQ.com/BTS Tire/QMI/Fatback's Tire Chev.	134	Running
19	8	33	Cale Gale #	Rheem Chevrolet	134	Running
20	26	99	Bryan Silas #	Rockingham Speedway Ford	134	Running
21	35	75	Caleb Holman #	Food Country USA/Morning Fresh Farms Chev.	134	Running
22	10	31	James Buescher	Exide Batteries Chevrolet	134	Running
23	28	01	Jake Crum	BanditChippers.com Chevrolet	132	Running
24	23	24	Max Gresham #	BugBand.net/Made in USA Brand Chevrolet	131	Running
25	13	13	Johnny Sauter	Hot Honeys/Curb Records Toyota	127	Running
26	25	10	Jennifer Jo Cobb	Driven2Honor.org Ram	126	Running
27	29	14	Brennan Newberry	The Jeremy Staat Foundation Chevrolet	125	Running
28	27	39	Ryan Sieg	Pull-A-Part Used Auto Parts Chevrolet	101	Engine
29	16	30	Nelson Piquet Jr.	Alpinestars Chevrolet	98	Accident
30	20	5	Paulie Harraka #	Child Help 1-800-4-A-CHILD Ford	84	Accident
31	30	60	Chad McCumbee	Turn One Racing Chevrolet	61	Overheating
32	32	84	Chris Fontaine	Glenden Enterprises Chevrolet	40	Engine
33	19	7	John King #	CONSOL Energy Toyota	24	Accident
34	36	38	Dennis Setzer	RSS Racing Chevrolet	19	Overheating
35	18	08	Ross Chastain #	Florida Watermelon Association Toyota	12	Engine
36	33	68	Clay Greenfield	@claygreenfield Ram	6	Power Steering

Sunoco Rookie of the Year Contender.

RACE COMMENTS: Before an estimated crowd of 25,000, Justin Lofton won the North Carolina Education Lottery 200, his first NASCAR Camping World Truck Series victory. Prior to the green flag, the following trucks dropped to the rear of the field for the reason indicated: #14 (engine change), #81 (adjustments outside impound), #92 (missed drivers meeting).

TIME OF RACE: 1 hour, 49 minutes, 51 seconds — AVERAGE SPEED: 109.786 mph — MARGIN OF VICTORY: 0.261 seconds — KEYSTONE 21 MEANS 21 POLE AWARD: Ty Dillon (181.616 mph. 29.733 secs.) — CAUTION FLAGS: 8 cautions for 36 laps — LAP LEADERS: 8 lead changes among 7 drivers. Dillon 1–25, Sieg 26–30, Buescher 31–40, Keselowski 41–66, Hornaday Jr. 67, Peters 68–84, Lofton 85–118, Keselowski 119–124, Lofton 125–134.

6 LUCAS OIL 200

June 1, 2012 — Dover International Speedway — 200 Laps – 200 Miles

Fin	Str	Car	Driver	Team	Laps	Status
1	13	11	Todd Bodine	Red Horse Racing Toyota	147	Running
2	11	29	Parker Kligerman	Cooper Standard Ram	147	Running
3	1	2	Kevin Harvick	Tide Chevrolet	147	Running
4	18	30	Nelson Piquet Jr.	Qualcomm Chevrolet	147	Running
5	5	33	Cale Gale #	Rheem Chevrolet	147	Running
6	6	3	Ty Dillon #	Bass Pro Shops/Allstate Chevrolet	147	Running
7	15	31	James Buescher	Koike Chevrolet	147	Running
8	10	88	Matt Crafton	Ideal Door/Menards Toyota	147	Running
9	8	17	Timothy Peters	Red Horse Racing Toyota	147	Running
10	16	6	Justin Lofton	CollegeComplete.com Chevrolet	147	Running
11	2	22	Joey Coulter	RCR/darrellgwynnfoundation.org Chevrolet	147	Running
12	9	32	Miguel Paludo	Duroline Brakes Chevrolet	147	Running
13	17	18	Brian Scott	Shore Lodge Toyota	147	Running
14	24	81	David Starr	AdvoCare/Zachry Toyota	147	Running
15	12	08	Ross Chastain #	Florida Watermelon Assn/Watermelon.org Toyota	147	Running
16	21	09	John Wes Townley #	Barberitos Toyota	147	Running
17	25	5	Paulie Harraka #	Wauters Motorsports Ford	147	Running
18	30	75	Caleb Holman #	Food Country USA Chevrolet	147	Running
19	7	27	Jeb Burton #	State Water Heaters Chevrolet	146	Running
20	19	98	Dakoda Armstrong #	EverFi.com Toyota	145	Running
21	27	70	Jeff Agnew	Team 7 Motorsports Chevrolet	145	Running
22	23	99	Bryan Silas #	Rockingham Speedway Ford	145	Running
23	29	84	Chris Fontaine	Glenden Enterprises Chevrolet	144	Running
24	4	13	Johnny Sauter	Hot Honeys/Curb Records Toyota	143	Running
25	35	57	Norm Benning	Norm Benning Racing Chevrolet	142	Running
26	33	10	Jennifer Jo Cobb	Driven2Honor.org Ram	137	Running
27	3	9	Ron Hornaday Jr.	Anderson's Maple Syrup Chevrolet	136	Accident
28	31	61	Wes Burton	Sam Pearce Racing/PHHUSA.org Ford	108	Accident
29	22	39	Ryan Sieg	RSS Racing Chevrolet	95	Accident
30	14	24	Max Gresham #	Made in USA Brand Chevrolet	88	Accident
31	28	07	Chris Jones	Wear Your Gear/Bobber.info Toyota	17	Overheating
32	32	93	Johnny Chapman	RSS Racing Chevrolet	14	Ignition
33	20	23	Jason White	GunBroker.com Ford	11	Engine
34	34	74	Mike Harmon	Koma Unwind Relaxation Drink Chevrolet	3	Ignition
35	26	38	Dennis Setzer	RSS Racing Chevrolet	2	Vibration

Sunoco Rookie of the Year Contender.

RACE COMMENTS: Before an estimated crowd of 28,000, Todd Bodine won the Lucas Oil 200, his 22nd NASCAR Camping World Truck victory. The race, which was scheduled for 200 laps, was shortened to 147 laps due to inclement weather.

TIME OF RACE: 1 hour, 48 minutes, 0 seconds — AVERAGE SPEED: 81.667 mph — MARGIN OF VICTORY: Under Caution — KEYSTONE LIGHT POLE AWARD: Kevin Harvick (158.235 mph. 22.751 secs.) — CAUTION FLAGS: 9 cautions for 46 laps — LAP LEADERS: 7 lead changes among 6 drivers. Harvick 1–29, Starr 30–32, Lofton 33–54, Harvick 55–121, Paludo 122–126, Bodine 127–139, Kligerman 140, Bodine 141–147.

7 WINSTAR WORLD CASINO 400

June 8, 2012 — Texas Motor Speedway — 167 Laps – 400 Miles

Fin	Str	Car	Driver	Team	Laps	Status
1	20	13	Johnny Sauter	Hot Honeys/Curb Records Toyota	167	Running
2	10	88	Matt Crafton	Menards/Goof Off Toyota	167	Running
3	11	22	Joey Coulter	RCR/Darrell Gwynn Foundation Chevrolet	167	Running
4	6	2	Brendan Gaughan	South Point Chevrolet	167	Running
5	8	30	Nelson Piquet Jr.	Qualcomm/Autotrac Chevrolet	167	Running
6	18	18	Jason Leffler	Dollar General Toyota	167	Running
7	3	3	Ty Dillon #	Bass Pro Shops/Tracker Boats Chevrolet	167	Running
8	16	33	Cale Gale #	Rheem Chevrolet	167	Running
9	1	6	Justin Lofton	CollegeComplete.com Chevrolet	167	Running
10	5	29	Parker Kligerman	Reese Towpower/Mopar Ram	167	Running
11	2	17	Timothy Peters	Toyota Toyota	167	Running
12	9	9	Ron Hornaday Jr.	SWM/AM/FM Energy Chevrolet	167	Running
13	17	81	David Starr	Build Your Future/Zachry Toyota	167	Running
14	15	32	Miguel Paludo	Unite for Diabetes/Duroline Brakes Chevrolet	167	Running
15	4	31	James Buescher	Koike.com Chevrolet	167	Running
16	23	08	Ross Chastain #	Watermelon/Holiday Inn Express Toyota	167	Running
17	13	23	Jason White	GunBroker.com Ford	167	Running
18	19	98	Dakoda Armstrong #	EverFi.com Toyota	167	Running
19	25	39	Ryan Sieg	Pull-A-Part Used Auto Parts Chevrolet	167	Running
20	34	14	Brandon Miller	NTS, Inc. Chevrolet	167	Running
21	21	24	Max Gresham #	Made in USA Brand Chevrolet	164	Running
22	30	57	Norm Benning	Norm Benning Racing Chevrolet	162	Running
23	26	84	B J McLeod	Boggy Creek Air Boat Rides Chevrolet	161	Running
24	31	65	Scott Stenzel	Making The Driver Chevrolet	160	Running
25	24	99	Bryan Silas #	Rockingham Speedway Ford	159	Running
26	27	93	Brent Raymer	RSS Racing Chevrolet	139	Suspension
27	12	09	John Wes Townley #	Toyota Care Toyota	128	Running
28	22	5	Paulie Harraka #	Wauters Motorsports Ford	69	Accident
29	32	73	Rick Crawford	Trans Pecos Trucking/Superseal Chevrolet	52	Accident
30	7	11	Todd Bodine	Toyota Care Toyota	31	Oil Pump
31	28	07	Johnny Chapman	Wear Your Gear/Bobber.info Toyota	25	Overheating
32	29	10	Jennifer Jo Cobb	Driven2Honor.org Ram	10	Engine
33	33	74	Mike Harmon	Koma Unwind Relaxation Drink Chevrolet	6	Overheating
34	35	0	Chris Lafferty	Driven2Honor.org Ram	3	Engine
35	14	27	Brandon Knupp	Hillman Racing Chevrolet	2	Ignition

Sunoco Rookie of the Year Contender.

RACE COMMENTS: Before an estimated crowd of 41,000, Johnny Sauter won the WinStar World Casino 400, his fifth NASCAR Camping World Truck Series victory. To start the race, prior to the green flag the following truck dropped to the rear of the field for the reasons indicated: #24 (backup truck).

TIME OF RACE: 2 hours, 1 minutes, 17 seconds — AVERAGE SPEED: 123.925 mph — MARGIN OF VICTORY: 2.101 seconds — KEYSTONE LIGHT POLE AWARD: Qualifying Canceled — CAUTION FLAGS: 7 cautions for 32 laps — LAP LEADERS: 13 lead changes among 6 drivers. Lofton 1–26, Buescher 27–33, Dillon 34–50, Buescher 51–54, Sauter 55–73, Buescher 74, White 75–81, Buescher 82–96, Lofton 97–125, Buescher 126–129, Dillon 130–134, Buescher 135–137, Crafton 138–145, Sauter 146–167.

8 UNOH 225

June 28, 2012 — Kentucky Speedway — 150 Laps – 225 Miles

Fin	Str	No	Driver	Team	Laps	Status
1	3	31	James Buescher	Exide Chevrolet	150	Running
2	17	19	Brad Keselowski	Brad Keselowski's Checkered Flag Foun. Ram	150	Running
3	4	3	Ty Dillon #	Bass Pro Shops/Tracker Boats Chevrolet	150	Running
4	1	88	Matt Crafton	Menards/Great Lakeswood Floors Toyota	150	Running
5	7	17	Timothy Peters	Red Horse Racing Toyota	150	Running
6	6	13	Johnny Sauter	Hot Honeys/Curb Records Toyota	150	Running
7	16	22	Joey Coulter	Steak-umm Chevrolet	150	Running
8	18	18	Jason Leffler	Dollar General Toyota	150	Running
9	11	9	Ron Hornaday Jr.	Hollywood Casino Chevrolet	150	Running
10	25	4	Kyle Larson	Chip Ganassi Racing Teams Mobile App Chevrolet	150	Running
11	12	23	Jason White	GunBroker.com Ford	150	Running
12	5	32	Miguel Paludo	Duroline Chevrolet	150	Running
13	26	98	Dakoda Armstrong #	EverFi.com Toyota	150	Running
14	10	6	Justin Lofton	CollegeComplete.com Chevrolet	150	Running
15	24	81	David Starr	Zachry Toyota	150	Running
16	29	39	Ryan Sieg	RSS Racing Chevrolet	150	Running
17	23	5	Paulie Harraka #	Wauters Motorsports Ford	150	Running
18	21	68	Clay Greenfield	@claygreenfield Ram	149	Running
19	8	29	Parker Kligerman	Drawtite Ram	149	Running
20	36	84	Chris Fontaine	Glenden Enterprises Chevrolet	148	Running
21	33	75	Caleb Holman #	Food Country USA Chevrolet	147	Running
22	31	14	Brennan Newberry	NTS/IronClad Performance Chevrolet	147	Running
23	34	02	Tyler Young #	RandCo Chevrolet	145	Running
24	15	2	Tim George Jr.	Applebee's Chevrolet	143	Running
25	9	33	Cale Gale #	Rheem Chevrolet	140	Running
26	28	99	Bryan Silas #	Advantage/Rockingham Speedway Ford	134	Running
27	30	07	Jeff Agnew	Wear Your Gear/Bobber.info Chevrolet	104	Vibration
28	13	11	Todd Bodine	Toyota Care Toyota	69	Accident
29	2	30	Nelson Piquet Jr.	Magic Brasil Chevrolet	68	Accident
30	19	24	Max Gresham #	Made in USA Brand Chevrolet	63	Engine
31	20	01	Jake Crum	Bandit Chippers Chevrolet	27	Accident
32	22	09	John Wes Townley #	Toyota Toyota	16	Accident
33	14	08	Ross Chastain #	South Carolina Watermelon Association Toyota	7	Engine
34	35	27	C E Falk III	Hillman Racing Chevrolet	6	Handling
35	27	93	Dennis Setzer	RSS Racing Chevrolet	4	Transmission
36	32	86	Scott Riggs	Clay Greenfield Motorsports Ram	3	Overheating

Sunoco Rookie of the Year Contender.

RACE COMMENTS: Before an estimated crowd of 25,000, James Buescher won the UNOH 225, his second NASCAR Camping World Truck Series victory. To start the race, prior to the green flag the following trucks dropped to the rear of the field for the reasons indicated: #3, 4 (engine change), #27 (back-up truck), #39, 81 (missing drivers meeting).

TIME OF RACE: 1 hour, 51 minutes, 16 seconds — AVERAGE SPEED: 121.33 mph — MARGIN OF VICTORY: 3.805 seconds — KEYSTONE LIGHT POLE AWARD: Matt Crafton (173.288 mph. 31.162 secs.) — CAUTION FLAGS: 7 cautions for 31 laps — LAP LEADERS: 8 lead changes among 4 drivers. Crafton 1–18, Silas 19, Crafton 20–26, Buescher 27–62, Crafton 63, Buescher 64–103, Crafton 104, Dillon 105–107, Buescher 108–150.

9 AMERICAN ETHANOL 200

July 14, 2012 — Iowa Speedway — 200 Laps – 175 Miles

Fin	Str	No	Driver	Team	Laps	Status
1	1	17	Timothy Peters	Toyota Toyota	200	Running
2	8	9	Ron Hornaday Jr.	Anderson's Pure Maple Syrup Chevrolet	200	Running
3	7	88	Matt Crafton	Menards/Ideal Door Toyota	200	Running
4	5	13	Johnny Sauter	Hot Honeys/Curb Records Toyota	200	Running
5	3	6	Justin Lofton	J.D. Heiskell & Co. Chevrolet	200	Running
6	9	18	Jason Leffler	Shore Lodge Toyota	200	Running
7	15	3	Ty Dillon #	Bass Pro Shops/Tracker Boats Chevrolet	200	Running
8	12	22	Joey Coulter	American Ethanol Chevrolet	200	Running
9	2	30	Nelson Piquet Jr.	Autotrac Chevrolet	200	Running
10	14	29	Parker Kligerman	Reese Towpower Ram	200	Running
11	17	97	Jeff Choquette	Liz Girl Logistics/Adrian Carriers Inc. Chevrolet	200	Running
12	11	11	Todd Bodine	Toyota Care Toyota	200	Running
13	10	32	Miguel Paludo	Duroline Chevrolet	200	Running
14	22	23	Jason White	GunBroker.com Ford	200	Running
15	18	2	Tim George Jr.	Applebee's Chevrolet	200	Running
16	20	08	Ross Chastain #	South Carolina Watermelon Association Toyota	200	Running
17	25	39	Ryan Sieg	RSS Racing Chevrolet	199	Running
18	23	75	Caleb Holman #	Food Country USA Chevrolet	199	Running
19	30	93	Dennis Setzer	RSS Racing Chevrolet	199	Running
20	29	09	John Wes Townley #	Toyota Toyota	197	Running
21	21	07	Jeff Agnew	Team 7 Chevrolet	197	Running
22	28	99	Bryan Silas #	Rockingham Speedway Ford	197	Running
23	31	65	Justin Jennings	LG Seeds Ford	196	Running
24	33	57	Norm Benning	Norm Benning Racing Chevrolet	192	Running
25	32	84	Chris Fontaine	Glenden Enterprises Chevrolet	189	Running
26	6	33	Cale Gale #	Rheem Chevrolet	181	Accident
27	16	98	Dakoda Armstrong #	EverFi.com Toyota	181	Accident
28	19	81	David Starr	Zachry Toyota	165	Oil Leak
29	36	10	Jennifer Jo Cobb	Driven2Honor.org Ram	155	Running
30	4	31	James Buescher	AccuDoc Chevrolet	135	Accident
31	26	27	Travis Miller	HotTorque.com Chevrolet	132	Running
32	35	15	Todd Shafer	thunderexhaust.com Toyota	71	Accident
33	13	5	Paulie Harraka #	Wauters Motorsports Ford	49	Accident
34	34	0	Chris Lafferty	Driven2Honor.org Ram	11	Power Steering
35	27	38	Chris Jones	RSS Racing Chevrolet	9	Brakes
36	24	14	Brennan Newberry	NTS/IronClad Performance Chevrolet	5	Accident

Sunoco Rookie of the Year Contender.

RACE COMMENTS: Before an estimated crowd of 24,000, Timothy Peters won the American Ethanol 200, his fourth NASCAR Camping World Truck Series victory. To start the race, prior to the green flag the following truck dropped to the rear of the field: #08 (unapproved adjustments during impound).

TIME OF RACE: 1 hour, 48 minutes, 54 seconds — AVERAGE SPEED: 96.419 mph — MARGIN OF VICTORY: 1.586 seconds — KEYSTONE LIGHT POLE AWARD: Timothy Peters (136.21 mph. 23.126 secs.) — CAUTION FLAGS: 7 cautions for 39 laps — LAP LEADERS: 6 lead changes among 3 drivers. Peters 1–9, Buescher 10–41, Peters 42–75, Buescher 76–134, Peters 135–168, Hornaday Jr. 169–190, Peters 191–200.

10 AMERICAN ETHANOL 225

July 21, 2012 — Chicagoland Speedway — 150 Laps – 225 Miles

Fin	Str	No	Driver	Team	Laps	Status
1	11	31	James Buescher	Fresh from Florida Gulf Seafood Chevrolet	150	Running
2	6	2	Brendan Gaughan	South Point Hotel & Casino Chevrolet	150	Running
3	4	17	Timothy Peters	Toyota Tundra Toyota	150	Running
4	9	88	Matt Crafton	Schrock Cabinetry/Menards Toyota	150	Running
5	17	29	Parker Kligerman	PlanitDiy.com/Laitner.com Ram	150	Running
6	8	33	Cale Gale #	Rheem Chevrolet	150	Running
7	14	9	Ron Hornaday Jr.	Anderson's Maple Syrup Chevrolet	150	Running
8	5	18	Jason Leffler	Dollar General/M&M's Toyota	150	Running
9	13	23	Jason White	JW Demolition/GunBroker.com Ford	150	Running
10	21	81	David Starr	NCCER/BYF Toyota	150	Running
11	22	73	Rick Crawford	SuperSeal/Lilly Trucking Chevrolet	150	Running
12	3	3	Ty Dillon #	Bass Pro Shops/Allstate Chevrolet	150	Running
13	19	08	Ross Chastain #	Illiana Watermelon Association Toyota	150	Running
14	16	09	John Wes Townley #	Family Farmers Toyota	150	Running
15	2	22	Joey Coulter	RCR/darrellgwynnfoundation.com Chevrolet	150	Running
16	20	98	Dakoda Armstrong #	EverFi.com/MUDD.com Toyota	150	Running
17	10	32	Miguel Paludo	Duroline Brakes Chevrolet	150	Running
18	7	11	Todd Bodine	Toyota Care Toyota	150	Running
19	18	5	Paulie Harraka #	Wauters Motorsports Ford	150	Running
20	28	92	Chad McCumbee	BTS Tire & Wheel/QMI Chevrolet	150	Running
21	1	6	Justin Lofton	Lofton Cattle Chevrolet	150	Running
22	15	13	Johnny Sauter	Hot Honeys/Curb Records Toyota	149	Running
23	34	10	Jennifer Jo Cobb	Driven2Honor.org Ram	144	Running
24	23	99	Bryan Silas #	Rockingham Speedway Ford	142	Running
25	36	57	Norm Benning	Norm Benning Racing Chevrolet	142	Running
26	12	30	Nelson Piquet Jr.	Polen Designs/AutoTrac Chevrolet	94	Accident
27	33	84	Chris Fontaine	Glenden Enterprises Chevrolet	92	Accident
28	25	68	Clay Greenfield	@claygreenfield RAM	90	Brakes
29	29	27	C E Falk III	HotTorque.com Chevrolet	72	Vibration
30	24	93	Ryan Sieg	RSS Racing Chevrolet	45	Engine
31	30	39	Chris Jones	RSS Racing Chevrolet	25	Engine
32	31	86	Blake Koch	Clay Greenfield Motorsports Ram	13	Vibration
33	27	38	Dennis Setzer	RSS Racing Chevrolet	10	Electrical
34	35	0	T.J. Bell	Driven2Honor.org Ram	3	Vibration
35	26	37	Jeff Green	RSS Racing Chevrolet	2	Rear Gear
36	32	07	Johnny Chapman	Wear Your Gear/Bobber.info Toyota	2	Vibration

Sunoco Rookie of the Year Contender.

RACE COMMENTS: Before an estimated crowd of 25,000, James Buescher won the American Ethanol 225, his third NASCAR Camping World Truck Series victory. To start the race, prior to the green flag the following trucks dropped to the rear of the field: #13 (missing drivers meeting), #17 (engine change), #29, 92 (unapproved adjustments during impound).

TIME OF RACE: 1 hour, 53 minutes, 6 seconds — AVERAGE SPEED: 119.363 mph — MARGIN OF VICTORY: 0.247 seconds — KEYSTONE LIGHT POLE AWARD: Justin Lofton (174.154 mph. 31.007 secs.) — CAUTION FLAGS: 7 cautions for 31 laps — LAP LEADERS: 16 lead changes among 10 drivers. Lofton 1–12, Gaughan 13–46, Hornaday Jr. 47, Paludo 48–52, Kligerman 53–58, Harraka 59–60, Gaughan 61–100, Coulter 101–103, Lofton 104, Dillon 105, Lofton 106–116, Dillon 117–132, Gaughan 133–141, Peters 142–143, Buescher 144–148, Peters 149, Buescher 150.

11 POCONO MOUNTAINS 125

August 4, 2012 — Pocono Raceway — 50 Laps – 125 Miles

Fin	Str	No	Driver	Team	Laps	Status
1	4	22	Joey Coulter	RCR/darrellgwynnfoundation.com Chevrolet	50	Running
2	5	31	James Buescher	Koike Aronson/Ransome Chevrolet	50	Running
3	1	30	Nelson Piquet Jr.	AutoTrac Chevrolet	50	Running
4	9	88	Matt Crafton	Jeld Wen/Menards Toyota	50	Running
5	16	18	Denny Hamlin	GNC Live Well/M&M's Toyota	50	Running
6	2	3	Ty Dillon #	Bass Pro Shops/Tracker Boats Chevrolet	50	Running
7	17	29	Parker Kligerman	Cooper Standard Ram	50	Running
8	11	09	John Wes Townley #	Toyota Care Toyota	50	Running
9	35	6	Justin Lofton	Millennium Private Jet Services/Lofton Cattle Chevrolet	50	Running
10	20	08	Ross Chastain #	Melon 1/SC Watermelon Association Toyota	50	Running
11	14	23	Jason White	GunBroker.com Ford	50	Running
12	18	98	Dakoda Armstrong #	EverFi.com Toyota	50	Running
13	3	32	Miguel Paludo	Duroline Brakes Chevrolet	50	Running
14	15	33	Cale Gale #	Rheem Chevrolet	50	Running
15	6	2	Tim George Jr.	Applebee's Chevrolet	50	Running
16	25	27	C E Falk III	HotTorque.com Chevrolet	49	Running
17	19	99	Bryan Silas #	Rockingham Speedway Ford	49	Running
18	23	84	Chris Fontaine	Glenden Enterprises Chevrolet	49	Running
19	10	9	Ron Hornaday Jr.	Joe Denette Motorsports Chevrolet	47	Running
20	34	57	Norm Benning	Norm Benning Racing Chevrolet	47	Running
21	32	59	Kyle Martel	PA Breast Cancer Coalition Chevrolet	47	Running
22	8	17	Timothy Peters	Toyota/Red Horse Racing Toyota	40	Running
23	27	28	Wes Burton	FDNY Racing Chevrolet	39	Accident
24	7	5	Paulie Harraka #	Wauters Motorsports Ford	38	Accident
25	30	82	Sean Corr	Leonard Bus Sales/American Heroes Racing/ Roush Yates Ford	37	Accident
26	12	11	Todd Bodine	Northeast Toyota Dealers Toyota	33	Accident
27	13	13	Johnny Sauter	Hot Honeys/Curb Records Toyota	28	Running
28	21	93	Dennis Setzer	RSS Racing Chevrolet	18	Handling
29	26	39	Ryan Sieg	RSS Racing Chevrolet	11	Engine
30	31	25	Brandon Knupp	Hillman Racing Chevrolet	8	Vibration
31	22	07	Jeff Agnew	Wear Your Gear/Bobber.info Toyota	7	Vibration
32	29	74	Scott Riggs	Kona Unwind Chevrolet	6	Overheating
33	36	75	Adam Edwards	Norm Benning Racing Chevrolet	5	Vibration
34	28	38	Chris Jones	RSS Racing Chevrolet	3	Vibration
35	33	0	Chris Lafferty	Driven2Honor.org Ram	1	Accident
36	24	10	Jennifer Jo Cobb	Driven2Honor.org Ram	0	Engine

Sunoco Rookie of the Year Contender.

RACE COMMENTS: Before an estimated crowd of 25,000, Joey Coulter won the Pocono Mountains 125, his first NASCAR Camping World Truck Series victory. Prior to the green flag, the following trucks dropped to the rear of the field for the reasons indicated: #6 (backup truck); #39 (engine change), #57 (adjustments outside impound).

TIME OF RACE: 1 hour, 1 minutes, 43 seconds — AVERAGE SPEED: 121.523 mph — MARGIN OF VICTORY: 1.224 seconds — KEYSTONE LIGHT POLE AWARD: Nelson Piquet Jr. (169.504 mph. 53.096 secs.) — CAUTION FLAGS: 3 cautions for 12 laps — LAP LEADERS: 7 lead changes among 5 drivers. Piquet Jr. 1–21, Buescher 22, Peters 23–24, White 25–26, Piquet Jr. 27–33, Buescher 34–38, Piquet Jr. 39–43, Coulter 44–50.

12 VFW 200

August 18, 2012 — Michigan International Speedway — 100 Laps – 200 Miles

Fin	Str	No	Driver	Team	Laps	Status
1	2	30	Nelson Piquet Jr.	AutoTrac Chevrolet	100	Running
2	12	23	Jason White	GunBroker.com Ford	100	Running
3	20	98	Dakoda Armstrong #	EverFi.com Toyota	100	Running
4	11	7	Parker Kligerman	Toyota/Red Horse Racing Toyota	100	Running
5	8	31	James Buescher	WolfPack Rentals Chevrolet	100	Running
6	5	3	Ty Dillon #	Bass Pro Shops/Tracker Boats Chevrolet	100	Running
7	1	22	Joey Coulter	Rip-It Energy Fuel Chevrolet	100	Running
8	10	29	Brad Keselowski	Cooper Standard Ram	100	Running
9	4	18	Kurt Busch	Shore Lodge Toyota	100	Running
10	3	32	Miguel Paludo	Duroline Chevrolet	100	Running
11	6	13	Johnny Sauter	Hot Honeys/Curb Records Toyota	100	Running
12	14	6	Justin Lofton	Lofton Cattle Chevrolet	100	Running
13	9	17	Timothy Peters	Toyota/Red Horse Racing Toyota	100	Running
14	23	99	Bryan Silas #	Rockingham Speedway Ford	100	Running
15	25	39	Ryan Sieg	RSS Racing Chevrolet	100	Running
16	13	88	Matt Crafton	Ideal Door/Menards Toyota	100	Running
17	22	9	Ron Hornaday Jr.	Joe Denette Motorsports Chevrolet	100	Running
18	21	08	Ross Chastain #	Melon 1/Engine Parts Plus Toyota	99	Running
19	18	14	Brennan Newberry	NTS/IronClad Performance Chevrolet	99	Running
20	17	33	Cale Gale #	Rheem Chevrolet	99	Running
21	7	2	Tim George Jr.	Applebee's Chevrolet	98	Running
22	29	10	Jennifer Jo Cobb	Driven2Honor.org RAM	96	Running
23	34	57	Norm Benning	Norm Benning Racing Chevrolet	94	Running
24	15	11	Todd Bodine	Toyota Care Toyota	49	Accident
25	16	09	John Wes Townley #	Toyota Care Toyota	45	Accident
26	26	07	Johnny Chapman	Wear Your Gear/Bobber.info Toyota	15	Overheating
27	32	27	Brandon Knupp	Hillman Racing Chevrolet	10	Transmission
28	31	74	Mike Harmon	Koma Unwind Chevrolet	9	Overheating
29	24	84	Chris Fontaine	Glenden Enterprises Chevrolet	6	Vibration
30	30	25	Stephen Leicht	Hillman Racing Chevrolet	6	Transmission
31	28	93	Dennis Setzer	RSS Racing Chevrolet	6	Overheating
32	19	5	Scott Riggs	Wauters Motorsports Chevrolet	4	Engine
33	27	38	Chris Jones	RSS Racing Chevrolet	4	Rear Gear
34	35	75	Josh Wise	Norm Benning Racing Chevrolet	1	Vibration
35	33	0	T.J. Bell	Driven2Honor.org Ford	1	Transmission

Sunoco Rookie of the Year Contender.

RACE COMMENTS: Before an estimated crowd of 35,000, Nelson Piquet Jr. won the VFW 200, his first NASCAR Camping World Truck Series victory. Prior to the green flag, the following truck dropped to the rear of the field for the reason indicated: #11 (unapproved adjustments).

TIME OF RACE: 1 hour, 26 minutes, 1 seconds — AVERAGE SPEED: 139.508 mph — MARGIN OF VICTORY: 8.082 seconds — KEYSTONE LIGHT POLE AWARD: Joey Coulter (184.101 mph. 39.109 secs.) — CAUTION FLAGS: 5 cautions for 17 laps — LAP LEADERS: 11 lead changes among 7 drivers. Coulter–pole, Piquet Jr 1–13, Keselowski 14–16, K. Busch 17–33, Piquet Jr. 34, K. Busch 35–39, Bodine 40–43, K. Busch 44–78, Dillon 79–81, Kligerman 82–83, Buescher 84–88, Piquet Jr. 89–100.

13 UNOH 200

August 22, 2012 — Bristol Motor Speedway — 200 Laps – 106.6 Miles

Fin	Str	No	Driver	Team	Laps	Status
1	2	17	Timothy Peters	Red Horse Racing Toyota	204	Running
2	9	7	Parker Kligerman	Toyota Toyota	204	Running
3	15	08	Ross Chastain #	Melon 1 Toyota	204	Running
4	8	22	Joey Coulter	Steak-umm Chevrolet	204	Running
5	11	2	Brendan Gaughan	South Point Chevrolet	204	Running
6	5	19	Ryan Blaney	Cooper Standard Ram	204	Running
7	28	31	James Buescher	Exide Chevrolet	204	Running
8	17	9	Ron Hornaday Jr.	Anderson's Pure Maple Syrup Chevrolet	204	Running
9	7	88	Matt Crafton	Menards/Great Lakes Toyota	204	Running
10	32	6	Justin Lofton	Millennium Private Jet Services/Lofton Cattle Chevrolet	204	Running
11	10	13	Johnny Sauter	Hot Honeys/Curb Records Toyota	204	Running
12	21	39	Ryan Sieg	RSS Racing Chevrolet	204	Running
13	19	81	David Starr	Chasco/Zachry Toyota	204	Running
14	27	23	Jason White	GunBroker.com Ford	204	Running
15	23	27	B J McLeod	Boggy Creek Air Boat Rides Chevrolet	204	Running
16	29	32	Miguel Paludo	Duroline Chevrolet	204	Running
17	22	18	Brian Scott	Dollar General Toyota	204	Running
18	6	30	Nelson Piquet Jr.	Drink B Chevrolet	204	Running
19	20	75	Caleb Holman #	Food Country USA/Wise Snacks/Pizza Plus Chevrolet	204	Running
20	13	02	Tyler Young #	Rando Chevrolet	203	Running
21	12	3	Ty Dillon #	Bass Pro Shops/Tracker Boats Chevrolet	202	Running
22	30	99	Bryan Silas #	Rockingham Speedway Ford	202	Running
23	24	92	Chad McCumbee	FleetHQ.com/BTS Tire & Wheel/QMI Chevrolet	202	Running
24	25	09	John Wes Townley #	Zaxby's Toyota	202	Running
25	4	29	Brad Keselowski	Reese Towpower Ram	201	Running
26	35	84	Russ Dugger	JPO Absorbents Chevrolet	200	Running
27	36	57	Norm Benning	Norm Benning Racing Chevrolet	196	Running
28	1	33	Cale Gale #	Rheem Chevrolet	193	Accident
29	16	01	Jake Crum	Bandit Chippers Chevrolet	187	Accident
30	18	98	Dakoda Armstrong #	EverFi.com Toyota	168	Running
31	3	11	Todd Bodine	Toyota Care Toyota	159	Accident
32	26	07	Jeff Agnew	Mark 4 Suzuki Chevrolet	91	Accident
33	34	93	Chris Jones	RSS Racing Chevrolet	81	Accident
34	14	86	Clay Greenfield	Titan Tool/Star Road-Guard Ram	53	Brakes
35	31	38	Dennis Setzer	RSS Racing Chevrolet	4	Brakes
36	33	5	Johnny Chapman	Wauters Motorsports Chevrolet	2	Electrical

Sunoco Rookie of the Year Contender.

RACE COMMENTS: Before an estimated crowd of 53,000, Timothy Peters won the UNOH 200, his fifth NASCAR Camping World Truck Series victory. Prior to the green flag, the following trucks dropped to the rear of the field for the reasons indicated: #93, 6 (unapproved adjustments); #86 (driver change).

TIME OF RACE: 1 hour, 21 minutes, 52 seconds — AVERAGE SPEED: 79.69 mph — MARGIN OF VICTORY: 0.465 seconds — KEYSTONE LIGHT POLE AWARD: Cale Gale (122.56 mph. 15.656 secs.) — CAUTION FLAGS: 6 cautions for 43 laps — LAP LEADERS: 1 lead changes among 1 drivers. Gale–pole, Peters 1–204.

14 JEFF FOXWORTHY'S GRIT CHIPS 200

August 31, 2012 — Atlanta Motor Speedway — 130 Laps – 200.2 Miles

Fin	Str	No	Driver	Team	Laps	Status
1	1	3	Ty Dillon #	Bass Pro Shops/NRA Chevrolet	130	Running
2	4	18	Kyle Busch	Dollar General Toyota	130	Running
3	3	31	James Buescher	Central Wire Chevrolet	130	Running
4	9	7	Parker Kligerman	Toyota/Red Horse Racing Toyota	130	Running
5	13	5	Aric Almirola	Courtesy Ford/Jordan Truck Sales Ford	130	Running
6	17	4	Kyle Larson	Chip Ganassi Racing Teams Chevrolet	130	Running
7	14	22	Joey Coulter	Armour Chevrolet	130	Running
8	5	30	Nelson Piquet Jr.	Drink B Chevrolet	130	Running
9	10	88	Matt Crafton	Roto-Rooter/Menards Toyot	130	Running
10	15	51	Kurt Busch	Bill Holt Chevrolet Chevrolet	130	Running
11	12	29	Ryan Blaney	Cooper Standard Ram	130	Running
12	6	13	Johnny Sauter	Hot Honeys/Curb Records Toyota	130	Running
13	8	17	Timothy Peters	Toyota/Red Horse Racing Toyota	130	Running
14	20	6	Justin Lofton	Lofton Cattle Chevrolet	130	Running
15	18	33	Cale Gale #	Ruud Chevrolet	130	Running
16	7	32	Miguel Paludo	Duroline Chevrolet	130	Running
17	23	39	Ryan Sieg	Pull-A-Part Used Auto Parts Chevrolet	130	Running
18	24	81	David Starr	AdvoCare Toyota	130	Running
19	22	09	John Wes Townley #	Zaxby's Toyota	129	Running
20	16	08	Ross Chastain #	Melon 1/Georgia Watermelon Association Toyota	129	Running
21	21	11	Todd Bodine	Toyota Care Toyota	129	Running
22	30	8	Max Gresham #	Made in USA/BugBand.net Chevrolet	129	Running
23	29	98	Dakoda Armstrong #	EverFi.com Toyota	128	Running
24	28	99	Bryan Silas #	Rockingham Speedway Ford	127	Running
25	26	92	Chad McCumbee	FleetHQ.com/BTS Tire & Wheel/QMI Chevrolet	127	Running
26	33	84	Chris Fontaine	Glenden Enterprises Chevrolet	126	Running
27	31	75	Caleb Holman #	Food Country USA/Sunset Farm Foods Chevrolet	74	Engine
28	2	2	Tim George Jr.	Applebee's Chevrolet	63	Accident
29	11	23	Jason White	GunBroker.com Ford	45	Accident
30	19	9	Ron Hornaday Jr.	AMFMEnergy.com/Anderson's Maple Syrup Chev.	43	Accident
31	35	93	Chris Jones	RSS Racing Chevrolet	25	Transmission
32	25	07	Johnny Chapman	Wear Your Gear/Bobber.info Toyota	17	Radiator
33	27	74	Scott Riggs	Koma Unwind Chevrolet	11	Ignition
34	34	27	Stephen Leicht	Boggy Creek Air Boat Rides Chevrolet	4	Engine
35	32	0	Blake Koch	RameyCars.com/Driven2Honor.org Ford	2	Overheating
36	36	38	Dennis Setzer	RSS Racing Chevrolet	2	Rear Gear

Sunoco Rookie of the Year Contender.

RACE COMMENTS: Before an estimated crowd of 28,300, Ty Dillon won the Jeff Foxworthy's Grit Chips 200, his first NASCAR Camping World Truck Series victory. To start the race, prior to the green flag no trucks dropped to the rear of the field.

TIME OF RACE: 1 hour, 27 minutes, 51 seconds — AVERAGE SPEED: 136.733 mph — MARGIN OF VICTORY: 3.227 seconds — KEYSTONE LIGHT POLE AWARD: Ty Dillon (177.357 mph. 31.259 secs.) — CAUTION FLAGS: 3 cautions for 16 laps — LAP LEADERS: 20 lead changes among 8 drivers. Dillon–pole, Ky. Busch 1–9, Dillon 10–35, Kligerman 36, Ky. Busch 37–45, Buescher 46–49, Ky. Busch 50–53, Buescher 54–55, Ky. Busch 56–57, Dillon 58–60, Ky. Busch 61–65, Dillon 66, Ky. Busch 67–83, Almirola 84, Coulter 85, Lofton 86–90, Gale 91, Ky. Busch 92–105, Dillon 106–109, Ky. Busch 110–124, Dillon 125–130.

15 AMERICAN ETHANOL 200 *presented by* HY-VEE

September 15, 2012 — Iowa Speedway — 200 Laps – 175 Miles

Fin	Str	No	Driver	Team	Laps	Status
1	2	29	Ryan Blaney	Cooper Standard Ram	200	Running
2	9	3	Ty Dillon #	Bass Pro Shops/NRA Chevrolet	200	Running
3	15	11	Todd Bodine	Toyota Care Toyota	200	Running
4	4	13	Johnny Sauter	Hot Honeys/Curb Records Toyota	200	Running
5	6	33	Cale Gale #	Rheem Chevrolet	200	Running
6	3	30	Nelson Piquet Jr.	DrinkB.com Chevrolet	200	Running
7	17	18	Drew Herring	Toyota/Dollar General Toyota	200	Running
8	18	97	Jeff Choquette	Adrian Carriers/Liz Girl Logistics Chevrolet	200	Running
9	12	88	Matt Crafton	Rip It Energy Fuel/Menards Toyota	200	Running
10	8	32	Miguel Paludo	Duroline Chevrolet	200	Running
11	22	08	Ross Chastain #	South Carolina Watermelon Association Toyota	200	Running
12	19	23	Jason White	GunBroker.com Ford	200	Running
13	14	22	Joey Coulter	RCR/Darrell Gwynn Foundation Chevrolet	199	Running
14	21	39	Ryan Sieg	RSS Racing Chevrolet	199	Running
15	16	09	John Wes Townley #	Zaxby's Toyota	199	Running
16	11	19	David Mayhew	MMI Wireless Services Ram	199	Running
17	5	31	James Buescher	Wolfpack Rentals Chevrolet	199	Running
18	24	99	Bryan Silas #	Rockingham Speedway Ford	198	Running
19	10	17	Timothy Peters	Toyota/Red Horse Racing Toyota	198	Running
20	26	65	Justin Jennings	LGSeeds.com Ford	198	Running
21	23	14	Brennan Newberry	NTS/Ironclad Performance Chevrolet	198	Running
22	25	2	Tim George Jr.	Applebee's Chevrolet	197	Running
23	1	7	Parker Kligerman	Toyota/Red Horse Racing Toyota	197	Running
24	32	84	Wayne Edwards	Enseva Chevrolet	196	Running
25	34	57	Norm Benning	Norm Benning Racing Chevrolet	194	Running
26	35	47	Benjamin Reynolds	Diversified Consulting Solutions Chevrolet	194	Running
27	20	4	August Grill	Turner Motorsports Chevrolet	188	Battery
28	33	96	Todd Peck	Stopain/Arthritis Foundation Chevrolet	179	Oil Leak
29	27	27	Ryan Lynch	Blankhood.com Chevrolet	173	Running
30	31	10	Jennifer Jo Cobb	Horejsi Graphics/Driven2Honor.org RAM	171	Radiator
31	13	6	Justin Lofton	Lofton Cattle Chevrolet	94	Accident
32	28	07	Caleb Roark	Bennigans/Montana Mikes Chevrolet	94	Accident
33	7	9	Ron Hornaday Jr.	Smokey Mountain Herbal Snuff Chevrolet	68	Accident
34	30	93	Chris Jones	RSS Racing Chevrolet	5	Brakes
35	36	0	Chris Lafferty	Horejsi Graphics Ford	3	Transmission
36	29	38	Dennis Setzer	RSS Racing Chevrolet	2	Overheating

Sunoco Rookie of the Year Contender.

RACE COMMENTS: Before an estimated crowd of 20,000, Ryan Blaney won the American Ethanol 200 presented by Hy-Vee, his first NASCAR Camping World Truck Series victory.

TIME OF RACE: 1 hour, 58 minutes, 56 seconds — AVERAGE SPEED: 88.285 mph — MARGIN OF VICTORY: 0.168 seconds — KEYSTONE LIGHT POLE AWARD: Parker Kligerman (137.507 mph. 22.908 secs.) — CAUTION FLAGS: 9 cautions for 54 laps — LAP LEADERS: 7 lead changes among 6 drivers. Kligerman 1–28, Buescher 29–35, Kligerman 36, Herring 37–55, Lofton 56–60, Kligerman 61–138, Sauter 139–150, Blaney 151–200.

16 KENTUCKY 201

September 21, 2012 — Kentucky Speedway — 134 Laps – 201 Miles

Fin	Str	No	Driver	Team	Laps	Status
1	8	31	James Buescher	Fraternal Order of Eagles Chevrolet	134	Running
2	5	7	Parker Kligerman	Toyota/Red Horse Racing Toyota	134	Running
3	3	3	Ty Dillon #	Bass Pro Shops/Tracker Boats Chevrolet	134	Running
4	1	22	Joey Coulter	RCR Chevrolet	134	Running
5	10	18	Brian Scott	Dollar General Toyota	134	Running
6	2	13	Johnny Sauter	Hot Honeys/Curb Records Toyota	134	Running
7	14	6	Justin Lofton	Lofton Cattle Chevrolet	134	Running
8	12	32	Miguel Paludo	Duroline Chevrolet	134	Running
9	11	88	Matt Crafton	Menards/Ideal Door Toyota	134	Running
10	23	09	John Wes Townley #	Zaxby's Toyota	134	Running
11	16	29	Ryan Blaney	Cooper Standard Ram	134	Running
12	6	30	Nelson Piquet Jr.	Drink B Chevrolet	134	Running
13	25	01	Jake Crum	Bandit Chippers Chevrolet	134	Running
14	22	9	Ron Hornaday Jr.	Chevy Truck Month Chevrolet	134	Running
15	34	57	Norm Benning	Norm Benning Racing Chevrolet	133	Running
16	30	10	Jennifer Jo Cobb	Driven2Honor.org Ram	127	Running
17	29	07	Jeff Agnew	Mark 4 Suzuki Chevrolet	123	Oil Pump
18	17	2	Tim George Jr.	Applebee's Chevrolet	118	Running
19	4	33	Cale Gale #	Rheem Chevrolet	115	Running
20	19	23	Jason White	GunBroker.com Ford	105	Accident
21	13	17	Timothy Peters	Toyota/Red Horse Racing Toyota	66	Accident
22	28	39	Ryan Sieg	RSS Racing Chevrolet	65	Engine
23	9	8	Max Gresham #	Made in USA Brand Chevrolet	62	Accident
24	33	27	Travis Miller	Hot Torque Chevrolet	54	Vibration
25	24	5	John King #	Food City/Fairway Ford	53	Accident
26	15	19	David Mayhew	MMI Ram	53	Brakes
27	18	14	Brennan Newberry	NTS/IronClad Performance Chevrolet	46	Accident
28	27	08	Ross Chastain #	SS/GLR Toyota	35	Vibration
29	26	99	Bryan Silas #	Rockingham Speedway Ford	33	Accident
30	7	11	Todd Bodine	Toyota Care Toyota	21	Accident
31	20	4	Dakoda Armstrong #	Drive for Savings Chevrolet	16	Engine
32	32	93	Johnny Chapman	RSS Racing Chevrolet	16	Rear End
33	21	38	Chris Jones	RSS Racing Chevrolet	4	Rear End
34	35	84	Chris Fontaine	JPO Absorbents Chevrolet	3	Engine
35	36	37	Dennis Setzer	RSS Racing Chevrolet	3	Vibration
36	31	0	Blake Koch	Driven2Honor.org Ford	0	Transmission

Sunoco Rookie of the Year Contender.

RACE COMMENTS: Before an estimated crowd of 20,000, James Buescher won the Kentucky 201, his fourth NASCAR Camping World Truck Series victory.

TIME OF RACE: 1 hour, 53 minutes, 43 seconds — AVERAGE SPEED: 106.053 mph — MARGIN OF VICTORY: 1.292 seconds — KEYSTONE LIGHT POLE AWARD: Joey Coulter (176.488 mph. 30.597 secs.) — CAUTION FLAGS: 7 cautions for 42 laps. — LAP LEADERS: 10 lead changes among 7 drivers. Coulter 1–17, Chastain 18, Silas 19–20, Scott 21–33, Buescher 34–42, Scott 43, Buescher 44–46, Blaney 47–59, Coulter 60–81, Agnew 82, Buescher 83–134.

17 SMITH'S 350

September 29, 2012 — Las Vegas Motor Speedway — 146 Laps – 350 Miles

Fin	Str	No	Driver	Team	Laps	Status
1	13	30	Nelson Piquet Jr.	OmniTracs/Iceberg/tdm transportes Chevrolet	146	Running
2	4	88	Matt Crafton	Menards Toyota	146	Running
3	1	22	Joey Coulter	RCR/Darrell Gwynn Foundation Chevrolet	146	Running
4	6	2	Brendan Gaughan	South Point Hotel & Casino Chevrolet	146	Running
5	10	11	Todd Bodine	Toyota Care Toyota	146	Running
6	15	31	James Buescher	Great Clips Chevrolet	146	Running
7	12	33	Cale Gale #	Rheem Chevrolet	146	Running
8	2	17	Timothy Peters	Toyota/Red Horse Racing Toyota	146	Running
9	3	18	David Mayhew	Dollar General Toyota	146	Running
10	5	3	Ty Dillon #	Bass Pro Shops/Tracker Boats Chevrolet	146	Running
11	7	32	Miguel Paludo	Duroline Chevrolet	146	Running
12	9	29	Grant Enfinger	Reese Towpower Ram	146	Running
13	16	23	Jason White	GunBroker.com Ford	146	Running
14	19	09	John Wes Townley #	Zaxby's Toyota	146	Running
15	17	98	Travis Pastrana	AM/PM Toyota	146	Running
16	21	99	Bryan Silas #	Rockingham Speedway Ford	146	Running
17	18	5	Ryan Reed	Racehead.com-RyansMission.org Ford	145	Running
18	33	57	Norm Benning	Norm Benning Racing Chevrolet	135	Running
19	14	7	Parker Kligerman	Toyota/Red Horse Racing Toyota	126	Accident
20	8	6	Justin Lofton	Imperial Valley Full Plate Chevrolet	114	Accident
21	11	13	Johnny Sauter	SealMaster Toyota	114	Accident
22	24	39	Ryan Sieg	RSS Racing Chevrolet	111	Alternator
23	22	14	Brennan Newberry	NTS Chevrolet	102	Accident
24	32	65	Chris Lafferty	Superseal Construction Products Chevrolet	27	Accident
25	23	08	Ross Chastain #	SC Watermelon Association Toyota	26	Suspension
26	28	27	Travis Miller	Hillman Racing Chevrolet	23	Overheating
27	20	9	Ron Hornaday Jr.	Smokey Mountain Herbal Snuff Chevrolet	20	Engine
28	30	10	Jennifer Jo Cobb	Horejsh Graphics Ram	19	Clutch
29	34	84	Chris Fontaine	Glenden Enterprise Chevrolet	13	Transmission
30	25	07	Johnny Chapman	Wear Your Gear/Bobber.info Toyota	11	Rear Gear
31	27	93	Dennis Setzer	RSS Racing Chevrolet	7	Vibration
32	26	25	B J McLeod	Boggy Creek Air Boat Rides Chevrolet	5	Overheating
33	29	38	Chris Jones	RSS Racing Chevrolet	4	Vibration
34	31	200	Clay Greenfield	Obregon Construction Ford	3	Overheating

Sunoco Rookie of the Year Contender.

RACE COMMENTS: Before an estimated crowd of 24,000, Nelson Piquet Jr. won the Smith's 350, his second NASCAR Camping World Truck Series victory. Prior to the green flag, the following truck dropped to the rear of the field for the reason indicated: #10 (missed drivers meeting).

TIME OF RACE: 1 hours, 57 minutes, 15 seconds — AVERAGE SPEED: 112.068 mph — MARGIN OF VICTORY: 0.223 seconds — KEYSTONE LIGHT POLE AWARD: Joey Coulter (176.632 mph. 30.572 secs.) — CAUTION FLAGS: 8 cautions for 33 laps. — LAP LEADERS: 17 lead changes among 8 drivers. Coulter–pole, Peters 1–18, Coulter 19–33, Kligerman 34–35, Enfinger 36, Kligerman 37–70, Piquet Jr. 71–76, Coulter 77, Dillon 78–80, Coulter 81–103, Dillon 104–105, Mayhew 106, Piquet Jr. 107–124, Crafton 125, Piquet Jr. 126–130, Coulter 131, Crafton 132–145, Piquet Jr. 146.

18 FRED'S 250 *powered by* COCA-COLA

October 6, 2012 — Talladega Superspeedway — 94 Laps – 250.04 Miles

Fin	Str	No	Driver	Team	Laps	Status
1	9	7	Parker Kligerman	Toyota/Red Horse Racing Toyota	94	Running
2	29	13	Johnny Sauter	Hot Honey's/Curb Records Toyota	94	Running
3	3	31	James Buescher	TMS Chevrolet	94	Running
4	1	3	Ty Dillon #	Bass Pro Shops/Tracker Boats Chevrolet	94	Running
5	8	17	Timothy Peters	Toyota/Red Horse Racing Toyota	94	Running
6	19	29	Ryan Blaney	DrawTite/Mopar Ram	94	Running
7	6	18	Kurt Busch	Dollar General Toyota	94	Running
8	23	51	German Quiroga Jr.	NET10 Wireless Toyota	94	Running
9	16	2	Tim George Jr.	Applebee's Chevrolet	94	Running
10	5	33	Cale Gale #	Rheem Chasing the Cure Chevrolet	94	Running
11	32	39	Ryan Sieg	Pull-A-Part Used Auto Parts Chevrolet	94	Running
12	15	99	Bryan Silas #	Rockingham Speedway Ford	94	Running
13	27	27	Cole Whitt	LittleJoesAutos.com Chevrolet	94	Running
14	11	22	Joey Coulter	Husky Liners Chevrolet	94	Running
15	31	57	Norm Benning	Norm Benning Racing Chevrolet	94	Running
16	22	68	Clay Greenfield	TitanTool.com Ram	94	Running
17	30	76	Ryan Hackett	J & R Supply Ford	94	Running
18	25	88	Matt Crafton	Goof Off/Menards Toyota	94	Running
19	21	32	Miguel Paludo	Duroline Chevrolet	94	Running
20	2	23	Jason White	GunBroker.com Ford	94	Running
21	35	93	Chris Jones	RSS Racing Chevrolet	94	Running
22	17	81	David Starr	Zachry Toyota	93	Accident
23	20	20	Rick Crawford	BRG Motorsport /Lilly Trucking Toyota	93	Accident
24	13	6	Justin Lofton	Lofton Cattle Chevrolet	93	Accident
25	18	09	John Wes Townley #	Zaxby's Toyota	93	Running
26	4	5	Aric Almirola	Jordan Truck Sales Ford	91	Running
27	36	10	Jennifer Jo Cobb	Driven2Honor.org/KOMA Unwind Ram	90	Running
28	10	9	Ron Hornaday Jr.	Anderson's Pure Maple Syrup Chevrolet	90	Running
29	12	84	Chris Fontaine	Glenden Enterprises Toyota	61	Accident
30	24	1	Donnie Neuenberger	Eagle Convenience Stores Chevrolet	59	Accident
31	14	30	Nelson Piquet Jr.	Alpinestars/Breast Cancer Awareness Chevrolet	59	Accident
32	34	07	Johnny Chapman	Wear Your Gear/Bobber.info Toyota	47	Accident
33	7	11	Todd Bodine	Toyota Care Toyota	46	Accident
34	33	08	Ross Chastain #	Melon 1 Toyota	45	Accident
35	26	74	Mike Harmon	Mike Harmon Racing Chevrolet	33	Fuel Pump
36	28	25	Brandon Knupp	Hillman Racing Chevrolet	2	Overheating

Sunoco Rookie of the Year Contender.

RACE COMMENTS: Before an estimated crowd of 43,000, Parker Kligerman won the Fred's 250 Powered by Coca-Cola, his first NASCAR Camping World Truck Series victory. Prior to the green flag, the following trucks dropped to the rear of the field for the reason indicated: #25 and 57 (unapproved adjustments).

TIME OF RACE: 1 hours, 56 minutes, 26 seconds — AVERAGE SPEED: 128.85 mph — MARGIN OF VICTORY: Under Caution — KEYSTONE POLE AWARD: Ty Dillon (177.291 mph. 54.013 secs.) — CAUTION FLAGS: 7 cautions for 26 laps — LAP LEADERS: 19 lead changes among 13 drivers. Dillon 1–8, White 9–10, Almirola 11–15, Neuenberger 16, Dillon 17–18, Almirola 19–21, Buescher 22–32, Chapman 33–34, Dillon 35–46, Neuenberger 47, Crafton 48, Dillon 49–51, Peters 52–53, K. Busch 54–55, Blaney 56–58, Sauter 59–61, Lofton 62–81, White 82–90, Buescher 91–92, Kligerman 93–94.

19 KROGER 200

October 27, 2012 — MARTINSVILLE SPEEDWAY — 200 Laps – 105.2 Miles

Fin	Str	No	Driver	Team	Laps	Status
1	5	51	Denny Hamlin	Toyota Toyota	200	Running
2	4	30	Nelson Piquet Jr.	Qualcomm/Bell Helmets Chevrolet	200	Running
3	15	22	Joey Coulter	RCR/Darrell Gwynn Foundation Chevrolet	200	Running
4	7	88	Matt Crafton	Zecol/Menards Toyota	200	Running
5	23	92	Scott Riggs	FleetHQ.com/BTS Tire & Wheel/QMI Chevrolet	200	Running
6	10	31	James Buescher	Great Clips Chevrolet	200	Running
7	1	17	Timothy Peters	Toyota/Strutmasters.com Toyota	200	Running
8	11	29	Ryan Blaney	DrawTite/Mopar Ram	200	Running
9	13	7	Parker Kligerman	Toyota/Camp Horsin' Around Toyota	200	Running
10	3	18	Brian Scott	Shore Lodge Toyota	200	Running
11	21	8	Max Gresham #	Made in USA Brand Chevrolet	200	Running
12	2	2	Kevin Harvick	Tide Pods Chevrolet	200	Running
13	27	23	Jason White	Grime Boss Ford	200	Running
14	8	13	Johnny Sauter	SealMaster/Curb Records Toyota	200	Running
15	20	32	Miguel Paludo	Duroline Chevrolet	200	Running
16	19	81	David Starr	Zachry Toyota	200	Running
17	24	5	Josh Richards	BulletLiner.com Ford	200	Running
18	26	09	John Wes Townley #	Romney-Ryan Toyota	200	Running
19	14	6	Justin Lofton	Lofton Cattle Chevrolet	200	Running
20	36	60	Peyton Sellers	St. Lawrence Radiology/N Fab Chevrolet	199	Running
21	9	07	Jeff Agnew	Mark 4 Suzuki Chevrolet	199	Running
22	12	11	Todd Bodine	Toyota Care Toyota	198	Running
23	31	08	Ross Chastain #	JDI Racing Toyota	198	Running
24	29	75	Caleb Holman #	Food Country USA/Sunset Farm Foods Chevrolet	198	Running
25	30	68	Clay Greenfield	Star Road/Guard Ram	198	Running
26	28	39	Ryan Sieg	Pull-A-Part Used Auto Parts Chevrolet	197	Running
27	33	93	Tim George Jr.	Applebee's Chevrolet	197	Running
28	6	3	Ty Dillon #	Bass Pro Shops/Tracker Boats Chevrolet	194	Running
29	32	99	Bryan Silas #	Rockingham Speedway Ford	193	Running
30	25	02	Tyler Young	Randco Industries Chevrolet	189	Running
31	35	57	Norm Benning	Norm Benning Racing Chevrolet	188	Running
32	17	27	Ryan Truex	The Classic at The Rock Chevrolet	158	Transmission
33	16	9	Ron Hornaday Jr.	AMFMEnergy.com/Armour/AKL Insurance Chev	136	Oil Pump
34	18	35	Matt Merrell	Win-Tron Racing/Merrell Lease Service Chevrolet	35	Transmission
35	22	33	Cale Gale #	Rheem Chasing the Cure Chevrolet	7	Transmission
36	34	84	Chris Fontaine	Glenden Enterprises Chevrolet	5	Clutch

Sunoco Rookie of the Year Contender.

RACE COMMENTS: Before an estimated crowd of 18,000, Denny Hamlin won the Kroger 200, his second NASCAR Camping World Truck Series victory. Prior to the green flag, the following trucks dropped to the rear of the field for the reason indicated: #51, 99, 39 (missing drivers meeting).

TIME OF RACE: 1 hour, 30 minutes, 43 seconds— AVERAGE SPEED: 69.579 mph — MARGIN OF VICTORY: 1.932 seconds — KEYSTONE LIGHT POLE AWARD: Timothy Peters (96.411 mph. 19.641 secs.) — CAUTION FLAGS: 7 cautions for 40 laps. — LAP LEADERS: 7 lead changes among 5 drivers. Peters 1–58, Harvick 59–94, Sauter 95, Harvick 96–151, Peters 152, Harvick 153–161, Crafton 162–194, Hamlin 195-200.

20 WINSTAR WORLD CASINO 350

November 2, 2012 — TEXAS MOTOR SPEEDWAY — 147 Laps – 350 Miles

Fin	Str	No	Driver	Team	Laps	Status
1	13	13	Johnny Sauter	SealMaster/Curb Records Toyota	147	Running
2	10	7	Parker Kligerman	Toyota/Camp Horsin' Around/Toyota	147	Running
3	1	30	Nelson Piquet Jr.	TAG Heuer Avant-Garde Eyewear Chevrolet	147	Running
4	3	18	Kyle Busch	Dollar General Toyota	147	Running
5	9	3	Ty Dillon #	Bass Pro Shops/Tracker Boats Chevrolet	147	Running
6	11	88	Matt Crafton	Menards/Tough Built Toyota	147	Running
7	5	22	Joey Coulter	OneMain Financial Chevrolet	147	Running
8	19	11	Todd Bodine	Toyota Care Toyota	147	Running
9	7	5	Aric Almirola	Rimrock Design Ford	147	Running
10	14	17	Timothy Peters	Toyota/Red Horse Racing Toyota	147	Running
11	2	31	James Buescher	Great Clips Chevrolet	147	Running
12	21	8	Max Gresham #	Made in USA Brand Chevrolet	146	Running
13	18	39	Ryan Sieg	Pull-A-Part, LLC Chevrolet	146	Running
14	4	32	Miguel Paludo	No.32 World Diabetes Day/Duroline Chevrolet	146	Running
15	12	33	Cale Gale #	Ruud Chevrolet	146	Running
16	8	09	John Wes Townley #	Zaxby's Toyota	146	Running
17	15	2	Brendan Gaughan	South Point Chevrolet	146	Running
18	17	4	Brandon McReynolds	Wolf Pack Rentals Chevrolet	146	Running
19	20	23	Jason White	Grime Boss/GunBroker.com Ford	146	Running
20	22	9	Ron Hornaday Jr.	SmokeyMtn.HerbalSnuff/SWMGunRunner Chev.	145	Running
21	27	81	David Starr	Zachry Toyota	145	Running
22	23	6	Justin Lofton	Lofton Cattle Chevrolet	145	Running
23	25	99	Bryan Silas #	Rockingham Speedway Ford	144	Running
24	6	19	David Mayhew	MMI/Steak & Grape Ram	144	Running
25	26	07	Jeff Agnew	Mark 4 Suzuki Chevrolet	142	Running
26	34	57	Norm Benning	riveteyelet.com Chevrolet	136	Running
27	36	10	Jennifer Jo Cobb	Driven2Honor.org Ram	69	Rear Axle
28	24	51	German Quiroga Jr.	NET10 Wireless Toyota	64	Engine
29	35	84	Russ Dugger	Vacuworx/JPO Absorbents Chevrolet	37	Rear Gear
30	16	29	Ryan Blaney	Cooper Standard Ram	31	Accident
31	31	08	Ross Chastain #	Wear Your Gear/Bobber.info Toyota	26	Suspension
32	33	27	Stephen Leicht	Chevrolet	15	Brakes
33	29	25	B J McLeod	Boggy Creek Air Boat Rides Chevrolet	9	Brakes
34	30	74	Scott Riggs	Koma Unwind Chevrolet	8	Rear Gear
35	32	93	Dennis Setzer	RSS Racing Chevrolet	6	Vibration
36	28	38	Chris Jones	RSS Racing Chevrolet	3	Vibration

Sunoco Rookie of the Year Contender.

RACE COMMENTS: Before an estimated crowd of 55,000, Johnny Sauter won the WinStar World Casino 350, his sixth NASCAR Camping World Truck Series victory. Prior to the green flag, the following trucks dropped to the rear for the reasons indicated: #9 (unapproved adjustments); #27 (missed drivers meeting).

TIME OF RACE: 1 hours, 25 minutes, 30 seconds — AVERAGE SPEED: 154.737 mph — MARGIN OF VICTORY: 2.199 seconds — KEYSTONE LIGHT POLE AWARD: Nelson Piquet Jr. (180.246 mph. 29.959 secs.) — CAUTION FLAGS: 2 cautions for 8 laps. — LAP LEADERS: 10 lead changes among 9 drivers. Piquet Jr. 1-35, Buescher 36-66, Gale 67-69, Piquet Jr. 70-99, Sauter 100-116, Crafton 117, Dillon 118, Paludo 119, White 120, Kligerman 121-136, Sauter 137-147.

21 LUCAS OIL 150

November 9, 2012 — Phoenix International Raceway — 150 Laps – 150 Miles

Fin	Str	No	Driver	Team	Laps	Status
1	3	18	Brian Scott	Dollar General Toyota	153	Running
2	6	4	Kyle Larson	Ganassi Earnhardt Racing Chevrolet	153	Running
3	17	22	Joey Coulter	American Eurocopter Chevrolet	153	Running
4	8	17	Timothy Peters	Toyota /Red Horse Racing Toyota	153	Running
5	2	29	Ryan Blaney	DrawTite/Mopar Ram	153	Running
6	14	39	Ryan Sieg	RSS Racing Chevrolet	153	Running
7	4	33	Cale Gale #	Rheem Heating, Cooling & Water Heating Chevrolet	153	Running
8	1	30	Nelson Piquet Jr.	Qualcomm/Autotrac Chevrolet	153	Running
9	11	27	Ryan Truex	LittleJoesAutos.com Chevrolet	153	Running
10	22	6	Justin Lofton	Lofton Cattle Chevrolet	153	Running
11	23	35	Matt Merrell	Merrell Lease Service Chevrolet	153	Running
12	13	19	David Mayhew	MMI/Steak & Grape Ram	153	Running
13	27	09	John Wes Townley #	Zaxby's Toyota	153	Running
14	15	32	Miguel Paludo	World Diabetes Day/Duroline Chevrolet	152	Running
15	21	3	Ty Dillon #	Bass Pro Shops/Tracker Boats Chevrolet	152	Running
16	32	99	Bryan Silas #	Rockingham Speedway Ford	152	Running
17	9	31	James Buescher	Exide Chevrolet	152	Running
18	33	08	Todd Peck	Stopain Cold/Arthritis Foundation Chevrolet	149	Running
19	34	57	Norm Benning	NormBenningRacing.com Chevrolet	148	Running
20	5	88	Matt Crafton	Fisher Nuts/Menards Toyota	144	Running
21	26	23	Jason White	GunBroker.com/Grime Boss Ford	136	Accident
22	10	9	Ron Hornaday Jr.	Anderson's Pure Maple Syrup/Bashas' Chevrolet	111	Running
23	19	2	Brendan Gaughan	South Point Hotel & Casino Chevrolet	109	Accident
24	18	51	German Quiroga Jr.	NET10 Wireless Toyota	109	Accident
25	16	13	Johnny Sauter	SealMaster/Curb Records Toyota	104	Running
26	30	74	Brian Weber	Koma Unwind Chevrolet	95	Rear Gear
27	7	7	Parker Kligerman	Toyota/Red Horse Racing Toyota	78	Accident
28	12	11	Todd Bodine	Toyota Care Toyota	48	Accident
29	36	5	John King	Fairway Frd Ford	43	Accident
30	20	97	Jeff Choquette	Adrian Carriers/Liz Girl Logistics Chevrolet	34	Accident
31	24	25	Stephen Leicht	Boggy Creek Air Boat Rides Chevrolet	22	Brakes
32	31	93	Dennis Setzer	RSS Racing Chevrolet	8	Brakes
33	25	07	Ross Chastain #	Watermelon.org Chevrolet	7	Ignition
34	35	84	Chris Fontaine	Glenden Enterprises Chevrolet	6	Brakes
35	28	38	Chris Jones	RSS Racing Chevrolet	4	Ignition
36	29	0	Blake Koch	Kmoa Unwind Ford	2	Suspension

Sunoco Rookie of the Year Contender.

RACE COMMENTS: Before an estimated crowd of 29,000 Brian Scott won the Lucas Oil 150, his second NASCAR Camping World Truck Series victory. Prior to the green flag, the following trucks dropped to the rear for the reasons indicated: #74 (driver change).

TIME OF RACE: 1 hours, 44 minutes, 49 seconds — AVERAGE SPEED:87.581 mph — MARGIN OF VICTORY:0.666 seconds — KEYSTONE LIGHT POLE AWARD: Nelson Piquet Jr. (134.439 mph. 26.778 secs.) — CAUTION FLAGS: 9 cautions for 46 laps — LAP LEADERS: 8 lead changes among 7 drivers. Piquet Jr. 1–8, Scott 9–53, Dillon 54–74, Scott 75, Truex 76–97, Lofton 98–105, Peters 106–108, Larson 109–151, Scott 152–153.

22 FORD ECOBOOST 200

November 16, 2012 — Homestead-Miami Speedway — 134 Laps – 201 Miles

Fin	Str	No	Driver	Team	Laps	Status
1	5	33	Cale Gale #	Rheem Chevrolet	140	Running
2	6	18	Kyle Busch	Dollar General Toyota 1	40	Running
3	11	22	Joey Coulter	Rip-It Chevrolet	140	Running
4	4	30	Nelson Piquet Jr.	flalottery.com Chevrolet	140	Running
5	7	32	Miguel Paludo	Duroline Brakes & Components Chevrolet	140	Running
6	10	13	Johnny Sauter	SealMaster/Curb Records Toyota	140	Running
7	1	7	Parker Kligerman	Toyota Toyota	140	Running
14	17		Timothy Peters	Toyota Toyota	140	Running
9	12	6	Justin Lofton	Mercury Chevrolet	140	Running
10	18	08	Ross Chastain #	Custom Cooling Toyota	140	Running
11	19	11	Todd Bodine	Toyota Tundra Endeavour Toyota	140	Running
12	9	88	Matt Crafton	Menards/IdealDoor Toyota	140	Running
13	17	31	James Buescher	Great Clips Chevrolet	140	Running
14	21	39	Ryan Sieg	Pull-A-Part, LLC Chevrolet	140	Running
15	28	51	German Quiroga Jr.	NET10 Wireless Toyota	139	Running
16	29	81	David Starr	Zachry Toyota	139	Running
17	22	23	Jason White	Gunbroker.com Ford	139	Running
18	30	2	Tim George Jr.	Appelbee's Chevrolet	139	Running
19	25	27	Jason Leffler	Sandy NJ Relief Fund Chevrolet	138	Running
20	8	9	Ron Hornaday Jr.	Smokey Mountain Herbal Snuff Chevrolet	138	Running
21	24	84	Mario Gosselin	Carport Empire/ProBuilt Chevrolet	138	Running
22	20	01	Jake Crum	Bandit Chippers Chevrolet	137	Running
23	13	8	Max Gresham #	Made In USA Brand Chevrolet	137	Running
24	26	07	Jeff Agnew	Wear Your Gear/Bobber.info Chevrolet	136	Running
25	3	3	Ty Dillon #	Bass Pro Shops/Tracker Boats Chevrolet	135	Running
26	36	25	Travis Miller	LittleJoesAutos.com Chevrolet	135	Running
27	2	4	Kyle Larson	Earnhardt Ganassi Racing Chevrolet	131	Accident
28	16	29	Ryan Blaney	Cooper Standard Ram	131	Accident
29	35	57	Norm Benning	Gardner Motor Group Chevrolet	131	Running
30	34	93	Ryan Lynch	BlankHood.com Chevrolet	130	Running
31	32	10	Jennifer Jo Cobb	Franky & Louie's Ram	129	Running
32	15	09	John Wes Townley #	Zaxby's Toyota	118	Running
33	33	99	Bryan Silas #	Rockingham Speedway Ford	43	Accident
34	23	20	Dusty Davis	SpeedyPolish/ThunderExhst/MilleniumVIP Toyota	28	Clutch
35	27	38	Chris Jones	RSS Racing Chevrolet	10	Brakes
36	31	0	Blake Koch	Driven2Honor.org Ford	3	Transmission

Sunoco Rookie of the Year Contender.

RACE COMMENTS: Before an estimated crowd of 23,000, Cale Gale won the Ford EcoBoost 200, his first NASCAR Camping World Truck Series victory.

TIME OF RACE: 1 hours, 43 minutes, 47 seconds — AVERAGE SPEED: 121.407 mph — MARGIN OF VICTORY: 0.014 seconds — KEYSTONE LIGHT POLE AWARD: Parker Kligerman (168.824 mph. 31.986 secs.) — CAUTION FLAGS: 5 cautions for 23 laps — LAP LEADERS: 11 lead changes among 7 drivers. Kligerman 1–5, Piquet Jr. 6–37, K. Busch 38–50, Larson 51–86, K. Busch 87, Piquet Jr. 88, Sauter 89, Bodine 90–93, Larson 94–105, Sauter 106–108, K. Busch 109–139, Gale 140.

NASCAR
HOME TRACKS 2012 REVIEW

UNOH
BATTLE AT THE BEACH

Short Track Stars to Light Up Daytona; Speedweeks 2013 to Include UNOH Battle at the Beach.

The bright lights of the "World Center of Racing" will shine on the stars of NASCAR's regional and touring series, as NASCAR announced Daytona International Speedway will host the inaugural UNOH Battle at the Beach on February 18–19, 2013.

The two-days of racing will be headlined by three non-points special events: the NASCAR K&N Pro Series, NASCAR Whelen Modified Tours, and the Late Model division of the NASCAR Whelen All-American Series.

A temporary oval will be set up on Daytona's Superstretch to host the races. It is tentatively slated to be approximately .4-mile.

"This is all about the stars of tomorrow vying for glory at Daytona International Speedway," said George Silbermann, NASCAR vice president of regional and touring series. "During two days and nights of intense competition, fans will be able to see today's aces of short track racing and some great young talent."

The event will include live television coverage on Speed.

The process for setting the field for the 2013 UNOH Battle At The Beach will be:

- Winners of 2012 NASCAR K&N Pro Series East and West events as well as the series champions will automatically be locked into that series' race at Daytona next year.
- Similarly, winners of 2012 NASCAR Whelen Modified Tour or NASCAR Whelen Southern Modified Tour

races and series champions will be locked into the Modified race next February at Daytona.

- The top 10 finishers in the 2012 NASCAR Whelen All-American Series Division I national standings will earn a starting spot in the 2013 Late Model race.
- In addition, the champions of the NASCAR Canadian Tire Series, NASCAR Toyota Series from Mexico, and Euro Racecar NASCAR Touring Series in 2012 will earn a protected starting spot in whichever one of the three 2013 Daytona races they choose to run.

- The remaining spots in the 2013 Daytona features will be filled through heat races during the two days of racing next February.

"Grassroots short track racing is the foundation of this great sport and we are thrilled to give these young drivers the opportunity to fight for a win at the 'World Center of Racing,'" said Daytona International Speedway President Joie Chitwood. "Many of NASCAR's greatest stars cut their teeth on short tracks around the country and we look forward to hosting the stars of tomorrow in 2013."

Chitwood also announced that Daytona has reached an agreement with a number of area hotels to secure special room rates for the event to make it more affordable for racers and fans to attend the UNOH Battle at the Beach.

Event entitlement sponsor, the University of Northwestern Ohio, has been heavily involved with NASCAR's grassroots racing programs. The school, which offers a degree in High Performance Motorsports, owns NASCAR-sanctioned Limaland Motorsports Park and is the sponsor of several NASCAR touring races.

KYLE LARSON

NASCAR K&N PRO SERIES EAST 2012 CHAMPION

E A S T

KYLE LARSON WON THE NASCAR K&N PRO SERIES EAST CHAMPIONSHIP IN HIS ROOKIE SEASON.

Kyle Larson's race to the NASCAR K&N Pro Series East championship proved to be historic for the sport as well as the 20-year-old, first-year driver. Larson not only became just the third competitor in series history to capture the championship as a true rookie, but he delivered Rev Racing and the Drive For Diversity initiative its first title at the NASCAR touring series level.

The most recent in a succession of open-wheel dirt racers to make the jump to NASCAR stock car racing, Larson found success right from the beginning, with a ninth-place finish at the challenging Bristol Motor Speedway in the season-opener. Through the rest of the 14-race season, the Elk Grove, CA, driver finished outside the top 10 just twice. His first top-five came in the third race of the campaign at

Richmond International Raceway and his first trip to Victory Lane was at the fast Gresham Motorsports Park half mile in his sixth K&N Pro Series East outing. After runner-up finishes at CNB Bank Raceway Park and the second K&N Pro Series combination race at Iowa Speedway, Larson captured his second checkered flag at New Hampshire Motor Speedway.

"I knew it was going to be a long-shot to win the championship," Larson said. "Every week after that, Brett (Moffitt) started having a lot of bad luck and Corey (LaJoie) and I started inching our way back into it. Then at the end, I guess I got a little lucky after the halfway point in the season."

He ascended to the points lead following a fifth-place effort at Dover International Speedway that moved him just a single tally ahead of Corey LaJoie with two races to go. Following a fourth-place finish at Greenville Pickens Speedway, Larson could clinch the title in the finale at Rockingham with a finish of sixth or better. With the help of some last-lap dramatics, Larson crossed the line sixth to secure the historic championship.

Not only did Larson have a championship-winning season, but he entered rare and elite company in his first year of K&N Pro

Series East competition. Larson joined Joey Logano and Ryan Truex as the only drivers in the 26-year history of the K&N Pro Series East to capture both the overall championship and the Sunoco Rookie of the Year honors in the same season.

"It's a really cool accomplishment, especially being my first year in stock cars," Larson said. "That's what makes it mean the most. Joey and Ryan were rookies and won the championship, but they had stock car experience. I'm a true rookie."

In a competitive class of rookies that numbered 46 in total, Larson waged a season-long battle for the first-year-driver title with Rev Racing teammate Bryan Ortiz. In the end Larson outdistanced Ortiz 114–107 in the standings with Jimmy Weller third at 65 points.

PERSONAL INFORMATION

Birth Date:	**July 31, 1992**
Hometown:	**Elk Grove, CA**
Marital Status:	**Single**
2012 Team:	**Rev Racing Toyota**
Car Owner:	**Max Siegel**
Crew Chief:	**Randy Goss**

CAREER RECORD

Year	Rank	Races	Wins	Poles	Top 5s	Top 10s
2012	1	14	2	1	8	12

NASCAR K&N PRO SERIES EAST
2012 CHAMPION KYLE LARSON SEASON RECORD

Date	Speedway	Location	Start	Finish	Status
March 17	Bristol Motor Speedway	Bristol, TN	6	9	Running
March 31	Greenville Pickens Speedway	Greenville, SC	2	17	Running
April 26	Richmond International Raceway	Richmond, VA	2	4	Running
May 19	Iowa Speedway	Newton, IA	5	6	Running
June 2	Bowman Gray Stadium	Winston-Salem, NC	1	5	Running
June 9	Gresham Motorsports Park	Jefferson, GA	4	1	Running
June 23	Langley Speedway	Hampton, VA	4	7	Running
July 14	CNB Bank Raceway Park	Clearfield, PA	6	2	Running
July 21	Columbus Motor Speedway	Columbus, OH	9	21	Running
Aug. 3	Iowa Speedway	Newton, IA	5	2	Running
Sept. 22	New Hampshire Motor Speedway	Loudon, NH	3	1	Running
Sept. 28	Dover International Speedway	Dover, DE	19	5	Running
Oct. 27	Greenville Pickens Speedway	Greenville, SC	2	4	Running
Nov. 3	Rockingham Speedway	Rockingham, NC	11	6	Running

COREY LAJOIE

It was a bittersweet year for Corey LaJoie, who turned in the best season of any driver in K&N Pro Series East history who did not win the championship. LaJoie rolled to a series-high five wins and 10 top fives across 14 races, but a late-season penalty stunted his title campaign.

BRETT MOFFITT

After finishing on the championship podium in each of his first three seasons, Brett Moffitt was half a mile away from his first title, but an accident on the last lap of the season finale at Rockingham dashed those hopes. Moffitt had wins at Richmond and Clearfield to go along with a series-high four poles.

CHASE ELLIOTT

Chase Elliott improved five positions in the final standings from his 2011 rookie campaign to his second season. The second-generation driver recorded his first career win at Iowa during the May combo race with the K&N Pro Series West. He also became the youngest pole winner in K&N Pro Series East history at Langley.

BRYAN ORTIZ

A sports car driver from Puerto Rico, Bryan Ortiz pushed his Rev Racing teammate, Kyle Larson, all season for the Sunoco Rookie of the Year title, and ended up second in the first-year driver standings by just seven points. Ortiz notched nine top-10 finishes as a true rookie, highlighted by a third-place effort at Bowman Gray.

NASCAR K&N PRO SERIES EAST 2012 TOP 50

Pos	Driver	Points	Starts	Wins	Top 5	Top 10
1	Kyle Larson *	536	14	2	8	12
2	Corey LaJoie	521	14	5	10	10
3	Brett Moffitt	512	14	2	8	10
4	Chase Elliott	500	14	1	6	9
5	Bryan Ortiz *	484	14	0	2	9
6	Eddie MacDonald	477	14	0	1	12
7	Darrell Wallace Jr.	470	14	1	6	7
8	Brandon Gdovic	470	14	0	4	9
9	Ben Kennedy	456	14	0	3	9
10	Sergio Pena	444	14	0	3	8
11	Ryan Gifford	413	14	0	2	3
12	Jimmy Weller *	412	14	0	0	2
13	Sam Hunt *	370	14	0	0	1
14	Jorge Arteaga *	333	13	0	0	2
15	Dylan Presnell *	279	11	0	0	2
16	Daniel Suarez	259	9	0	1	3
17	Travis Pastrana *	258	9	0	1	4
18	CJ Faison *	240	9	0	0	2
19	Cale Conley	235	9	1	3	4
20	Jesse Little *	210	7	0	2	2
21	Andrew Smith	205	7	0	1	2
22	Carlos Iaconelli *	179	8	0	0	0
23	Ryan Blaney *	146	5	0	2	2
24	Dale Quarterley	142	6	0	0	1
25	Harrison Rhodes *	134	5	0	1	2
26	Clay Campbell	133	5	0	0	0
27	Chad Boat	118	6	0	0	0
28	Enrique Contreras III *	111	4	0	0	0
29	John Salemi	111	5	0	0	0
30	Michael McGuire *	104	3	0	0	3
31	Dylan Kwasniewski	103	3	0	1	2
32	Chad Finchum *	96	4	0	0	1
33	Ali Jackson *	89	3	0	0	0
34	Akinori Ogata *	84	4	0	0	0
35	Jacob Wallace *	81	3	0	0	0
36	Scott Saunders *	79	3	0	0	0
37	Nelson Piquet Jr. *	75	2	1	1	1
38	Larry Barford Jr. *	72	3	0	0	0
39	Rafael Vallina *	70	3	0	0	0
40	Derek Ramstrom	69	2	0	1	1
41	Jorge Contreras Jr. *	69	3	0	0	0
42	Travis Miller *	59	2	0	0	0
43	Jeff Anton	57	2	0	0	0
44	Austin Hill *	55	2	0	0	0
45	Nicholas Sweet *	53	2	0	0	0
46	Chuck Buchanan	52	3	0	0	0
47	Tyler Reddick *	47	1	1	1	1
48	Stephen Nasse *	46	2	0	0	0
49	Steven Legendre *	45	3	0	0	0
50	Spencer Gallagher	43	2	0	0	0

* Denotes Sunoco Rookie of the Year Contender

NASCAR HOME TRACKS

NASCAR K&N PRO SERIES EAST COORS LIGHT POLE AWARD (1987-2012)

Year	Driver	Year	Driver	Year	Driver
1987	Billy Clark	1996	Andy Santerre	2005	Matt Kobyluck
1988	Kelly Moore	1997	Mike Stefanik	2006	Sean Caisse
1989	Joe Bessey	1998	Tom Carey	2007	Sean Caisse
1990	Ricky Craven	1999	Tom Carey	2008	Peyton Sellers
1991	Ricky Craven	2000	Tracy Gordon	2009	Matt DiBenedetto
1992	Kelly Moore	2001	Mike Olsen	2010	Brett Moffitt
1993	Robbie Crouch	2002	Martin Truex Jr.	2011	Max Gresham
1994	Tom Rosati	2003	Martin Truex Jr.	2012	Brett Moffitt
1995	Dave Dion	2004	Dave Dion		

NASCAR K&N PRO SERIES EAST SUNOCO ROOKIE OF THE YEAR (1988-2012)

Year	Driver	Year	Driver	Year	Driver
1988	Joe Bessey	1997	Tracy Gordon	2006	Ruben Pardo
1989	Ron Lamell	1998	Jeff Taylor	2007	Joey Logano
1990	Ricky Craven	1999	Mike Bruno	2008	Austin Dillon
1991	Tony Hirschman	2000	Mike Johnson	2009	Ryan Truex
1992	Curtis Markham	2001	Brian Hoar	2010	Darrell Wallace Jr.
1993	Andy Santerre	2002	Robbie Harrison	2011	Alex Bowman
1994	Jerry Marquis	2003	Ryan Moore	2012	Kyle Larson
1995	Brandon Butler	2004	Ryan Seaman		
1996	Brad Leighton	2005	Sean Caisse		

NASCAR K&N PRO SERIES EAST MOST POPULAR DRIVER (1987-2012)

Year	Driver	Year	Driver	Year	Driver
1987	Chuck Bown,	1996	Brandon Butler	2005	Andy Santerre
1988	Dick McCabe	1997	Mike Stefanik	2006	Matt Kobyluck
1989	Jamie Aube	1998	Tom Carey	2007	Jeffrey Earnhardt
1990	Ricky Craven	1999	Dave Dion	2008	Ricky Carmichael
1991	Ricky Craven	2000	Brad Leighton	2009	Steve Park
1992	Mike McLaughlin	2001	Mike Olsen	2010	Ryan Truex
1993	Mike McLaughlin	2002	Andy Santerre	2011	Chase Elliott
1994	Andy Santerre	2003	Andy Santerre	2012	Chase Elliott
1995	Mike Stefanik	2004	Mike Stefanik		

NASCAR K&N PRO SERIES EAST CAREER WINS (1987-2012)

Driver	Wins	Driver	Wins	Driver	Wins	Driver	Wins
Kelly Moore	27	Sean Caisse	7	Larry Caron	2	Kip Stockwell	1
Brad Leighton	24	Dale Quarterley	6	Billy Clark	2	Rick Fuller	1
Andy Santerre	23	Mike Olsen	6	Pete Silva	2	Kim Baker	1
Dale Shaw	19	Eddie MacDonald	6	Ryan Moore	2	Dennis Demers	1
Matt Kobyluck	16	Darrell Wallace Jr.	6	Kyle Larson	2	Denny Doyle	1
Bobby Dragon	14	Bryan Wall	5	Bruce Haley	1	Joey McCarthy	1
Ricky Craven	13	Martin Truex Jr.	5	Mike Weeden	1	Brian Hoar	1
Dave Dion	13	Joey Logano	5	Tommy Houston	1	Bryon Chew	1
Tracy Gordon	12	Ryan Truex	5	Ralph Nason	1	Tim Andrews	1
Mike Stefanik	12	Corey LaJoie	5	Rick Martin	1	Ruben Pardo	1
Ted Christopher	10	Stub Fadden	4	Ken Bouchard	1	Rogelio Lopez	1
Jamie Aube	9	Butch Leitzinger	4	Bobby Gada	1	Austin Dillon	1
Brett Moffitt	9	Brian Ickler	4	Tony Hirschman	1	Trevor Bayne	1
Joe Bessey	8	Max Gresham	4	Brian Ross	1	Aric Almirola	1
Robbie Crouch	8	Joey Kourafas	3	Ken Schrader	1	Peyton Sellers	1
Dick McCabe	8	Steve Park	3	John Preston	1	Kyle Busch	1
Mike Rowe	8	Matt DiBenedetto	3	Martin Truex Sr.	1	Andrew Ranger	1
Jerry Marquis	7	Sergio Peña	3	Glenn Sullivan	1	Ty Dillon	1
Mike McLaughlin	7	Chuck Bown	2	Keith Lamell	1	Nelson Piquet Jr.	1
Tom Carey	7	Jimmy Spencer	2	Tom Rosati	1	Chase Elliott	1
Mike Johnson	7	Tom Bolles	2	Jeff Fuller	1	Cale Conley	1
						Tyler Reddick	1

NASCAR K&N PRO SERIES EAST CHAMPS AND LEADERS (1987-2012)

1987
Joey Kourafas	2530
Chuck Bown	2525
Bobby Dragon	2459
Kelly Moore	2406
Billy Clark	2280
Dick McCabe	2228
Mike Weeden	2221
Dale Shaw	1998
Larry Caron	1904
Bob Healey	1857

1988
Jamie Aube	2752
Dick McCabe	2716
Dale Shaw	2689
Chuck Bown	2575
Kelly Moore	2569
Joe Bessey	2251
Stub Fadden	2231
Jimmy Burns	2120
Pete Silva	2117
Larry Caron	2086

1989
Jamie Aube	2382
Kelly Moore	2355
Billy Clark	2316
Dana Patten	2306
Joey Kourafas	2214
Dick McCabe	2172
Ron Lamell	2070
Dave Davis	2049
Joe Bessey	2018
Bruce Haley	1986

1990
Jamie Aube	2097
Mike Rowe	1954
Ricky Craven	1942
Joey Kourafas	1936
Billy Clark	1868
Kelly Moore	1828
Mike Weeden	1785
Bruce Haley	1773
Dick McCabe	1710
Ron Lamell	1671

1991
Ricky Craven	2728
Dick McCabe	2459
Billy Clark	2350
Jamie Aube	2306
Kelly Moore	2303
Joey Kourafas	2257
Tony Hirschman	2241
Stub Fadden	2206
Mike Rowe	2189
Dale Shaw	2098

1992
Dick McCabe	1988
Joe Bessey	1982
Kelly Moore	1958
Mike McLaughlin	1955
Stub Fadden	1795
Curtis Markham	1787
Babe Branscombe	1676
Tony Hirschman	1675
Bobby Dragon	1654
Dale Shaw	1637

1993
Dick McCabe	2466
Kelly Moore	2409
Mike McLaughlin	2349
Curtis Markham	2260
Bob Dragon	2239
Jamie Aube	2145
Stub Fadden	2115
Robbie Crouch	2112
Robbie Crouch	1991
Andy Santerre	1973

1994
Dale Shaw	2613
Kelly Moore	2463
Andy Santerre	2412
Dick McCabe	2389
Bobby Dragon	2380
Stub Fadden	2302
Martin Truex Sr	2296
Tom Bolles	2210
Tom Rosati	2199
Robbie Crouch	2133

1995
Kelly Moore	2730
Mike Stefanik	2621
Andy Santerre	2583
Dave Dion	2505
Tom Bolles	2493
Robbie Crouch	2444
Jerry Marquis	2383
Dale Shaw	2369
Brian Ross	2360
Stub Fadden	2336

1996
Dave Dion	2803
Andy Santerre	2687
Dale Shaw	2654
Kelly Moore	2637
Brad Leighton	2596
Mike Stefanik	2523
Robbie Crouch	2415
Tom Bolles	2380
Brandon Butler	2321
Stub Fadden	2243

1997
Mike Stefanik	3033
Jerry Marquis	2968
Dave Dion	2941
Andy Santerre	2879
Brad Leighton	2873
Kelly Moore	2686
Bobby Dragon	2658
Tom Bolles	2622
Mike Olsen	2558
Stub Fadden	2404

1998
Mike Stefanik	2554
Brad Leighton	2383
Kelly Moore	2265
Jerry Marquis	2245
Tom Carey	2227
Bryan Wall	2198
Tracy Gordon	2191
Dave Dion	2142
Mike Olsen	2061
Martin Truex Jr.	1988

NASCAR HOME TRACKS

1999

Brad Leighton	2805
Tracy Gordon	2637
David Dion	2497
Mike Olsen	2424
Tom Carey Jr.	2415
Bryan Wall	2342
Kelly Moore	2315
Dennis Demers	2200
Jamie Aube	2135
Dennis Doyle	2093

2000

Brad Leighton	2697
Dale Shaw	2478
Tracy Gordon	2462
Dave Dion	2395
Mike Olsen	2376
Bryan Wall	2307
Dennis Demers	2261
Mike Johnson	2211
Jamie Aube	2073
Bobby Dragon	2030

2001

Mike Olsen	3031
Mike Johnson	2819
Dale Shaw	2771
Bryan Wall	2770
Dale Quarterley	2765
Kelly Moore	2758
Tracy Gordon	2647
Martin Truex Jr.	2630
Brad Leighton	2590
Dennis Demers	2563

2002

Andy Santerre	2844
Matt Kobyluck	2835
Brad Leighton	2808
Kelly Moore	2668
Tracy Gordon	2612
Dale Quarterley	2566
Dale Shaw	2528
Mike Johnson	2491
Greg Schaefer	2465
Mike Olsen	2446

2003

Andy Santerre	2652
Mike Stefanik	2446
Mike Johnson	2390
Brian Hoar	2386
Kelly Moore	2381
Joey McCarthy	2358
Dale Quarterley	2349
Eddie MacDonald	2297
Mike Olsen	2271
Matt Kobyluck	2233

2004

Andy Santerre	2139
Mike Olsen	1933
Dale Quarterley	1908
Kelly Moore	1833
Mike Stefanik	1824
Ryan Moore	1800
Matt Kobyluck	1781
Joey McCarthy	1737
Mike Johnson	1721
Brian Hoar	1696

2005

Andy Santerre	2120
Mike Stefanik	2078
Matt Kobyluck	1980
Mike Olsen	1933
Ryan Moore	1859
Bryon Chew	1737
Sean Caisse	1682
Brian Hoar	1666
Eddie MacDonald	1647
Mike Johnson	1621

2006

Mike Olsen	1823
Sean Caisse	1699
Bryon Chew	1656
Brian Hoar	1656
Matt Kobyluck	1551
Joey McCarthy	1458
Mike Johnson	1437
Ruben Pardo	1390
Jeff Anton	1353
Chas Lewandowski	1319

2007

Joey Logano	2123
Sean Caisse	1957
Peyton Sellers	1862
Matt Kobyluck	1840
Jeffrey Earnhardt	1736
Mike Olsen	1721
Rogelio Lopez	1671
Jamie Hayes	1661
Marc Davis	1654
Jeff Anton	1630

2008

Matt Kobyluck	2226
Austin Dillon	1916
Jesus Hernandez	1857
Trevor Bayne	1855
Marc Davis	1812
Ricky Carmichael	1745
Eddie MacDonald	1733
Peyton Sellers	1732
Steve Park	1727
Brian Ickler	1644

2009

Ryan Truex	1719
Eddie MacDonald	1685
Brett Moffitt	1625
Jody Lavender	1587
Steve Park	1571
Matt Kobyluck	1567
Alan Tardiff	1416
Dustin Delaney	1395
Ryan Duff	1384
Alex Kennedy	1324

2010

Ryan Truex	1662
Brett Moffitt	1528
Darrell Wallace Jr.	1467
Cole Whitt	1420
Eddie MacDonald	1368
DJ Shaw	1318
Kevin Swindell	1305
Max Gresham	1303
Ryan Gifford	1290
Matt Kobyluck	1290

2011

Max Gresham	1937
Darrell Wallace Jr.	1871
Brett Moffitt	1851
Matt DiBenedetto	1741
Sergio Peña	1657
Alex Bowman	1642
Eddie MacDonald	1636
Corey LaJoie	1548
Chase Elliott	1510
Ryan Gifford	1509

2012

Kyle Larson	536
Corey LaJoie	521
Brett Moffitt	512
Chase Elliott	500
Bryan Ortiz	484
Eddie MacDonald	477
Darrell Wallace Jr.	470
Brandon Gdovic	470
Ben Kennedy	456
Sergio Peña	444

NASCAR K&N PRO SERIES EAST 2012 RACE RESULTS

1 BRISTOL MOTOR SPEEDWAY 03/17/2012

Fin	Str	Driver	Team	Laps	Status
1	1	Nelson Piquet Jr.	Fox Sports Toyota	127	Running
2	9	Ryan Blaney *	Widow Wax/SealWrap/Heavy Duty Toyota	127	Running
3	7	Ryan Gifford	Universal Technical Institute/NTI Toyota	127	Running
4	13	Andrew Smith	SavannahPawn.com Chevrolet	127	Running
5	3	Derek Ramstrom	Matthews Truck Service/Titech Chevrolet	127	Running
6	12	Ben Kennedy	Emco Gears/Mac Tools Chevrolet	127	Running
7	25	Chad Finchum *	Texas Roadhouse/Spraker Racing Toyota	127	Running
8	4	Michael McGuire *	Wood's Towing & Transportation Toyota	127	Running
9	6	Kyle Larson *	Universal Technical Institute/NTI Toyota	127	Running
10	10	Chase Elliott	Aaron's/HendrickCars.com Chevrolet	127	Running
11	14	David Mayhew	MMI Services/Ron's Rear Ends Chevrolet	127	Running
12	19	Travis Pastrana *	Boost Mobile Toyota	127	Running
13	15	Jimmy Weller *	Integrated Metal Products Toyota	127	Running
14	33	Bryan Ortiz *	Toyota Racing Development Toyota	127	Running
15	21	Daniel Suarez	Telcel/Finsa/Roca Acero Toyota	127	Running
16	29	Scott Saunders *	Inox Supreme Lube/Standout Wraps Dodge	127	Running
17	28	Spencer Gallagher	Allegiant Air Chevrolet	127	Running
18	2	Darrell Wallace Jr.	Coca-Cola Toyota	127	Running
19	22	Dale Quarterley	Van Dyk Baler Chevrolet	127	Running
20	16	Sergio Pena	NASCAR Technical Institute/UTI Toyota	127	Running
21	18	Brandon Gdovic	Aquis Communications/ComServe Dodge	126	Running
22	11	Corey LaJoie	Sims Metal Management Ford	125	Running
23	20	Dylan Presnell *	American Mountain Rentals/Amtrol Toyota	125	Running
24	32	Sam Hunt *	Oakley/Bruster's Ice Cream Dodge	125	Running
25	26	Carlos Iaconelli *	Bienvenidos a NASCAR/Mayor Cars Toyota	124	Running
26	31	John Salemi	John Salemi Racing Toyota	120	Running
27	5	CJ Faison *	Generation Rescue Chevrolet	117	Accident
28	23	Eddie MacDonald	Grimm Construction Toyota	117	Accident
29	27	Blake Jones *	Teddy Jones Racing Chevrolet	111	Running
30	24	Jorge Arteaga *	Rev Racing Toyota	96	Running
31	35	Ray Courtemanche Jr. *	BonzaiRacing.ca Chevrolet	90	Running
32	8	Brett Moffitt	UTI/NASCAR Technical Institute Toyota	69	Oil Leak
33	34	Candace Muzny *	Arrow Wrecker Service Toyota	63	Accident
34	17	Chad Boat	Curb Records/Celebrity Fight Night Chevrolet	26	Overheating
35	30	Jorge Contreras Jr. *	Grupo CEDVA Dodge	0	DNS

* Denotes Sunoco Rookie of the Year Contender

TIME OF RACE: 1 hrs., 2 mins, 6 secs — Average Speed: 65.402 mph — Caution Flags: 6 for 33 laps — Lap Leaders: Nelson Piquet Jr. 1-35, Chase Elliott 36-75, Ryan Blaney * 76, Corey LaJoie 77-100, Nelson Piquet Jr. 101-127.

2 GREENVILLE PICKENS SPEEDWAY 03/31/2012

Fin	Str	Driver	Team	Laps	Status
1	1	Darrell Wallace Jr.	Coca-Cola Toyota	150	Running
2	9	Corey LaJoie	Sims Metal Management Ford	150	Running
3	16	Brandon Gdovic	Aquis Communications/ComServe Toyota	150	Running
4	21	Brett Moffitt	Kobe Toyopet Toyota	150	Running
5	8	Eddie MacDonald	Grimm Construction Chevrolet	150	Running
6	10	Chase Elliott	Aaron's/HendrickCars.com Chevrolet	150	Running
7	29	Dylan Kwasniewski	Rockstar/Royal Purple Toyota	150	Running
8	25	Dylan Presnell *	American Mountain Rentals/Amtrol Chevrolet	150	Running
9	14	Ben Kennedy	MAC Tools Chevrolet	150	Running
10	5	Daniel Suarez	Telcel/Finsa/Roca Acero Toyota	150	Running
11	7	Bryan Ortiz *	Toyota Racing Development Toyota	150	Running
12	12	Chad Finchum *	Texas Roadhouse/Spraker Racing Toyota	150	Running
13	11	Ryan Gifford	Universal Technical Institute/NTI Toyota	149	Running
14	20	Sam Hunt *	Oakley/Bruster's Ice Cream Dodge	149	Running
15	26	CJ Faison *	Generation Rescue Chevrolet	149	Running
16	28	Jacob Wallace *	El Toro Loco Chevrolet	149	Running
17	2	Kyle Larson *	Rev Racing Toyota	148	Running
18	24	Scott Saunders *	Inox Supreme Lube/Standout Wraps Dodge	148	Running
19	4	Carlos Iaconelli *	Bienvenidos a NASCAR/Mayor Cars Toyota	148	Running
20	3	Travis Pastrana *	Nitro Circus The Movie Toyota	148	Running
21	19	Dale Quarterley	Van Dyk Baler Chevrolet	147	Running
22	23	Jimmy Weller *	Integrated Metal Products Toyota	147	Running
23	27	Blake Jones *	Teddy Jones Racing Chevrolet	146	Running
24	13	Andrew Smith	Octane/SavannahPawn.com Chevrolet	146	Running
25	15	Jorge Arteaga *	Rev Racing Toyota	145	Running
26	17	Chad Boat	Curb Records/Celebrity Fight Night Chevrolet	141	Running
27	6	Duarte Ferreira *	LS Sports/Sonagol Toyota	127	Running
28	18	Cale Conley	PMC/Health Bridge Imaging Toyota	48	Electrical
29	22	Sergio Pena	JMS/Goodyear Toyota	3	Engine

* Denotes Sunoco Rookie of the Year Contender

TIME OF RACE: 1 hrs., 10 mins, 59 secs — Average Speed: 63.395 mph — Caution Flags: 6 for 27 laps — Lap Leaders: Darrell Wallace Jr. 1-127, Brett Moffitt 128, Darrell Wallace Jr. 129-150.

3 RICHMOND INTERNATIONAL RACEWAY 04/26/2012

Fin	Str	Driver	Team	Laps	Status
1	1	Brett Moffitt	Kobe Toyopet Toyota	103	Running
2	10	Chase Elliott	Aaron's/HendrickCars.com Chevrolet	103	Running
3	8	Corey LaJoie	Virginia Motor Spdwy/Sims Metal Ford	103	Running
4	2	Kyle Larson *	Langley Speedway Toyota	103	Running
5	7	Brandon Gdovic	Aquis Communications/ComServe Toyota	103	Running
6	3	Ben Kennedy	Blue Ox Chevrolet	103	Running
7	16	Bryan Ortiz *	Toyota Racing Development Toyota	103	Running
8	11	Eddie MacDonald	Grimm Construction/UNOH Chevrolet	103	Running
9	13	Sergio Pena	JMS Toyota	103	Running
10	18	Michael McGuire *	Woods Towing & Transportation Toyota	103	Running
11	15	Jesse Little *	Hurst Motorsports/Team Little Racing Chevrolet	103	Running
12	21	Jimmy Weller *	Integrated Metal Products Toyota	103	Running
13	20	Andrew Smith	Octane/SavannahPawn.com Chevrolet	103	Running
14	28	Derek Ramstrom	Matthews Truck Service/Titech Chevrolet	103	Running
15	33	Jorge Arteaga *	Precon Marine Toyota	103	Running
16	30	Enrique Contreras III *	Viva La Raza Racing Toyota	103	Running
17	6	Nelson Piquet Jr.	Fox Sports Toyota	103	Running
18	25	Dylan Presnell *	American Mountain Rentals/Amtrol Chevrolet	103	Running
19	24	Scott Saunders *	Inox Lube/Piston Energy Drink Dodge	103	Running
20	27	Stephen Nasse *	All American Cncrt/StephenNasse.com Toyota	103	Running
21	5	Ryan Gifford	Universal Technical Institute/NTI Toyota	103	Running
22	22	Ryan Blaney *	SealWrap/Heavy Duty Toyota	103	Running
23	4	Travis Pastrana *	iRacing Toyota	103	Running
24	19	CJ Faison *	Generation Rescue Chevrolet	103	Running
25	29	Sam Hunt *	Ruth's Chris/Oaklely Tank Lines Dodge	103	Running
26	35	John Salemi	John Salemi Racing Toyota	103	Running
27	26	Rafael Vallina *	Viva La Raza Racing Toyota	103	Running
28	9	Darrell Wallace Jr.	Joe Gibbs Racing Toyota	102	Running
29	14	Daniel Suarez	Telcel/Finsa/Roca Acero Toyota	88	Accident
30	34	Jorge Contreras Jr. *	Grupo CEDVA/Champion Racing Oil Dodge	88	Accident
31	17	Chad Boat	Curb Records/Celebrity Fight Night Chevrolet	88	Running
32	32	Dale Quarterley	Van Dyk Baler Chevrolet	77	Running
33	23	Carlos Iaconelli *	Bienvenidos a NASCAR/Mayor Cars Toyota	54	Accident
34	36	Chuck Buchanan	Spring Drug/Pepper's Grill Chevrolet	49	Running
35	12	Duarte Ferreira *	LS Sports/Sonagol Toyota	45	Accident
36	31	Chad Finchum *	Texas Roadhouse/Spraker Racing Toyota	16	Engine

* Denotes Sunoco Rookie of the Year Contender

TIME OF RACE: 1 hrs., 3 mins, 19 secs — Average Speed: 73.203 mph — Caution Flags: 8 for 35 laps — Lap Leaders: Brett Moffitt 1-71, Ryan Gifford 72-75, Brett Moffitt 76, Ryan Gifford 77-83, Brett Moffitt 84-103.

4 IOWA SPEEDWAY 05/19/2012

Fin	Str	Driver	Team	Laps	Status
1	15	Chase Elliott	Aaron's/HendrickCars.com Chevrolet	154	Running
2	4	Ryan Blaney *	SealWrap/Heavy Duty Toyota	154	Running
3	13	Cale Conley	PMC/Health Bridge Imaging Toyota	154	Running
4	11	Travis Pastrana *	Nitro Circus The Movie 3D Toyota	154	Running
5	1	Brett Moffitt	Castle Packs Power Toyota	154	Running
6	5	Kyle Larson *	L&M Ethanol Toyota	154	Running
7	3	Sergio Pena	NASCAR Technical Institute/UTI Toyota	154	Running
8	17	Dylan Kwasniewski	Royal Purple/Rockstar Ford	154	Running
9	25	Greg Pursley	Gene Price Motorsports/Star Nursery Ford	154	Running
10	18	Eddie MacDonald	Grimm Construction/UNOH Chevrolet	154	Running
11	14	Brandon Gdovic	Aquis Communications/ComServe Dodge	154	Running
12	7	Bryan Ortiz *	Toyota Racing Development Toyota	154	Running
13	27	Jonathon Gomez	Century Boatland Chevrolet	154	Running
14	26	Chad Boat	Curb Records/Celebrity Fight Night Chevrolet	154	Running
15	12	Jason Bowles	Inox Lube/Piston Energy Drinks Dodge	154	Running
16	19	Daniel Suarez	Telcel/Finsa/Roca Aero Toyota	154	Running
17	35	Michael Self	Rockwell/Golden Gate Meat Chevrolet	154	Running
18	6	Corey LaJoie	Dewey Automotive/Sims Metal Ford	154	Running
19	29	Dylan Presnell *	American Mountain Rentals/Amtrol Toyota	153	Running
20	24	Travis Miller *	X Team Racing Toyota	153	Running
21	8	Ryan Gifford	Universal Technical Institute/NTI Toyota	153	Running
22	21	Jesse Little *	Hurst Mtspts/Team Little Racing Chevrolet	153	Running
23	32	Alex Kennedy	JPO Absorbants/Spraker Racing Chevrolet	153	Running
24	28	Derek Thorn	Sunrise Ford/Lucas Oil/Eibach Ford	153	Running
25	31	Cameron Hayley *	Cabinets By Hayley Toyota	153	Running
26	36	CJ Faison *	Generation Rescue Chevrolet	153	Running
27	23	Jimmy Weller *	Integrated Metal/Geneva-Liberty Toyota	153	Running
28	34	Daryl Harr	iWorld Connect Chevrolet	152	Running
29	30	Austin Dyne *	William Rast/Sunrise Ford/Lucas Ford	151	Running
30	22	Ben Kennedy	Emco Gears/Mac Tools Chevrolet	143	Accident
31	10	Carlos Iaconelli *	Delavaco/Mayor Cars Toyota	122	Accident
32	16	Andrew Smith	Octane/America's Best Value Inn Chevrolet	113	Overheating
33	20	Eric Holmes	NAPA Auto Parts Toyota	57	Handling
34	9	David Mayhew	MMI Services/Ron's Rear Ends Chevrolet	54	Accident
35	33	Sam Hunt *	Oakley Tank Lines/ Montana Mike's Dodge	36	Accident
36	2	Darrell Wallace Jr.	Coca-Cola Toyota	26	Accident

* Denotes Sunoco Rookie of the Year Contender

TIME OF RACE: 1 hrs., 43 mins, 18 secs — Average Speed: 78.267 mph (record)— Caution Flags: 6 for 35 laps — Lap Leaders: Brett Moffitt 1-144, Chase Elliott 145-154.

5 BOWMAN GRAY STADIUM 06/02/2012

Fin	Str	Driver	Team	Laps	Status
1	2	Corey LaJoie	Thermal Control/Sims Metal Mgmt Ford	153	Running
2	5	Darrell Wallace Jr.	Coca-Cola Toyota	153	Running
3	8	Bryan Ortiz *	Toyota Racing Development Toyota	153	Running
4	14	Harrison Rhodes *	Chick-fil-A/G-Oil Chevrolet	153	Running
5	1	Kyle Larson *	Rev Racing Toyota	153	Running
6	6	Chase Elliott	Aaron's/HendrickCars.com Chevrolet	153	Running
7	12	Brandon Gdovic	Aquis Communications/ComServe Dodge	153	Running
8	16	Ben Kennedy	G-Oil Chevrolet	153	Running
9	7	Brett Moffitt	Don Valley North Toyota Dealership Toyota	153	Running
10	10	Eddie MacDonald	Grimm Construction Chevrolet	153	Running
11	18	Jorge Arteaga *	Rev Racing Toyota	153	Running
12	11	Carlos Iaconelli *	Delavaco/Power One Capital Toyota	153	Running
13	19	Jimmy Weller *	Integrated Metal Products Toyota	153	Running
14	21	Travis Pastrana *	iRacing Toyota	153	Running
15	15	Sam Hunt *	ComServ/Bruster's Ice Cream Toyota	152	Running
16	20	Jorge Contreras Jr. *	Grupo CEDVA/Champion Racing Oil Dodge	148	Running
17	3	Sean Caisse	MacDonald Motorsports Dodge	148	Running
18	9	Ryan Gifford	Universal Technical Institute/NTI Toyota	148	Running
19	4	Sergio Pena	Aisin AW Toyota	129	Engine
20	17	Dale Quarterley	Van Dyk Baler Chevrolet	107	Accident
21	22	Dylan Presnell *	American Mountain Rentals/Amtrol Toyota	88	Engine
22	13	Daniel Suarez	Telcel/Finsa/Roca Acero Toyota	46	Accident

* Denotes Sunoco Rookie of the Year Contender

TIME OF RACE: 0 hrs., 59 mins, 51 secs — Average Speed: 38.346 mph — Caution Flags: 10 for 59 laps — Lap Leaders: Corey LaJoie 1, Kyle Larson * 2-36, Corey LaJoie 37-153.

6 GRESHAM MOTORSPORTS PARK 06/09/2012

Fin	Str	Driver	Team	Laps	Status
1	4	Kyle Larson *	Rev Racing Toyota	150	Running
2	1	Cale Conley	PMC/Health Bridge Imaging Toyota	150	Running
3	3	Brett Moffitt	Saitama Toyopet Toyota	150	Running
4	5	Corey LaJoie	LaJoie Scrap/Sims Metal Mgmt Ford	150	Running
5	8	Ben Kennedy	Slack Auto Parts Chevrolet	150	Running
6	7	Sergio Pena	Saitama Toyopet Toyota	150	Running
7	6	Darrell Wallace Jr.	Joe Gibbs Racing Toyota	150	Running
8	27	Eddie MacDonald	Grimm Construction Chevrolet	150	Running
9	23	Andrew Smith	Octane/SavannahPawn.com Chevrolet	150	Running
10	24	CJ Faison *	Generation Rescue Chevrolet	150	Running
11	25	Carlos Iaconelli *	Delavaco/Power One Capital Toyota	150	Running
12	22	Sam Hunt *	Oakley Tank Lines/Bruster's Dodge	150	Running
13	29	Rafael Vallina *	Viva La Raza Racing Toyota	150	Running
14	12	Chase Elliott	Aaron's/HendrickCars.com Chevrolet	150	Running
15	26	Akinori Ogata *	Kajima Dodge	150	Running
16	19	Jimmy Weller *	Integrated Metal Products Toyota	150	Running
17	13	Jesse Little *	Hurst Mtspts/Team Little Racing Chevrolet	148	Running
18	2	Dylan Kwasniewski	Rockstar/Royal Purple Toyota	140	Handling
19	15	Daniel Suarez	Telcel/Finsa/Roca Acero Toyota	139	Accident
20	9	Brandon Gdovic	Aquis Communications/ComServe Toyota	137	Accident
21	20	Dylan Presnell *	Amtrol/American Mountain Rentals Toyota	137	Accident
22	18	Stephen Nasse *	All American Cncrt/StephenNasse.com Toyota	131	Engine
23	14	Jorge Arteaga *	Rev Racing Toyota	124	Engine
24	21	Enrique Contreras III *	Viva La Raza Racing Toyota	124	Accident
25	16	Chad Finchum *	Texas Roadhouse/Spraker Racing Toyota	116	Accident
26	28	Clay Campbell	Mountain Dew/Spraker Racing Chevrolet	82	Handling
27	10	Bryan Ortiz *	Toyota Racing Development Toyota	74	Accident
28	17	Ryan Gifford	Universal Technical Institute/NTI Toyota	74	Accident
29	11	Chad Boat	Curb Records/Celebrity Fight Night Chevrolet	10	Accident

* Denotes Sunoco Rookie of the Year Contender

TIME OF RACE: 1 hrs., 18 mins, 23 secs — Average Speed: 57.410 mph — Caution Flags: 9 for 48 laps — Lap Leaders: Cale Conley 1-145, Kyle Larson * 146-150.

7 LANGLEY SPEEDWAY 06/23/2012

Fin	Str	Driver	Team	Laps	Status
1	2	Corey LaJoie	Direct Wood Prod/Sims Metal Mgmt Ford	175	Running
2	3	Brett Moffitt	Universal Technical Institute/NTI Toyota	175	Running
3	1	Chase Elliott	Aaron's/HendrickCars.com Chevrolet	175	Running
4	9	Brandon Gdovic	Aquis Communications/ComServe Toyota	175	Running
5	6	Sergio Pena	NASCAR Technical Institute/UTI Toyota	175	Running
6	10	Bryan Ortiz *	Toyota Racing Development Toyota	175	Running
7	4	Kyle Larson *	L&M Ethanol/Rev Racing Toyota	175	Running
8	12	Travis Pastrana *	iRacing Toyota	175	Running
9	17	Eddie MacDonald	Grimm Construction Chevrolet	175	Running
10	18	Jorge Arteaga *	Rev Racing Toyota	175	Running
11	15	Dylan Presnell *	Amtrol Toyota	175	Running
12	22	Jimmy Weller *	Integrated Metal Products Toyota	175	Running
13	11	Sam Hunt *	RaceAlert/Oakley Tank Lines Toyota	175	Running
14	16	Jacob Wallace *	Bank Street Cafe Chevrolet	175	Running
15	21	Ali Jackson *	Celtic Waste Dodge	175	Running
16	5	Darrell Wallace Jr.	Joe Gibbs Racing Toyota	175	Running
17	13	Kenny Forbes *	Forbes Racecars/Old Dominion Pkgng Chevrolet	175	Running
18	8	Ryan Gifford	UTI/NASCAR Technical Institute Toyota	174	Running
19	14	Harrison Rhodes *	Spraker Racing/Chick-Fil-A Chevrolet	173	Running
20	20	Akinori Ogata *	ENEOS Motor Oil Toyota	167	Running
21	7	Ben Kennedy	Ben Kennedy Racing Chevrolet	148	Fuel Pump
22	19	Rick Gdovic	Aquis Communications/ComServe Dodge	23	Rear Seal

* Denotes Sunoco Rookie of the Year Contender

TIME OF RACE: 1 hrs., 9 mins, 58 secs — Average Speed: 59.428 mph — Caution Flags: 8 for 43 laps — Lap Leaders: Elliott 1-20, Corey LaJoie 21-48, Brett Moffitt 49-134, Corey LaJoie 135, Brett Moffitt 136-164, Corey LaJoie 165-175.

8 CNB BANK RACEWAY PARK 06/23/2012

Fin	Str	Driver	Team	Laps	Status
1	1	Brett Moffitt	Don Valley North Toyota Dealership Toyota	153	Running
2	6	Kyle Larson *	Rev Racing Toyota	153	Running
3	4	Ben Kennedy	G-Oil Chevrolet	153	Running
4	9	Ryan Gifford	Universal Technical Institute/NTI Toyota	153	Running
5	7	Bryan Ortiz *	Toyota Racing Development Toyota	153	Running
6	13	Eddie MacDonald	Grimm Construction Chevrolet	153	Running
7	21	Brandon Gdovic	Aquis Communications/ComServe Toyota	153	Running
8	10	Harrison Rhodes *	Chick-fil-A Toyota	153	Running
9	14	Benny Gordon	Samuel Metals/VSI Racing Toyota	153	Running
10	16	Tim Bainey Jr.	Window World/DelGrosso Chevrolet	153	Running
11	20	John Salemi	John Salemi Racing Toyota	153	Running
12	19	Clay Campbell	Mountain Dew/Spraker Racing Chevrolet	153	Running
13	15	Jorge Arteaga *	Sign Innovations Toyota	152	Running
14	17	Nathan Russell *	VSI Racing/Russell Stone Products Chevrolet	152	Running
15	8	Chase Elliott	Aaron's/HendrickCars.com Chevrolet	151	Running
16	23	Grant Winchester *	RNB Champion Oil/TW Pure Water Toyota	145	Electrical
17	5	Sergio Pena	Gunma Toyopet Toyota	136	Electrical
18	11	Sam Hunt *	Race Alert/Oakley Tank Lines Toyota	95	Accident
19	12	Jimmy Weller *	Integrated Metal Products Toyota	94	Mechanical
20	22	Chuck Buchanan *	Spring Drug/Pepper's Grill Chevrolet	73	Running
21	18	Jacob Wallace *	Petro South Chevrolet	56	Suspension
22	3	Darrell Wallace Jr.	Joe Gibbs Racing Toyota	50	Accident
23	2	Corey LaJoie	Sims Metal Management/Team Onion Ford	8	Accident

* Denotes Sunoco Rookie of the Year Contender

TIME OF RACE: 1 hrs., 17 mins, 4 secs — Average Speed: 61.941 mph — Caution Flags: 8 for 38 laps — Lap Leaders: Brett Moffitt 1-153.

9 COLUMBUS MOTOR SPEEDWAY 07/21/2012

Fin	Str	Driver	Team	Laps	Status
1	2	Cale Conley	Network W. Va./Health Bridge Imaging Toyota	150	Running
2	5	Brett Moffitt	Aisin Toyota	150	Running
3	7	Darrell Wallace Jr.	Joe Gibbs Racing Toyota	150	Running
4	10	Sergio Pena	Advics Toyota	150	Running
5	3	Daniel Suarez	Telcel/Finsa/Roca Acero Toyota	150	Running
6	6	Bryan Ortiz *	Toyota Racing Development Toyota	150	Running
7	1	Ben Kennedy	G-Oil Chevrolet	150	Running
8	15	Jimmy Weller *	Integrated Metal Products Toyota	150	Running
9	11	Brandon Gdovic	Aquis Communications/ComServe Toyota	150	Running
10	14	Eddie MacDonald	Grimm Construction Chevrolet	150	Running
11	18	Sam Hunt *	Oakley Tank Lines/Bruster's Dodge	150	Running
12	19	Clay Campbell	Mountain Dew/Spraker Racing Chevrolet	150	Running
13	17	Ryan Gifford	Universal Technical Institute/NTI Toyota	149	Running
14	20	Ali Jackson *	Celtic Waste Dodge	149	Running
15	8	Chase Elliott	Aaron's/HendrickCars.com Chevrolet	148	Running
16	21	Tim Bell *	Make Direct Chevrolet	148	Running
17	4	Corey LaJoie	Sims Metal Management Ford	148	Running
18	13	Austin Hill *	MacDonald Motorsports Toyota	147	Running
19	12	Carlos Iaconelli *	Delavaco Toyota	146	Running
20	22	Xavi Razo *	Troy Williams Racing Chevrolet	146	Running
21	9	Kyle Larson *	Rev Racing Toyota	143	Running
22	16	Jorge Arteaga *	Rev Racing Toyota	108	Accident

* Denotes Sunoco Rookie of the Year Contender

TIME OF RACE: 52 mins, 6 secs — Average Speed: 57.524 mph — Caution Flags: 6 for 35 laps — Lap Leaders: Cale Conley 1-150.

10 IOWA SPEEDWAY 08/03/2012

Fin	Str	Driver	Team	Laps	Status
1	2	Corey LaJoie	Dewey Automotive/Sims Metal Ford	150	Running
2	5	Kyle Larson *	L&M Ethanol Toyota	150	Running
3	3	Sergio Pena	Don Valley North Toyota Dealership Toyota	150	Running
4	4	Chase Elliott	Aaron's/HendrickCars.com Chevrolet	150	Running
5	6	Brett Moffitt	Aisin Toyota	150	Running
6	7	Travis Pastrana *	iRacing Toyota	150	Running
7	1	Cale Conley	PMC/Health Bridge Imaging Toyota	150	Running
8	21	Eddie MacDonald	Grimm Construction Chevrolet	150	Running
9	22	Michael Self	Rockwell/Golden Gate Meat Chevrolet	150	Running
10	11	Daniel Suarez	Telcel/Finsa/Roca Aero Toyota	150	Running
11	24	Jorge Arteaga *	Rev Racing Toyota	150	Running
12	15	Cameron Hayley *	Cabinets By Hayley Toyota	150	Running
13	19	Darrell Wallace Jr.	Z-Line Designs Toyota	150	Running
14	8	Bryan Ortiz *	Toyota Racing Development Toyota	150	Running
15	27	Travis Miller *	X Team Racing Toyota	150	Running
16	17	Jimmy Weller *	Integrated Metal Products Toyota	150	Running
17	26	Chad Boat	Curb Records/Celebrity Fight Night Chevrolet	149	Running
18	25	Eric Holmes	NAPA Auto Parts Toyota	149	Running
19	28	David Mayhew	MMI Services/Ron's Rear Ends Chevrolet	149	Running
20	20	Greg Pursley	GPM/Star Nursery/Real Water Ford	149	Running
21	18	CJ Faison *	Generation Rescue Chevrolet	149	Running
22	33	Ryan Philpott	51 FIFTY Energy Drink Ford	148	Running
23	23	Jonathon Gomez	Century Boatland Chevrolet	147	Running
24	34	Sam Hunt *	Oakley Tank Lines/Bruster's Toyota	147	Running
25	30	Brandon Gdovic	Aquis Communications/ComServe Toyota	147	Running
26	36	Carl Harr	WestWorld Computers Chevrolet	145	Running
27	29	Dylan Kwasniewski	Rockstar/Royal Purple Ford	139	Running
28	13	Ben Kennedy	G-Oil/Hawkeye Graphics Chevrolet	137	Accident
29	14	Derek Thorn	Sunrise Ford/Lucas Oil/Eibach Ford	136	Running
30	12	Matt DiBenedetto	Toyota Tech College/Tokyo Toyota	133	Accident
31	31	Akinori Ogata *	Eneos Motor Oil Toyota	132	Accident
32	35	Dylan Presnell *	American Mountain Rentals/Amtrol Toyota	131	Accident
33	16	Ryan Gifford	Universal Technical Institute/NTI Toyota	77	Oil Leak
34	9	Ryan Blaney *	SealWrap/Heavy Duty Toyota	75	Engine
35	10	Brennan Newberry	NTS Chevrolet	53	Accident
36	32	Austin Dyne *	William Rast/Sunrise Ford/Lucas Ford	24	Engine

* Denotes Sunoco Rookie of the Year Contender

TIME OF RACE: 1 hrs., 28 mins, 36 secs — Average Speed: 88.883 mph (record) — Caution Flags: 5 for 25 laps — Lap Leaders: Cale Conley 1-4, Corey LaJoie 5-77, Brett Moffitt 78-80, Corey LaJoie 81-130, Kyle Larson * 131-139, Corey LaJoie 140-150.

11 NEW HAMPSHIRE MOTOR SPEEDWAY 09/22/2012

Fin	Str	Driver	Team	Laps	Status
1	3	Kyle Larson *	Rev Racing Toyota	100	Running
2	4	Corey LaJoie	Riverside Precision Sheet Metal/Sims Ford	100	Running
3	6	Darrell Wallace Jr.	Joe Gibbs Racing Toyota	100	Running
4	10	Dylan Kwasniewski	Royal Purple Toyota	100	Running
5	5	Chase Elliott	Aaron's/HendrickCars.com Chevrolet	100	Running
6	33	Bryan Ortiz *	Puerto Rico Does It Better Toyota	100	Running
7	14	Travis Pastrana *	iRacing.com Toyota	100	Running
8	18	Eddie MacDonald	Grimm Construction Chevrolet	100	Running
9	27	Dale Quarterley	Van Dyk Baler Chevrolet	100	Running
10	11	Michael McGuire *	Woods Towing & Transportation Toyota	100	Running
11	15	Jimmy Weller *	Integrated Metal Products Toyota	100	Running
12	9	Ryan Gifford	NASCAR Tech Inst 10th Anniv/UTI Toyota	100	Running
13	31	Brandon Gdovic	Aquis Communications/ComServe Toyota	100	Running
14	17	Enrique Contreras III *	Viva La Raza Racing Toyota	100	Running
15	16	Daniel Suarez	Acapulco/Roca Aero Toyota	100	Running
16	1	Brett Moffitt	Nitro Circus The Movie 3D Toyota	100	Running
17	22	Jeff Anton	ECR/RaceShopFloors.com Chevrolet	100	Running
18	35	John Salemi	John Salemi Racing Toyota	99	Running
19	23	Austin Theriault *	Mainely Motorsports TV Ford	99	Running
20	25	Sam Hunt *	Race Alert/Oakley Tank LinesToyota	99	Running
21	24	Clay Campbell	Mountain Dew/Spraker Racing Chevrolet	97	Suspension
22	20	Nicholas Sweet *	Gilbane Chevrolet	93	Running
23	12	Jesse Little *	Coulter Mtrspts/Team Little Racing Chevrolet	93	Running
24	2	Sergio Pena	NRC/NISCO Toyota	91	Accident
25	8	Ben Kennedy	G-Oil Chevrolet	91	Accident
26	19	CJ Faison *	Elevate Youth Group Chevrolet	91	Accident
27	28	Steven Legendre *	Kendell Legendre Racing Chevrolet	91	Accident
28	32	Spencer Gallagher	Allegiant Air Chevrolet	91	Accident
29	13	Dylan Presnell *	American Mountain Rentals/Amtrol Toyota	91	Accident
30	21	Jorge Arteaga *	DogHouse Systems Toyota	80	Accident
31	30	Carlos Iaconelli *	Bienvenidos A NASCAR Toyota	78	Accident
32	29	Hector Aguirre *	GAMA/Champion Oil/TWR Chevrolet	75	Alternator
33	26	Harrison Rhodes *	MacDonald Motorsports Toyota	46	Accident
34	36	Tim Bell *	Make Direct Chevrolet	43	Accident
35	7	Cale Conley	PMC/Health Bridge Imaging Toyota	25	Accident
36	34	Akinori Ogata *	Eneos Motor Oil Toyota	19	Accident

* Denotes Sunoco Rookie of the Year Contender

TIME OF RACE: 1 hrs., 20 mins, 29 secs — Average Speed: 78.873 mph — Caution Flags: 6 for 23 laps — Lap Leaders: Brett Moffitt 1-24, Corey LaJoie 25-26, Brett Moffitt 27-62, Corey LaJoie 63-85, Kyle Larson * 86-100.

12 DOVER INTERNATIONAL SPEEDWAY 09/26/2012

Fin	Str	Driver	Team	Laps	Status
1	2	Corey LaJoie	Sims Metal Management Ford	154	Running
2	1	Darrell Wallace Jr.	Joe Gibbs Racing Toyota	154	Running
3	7	Brandon McReynolds *	Turner Motorsports Chevrolet	154	Running
4	15	Ben Kennedy	G-Oil Chevrolet	154	Running
5	19	Kyle Larson *	Rev Racing Toyota	154	Running
6	9	Bryan Ortiz *	Puerto Rico Does It Better Toyota	154	Running
7	10	CJ Faison *	Little Caesars/Carl Deputy Bldrs. Chevrolet	154	Running
8	14	Jimmy Weller *	Integrated Metal Products Toyota	154	Running
9	20	Dylan Presnell *	Amtrol/American Mountain Rentals Toyota	154	Running
10	23	Brandon Gdovic	Windstax.com/Aquis Communications Toyota	153	Running
11	13	Eddie MacDonald	Grimm Construction Chevrolet	153	Running
12	5	Sergio Pena	TOYOTA BOSHOKU Toyota	153	Running
13	28	Nicholas Sweet *	Team Fox Foundation Dodge	152	Running
14	24	Jeff Anton	East Coast Resurfacing Chevrolet	151	Running
15	16	Ryan Gifford	NASCAR Tech Institute 10th Anniv./UTI Toyota	151	Running
16	27	Clay Campbell	Mountain Dew/Spraker Racing Chevrolet	150	Running
17	21	Larry Barford Jr. *	Trauma Doc Chevrolet	149	Running
18	4	Brett Moffitt	Nitro City Resort Toyota	147	Running
19	22	Sam Hunt *	Windstax.com/Aquis Communications Toyota	147	Running
20	25	Hector Aguirre *	TWR/Champion Oil Toyota	144	Running
21	18	Dale Quarterley	Van Dyk Baler Chevrolet	127	Accident
22	11	Jesse Little *	Hurst Motorsports Chevrolet	104	Accident
23	3	Jorge Arteaga *	DogHouse Systems Toyota	55	Accident
24	12	Cale Conley	PMC/Health Bridge Imaging Toyota	51	Accident
25	8	Ryan Blaney *	SealWrap/Heavy Duty Toyota	51	Accident
26	17	Andrew Smith	Octane/SavannahPawn.com Chevrolet	42	Accident
27	6	Chase Elliott	Aaron's/HendrickCars.com Chevrolet	27	Accident
28	26	John Salemi	John Salemi Racing Toyota	13	Oil Leak

* Denotes Sunoco Rookie of the Year Contender

TIME OF RACE: 1 hrs., 47 mins, 19 secs — Average Speed: 86.100 mph — Caution Flags: 8 for 35 laps — Lap Leaders: Wallace Jr. 1-56, Brett Moffitt 57-112, Corey LaJoie 113-154.

13 GREENWILLE PICKENS SPEEDWAY 10/27/2012

Fin	Str	Driver	Team	Laps	Status
1	4	Corey LaJoie	Sims Metal Management Ford	146	Running
2	3	Chase Elliott	Aaron's/HendrickCars.com Chevrolet	146	Running
3	20	Jesse Little *	Coulter Mtrsprts/Team Little Racing Chevrolet	146	Running
4	2	Kyle Larson *	Rev Racing Toyota	146	Running
5	7	Brandon Gdovic	Aquis Communicatons/Windstax.com Toyota	146	Running
6	6	Bryan Ortiz *	Toyota Racing Development Toyota	146	Running
7	15	Sam Hunt *	Team Kyle/Oakley Tank Lines Toyota	146	Running
8	1	Brett Moffitt	Kobe Toyopet Toyota	146	Running
9	9	Sergio Pena	Kobe Toyopet Toyota	146	Running
10	5	Eddie MacDonald	Grimm Construction Chevrolet	146	Running
11	22	Enrique Contreras III *	Viva La Raza Racing Toyota	146	Running
12	12	Ryan Gifford	NASCAR Tech Institute 10th Anniv./UTI Toyota	146	Running
13	10	Darrell Wallace Jr.	Joe Gibbs Racing Toyota	145	Accident
14	24	Brandon Jones *	Rheem Chevrolet	145	Accident
15	13	Austin Hill *	A&D Welding/MacDonald Motorsports Toyota	145	Running
16	8	Ben Kennedy	G-Oil Chevrolet	145	Running
17	16	Jorge Arteaga *	DogHouse Toyota	144	Running
18	14	Jason Hathaway *	King Brewery/Choko Apparel Chevrolet	142	Running
19	25	Larry Barford Jr. *	Trauma Doc Chevrolet	141	Running
20	21	Ali Jackson *	Celtic Waste Dodge	139	Running
21	11	Jimmy Weller *	Integrated Metal Products Toyota	137	Running
22	19	Andrew Smith	Octane/SavannahPawn.com Chevrolet	40	Suspension
23	17	Travis Pastrana *	Nitro Circus The Movie 3D Toyota	0	DNS
24	18	Cale Conley	PMC/Health Bridge Imaging Toyota	0	DNS
25	23	Steven Legendre *	Kendell Legendre Racing Chevrolet	0	DNS

* Denotes Sunoco Rookie of the Year Contender

TIME OF RACE: 1 hrs., 13 mins, 8 secs — Average Speed: 59.891 mph — Caution Flags: 6 for 30 laps — Lap Leaders: Brett Moffitt 1-144, Corey LaJoie 145-146.

14 ROCKINGHAM SPEEDWAY 11/03/2012

Fin	Str	Driver	Team	Laps	Status
1	6	Tyler Reddick *	Broken Bow Dodge	100	Running
2	4	Corey LaJoie	Sims Metal/LaJoie Scrap Metal Ford	100	Running
3	2	Darrell Wallace Jr.	Joe Gibbs Racing Toyota	100	Running
4	3	Coleman Pressley	Acapulco/Jasper Engines Toyota	100	Running
5	7	Jesse Little *	Charlotte Checkers Hockey Chevrolet	100	Running
6	11	Kyle Larson *	Toyota Racing Development Toyota	100	Running
7	21	Ryan Gifford	NASCAR Tech Institute 10th Anniv.\UTI Toyota	100	Running
8	27	Sergio Pena	Chiba Toyopet Toyota	100	Running
9	8	Ben Kennedy	G-Oil Chevrolet	100	Running
10	22	Eddie MacDonald	Grimm Construction Chevrolet	100	Running
11	1	CJ Faison *	Little Caesar's Pizza Chevrolet	100	Running
12	15	Chase Elliott	Aaron's/HendrickCars.com Chevrolet	100	Running
13	10	Bryan Ortiz *	Toyota Racing Development Toyota	100	Running
14	12	Jimmy Weller *	Integrated Metal Products Toyota	100	Running
15	19	Brandon Gdovic	Windstax.com/Aquis Communications Toyota	100	Running
16	13	Steven Legendre *	Kendell Legendre Racing Chevrolet	100	Running
17	23	Tim George Jr.	Applebee's/Spraker Racing Chevrolet	100	Running
18	24	Frank Deiny *	Kiker Tree Service Chevrolet	100	Running
19	14	Jack Clarke *	Marussia/KSS Design/APO Toyota	100	Running
20	29	Noel Dowler *	Frontline Designs/Apollo Motorsports Chevrolet	100	Running
21	5	Brett Moffitt	Chiba Toyopet Toyota	99	Accident
22	18	Harrison Rhodes *	Hands & Feet Project Dodge	99	Running
23	28	Beto Monteiro	MMKT Sports Marketing/TWR Pure Water Toyota	99	Running
24	16	Larry Barford Jr. *	Trauma Doc Chevrolet	99	Running
25	9	Cale Conley	Tait Towers/Rock-It Cargo Toyota	97	Running
26	25	Sam Hunt *	Windstax.com/Oakley Tank Lines Toyota	96	Running
27	20	Jorge Arteaga *	DogHouse Systems Toyota	77	Accident
28	17	Dylan Presnell *	Amtrol Toyota	77	Accident
29	26	Rafael Vallina *	Chihuahua Vive/Ah Chihuahua Mexico Toyota	42	Accident
30	30	Chuck Buchanan	Spring Drug Chevrolet	9	Accident

* Denotes Sunoco Rookie of the Year Contender

TIME OF RACE: 1 hrs., 6 mins, 4 secs — Average Speed: 90.817 mph — Caution Flags: 5 for 13 laps — Lap Leaders: Darrell Wallace Jr. 1-51, Jesse Little * 52-84, Brett Moffitt 85-99, Tyler Reddick * 100.

DYLAN KWASNIEWSKI

NASCAR K&N PRO SERIES WEST 2012 CHAMPION

WEST

KWASNIEWSKI BECAME THE YOUNGEST NASCAR K&N PRO SERIES WEST CHAMP

Dylan Kwasniewski came away with the 2012 championship in one of the closest title battles in the history of the NASCAR K&N Pro Series West.

Kwasniewski edged his teammate at Gene Price Motorsports, Greg Pursley, by six points to become the youngest series champion – at 17 years, 5 months, 10 days old.

It marks one more record for the young Las Vegas driver – who in 2011 had become the youngest race winner and youngest pole winner in series history, along with being the youngest to win the Sunoco Rookie of the Year Award.

"My dad started all this for me and this championship is for him," Kwasniewski said of his father, who passed away in 2010. "All of this started with my dad. This was his legacy and I wanted to make sure this happened for him."

Kwasniewski drove the No. 03 Rockstar/Royal Purple Ford to three wins, five poles, 12 top fives and 15 top 10s in 15 series starts in 2012. His wins came at Stockton (CA) 99 Speedway; Iowa Speedway in Newton, Iowa; and All American Speedway in Roseville, CA. He was the top qualifier at Stockton; The Bullring at Las Vegas Motor Speedway; Colorado National Speedway in Dacono, CO; NAPA Speedway in Albuquerque, NM; and at Roseville.

The two Gene Price Motorsports drivers swapped the points lead back-and-forth through the season. Kwasniewski became the youngest driver to lead the championship standings when he moved into the top spot following his win at Stockton in May. Pursley remained consistent and took over the points lead after a win in July, but Kwasniewski's victory at Roseville in October propelled him back into first place. Kwasniewski held a slim two-point edge heading into the season finale at Phoenix International Raceway – where he finished second, while Pursley was sixth.

"All we had to do was finish in front of Greg and that's what we did," Kwasniewski said.

In two seasons of competing in the NASCAR K&N Pro Series West, Kwasniewski has put together a record of five wins, seven poles, 20 top fives and 24 top 10s in 28 starts. He has also been part of NASCAR's Next9 program, an industry initiative designed to spotlight the sport's next wave of national-series stars.

Kwasniewski became the first 15-year-old to compete on the circuit when he made his series debut in April of 2011. His prior racing resume included competition in a variety of race cars as a youth, beginning with go-karts at the age of 5. Along the way, he raced in Bandolero Bandits, Legends cars, Late Models and Modifieds.

PERSONAL INFORMATION

Birth Date:	**May 31, 1995**
Hometown:	**Las Vegas, NV**
Marital Status:	**Single**
2012 Team:	**Gene Price Motorsports**
Car Owner:	**Gene Price**
Crew Chief:	**Jeff Jefferson**

CAREER RECORD

Year	Rank	Races	Wins	Poles	Top 5s	Top 10s
2011	5	13	2	2	8	9
2012	1	15	3	5	12	15
TOTALS		**28**	**5**	**7**	**20**	**24**

NASCAR K&N PRO SERIES WEST
2012 CHAMPION DYLAN KWASNIEWSKI SEASON RECORD

Date	Speedway	Location	Start	Finish	Status
March 3	Phoenix International Raceway	Avondale, AZ	4	2	Running
April 14	Havasu 95 Speedway	Lake Havasu City, AZ	2	3	Running
April 28	Miller Motorsports Park	Tooele, UT	6	4	Running
May 5	Stockton 99 Speedway	Stockton, CA	1	1	Running
May 19	Iowa Speedway	Newton, IA	2	1	Running
May 26	Brainerd International Raceway	Brainerd, MN	1	2	Running
June 2	The Bullring at LVMS	Las Vegas, NV	1	2	Running
June 23	Sonoma	Sonoma, CA	2	5	Running
July 14	Evergreen Speedway	Monroe, WA	2	7	Running
July 28	Colorado National Speedway	Dacono, CO	1	5	Running
Aug. 3	Iowa Speedway	Newton, IA	9	9	Running
Aug. 26	Portland International Raceway	Portland, OR	11	2	Running
Sept. 29	NAPA Speedway	Albuquerque, NM	1	9	Running
Oct. 13	All American Speedway	Roseville, CA	1	1	Running
Nov. 10	Phoenix International Raceway	Avondale, AZ	4	2	Running

GREG PURSLEY

Greg Pursley finished second in the final standings after a close championship battle in 2012. Pursley, whose 2011 championship was fueled by a dominant run early in the season, came on strong through the middle of the 2012 campaign. He ultimately came up six points short, however, despite scoring four wins and four poles.

DEREK THORN

Derek Thorn established himself as a championship contender in his first full season of competing in the series in 2012. He remained in the running for the title through the final event of the year. En route to his third-place finish in the championship standings, Thorn notched two wins and a pole.

ERIC HOLMES

Three-time series champion Eric Holmes finished fourth in the final standings for 2012. It marked the sixth time in seven years he has finished fourth or better in series points. With his victory in Monroe, WA, it also marked his seventh straight season to score at least one series win.

DAVID MAYHEW

David Mayhew came away with a top-five finish in the championship standings for 2012, despite missing a race while competing in a NASCAR Camping World Truck Series event. In addition to his win in the series' season opener, Mayhew also won two poles over the course of the season.

NASCAR K&N PRO SERIES WEST CAREER WINS (1954-2012)

Driver	Wins	Driver	Wins	Driver	Wins	Driver	Wins	Driver	Wins
Jack McCoy	54	Mike David	7	Marty Kinerk	3	John Anderson	1	Luis Martinez Jr.	1
Ray Elder	47	Don Noel	7	Jack McCoy	3	Brandon Ash	1	Scott Miller	1
Hershel McGriff	35	Steve Portenga	7	Eric Norris	3	Buck Baker	1	Jerry Nadeau	1
Jim Insolo	25	Sean Woodside	7	Richard Petty	3	Ivan Baldwin	1	Norm Nelson	1
Bill Amick	21	Doug George	6	Michael Self	3	Jeff Barkshire	1	Roger Penske	1
Eddie Gray	20	Kevin Harvick	6	Gary Smith	3	Johnny Benson	1	Bob Perry	1
Bill Schmitt	19	Ron Hornaday Jr.	6	Dirk Stephens	3	Ryan Blaney	1	Sammy Potashnick	1
Eric Holmes	17	Harry Jefferson	6	Herb Thomas	3	Geoff Bodine	1	Clyde Prickett	1
Bill Sedgwick	17	Jim Cook	5	Joe Bean	2	Neil Bonnett	1	Andrew Ranger	1
Austin Cameron	15	Dan Gurney	5	Gary Collins	2	John Borneman	1	Dick Rathman	1
Parnelli Jones	15	Dylan Kwasniewski	5	Ernie Cope	2	Jim Boyd	1	Fireball Roberts	1
Roy Smith	15	Chad Little	5	Darel Dieringer	2	Bob Caswell	1	Art Roth	1
Dick Bown	14	Chuck Meekins	5	Jason Fensler	2	Bill Cheesbourg	1	Marshall Sargent	1
Butch Gilliland	13	Marvin Panch	5	Tim Flock	2	Ricky Craven	1	Peyton Sellers	1
Ron Hornaday Sr.	13	Johnny Steele	5	Ruben Garcia	2	Dale Earnhardt	1	John Soares Jr.	1
Greg Pursley	13	Ernie Stierly	5	Carl Joiner	2	Bill Elliott	1	John Soares Sr.	1
Lloyd Dane	12	Derrike Cope	4	Burney Lamar	2	Larry Gunselman	1	Todd Souza	1
Danny Letner	12	Bobby Dotter	4	Joey Logano	2	Royce Hagerty	1	David Starr	1
Scotty Cain	11	Cliff Garner	4	Patrick Long	2	Harold Hardesty	1	Chuck Stevenson	1
Ron Eaton	11	David Gilliland	4	Rick McCray	2	Tavo CT Hellmund	1	George Stuart	1
Marvin Porter	11	Lance Hooper	4	Sumner McKnight	2	Andy Houston	1	Brett Thompson	1
Jim Reed	11	David Mayhew	4	Andrew Myers	2	Vic Irvan	1	Brian Vickers	1
Jim Robinson	11	Kevin Richards	4	Neal Newberry	2	Dave James	1	Auggie Vidovich	1
Ken Schrader	11	Bob Ross	4	Clyde Palmer	2	Jason Jefferson	1	Jim Walker	1
Mike Chase	10	Allen Adkins	3	Clem Proctor	2	Jeff Jefferson	1	Michael Waltrip	1
Jason Bowles	9	Bobby Allison	3	Mark Reed	2	Jack Jeffery	1	Art Watts	1
Rick Carelli	9	Johnny Borneman	3	Jim Reich	2	Bob Kauf	1	Danny Weinberg	1
Scott Lynch	9	Chuck Bown	3	John Rostek	2	John Kieper	1	Dempsey Wilson	1
Eddie Pagan	9	Danny Graves	3	Jim Thirkettle	2	Frank Kimmel	1	Rich Woodland Jr.	1
Mike Duncan	8	Paulie Harraka	3	Derek Thorn	2	John Krebs	1	Cale Yarborough	1
Sonny Easley	8	Brian Ickler	3	Chuck Wahl	2	Mark Krogh	1		
Brendan Gaughan	8	Jim Inglebright	3	Mike Wallace	2	Kuzie Kuzmanich	1		
Jim Bown	7	Gary Johnson	3	Tim Williamson	2	Tiny Lund	1		

NASCAR K&N PRO SERIES WEST COORS LIGHT POLE AWARD WINNERS (1971-2012)

Year	Winner	Year	Winner	Year	Winner	Year	Winner
1971	Ray Elder	1982	Ron Eaton	1993	Rick Carelli	2004	Mike Duncan
1972	Hershel McGriff	1983	Jim Bown	1994	Ron Hornaday Jr.	2005	Mike Duncan
1973	Jack McCoy	1984	Hershel McGriff	1995	Doug George	2006	Eric Holmes
1974	Jack McCoy	1985	Hershel McGriff	1996	Mark Krogh	2007	Mike Duncan
1975	Jim Insolo	1986	Derrike Cope	1997	Sean Woodside	2008	Eric Holmes
1976	Gary Johnson	1987	Hershel McGriff	1998	Kevin Harvick	2009	Jason Bowles
1977	Chuck Bown	1988	Chad Little	1999	Mike Wallace	2010	David Mayhew
1978	Ray Elder	1989	Bill Sedgwick	2000	Brendan Gaughan	2011	Greg Pursley
1979	Tim Williamson	1990	Bill Sedgwick	2001	Sean Woodside	2012	Dylan Kwasniewski
1980	Ron Eaton	1991	Bill Sedgwick	2002	Austin Cameron		
1981	Roy Smith	1992	Ron Hornaday Jr.	2003	Scott Lynch		

NASCAR K&N PRO SERIES WEST 2012 TOP 50 (1950-2012)

Pos	Driver	Points	Starts	Wins	Top 5	Top 10
1	Dylan Kwasniewski	622	15	3	12	15
2	Greg Pursley	616	15	4	10	14
3	Derek Thorn	568	15	2	10	12
4	Eric Holmes	557	15	1	8	12
5	David Mayhew	548	14	1	8	14
6	Michael Self	541	15	3	8	9
7	Cameron Hayley *	493	15	0	5	9
8	Austin Dyne *	487	14	0	2	8
9	Jonathon Gomez	478	14	0	3	8
10	Ryan Philpott	420	14	0	0	3
11	Carl Harr	412	13	0	0	5
12	Daryl Harr	400	13	0	0	2
13	John Wood	378	13	0	0	2
14	Dylan Hutchison *	316	11	0	0	2
15	Travis Milburn	272	10	0	0	0
16	Braeden Havens *	265	8	0	0	3
17	Jack Sellers	245	10	0	0	0
18	Taylor Cuzick *	224	6	0	1	2
19	Brett Thompson	216	5	0	0	1
20	Ronnie Jay *	170	5	0	0	1
21	Billy Kann	133	5	0	0	0
22	Cassie Gannis *	130	5	0	0	0
23	Anthony Giannone *	127	5	0	0	0
24	Josh Reaume *	115	3	0	0	0
25	Dallas Montes *	111	3	0	1	2
26	Chris Evans *	109	3	0	0	0
27	Ben Kennedy	102	3	0	0	2
28	Brian Wong	98	3	0	0	1
29	Jessica Brunelli *	96	3	0	0	0
30	Austin Cameron	91	3	0	1	2
31	Scott Ivie	89	3	0	0	1
32	Tommy Regan *	89	4	0	0	0
33	David Gilliland	82	2	1	1	2
34	Justin Funkhouser	82	4	0	0	0
35	Jason Fensler	81	3	0	1	1
36	Jim Inglebright	75	2	0	1	2
37	Zack Huffman *	68	3	0	0	0
38	Chase Elliott	67	2	0	1	1
39	Kelly Admiraal *	67	2	0	0	0
40	Ryan Partridge *	65	2	0	0	1
41	Brennan Newberry	62	2	0	0	0
42	Kyle Kelley	54	2	0	0	0
43	Mike Haslam *	54	2	0	0	0
44	Hannah Newhouse *	53	1	0	0	1
45	Kyle Heckman *	52	2	0	0	0
46	Isaac Sherman *	51	2	0	0	0
47	Tim Spurgeon *	46	2	0	0	0
48	Robbie Brand	45	1	0	0	0
49	Daniel Graeff *	44	2	0	0	0
50	Jack Clarke *	43	1	0	0	0

* Denotes Sunoco Rookie of the Year contender

NASCAR K&N PRO SERIES WEST SUNOCO ROOKIE OF THE YEAR (1971-2012)

Year	Driver	Year	Driver
1971	Dick Kranzler	1992	Rick Carelli
1972	Carl Adams	1993	Dirk Stephens
1973	Richard White	1994	Doug George
1974	Markey James	1995	Ernie Cope
1975	Don Puskarich	1996	Lance Hooper
1976	Gary Johnson	1997	Gary Smith
1977	Pat Mintey	1998	Austin Cameron
1978	Rick McCray	1999	Jason Small
1979	Tim Williamson	2000	Mike Duncan
1980	Don Waterman	2001	Mark Reed
1981	Jim Bown	2002	Mike David
1982	Jim Reich	2003	Scott Lynch
1983	Ron Esau	2004	David Gilliland
1984	Derrike Cope	2005	Andrew Lewis
1985	Glen Steurer	2006	Peyton Sellers
1986	Chad Little	2007	Jason Bowles
1987	Roman Calczynski	2008	Jeff Barkshire
1988	Bob Howard	2009	Paulie Harraka
1989	Bill Sedgwick	2010	Luis Martinez Jr.
1990	Mike Chase	2011	Dylan Kwasniewski
1991	Billy Jac Shaw	2012	Austin Dyne

NASCAR K&N PRO SERIES WEST MOST POPULAR DRIVER (1965-2012)

Year	Driver	Year	Driver
1965	Ray Elder	1989	Hershel McGriff
1966	Ray Elder	1990	Hershel McGriff
1967	Marshall Sargent	1991	Hershel McGriff
1968	Ray Elder	1992	Hershel McGriff
1969	Ray Elder	1993	Rick Carelli
1970	Ray Elder	1994	Ron Hornaday Jr.
1971	Ray Elder	1995	Ernie Cope
1972	Ray Elder	1996	Larry Gunselman
1973	Ray Elder	1997	Butch Gilliland
1974	Ray Elder	1998	Scott Gaylord
1975	Ray Elder	1999	Butch Gilliland
1976	Jim Insolo	2000	Bobby Dotter
1977	Chuck Bown	2001	Brendan Gaughan
1978	Jim Insolo	2002	Scott Gaylord
1979	Jim Insolo	2003	Austin Cameron
1980	David Pearson	2004	Austin Cameron
1981	Hershel McGriff	2005	Sarah Fisher
1982	Hershel McGriff	2006	Austin Cameron
1983	Hershel McGriff	2007	Mike Duncan
1984	Hershel McGriff	2008	Moses Smith
1985	Hershel McGriff	2009	Moses Smith
1986	Hershel McGriff	2010	Moses Smith
1987	Hershel McGriff	2011	Moses Smith
1988	Hershel McGriff	2012	Cassie Gannis

NASCAR K&N PRO SERIES WEST CHAMPS & LEADERS (1954-2012)

1954
Lloyd Dane 1530 · Danny Letner 1292 · Marvin Panch 1042 · Ben Gregory 982 · John Soares 974 · Bob Caswell 888 · Allen Adkins 858 · Tony Nelson 842 · Joe Valente 686 · Woody Brown 666

1955
Danny Letner 2056 · Allen Adkins 1594 · Marvin Panch 1524 · Bill West 1500 · Ed Brown 1164 · Lloyd Dane 1064 · Bill Amick 944 · Bill Stamer 866 · Sherman Clark 760 · George Seeger 738

1956
Lloyd Dane 4476 · Chuck Meekins 4318 · Eddie Pagan 4060 · Clyde Palmer 3002 · Jim Blomgren 2670 · Bob Ross 2510 · Jim Cook 1996 · Dick Getty 1966 · Howard Phillippi 1840 · John Kieper 1806

1957
Lloyd Dane 3574 · Eddie Pagan 3556 · Scott Cain 3032 · Dick Getty 2606 · Eddie Gray 2096 · Bob Ross 2004 · Danny Graves 1942 · Parnelli Jones 1902 · George Seger 1738 · Jim Blomgren 1608

1958
Eddie Gray 1821 · Lloyd Dane 1663 · Bob Keefe 1536 · Parnelli Jones 1140 · Jim Cook 1107 · Lucky Long 1068 · Mike Batinich 918 · Dave James 760 · Danny Graves 754 · Marshall Sargent 738

1959
Bob Ross 1428 · Lloyd Dane 1280 · Scott Cain 1118 · Marvin Porter 1112 · Parnelli Jones 1070 · Eddie Gray 1036 · Johnny Porter 1024 · Lucky Long 992 · Mel Larson 976 · Bob Perry 802

1960
Marvin Porter 1476 · Don Noel 1464 · Lloyd Dane 1296 · Bruce Worrell 1266 · Eddie Gray 1258 · Dick Smith 1106 · Bob Perry 1096 · Scott Cain 1076 · Al Self 1068 · Jim Blomgren 1064

1961
Eddie Gray 2480 · Eddie Pagan 2074 · Don Noel 2064 · Lloyd Dane 1972 · Jim Cook 1810 · Bob Perry 1650 · Jack Norton 1500 · Danny Weinberg 1428 · Bruce Worrell 1416 · Jim Blomgren 1414

1962
Eddie Gray 1364 · Ron Hornaday 1328 · Don Noel 1272 · Lloyd Dane 1204 · Eddie Pagan 1140 · Danny Weinberg 1060 · Jim Blomgren 892 · Bill Clifton 752 · Scott Cain 692 · Clarence Brand 668

1963
Ron Hornaday 1424 · Bob Perry 1420 · Jim Cook 1140 · Don Noel 1052 · Bruce Worrell 996 · Jack McCoy 848 · Darel Dieringer 800 · Joe Weatherly 768 · Eddie Pagan 720 · Eddie Gray 688

1964
Ron Hornaday 4706 · Bill Amick 4242 · Ed Brown 3408 · Dick Bown 3122 · Jack McCoy 3040 · Carl Joiner 2724 · Kuzie Kuzmanich 2232 · Larry Bell 2160 · Scott Cain 1998 · Johnny Steele 1954

1965
Bill Amick 3036 · Marvin Porter 3030 · Johnny Steele 2894 · Jack McCoy 2480 · Ed Brown 2316 · Dave James 2112 · Cliff Garner 1898 · Scott Cain 1854 · Carl Joiner 1732 · Ron Hornaday 1642

1966
Jack McCoy 2552 · Ray Elder 2534 · Johnny Steele 2130 · Dave James 2100 · Scott Cain 2000 · Marvin Porter 1858 · Jerry Oliver 1836 · Frank Burnett 1674 · Jim Cook 1660 · Ren Reugebrink 1546

1967
Scott Cain 3326 · Ray Elder 2888 · Jim Cook 2688 · Cliff Garner 2566 · Johnny Steele 2468 · Jack McCoy 2432 · Dave James 2216 · Don Noel 2176 · Jerry Oliver 1922 · Clyde Prickett 1920

1968
Scott Cain 1051 · Ray Elder 1049 · Jim Cook 1030 · Paul Dorrity 985 · Johnny Steele 941 · Sam Rose 933 · Clyde Prickett 902 · Jack McCoy 889 · Harold Hardesty 723 · Bob Link 631

1969
Ray Elder 1060 · Jack McCoy 1022 · Marty Kinerk 1014 · Jim Cook 972 · Scott Cain 944 · Johnny Steele 932 · Dick Bown 804 · Kevin Terris 774 · Bob England 768 · Jerry Oliver 726

1970
Ray Elder 1024 · Jack McCoy 1004 · Dick Bown 992 · Jerry Oliver 971 · Bob England 934 · Frank James 926 · George Tallas 813 · Johnny Steele 686 · John Soares 657 · Scott Cain 612

1971
Ray Elder 1471 · Jack McCoy 1304 · Jim Insolo 1264 · Bob England 1224 · John Soares 1067 · Jim Cook 988 · Robert Kauf 908 · Jerry Barnett 903 · Hershel McGriff 843 · Frank James 807

1972
Ray Elder 2782 · Hershel McGriff 2742 · Dick Bown 2434 · Jack McCoy 2370 · John Soares 2324 · Carl Adams 2289 · Chuck Bown 2200 · JC Danielsen 2178 · Dick Kranzler 2075 · Ron Gautsche 2074

1973
Jack McCoy 1673 · Sonny Easley 1619 · Ray Elder 1618 · Dick Bown 1604 · Richard White 1587 · Ron Gautsche 1503 · Jim Insolo 1414 · Carl Adams 1357 · Chuck Bown 1272 · John Soares 1160

1974
Ray Elder 1942 · Jack McCoy 1884 · Jim Insolo 1849 · Ron Gautsche 1837 · Sonny Easley 1836 · Markey James 1617 · Jim Boyd 1595 · George Behlman 1574 · John Dineen 1554 · Ernie Stierly 1387

1975
Ray Elder 1327 · Sonny Easley 1142 · Chuck Wahl 1102 · Don Puskarich 1027 · Dennis Wilson 1006 · Jim Boyd 998 · Jim Insolo 988 · Richard White 865 · Bill Schmitt 778 · Ron Gautsche 743

1976
Chuck Bown 937 · Ernie Stierly 827 · Gary Johnson 813 · Chuck Wahl 752 · Richard White 738 · Sumner McKnight 722 · Glen Francis 716 · Ron Gautsche 653 · Bill Schmitt 592 · John Kieper 506

1977
Bill Schmitt 1526 · Chuck Bown 1415 · Richard White 1355 · Gary Johnson 1284 · Pat Mintey 1214 · Ernie Stierly 1112 · John Borneman 991 · Sumner McKnight 987 · Bill Baker 835 · Don Graham 794

1978
Jim Insolo 1065 · Bill Schmitt 1014 · Richard White 954 · Ray Elder 953 · Harry Goularte 922 · John Borneman 903 · Rick McCray 835 · Don Graham 811 · Pat Mintey 753 · John Krebs 751

1979
Bill Schmitt 748 · Tim Williamson 743 · Jim Insolo 699 · Richard White 691 · Jim Robinson 653 · Rick McCray 621 · Robert Tartaglia 498 · Pat Mintey 447 · Sharon Bishop 410 · Roy Smith 405

1980
Roy Smith 486 · Bill Schmitt 478 · Jim Robinson 462 · Rick McCray 439 · Don Waterman 434 · Hershel McGriff 405 · Don Puskarich 390 · Robert Tartaglia 373 · Glen Ward 346 · Steve Pfeifer 325

1981
Roy Smith 677 · Jim Robinson 658 · Jim Bown 620 · Don Waterman 615 · Jim Bown 606 · Hershel McGriff 581 · Pat Mintey 530 · Gene Thonesen 495 · Don Puskarich 394 · Rick McCray 372

1982
Roy Smith 607 · Jim Reich 592 · Jim Bown 586 · Jim Robinson 581 · Bill Schmitt 579 · Rick McCray 565 · Don Waterman 561 · John Krebs 511 · Randy Becker 484 · Hershel McGriff 438

1983
Jim Robinson 498 · Bill Schmitt 438 · Hershel McGriff 438 · Jim Bown 435 · Don Waterman 435 · Doug Wheeler 409 · Pat Mintey 408 · Sumner McKnight 407 · Ron Esau 401 · Bob Kennedy 378

1984
Jim Robinson 530 · Derrike Cope 526 · Sumner McKnight 512 · Jim Bown 493 · Ron Esau 492 · Bill Schmitt 484 · Harry Goularte 455 · Ruben Garcia 455 · 9 Jim Krebs 422 · 10 Hershel McGriff 410

1985
Jim Robinson 584 · Hershel McGriff 565 · Ruben Garcia 561 · Glen Steurer 543 · Blair Aiken 518 · Jim Bown 511 · Bill Osborn 506 · Bill Schmitt 494 · Derrike Cope 492 · John Soares 470

1986
Hershel McGriff 408 · Chad Little 392 · Bill Schmitt 376 · Jim Robinson 368 · Terry Petris 366 · Ruben Garcia 357 · Glen Steurer 342 · John Krebs 308 · Derrike Cope 269 · Brad Tidrick 261

1987
Chad Little 412 · Hershel McGriff 362 · Roy Smith 345 · Ruben Garcia 342 · Bill Schmitt 342 · Jim Robinson 339 · Harry Goularte 330 · Bob Howard 313 · Roman Calczynski 278 · 10 Jack Sellers 277

1988
Roy Smith 418 · Bill Schmitt 381 · Chad Little 368 · JC Danielsen 329 · Hershel McGriff 328 · Jim Bown 313 · Scott Gaylord 309 · Bob Howard 298 · Sumner McKnight 271

1989
Bill Schmitt 1845 · Bill Sedgwick 1789 · Roy Smith 1766 · Hershel McGriff 1666 · Rick McCray 1613 · John Krebs 1524 · Jack Sellers 1412 · Robert Sprague 1344 · Bob Walker 1334 · Butch Gilliland 1304

1990
- Bill Schmitt . . . 1342
- Bill Sedgwick . . . 1341
- Mike Chase . . . 1278
- Terry Fisher . . . 1205
- John Krebs . . . 1183
- Robert Sprague . . . 1128
- Butch Gilliland . . . 1107
- Jack Sellers . . . 1018
- Rick Mackey . . . 994
- Bob Walker . . . 947

1991
- Bill Sedgwick . . . 1509
- Bill Schmitt . . . 1435
- Butch Gilliland . . . 1413
- Hershel McGriff . . . 1353
- John Krebs . . . 1259
- Rick Scribner . . . 1211
- Billy Jac Shaw . . . 1187
- Robert Sprague . . . 1173
- Mike Chase . . . 1172
- Jack Sellers . . . 1106

1992
- Bill Sedgwick . . . 1817
- Bill Schmitt . . . 1811
- Rick Carelli . . . 1765
- John Krebs . . . 1742
- Ron Hornaday Jr. . . . 1722
- Butch Gilliland . . . 1660
- Rick Scribner . . . 1517
- Jack Sellers . . . 1290
- Chuck Welch . . . 1141
- Rich Woodland Jr. . . . 1047

1993
- Rick Carelli . . . 2390
- Dirk Stephens . . . 2292
- Bill Sedgwick . . . 2008
- Wayne Jacks . . . 1888
- Jack Sellers . . . 1833
- Rick Scribner . . . 1676
- Chuck Welch . . . 1448
- Butch Gilliland . . . 1416
- Hershel McGriff . . . 1269
- Tony Hunt . . . 1151

1994
- Mike Chase . . . 2190
- Ron Hornaday Jr. . . . 2162
- John Krebs . . . 2016
- Jeff Davis . . . 1958
- Doug George . . . 1932
- Joe Heath . . . 1812
- Wayne Jacks . . . 1768
- Jack Sellers . . . 1611
- Rich Woodland Jr. . . . 1430
- Chuck Welch . . . 1420

1995
- Doug George . . . 2295
- Ernie Cope . . . 2143
- Butch Gilliland . . . 2074
- Dan Obrist . . . 1988
- Rich Woodland Jr. . . . 1865
- Scott Gaylord . . . 1839
- LJ Pryor . . . 1730
- Wayne Jacks . . . 1726
- Bill McAnally . . . 1622
- Garrett Evans . . . 1433

1996
- Lance Hooper . . . 2185
- Jeff Krogh . . . 2155
- Larry Gunselman . . . 2070
- Mark Krogh . . . 1907
- Scott Gaylord . . . 1883
- Rich Woodland Jr. . . . 1841
- Joe Bean . . . 1789
- Butch Gilliland . . . 1675
- Bill McAnally . . . 1623
- Pete Graham . . . 1404

1997
- Butch Gilliland . . . 2190
- Sean Woodside . . . 2113
- Gary Smith . . . 2101
- Larry Gunselman . . . 1833
- Kevin Culver . . . 1795
- Scott Gaylord . . . 1706
- Bill McAnally . . . 1677
- John Kinder . . . 1377
- St James Davis . . . 1363
- Dan Obrist . . . 1115

1998
- Kevin Harvick . . . 2315
- Sean Woodside . . . 2216
- Gary Smith . . . 1945
- Austin Cameron . . . 1909
- Kevin Richards . . . 1897
- Butch Gilliland . . . 1888
- Kelly Tanner . . . 1821
- Tony Toste . . . 1793
- Scott Gaylord . . . 1748
- Jeff Davis . . . 1745

1999
- Sean Woodside . . . 2075
- Austin Cameron . . . 1981
- Joe Bean . . . 1955
- Kevin Richards . . . 1910
- Steve Portenga . . . 1889
- Jason Small . . . 1845
- Mike Chase . . . 1838
- Brandon Ash . . . 1831
- Sammy Potashnick . . . 1830
- Butch Gilliland . . . 1821

2000
- Brendan Gaughan . . . 1956
- Bobby Dotter . . . 1792
- Steve Portenga . . . 1748
- John Metcalf . . . 1705
- Kevin Richards . . . 1683
- Bill Sedgwick . . . 1659
- Eric Norris . . . 1621
- Mike Duncan . . . 1604
- Joe Bean . . . 1579
- Scott Gaylord . . . 1568

2001
- Brendan Gaughan . . . 2257
- Mark Reed . . . 2197
- Austin Cameron . . . 2048
- Steve Portenga . . . 1988
- Eric Norris . . . 1945
- Sean Woodside . . . 1914
- Johnny Borneman . . . 1873
- Scott Gaylord . . . 1861
- Brandon Ash . . . 1852
- Bill Sedgwick . . . 1811

2002
- Eric Norris . . . 1665
- Kevin Richards . . . 1546
- Austin Cameron . . . 1542
- Johnny Borneman . . . 1459
- Mike Duncan . . . 1459
- Brandon Ash . . . 1417
- Mike David . . . 1383
- Scott Gaylord . . . 1382
- Greg Pursley . . . 1364
- Brett Thompson . . . 1339

2003
- Scott Lynch . . . 1890
- Mike Duncan . . . 1876
- Steve Portenga . . . 1857
- Kevin Richards . . . 1734
- Scott Gaylord . . . 1733
- Jim Inglebright . . . 1672
- Mark Reed . . . 1663
- Johnny Borneman . . . 1657
- Brett Thompson . . . 1634
- Gene Woods . . . 1458

2004
- Mike Duncan . . . 2090
- Austin Cameron . . . 2074
- David Gilliland . . . 1915
- Scott Gaylord . . . 1900
- Scott Lynch . . . 1877
- Mike David . . . 1803
- Daryl Harr . . . 1711
- Carl Harr . . . 1666
- Tim Woods III . . . 1642
- Jose Luis Ramirez . . . 1534

2005
- Mike Duncan . . . 1665
- Steve Portenga . . . 1546
- Scott Lynch . . . 1542
- David Gilliland . . . 1459
- Mike David . . . 1459
- Brett Thompson . . . 1417
- Scott Gaylord . . . 1383
- Tim Woods III . . . 1382
- Andrew Myers . . . 1364
- Andrew Lewis . . . 1339

2006
- Eric Holmes . . . 1889
- Mike David . . . 1806
- Mike Duncan . . . 1762
- Steve Portenga . . . 1720
- Peyton Sellers . . . 1675
- Jim Inglebright . . . 1657
- Scott Gaylord . . . 1644
- Austin Cameron . . . 1631
- Brian Ickler . . . 1591
- Johnny Borneman . . . 1569

2007
- Mike David . . . 2013
- Mike Duncan . . . 1899
- Jason Bowles . . . 1871
- Brian Ickler . . . 1838
- Johnny Borneman . . . 1813
- Justin Lofton . . . 1742
- Eric Hardin . . . 1712
- Brett Thompson . . . 1683
- Alex Haase . . . 1653
- Eric Richardson . . . 1 617

2008
- Eric Holmes . . . 2098
- Jason Bowles . . . 2050
- Jeff Barkshire . . . 1955
- Mike David . . . 1919
- Jim Inglebright . . . 1840
- Moses Smith . . . 1823
- Austin Cameron . . . 1770
- David Mayhew . . . 1724
- Johnny Borneman . . . 1699
- Jason Patison . . . 1630

2009
- Jason Bowles . . . 2158
- Eric Holmes . . . 2035
- Greg Pursley . . . 1978
- Paulie Harraka . . . 1951
- Brett Thompson . . . 1805
- David Mayhew . . . 1799
- Moses Smith . . . 1766
- Blake Koch . . . 1726
- Jim Warn . . . 1590
- Jamie Dick . . . 1423

2010
- Eric Holmes . . . 1945
- David Mayhew . . . 1822
- Paulie Harraka . . . 1707
- Moses Smith . . . 1678
- Greg Pursley . . . 1641
- Jonathon Gomez . . . 1630
- Luis Martinez Jr. . . . 1593
- Michael Self . . . 1552
- Todd Souza . . . 1496
- Travis Milburn . . . 1412

2011
- Greg Pursley . . . 2324
- Eric Holmes . . . 2062
- Moses Smith . . . 1980
- Luis Martinez Jr. . . . 1942
- Dylan Kwasniewski . . . 1856
- Brett Thompson . . . 1824
- Michael Self . . . 1807
- Daryl Harr . . . 1661
- Ryan Philpott . . . 1660
- Carl Harr . . . 1532

2012
- Dylan Kwasniewski . . . 622
- Greg Pursley . . . 616
- Derek Thorn . . . 568
- Eric Holmes . . . 557
- David Mayhew . . . 548
- Michael Self . . . 541
- Cameron Hayley . . . 493
- Austin Dyne . . . 487
- Jonathon Gomez . . . 478
- Ryan Philpott . . . 420

NASCAR K&N PRO SERIES WEST 2012 RACE RESULTS

1 PHOENIX INTERNATIONAL RACEWAY 03/03/2012

Fin	Str	Driver	Team	Laps	Status
1	1	David Mayhew	MMI Services/Ron's Rear Ends Chevrolet	50	Running
2	4	Dylan Kwasniewski	Rockstar/Royal Purple Ford	50	Running
3	2	Daniel Suarez	Telcel/Finsa/Rocaacero Toyota	50	Running
4	12	Greg Pursley	Gene Price Motorsports/Star Nursery Ford	50	Running
5	10	Derek Thorn	Sunrise Ford/Lucas Oil/Eibach Ford	50	Running
6	3	Carlos Iaconelli *	Bienvenidos a NASCAR/Mayor Cars Toyota	50	Running
7	17	Chad Boat	Celebrity Fight Night Chevrolet	50	Running
8	7	Eric Holmes	NAPA Auto Parts Toyota	50	Running
9	13	David Gilliland	Sunrise Ford/Lucas Oil/Eibach Ford	50	Running
10	16	DJ Kennington	Northern Provisional Pipelines Toyota	50	Running
11	8	Ben Kennedy	NAPA Filters Toyota	50	Running
12	20	Brett Thompson	Rich Thompson Trucking Chevrolet	50	Running
13	27	Daryl Harr	i World Connect Chevrolet	50	Running
14	19	Travis Milburn	Cooks /Holleran's Perf. Toyota	50	Running
15	5	Brennan Newberry	NTS Chevrolet	50	Running
16	18	Ryan Philpott	Philpott Race Cars Ford	50	Running
17	9	Chase Elliott	Hendrickcars.com/Aaron's Chevrolet	49	Accident
18	14	Michael Self	Golden Gate Meat Co/RCR Chevrolet	49	Running
19	22	Isaac Sherman *	Holleran's Performance Toyota	49	Running
20	26	Carl Harr	West World Computers Chevrolet	49	Running
21	24	Brady Flaherty	Social Apex Ford	48	Running
22	6	Cameron Hayley *	NAPA Gold Filters Toyota	48	Running
23	23	Dylan Hutchison *	Bay Bio Diesel Chevrolet	48	Running
24	15	Jonathon Gomez	Century Boatland/Approved Memory Chevrolet	47	Running
25	25	Trevor Cristiani *	Fast Lube Plus Ford	47	Running
26	28	John Wood	Holleran's/Pegasus Trnsprt & Towing Ford	47	Running
27	21	Billy Kann	Interstate Batteries Toyota	47	Running
28	29	Justin Funkhouser	Mobile Gold Buyers/Holleran's Chevrolet	47	Running
29	30	Jack Sellers	Bay Bio Diesel Chevrolet	46	Running
30	11	Johnny Borneman	Twisted X Boots/Red Line Oil Chevrolet	41	Electrical

* Denotes Sunoco Rookie of the Year Contender

TIME OF RACE: 27 mins, 24 secs — Average Speed: 109.489 mph (record) — Caution Flags: 1 for 3 laps — Lap Leaders: David Mayhew 1-50.

2 HAVASU 95 SPEEDWAY 04/14/2012

Fin	Str	Car	Driver	Team	Laps	Status
1	1	6	Derek Thorn	Sunrise Ford/Lucas Oil/Eibach Ford	150	Running
2	7	17	David Mayhew	MMI Services/Ron's Rear Ends Chevrolet	150	Running
3	2	03	Dylan Kwasniewski	Rockstar/Royal Purple Ford	150	Running
4	4	21	Michael Self	Golden Gate Meat Co/RCR Chevrolet	150	Running
5	8	20	Eric Holmes	NAPA Auto Parts Toyota	150	Running
6	6	24	Cameron Hayley *	Cabinets By Hayley/NAPA Batteries Toyota	150	Running
7	9	9	Austin Dyne *	William Rast/Sunrise Ford/Lucas Ford	150	Running
8	15	61	Braeden Havens *	Western Rail Inc/Hilliard Chevrolet	150	Running
9	11	07	Ryan Partridge *	PPL Motorsports Ford	150	Running
10	3	26	Greg Pursley	London Bridge Resort/Star Nursery Ford	150	Running
11	12	71	Daryl Harr	i World Connect Chevrolet	150	Running
12	14	5	Dylan Hutchison *	Bay Bio Diesel/Johnnie Walker Chevrolet	150	Running
13	5	22	Jonathon Gomez	Century Boatland Chevrolet	149	Running
14	19	2	Carl Harr	West World Computers Chevrolet	149	Running
15	20	01	Cassie Gannis *	Quick Lane@San Tan Ford/Majerle's Ford	149	Running
16	13	37	Robbie Brand	Socal Autobody/No Limits Hair/Chili's Chevrolet	147	Running
17	10	52	Ryan Philpott	Philpott Race Cars Ford	146	Running
18	17	36	John Wood	Pegasus Transport & Towing Ford	143	Running
19	18	14	Travis Milburn	Cooks /Holleran's Perf. Toyota	133	Running
20	22	15	Jack Sellers	Bay Bio Diesel Chevrolet	113	Accident
21	16	30	Ronnie Jay *	Holleran's Performance Dodge	46	Electrical
22	21	38	Justin Funkhouser	Holleran's Performance Chevrolet	30	Electrical

* Denotes Sunoco Rookie of the Year Contender

TIME OF RACE: 59 mins, 30 secs — Average Speed: 37.815 mph (record) — Caution Flags: 8 for 48 laps — Lap Leaders: Derek Thorn 1-76, Dylan Kwasniewski 77-81, Derek Thorn 82-92, Dylan Kwasniewski 93, Derek Thorn 94-104, Dylan Kwasniewski 105-107, Derek Thorn 108-150.

3 MILLER MOTORSPORTS PARK 04/28/2012

Fin	Str	Car	Driver	Team	Laps	Status
1	1	26	Greg Pursley	Gene Price Motorsports/Star Nursery Ford	50	Running
2	2	20	Eric Holmes	NAPA Auto Parts Toyota	50	Running
3	9	9	Austin Dyne *	William Rast/Sunrise Ford/Lucas Ford	50	Running
4	6	03	Dylan Kwasniewski	Rockstar/Royal Purple Ford	50	Running
5	15	12	Austin Cameron	AC Motorsports Toyota	50	Running
6	19	47	Scott Ivie	MSI Development Inc. Toyota	50	Running
7	13	19	Kyle Heckman *	MMI Services/Ron's Rear Ends Chevrolet	50	Running
8	8	24	Cameron Hayley *	Cabinets By Hayley/NAPA Batteries Toyota	50	Running
9	4	17	David Mayhew	MMI Services/Ron's Rear Ends Chevrolet	50	Running
10	20	2	Carl Harr	West World Computers Chevrolet	50	Running
11	11	89	Brian Wong	Go HD/Moutai/Mash TV Toyota	50	Running
12	3	6	Derek Thorn	Sunrise Ford/Lucas Oil/Eibach Ford	50	Running
13	23	36	John Wood	Holleran Perf./Pegasus Trans. Ford	50	Running
14	16	42	Taylor Cuzick *	Freightliner of Arizona Ford	50	Running
15	10	22	Jonathon Gomez	Century Boatland Chevrolet	50	Running
16	14	52	Ryan Philpott	Philpott Race Cars Ford	50	Running
17	5	31	Mike Skeen *	Carlisle Construction/Hawk Perf Chevrolet	49	Running
18	7	21	Michael Self	MMP/Rockwell Watches Chevrolet	49	Running
19	12	7	Kyle Kelley	Jamison Eng/UPR.com/Apex Chevrolet	48	Running
20	17	61	Brett Thompson	RTTI/Jerome Truck Serv. Chevrolet	47	Running
21	18	71	Daryl Harr	i World Connect Chevrolet	47	Running
22	21	5	Dylan Hutchison *	Bay Bio Diesel/Johnnie Walker Chevrolet	43	Running
23	25	01	Cassie Gannis *	itxtdeals.com Ford	41	Running
24	24	15	Jack Sellers	Bay Bio Diesel Chevrolet	39	Ignition
25	22	07	Josh Reaume *	Colonial Countertops Ford	38	Ignition
26	27	14	Travis Milburn	Cooks/Holleran's Perf. Ford	19	Fuel Pump
27	26	38	Justin Funkhouser	Holleran's Performance Chevrolet	0	Engine

* Denotes Sunoco Rookie of the Year Contender

TIME OF RACE: 1 hrs., 39 mins, 25 secs — Average Speed: 66.387 mph (record) — Caution Flags: 2 for 10 laps — Lap Leaders: Greg Pursley 1-21, Eric Holmes 22, Dylan Kwasniewski 23, David Mayhew 24-25, Austin Dyne * 26-48, Greg Pursley 49-50.

4 STOCKTON 99 SPEEDWAY 05/05/2012

Fin	Str	Car	Driver	Team	Laps	Status
1	1	03	Dylan Kwasniewski	Rockstar/Royal Purple Ford	155	Running
2	3	20	Eric Holmes	NAPA Auto Parts Toyota	155	Running
3	8	17	David Mayhew	MMI Services/Ron's Rear Ends Chevrolet	155	Running
4	2	26	Greg Pursley	Gene Price Motorsports/Star Nursery Ford	155	Running
5	14	59	Jason Fensler	Beat Cancer/MTFX Graphics Chevrolet	155	Running
6	7	22	Jonathon Gomez	Century Boatland Chevrolet	155	Running
7	6	6	Derek Thorn	Sunrise Ford/Lucas Oil/Eibach Ford	155	Running
8	17	9	Austin Dyne *	William Rast/Sunrise Ford/Lucas Ford	155	Running
9	11	88	Jessica Brunelli *	Pick-N-Pull Chevrolet	155	Running
10	24	30	Ronnie Jay *	Holleran's Performance Dodge	155	Running
11	15	15	Dylan Hutchison *	Bay Bio Diesel/Johnnie Walker Chevrolet	155	Running
12	13	71	Daryl Harr	i World Connect Chevrolet	155	Running
13	9	61	Braeden Havens *	Western Rail/Power Systems Chevrolet	155	Running
14	16	14	Travis Milburn	Cooks /Holleran's Perf. Toyota	155	Running
15	4	24	Cameron Hayley *	Cabinets by Hayley Toyota	155	Running
16	18	2	Carl Harr	West World Computers Chevrolet	154	Running
17	20	07	Justin Funkhouser	K&L Body & Frame Ford	153	Running
18	19	36	John Wood	Pegasus Transport & Towing Ford	153	Running
19	23	01	Cassie Gannis *	itxtdeals.com Ford	152	Running
20	5	21	Michael Self	Rockwell/Golden Gate Meat Chevrolet	150	Running
21	21	5	Jack Sellers	Bay Bio Diesel Chevrolet	129	Handling
22	22	38	Tommy Regan *	Holleran's Performance Chevrolet	57	Engine
23	12	52	Ryan Philpott	Philpott Race Cars Ford	43	Overheating
24	10	16	Jacob Gomes	Sunny Valley Smoked Meats Chevrolet	40	Overheating

* Denotes Sunoco Rookie of the Year Contender

TIME OF RACE: 59 mins, 32 secs — Average Speed: 39.054mph — Caution Flags: 7 for 59 laps — Lap Leaders: Dylan Kwasniewski 1-155.

5 IOWA SPEEDWAY 05/19/2012

Fin	Str	Car	Driver	Team	Laps	Status
1	15	9	Chase Elliott	Aaron's/HendrickCars.com Chevrolet	154	Running
2	4	10	Ryan Blaney *	SealWrap/Heavy Duty Toyota	154	Running
3	13	47	Cale Conley	PMC/Health Bridge Imaging Toyota	154	Running
4	11	99	Travis Pastrana *	Nitro Circus The Movie 3D Toyota	154	Running
5	1	11	Brett Moffitt	Castle Packs Power Toyota	154	Running
6	5	69	Kyle Larson *	L&M Ethanol Toyota	154	Running
7	3	1	Sergio Pena	NASCAR Technical Institute/UTI Toyota	154	Running
8	17	03	Dylan Kwasniewski	Royal Purple/Rockstar Ford	154	Running
9	25	26	Greg Pursley	Gene Price Motorsports/Star Nursery Ford	154	Running
10	18	7	Eddie MacDonald	Grimm Construction/UNOH Chevrolet	154	Running
11	14	46	Brandon Gdovic	Aquis Communications/ComServe Dodge	154	Running
12	7	4	Bryan Ortiz *	Toyota Racing Development Toyota	154	Running
13	27	22	Jonathon Gomez	Century Boatland Chevrolet	154	Running
14	26	98	Chad Boat	Curb Records/Celebrity Fight Night Chevrolet	154	Running
15	12	49	Jason Bowles	Inox Lube/Piston Energy Drinks Dodge	154	Running
16	19	14	Daniel Suarez	Telcel/Finsa/Roca Aero Toyota	154	Running
17	35	21	Michael Self	Rockwell/Golden Gate Meat Chevrolet	154	Running
18	6	07	Corey LaJoie	Dewey Automotive/Sims Metal Ford	154	Running
19	29	83	Dylan Presnell *	American Mountain Rentals/Amtrol Toyota	153	Running
20	24	16	Travis Miller *	X Team Racing Toyota	153	Running
21	8	2	Ryan Gifford	Universal Technical Institute/NTI Toyota	153	Running
22	21	97	Jesse Little *	Hurst Mtspts/Team Little Racing Chevrolet	153	Running
23	32	37	Alex Kennedy	JPO Absorbants/Spraker Racing Chevrolet	153	Running
24	28	6	Derek Thorn	Sunrise Ford/Lucas Oil/Eibach Ford	153	Running
25	31	24	Cameron Hayley *	Cabinets By Hayley Toyota	153	Running
26	36	39	CJ Faison *	Generation Rescue Chevrolet	153	Running
27	23	31	Jimmy Weller *	Integrated Metal/Geneva-Liberty Toyota	153	Running
28	34	41	Daryl Harr	i World Connect Chevrolet	152	Running
29	30	91	Austin Dyne *	William Rast/Sunrise Ford/Lucas Ford	151	Running
30	22	96	Ben Kennedy	Emco Gears/Mac Tools Chevrolet	143	Accident
31	10	51	Carlos Iaconelli *	Delavaco/Mayor Cars Toyota	122	Accident
32	16	62	Andrew Smith	Octane/America's Best Value Inn Chevrolet	113	Overheating
33	20	20	Eric Holmes	NAPA Auto Parts Toyota	57	Handling
34	9	17	David Mayhew	MMI Services/Ron's Rear Ends Chevrolet	54	Accident
35	33	23	Sam Hunt *	Oakley Tank Lines/ Montana Mike's Dodge	36	Accident
36	2	18	Darrell Wallace Jr.	Coca-Cola Toyota	26	Accident

* Denotes Sunoco Rookie of the Year Contender

TIME OF RACE:1 hrs., 43 mins, 18 secs — Average Speed: 78.267 mph (record) — Caution Flags: 6 for 35 laps — Lap Leaders: Brett Moffitt 1-144, Chase Elliott 145-154.

6 BRAINERD INTERNATIONAL RACEWAY 05/26/2012

Fin	Str	Car	Driver	Team	Laps	Status
1	9	21	Michael Self	Rockwell/Golden Gate Meat/Bay Bio Chevrolet	50	Running
2	1	03	Dylan Kwasniewski	Royal Purple/Rockstar Ford	50	Running
3	2	26	Greg Pursley	GPM/Star Nursery/ Real Water Ford	50	Running
4	4	6	Derek Thorn	Sunrise Ford/Lucas Oil/Eibach Ford	50	Running
5	3	17	David Mayhew	MMI Services/Ron's Rear Ends Chevrolet	50	Running
6	5	20	Eric Holmes	NAPA Auto Parts Toyota	50	Running
7	8	22	Jonathon Gomez	Century Boatland Chevrolet	50	Running
8	6	9	Austin Dyne *	William Rast/Sunrise Ford/Lucas Ford	50	Running
9	14	5	Dylan Hutchison *	Bay Bio Diesel/Johnnie Walker Chevrolet	49	Running
10	10	2	Carl Harr	West World Computers Chevrolet	49	Running
11	12	71	Daryl Harr	i World Connect Chevrolet	49	Running
12	7	24	Cameron Hayley *	Cabinets by Hayley Toyota	49	Running
13	11	61	Brett Thompson	RTTI/Jerome Truck Serv. Chevrolet	48	Running
14	13	52	Ryan Philpott	Philpott Race Cars Ford	48	Running
15	16	36	John Wood	Pegasus Trans & Tow/Holleran's Perf. Dodge	47	Running
16	17	15	Jack Sellers	Bay Bio Diesel Chevrolet	47	Running
17	18	90	Chris Evans *	GASS Toyota	44	Running
18	15	14	Ronnie Jay *	Cooks/Holleran's Perf./PTW Repair Ford	31	Transmission
19	19	54	Anthony Giannone *	K&N Air Fillters/MGP Chevrolet	6	Accident

* Denotes Sunoco Rookie of the Year Contender

TIME OF RACE: 1 hrs., 32 mins, 48 secs — Average Speed: 80.819mph (record) — Caution Flags: 1 for 4 laps — Lap Leaders: Greg Pursley 1-2, Dylan Kwasniewski 3-11, Greg Pursley 12-16, Dylan Kwasniewski 17-20, Eric Holmes 21, David Mayhew 22, Greg Pursley 23-29, Dylan Kwasniewski 30-48, Michael Self 49-50.

7 BULLRING AT LAS VEGAS MOTOR SPEEDWAY 06/02/2012

Fin	Str	Car	Driver	Team	Laps	Status
1	3	26	Greg Pursley	GPM/Star Nursery/Real Water Ford	200	Running
2	1	03	Dylan Kwasniewski	Royal Purple/Rockstar Ford	200	Running
3	6	22	Jonathon Gomez	Century Boatland Chevrolet	200	Running
4	11	17	David Mayhew	MMI Services/Ron's Rear Ends Chevrolet	200	Running
5	2	24	Cameron Hayley *	Cabinets by Hayley Toyota	200	Running
6	16	74	Tim Bell *	Creation Cope Racing Chevrolet	200	Running
7	14	9	Austin Dyne *	William Rast/Sunrise Ford/Lucas Ford	200	Running
8	12	5	Dylan Hutchison *	Bay Bio Diesel/Johnnie Walker Chevrolet	200	Running
9	18	42	Taylor Cuzick *	Freightliner of Arizona Chevrolet	200	Running
10	13	52	Ryan Philpott	Philpott Race Cars Ford	200	Running
11	23	2	Carl Harr	West World Computers Chevrolet	200	Running
12	8	61	Braeden Havens *	Western Rail Inc/Hilliard Chevrolet	199	Running
13	21	15	Jack Sellers	Bay Bio Diesel Chevrolet	199	Running
14	5	6	Derek Thorn	Sunrise Ford/Lucas Oil/Eibach Ford	196	Running
15	10	88	Jessica Brunelli *	Pick-N-Pull Chevrolet	196	Running
16	17	14	Travis Milburn	Cooks /Holleran's Perf. Chevrolet	190	Running
17	7	21	Michael Self	Rockwell/Golden Gate Meat Chevrolet	184	Accident
18	22	30	Mike Haslam *	Alpine Mtrs Gp/Western Mailing Dodge	180	Accident
19	4	20	Eric Holmes	NAPA Auto Parts Toyota	141	Engine
20	19	71	Daryl Harr	i World Connect Chevrolet	89	Engine
21	15	73	Ali Jackson *	Celtic Waste Chevrolet	51	Accident
22	25	36	John Wood	Pegasus Transport & Towing Ford	49	Accident
23	9	59	Jason Fensler	Beat Cancer/MTFX Graphics Chevrolet	42	Engine
24	20	07	Cassie Gannis *	PPL Motorsports Ford	32	Ignition
25	24	18	Billy Kann	Interstate Batteries Toyota	25	Engine
26	26	44	Ronnie Jay *	Holleran's Performance Toyota	16	Overheating

* Denotes Sunoco Rookie of the Year Contender

TIME OF RACE: 1 hrs., 23 mins — Average Speed: 54.217 mph (record) — Caution Flags: 10 for 52 laps — Lap Leaders: Dylan Kwasniewski 1-11, Greg Pursley 12-159, Dylan Kwasniewski 160-192, Greg Pursley 193-200.

8 SONOMA RACEWAY 06/23/2012

Fin	Str	Car	Driver	Team	Laps	Status
1	7	25	David Gilliland	Pick-N-Pull Chevrolet	64	Running
2	6	6	Derek Thorn	Sunrise Ford/Lucas Oil/Eibach Ford	64	Running
3	1	26	Greg Pursley	GPM/Star Nursery/Real Water Ford	64	Running
4	14	1	Jim Inglebright	Federated Auto Parts Chevrolet	64	Running
5	2	03	Dylan Kwasniewski	Royal Purple/Rockstar Ford	64	Running
6	4	21	Michael Self	Rockwell/Golden Gate Meat Chevrolet	64	Running
7	11	22	Jonathon Gomez	Century Boatland Chevrolet	64	Running
8	17	12	Austin Cameron	AC Motorsports Toyota	64	Running
9	5	17	David Mayhew	Madorom/Steak & Grape Chevrolet	64	Running
10	8	24	Cameron Hayley *	Cabinets by Hayley Toyota	64	Running
11	15	14	Travis Milburn	Cooks/Holleran's Perf. Ford	64	Running
12	20	88	Jessica Brunelli *	Pick-N-Pull Chevrolet	64	Running
13	10	9	Austin Dyne *	William Rast/Sunrise Ford/Lucas Ford	64	Running
14	22	52	Ryan Philpott	51 FIFTY Energy Drink Ford	64	Running
15	12	31	Eric Norris	Kickstart Kids Chevrolet	63	Running
16	13	65	Stan Silva Jr.	A&S Metals/Stan Silva Jr Trucking Chevrolet	63	Running
17	19	51	Carlos Vieira *	51 FIFTY Energy Drink Toyota	62	Running
18	25	04	Hershel McGriff	Park Corporation Chevrolet	61	Running
19	21	90	Chris Evans *	GASS Toyota	60	Running
20	28	07	Daniel Graeff *	Children's Tumor Foundation Ford	60	Running
21	26	44	Tommy Regan *	Ultra Lube Toyota	52	Running
22	24	36	John Wood	Pegasus Transport & Towing Dodge	48	Engine
23	3	20	Eric Holmes	NAPA Auto Parts Toyota	45	Engine
24	30	47	Scott Ivie	MSI Development Inc. Ford	37	Rear End
25	18	86	Tim Spurgeon *	Kleen Blast/David's Racing Products Ford	36	Accident
26	29	38	Dave Smith	Sonoma Harvest Critelli Olive Oil Ford	22	Transmission
27	27	15	Jack Sellers	Bay Bio Diesel Chevrolet	18	Brakes
28	23	5	Dylan Hutchison *	Bay Bio Diesel/Johnnie Walker Chevrolet	18	Transmission
29	16	19	Kyle Heckman *	MMI Services/Ron's Rear Ends Chevrolet	5	Rear End
30	9	61	Johnny Borneman	Red Line Oil Chevrolet	1	Clutch

* Denotes Sunoco Rookie of the Year Contender

TIME OF RACE: 1 hrs., 50 mins,50 secs — Average Speed: 68.947 mph — Caution Flags: 4 for 14 laps — Lap Leaders: Greg Pursley 1-23, David Mayhew 24-30, Eric Holmes 31-43, David Gilliland 44-64.

9 EVERGREEN SPEEDWAY 07/14/2012

Fin	Str	Car	Driver	Team	Laps	Status
1	3	20	Eric Holmes	NAPA Auto Parts Toyota	150	Running
2	4	21	Michael Self	Rockwell/Golden Gate Meat Chevrolet	150	Running
3	7	6	Derek Thorn	Sunrise Ford/Lucas Oil/Eibach Ford	150	Running
4	8	22	Jonathon Gomez	Century Boatland Chevrolet	150	Running
5	5	17	David Mayhew	MMI Services/Ron's Rear Ends Chevrolet	150	Running
6	1	26	Greg Pursley	GPM/Star Nursery/ Real Water Ford	150	Running
7	2	03	Dylan Kwasniewski	GPM/Rockstar/Royal Purple Ford	150	Running
8	11	71	Daryl Harr	i World Connect Chevrolet	150	Running
9	10	52	Ryan Philpott	Philpott Race Cars Ford	150	Running
10	18	2	Carl Harr	West World Computers Chevrolet	150	Running
11	9	61	Braeden Havens *	UNIPAR/Hilliard Chevrolet	150	Running
12	15	47	Justin Philpott *	MSI Development Inc Toyota	150	Running
13	14	9	Austin Dyne *	William Rast/Sunrise Ford/Lucas Ford	150	Running
14	12	42	Taylor Cuzick *	Freightliner of Arizona Chevrolet	150	Running
15	19	07	Josh Reaume *	Colonial Countertops Chevrolet	150	Running
16	16	36	Mike Haslam *	VegasCustomClassicCars.com Dodge	150	Running
17	13	5	Dylan Hutchison *	Bay Bio Diesel/Johnnie Walker Chevrolet	147	Running
18	17	15	Jack Sellers	Bay Bio Diesel Chevrolet	147	Running
19	6	24	Cameron Hayley *	Cabinets by Hayley Toyota	146	Running
20	21	38	Zack Huffman *	Holleran's Performance Ford	139	Running
21	22	54	Anthony Giannone *	K&N Air Filters/MGP Chevrolet	130	Running
22	20	14	John Wood	Cooks /Holleran's Perf. Toyota	129	Accident
23	23	55	Bobby Hillis	First Impression Press/Hinkley Lighting Dodge	21	Brakes

* Denotes Sunoco Rookie of the Year Contender

TIME OF RACE: 1 hrs., 30 mins, 2 secs — Average Speed: 64.576 mph — Caution Flags: 5 for 29 laps — Lap Leaders: Greg Pursley 1-37, Eric Holmes 38-82, Michael Self 83-130, Eric Holmes 131-150.

10 COLORADO NATIONAL SPEEDWAY 07/28/2012

Fin	Str	Car	Driver	Team	Laps	Status
1	2	26	Greg Pursley	GPM/Star Nursery/Real Water Ford	153	Running
2	8	6	Derek Thorn	Sunrise Ford/Lucas Oil/Eibach Ford	153	Running
3	5	24	Cameron Hayley *	Cabinets by Hayley Toyota	153	Running
4	4	21	Michael Self	Rockwell/Golden Gate Meat Chevrolet	153	Running
5	1	03	Dylan Kwasniewski	GPM/Rockstar/Royal Purple Ford	153	Running
6	7	55	Michael Waltrip	NAPA Knows How To Care Toyota	153	Running
7	6	20	Eric Holmes	NAPA Auto Parts Toyota	153	Running
8	3	17	David Mayhew	MMI Services/Ron's Rear Ends Chevrolet	153	Running
9	11	96	Ben Kennedy	G-Oil/NAPA Toyota	153	Running
10	10	61	Braeden Havens *	UNIPAR/Hilliard Chevrolet	153	Running
11	18	2	Carl Harr	West World Computers Chevrolet	153	Running
12	14	9	Austin Dyne *	William Rast/Sunrise Ford/Lucas Ford	153	Running
13	17	14	Travis Milburn	Cooks /Holleran's Perf. Chevrolet	150	Running
14	19	36	John Wood	Holleran Perf./Pegasus Trans. Dodge	150	Running
15	9	22	Jonathon Gomez	Century Boatland Chevrolet	149	Running
16	21	18	Billy Kann	Interstate Batteries Toyota	149	Running
17	23	38	Zack Huffman *	Holleran's Performance Ford	149	Running
18	15	42	Taylor Cuzick *	Freightliner of Arizona Chevrolet	147	Accident
19	22	54	Anthony Giannone *	K&N Air Filters/MGP Chevrolet	147	Running
20	12	5	Dylan Hutchison *	Bay Bio Diesel/Johnnie Walker Chevrolet	140	Running
21	16	71	Daryl Harr	i World Connect Chevrolet	138	Running
22	13	52	Ryan Philpott	Philpott Race Cars Ford	137	Running
23	20	15	Jack Sellers	Bay Bio Diesel Chevrolet	134	Running
24	24	07	Daniel Graeff *	Children's Tumor Foundation Ford	98	Accident

* Denotes Sunoco Rookie of the Year Contender

TIME OF RACE: 1 hrs., 2 mins, 38 secs — Average Speed: 54.963 mph — Caution Flags: 6 for 31 laps — Lap Leaders: Dylan Kwasniewski-grid. Greg Pursley 1-153.

11 IOWA SPEEDWAY 08/03/2012

Fin	Str	Car	Driver	Team	Laps	Status
1	2	07	Corey LaJoie	Dewey Automotive/Sims Metal Ford	150	Running
2	5	6	Kyle Larson *	L&M Ethanol Toyota	150	Running
3	3	1	Sergio Pena	Don Valley North Toyota Dealership Toyota	150	Running
4	4	9	Chase Elliott	Aaron's/HendrickCars.com Chevrolet	150	Running
5	6	11	Brett Moffitt	Aisin Toyota	150	Running
6	7	99	Travis Pastrana *	iRacing Toyota	150	Running
7	1	47	Cale Conley	PMC/Health Bridge Imaging Toyota	150	Running
8	21	71	Eddie MacDonald	Grimm Construction Chevrolet	150	Running
9	22	21	Michael Self	Rockwell/Golden Gate Meat Chevrolet	150	Running
10	11	74	Daniel Suarez	Telcel/Finsa/Roca Aero Toyota	150	Running
11	24	8	Jorge Arteaga *	Rev Racing Toyota	150	Running
12	15	24	Cameron Hayley *	Cabinets By Hayley Toyota	150	Running
13	19	18	Darrell Wallace Jr.	Z-Line Designs Toyota	150	Running
14	8	4	Bryan Ortiz *	Toyota Racing Development Toyota	150	Running
15	27	15	Travis Miller *	X Team Racing Toyota	150	Running
16	17	31	Jimmy Weller *	Integrated Metal Products Toyota	150	Running
17	26	98	Chad Boat	Curb Records/Celebrity Fight Night Chevrolet	149	Running
18	25	20	Eric Holmes	NAPA Auto Parts Toyota	149	Running
19	28	17	David Mayhew	MMI Services/Ron's Rear Ends Chevrolet	149	Running
20	20	26	Greg Pursley	GPM/Star Nursery/Real Water Ford	149	Running
21	18	39	CJ Faison *	Generation Rescue Chevrolet	148	Running
22	33	52	Ryan Philpott	51 FIFTY Energy Drink Ford	147	Running
23	23	22	Jonathon Gomez	Century Boatland Chevrolet	147	Running
24	34	23	Sam Hunt *	Oakley Tank Lines/Bruster's Toyota	147	Running
25	30	46	Brandon Gdovic	Aquis Communications/ComServe Toyota	147	Running
26	36	72	Carl Harr	WestWorld Computers Chevrolet	145	Running
27	29	03	Dylan Kwasniewski	Rockstar/Royal Purple Ford	139	Running
28	13	96	Ben Kennedy	G-Oil/Hawkeye Graphics Chevrolet	137	Accident
29	14	66	Derek Thorn	Sunrise Ford/Lucas Oil/Eibach Ford	136	Running
30	12	01	Matt DiBenedetto	Toyota Tech College/Tokyo Toyota	133	Accident
31	31	49	Akinori Ogata *	Eneos Motor Oil Toyota	132	Accident
32	35	83	Dylan Presnell *	American Mountain Rentals/Amtrol Toyota	131	Accident
33	16	2	Ryan Gifford	Universal Technical Institute/NTI Toyota	77	Oil Leak
34	9	10	Ryan Blaney *	SealWrap/Heavy Duty Toyota	75	Engine
35	10	29	Brennan Newberry	NTS Chevrolet	53	Accident
36	32	91	Austin Dyne *	William Rast/Sunrise Ford/Lucas Ford	24	Engine

* Denotes Sunoco Rookie of the Year Contender

TIME OF RACE: 1 hrs., 28 mins, 36 secs — Average Speed: 88.883 mph (record) — Caution Flags: 5 for 25 laps — Lap Leaders: Cale Conley 1-4, Corey LaJoie 5-77, Brett Moffitt 78-80, Corey LaJoie 81-130, Kyle Larson * 131-139, Corey LaJoie 140-150.

12 PORTLAND INTERNATIONAL RACEWAY 08/26/2012

Fin	Str	Car	Driver	Team	Laps	Status
1	1	26	Greg Pursley	GPM/Star Nursery/Real Water Ford	63	Running
2	3	21	Michael Self	Rockwell/Golden Gate Meat Chevrolet	63	Running
3	2	20	Eric Holmes	NAPA Auto Parts Toyota	63	Running
4	11	03	Dylan Kwasniewski	Royal Purple/Rockstar Ford	63	Running
5	4	6	Derek Thorn	Sunrise Ford/Lucas Oil/Eibach Ford	63	Running
6	5	17	David Mayhew	MMI/Steak & Grape Chevrolet	63	Running
7	8	89	Brian Wong	Livery Design Gruppe Toyota	63	Running
8	12	32	Dale Quarterley	Action Equipment Ford	63	Running
9	9	1	Jim Inglebright	Federated Auto Parts Chevrolet	63	Running
10	7	9	Austin Dyne *	William Rast/Sunrise Ford/Lucas Ford	63	Running
11	14	61	Brett Thompson	RTTI/Jerome Truck Serv. Chevrolet	63	Running
12	13	22	Jonathon Gomez	Century Boatland Chevrolet	63	Running
13	24	47	Scott Ivie	MSI Development Inc. Ford	63	Running
14	23	25	Tom Klauer *	Naake-Klauer Motorsports Chevrolet	62	Running
15	18	7	Kyle Kelley	Jamison Eng/UPR.com/Apex Chevrolet	61	Running
16	16	90	Chris Evans *	GASS Toyota	61	Running
17	21	86	Tim Spurgeon *	Kleen Blast/David's Racing Products Ford	60	Running
18	20	09	Josh Reaume *	Colonial Countertops Chevrolet	60	Running
19	26	36	John Wood	Holleran Perf./Pegasus Trans. Dodge	60	Running
20	29	07	Eddie Nakato *	AR Auto Service Ford	59	Running
21	19	52	Ryan Philpott	Philpott Race Cars Ford	54	Running
22	6	24	Cameron Hayley *	NAPA Batteries/Cabinets by Hayley Toyota	54	Running
23	17	71	Daryl Harr	i World Connect Chevrolet	52	Running
24	30	53	Mike Olsen	Action Equipment Dodge	38	Engine
25	15	14	Travis Milburn	Cooks /Holleran's Perf. Ford	34	Engine
26	25	2	Carl Harr	West World Computers Chevrolet	31	Rear End
27	28	38	Zack Huffman *	Holleran's Performance Ford	28	Engine
28	10	12	Austin Cameron	AC Motorsports Toyota	24	Suspension
29	27	15	Jack Sellers	Bay Bio Diesel Chevrolet	21	Radiator
30	22	5	Dylan Hutchison *	Bay Bio Diesel/Johnnie Walker Chevrolet	20	Transmission

* Denotes Sunoco Rookie of the Year Contender

TIME OF RACE: 1 hrs., 53 mins, 59 secs — Average Speed: 65.231 mph — Caution Flags: 4 for 15 laps — Lap Leaders: Greg Pursley 1-63.

13 NAPA SPEEDWAY 09/29/2012

Fin	Str	Car	Driver	Team	Laps	Status
1	7	6	Derek Thorn	Sunrise Ford/Lucas Oil/Eibach Ford	153	Running
2	2	17	Dallas Montes *	MMI Services/Ron's Rear Ends Chevrolet	153	Running
3	6	20	Eric Holmes	NAPA Auto Parts Toyota	153	Running
4	8	42	Taylor Cuzick *	Freightliner of Arizona Ford	153	Running
5	13	9	Austin Dyne *	William Rast/Sunrise Ford/Lucas Ford	153	Running
6	11	60	Hannah Newhouse *	Car Store/Brasher's/RTTI Chevrolet	153	Running
7	12	61	Braeden Havens *	Western Rail Inc/Hilliard Chevrolet	153	Running
8	10	26	Greg Pursley	GPM/Star Nursery/Real Water Ford	153	Running
9	1	03	Dylan Kwasniewski	Royal Purple/Rockstar Ford	153	Running
10	18	2	Carl Harr	West World Computers Chevrolet	153	Running
11	17	83	Kelly Admiraal *	William Scotsman/Western Camp Chevrolet	151	Running
12	3	21	Michael Self	Rockwell/Golden Gate Meat Chevrolet	150	Running
13	19	36	John Wood	Holleran Perf./Pegasus Trans. Dodge	150	Running
14	22	14	Ronnie Jay *	Holleran's Perf/Philpott Racecars Chevrolet	149	Running
15	5	24	Cameron Hayley *	NAPA Batteries/Cabinets by Hayley Toyota	149	Running
16	4	54	Anthony Giannone *	K&N Air Filters/ MGP Chevrolet	148	Running
17	20	18	Billy Kann	Interstate Batteries Toyota	148	Running
18	15	38	Isaac Sherman *	Supercuts/Motiva/Car Crafters Ford	148	Running
19	9	71	Daryl Harr	i World Connect Chevrolet	147	Running
20	16	74	Jack Clarke *	Marussia/KSS Design/APO Dodge	140	Running
21	14	52	Ryan Philpott	Philpott Race Cars Ford	40	Overheating
22	21	30	Sean Guthrie *	Holleran's Perf/Car Crafters Ford	11	Ignition

* Denotes Sunoco Rookie of the Year Contender

TIME OF RACE: 1 hrs., 5 mins, 35 secs — Average Speed: 69.987 mph — Caution Flags: 4 for 20 laps — Lap Leaders: Dylan Kwasniewski 1-86, Derek Thorn 87-153.

14 ALL AMERICAN SPEEDWAY 10/13/2012

Fin	Str	Car	Driver	Team	Laps	Status
1	1	03	Dylan Kwasniewski	Royal Purple/Rockstar Ford	150	Running
2	4	20	Eric Holmes	NAPA Auto Parts Toyota	150	Running
3	8	17	David Mayhew	MMI Services/Ron's Rear Ends Chevrolet	150	Running
4	2	6	Derek Thorn	Sunrise Ford/Lucas Oil/Eibach Ford	150	Running
5	3	24	Cameron Hayley *	NAPA Batteries/Cabinets by Hayley Toyota	150	Running
6	6	16	Jamie Krzysik *	Oculus Trnspt/Northwoods Hauling Toyota	150	Running
7	7	14	Travis Milburn	Cooks Collision Chevrolet	150	Running
8	15	31	Dallas Montes *	Golden Gate Meat/Lynch Oil Chevrolet	150	Running
9	11	51	Mike David	51 FIFTY Energy Drink Toyota	150	Running
10	12	22	Jonathon Gomez	Century Boatland Chevrolet	150	Running
11	17	61	Braeden Havens *	Western Rail Inc/Hilliard Chevrolet	150	Running
12	20	9	Austin Dyne *	William Rast/Sunrise Ford/Lucas Oil Ford	150	Running
13	13	26	Greg Pursley	GPM/Star Nursery/ Real Water Ford	150	Running
14	23	07	Ryan Partridge *	PPL Motorsports Ford	149	Running
15	5	99	Markus Niemela *	Bad Piggies Toyota	149	Running
16	21	2	Carl Harr	West World Computers Chevrolet	149	Running
17	16	71	Daryl Harr	i World Connect Chevrolet	149	Running
18	22	36	John Wood	Holleran Perf./Pegasus Trans. Dodge	147	Running
19	24	38	Tommy Regan *	Ultra Lube/National Tool Warehouse Ford	146	Running
20	18	5	Dylan Hutchison *	Bay Bio Diesel/Johnnie Walker Chevrolet	143	Running
21	19	52	Ryan Philpott	51 Fifty Energy Drink/Moto EFX Ford	136	Running
22	9	21	Michael Self	Rockwell/Golden Gate Meat Chevrolet	135	Running
23	10	59	Jason Fensler	Swartz Diesel/Cancer Awareness Chevrolet	101	Accident
24	14	73	Julien Jousse *	Barbarac Ice Cream Chevrolet	9	Radiator

* Denotes Sunoco Rookie of the Year Contender

TIME OF RACE: 1 hrs., 3 mins, 9 secs — Average Speed: 47.458 mph — Caution Flags: 10 for 58 laps — Lap Leaders: Kwasniewski -grid, Derek Thorn 1-14, Eric Holmes 15, Derek Thorn 16-32, Eric Holmes 33-118, Dylan Kwasniewski 119-150.

15 PHOENIX INTERNATIONAL RACEWAY 11/10/2012

Fin	Str	Car	Driver	Team	Laps	Status
1	2	21	Michael Self	Rockwell/Golden Gate Meat Chevrolet	50	Running
2	4	03	Dylan Kwasniewski	Royal Purple/Rockstar Ford	50	Running
3	1	47	Cale Conley	Tait Towers/Rock-It Cargo Toyota	50	Running
4	7	94	Chase Elliott	Hendrickcars.com/Aaron's Chevrolet	50	Running
5	9	24	Cameron Hayley *	Cabinets by Hayley Toyota	50	Running
6	11	26	Greg Pursley	GPM/Star Nursery/ Real Water Ford	50	Running
7	20	17	David Mayhew	MMI Services/Ron's Rear Ends Chevrolet	50	Running
8	6	4	Bryan Ortiz *	Putinka Vodka Toyota	50	Running
9	5	61	Brett Thompson	RTTI/61 Logistics Chevrolet	50	Running
10	10	96	Ben Kennedy	NAPA Filters Toyota	50	Running
11	18	10	Dallas Montes *	Bakersfield Jam/Lynch Oil Toyota	50	Running
12	17	16	Jonathon Gomez	Telcel America/Acapulco Chevrolet	50	Running
13	15	9	Austin Dyne *	William Rast/Sunrise Ford/Lucas Oil Ford	50	Running
14	22	42	Taylor Cuzick *	Freightliner of Arizona Chevrolet	50	Running
15	13	60	Braeden Havens *	Western Rail Inc/Hilliard Chevrolet	50	Running
16	16	89	Brian Wong	PECO Car Wash Systems Toyota	50	Running
17	12	52	Ryan Philpott	51 Fifty Energy Drink/Moto EFX Ford	50	Running
18	21	54	Anthony Giannone *	K&N Air Filters/ MGP Chevrolet	50	Running
19	24	71	Daryl Harr	i World Connect Chevrolet	50	Running
20	27	20	Eric Holmes	NAPA Auto Parts Toyota	50	Running
21	19	22	Cassie Gannis *	Mancavesite.org Chevrolet	50	Running
22	26	18	Billy Kann	Interstate Batteries Toyota	50	Running
23	25	14	Travis Milburn	Cooks Collision Toyota	49	Running
24	28	2	Carl Harr	West World Computers Chevrolet	49	Running
25	23	38	Tommy Regan *	Ultra Lube/National Tool Warehouse Ford	48	Running
26	29	30	John Wood	Holleran's Performance Toyota	48	Running
27	3	6	Derek Thorn	Sunrise Ford/Lucas Oil/Eibach Ford	47	Running
28	14	83	Kelly Admiraal *	Honoring The Fallen Tribute Car Chevrolet	40	Running
29	8	8	Johnny Borneman	Twisted X Boots/Red Line Oil Chevrolet	11	Accident
30	30	36	Griffin Steinfeld *	Our Military Kids Ford	4	Clutch

* Denotes Sunoco Rookie of the Year Contender

TIME OF RACE: 28 mins, 19 secs — Average Speed: 105.945 mph — Caution Flags: 2 for 5 laps — Lap Leaders: Cale Conley-grid, Michael Self 1-50.

NASCAR HOME TRACKS
D.J. KENNINGTON
NASCAR CANADIAN TIRE SERIES 2012 CHAMPION

NASCAR CANADIAN TIRE SERIES

Presented by **Mobil 1**

PERSONAL INFORMATION

Birth Date:	**July 15, 1977**
Hometown:	**St. Thomas, Ontario**
Marital Status:	**Married (Jaime)**
2012 Team:	**DJK Racing**
Car Owner:	**Doug Kennington**
Crew Chief:	**Dave Wight**

CAREER RECORD

Year	Rank	Races	Wins	Poles	Top 5s	Top 10s
2007	2	12	2	1	8	9
2008	3	13	0	0	9	11
2009	2	13	2	2	9	10
2010	1	13	5	5	9	11
2011	2	12	2	1	8	10
2012	1	12	7	1	11	11
TOTALS		**75**	**18**	**10**	**54**	**62**

D.J. KENNINGTON CAPTURED HIS SECOND NASCAR CANADIAN TIRE SERIES CHAMPIONSHIP

D.J. Kennington made good on his promise. The quest for the 2012 NASCAR Canadian Tire Series presented by Mobil 1 championship began in December 2011 at the NASCAR Touring Series Awards when Kennington informed 2011 series champion Scott Steckly that, at the stroke of midnight, the new season had begun.

It proved to be a historic season for the St. Thomas, Ontario, driver. After collecting a pair of top-five finishes on road courses to open the season, Kennington and the Castrol Edge/Mahindra Tractors Dodge team went to work.

Collecting his first win of the season at the Speedway at Canadian Tire Motorsport Park in Bowmanville, Ontario, Kennington triggered a sequence of events not commonly accomplished in NASCAR. After getting that initial victory, Kennington picked up wins at his home track of Delaware (Ontario) Speedway and Motoplex Speedway and Event Park in Vernon, B.C., to run his winning streak to three races in a row. A bit of luck took the streak to four in a row in a road-course race in Edmonton, Alberta. Contact between the race leaders opened the door for Kennington – running in third – to sneak through for just his second career win on a road course.

The opportunity at history came at Auto Clearing Motor Speedway in Saskatoon, Saskatchewan – an oval where Kennington is most comfortable. A strong finish resulted in a fifth straight victory. With the win, Kennington joined legendary West Coast driver Herschel McGriff (NASCAR K&N Pro Series West – 1972), NASCAR Hall of Famer Richie Evans (NASCAR Whelen Modified Tour – 1985), longtime NASCAR Sprint Cup Series competitor Ricky Craven (NASCAR K&N Pro Series East – 1991) and nine-time NASCAR champion Mike Stefanik (NASCAR Whelen Modified Tour – 1997) as winners of five straight races in the modern era of the currently NASCAR-sanctioned touring series. Two more top fives followed in Quebec road-course events at Trois-Rivieres and Montreal.

The only bobble for Kennington, who also won the 2010 series title, was a 21st-place effort on Sept. 8 at Barrie (Ontario) Speedway where his evening was undone by a fuel pump failure. However, he bounced right back and closed out the year with back-to-back wins at Nova Scotia's Riverside International Speedway and Kawartha Speedway in Fraserville, Ontario.

All told, Kennington earned victories in six of the seven scheduled races on ovals and the Edmonton road-course win to set a series record for wins in a season. His career victory total now stands at 18, which is tops on the all-time list for the young series. To go along with his seven victories, Kennington scored 11 top fives, 11 top 10s and one pole position en route to his second NASCAR Canadian Tire Series championship.

NASCAR CANADIAN TIRE SERIES
2012 CHAMPION D.J. KENNINGTON SEASON RECORD

Date	Speedway	Location	Start	Finish	Status
May 20	Canadian Tire Motorsport Park (Road Course)	Bowmanville, Ontario	4	2	Running
June 3	Circuit ICAR	Mirabel, Quebec	2	5	Running
June 16	Canadian Tire Motorsport Park (Oval)	Bowmanville, Ontario	5	1	Running
June 23	Delaware Speedway	Delaware, Ontario	1	1	Running
July 14	Motoplex Speedway	Vernon, British Columbia	3	1	Running
July 22	Edmonton City Centre Airport	Edmonton, Alberta	6	1	Running
July 25	Auto Clearing Motor Speedway	Saskatoon, Saskatchewan	5	1	Running
Aug. 5	Circuit de Trois-Rivieres	Trois-Rivieres, Quebec	5	5	Running
Aug. 18	Circuit Gilles Villeneuve	Montreal, Quebec	3	5	Running
Sept. 9	Barrie Speedway	Barrie, Ontario	6	21	Running
Sept. 15	Riverside International Speedway	Antigonish, Nova Scotia	5	1	Running
Sept. 22	Kawartha Speedway	Fraserville, Ontario	4	1	Running

2

J.R. FITZPATRICK

J.R. Fitzpatrick turned in his most consistent season north of the border, but the dominance of D.J. Kennington was too much. Fitzpatrick collected road-course wins at Canadian Tire Motorsport Park and Circuit Gilles Villeneuve. He paced the series with four pole positions and led a series-high 809 laps.

3

ANDREW RANGER

Two-time series champion Andrew Ranger returned to fulltime competition in the series after running in selected events in 2010 and 2011. He continued his mastery of road courses with wins at Circuit ICAR and Circuit de Trois-Rivières. Thirteen of his 16 career wins have come in road-racing events.

4

SCOTT STECKLY

Scott Steckly, a two-time series champ, scored another solid season, but was not up to his own high standards. It was his fifth straight season of finishing in the top four in points, but for the first time in his six-year series career he failed to reach Victory Lane. He did, however, notch eight top-five finishes in 12 outings.

5

RON BEAUCHAMP JR.

Ron Beauchamp Jr. is one of four drivers to start every race (75) in series history and registered a top-five finish in points for the second time. He collected a pole win at Motoplex Speedway and has garnered at least one pole position in three of the last four seasons.

NASCAR CANADIAN TIRE SERIES CAREER WINS (2007-2012)

Driver	Wins	Driver	Wins	Driver	Wins	Driver	Wins
D.J. Kennington	18	J.R. Fitzpatrick	8	Kerry Micks	3	Jason Hathaway	1
Andrew Ranger	16	Don Thomson Jr.	7	Pete Shepherd III	3	Derek Lynch	1
Scott Steckly	11	Mark Dilley	3	Robin Buck	2	Alex Tagliani	1
						Dave Whitlock	1

NASCAR CANADIAN TIRE SERIES 2012 FINAL DRIVER STANDINGS

Pos	Driver	Points	Starts	Wins	Top 5	Top 10
1	D.J. Kennington	517	12	7	11	11
2	J.R. Fitzpatrick	490	12	2	9	10
3	Andrew Ranger	482	12	2	7	10
4	Scott Steckly	471	12	0	8	11
5	Ron Beauchamp Jr.	422	12	0	1	8
6	L.P. Dumoulin	396	12	0	3	7
7	Jason Hathaway	390	12	0	4	6
8	Martin Roy *	383	12	0	2	6
9	Jason White	375	12	0	1	3
10	Noel Dowler	355	12	0	1	5
11	Mike Scholz *	297	12	0	0	0
12	Jeff Lapcevich	265	8	0	1	5
13	Mark Dilley	255	7	0	3	5
14	Larry Jackson *	248	9	0	0	1
15	Hugo Vannini	221	9	0	0	0
16	Ray Courtemanche Jr. *	214	9	0	0	0
17	Joey McColm	203	8	0	0	1
18	Kerry Micks	190	6	0	0	3
19	Howie Scannell Jr.	187	7	0	0	0
20	Steve Mathews	181	6	0	1	2
21	Jarrad Whissell	180	7	0	0	1
22	Isabelle Tremblay	171	6	0	0	2
23	Robin Buck	167	5	0	2	3
24	Pete Shepherd III	155	4	1	3	3
25	Dave Connelly	151	6	0	0	0
26	Trevor Seibert	131	4	0	1	2
27	Derek White	123	5	0	0	0
28	Ryley Seibert *	119	4	0	0	1
29	Steve Côté *	114	4	0	0	1
30	Dexter Stacey	107	5	0	1	1
31	Peter Klutt	100	3	0	0	0
32	Dave Coursol *	87	3	0	0	0
33	J.F. Dumoulin	85	3	0	0	2
34	James Van Domselaar	79	3	0	0	0
35	Elie Arseneau *	78	4	0	0	0
36	Jim White	76	2	0	1	2
37	Donald Chisholm	73	2	0	0	2
38	Alex Labbe *	65	3	0	0	1
39	Bob De Lorme *	59	2	0	0	0
40	David Thorndyke	58	2	0	0	0
41	Kevin Dowler *	54	2	0	0	0
42	Jason Hankewich *	51	2	0	0	0
43	Patrice Brisebois	49	2	0	0	0
44	Timmy Hill	38	1	0	0	1
45	Austin Dillon	37	1	0	0	1
46	Michel Pilon	37	1	0	0	0
47	Nick Jewell *	35	1	0	0	1
48	Xavier Coupal *	35	1	0	0	1
49	Benoit Theetge *	32	2	0	0	0
50	Francois Lessard *	31	1	0	0	0
51	Dan Shirley *	30	1	0	0	0
52	Todd Nichol	26	1	0	0	0
53	Nathan Weenk	26	1	0	0	0
54	Kelly Admiraal *	23	1	0	0	0
55	Max Papis	23	1	0	0	0
56	Brandon White *	8	0	0	0	0

* Rookie of the Year Contender

NASCAR CANADIAN TIRE SERIES POLE WINNERS (2007-2012)

J.R. Fitzpatrick 11	Scott Steckly 8	Alex Tagliani 3	Louis-Philippe Dumoulin 1
Andrew Ranger 11	Ron Beauchamp Jr. 4	Steve Mathews 2	Peter Gibbons 1
Don Thomson Jr. 11	Mark Dilley 3	Pete Shepherd III 2	Anthony Simone 1
D.J. Kennington 10	Kerry Micks 3	Jason Bowles 1	

NASCAR CANADIAN TIRE SERIES ROOKIES OF THE YEAR (2008-2012)

2008 . . . . .Jason White	2010 . . . . .Derek White	2012 . . . . Martin Roy
2009 . . . . .Joey Hanssen	2011 . . . . .L.P. Dumoulin	

NASCAR CANADIAN TIRE SERIES MOST POPULAR DRIVERS (2007-2012)

2007 . . . . J.R. Fitzpatrick	2009 . . . . Andrew Ranger	2011 . . . . .Jason White
2008 . . . . .D.J. Kennington	2010 . . . . Andrew Ranger	2012 . . . . .Ray Courtemanche Jr.

NASCAR HOME TRACKS

NASCAR CANADIAN TIRE SERIES CHAMPS AND LEADERS (2007–2012)

2007		2008		2009		2010		2011		2012	
Andrew Ranger	1896	Scott Steckly	2070	Andrew Ranger	2190	D.J. Kennington	2117	Scott Steckly	1960	D.J. Kennington	517
D.J. Kennington	1793	Don Thomson Jr.	2046	D.J. Kennington	2023	J.R. Fitzpatrick	2030	D.J. Kennington	1881	J.R. Fitzpatrick	490
Peter Gibbons	1770	D.J. Kennington	1972	Ron Beauchamp Jr.	2023	Scott Steckly	2022	J.R. Fitzpatrick	1774	Andrew Ranger	482
Don Thomson Jr.	1739	Andrew Ranger	1853	Scott Steckly	1953	Don Thomson Jr.	2006	Kerry Micks	1754	Scott Steckly	471
Derek Lynch	1713	Kerry Micks	1828	Kerry Micks	1942	Kerry Micks	1977	Don Thomson Jr.	1731	Ron Beauchamp Jr.	422
J.R. Fitzpatrick	1710	Mark Dilley	1819	Don Thomson Jr.	1841	Jason Hathaway	1826	Mark Dilley	1631	LP Dumoulin	396
Kerry Micks	1696	J.R. Fitzpatrick	1813	Jason Hathaway	1819	Ron Beauchamp Jr.	1731	Ron Beauchamp Jr.	1571	Jason Hathaway	390
Mark Dilley	1688	Peter Gibbons	1770	Anthony Simone	1800	Mark Dilley	1701	Jason White	1499	Martin Roy	383
Jason Hathaway	1631	Jason Hathaway	1736	Mark Dilley	1767	Anthony Simone	1601	Jason Hathaway	1450	Jason White	375
Scott Steckly	1630	Brad Graham	1720	Dave Whitlock	1746	Dexter Stacey	1528	Dexter Stacey	1396	Noel Dowler	355

NASCAR CANADIAN TIRE SERIES 2012 RACE RESULTS

1 CANADIAN TIRE MOTORSPORTS PARK ROAD COURSE 05/20/2012

Fin	Str	Driver	Team	Laps	Status
1	2	J.R. Fitzpatrick	Equipment Express Chevrolet	51	Running
2	4	D.J. Kennington	Castrol Edge/Mahindra Tractors Dodge	51	Running
3	1	Scott Steckly	Canadian Tire Dodge	51	Running
4	3	Andrew Ranger	Dodge/GC Motorsports Dodge	51	Running
5	10	Louis-Philippe Dumoulin	WeatherTech Canada/Bellemare Dodge	51	Running
6	6	Jason Hathaway	Snap-on Tools/Vortex Brake Pads Dodge	51	Running
7	7	Kerry Micks	PartSource Ford	51	Running
8	9	Jeff Lapcevich	Tim Hortons Dodge	51	Running
9	11	Robin Buck	Quaker State Dodge	51	Running
10	8	Peter Klutt	Legendary Motorcar Chevrolet	51	Running
11	5	Ron Beauchamp Jr.	Mopar/Mobil 1 Dodge	51	Running
12	13	Jason White	A&W/Bower & Wilkins Dodge	51	Running
13	17	Howie Scannell Jr.	Trailers by Jim Bray Dodge	51	Running
14	22	Derek White	Burger Barn Chevrolet	51	Running
15	23	Dave Coursol *	Carquest Canada Dodge	51	Running
16	20	Larry Jackson *	B&B Decals/Speedy Auto Service Dodge	51	Running
17	26	David Thorndyke	Thorsons EVT Chevrolet	50	Running
18	16	Martin Roy *	Veloce/Gamache Truck Center Dodge	50	Running
19	14	Jarrad Whissell	SMS Equipment/Komatsu Ford	48	Running
20	18	Steven Mathews	Bill Mathews Motors Ford	43	Off Track
21	19	Isabelle Tremblay	Frank Lyman Design Dodge	28	Rear End
22	12	Steve Cote *	White Motorsports Chevrolet	24	Off Track
23	27	Hugo Vannini	Vannini Motorsports Ford	24	Running
24	24	Michael Scholz *	Jiffy Car Wash/Watchfinder.ca Chevrolet	21	Running
25	25	Joey McColm	@JoeyMcColm Dodge	17	Off Track
26	15	Noel Dowler	EMCO-Kohler/Rheem Dodge	14	Off Track
27	21	Ray Courtemanche Jr. *	Construction Danam Bonzai Dodge	1	Off Track

* Rookie of the Year contender

TIME OF RACE: 1 hrs., 41 mins, 8 secs — Average Speed: 74.402 mph — Caution Flags: 3 for 11 laps — Lap Leaders: JR Fitzpatrick 1-15, Ron Beauchamp 16, Ron Beauchamp Jr. 17-20, Robin Buck 21-23, JR Fitzpatrick 24-38, Scott Steckly 39, DJ Kennington 40-41, JR Fitzpatrick 42-43, DJ Kennington 44, JR Fitzpatrick 45-51.

2 CIRCUIT ICAR 06/03/2012

Fin	Str	Driver	Team	Laps	Status
1	16	Andrew Ranger	Dodge/GC Motorsports Dodge	31	Running
2	3	JR Fitzpatrick	Equipment Express Chevrolet	31	Running
3	1	Scott Steckly	Canadian Tire Dodge	31	Running
4	12	Louis-Philippe Dumoulin	WeatherTech Canada/Bellemare Dodge	31	Running
5	2	D.J. Kennington	Castrol Edge/Mahindra Tractors Dodge	31	Running
6	25	Alex Labbe *	VR Victoriaville Dodge	31	Running
7	26	J.F. Dumoulin	ACASS/Bellemare/Marac Dodge	31	Running
8	9	Jeff Lapcevich	Tim Hortons Dodge	31	Running
9	5	Ron Beauchamp Jr.	Mopar/Mobil 1 Dodge	31	Running
10	21	Martin Roy *	Veloce/Gamache Truck Center Dodge	31	Running
11	13	Steve Cote	White Motorsports Chevrolet	31	Running
12	20	Larry Jackson *	B&B Decals/Speedy Auto Service Dodge	31	Running
13	6	Jason White	A&W/Bower&Wilkins Dodge	31	Running
14	19	Dave Coursol *	Carquest Canada Dodge	31	Running
15	24	Ray Courtemanche Jr. *	Construction Danam Bonzai Dodge	31	Running
16	17	Howie Scannell Jr.	Trailers by Jim Bray Dodge	31	Running
17	14	Hugo Vannini	VTI Motorsports Ford	31	Running
18	10	Noel Dowler	EMCO-Kohler/Rheem Dodge	31	Running
19	29	Michel Pilon	Aquacoupe Technologie Chevrolet	31	Running
20	22	Jarrad Whissell	SMS Equipment/Komatsu Ford	31	Running
21	4	Kerry Micks	Leland/BDI/PartSource Ford	30	Running
22	23	Mike Scholz *	Jiffy Car Wash/Watchfinder.ca Chevrolet	29	Off Track
23	7	Jason Hathaway	Snap-on Tools/Vortex Brake Pads Dodge	24	Running
24	18	Derek White	Burger Barn Chevrolet	23	Off Track
25	11	Isabelle Tremblay	Frank Lyman Design Dodge	15	Rear End
26	15	Robin Buck	Quaker State Dodge	6	Off Track
27	8	Dexter Stacey	WJS Motorsports Dodge	5	Off Track
28	27	Elie Arseneau *	Prime Racing/Circuit ICAR Chevrolet	4	Suspension
29	28	Dave Connelly	Schneider's/Metro Dodge	1	Suspension

* Rookie of the Year contender

TIME OF RACE: 1 hr., 12 min., 18 sec. — Average Speed: 54.359 mph — Caution Flags: 4 for 10 laps — Lap Leaders: DJ Kennington 1-6, Andrew Ranger 7-31.

3 SPEEDWAY AT CANADIAN TIRE MOTORSPORT PARK 06/16/2012

Fin	Str	Driver	Team	Laps	Status
1	5	D.J. Kennington	Castrol Edge/Mahindra Tractors Dodge	200	Running
2	7	Mark Dilley	PartSource/BDI/Leland Ford	200	Running
3	3	J.R. Fitzpatrick	Equipment Express Chevrolet	200	Running
4	8	Jeff Lapcevich	Tim Hortons Dodge	200	Running
5	6	Jason Hathaway	Snap-on Tools/Vortex Brake Pads Dodge	200	Running
6	2	Steve Mathews	Bill Mathews Motors Ford	200	Running
7	4	Andrew Ranger	Dodge/GC Motorsports Dodge	200	Running
8	10	Ron Beauchamp Jr.	Mopar/Mobil 1 Dodge	200	Running
9	11	Steve Côté *	White Motorsports Chevrolet	199	Running
10	20	Noel Dowler	EMCO-Kohler/Rheem Dodge	199	Running
11	15	Jason White	A&W/Bower&Wilkins Dodge	199	Running
12	14	L.P. Dumoulin	WeatherTech Canada/Bellemare Dodge	198	Running
13	16	Joey McColm	CarNationCanada.com Dodge	196	Running
14	4	Scott Steckly	Canadian Tire Dodge	194	Running
15	19	Ray Courtemanche Jr. *	Construction Danam Bonzai Dodge	193	Running
16	1	Pete Shepherd III	National Exhaust Dodge	158	Axle
17	12	Larry Jackson *	B&B Decals/Speedy Auto Service Dodge	144	Running
18	18	Hugo Vannini	VTI Motorsports Ford	128	Engine
19	13	Martin Roy *	Veloce/Gamache Truck Center Dodge	83	Oil Line
20	17	Howie Scannell Jr.	Trailers by Jim Bray Dodge	34	Overheating
21	21	Mike Scholz *	Jiffy Car Wash/Watchfinder.ca Chevrolet	5	Clutch

TIME OF RACE: 1 hrs., 35 min, 1 secs — Average Speed: 63.147 mph — Caution Flags: 5 for 36 laps — Lap Leaders: Pete Shepherd III 1-41, J.R. Fitzpatrick 42-55, D.J. Kennington 56-62, L.P. Dumoulin 63-70, D.J. Kennington 71-200.

4 DELAWARE SPEEDWAY 06/23/2012

Fin	Str	Driver	Team	Laps	Status
1	1	D.J. Kennington	Castrol Edge/Mahindra Tractors Dodge	200	Running
2	4	Scott Steckly	Canadian Tire Dodge	200	Running
3	10	Jason Hathaway	Snap-on Tools/Vortex Brake Pads Dodge	200	Running
4	7	Andrew Ranger	Dodge/GC Motorsports Dodge	200	Running
5	6	Pete Shepherd III	National Exhaust Dodge	200	Running
6	20	Jason White	A&W/Bower&Wilkins Dodge	199	Running
7	8	Mark Dilley	PartSource/BDI/Leland Ford	198	Running
8	12	Joey McColm	CarNationCanada.com Dodge	198	Running
9	16	Noel Dowler	EMCO-Kohler/Rheem Dodge	198	Running
10	14	L.P. Dumoulin	WeatherTech Canada/Bellemare Dodge	198	Running
11	5	Ron Beauchamp Jr.	Mopar/Mobil 1 Dodge	196	Running
12	17	Martin Roy *	Veloce/Gamache Truck Center Dodge	196	Running
13	18	Dave Connelly	Schneider's/Metro Dodge	195	Running
14	3	J.R. Fitzpatrick	Equipment Express Chevrolet	194	Running
15	15	Howie Scannell Jr.	Trailers by Jim Bray Dodge	194	Running
16	21	Ray Courtemanche Jr. *	Construction Danam Bonzai Dodge	189	Running
17	2	Steve Mathews	Bill Mathews Motors Ford	181	Suspension
18	13	Larry Jackson *	B&B Decals/Speedy Auto Service Dodge	134	Suspension
19	9	Jeff Lapcevich	Tim Hortons Dodge	117	Running
20	11	Steve Côté *	White Motorsports Chevrolet	91	Engine
21	22	Mike Scholz *	Jiffy Car Wash/Watchfinder.ca Chevrolet	16	Engine
22	19	Hugo Vannini	VTI Motorsports Ford	5	Suspension

* Rookie of the Year contender

TIME OF RACE: 1 hrs., 22 mins, 15 secs — Average Speed: 72.948 mph — Caution Flags: 4 for 34 laps — Lap Leaders: D.J. Kennington 1-55, J.R. Fitzpatrick 56, Steve Mathews 57-65, J.R. Fitzpatrick 66-156, D.J. Kennington 157-200.

5 MOTOPLEX SPEEDWAY 07/14/2012

Fin	Str	Driver	Team	Laps	Status
1	3	D.J. Kennington	Castrol Edge/Mahindra Tractors Dodge	300	Running
2	6	Jason Hathaway	Snap-on Tools/Rockstar/Vortex Dodge	300	Running
3	2	Scott Steckly	Canadian Tire Dodge	300	Running
4	5	J.R. Fitzpatrick	Equipment Express Chevrolet	300	Running
5	11	Jason White	A&W/Sturgis North 2012 Dodge	300	Running
6	13	Martin Roy *	Veloce/Battery Expert Dodge	300	Running
7	7	Jim White	Sun Ridge Equipment Dodge	300	Running
8	1	Ron Beauchamp Jr.	Mopar/Mobil 1 Dodge	300	Running
9	10	L.P. Dumoulin	WeatherTech Canada/Bellemare Dodge	300	Running
10	16	Noel Dowler	EMCO-Kohler/Rheem Dodge	300	Running
11	8	Andrew Ranger	GC Mtrspts/Dodge/Canada Co Dodge	299	Running
12	12	Trevor Seibert	Lake Excavating Dodge	299	Running
13	4	Mark Dilley	Leland/BDI/PartSource Ford	299	Running
14	19	Bob De Lorme *	Deerfoot Mechanical Chevrolet	295	Running
15	17	James Van Domselaar	Steel-Craft Door Products Chevrolet	290	Running
16	18	Mike Scholz *	Jiffy Car Wash/Watchfinder.ca Chevrolet	268	Running
17	14	Jarrad Whissell	SMS Equipment/Komatsu Chevrolet	257	Rear End
18	9	Ryley Seibert *	Lake Excavating Ford	141	Electrical
19	15	Kevin Dowler *	Whitemud Mech./EMCO Dodge	116	Handling
20	20	Jason Hankewich *	Digger Racing Chevrolet	80	Suspension

* Rookie of the Year contender

TIME OF RACE: 2 hrs., 0 mins, 58 secs — Average Speed: 74.401 mph — Caution Flags: 7 for 52 laps — Lap Leaders: Scott Steckly 1, Ron Beauchamp Jr. 2-4, D.J. Kennington 5-16, J.R. Fitzpatrick 17-37, D.J. Kennington 38-50, J.R. Fitzpatrick 51, D.J. Kennington 52, J.R. Fitzpatrick 53-116, D.J. Kennington 117-158, Scott Steckly 159-172, J.R. Fitzpatrick 173-179, D.J. Kennington 180-182, Andrew Ranger 183-188, D.J. Kennington 189-193, Andrew Ranger 194-200, Scott Steckly 201-248, D.J. Kennington 249-300.

6 EDMONTON CITY CENTRE AIRPORT 07/22/2012

Fin	Str	Driver	Team	Laps	Status
1	6	D.J. Kennington	Castrol Edge/Mahindra Tractors Dodge	31	Running
2	8	Jason Hathaway	Snap-on Tools/Vortex Brake Pads Dodge	31	Running
3	10	Trevor Seibert	Lake Excavating/EMCO Waterworks Dodge	31	Running
4	1	Scott Steckly	Canadian Tire Dodge	31	Running
5	13	Martin Roy *	Veloce/Gamache Truck Center Dodge	31	Running
6	7	Kerry Micks	Leland/BDI/PartSource Ford	31	Running
7	2	Andrew Ranger	Pizza 73/GC Motorsports Dodge	31	Running
8	9	Ron Beauchamp Jr.	Mopar/Mobil 1 Dodge	31	Running
9	11	Jarrad Whissell	SMS Equipment/Komatsu Ford	31	Running
10	12	Ryley Seibert *	Lake Excavating Dodge	31	Running
11	17	Noel Dowler	EMCO-Kohler/Rheem Dodge	31	Running
12	5	Robin Buck	Quaker State Dodge	31	Running
13	18	Joey McColm	Bubbles Car Wash Dodge	31	Running
14	15	Jason White	A&W/Bower&Wilkins Dodge	31	Running
15	14	Kevin Dowler *	Whitemud Mech./EMCO Dodge	31	Running
16	21	Mike Scholz *	Jiffy Car Wash/Watchfinder.ca Chevrolet	30	Running
17	3	J.R. Fitzpatrick	Equipment Express Chevrolet	29	Accident
18	20	Todd Nichol	West World Motorsports Chevrolet	14	Suspension
19	16	James Van Domselaar	Steel-Craft Door Products Chevrolet	14	Suspension
20	4	L.P. Dumoulin	WeatherTech Canada/Bellemare Dodge	3	Transmission
21	19	Kelly Admiraal *	Willam Scottsman Chevrolet	3	Off Track

* Rookie of the Year contender

TIME OF RACE: 0 hrs., 59 mins, 43 secs — Average Speed: 70.268 mph — Caution Flags: 2 for 4 laps — Lap Leaders: Scott Steckly 1-29, D.J. Kennington 30-31.

7 AUTO CLEARING MOTOR SPEEDWAY 07/25/2012

Fin	Str	Driver	Team	Laps	Status
1	5	D.J. Kennington	Castrol Edge/Mahindra Tractors Dodge	250	Running
2	2	Mark Dilley	Leland/BDI/PartSource Ford	250	Running
3	1	J.R. Fitzpatrick	Equipment Express Chevrolet	250	Running
4	7	Scott Steckly	Canadian Tire Dodge	250	Running
5	12	Jim White	AW Millwrights/New Life Feeds Dodge	250	Running
6	8	Andrew Ranger	Pizza 73/GC Motorsports Dodge	250	Running
7	11	L.P. Dumoulin	WeatherTech Canada/Bellemare Dodge	250	Running
8	6	Ron Beauchamp Jr.	Mopar/Exide/Mobil 1 Dodge	250	Running
9	14	Nick Jewell *	Prairie Dodge Dealers/Sikkens Dodge	249	Running
10	3	Martin Roy *	Veloce/Battery Expert Dodge	248	Running
11	22	Jarrad Whissell	SMS Equipment/Komatsu Ford	246	Running
12	16	Mike Scholz *	Jiffy Car Wash/Watchfinder.ca Chevrolet	245	Running
13	17	Ryley Seibert *	Lake Excavating Ford	245	Running
14	13	Dan Shirley *	Saskatoon Co-op/Turtle Wax Chevrolet	245	Running
15	15	Bob De Lorme *	Deerfoot Mechanical Chevrolet	244	Running
16	18	Noel Dowler	EMCO-Kohler/Rheem Dodge	243	Running
17	21	Jason Hankewich *	Hankewich Motorsports Dodge	243	Running
18	4	Nathan Weenk	Mid West Combustion Chevrolet	238	Running
19	19	James Van Domselaar	Steel-Craft Door Products Chevrolet	231	Running
20	20	Jason White	A&W/Bower&Wilkins Dodge	214	Running
21	9	Jason Hathaway	Snap-on Tools/Rockstar/Vortex Dodge	195	Suspension
22	10	Trevor Seibert	Lake Excavating Dodge	148	Engine

* Rookie of the Year contender

TIME OF RACE: 1 hrs., 24 mins, 12 secs — Average Speed: 59.323 mph — Caution Flags: 6 for 46 lap — Lap Leaders: J.R. Fitzpatrick 1-78, Scott Steckly 79-131, J.R. Fitzpatrick 132-138, D.J. Kennington 139-160, Jason Hathaway 161-194, D.J. Kennington 195-250.

8 CIRCUIT DE TROIS-RIVIERES 08/05/2012

Fin	Str	Driver	Team	Laps	Status
1	3	Andrew Ranger	Dodge/GC Motorsports Dodge	44	Running
2	1	L.P. Dumoulin	WeatherTech Canada/Bellemare Dodge	44	Running
3	2	J.R. Fitzpatrick	Equipment Express Chevrolet	44	Running
4	9	Robin Buck	Quaker State Dodge	44	Running
5	5	D.J. Kennington	Castrol Edge/Mahindra Tractors Dodge	44	Running
6	10	J.F. Dumoulin	Bernier Crepeau/Bellmare Dodge	44	Running
7	4	Scott Steckly	Canadian Tire Dodge	44	Running
8	6	Ron Beauchamp Jr.	Mopar/Exide/Mobil 1 Dodge	44	Running
9	30	Jeff Lapcevich	Tim Hortons Dodge	44	Running
10	19	Isabelle Tremblay	Frank Lyman Design Dodge	44	Running
11	12	Peter Klutt	Legendary Motorcar Chevrolet	44	Running
12	13	Kerry Micks	Leland/BDI/PartSource Ford	44	Running
13	22	Francois Lessard *	Ispeedzone Chevrolet	44	Running
14	23	Derek White	BFB Chevrolet	44	Running
15	11	Jason Hathaway	Snap-on Tools/Vortex/Rockstar Dodge	43	Running
16	16	Howie Scannell Jr.	VR Emond/B&B Decals Dodge	43	Running
17	18	Hugo Vannini	VTI Motorsports Ford	43	Running
18	28	Mike Scholz *	Jiffy Car Wash/Watchfinder.ca Chevrolet	43	Running
19	17	Noel Dowler	EMCO-Kohler/Rheem Dodge	43	Running
20	29	David Thorndyke	Thorsons EVT Chevrolet	43	Running
21	21	Jason White	Bowers&Wilkins at FutureShop Dodge	43	Running
22	24	Patrice Brisebois	L'Equipeur Dodge	42	Running
23	31	Dexter Stacey	WJS Motorsports Dodge	41	Running
24	7	Martin Roy *	Veloce/Gamache Truck Center Dodge	39	Running
25	20	Dave Coursol *	Carquest Canada Dodge	37	Running
26	27	Ray Courtemanche Jr. *	Construction Danam Bonzai Dodge	20	Transmission
27	26	Larry Jackson *	B&B Decals/Speedy Auto Service Dodge	19	Transmission
28	15	Benoit Theetge *	Camasino Chevrolet	17	Accident
29	25	Dave Connelly	Schneider's/Metro Dodge	12	Accident
30	8	Elie Arseneau *	Prime Racing/Circuit ICAR Dodge	11	Axle
31	14	Alex Labbe *	VR Victoriaville Dodge	11	Rear End

* Rookie of the Year contender

TIME OF RACE: 1 hrs., 7 mins, 11 secs — Average Speed: 60.122 mph — Caution Flags: 3 for 9 laps — Lap Leaders: L.P. Dumoulin 1-3, J.R. Fitzpatrick 4-9, Andrew Ranger 10-44.

9 CIRCUIT GILLES VILLENEUVE 08/18/2012

Fin	Str	Driver	Team	Laps	Status
1	1	J.R. Fitzpatrick	Equipment Express Chevrolet	23	Running
2	2	Andrew Ranger	Dodge/GC Motorsports Dodge	23	Running
3	6	Robin Buck	Quaker State Dodge	23	Running
4	5	Scott Steckly	Canadian Tire Dodge	23	Running
5	3	D.J. Kennington	Castrol Edge/Mahindra Tractors Dodge	23	Running
6	11	Timmy Hill	Affichage.ca Dodge	23	Running
7	9	Austin Dillon	Fitzpatrick Motorsports Chevrolet	23	Running
8	8	Trevor Seibert	Lake Excavating/EMCO Waterworks Dodge	23	Running
9	20	Xavier Coupal *	Dr. Tint/FRS Dodge	23	Running
10	7	Kerry Micks	Leland/BDI/PartSource Ford	23	Running
11	23	Peter Klutt	Legendary Motorcar Chevrolet	23	Running
12	10	Martin Roy *	Veloce/Battery Expert Dodge	23	Running
13	16	Jason White	Bowers&Wilkins at Future Shop Dodge	23	Running
14	13	Ron Beauchamp Jr.	Mopar/Exide/Mobil 1 Dodge	23	Running
15	33	Steve Mathews	Bill Mathews Motors Ford	23	Running
16	26	Ryley Seibert *	Lake Excavating Dodge	23	Running
17	25	Patrice Brisebois	L'Equipeur Dodge	23	Running
18	30	Noel Dowler	EMCO-Kohler/Rheem Dodge	23	Running
19	15	Jeff Lapcevich	Tim Hortons Dodge	23	Running
20	22	Elie Arseneau *	Prime Racing/Circuit ICAR Dodge	23	Running
21	27	Hugo Vannini	VTI Motorsports Ford	23	Running
22	32	Larry Jackson *	B&B Decals/Speedy Auto Service Dodge	23	Running
23	34	Derek White	Headrush Chevrolet	23	Running
24	21	Howie Scannell Jr.	K&K Ins./VR Emond Dodge	23	Running
25	31	Mike Scholz *	Jiffy Car Wash/Watchfinder.ca Chevrolet	23	Running
26	18	Jason Hathaway	Snap-on Tools/Vortex/Rockstar Dodge	22	Running
27	19	Jarrad Whissell	SMS Equipment/Komatsu Chevrolet	22	Running
28	17	Benoit Theetge *	Camasino Chevrolet	22	Running
29	24	Joey McColm	Espar Dodge	21	Accident
30	14	Alex Labbe *	VR Victoriaville Dodge	18	Engine
31	29	Dexter Stacey	WJS Motorsports Dodge	16	Engine
32	28	Ray Courtemanche Jr. *	Construction Danam Bonzai Dodge	11	Radiator
33	4	L.P. Dumoulin	WeatherTech Canada/Bellemare Dodge	6	Engine
34	12	J.F. Dumoulin	Bernier Crepeau/Bellemare Dodge	6	Axle

* Rookie of the Year contender

TIME OF RACE: 1 hrs., 4 mins, 7 secs — Average Speed: 58.307 mph — Caution Flags: 4 for 11 laps — Lap Leaders: J.R. Fitzpatrick 1-11, Andrew Ranger 12, J.R. Fitzpatrick 13-23.

10 BARRIE SPEEDWAY 09/09/2012

Fin	Str	Driver	Team	Laps	Status
1	8	Pete Shepherd III	National Exhaust Dodge	307	Running
2	11	Andrew Ranger	Dodge/GC Motorsports Dodge	307	Running
3	16	Noel Dowler	EMCO-Kohler/Rheem Dodge	307	Running
4	1	Steve Mathews	Bill Mathews Motors Ford	307	Running
5	20	Dexter Stacey	WJS Motorsports Dodge	307	Running
6	4	J.R. Fitzpatrick	Equipment Express Chevrolet	307	Running
7	2	Ron Beauchamp Jr.	Mopar/Exide/Mobil 1 Dodge	307	Running
8	7	Jason Hathaway	Snap-on Tools/Vortex/Rockstar Dodge	307	Running
9	3	Scott Steckly	Canadian Tire Dodge	306	Running
10	18	Larry Jackson *	Nat'l Tomlinson Tire Rec./RC Trailers Dodge	305	Running
11	13	L.P. Dumoulin	WeatherTech Canada/Bellemare Dodge	303	Running
12	9	Jeff Lapcevich	Tim Hortons Dodge	301	Running
13	12	Joey McColm	Espar Dodge	300	Running
14	17	Dave Connelly	Schneider's/Metro Dodge	299	Running
15	22	Mike Scholz *	Jiffy Car Wash/Watchfinder.ca Chevrolet	298	Running
16	15	Isabelle Tremblay	Frank Lyman Design Dodge	298	Running
17	14	Jason White	Bowers&Wilkins at Future Shop Dodge	297	Running
18	10	Martin Roy *	Veloce/Battery Expert Dodge	286	Running
19	21	Ray Courtemanche Jr. *	Porto Cabral/Const. Danam Bonzai Dodge	285	Running
20	5	Mark Dilley	Leland/BDI/PartSource Ford	282	Transmission
21	6	D.J. Kennington	Castrol Super Clean Dodge	280	Running
22	19	Hugo Vannini	VTI Motorsports Ford	132	Accident

* Rookie of the Year contender

TIME OF RACE: 1 hrs., 58 mins, 39 secs — Average Speed: 51.697 mph — Caution Flags: 13 for 125 laps — Lap Leaders: Steve Mathews 1-3, Scott Steckly 4-26, J.R. Fitzpatrick 27-139, Pete Shepherd III 140-156, Mark Dilley 157-162, Martin Roy * 163-164, Mark Dilley 165-178, J.R. Fitzpatrick 179-206, Scott Steckly 207-293, Steve Mathews 294-305, Pete Shepherd III 306-307.

11 RIVERSIDE INTERNATIONAL SPEEDWAY 09/15/2012

Fin	Str	Driver	Team	Laps	Status
1	5	D.J. Kennington	Castrol Edge/Mahindra Tractors Dodge	300	Running
2	1	J.R. Fitzpatrick	Equipment Express Chevrolet	300	Running
3	4	Mark Dilley	Leland/BDI/PartSource Ford	300	Running
4	2	Scott Steckly	Canadian Tire Dodge	300	Running
5	8	Ron Beauchamp Jr.	Mopar/Exide/Mobil 1 Dodge	300	Running
6	9	Donald Chisholm	Keltic Ford/Nova Construction Ford	300	Running
7	10	Jason White	Bowers&Wilkins at Future Shop Dodge	300	Running
8	6	Martin Roy *	Lemken/Batteries Expert Dodge	299	Running
9	18	Noel Dowler	EMCO-Kohler/Rheem Dodge	298	Running
10	14	Isabelle Tremblay	Frank Lyman Design Dodge	298	Running
11	11	L.P. Dumoulin	WeatherTech Canada/Bellemare Dodge	297	Running
12	7	Andrew Ranger	Dodge/David Brown Transport Dodge	295	Running
13	12	Larry Jackson *	Nat'l Tomlinson Tire Rec./RC Trailers Dodge	287	Running
14	15	Ray Courtemanche Jr. *	Porto Cabral/Const. Danam Bonzai Dodge	249	Running
15	16	Mike Scholz *	Jiffy Car Wash/Watchfinder.ca Chevrolet	241	Suspension
16	17	Hugo Vannini	VTI Motorsports Ford	88	Accident
17	3	Jason Hathaway	Snap-on Tools/Vortex/Rockstar Dodge	72	Engine
18	13	Kerry Micks	Leland/BDI/PartSource Ford	4	Electrical
19	19	Dave Connelly	Schneider's/Metro Dodge	3	Suspension
20	20	Joey McColm	Snap-on Tools Dodge	1	Ignition

* Rookie of the Year contender

TIME OF RACE: 1 hrs., 36 mins, 14 secs — Average Speed: 62.286 mph — Caution Flags: 6 for 43 laps — Lap Leaders: J.R. Fitzpatrick 1-67, D.J. Kennington 68-97, J.R. Fitzpatrick 98, Martin Roy * 99-109, D.J. Kennington 110-190, J.R. Fitzpatrick 191-220, D.J. Kennington 221, J.R. Fitzpatrick 222-224, D.J. Kennington 225-300.

12 KAWARTHA SPEEDWAY 09/22/2012

Fin	Str	Driver	Team	Laps	Status
1	4	D.J. Kennington	Castrol Edge/Mahindra Tractors Dodge	255	Running
2	3	Andrew Ranger	GC Motorsports/Surgenor Dodge	255	Running
3	1	J.R. Fitzpatrick	Equipment Express Chevrolet	255	Running
4	5	Pete Shepherd III	National Exhaust Dodge	255	Running
5	12	Martin Roy *	Gamache/Batteries Expert Dodge	255	Running
6	2	Scott Steckly	Canadian Tire Dodge	255	Running
7	7	Mark Dilley	PartSource/Leland Ford	255	Running
8	10	Jeff Lapcevich	Tim Hortons Dodge	255	Running
9	6	Donald Chisholm	Keltic Ford/Nova Construction Ford	255	Running
10	15	L.P. Dumoulin	WeatherTech Canada/Bellemare Dodge	255	Running
11	8	Ron Beauchamp Jr.	Mopar/Exide/Mobil 1 Dodge	255	Running
12	14	Jason Hathaway	Snap-on Tools/Vortex/Rockstar Dodge	255	Running
13	9	Larry Jackson *	Nat'l Tomlinson Tire/B&B Decals Dodge	255	Running
14	18	Jason White	Bowers&Wilkins at Future Shop Dodge	255	Running
15	27	Dave Connelly	Schneider's/Metro Dodge	254	Running
16	19	Isabelle Tremblay	Frank Lyman Design Dodge	253	Running
17	13	Howie Scannell Jr.	Nat'l Tomlinson Tire/Trailers by Jim Bray Dodge	251	Running
18	22	Ray Courtemanche Jr. *	Porto Cabral/Const. Danam Bonzai Dodge	249	Running
19	25	Hugo Vannini	VTI Motorsports Ford	243	Running
20	20	Elie Arseneau *	Prime Racing/Circuit ICAR Dodge	232	Running
21	16	Max Papis	AW Millwrights/Nano Spark Dodge	219	Running
22	17	Derek White	White Motorsports Chevrolet	203	Fuel Pump
23	11	Steve Mathews	Bill Mathews Motors Ford	195	Suspension
24	24	Noel Dowler	EMCO-Kohler/Rheem Dodge	186	Accident
25	28	Jarrad Whissell	SMS Equipment/Komatsu Chevrolet	88	Accident
26	23	Mike Scholz *	Jiffy Car Wash/Watchfinder.ca Chevrolet	80	Rear End
27	21	Dexter Stacey	WJS Motorsports Dodge	45	Oil Leak
28	26	Joey McColm	Espar Dodge	7	Engine

* Rookie of the Year contender

TIME OF RACE: 1 hrs., 51 mins, 27 secs — Average Speed: 51.480 mph — Caution Flags: 8 for 65 laps — Lap Leaders: .R. Fitzpatrick 1-118, Jason Hathaway 119-132, J.R. Fitzpatrick 133-230, D.J. Kennington 231-255.

JORGE GOETERS

NASCAR TOYOTA SERIES 2012 CHAMPION

It can't be denied that winning a championship takes a lot of skill, and some luck. Jorge Goeters used a dose of each en route to the 2012 NASCAR Toyota Series championship in Mexico.

The veteran out of Mexico City began the season with a pair of top-five finishes, but a 20th-place finish at Querétaro dug the first of two holes from out of which Goeters would have to climb on the year. A May win at Puebla took him back to the top of the standings, but a season-worst finish of 22nd at the July Mexico City event created the second hurdle – one which Goeters would spend virtually the rest of the season looking to clear.

Despite reeling off five consecutive top-10 finishes, including his second win of the season in September at Monterrey, Goeters still trailed Daniel Suárez in points, but a drastic change was on the horizon. In the series' inaugural visit to Chihuahua in October, Suarez looked ready to pad his advantage by dominating the early portion of the event but, as luck would have it, a suspension problem turned his car into the Turn 4 wall. As a result, Goeters reclaimed the points lead and went into the season finale with an 18-point advantage – a lead he only added to when all was said and done.

On the season, Goeters claimed two victories with nine top-five and 12 top-10 finishes to claim his second NASCAR Toyota Series title, but first under the NASCAR banner.

PERSONAL INFORMATION

Birth Date:	**June 26, 1970**
Hometown:	**Mexico City, Mexico**
2012 Team:	**Canel's Racing**
Car Owner:	**Juan Pablo Garcia**
Crew Chief:	**Ramon Fidalgo**

CAREER RECORD

Year	Rank	Starts	Wins	Poles	Top 5s	Top 10s
2007	6	14	1	1	8	9
2008	6	14	0	1	4	9
2009	3	14	1	2	6	9
2010	5	14	2	2	6	6
2011	3	14	2	2	5	10
2012	1	14	2	0	9	12
TOTALS		**80**	**8**	**8**	**38**	**55**

NASCAR TOYOTA SERIES
2012 CHAMPION JORGE GOETERS SEASON RECORD

Date	Speedway	Location	Start	Finish	Status
May 25	Autódromo de Monterrey (road course)	Monterrey, Mexico	7	3	Running
April 15	Autódromo Potosino	San Luis Potosí, Mexico	14	4	Running
April 28	Nuevo Autódromo de Querétaro	Querétaro, Mexico	7	20	Running
May 12	Autódromo Hermanos Rodríguez	Mexico City, Mexico	14	4	Running
May 27	Autódromo Miguel E. Abed	Puebla, Mexico	10	1	Running
June 17	Nuevo Autódromo de Aguascalientes	Aguascalientes, Mexico	3	3	Running
July 8	Autódromo Hermanos Rodríguez	Mexico City, Mexico	14	22	Running
July 29	Autódromo Potosino	San Luis Potosí, Mexico	13	4	Running
Aug. 12	Nuevo Autódromo de Querétaro	Querétaro, Mexico	7	6	Running
Aug. 26	Nuevo Autódromo de Aguascalientes	Aguascalientes, Mexico	4	3	Running
Sept. 9	Autódromo Miguel E. Abed	Puebla, Mexico	8	2	Running
Sept. 30	Autódromo de Monterrey (oval)	Monterrey, Mexico	9	1	Running
Oct. 28	El Dorado Speedway	Chihuahua, Mexico	7	8	Running
Nov. 11	Autódromo Hermanos Rodríguez	Mexico City, Mexico	6	8	Running

2

HOMERO RICHARDS

Homero Richards finished second in the final point standings for the second straight year after an inconsistent season. He followed up his five-win season in 2011 with a pair of triumphs in 2012. Those victories came at Querétaro in April and Mexico City in the November season finale.

3

DANIEL SUÁREZ

Daniel Suárez, at 20 years of age, established himself as a championship contender from the very beginning of the year. He claimed his first series win in May at Mexico City and won again in the August Querétaro date. His championship dreams were dashed by a suspension problem in the season's next-to-last race.

4

RUBÉN PARDO

Rubén Pardo bounced back from a 14th-place points effort in 2011. He collected his first series victory since September 2005 when he took the checkered flag in October at the inaugural Chihuahua race. He also scored six top-five and nine top-10 finishes.

5

ANTONIO PÉREZ

Antonio Pérez scored his first top-10 finish in points since a fourth-place effort in 2010. He got out of the gate quickly with a win at San Luis Potosí in the season's second race and followed it up with a June victory at Aguascalientes. On the year, he registered three top fives and nine top 10s.

NASCAR TOYOTA SERIES 2012 RESULTS

Pos	Driver	Points	Starts	Wins	Top 5	Top 10
1	Jorge Goeters	539	14	2	9	12
2	Homero Richards	505	14	2	6	9
3	Daniel Suárez	504	14	2	9	9
4	Rubén Pardo	478	14	1	6	9
5	Antonio Pérez	472	14	2	3	9
6	Hugo Oliveras	461	14	1	4	8
7	Patrick Goeters	461	14	0	3	9
8	Rafael Martínez	447	14	1	5	8
9	José Luis Ramírez	446	14	0	0	8
10	Rubén Rovelo	437	14	2	5	6
11	Abraham Calderón	436	14	0	5	7
12	Freddy Tame Jr.	433	14	0	2	6
13	Rogelio López	429	14	1	4	7
14	Rubén García Jr. *	416	14	0	1	7
15	Salvador Durán	410	14	0	2	4
16	Irwin Vences	409	14	0	1	6
17	Carlos Peralta	406	14	0	0	3
18	Juan Carlos Blum *	345	13	0	0	2
19	Elliot Van Rankin	342	14	0	1	4
20	Luis Felipe Montaño	330	14	0	1	1
21	Rafael Vallina	322	14	0	0	0
22	Pepe Montaño	317	14	0	0	0
23	Victor Barrales	312	14	0	0	0
24	Alejandro Capín	311	14	0	1	1
25	Héctor Félix	310	14	0	0	1
26	Óscar Ruíz	309	14	0	0	0
27	Israel Jaitovich	309	14	0	0	0
28	Rodrigo Marbán	292	14	0	0	0
29	Rodrigo Peralta *	215	9	0	0	1
30	Alejandro Villasana *	194	8	0	0	0
31	Javier Fernandez *	184	11	0	0	0
32	Jorge Contreras Jr.	158	9	0	0	0
33	Héctor Aguirre *	155	7	0	2	2
34	Carlos Contreras	134	6	0	0	1
35	Óscar Peralta	118	7	0	0	0
36	Rubén García	54	3	0	0	0
37	Oscar Torres Jr. *	37	2	0	0	0
38	Waldemar Coronas *	31	1	0	0	0
39	José González	31	1	0	0	0
40	Enrique Contreras III	27	2	0	0	0
41	Rodrigo Echeverría *	25	2	0	0	0
42	Xavier Razo	24	1	0	0	0
43	Nelson Canache	16	1	0	0	0
44	Mike Sanchez	10	0	0	0	0
45	Carlos Anaya	8	1	0	0	0

* Rookie of the Year Contender

NASCAR TOYOTA SERIES CAREER WINS (2004-2012)

Driver	Wins	Driver	Wins	Driver	Wins	Driver	Wins
Rogelio López	21	Antonio Pérez	11	Carlos Contreras	2	Ricardo Pérez de Lara	1
Germán Quiroga	17	Homero Richards	11	Hugo Oliveras	2	Fernando Plata	1
Rafael Martínez	16	Rubén Rovelo	6	Daniel Suárez	2	José Luis Ramírez	1
Jorge Goeters	13	Patrick Goeters	4	Freddy Tame	2	Cesar Tiberio	1
Carlos Pardo	11	Rubén Pardo	4	Waldermar Coronas	1		

NASCAR TOYOTA SERIES ROOKIES OF THE YEAR (2004-2012)

2004	Ignacio Alvarado	2007	Mike Sanchez	2010	Daniel Suárez
2005	Patricio Jourdain	2008	Irwin Vences	2011	Enrique Contreras III
2006	Antonio Pérez	2009	Alejandro Capín	2012	Rubén García Jr.

NASCAR TOYOTA SERIES MOST POPULAR DRIVERS (2008-2012)

2008	Carlos Contreras	2010	Jorge Arteaga	2012	Pepe Montaño
2009	Jorge Arteaga	2011	Jorge Arteaga		

NASCAR TOYOTA SERIES POLE POSITIONS (2004-2012)

Driver		Driver		Driver		Driver	
Rogelio López	20	Ruben Rovelo	5	Fernando Plata	2	Rubén García Jr.	1
Jorge Goeters	17	Antonio Pérez	4	Jorge Arteaga	1	José Garfías	1
Homero Richards	13	Patrick Goeters	4	Abraham Calderón	1	Sebastian Ocaranza Sr	1
Rafael Martínez	9	José Luis Ramírez	3	Gianfranco Cane	1	Hugo Oliveras	1
Carlos Pardo	9	Carlos Contreras	2	Alejandro Capín	1	Fernando Plata	1
Germán Quiroga	7	Ruben Pardo	2	Salvador Durán	1	Mara Reyes	1
Daniel Suárez	6	Freddy Tame	2	Rubén García Novoa	1		

NASCAR TOYOTA SERIES CHAMPS AND LEADERS (2004–2012)

2004

Carlos Pardo	2328
Rubén Pardo	2237
Rogelio López	2201
Jorge Goeters	2045
Fernando Plata	2026
Mara Reyes	1942
Carlos Contreras	1941
Oscar Ruíz	1887
Héctor Sánchez	1857
Luis F. Montaño	1815

2005

Jorge Goeters	2320
Rogelio López	2272
Carlos Pardo	1999
Patrick Goeters	1995
Rafael Martínez	1920
Oscar Ruíz	1883
Ruben García Novoa	1873
Mara Reyes	1863
Ricardo Pérez de Lara	1840
Luis F. Montaño	1710

2006

Rogelio López	2204
Ruben García Novoa	2079
Carlos Pardo	2026
Ruíz de Azua	1983
Freddy Tame	1946
Carlos Peralta	1889
Ricardo Pérez de Lara	1874
Fernando Plata	1866
Rubén Pardo	1816
Rafael Martínez	1701

2007

Rafael Martínez	2300
Germán Quiroga	2296
Patrick Goeters	1996
Carlos Peralta	1948
Antonio Pérez	1936
Jorge Goeters	1931
Rubén Rovelo	1918
Carlos Pardo	1900
Freddy Tame	1892
Ricardo Pérez de Lara	1857

2008

Antonio Pérez	2182
Germán Quiroga	2153
Rafael Martínez	2046
Homero Richards	1997
Carlos Pardo	1968
Jorge Goeters	1896
Rubén Rovelo	1891
Patrick Goeters	1881
Carlos Peralta	1864
Luis F. Montaño	1810

2009

Germán Quiroga	2273
Rogelio López	1992
Jorge Goeters	1987
Rafael Martínez	1962
Rubén Pardo	1946
Homero Richards	1946
Rubén Rovelo	1924
Hugo Oliveras	1831
Patrick Goeters	1783
Carlos Peralta	1764

2010

Germán Quiroga	2173
Homero Richards	2023
Rafael Martínez	1966
Antonio Pérez	1941
Jorge Goeters	1880
Rubén Rovelo	1831
José Luis Ramírez	1812
Jorge Arteaga	1803
Rogelio López	1791
Patrick Goeters	1743

2011

Germán Quiroga	2272
Homero Richards	1986
Jorge Goeters	1942
Rubén Rovelo	1924
José Luis Ramírez	1893
Rogelio López	1885
Rafael Martínez	1867
Patrick Goeters	1818
Daniel Suárez	1769
Abraham Calderón	1752

2012

Jorge Goeters	539
Homero Richards	505
Daniel Suárez	504
Rubén Pardo	478
Antonio Pérez	472
Hugo Oliveras	461
Patrick Goeters	461
Rafael Martínez	447
José Luis Ramírez	446
Rubén Rovelo	437

NASCAR TOYOTA SERIES 2012 RACE RESULTS

1 AUTÓDROMO MONTERREY 03/25/2012

Fin	Str	Driver	Team	Laps	Status
1	2	Rubén Rovelo	TELMEX Toyota	63	Running
2	1	Abraham Calderón	HDI Seguros Toyota	63	Running
3	7	Jorge Goeters	Canels/LUK/XTreme Mazda	63	Running
4	6	Patrick Goeters	AC Delco/Finsa Chevrolet	63	Running
5	4	Rogelio López	CI Banco Toyota	63	Running
6	17	Antonio Pérez	TELMEX Chevrolet	63	Running
7	32	Rodrigo Peralta *	Tame Racing Toyota	63	Running
8	27	Rubén Garcia Jr. *	HDI Seguros Toyota	63	Running
9	23	Carlos Peralta	La Costeña/Café Oro Toyota	63	Running
10	22	Héctor Félix	Logistica Aduanal Racing Toyota	63	Running
11	18	Israel Jaitovich	Casas Geo Mazda	63	Running
12	3	Daniel Suárez	TELCEL Dodge	63	Running
13	30	Víctor Barrales	Global Lube/Italika Toyota	62	Running
14	29	Juan Carlos Blum *	FCV Racing Dodge	62	Running
15	19	Elliot Van Rankin	Tame Racing Toyota	61	Running
16	25	Rafael Vallina	Fenix Racing Chevrolet	59	Running
17	15	José Luis Ramírez	Rayere/Prestoflam Chevrolet	57	Running
18	14	Salvador Durán	TELCEL/FedEx Dodge	56	Running
19	33	Rodrigo Marbán	BC&B/Saborex Toyota	56	Running
20	11	Freddy Tame Jr.	La Costeña/Café Oro Toyota	51	Running
21	24	Xavier Razo *	H&H High Speed Ford	49	Running
22	12	Hugo Oliveras	Monster Energy/Bosch Toyota	45	Accident
23	8	Homero Richards	NEXTEL/Kellogg's Toyota	45	Accident
24	13	Rubén Pardo	Citizen/Fram/Prestone Toyota	45	Accident
25	16	Luis Felipe Montaño	AIRHO/Ultra Toyota	45	Accident
26	5	Irwin Vences	Chick's Dodge	44	Accident
27	10	Rafael Martínez	Canels/LUK/XTreme Mazda	44	Accident
28	21	Alejandro Capín	SYD-RPM Motorsport Toyota	44	Accident
29	28	Rodrigo Echeverría *	Banco Afirme Toyota	29	Accident
30	31	Héctor Aguirre *	AVM3 Chevrolet	29	Accident
31	26	Óscar Ruíz	Provamp Toyota	24	Mechanical
32	20	Pepe Montaño	MT Sports Marketing Toyota	24	Mechanical
33	9	Carlos Contreras	Seguros Banorte Toyota	19	Mechanical

* Rookie of the Year Contender

TIME OF RACE: 2 hrs., 8 mins, 4 secs — Average Speed: 58.678 mph — Caution Flags: 4 for 23 laps — Lap Leaders: Abraham Calderón 1-14, Rubén Rovelo 15-25, Xavier Razo * 26-28, Jorge Goeters 29-33, Rubén Rovelo 34-53, Daniel Suárez 54-59, Rubén Rovelo 60-63.

2 AUTÓDROMO POTOSINO 04/15/2012

Fin	Str	Driver	Team	Laps	Status
1	5	Antonio Pérez	TELMEX Chevrolet	250	Running
2	16	Rafael Martínez	Canel's/FICREA/LuK Mazda	250	Running
3	1	Daniel Suárez	TELCEL Dodge	250	Running
4	14	Jorge Goeters	Canel's/FICREA/LuK Mazda	250	Running
5	4	Homero Richards	Estrella Roja/Kelloggs Ford	250	Running
6	7	Rogelio López	CI Banco Toyota	250	Running
7	10	Patrick Goeters	AC Delco/Finsa Chevrolet	250	Running
8	3	José Luis Ramírez	Rayere/Prestoflam Chevrolet	250	Running
9	11	Rubén Rovelo	TELMEX Toyota	250	Running
10	20	Freddy Tame Jr.	La Costeña/Café Oro Toyota	250	Running
11	13	Salvador Durán	TELCEL/FedEx Dodge	250	Running
12	22	Pepe Montaño	MT Sports Marketing Toyota	250	Running
13	26	Carlos Peralta	La Costeña/Café Oro Toyota	250	Running
14	19	Irwin Vences	Chick's Dodge	250	Running
15	17	Rodrigo Peralta *	Tame Racing Toyota	249	Running
16	21	Alejandro Capín	RPM Motorsport Toyota	249	Running
17	6	Abraham Calderón	HDI/Finsa Toyota	247	Running
18	28	Óscar Ruíz	Mikel's Toyota	247	Running
19	24	Juan Carlos Blum *	Planet Pit Dodge	247	Running
20	8	Alejandro Villasana *	RPM Motorsport Toyota	247	Running
21	23	Rafael Vallina	Fenix Racing Chevrolet	245	Running
22	18	Jorge Contreras Jr.	Cedva Racing Team Toyota	245	Running
23	12	Rubén Pardo	Citizen/Fram/Prestone Toyota	245	Running
24	30	Israel Jaitovich	Grupo Roo Mazda	242	Running
25	29	Héctor Félix	Logistica Aduanal Racing Toyota	241	Accident
26	33	Rodrigo Marbán	BC&B/Saborex Toyota	239	Running
27	2	Rubén Garcia Jr. *	HDI Seguros Toyota	238	Accident
28	25	Héctor Aguirre *	AVM3 Chevrolet	216	Running
29	27	Elliot Van Rankin	Tame Racing Toyota	196	Mechanical
30	34	Óscar Peralta	Pronto/Benedik Toyota	194	Running
31	31	Víctor Barrales	Global Lube/Italika Toyota	188	Mechanical
32	9	Hugo Oliveras	Monster Energy/Bosch Toyota	166	Mechanical
33	15	Luis Felipe Montaño	AIRHO/Ultra Toyota	143	Running
34	32	Rodrigo Echeverría *	SC Racing Toyota	39	Mechanical

* Rookie of the Year Contender

TIME OF RACE: 2 hrs., 22 mins, 48 secs — Average Speed: 52.521 mph — Caution Flags: 7 for 39 laps — Lap Leaders: Daniel Suárez 1-6, Homero Richards 7-36, Antonio Pérez 37-126, Patrick Goeters 127-137, Daniel Suárez 138-156, Rafael Martínez 157-171, Antonio Pérez 172-176, Rafael Martínez 177-237, Antonio Pérez 238-239, Rafael Martínez 240, Antonio Pérez 241-250.

3 NUEVO AUTÓDROMO DE QUERÉTARO 04/29/2012

Fin	Str	Driver	Team	Laps	Status
1	2	Homero Richards	NEXTEL/Kellogg's Toyota	166	Running
2	11	Daniel Suárez	TELCEL Dodge	166	Running
3	28	Rogelio López	CI Banco Toyota	166	Running
4	5	Irwin Vences	Chick's Dodge	166	Running
5	14	Alejandro Capín	RPM Motorsport Toyota	166	Running
6	1	José Luis Ramírez	Rayere/Prestoflam Chevrolet	166	Running
7	6	Rubén Garcia Jr. *	HDI Seguros/Imagen Toyota	166	Running
8	20	Rubén Pardo	Citizen/Fram/Prestone Toyota	166	Running
9	3	Elliot Van Rankin	Tame Racing Toyota	166	Running
10	19	Carlos Peralta	La Costeña/Café Oro Toyota	166	Running
11	10	Juan Carlos Blum *	Planet Pit Dodge	166	Running
12	23	Freddy Tame Jr.	La Costeña/Café Oro Toyota	166	Running
13	13	Waldemar Coronas *	SC Racing Toyota	166	Running
14	12	Luis Felipe Montaño	AIRHO/Ultra Toyota	166	Running
15	7	Hugo Oliveras	Monster Energy/Bosch Toyota	166	Running
16	22	Israel Jaitovich	Grupo Roo Mazda	166	Running
17	32	Víctor Barrales	Global Lube/Gel Gomina/Italika Toyota	166	Running
18	31	Rodrigo Marbán	BC&B/Saborex Toyota	165	Running
19	15	Patrick Goeters	AC Delco/Finsa Chevrolet	164	Running
20	8	Jorge Goeters	Canel's/FICREA/LuK Mazda	161	Running
21	26	Rubén Rovelo	TELMEX Toyota	160	Running
22	18	Salvador Durán	TELCEL/FedEx Dodge	157	Running
23	4	Rafael Martínez	Canel's/FICREA/LuK Mazda	155	Running
24	25	Antonio Pérez	TELMEX Chevrolet	146	Running
25	29	Óscar Ruíz	Mikel›s Toyota	146	Running
26	21	Jorge Contreras Jr.	Cedva Racing Team Toyota	139	Running
27	24	Pepe Montaño	MT Sports Marketing Toyota	129	Running
28	9	Alejandro Villasana *	RPM Motorsport Toyota	124	Mechanical
29	30	Héctor Félix	Logistica Aduanal Racing Toyota	104	Running
30	34	Javier Fernandez *	Car Motion Motorsport Toyota	101	Mechanical
31	16	Rafael Vallina	Fenix Racing Chevrolet	50	Accident
32	33	Óscar Peralta	Harley-Davidson/MetroRed Toyota	41	Mechanical
33	17	Rodrigo Peralta *	Price Shoes Toyota	31	Mechanical
34	27	Abraham Calderón	HDI/Finsa Toyota	3	Accident

* Rookie of the Year Contender

TIME OF RACE: 2 hrs., 24 mins, 10 secs — Average Speed: 51.815 mph — Caution Flags: 9 for 40 laps — Lap Leaders: José Luis Ramírez 1-8, Homero Richards 9-39, José Luis Ramírez 40-41, Irwin Vences 42-64, Elliot Van Rankin 65-80, Rogelio López 81-114, Irwin Vences 115-128, Homero Richards 129-166.

4 AUTÓDROMO HERMANOS RODRÍGUEZ 05/12/2012

Fin	Str	Driver	Team	Laps	Status
1	5	Daniel Suárez	TELCEL Dodge	161	Running
2	26	Rafael Martínez	Canel's/FICREA/LuK Mazda	161	Running
3	2	Homero Richards	NEXTEL/H&H Toyota	161	Running
4	14	Jorge Goeters	Canel's/FICREA/LuK Mazda	161	Running
5	6	Rubén Rovelo	TELMEX Toyota	161	Running
6	20	Rubén Pardo	Citizen/Fram/Prestone Toyota	161	Running
7	8	Antonio Pérez	TELMEX Chevrolet	161	Running
8	1	Rogelio López	CI Banco Toyota	161	Running
9	7	José Luis Ramírez	Rayere/Prestoflam Chevrolet	161	Running
10	24	Irwin Vences	Chick's Dodge	161	Running
11	11	Rubén Garcia Jr. *	HDI Seguros Toyota	161	Running
12	4	Abraham Calderón	HDI/Finsa Toyota	161	Running
13	19	Freddy Tame Jr.	La Costeña/Café Oro Toyota	161	Running
14	12	Patrick Goeters	AC Delco/Finsa Chevrolet	161	Running
15	10	Rodrigo Peralta *	Price Shoes Toyota	160	Running
16	21	Pepe Montaño	Toyota/Goodyear Toyota	160	Running
17	32	Rodrigo Marbán	BC&B/Saborex Toyota	159	Running
18	28	Óscar Peralta	Harley-Davidson/GMI Toyota	159	Accident
19	15	Luis Felipe Montaño	AIRHO/Ultra Toyota	158	Running
20	29	Óscar Ruíz	Mikel›s Toyota	158	Running
21	13	Hugo Oliveras	Monster Energy/Bosch Toyota	158	Running
22	9	Carlos Peralta	La Costeña/Café Oro Toyota	158	Running
23	22	Víctor Barrales	Global Lube/Italika Toyota	153	Running
24	30	Israel Jaitovich	Grupo Roo Mazda	153	Running
25	16	Elliot Van Rankin	Von Haucke/Sanirent Toyota	152	Accident
26	23	Salvador Durán	TELCEL/FedEx Dodge	152	Accident
27	17	Alejandro Capín	RPM Motorsport Toyota	151	Accident
28	27	Alejandro Villasana *	RPM Motorsport Toyota	150	Running
29	34	Rafael Vallina	Fenix Racing Chevrolet	149	Running
30	31	Héctor Félix	Logistica Aduanal Racing Toyota	142	Running
31	3	Juan Carlos Blum *	Planet Pit Dodge	141	Mechanical
32	25	Enrique Contreras III	Fenix Racing Toyota	137	Mechanical
33	18	Jorge Contreras Jr.	Cedva Racing Team Toyota	34	Mechanical
34	33	Javier Fernandez *	Car Motion Motorsport Toyota	33	Accident

* Rookie of the Year Contender

TIME OF RACE: 2 hrs., 31 mins, 46 secs — Average Speed: 63.650 mph — Caution Flags: 7 for 32 laps — Lap Leaders: Rogelio López 1-19, Homero Richards 20-106, Rogelio López 107-108, Hugo Oliveras 109-112, Patrick Goeters 113-117, Daniel Suárez 118-161.

5 AUTÓDROMO INTERNACIONAL MIGUEL E. ABED 05/27/2012

Fin	Str	Driver	Team	Laps	Status
1	10	Jorge Goeters	Canel's/FICREA/LuK Mazda	129	Running
2	6	Héctor Aguirre *	H&H High Speed Toyota	129	Running
3	14	Patrick Goeters	AC Delco/Finsa Chevrolet	129	Running
4	19	Rubén Pardo	Citizen/Fram/Prestone Toyota	129	Running
5	12	Luis Felipe Montaño	AIRHO/Ultra Toyota	129	Running
6	1	Rubén Garcia Jr. *	HDI/Seguros/Imagen Toyota	129	Running
7	17	Carlos Peralta	La Costeña/Café Oro Toyota	129	Running
8	4	José Luis Ramírez	Rayere/Prestoflam Chevrolet	129	Running
9	21	Freddy Tame Jr.	La Costeña/Café Oro Toyota	129	Running
10	13	Hugo Oliveras	Monster Energy/Bosch Toyota	129	Running
11	26	Rubén Rovelo	TELMEX Toyota	129	Running
12	18	Alejandro Villasana *	Suspension Y Direccion Toyota	129	Running
13	15	Elliot Van Rankin	Von Haucke/Sanirent Toyota	129	Running
14	5	Rafael Martínez	Canel's/FICREA/LuK Mazda	129	Running
15	27	Israel Jaitovich	Grupo Roo Mazda	129	Running
16	8	Antonio Pérez	TELMEX Chevrolet	129	Running
17	7	Homero Richards	NEXTEL/H&H Toyota	129	Running
18	20	Salvador Durán	TELCEL/FedEx Dodge	128	Running
19	32	Rafael Vallina	Fenix Racing Chevrolet	126	Running
20	9	Rodrigo Peralta *	Tame Racing Toyota	126	Running
21	11	Alejandro Capín	Suspension Y Direccion Toyota	126	Running
22	28	Rodrigo Marbán	BC&B/Saborex Toyota	126	Running
23	33	Javier Fernandez *	Car Motion Motorsport Toyota	126	Running
24	23	Óscar Ruíz	Mikel›s Toyota	125	Running
25	16	Daniel Suárez	TELCEL Dodge	124	Accident
26	29	Víctor Barrales	Global Lube/Italika Toyota	123	Running
27	25	Irwin Vences	Chick›s Dodge	121	Accident
28	24	Héctor Félix	Logistica Aduanal Racing Toyota	111	Running
29	3	Abraham Calderón	HDI/Gesti/Picsa Toyota	100	Mechanical
30	31	Óscar Peralta	Harley-Davidson/MetroRed/GMI Toyota	87	Mechanical
31	2	Rogelio López	CI Banco/Boing Toyota	81	Running
32	22	Pepe Montaño	Toyota/Goodyear Toyota	79	Running
33	30	Jorge Contreras Jr.	Cedva Racing Team Toyota	19	Mechanical

* Rookie of the Year Contender

TIME OF RACE: 2 hrs., 5 mins, 51 secs — Average Speed: 76.877 mph — Caution Flags: 7 for 21 laps — Lap Leaders: José Luis Ramírez 1-7, Rubén Garcia Jr. * 8-13, Rogelio López 14-52, Homero Richards 53-54, Abraham Calderón 55, Homero Richards 56-71, Jorge Goeters 72-129.

6 AUTÓDROMO INTERNACIONAL DE AGUASCALIENTES 06/17/2012

Fin	Str	Driver	Team	Laps	Status
1	2	Antonio Pérez	TELMEX Chevrolet	171	Running
2	21	Daniel Suárez	TELCEL Dodge	171	Running
3	3	Jorge Goeters	Canel's/FICREA/LuK Mazda	171	Running
4	9	Rafael Martínez	Canel's/FICREA/LuK Mazda	171	Running
5	7	Rubén Pardo	Citizen/Fram Toyota	171	Running
6	20	Homero Richards	NEXTEL/H&H Toyota	171	Running
7	5	Rubén Garcia Jr. *	HDI Seguros/Imagen Toyota	171	Running
8	8	Patrick Goeters	AC Delco/Finsa Chevrolet	171	Running
9	16	Freddy Tame Jr.	La Costeña/Café Oro Toyota	171	Running
10	13	Juan Carlos Blum *	Sheets Energy/Pitbull Dodge	171	Running
11	6	Hugo Oliveras	Monster Energy/Bosch Toyota	171	Running
12	14	Irwin Vences	Chick's Dodge	171	Running
13	15	Elliot Van Rankin	Von Haucke/Sanirent Toyota	170	Running
14	12	Salvador Durán	TELCEL/FedEx Dodge	170	Running
15	11	Abraham Calderón	Gesti/Constructora Williams/HDI Toyota	170	Running
16	10	Rubén Rovelo	TELMEX Toyota	169	Running
17	30	Héctor Félix	Logistica Aduanal Racing Toyota	168	Running
18	27	Rodrigo Marbán	BC&B/Saborex Toyota	168	Running
19	32	Javier Fernandez *	Car Motion Motorsport Toyota	167	Running
20	28	Víctor Barrales	Global Lube/Gel Gomina/Italika Toyota	162	Running
21	23	Óscar Ruíz	SyD/Mikels Toyota	157	Running
22	22	Rafael Vallina	Coca-Cola/Bokados/Mobil 1 Chevrolet	151	Mechanical
23	25	Carlos Peralta	La Costeña/Café Oro Toyota	137	Running
24	18	Luis Felipe Montaño	AIRHO/Ultra Toyota	136	Running
25	24	Pepe Montaño	Toyota/Goodyear Toyota	125	Mechanical
26	1	Rogelio López	CI Banco/Boing Toyota	123	Running
27	17	Alejandro Capín	Suspension Y Direccion Toyota	101	Mechanical
28	4	José Luis Ramírez	Rayere/Prestoflam Chevrolet	90	Mechanical
29	29	Enrique Contreras III	Fenix Racing Toyota	89	Accident
30	26	Israel Jaitovich	Grupo Roo Mazda	48	Excluded
31	31	Óscar Peralta	Harley-Davidson/GMI Toyota	31	Accident
32	19	Jorge Contreras Jr.	Cedva Racing Team Toyota	24	Mechanical

* Rookie of the Year Contender

TIME OF RACE: 1 hrs., 48 mins, 9 secs — Average Speed: 83.010 mph — Caution Flags: 6 for 38 laps — Lap Leaders: Rogelio López 1-6, Antonio Pérez 7-38, José Luis Ramírez 39-40, Antonio Pérez 41-43, José Luis Ramírez 44-46, Antonio Pérez 47-62, Pepe Montaño 63-68, Antonio Pérez 69-83, Daniel Suárez 84-101, Antonio Pérez 102-104, Daniel Suárez 105-130, Antonio Pérez 131-143, Daniel Suárez 144, Antonio Pérez 145-157, Daniel Suárez 158-159, Antonio Pérez 160-161, Daniel Suárez 162-164, Antonio Pérez 165-171

7 AUTÓDROMO HERMANOS RODRÍGUEZ 07/08/2012

Fin	Str	Driver	Team	Laps	Status
1	7	Hugo Oliveras	Monster Energy/Bosch Toyota	150	Running
2	3	Rogelio López	CI Banco/Boing Toyota	150	Running
3	12	Abraham Calderón	Gesti/Constructora Williams/HDI Toyota	150	Running
4	1	Homero Richards	NEXTEL/H&H Toyota	150	Running
5	2	Daniel Suárez	TELCEL Dodge	150	Running
6	5	Patrick Goeters	AC Delco/Finsa Chevrolet	149	Running
7	27	Irwin Vences	Chick's Dodge	149	Running
8	8	José Luis Ramírez	Rayere/Prestoflam Chevrolet	149	Running
9	29	Juan Carlos Blum *	Oleofinos/Pitbull Ford	149	Running
10	19	Elliot Van Rankin	Von Haucke/Sanirent Ford	149	Running
11	25	Luis Felipe Montaño	AIRHO/Ultra Toyota	149	Running
12	17	Freddy Tame Jr.	La Costeña/Café Oro Toyota	149	Running
13	4	Carlos Peralta	La Costeña/Café Oro Toyota	149	Running
14	16	Alejandro Villasana *	Tame Racing Ford	149	Running
15	22	Salvador Durán	TELCEL/FedEx Dodge	148	Running
16	24	Rodrigo Marbán	BC&B/Saborex Toyota	147	Running
17	15	Rafael Martínez	Canel's/FICREA/LuK Mazda	147	Running
18	9	Rubén Garcia Jr. *	HDI/Seguros/Imagen Toyota	147	Running
19	30	Jorge Contreras Jr.	Cedva Racing Team Toyota	146	Running
20	6	Rubén Pardo	Citizen/Fram Toyota	146	Running
21	28	Israel Jaitovich	Grupo Roo Mazda	145	Running
22	14	Jorge Goeters	Canel's/FICREA/LuK Mazda	145	Running
23	32	Javier Fernandez *	Car Motion Motorsport Toyota	144	Running
24	18	Pepe Montaño	Toyota/Goodyear Toyota	143	Running
25	21	Héctor Félix	Logistica Aduanal Racing Toyota	142	Running
26	23	Alejandro Capín	Suspension Y Direccion Toyota	141	Running
27	11	Héctor Aguirre *	H&H Toyota	140	Running
28	31	Víctor Barrales	Global Lube/Italika Toyota	140	Running
29	26	Rubén Rovelo	TELMEX Toyota	134	Running
30	20	Rafael Vallina	Coca-Cola/Bokados/Mobil 1 Chevrolet	124	Running
31	10	Antonio Pérez	TELMEX Chevrolet	91	Running
32	13	Óscar Ruíz	SyD/Mikels Toyota	40	Mechanical

* Rookie of the Year Contender

TIME OF RACE: 1 hrs., 46 mins, 56 secs — Average Speed: 84.165 mph — Caution Flags: 3 for 10 laps — Lap Leaders: Homero Richards 1-73, Abraham Calderón 74-99, Rogelio López 100-123, Homero Richards 124-127, Hugo Oliveras 128-150.

8 AUTÓDROMO POTOSINO 07/29/2012

Fin	Str	Driver	Team	Laps	Status
1	21	Rafael Martínez	Canel's/FICREA/LuK Mazda	258	Running
2	2	Daniel Suárez	TELCEL Dodge	258	Running
3	11	Héctor Aguirre *	GAMA Toyota	258	Running
4	13	Jorge Goeters	Canel's/FICREA/LuK Mazda	258	Running
5	20	Salvador Durán	TELMEX Toyota	258	Running
6	5	Abraham Calderón	Gesti/Constructora Williams/HDI Toyota	258	Running
7	4	Antonio Pérez	TELMEX Chevrolet	258	Running
8	14	Rubén Pardo	Citizen/Fram Toyota	258	Running
9	9	José Luis Ramírez	Rayere/Prestoflam Chevrolet	258	Running
10	10	Hugo Oliveras	Monster Energy/Bosch Toyota	258	Running
11	27	Óscar Ruíz	SyD/Mikels Toyota	258	Running
12	31	Pepe Montaño	Toyota/Goodyear Toyota	258	Running
13	19	Rafael Vallina	Coca-Cola/Bokados/Mobil 1 Chevrolet	258	Running
14	32	Víctor Barrales	Global Lube/Italika Toyota	256	Running
15	17	Juan Carlos Blum *	Oleofinos/Pitbull Ford	255	Running
16	30	Israel Jaitovich	Grupo Roo Mazda	254	Running
17	12	Rogelio López	CI Banco/Boing Toyota	251	Accident
18	29	Luis Felipe Montaño	AIRHO/Ultra Toyota	251	Running
19	1	Homero Richards	NEXTEL/H&H Toyota	250	Accident
20	18	Alejandro Villasana *	Tame Racing Ford	246	Running
21	7	Patrick Goeters	AC Delco/Finsa Chevrolet	239	Mechanical
22	23	Carlos Peralta	La Costeña/Café Oro Toyota	239	Running
23	15	Freddy Tame Jr.	La Costeña/Café Oro Toyota	237	Running
24	3	Rubén Garcia Jr. *	HDI Seguros/Imagen Toyota	232	Running
25	8	Jorge Contreras Jr.	Cedva Racing Team Toyota	227	Mechanical
26	6	Rubén Rovelo	TELCEL/FedEx Dodge	226	Accident
27	22	Oscar Torres Jr. *	DAR Refaccionarias Toyota	198	Running
28	24	Alejandro Capín	Suspension Y Direccion Toyota	182	Accident
29	25	Héctor Félix	Logistica Aduanal Racing Toyota	167	Mechanical
30	16	Irwin Vences	Chick›s Dodge	155	Running
31	26	Elliot Van Rankin	Von Haucke/Sanirent Ford	150	Mechanical
32	33	Javier Fernandez *	Car Motion Motorsport Toyota	127	Accident
33	28	Rodrigo Marbán	BC&B/Saborex Toyota	31	Mechanical

* Rookie of the Year Contender

TIME OF RACE: 2 hrs., 40 mins, 29 secs — Average Speed: 48.229 mph — Caution Flags: 15 for 80 laps — Lap Leaders: Homero Richards 1-12, Daniel Suárez 13-17, Homero Richards 18-46, Rogelio López 47-140, Abraham Calderón 141-148, Daniel Suárez 149-203, Rafael Martínez 204-223, Homero Richards 224-249, Rafael Martínez 250-258.

9 NUEVO AUTÓDROMO DE QUERÉTARO 08/12/2012

Fin	Str	Driver	Team	Laps	Status
1	1	Daniel Suárez	TELCEL Dodge	157	Running
2	11	Hugo Oliveras	Monster Energy/Bosch Toyota	157	Running
3	19	Rafael Martínez	Canel's/FICREA/LuK Mazda	157	Running
4	6	Rubén Rovelo	TELCEL/FedEx Dodge	157	Running
5	20	Abraham Calderón	Gesti/HDI Seguros/Mikels Toyota	157	Running
6	7	Jorge Goeters	Canel's/FICREA/LuK Mazda	157	Running
7	4	José Luis Ramírez	Rayere/Prestoflam Chevrolet	157	Running
8	3	Antonio Pérez	TELMEX Chevrolet	157	Running
9	17	Freddy Tame Jr.	La Costeña/Café Oro Toyota	157	Running
10	5	Rubén Garcia Jr. *	HDI Seguros/Imagen Toyota	157	Running
11	26	Irwin Vences	Chick's Dodge	157	Running
12	23	Salvador Durán	TELMEX Toyota	157	Running
13	14	Alejandro Capín	Suspension Y Direccion Toyota	157	Running
14	27	Luis Felipe Montaño	AIRHO/Ultra Toyota	157	Running
15	16	Óscar Ruíz	SyD/Mikels Toyota	157	Running
16	18	Héctor Félix	Logistica Aduanal Racing Toyota	157	Running
17	12	Juan Carlos Blum *	Oleofinos/Pitbull Ford	157	Running
18	31	Rafael Vallina	Coca-Cola/Bokados/Mobil 1 Chevrolet	157	Running
19	13	Rubén Pardo	Citizen/Fram Toyota	157	Running
20	8	Carlos Peralta	La Costeña/Café Oro Toyota	155	Running
21	25	Pepe Montaño	Toyota/Goodyear Toyota	155	Running
22	22	Israel Jaitovich	Grupo Roo Mazda	155	Running
23	2	Homero Richards	NEXTEL/H&H Toyota	155	Running
24	30	Javier Fernandez *	Car Motion Motorsport Toyota	154	Running
25	15	Rogelio López	CI Banco/Boing Toyota	152	Running
26	21	Víctor Barrales	Global Lube/Italika Toyota	152	Running
27	10	Elliot Van Rankin	Von Haucke/Sanirent Ford	147	Accident
28	29	Óscar Peralta	Harley-Davidson/MetroRed Toyota	133	Mechanical
29	32	Jorge Contreras Jr.	Cedva Racing Team Toyota	111	Accident
30	9	Héctor Aguirre *	H&H Toyota	95	Mechanical
31	28	Rodrigo Marbán	BC&B/Saborex Toyota	88	Mechanical
32	24	Patrick Goeters	AC Delco/Finsa Chevrolet	16	Mechanical

* Rookie of the Year Contender

TIME OF RACE: 1 hrs., 53 mins, 38 secs — Average Speed: 62.174 mph — Caution Flags: 6 for 28 laps — Lap Leaders: Daniel Suárez 1-4, Homero Richards 5-97, Daniel Suárez 98-102, Antonio Pérez 103-110, Daniel Suárez 111-113, Hugo Oliveras 114-143, Daniel Suárez 144, Hugo Oliveras 145, Daniel Suárez 146, Hugo Oliveras 147-151, Daniel Suárez 152-157.

10 AUTÓDROMO INTERNACIONAL DE AGUASCALIENTES 08/26/2012

Fin	Str	Driver	Team	Laps	Status
1	2	Rubén Rovelo	TELCEL/FedEx Dodge	171	Running
2	1	Daniel Suárez	TELCEL Dodge	171	Running
3	4	Jorge Goeters	Canel's/FICREA/LuK Mazda	171	Running
4	6	Rubén Pardo	Citizen/Fram Toyota	171	Running
5	15	Salvador Durán	TELMEX Toyota	171	Running
6	7	Homero Richards	NEXTEL/H&H Toyota	171	Running
7	5	Hugo Oliveras	Monster Energy/Bosch Toyota	171	Running
8	9	Irwin Vences	Chick's Toyota	171	Running
9	12	Abraham Calderón	Gesti/HDI Seguros/Mikels Toyota	171	Running
10	17	Patrick Goeters	AC Delco/Finsa Chevrolet	171	Running
11	23	Luis Felipe Montaño	AIRHO/Ultra Toyota	171	Running
12	11	José Luis Ramírez	Rayere/Prestoflam Chevrolet	171	Running
13	13	Freddy Tame Jr.	La Costeña/Café Oro Toyota	171	Running
14	19	Juan Carlos Blum *	Oleofinos/Pitbull Ford	170	Running
15	10	Rogelio López	CI Banco/Boing Toyota	170	Running
16	8	Carlos Peralta	La Costeña/Café Oro Toyota	170	Running
17	21	Héctor Félix	Logistica Aduanal Racing Toyota	170	Running
18	25	Carlos Contreras	NEXTEL Racing Toyota	169	Running
19	27	Rafael Vallina	Coca-Cola/Bokados/Mobil 1 Chevrolet	169	Running
20	3	Antonio Pérez	TELMEX Chevrolet	169	Running
21	31	Víctor Barrales	Global Lube/Italika Toyota	168	Running
22	22	Pepe Montaño	Toyota/Goodyear Toyota	167	Running
23	34	Alejandro Villasana *	Tame Racing Ford	167	Running
24	24	Oscar Torres Jr. *	DAR Refaccionarias Toyota	167	Running
25	28	Israel Jaitovich	Grupo Roo Mazda	162	Running
26	26	Rubén Garcia Jr. *	HDI Seguros/Imagen Toyota	154	Running
27	16	Alejandro Capín	Suspension Y Direccion Toyota	142	Running
28	33	Jorge Contreras Jr.	Cedva Racing Team Toyota	141	Accident
29	35	Rodrigo Marbán	BC&B/Saborex Toyota	141	Running
30	29	Óscar Ruíz	SyD/Mikels Toyota	129	Accident
31	18	Rafael Martínez	Canel›s/FICREA/LuK Mazda	111	Accident
32	30	Rubén García	HDI Seguros/Imagen Toyota	111	Accident
33	14	Rodrigo Peralta *	Tame Racing Toyota	60	Accident
34	20	Elliot Van Rankin	Von Haucke/Sanirent Ford	50	Accident
35	32	Javier Fernandez *	Car Motion Motorsport Toyota	15	Mechanical

* Rookie of the Year Contender

TIME OF RACE: 2 hrs., 9 mins, 0 secs — Average Speed: 69.593 mph — Caution Flags: 8 for 38 laps — Lap Leaders: Daniel Suárez 0, Antonio Pérez 1-8, Daniel Suárez 9-12, Rubén Rovelo 13, Daniel Suárez 14-20, Rubén Rovelo 21-23, Daniel Suárez 24-33, Antonio Pérez 34-35, Daniel Suárez 36-55, José Luis Ramírez 56-58, Antonio Pérez 59, José Luis Ramírez 60-64, Homero Richards 65-67, Antonio Pérez 68-71, Jorge Goeters 72-78, Antonio Pérez 79-82, Rubén Rovelo 83-105, Antonio Pérez 106, Rubén Rovelo 107, Antonio Pérez 108-143, Daniel Suárez 144-145, Antonio Pérez 146-149, Daniel Suárez 150, Antonio Pérez 151, Rubén Rovelo 152-171.

11 AUTÓDROMO INTERNACIONAL MIGUEL E. ABED 09/09/2012

Fin	Str	Driver	Team	Laps	Status
1	1	Rogelio López	CI Banco/Boing Toyota	120	Running
2	8	Jorge Goeters	Canel's/FICREA/LuK Mazda	120	Running
3	12	Rubén Pardo	Citizen/Fram Toyota	120	Running
4	11	Hugo Oliveras	Monster Energy/Bosch Toyota	120	Running
5	6	Abraham Calderón	Gesti/HDI Seguros/Mikels Toyota	120	Running
6	7	Rafael Martínez	Canel's/FICREA/LuK Mazda	120	Running
7	4	José Luis Ramírez	Rayere/Prestoflam Chevrolet	120	Running
8	3	Homero Richards	NEXTEL/H&H Toyota	120	Running
9	10	Patrick Goeters	AC Delco/Finsa Chevrolet	120	Running
10	9	Irwin Vences	Chick's Toyota	120	Running
11	15	Rodrigo Peralta *	Tame Racing Toyota	120	Running
12	28	Rafael Vallina	Coca-Cola/Bokados/Mobil 1 Chevrolet	120	Running
13	23	Pepe Montaño	Toyota/Goodyear Toyota	120	Running
14	16	Carlos Peralta	La Costeña/Café Oro Toyota	120	Running
15	5	Daniel Suárez	TELCEL Dodge	120	Running
16	21	Alejandro Capín	Suspension Y Direccion Toyota	120	Running
17	13	Rubén Garcia Jr. *	HDI Seguros/Imagen Toyota	120	Running
18	29	Rubén García	HDI Seguros/Imagen Toyota	120	Running
19	25	Víctor Barrales	Global Lube/Italika Toyota	120	Running
20	32	Héctor Félix	Logistica Aduanal Racing Toyota	120	Running
21	31	Óscar Peralta	Harley-Davidson/MetroRed/GMI Toyota	120	Running
22	24	Salvador Durán	TELMEX Toyota	120	Running
23	14	Juan Carlos Blum *	Oleofinos/Pitbull Ford	119	Running
24	17	Carlos Contreras	NEXTEL Racing Toyota	119	Running
25	2	Antonio Pérez	TELMEX Chevrolet	115	Accident
26	30	Rodrigo Marbán	BC&B/Saborex Toyota	115	Running
27	26	Freddy Tame Jr.	La Costeña/Café Oro Toyota	113	Running
28	22	Elliot Van Rankin	Von Haucke/Sanirent Ford	109	Running
29	20	Rubén Rovelo	TELCEL/FedEx Dodge	107	Accident
30	33	Javier Fernandez *	Car Motion Motorsport Toyota	101	Running
31	27	Israel Jaitovich	Grupo Roo Mazda	100	Penalty
32	34	Óscar Ruíz	SyD/Mikels Toyota	83	Mechanical
33	18	Héctor Aguirre *	Tame Racing Ford	48	Accident
34	19	Luis Felipe Montaño	AIRHO/Ultra Toyota	16	Accident

* Rookie of the Year Contender

TIME OF RACE: 2 hrs., 9 mins, 22 secs — Average Speed: 69.570 mph — Caution Flags: 9 for 30 laps — Lap Leaders: Rogelio López 1-2, Antonio Pérez 3-6, Rogelio López 7-18, Rafael Martínez 19-22, Jorge Goeters 23-30, Hugo Oliveras 31-39, Rogelio López 40-44, Rafael Martínez 45-48, Rogelio López 49-50, Hugo Oliveras 51-54, José Luis Ramírez 55, Hugo Oliveras 56-59, José Luis Ramírez 60-66, Rafael Martínez 67-69, José Luis Ramírez 70-71, Rafael Martínez 72, José Luis Ramírez 73, Rafael Martínez 74-75, José Luis Ramírez 76, Rogelio López 77-84, Jorge Goeters 85, Rogelio López 86, Jorge Goeters 87, Rogelio López 88-96, Homero Richards 97, Jorge Goeters 98-100, Rogelio López 101, Jorge Goeters 102-112, Rogelio López 113-120.

12 AUTÓDROMO MONTERREY 09/30/2012

Fin	Str	Driver	Team	Laps	Status
1	9	Jorge Goeters	Canel's/FICREA/LuK Mazda	150	Running
2	5	Patrick Goeters	AC Delco/Finsa Chevrolet	150	Running
3	2	Daniel Suárez	TELCEL Dodge	150	Running
4	19	Freddy Tame Jr.	La Costeña/Café Oro Toyota	150	Running
5	3	Homero Richards	NEXTEL/H&H Toyota	150	Running
6	8	Antonio Pérez	TELMEX Chevrolet	150	Running
7	23	Irwin Vences	Chick's Toyota	150	Running
8	10	Hugo Oliveras	Monster Energy/Bosch Toyota	150	Running
9	25	Elliot Van Rankin	Von Haucke/Sanirent Ford	150	Running
10	11	Salvador Durán	TELMEX Toyota	150	Running
11	24	Carlos Peralta	La Costeña/Café Oro Toyota	150	Running
12	17	Rubén Pardo	Citizen/Fram Toyota	150	Running
13	21	Juan Carlos Blum *	Oleofinos/Pitbull Ford	150	Running
14	30	Óscar Ruíz	SyD/Mikels Toyota	150	Running
15	7	Rubén Rovelo	TELCEL/FedEx Dodge	148	Running
16	1	José Luis Ramírez	Rayere/Prestoflam Chevrolet	147	Running
17	27	Israel Jaitovich	Grupo Roo Mazda	147	Running
18	29	Rodrigo Marbán	BC&B/Saborex Toyota	146	Running
19	26	Rafael Vallina	Coca-Cola/Bokados/Mobil 1 Chevrolet	146	Running
20	15	Alejandro Villasana *	Tame Racing Ford	145	Running
21	31	Carlos Contreras	NEXTEL Racing Toyota	141	Running
22	28	Víctor Barrales	Global Lube/Italika Toyota	140	Running
23	22	Abraham Calderón	Gesti/HDI Seguros/Mikels Toyota	134	Accident
24	6	Rubén Garcia Jr. *	HDI Seguros/Imagen Toyota	134	Accident
25	18	Héctor Félix	Logistica Aduanal Racing Toyota	122	Running
26	12	Rodrigo Peralta *	Tame Racing Toyota	113	Running
27	16	Rafael Martínez	Canel's/FICREA/LuK Mazda	113	Mechanical
28	13	Alejandro Capín	Suspension Y Direccion Toyota	106	Mechanical
29	20	Luis Felipe Montaño	AIRHO/Ultra Toyota	71	Accident
30	4	Rogelio López	CI Banco/Boing Toyota	57	Accident
31	14	Pepe Montaño	Toyota/Goodyear Toyota	48	Mechanical

* Rookie of the Year Contender

TIME OF RACE: 2 hrs., 38 mins, 40 secs — Average Speed: 112.765 mph — Caution Flags: 9 for 38 laps — Lap Leaders: José Luis Ramírez grid, Daniel Suárez 1-2, José Luis Ramírez 3-40, Rafael Martínez 41-52, Salvador Durán 53-66, Rafael Martínez 67-82, Antonio Pérez 83-117, Carlos Contreras 118-121, Óscar Ruíz 122-127, Jorge Goeters 128-150.

13 EL DORADO SPEEDWAY 10/28/2012

Fin	Str	Driver	Team	Laps	Status
1	2	Rubén Pardo	Citizen/Fram Toyota	250	Running
2	1	Rubén Rovelo	TELCEL/FedEx Dodge	250	Running
3	15	Antonio Pérez	TELMEX Chevrolet	250	Running
4	6	Freddy Tame Jr.	La Costeña/Café Oro Toyota	250	Running
5	10	Hugo Oliveras	Monster Energy/Bosch Toyota	250	Running
6	17	Carlos Contreras	NEXTEL Racing Toyota	250	Running
7	11	Salvador Durán	TELMEX Toyota	250	Running
8	7	Jorge Goeters	Canel's/FICREA/LuK Mazda	250	Running
9	22	Rafael Martínez	Canel's/FICREA/LuK Mazda	249	Running
10	4	Rubén Garcia Jr. *	HDI Seguros/Imagen Toyota	249	Running
11	16	Homero Richards	NEXTEL/H&H Toyota	247	Running
12	8	Héctor Félix	Logistica Aduanal Racing Toyota	247	Running
13	9	Patrick Goeters	AC Delco/Finsa Chevrolet	246	Running
14	12	Carlos Peralta	La Costeña/Café Oro Toyota	246	Running
15	26	Rafael Vallina	Coca-Cola/Bokados/Mobil 1 Chevrolet	246	Running
16	29	Óscar Ruíz	SyD/Mikels Toyota	245	Running
17	30	Javier Fernandez *	Car Motion Motorsport Toyota	243	Running
18	24	Luis Felipe Montaño	AIRHO/Ultra Toyota	243	Mechanical
19	5	Rogelio López	CI Banco/Boing Toyota	241	Running
20	28	Víctor Barrales	Global Lube/Italika Toyota	241	Running
21	20	Pepe Montaño	Toyota/Goodyear Toyota	241	Running
22	21	Abraham Calderón	Gesti/HDI Seguros/Mikels Toyota	226	Running
23	27	Israel Jaitovich	Grupo Roo Mazda	226	Penalty
24	19	Juan Carlos Blum *	Oleofinos/Pitbull Ford	219	Running
25	31	Rodrigo Marbán	BC&B/Saborex Toyota	199	Mechanical
26	18	Alejandro Capín	Suspension Y Direccion Toyota	193	Accident
27	13	Irwin Vences	Chick›s Toyota	188	Mechanical
28	14	Nelson Canache	Venezuela Toyota	170	Accident
29	23	Elliot Van Rankin	Von Haucke/Sanirent Ford	144	Accident
30	3	Daniel Suárez	TELCEL Dodge	130	Accident
31	25	José Luis Ramírez	Rayere/Prestoflam Chevrolet	113	Mechanical

* Rookie of the Year Contender

TIME OF RACE: 2 hrs., 3 mins, 32 secs — Average Speed: 75.890 mph — Caution Flags: 7 for 49 laps — Lap Leaders: Rubén Rovelo 1, Daniel Suárez 2-116, Rubén Rovelo 117, Rubén Garcia Jr. * 118, Antonio Pérez 119-126, Rubén Pardo 127-180, Antonio Pérez 181-183, Rubén Pardo 184-202, Rubén Rovelo 203-222, Rubén Pardo 223-250.

14 AUTÓDROMO HERMANOS RODRÍGUEZ 11/11/2012

Fin	Str	Driver	Team	Laps	Status
1	1	Homero Richards	NEXTEL/H&H Toyota	150	Running
2	12	Abraham Calderón	HDI Seguros/Mikels Toyota	150	Running
3	21	Rubén Garcia Jr. *	HDI Seguros/Imagen Toyota	150	Running
4	4	Elliot Van Rankin	Von Haucke/Sanirent Ford	150	Running
5	10	Rubén Pardo	Citizen/Fram Toyota	150	Running
6	2	Antonio Pérez	TELMEX Chevrolet	149	Running
7	19	Rogelio López	CI Banco/Boing Toyota	149	Running
8	6	Jorge Goeters	Canel's/FICREA/LuK Mazda	149	Running
9	20	Patrick Goeters	AC Delco/Finsa Chevrolet	149	Running
10	5	Rafael Martínez	Canel's/FICREA/LuK Mazda	149	Running
11	13	José Luis Ramírez	Rayere/Prestoflam Chevrolet	149	Running
12	14	Pepe Montaño	Toyota/Goodyear Toyota	149	Running
13	18	José González	Akron/Ultra/Excelerate Toyota	149	Running
14	8	Hugo Oliveras	Monster Energy/Bosch Toyota	149	Running
15	9	Irwin Vences	Chick›s Toyota	149	Running
16	7	Carlos Peralta	La Costeña/Café Oro Toyota	149	Running
17	17	Alejandro Capín	Suspension Y Direccion Toyota	148	Running
18	23	Freddy Tame Jr.	La Costeña/Café Oro Toyota	148	Running
19	30	Óscar Ruíz	Suspension Y Direccion Toyota	148	Running
20	11	Rubén Rovelo	TELCEL/FedEx Dodge	148	Running
21	15	Rodrigo Peralta *	Tame Racing Toyota	147	Running
22	24	Salvador Durán	TELMEX Toyota	147	Running
23	29	Héctor Félix	Logistica Aduanal Racing Toyota	147	Running
24	28	Víctor Barrales	Global Lube/Gel Gomina/Italika Toyota	147	Running
25	3	Daniel Suárez	TELCEL Dodge	146	Running
26	32	Rodrigo Marbán	BC&B/Saborex Toyota	146	Running
27	16	Juan Carlos Blum *	Oleofinos/Pitbull Ford	146	Running
28	33	Rubén García	HDI Seguros/Imagen Toyota	144	Running
29	25	Carlos Contreras	NEXTEL Racing Toyota	141	Running
30	22	Rafael Vallina	Coca-Cola/Bokados/Mobil 1 Chevrolet	134	Mechanical
31	26	Luis Felipe Montaño	AIRHO/Polaroid/Adrenalina Extreme Toyota	121	Running
32	27	Israel Jaitovich	Grupo Roo/Global Lube Mazda	105	Mechanical
33	31	Javier Fernandez *	Car Motion Motorsport Toyota	53	Mechanical

* Rookie of the Year Contender

TIME OF RACE: 1 hrs., 37 mins, 41 secs — Average Speed: 92.134 mph — Caution Flags: 1 for 3 laps — Lap Leaders: Homero Richards 1-104, Elliot Van Rankin 105-115, Homero Richards 116-150.

DOUG COBY

NASCAR WHELEN MODIFIED TOUR 2012 CHAMPION

PERSONAL INFORMATION

Birth Date:	**August 18, 1979**
Hometown:	**Milford, CT**
Marital Status:	**Single**
2012 Team:	**Reynolds Auto Wrecking/**
	Furnace & Duct Supply Chevrolet
Car Owner:	**Wayne Darling**
Crew Chief:	**John McKenna**

CAREER RECORD

Year	Rank	Races	Wins	Poles	Top 5s	Top 10s
2002	59	3	0	0	0	0
2003	14	15	0	0	0	3
2004	12	19	0	1	0	5
2005	7	18	0	0	6	9
2006	14	15	1	0	2	4
2007	37	6	0	0	2	2
2008	35	5	0	0	3	3
2009	18	11	0	1	2	5
2010	27	8	0	0	2	4
2011	5	16	1	2	4	10
2012	1	14	5	0	8	11
TOTALS		**130**	**7**	**4**	**29**	**56**

DOUG COBY PUT TOGETHER A BREAKTHROUGH CAMPAIGN IN HIS 11TH SEASON TO CAPTURE THE NASCAR WHELEN MODIFIED CHAMPIONSHIP.

Doug Coby, from Milford, CT, had made 116 starts with multiple teams across 10 seasons in which he competed both full- and part-time on the Whelen Modified Tour. He had two wins during that time. But 2012 was a whole different story.

After finishing eighth in the opener at Thompson International Speedway, Coby reeled off a streak of seven-consecutive podium finishes, including four wins. He drove the No. 52 Chevrolet to Victory Lane for the first time in Stafford Motor Speedway's Spring Sizzler, then took home the checkered flag in the May and August Stafford events with a triumph at Waterford Speedbowl in between. The statement was sent early and often – for the first time in his career, Coby was a serious championship challenger.

Despite the wildly-successful start, Coby can't put his finger on a time or place where he became comfortable with the realization that they were championship contenders. "We had never won a championship before, so I don't think any of us knew what it took to be a championship-caliber team," Coby said. "We were always thinking, 'Do we have the right people, do we have the right equipment, do we have the right driver, are we making the right decisions with tires?"

The second half of the campaign provided considerably more challenges than the first. A lead that rose as high as 41 points following the third Stafford win was cut down to just nine following the team's only DNF of the year at Riverhead Raceway, the third of three-straight finishes outside the top 10. "We had those three bad races in a row, and you couldn't have predicted that, because we were running well at every track up to that point," Coby said.

There's no better way to turn around bad luck than with a win, however, and that's just what Coby did at New Hampshire Motor Speedway in September when he secured his first career "Magic Mile" victory. From there he closed the deal with a pair of top 10s. "I kind of thought that if we could make it through the summer stretch of Stafford, Thompson and

Loudon that we would be in pretty good contention for the championship, but you really never know."

All told, Coby delivered the first NASCAR touring series title to car owner Wayne Darling with five wins and 11 top 10s across the 14-race season.

"I don't necessarily know when it is that you realize you have a championship-caliber team where you're going to win a championship until the checkered flag flies at Thompson at the end of the year. All I know is this year we were the best of the bunch and my guys are really deserving of it."

NASCAR WHELEN MODIFIED TOUR
2012 CHAMPION DOUG COBY SEASON RECORD

Date	Speedway	Location	Start	Finish	Status
April 15	Thompson International Speedway	Thompson, CT	19	8	Running
April 29	Stafford Motor Speedway	Stafford, CT	7	1	Running
May 12	Monadnock Speedway	Winchester, NH	2	2	Running
May 25	Stafford Motor Speedway	Stafford, CT	5	1	Running
June 23	Waterford Speedbowl	Waterford, CT	3	1	Running
July 14	New Hampshire Motor Speedway	Loudon, NH	3	3	Running
Aug. 3	Stafford Motor Speedway	Stafford, CT	6	1	Running
Aug. 9	Thompson International Speedway	Thompson, CT	14	3	Running
Aug. 22	Bristol Motor Speedway	Bristol, TN	11	11	Running
Sept. 9	Thompson International Speedway	Thompson, CT	4	13	Running
Sept. 15	Riverhead Raceway	Riverhead, NY	7	22	Engine
Sept. 22	New Hampshire Motor Speedway	Loudon, NH	2	1	Running
Sept. 30	Stafford Motor Speedway	Stafford, CT	11	9	Running
Oct. 14	Thompson International Speedway	Thompson, CT	9	6	Running

2

3

4

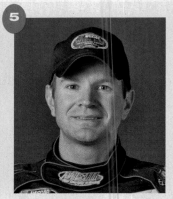

5

RYAN PREECE

Ryan Preece finished as the championship runner-up for the second time in his six-year Whelen Modified Tour career. Preece's season was highlighted by wins at both bullrings – Monadnock and Riverhead – as well as five additional podium finishes across 14 events. He also recorded a tour-high six Coors Light Pole Awards.

RON SILK

Ron Silk was unable to defend his 2011 Whelen Modified Tour title, but he did find Victory Lane twice with triumphs in the opener at Thompson and the annual combination race with the Whelen Southern Modified Tour at Bristol. Silk led all drivers with nine top fives and earned a pair of poles.

DONNY LIA

Donny Lia captured the Whelen Modified Tour championships in each of his two previous full-time seasons, but after a two year absence from the tour, he had to settle for a fourth-place finish in 2012. Lia found Victory Lane in August at Thompson and was the pole winner at New Hampshire in September.

TODD SZEGEDY

Todd Szegedy continued his remarkable run of consistency when he finished in the top five in the Whelen Modified Tour final standings for the seventh season in a row. The 2003 titlist, Szegedy registered eight top-five finishes, including a runner-up effort in the combo race at Bristol and four additional podiums.

NASCAR WHELEN MODIFIED TOUR 2012 SEASON STANDINGS

Pos	Driver Name	Points	Starts	Wins	Top 5	Top 10	Pos	Driver Name	Points	Starts	Wins	Top 5	Top 10	Pos	Driver Name	Points	Starts	Wins	Top 5	Top 10
1	Doug Coby	556	14	5	8	11	19	Wade Cole	349	14	0	0	1	37	Cole Powell *	41	2	0	0	0
2	Ryan Preece	545	14	2	8	10	20	Bobby Santos	310	9	2	4	5	38	Howie Brode	40	1	0	1	1
3	Ron Silk	533	14	2	9	10	21	Woody Pitkat	301	9	0	1	6	39	Mike Christopher	36	2	0	0	0
4	Donny Lia	493	14	1	4	9	22	Ken Heagy	298	13	0	0	1	40	John Jensen *	36	2	0	0	0
5	Todd Szegedy	476	14	0	8	9	23	Jon McKennedy	248	9	0	0	3	41	Zane Zeiner	35	1	0	0	1
6	Eric Beers	469	14	0	3	7	24	Keith Rocco *	246	8	0	1	5	42	Frank Vigliarolo Jr.	31	1	0	0	0
7	Justin Bonsignore	460	14	1	5	8	25	Richie Pallai Jr.	214	8	0	0	0	43	Ed Brunnhoelzl III *	28	1	0	0	0
8	Jimmy Blewett	459	14	0	4	6	26	Johnny Bush	149	6	0	0	0	44	Renee Dupuis	26	1	0	0	0
9	Ted Christopher	452	14	0	5	7	27	Gary McDonald	126	6	0	0	0	45	Jerry Marquis	22	1	0	0	0
10	Ron Yuhas Jr.	439	14	0	2	5	28	Rob Fuller	106	5	0	0	0	46	Steve Masse	21	1	0	0	0
11	Mike Stefanik	421	13	1	4	8	29	Andy Seuss	99	4	0	0	1	47	Brian Schofield	21	1	0	0	0
12	Rowan Pennink	412	13	0	2	6	30	Steve Dickey *	71	4	0	0	0	48	Shawn Solomito *	20	1	0	0	0
13	Eric Berndt	399	14	0	0	2	31	Tom Rogers Jr.	70	2	0	0	1	49	Tony Ferrante Jr.	18	1	0	0	0
14	Patrick Emerling	398	14	0	0	2	32	Matt Hirschman	70	2	0	0	2	50	Kyle Spencer *	18	1	0	0	0
15	Ed Flemke Jr.	380	14	0	0	1	33	Tommy Barrett Jr. *	62	2	0	0	1	51	Corey LaJoie *	17	1	0	0	0
16	Jamie Tomaino	379	14	0	0	2	34	Kevin Goodale	62	3	0	0	0	52	Ryan Blaney *	11	1	0	0	0
17	Eric Goodale	374	14	0	0	3	35	Daniel Hemric *	57	2	0	0	0		* Denotes Rookie of the Year Contender					
18	Bryon Chew	364	13	0	0	3	36	Ryan Newman	54	2	0	1	1							

NASCAR WHELEN MODIFIED TOUR MOST POPULAR DRIVER (1985-2012)

1985	Mike McLaughlin	1995	Steve Park	2005	Tony Hirschman
1986	Jamie Tomaino	1996	Steve Park	2006	Tony Hirschman
1987	Jamie Tomaino	1997	Mike Stefanik	2007	Todd Szegedy
1988	Reggie Ruggiero	1998	Mike Stefanik	2008	Ted Christopher
1989	Reggie Ruggiero	1999	Reggie Ruggiero	2009	Ted Christopher
1990	Satch Worley	2000	Rick Fuller	2010	Ted Christopher
1991	Satch Worley	2001	Mike Stefanik	2011	Justin Bonsignore
1992	Jeff Fuller	2002	Ed Flemke Jr.	2012	Ryan Preece
1993	Jeff Fuller	2003	Tom Baldwin Sr.		
1994	Jeff Fuller	2004	Tom Baldwin Sr.		

NASCAR WHELEN MODIFIED TOUR SUNOCO ROOKIE OF THE YEAR (1999-2012)

1999	Dave Pecko	2004	Ken Barry	2009	Eric Goodale
2000	Michael Boehler	2005	Tyler Haydt	2010	Justin Bonsignore
2001	Ricky Miller	2006	James Civali	2011	Patrick Emerling
2002	Todd Szegedy	2007	Richard Savary	2012	Keith Rocco
2003	Donny Lia	2008	Glen Reen		

NASCAR WHELEN MODIFIED TOUR COORS LIGHT POLE AWARD (1994-2012)

1994	Jeff Fuller	1999	Tony Hirschman	2004	Donny Lia	2009	Ted Christopher
1995	Steve Park	2000	Rob Summers	2005	Tony Hirschman	2010	Bobby Santos
1996	Steve Park	2001	Mike Ewanitsko	2006	Tony Hirschman	2011	Bobby Santos
1997	Tim Connolly	2002	Nevin George	2007	Donny Lia	2012	Ryan Preece
1998	Mike Stefanik	2003	Tony Hirschman	2008	Eric Beers		

NASCAR HOME TRACKS

NASCAR WHELEN MODIFIED TOUR CAREER WINS (1985-2012)

Driver	Wins	Driver	Wins	Driver	Wins	Driver	Wins
Mike Stefanik	72	John Blewett III	10	Tommy Cravenho	3	John Bryant	1
Reggie Ruggiero	44	Tim Connolly	9	Doug Heveron	3	Corky Cookman	1
Ted Christopher	42	Jan Leaty	9	Jamie Tomaino	3	Rick Donnelly	1
Tony Hirschman	35	Ron Silk	9	Eric Beers	2	Richie Gallup	1
Jeff Fuller	31	Bobby Santos	8	Dave Berghman	2	Doug Hoffman	1
Mike Ewanitsko	28	Brian Ross	7	Justin Bonsignore	2	Don Howe	1
Rick Fuller	20	Chuck Hossfeld	7	George Brunnhoelzl Jr.	2	L.W. Miller	1
Jerry Marquis	19	Doug Coby	7	Nevin George	2	Ray Miller	1
Ed Flemke Jr.	17	Tom Baldwin	6	Matt Hirschman	2	Ricky Miller	1
Todd Szegedy	17	Charlie Jarzombek	6	Dan Jivanelli	2	Bob Park	1
Mike McLaughlin	16	Jimmy Blewett	5	Chris Kopec	2	Charlie Pasteryak	1
Steve Park	16	Ryan Preece	5	Satch Worley	2	Rowan Pennink	1
Donny Lia	16	James Civali	4	John Blewett Jr.	1	Dale Quarterley	1
Jimmy Spencer	15	Ryan Newman	4	Tom Bolles	1	Glen Reen	1
Richie Evans	12	Wayne Anderson	3	Ken Bouchard	1	Erick Rudolph	1
George Kent	12	Brett Bodine	3	Ed Brunnhoelzl Jr.	1		

NASCAR WHELEN MODIFIED TOUR CHAMPS AND LEADERS (1985–2012)

1985
Richie Evans 4215
Mike McLaughlin 4092
George Kent 4011
Jeff Fuller 3951
Brian Ross 3912
Jamie Tomaino 3675
Doug Heveron 3469
Jimmy Spencer 3178
Jerry Cranmer 2539
Corky Cookman 2354

1986
Jimmy Spencer 3866
Jamie Tomaino 3655
George Kent 3562
Ken Bouchard 3467
Brian Ross 3413
Mike McLaughlin 3343
Jeff Fuller 3292
Corky Cookman 3136
Reggie Ruggiero 2889
Dave Rezendes 2409

1987
Jimmy Spencer 4176
Reggie Ruggiero 4077
Mike McLaughlin 4023
Jeff Fuller 4011
George Kent 3797
Tom Baldwin 3623
Mike Stefanik 3607
Jamie Tomaino 3512
Dave Rezendes 3433
Carl Pasteryak 3219

1988
Mike McLaughlin 3611
Reggie Ruggiero 3456
Brian Ross 3441
Rick Fuller 3201
Jeff Fuller 3173
Jamie Tomaino 3142
Tom Baldwin 3137
Tom Bolles 3064
Carl Pasteryak 2703
George Kent 2556

1989
Mike Stefanik 3941
Reggie Ruggiero 3935
Tony Hirschman 3921
Mike McLaughlin 3796
Jamie Tomaino 3456
Tom Bolles 3409
George Kent 3367
Doug Heveron 3350
Tom Baldwin 3270
Rick Fuller 3250

1990
Jamie Tomaino 3077
Mike Stefanik 2947
Satch Worley 2930
Rick Fuller 2897
Tony Hirschman 2859
Reggie Ruggiero 2840
George Kent 2785
Doug Heveron 2730
Tom Baldwin 2688
Jeff Fuller 2681

1991
Mike Stefanik 3692
Jeff Fuller 3253
Reggie Ruggiero 3186
Doug Heveron 3182
George Brunnhoelzl . . . 3062
Rick Fuller 3045
George Kent 2999
Satch Worley 2973
Jamie Tomaino 2860
Tom Baldwin 2756

1992
Jeff Fuller 3256
Reggie Ruggiero 2942
Tom Baldwin 2829
Steve Park 2820
Satch Worley 2817
Wayne Anderson 2804
Doug Heveron 2722
Rick Fuller 2717
Jan Leaty 2581
Tom Bolles 2514

1993
Rick Fuller 2521
Reggie Ruggiero 2428
Jan Leaty 2349
Jeff Fuller 2335
Doug Heveron 2281
Tom Baldwin 2168
Satch Worley 2203
Wayne Anderson 2174
Steve Park 2136
Charlie Pasteryak 2121

1994
Wayne Anderson 3139
Reggie Ruggiero 3119
Jeff Fuller 2894
Steve Park 2877
Charlie Pasteryak 2837
Rick Fuller 2761
Carl Pasteryak 2761
Bruce D'Alessandro . . . 2627
Ed Flemke Jr. 2583
Tony Ferrante Jr. 2575

1995
Tony Hirschman 3022
Steve Park 3019
Rick Fuller 2931
Mike Ewanitsko 2895
Mike Stefanik 2833
Ed Flemke Jr. 2808
Charlie Pasteryak 2803
Jan Leaty 2759
Tommy Cravenho 2683
Satch Worley 2649

1996
Tony Hirschman 2919
Steve Park 2907
Rick Fuller 2698
Jan Leaty 2689
Mike Stefanik 2669
Tim Connolly 2664
Jerry Marquis 2649
Ed Flemke Jr. 2568
Tom Baldwin 2501
Tony Ferrante Jr. 2387

1997
Mike Stefanik 3624
Tim Connolly 3307
Rick Fuller 3292
Tony Hirschman 3118
Tommy Cravenho 3089
Mike Ewanitsko 3085
Jan Leaty 3005
Charlie Pasteryak 2985
Ed Flemke Jr. 2902
Dan Avery 2877

1998
Mike Stefanik 3725
Mike Ewanitsko 3415
Reggie Ruggiero 3114
Chris Kopec 2937
Tim Connolly 2922
Ed Flemke Jr. 2908
Tony Hirschman 2882
Tommy Cravenho 2788
Jamie Tomaino 2773
Charlie Pasteryak 2733

1999
Tony Hirschman 3361
Mike Ewanitsko 2958
Tim Connolly 2931
Jamie Tomaino 2810
Rick Fuller 2803
Chris Kopec 2795
Tommy Cravenho 2788
Charlie Pasteryak 2773
Tony Ferrante Jr. 2682
Reggie Ruggiero 2670

2000
Jerry Marquis 2642
Reggie Ruggiero 2606
Rick Fuller 2508
Tim Connolly 2329
Ted Christopher 2326
Tommy Cravenho 2233
John Blewett III 2209
Charlie Pasteryak 2174
Ed Flemke Jr. 2106
Mike Ewanitsko 2025

2001
Mike Stefanik 2993
Jerry Marquis 2968
John Blewett III 2891
Tommy Cravenho 2691
Charlie Pasteryak 2625
Ted Christopher 2606
Rick Fuller 2602
Reggie Ruggiero 2498
Mike Ewanitsko 2488
Tony Hirschman 2397

2002
Mike Stefanik 2678
Ted Christopher 2628
Chuck Hossfeld 2606
Jerry Marquis 2594
Rick Fuller 2585
Ed Flemke Jr. 2562
Todd Szegedy 2497
Nevin George 2478
John Blewett III 2377
Jamie Tomaino 2370

2003
Todd Szegedy 2716
Chuck Hossfeld 2684
John Blewett III 2610
Ted Christopher 2520
Jerry Marquis 2501
Tony Hirschman 2403
Rick Fuller 2344
Ed Flemke Jr. 2235
Jamie Tomaino 2204
Donny Lia 2040

2004
Tony Hirschman 2915
Ed Flemke Jr. 2811
Jerry Marquis 2634
Ted Christopher 2512
Rick Fuller 2472
Jamie Tomaino 2466
Chuck Hossfeld 2457
Donny Lia 2400
Ken Barry 2397
Zach Sylvester 2317

2005
Tony Hirschman 2749
Ted Christopher 2731
Chuck Hossfeld 2666
Jerry Marquis 2647
Eric Beers 2470
Donny Lia 2469
Doug Coby 2327
Rick Fuller 2236
Mike Christopher 2202
Zach Sylvester 2178

2006
Mike Stefanik 2457
Ed Flemke Jr. 2248
Ted Christopher 2247
Tony Hirschman 2170
Todd Szegedy 2165
Jerry Marquis 2096
James Civali 2087
Donny Lia 2029
Zach Sylvester 1997
Eric Beers 1888

2007
Donny Lia 2471
Todd Szegedy 2291
Matt Hirschman 2260
Ron Silk 2257
Ted Christopher 2187
James Civali 2178
Mike Stefanik 2077
Jimmy Blewett 1883
Jamie Tomaino 1872
Ed Flemke Jr. 1851

2008
Ted Christopher 2441
Matt Hirschman 2314
Todd Szegedy 2260
Chuck Hossfeld 2251
Ron Silk 2158
Eric Beers 2115
Mike Stefanik 2102
Rowan Pennink 2016
Jimmy Blewett 1969
Ryan Preece 1948

2009
Donny Lia 2020
Ryan Preece 2004
Ted Christopher 1931
Rowan Pennink 1867
Todd Szegedy 1823
Chris Pasteryak 1691
Mike Stefanik 1650
Eric Beers 1645
Woody Pitkat 1621
Ed Flemke Jr. 1602

2010
Bobby Santos 2180
Mike Stefanik 2153
Ted Christopher 2102
Ron Silk 2096
Todd Szegedy 1957
Ryan Preece 1953
Eric Goodale 1933
Erick Rudolph 1753
Eric Beers 1752
Chuck Hossfeld 1704

2011
Ron Silk 2443
Todd Szegedy 2367
Eric Beers 2309
Rowan Pennink 2219
Doug Coby 2214
Matt Hirschman 2163
Justin Bonsignore . . . 2141
Bobby Santos 2133
Ted Christopher 2053
Erick Rudolph 2051

2012
Doug Coby 556
Ryan Preece 545
Ron Silk 533
Donny Lia 493
Todd Szegedy 476
Eric Beers 469
Justin Bonsignore . . . 460
Jimmy Blewett 459
Ted Christopher 452
Ron Yuhas Jr. 439

NASCAR WHELEN MODIFIED TOUR 2012 RACE RESULTS

1 THOMPSON INTERNATIONAL 04/15/2012

Fin	Str	Driver	Team	Laps	Status
1	8	Ron Silk	Reynolds Auto Wrkg/Schnitzer Chevrolet	159	Running
2	12	Ted Christopher	Al-Lee Installations Chevrolet	159	Running
3	7	Mike Stefanik	Robert B. Our Co. Chevrolet	159	Running
4	16	Jimmy Blewett	John Blewett Inc./Ling Trucking Chevrolet	159	Running
5	10	Donny Lia	Mystic Missile Racing Dodge	159	Running
6	21	Jamie Tomaino	Supreme Manufacturing Chevrolet	159	Running
7	14	Patrick Emerling	Emerling Ford Chevrolet	159	Running
8	19	Doug Coby	Reynolds Auto Wrkg/Sims Chevrolet	159	Running
9	26	Wade Cole	Perf. Engines/Kendall Oil/Ryan's Chevrolet	159	Running
10	5	Rowan Pennink	Monk Mechanics Hand Cleaner Chevrolet	159	Running
11	17	Ed Flemke Jr.	Ron Bouchard Autos/Raceworks TV Chevrolet	158	Running
12	13	Kevin Goodale	Riverhead Building Supply Chevrolet	158	Running
13	2	Justin Bonsignore	M3 Technology Chevrolet	149	Accident
14	22	Richie Pallai Jr.	CARQUEST Filters/Bosch Spark Plugs Chevrolet	130	Running
15	20	Woody Pitkat	Spectro Peformance Oil Chevrolet	129	Running
16	1	Ryan Preece	Diversified Metals/R.B. Enterprises Ford	125	Accident
17	3	Bobby Santos	Imperial Cars/Tinio Corp. Chevrolet	124	Accident
18	6	Ron Yuhas Jr.	Fast Track Electric/DreamRide.org Chevrolet	122	Accident
19	25	Bryon Chew	Buzz Chew Chevrolet/GT Vodka Chevrolet	122	Running
20	27	Daniel Hemric *	Hill Enterprises/Coors Light Pontiac	121	Electrical
21	24	Eric Beers	Howrith Freightliner/John Blewett Inc. Ford	118	Suspension
22	4	Keith Rocco *	Cape Cod Copper/Silver Dollar Const. Chevrolet	88	Accident
23	11	Eric Goodale	Riverhead Building Supply Chevrolet	87	Accident
24	15	Eric Berndt	Cape Cod Agts/ North End Auto Parts Chevrolet	86	Accident
25	23	Rob Fuller	Draco Spring Ford	86	Accident
26	18	Tony Ferrante Jr.	Ferrante & Co. Chevrolet	85	Accident
27	9	Todd Szegedy	Dunleavy Repair/A&J Romano Const. Ford	78	Accident
28	28	Ken Heagy	Buoy One Seafood/MacLad Drywall Chevrolet	75	Engine
29	29	John Jensen *	Perf. Engines/Kendall Oil/Ryan's Chevrolet	42	Engine

* Denotes Sunoco Rookie of the Year Contender

TIME OF RACE: 1 hrs., 24 mins, 42 secs — Average Speed: 70.396 mph — Caution Flags: 12 for 45 laps — Lap Leaders: Ryan Preece 1-84, Bobby Santos 85-86, Ryan Preece 87-88, Donny Lia 89-129, Rowan Pennink 130-137, Ron Silk 138-159.

2 STAFFORD MOTOR SPEEDWAY 04/29/2012

Fin	Str	Driver	Team	Laps	Status
1	7	Doug Coby	Reynolds Auto Wrkg/Sims Chevrolet	200	Running
2	1	Ryan Preece	Diversified Metals/R.B. Enterprises Ford	200	Running
3	9	Keith Rocco *	Wheelers Auto/Silver Dollar Const. Chevrolet	200	Running
4	8	Ron Silk	Reynolds Auto Wrkng/Schnitzer Chevrolet	200	Running
5	10	Jimmy Blewett	John Blewett Inc./Ling Trucking Chevrolet	200	Running
6	5	Justin Bonsignore	M3 Technology Ford	200	Running
7	11	Ron Yuhas Jr.	Hughes Motors/DreamRide.org Chevrolet	200	Running
8	20	Woody Pitkat	Spectro Peformance Oil Chevrolet	200	Running
9	4	Mike Stefanik	Robert B. Our Co. Chevrolet	200	Running
10	25	Bryon Chew	Buzz Chew Chevrolet/GT Vodka Chevrolet	200	Running
11	14	Daniel Hemric *	Hill Enterprises/Coors Light Pontiac	200	Running
12	12	Todd Szegedy	Dunleavy Repair/A&J Romano Const. Ford	200	Running
13	13	Rowan Pennink	Monk Mechanics Hand Cleaner Chevrolet	200	Running
14	6	Donny Lia	Mystic Missile Racing Dodge	200	Running
15	3	Eric Berndt	Cape Cod Aggregrates/ North End Auto Parts	200	Running
16	21	Richie Pallai Jr.	CARQUEST Filters/Bosch Spark Plugs Chevrolet	199	Running
17	17	Ed Flemke Jr.	Ron Bouchard Autos/Raceworks TV Chevrolet	199	Running
18	18	Eric Goodale	Riverhead Building Supply Chevrolet	199	Running
19	22	Jamie Tomaino	Supreme Manufacturing Chevrolet	198	Running
20	19	Patrick Emerling	Emerling Ford Chevrolet	197	Running
21	27	Ken Heagy	Buoy One Seafood/MacLad Drywall Chevrolet	193	Running
22	15	Ted Christopher	Al-Lee Installations Chevrolet	187	Vibration
23	26	John Jensen *	Perf. Engines/Kendall Oil/Ryan's Chevrolet	183	Running
24	16	Eric Beers	Howrith Freightliner/John Blewett Inc. Ford	164	Steering
25	28	Gary McDonald	Lakeland Landscape/TRC Electric Chevrolet	154	Running
26	24	Wade Cole	Perf. Engines/Kendall Oil/Ryan's Chevrolet	114	Running
27	2	Corey LaJoie *	LaJoie Scrap Metal/Joie of Seating Chevrolet	103	Suspension
28	23	Kevin Goodale	Riverhead Building Supply Chevrolet	50	Brakes

* Denotes Sunoco Rookie of the Year Contender

TIME OF RACE: 1 hrs., 5 mins, 2 secs — Average Speed: 92.260 mph — Caution Flags: 6 for 33 laps— Lap Leaders: Ryan Preece 1-98, Eric Berndt 99-109, Ryan Preece 110-111, Doug Coby 112-200.

3 MONADNOCK SPEEDWAY 05/12/2012

Fin	Str	Driver	Team	Laps	Status
1	1	Ryan Preece	Diversified Metals /R.B. Enterprises Ford	175	Running
2	2	Doug Coby	Reynolds Auto Wrkg/Furnace & Duct Chevrolet	175	Running
3	3	Todd Szegedy	Dunleavy Repair/A&J Romano Const. Ford	175	Running
4	14	Justin Bonsignore	M3 Technology Chevrolet	175	Running
5	8	Ron Silk	Reynolds Auto Wrkg/Schnitzer Chevrolet	175	Running
6	17	Donny Lia	Mystic Missile Racing Dodge	175	Running
7	9	Mike Stefanik	Sheraton Harborside Portsmouth Chevrolet	175	Running
8	22	Eric Beers	Howrith Freightliner/John Blewett Inc Ford	175	Running
9	20	Ed Flemke Jr.	Ron Bouchard's Autos/Raceworks TV Chevrolet	175	Running
10	6	Keith Rocco *	Cape Cod Copper/Silver Dollar Const. Chevrolet	175	Running
11	19	Jamie Tomaino	Supreme Manufacturing Chevrolet	175	Running
12	5	Ted Christopher	Al-Lee Installations Chevrolet	175	Running
13	16	Jimmy Blewett	John Blewett Inc./Ling Trucking Chevrolet	175	Running
14	12	Andy Seuss	Rockingham Boat/Lee Vinal Excavating Chevrolet	174	Running
15	24	Ken Heagy	Buoy One Seafood/MacLad Drywall Chevrolet	174	Running
16	7	Ron Yuhas Jr.	Hughes Motors/DreamRide.org Chevrolet	174	Running
17	10	Bryon Chew	Buzz Chew Chevrolet/GT Vodka Chevrolet	174	Running
18	21	Renee Dupuis	Union Insurance Group Chevrolet	172	Running
19	25	Gary McDonald	Lakeland Landscape /TRC Electric Pontiac	171	Running
20	11	Patrick Emerling	Emerling Chevrolet Ford	136	Accident
21	13	Eric Berndt	Cape Cod Agts/North End Auto Parts Chevrolet	136	Running
22	15	Jerry Marquis	Cliff Nelson/AARN/LIModManiac Chevrolet	134	Suspension
23	4	Jon McKennedy	Hill Enterprises/Coors Light Pontiac	124	Accident
24	18	Eric Goodale	Riverhead Building Supply Chevrolet	97	Engine
25	23	Wade Cole	Perf. Engines/Kendall Oil/Ryan's Chevrolet	81	Overheating
26	26	Kyle Spencer *	Perf. Engines/Kendall Oil/Ryan's Chevrolet	42	Suspension

* Denotes Sunoco Rookie of the Year Contender

TIME OF RACE: 1 hrs., 1 mins, 47 secs — Average Speed: 42.487 mph — Caution Flags: 10 for 60 laps — Lap Leaders: Ryan Preece 1-175.

4 STAFFORD MOTOR SPEEDWAY 05/25/2012

Fin	Str	Driver	Team	Laps	Status
1	5	Doug Coby	Reynolds Auto Wrkg/Furnace & Duct Chevrolet	125	Running
2	1	Bobby Santos	Imperial Cars/Tinio Corp. Chevrolet	125	Running
3	9	Ron Silk	Reynolds Auto Wrkg/Schnitzer Chevrolet	125	Running
4	14	Todd Szegedy	Dunleavy Repair/A&J Romano Const. Ford	125	Running
5	6	Rowan Pennink	Monk Mechanics Hand Cleaner Chevrolet	125	Running
6	16	Keith Rocco *	Wheelers Auto/Silver Dollar Const. Chevrolet	125	Running
7	11	Ted Christopher	Al-Lee Installations Chevrolet	125	Running
8	21	Woody Pitkat	TSi Harley Davidson/Spectro Oils of America Ford	125	Running
9	13	Jimmy Blewett	John Blewett Inc/Reynolds Auto Wkng/ Ling Trucking Chevrolet	125	Running
10	20	Justin Bonsignore	M3 Technology Chevrolet	125	Running
11	4	Ryan Preece	Sanderson MacLeod/Monster Energy/ Diversified Mtls Ford	125	Running
12	15	Ron Yuhas Jr.	Haymond Law Firm/DreamRide.org Chevrolet	125	Running
13	8	Eric Beers	Horwith Freightliner/John Blewett Inc Ford	125	Running
14	18	Ed Flemke Jr.	Ron Bouchard's Autos/Raceworks TV Chevrolet	125	Running
15	2	Eric Berndt	Cape Cod Agts/North End Auto Parts Chevrolet	125	Running
16	12	Eric Goodale	Riverhead Building Supply Chevrolet	125	Running
17	10	Patrick Emerling	Emerling Chevrolet Chevrolet	125	Running
18	23	Jon McKennedy	Hill Enterprises/Coors Light Pontiac	125	Running
19	3	Bryon Chew	Buzz Chew Chevrolet/The Elbow East Restaurant Chevrolet	125	Running
20	7	Donny Lia	Mystic Missile Racing Dodge	125	Running
21	22	Ken Heagy	Buoy One Seafood/MacLad Drywall Ford	125	Running
22	26	Gary McDonald	Lakeland Landscape /TRC Electric Pontiac	124	Running
23	25	Wade Cole	Perf. Engines/Kendall Oil,/Ryan's Chevrolet	124	Running
24	19	Richie Pallai Jr.	CARQUEST Filters/Bosch Spark Plugs Chevrolet	124	Running
25	17	Jamie Tomaino	Supreme Manufacturing Chevrolet	123	Running
26	24	Mike Stefanik	Robert B. Our Co. Chevrolet	2	Engine

* Denotes Sunoco Rookie of the Year Contender

TIME OF RACE: 51 mins, 46 secs — Average Speed: 77.440 mph — Caution Flags: 5 for 21 laps — Lap Leaders: Bobby Santos 1-117, Doug Coby 118-125.

5 WATERFORD SPEEDBOWL 06/23/2012

Fin	Str	Driver	Team	Laps	Status
1	3	Doug Coby	Reynolds Auto Wrkg/Furnace & Duct Chevrolet	163	Running
2	4	Justin Bonsignore	M3 Technology Chevrolet	163	Running
3	7	Ryan Preece	Diversified Metals/R.B. Enterprises Ford	163	Running
4	11	Ron Yuhas Jr.	DreamRide.org/Hughes Motors Chevrolet	163	Running
5	8	Donny Lia	Mystic Missile Racing Dodge	163	Running
6	6	Rowan Pennink	Monk Mechanics Hand Cleaner Chevrolet	163	Running
7	16	Eric Beers	Horwith Freightliner/John Blewett Inc Ford	163	Running
8	12	Keith Rocco *	Belltown Motors/Macara/Big A Chevrolet	163	Running
9	1	Ted Christopher	Al-Lee Installations Chevrolet	163	Running
10	15	Jon McKennedy	Hill Enterprises/Coors Light Pontiac	163	Running
11	5	Ron Silk	Reynolds Auto Wrecking/Mr. Rooter Chevrolet	163	Running
12	17	Eric Berndt	North End Auto Parts/Cape Cod Agts Chevrolet	163	Running
13	18	Jimmy Blewett	John Blewett Inc./Ling Trucking Chevrolet	160	Running
14	9	Bryon Chew	Buzz Chew Chevrolet/Elbow East Chevrolet	160	Running
15	24	Wade Cole	Perf. Engines/Kendall Oil,/Ryan's Chevrolet	156	Running
16	14	Jamie Tomaino	Supreme Manufacturing Chevrolet	155	Accident
17	23	Johnny Bush	Perf. Engines/Kendall Oil,/Ryan's Chevrolet	153	Mechanical
18	21	Ken Heagy	Buoy One Seafood/MacLad Drywall Chevrolet	111	Running
19	2	Todd Szegedy	Dunleavy Repair/A&J Romano Const. Ford	102	Accident
20	20	Ed Flemke Jr.	Ron Bouchard's Autos/Raceworks TV Chevrolet	101	Accident
21	13	Patrick Emerling	Emerling Chevrolet Dealership Chevrolet	101	Accident
22	19	Mike Stefanik	Town-line farms/Xtreme Auto Chevrolet	67	Mechanical
23	22	Gary McDonald	Lakeland Landscape /TRC Electric Pontiac	59	Front End
24	10	Eric Goodale	Riverhead Building Supply Chevrolet	39	Electrical

* Denotes Sunoco Rookie of the Year Contender

TIME OF RACE: 53 mins, 3 secs — Average Speed: 68.211 mph — Caution Flags: 4 for 26 laps — Lap Leaders: Ted Christopher 1-44, Doug Coby 45-145, Ryan Preece 146, Doug Coby 147-163.

6 NEW HAMPSHIRE MOTOR SPEEDWAY 07/14/2012

Fin	Str	Driver	Team	Laps	Status
1	9	Mike Stefanik	Canto & Sons Pvng/Robert B Our Co Ford	100	Running
2	1	Ron Silk	Reynolds Auto Wrkg/Schnitzer Chevrolet	100	Running
3	3	Doug Coby	Reynolds Auto Wrecking Chevrolet	100	Running
4	12	Eric Beers	Horwith Freightliner/John Blewett Inc Ford	100	Running
5	10	Todd Szegedy	Dunleavy Repair/A&J Romano Const. Ford	100	Running
6	7	Rowan Pennink	Monk Mechanics Hand Cleaner Chevrolet	100	Running
7	15	Andy Seuss	Rockingham Boat/Summit Signs/ Lee Vinyl Chevrolet	100	Running
8	19	Donny Lia	Mystic Missile Racing Dodge	100	Running
9	13	Zane Zeiner	ATC/Spacefitters Dodge	100	Running
10	18	Woody Pitkat	Spectro Oils of America Ford	100	Running
11	17	Bobby Santos	Imperial Cars/Tinio Corp. Chevrolet	100	Running
12	2	Ryan Preece	Diversified Metals/R.B.Enterp/Wales Irish Pub Ford	100	Running
13	22	Patrick Emerling	Emerling Chevrolet Dealership Chevrolet	100	Running
14	8	Bryon Chew	Buzz Chew Chevrolet/Elbow East Restaurant	100	Running
15	4	Eric Berndt	Cape Cod Agts/North End Auto Parts Chevrolet	100	Running
16	23	Jimmy Blewett	John Blewett Inc./Ling Trucking Chevrolet	100	Running
17	25	Rob Fuller	Draco Spring Ford	99	Running
18	20	Ed Flemke Jr.	Ron Bouchard's Autos/Raceworks TV Chevrolet	99	Running
19	28	Wade Cole	Perf. Engines/Kendall Oil/Ryan's Chevrolet	99	Running
20	29	Johnny Bush	Perf. Engines/Kendall Oil/Ryan's Chevrolet	99	Running
21	16	Eric Goodale	Perimeters for the Home Chevrolet	97	Running
22	6	Keith Rocco *	Cape Cod Copper/Silver Dollar Const. Chevrolet	94	Running
23	33	Steve Dickey *	Harold Estes Lumber/Old School Choppers Chevrolet	84	Suspension
24	30	Gary McDonald	Lakeland Landscape /TRC Electric Pontiac	81	Running
25	21	Ron Yuhas Jr.	DreamRide.org/Hughes Motors Chevrolet	68	Running
26	26	Jon McKennedy	Hill Enterprises/Coors Light/LaBleu Water Pontiac	62	Accident
27	14	Richie Pallai Jr.	CARQUEST Filters Chevrolet	60	Accident
28	27	Justin Bonsignore	M3 Technology Chevrolet	60	Accident
29	24	Ted Christopher	Al-Lee Installations Chevrolet	51	Accident
30	5	Ryan Newman	Menards/Aggressive Hydraulics Chevrolet	48	Accident
31	32	Ken Heagy	Buoy One Seafood/Green Island Distributors Ford	47	Engine
32	34	Mike Christopher	Connecticut Trailers Dodge	47	Overheating
33	11	Ryan Blaney *	Mohawk Northeast Chevrolet	37	Accident
34	31	Jamie Tomaino	Supreme Manufacturing Chevrolet	0	Engine

* Denotes Sunoco Rookie of the Year Contender

TIME OF RACE: 1 hrs., 17 mins, 24 secs — Average Speed: 82.016 mph — Caution Flags: 7 for 26 laps— Lap Leaders: Ron Silk 1-51, Mike Stefanik 52-53, Ron Silk 54-57, Mike Stefanik 58-59, Ron Silk 60, Mike Stefanik 61, Ron Silk 62-71, Mike Stefanik 72-73, Ron Silk 74-76, Mike Stefanik 77-78, Ron Silk 79-81, Mike Stefanik 82-83, Ron Silk 84-86, Mike Stefanik 87-88, Ron Silk 89-93, Mike Stefanik 94, Ron Silk 95-96, Mike Stefanik 97-100.

7 STAFFORD MOTOR SPEEDWAY 08/03/2012

Fin	Str	Driver	Team	Laps	Status
1	6	Doug Coby	Reynolds Auto Wrkg/Furnace & Duct Chevrolet	150	Running
2	11	Jimmy Blewett	John Blewett Inc./Ling Trucking Chevrolet	150	Running
3	13	Todd Szegedy	Dunleavy Repair/A&J Romano Const. Ford	150	Running
4	5	Eric Beers	Horwith Freightliner/John Blewett Inc. Ford	150	Running
5	10	Ted Christopher	Sherm's Towing/M&T Enterprises Chevrolet	150	Running
6	1	Ryan Preece	Sanderson MacLeod/Palmer Paving Ford	150	Running
7	18	Jon McKennedy	Hill Enterprises/Coors Light Pontiac	150	Running
8	22	Woody Pitkat	Spectro Oils of America Ford	150	Running
9	2	Eric Goodale	Riverhead Building Supply Chevrolet	150	Running
10	27	Justin Bonsignore	M3 Technology Chevrolet	150	Running
11	4	Ron Yuhas Jr.	DreamRide.org/Hughes Motors Chevrolet	150	Running
12	8	Rowan Pennink	Monk Mechanics Hand Cleaner Chevrolet	150	Running
13	20	Patrick Emerling	Emerling Chevrolet Dealership Chevrolet	149	Running
14	25	Johnny Bush	Perf. Engines/Kendall Oil/Ryan's Chevrolet	147	Running
15	23	Wade Cole	Perf. Engines/Kendall Oil/Ryan's Chevrolet	147	Running
16	3	Donny Lia	Mystic Missile Racing Dodge	147	Running
17	21	Ken Heagy	Buoy One Seafood/MacLad Drywall Ford	147	Running
18	12	Ed Flemke Jr.	Ron Bouchard's Autos/Raceworks TV Chevrolet	146	Ignition
19	16	Mike Stefanik	Canto & Sons Paving/Willy's Towing Ford	141	Running
20	17	Eric Berndt	North End Auto Parts/Cape Cod Agts Chevrolet	135	Running
21	26	Jamie Tomaino	Supreme Manufacturing Chevrolet	135	Running
22	15	Ron Silk	Reynolds Auto Wrkg/Schnitzer Chevrolet	113	Fuel Pump
23	14	Steve Masse *	Cape Cod Copper/Silver Dollar Const. Chevrolet	85	Suspension
24	9	Bryon Chew	Buzz Chew Chevrolet/Elbow East Chevrolet	82	Accident
25	24	Gary McDonald	Lakeland Landscape /TRC Electric Pontiac	45	Mechanical
26	19	Richie Pallai Jr.	CARQUEST Filters Chevrolet	43	Accident
27	7	Bobby Santos	Imperial Cars/Tinio Corp. Chevrolet	29	Mechanical

* Denotes Sunoco Rookie of the Year Contender

TIME OF RACE: 1 hrs., 5 mins, 57 secs — Average Speed: 68.234 mph — Caution Flags: 6 for 30 laps — Lap Leaders: Ryan Preece 1-22, Eric Beers 23-48, Doug Coby 49-150.

8 THOMPSON INTERNATIONAL SPEEDWAY 08/09/2012

Fin	Str	Driver	Team	Laps	Status
1	9	Donny Lia	Mystic Missile Racing Dodge	150	Running
2	4	Ron Silk	Calverton Tree Farm/T.S. Haulers Chevrolet	150	Running
3	14	Doug Coby	Reynolds Auto Wrkg/Furnace & Duct Chevrolet	150	Running
4	3	Ted Christopher	Cape Cod Copper/Silver Dollar Const. Chevrolet	150	Running
5	1	Mike Stefanik	Barnyard Racing/Sunoco Racing Fuel Ford	150	Running
6	7	Rowan Pennink	Monk Mechanics Hand Cleaner Chevrolet	150	Running
7	8	Jimmy Blewett	John Blewett Inc./Ling Trucking Chevrolet	150	Running
8	2	Bobby Santos	Imperial Cars/Tinio Corp. Chevrolet	150	Running
9	12	Ron Yuhas Jr.	DreamRide.org/Complete Construction Chevrolet	150	Running
10	6	Todd Szegedy	Dunleavy Repair/A&J Romano Const. Ford	150	Running
11	11	Eric Beers	Horwith Freightliner/John Blewett Inc Ford	150	Running
12	17	Patrick Emerling	Emerling Chevrolet Dealership Chevrolet	150	Running
13	18	Jamie Tomaino	Supreme Manufacturing Chevrolet	150	Running
14	25	Jon McKennedy	Hill Enterprises/Coors Light Pontiac	150	Running
15	5	Rob Fuller	Draco Spring Ford	149	Running
16	22	Ken Heagy	Buoy One Seafood/MacLad Drywall Ford	149	Running
17	21	Ryan Preece	East West Marine Ford	147	Running
18	24	Johnny Bush	Perf Engines/Kendall Oil/Ryan's Chevrolet	145	Running
19	13	Eric Berndt	Cape Cod Agts/North End Auto Parts Chevrolet	100	Mechanical
20	19	Ed Flemke Jr.	Ron Bouchard's Autos/Raceworks TV Chevrolet	93	Running
21	16	Bryon Chew	Buzz Chew Chevrolet/Elbow East Chevrolet	91	Mechanical
22	20	Woody Pitkat	Spectro Oils of America Ford	87	Accident
23	23	Wade Cole	Perf Engines/Kendall Oil/Ryan's Chevrolet	61	Running
24	10	Eric Goodale	Riverhead Building Supply Chevrolet	16	Mechanical
25	15	Justin Bonsignore	M3 Technology Chevrolet	15	Accident

* Denotes Sunoco Rookie of the Year Contender

TIME OF RACE: 1 hrs., 9 mins, 50 secs — Average Speed: 80.549 mph — Caution Flags: 8 for 34 laps — Lap Leaders: Mike Stefanik 1-74, Todd Szegedy 75-94, Ron Silk 95-128, Donny Lia 129-150.

9 BRISTOL MOTOR SPEEDWAY 08/22/2012

Fin	Str	Driver	Team	Laps	Status
1	1	Ron Silk	Calverton Tree Farm/TS Haulers Chevrolet	150	Running
2	3	Todd Szegedy	UNOH/Dunleavy Repair Ford	150	Running
3	6	Ryan Preece	East-West Marine Ford	150	Running
4	12	Justin Bonsignore	M3 Technology Chevrolet	150	Running
5	22	Ron Yuhas Jr.	DreamRide.org/Hughes Motors Chevrolet	150	Running
6	10	George Brunnhoelzl III	Phoenix Pre-Owned Chevrolet	150	Running
7	31	Danny Bohn *	Rifenburg Construction/Rustoleum Chevrolet	150	Running
8	29	Ken Heagy	Buoy One Seafood/MacLad Drywall Supply Chevrolet	150	Running
9	35	Tom Stinson	Cowardin Jewelers/M&M Painting Chevrolet	150	Running
10	33	Michael Speeney *	MRI Graphics/Presto Painters Tape Chevrolet	150	Running
11	27	Jonny Kievman	A Best Forklift Chevrolet	150	Running
12	5	Jon McKennedy	Hill Enterprises/Coors Light/Mtn. River Trucking	149	Running
13	8	Eric Goodale	Riverhead Building Supply Chevrolet	149	Running
14	25	Kyle Ebersole *	Ebersole Excavating Inc. Chevrolet	147	Running
15	9	Bryon Chew	Buzz Chew Chevrolet/Elbow East Chevrolet	147	Running
16	34	Jamie Tomaino	Supreme Manufacturing Chevrolet	146	Running
17	13	Doug Coby	Reynolds Auto Wkng./Furnace & Duct Chevrolet	138	Running
18	30	Eric Berndt	Cape Cod Agts./North End Auto Parts Chevrolet	138	Running
19	7	Ryan Newman	Menards/Aggressive Hydraulics Chevrolet	130	Running
20	28	Jason Myers	Trantham Moorefield/Wendell Edwards Ford	122	Running
21	18	Eric Beers	Horwith Freightliner/John Blewett Inc. Ford	119	Running
22	16	Cole Powell *	Copp's Tricar/Fountain Motorsports Chevrolet	116	Accident
23	2	Donny Lia	Mystic Missile Racing Dodge	116	Running
24	20	Jimmy Blewett	John Blewett Inc./Atlantic Sprinkler Chevrolet	114	Accident
25	11	Patrick Emerling	Emerling Chevrolet Chevrolet	108	Running
26	4	Ted Christopher	Cape Cod Copper/Silver Dollar Const. Chevrolet	105	Accident
27	32	Ed Flemke Jr.	Ron Bouchard Auto/RaceWorks TV Chevrolet	101	Accident
28	23	Andy Seuss	RAHMOC Racing Engines/Phoenix Pre-Owned	101	Running
29	15	Frank Fleming	Autos By Nelson/Jerry Hunt Auto Sales/Perkins Ford	56	Running
30	26	Gary Fountain Sr. *	Andy Petree Racing Chevrolet	49	Accident
31	36	Wade Cole	Performance Engines/Kendall Oil/Ryan's Chevrolet	24	Running
32	14	Burt Myers	Enforcer One Ext./Citrusafe/Adams Towing Ford	3	Accident
33	24	Mike Stefanik	Canto Paving/Robert B. Our Const. Ford	3	Accident
34	19	Rowan Pennink	Monk Mechanics Hand Cleaner Chevrolet	3	Accident
35	21	John Smith	Havoline Plus Svc/Shady Grady Rcng. Chevrolet	3	Accident
36	17	Tim Brown	Hayes Jewelers/T&C Motorsports Chevrolet	3	Accident

* Denotes Sunoco Rookie of the Year Contender

TIME OF RACE: 1 hrs., 16 mins, 34 secs — Average Speed: 62.299 mph — Caution Flags: 8 for 54 laps — Lap Leaders: Silk GRID, Todd Szegedy 1-12, Ted Christopher 13-58, Todd Szegedy 59-126, Ron Silk 127-150.

10 THOMPSON INTERNATIONAL SPEEDWAY 09/09/2012

Fin	Str	Driver	Team	Laps	Status
1	2	Justin Bonsignore	M3 Technology Chevrolet	82	Running
2	3	Bobby Santos	ImperialCars.com/Tinio Corp. Chevrolet	82	Running
3	1	Ryan Preece	East West Marine/Diversified Metals Ford	82	Running
4	6	Todd Szegedy	UNOH/Dunleavy Repair Ford	82	Running
5	7	Ted Christopher	Cape Cod Copper/Silver Dollar Const. Chevrolet	82	Running
6	8	Mike Stefanik	Cady's Tavern/Town Line Farms Ford	82	Running
7	13	Donny Lia	Mystic Missile Racing Dodge	82	Running
8	10	Eric Beers	Horwith Freightliner/John Blewett Inc Ford	82	Running
9	11	Eric Berndt	Cape Cod Agts/North End Auto Parts Chevrolet	82	Running
10	17	Richie Pallai Jr.	Bosch Spark Plugs Chevrolet	82	Running
11	19	Eric Goodale	Riverhead Building Supply Chevrolet	82	Running
12	21	Jamie Tomaino	Supreme Manufacturing Chevrolet	82	Running
13	4	Doug Coby	Reynolds Auto Wrkg/Furnace & Duct Chevrolet	82	Running
14	16	Ron Yuhas Jr.	Fast Track Elect./Complete Const. Chevrolet	82	Running
15	18	Patrick Emerling	Emerling Chevrolet Dealership Chevrolet	82	Running
16	23	Wade Cole	Perf Engines/Kendall Oil/Ryan's Chevrolet	82	Running
17	20	Bryon Chew	Buzz Chew Chevrolet/Elbow East Chevrolet	82	Running
18	9	Ron Silk	Calverton Tree Farm/T.S. Haulers Chevrolet	81	Accident
19	5	Rowan Pennink	Monk Mechanics Hand Cleaner Chevrolet	81	Running
20	14	Jimmy Blewett	John Blewett Inc./Ling Trucking Chevrolet	80	Running
21	15	Ed Flemke Jr.	Ron Bouchard's Autos/Raceworks TV Chevrolet	76	Running
22	12	Jon McKennedy	Hill Enterprises/Coors Light Pontiac	72	Rear End
23	24	Brian Schofield	Perf Engines/Kendall Oil/Ryan's Chevrolet	56	Suspension
24	22	Ken Heagy	Buoy One Seafood/MacLad Drywall Chevrolet	47	Suspension

* Denotes Sunoco Rookie of the Year Contender

TIME OF RACE: 0 hrs., 36 mins, 32 secs — Average Speed: 84.170 mph — Caution Flags: 3 for 14 laps — Lap Leaders: Ryan Preece 1-67, Justin Bonsignore 68-82.

11 RIVERHEAD RACEWAY 09/15/2012

Fin	Str	Driver	Team	Laps	Status
1	1	Ryan Preece	East West Marine/Diversified Metals Ford	203	Running
2	10	Justin Bonsignore	M3 Technology Chevrolet	203	Running
3	4	Todd Szegedy	Delicacies Gourmet/Dunleavy Repair Ford	203	Running
4	11	Howie Brode	Long Island Freightliner Chevrolet	203	Running
5	12	Ted Christopher	Eastport Feeds Chevrolet	203	Running
6	6	Tom Rogers Jr.	Planet Earth Recycling & Recovery Chevrolet	203	Running
7	2	Eric Goodale	Riverhead Building Supply Chevrolet	203	Running
8	5	Donny Lia	Mystic Missile Racing Dodge	203	Running
9	9	Ron Silk	T.S. Haulers/Calverton Tree Farm Chevrolet	203	Running
10	16	Eric Berndt	Cape Cod Agts/North End Auto Parts Chevrolet	203	Running
11	18	Eric Beers	Horwith Freightliner/John Blewett Inc Ford	203	Running
12	13	Jimmy Blewett	John Blewett Inc./T.S. Haulers Chevrolet	203	Running
13	17	Frank Vigliarolo	Frankie's Towing Chevrolet	201	Running
14	19	Rowan Pennink	Monk Mechanics Hand Cleaner Chevrolet	201	Running
15	22	Wade Cole	Perf Engines/Kendall Oil/Ryan's Chevrolet	200	Running
16	20	Ed Brunnhoelzl III *	CLN/AARN/LIModManiac Chevrolet	199	Running
17	15	Ed Flemke Jr.	Ron Bouchard's Autos/Raceworks TV Chevrolet	199	Running
18	21	Ron Yuhas Jr.	Hughes Motors/Complete Const. Chevrolet	195	Suspension
19	23	Jamie Tomaino	Supreme Manufacturing Chevrolet	192	Suspension
20	14	Patrick Emerling	Emerling Chevrolet Dealership Chevrolet	184	Running
21	3	Jon McKennedy	Hill Enterprises/Coors Light Pontiac	148	Steering
22	7	Doug Coby	Reynolds Auto Wrkg/Furnace & Duct Chevrolet	60	Engine
23	8	Ken Heagy	Two Brothers Scrap Metal Chevrolet	53	Mechanical

* Denotes Sunoco Rookie of the Year Contender

TIME OF RACE: 0 hrs., 56 mins, 49 secs — Average Speed: 53.593 mph — Caution Flags: 7 for 45 laps — Lap Leaders: Ryan Preece 1-77, Eric Goodale 78-112, Ryan Preece 113-203.

12 NEW HAMPSHIRE MOTOR SPEEDWAY 09/22/2012

Fin	Str	Driver	Team	Laps	Status
1	2	Doug Coby	Reynolds Auto Wrecking Chevrolet	100	Running
2	1	Donny Lia	Mystic Missile Racing Dodge	100	Running
3	3	Ron Silk	TS Haulers / Calverton Tree Farm Chevrolet	100	Running
4	6	Ryan Newman	Menards/Aggressive Hydraulics Chevrolet	100	Running
5	11	Rowan Pennink	Monk Mechanics Hand Cleaner Chevrolet	100	Running
6	16	Eric Beers	Horwith Freightliner/John Blewett Inc Ford	100	Running
7	13	Richie Pallai Jr.	CARQUEST Filters Chevrolet	100	Running
8	20	Matt Hirschman	Heritage Wide Plank Flooring Chevrolet	100	Running
9	12	Ron Yuhas Jr.	Hughes Motors/Complete Const. Chevrolet	100	Running
10	4	Ryan Preece	East West Marine/Diversified Metals Ford	100	Running
11	15	Eric Berndt	Cape Cod Agts/North End Auto Parts Chevrolet	100	Running
12	18	Patrick Emerling	Emerling Chevrolet Dealership Chevrolet	100	Running
13	24	Ed Flemke Jr.	Ron Bouchard's Autos/Raceworks TV Chevrolet	100	Running
14	22	Woody Pitkat	Hill Enterprises/Coors Light Pontiac	100	Running
15	27	Jamie Tomaino	Supreme Manufacturing Chevrolet	100	Running
16	19	Cole Powell *	Tricar/Copps BuildAll Chevrolet	100	Running
17	5	Ted Christopher	Cape Cod Copper/Silver Dollar Const. Chevrolet	99	Accident
18	9	Eric Goodale	Perimeters for the Home Chevrolet	99	Accident
19	30	Wade Cole	Perf. Engines/Kendall Oil,/Ryan's Chevrolet	98	Running
20	28	Mike Christopher	Conn. Trailers/Martino & Benzer Dodge	98	Running
21	31	Johnny Bush	Two Brothers Scrap Metal Chevrolet	98	Running
22	23	Bryon Chew	Buzz Chew Chevrolet/Elbow East Chevrolet	97	Running
23	7	Jimmy Blewett	John Blewett Inc/Atlantic Sprinkler Chevrolet	95	Running
24	14	Andy Seuss	Lee Vinal Excavation/GEX Chevrolet	94	Running
25	8	Justin Bonsignore	M3 Technology Chevrolet	92	Running
26	21	Todd Szegedy	Dunleavy Repair/A&J Romano Const. Ford	92	Running
27	26	Ken Heagy	Buoy One Seafood/MacLad Drywall Chevrolet	92	Running
28	17	Bobby Santos	ImperialCars.com/Tinio Corp. Chevrolet	59	Suspension
29	10	Mike Stefanik	Canto & Sons Pvng/Robert B Our Co Ford	32	Engine
30	29	Steve Dickey *	Perf. Engines/Kendall Oil,/Ryan's Chevrolet	30	Handling
31	25	Rob Fuller	Draco Spring Ford	7	Accident

* Denotes Sunoco Rookie of the Year Contender

TIME OF RACE: 1 hrs., 5 mins, 34 secs — Average Speed: 96.817 mph — Caution Flags: 5 for 17 laps — Lap Leaders: Donny Lia 1-3, Ryan Preece 4, Donny Lia 5, Ryan Preece 6-11, Ron Silk 12, Ryan Preece 13-14, Ron Silk 15, Ryan Preece 16, Ron Silk 17, Ryan Preece 18-19, Donny Lia 20-23, Ron Silk 24, Donny Lia 25, Doug Coby 26, Donny Lia 27, Doug Coby 28, Donny Lia 29-45, Patrick Emerling 46, Donny Lia 47-61, Doug Coby 62-68, Donny Lia 69-73, Doug Coby 74-76, Ted Christopher 77-83, Doug Coby 84-100.

13 STAFFORD MOTOR SPEEDWAY 09/30/2012

Fin	Str	Driver	Team	Laps	Status
1	2	Bobby Santos	ImperialCars.com/Tinio Corp. Chevrolet	150	Running
2	4	Woody Pitkat	Hill Enterprises/Coors Light Pontiac	150	Running
3	1	Jimmy Blewett	John Blewett Inc./Ed Bennett Properties Chevrolet	150	Running
4	3	Ron Silk	T.S.Haulers/Calverton Tree Farm Chevrolet	150	Running
5	10	Ryan Preece	East West Marine/Diversified Metals Ford	150	Running
6	17	Mike Stefanik	Canto & Sons/Robert B. Our Co. Ford	150	Running
7	9	Donny Lia	Mystic Missile Racing Dodge	150	Running
8	8	Bryon Chew	Buzz Chew Chevrolet/Elbow East Chevrolet	150	Running
9	11	Doug Coby	Reynolds Auto Wrkg/Furnace & Duct Chevrolet	150	Running
10	6	Matt Hirschman	Heritage Wide Plank Flooring Chevrolet	150	Running
11	13	Justin Bonsignore	M3 Technology Chevrolet	150	Running
12	14	Ron Yuhas Jr.	Fast Track Electrical/Complete Construction Chevrolet	150	Running
13	7	Eric Beers	Horwith Freightliner/John Blewett Inc Ford	150	Running
14	16	Richie Pallai Jr.	CARQUEST Filters Chevrolet	150	Running
15	12	Rowan Pennink	Monk Mechanics Hand Cleaner Chevrolet	150	Running
16	24	Jamie Tomaino	Supreme Manufacturing Chevrolet	150	Running
17	21	Eric Goodale	Riverhaed Bldg Supply Chevrolet	150	Running
18	23	Ed Flemke Jr.	Ron Bouchard's Autos/Raceworks TV Chevrolet	149	Running
19	15	Tommy Barrett Jr. *	Friends of Teto Racing/Make-A-Wish Chevrolet	149	Running
20	20	Ted Christopher	Eastport Feeds Chevrolet	149	Running
21	19	Eric Berndt	North End Auto Parts/Cape Cod Agts Chevrolet	148	Running
22	25	Wade Cole	Perf Engines/Kendall Oil/Ryan's Chevrolet	142	Running
23	5	Todd Szegedy	Dunleavy Repair/A&J Romano Const. Ford	128	Running
24	26	Steve Dickey *	Perf Engines/Kendall Oil/Ryan's Chevrolet	70	Clutch
25	22	Patrick Emerling	Emerling Chevrolet Dealership Chevrolet	50	Steering
26	18	Keith Rocco *	J & R Precast/Vivieros Insurance Ford	10	Engine

* Denotes Sunoco Rookie of the Year Contender

TIME OF RACE: 1 hrs., 0 mins, 26 secs — Average Speed: 74.462 mph — Caution Flags: 4 for 24 laps — Lap Leaders: Jimmy Blewett 1-2, Ron Silk 3-16, Woody Pitkat 17-144, Bobby Santos 145-150

14 THOMPSON INTERNATIONAL SPEEDWAY 10/14/2012

Fin	Str	Driver	Team	Laps	Status
1	2	Bobby Santos	Imperialcars.com/Tino Corp. Chevrolet	150	Running
2	4	Ryan Preece	East West Marine/Diversified Metals Ford	150	Running
3	14	Todd Szegedy	Dunleavy Repair/A&J Romano Const. Ford	150	Running
4	6	Mike Stefanik	Town Line Farm/Cady's Tavern Chevrolet	150	Running
5	7	Eric Beers	Horwith Freightliner/John Blewett Inc Ford	150	Running
6	9	Doug Coby	Reynolds Auto Wrkg/Furnace & Duct Chevrolet	150	Running
7	15	Tommy Barrett Jr. *	Friends of Teto Racing/Make-A-Wish Chevrolet	150	Running
8	18	Patrick Emerling	Emerling Chevrolet Dealership Chevrolet	150	Running
9	19	Keith Rocco *	Cape Cod Copper/Silver Dollar Const. Chevrolet	150	Running
10	11	Woody Pitkat	Hill Enterprises/Coors Light Pontiac	150	Running
11	3	Ron Silk	T.S.Haulers/Calverton Tree Farm Chevrolet	150	Running
12	21	Tom Rogers Jr.	Planet Earth Recycling & Recovery Chevrolet	150	Running
13	23	Ted Christopher	M&T Enterprises Ford	150	Running
14	13	Bryon Chew	Buzz Chew Chevrolet/Elbow East Chevrolet	150	Running
15	1	Eric Berndt	Cape Cod Agts/North End Auto Parts Chevrolet	150	Running
16	8	Jimmy Blewett	John Blewett Inc./Ed Bennett Prop. Chevrolet	150	Running
17	20	Ron Yuhas Jr.	Hughes Motors/Complete Construction Chevrolet	150	Running
18	12	Donny Lia	Mystic Missile Racing Dodge	150	Running
19	5	Justin Bonsignore	M3 Technology Chevrolet	150	Running
20	22	Jamie Tomaino	Supreme Manufacturing Chevrolet	148	Engine
21	28	Wade Cole	Perf. Engines/Kendall Oil,/Ryan's Chevrolet	148	Running
22	25	Ed Flemke Jr.	Ron Bouchard's Autos/Raceworks TV Chevrolet	146	Running
23	27	Eric Goodale	Riverhead Building Supply Chevrolet	145	Running
24	32	Shawn Solomito *	Acme Sanitary Svc/Empower Capital Chevrolet	137	Running
25	30	Johnny Bush	Two Brothers Scrap Metal Chevrolet	136	Running
26	16	Rob Fuller	Draco Springs Ford	123	Accident
27	29	Ken Heagy	Buoy One Seafood/MacLad Drywall Ford	88	Running
28	31	Steve Dickey *	Perf. Engines/Kendall Oil,/Ryan's Chevrolet	64	Oil Pressure
29	24	Rowan Pennink	Monk Mechanics Hand Cleaner Chevrolet	50	Suspension
30	17	Kevin Goodale	Heritage Wide Plank Flooring Chevrolet	41	Accident
31	26	Cole Powell *	Tricar/Copps BuildAll Chevrolet	34	Accident
32	10	Andy Seuss	Rahmoc Racing Eng/Phoenix Pre-Owned Chevrolet	29	Accident

* Denotes Sunoco Rookie of the Year Contender

TIME OF RACE: 1 hrs., 15 mins, 39 secs — Average Speed: 74.356 mph — Caution Flags: 8 for 38 laps— Lap Leaders: Eric Berndt 1-2, Ryan Preece 3-48, Donny Lia 49-82, Ryan Preece 83-92, Todd Szegedy 93-129, Bobby Santos 130-150.

GEORGE BRUNNHOELZL III

NASCAR WHELEN SOUTHERN MODIFIED TOUR 2012 CHAMPION

GEORGE BRUNNHOELZL III IS FAST BECOMING A LEGEND IN THE NASCAR WHELEN SOUTHERN MODIFIED TOUR.

PERSONAL INFORMATION

Birth Date:	October 28, 1982
Hometown:	West Babylon, NY
Marital Status:	Married (Heather)
2012 Team:	No. 09 Phoenix Pre-owned/ Triad Auto Sales Chevrolet
Car Owner:	Howard Harvey

CAREER RECORD

Year	Races	Wins	Top 5s	Top 10s
2006	2	0	0	0
2007	12	0	1	7
2008	11	1	6	7
2009	14	5	13	13
2010	3	0	1	1
2011	14	5	12	14
2012	11	6	6	11
Totals	**67**	**17**	**39**	**53**

Brunnhoelzl, from West Babylon, NY, separated himself from the rest of the competition when he captured his third Whelen Southern Modified Tour crown in 2012. Brunnhoelzl now has the most titles in the eight-year history of the southern tour, one more than Junior Miller, who earned the first two in 2005-06.

"They're all special, but this one is probably the most special just because of everything that happened off the track this year with the birth of my daughter," Brunnhoelzl said. "Life in general was awesome this year. That definitely makes a difference."

Brunnhoelzl's daughter Riley was born just a handful of days before he won the Fire-cracker 150 at Caraway on July 6.

Statistically, Brunnhoelzl's season might compare to each of his two previous Whelen Southern Modified Tour championship years, but nothing about the year was similar to the previous ones following the birth of his daughter. With all that was going on in his personal life, Brunnhoelzl had to hit the proverbial internal switch when it was time to go racing.

"When you get done with work for the day, I want to go home and hold my kid and sit there on the couch holding her. It makes it more difficult when you're not (at home) – you want to be there," Brunnhoelzl said. "You relax a little bit more during the week, but when you get to the race track it's business as usual."

Brunnhoelzl, who turned 30 just after the season concluded, has not only put together championship-winning seasons in three of the last four years, but he's done it in dominating fashion. His first title came in 2009, and after stepping away from the tour in 2010, he returned to capture the crown twice more. In those three championship campaigns Brunnhoelzl has won a combined 16 of 39 races with 16 poles.

The 2012 title run was perhaps even more dominant that the first two. Brunnhoelzl took the checkered flag in six of 11 events on the schedule and led nearly 60-percent of all laps contested by the Whelen Southern Modified Tour during the season. During one four-race stretch Brunnhoelzl led 598 out of 664 circuits.

A winner in the season-opener at Caraway, Brunnhoelzl took home the checkers in five of the first seven events – including his sought-after first triumph at historic Bowman Gray – and never trailed in the points standings. He closed the season the same way he began it – in Victory Lane – when he also registered his first win on the quarter-mile track at Charlotte.

NASCAR WHELEN SOUTHERN MODIFIED TOUR 2012 CHAMPION GEORGE BRUNNHOELZL III SEASON RECORD

Date	Speedway	Location	Start	Finish	Status
Mar. 31	Caraway Speedway	Asheboro, NC	1	1	Running
April 7	Caraway Speedway	Asheboro, NC	7	7	Running
April 14	South Boston Speedway	South Boston, VA	3	8	Running
April 21	Caraway Speedway	Asheboro, NC	1	1	Running
July 6	Caraway Speedway	Asheboro, NC	1	1	Running
Aug. 4	Bowman Gray Stadium	Winston-Salem, NC	2	1	Running
Aug. 22	Bristol Motor Speedway	Bristol, TN	2	1	Running
Sept. 1	Langley Speedway	Hampton, VA	5	10	Running
Sept. 9	Thompson Intl. Speedway	Thompson, CT	7	8	Running
Oct. 6	Caraway Speedway	Asheboro, NC	1	10	Running
Oct. 11	Charlotte Motor Speedway	Concord, NC	1	1	Running

NASCAR HOME TRACKS

2

DANNY BOHN

The Sunoco Rookie of the Year, Danny Bohn made an immediate impact during his first season. The Freehold, NJ, driver recorded the best points finish in tour history for a rookie, and his solid close to the campaign was highlighted by a win at the final visit of the season to Caraway Speedway.

3

JASON MYERS

Jason Myers, a third-generation driver from Walnut Cove, NC, enjoyed his best season of competition. One of the sport's true iron men, the veteran has started all but one race since the tour began in 2005. Myers' season peaked with a victory at Langley Speedway.

4

TIM BROWN

A consistent contender who has one of the largest fan followings, Tim Brown has finished in the top five in the final points standings six times in the eight seasons of the tour. From Yadkinville, NC, Brown had a pole and five top-five finishes in 2012.

5

ANDY SEUSS

Not many title contenders are happy finishing in fifth place, but after the start Andy Seuss had in 2012, he will take it. The Hampstead, NH, native began the season with two DNFs in the first three races, but rebounded to finish the season with eight top-10 runs highlighted by a win at Thompson.

NASCAR WHELEN SOUTHERN MODIFIED TOUR 2012 FINAL POINT STANDINGS

Pos	Driver	Points	Starts	Wins	Top 5	Top 10	Pos	Driver	Points	Starts	Wins	Top 5	Top 10	Pos	Driver	Points	Starts	Wins	Top 5	Top 10
1	George Brunnhoelzl III	468	11	6	6	11	16	L W Miller	221	6	0	4	4	31	Donnie Lacks	53	1	0	0	0
2	Danny Bohn	415	11	1	6	8	17	Mike Norman	221	7	0	0	1	32	Jeremy Gerstner	52	1	0	0	0
3	Jason Myers	412	11	1	6	9	18	AJ Winstead	177	6	0	0	0	33	Brian Weber	49	2	0	0	0
4	Tim Brown	393	11	0	5	6	19	Gary Fountain	163	6	0	0	1	34	Matt Hirschman	42	1	0	1	1
5	Andy Seuss	388	11	1	5	8	20	Jonny Kievman	154	5	0	1	1	35	Rob Fuller	41	1	0	1	1
6	Kyle Ebersole	381	11	0	3	7	21	Brandon Ward	148	4	1	3	3	36	Patrick Emerling	38	1	0	0	1
7	Frank Fleming	366	11	0	1	4	22	Cole Powell	137	4	0	1	3	37	Steve Masse	38	1	0	0	1
8	Thomas Stinson	357	11	0	1	5	23	Daniel Hemric	117	3	0	1	3	38	Ryan Newman	37	1	0	0	1
9	John Smith	357	11	0	2	6	24	Rich Kuiken	108	4	0	0	1	39	Ted Christopher	37	1	0	0	1
10	Burt Myers	353	10	0	2	7	25	Renee Dupuis	87	3	0	0	1	40	Jimmy Zacharias	33	1	0	0	0
11	Joe Scarbrough	310	10	0	0	3	26	JR Bertuccio Jr.	84	3	0	0	0	41	Chuck Hossfeld	30	1	0	0	0
12	Michael Speeney	309	10	0	2	3	27	Ryan Preece	75	2	0	1	1	42	Ken Bouchard	29	1	0	0	0
13	Gary Putnam	294	10	0	0	2	28	Jon McKennedy	65	2	0	0	1	43	Darryl Lacks	28	1	0	0	0
14	Bryan Dauzat	247	8	0	0	1	29	Dalton Baldwin	59	2	0	0	0	44	Johnny Sutton	28	1	0	0	0
15	Brian Loftin	245	7	1	3	4	30	Corey LaJoie	57	2	0	0	0	45	Carl Long	26	0	0	0	0

NASCAR WHELEN SOUTHERN MODIFIED TOUR MOST POPULAR DRIVERS (2005-2012)

2005 . . . . Junior Miller	2008 . . . . Bobby Hutchins	2011 . . . . Jason Myers
2006 . . . . Junior Miller	2009 . . . . Andy Seuss	2012 . . . . Danny Bohn
2007 . . . . L.W. Miller	2010 . . . . Burt Myers	

NASCAR WHELEN SOUTHERN MODIFIED TOUR COORS LIGHT POLE AWARD (2005-2012)

2005 . . . . Jay Hedgecock	2007 . . . . Burt Myers	2009 . . . . . . George Brunnhoelzl III	2011 . . . . George Brunnhoelzl III
2006 . . . . Burt Myers	2008 . . . . Tim Brown	2010 . . . . James Civali	2012 . . . . George Brunnhoelzl III

NASCAR WHELEN SOUTHERN MODIFIED TOUR ROOKIES OF THE YEAR (2005-2012)

2005 . . . . Wesley Swartout	2008 . . . . Buddy Emory	2011 . . . . Austin Pack
2006 . . . . None	2009 . . . . None	2012 . . . . Danny Bohn
2007 . . . . None	2010 . . . . Greg Butcher	

NASCAR WHELEN SOUTHERN MODIFIED TOUR CAREER WINS (2005-2012)

Driver	Wins	Driver	Wins	Driver	Wins	Driver	Wins
George Brunnhoelzl III	17	Burt Myers	8	Danny Bohn	1	Corey LaJoie	1
L.W. Miller	13	Tim Brown	7	Frank Fleming	1	John Smith	1
Brian Loftin	12	Ted Christopher	6	Luke Fleming	1	Brandon Ward	1
Andy Seuss	12	James Civali	2	Jay Hedgecock Jr.	1		
Junior Miller	10	Jason Myers	2	Brian King	1		

NASCAR WHELEN SOUTHERN MODIFIED TOUR CHAMPS & LEADERS (2005–2012)

2005	
Junior Miller	1904
Burt Myers	1872
Brian Loftin	1844
Tim Brown	1752
Michael Clifton	1740
Jay Hedgecock Jr.	1680
Jay Foley	1669
Frank Fleming	1655
Brian Pack	1585
Bobby Hutchens	1579

2006	
Junior Miller	2098
Tim Brown	2092
LW Miller	1924
Burt Myers	1913
Brian King	1824
Jason Myers	1788
Brian Pack	1778
Bobby Hutchens	1760
Gene Pack	1705
Frank Fleming	1534

2007	
LW Miller	1930
Tim Brown	1905
Burt Myers	1798
Junior Miller	1766
Brian King	1718
Jason Myers	1694
Frank Fleming	1692
George Brunnhoelzl III	1609
Brian Pack	1593
Gene Pack	1475

2008	
Brian Loftin	1780
Tim Brown	1750
LW Miller	1698
Andy Seuss	1617
Jason Myers	1562
Frank Fleming	1552
George Brunnhoelzl III	1540
John Smith	1398
Burt Myers	1355
Rich Kuiken Jr.	1256

2009	
George Brunnhoelzl III	2385
Andy Seuss	2205
Burt Myers	2138
Brian Loftin	2090
Frank Fleming	2044
Jason Myers	2016
John Smith	1823
Gene Pack	1762
Buddy Emory	1602
LW Miller	1457

2010	
Burt Myers	1609
LW Miller	1578
James Civali	1575
Andy Seuss	1566
John Smith	1555
Zach Brewer	1429
Jason Myers	1427
Frank Fleming	1365
Brandon Hire	1348
Gene Pack	1293

2011	
George Brunnhoelzl III	2415
Andy Seuss	2231
Jason Myers	2103
Tim Brown	2067
John Smith	2043
Frank Fleming	1988
LW Miller	1984
Austin Pack	1875
Burt Myers	1854
Thomas Stinson	1570

2012	
George Brunnhoelzl III	468
Danny Bohn	415
Jason Myers	412
Tim Brown	393
Andy Seuss	388
Kyle Ebersole	381
Frank Fleming	366
Thomas Stinson	357
John Smith	357
Burt Myers	353

NASCAR WHELEN SOUTHERN MODIFIED TOUR 2012 RACE RESULTS

1 CARAWAY SPEEDWAY 03/31/2012

Fin	Str	Driver	Team	Laps	Status
1	1	George Brunnhoelzl III	Phoenix Pre-Owned Chevrolet	150	Running
2	4	Jason Myers	Trantham Moorefield/Wendell Edwards Ford	150	Running
3	3	L W Miller	Tax Sleyer/Speedco Chevrolet Chevrolet	150	Running
4	6	Brandon Ward	Clemmons Speed Shop/Hire's Automotive Chevrolet	150	Running
5	14	John Smith	Shady Grady Racing Chevrolet	150	Running
6	13	Daniel Hemric *	Hill Enterprises/Coors Light/LeBleu Water Pontiac	149	Running
7	9	Brian Loftin	QMF Metal & Electronic Sol/L & K Trans Chevrolet	149	Running
8	5	Burt Myers	Adams Towing/Citrusafe Ford	149	Running
9	19	Gary Fountain *	Andy Petree Racing/Race Car Engineering Chevrolet	149	Running
10	18	Rich Kuiken	Flowmasters Testing & Balancing Chevrolet	148	Running
11	10	JR Bertuccio Jr.	Gershow Recycling Chevrolet	148	Running
12	7	Danny Bohn *	Rifenburg Construction/Rustoleum Chevrolet	146	Running
13	2	Tim Brown	Hayes Jewelers/T&C Motorsports Chevrolet	144	Running
14	11	Frank Fleming	Jerry Hunt Auto & Truck Sales/Adams Towing Ford	142	Running
15	17	AJ Winstead *	Clark American Sanders Chevrolet	124	Running
16	23	Michael Speeney *	UNC Charlotte Motorsports Chevrolet	96	Engine
17	12	Andy Seuss	Phoenix Pre-Owned Chevrolet	94	Accident
18	16	Jonny Kievman	A Best Forklift Chevrolet	94	Accident
19	22	Joe Scarbrough *	Hyperion Stud Chevrolet	87	Accident
20	24	Mike Norman	Auto Solution Mag/Perfection Exhaust Ford	79	Accident
21	21	Gary Putnam	Stock Car Steel Chevrolet	78	Suspension
22	20	Bryan Dauzat	O B Builders Inc Chevrolet	78	Radiator
23	15	Thomas Stinson	Cowardin Jewelers/United Solar Chevrolet	77	Accident
24	8	Kyle Ebersole *	Ebersole Excavating Inc Chevrolet	40	Suspension

* Denotes Rookie of the Year Contender

TIME OF RACE: 1 hrs., 6 mins, 53 secs — Average Speed: 61.226 mph— Caution Flags: 8 for 37 laps — Lap Leaders: George Brunnhoelzl III 1-150.

2 CARAWAY SPEEDWAY 04/07/2012

Fin	Str	Driver	Team	Laps	Status
1	3	Brian Loftin	L & R Transmissions/QMF Metal Solutions Chevrolet	150	Running
2	4	LW Miller	Tax Sleyer/Speedco/Lucas Oil Chevrolet	150	Running
3	5	Daniel Hemric *	Hill Enterprises/Coors Light/LeBleu Water Pontiac	150	Running
4	1	Tim Brown	Hayes Jewelers/T&C Motorsports Chevrolet	150	Running
5	12	Danny Bohn *	Rifenburg Construction/Rustoleum Chevrolet	150	Running
6	16	Patrick Emerling *	Emerling Chevrolet Chevrolet	150	Running
7	7	George Brunnhoelzl III	Phoenix Pre-Owned/Triad Auto Sales Chevrolet	150	Running
8	9	Jason Myers	Trantham Moorefield/Wendell Edwards Ford	150	Running
9	6	Burt Myers	Citrusafe/Adams Towing Ford	150	Running
10	10	Andy Seuss	Phoenix Pre-Owned Chevrolet	150	Running
11	8	Thomas Stinson	United Solar Graphics Chevrolet	150	Running
12	14	Kyle Ebersole *	Ebersole Excavating Inc Chevrolet	150	Running
13	19	Michael Speeney *	UNC Charlotte Motorsports Chevrolet	150	Running
14	17	Rich Kuiken	Flowmasters Testing & Balancing Chevrolet	150	Running
15	2	Frank Fleming	Lewisville Mtr Co/Perkins & Assoc Ford	149	Running
16	21	Mike Norman	Lewisville Mtr Co/Combs Wholesale Produce Ford	149	Running
17	11	John Smith	Shady Grady Racing Chevrolet	149	Running
18	15	Gary Putnam	Stock Car Steel Chevrolet	148	Running
19	13	JR Bertuccio Jr.	Gershow Recycling Chevrolet	135	Clutch
20	18	Gary Fountain *	Fountain Motorsports/Andy Petree Racing Chevrolet	128	Running
21	22	Bryan Dauzat	O B Builders Inc Chevrolet	126	Running
22	20	Joe Scarbrough *	Hyperion Stud Chevrolet	69	Power Steering

* Denotes Rookie of the Year Contender

TIME OF RACE: 1 hrs., 10 mins, 57 secs — Average Speed: 57.717 mph — Caution Flags: 6 for 34 laps — Lap Leaders: Tim Brown 1-3, Frank Fleming 4-47, Brian Loftin 48-150.

3 SOUTH BOSTON SPEEDWAY 04/14/2012

Fin	Str	Driver	Team	Laps	Status
1	7	Brandon Ward	Konnoak Giant/Hire's Automotive Chevrolet	150	Running
2	4	Andy Seuss	Phoenix Pre-Owned Chevrolet	150	Running
3	13	Danny Bohn *	Rifenburg Construction/Rustoleum Chevrolet	150	Running
4	6	Kyle Ebersole *	Ebersole Excavating Inc Chevrolet	150	Running
5	1	LW Miller	Tax Sleyer/Speedco/Lucas Oil Chevrolet	150	Running
6	8	Thomas Stinson	United Solar Graphics/Cowardin Jewelers Chevrolet	150	Running
7	17	Burt Myers	Citrusafe/Adams Towing Ford	150	Running
8	3	George Brunnhoelzl III	Phoenix Pre-Owned/Triad Auto Sales Chevrolet	150	Running
9	20	Renee Dupuis	Union Insurance Group Chevrolet	150	Running
10	9	John Smith	Shady Grady Racing Chevrolet	150	Running
11	2	Tim Brown	Hayes Jewelers/T&C Motorsports Chevrolet	150	Running
12	11	Frank Fleming	Autos By Nelson/Perkins & Assoc/Lewisville Ford	150	Running
13	14	Jonny Kievman	A Best Forklift Chevrolet	150	Running
14	19	Chuck Hossfeld	Hill Enterprises/Coors Light/LeBleu Water Pontiac	150	Running
15	23	Gary Putnam	Stock Car Steel Chevrolet	150	Running
16	26	Darryl Lacks *	Bass Automotive Trans Parts/Auto Eng Spec Chevrolet	150	Running
17	18	Mike Norman	PestX Exterminating/Auto Sol. Magazine Ford	135	Running
18	12	JR Bertuccio Jr.	Gershow Recycling Chevrolet	124	Running
19	25	Donnie Lacks *	Bass Automotive Trans Parts/Auto Eng Spec Chevrolet	124	Accident
20	5	Jason Myers	Moorefield/Trantham/Wendell Edwards Ford	89	Accident
21	22	AJ Winstead *	Clark American Sanders Chevrolet	64	Overheating
22	21	Joe Scarbrough *	Hyperion Stud Chevrolet	52	Power Steering
23	10	Brian Loftin	L & R Transmissions/QMF Metal Solutions Chevrolet	40	Rear End
24	15	Bryan Dauzat	O B Builders Inc Chevrolet	28	Suspension
25	16	Michael Speeney *	UNC Charlotte Motorsports Chevrolet	18	Accident
26	24	Gary Fountain *	Fountain Motorsports/Andy Petree Racing Chevrolet	18	Accident
27	27	Rich Kuiken	Flow Masters Testing & Balancing Chevrolet	2	Engine

* Denotes Rookie of the Year Contender

TIME OF RACE: 1 hrs., 6 mins, 25 secs — Average Speed: 54.203 mph — Caution Flags: 8 for 40 laps — Lap Leaders: L W Miller 1-2, George Brunnhoelzl III 3-131, Brandon Ward 132-150.

4 CARAWAY SPEEDWAY 04/21/2012

Fin	Str	Driver	Team	Laps	Status
1	1	George Brunnhoelzl III	Phoenix Pre-Owned Chevrolet	160	Running
2	8	L W Miller	TaxSlayer.com/Speedco Chevrolet	160	Running
3	10	Jason Myers	Trantham Moorefield/Wendell Edwards Ford	160	Running
4	5	Kyle Ebersole *	Ebersole Excavating Inc Chevrolet	160	Running
5	18	Michael Speeney *	UNC Charlotte Motorsports Chevrolet	160	Running
6	16	Daniel Hemric *	Hill Enterprises/Coors Light/Anna Bells of RC Pontiac	160	Running
7	6	Thomas Stinson	United Solar Graphics/Cowardin Jewelers Chevrolet	160	Running
8	14	Bryan Dauzat	O B Builders Inc Chevrolet	160	Running
9	3	Frank Fleming	Jerry Hunt Auto & Truck Sales/Adams Towing Ford	160	Running
10	4	Burt Myers	Citrusafe/Adams Towing Ford	160	Running
11	2	Danny Bohn *	Rifenburg Construction/Rustoleum Chevrolet	159	Running
12	7	Brian Loftin	L & R Transmissions/QMF Metal Solutions Chevrolet	159	Running
13	19	Gary Fountain *	Racecar Engineering/Bruns Construction Chevrolet	159	Running
14	9	Tim Brown	Hayes Jewelers/T&C Motorsports Chevrolet	155	Running
15	20	Gary Putnam	Stock Car Steel Chevrolet	150	Running
16	12	Renee Dupuis	Union Insurance Group Chevrolet	150	Running
17	13	Rich Kuiken	Flow Masters Testing & Balancing Chevrolet	150	Running
18	21	Mike Norman	McDonalds/Combs Wholesale Produce Chevrolet	148	Running
19	11	John Smith	Shady Grady Racing Chevrolet	139	Brakes
20	22	Joe Scarbrough *	Atlantic Solar Solutions Chevrolet	99	Engine
21	15	Corey LaJoie	LaJoie's Auto Wrecking Chevrolet	75	Accident
22	17	Andy Seuss	Phoenix Pre-Owned Chevrolet	25	Accident

* Denotes Rookie of the Year Contender

TIME OF RACE: 1 hrs., 22 mins, 52 secs — Average Speed: 52.711 mph — Caution Flags: 11 for 45 laps — Lap Leaders: George Brunnhoelzl III 1-42, Brian Loftin 43-62, George Brunnhoelzl III 63-160.

5 CARAWAY SPEEDWAY 07/06/2012

Fin	Str	Driver	Team	Laps	Status
1	1	George Brunnhoelzl III	Phoenix Pre-Owned Chevrolet	150	Running
2	4	Brandon Ward	Crane & Rigging/Konnoak Gaint Service Chevrolet	150	Running
3	9	Danny Bohn *	Rifenburg Construction/Rustoleum Chevrolet	150	Running
4	2	Brian Loftin	QMF Metal & Electronic Sol/L & K Trans Chevrolet	150	Running
5	10	Jason Myers	Trantham Moorefield/Wendell Edwards Ford	150	Running
6	12	Jon McKennedy	Coors Light/Anna Bell/Mtn. River Trucking Pontiac	150	Running
7	15	John Smith	Asheboro Recycling/Havoline Xpress Lube Chevrolet	150	Running
8	18	Michael Speeney *	MRI Graphics Chevrolet	150	Running
9	3	Tim Brown	Hayes Jewelers/T&C Motorsports Chevrolet	150	Running
10	16	Joe Scarbrough *	Hyperion Stud Chevrolet	150	Running
11	13	Frank Fleming	Autos By Nelson/Lewisville Motors Chevrolet	149	Running
12	20	Gary Putnam	Stock Car Steel Chevrolet	149	Running
13	6	Kyle Ebersole *	Ebersole Excavating Inc Chevrolet	149	Running
14	11	Thomas Stinson	Cowardin Jewelers/United Solar Chevrolet	149	Running
15	7	Burt Myers	Citrusafe/Adams Towing Ford	148	Running
16	17	Bryan Dauzat	O B Builders Inc Chevrolet	148	Running
17	19	Cole Powell	Copp's Tricar Chevrolet	147	Running
18	14	Andy Seuss	Phoenix Pre-Owned Chevrolet	142	Accident
19	5	L W Miller	Tax Sleyer/Speedco/Lucas Oil Chevrolet	142	Accident
20	21	Mike Norman	Auto Solution Mag/Perfection Exhaust Ford	128	Clutch
21	8	Gary Fountain *	Andy Petree Racing/Race Car Engineering Chevrolet	42	Accident

* Denotes Rookie of the Year Contender

TIME OF RACE: 0 hrs., 58 mins, 41 secs — Average Speed: 69.781 mph — Caution Flags: 6 for 27 laps — Lap Leaders: George Brunnhoelzl III 1-150.

6 BOWMAN GRAY STADIUM 08/04/2012

Fin	Str	Driver	Team	Laps	Status
1	2	George Brunnhoelzl III	Phoenix Pre-Owned Chevrolet	204	Running
2	3	Tim Brown	Hayes Jewelers/T&C Motorsports Chevrolet	204	Running
3	22	Cole Powell*	Copp's Tricar/Fountain Motorsports Chevrolet	204	Running
4	4	Jason Myers	Trantham Moorefield/Wendell Edwards Ford	204	Running
5	12	Andy Seuss	RAHMOC Racing Engines Chevrolet	204	Running
6	11	Kyle Ebersole *	Ebersole Excavating Inc Chevrolet	204	Running
7	7	Frank Fleming	AutosByNelson/Lewisville Mt./Perkins & Assoc. Ford	204	Running
8	16	Mike Norman	Auto Solution Mag/North Pt Chrysler/McDonalds Ford	204	Running
9	1	Burt Myers	Citrusafe/Adams Towing Ford	204	Running
10	13	Danny Bohn *	Rifenburg Construction/Rustoleum Chevrolet	204	Running
11	5	Ryan Preece	Long Island Mod. Maniac/NAPA of Canton Chevrolet	203	Running
12	21	Joe Scarbrough *	Hyperion Stud/Atlantic Solar Chevrolet	203	Running
13	17	L W Miller	TaxSlayer.com/Speedco/Lucas Oil Chevrolet	201	Running
14	20	Michael Speeney *	MRI Graphics Chevrolet	198	Running
15	15	Bryan Dauzat	O B Builders Inc Chevrolet	185	Running
16	6	John Smith	Havoline Plus Xpress Lube/Shady Grady Chevrolet	159	Accident
17	8	Jon McKennedy	Hill Enterprises/Coors Light/Anna Bells of RC Pontiac	145	Engine
18	14	Jonny Kievman	A Best Forklift Chevrolet	145	Engine
19	24	Jeremy Gerstner *	GMR Lawn Care, Kooks Headers Chevrolet	89	Electrical
20	25	Brian Weber *	Koma Unwind Relaxation Drink Chevrolet	73	Handling
21	19	Gary Putnam	Stock Car Steel Chevrolet	72	Engine
22	9	Brian Loftin	QMF Metal & Electronic Sol/L & K Trans Chevrolet	56	Engine
23	10	Thomas Stinson	Cowardin Jewelers/United Solar Chevrolet	56	Suspension
24	23	AJ Winstead *	Clark American Sanders/Health Diagnostic Chevrolet	35	Accident
25	18	Brandon Ward	Crane&Rigging/Q104/Kenny Powell Mtrspt. Chevrolet	32	Accident

* Denotes Rookie of the Year Contender

TIME OF RACE: 1 hrs., 21 mins, 57 secs — Average Speed: 37.340 mph — Caution Flags: 13 for 84 laps — Lap Leaders: Burt Myers 1-25, George Brunnhoelzl III 26-204.

NASCAR HOME TRACKS

7 BRISTOL MOTOR SPEEDWAY 08/22/2012

Fin	Str	Driver	Team	Laps	Status
1	1	Ron Silk	Calverton Tree Farm/TS Haulers Chevrolet	150	Running
2	3	Todd Szegedy	UNOH/Dunleavy Repair Ford	150	Running
3	6	Ryan Preece	East-West Marine Ford	150	Running
4	12	Justin Bonsignore	M3 Technology Chevrolet	150	Running
5	22	Ron Yuhas Jr.	DreamRide.org/Hughes Motors Chevrolet	150	Running
6	10	George Brunnhoelzl III	Phoenix Pre-Owned Chevrolet	150	Running
7	31	Danny Bohn *	Rifenburg Construction/Rustoleum Chevrolet	150	Running
8	29	Ken Heagy	Buoy One Seafood/MacLad Drywall Supply Chevrolet	150	Running
9	35	Tom Stinson	Cowardin Jewelers/M&M Painting Chevrolet	150	Running
10	33	Michael Speeney	*MRI Graphics/Presto Painters Tape Chevrolet	150	Running
11	27	Jonny Kievman	A Best Forklift Chevrolet	150	Running
12	5	Jon McKennedy	Hill Enterprises/Coors Light/Mtn. River Trucking	149	Running
13	8	Eric Goodale	Riverhead Building Supply Chevrolet	149	Running
14	25	Kyle Ebersole *	Ebersole Excavating Inc. Chevrolet	147	Running
15	9	Bryon Chew	Buzz Chew Chevrolet/Elbow East Chevrolet	147	Running
16	34	Jamie Tomaino	Supreme Manufacturing Chevrolet	146	Running
17	13	Doug Coby	Reynolds Auto Wkng./Furnace & Duct Chevrolet	138	Running
18	30	Eric Berndt	Cape Cod Agts./North End Auto Parts Chevrolet	138	Running
19	7	Ryan Newman	Menards/Aggressive Hydraulics Chevrolet	130	Running
20	28	Jason Myers	Trantham Moorefield/Wendell Edwards Ford	122	Running
21	18	Eric Beers	Horwith Freightliner/John Blewett Inc. Ford	119	Accident
22	16	Cole Powell *	Copp's Tricar/Fountain Motorsports Chevrolet	116	Accident
23	2	Donny Lia	Mystic Missile Racing Dodge	116	Running
24	20	Jimmy Blewett	John Blewett Inc./Atlantic Sprinkler Chevrolet	114	Accident
25	11	Patrick Emerling	Emerling Chevrolet Chevrolet	108	Running
26	4	Ted Christopher	Cape Cod Copper/Silver Dollar Const. Chevrolet	105	Accident
27	32	Ed Flemke Jr.	Ron Bouchard Auto/RaceWorks TV Chevrolet	101	Accident
28	23	Andy Seuss	RAHMOC Racing Engines/Phoenix Pre-Owned	101	Accident
29	15	Frank Fleming	Autos By Nelson/Jerry Hunt Auto Sales/Perkins Ford	56	Running
30	26	Gary Fountain Sr. *	Andy Petree Racing Chevrolet	49	Accident
31	36	Wade Cole	Performance Engines/Kendall Oil/Ryan's Chevrolet	24	Running
32	14	Burt Myers	Enforcer One Ext./Citrusafe/Adams Towing Ford	3	Accident
33	24	Mike Stefanik	Canto Paving/Robert B. Our Const. Ford	3	Accident
34	19	Rowan Pennink	Monk Mechanics Hand Cleaner Chevrolet	3	Accident
35	21	John Smith	Havoline Plus Svc/Shady Grady Rcng. Chevrolet	3	Accident
36	17	Tim Brown	Hayes Jewelers/T&C Motorsports Chevrolet	3	Accident

* Denotes Sunoco Rookie of the Year contender

TIME OF RACE: 1 hrs., 16 mins, 34 secs — Average Speed: 62.299 mph — Caution Flags: 8 for 54 laps — Lap Leaders: Ron Silk GRID, Todd Szegedy 1-12, Ted Christopher 13-58, Todd Szegedy 59-126, Ron Silk 127-150.

8 LANGLEY SPEEDWAY 09/01/2012

Fin	Str	Driver	Team	Laps	Status
1	7	Jason Myers	Wendell Edwards/Flat Rock Grill Ford	150	Running
2	11	Frank Fleming	Lewisville Mtr Co/Perkins & Assoc Ford	150	Running
3	4	Andy Seuss	RAHMOC Racing Engines Chevrolet	150	Running
4	10	John Smith	Havoline Plus Xpress Lube/Shady Grady Chevrolet	150	Running
5	3	Tim Brown	Hayes Jewelers/T&C Motorsports Chevrolet	150	Running
6	6	Kyle Ebersole *	Ebersole Excavating Inc Chevrolet	150	Running
7	9	Thomas Stinson	Cowardin Jewelers/United Solar/Dennis' Tow Chevrolet	150	Running
8	15	Gary Putnam	Stock Car Steel Chevrolet	149	Running
9	12	Joe Scarbrough *	Dreadnought Shaving/Atlantic Solar Chevrolet	146	Running
10	5	George Brunnhoelzl III	Phoenix Pre-Owned Chevrolet	145	Running
11	13	Bryan Dauzat	O B Builders Inc Chevrolet	143	Running
12	2	Corey LaJoie	Adams Towing/Citrusafe/UHOH Showdown Ford	108	Transmission
13	8	Michael Speeney	*MRI Graphics/Presto Painters Tape Chevrolet	108	Suspension
14	14	Mike Norman	DMC Auto Exchange/Auto Sol. Mag./Lewisville Mtr. Ford	107	Accident
15	1	Danny Bohn *	Rifenburg Construction/Rustoleum Chevrolet	2	Rear End

* Denotes Rookie of the Year Contender

TIME OF RACE: 54 mins, 3 secs — Average Speed: 65.772 mph — Caution Flags: 4 for 17 laps — Lap Leaders: Tim Brown 1-6, George Brunnhoelzl III 7-22, Corey LaJoie 23-37, Jason Myers 38-51, Corey LaJoie 52-107, Tim Brown 108-115, Jason Myers 116-150.

9 THOMPSON INTERNATIONAL SPEEDWAY 09/09/2012

Fin	Str	Driver	Team	Laps	Status
1	3	Andy Seuss	Phoenix Pre-Owned Chevrolet	75	Running
2	8	Matt Hirschman	Heritage Wide Plank Flooring Chevrolet	75	Running
3	1	Rob Fuller	Draco Springs Ford	75	Running
4	5	Burt Myers	Citrusafe/NAPA/Adams Towing Ford	75	Running
5	2	Tim Brown	Hayes Jewelers/T&C Mtrsports Chevrolet	75	Running
6	4	Steve Masse *	R&R Landscaping Chevrolet	75	Running
7	6	Danny Bohn *	Rifenburg Const/Rustoleum Chevrolet	75	Running
8	7	George Brunnhoelzl III	Phoenix Pre-Owned Chevrolet	75	Running
9	9	John Smith	Havoline Plus/Shady Grady Racing Chevrolet	75	Running
10	17	Cole Powell *	Copp's Buildall/Tricar/Fountain Chevrolet	75	Running
11	14	Jimmy Zacharias	*Wilbur Auto Sales Chevrolet	75	Running
12	10	Jason Myers	Trantham Moorefield/Wendell Edwards Ford	75	Running
13	15	Thomas Stinson	Cowardin Jewelers/United Solar/Dennis' Tow Chevrolet	74	Running
14	12	Gary Putnam	Stock Car Steel Chevrolet	74	Running
15	19	Ken Bouchard	Ron Bouchard's Auto Stores Chevrolet	74	Running
16	18	Frank Fleming	AutosByNelson.com/Lewisville Mtr./Adams Towing Ford	74	Running
17	21	Michael Speeney	*MRI Graphics Chevrolet	74	Running
18	20	Joe Scarbrough *	Dreadnought Shaving/Atlantic Solar Chevrolet	73	Running
19	13	Kyle Ebersole *	Ebersole Excavating Inc. Ford	73	Running
20	11	Renee Dupuis	Ed Bennett Properties Chevrolet	73	Running
21	16	AJ Winstead *	Health Diagnostic Chevrolet	54	Engine

* Sunoco Rookie of the Year contender

TIME OF RACE: 0 hrs., 26 mins, 52 secs — Average Speed: 104.684 mph — Caution Flags: 1 for 3 laps — Lap Leaders: Tim Brown 1-13, Burt Myers 14-23, Andy Seuss 24-75.

10 CARAWAY SPEEDWAY 10/06/2012

Fin	Str	Driver	Team	Laps	Status
1	6	Danny Bohn *	Rifenburg Construction/Rustoleum Chevrolet	150	Running
2	3	Brian Loftin	L & R Transmissions/QMF Metal Solutions Chevrolet	150	Running
3	4	Kyle Ebersole *	Ebersole Excavating Inc Chevrolet	150	Running
4	2	Jason Myers	Trantham Moorefield/Wendell Edwards Ford	150	Running
5	7	Tim Brown	Hayes Jewelers/T&C Motorsports Chevrolet	150	Running
6	14	Joe Scarbrough *	Hyperion Stud/Atlantic Solar Chevrolet	150	Running
7	11	Thomas Stinson	Cowardin Jewelers/United Solar/Dennis' Tow Chevrolet	150	Running
8	5	Andy Seuss	Phoenix Pre-Owned Chevrolet	150	Running
9	10	John Smith	Shady Grady Racing Chevrolet	150	Running
10	1	George Brunnhoelzl III	Phoenix Pre-Owned Chevrolet	146	Running
11	8	Burt Myers	Citrusafe/Adams Towing Ford	144	Running
12	16	Gary Putnam	Stock Car Steel Chevrolet	142	Running
13	12	AJ Winstead *	Health Diagnostic Chevrolet	138	Running
14	9	Frank Fleming	Autos By Nelson/Perkins & Assoc./Lewisville Ford	138	Running
15	15	Dalton Baldwin *	Main Street Automotive Chevrolet	104	Mechanical
16	13	Michael Speeney	*MRI Graphics Chevrolet	20	Engine

* Sunoco Rookie of the Year contender

TIME OF RACE: 0 hrs., 54 mins, 32 secs — Average Speed: 75.092 mph — Caution Flags: 4 for 16 laps — Lap Leaders: Brunnhoelzl III 1-13, Brian Loftin 14-142, Danny Bohn * 143-150.

11 CHARLOTTE MOTOR SPEEDWAY QUARTER-MILE 10/11/2012

Fin	Str	Driver	Team	Laps	Status
1	1	George Brunnhoelzl III	Phoenix Pre-Owned Chevrolet	150	Running
2	2	Ryan Preece	L.I. Mod Maniac/Mizzy Construction Chevrolet	150	Running
3	3	Burt Myers	Citrusafe/Adams Towing Ford	150	Running
4	4	Danny Bohn *	Rifenburg Const/Rustoleum Chevrolet	150	Running
5	8	Andy Seuss	RAHMOC Racing Engines Chevrolet	150	Running
6	6	Kyle Ebersole *	Ebersole Excavating Inc Chevrolet	150	Running
7	7	Ted Christopher	Mtn. River Trucking/Coors Light/Hilli Ent. Pontiac	150	Running
8	10	Frank Fleming	AutosByNelson.com/Lewisville Mtr. Ford	150	Running
9	12	Jason Myers	Trantham Moorefield/Wendell Edwards Ford	150	Running
10	10	Gary Putnam	Stock Car Steel Chevrolet	150	Running
11	9	Tim Brown	Hayes Jewelers/T&C Motorsports Chevrolet	150	Running
12	11	Jonny Kievman	A Best Forklift Chevrolet	150	Running
13	19	Thomas Stinson	Cowardin Jewelers/Untd. Solar/Dennis' Chevrolet	150	Running
14	13	Dalton Baldwin *	Main Street Automotive Chevrolet	149	Running
15	17	Bryan Dauzat	O B Builders Inc Chevrolet	149	Running
16	18	Johnny Sutton	Betts Racing Engines Chevrolet	147	Running
17	14	John Smith	G-Oil/Shady Grady Racing Chevrolet	137	Running
18	15	AJ Winstead *	Clark American Sanders Chevrolet	94	Running
19	20	Brian Weber *	Koma Unwind Relaxation Drink Chevrolet	79	Running
20	16	Joe Scarbrough *	Hyperion Stud/Atlantic Solar Chevrolet	46	Motor

* Sunoco Rookie of the Year contender

TIME OF RACE: 50 mins, 53 secs — Average Speed: 44.219 mph — Caution Flags: 5 for 19 laps — Lap Leaders: George Brunnhoelzl III 1-150.

NASCAR WHELEN

NATIONAL CHAMPIONS (1982-2012)

Year	Champion	Year	Champion
1982	Tom Hearst, Muscatine, IA	1998	Ed Kosiski, Omaha, NE
1983	Mike Alexander, Franklin, TN	1999	Jeff Leka, Buffalo, IL
1984	David Into, Hardeeville, SC	2000	Gary Webb, Bluegrass, IA
1985	Doug McCoun, Prunedale, CA	2001	Ted Christopher, Plainville, CT
1986	Joe Kosiski, Omaha, NE	2002	Peter Daniels, Lebanon, NH
1987	Roger Dolan, Lisbon, IA	2003	Mark McFarland, Winchester, VA
1988	Robert Powell, Moncks Corner, SC	2004	Greg Pursley, Santa Clarita, CA
1989	Larry Phillips, Springfield, MT	2005	Peyton Sellers, Danville, VA
1990	Max Prestwood, Lenoir, NC	2006	Philip Morris, Ruckersville, VA
1991	Larry Phillips, Springfield, MT	2007	Steve Carlson, Black River Falls, WS
1992	Larry Phillips, Springfield, MT	2008	Philip Morris, Ruckersville, VA
1993	Barry Beggarly, Pelham, NC	2009	Philip Morris, Ruckersville, VA
1994	David Rogers, Orlando, FL	2010	Keith Rocco, Wallingford, CT
1995	Larry Phillips, Springfield, MT	2011	Philip Morris, Ruckersville, VA
1996	Larry Phillips, Springfield, MT	2012	Lee Pulliam, Semora, NC
1997	Dexter Canipe, Claremont, NC		

2001 NASCAR Whelen All-American Series champion Ted Christopher.

DIVISION ALL-TIME CHAMPIONS (1982-2012)

Rank	Driver	NASCAR Championships
1	Joe Kosiski	17 (Sunset - 1985, 1989-1992, 1994, 1997, 1999, 2000; Park Jefferson - 1989, 1991-92; I-80 - 2001-02, 2005; I-70 - 1986, Lakeside - 1986)
2	Jeff Strunk	14 (Grandview - 2000, 2002-05, 2007-09, 2011; Big Diamond - 1994-97)
3	Jeff Aikey	13 (Farley - 1996, 1998-2001, 2003-04; Butler County - 1999-2000; Dubuque - 2003-04; Hamilton County - 1995; West Liberty - 1997)
4	Larry Phillips	12 (Lebanon I-44 - 1993-96, 1998; Bolivar - 1994-95, 1997-99; Lakeside - 1991-92)
	Mike Love	12 (Lanier - 1986-89, 1991-92, 1996; Anderson - 1986-87, 1989; Lavonia - 1991)
	Ed Kosiski	12 (Adams County - 1986, 1988, 1996-97, 2000; Eagle - 1988, 1990, 1998-99; Sunset - 1995-96; I-80 - 2005)
	Andy Bozell	12 (Kalamazoo - 1994, 1998-2005, 2007-08, 2010)
	Ted Christopher	12 (Stafford - 1987, 1996, 2000-01, 2004, 2007, 2009, 2012; Thompson - 1988-89, 2002, 2010)
	Donny Reuvers	12 (Elko - 2000, 2005-11; Raceway Park - 2002, 2005-07)
10	Steve Boley	11 (West Liberty - 1991-93, 1996, 1998; Dubuque - 1992-93, 1998; Farley - 1992, 1994, 2005)
	Kyle Berck	11 (Mid-Continent - 1989, 1991-93; Sunset - 1993, 1998; Eagle - 1994, 2000; Crawford County - 1997; Adams County - 1998; I-80 - 2003)
	Terry Gallaher	11 (Capital - 1986, 1988-91, 1995-96; Quincy - 1985, 1988, 1991; Moberly - 1993)
13	Carl Trimmer	10 (Tucson, 1993-99, 2001; Raven - 1987-88)
	Kevin Nuttleman	10 (LaCrosse - 1990-92, 1994, 1999-2000, 2002, 2005-06, 2009)
	Raymond Guss Jr.	10 (Farley - 1989-90, 1995, 1997; Dubuque - 1989, 1991, 1995; West Liberty - 1989-90; Peoria - 2004)
16	Steve Kosiski	9 (Sunset - 1986-88; Park Jefferson - 1986-87; Eagle - 1986, 1989; Adams County - 1989; Crawford County - 1999)
	Gary Webb	9 (Dubuque - 1999-2002; Peoria - 1988-89; Farley - 1993; West Liberty - 2000; Grant County - 2005)
	Bobby Gahan	9 (All-Star - 1994, 1996, 1998, 2000, 2004, 2007; Lee USA - 1997-99)
	Chris Spieker	9 (Adams County - 2001, 2003-09)
	Philip Morris	9 (Motor Mile - 1997, 2001, 2005-09; South Boston - 2003, 2011)
	Tim Brown	9 (Bowman Gray - 1996-98; 2002, 2004-05; 2008-09, 2012)
22	Robert Hogge IV	8 (Watsonville - 1997-99, 2003; Antioch - 1995-96; Altamont - 1996; San Jose - 1998)
	David Byrd	8 (Stockton 99 - 1994, 1996-97, 2004; Altamont - 1995, 2006; Watsonville - 1994-95)
	Barry Beggarly	8 (Orange County - 1991, 1993-94, 2000; Ace - 1990, 1993, 1996; South Boston - 1988)
	Jeff Agnew	8 (Motor Mile - 1992, 1994-95; Lonesome Pine - 1991-92; Kingsport - 1996-97; Pulaski County - 1991)
	Max Prestwood Jr.	8 (Hickory - 1984-85, 1990, 1995; Tri-County - 1990, 1995-96, 1998)
	David Chase	8 (Adams County - 1987, 1990, 1992, 1994-95, 1999; Eagle - 1987, 1992)
	Roger Dolan	8 (1983, 1985-87; Hawkeye Downs - 1985, 1987; Farley - 1983; West Liberty - 1987)
29	Eddie Johnson	7 (Southside - 1985, 1996, 1998, 2000; Old Dominion - 1987, 1991; Langley - 1993)
	David Blankenship	7 (South Boston - 1984, 1989-1990, 1993, 1997-98; Orange County - 1985)
	Ricky Bilderback	7 (Rockford - 2001-07)
	Bobby Wilberg	7 (Rockford - 1991, 1995-2000)
	Steve Murgic	7 (Raceway - 1988, 1991, 1997-2001)
	Mark Burgtorf	7 (Quincy - 1992-96; Moberly - 1994-95)
	Charles Powell III	7 (Myrtle Beach, 1994-96, 1998; Summerville - 1984-85, 1987)
	Jerry Marquis	7 (Monadnock - 1990-92; Riverside - 1991-93; Stafford - 1999)
	Phillip Warren	7 (Langley - 1994-95, 1997, 2000-01; Southside - 1999; South Hampton - 2004)
	Ronald Wylie	7 (Holland - 1988, 1991-92, 1995-98)

Track champions for Division I at NASCAR-sanctioned tracks

ALL-AMERICAN SERIES

TOP 24 MOST WINS IN A SEASON (1982-2012)

Year	Driver	Wins	Year	Driver	Wins
1989	Ray Guss Jr.	38	1993	Dennis Setzer	27
1992	Larry Phillips	38	1994	Larry Phillips	27
1990	Max Prestwood Jr.	35	1995	Greg Biffle	27
1990	Ray Guss Jr.	34	1982	Tom Hearst	26
1987	Roger Dolan	33	1988	Dale Fischlein	26
1991	Larry Phillips	32	1992	Steve Hendren	25
1995	Larry Phillips	32	1994	Charlie Cragan	25
1983	Mike Alexander	31	1991	Ray Guss Jr.	24
1986	Joe Kosiski	29	2011	Keith Rocco	24
1983	Richie Evans	28	1984	David Into	23
1985	Doug McCoun	27	1988	Robert Powell	23
1986	Roger Dolan	27			
1993	Barry Beggarly	27	Most wins in one season; NASCAR Div. I		

FINALIST PROGRAM

Beginning in 2010, NASCAR recognized the top drivers in Divisions II-V with the NASCAR Finalist Program. The top three in each division are recognized for their accomplishments.

2011 ASPHALT

DIVISION II

Shawn Balluzzo	Langley Speedway
Ricky Martin	Raceway Park
Dan Glister	LaCrosse Speedway

DIVISION III

Shawn Murray	Barrie Speedway
John Ketron	Kingsport Speedway
Matt Galko	All American Speedway

DIVISION IV

Jack Nugent	Colorado National Speedway
Ken Cassidy Jr.	Waterford Speedbowl
Glenn Colvin	Waterford Speedbowl

DIVISION V

Danny Field	Thompson Int'l Speedway
Doug Schmitz	Raceway Park
Jason Heitz	Raceway Park

2011 DIRT

DIVISION II

Jess Sobbing	I-80 Speedway
Chuck Schutz	Grandview Speedway
Dennis Cook	Grandview Speedway

DIVISION III

Brad Derry	I-80 Speedway
Jason Rold	Adams County Speedway
Terry Hardisty	I-80 Speedway

DIVISION IV

Matt McAtee	Adams County Speedway
Pat Shifflett	Adams County Speedway
Jeremy Auten	Adams County Speedway

DIVISION V

Bill Gibson	Adams County Speedway
Blaine Petersen	Adams County Speedway
Jerod Weston	Adams County Speedway

2010 ASPHALT

DIVISION II

Danny Johnson	Raceway Park
Ricky Martin	Raceway Park
Woody Pitkat	Stafford Motor Speedway

DIVISION III

Tommy Barrett	Stafford Motor Speedway
Christopher Barrett	All American Speedway
Mickey Owens	All American Speedway

DIVISION IV

Rob Roush	Rockford Speedway
Tim Hollen	Raceway Park
Danny Field	Waterford Speedbowl

DIVISION V

Brian Adams	Raceway Park
Doug Schmitz	Raceway Park
Patrick Bennett	Raceway Park

2010 DIRT

DIVISION II

Jess Sobbing	I-80 Speedway
Ronald Kline	Grandview Speedway
Chuck Schutz	Grandview Speedway

DIVISION III

Brad Derry	I-80 Speedway
Greg Miller	Adams County Speedway
Jeremy Swanson	Adams County Speedway

DIVISION IV

Jamie Spanel	I-80 Speedway
Pat Shifflett	Adams County Speedway
Justin Soule	I-80 Speedway

DIVISION V

Andy Wilkinson	Junction Motor Speedway
Rich Dzelek Jr.	Superior Speedway
Scott Smith	Junction Motor Speedway

NASCAR WHELEN ALL-AMERICAN SERIES
LEE PULLIAM

NASCAR WHELEN ALL-AMERICAN SERIES 2012 NATIONAL CHAMPION

Lee Pulliam's meteoric rise from raw rookie to national prominence is complete.

Lee Pulliam, 24, of Semora, NC, won the coveted NASCAR Whelen All-American Series national championship in his sixth year of racing and fourth year driving pavement Late Models.

"I was just a little kid wanting to be a race car driver one day," Pulliam said. "This year that little kid's dream came true."

Pulliam's 2012 national championship racing record in 36 starts is 22 wins, 30 top fives and 32 top 10s. His wins were spread among four tracks, including 10 at Motor Mile, nine at South Boston (VA) Speedway, two at Caraway Speedway in Sophia, NC, and one at Southern National Motorsports Park in Kenly, NC. He also won Virginia's NASCAR Whelen All-American Series State Championship.

"When I finished third in points last year I stood on the stage at the banquet behind two national champions, Philip Morris and Keith Rocco. I respect them and look up to both of them," Pulliam said.

Motor Mile and South Boston opened their seasons in March but Pulliam didn't get on track until the first weekend in May. He was suspended by NASCAR until May 1 for an incident at the end of the 2011 season. Pulliam used the 2012 season to turn his career around and fulfill the potential of his third-place national ranking a year ago.

"I got a second chance," Pulliam said. "Not being able to compete reminded me how much I love short track racing."

Pulliam began his racing career in the Limited Sportsman division at South Boston in 2007 and moved to Late Models in 2009. He was rookie of the year in both divisions and won the Limited Sportsman division championship in 2008. He is a three-time winner of the Most Popular Driver Award at South Boston and won his first career NASCAR Late Model track title at Motor Mile in 2011.

In the 31-year history of the NASCAR Whelen All-American Series, Pulliam is the 22nd driver to win the national championship.

PERSONAL INFORMATION

Birth Date:	**April 5, 1988**
Hometown:	**Semora, NC**
2012 Team:	**No. 1 Pulliam Motorsports Chevrolet**
Car Owner:	**Harold Pulliam**

CAREER RECORD

Year	Starts	Wins	Top 5s	Top 10s	Ntl. Stand.
2009	21	1	4	10	191
2010	21	5	14	15	26
2011	32	18	28	30	3
2012	36	22	30	32	1
Totals:	110	46	76	87	

KEITH ROCCO
Second-Place Finisher

Keith Rocco continues to be one of the most consistent and successful drivers in the NASCAR Whelen All-American Series. Rocco, 27, of Wallingford, CT, the series' 2010 national champion, also posted runner-up finishes in 2011 and 2009. Over the past six years, Rocco has finished no lower than fourth in national ranking and accumulated 91 wins in 245 starts.

Rocco competes in pavement Modifieds. He won eight times at Waterford (CT) Speedbowl, four times at Stafford Motor Speedway in Stafford Springs, CT, and twice at Thompson (CT) International Speedway. He overcame injury to contend for the 2012 national title. He dislocated his left wrist and broke a radial bone in an accident at Thompson on July 29. The injuries required surgery.

"I'm happy we were able to pull off second place this year," Rocco said. "We had about four weeks racing three nights a week where I was starting races then making a driver change at the first caution."

Rocco's 43-race record this year includes 14 wins, 26 top fives and 32 top 10s.

C.E. FALK III
Third-Place Finisher

C.E. Falk III continued a methodical march toward the top of the NASCAR Whelen All-American Series this year. Falk, 24, of Virginia Beach, VA, placed a career-high third in the 2012 national point race. He placed fourth last year, fifth in 2010 and sixth in 2009.

"I'm on a mission to do better every year and a mission to win the next race," Falk said. "It's pretty cool to keep improving."

Falk won at four tracks during the season, including 10 at Langley Speedway in Hampton, VA, and two each at South Boston (VA) Speedway, Motor Mile Speedway in Radford, VA, and Southern National Motorsports Park in Kenly, NC. He finished second to Pulliam in the Virginia point race.

Key to his advancement to third in final standings was a pair of wins at Langley on the final weekend of the season. That helped him slip by Tennessee state champion Nate Monteith and into third by a two-point margin. Falk's racing record for the season is 16 wins, 25 top fives and 27 top 10s in 30 starts.

NASCAR HOME TRACKS

Brian Parker is joined by Linda Harbuck and track announcer Bryce Hall in victory lane at Salina (OK) Highbanks Speedway. Parker is the 2012 NASCAR WHELEN ALL-AMERICAN SERIES NATIONAL ROOKIE OF THE YEAR presented by Jostens. *Courtesy SHS.*

NASCAR WHELEN ALL-AMERICA SERIES NATIONAL ROOKIE OF THE YEAR AWARD

Brian Parker made a radical departure from his racing routine this year and the move brought him multiple NASCAR titles. Parker, 32, of Collinsville, OK, is the 2012 NASCAR Whelen All-American Series National Rookie of the Year presented by Jostens. He is also the Oklahoma State Champion, Oklahoma Rookie of the Year and the Salina (OK) Highbanks Speedway Track Champion. He won the rookie point race 479-451 over Vince Quenneville, who races at Devil's Bowl Speedway in West Haven, VA.

"This is an awesome accomplishment," Parker said. "Wade Cagle asked me if I'd like to drive his car for points at Salina this year. I've been racing for 17 years and never raced for points. I said 'Let's do it.' All we wanted to do this year was go out and win races. We didn't expect this much success."

Parker, a drafting and design engineer, has enjoyed a long and successful career building and racing support division cars such as Street Stocks, Factory Stocks and Grand Nationals. Known as a traveling racer, 2012 was the first season he settled in to focus on racing at Salina each Saturday night.

Parker is also Salina's 2012 Grand National Division Track Champion.

STATE & PROVINCIAL 2012 ROOKIE OF THE YEAR AWARDS

State/Prov.	Driver Name	Track	Starts	Wins	Top 5	Top 10	Points
Alberta	Shania Laforce	Edmonton International Raceway	11	0	10	11	72
California	Jason Bamberg	Stockton 99 Speedway	18	3	13	15	403
Colorado	Eric Meisner	Colorado National Speedway	12	0	0	3	166
Connecticut	Ed Puleo	Waterford Speedbowl	19	0	0	13	406
Idaho	Casey Pehrson	Magic Valley Speedway	20	4	16	19	298
Illinois	Matthew Clossey	Rockford Speedway	17	1	6	11	281
Iowa	Daulton Maassen	Adams County Speedway	16	0	0	9	286
Louisiana	Brandon Kelley	Revolution Park Racing and Entertainment Complex	12	11	11	12	227
Maine	Corey Bubar	Beech Ridge Motor Speedway	13	1	3	6	283
Michigan	Jamison Russell	Kalamazoo Speedway	11	0	0	2	136
Minnesota	Derek Lemke	Elko Speedway/Raceway Park	18	0	3	9	332
Nebraska	Cory Dumpert	Junction Motor Speedway	15	1	5	9	289
Nevada	Cole Custer	Las Vegas Motor Speedway	2	0	2	2	38
New Hampshire	Scott MacMichael	Canaan Fair Speedway	19	0	9	14	384
New York	Tommy Catalano	Spencer Speedway	25	0	9	19	336
North Carolina	Ricky Jones	Southern National Motorsports Park	22	0	3	13	334
Ohio	Jake Reufer	Limaland Motorsports Park	14	2	11	12	354
Oklahoma	Brian Parker	Salina Highbanks Speedway	19	7	13	17	479
Ontario	Shawn Murray	Barrie Speedway	34	4	14	28	408
Pennsylvania	Teddy Gibala	Motordrome Speedway	16	0	1	10	182
South Carolina	Sam Scarpelli Jr.	Myrtle Beach Speedway	11	0	0	1	134
Tennessee	Austin Peters	Kingsport Speedway	20	0	0	12	390
Texas	Bayley Currey	Thunderhill Raceway	25	3	13	19	337
Vermont	Vince Quenneville	Devil's Bowl Speedway	18	5	11	15	451
Virginia	Tyler Hughes	Old Dominion Speedway	18	1	11	17	353
Washington	Molly Helmuth	Evergreen Speedway	11	0	2	7	208
Wisconsin	John Olson	LaCrosse Fairgrounds Speedway	17	0	0	0	214

UNOH ULTIMATE MECHANIC CHALLENGE AWARD

Mark Ruhmann is the 2012 NASCAR Whelen All-American Series UNOH Ultimate Mechanic Challenge Award winner. Ruhmann, 45, of Rural Hall, NC, is crew chief for Tim Brown. Brown won his record ninth NASCAR Modified track championship at Bowman Gray Stadium in Winston-Salem, NC.

With his brother, Ben, Brown's team was established in 1991. Ruhmann joined them as a rookie crewman a season later. He became crew chief in 2009. This year Brown broke a tie of the record eight track championships with the long-retired Ralph Brinkley. Brinkley's record stood for 26 years. Brown's team also matched its all-time record of eight wins in a single season this year. In addition to the eight wins, Brown posted 13 top fives and 18 top 10s in 24 starts.

NASCAR WHELEN ALL-AMERICAN SERIES FINALIST PROGRAM

The NASCAR Finalist national recognition program focuses on the divisions outside of the Division I at each NASCAR Whelen All-American Series track. Points are kept separately for dirt and asphalt tracks. A NASCAR-licensed driver's best 14 finishes are counted toward their final points total for the year. Each track in the NASCAR Whelen All-American Series designates its top division as its Division I, and assigns its remaining divisions a designation of II, III, IV or V. The Finalist Program was established to recognize the drivers in those latter divisions.

DIVISION II ASPHALT FINALISTS

1	Woody Pitkat	Stafford Motor Speedway/Thompson Int'l Speedway
2	Jeff Garrison	Bowman Gray Stadium/Hickory Motor Speedway
3	Ricky Martin	Raceway Park

DIVISION III ASPHALT FINALISTS

1	Scott Sundeen	Thompson Int'l Speedway
2	Jesse Gleason	Thompson Int'l Speedway
3	Charlie Smith	Barrie Speedway

DIVISION IV ASPHALT FINALISTS

1	Ken Cassidy Jr.	Waterford Speedbowl
2	Bobby Frisch	Rockford Speedway
3	Matt Wieg	Lake County Speedway

DIVISION V ASPHALT FINALISTS

1	Jack Purcell	Raceway Park/Elko Speedway
2	Greg Staggers	Motordrome Speedway
3	Blake Dorweiler	Raceway Park/Elko Speedway

DIVISION II DIRT FINALISTS

1	Chuck Schutz Jr.	Grandview Speedway
2	Dylan Smith	I-80 Speedway
3	Shawn Valenti	Limaland Motorsports Park

DIVISION III DIRT FINALISTS

1	Brad Brightbill	Grandview Speedway
2	Craig Whitmoyer	Grandview Speedway
3	Jared Umbenhauer	Grandview Speedway

DIVISION IV DIRT FINALISTS

1	Jesse Sobbing	I-80 Speedway/Adams County Speedway
2	Jeffrey Jones	I-80 Speedway/Adams County Speedway/Junction Motor Speedway
3	Brian Kosiski	I-80 Speedway/Adams County Speedway/Junction Motor Speedway

DIVISION V DIRT FINALISTS

1	Matt McAtee	Adams County Speedway
2	Jeremy Auten	Adams County Speedway
3	Jeremy Purdy	Adams County Speedway

2012 WENDELL SCOTT TRAILBLAZER AWARD

The late Wendell Scott won the NASCAR Virginia championship in the NASCAR Sportsman Division in 1959 and became the first African-American to win a NASCAR Sprint Cup race in 1964 with his victory at Speedway Park in Jacksonville, FL.

TREY GIBSON

Trey Gibson is the recipient of the 2012 Wendell Scott Trailblazer Award. The Wendell Scott Trailblazer Award is an annual award that is presented to an outstanding minority or female driver competing in the NASCAR Whelen All-American Series.

Gibson, 20, of Easley, SC, raced fulltime in NASCAR Whelen All-American Series Late Models at Hickory (NC) Motor Speedway in 2012. He finished sixth in track points with a record of one win, 12 top fives and 16 top 10s in 21 starts.

Off track, Gibson is a popular representative of Drive for Diversity and NASCAR racing in general. When speaking to young people he is an advocate for education and determination as the route to achieve goals. He expanded his community outreach as a participant in the Diversity In Motion Youth Camp at Winston-Salem (NC) State University and the Charlotte (NC) Speed Street Festival.

Gibson is a second-year driver for Rev Racing as part of the NASCAR-supported Drive for Diversity program. As his racing schedule permits, Gibson is a spotter for Ryan Gifford, one of Rev Racing's NASCAR K&N Pro Series drivers. Rev Racing is owned and managed by Max Siegel and headquartered in Concord, NC.

NASCAR WHELEN ALL-AMERICAN SERIES
NATIONAL TOP 500 FEATURE DIVISION POINT LEADERS 2012

Pos	Driver	Track	Points
1	Lee Pulliam	Southern Natl, Kingsport, Motor Mile, Caraway, S	794
2	Keith Rocco	Waterford, Thompson, Stafford	748
3	C E Falk III	S Boston, Caraway, Langley, Southern Natl, Motor	728
4	Nate Monteith	Southern Natl, Greenville, Kingsport	726
5	Ryan Preece	Stafford, Thompson, Riverhead	724
6	Ted Christopher	Riverhead, Stafford, Thompson	716
7	Duane Howard	Grandview	713
8	Deac Mccaskill	S Boston, Southern Natl	706
9	Adam Royle	Elko	685
10	Tim Brown	Bowman	672
11	Woody Pitkat	Thompson, Stafford	671
12	Tommy Lemons Jr.	S Boston, Southern Natl, Caraway, Myrtle, Motor	666
13	Jason O'brien	Adams, I-80	661
14	Wayne Helliwell Jr.	Canaan, Lee	650
15	Jase Kaser	Junction, I-80	647
16	Matt Bowling	Motor Mile, Langley, Kingsport, Caraway, S Boston	638
17	Anthony Anders	Myrtle, Greenville, Kingsport, Hickory	632
18	Frank Deiny Jr.	Southern Natl, S Boston, Motor Mile	621
19	Josh Berry	Motor Mile	601
20	Scott Winters	Stockton, All American	596
21	Donny Reuvers	Elko	596
22	Shawn Solomito	Riverhead	595
23	Jonathan Brown	Bowman	592
24	Danny Bohn	Bowman	592
25	Doug Manmiller	Grandview	586
26	Tyler Chadwick	Waterford	584
27	Jason Myers	Bowman	576
28	Matt Goede	Elko	575
29	Chris Spieker	Adams, I-80	572
30	Burt Myers	Bowman	570
31	Dwayne Baker	Barrie	567
32	Austin Mcdaniel	Hickory	567
33	Howie Brode	Riverhead	566
34	Jc Wyman	Adams, I-80	565
35	Lee Jeffreys	Bowman	564
36	Zeke Shell	Kingsport	562
37	Jeff Pearl	Waterford	562
38	Tom Rogers Jr.	Riverhead	560
39	Todd Korish	Lacrosse	558
40	Peyton Sellers	Motor Mile, S Boston, Langley	557
41	Joe Aramendia	Thunderhill, Houston	553
42	Shawn Pfaff	Lacrosse	552
43	Justin Zeitner	I-80, Adams	548
44	Dean Ward	Bowman	547
45	Chad Walen	Elko, Raceway	544
46	Rob Janovic Jr.	Waterford	537
47	Randy Butner	Bowman	535
48	Adam Long	Hickory, Kingsport, Motor Mile	531
49	John Smith	Bowman	530
50	J Herbst	Lacrosse	528
51	Greg Edwards	Langley, S Boston, Southern Natl	528
52	Craig Von Dohren	Grandview	526
53	Michael Hardin	S Boston, Southern Natl, Old Dominion	524
54	Brent Kirchner	Lacrosse	524
55	Jeff Strunk	Grandview	521
56	Jason Schneider	Elko	519
57	Doug Godsey	Southern Natl, Caraway, Langley	515
58	Paul Nogradi Jr.	Southern Natl, Kingsport	507
59	Austin Self	S Boston, Langley, Southern Natl, Motor Mile	502
60	Ed Brunnhoelzl III	Riverhead	495
61	Keith Mcleod	Barrie	489
62	Jesse Lefevers	Hickory	489
63	Bill Leighton Jr.	I-80, Adams	484
64	Paul Glendenning	I-80, Adams	484
65	Bruce Yackey	Colorado	483
66	Gord Shepherd	Barrie	480
67	Brian Parker	Salina	479
68	Ron Proctor	Devil's Bowl	479
69	Bradley Powell	Lacrosse	477
70	Tom Abele Jr.	Thompson, Waterford	476
71	Lee Tissot	Kingsport	475
72	Kyle James	Waterford	473
73	John Hampel	Adams	470
74	Jeff Rocco	Stafford, Waterford	470
75	Chad Pendleton	Kil-Kare, Columbus	462
76	Wes Falk	Motor Mile, Southern Natl, S Boston, Langley	461
77	Toby Porter	Greenville	458
78	David Polenz	S Boston, Old Dominion, Motor Mile	457
79	Mike Looney	Kingsport, Motor Mile	457
80	Brandon Brown	Old Dominion, Motor Mile, Southern Natl	456
81	Justin Milliken	Southern Natl, Myrtle	455
82	Mike Gular	Grandview	452
83	Vince Quenneville	Devil's Bowl	451
84	Michael Clifton	Bowman	451

Pos	Driver	Track	Points
85	Dennis Holdren	Motor Mile, S Boston	450
86	Hunter Bates	Canaan, Devil's Bowl	448
87	Ron Quesnelle	Barrie	448
88	Michael Gervais Jr.	Stafford	446
89	Blake Jones	Kingsport	446
90	Andrew Kosiski	I-80, Junction	446
91	Neil Brown	Motordrome	442
92	Joe Duvall	Salina	442
93	Jerry Gille	Rockford	442
94	Kerry Malone	Thompson	442
95	Ryan Stiltner	Kingsport	442
96	Russ Hersey Jr.	Lee, Monadnock	441
97	Josh Wimbish	Hickory	441
98	Allan Inglis	Barrie	440
99	Mike Carlson	Lacrosse	440
100	Austin Thaxton	S Boston	440
101	Michael Rouse Jr.	Southern Natl	439
102	Matt Buller	Junction, I-80	438
103	Matthew Henderson	Lacrosse	438
104	Rich Lindgren	All American, Stockton	437
105	John F Fortin	Riverhead	437
106	Joe Gada	Stafford, Waterford	436
107	Kyle Berck	I-80	435
108	Terry Dease	Southern Natl	432
109	Mike Darne	Caraway, Concord, Southern Natl, Motor Mile, S	431
110	Timmy Solomito	Riverhead	423
111	Nichole Morgillo	Stafford, Waterford	422
112	John Beatty Jr.	Riverhead	422
113	Daniel Pope II	Kingsport, Motor Mile	417
114	Marc Peters	Junction	417
115	Matt Berger	Rockford	416
116	Adam Degenhardt	Lacrosse	415
117	Todd Ceravolo	Waterford, Thompson	413
118	Cole Howland	Lacrosse	412
119	Ronnie Clifton	Bowman	412
120	Dick Dunlevy Jr.	Kil-Kare, Columbus	411
121	Darrell Gilchrist	Southern Natl, S Boston	411
122	Billy Murphy	Junction	411
123	Bryan Roach	Raceway, Elko	411
124	Bobby Justus	Columbus, Kil-Kare	409
125	Trey Gibson	Greenville, Hickory	409
126	Leon Gonyo	Devil's Bowl	409
127	Shawn Murray	Barrie	408
128	Jessey Mueller	Devil's Bowl	408
129	Ed Puleo	Waterford	406
130	Rusty Smith	Spencer	405
131	Brian Bergakker	Kalamazoo	405
132	Danny Cates	Stafford	404
133	Sam Yarbrough	Myrtle	403
134	Jason Bamberg	All American, Stockton	403
135	Garry Wiltrout	Motordrome, Lake Erie	400
136	Joe Roberts	Devil's Bowl	399
137	Todd Sherman	Limaland	398
138	Hayden Woods	Kingsport, Motor Mile	396
139	Jon Reynolds Jr.	Rockford	395
140	Barry Awtey	Motordrome	395
141	Hunter Devers	S Boston, Motor Mile, Southern Natl	394
142	Austin Peters	Kingsport	390
143	Doug Liberman	Old Dominion	389
144	Steve Carlson	Lacrosse	387
145	Marty Ward Jr.	Greenville	386
146	Andy Bozell Sr.	Kalamazoo	386
147	Royce Peters	Kingsport	386
148	Todd Owen	Stafford	385
149	Scott Macmichael	Monadnock, Canaan	384
150	Thayne Hallyburton	Barrie	384
151	Austin Pack	Bowman	383
152	Alex Bell	Devil's Bowl	381
153	Randy Foote	Adams	381
154	Casey Wyatt	Langley	380
155	Jeran Frailey	Salina	379
156	Bill Kimball Jr.	Monadnock	377
157	Alex Humphrey	Junction	376
158	Leon Zeitner	I-80, Adams	375
159	Danny Womack	Salina	375
160	Naima Lang	Evergreen	374
161	Shayne Lockhart	Langley	372
162	Ryan Wilson	Caraway, Southern Natl	372
163	George Skora III	Motordrome, Lake Erie, Holland	370
164	Dylan Lupton	Southern Natl, Motor Mile, S Boston, Las Vegas	366
165	John Bridges	Junction	365
166	Brent Larson	Cedar Lake	364
167	David Catalano	Spencer, Holland	363
168	Joel Theisen	Elko	361

Pos	Driver	Track	Points
169	Eric Withers	Kil-Kare, Columbus	360
170	Josh Cahill	Columbus, Kil-Kare	360
171	Dan Savage	Colorado	360
172	Wayne Freimund	Rockford	359
173	Billy Mohn	Elko, Raceway	358
174	Donnie Lashua	Canaan	358
175	Tom Burbage Jr.	Southern Natl	358
176	Mark Lamoreaux	Elko, Lacrosse, Raceway	357
177	Jason Aggugliaro	Riverhead	356
178	Jake Reufer	Limaland	354
179	Jeremy Sorel	Hickory	354
180	Derrick Lancaster	Motor Mile	354
181	David Sapienza	Riverhead	354
182	Tyler Hughes	Old Dominion	353
183	Danny Edwards Jr.	Langley, Southern Natl	352
184	Joey Garofalo	Elko	352
185	Cody Thompson	All American, Stockton	351
186	Mark Wertz	Langley, Southern Natl	350
187	Joe Perry	Waterford	350
188	Paddy Rodenbeck	Southern Natl, Motor Mile	348
189	Bradley Babb	B Ridge	347
190	Michael Hanson	Raceway, Elko	346
191	Rick Smith	Colorado	345
192	Eric Berndt	Stafford	345
193	Mack Little III	Concord, Caraway, S Boston	344
194	Terry Hull	Limaland	344
195	Jeremy Mcdowell	Myrtle	341
196	Dennis Perry Jr.	Thompson	340
197	Jamey Lee	Myrtle	338
198	Bayley Currey	Houston, Thunderhill	337
199	Tommy Catalano	Spencer, Holland	336
200	Micah Veleba	I-80, Junction	336
201	Nick Lyons	Stockton, All American	336
202	Eddie Hawkins	Holland, Spencer	336
203	Kevin Timmerman	Spencer	334
204	Ricky Jones	Southern Natl	334
205	Rick Hanestad	Cedar Lake	333
206	Steve Black	Motordrome	332
207	Derek Lemke	Elko, Raceway	332
208	Andy Jankowiak	Holland, Chemung	330
209	Chris Fleming	Bowman	330
210	Tim Cooney	Adams	330
211	Junior Miller	Bowman	328
212	Nik Romano	Stockton	328
213	Rusty Skewes	S Boston, Motor Mile	328
214	Meme Desantis	Grandview	327
215	Mitch Garfield	Rockford	327
216	Shannon Scott	Salina	327
217	Ray Muncy	Columbus	325
218	Ronald Hill	S Boston	324
219	Brad Queen	Houston	323
220	Nick Barstad	Elko, Raceway	323
221	Brian Moczygemba	Houston, Thunderhill	322
222	Mike Collins	I-80, Adams	322
223	Charlie Colby	B Ridge	320
224	Pietro Fittipaldi	Hickory	320
225	Scott Gafforini	Las Vegas	319
226	Paul White	Houston	319
227	Kristopher Mckean	M Valley	315
228	Mike Leaty	Spencer	314
229	Davey Callihan	Old Dominion	314
230	Jerimy Wagner	Lacrosse	314
231	Steven Anderson	Elko	313
232	Tony Hanbury	Spencer	312
233	Adam Deines	Colorado	312
234	David Lewis	Barrie	312
235	Sean Foster	Stafford	311
236	Don Colpritt Jr.	B Ridge	311
237	Wayne Hale	Kingsport	310
238	Matt Galko	Stafford	310
239	Jeff Shiflett	Langley, Southern Natl	310
240	Bill Niles	Lacrosse	310
241	Thomas Tombarello Jr.	Lee	309
242	Kyle Moon	Hickory	308
243	Chris Atkinson	Colorado	308
244	Thomas Neal	Bowman	308
245	Ryan Beeman	Spencer	306
246	Brian Sullivan	Stafford	306
247	Terry Carroll	Motor Mile, Southern Natl, Langley, S Boston	306
248	Bill Rodgers	B Ridge	305
249	Keith Carzello	Monadnock	305
250	Bruce Anderson Jr.	S Boston, Caraway	304
251	Kelly Mann	Evergreen	302
252	Chris Bergeron	Canaan	301

NASCAR WHELEN ALL-AMERICAN SERIES

NATIONAL TOP 500 FEATURE DIVISION POINT LEADERS 2012

Pos	Driver	Track	Points
253	Aaron Ricker	B Ridge	300
254	Tyler Alati	Canaan	299
255	Phil Bozell	Kalamazoo	298
256	Bobby Timmons	B Ridge	297
257	Trenton Jackson	Adams	297
258	David Oliver	B Ridge	297
259	Jay Linstroth	All American, Stockton	296
260	Jason Philpot	Stockton, All American	296
261	Andy Sole	Evergreen	296
262	Robert Tyler	Caraway	295
263	Billy Shannon	Kalamazoo	295
264	Alan Tardiff	B Ridge	295
265	Cody Sargen	Devil's Bowl	294
266	Jeff Bozell	Kalamazoo	294
267	Melvin Langley	Southern Natl	294
268	Michael Landry	B Ridge	293
269	Chad Mahder	Cedar Lake	293
270	Chad Harris	Motor Mile	292
271	Al Stone III	Waterford	292
272	Dan Avery	Stafford	290
273	Hannah Newhouse	M Valley	289
274	Joe Kendall	Monadnock	289
275	Cory Dumpert	Junction	289
276	Bruce Jaycox	Canaan	288
277	Kenny Brooks	Concord	287
278	Jeff Haskins	Devil's Bowl	286
279	Curt Brainard	Stafford	286
280	Daulton Maassen	Adams	286
281	Casey Pehrson	M Valley	285
282	Robert Jeffreys	Bowman	285
283	Chris Mcguire	Riverhead	285
284	John Beinlich	Rockford	285
285	Andrew Thomas	Concord, Motor Mile	284
286	Emily Packard	Canaan	284
287	Tony Black	Bowman	284
288	Corey Bubar	B Ridge	283
289	Richard Bly Jr.	Canaan	283
290	Dan Mckeage	B Ridge	282
291	Jeff Gallup	Thompson, Waterford	282
292	Mackena Bell	Hickory	282
293	Robert Bruce	Old Dominion	281
294	Matthew Clossey	Rockford	281
295	John Kaanta	Cedar Lake	280
296	Keith Bumgarner	Hickory	279
297	Jacob Gille	Rockford	279
298	Mike Brown	Barrie	278
299	Denton Buller	Junction	278
300	Eric Winslow	Caraway, S Boston	278
301	Ian Webster	Houston	277
302	Luke Krick	Kalamazoo	276
303	Steve Laursen	Cedar Lake	275
304	P J Stergios	Lee	275
305	Randy Bull	Barrie	274
306	Kenny Darch	Riverhead	274
307	Mike Wroblewski	Salina	272
308	James Monahan	Waterford	272
309	Mark Shook	Kalamazoo	272
310	Brent Elliott	Bowman	271
311	Chase Grigsby	All American, Stockton	271
312	Kyle Weiss	Grandview	270
313	Matthew Lees	Spencer	269
314	Mike Netishen	Lee	268
315	Jamie Proctor	Devil's Bowl	268
316	Sterling Perkins	Adams	268
317	Mark Poole	Motordrome	267
318	Burgess White	Kil-Kare, Columbus	265
319	Doni Wanat	Evergreen	264
320	Rick Burns	Raceway, Elko	264
321	Glen Reen	Stafford	264
322	Bobby Henry	Motordrome, Lake Erie	263
323	Jon Kellner	Grandview	261
324	Sam Fullone	Lake Erie, Motordrome	260
325	Ryan Grim	Grandview	260
326	Keegan Walmer	Stockton, All American	260
327	Michael Leal	Adams	260
328	Quin Houff	Motor Mile, S Boston	260
329	William Browning	Columbus	258
330	Daniel Stebbins	Monadnock	258
331	Joseph Brown	Bowman	256
332	Daryl Lewis Jr.	Spencer	256
333	Eric Leclair	Stafford, Thompson, Monadnock	256
334	Glenn Gault Jr.	Lake Erie, Motordrome	254
335	Brad Robbins	Bowman	254

Pos	Driver	Track	Points
336	Tony Anderson	Limaland	254
337	Travis Dickes	I-80	252
338	Fred Miller III	Adams	252
339	Wes Miller	Stockton	251
340	Jarrad Miller	Grandview	251
341	Jeff Knight	Evergreen	251
342	William Camara	Stockton	251
343	Darren Bucklen	Colorado	250
344	Tom Bolles	Stafford	250
345	Randall Roberts	Myrtle	250
346	Kevin Hirthler	Grandview	249
347	Brian Chapin	Monadnock	249
348	Darren Robertson	Colorado	248
349	Larry Schild III	Houston	248
350	Adam Norton	Monadnock, Thompson	247
351	Allen Rider Jr.	Stockton	247
352	Chris Eggleston	Colorado	246
353	Dennis Rock Jr.	Las Vegas	246
354	James Jackson	Southern Natl, Langley	246
355	Paul Paine	Elko	244
356	Cory Seeling	Limaland	244
357	Dallas Trombley	Canaan	244
358	Michael Ordway Jr.	Lee	243
359	Harley Jankowski	Lacrosse	243
360	Brett Hansen	Salina	242
361	Glen Burke	Las Vegas	242
362	Daniel Moore	Evergreen	241
363	Howard Muncy	Columbus	241
364	Kody Weisner	Limaland	240
365	Kres Vandyke	Kingsport	240
366	Terry Meitzler	Grandview	240
367	Tim Nelson	Lacrosse	240
368	Jonathan Smith	Motor Mile	240
369	Austin Nason	Rockford	239
370	Corey Zeitner	I-80, Adams	238
371	Todd Harrington	Kalamazoo	234
372	Jason Morman	Houston, Thunderhill	234
373	Vincent Biondolillo	Riverhead	234
374	Rick Pannell	Kingsport	234
375	Bob Sibila Jr.	Kil-Kare, Columbus	232
376	Matt Cox	Myrtle	232
377	Roger Avants	Colorado	232
378	Kyle Dumpert	Junction	232
379	Joey Trent	Kingsport	232
380	Andy Lewis	Spencer	231
381	Ricky Bilderback	Rockford	231
382	Frank Ruocco	Stafford	230
383	Matt Piercy	Hickory	230
384	Molly Rhoads	Elko	230
385	Mike Brooks	Kalamazoo	229
386	Christopher Clyne	Las Vegas, Motor Mile	229
387	Jeb Burton	S Boston	229
388	Tyler Fiscus	Canaan	228
389	Brandon Kelley	Revolution	227
390	Bucky Demers	Canaan	227
391	Joe Williams	Devil's Bowl	227
392	Sparky Maciver	Lee	227
393	Gary Glenn	Stockton, All American	226
394	Kris Bowen	Concord, Motor Mile, S Boston	226
395	Tom Svoboda	Junction	226
396	Richard Storm	Old Dominion	226
397	Nick Clements	Lacrosse	226
398	Stephen Berry Jr.	B Ridge	225
399	Keith Mckinnon	B Ridge	224
400	Rick Andersen Jr.	All American, Stockton	224
401	Roy Manary	Barrie	224
402	Tommy Peregoy	S Boston	222
403	Duane Shreeves	Langley	222
404	Doug Davidson	Evergreen	220
405	Greg Welborn	Myrtle, Greenville	220
406	Andy Smith	Devil's Bowl	218
407	Ray Swinehart	Grandview	217
408	Donald Norris Jr.	Grandview	217
409	Matt Zwingelberg	Colorado	216
410	Trent Hellenga	Kalamazoo	216
411	Ralph Carnes	Greenville	216
412	Ryan Gath	Lee	216
413	Jesse Little	Hickory, S Boston, Greenville, Motor Mile	216
414	Justin Cooper	Adams	216
415	Adam Gada	Stafford, Waterford	216
416	Tom Hughs	Evergreen	215
417	Jeremy Burns	Hickory, Greenville	214
418	Randy Chupp	Kalamazoo	214

Pos	Driver	Track	Points
419	John Olson	Lacrosse	214
420	Craig Preble	I-80	213
421	Kyle Poodiack	Monadnock	213
422	Jeff Brown Jr.	Motordrome, Lake Erie	213
423	Casey Lindell	Salina	211
424	Tyler Stump	Limaland	210
425	Arthur Heino Jr.	Monadnock	209
426	Josh Oakley	S Boston	209
427	Molly Helmuth	Evergreen	208
428	Stuart Ricks	Myrtle	208
429	Tyler Hill	Hickory	208
430	Ronnie Bassett Jr.	Hickory, Southern Natl	207
431	Rick Senneker	Kalamazoo	206
432	Casey Luedeke	Limaland	206
433	Brian Vause	Myrtle	206
434	Josh Krug	I-80, Adams	204
435	Bobby Babb Jr.	B Ridge	202
436	AJ Panessiti	Canaan	202
437	John Mamula	All American, Stockton	202
438	Nick Boivin	Thompson, Stafford	202
439	Toby Lindell	Salina	200
440	Craig Lutz	Thompson, Waterford	198
441	Bradley Tilton	Colorado	198
442	Tommy Scheetz Jr.	Grandview	198
443	Dustin Storm	Old Dominion, S Boston	197
444	Philip Morris	S Boston, Motor Mile	196
445	Michael Kidd	Motor Mile	196
446	Allen Williams	M Valley	195
447	Dan Moore Jr.	Hickory, Caraway	194
448	Greg Sheppard	Motor Mile	194
449	Doug Rodanhisler	Kalamazoo	194
450	Brad Vanhouten	Riverhead	192
451	Bill Hebing Jr.	Spencer	191
452	Johnny Jenkins	Kil-Kare, Columbus	190
453	Daniel Shirley	M Valley	190
454	Todd Dougherty	Kalamazoo	190
455	Bryan Keske	Raceway, Elko	190
456	Jt Schild	Houston	190
457	Brian Loftin	Bowman	190
458	Les Keyser	Lee	189
459	Dave Moon	Old Dominion	188
460	Dave Brigati	Riverhead	188
461	Cris Muhler	Colorado	188
462	Jason Boyd	Houston	188
463	Matt Gallo	Stafford, Waterford	188
464	Pat Doar	Cedar Lake	186
465	Jake Engie	Myrtle	186
466	Greg Nippoldt	Cedar Lake	186
467	Gene Kepley	Caraway	186
468	Allen Fellows	Canaan	186
469	Rick Egersdorf	Cedar Lake	186
470	Jerry Bowersock	Limaland	185
471	Alex Yontz	Myrtle, Caraway	185
472	Dominic Ursetta	Colorado	184
473	Brad Missimer	Grandview	184
474	Nate Christman	Grandview	184
475	Jesse Runkle	Colorado	184
476	Shawn Thibeault	Waterford, Stafford, Thompson	184
477	Wayne Arute	Thompson	184
478	Chris Esposito	Grandview	182
479	Teddy Gibala	Motordrome	182
480	Mark Christian	Kingsport	182
481	Larry Gelinas	B Ridge	180
482	Jason Bruno	Devil's Bowl	180
483	Joe Deguevara	Las Vegas	180
484	Jacob Boerman	Spencer	180
485	Andre Pepin	Barrie	180
486	Kelly Moore	B Ridge	179
487	Shawn Stansell	Kil-Kare	178
488	Robert Root	Greenville	178
489	Harrison Rhodes	Motor Mile, Caraway, Southern Natl	178
490	Jim Carlson	Cedar Lake	178
491	Michael Regelman	Stockton	177
492	Don King Jr.	Holland, Chemung	177
493	Rick Sibila	Barberton	176
494	Bob Weber	Lake Erie, Holland, Motordrome	176
495	Kendel Woll	M Valley	176
496	Shawn Reimert	Grandview	176
497	Addison Meitzler	Grandview	174
498	Craig Stallard	Motor Mile	174
499	Chandler Le Van	Hickory	174
500	Jimmy Zacharias	Chemung, Thompson	173

NASCAR WHELEN ALL-AMERICAN SERIES 2012 TRACK LISTINGS

2012 Track Name	City	State	Track Phone	Office Phone	Web Address
Adams County Speedway	Corning	IA	(641) 322-4184	(641) 322-4700	www.acspeedway.com
All American Speedway	Roseville	CA	(916) 786-2025	(916) 786-2023	www.allamericanspeedway.com
Barberton Raceway Park	Norton	OH	(440) 867-5394	(440) 867-5394	www.barbertonracewaypark.com
Barrie Speedway	Oro	ON	(705) 487-0279	(705) 487-0279	www.barriespeedway.com
Beech Ridge Motor Speedway	Scarborough	ME	(207) 885-5800	(207) 885-0111	www.beechridge.com
Bowman Gray Stadium	Winston-Salem	NC	(336) 679-8118	(336) 679-2008	www.bowmangrayracing.com
Canaan Fair Speedway	Canaan	NH	(802) 274-8823	(603) 523-4502	www.canaanspeedways.com
Caraway Speedway	Sophia	NC	(336) 629-5803	(336) 629-5848	www.carawayspeedway.com
Cedar Lake Speedway	New Richmond	WI	(715) 248-7719	(651) 466-8159	www.cedarlakespeedway.com
Chemung Speedrome	Chemung	NY	(607) 529-9998	(607) 734-1987	www.chemungspeedrome.net
Colorado National Speedway	Dacono	CO	(303) 828-0116	(303) 828-0116	www.coloradospeedway.com
Columbus Motor Speedway	Columbus	OH	(614) 491-1047		www.columbusspeedway.com
Concord Speedway	Concord	NC	(704) 782-4221	(704) 782-4221	www.concordspeedway.net
Devil's Bowl Speedway	West Haven	VT	(802) 265-3112	(802) 265-3112	www.devilsbowlspeedwayvt.com
Edmonton International Raceway	Wetaskiwin	AB	(780) 352-8054	(780) 467-9276	www.edmontonraceway.com
Elko Speedway	Elko	MN	(952) 461-7223	(952) 894-3200	www.elkospeedway.com
Evergreen Speedway	Monroe	WA	(360) 805-6100	(360) 805-6100	www.evergreenspeedway.com
Grandview Speedway	Bechtelsville	PA	(610) 754-7688	(610) 754-7688	www.grandviewspeedway.com
Greenville Pickens Speedway	Easley	SC	(864) 269-0852		www.greenvillepickens.com
Hickory Motor Speedway	Newton	NC	(828) 464-3655	(828) 464-3655	www.hickorymotorspeedway.com
Holland Motorsports Complex	Holland	NY	(716) 418-7223	(716) 418-7223	www.hollandspeedway.com
Houston Motorsports Park	Houston	TX	(281) 458-1972	(281) 458-1972	www.houstonmotorsportspark.com
I-80 Speedway	Greenwood	NE	(402) 659-3301	(402) 342-3453	www.neraceraypark.com
Junction Motor Speedway	McCool Junction	NE	(402) 724-3100	(402) 773-5538 ext 539	www.junctionmotorspeedway.com
Kalamazoo Speedway	Kalamazoo	MI	(269) 692-2423	(269) 692-2423	www.kalamazoospeedway.com
Kil-Kare Speedway	Xenia	OH	(937) 429-2961	(937) 426-2764	www.kilkare.com
Kingsport Speedway	Kingsport	TN	(423) 817-0925	(423) 288-5992	www.newkingsportspeedway.com
LaCrosse Fairgrounds Speedway	West Salem	WI	(608) 786-1525	(608) 786-1525	www.lacrossespeedway.com
Lake County Speedway	Painesville	OH	(440) 354-3505		www.lakecountyspeedway.com
Lake Erie Speedway	Erie	PA	(814) 725-3303	(814) 725-3303	www.lakeeriespeedway.com
Langley Speedway	Hampton	VA	(757) 865-7223	(757) 865-7223	www.langley-speedway.com
Lee USA Speedway	Lee	NH	(978) 462-4252	(978) 462-0008	www.leeusaspeedway.com
Limaland Motorsports Park	Lima	OH	(419) 339-6249	(419) 998-3168	www.limaland.com
Magic Valley Speedway	Twin Falls	ID	(208) 734-3700	(208) 734-3700	www.magicvalleyspeedway.com
Monadnock Speedway	Winchester	NH	(603) 239-4067	(603) 239-4067	www.monadnockspeedway.com
Motor Mile Speedway	Radford	VA	(540) 639-1700	(540) 639-1700	www.motormilespeedway.com
Motordrome Speedway	Smithton	PA	(724) 872-7555	(724) 872-7555	www.motordrome.com
Myrtle Beach Speedway	Myrtle Beach	SC	(843) 236-0500	(843) 236-0500	www.myrtlebeachspeedway.com
Odessa Champion Motor Speedway	Odessa	TX	(432) 563-1715		www.championmotorspeedway.com
Old Dominion Speedway	Manassas	VA	(703) 361-7753	(703) 361-7753	www.olddominionspeedway.com
Raceway Park	Shakopee	MN	(952) 445-2257	(952) 445-2257	www.goracewaypark.com
Revolution Park Racing & Entertainment Complex	Monroe	LA	(318) 312-7223		www.revolutionparkentertainment.com
Riverhead Raceway	Riverhead	NY	(631) 842-7223	(631) 727-0010	www.riverheadraceway.com
Rockford Speedway	Loves Park	IL	(815) 633-1500	(815) 633-0735	www.rockfordspeedway.com
Salina Highbanks Speedway	Pryor	OK	(918) 434-7223	(918) 434-7223	www.salinahighbanksspeedway.com
South Boston Speedway	South Boston	VA	(434) 572-4947	(434) 572-4947	www.southbostonspeedway.com
Southern National Motorsports Park	Lucama	NC	(919) 284-1114	(919) 284-1114	www.snmpark.com
Spencer Speedway	Williamson	NY	(315) 589-3018	(315) 589-3018	www.spencerspeedway.org
Stafford Motor Speedway	Stafford Springs	CT	(860) 684-2783	(860) 684-2783	www.staffordmotorspeedway.com
Stockton 99 Speedway	Stockton	CA	(209) 466-9999	(209) 466-9999	www.stockton99.com
The Bullring at Las Vegas Motor Speedway	Las Vegas	NV	(702) 644-4444	(702) 632-8213	www.lvms.com
Thompson International Speedway	Thompson	CT	(860) 923-2280	(860) 923-2280	www.thompsonspeedway.com
Thunderhill Raceway	Kyle	TX	(512) 507-1486	(512) 507-1486	www.thunderhillraceway.com
Waterford Speedbowl	Waterford	CT	(860) 442-1585	(860) 442-1585	www.speedbowl.com

NASCAR HOME TRACKS

ALBERTA TOP 10

1 ERICA THIERING
POINTS: 145

STARTS: *11* **WINS:** *5* **TOP 5:** *11* **TOP 10:** *11*

Edmonton's Erica Thiering earned the Alberta provincial title with five wins and 11 top-five finishes in all 11 starts. This year's win is her fourth provincial championship in the last five years.

2-10

Pos	Driver Name	Track	Starts	Wins	T-5	T-10	Points
2	Ian Wilson	Edmonton	10	4	8	10	106
3	Shania Laforce	Edmonton	11	0	10	11	72
4	Rob Mason	Edmonton	11	0	7	11	54
5	Tom Gislason	Edmonton	5	0	4	5	42
6	Ian Admiraal	Edmonton	3	1	3	3	41
7	Kel Rudy	Edmonton	5	1	3	5	31
8	Kelly Admiraal	Edmonton	4	0	2	4	30
9	Dana Wick	Edmonton	5	0	5	5	16
10	Dennis Laforce	Edmonton	2	0	2	2	14
11	Brad Jensen	Edmonton	1	0	0	1	6
12	Brian Strachen	Edmonton	1	0	0	1	4

EDMONTON INTERNATIONAL RACEWAY

4 Kms West of Hwy 2A + Hwy 13 Junction/Wetaskiwin, AB — (780) 352-8054 — www.edmontonraceway.com **Saturday/.25 mile paved**

Super Stock

1	ERICA THIERING	678	6	IAN ADMIRAAL	277
2	ROB MASON	568	7	KEL RUDY	261
3	SHANIA LAFORCE	563	8	DANA WICK	249
4	IAN WILSON	490	9	KELLY ADMIRAAL	207
5	TOM GISLASON	351	10	DENNIS LAFORCE	207

Feature Stock

1	DEVON RENDALL	912	6	RYAN KNOWLES	562
2	RHYS HILL	886	7	ALAR AKSBERG	543
3	RICK PARENTEAU	792	8	AL STRONG	542
4	TYRELL BRENNEMAN	784	9	MICHAEL CARTER	539
5	RYAN PLESMAN	673	10	DOUG THOMSON	499

Late Model

1	ERICA THIERING	274	6	BRIAN MCCAUGHAN	53
2	LYNDON FRITZ	251	7	CURT HAZLETT	47
3	CHASE MCCAUGHAN	179	8	IAN WILSON	45
4	DARYL STEELE	134	9	SHANIA LAFORCE	45
5	SYDNEY MCCAUGHAN	81	10	BRAD JENSEN	41

Thunder Car

1	ART EILANDER	805	6	DANIEL DAVIDSON	377
2	DAVID RENDALL	802	7	RODNEY PAHL	370
3	KEITH PAHL	698	8	LEE WERNER	338
4	GORDON ANDERSON	695	9	MARK BURTON	330
5	DON LAWRENCE	505	10	TYLER NEMEC	275

Modified

1	TERRY DOWLER	459	6	ASHLEY MCINTOSH	330
2	DEAN CRAIG	432	7	SHONE LAING	326
3	DAVE MCINTOSH	379	8	KEN RIVAIT	324
4	KAREY STULAR	350	9	ASH LANE	285
5	CODY LANG	335	10	BRAD WILSON	239

CALIFORNIA TOP 10

1 SCOTT WINTERS
POINTS: 596

STARTS: *32* **WINS:** *16* **TOP 5:** *28* **TOP 10:** *29*

Scott Winters of Tracy, California, rode two individual track championships to the California state championship with 16 wins and 28 top fives in 32 combined starts. This is his first state championship.

2-10

Pos	Driver Name	Track	Starts	Wins	T-5	T-10	Points
2	Rich Lindgren	Stockton, All American	19	3	16	18	437
3	Jason Bamberg	Stockton, All American	18	3	13	15	403
4	Cody Thompson	Stockton, All American	21	1	9	15	351
5	Nick Lyons	All American, Stockton	23	0	9	21	336
6	Nik Romano	Stockton	20	0	11	17	328
7	Jay Linstroth	Stockton, All American	16	2	9	11	296
8	Jason Philpot	Stockton, All American	14	2	11	12	296
9	Chase Grigsby	Stockton, All American	19	1	5	15	271
10	Keegan Walmer	Stockton, All American	17	0	3	13	260

ALL AMERICAN SPEEDWAY

800 All America City Blvd./Roseville,CA/95678 — (916) 786-2025 — www.allamericanspeedway.com **Saturday/.292 mile paved**

Modified

1	SCOTT WINTERS	396	6	GARY GLENN	240
2	RICH LINDGREN	367	7	CODY THOMPSON	188
3	JASON BAMBERG	287	8	JOHN MAMULA	160
4	CHASE GRIGSBY	283	9	RICK ANDERSEN JR.	152
5	JASON PHILPOT	256	10	JAY LINSTROTH	128

Bomber

1	DAVID THOMPSON	576	6	JOE RHODES	394
2	ERICK RAY	553	7	HARRY LAMBERT	326
3	RICHARD PEREZ	477	8	KENNY BEAUMONT SR.	302
4	CHRIS PAULSON	474	9	RICK ANABLE-MANSUETI	262
5	ERIC BOCKSBERGER	442	10	MO ABHAT	244

Street Stock

1	MICKEY OWENS	501	6	BYRON GONZALES	282
2	KEVIN OWENS	461	7	MEL WILSON	272
3	MATT CAMP	433	8	MARK BLANTON	262
4	RICHARD POPPERT JR.	348	9	DAVID SILVA	237
5	ERIC PRICE	284	10	LONNIE LEONARD	182

Late Model

1	MATT SCOTT	233	6	MINDY MCCORD	140
2	CHRIS SCRIBNER	220	7	BOBBY BUTLER	106
3	RON CHUNN	185	8	ROGER DAVISON	92
4	TRAVIS MILBURN	156	9	MICHAEL ROMAN	86
5	CHRISTOPHER LAMBERT	150	10	CHUCK GLICK	80

NASCAR HOME TRACKS

STOCKTON 99 SPEEDWAY

4105 North Wilson Way/Stockton, CA/95202 — (209) 466-9999 — www.stockton99.com **Saturday/ .25 mile paved**

Modified
1	SCOTT WINTERS	830
2	NIK ROMANO	798
3	NICK LYONS	784
4	WILLIAM CAMARA	710
5	ALLEN RIDER JR.	602
6	WES MILLER	460
7	MIKE REGELMAN	412
8	JESSICA CLARK	402
9	PJ PEDRONCELLI JR.	398
10	DAVID CROUCH	398

Pure Stock
1	TYLER GUZMAN	535
2	RODNEY TRIPP	530
3	BRANDON JONES	520
4	DARIN ADLER	474
5	RICK IRWIN	458
6	GUIDO BINDI JR.	441
7	SAMANTHA WILLIAMS	423
8	ROY LUFT	411
9	CHRIS CORDER	380
10	BEN LEWIS	378

Basic 4 Cylinder
1	JOSEPH REICHMUTH	679
2	DAVID KONG	641
3	BRAD MAST	622
4	SHANNON RUMSEY	530
5	JENNIFER CORDER	526
6	MARK JACKE	460
7	CHRIS CORDER	364
8	JUSTIN TERRY	302
9	CHRISTOPHER BOONE	172
10	MATT ANDERSON	146

Super Stock
1	JASON AGUIRRE	514
2	ROBBIE KNITTEL	500
3	RICH HARPER	452
4	AARON COONFIELD	412
5	MIKE GRAHAM	316
6	GARLAND TYLER	241
7	TRAVIS TUCKER	238
8	BROCK MONROE	195
9	CHAD HOLMAN	144
10	MATT ERICKSON	142

Late Model
1	JEFF BELLETTO	768
2	MATT SCOTT	740
3	NIC BELLETTO	700
4	LUIS TYRRELL	692
5	MIKE BEELER	680
6	MATT ERICKSON	582
7	JUSTIN PHILPOTT	518
8	ADAM COONFIELD	498
9	STANISLAV OSTERLUND	464
10	MINDY MCCORD	264

COLORADO TOP 10

1 BRUCE YACKEY POINTS: 483

STARTS: *13* **WINS:** *7* **TOP 5:** *12* **TOP 10:** *12*

From Greeley, Colorado, Bruce Yackey captured the state championship in Colorado with seven wins and top fives in 12 of 13 starts. This is the fourth state championship for Bruce.

2-10

Pos	Driver Name	Track	Starts	Wins	T-5	T-10	Points
2	Dan Savage	Colorado	13	0	6	12	360
3	Rick Smith	Colorado	13	3	7	9	345
4	Adam Deines	Colorado	13	0	6	10	312
5	Chris Atkinson	Colorado	13	0	4	10	308
6	Darren Bucklen	Colorado	13	0	2	7	250
7	Darren Robertson	Colorado	11	0	3	8	248
8	Chris Eggleston	Colorado	10	2	6	7	246
9	Roger Avants	Colorado	9	0	3	9	232
10	Matt Zwingelberg	Colorado	13	0	3	5	216

COLORADO NATIONAL SPEEDWAY

4281 Graden Blvd/Dacono, CO/80514 — (303) 828-0116 — www.coloradospeedway.com **Saturday/.375 mile paved**

Late Model
1	BRUCE YACKEY	618
2	RICK SMITH	525
3	DAN SAVAGE	516
4	CHRIS ATKINSON	473
5	ADAM DEINES	434
6	DARREN ROBERTSON	379
7	MATT ZWINGELBERG	359
8	DARREN BUCKLEN	347
9	BRADLEY TILTON	333
10	ROGER AVANTS	321

Super Stock
1	MICHAEL COX	536
2	JOHN HUMPHREY	487
3	JASON MORRIS	473
4	KYLE PATEE	368
5	RIC LOTHERT	353
6	JOSH PARKER	310
7	DARRELL SMITH JR.	310
8	KEVIN KELLER	273
9	JACK NUGENT	243
10	HARRY LIVERMORE JR.	214

Figure 8
1	JOE MARTINEZ	537
2	JEREME WALL	504
3	NICK MARTINEZ	484
4	JUSTIN MCKEACHIE	481
5	AL DURAN	437
6	JOHN JOHNSON	398
7	LANCE PROCTOR	373
8	HARRY LIVERMORE JR.	330
9	DAVE SMITH	328
10	LUKE ZIKE	325

Sportsman
1	LEE KEMMIT	455
2	JEFFREY WALBAUM	422
3	BRUCE BORCHARDT	389
4	WADE GROVE	338
5	JOSH MERANDA	267
6	TOMMY ROE	256
7	JEFF WEBB	227
8	ADAM GASTINEAU	197
9	STEPHANIE BROWN	187
10	ALAN CARTER	173

Pro Truck
1	JUSTIN SIMONSON	396
2	ROGER AVANTS	396
3	CHRIS LEAF	348
4	MATT BURTON	334
5	RUDY VANDERWAL	334
6	TROY WITTHAR	291
7	STEPHEN JOHNSON	257
8	SCOTT RHOADES	252
9	JEREMY BARCLAY	245
10	BILLY HARKINS	228

CONNECTICUT TOP 10

1 KEITH ROCCO POINTS: 748

STARTS: *43* **WINS:** *14* **TOP 5:** *26* **TOP 10:** *32*

The competitive state title in Connecticut went to Keith Rocco of Wallingford, Connecticut, on the strength of 14 wins and 32 top 10s in 43 starts. Keith has topped the Modified competition at Connecticut's three short tracks for five straight seasons.

2-10

Pos	Driver Name	Track	Starts	Wins	T-5	T-10	Points
2	Ryan Preece	Thompson, Riverhead, Stafford	36	12	29	31	706
3	Ted Christopher	Thompson, Riverhead, Stafford	31	6	27	29	671
4	Woody Pitkat	Thompson, Stafford	30	6	21	25	671
5	Tyler Chadwick	Waterford	19	4	13	16	584
6	Jeff Pearl	Waterford	19	2	13	17	562
7	Rob Janovic Jr.	Waterford	19	1	12	14	537
8	Tom Abele Jr.	Waterford, Thompson	20	0	10	15	476
9	Kyle James	Waterford	19	1	10	12	473
10	Jeff Rocco	Stafford, Waterford	21	0	7	14	470

STAFFORD MOTOR SPEEDWAY

55 West Street/Stafford Springs, CT/06076 — (860) 684-2783 — www.staffordmotorspeedway.com   **Friday/.50 mile paved**

SK Modified
1	TED CHRISTOPHER	744	6	KEITH ROCCO	556
2	WOODY PITKAT	710	7	ERIC BERNDT	534
3	MICHAEL GERVAIS JR.	630	8	TODD OWEN	512
4	RYAN PREECE	598	9	MATT GALKO	490
5	DANNY CATES	568	10	SEAN FOSTER	488

Limited Late Model
1	CORY CASAGRANDE	844	6	ANDREW HAYES	690
2	JOSH WOOD	832	7	DAVID ARUTE	650
3	DJ BURNHAM	740	8	JUSTIN BREN	606
4	DENNIS BOTTICELLO	698	9	JOE NOGIEC	592
5	JESSE HINZE	698	10	BRIAN CLEMENT	548

Dare Stock
1	CLIFF SAUNDERS	850	6	AL SAUNDERS	690
2	AUSTIN BESSETTE	828	7	JOHNNY WALKER	678
3	KYLE CASAGRANDE	742	8	JEREMY LAVOIE	598
4	KRIS FLUCKIGER	740	9	JIM CARROLL	534
5	MONTE GIBBS	702	10	DOUGLAS PHELPS	532

Late Model
1	WOODY PITKAT	732	6	ADAM GRAY	620
2	MIKE QUINTILIANO	696	7	MARK ST HILAIRE	618
3	JIM PETERSON	674	8	PATRICK TOWNSEND JR.	562
4	TOM FEARN	636	9	KEVIN GAMBACORTA	510
5	COREY HUTCHINGS	632	10	EDWARD RICARD	506

SK Lights
1	ZACHARY ASZKLAR	766	6	RONNIE WILLIAMS	664
2	BOB CHARLAND	758	7	HARRY WHEELER	662
3	TONY MEMBRINO JR.	756	8	PAYTON HENRY	658
4	DYLAN KOPEC	722	9	TYLER HINES	650
5	JOEY FERRIGNO	684	10	JAY GOFF	636

THOMPSON INTERNATIONAL SPEEDWAY

205 East Thompson Road/Thompson, CT/06277 — (860) 923-2280 — www.thompsonspeedway.com   **Thursday/.625 mile paved**

Sunoco Modified
1	RYAN PREECE	922	6	TODD CERAVOLO	520
2	KERRY MALONE	808	7	KEITH ROCCO	456
3	DENNIS PERRY JR.	656	8	WAYNE ARUTE	434
4	TED CHRISTOPHER	644	9	ERIC LECLAIR	390
5	WOODY PITKAT	576	10	JIM SMITH	378

Mini Stocks
1	CHAD BAXTER	780	6	MICHAEL VIENS	594
2	ERIC BOURGEOIS	772	7	NICK ANDERSON	588
3	STEVE VIOLETTE	716	8	DAVE TRUDEAU	584
4	JOE BAXTER	700	9	TRAVIS JURCIK	526
5	STEVE MICHALSKI	600	10	BRAD CADDICK	464

Super Late Model
1	DEREK RAMSTROM	240	6	GEORGE BESSETTE	178
2	JIM BANFIELD	234	7	COLBEY FOURNIER	170
3	MIKE O'SULLIVAN	224	8	DARYL STAMPFL	170
4	LARRY GELINAS	206	9	GLENN TYLER	152
5	DICK HOULIHAN	192	10	JAKE VANADA	150

Thompson Modified
1	JOHN LOWINSKI-LOH JR.	876	6	GLENN BOSS	406
2	JAY SUNDEEN	814	7	RYAN MORGAN	390
3	BRIAN TAGG	778	8	COREY BARRY	82
4	CHAD LABASTIE	760	9	PAYTON HENRY	80
5	DANNY GAMACHE JR.	702	10	DENIS LEGERE	78

Late Models
1	TOMMY O'SULLIVAN	868	6	RYAN WATERMAN	542
2	JOHN FALCONI	796	7	ROBERT O'CONNELL	460
3	RANDY TUCKER	722	8	MARC PALMISANO	402
4	MIKE SCORZELLI	708	9	JARED MATERAS	324
5	DAMON TINIO	706	10	WAYNE COURY	280

Lite Modified
1	CAM MCDERMOTT	844	6	JOE BOIVIN	232
2	TROY TALMAN	738	7	JOHN STUDLEY	190
3	NIKKI OUELLETTE	682	8	COREY BARRY	184
4	ERIC LECLAIR	594	9	DYLAN KOPEC	142
5	SHAWN BRULE	472	10	HARRY WHEELER	70

Limited Sportsman
1	SCOTT SUNDEEN	790	6	THOMAS SHEA	578
2	JESSE GLEASON	764	7	LLOYD ANDERSON JR.	514
3	JASON CHICOLAS	740	8	MIKE PALIN	496
4	STEVE KENNEWAY	712	9	KEVIN BOWE	470
5	COREY FANNING	676	10	ARTHUR MORAN III	444

WATERFORD SPEEDBOWL

1080 Hartford Turnpike/Waterford, CT/06385 — (860) 442-1585 — www.speedbowl.com   **Saturday/ .375 mile asphalt**

SK Modified
1	TYLER CHADWICK	887	6	JEFF ROCCO	751
2	JEFF PEARL	848	7	KEITH ROCCO	738
3	ROB JANOVIC JR.	839	8	ED PULEO	696
4	TOM ABELE JR.	775	9	JOE GADA	676
5	KYLE JAMES	759	10	NICHOLE MORGILLO	662

Mini Stock
1	KEN CASSIDY JR.	1040	6	BILL LEONARD	766
2	JEFF CEMBRUCH	905	7	WAYNE BURROUGHS JR.	681
3	RAY CHRISTIAN III	854	8	SEAN CARON	671
4	IAN BREW	812	9	JOE FOGARASI	646
5	GARRETT DENTON	807	10	DOUG CURRY	642

SK Light
1	PAUL FRENCH	396	6	ALAN BENINCASO	252
2	TYLER JACKSON	389	7	LAWRENCE GOSS	248
3	COREY BARRY	371	8	CAM MCDERMOTT	244
4	CHRISTOPHER IGNAZIO	356	9	CHRIS CORRELL	228
5	JASON FERREIRA	272	10	SHAYNE PRUCKER	200

Late Model
1	DILLON MOLTZ	815	6	ANTHONY FLANNERY IV	687
2	BRUCE THOMAS JR.	787	7	ED GERTSCH JR.	556
3	RICHARD STASKOWSKI	778	8	MIKE SWEENEY JR.	528
4	JASON PALMER	731	9	KEITH ROCCO	525
5	JEFF SMITH	729	10	RICHARD DURANTI	504

Street Stock
1	WALT HOVEY JR.	892	6	COREY HUTCHINGS	743
2	JOSH GALVIN	816	7	PHIL EVANS	726
3	DANIEL DARNSTAEDT	814	8	TED DUPRE	712
4	CHRIS MEYER	810	9	NORMAN ROOT	654
5	JOE ARENA	803	10	BILL MCNEIL	624

NASCAR HOME TRACKS

IDAHO TOP 10

1 KRISTOPHER MCKEAN
POINTS: 319

STARTS: *19* WINS: *7* TOP 5: *17* TOP 10: *18*

Seven wins and 17 top fives in 19 races earned Kristopher McKean the Idaho Whelen All-American Series crown. It is the Jerome, Idaho, natives first state title.

2-10

Pos	Driver Name	Track	Starts	Wins	T-5	T-10	Points
2	Casey Pehrson	M Valley	20	4	16	19	298
3	Hannah Newhouse	M Valley	20	5	15	20	295
4	Allen Williams	M Valley	20	1	9	20	201
5	Daniel Shirley	M Valley	15	2	10	14	190
6	Kendel Woll	M Valley	16	0	9	16	176
7	Dan Pehrson	M Valley	13	0	10	13	156
8	Willie Dalton	M Valley	19	1	2	18	139
9	Spencer Meyer	M Valley	14	0	3	14	118
10	Steve Edens	M Valley	12	0	5	11	100

MAGIC VALLEY SPEEDWAY
1 Mile West of the Twin Falls Airport/Twin Falls, ID /83301 — (208) 734-3700 — www.magicvalleyspeedway.com

Saturday/.333 mile paved

Super Stock
1	KRISTOPHER MCKEAN	321
2	CASEY PEHRSON	306
3	HANNAH NEWHOUSE	299
4	ALLEN WILLIAMS	207
5	DANIEL SHIRLEY	190
6	KENDEL WOLL	176
7	DAN PEHRSON	156
8	WILLIE DALTON	141
9	SPENCER MEYER	118
10	STEVE EDENS	100

Street Stock
1	ERNIE HALL	418
2	PAUL BROWNE	352
3	JASON TODD	263
4	MITCHELL PEHRSON	259
5	DALE MILES	207
6	JAY MCDONALD	175
7	RUSSELL DALTON	151
8	JUSTIN BOYD	129
9	BILLI MILES	113
10	JUSTIN MEYER	88

Hornets
1	JEFF PECK	233
2	LANE WALKER	224
3	CHAD EVERETT	174
4	JASON QUALE	125
5	JAMES COLE	121
6	JOSH BLACK	106
7	EDDY COLE	80
8	BRANDAN GRECO	79
9	KRISTOPHER MCKEAN	51
10	RAY BOOTS JR.	39

Thunder Dog
1	JEFF PECK	674
2	DOUGLAS BROWNFIELD	649
3	KRISTOPHER MCKEAN	492
4	CHAD EVERETT	207
5	JOSH BLACK	176
6	DAVID ANDREWS	129
7	VINNY ORR	86
8	WILLIAM STANLEY	70
9	ANTHONY MEYER	49
10	EDDY COLE	28

ILLINOIS TOP 10

1 JERRY GILLE
POINTS: 442

STARTS: *19* WINS: *2* TOP 5: *16* TOP 10: *19*

With a pair of wins and top 10s in all 19 outings Jerry Gille took home his second career Illinois championship. The Roscoe, Illinois, native is the first racer to be a two-time state champion.

2-10

Pos	Driver Name	Track	Starts	Wins	T-5	T-10	Points
2	Matt Berger	Rockford	18	2	10	17	416
3	Jon Reynolds Jr.	Rockford	19	1	14	15	395
4	Wayne Freimund	Rockford	19	1	9	16	359
5	Mitch Garfield	Rockford	19	1	6	15	327
6	John Beinlich	Rockford	19	1	4	15	285
7	Matthew Clossey	Rockford	17	1	6	11	281
8	Jacob Gille	Rockford	16	1	7	12	279
9	Austin Nason	Rockford	19	1	1	10	239
10	Ricky Bilderback	Rockford	14	1	6	8	231

ROCKFORD SPEEDWAY
1601 West Lane Road/Loves Park, IL/61111 — (815) 633-1500 — www.rockfordspeedway.com

Saturday/.292 mile paved

Late Model
1	JERRY GILLE	1017
2	JON REYNOLDS JR.	930
3	MATT BERGER	867
4	WAYNE FREIMUND	832
5	MITCH GARFIELD	803
6	JOHN BEINLICH	739
7	AUSTIN NASON	717
8	MATTHEW CLOSSEY	684
9	JACOB GILLE	664
10	MARK HARTLINE	610

All American Sportsman
1	DOUG BENNETT	798
2	JUSTIN SELLERS	721
3	JOHNNY ROBINSON	699
4	BRETT MCCOY	692
5	SCOTT LAWVER	632
6	DARYL GERKE	593
7	ROB GOODMAN	544
8	PATRICK FEATHERSTON II	502
9	BOB MOELLER	453
10	TIM JENDRYCKI	433

Road Runner
1	BOBBY FRISCH	903
2	DENNIS SMITH JR.	757
3	ARLYN ROUSH	732
4	HOWIE WARE	703
5	ADAM CARTWRIGHT	642
6	JASON VAN HISE	630
7	DEREK NICHOL	619
8	BRIAN MAYER	614
9	RAY HARDESTY	565
10	GENE MAROCCO	558

American Shorttracker
1	JOE LAMARCA	808
2	GEORGE SPARKMAN	753
3	NICK CINA JR.	737
4	SCOTTY HOEFT	710
5	CHRIS JONES	664
6	KYLE LAPIER	587
7	RACHEL SPARKMAN	539
8	DAVID RUSSELL JR.	514
9	ZACH RODRIGUEZ	491
10	NICK LETSINGER	480

IOWA TOP 10

1 JC WYMAN
POINTS: 515

STARTS: *16* WINS: *3* TOP 5: *11* TOP 10: *14*

With three wins and 14 top 10s in 16 starts Griswold, Iowa's JC Wyman captured the state crown. This is JC's first Iowa state title.

2-10

Pos	Driver Name	Track	Starts	Wins	T-5	T-10	Points
2	Jason O'Brien	Adams, I-80	16	5	10	13	477
3	John Hampel	Adams	16	2	10	15	470
4	Paul Glendenning	Adams	16	0	11	15	470
5	Chris Spieker	Adams, I-80	16	2	10	12	424
6	Randy Foote	Adams	16	1	5	12	381
7	Tim Cooney	Adams	16	0	1	11	330
8	Trenton Jackson	Adams	12	1	6	9	297
9	Daulton Maassen	Adams	16	0	0	9	286
10	Sterling Perkins	Adams	16	0	1	8	268

ADAMS COUNTY SPEEDWAY

1200 John Street/Corning, IA/50841 — (641) 322-4184 — www.acspeedway.com

Saturday/.50 mile dirt

Late Model
1	JC WYMAN	515
2	JASON O'BRIEN	477
3	JOHN HAMPEL	470
4	PAUL GLENDENNING	470
5	CHRIS SPIEKER	424
6	RANDY FOOTE	381
7	TIM COONEY	330
8	TRENTON JACKSON	297
9	DAULTON MAASSEN	286
10	STERLING PERKINS	268

Pro Stock
1	GREG MILLER	374
2	JASON ROLD	361
3	TONY HARDISTY	347
4	CRAIG GARNER	324
5	BRAD DERRY	323
6	CLAY MERCER	263
7	KEVIN SHARP	212
8	JOE ZADINA	190
9	CHAD HELVIE	169
10	JEFF ORR II	112

Hobby Stock
1	JEREMY AUTEN	581
2	MATT MCATEE	532
3	JEREMY PURDY	501
4	RICK RITCHIE	483
5	DAVID WEEDA	480
6	BRETT SINK	471

Modified
1	JARED STIENS	419
2	BRIAN FOOTE	408
3	JESSE DENNIS	380
4	JOHN DAVIS	361
5	TODD VAN EATON	344
6	ERIC HANNA	328
7	DAN MUELLER	323
8	KIRBY STIENS	303
9	LARRY FOOTE	257
10	RYAN STIENS	250

B Modified
1	JEROD WESTON	570
2	JEFFREY JONES	519
3	BLAINE PETERSEN	501
4	RON BALLINGER JR.	436
5	BRET SHEPPARD	391
6	JOSH COOPER	298
7	CHRIS VANNAUSDLE	292
8	JOSH SINK	278
9	SHAWN KRALIK	250
10	TIM SUTTER	234
7	THOMAS MYERS	424
8	ANDY DAVISON	383
9	KENNY CHAMP	368
10	JOE MURPHY	322

LOUISIANA TOP 10

1 BRANDON KELLEY — POINTS: 227

STARTS: *12* **WINS:** *11* **TOP 5:** *11* **TOP 10:** *12*

Brandon Kelley, of Porter, Texas, turned in a near-perfect season in Louisiana with 11 wins in 12 starts to wear the state crown. This is also Brandon's first state championship.

2-10

Pos	Driver Name	Track	Starts	Wins	T-5	T-10	Points
2	Cole Fancher	Revolution	12	0	10	12	130
3	Donny Kelley	Revolution	10	0	7	10	98
4	Kevin Hogard	Revolution	11	0	8	11	94
5	Michael Hudson	Revolution	8	0	6	8	88
6	Ryan Humphrey	Revolution	10	0	7	10	84
7	Mark Underwood	Revolution	6	1	4	6	51
8	Kody Brusso	Revolution	6	0	2	6	34
9	Gary Sullivan	Revolution	2	0	1	2	18
10	Chris Ehrhardt	Revolution	2	0	0	2	16

REVOLUTION PARK RACING AND ENTERTAINMENT COMPLEX

8850 Frontage Road/Monroe, LA/71211 — (318) 312-7223 — www.revolutionparkentertainment.com

Saturday/.375 mile concrete

Late Model
1	BRANDON KELLEY	985
2	COLE FANCHER	806
3	KEVIN HOGARD	764
4	DONNY KELLEY	658
5	MICHAEL HUDSON	535
6	RYAN HUMPHREY	525
7	KODY BRUSSO	343
8	CHRIS EHRHARDT	340
9	MARK UNDERWOOD	296
10	RONNIE HUMPHREY	167

Compacts
1	KORY KULP	516
2	CODY STEEN	466
3	DALTON SMITH	440
4	TYLER JACKSON	268
5	RICKY FORTENBERRY	228
6	KYLE KULP	186

Thunder Car
1	DENNIS CARPENTER	706
2	JOHN PAUL CARPENTER	670
3	JOE SMITH	638
4	RONNIE WOODS JR.	584
5	BUBBA GOWAN	560
6	HUNTER STREET	366
7	RICK KEMP	302
8	JERRY MCMASTER	294
9	EARL KULP	270
10	ASHLIN HUMPHREY	238
7	BUBBA GOWAN FAIRCLOTH	182
8	BUBBA GOWAN	178
9	JERRY MCMASTER	176
10	DUSTIN TRIM	88

MAINE TOP 10

1 BRADLEY BABB — POINTS: 347

STARTS: *13* **WINS:** *1* **TOP 5:** *6* **TOP 10:** *10*

Bradley Babb of Windham, Maine, earned the Maine State Championship with a win and 10 top 10s in 13 races. A third-generation racer, he is the first to earn a state championship.

2-10

Pos	Driver Name	Track	Starts	Wins	T-5	T-10	Points
2	Charlie Colby	B Ridge	12	2	4	9	320
3	Don Colpritt Jr.	B Ridge	13	1	4	8	311
4	Bill Rodgers	B Ridge	13	1	4	8	305
5	Aaron Ricker	B Ridge	13	0	3	9	300
6	Bobby Timmons	B Ridge	13	1	5	7	297
7	David Oliver	B Ridge	13	1	4	7	297
8	Alan Tardiff	B Ridge	13	1	4	8	295
9	Michael Landry	B Ridge	13	1	3	8	293
10	Corey Bubar	B Ridge	13	1	3	6	283

BEECH RIDGE MOTOR SPEEDWAY

70 Holmes Road/Scarborough, ME/04074 — (207) 885-5800 — www.beechridge.com

Saturday/.33 mile paved

Pro Series
1	BRADLEY BABB	570
2	BILL RODGERS	559
3	AARON RICKER	558
4	MICHAEL LANDRY	554
5	CHARLIE COLBY	546
6	BOBBY TIMMONS	545
7	DON COLPRITT JR.	542
8	COREY BUBAR	540
9	ALAN TARDIFF	539
10	DAVID OLIVER	532

Road Runner
1	EVAN ARMINGTON	753
2	DAVID CAMERON	728
3	BRANDON BARKER	721
4	SHAWN BRACKETT	695
5	ADAM RICCI	641
6	CLAYTON LOUBIER III	605
7	DAVID TURNER	602
8	NATE CALDWELL	466
9	ED PIERCE	297
10	WILLIAM WEBBER	169

Sport Series
1	DONNY MORSE JR.	629
2	MATT DOW	613
3	FRANK WEAR	564
4	SALLY GHERARDI HATCH	563
5	GARRETT HALL	557
6	BRANDON INGALLS	553
7	DALTON GAGNON	551
8	PHIL PINKHAM	544
9	DAVID LANGLAIS	537
10	NATHAN LEAVITT	533

Wildcats
1	NICHOLAS CUSACK	689
2	COLE WATSON	679
3	JASON GAMMON	665
4	KEITH STUART	657
5	DAN BEAN	645
6	DAVID VAUGHN	618
7	BRIAN CASWELL	588
8	DONNIE DINSMORE	567
9	LEWIS ANDERSON	539
10	JAIRET HARRISON	510

NASCAR HOME TRACKS

MICHIGAN TOP 10

1 BRIAN BERGAKKER POINTS: 405

STARTS: *13* **WINS:** *3* **TOP 5:** *10* **TOP 10:** *12*

Brian Bergakker of Lowell, Michigan, captured three wins and 12 top 10s in 13 outings, earning top honors in the state of Michigan. It is his first state championship.

2-10

Pos	Driver Name	Track	Starts	Wins	T-5	T-10	Points
2	Andy Bozell Sr.	Kalamazoo	13	0	11	12	386
3	Phil Bozell	Kalamazoo	12	2	7	8	298
4	Billy Shannon	Kalamazoo	13	1	3	9	295
5	Jeff Bozell	Kalamazoo	13	0	2	12	294
6	Luke Krick	Kalamazoo	13	0	5	9	276
7	Mark Shook	Kalamazoo	13	0	5	8	272
8	Todd Harrington	Kalamazoo	11	2	3	6	234
9	Mike Brooks	Kalamazoo	13	1	1	6	229
10	Trent Hellenga	Kalamazoo	9	0	2	7	216

KALAMAZOO SPEEDWAY

7656 Ravine Road/Kalamazoo, MI/49009 — (269) 692-2423 — www.kalamazoospeedway.com   **Saturday /.375 mile paved**

Late Model
1	BRIAN BERGAKKER	1788
2	ANDY BOZELL SR.	1775
3	PHIL BOZELL	1464
4	MARK SHOOK	1405
5	BILLY SHANNON	1391
6	JEFF BOZELL	1354
7	LUKE KRICK	1303
8	RANDY CHUPP	1291
9	MIKE BROOKS	1154
10	TRENT HELLENGA	1060

Mini Stock
1	FRANK STAGER	1687
2	NOAH GALLANDT	1351
3	BILLY BUSSEMA	1288
4	RICK VANCLEAVE	1080
5	ANDREW BREST	990
6	DOUG SMITH	957
7	ROBERT MASON	933
8	MATTHEW GROSS	703
9	RICHARD GALE	699
10	GEORGE WATTS	646

Cyber Stock
1	JERRY JANSEN JR.	1799
2	DALE LEONARD	1641
3	WAYNE STACK	1613
4	JACK COOK	1574
5	BARRY JENKINS JR.	1520
6	BRIAN GREGERSEN	1342
7	NICK DELONGPRE	1271
8	LOGAN KNIGHT	1252
9	WALTER NIELSON IV	1156

Super Stock
1	KENNY HEAD	1688
2	BRANDON LYONS	1629
3	CHRIS SHANNON	1468
4	RYAN WHEELER	1353
5	MATT CORLISS	1342
6	DARREN LANE	1235
7	LINDSEY KATZ	1207
8	KELLI JO HOFACKER	1102
9	CHRIS ORR	1079
10	JAKE HOPWOOD	1008

Pro Stock
1	LLOYD BROOKS, IV	1852
2	TYLER HUFFORD	1809
3	KEITH WILFONG	1617
4	BRENT HOOK	1574
5	ZACK COOK	1562
6	GREG HAYNES	1534
7	BRYAN NOBLE	1406
8	DANNY OXFORD	1093
9	RON LANDIS	1062
10	JIMMY WHEATON	1020

MINNESOTA TOP 10

1 ADAM ROYLE POINTS: 685

STARTS: *18* **WINS:** *7* **TOP 5:** *16* **TOP 10:** *18*

With seven wins, and top 10s in all 18 races, Adam Royle of Northfield, Minnesota, secured his third Minnesota state title and a ninth-place finish in the national standings. This is his second state crown in a row, and third in the last four years.

2-10

Pos	Driver Name	Track	Starts	Wins	T-5	T-10	Points
2	Donny Reuvers	Elko	18	2	15	17	596
3	Matt Goede	Elko	18	1	12	17	575
4	Chad Walen	Elko, Raceway	35	15	22	33	544
5	Jason Schneider	Elko	18	1	10	15	519
6	Bryan Roach	Raceway, Elko	29	1	18	26	411
7	Joel Theisen	Elko	17	1	5	10	361
8	Billy Mohn	Elko, Raceway	20	0	6	11	358
9	Joey Garofalo	Elko	15	0	0	12	352
10	Michael Hanson	Elko, Raceway	19	0	4	8	346

ELKO SPEEDWAY

26350 France Avenue/Elk, MN/55020 — (952) 461-7223 — www.elkospeedway.com   **Saturday/.375 mile paved**

Super Late Model
1	DONNY REUVERS	1339
2	MATT GOEDE	1313
3	ADAM ROYLE	1308
4	CHAD WALEN	1253
5	JASON SCHNEIDER	1228
6	JOEL THEISEN	1087
7	BILLY MOHN	1035
8	RICK BURNS	939
9	NICK BARSTAD	917
10	MICHAEL HANSON	910

Thunder Car
1	STEVE ANDERSON	871
2	DUSTY MANN	852
3	DILLON SELLNER	832
4	CONRAD JORGENSON	826
5	SCOTT KING	788
6	GREGORY BORCHARDT	781
7	TED REUVERS	756
8	KYLE KIRBERGER	752
9	MICHAEL GILOMEN	735
10	ERIC CAMPBELL	718

Mini Stock
1	JACK PURCELL	526
2	AARON HOPKINS	511
3	JOHN VANDENHEUVEL	489
4	JUSTIN SCHELITZCHE	444
5	BLAKE DORWEILER	440
6	MATT BUSSON	423
7	TREVOR THOMPSON	212
8	BRIAN ADAMS	175
9	TODD TACHENY	167
10	TYLER CHRISTENSEN	159

Big 8 Sportsman
1	JAKE RYAN	1069
2	CHRIS MAREK	1063
3	JON LEMKE	1035
4	LAWRENCE BERTHIAUME	957
5	TRAVIS STANLEY	949
6	NICK BEAVER	932
7	DOUG BROWN	868
8	MICHAEL BEAMISH	848
9	MIKE PEDERSON	822
10	MITCH WEISS	656

Power Stock
1	JOHN LEBENS	984
2	THOMAS DOTEN	974
3	TAYLOR GOLDMAN	919
4	JOSIAH KING	900
5	PAUL HAMILTON	883
6	DAVE GOLDMAN	851
7	BRYAN WROLSTAD	810
8	LARRY SCOTT JR.	690
9	DAN BOHNSACK	646
10	SHAWN EVANS	470

RACEWAY PARK

6528 Hwy 101/Shakopee, MN/55379 — (952) 445-2257 — www.goracewaypark.com   **Sunday/.25 mile paved**

Late Model
1	CHAD WALEN 1480	6	JERRY ZIEMIECKI 980
2	TOM QUADE 1208	7	BRYAN SYER-KESKE 849
3	RYAN KAMISH. 1163	8	GARY PETRASH 536
4	JOE PRUSAK 1031	9	TROY TUMA 418
5	MARK LAMOREAUX 986		

Hobby Stock
1	BRENT KANE 1122	6	LOUIE ANSOLABEHERE 904
2	DUSTY MANN 1089	7	DREW SKAJA 885
3	JEREMY WOLFF 1058	8	JOHN HEATH 875
4	MATT STANLEY 968	9	MARK HAWES. 800
5	TINA DAVIS 924	10	JACOB GOEDE 799

Mini Stock
1	JACK PURCELL 1071	6	BRANDON PLEKKENPOL . . . 918
2	JASON HEITZ 1000	7	MICHAEL WACHS, JR 916
3	BLAKE DORWEILER 984	8	TREVOR THOMPSON 839
4	JUSTIN SCHELITZCHE 983	9	TOM SIBILA 837
5	TODD TACHENY 965	10	RYLEE REANN MICHAELSON 812

Figure 8
1	RICKY MARTIN 1657	6	RICHARD MARTIN 1553
2	JOHN LEBENS 1605	7	TODD WILSON 1525
3	MARK BRONSTAD. 1597	8	TODD TACHENY 1504
4	DANNY JOHNSON. 1586	9	DENNIS BARTA 1494
5	MATT DICKEY 1565	10	JOEL JOHNSTON 1376

Bomber
1	MIKE STOER 998	6	MONTGOMERY KNOLL 902
2	RYAN VARNER 969	7	KYLE CAMPBELL 877
3	ERIC PRINDLE. 934	8	NATHAN BORCHARDT. . . . 820
4	JUSTIN KOTCHEVAR 931	9	TIM HOLLEN 771
5	KENNY SCHUG 909	10	DAVE MONTOUR 763

Short Trackers
1	TODD KAMISH 1145	6	MATTHEW SCHAAR 979
2	CHARLIE PEHRSON 1079	7	KEITH PAULSRUD 889
3	JUSTIN SCHELITZCHE 1053	8	KEVIN BEAMISH. 825
4	MIKE DIMMICK 1031	9	RICHIE SPRINGBORN 787
5	DAVE REED 1001	10	JEREMY ROCHE. 774

NEBRASKA TOP 10

1 JASE KASER   POINTS: 647

STARTS: 30 **WINS:** 9 **TOP 5:** 21 **TOP 10:** 26

With nine wins and 26 top 10s in 30 combined starts Jase Kaser of Lincoln, Nebraska, raced to his first state championship. A rookie, Jase finished 15th in the Whelen All-American Series national standings.

2-10

Pos	Driver Name	Track	Starts	Wins	T-5	T-10	Points
2	Andrew Kosiski	I-80, Junction	27	0	7	18	446
3	Matt Buller	I-80, Junction	18	2	11	15	438
4	Kyle Berck	I-80	12	5	10	12	435
5	Marc Peters	Junction	17	1	9	15	417
6	Billy Murphy	Junction	17	1	10	15	411
7	Bill Leighton Jr.	I-80, Adams	13	2	6	12	382
8	Alex Humphrey	Junction	17	0	9	13	376
9	Jason O'Brien	Adams, I-80	13	0	8	12	372
10	John Bridges	Junction	17	1	6	13	365

1-80 SPEEDWAY

13909 238th Street/Greenwood, NE/68366 — (402) 659-3301 — www.neracewaypark.com   **Friday/.40 mile dirt**

Super Late Model
1	KYLE BERCK 828	6	LEON ZEITNER 698
2	BILL LEIGHTON JR. 794	7	MIKE COLLINS 632
3	JASON O'BRIEN. 794	8	JUSTIN ZEITNER 622
4	JASE KASER 766	9	JOSH KRUG 614
5	CHRIS SPIEKER 732	10	JOHN NICHOLSON 568

B Modified
1	BILL FLEGG 792	6	JEREMY LEITING 698
2	JESSE SOBBING 784	7	JEFFREY JONES 670
3	DENNIS COOK. 748	8	PRESTON GIGAX 640
4	BRIAN KOSISKI 738	9	KEVIN WAGNER 588
5	CODY OLSEN 718	10	DEREK ODEN 514

Pro-Am
1	BRAD DERRY 768	6	NICK STEIER 601
2	DON MOHR 751	7	CHAD SANDERS. 583
3	RICK NEGRETE 739	8	NICK HERMSEN 563
4	CURT DRAKE 675	9	RAY DESSEL 499
5	TIM PODRAZA. 661	10	TIM DRAKE 415

Modified
1	DYLAN SMITH. 897	6	DUSTIN JARILLO 600
2	JESSE DENNIS 841	7	CLINT HOMAN 589
3	MARK LEITING 692	8	JAMES MORIN 456
4	BUZZ WILSON 628	9	DAN RHILEY. 441
5	PHILIP LOSEKE 601	10	JIM COLE 426

Hornets
1	JAMIE SPANEL 800	6	SKIP BROWN 684
2	DAN MARKHAM 788	7	SCOTT BROWN 675
3	DAVID CHRISTENSEN 755	8	WAYNE STRICKLETT 642
4	TAMMY CLARK 735	9	DAN ALEXANDER 583
5	KELLY JOHNSON 729	10	JON ROWE 538

Grand Nationals
1	MICAH BROWN 791	6	TROY DALY 614
2	JACOB BROWN 768	7	STEVE MCCONNELL. 594
3	CORY DUMPERT 730	8	JOE ROBEY 585
4	TODD HIPNAR. 724	9	SCOTT LANE 524
5	KYLE DUMPERT 724	10	JASON WALLACE 497

JUNCTION MOTOR SPEEDWAY

1206 Road 4/McCool Junction, NE/68401 — (402) 724-3100 — www.junctionmotorspeedway.com   **Saturday/.375 mile dirt**

Late Model
1	JASE KASER 643	6	ANDREW KOSISKI 578
2	MARC PETERS 597	7	JOHN BRIDGES 571
3	BILLY MURPHY 593	8	MICAH VELEBA 548
4	MATT BULLER. 591	9	DENTON BULLER 510
5	ALEX HUMPHREY 579	10	TOM SVOBODA 504

B-Modified
1	TONY ROST 509	6	JEREMY LEITING 472
2	BRIAN KOSISKI 494	7	TYLER MARK 424
3	DUSTY BLAKE 483	8	EDD HUXOLL 381
4	BRENT KASSIK 477	9	CORY HUTCHISON 376
5	ROCKY ZIMMERMAN 474	10	KEVIN BETZEN 375

Modified
1	MARK LEITING 479	6	SCOTT SMITH. 380
2	ROBERT BRINKMAN 468	7	SHANE STUTZMAN 369
3	ANDY WILKINSON 447	8	EDD HUXOLL 366
4	DARREN MEINKE 435	9	JUSTIN BELL 329
5	STACI STAVA 417	10	PHILIP LOSEKE 329

Hobby Stock
1	TRAVIS THELANDER. 526	6	KYLE HEIN 332
2	SHANE SCHNEIDER 504	7	JUSTIN MEYER 239
3	JEFF TIMMERMANS 498	8	BRENT VAN DIEST. 112
4	DEREK KONERT 469	9	AJ HANSEN 104
5	DILLON BURKLUND 352	10	ANDREW LOVEGROVE 69

4 Cylinder
1	STEVE MOOCK 502	4	CASEY BAGWELL 467	7	JIM BAUMER 140	10	JORDAN UEHLING. 101
2	RICHARD CROW 493	5	DALTON SIEBKE 444	8	TERRY PEARSON 127		
3	EDD HUXOLL 486	6	CHAD CARLSON 381	9	DAN MARKHAM 114		

NEVADA TOP 10

1 SCOTT GAFFORINI POINTS: 319

STARTS: 12 **WINS:** 7 **TOP 5:** 10 **TOP 10:** 11

Scott Gafforini secured the Nevada championship with eight wins and 11 top fives in 14 races. This is the Henderson, Nevada, native's second state title.

2-10

Pos	Driver Name	Track	Starts	Wins	T-5	T-10	Points
2	Dennis Rock Jr.	Las Vegas	12	0	6	12	246
3	Glen Burke	Las Vegas	12	0	8	12	242
4	Christopher Clyne	Las Vegas	10	1	6	9	225
5	Joe Deguevara	Las Vegas	11	0	1	10	180
6	John Thomson	Las Vegas	12	0	1	8	144
7	Stan Mullis	Las Vegas	12	0	0	7	122
8	David Anderson	Las Vegas	5	0	3	5	106
9	Mark Shackleford	Las Vegas	5	0	2	5	100
10	Steve Anderson	Las Vegas	5	0	1	5	100

THE BULLRING AT LAS VEGAS MOTOR SPEEDWAY

7000 Las Vegas Blvd. North/Las Vegas, NV/89115 — (702) 644-4444 — www.lvms.com   **Saturday/.375 mile paved**

Super Late Model
1	SCOTT GAFFORINI	352
2	DENNIS ROCK JR.	274
3	GLEN BURKE	268
4	CHRIS CLYNE	256
5	JOE DEGUEVARA	182
6	JOHN THOMSON	160
7	DAVID ANDERSON	132
8	STAN MULLIS	130
9	STEVE ANDERSON	126
10	ALEX HAASE	101

Bomber
1	PETE MEYER	619
2	JASON KISER	594
3	MICHAEL TAKAMI	509
4	WADE PEARSON	504
5	MARTIN SULLINS JR.	453
6	NATHAN BOSS	450
7	DALLAS SIMONETTE	420
8	JUDY ROWE	362
9	JASON SULLINS-HAMETT	355
10	JIM MERLINO	342

Super Stock
1	JAMES WINGARD	554
2	PATRICK O'HANLEY	548
3	CHUCK BURGESS	514
4	KAYLI BARKER	514
5	KOLLEEN DRESSER	501
6	MIKE MCKEARN	469
7	JAMES LAUK	273
8	STEVE SMITH	245
9	VINNY RAUCCI	199
10	BARBARA BORKOWSKI	147

NEW HAMPSHIRE TOP 10

1 WAYNE HELLIWELL JR. POINTS: 650

STARTS: 31 **WINS:** 16 **TOP 5:** 26 **TOP 10:** 29

With 16 wins and 29 top 10s in 31 races, Wayne Helliwell Jr. cruised to the New Hampshire state title. It was the third-consecutive Whelen All-American Series championship for the Dover, New Hampshire, native.

2-10

Pos	Driver Name	Track	Starts	Wins	T-5	T-10	Points
2	Russ Hersey Jr.	Lee, Monadnock	16	7	14	15	441
3	Scott Macmichael	Canaan, Monadnock	19	0	9	14	384
4	Bill Kimball Jr.	Monadnock	15	1	14	14	377
5	Donnie Lashua	Canaan	17	0	9	14	358
6	Thomas Tombarello Jr.	Lee	15	3	12	14	309
7	Keith Carzello	Monadnock	15	1	7	14	305
8	Chris Bergeron	Canaan	14	1	8	10	301
9	Tyler Alati	Canaan	17	1	5	11	299
10	Joe Kendall	Monadnock	15	1	10	12	289

CANAAN FAIR SPEEDWAY

18 Orange Road/Canaan,NH/03741 — (802) 274-8823 — www.canaanspeedways.com   **Saturday/.333 mile asphalt**

Late Model
1	WAYNE HELLIWELL JR.	723
2	DONNIE LASHUA	641
3	SCOTT MACMICHAEL	640
4	EMILY PACKARD	611
5	TYLER ALATI	582
6	CHRIS BERGERON	579
7	DALLAS TROMBLEY	504
8	TYLER FISCUS	501
9	BUCKY DEMERS	498
10	ALLEN FELLOWS	496

Super Street
1	TREVER PERREAULT	599
2	BOB LABINE	588
3	RICH DUBEAU	586
4	KAYLA CAZARES	566
5	MATTHEW MORRILL	502
6	SID LAQUIRE JR.	301
7	MARK POTTER	242
8	CHRIS MCKINSTRY	170
9	JUNIOR MARTIN JR.	130
10	NATHAN A YOUNG	124

Pro Stock
1	JEREMY DAVIS	500
2	WALTER HAMMOND JR.	500
3	DONNIE LASHUA	455
4	KEITH PATNODE	389
5	DAVID A DAVIS	382
6	SULO BURBANK	316
7	KEVIN MENARD	259
8	BRIAN HENRY	257
9	DAVID BLY	248
10	KENNY CANTLIN	232

LEE USA SPEEDWAY

Route 380 Calef Hwy./Lee, NH/03824 — (978) 462-4252 — www.leeusaspeedway.com   **Friday/.375 mile paved**

Super Modified
1	THOMAS TOMBARELLO JR.	805
2	WAYNE HELLIWELL JR.	780
3	P J STERGIOS	750
4	MIKE NETISHEN	748
5	LES KEYSER	692
6	MICHAEL ORDWAY JR.	681
7	SPARKY MACIVER	675
8	RYAN GATH	646
9	TONY CARROLL	605
10	MIKE SPURLING	507

Ironman
1	JAKE RHEAUME	927
2	DANIELLE SIMONEAU	892
3	EVAN HORVATH	823
4	TYLER MITCHELL	655
5	WAYNE PURINGTON	529
6	CHRIS MURRAY	491
7	TRAVIS HOLLINS	467
8	HANNAH SHAW	437
9	RYAN PITKIN	392
10	SHANE HORVATH	383

Late Model Sportsman
1	PHILIP BARIL JR.	826
2	MICHELE FUSHPANSKI	717
3	TIMMY JOHNSON	684
4	TONY KAWEISZA	664
5	KYLE ROY	647
6	PATRICK STEWART	620
7	JASON WELCH	521
8	DOC PIPER	518
9	RAY DINSMORE III.	515
10	CHRISTOPHER TITCOMB	428

Hobby Stock
1	JIM SHOREY	880
2	PATRICK TANGUAY	776
3	JIM PIASECZNY	772
4	KENNY SCOTT JR.	761
5	PAUL PALEN	753
6	NIKO MANIATIS	736
7	RON WASHBURN	721
8	CHRIS JACOBSON	677
9	BRIAN THOMPSON	642
10	KYLE SAWYER	615

MONADNOCK SPEEDWAY

840 Keene Road/Winchester, NH/03470 — (603) 239-4067 — www.monadnockspeedway.com **Saturday/.25 mile paved**

Sport Modified
1	RUSS HERSEY JR.	708
2	BILL KIMBALL JR.	678
3	KEITH CARZELLO	606
4	JOE KENDALL	590
5	DANIEL STEBBINS	564
6	BRIAN CHAPIN	550
7	KYLE POODIACK	514
8	ERIC LECLAIR	484
9	JEFFREY BECKWITH	454
10	JEREMY MCCUTCHEON	400

Lighting Stock
1	CRAIG CHAFFEE	532
2	DICKIE HOULE	530
3	CJ JOHNSON	488
4	RICHARD WHIPPLE	430
5	TIMOTHY PAQUETTE	416
6	PAT HOULE	402
7	HILLARY RENAUD	370
8	MATTHEW SOMERVILLE	368
9	DARREN JACOBS	364
10	ERIC SILVERNALE	330

Thunder Stock
1	JAMES THOMPSON	500
2	JOE ETHIER	496
3	EDWARD LOFLAND	490
4	BARRY SCHONBORG	406
5	RYAN RIVET	390
6	MARSHALL USHER	348

Super Stock
1	JOHN LAVOIE	728
2	JASON LAFLEUR	716
3	DAVID STRIEBEL	656
4	DANA SHEPARD	602
5	ANDREW DURAND	590
6	NANCY MUNI-RUOT	578
7	STUART WHEELDEN	378
8	KENNETH SPRINGER	244
9	BILL JOHNSTON	214
10	CHRISTOPHER COOK	146

Mini Stock
1	KIMBERLEY RIVET	694
2	BETH ADAMS	668
3	JULIA RAYMOND	610
4	MIKE STEBBINS	588
5	ROBERT THOMPSON	564
6	JOE ROGERS	540
7	ADAM MANLEY	522
8	KEVIN MCKNIGHT JR.	504
9	ALECIA FOHLIN	500
10	CHRIS MCTAGGART	426
7	JON GODDARD	326
8	HOWARD SHEATS	242
9	DOUGLAS GUY	242
10	SETH PETALAS	238

NEW YORK TOP 10

1 SHAWN SOLOMITO POINTS: 595

STARTS: 21 **WINS:** 3 **TOP 5:** 14 **TOP 10:** 17

Three wins and 17 top 10s in 21 Modified starts secured the New York State Championship for Islip, New York's, Shawn Solomito. This is his first Whelen All-American Series state title.

2-10

Pos	Driver Name	Track	Starts	Wins	T-5	T-10	Points
2	Howie Brode	Riverhead	21	0	12	20	566
3	Tom Rogers Jr.	Riverhead	20	8	12	13	560
4	Ed Brunnhoelzl III	Riverhead	21	1	8	16	495
5	Ted Christopher	Thompson, Riverhead, Stafford	17	1	13	14	493
6	John F Fortin	Riverhead	17	1	7	12	437
7	Timmy Solomito	Riverhead	20	1	9	12	423
8	John Beatty Jr.	Riverhead	18	0	4	13	422
9	Rusty Smith	Spencer	13	3	10	13	405
10	David Catalano	Spencer, Holland	22	3	11	16	363

CHEMUNG SPEEDROME

605 Wyncoop Creek Road/Chemung, NY/14825 — (607) 529-9998 — www.chemungspeedrome.net **Sunday/ .375 mile dirt paved**

Sunoco Modifieds
1	TJ ZACHARIAS	380
2	JIMMY ZACHARIAS	361
3	MATT CLEMENS	348
4	MICHAEL ODWAZNY	341
5	ANDY JANKOWIAK	302
6	BOB MOSHER	283
7	JODY BUCKLEY	198
8	DON KING JR.	182
9	BRITTANY JACK	86
10	TERRY ZACHARIAS	81

4-Cylinders
1	GENE PURVIS JR.	379
2	FRANK MORICH	370

Super Stocks
1	CRICKET CLONCH	361
2	TERRY POTRZEBOWSKI	353
3	JOHN LANE	343
4	JOE LANE JR.	306
5	CHUCK NICHOLS	284
6	DERRICK TARBOX	212
7	CODY MARSHALL	186
8	HANK BUCHANAN	179
9	BRITTANY JACK	119
10	JIM HOUSE JR.	81
3	BUBBA PETERS	98

HOLLAND MOTORSPORTS COMPLEX

11586 Holland Glenwood Road/Holland, NY/14080 — (716) 418-7223 — www.hollandspeedway.com **Saturday/.375 mile paved**

Pro Modified
1	ANDY JANKOWIAK	299
2	DAVID CATALANO	265
3	TOMMY CATALANO	226
4	OWEN BEDNASZ	218
5	JOE EVANS	214
6	DON KING JR.	182
7	JOE CARBONE	157
8	NEAL DIETZ JR.	143
9	JAKE VERNON	142
10	AMY CATALANO	98

Hornet
1	JEFF SZAFRANEC	550
2	CHRIS POWERS	531
3	BEN RUSSO	510
4	TONY CARBONE	486
5	LOU CARBONE	482
6	BILL LUTZ	457
7	SAMANTHA LUTZ	425
8	ROBERT MARZEC	321
9	JOHN BLINSTON	278
10	JENNIFER TERMER	269

Charger
1	JIM LOFFREDO	399
2	DAVE WILSON JR.	390
3	KRIS HAMANN	345
4	JERRY KOSMOWSKI	337
5	RICH CARNES SR.	275
6	MARTY HUGHES	272
7	TOM NORTHEM	263
8	SHAWN LAFFERTY	236
9	JASON ADAMS	208
10	ZACH MYERS	181

Figure 8
1	JASON ADAMS	140
2	ROBERT MARZEC	132
3	BILL LUTZ	108
4	BUTCH PALMER	86
5	KYLE SKONEY	76
6	DALE MCCOOL	48
7	JOE MASTROCICCO III	34
8	DAVID WARRIOR	32
9	ERIC RICH	32
10	JACK WARRIOR JR.	26

RIVERHEAD RACEWAY

1797 Old Country Road/Riverhead, NY/11901 — (631) 842-7223 — www.riverheadraceway.com **Saturday/.25 mile paved**

Modified
1	SHAWN SOLOMITO	504
2	HOWIE BRODE	494
3	TOM ROGERS JR.	418
4	TED CHRISTOPHER	418
5	ED BRUNNHOELZL III	370
6	JOHN F FORTIN	348
7	TIMMY SOLOMITO	335
8	JOHN BEATTY JR.	320
9	JASON AGUGLIARO	308
10	DAVID SAPIENZA	298

Figure 8
1	MIKE MUJSCE SR.	416
2	ARNE PEDERSEN	414
3	KENNETH HYDE JR.	408
4	TOM FERRARA	396
5	ROGER MAYNOR	324
6	TIMMY MULQUEEN	324
7	TIM FARRELL	214
8	GEORGE SEUS	210
9	MICHAEL SMITH	182
10	SCOTT PEDERSEN	168

Late Model
1	MIKE BOLOGNA	462
2	BUZZY ERIKSEN JR.	426
3	SHAWN PATRICK	426
4	CHRIS LASPISA	420
5	SCOTT KULESA	416
6	KEVIN METZGER	402
7	ARNE PEDERSEN	364
8	DENNIS KRUPSKI	354
9	R J OXEE	302
10	JEREMY MCDERMOTT	168

Charger
1	JEREMY MCDERMOTT	546
2	ERIC ZEH	534
3	CHRIS TURBUSH	520
4	JOHN BAKER	516
5	CARL LEHMANN JR.	510
6	RAY MINIERI	492
7	CORY OSLAND	456
8	BRIAN DOYLE	366
9	JAYSON WHITE	366
10	DEREK STACHECKI	274

NASCAR HOME TRACKS

SPENCER SPEEDWAY

3011 Ridge Road/Williamson, NY/14589 — (315) 589-3018 — www.spencerspeedway.org

Friday/.50 mile paved

Sunoco Modified

1	RUSTY SMITH	847
2	KEVIN TIMMERMAN	759
3	MIKE LEATY	750
4	TONY HANBURY	713
5	RYAN BEEMAN	710
6	EDDIE HAWKINS	677
7	MATTHEW LEES	656
8	DARYL LEWIS JR.	634
9	TOMMY CATALANO	623
10	ANDY LEWIS	613

Super Stocks

1	TERRY CHEETHAM	878
2	MITCHELL WRIGHT	795
3	BRANDON LARNER	532
4	WILLIE STRUSZ	486
5	WILLIAM GLEASON	442
6	BRIAN GORDON	310
7	STEVE MALIN	217
8	JOHN AVERY	149
9	JOHN LANE	54
10	KRIS HILLEGEER	52

Super Sixes

1	BRIAN HALLETT	895
2	BRANDON ALLEN	729
3	ERICK RUFFELL	714
4	TIM FARO	702
5	ADAM VANHALL	684
6	VAN GRANT	677
7	HUGH VINE JR.	642
8	RICK WILSON JR.	630
9	DENNIS COYLE	390
10	JEFF DAVIS	360

Scorpins

1	MICHAEL BRADSHAW	869
2	KEVIN BERTOLONE	773
3	JOSEPH CLARK	731
4	ZACH WILLIS	725
5	SHAUN FRAREY	702
6	ALISON KNOEPFLER	696
7	DAVE BRADSHAW	677
8	RUSSELL PEETS	665
9	BETH DENNIE	659
10	BRO BRADSHAW	569

NORTH CAROLINA TOP 10

1 DEAC McCASKILL POINTS: 706

STARTS: *26* **WINS:** *17* **TOP 5:** *23* **TOP 10:** *25*

Deac McCaskill of Raleigh, North Carolina, compiled 17 wins and 23 top fives in 26 starts to earn the state title in North Carolina. This was Deac's first championship of the Tar Heel State.

2-10

Pos	Driver Name	Track	Starts	Wins	T-5	T-10	Points
2	Tim Brown	Bowman	24	8	13	18	672
3	Jonathan Brown	Bowman	24	2	11	18	592
4	Danny Bohn	Bowman	22	2	12	16	592
5	Jason Myers	Bowman	24	0	13	19	576
6	Burt Myers	Bowman	24	2	9	17	570
7	Austin McDaniel	Hickory	22	9	20	21	567
8	Lee Jeffreys	Bowman	24	0	9	19	564
9	Dean Ward	Bowman	20	3	8	16	547
10	Randy Butner	Bowman	24	1	7	18	535

BOWMAN GRAY STADIUM

1250 South Martin Luther King Jr. Drive/Winston-Salem, NC/27107 — (336) 679-8118 — www.bowmangrayracing.com

Saturday/.25 mile paved

Modified

1	TIM BROWN	711
2	JASON MYERS	691
3	JONATHAN BROWN	679
4	DANNY BOHN	648
5	BURT MYERS	638
6	LEE JEFFREYS	629
7	JOHN SMITH	608
8	RANDY BUTNER	597
9	MICHAEL CLIFTON	584
10	DEAN WARD	552

Stadium Stock

1	CHARLES CURRY	736
2	CHUCK WALL III	674
3	A J SANDERS JR.	658
4	DEREK TAYLOR	658
5	ROB YOUNG	590
6	CHRIS ALLISON	584
7	CHASE HUNT	554
8	SHANE SOUTHARD	550
9	JOSEPH SWANSON	544
10	TED MICKALOWSKI	538

Sportsman

1	DEREK STOLTZ	684
2	JEFF GARRISON	683
3	MICHAEL ADAMS	622
4	ZACK CLIFTON	571
5	TAYLOR BRANCH	566
6	KENNY BOST JR.	563
7	JOHN LAIN	550
8	DAVID ADAMS	516
9	BRYANT ROBERTSON	509
10	KYLE SOUTHERN	507

Street Stock

1	BILLY GREGG	756
2	JOHN HOLLEMAN IV	734
3	DAVID SUMNER	714
4	DOUG WALL	686
5	DANIEL FISHEL	638
6	K J STIMPSON JR.	628
7	STEPHEN BAKER	588
8	TIM VADEN	552
9	WHITNEY CLIFTON	542
10	BRIAN WALL	414

CARAWAY SPEEDWAY

2518 Racetrack Road Ext/Sophia, NC/27350 — (336) 629-5803 — www.carawayspeedway.com

Saturday/.455 mile asphalt

Late Model

1	MACK LITTLE III	774
2	RYAN WILSON	750
3	ROBERT TYLER	738
4	GENE KEPLEY	636
5	DAN MOORE JR.	518
6	ALEX YONTZ	308
7	PETE STEWART	302
8	RANDY BENSON	300
9	TOMMY LEMONS JR.	236
10	JAY PAYNE	232

Mini Truck

1	TYLER MCDONALD	444
2	CHRIS MCDONALD	430
3	DAVID HOUCK JR.	230
4	STEVE COLLINS	138
5	ANTHONY BENNETT	94
6	JUNIOR CHRISCOE JR.	46
7	TONEY HENDERSON	44
8	DAVID WENHART	42

Limited Late Model

1	RYAN BROWN	520
2	CARL AUMAN	476
3	JUSTIN NEWLIN	430
4	TYLER JORDAN	410
5	PAUL WARK	338
6	JUNIOR KENDRICK	264
7	ANNABETH BARNES	212
8	SCOTT BROADFIELD	208
9	JAMES MARKWELL	192
10	HEATH CAUSEY	170

Mini Stock

1	ANDREW SANDERS	556
2	JOHNNY BAKER	522
3	JOHN DAVIS	390
4	ALLEN HORNADAY	372
5	MICHAEL LOWERY	326
6	MICHAEL KITCHIN	288
7	ZACK BRALLEY	268
8	JOHNNY WARR	254
9	JASON TUTTEROW	200
10	MICHAEL WELLS	184

CONCORD SPEEDWAY

3400 Concord Speedway Drive/Concord, NC/28025 — (704) 782-4221 — www.concordspeedway.net

Saturday/.50 mile paved

Late Model

1	KENNY BROOKS	363
2	ANDREW THOMAS	341
3	JEFF MELTON	305
4	JERRY MIRACLE	217
5	BRYAN DAUZAT	211
6	LARRY BENZ	193
7	TONY PASQUARELLO	188
8	JAY PAYNE	110
9	COLE CUSTER	107
10	NICK DRAKE	100

Fast & Furious Fours

1	ADAM MORGAN	268
2	CHRIS PARHAM	247
3	TERRY PARHAM	236
4	DAVID LAYTON	183
5	MIKE LOOMIS	179
6	TRACY MULLIS	140
7	ERIC HARRINGTON	99
8	KYLE LYNCH	74
9	WAYNE HARRINGTON JR.	70
10	ALAN SAXON	41

Street Stock

1	SONNY SCHOFFEN	312
2	COOPER FAASSEN	259
3	CHARLES HUTTO	248
4	RON FLYNN	236
5	RYAN PENCEK	161
6	CHARLES FAASSEN	157
7	STEVE DAVIS	122
8	BRIAN LOVE	116
9	BRYAN THOMAS	113
10	RANDY MCANULTY	99

NASCAR HOME TRACKS

HICKORY MOTOR SPEEDWAY

3130 Highway 70 S.E./Newton, NC/28658 — (828) 464-3655 — www.hickorymotorspeedway.com

Saturday/.363 mile asphalt

Late Model Stock
1	AUSTIN MCDANIEL	1012
2	JESSE LEFEVERS	904
3	JOSH WIMBISH	884
4	JEREMY SOREL	810
5	PIETRO FITTIPALDI	758
6	TREY GIBSON	756
7	MATT PIERCY	660
8	MACKENA BELL	606
9	KYLE MOON	558
10	TYLER HILL	482

Street Stock
1	KEVIN EBY	922
2	MARSHALL SUTTON	870
3	ROY SMITH	790
4	SAMUEL THOMPSON	720
5	MIKE NEWTON	702
6	MARK WHITTEN	616
7	JASON STANLEY	396
8	JOHN JONES, IV.	308
9	KEVIN TOWNSEND	216
10	BARON KURITZKY	194

4 Cylinder
1	TODD HARRINGTON	496
2	NATHANIEL KANUPP	436
3	DONN WARDO	424
4	DONNIE HARMON	368
5	ROB LEWIS	344
6	CALEB SISK	272
7	PATRICK SHIFLETT	124
8	RANDY CANIPE	84
9	DEVON HAUN	48
10	SHANE CANIPE	48

Hobbies
1	JASON BYRD	234
2	DAVID HASSON	222
3	RONALD MCNEILL	216
4	TYLER MCKINNEY	148
5	CHAD MCKINNEY	146
6	PAUL WYATT	126
7	COLE KILLIAN	126

Limited
1	SHANE LEE	860
2	JEREMY PELFREY	790
3	TRAVIS BYRD	708
4	ZACH BRUENGER	698
5	CHRISTIAN CALVO	592
6	CHARLIE WATSON	582
7	MONTY COX	580
8	ARNOLD MOORE III	550
9	JOSH BRALLEY	468
10	LANDON HUFFMAN	456

Trucks
1	JASON COCHRAN	478
2	JEREMY BIRCH	476
3	WHITNEY LAIL	408
4	TREY PITTS	290
5	CHASE CAMPBELL	286
6	THOMAS BEANE	180
7	DANIEL FREEMAN	150
8	BRAD COX	138
9	TREVOR HIGNUTT	138
10	RICKY DENNIE JR.	134

Renegades
1	DARBY CROUCH	450
2	BARNEY ARNETTE	432
3	EDDIE RUSS	420
4	GREG AUSTIN	374
5	CARROLL MCKINNEY	368
6	KYLE DIVANNA	340
7	BRADFORD NELSON	304
8	STEVE GRIFFITH	296
9	KENNETH ROBERTS	184
10	DARREN DICKINSON	178

SOUTHERN NATIONAL MOTORSPORTS PARK

8071 Newsome Mill Road/Lucama, NC/27851 — (919) 284-1114 — www.snmpark.com

Saturday/ .40 mile asphalt

Late Model
1	DEAC MCCASKILL	791
2	TERRY DEASE	498
3	MICHAEL ROUSE JR.	483
4	DOUG GODSEY	463
5	AUSTIN SELF	372
6	BRANDON BROWN	368
7	RICKY JONES	356
8	TOM BURBAGE JR.	296
9	MELVIN LANGLEY	296
10	PADDY RODENBECK	268

Charger
1	BUCKSHOT JONES	191
2	GERALD BENTON	141
3	DAVID WARREN	98
4	RONALD RENFROW JR.	81
5	JUSTIN MARSHBURN	66
6	WOODY ELLINGTON	56
7	LARRY PENNY	52
8	TRAVIS ROBERSON	46
9	TERRY CLINE	33
10	ALTON COOMBS	30

Street Stock
1	GARY LEDBETTER JR.	94
2	GREGG BARNETT	79
3	HENRY BARNES	60
4	CHET CHRISTMAN	38
5	WAYNE GOSS	26
6	JONAS HOWARD	24
7	DAVID FOREMAN	12
8	MACK PARKER	12
9	KYLE SMITH	10
10	FRANK RIEGEL	10

Limited Late Model
1	LOUIS WHITE	427
2	CLAY JONES	383
3	JOE HEIGL	273
4	DOUG BAREFOOT	210
5	ADAM MURRAY	185
6	JD EVERSOLE III.	180
7	BUDDY ISLES	156
8	CORY WALKER	130
9	DONALD BRACE	122
10	ADAM RESNICK	112

U Car
1	CHAD WALL	348
2	AARON MILLER	331
3	DUANE WALKER	254
4	TRAVIS MILLER	192
5	TYLER HORNE	189
6	DAVID WIGGINS	168
7	JASON MILLER	164
8	EDDIE HOWARD	144
9	LYNN WALLER	128
10	MICKEY CONNOR	106

Mini Mod
1	JASON HORNE	152
2	LEE KOZIKOWSKI	135
3	TRAVIS GREEN	94
4	MICHAEL O'BRIEN	83
5	TODD LANGLEY	60
6	ADAM MURRAY	57
7	JEREMY BOHNE	46
8	KENNY JOHNSON	42
9	NICHOLAS FULGHUM	40
10	HUNTER BAILEY	34

OHIO TOP 10

1 CHAD PENDLETON   POINTS: 462

STARTS: *20* **WINS:** *4* **TOP 5:** *16* **TOP 10:** *20*

With four wins and top 10s in all 20 starts Chad Pendleton of Columbus, Ohio, took home his first Ohio state championship. The Buckeye State has featured different champions in each of the last six seasons.

2-10

Pos	Driver Name	Track	Starts	Wins	T-5	T-10	Points
2	Dick Dunlevy Jr.	Kil-Kare, Columbus	25	16	25	25	411
3	Bobby Justus	Kil-Kare, Columbus	28	3	19	26	409
4	Todd Sherman	Limaland	14	6	12	13	398
5	Eric Withers	Columbus, Kil-Kare	18	2	8	16	360
6	Josh Cahill	Columbus, Kil-Kare	19	2	8	17	360
7	Jake Reufer	Limaland	14	2	11	12	354
8	Terry Hull	Limaland	14	2	8	13	344
9	Ray Muncy	Columbus	16	1	8	14	325
10	Burgess White	Columbus, Kil-Kare	18	1	6	13	265

BARBERTON RACEWAY PARK

3363 Clark Mill Road/Norton, OH/44203 — (440) 867-5394 — www.barbertonracewaypark.com

Friday/.25 mile paved

Late Model
1	DON HARVEY JR.	1113	6	MIKE MAZZAGATTI	574
2	RICK SIBILA	1000	7	DOUG SOMMERS	299
3	JEFF TAYLOR	788	8	GENE MOLNAR	280
4	DAVID MARTIN	753	9	DWAIN WILLIS	225
5	COLE HOLTREY	619	10	MIKE MILLER	219

Mini Truck
1	DAN BURDEN	890	6	TODD SHULTZ	522
2	DENNIS GARRETT	801	7	LOGAN COLLMAR	438
3	CYLER BERTRAM	619	8	JUSTIN BADGETT	417
4	DENNIS GARRETT JR.	588	9	BRIAN POLING	314
5	TROY CAMPBELL	545	10	DAVID WAGNER	275

Pure Stock
1	BRIAN POLING	1185	6	BRIAN MILLER	632
2	DEBRA THOMAS	1104	7	AJ VASILLIU	579
3	AUSTIN HARVEY	903	8	TIM FARRAR	558
4	PAUL MANGUM	844	9	BILL JANE	543
5	LEEZA MOORE	782	10	RANDY CECIL	531

Sportsman
1	MARK LUSHES	1183	6	JOE COURSEN	303
2	CHRIS MICK	1085	7	WAYNE MOUNTS	272
3	AARON PRATER	559	8	SCOTT CURTO	252
4	JOHN BREEHL	503	9	CHAD LEMMERMAN	134
5	RICHARD PRICE II	471	10	TOM WRIGHT JR.	112

Hobby Stock
1	DENNIS WOOD	1374	6	PATRICK MADISON	353
2	KENNETH PRICE	1089	7	JESSE PATTERSON	316
3	TOM POWELL	716	8	ADAM WHITE	298
4	RICK PERECES	631	9	MAX GEE	236
5	JASON WRIGHT	546	10	CHET COLLMAR JR.	74

COLUMBUS MOTOR SPEEDWAY

1841 Williams Road/Columbus, OH/43207 — (614) 491-1047 — www.columbusspeedway.com

Saturday/.333 mile paved

Late Model
1	CHAD PENDLETON	1389	6	RAY MUNCY	1163
2	BOBBY JUSTUS	1376	7	HOWARD MUNCY	1098
3	ERIC WITHERS	1292	8	BURGESS WHITE	1039
4	JOSH CAHILL	1205	9	JIM HURSEY	861
5	BILL BROWNING	1189	10	JACOB MUNCY	571

Sports Stock
1	JOE HENSEL	1492	6	STEVE KARNES	1302
2	MIKE LITCHFIELD	1435	7	PHIL GUSSLER JR.	1228
3	RALPH VINSON	1423	8	JEREMIAH ENGLISH	969
4	KENNY SIMPSON	1388	9	DAVID JAMES	766
5	BILL RAMEY	1306	10	BRUCE SNIDER	750

Modified
1	GEORGE LINDSAY	1578	6	DAVE DISINGER	1279
2	BUDDY TOWNSEND	1491	7	CHAD PENDLETON	1170
3	KYLE PURVIS	1462	8	BRIAN WHETNALL	1006
4	SEAN MACNEALY	1361	9	BOB EATON	960
5	DARYL MCKAY	1304	10	PAUL BAKER	958

Compacts
1	JIM MCELFRESH	1362	6	RYAN SMITH	1085
2	MICHAEL ROBISON	1352	7	JOSH MECUM	1025
3	COREY KYER	1260	8	CHRISTIAN BULLOCK	1011
4	RANDY ROGERS	1204	9	BILL OTT	989
5	ROB SMITH	1113	10	CHARLIE HOEPKER	979

KIL-KARE SPEEDWAY

1166 Dayton-Xenia Road/Xenia, OH/45385 — (937) 429-2961 — www.kilkare.com

Friday/.375 mile paved

Late Model
1	DICK DUNLEVY JR.	1589	6	RUSSELL BOBB	1001
2	BOB SIBILA JR.	1389	7	BOBBY JUSTUS	698
3	TERRY SCHERZ	1340	8	JUSTIN ALSIP	596
4	SHAWN STANSELL	1165	9	CAL BUSCH	446
5	TONY BRUNKE	1152	10	MIKE HOLLAND	226

Compacts
1	BO HOELSCHER JR.	1503	6	NICK BARRETT	1244
2	STEVE BARNHART	1338	7	JOE HOELSCHER	1203
3	AMBER SITES	1280	8	RYAN BARRETT	1129
4	PAUL HOLLEY	1277	9	RYAN TAMBURRO	896
5	BRYAN LYNCH	1251	10	TONY COTTRILL	677

Modifieds
1	RYAN FLEMING	1537	6	RODNEY KREUSCH	628
2	WILLIAM BURBA	1466	7	BRAD WILLIAMS	538
3	DARYL MCKAY	1414	8	JOHN DONOVAN	533
4	MIKE CARROLL	1051	9	JAMIE SITES	495
5	GRANT GAMBLE	986	10	DEREK BARNETTE	473

Sport Stocks
1	TYLER MAHAFFEY	1459	6	JAY LAKINS JR.	812
2	DAVID STUMP	1372	7	TRAVIS DIGGES	792
3	JAMIE SITES	1370	8	WILLIAM GREGORY	454
4	JOSH LONGSTRETH	1351	9	RODNEY KREUSCH	440
5	JOE HENSEL	815	10	PHIL GUSSLER JR.	400

LAKE COUNTY SPEEDWAY

500 Fairport Nursery Road/Painesville, OH/44077 — (440) 354-3505 — www.lakecountyspeedway.com

Saturday/.20 mile asphalt

Limited Late Model
1	BUZZ BATES	2166	6	DAVEY LAWSON	585
2	CHARLES DURST	1768	7	DON KRAMER	545
3	KEITH PLATZ JR.	1440	8	BILLY STREHLE	432
4	BILL WELCH	1126	9	DALE MARKIEWICZ SR.	324
5	BILLY ROBERTS	746	10	RODNEY SAUNDERS	280

Figure 8
1	MIKE REED	2418	6	KEVIN MALEK	931
2	CHUCK SADAR	1995	7	JUSTIN BEVER	915
3	MIKE DAVIS	1955	8	STEVE SANDLI	901
4	JOE MARCH	1199	9	CHAD TEKAVIC	876
5	CHAD DAVIS	1160	10	RANDY LETTE	858

Renegade Eight
1	MIKE REED	2300	6	ALLEN FILKINS	1132
2	RYAN BRENNER	1962	7	CHRIS MORGAN	707
3	ALLEN FILKINS JR.	1901	8	AARON VAN DALEN	587
4	CW DUNHAM	1321	9	JOHN YECKLEY	425
5	JACK HRIBAR	1256	10	BO MARTIN	423

Street Stock
1	JOSH WAY	2191	6	BILL JOHNSON	1218
2	JAKE SHIPMAN	2162	7	FRED MCCORD	967
3	SCOTT SKUFCA	1949	8	MATT WIEGAND	826
4	JOHNNY CANTER III	1867	9	JOE TILLERY	810
5	RODNEY REYNOLDS	1586	10	EARL GOLDY HEDRICK	699

Factory Four
1	MATT WIEGAND	2340	6	ROCKY NAILS	1482
2	KELLY HORST	1921	7	DAVID GUYNN SR.	1452
3	TJ SCHINKE	1855	8	JACK HRIBAR	1355
4	BEN CALL	1845	9	JOE COMBS	1309
5	MIKE LIDDY	1611	10	TIM CLOUTMAN	1277

LIMALAND MOTORSPORTS PARK

1500 Dutch Hollow Road/Lima, OH/45807 — (419) 339-6249 — www.limaland.com

Friday/.25 mile dirt

Modifieds

1	TODD SHERMAN	1530	6	CASEY LUEDEKE	1282
2	TERRY HULL	1478	7	TYLER STUMP	1270
3	JAKE REUFER	1474	8	CORY SEELING	1264
4	KODY WEISNER	1336	9	CHAD ROSENBECK	1222
5	TONY ANDERSON	1330	10	RYAN O'DETTE	1196

Thunderstocks

1	SHAWN VALENTI	1572	6	ANDY KING	1226
2	TONY ANDERSON	1526	7	BRYAN MARTIN	1222
3	CHRIS DOUGLAS	1436	8	RANDY CROSSLEY	1208
4	JEFF KOSLAKIEWICZ	1426	9	KEITH SHOCKENCY	1192
5	BILLY SIFERD	1402	10	FRANK PALADINO	1068

OKLAHOMA TOP 10

1 BRIAN PARKER POINTS: 479

STARTS: 19 **WINS:** 7 **TOP 5:** 13 **TOP 10:** 17

Seven wins and 19 top 10s in 21 outings secured the state championship for Brad Parker of Collinsville, Oklahoma. He was also the state and national Rookie of the Year.

2-10

Pos	Driver Name	Track	Starts	Wins	T-5	T-10	Points
2	Joe Duvall	Salina	19	2	15	18	442
3	Jeran Frailey	Salina	18	1	10	17	379
4	Danny Womack	Salina	19	2	10	17	375
5	Shannon Scott	Salina	19	1	9	15	327
6	Mike Wroblewski	Salina	18	0	6	9	272
7	Brett Hansen	Salina	17	0	4	9	242
8	Casey Lindell	Salina	16	1	1	8	211
9	Toby Lindell	Salina	17	0	0	8	200
10	Jeremy Rasmussen	Salina	7	0	5	5	164

SALINA HIGHBANKS SPEEDWAY

3164 East Highway 20/Pryor, OK/74361 — (918) 434-7223 — www.salinahighbanksspeedway.com

Saturday/.375 mile dirt

Modified

1	BRIAN PARKER	1927	6	MIKE WROBLEWSKI	1534
2	JOE DUVALL	1901	7	BRETT HANSEN	1454
3	JERAN FRAILEY	1746	8	TOBY LINDELL	1338
4	DANNY WOMACK	1711	9	CASEY LINDELL	1313
5	SHANNON SCOTT	1621	10	CHRISTOPHER THEODORE	800

360 Modified

1	RANDY FRAILEY	1963	6	PAUL BEYER	1797
2	JUSTIN SHOEMAKER	1908	7	BRANDON WILSON	1717
3	KEITH CAMPBELL	1908	8	JD JACKSON	1716
4	JERRY WAGNER	1851	9	JOHN MONTGOMERY	1686
5	MIKE NORTHRUP	1834	10	JAMES LITTLE	1447

Factory Stock

1	KINZER EDWARDS	2013	6	ERICK SHIVE	1354
2	RIKKI SCOTT	1660	7	BRANDON JARVIS	1165
3	BUTCH DODD	1579	8	JACKY GRIFFIN	1007
4	WILLIAM PARKER	1534	9	TAYLOR HALPAIN	999
5	JOE WATT	1403	10	MICHAEL RYALS	969

Grand National

1	BRIAN PARKER	2003	6	JONATHAN MITCHELL	1502
2	DUSTIN DAVIS	1956	7	DOUG HULS	1270
3	DARIN RIGNEY	1918	8	JOHN TURNER	1258
4	RANDY MOSES SR.	1862	9	DALE RICHARDSON JR.	1222
5	STEVE TOALSON	1618	10	RANDY MOSES II	1168

Pure Stock

1	CHRIS JENKINS	2055	6	COLBY NORTH	1564
2	SUSAN STAND	1897	7	DUSTY COLES	1564
3	DYLAN CANTWELL	1808	8	ROBERT MUHLHAUSER	1383
4	KIRK KVITTUM	1638	9	JACOBY FRAILEY	1352
5	ROY EDENFIELD	1635	10	JIM WALKER JR.	1342

ONTARIO TOP 10

1 DWAYNE BAKER POINTS: 567

STARTS: 35 **WINS:** 15 **TOP 5:** 28 **TOP 10:** 34

The province of Ontario championship was captured with 15 wins and an amazing display of consistency that saw Dwayne Baker of Stayner, Ontario, finish in the top 10 in 34 of 35 starts. He became the first driver to earn two Ontario championships.

2-10

Pos	Driver Name	Track	Starts	Wins	T-5	T-10	Points
2	Keith Mcleod	Barrie	28	7	22	26	489
3	Gord Shepherd	Barrie	34	4	29	32	480
4	Ron Quesnelle	Barrie	35	2	25	35	448
5	Allan Inglis	Barrie	35	2	25	33	440
6	Shawn Murray	Barrie	34	4	14	28	408
7	Thayne Hallyburton	Barrie	34	0	16	33	384
8	David Lewis	Barrie	33	0	5	22	312
9	Mike Brown	Barrie	24	0	3	19	278
10	Randy Bull	Barrie	17	0	4	15	274

BARRIE SPEEDWAY

240 Eighth Line South/Oro, ON/L0L 2X0 — (705) 487-0279 — www.barriespeedway.com

Saturday/.333 mile paved

Late Model

1	DWAYNE BAKER	1513	6	SHAWN MURRAY	1272
2	RON QUESNELLE	1417	7	KEITH MCLEOD	1174
3	ALLAN INGLIS	1378	8	DAVID LEWIS	1092
4	GORD SHEPHERD	1364	9	ROY MANARY	1056
5	THAYNE HALLYBURTON	1293	10	GLENN LLOYD	954

Thunder

1	RICK WALT	894	6	JIM BELESKEY	700
2	DAVE DOUCETTE	827	7	DESIREE WALT	655
3	LEONARD JOHNSTON	799	8	BRIAN MURRAY	608
4	TRAVIS HALLYBURTON	750	9	PETER MARQUARDT	536
5	DARRYL ST ONGE	743	10	DOUG SHAKELL	494

Division III

1	CHARLIE SMITH	843	6	RYAN TOON	700
2	ADAM MISENER	831	7	DEAN CURRY	606
3	WILLIAM DAVIES	726	8	RYAN HARDY	532
4	JUSTIN HOLMES	725	9	RALPH SIKES	532
5	BILLY MELENHORST	714	10	LARRY WOODWARD	503

PENNSYLVANIA TOP 10

1 DUANE HOWARD POINTS: 713

STARTS: *19* **WINS:** *9* **TOP 5:** *16* **TOP 10:** *19*

Duane Howard, of Oley, Pennsylvania, had nine wins and top-10 finishes in all 19 outings on his way to the state championship. In six seasons of crowning champions in the Keystone State, Duane has won three.

2-10

Pos	Driver Name	Track	Starts	Wins	T-5	T-10	Points
2	Doug Manmiller	Grandview	19	2	10	18	586
3	Craig Von Dohren	Grandview	19	0	8	17	526
4	Jeff Strunk	Grandview	19	1	11	16	521
5	Mike Gular	Grandview	19	0	6	13	452
6	Neil Brown	Motordrome	16	8	12	14	442
7	Garry Wiltrout	Lake Erie, Motordrome	18	2	8	16	400
8	Barry Awtey	Motordrome	16	1	13	15	395
9	George Skora III	Motordrome, Lake Erie	15	5	14	15	356
10	Steve Black	Motordrome	16	2	10	14	332

GRANDVIEW SPEEDWAY

87 Wilt Road/Bechtelsville, PA/19505 — (610) 754-7688 — www.grandviewspeedway.com

Saturday/.333 mile dirt

Modifieds
1	DUANE HOWARD	5514	
2	DOUG MANMILLER	4890	
3	CRAIG VON DOHREN	4573	
4	JEFF STRUNK	4527	
5	MIKE GULAR	4193	
6	MEME DESANTIS	3166	
7	KYLE WEISS	3121	
8	TERRY MEITZLER	3010	
9	RYAN GRIM	2934	
10	KEVIN HIRTHLER	2852	

Sportsman
1	JARED UMBENHAUER	4604
2	BRAD BRIGHTBILL	4452
3	CRAIG WHITMOYER	4155
4	DAVE DISSINGER	4033
5	PAUL KLINE	4021
6	JOE FUNK III	3909
7	KYLE BORROR	3786
8	BRIAN HIRTHLER	3631
9	BOBBY LILICK	3541
10	KEVIN BEACH	3463

Limited Late Model
1	CHUCK SCHUTZ JR.	5225
2	DANNY SNYDER	4864
3	RON KLINE	4766
4	JASON MILLER	4509
5	MIKE KELLNER	4376
6	RICK TODOROW	4248
7	KORY FLEMING	4235
8	STEVE NEDEROSTEK	4234
9	WAYNE PFEIL	4111
10	LOU EGRIE	4001

LAKE ERIE SPEEDWAY

10700 Delmas Drive/Erie, PA/16428 — (814) 725-3303 — www.lakeeriespeedway.com

Saturday/.375 mile asphalt

Late Model
1	GEORGE SKORA III	648
2	SAM FULLONE	610
3	JEFF BROWN JR.	497
4	SCOTT SKORA	464
5	GLENN GAULT JR.	335
6	RICHARD ARNDT	290
7	SCOTT WYLIE	232
8	JOHN GALLAGHER	216
9	DAVE HEITZHAUS	195
10	DAN LEWIS	172

Modified
1	DAVE MCAVOY	606
2	ERIC MCCRAY	580
3	RANDY CULVER	573
4	MIKE NEUBAUER	514
5	DENNIS HAGG JR.	492
6	CHRIS BRIGGS	485
7	CARTER MOOK	484
8	SCOTT WYLIE	469
9	DALE MURDOCK	450
10	JAMIE HEBNER	411

Street Stock
1	KAITY KICINSKI	707
2	DAVE KRAWCZYK	696
3	JOHN DENNY	656
4	RICH MILLER	624
5	CHRIS CROSSMAN	504
6	TRAVIS RAMMELT	499
7	ED MCCONNELL	484
8	VERN HEDDERICK	459
9	JACK HALL	453
10	TIM ARTHUR	444

Compact
1	DAN BITTINGER	816
2	JIM TOBIN	804
3	SHANE FORSTER	648
4	TJ COLBY	591
5	STEPHANIE AKERLY	576
6	BRIAN CARLSON	572
7	GARRETT RAMMELT	566
8	DOUG HADLEY	523
9	KYLE ROURKE	483
10	BOB MOORE	466

MOTORDROME SPEEDWAY

164 Motordrome Road/Smithton, PA/15479 — (724) 872-7555 — www.motordrome.com

Friday/.50 mile paved

Pro Late Model
1	NEIL BROWN	844
2	BARRY AWTEY	829
3	GARRY WILTROUT	808
4	STEVE BLACK	764
5	TEDDY GIBALA	663
6	MARK POOLE	651
7	JOHN KOMARINSKI	627
8	BOBBY HENRY	617
9	ADAM KOSTELNIK	568
10	SCOTT STERN	483

Modified
1	GEORGE P NICOLA	807
2	BILLY HRIBAR JR.	793
3	LOU BOTTI	693
4	BERNIE MCQUILLAN	606
5	JASON BUSCH	581
6	JOEY SCHOOL	562
7	DAN STAGGERS	562
8	JON SCOTT	534
9	TROY KNIGHT	519
10	VINCE KAIDER	297

Charger
1	JONATHAN HILEMAN	764
2	ZANE FERRELL	753
3	RON EIFORD III	728
4	ANTHONY AIELLO	715
5	JON SCOTT	705
6	ROGER BRYAN	657
7	JOE BALLOUGH	613
8	MARY CATHERINE SHIMKO	554
9	MIKE GEORGE	519
10	SCOTT HILEMAN	505

Street Stock
1	MATT SEVER JR.	842
2	SHAWN PHILLIPS	806
3	AJ POLJAK	800
4	DINK COLARUSSO	706
5	MIKE BAKALON	697
6	TERRY SCHWARTZ	583
7	BILL ASHTON	562
8	SCOTT AIELLO	560
9	ANDREW KOSTELNIK	548
10	GEORGE T NICOLA SR.	509

Super Compact
1	GREG STAGGERS	792
2	CHRIS KNIGHT	753
3	STEVE LONG	744
4	KYLE KOMARINSKI	703
5	JEREMY HILL	702
6	JESSICA KNIGHT	672
7	MARK TRINGES JR.	646
8	BRIAN NOEL	627
9	JOHN SYMSEK	596
10	STEPHEN SHELPMAN	579

SOUTH CAROLINA TOP 10

1 ANTHONY ANDERS POINTS: 581

STARTS: *29* **WINS:** *6* **TOP 5:** *23* **TOP 10:** *28*

With a pair of wins and top 10s in all 13 starts, Anthony Anders of Easley, South Carolina, drove to the top of the state standings.

2-10

Pos	Driver Name	Track	Starts	Wins	T-5	T-10	Points
2	Toby Porter	Greenville	21	13	20	21	458
3	Justin Milliken	Myrtle	13	3	8	12	413
4	Sam Yarbrough	Myrtle	13	3	9	12	403
5	Marty Ward Jr.	Greenville	21	4	20	20	386
6	Jeremy Mcdowell	Myrtle	13	3	9	9	341
7	Jamey Lee	Myrtle	13	0	7	11	338
8	Randall Roberts	Myrtle	13	0	1	7	250
9	Matt Cox	Myrtle	12	0	2	5	232
10	Greg Welborn	Myrtle, Greenville	16	0	1	14	220

GREENVILLE PICKENS SPEEDWAY
3800 Calhoun Memorial Hwy./Easley, SC/29640 — (864) 269-0852 — www.greenvillepickens.com **Saturday/.50 mile paved**

Late Model Stock
1 TOBY PORTER 1018
2 MARTY WARD JR. 968
3 ROBERT ROOT 724
4 ANTHONY ANDERS 716
5 TASHA KUMMER 670
6 RALPH CARNES 454
7 GREG WELBORN 392
8 JOEY COLLINS JR. 368
9 JEREMY BURNS 364
10 WILL BURNS 314

Charger
1 MIKE MOTE 970
2 JAMES JOHNSON 924
3 MICHAEL MOTE 878
4 ANDY NORRIS 818
5 DALE WALKER 724
6 ZACH PRESSLEY 668
7 TIM CROWE 558
8 BRYAN DAVIS 452
9 CHUCKIE GREER 426
10 DANNY GILBERT 356

Pure Stock
1 DAVID RADER 930
2 FREDDY HALE JR. 730
3 MARK GIBSON 670
4 FURMAN CRAFT 548
5 TYLER GIBSON 542
6 KIRK GIBSON 398
7 DYLAN CROWE 226
8 MITCH BARRETT 130
9 CODY HILL 88
10 JD GRIFFITH 46

Sportsman
1 RYAN WALKER 988
2 MICHAEL ALTOP 826
3 TIM LOLLIS 768
4 GENE BURNETT 574
5 RANDY BALLEW II 466
6 CHRIS CHASTAIN 464
7 JAMIE ALTOP 292
8 JON MARTIN 198
9 JAMIE TATE 50
10 RICHARD LAINO 44

Renegades
1 KYLE BALLEW 980
2 TRAVIS COX 918
3 JEREMY DRUMMOND 864
4 DANIEL JAMESON 792
5 BRAD BURNS 788
6 BOBBY EMORY JR. 750
7 SCOTTY TYNER 744
8 BRANDON FOX 580
9 DALE STANCIL JR. 530
10 ANDREW CORDELL 424

4 Cylinder
1 JAMES MADDEN 688
2 ROBERT FLOYD 680
3 TOMMY DAVIS 674
4 RAY MULLINAX 642
5 BUCK SIMMONS 612
6 AUSTIN HEIL 558
7 DANNY HEIL 526
8 DAVID RADER 432
9 CHAD TAVERNIA 384
10 SARA MADDEN 384

MYRTLE BEACH SPEEDWAY
455 Hospitality Lane/Myrtle Beach, SC/29579 — (843) 236-0500 — www.myrtlebeachspeedway.com **Saturday/.50 mile paved**

Late Model
1 ANTHONY ANDERS 450
2 JUSTIN MILLIKEN 429
3 SAM YARBROUGH 417
4 JEREMY MCDOWELL 355
5 JAMEY LEE 352
6 RANDALL ROBERTS 270
7 MATT COX 234
8 STUART RICKS 220
9 BRIAN VAUSE 214
10 JAKE ENGLE 194

Mini Stock
1 MICHAEL MCKINNON 220
2 ADAM FULFORD 167
3 WILLIE FULFORD 133
4 ERIC MCKINNON 92
5 DUB FULFORD JR. 87
6 RANDY HEWETT 86
7 KEVIN JACKSON 85
8 GARY FULFORD 72
9 BAILEY MILES 62
10 DAVID WARD 54

Charger
1 MARK HALE 207
2 KEVIN BARNHILL 169
3 LUCAS WILLIAMS JR. 151
4 ERIC JOYNER 110
5 JOE ARMAKOVITCH 108
6 ED RAY 58
7 BRIAN NOBLIN 54
8 SCOTT BUFF 48
9 CAMERON HARRINGTON 28
10 DAN BRYANT 28

TENNESSEE TOP 10

1 NATE  MONTEITH POINTS: 726

STARTS: *20* **WINS:** *10* **TOP 5:** *18* **TOP 10:** *18*

Nate Monteith of Blountville, Tennessee, captured his second consecutive Tennessee state crown with 10 wins, 10 poles and 18 top fives in 20 events. As well, he finished fourth in the national standings this year.

2-10

Pos	Driver Name	Track	Starts	Wins	T-5	T-10	Points
2	Zeke Shell	Kingsport	20	2	11	16	562
3	Paul Nogradi Jr.	Kingsport	20	1	8	14	507
4	Lee Tissot	Kingsport	19	1	11	12	475
5	Blake Jones	Kingsport	16	0	7	14	446
6	Anthony Anders	Myrtle, Greenville, Kingsport	16	0	8	14	446
7	Ryan Stiltner	Kingsport	20	0	5	16	442
8	Daniel Pope II	Kingsport	14	3	9	11	395
9	Austin Peters	Kingsport	20	0	0	12	390
10	Hayden Woods	Kingsport	20	0	3	11	388

NASCAR HOME TRACKS

KINGSPORT SPEEDWAY

2961 N. John B. Dennis Highway/Kingsport, TN/37660 — (423) 817-0925 — www.newkingsportspeedway.com **Friday/.333 mile concrete**

Late Model

1	NATE MONTEITH	539	6	AUSTIN PETERS	412
2	ZEKE SHELL	489	7	ROYCE PETERS	407
3	PAUL NOGRADI JR.	467	8	HAYDEN WOODS	406
4	RYAN STILTNER	432	9	ANTHONY ANDERS	389
5	LEE TISSOT	431	10	BLAKE JONES	388

Pure 4

1	JOHN KETRON	449	6	GLENN HUGHES	336
2	JASON KETRON	447	7	JEREMY HUGHES	325
3	CHRIS NEELEY	434	8	KENNY ABSHER	298
4	KEITH HELTON	394	9	BILLY KETRON	288
5	DAVE TRENT	348	10	TODD CROSS	263

Street Stock

1	ROGER NEECE	438	6	PAUL SHULL	271
2	ROB AUSTIN	409	7	RICK SMITH	242
3	CHRIS TUNNELL	363	8	JOHN HARRELL	210
4	JARED BROADBENT	355	9	ROBY ORR	203
5	TONY WARD	338	10	TONY VANCE	186

Division IV

1	JIMMY HILLARD	468	6	DANNY PLESS	274
2	TIM ABELSETH	430	7	AUSTIN GRAY	251
3	ROBIN HUGHES	421	8	LEE SHULTZ	163
4	DYLAN BATES	405	9	PIE SHORT	162
5	TAMMY CROSS	327			

TEXAS TOP 10

1 JOE ARAMENDIA   POINTS: 553

STARTS: 27 WINS: 18 TOP 5: 25 TOP 10: 26

With a 216-point advantage in the standings, the highest margin of victory in 2012, Joe Aramendia of Seguin, Texas, regained his perch atop the state standings with 18 wins and 25 top fives in 27 starts. A dual-track champion this year, this is Joe's fourth Lone Star state title in the last five seasons.

2-10

Pos	Driver Name	Track	Starts	Wins	T-5	T-10	Points
2	Bayley Currey	Thunderhill, Houston	25	3	13	19	337
3	Brad Queen	Houston	12	1	9	10	323
4	Brian Moczygemba	Thunderhill, Houston	25	0	13	21	322
5	Paul White	Houston	12	1	7	11	319
6	Ian Webster	Houston	14	1	6	10	277
7	Larry Schild III	Houston	11	0	7	8	248
8	Jason Morman	Houston, Thunderhill	14	0	3	7	234
9	JT Schild	Houston	14	0	1	7	190
10	Jason Boyd	Houston	9	0	2	7	188

HOUSTON MOTORSPORTS PARK

11620 North Lake Houston Parkway/Houston, TX/77044 — (281) 458-1972 — www.houstonmotorsportspark.com **Saturday/.375 mile asphalt/concrete**

Modified

1	JOE ARAMENDIA	460	6	BAYLEY CURREY	286
2	BRAD QUEEN	360	7	LARRY SCHILD III	273
3	PAUL WHITE	344	8	JASON MORMAN	256
4	BRIAN MOCZYGEMBA	309	9	JASON BOYD	211
5	IAN WEBSTER	292	10	JT SCHILD	211

Division 360 Trucks

1	MASON TEAGUE	604	6	JIM NIDES	439
2	KYLE BOOKS	556	7	JUSTIN-PAUL STEINER	394
3	MICHAEL KOURKOUBES	500	8	SEAN-MICHAEL STEINER	391
4	LYNN HARDY JR.	452	9	CHRIS DAVID	343
5	CARY STAPP	445	10	KEVIN WISEMAN	323

Stock Cars

1	DAVID WEBSTER	383	6	BJ ATCHISON	150
2	NATHAN DEMSKI	273	7	LYNN HARDY JR.	144
3	DAVID COBB	248	8	MIKE MOGENSEN	123
4	DALE DEMSKI	211	9	ERIK OLSZEWSKI	106
5	TRAVIS ELLIOTT	171	10	LORI LINDLEY	105

ODESSA CHAMPION MOTOR SPEEDWAY

12300 West Highway 80 East/Odessa, TX/79762 — (432) 563-1715 — www.championmotorspeedway.com **Saturday/.375 mile dirt**

Modified

1	TRENT CRAWFORD	518	6	KENNETH GRAVES	203
2	HUNTER RUSSELL	457	7	YOGI THATCH	164
3	RONNIE SEBREE	337	8	PHILIP HOUSTON	143
4	VERL KENYON	251	9	JIM THORP	66
5	ERIC HUGHES	235	10	CALEB STONE	38

Street Stock

1	RYAN WILKERSON	570	6	DALTON RILEY	269
2	RANDY MADRY	502	7	RUSSELL MASEY	234
3	FRANK MORGAN	452	8	CLINT PELZEL	216
4	BRIAN SPANN	362	9	JOHN JACKSON	216
5	BRIAN COMER	291	10	CODY TODD	203

Sport Modified

1	CHANCE MCDANIEL	563	6	TIM RIDGEWAY	285
2	WILL POSTON	491	7	MICHAEL MARASCHICK	272
3	JEREMY TEMPLETON	346	8	RJ FRANTZ	237
4	RICKEY BEARD	344	9	JOHN ROSS	235
5	DERIK ROYS	331	10	CALIN ROYS	217

IStock

1	LEWIS HAMMOND	521	6	WILLIE FREE	232
2	JACK MILES	495	7	CARY WHITE	216
3	LP O'NEAL	400	8	STEVE EMMONS	196
4	HUNTER RUSSELL	362	9	TONY FISHER	170
5	GARY KERR JR.	302	10	KENNETH GRAVES	162

Dwarf

1	KELVIN CHANDLER	269	6	JOE JACKSON	141
2	EDDIE TEMPLETON	240	7	JERRY JACKSON	136
3	TERRY MCCREERY	213	8	ROCH BELLAMY	107
4	DARREN AKIN	212	9	GARY JACKSON	100
5	JJ JACKSON	171	10	RICKY WINKS	71

Hobby Stock

1	JR PATMAN	537	6	JILL CODY THOMPSON	276
2	EDDIE JOHNSON	532	7	STEVE EMMONS	274
3	SHELBY JONES	476	8	CHRIS SEPEDA	208
4	JAMES KEMP	364	9	WARREN GRAVES	205
5	BRANDON ROSS	279	10	LEE RILEY	168

NASCAR HOME TRACKS

THUNDERHILL RACEWAY
24801 IH – 35/Kyle, TX/78640 — (512) 507-1486 — www.thunderhillraceway.com

Saturday/.375 mile paved

Modified

1	JOE ARAMENDIA	206	6	ROBERT WALTON	36
2	HEATH STEWART	107	7	DILLON SPREEN	28
3	BAYLEY CURREY	81	8	BRAD NAUMANN	26
4	BRIAN MOCZYGEMBA	56	9	MICHAEL UMSCHEID	25
5	TODD MCLEMORE	44	10	BRUCE BEDDOE	24

Super Stock

1	TRACY TSCHOERNER	158	6	JOEY TSCHOERNER	54
2	TOMMY GURAL	140	7	PAUL WATSON	32
3	BRANDON SPREEN	131	8	MICKEY MCKIM	20
4	ARDEN SMITH	113	9	TERRY TSCHOERNER	19
5	MATT GOULAIS	64	10	DAN DECKER	16

Late Model

1	BRIAN MOCZYGEMBA	176	6	HEATHER ABLES	38
2	BOBBY TEER JR.	152	7	JOHN HERNANDEZ	26
3	MIKE REININGER	101	8	RICK POLLARO	24
4	LOGAN BEARDEN	97	9	MICHAEL POLLARO	24
5	KENNETH HURLEY	69	10	ROBERT BARKER	20

Trucks

1	MASON TEAGUE	156	6	RICK POLLARO	79
2	ROBERT STEWART	122	7	CARY STAPP	54
3	JEFF O'NEILL	119	8	BRYON REED	51
4	SHAWN LEHMAN	104	9	JIM ALBERT	39
5	JOEY JENKINS	100	10	MARK CHRUDIMSKY	36

VERMONT TOP 10

1 RON PROCTOR POINTS: 479

STARTS: 18 **WINS:** 3 **TOP 5:** 12 **TOP 10:** 18

Ron Proctor of Charlton, New York, had three wins as well as top 10s in all 18 starts to secure the state title in Vermont. This is his second championship in a row.

2-10

Pos	Driver Name	Track	Starts	Wins	T-5	T-10	Points
2	Vince Quenneville	Devil's Bowl	18	5	11	15	451
3	Leon Gonyo	Devil's Bowl	18	1	11	16	409
4	Jessey Mueller	Devil's Bowl	18	2	10	15	408
5	Joe Roberts	Devil's Bowl	18	1	11	17	399
6	Hunter Bates	Devil's Bowl	18	2	9	14	386
7	Alex Bell	Devil's Bowl	18	3	8	13	381
8	Cody Sargen	Devil's Bowl	18	0	3	12	294
9	Jeff Haskins	Devil's Bowl	18	0	1	12	286
10	Jamie Proctor	Devil's Bowl	18	0	3	12	268

DEVIL'S BOWL SPEEDWAY
2743 Route 22A/West Haven, VT/05743 — (802) 265-3112 — www.devilsbowlspeedwayvt.com

Friday/.50 mile paved

Division Modified

1	RON PROCTOR	898	6	ALEX BELL	806
2	VINCE QUENNEVILLE	865	7	HUNTER BATES	790
3	JESSEY MUELLER	828	8	CODY SARGEN	688
4	LEON GONYO	823	9	JAMIE PROCTOR	685
5	JOEY ROBERTS	810	10	JEFF HASKINS	677

Renegade

1	ROBERT GORDON	868	6	ROBIN CUMMINGS	215
2	RYAN KEITH	850	7	BOB MONROE	156
3	JEREMY JONES	661	8	RANDY MILLER	79
4	BILL DUPREY	658	9	LANCE RABTOY	52
5	FRANK MONROE	385	10	RICK DONER	39

Late Model

1	CRAIG BUSHEY	751	6	ROBERT BRYANT JR.	571
2	MATT WHITE	684	7	NORM ANDREWS	488
3	BRYAN TOWN	675	8	JESSE CARRIS	355
4	DAN PETRONIS II	638	9	JOHNNY CHESTNUT	346
5	KEVIN ELLIOTT	628	10	JOEY LAQUERRE	322

Bomber

1	JOSH MASTERSON	861	6	GARRETT GIVEN	593
2	BOBBY LAVAIR	796	7	DAN COLLINS	585
3	RAY GERMAIN	787	8	MATT MONAGHAN	533
4	HAROLD LAVAIR JR.	752	9	JOHN MCCARRON	500
5	GERALD LAFLAM	639	10	JAKE NOBLE	439

VIRGINIA TOP 10

1 LEE PULLIAM POINTS: 776

STARTS: 25 **WINS:** 19 **TOP 5:** 23 **TOP 10:** 24

With 17 wins and 23 top fives in 25 starts, Lee Pulman of Semora, North Carolina, secured his first Virginia state title.

2-10

Pos	Driver Name	Track	Starts	Wins	T-5	T-10	Points
2	C E Falk III	S Boston, Langley, Motor Mile	23	14	20	22	700
3	Tommy Lemons Jr.	Motor Mile, S Boston	22	2	15	17	606
4	Matt Bowling	Langley, Motor Mile, S Boston	29	2	19	27	602
5	Josh Berry	Motor Mile	18	1	15	17	601
6	Frank Deiny Jr.	S Boston, Motor Mile	19	1	12	17	581
7	Peyton Sellers	S Boston, Motor Mile, Langley	23	3	14	20	557
8	Greg Edwards	S Boston, Langley	17	2	14	16	496
9	David Polenz	Motor Mile, S Boston, Old Dominion	22	3	14	17	457
10	Wes Falk	Langley, Motor Mile, S Boston	21	1	13	14	457

NASCAR HOME TRACKS

LANGLEY SPEEDWAY

3165 North Armistead Ave./Hampton, VA/23666 — (757) 865-7223 — www.langley-speedway.com

Saturday/.396 mile paved

Late Model
1	GREG EDWARDS	382	6	DANNY EDWARDS JR.	306
2	WES FALK	365	7	MARK WERTZ	287
3	SHAYNE LOCKHART	331	8	JEFF SHIFLETT	286
4	CASEY WYATT	330	9	TERRY CARROLL	253
5	C E FALK III	320	10	DUANE SHREEVES	250

Grand Stock
1	RICKY DERRICK	338	6	ANDREW CONDREY	242
2	TOMMY SWEENEY	303	7	RODNEY BOYD	231
3	PAUL LUBNO	286	8	CARL LIVINGSTON	231
4	MARK CLAAR SR.	279	9	SHAWN SCOVEL	223
5	MARK FRYE	251	10	MICHAEL WATERS	219

Super Truck
1	ROBBIE DAVIS	275	6	CHASE MCADAMS	211
2	TROY TURNAGE	269	7	JACOB CARR	192
3	THOMAS NIXON JR.	260	8	BILL WALLACE	190
4	CHRIS BECHTEL	219	9	CHRIS MUNGER	154
5	BUCK MUNGER	212	10	CORY MILLARD	144

Modified
1	SHAWN BALLUZZO	403	6	CAMERON PATRICK	304
2	MIKE RUDY	386	7	DANNY HARRELL	292
3	ANTHONY KINCAID	363	8	TODD VANGUILDER	192
4	MATT SLYE	336	9	CASEY WYATT	180
5	ROBERT BABB	327	10	CURTIS HUGHES	178

Super Street
1	RENNO MARCHETTI IV	285	6	SEAN CALWAY	236
2	JOHN PEREIRA	280	7	LARRY VENABLE	221
3	DALE PARRO	271	8	THOMAS WILSON	193
4	RYAN NESTER	271	9	JERRY LAMONTAGNE	107
5	ROD BUSITZKY	249	10	JORDAN WOOD	103

MOTOR MILE SPEEDWAY

6749 Lee Highway/Radford, VA/24141 — (540) 639-1700 — www.motormilespeedway.com

Saturday/.416 mile paved

Late Model Stock Car
1	JOSH BERRY	666	6	DERRICK LANCASTER	424
2	FRANK DEINY JR.	634	7	CHAD HARRIS	360
3	LEE PULLIAM	561	8	RUSTY SKEWES	338
4	TOMMY LEMONS JR.	528	9	JONATHAN SMITH	310
5	MIKE LOONEY	452	10	QUIN HOUFF	300

Mod-4
1	ROCKY YATES	184	6	DREW HOLDREN	90
2	DOODLE LANG III	148	7	TED HAMB	60
3	CHARLES WILLIAMS	140	8	HAILEY HOLDREN	46
4	DENNIS SLOAN JR.	126	9	WAYNE CORPREW	44
5	BRITTANY COCKRAM	96	10	KEVIN KENLEY	36

Limited Sportsman
1	PRESTON MCGHEE	348	6	GARRETT BUNCH JR.	266
2	SCOTT LANCASTER	335	7	BRYAN REEDY	246
3	MATT TAYLOR	321	8	STEVEN WEEKS	204
4	KARL BUDZEVSKI	312	9	TRAVIS HURT	172
5	KYLE DUDLEY	296	10	KYLE BARNES	156

Street Stock
1	BARRY GREGORY	140	6	TIM HALE	52
2	JERRY HOLLANDSWORTH	128	7	MATTHEW GUSLER	50
3	DR. SHERYL CARLS	128	8	CHAD CONNER	38
4	JESSICA HARMAN	70	9	TONY VANCE	30
5	BRENT BELL	56	10	DUSTIN WALKER	22

OLD DOMINION SPEEDWAY

10611 Dumfries Road/Manassas, VA/20112 — (703) 361-7753 — www.olddominionspeedway.com

Saturday/.375 mile paved

Late Model
1	DOUG LIBERMAN	395	6	ROBERT BRUCE	281
2	DAVID POLENZ	381	7	RICHARD STORM	226
3	TYLER HUGHES	355	8	MIKE DARNE	223
4	DAVEY CALLIHAN	318	9	DAVE MOON	188
5	MICHAEL HARDIN	286	10	PAUL GREEN	158

U Cars
1	SCOTT GORE	261	6	DAVID GONCE	208
2	STEVE BRADY	250	7	JESSIE POLENZ	177
3	CRAIG OGLEVEE	240	8	MIKE WEBB JR.	162
4	NATHAN BRASZ	237	9	RUSTY POLAND	122
5	MARCUS LAMBERT	224	10	JEFF BUDWASH	117

Mini Mod
1	KEITH RILEY	126	6	MORGAN DUNCAN	50
2	MIKE CARTE	123	7	KEVIN DAVIS	44
3	TODD JOHNSTON	86	8	SKYLAR FELKNER	37
4	BOBBY ABLE JR.	58	9	NICK JOHNSTON	36
5	LARRY FUCHS JR.	54	10	DAVID REID	28

Mad Mod
1	TANNER RUMBURG	66	6	MARK CROPP	28
2	HUNTER SLAYTON	58	7	MARTY HANBURY	26
3	ROBERT CONNER	57	8	TANNER AMAN	24
4	JOE SCARBROUGH	44	9	LAUREN EDGERTON	16
5	JIMMY HUMBLET	32	10	CHRIS HUMBLET	14

SOUTH BOSTON SPEEDWAY

1188 James D Hagood Highway/South Boston, VA/24592 — (434) 572-4947 — www.southbostonspeedway.com

Saturday/.40 mile asphalt

Late Model
1	MATT BOWLING	531	6	RONALD HILL	308
2	PEYTON SELLERS	513	7	BRUCE ANDERSON JR.	272
3	LEE PULLIAM	441	8	JEB BURTON	229
4	AUSTIN THAXTON	424	9	TOMMY PEREGOY	222
5	DENNIS HOLDREN	368	10	JOSH OAKLEY	209

Mad Modified
1	HUNTER SLAYTON	146	6	LAUREN EDGERTON	51
2	JAMES HUMBLET	86	7	MICHAEL JOHNSON	48
3	KYLE WOOD	74	8	MIKE RUDY	41
4	TANNER RUMBURG	70	9	JOE SCARBROUGH	34
5	ROBERT CONNER	60	10	JOSEPH OVERSTREET	34

Limited Sportsman
1	BOBBY MCCARTY	349	6	CHARLES BARNES	150
2	DANNY WILLIS JR.	328	7	TOMMY PEREGOY	147
3	BLAKE STALLINGS	276	8	DANIEL MOSS	126
4	MIKE JONES JR.	252	9	G R WALDROP	98
5	MIKE MARESCA JR.	228	10	CHRIS THROCKMORTON	74

Pure Stock
1	TREY CREWS III	434	6	BRUCE MAYO	236
2	JOE ALLRED III	395	7	ERIC CREWS	234
3	RANDY HUPP	370	8	COURTNEY CROSBY	214
4	STUART CREWS	282	9	LIBBY PRIVETTE	194
5	JAKE BROWN	280	10	DANIEL CREWS	189

NASCAR HOME TRACKS

WASHINGTON TOP 10

1 NAIMA LANG POINTS: 374

STARTS: *12* **WINS:** *4* **TOP 5:** *8* **TOP 10:** *11*

Naima Lang of Lynwood, Washington, won the state championship on the strength of four wins and 11 top 10s in 12 outings. This is the fourth time in the last five years that Naima has represented the state of Washington as champion.

2-10

Pos	Driver Name	Track	Starts	Wins	T-5	T-10	Points
2	Kelly Mann	Evergreen	12	2	8	9	302
3	Andy Sole	Evergreen	12	0	6	11	296
4	Doni Wanat	Evergreen	12	0	5	9	264
5	Jeff Knight	Evergreen	12	1	4	8	251
6	Daniel Moore	Evergreen	11	1	5	7	241
7	Doug Davidson	Evergreen	11	0	3	7	220
8	Tom Hughs	Evergreen	10	1	4	6	215
9	Molly Helmuth	Evergreen	11	0	2	7	208
10	John Lathrop Jr.	Evergreen	12	0	0	3	150

EVERGREEN SPEEDWAY

14405 179th Avenue Southeast Building 305/Monroe, WA/98272 — (360) 805-6100 — www.evergreenspeedway.com   **Saturday/.375 and .625 mile paved**

Super Late Model

1	NAIMA LANG	532	6	DANIEL MOORE	400
2	ANDY SOLE	470	7	DOUG DAVIDSON	384
3	KELLY MANN	468	8	MOLLY HELMUTH	362
4	DONI WANAT	440	9	TOM HUGHS	338
5	JEFF KNIGHT	420	10	JOHN LATHROP JR.	326

Mini Stock

1	JON ROBERTS	657	6	TRAVIS WOODWARD	491
2	MICHAEL FRITZ	578	7	MIKE HESSLER	487
3	ANDREW SCHUKAR	575	8	DEVIN KESSLER	446
4	CHUCK RICHARD	520	9	MARK CREAGER	375
5	NAT BARBER	509	10	SCOTT BURBY	308

Street Stocks

1	FRANK COWGILL	643	6	JEFF MILLER	546
2	STEVE PTACEK	608	7	DARREL LUTOVSKY	449
3	KENNY ERICKSON	589	8	SCOTT GIEBEL	421
4	JIM FOTI	584	9	ERIC GIMMAKA	380
5	TIM WIDENER	561	10	NIKKI BRISTOL	323

Super Figure Eight

1	JAKE REPIN	525	6	SETH FUNDEN	319
2	STEVE PETERS	495	7	MIKE MIDDLETON	286
3	QUENTON BORRESON	364	8	PATRICK CLARK	225
4	GREG SCOTT	353	9	STEVE SCHOENFELDT	206
5	BRIAN GUNDERSON	341	10	RYAN GUNDERSON	195

WISCONSIN TOP 10

1 TODD KORISH POINTS: 558

STARTS: *17* **WINS:** *0* **TOP 5:** *12* **TOP 10:** *17*

Todd Korish of Holmen, Wisconsin, tallied top-10 finishes in all 17 of his outings to win the Wisconsin State Championship.

2-10

Pos	Driver Name	Track	Starts	Wins	T-5	T-10	Points
2	Shawn Pfaff	Lacrosse	17	0	12	17	552
3	J Herbst	Lacrosse	17	4	12	14	528
4	Brent Kirchner	Lacrosse	17	2	8	16	524
5	Bradley Powell	Lacrosse	17	3	8	13	477
6	Mike Carlson	Lacrosse	17	0	6	11	440
7	Matthew Henderson	Lacrosse	17	0	7	12	438
8	Adam Degenhardt	Lacrosse	15	1	4	14	415
9	Cole Howland	Lacrosse	17	2	3	9	412
10	Steve Carlson	Lacrosse	12	3	9	10	387

CEDAR LAKE SPEEDWAY

2275 County Road CC/New Richmond, WI/54017 — (715) 248-7719 — www.cedarlakespeedway.com   **Saturday/.375 mile dirt**

Midwest Modified

1	BRENT LARSON	364	6	PAT DOAR	186
2	RICK HANESTAD	333	7	GREG NIPPOLDT	186
3	CHAD MAHDER	293	8	RICK EGERSDORF	186
4	JOHN KAANTA	280	9	JIM CARLSON	178
5	STEVE LAURSEN	275	10	MIKE NUTZMANN	160

Midwest Modified

1	RYAN OLSON	350	6	DOUGLAS TOEPPER	164
2	JOSH BAZEY	268	7	CODY WOLKOWSKI	150
3	SCOTT SPLITTSTOESSER	198	8	ERIC HERBISON	138
4	JEREMY HOULE	171	9	JORDAN HESSLER	132
5	TONY SCHILL	164	10	DAVID SWEARINGEN	122

Division II

1	BRENT LARSON	279	6	JAKE MILLER	130
2	JASON GROSS	250	7	CORY WILLIAMS	118
3	CRAIG THATCHER	241	8	RICK KOBS	113
4	SCOTT SPLITTSTOESSER	178	9	SCOTT DUVAL	111
5	BRANDON JENSEN	171	10	DOUG GUSTAFSON	110

Pro Stocks

1	CORY DAVIS	251	6	LARRY FITZSIMMONS	156
2	ADAM AYOTTE	219	7	MIKE WEBER	150
3	CODY CAMPEAU	186	8	SHAWN KAMMERUD	131
4	MIKE MUELLER	185	9	MIKE HESSELINK	124
5	RICH BISHOP	176	10	JEFF HEINTZ	123

LACROSSE FAIRGROUNDS SPEEDWAY

N4985 County Rd /West Salem, WI/54669 — (608) 786-1525 — www.lacrossespeedway.com   **Saturday/0.545 and .25 mile paved**

Late Models

1	TODD KORISH	856	6	MIKE CARLSON	686
2	SHAWN PFAFF	838	7	MATTHEW HENDERSON	685
3	BRENT KIRCHNER	821	8	COLE HOWLAND	648
4	J HERBST	799	9	STEVE CARLSON	644
5	BRAD POWELL	793	10	ADAM DEGENHARDT	635

Thunderstox

1	TOM LUETHE	1089	6	DAVID CAVIN	1009
2	DAKOTA MILLER	1086	7	JACINDA PFAFF	954
3	JORDAN MYERS	1052	8	MARK CHALLET	924
4	JASON BOLSTER	1041	9	BERT YOUNG	908
5	NATHAN WHITE	1019	10	ADAM MOORE	842

Sportsman

1	RANDY HUMFELD	867	6	STEVE BACHMAN	652
2	GREG SCHECK	841	7	JACK LITSHEIM	635
3	JAKE ARNESON	824	8	BILL MARTIN	626
4	MATT INGLETT	809	9	BRIAN HESSELBERG	601
5	AARON HASS	691	10	JERROD LOGING	577

NASCAR HOME TRACKS

ANDER VILARINO

EURO RACECAR, NASCAR TOURING SERIES 2012 CHAMPION

PERSONAL INFORMATION

Birth Date:	**November 6, 1979**
Hometown:	**San Sebastián, Spain**
2012 Team:	**No. 2 TFT-Banco Santander**
	Chevrolet Camaro
Car Owner:	**Ander Vilarino**

CAREER RECORD

Year	Races	Wins	Top 5s	Top 10s
2012	12	6	9	12
Totals	**12**	**6**	**9**	**12**

The partnership between EURO RACECAR and NASCAR had not yet been forged when Ander Vilarino first set his sights on a NASCAR title.

In October 2011 at the Finals of the EURO RACECAR, NASCAR Touring Series in Le Mans, France, Vilarino triumphed on the Bugatti circuit and, along with his TFT-Banco Santander Chevrolet team, began plotting a course for the 2012 championship. For the Spaniard, only one outcome would suffice – to enter the history books as the inaugural EURO RACECAR, NASCAR Touring Series champion.

Fast forward to October 2012 when Le Mans, again, proved a happy hunting ground for the driver from San Sebastian in Spain's Basque Country. In the same town where his racing career began 16 years earlier, Vilarino fulfilled his goal by claiming the coveted crown after a season in which he led the standings wire-to-wire while fending off challenges from Romain Thievin and Javier Villa.

He dominated the season-opening Nogaro 200 in France by securing pole position and wins in both the Sprint and Endurance competitions. A third consecutive victory came in the Sprint portion of Great Britain's Brands Hatch 200 followed up with a runner-up finish in the Endurance race. He won again at the Spa 200 in Belgium and twice more at the Semi-Finals in Valencia, Spain. With the exception of his conservative showing at the Le Mans Finals, Vilarino outscored his rivals at every circuit, including the Tours Speedway Oval – Europe's first NASCAR-sanctioned oval-track event.

On the season, Vilarino amassed six victories, five pole wins, nine top-five and 12 top-10 finishes.

EURO RACECAR, NASCAR TOURING SERIES 2012 RUNNERS UP

2ND
ROMAIN THIEVIN

Romain Thievin was in the hunt for the inaugural EURO RACECAR, NASCAR Touring Series championship right up to the final race. Despite not collecting a win this season, his consistency with 10 top-five and 12 top-10 finishes kept him alive before losing out to Ander Vilarino by just 16 points.

3RD
JAVIER VILLA

Javier Villa claimed the series' Junior Trophy that is designated for drivers under 25 years of age. As the de facto Rookie of the Year, he picked up an endurance victory at Great Britain's Brands Hatch Circuit. He also scored eight top-five and nine top-10 finishes.

OPEN DIVISION

OPEN-DIVISION CHAMPION
SIMON ESCALLIER

Simon Escallier dominated the Open Division en route to the championship. The 23-year-old collected five wins, seven top fives and seven 10s in 12 starts. He also had two poles. Escallier swept the Sprint and Endurance events at the Ricardo Tormo circuit in Valencia, Spain. Driving for No. 19 Racing Club Partners, Escallier paired with Elite Division driver Stephane Romecki.

RUNNER-UP
ALAIN GRAND

Alain Grand finished second in the Open Division and collected the Legends trophy, given to the top Open driver 50-years-old and older. The Frenchman had six top fives and 10 top 10s in 12 starts. He also paired with Fournillier to finish third in the team championship with the No. 11 Overdrive-McDonald's team.

ELITE DIVISION CHAMPIONSHIP SEASON 2012 FINAL

Pos.	No.	Drivers	Points	Diff.	Poles	Victories	Top 5	Top 10
1	2	Ander Vilarino	667	Leader	2	6	9	12
2	99	Romain Thievin	651	-16	1	0	10	12
3	64	Javier Villa	603	-64	2	1	8	9
4	5	Antoine Lioen	567	-100	0	0	6	9
5	25	Romain Iannetta	566	-101	0	1	6	8
6	17	Wilfried Boucenna	563	-104	0	0	6	9
7	11	Romain Fournillier	548	-119	1	0	2	10
8	6	Anthony Garbarino	528	-139	0	0	0	7
9	44	Freddy Nordstrom	512	-155	0	0	1	7
10	55	Bruno Cosin	483	-184	0	0	1	3
11	22	Stéphane Jaggi	461	-206	0	0	0	1
12	46	Nathalie Maillet	445	-222	0	0	0	2
13	15	Vincent Gonneau	431	-236	0	0	0	3
14	100	Stéphane Sabates	398	-269	0	0	0	0
15	28	Franck Violas	372	-295	0	0	0	0
16	42	Carole Perrin	367	-300	0	0	1	3
17	14	Jospeh Cozzella	331	-336	0	0	0	0
18	33	Dimitri Enjalbert	272	-395	0	0	2	6
19	88	Valentin Simonet	218	-449	0	0	0	1
20	18	Yann Zimmer	201	-466	0	0	1	2
21	88	Olivier Pernaut	181	-486	0	0	0	0
22	7	Harry Vaulkhard	178	-489	0	0	0	2
23	85	Nicolas Gaudin	164	-503	0	0	0	0
24	18	James Winslow	104	-563	0	0	2	2
25	14	Grégory Guilvert	77	-590	0	0	1	2
26	7	Manu Brigand	69	-598	0	0	0	1
27	38	Martin Van Hove	58	-609	0	0	0	1
28	81	Niall Quinn	50	-617	0	0	0	0
29	81	Joao Teixeira	25	-642	0	0	0	0
30	48	Nigel Greensall	24	-643	0	0	0	0
31	6	Gaël Castelli	0	-667	0	2	2	2
32	96	Ben Kennedy	0	-667	0	1	1	1
33	14	Eric Helary	0	-667	0	1	1	1
34	100	Yvan Muller	0	-667	0	1	1	1
35	19	Stéphane Romecki	0	-667	0	0	1	3
36	29	Nicolas Dekejser	0	-667	0	0	1	2
37	33	Azor Duenas	0	-667	0	0	0	1
38	81	Didier Lescos	0	-667	0	0	0	0
39	33	Frederic Johais	0	-667	0	0	0	0

OPEN-DIVISION CHAMPIONSHIP SEASON 2012 FINAL

Pos.	No.	Drivers	Points	Diff.	Poles	Victories	Top 5	Top 10
1	19	Simon Escallier	617	Leader	2	5	7	7
2	11	Alain Grand	573	-44	0	0	6	10
3	25	Gérald Cormon	567	-50	0	0	5	8
4	15	Vincent Gonneau	554	-63	1	3	6	8
5	5	Joaquin Gabarron	554	-63	0	0	4	9
6	44	Tanguy Ide	549	-68	0	0	7	9
7	99	David Perisset	524	-93	0	0	1	7
8	22	Léonard Vernet	521	-96	0	0	2	5
9	100	Stéphane Sabates	500	-117	0	0	1	4
10	33	Vito Rodrigues	457	-160	0	0	0	3
11	28	Franck Violas	455	-162	0	0	1	4
12	14	Joseph Cozzella	451	-166	0	0	0	2
13	46	Christophe De Fierlant	441	-176	0	0	1	3
14	55	Jérôme Laurin	439	-178	0	0	1	6
15	2	Eric Quintal	437	-180	0	0	1	6
16	88	Philippe Marie	391	-226	1	0	4	4
17	17	Philippe Baudiniere	339	-278	0	0	0	2
18	38	Martin Van Hove	232	-385	1	2	4	4
19	42	Zihara Esteban	192	-425	0	0	0	1
20	42	Adriano Medeiros	156	-461	0	1	2	3
21	85	Jack Gaudin	151	-466	0	0	0	1
22	29	Neil Tressler	117	-500	0	0	0	0
23	6	Ben Anderson	81	-536	0	0	2	2
24	64	Cedric Deman	71	-546	0	0	0	1
25	64	Pascal Renaudat	71	-546	0	0	1	1
26	7	Jean Luc Zajfert	68	-549	0	0	0	1
27	88	Eric Van De Vyver	65	-552	0	0	0	1
28	21	Stéphane Enout	62	-555	0	0	0	1
29	81	Enzo Pastor	58	-559	0	0	0	1
30	7	Nigel Vaulkhard	57	-560	0	0	0	0
31	48	Eric Menini	51	-566	0	0	0	0
32	42	Bertrand Migout	50	-567	0	0	0	0
33	6	Sebastien Baron	32	-585	0	0	0	0
34	81	Joao Teixeira	31	-586	0	0	0	0
35	6	Oscar Pereira	25	-592	0	0	0	0
36	6	Donald Reignoux	0	-617	0	0	0	0
37	2	Marc Duez	0	-617	0	1	2	2
38	33	Frederick Johais	0	-617	0	1	2	2
39	6	Loic Deman	0	-617	1	1	1	1
40	96	Olivier Porta	0	-617	1	2	2	2
41	18	Josh Burdon	0	-617	0	0	1	1
42	81	Didier Lescos	0	-617	0	0	0	2
46	64	Olivier Bacle	0	-617	0	0	0	0
43	29	Benoit Dekejser	0	-617	0	0	0	0
44	6	Anthony Garbarino	0	-617	0	0	0	0
45	64	Diego Duez	0	-617	0	0	0	0
46	64	Diego Duez	0	-521	0	0	0	0

TEAMS CHAMPIONSHIP SEASON 2012 FINAL

Pos.	No.	Drivers	Points	Diff.
1	99	Still Racing – Exotics Racing (Thievin/Perisset)	1238	Leader
2	5	Rapido Racing (Lioen/Gabarron)	1182	-56
3	11	Overdrive - Mc Donald's (Fournillier/Grand)	1180	-58
4	25	Orhes Compétition 1 (Iannetta/Cormon)	1157	-81
5	2	TFT – Banco Santander (Vilarino/Quintal)	1141	-97
6	44	Orhes Compétition 2 (Nordstrom/Ide)	1125	-113
7	22	Overdrive - Moser Vernet (Jaggi/Vernet)	1030	-208
8	33	Overdrive - Etape Auto (Enjalbert/Rodrigues)	1008	-230
9	100	Still Racing - Convergence (Sabates)	990	-248
10	15	Gonneau Racing (Gonneau)	985	-253
11	14	Still Racing - JDC Finances (Cozzella)	956	-282
12	17	Pole Position - AIS (Boucena/Baudinière)	949	-289
13	55	Pole Position 81 (Cosin/Laurin)	948	-290
14	46	Racing Club Partners (Maillet/De Fierlant)	886	-352
15	28	RDV Compétition (Violas)	827	-411
16	42	Autosport 42 (Perrin/Medeiros/Esteban)	792	-446
17	88	Orhes Compétition 3 (Simonet/Marie)	785	-453
18	6	Performance Engineering (Garbarino/Anderson)	747	-491
19	64	Gonneau Racing 2 (Villa/Deman/Renaudat)	703	-535
20	96	TFT (Villa/Kennedy/VanHove)	690	-548
21	19	Scorpus 2 (Romecki/Escallier)	654	-584
22	18	Scorpus M&M's (Winslow/Zimmer/Escallier)	560	-678
23	81	Pole Position 81 - 2 (Quinn/Pastor)	424	-814
24	7	Pacifique House (Vaulkhard/Tressler)	393	-845
25	85	VTS 85 (Gaudin/Gaudin)	315	-923
26	21	Orhes Compétition 4 (Pernaut/Enout)	117	-1121
27	48	One (Greensall/Menini)	75	-1163

EURO RACECAR, NASCAR TOURING SERIES 2012 RACE RESULTS

NOGARO 200 — Circuit Paul Armagnac — 2.088 Miles — 4/8-9/2012

1 SPRINT RACE RESULTS

Pos	Car	Driver	Laps
1	2	Ander Vilarino	14
2	99	Romain Thievin	14
3	33	Dimitri Enjalbert	14
4	64	Javier Vila	14
5	25	Romain Iannetta	14
6	11	Romain Foumillier	14
7	14	Gregory Guilvert	14
8	15	Vincent Gonneau	14
9	17	Wilfried Boucenna	14
10	7	Harry Vaulkhard	14
11	42	Carole Perrin	14
12	55	Bruno Cosin	14
13	5	Antoine Lioen	14
14	88	Valentin Simonet	14
15	44	Freddy Nordstroem	14
16	22	Stephane Jaggi	14
17	46	Nathalie Maillet	14
18	100	Stephane Sabates	14
19	81	Joao Teixeira	13
20	48	Nigel Greensall	12
21	85	Nicolas Gaudin	8
22	21	Olivier Pernaut	3
23	6	Anthony Garbarino	1

2 ENDURANCE RACE RESULTS

Pos	Car	Driver	Laps
1	2	Ander Vilarino	18
2	64	Javier Villa	18
3	99	Romain Thievin	18
4	14	Gregory Guilvert	18
5	17	Wilfried Boucenna	18
6	11	Romain Foumillier	18
7	5	Antoine Lioen	18
8	42	Carole Perrin	18
9	44	Freddy Nordstrom	18
10	88	Valentin Simonet	18
11	21	Olivier Pernaut	18
12	7	Harry Vaulkhard	18
13	46	Nathalie Maillet	18
14	22	Stéphane Jaggi	18
15	100	Stéphane Sabates	17
16	25	Romain Iannetta	17
17	55	Bruno cosin	16
18	6	Anthony Garbarino	15
19	33	Dimitri Enjalbert	13
20	15	Vincent Gonneau	5
21	48	Nigel Greensall	1
22	28	Franck Violas	0
23	85	Nicolas Gaudin	0

BRANDS HATCH 200 — Brands Hatch Circuit — 1.198 Miles — 5/19-20/2012

1 SPRINT RACE RESULTS

Pos.	No.	Driver	Team	Laps
1	2	Ander Vilarino	TFT-Banco Santander	25
2	99	Romain Thiévin	Still Racing - Exotics Racing	25
3	64	Javier Villa	TFT	25
4	18	James Winslow	Scorpus Racing	25
5	25	Romain Iannetta	Orhes Competition	25
6	5	Antoine Lioen	Rapido Racing	25
7	33	Dimitri Enjalbert	OverDrive	25
8	44	Freddy Nordstrom	Orhes Competition	25
9	11	Romain Fournillier	OverDrive - McDonald's	25
10	7	Harry Vaulkhard	Pacific House	25
11	17	Willy Boucenna	Pole Position 81	25
12	42	Carole Perrin	Autosport 42	25
13	15	Vincent Gonneau	Gonneau Racing	25
14	55	Bruno Cosin	Pole Position 81	25
15	6	Anthony Garbarino	Rapido Racing	25
16	28	Franck Violas	RDV Competition	24
17	100	Stéphane Sabates	Still Racing-Convergence	23
18	14	Joseph Cozella	Still Racing-JDC Finances	23
19	46	Nathalie Maillet	Racing Club Partner	16

2 ENDURANCE RACE RESULTS

Pos.	No.	Driver	Team	Laps
1	64	Javier Villa	TFT	24
2	2	Ander Vilarino	TFT-Banco Santander	24
3	99	Romain Thiévin	Still Racing - Exotics Racing	24
4	5	Antoine Lioen	Rapido Racing	24
5	17	Willy Boucenna	Pole Position 81	24
6	44	Freddy Nordstrom	Orhes Competition	24
7	33	Dimitri Enjalbert	OverDrive	24
8	42	Carole Perrin	Autosport 42	24
9	25	Romain Iannetta	Orhes Competition	24
10	11	Romain Fournillier	OverDrive - McDonald's	24
11	15	Vincent Gonneau	Gonneau Racing	24
12	6	Anthony Garbarino	Rapido Racing	24
13	55	Bruno Cosin	Pole Position 81	24
14	7	Harry Vaulkhard	Pacific House	24
15	88	Valentin Simonet	Orhes Competition	24
16	46	Nathalie Maillet	Racing Club Partner	24
17	81	Nial Quinn	Pole Position 81	24
18	100	Stéphane Sabates	Still Racing-Convergence	23
19	22	Stéphane Jaggi	Over Drive-Moser Vernet	22
20	18	James Winslow	Scorpus Racing	20
21	14	Joseph Cozella	Still Racing-JDC Finances	17

SPA 200 — Circuit of Spa- Francorchamps — 4.353 Miles — 6/9-10/2012

1 SPRINT RACE RESULTS

Pos.	No.	Driver	Team	Laps
1	2	Ander Vilarino	TFT-Banco Santander	10
2	99	Romain Thiévin	Still Racing-Exotics Racing	10
3	42	Carole Perrin	Autosport 42	10
4	18	James Winslow	Scorpus Racing	10
5	5	Antoine Lioen	Rapido Racing	10
6	33	Dimitri Enjalbert	OverDrive	10
7	44	Freddy Nordström	Orhès Compétition	10
8	46	Nathalie Maillet	Racing Club Partner	10
9	6	Anthony Garbarino	Rapido Racing	10
10	38	Martin Van Hove	TFT	10
11	15	Vincent Gonneau	Gonneau Racing	10
12	88	Valentin Simonet	Orhès Compétition	10
13	22	Stéphane Jaggi	OverDrive-Moser Vernet	10
14	100	Stéphane Sabates	Still Racing-Convergence	10
15	84	Franck Violas	RDV Compétition	10
16	55	Bruno Cosin	Pole Position 81	9
17	14	Joseph Cozella	Still Racing-JDC Finances	9
18	11	Romain Fournillier	OverDrive-McDonald's	9
19	64	Javier Villa	Gonneau Racing	7
20	25	Romain Ianetta	Orhès Compétition	6
21	7	Harry Vaulkhard	Pacific House	2
22	17	Wilfried Boucenna	Pole Position 81	1

2 ENDURANCE RACE RESULTS

Pos.	No.	Driver	Team	Laps
1	2	Ander Vilarino	TFT-Banco Santander	20
2	15	Vincent Gonneau	Gonneau Racing	20
3	25	Romain Ianetta	Orhès Compétition	20
4	44	Freddy Nordström	Orhès Compétition	20
5	88	Valentin Simonet	Orhès Compétition	20
6	11	Romain Fournillier	OverDrive	20
7	55	Bruno Cosin	Pole Position 81	20
8	99	Romain Thiévin	Still Racing-Exotics Racing	20
9	5	Antoine Lioen	Rapido Racing	20
10	33	Dimitri Enjalbert	OverDrive	20
11	100	Stéphane Sabates	Still Racing Convergence	20
12	64	Javier Villa	Gonneau Racing	20
13	14	Joseph Cozella	Still Racing-JDC Finances	20
14	17	Wilfried Boucenna	Pole Position 81	19
15	42	Carole Perrin	Autosport 42	19
16	84	Franck Violas	RDV Compétition	19
17	22	Stéphane Jaggi	OverDrive-Moser Vernet	19
18	38	Martin Van Hove	TFT	11
19	6	Anthony Garbarino	Rapido Racing	8
20	7	Harry Vaulkhard	Pacific House	5
21	46	Nathalie Maillet	Racing Club Partner	1
22	18	James Winslow	Scorpus Racing	0

MICHELIN 100 — Tours Speedway — 0.375 mile — 7/7/2012

Pos.	No.	Driver	Team	Laps	Diff.	Best Time
1	96	Ben Kennedy	TFT – Whelen	100	18.550	
2	33	Dimitri Enjalbert	OverDrive	100	1.427	18.203
3	99	Romain Thievin	Still Racing/Exotics Racing	100	1.980	18.618
4	5	Antoine Lioen	Rapido Racing	100	3.228	18.700
5	18	Yann Zimmer	Scorpus Racing - M&M's	100	4.580	18.750
6	11	Romain Fournillier	OverDrive - Mc Donald's	100	4.895	18.735
7	55	Bruno Cosin	Pole Position 81	100	5.078	18.462
8	2	Ander Vilarino	TFT - Banco Santander	100	5.776	18.638
9	6	Anthony Garbarino	Rapido Racing	100	10.293	18.903
10	7	Manu Brigand	Rapido Racing	98	2 Laps	18.450
11	64	Javier Villa	Gonneau Racing	98	2 Laps	18.506
12	42	Carole Perrin	Autosport 42	95	5 Laps	17.835
13	88	Valentin Simonet	Orhes Competition	92	8 Laps	18.601
14	17	Willy Boucenna	Pole Position 81 - AIS	91	9 Laps	18.977
15	14	Eric Helary	Still Racing - JDC Finances	90	10 Laps	18.409
16	44	Freddy Nordstrom	Orhes Competition	90	10 Laps	19.009
17	100	Yvan Muller	Still Racing - Convergence	85	15 Laps	18.774
18	22	Stephane Jaggi	OverDrive - Moser Vernat	77	23 Laps	19.334
19	25	Romain Iannetta	Orhes Competition	74	26 Laps	18.144

TOURS EVENEMENTS 100 — Tours Speedway — 0.375 mile — 7/8/2012

Pos.	No.	Driver	Team	Laps	Diff.	Best Time
1	14	Eric Helary	Still Racing - JDC Finances	104	17.438	
2	2	Ander Vilarino	TFT - Banco Santander	104	0.490	17.410
3	100	Yvan Muller	Still Racing - Convergence	104	1.574	17.640
4	17	Willy Boucenna	Pole Position 81 - AIS	104	2.059	17.469
5	5	Antoine Lioen	Rapido Racing	104	4.717	17.792
6	6	Anthony Garbarino	Rapido Racing	104	7.851	17.915
7	11	Romain Fournillier	OverDrive - Mc Donald's	104	10.676	17.543
8	22	Stephane Jaggi	OverDrive - Moser Vernat	104	13.081	18.370
9	44	Freddy Nordstrom	Orhes Competition	101	3 Laps	17.736
10	99	Romain Thievin	Still Racing/Exotics Racing	97	7 Laps	17.501
11	18	Yann Zimmer	Scorpus Racing - M&M's	95	9 Laps	17.515
12	7	Manu Brigand	Rapido Racing	95	9 Laps	17.498
13	33	Dimitri Enjalbert	OverDrive	95	9 Laps	17.499
14	96	Ben Kennedy	TFT - Wheelen	72	32 Laps	17.424
15	64	Javier Villa	Gonneau Racing	72	32 Laps	17.266
16	42	Carole Perrin	Autosport 42	60	44 Laps	17.421
17	88	Valentin Simonet	Orhes Competition	44	60 Laps	17.459
18	25	Romain Iannetta	Orhes Competition	17	87 Laps	17.740
19	28	Franck Violas	RDV Competition	10	94 Laps	18.436

SEMIFINALS — Circuit Ricardo Tormo — 2.517 miles — 9/29-30/2012

1 SPRINT RACE RESULTS

Pos.	No.	Driver	Team	Laps
1	2	Ander Vilarino	TFT-Banco Santander	15
2	64	Javier Villa	Gonneau Racing	15
3	99	Romain Thiévin	Still Racing-Exotics Racing	15
4	5	Antoine Lioen	Rapido Racing	15
5	17	Willy Boucenna	Pole Position 81	15
6	44	Freddy Nordstrom	Orhes Competition	15
7	33	Azor Duenas	Over Drive	15
8	19	Stéphane Romecki	Scorpus Racing-M&M's	15
9	6	Anthony Garbarino	Rapido Racing	15
10	25	Romain Iannetta	Orhes Competition	15
11	46	Nathalie Maillet	Racing Club Partner	15
12	22	Stéphane Jaggi	Over Drive-Moser Vernet	15
13	42	Carole Perrin	Autosport 42	15
14	100	Stéphane Sabates	Still Racing-Convergence	15
15	28	Franck Violas	RDV Competition	15
16	81	Didier Lescos	Pole Position 81	14
17	14	Joseph Cozella	Still Racing-JDC Finances	14
18	88	Olivier Pernaut	Orhes Competition	14
19	18	Yann Zimmer	Scorpus Racing-M&M's	12
20	11	Romain Fournillier	Over Drive-McDonald's	12
21	55	Bruno Cosin	Pole Position 81	7
22	15	Vincent Gonneau	Gonneau Racing	1

2 ENDURANCE RACE RESULTS

Pos.	No.	Driver	Team	Laps
1	2	Ander Vilarino	TFT-Banco Santander	17
2	99	Romain Thiévin	Still Racing-Exotics Racing	17
3	64	Javier Villa	Gonneau Racing	17
4	25	Romain Iannetta	Orhes Competition	17
5	5	Antoine Lioen	Rapido Racing	17
6	6	Anthony Garbarino	Rapido Racing	17
7	17	Willy Boucenna	Pole Position 81	17
8	11	Romain Fournillier	Over Drive-McDonald's	17
9	19	Stéphane Romecki	Scorpus Racing-M&M's	17
10	18	Yann Zimmer	Scorpus Racing-M&M's	17
11	88	Olivier Pernaut	Orhes Competition	17
12	33	Azor Duenas	Over Drive	17
13	46	Nathalie Maillet	Racing Club Partner	17
14	44	Freddy Nordstrom	Orhes Competition	17
15	55	Bruno Cosin	Pole Position 81	17
16	22	Stéphane Jaggi	Over Drive-Moser Vernet	17
17	81	Didier Lescos	Pole Position 81	17
18	42	Carole Perrin	Autosport 42	17
19	100	Stéphane Sabates	Still Racing-Convergence	17
20	28	Franck Violas	RDV Competition	17
21	14	Joseph Cozella	Still Racing-JDC Finances	15
22	15	Vincent Gonneau	Gonneau Racing	11

FINALS — Circuit Le Mans Bugatti — 2.655 miles — 10/13-14/2012

1 SPRINT RACE RESULTS

Pos.	No.	Driver	Team	Laps
1	6	Gael Castelli	Rapido Racing	13
2	99	Romain Thiévin	Still Racing - Exotics Racing	13
3	25	Romain Iannetta	Orhes Competition	13
4	55	Bruno Cosin	Pole Position 81	11
5	11	Romain Fournillier	OverDrive - McDonald's	11
6	64	Javier Villa	Gonneau Racing	11
7	2	Ander Vilarino	TFT-Banco Santander	11
8	96	Anthony Garbarino	TFT - Alpes Carrelage	11
9	29	Nicolas Dekejser	Racing Club Partner	11
10	19	Stéphane Romecki	Scorpus Racing	11
11	17	Willy Boucenna	Pole Position 81	11
12	33	Frédéric Johais	OverDrive	11
13	15	Vincent Gonneau	Gonneau Racing	11
14	46	Nathalie Maillet	Racing Club Partner	11
15	5	Antoine Lioen	Rapido Racing	11
16	22	Stéphane Jaggi	OverDrive - Moser Vernet	11
17	28	Franck Violas	RDV Competition	11
18	85	Nicolas Gaudin	VTS 85	11
19	14	Joseph Cozella	Still Racing - JDC Finances	11
20	44	Freddy Nordstrom	Orhes Competition	10
21	100	Stéphane Sabates	Still Racing - Convergence	6

2 ENDURANCE RACE RESULTS

Pos.	No.	Driver	Team	Laps
1	6	Gael Castelli	Rapido Racing	13
2	99	Romain Thiévin	Still Racing - Exotics Racing	13
3	25	Romain Iannetta	Orhes Competition	13
4	29	Nicolas Dekejser	Racing Club Partner	13
5	17	Willy Boucenna	Pole Position 81	13
6	64	Javier Villa	Gonneau Racing	13
7	96	Anthony Garbarino	TFT - Alpes Carrelage	13
8	11	Romain Fournillier	OverDrive - McDonald's	13
9	5	Antoine Lioen	Rapido Racing	13
10	2	Ander Vilarino	TFT-Banco Santander	13
11	46	Nathalie Maillet	Racing Club Partner	13
12	19	Stéphane Romecki	Scorpus Racing-M&M's	13
13	15	Vincent Gonneau	Gonneau Racing	13
14	33	Frédéric Johais	OverDrive	13
15	55	Bruno Cosin	Pole Position 81	13
16	44	Freddy Nordstrom	Orhes Competition	13
17	22	Stéphane Jaggi	OverDrive - Moser Vernet	13
18	85	Nicolas Gaudin	VTS 85	13
19	28	Franck Violas	RDV Competition	12
20	14	Joseph Cozella	Still Racing - JDC Finances	12
21	100	Stéphane Sabates	Still Racing - Convergence	10
22	18	Jean-Charles Battut	Scorpus Racing-M&M's	0

GRAND-AM ROLEX SPORTS CAR SERIES

GRAND-AM ROAD RACING™

SCOTT PRUETT AND MEMO ROJAS

DAYTONA PROTOTYPE 2012 CHAMPIONS

SCOTT PRUETT AND MEMO ROJAS COMBINED TO GIVE CHIP GNASSI RACING ITS THIRD CONSECUTIVE CHAMPIONSHIP.

At 52, Scott Pruett is showing no signs of slowing down. The native of Sacramento joined Memo Rojas in giving Chip Ganassi Racing its third consecutive Daytona Prototype championship in the GRAND-AM Rolex Sports Car Series. It was the fourth title in five years for the drivers of the No. 01 TELMEX BMW/Riley. It was also the fifth DP crown for Pruett, who joined Max Papis in taking honors in 2004.

Pruett and Rojas won races at Road America and Montreal, and finished on the podium eight times in 13 races. The latter triumph – at Circuit Gilles Villeneuve – was a milestone 150th victory for the Ganassi organization in IndyCar, NASCAR and sports cars.

Pruett is the leading winner in Rolex Series competition with 39 victories – all but one in the premier DP class. Rojas has quietly advanced to second on the all-time list with 25 victories. The 31-year-old resident of Mexico City won championships in four of his six seasons of GRAND-AM competition.

After scoring 14 victories over the past two seasons, the Ganassi team struggled to keep the pace of the teams running the new Corvette

DPs. Max Angelelli and Ricky Taylor were three-time winners for SunTrust Racing while Richard Westbrook led Spirit of Daytona to its first three triumphs, leading the charge for eight victories for the new Corvette DPs.

The season began in frustration. Joined by Graham Rahal and Joey Hand, the team opened the year with a disappointing sixth-place finish in the 50th Rolex 24 at Daytona won by Michael Shank Racing. Pruett and Rojas followed with podium finishes at Homestead-Miami Speedway and Barber Motorsports Park, but the new Corvette DPs stole the thunder with back-to-back victories.

The low point of the season came on lap 81 of the fourth race of the season at New Jersey Motorsports Park. Pruett tangled with Alex Gurney's "Red Dragon" GAINSCO Corvette DP while battling for second. That eliminated both cars, and dropped the Ganassi duo to fifth in the standings – behind Starworks Motorsport's Ryan Dalziel and Enzo Potolicchio.

They were down, but far from out. A third-place finish in the next round at Detroit's Belle Isle circuit moved the Ganassi duo up to fourth; Pruett then finished a close second to Westbrook at Mid-Ohio, and the Ganassi team was back in front.

There was no letting up. A victory at Road Atlanta padded the lead, continuing a run in which Pruett and Rojas finished in the top four in seven consecutive races. The Montreal victory upped the lead to 18 points, all but icing the championship.

Corvettes dominated the final two rounds, but Ganassi's charges finished a respective sixth and seventh to win the title by a comfortable 12 points over Dalziel.

PERSONAL INFORMATION
SCOTT PRUETT

Birth Date:	**March 24, 1960**
Hometown:	**Sacramento, CA**
Team:	**Chip Ganassi Racing with Felix Sabates**
Owners:	**Chip Ganassi, Felix Sabates**
Team Manager:	**Tim Keene**

CAREER RECORD

Year	Class	Finish	Races	Wins	Poles	Podiums
2001	GTS	-	1	0	0	0
2002	GTS	12	1	0	0	1
2004	DP	1	12	4	4	8
2005	DP	2	14	3	2	8
2006	DP	2	14	5	3	8
2007	DP	2	14	2	1	8
2008	DP	1	14	6	1	8
2009	DP	2	12	2	1	8
2010	DP	1	12	9	1	11
2011	DP	1	12	5	0	10
2012	DP	1	13	2	1	8
Total			**106**	**38**	**13**	**78**

PERSONAL INFORMATION
MEMO ROJAS

Birth Date:	**Aug. 18, 1981**
Hometown:	**Mexico City, Mexico**
Team:	**Chip Ganassi Racing with Felix Sabates**
Owners:	**Chip Ganassi, Felix Sabates**
Team Manager:	**Tim Keene**

CAREER RECORD

Year	Class	Finish	Races	Wins	Poles	Podiums
2007	DP	4	14	1	0	7
2008	DP	1	14	6	1	8
2009	DP	2	12	2	3	8
2010	DP	1	12	9	4	11
2011	DP	1	12	5	0	10
2012	DP	1	13	2	0	8
Total			**52**	**25**	**8**	**52**

GRAND-AM ROLEX SPORTS CAR SERIES DAYTONA PROTOTYPE
2012 CHAMPIONS SCOTT PRUETT/MEMO ROJAS SEASON RECORD

Date	Speedway	Location	Start	Finish	Status
Jan. 28-29	Daytona International Speedway	Daytona Beach, FL	13	6	Running
March 31	Barber Motorsports Park	Birmingham, AL	4	3	Running
April 29	Homestead-Miami Speedway	Homestead, FL	4	2	Running
May 13	New Jersey Motorsports Park	Millville, NJ	3	10	Accident
June 2	Raceway at Belle Isle Park	Detroit, MI	5	3	Running
June 9	Mid-Ohio Sports Car Course	Lexington, OH	6	2	Running
June 23	Road America	Elkhart Lake, WS	1	1	Running
July 1	Watkins Glen International (long course)	Watkins Glen, NY	1	4	Running
July 27	Indianapolis Motor Speedway	Indianapolis IN	8	2	Running
Aug. 11	Watkins Glen International (short)	Watkins Glen, NY	3	5	Running
Aug. 18	Circuit Gilles Villeneuve	Montreal, Quebec, Canada	2	1	Running
Sept. 9	Mazda Raceway Laguna Seca	Monterey, CA	5	6	Running
Sept. 29	Lime Rock Park	Lakeville, CT	2	7	Running

2

RYAN DALZIEL

Hometown: Coatbridge, Scotland
Date of Birth: April 12, 1982

Ryan Dalziel found himself in a season-long battle with veteran Chip Ganassi Racing for the 2012 DP title, coming up 12 points shy. The year came down to the inaugural Brickyard Grand Prix, where Dalziel spun after controversial contact with superstar Juan Pablo Montoya – driving the second Ganassi DP. Dalziel followed up Indy with a victory at Watkins Glen, but the damage was done.

Dalziel opened the year by winning the pole and finishing second in the Rolex 24 at Daytona, and also finished second at New Jersey and Road America.

Running in three championships on two continents for Starworks, Dalziel won his class in the 24 Hours of Le Mans, 12 Hours of Sebring and Petit Le Mans, along with class triumphs at Long Beach, Baltimore and Brazil. While he came up short for the DP crown, he won the FIA World Endurance LMP2 championship.

3

DARREN LAW

Hometown: Phoenix, AZ
Date of Birth: April 4, 1968

In a major strategy change, Action Express Racing split long-time co-drivers Darren Law and David Donohue after four races in 2012. Law moved to the team's No. 9 Corvette DP, co-driving with Joao Barbosa. The move immediately paid dividends as Law and Barbosa won in GRAND-AM's first visit to Detroit Belle Isle, winning over the sister car of Donohue and Terry Borcheller in the shadows of General Motors' world headquarters. Law and Barbosa followed up with a victory in the Sahlen's Six Hours of Watkins Glen.

Law has never missed a race since the Rolex Series debuted in 2000. He will keep that streak intact in the 2013 Rolex 24 with GAINSCO/Bob Stallings Racing, but is without an announced ride after the opener.

4

DAVID DONOHUE

Hometown: Malvern, PA
Date of Birth: Jan. 5, 1967

After co-driving with Darren Law since 2004 with Brumos Porsche and Action Express Racing, an early-season strategy change saw Donohue paired with four different co-drivers over the final nine races.

Donohue managed to keep the new No. 5 Corvette DP near the front throughout the season, scoring four podium finishes among eight top-five outings. A highlight was second behind Law, at Detroit's Belle Isle, in Donohue's first race co-driving with Terry Borcheller. Another key outing was at Montreal, where he joined Canadian veteran Paul Tracy in a third-place finish.

The end of the season saw Donohue without a ride for 2013. While he's not ready to call it quits, he noted that his run in the DPs were longer than his father – the legendary Mark Donohue – racing for Team Penske.

5

ALEX POPOW

Hometown: Lecheria, Venezuela
Date of Birth: Nov. 9, 1975

Alex Popow came into his own in 2012. He opened the year with a second-place finish in the Rolex 24 at Daytona, and followed it up with an ALMS PC class victory in the 12 Hours of Sebring, driving two different cars for Peter Baron's South Florida-based Starworks Motorsport.

The best was yet to come. Popow joined four-time Champ Car titlist Sebastien Bourdais in winning the Brickyard Grand Prix, GRAND-AM's first race at historic Indianapolis Motor Speedway. The victory also boosted Popow to the inaugural driver's title in the North American Endurance Championship presented by VISITFLORIDA.com. Popow and Bourdais then finished second at Watkins Glen.

Popow ended the year by winning the Jim Trueman Award recognizing GRAND-AM's top Pro-Am driver. He also won his class at Long Beach, Road America, Baltimore and Petit Le Mans to take the ALMS title.

2012 DAYTONA PROTOTYPE DRIVER STANDINGS (TOP-10)

Pos.	Driver	Pts.	Races	Wins	Podiums
1	Memo Rojas	379	13	2	8
	Scott Pruett	379	13	2	8
2	Ryan Dalziel	367	13	1	6
3	Darren Law	355	13	2	3
4	David Donohue	348	13	0	4
5	Alex Popow	346	13	1	3
6	Max Angelelli	343	13	3	4
	Ricky Taylor	343	13	3	4
7	Joao Barbosa	342	13	2	2
8	Alex Gurney	340	13	0	5
	Jon Fogarty	340	13	0	5
9	Oswaldo Negri Jr.	334	13	1	1
	John Pew	334	13	1	3
10	Richard Westbrook	205	13	3	3

ROLEX SPORTS CAR SERIES ROOKIE OF THE YEAR WINNERS (2006-2012)

2006 . . . . .Mike Rockenfeller	2009 . . . . Romain Dumas and Timo Bernhard
2007 . . . . Dirk Werner	2010 . . . . Jonathan Bomarito
2008 . . . . Tim George Jr.	2011 . . . . Henri Richard

2012 . . . . Dr. Jim Norman

JIM TRUEMAN AWARD WINNERS (2006-2012)

2006	Mark Patterson
2007	Tracy Krohn
2008	JC France
2009	Mark Patterson
2010	John Pew
2011	John Pew
2012	Alex Popow

BOB AKIN AWARD WINNERS (2006-2012)

(Given annually to the top Pro-Am drivers in the Rolex Series DP and GT classes)

2006	Marc Bunting
2007	Emil Assentato
2008	Tim George Jr.
2009	Leh Keen
2010	Emil Assentato
2011	Wayne Nonnamaker
2012	Emil Assentato

ROLEX SPORTS CAR SERIES CHAMPIONS

DP Drivers

Year	
2012	Scott Pruett & Memo Rojas
2011	Scott Pruett & Memo Rojas
2010	Scott Pruett & Memo Rojas
2009	Alex Gurney & Jon Fogarty
2008	Scott Pruett & Memo Rojas
2007	Alex Gurney & Jon Fogarty
2006	Jörg Bergmeister
2005	Max Angelelli & Wayne Taylor
2004	Scott Pruett & Max Papis
2003	Terry Borcheller

DP Teams

Year	
2012	No. 01 TELMEX Chip Ganassi Racing
2011	No. 01 TELMEX Chip Ganassi Racing
2010	No. 01 TELMEX Chip Ganassi Racing
2009	No. 99 GAINSCO/Bob Stallings Racing
2008	No. 01 TELMEX Chip Ganassi Racing
2007	No. 99 GAINSCO/Bob Stallings Racing
2006	No. 01 CompUSA Chip Ganassi Racing
2005	No. 10 SunTrust Racing
2004	No. 01 CompUSA Chip Ganassi Racing
2003	No. 54 Bell Motorsports

DP Engine Manufacturers

Year	
2012	Chevrolet
2011	BMW
2010	BMW
2009	Ford
2008	Pontiac
2007	Pontiac
2006	Lexus
2005	Pontiac
2004	Pontiac
2003	Porsche

DP Chassis Constructors

Year	
2012	Riley
2011	Riley
2010	Riley
2009	Riley
2008	Riley
2007	Riley
2006	Riley
2005	Riley
2004	Riley
2003	Fabcar

GT Drivers

Year	
2012	Jeff Segal & Emil Assentato
2011	Andrew Davis & Leh Keen
2010	Jeff Segal & Emil Assentato
2009	Dirk Werner & Leh Keen
2008	Paul Edwards & Kelly Collins
2007	Dirk Werner
2006	Andy Lally & Marc Bunting
2005	Craig Stanton
2004	Bill Auberlen
2003	Cort Wagner & Brent Martini
2002	Bill Auberlen & Cort Wagner
2001	Darren Law

GT Teams

Year	
2012	No. 69 AIM Autosport Team FXDD w/ Ferrari
2011	No. 59 Brumos Racing
2010	No. 69 SpeedSource
2009	No. 87 Farnbacher Loles Racing
2008	No. 07 Banner Racing
2007	No. 87 Farnbacher Loles Racing
2006	No. 65 TRG
2005	No. 65 TRG
2004	No. 21 BMW Team PTG
2003	No. 33 Scuderia Ferrari of Washington
2002	No. 33 Scuderia Ferrari of Washington
2001	No. 81 G&W Motorsports

GT Manufacturers

Year	
2012	Ferrari
2011	Chevrolet
2010	Mazda
2009	Porsche
2008	Pontiac
2007	Porsche
2006	Pontiac
2005	Porsche
2004	BMW
2003	Ferrari

SGS Drivers

Year	
2004	Marc Bunting & Andy Lally

SGS Team

Year	
2004	No. 38 TPC Racing

SGS MANUFACTURER

Year	
2004	Porsche

GTS Drivers

Year	
2003	Tommy Riggins & Dave Machavern
2002	Chris Bingham
2001	Chris Bingham

GTS Manufacturer

Year	
2003	Ford

SRP/SR Drivers

Year	
2002	Didier Theys (SRP)
2001	James Weaver (SRP)
2000	James Weaver (SR)

SRP/SR Teams

Year	
2002	No. 16 Dyson Racing Team (SRP)
2001	No. 16 Dyson Racing Team (SRP)
2000	No. 16 Dyson Racing Team (SR)

SRPII/SRII Drivers

Year	
2002	Terry Borcheller (SRPII)
2001	Andy Lally (SRPII)
2000	Larry Oberto & Ryan Hampton (SRII)

SRPII/SRII Teams

Year	
2002	No. 8 Rand Racing (SRPII)
2001	No. 21 Archangel Motorsport Services (SRPII)
2000	No. 22 Archangel Motorsport Services (SRII)

AGT Drivers

Year	
2002	Kerry Hitt
2001	Craig Conway & Doug Goad
2000	Doug Mills

AGT Teams

Year	
2002	No. 46 Morgan Dollar Motorsports
2001	No. 09 Flis Motorsports
2000	No. 09 Spirit of Daytona

GTO Drivers

Year	
2000	Terry Borcheller & Ron Johnson

GTO Team

Year	
2000	No. 5 Saleen-Allen Speedlab

GTU Driver

Year	
2000	Mike Fitzgerald

GTU Team

Year	
2000	No. 81 G&W Motorsports

GRAND-AM ROAD RACING

GRAND-AM ROLEX SPORTS CAR SERIES
EMIL ASSENTATO AND JEFF SEGAL

GRAND TOURING 2012 CHAMPIONS

THREE RACE WINS AND EIGHT PODIUMS PROPELLED JEFF SEGAL AND EMIL ASSENTATO TO THE GRAND-AM ROLEX SPORTS CAR SERIES GT CHAMPIONSHIP.

Jeff Segal and Emil Assentato didn't have to wait long to get a Ferrari back into victory lane in GRAND-AM Rolex Sports Car Series competition in 2012. The co-drivers of the No. 69 AIM Autosport Team FXDD Ferrari 458 picked up their first win of the season in just their third race with a dominating performance at Homestead-Miami Speedway, and then followed that up with another win at New Jersey Motorsports Park one race later. When all was said and done Segal and Assentato rode to three race wins and an impressive eight podium finishes in 13 starts to win the GT championship by 27 points over Robin Liddell.

It was a tremendous accomplishment for an AIM Autosport team that announced just three months prior to the season-opening Rolex 24 at Daytona that they would join forces with Ferrari and move to the GT ranks after spending six years in the Daytona Prototype class. Not only did the team make the transition to GT, but they also became the first team to campaign the new Ferrari 458, which was built specifically for Rolex Series competition, and the only team to compete with the car for the full season.

That proved to be an advantage for Segal and Assentato. After starting off the year with a solid eighth-place finish in the Rolex 24 At Daytona, the co-drivers went on a three-month tear that made them championship favorites sooner than later. That seven-race stretch included six podium finishes and three wins, the first podium finish for the Ferrari 458 (Barber Motorsports Park) and the first win (Homestead).

Over that stretch the team's lone non-podium finish came in the inaugural race at Belle Isle Park. Even then, a fourth-place finish was still enough for AIM Autosport to continue to distance itself from the competition. It wasn't until Indianapolis Motor Speedway in July that Segal and Assentato gave up some ground in the points pace race.

A fifth-place finish in the Brickyard Grand Prix, followed by a first lap crash at Watkins Glen gave Liddell, as well as other GT contenders Paul Dalla Lana and SpeedSource co-drivers Sylvain Tremblay and Jonathan Bomarito a glimmer hope. But as they had done all season long, Segal and Assentato rebounded with back-to-back second-place finishes at Circuit Gilles Villeneuve and Mazda Raceway Laguna Seca.

An eighth-place finish in the season finale at Lime Rock Park was more than enough to finish the job as AIM Autosport, Segal and Assentato, and Ferrari swept the GT class championships. Not a bad debut for a car on its maiden voyage and a team making its GT class debut.

AIM Autosport will grow to two cars for the 2013 season with sports car and NASCAR veteran Max Papis joining Segal, and Ferrari ace Anthony Lazzaro joining Assentato for an attempt to repeat as GT champions.

PERSONAL INFORMATION
EMIL ASSENTATO

Birth Date:	**May 21, 1949**
Hometown:	**New York, NY**
2012 Team:	**AIM Autosport Team FXDD with Ferraris**
Car Owners:	**Ian Willis, Andrew Bordin**
Crew Chief:	**Matt Wivell**

CAREER RECORD

Year	Class	Finish	Races	Wins	Poles	Podiums
2000	GTU	10	5	0	0	0
2001	GT	28	4	0	0	0
2002	GT	41	2	0	0	1
2003	GT	29	4	0	0	0
2004	GT	7	12	0	0	1
2005	GT	17	11	0	0	1
2006	GT	38	3	0	0	0
2007	GT	10	13	0	0	1
2008	GT	12	13	1	0	1
2009	GT	7	12	2	0	3
2010	GT	1	12	2	0	5
2011	GT	5	12	0	0	4
2012	GT	1	13	3	0	8
Total			**116**	**8**	**0**	**25**

PERSONAL INFORMATION
JEFF SEGAL

Birth Date:	**April 27, 1985**
Hometown:	**Philadelphia, PA**
2012 Team:	**AIM Autosport Team FXDD with Ferraris**
Car Owners:	**Ian Willis, Andrew Bordin**
Crew Chief:	**Matt Wivell**

CAREER RECORD

Year	Class	Finish	Races	Wins	Poles	Podiums
2003	GT	-	1	0	0	1
2004	GT	22	3	0	0	0
2005	GT	57	3	0	0	0
2007	GT	43	3	0	0	0
2008	GT	14	12	1	1	1
2009	GT	7	11	2	0	3
2010	GT	1	12	2	1	5
2011	GT	5	12	0	0	4
2012	GT	1	13	3	0	8
Total			**45**	**8**	**2**	**22**

GRAND-AM ROLEX SPORTS CAR SERIES GRAND TOURING
2012 CHAMPIONS EMIL ASSENTATO/JEFF SEGAL SEASON RECORD

Date	Speedway	Location	Start	Finish	Status
Jan. 28-29	Daytona International Speedway	Daytona Beach, FL	2	8	Running
March 31	Barber Motorsports Park	Birmingham, AL	2	2	Running
April 29	Homestead-Miami Speedway	Homestead, FL	4	1	Running
May 13	New Jersey Motorsports Park	Millville, NJ	9	1	Running
June 2	Raceway at Belle Isle Park	Detroit, MI	12	4	Running
June 9	Mid-Ohio Sports Car Course	Lexington, OH	6	2	Running
June 23	Road America	Elkhart Lake, WI	1	1	Running
July 1	Watkins Glen International (long course)	Watkins Glen, NY	3	3	Running
July 27	Indianapolis Motor Speedway	Indianapolis IN	7	5	Running
Aug. 11	Watkins Glen International (short)	Watkins Glen, NY	4	7	Running
Aug. 18	Circuit Gilles Villeneuve	Montreal, Quebec, Canada	5	2	Running
Sept. 9	Mazda Raceway Laguna Seca	Monterey, CA	5	2	Running
Sept. 29	Lime Rock Park	Lakeville, CT	13	8	Running

2

ROBIN LIDDELL
Hometown: Edinburgh, Scotland
Birth Date: Feb. 28, 1974

Despite losing his co-driver John Edwards for two races due to a leg injury, Robin Liddell put together a strong season that any other year may have been good enough for the GT title. Although he ultimately finished in the runner-up spot, 27 points behind the Ferrari duo of Jeff Segal and Emil Assentato, Liddell put up quite a fight, winning three of the final six races to tie the class lead.

The Stevenson Motorsports driver also earned seven podium finishes, including four consecutive podiums early in the year. Liddell has plenty of momentum to build on heading into the 2013 season as he hopes to earn his first GT title.

3

PAUL DALLA LANA
Hometown: Toronto, Ontario, Canada
Birth Date: Feb. 1, 1966

It was a career year in the Rolex Series for Paul Dalla Lana in 2012. One year after winning the Continental Tire Sports Car Challenge GS title and being named by BMW as the manufacturer's top privateer driver, Dalla Lana followed that up with his highest Rolex Series points finish to date.

Carried by a stretch of nine consecutive top-five finishes, Dalla Lana was a threat for a podium each week, and found himself on the top step twice (Mid-Ohio, Watkins Glen) alongside co-driver Bill Auberlen.

Finishes of 10th or worse in the final three events ultimately prevented Dalla Lana from competing for the GT title, but coming off his best season to date there's no reason to think he can't contend again in 2013.

4

SYLVAIN TREMBLAY
Hometown: Coral Springs, FL
Birth Date: Aug. 9, 1965

JONATHAN BOMARITO
Hometown: Monterey, CA
Birth Date: Jan. 23, 1982

Sylvain Tremblay and Jonathan Bomarito carried the Mazda banner for much of the 2012 season earning the manufacturer a victory at Barber Motorsports Park and three additional podiums (Belle Isle, Road America, Indianapolis). It was a farewell tour so to speak for the SpeedSource team's rotary-engined Mazda RX-8 as the team will switch to a Mazda6 in the Rolex Series' new GX class in 2013, but Tremblay and Bomarito still contended for podium finishes every week.

After a sixth-place finish in the Rolex 24 at Daytona to start the season, the teammates went on to win at Barber to put themselves in the thick of the points battle early in the season. A string of four top-five finishes in five races solidified that position as Tremblay and Bomarito went on to be the highest finishing Mazda drivers in the GT class.

5

ANDREW DAVIS
Hometown: Athens, GA
Birth Date: Nov. 2, 1977

LEH KEEN
Hometown: Dublin, GA
Birth Date: July 22, 1983

Driving the iconic No. 59 Brumos Racing Porsche GT3, Andrew Davis and Leh Keen continued to show why Brumos Racing is always in the thick of the championship race. Despite going winless on the season, the 2011 GT champs rode consistency to a fifth-place finish in GT points with four podium finishes and just two finishes outside of the top-10.

The year kicked off with a pole position and podium finish in the Rolex 24 at Daytona, followed by another podium at Barber Motorsports Park, but a stretch of four consecutive races outside of the top-five was not enough to keep up with the championship-winning AIM Autosport Ferrari team despite a strong finish to the season.

Still, with back-to-back top-five points finishes since the team returned to the GT class in 2011, Brumos Racing and Davis and Keen will be considered contenders again in 2013.

GRAND TOURING VICTORIES

Pos.	Drivers	Wins	Pos.	Drivers	Wins	Pos.	Drivers	Wins	Pos.	Drivers	Wins
1	Bill Auberlen	21	6	Kelly Collins	12	11	Nick Ham	8	18	Boris Said	6
2	Andy Lally	20	7	Sylvain Tremblay	11		Justin Marks	8		Wolf Henzler	6
3	Robin Liddell	18	8	Brent Martini	9		Jeff Segal	8	20	Randy Pobst	5
4	Paul Edwards	15		Leh Keen	9		Emil Assentato	8		Dirk Werner	5
5	Cort Wagner	13		Andrew Davis	9	15	Marc Bunting	7		Joey Hand	5
							RJ Valentine	7			
							Spencer Pumpelly	7			

GRAND TOURING PODIUMS

Pos.	Drivers	Podiums	Pos.	Drivers	Podiums	Pos.	Drivers	Podiums	Pos.	Drivers	Podiums
1	Andy Lally	41	7	Andrew Davis	26	12	RJ Valentine	18	17	Justin Marks	15
2	Robin Liddell	38	8	Leh Keen	25	13	Marc Bunting	17		Wolf Henzler	15
3	Paul Edwards	36	9	Spencer Pumpelly	23	14	Joey Hand	16	19	Randy Pobst	14
4	Kelly Collins	33	10	Emil Assentato	22		Cort Wagner	16	20	Bryce Miller	13
5	Bill Auberlen	31		Jeff Segal	22		Nick Ham	16			
6	Sylvain Tremblay	30	11	Dirk Werner	21						

2012 GRAND TOURING TOP-50 DRIVERS

Pos.	Driver	Pts.	Races	Wins	Podiums	Pos.	Driver	Pts.	Races	Wins	Podiums
1	Emil Assentato	387	13	3	8	26	Ronnie Bremer	122	5	0	1
	Jeff Segal	387	13	3	8	27	Tom Long	113	6	0	0
2	Robin Liddell	360	13	3	7	28	J van Overbeek	102	4	0	1
3	Paul Dalla Lana	339	13	2	4	29	Guy Cosmo	88	4	0	0
4	Jonathan Bomarito	336	13	1	4	30	Joe Sahlen	86	4	0	0
	Sylvain Tremblay	336	13	1	4	31	Scott Maxwell	77	4	0	0
5	Andrew Davis	329	13	0	4	32	Mike Hedlund	70	3	0	0
	Leh Keen	329	13	0	4	33	Robert Kauffman	69	4	0	0
6	Dane Cameron	324	13	1	3	34	Alessandro Balzan	58	2	0	0
	Wayne Nonnamaker	324	13	1	3	35	Matt Bell	56	3	0	0
7	Andy Lally	323	13	2	4	36	Ben Keating	56	3	0	0
	John Potter	323	13	2	4	37	Jeroen Bleekemolen	55	2	0	0
8	John Edwards	306	11	3	6	38	Claudio Burtin	55	3	0	0
9	Charles Espenlaub	280	13	0	0		Martin Ragginger	55	3	0	0
	Charles Putman	280	13	0	0	39	Olivier Beretta	54	2	0	0
10	Bill Auberlen	277	10	2	4	40	Anthony Lazzaro	53	2	0	0
11	Eric Curran	270	13	0	1	41	Rui Aguas	53	3	0	0
12	Boris Said	270	13	0	1	42	Eduardo Costabal	52	3	0	0
13	Dion von Moltke	241	13	0	1		Eliseo Salazar	52	3	0	0
14	Joe Nonnamaker	232	13	0	0	43	Wolf Henzler	48	2	0	1
15	Jordan Taylor	221	9	0	0	44	Jan Heylen	45	3	0	0
16	Patrick Lindsey	199	11	0	0	45	Scott Sharp	42	2	0	0
17	Will Nonnamaker	189	11	0	0	46	Emilio DiGuida	39	2	0	0
18	Spencer Pumpelly	184	8	0	1	47	Ryan Eversley	37	2	0	0
19	Joe Foster	177	10	0	0	48	Ed Brown	36	2	0	0
20	Paul Edwards	174	7	1	1		Jorg Bergmeister	36	2	0	0
21	Jim Norman	168	10	0	0	49	Rene Rast	35	1	1	1
22	Eric Foss	161	9	0	0		Richard Lietz	35	1	1	1
23	Steven Bertheau	142	6	0	1	50	Santiago Orjuela	34	2	0	0
24	Patrick Dempsey	138	8	0	0						
25	Billy Johnson	125	5	0	0						

GRAND-AM ROLEX SPORTS CAR SERIES 2012 RACE RESULTS

1 ROLEX 24 AT DAYTONA

Daytona International Speedway — January 28-29, 2012 — 3.56-mile, 12-turn stadium road course — 24 Hours

Pos.	Stc	No.	Class	Pic	Drivers	Car	Laps
1	6	60	DP	1	John Pew, Oswaldo Negri Jr, AJ Allmendinger, Justin Wilson	Liveon.com Ford/Riley	761
2	1	8	DP	2	Enzo Potolicchio, Ryan Dalziel, Alex Popow Lucas Luhr	Motorola Ford/Riley	761
3	8	6	DP	3	Michael McDowell, Felipe Nasr, Jorge Goncalvez, Gustavo Yacaman	Michael Shank Racing w/ Curb Agajanian Ford/Riley	761
4	3	02	DP	4	Scott Dixon, Juan Pablo Montoya, Dario Franchitti, Jamie McMurray	Target/TELMEX BMW/Riley	760
5	14	5	DP	5	Darren Law, David Donohue, Christian Fittipaldi	Action Express Racing Corvette DP	758
6	13	01	DP	6	Scott Pruett, Memo Rojas, Graham Rahal, Joey Hand	TELMEX BMW/Riley	757
7	10	77	DP	7	Brian Frisselle, Burt Frisselle, Jim Lowe, Paul Tracy, Billy Johnson	COMBOS/Circle K Ford Dallara	748
8	5	90	DP	8	Antonio Garcia, Richard Westbrook, Oliver Gavin, Jan Magnussen	Spirit of Daytona Corvette DP	746
9	7	9	DP	9	Terry Borcheller, JC France, Joao Barbosa, Max Papis	Action Express Racing Corvettet DP	739
10	9	2	DP	10	Michael Valiante, Ryan Hunter-Reay, Andy Andretti, Scott Mayer	Motorola Ford/Riley	736
11	3	44	GT	1	John Potter, Andy Lally, Richard Lietz, Rene Rast	Magnus Racing Porsche GT3	727
12	39	67	GT	2	Steven Bertheau, Marc Goossens, Wolf Henzler, Spencer Pumpelly, Jeroen Bleekemolen	Sargent & Lundy Porsche GT3	727
13	1	59	GT	3	Leh Keen, Andrew Davis, Hurley Haywood, Marc Lieb	The Brumos Companies Porsche GT3	726
14	15	57	GT	4	Robin Liddell, John Edwards, Ronnie Bremer	Stevenson Auto Group Camaro GT.R	726
15	10	63	GT	5	Toni Vilander, Olivier Beretta, Andrea Bertolini	Risi Competizione w/ American Canadian Ferrari 458	726
16	24	70	GT	6	James Hinchcliffe, Sylvain Tremblay, Jonathan Bomarito, Marino Franchitti	Speedsource/ModSpace/Castrol Mazda RX-8	722
17	17	66	GT	7	Dominik Farnbacher, Ben Keating, Patrick Pilet, Allan Simonsen	Viper Exchange Porsche GT3	721
18	2	69	GT	8	Emil Assentato, Jeff Segal, Nick Longhi, Anthony Lazzaro	FXDD Ferrari 458	716
19	12	76	DP	11	Tracy Krohn, Nic Jonsson, Ricardo Zonta, Colin Braun	Krohn Racing Ford Lola	713
20	7	88	GT	9	Jordan Taylor, Paul Edwards, Matthew Marsh, Tom Milner	Authaus/Flex-Box Camaro GT.R	713
21	26	40	GT	10	Joe Foster, Patrick Dempsey, Tom Long, Charles Espenlaub, Charles Putman	Visit Florida Mazda RX-8	713
22	20	32	GT	11	Nicolas Armindo, Shane Lewis, Bret Curtis, James Sofronas	Positive Output Porsche GT3	713
23	5	42	GT	12	Dane Cameron, Wayne Nonnamaker, Joe Nonnamaker, Will Nonnamaker	Theracesite.com Mazda RX-8	711
24	11	03	GT	13	Scott Sharp, J van Overbeek, Ed Brown, Guy Cosmo	Tequila Patron Ferrari 458	707
25	23	24	GT	14	Michael Avenatti, Bob Faieta, Cort Wagner, Bill Sweedler, Fred Poordad	McKenna Porsche/Battery Tender	707
26	4	45	GT	15	Jorg Bergmeister, Patrick Long, Mike Rockenfeller, Seth Neiman	Flying Lizard Motorsorts w/ Wright Motorsports Porsche GT3	706
27	19	93	GT	16	Bill Auberlen, Paul Dalla Lana, Michael Marsal, Dirk Werner, Dirk Muller	Turner Motorsport BMW M3	691
28	6	23	GT	17	Cooper MacNeil, Butch Leitzinger, Emmanuel Collard, Marco Holzer	WeatherTech Porsche GT3	689
29	13	26	GT	18	Sean Edwards, Carlos Kauffmann, Henrique Cisneros, Nick Tandy	MOMO Porsche GT3	689
30	34	64	GT	19	Gaetano Ardagna, Eduardo Costabal, Emilio DiGuida, Eliseo Salazar, Santiago Orjuela	TRG Porsche GT3	688
31	18	22	GT	20	Kevin Roush, Randy Blaylock, Joe White, Darryl O' Young, Brett Van Blankers	The Ridge Motorsports Park Porsche GT3	681
32	11	50	DP	12	Byron Defoor, Brian Johnson, Elliott Forbes-Robinson, Jim Pace, Carlos de Quesada	50+Predator/Alegra BMW/Riley	672
33	4	99	DP	13	Jon Fogarty, Alex Gurney, Memo Gidley	GAINSCO Auto Insurance Corvette DP	672
34	36	82	GT	21	John Fergus, Dick Greer, John Finger, Mark Hotchkis, Owen Trinkler	Wendy's Porsche GT3	665
35	25	56	GT	22	Robert Kauffman, Michael Waltrip, Travis Pastrana, Rui Aguas	RK Motors Ferrari 458	645
36	38	65	GT	23	Spencer Cox, Mike Hedlund, Jack McCarthy Jr, Jim Michaelian, Joe Castellano	TRG Porsche GT3	643
37	44	68	GT	24	Chris Cumming, Ben Keating, Damien Faulkner, Carlos Gomez, Kevin Estre	TRG Porsche GT3	640
38	28	55	GT	25	Douglas Grunnet, Frank Del Vecchio, Scott McKee, Randy Pobst, Tony Kester	ALM Materials Handling	626
39	31	18	GT	26	Mark Thomas, Bill Lester, John McCutchen, Davy Jones	Muehlner Motorsports Porsche GT3	609
40	35	41	GT	27	Don Kitch Jr, Daniel Rogers, Rick Johnson, Scott Maxwell, Ian James	Fishingcapital.com/Bass2BillFish/ Team Seattle Mazda RX-8	608
41	30	12	GT	28	Scott Rettich, Jon Miller, Hal Prewitt, Matt Schneider, Darryl Shoff	PDI Communication Systems Porsche GT3	604
42	42	19	GT	29	Derek Whitis, Rhett O'Doski, Ian Nater, Scott Dollahite, Marco Seefried	Muehlner Motorsports America Porsche GT3	599
43	12	75	GT	30	Al Carter, Hugh Plumb, Matt Bell, Eric Curran	Stevenson Auto Group Camaro GT.R	577
44	21	51	GT	31	Ian Baas, Dion von Moltke, Jim Norman, Nelson Canache, Emanuele Pirro	APR Tuned/Parathyroid.com/PR Newswire Audi R8	447
45	14	74	GT	32	Humaid Masaood, Steven Kane, Saeed Al Mehairi	Oryx Racing Audi R8	432
46	8	17	GT	33	Martin Ragginger, Jack Baldwin, Claudio Burtin, Bryan Sellers, Sebastian Asch	FOAMETIX Porsche GT3	424
47	33	20	GT	34	David Murry, Gunter Schaldach, Franz Engstler, Jade Buford	Liqui Moly Porsche GT3	416
48	40	34	GT	35	Michael DeFontes, Miro Konopka, Phil Fogg, Jan Vonka, Ronald van de Laar	GlobalBarterCorp.com Porsche GT3	383
49	16	4	GT	36	Ron Yarab Jr, Daniel Graeff, Ryan Eversley, Justin Bell	eBay Motors/Children's Tumor Foundation/Racing4Research Porsche GT3	310
50	37	36	GT	37	Taylor Hacquard, Jarett Andretti, Anders Krohn, John Andretti	Window World/PMFirst.com/ Mazdaspeed	270
51	22	15	GT	38	Jeffrey Earnhardt, Chris Cook, Doug Harrington, Timmy Hill, John Ware Jr.	Poynt Ford Mustang GT	256
52	9	48	GT	39	Bryce Miller, Sascha Maassen, Rob Bell, Mark Wilkins	Chopard Porsche GT3	224
53	41	46	GT	40	Max Ryan, Michael Baughman, Jeff Nowicki, Armand Fumal, Ivo Breukers	Dynamat/Hub Garage Corvette	172
54	45	62	GT	41	Gianmaria Bruni, Raphael Matos	Risi Competizione Ferrari 458	154
55	27	87	GT	42	Maxime Soulet, Emilio Valverde, Jan Heylen, Tony Ave	3-Dimensional.com Dodge Viper	101
56	29	94	GT	43	Paul Dalla Lana, Boris Said, Billy Johnson	Turner Motorsport BMW M3	86
57	32	43	GT	44	Will Nonnamaker	Theracesite.com Mazda RX-8	21
58	2	10	DP	14	Max Angelelli, Ricky Taylor, Ryan Briscoe	SunTrust Corvette DP	14

LENGTH OF RACE: 24:00:36.793 — MARGIN OF VICTORY: 5.198 seconds — CAUTIONS: 14 for 64 laps — AVERAGE SPEED (DP): 112.834 mph — AVERAGE SPEED (GT): 107.700 mph — POLESITTER(DP): Ryan Dalziel, No. 8 Motorola Ford/Riley – 1:41.119 (126.742 mph) — POLESITTER(GT): Andrew Davis, No. 59 The Brumos Companies Porsche GT3 – 1:49.342 (117.210 mph) — BEST LAP TIME (DP): Ryan Dalziel, No. 8 Motorola Ford/Riley – 1:41.470 (126.303 mph) — BEST LAP TIME (GT): Marco Holzer, No. 23 WeatherTech Porsche GT3 Cup – 1:48.410 (118.218 mph)

TOP 3 DP POINTS	Points
1 – Ozz Negri, John Pew, AJ Allmendinger, Justin Wilson	35
2 – Enzo Potolicchio, Ryan Dalziel, Alex Popow, Lucas Luhr, Allan McNish	32
3 – Michael McDowell, Felipe Nasr, Jorge Goncalvez, Gustavo Yacaman	30

TOP 3 GT POINTS	Points
1 – Andy Lally, John Potter, Richard Lietz, Rene Rast	35
2 – Steven Bertheau, Marc Goossens, Wolf Henzler, Spencer Pumpelly, Jeroen Bleekemolen	32
3 – Leh Keen, Andrew Davis, Hurley Haywood, Marc Lieb	30

2 PORSCHE 250 AT BARBER

Barber Motorsports Park — Birmingham, AL — March 31, 2012 — 2.3-mile, 17-turn stadium road course — 2 Hours, 45 Minutes

Pos.	Sic	No.	Class	Pic	Drivers	Car	Laps
1	1	90	DP	1	Antonio Garcia, Richard Westbrook	Spirit of Daytona Corvette DP	103
2	2	99	DP	2	Jon Fogarty, Alex Gurney	GAINSCO Auto Insurance Corvette DP	103
3	4	01	DP	3	Scott Pruett, Memo Rojas	TELMEX BMW/Riley	103
4	6	8	DP	4	Enzo Potolicchio, Ryan Dalziel	Duncan Ford/Riley	103
5	9	10	DP	5	Max Angelelli, Ricky Taylor	SunTrust Corvette DP	103
6	7	2	DP	6	Alex Popow, Lucas Luhr	Soloson Import Ford/Riley	102
7	8	9	DP	7	JC France, Joao Barbosa	Action Express Racing Corvette DP	101
8	5	60	DP	8	John Pew, Oswaldo Negri Jr.	Liveon.com Ford/Riley	100
9	17	70	GT	1	Sylvain Tremblay, Jonathan Bomarito	Mazdaspeed Mazda RX-8	98
10	11	69	GT	2	Emil Assentato, Jeff Segal	FXDD Ferrari 458	97
11	16	59	GT	3	Leh Keen, Andrew Davis	The Brumos Companies Porsche GT3	97
12	19	44	GT	4	John Potter, Andy Lally	Magnus Racing Porsche GT3	97
13	27	94	GT	5	Bill Auberlen, Paul Dalla Lana	Turner Motorsport BMW M3	97
14	10	88	GT	6	Jordan Taylor, Apopka, FL Paul Edwards	Autohaus Motorsports Camaro GT.R	97
15	12	57	GT	7	Robin Liddell, Ronnie Bremer	Stevenson Auto Group Camaro GT.R	97
16	14	41	GT	8	Charles Putman, Charles Espenlaub	Visit Florida Mazda RX-8	97
17	18	42	GT	9	Dane Cameron, Wayne Nonnamaker	Theracesite.com Mazda RX-8	97
18	26	67	GT	10	Steven Bertheau, Spencer Pumpelly	Sargent & Lundy Porsche GT3	97
19	28	51	GT	11	Dion von Moltke, Jim Norman	Parathyroid.com/PR Newswire Audi R8	97
20	15	31	GT	12	Boris Said, Eric Curran	Whelen Engineering Corvette	97
21	21	40	GT	13	Joe Foster, Patrick Dempsey	Visit Florida/Share A Little Sunshine Mazda RX-8	96
22	13	73	GT	14	Patrick Lindsey, Eric Foss	Neo Synthetic Oil Porsche GT3	95
23	20	74	GT	15	Humaid al Masaood, Steven Kane	Oryx Racing Audi R8	95
24	22	43	GT	16	Wayne Nonnamaker, Joe Nonnamaker	Theracesite.com Mazda RX-8	95
25	25	49	GT	17	Joe Sahlen, Will Nonnamaker	Western New York Flash Mazda RX-8	95
26	24	15	GT	18	Jeffrey Earnhardt, Chris Cook	Poynt.com Mustang Boss	94
27	3	5	DP	9	Darren Law, David Donohue	Action Express Racing Corvette DP	80
28	23	68	GT	19	Emilio DiGuida	Grupo SK 18 Porsche GT3	11

LENGTH OF RACE: 2:45:53.350 — MARGIN OF VICTORY: 2.326 seconds — CAUTIONS: 4 for 17 laps — AVERAGE SPEED (DP): 86.116 mph — AVERAGE SPEED (GT): 81.458 mph — POLESITTER(DP): Richard Westbrook, No. 90 Spirit of Daytona Corvette DP – 1:21.420 (101.695 mph) — POLESITTER(GT): Paul Edwards, No. 88 Autohaus Motorsports Camaro GT.R – 1:30.762 (91.228 mph) — BEST LAP TIME (DP): Richard Westbrook, No. 90 Spirit of Daytona Corvette DP – 1:22.245 (100.695 mph) — BEST LAP TIME (GT): Spencer Pumpelly, No. 67 TRG Porsche GT3 – 1:31.289 (90.701 mph)

TOP 3 DP POINTS	POINTS	TOP 3 GT POINTS	POINTS
1 – Enzo Potolicchio, Ryan Dalziel	60	1 – Andy Lally, John Potter	63
2 – Ozz Negri, John Pew	58	2 –Sylvain Tremblay, Jonathan Bomarito	60
3 – Richard Westbrook, Antonio Garcia	57	3 – Leh Keen, Andrew Davis	60

3 GRAND PRIX OF MIAMI AT HOMESTEAD-MIAMI

Homestead- Miami Speedway — Homestead, FL — April 29, 2012 — 2.3-mile, 11-turn stadium road course — 2 Hours, 45 Minutes

Pos.	Sic	No.	Class	Pic	Drivers	Car	Laps
1	9	10	DP	1	Max Angelelli, Ricky Taylor	SunTrust Corvette DP	54
2	4	01	DP	2	Scott Pruett, Memo Rojas	TELMEX BMW/Riley	54
3	6	5	DP	3	Darren Law, David Donohue	Action Express Racing Corvette DP	54
4	7	2	DP	4	Alex Popow, Lucas Luhr	Soloson Imports Ford/Riley	54
5	3	90	DP	5	Richard Westbrook, Antonio Garcia	Spirit of Daytona Corvette DP	54
6	13	69	GT	1	Emil Assentato, Jeff Segal	FXDD Ferrari 458	54
7	18	42	GT	2	Dane Cameron, Wayne Nonnamker	Theracesite.com Mazda RX-8	54
8	15	57	GT	3	Robin Liddell, Ronnie Bremer	Stevenson Auto Group Camaro GT.R	54
9	14	67	GT	4	Steven Bertheau, Spencer Pumpelly	Sargent & Lundy Porsche GT3	54
10	17	94	GT	5	Bill Auberlen, Paul Dalla Lana, Billy Johnson	Turner Motorsport BMW M3	54
11	12	59	GT	6	Leh Keen, Andrew Davis	The Brumos Companies Porsche GT3	54
12	10	44	GT	7	John Potter, Andy Lally	Magnus Racing Porsche GT3	54
13	23	68	GT	8	Emilio DiGuida, Jeroen Bleekemolen	Grupo SK 18 Porsche GT3	54
14	16	88	GT	9	Jordan Taylor, Paul Edwards	Autohaus Motorsports Camaro GT.R	54
15	27	93	GT	10	Paul Dalla Lana, Billy Johnson, Boris Said	Turner Motorsport BMW M3	54
16	26	73	GT	11	Patrick Lindsey, Eric Foss	Neo Synthetic Oil Porsche GT3	54
17	11	70	GT	12	Sylvain Tremblay, Jonathan Bomarito	Mazdaspeed Mazda RX-8	54
18	1	8	DP	6	Enzo Potolicchio, Ryan Dalziel	Duncan Ford/Riley	53
19	2	60	DP	7	John Pew, Ozz Negri	Liveon.com Ford/Riley	53
20	25	03	GT	13	Ed Brown, Guy Cosmo	Tequila Patron Ferrari 458	53
21	20	40	GT	14	Joe Foster, Patrick Dempsey, Tom Long	Visit Florida Mazda RX-8	53
22	19	41	GT	15	Charles Putman, Charles Espenlaub	Bass 2 Bill Fish Mazda RX-8	53
23	28	21	GT	16	Sebastian Martinez, Julian Martinez, Mario Monroy	M2 Autosport Mazda RX-8	52
24	21	51	GT	17	Dion von Moltke, Jim Norman, Ian Baas	APR Tuned Audi R8	52
25	24	31	GT	18	Boris Said, Eric Curran	Whelen Engineering Corvette	47
26	8	9	DP	8	Terry Borcheller, JC France, Joao Barbosa	Action Express Racing Corvette DP	39
27	5	99	DP	9	Jon Fogarty, Alex Gurney	GAINSCO Auto Insurance Corvetet DP	16
28	22	43	GT	19	Joe Nonnamaker, Will Nonnamaker	Theracesite.com Mazda RX-8	9

LENGTH OF RACE: 1:53:09.242 (rain shortened) — MARGIN OF VICTORY: 0.603 seconds — CAUTIONS: 3 for 24 laps — AVERAGE SPEED (DP): 65.857 mph — AVERAGE SPEED (GT): 65.906 mph — POLESITTER(DP): Set by points (rain) — POLESITTER(GT): Set by points (rain) — BEST LAP TIME (DP): Richard Westbrook, No.90 Spirit of Daytona Corvette DP – 1:25.063 (97.340 mph) — BEST LAP TIME (GT): Sylvain Tremblay, No. 70 SpeedSource Mazda RX-8 – 1:29.886 (92.117 mph)

TOP 3 DP POINTS	POINTS	TOP 3 GT POINTS	POINTS
1 – Scott Pruett, Memo Rojas	87	1 – Jeff Segal, Emil Assentato	90
2 – Alex Popow, Lucas Luhr	85	2 – Andy Lally, John Potter	87
3 – Ryan Dazliel, Enzo Potolicchio	85	3 – Andrew Davis, Leh Keen	85

4 GLOBAL BARTER 250 AT NEW JERSEY

New Jersey Motorsports Park — Millville, NJ — May 13, 2012 — 2.25-mile, 12-turn natural road course — 2 Hours, 45 Minutes

Pos.	Sic	No.	Class	Pic	Drivers	Car	Laps
1	1	10	DP	1	Max Angelelli, Ricky Taylor	SunTrust Corvette DP	117
2	6	8	DP	2	Enzo Potolicchio, Ryan Dalziel	Starworks Motorsport Ford/Riley	117
3	7	60	DP	3	John Pew, Oswaldo Negri Jr.	LiveOn Ford/Riley	117
4	5	5	DP	4	Darren Law, David Donohue	Action Express Racing Corvette DP	117
5	10	90	DP	5	Michael Valiante, Richard Westbrook	Spirit of Daytona Corvette DP	117
6	9	2	DP	6	Alex Popow, Lucas Luhr	Starworks Motorsport Ford/Riley	116
7	4	9	DP	7	Terry Borcheller, Joao Barbosa	Action Express Racing Corvette DP	114
8	9	69	GT	1	Emil Assentato, Jeff Segal	FXDD Ferrari 458	111
9	1	57	GT	2	Robin Liddell, John Edwards	Stevenson Auto Group Camaro GT.R	111
10	11	44	GT	3	John Potter, Andy Lally	Magnus Racing Porsche GT3	111
11	12	94	GT	4	Paul Dalla Lana, Billy Johnson	Turner Motorsport BMW M3	111
12	7	88	GT	5	Jordan Taylor, Paul Edwards	Autohaus Motorsports Camaro GT.R	111
13	5	42	GT	6	Dane Cameron, Wayne Nonnamaker	Theracesite.com Mazda RX-8	111
14	2	70	GT	7	Sylvain Tremblay, Jonathan Bomarito	Mazdaspeed Mazda RX-8	111
15	6	31	GT	8	Boris Said, Eric Curran	Whelen Engineering Corvette	111
16	3	59	GT	9	Leh Keen, Andrew Davis	The Brumos Companies Porsche GT3	110
17	16	67	GT	10	Steven Bertheau, Spencer Pumpelly	Sargent & Lundy Porsche GT3	110
18	15	41	GT	11	Charles Putman, Charles Espenlaub	Bass2BillFish Mazda RX-8	110
19	8	73	GT	12	Patrick Lindsey, Eric Foss	Horton Autosport Porsche GT3	108
20	4	08	GT	13	Elivan Goulart, Jason Lee	SCDA1.com Audi R8	108
21	8	77	DP	8	Jim Lowe, Paul Tracy	Drive4COPD Ford Dallara	108
22	13	51	GT	14	Dion von Moltke, Jim Norman	APR Tuned Audi R8	107
23	14	43	GT	15	Joe Nonnamaker, Will Nonnamaker	Theracesite.com Mazda RX-8	102
24	10	40	GT	16	Tom Long, Scott Maxwell	Visit Florida Mazda RX-8	100
25	2	99	DP	9	Jon Fogarty, Alex Gurney	GAINSCO Auto Insurance Corvette DP	83
26	3	01	DP	10	Scott Pruett, Memo Rojas	TELMEX BMW/Riley	80

LENGTH OF RACE: 2:45:34.839 — MARGIN OF VICTORY: 4.988 seconds — CAUTIONS: 2 for 7 laps — AVERAGE SPEED (DP): 95.681 mph — AVERAGE SPEED (GT): 90.187 mph — POLESITTER(DP): Ricky Taylor, No. 10 SunTrust Racing Corvette DP – 1:15.091 (107.869 mph) — POLESITTER(GT): John Edwards, No. 57 Stevenson Automotive Group Chevrolet Camaro – 1:21.834 (98.981 mph) — BEST LAP TIME (DP): Joao Barbosa, No. 9 Action Express Racing Corvette DP – 1:17.140 (105.004 mph) — BEST LAP TIME (GT): Jordan Taylor, No. 88 Autohaus Motorsports Chevrolet Camaro – 1:22.877 (97.735 mph)

TOP 3 DP POINTS	POINTS	TOP 3 GT POINTS	POINTS
1 – Enzo Potolicchio, Ryan Dalziel	117	1 – Emil Assentato, Jeff Segal	125
2 – Max Angelelli, Ricky Taylor	113	2 – Andy Lally, John Potter	117
3 – John Pew, Ozz Negri	112	3 – Robin Liddell	114

5 CHEVROLET GRAND-AM DETROIT 200 AT BELLE ISLE

Raceway At Belle Isle Park — Detroit, MI — June 2, 2012 — 2.1-mile, 14-turn temporary street course — 2 Hours

Pos.	Sic	No.	Class	Pic	Drivers	Car	Laps
1	4	9	DP	1	Darren Law, Joao Barbosa	Action Express Racing Corvette DP	72
2	3	5	DP	2	Terry Borcheller, David Donohue	Action Express Racing Corvette DP	72
3	5	01	DP	3	Scott Pruett, Memo Rojas	TELMEX BMW/Riley	72
4	1	99	DP	4	Jon Fogarty, Alex Gurney	GAINSCO Auto Insurance Corvette DP	72
5	9	60	DP	5	John Pew, Oswaldo Negri Jr.	LiveOn Ford/Riley	72
6	8	8	DP	6	Enzo Potolicchio, Ryan Dalziel	Duncan Ford/Riley	72
7	7	2	DP	7	Alex Popow, Lucas Luhr	Soloson Ford/Riley	72
8	10	7	DP	8	Scott Mayer, Colin Braun	Starworks Motorsport Ford/Riley	71
9	15	88	GT	1	Jordan Taylor, Paul Edwards	Autohaus Motorsports Camaro GT.R	70
10	18	70	GT	2	Sylvain Tremblay, Jonathan Bomarito	Mazdaspeed Mazda RX-8	70
11	12	57	GT	3	Robin Liddell, John Edwards	Stevenson Auto Group Camaro GT.R	70
12	22	69	GT	4	Emil Assentato, Jeff Segal	FXDD Ferrari 458	70
13	20	94	GT	5	Bill Auberlen, Paul Dalla Lana	Turner Motorsport BMW M3	70
14	19	44	GT	6	John Potter, Andy Lally	Magnus Racing Porsche GT3	70
15	11	03	GT	7	Scott Sharp, Guy Cosmo	Tequila Patron Ferrari 458	70
16	17	42	GT	8	Dane Cameron, Wayne Nonnamaker	Theracesite.com Mazda RX-8	69
17	26	43	GT	9	Wayne Nonnamaker, Joe Nonnamaker	Theracesite.com Mazda RX-8	69
18	21	73	GT	10	Patrick Lindsey, Eric Foss	Angels for Atticus/Neo Synthetic Oils Porsche GT3	68
19	14	51	GT	11	Dion von Moltke, Jim Norman	APR Tuned Audi R8	68
20	16	31	GT	12	Boris Said, Eric Curran	Whelen Engineering Corvette	67
21	13	59	GT	13	Leh Keen, Andrew Davis	The Brumos Companies Porsche GT3	66
22	6	90	DP	9	Richard Westbrook, Michael Valiante	Spirit of Daytona Corvette DP	65
23	23	67	GT	14	Steven Bertheau, Spencer Pumpelly	Sargent & Lundy Porsche GT3	63
24	24	41	GT	15	Charles Putman, Charles Espenlaub	Bass2BillFish Mazda RX-8	62
25	25	40	GT	16	Joe Foster, Patrick Dempsey	Visit Florida Mazda RX-8	61
26	2	10	DP	10	Max Angelelli, Ricky Taylor	SunTrust Racing Corvette DP	39
27	27	46	GT	17	Michael Baughman, Jeff Nowicki	Matick Chevrolet Corvette	13

LENGTH OF RACE: 2:00:57.049 — MARGIN OF VICTORY: 0.440 seconds — CAUTIONS: 4 for 14 laps — AVERAGE SPEED (DP): 74.807 mph — AVERAGE SPEED (GT): 72.120 mph — POLESITTER(DP): Jon Fogarty, No. 99 GAINSCO Auto Insurance Corvette DP – 1:22.369 seconds (90.908 mph) — POLESITTER(GT): Guy Cosmo, No. 03 Tequila Patron Ferrari 458 – 1:27.967 seconds (85.123 mph) — BEST LAP TIME (DP): Joao Barbosa, No. 9 Action Express Racing Corvette DP – 1:21.552 seconds (91.819 mph) — BEST LAP TIME (GT):): Guy Cosmo, No. 03 Tequila Patron Ferrari 458 – 1:27.589 seconds (85.490 mph)

TOP 3 DP POINTS	POINTS	TOP 3 GT POINTS	POINTS
1 – Enzo Potolicchio, Ryan Dalziel	142	1 – Emil Assentato, Jeff Segal	153
2 – Darren Law	141	2 – Robin Liddell	144
3 – John Pew, Ozz Negri; Memo Rojas, Scott Pruett; David Donohue	138	3 – Andy Lally, John Potter	142

6 EMCO GEARS CLASSIC AT MID-OHIO

Mid-Ohio Sports Car Course — Lexington, OH — June 9, 2012 — 2.258-mile, 13-turn natural road course — 2 Hours, 45 Minutes

Pos.	Sic	No.	Class	Pic	Drivers	Car	Laps
1	2	90	DP	1	Richard Westbrook, Michael Valiante	Spirit of Daytona Corvette DP	111
2	6	01	DP	2	Scott Pruett, Memo Rojas	TELMEX BMW/Riley	111
3	4	5	DP	3	Terry Borcheller, David Donohue	Action Express Racing Corvette DP	111
4	8	2	DP	4	Alex Popow, Lucas Luhr	Soloson Ford/Riley	111
5	9	8	DP	5	Enzo Potolicchio, Ryan Dalziel	Duncan Ford/Riley	111
6	5	9	DP	6	Darren Law, Joao Barbosa	Action Express Racing Corvette DP	111
7	1	99	DP	7	Jon Fogarty, Alex Gurney	GAINSCO Auto Insurance Corvette DP	110
8	7	60	DP	8	John Pew, Oswaldo Negri Jr.	LiveOn Ford/Riley	109
9	17	94	GT	1	Bill Auberlen, Paul Dalla Lana	Turner Motorsport BMW M3	106
10	15	69	GT	2	Emil Assentato, Jeff Segal	FXDD Ferrari 458	106
11	10	57	GT	3	Robin Liddell, John Edwards	Stevenson Auto Group Camaro GT.R	106
12	16	70	GT	4	Sylvain Tremblay, Jonathan Bomarito	Mazdaspeed Mazda RX-8	106
13	18	44	GT	5	Andy Lally, John Potter	Magnus Racing Porsche GT3	106
14	14	42	GT	6	Dane Cameron, Wayne Nonnamaker	Theracesite.com Mazda RX-8	106
15	11	59	GT	7	Leh Keen, Andrew Davis	The Brumos Companies Porsche GT3	106
16	24	67	GT	8	Steven Bertheau, Spencer Pumpelly	Sargent & Lundy Porsche GT3	106
17	12	88	GT	9	Jordan Taylor, Paul Edwards	Autohaus Motorsports Camaro GT.R	106
18	19	40	GT	10	Joe Foster, Patrick Dempsey	Visit Florida Mazda RX-8	106
19	21	41	GT	11	Charles Putman, Charles Espenlaub	Bass2BillFish Mazda RX-8	106
20	22	43	GT	12	Wayne Nonnamaker, Joe Nonnamaker	Theracesite.com	105
21	20	51	GT	13	Dion von Moltke, Jim Norman	APR Tuned Audi R8	105
22	13	31	GT	14	Boris Said, Eric Curran	Whelen Engineering Corvette	104
23	23	49	GT	15	Joe Sahlen, Will Nonnamaker	Western New York Flash Mazda RX-8	103
24	3	10	DP	9	Max Angelelli, Ricky Taylor	SunTrust Racing Corvette DP	100
25	26	73	GT	16	Patrick Lindsey, Eric Foss	Horton Autosport Porsche GT3	81
26	25	72	GT	17	Milton Grant	Courtyard Hotel Porsche GT3	10

LENGTH OF RACE: 2:45:52.182 — MARGIN OF VICTORY: 0.236 seconds — CAUTIONS: 3 for 12 laps — AVERAGE SPEED (DP): 91.121 mph — AVERAGE SPEED (GT): 86.485 mph — POLESITTER(DP): Jon Fogarty, No. 99 GAINSCO Auto Insurance Corvette DP – 1:18.079 (104.110 mph) — POLESITTER(GT): John Edwards, No. 57 Stevenson Auto Group Camaro GT.R – 1:25.083 (95.540 mph) — BEST LAP TIME (DP): Alex Gurney, No. 99 GAINSCO Auto Insurance Corvette DP – 1:18.529 (103.513 mph) — BEST LAP TIME (GT): Jeff Segal, No. 69 AIM Autosport Team FXDD Ferrari 458 – 1:24.746 (95.920 mph)

TOP 3 DP POINTS	POINTS	TOP 3 GT POINTS	POINTS
1 – Scott Pruett, Memo Rojas	170	1 – Emil Assentato, Jeff Segal	185
2 – Enzo Potolicchio, Ryan Dalziel; David Donohue	168	2 – Robin Liddell	174
3 – Richard Westbrook	167	3 – Andy Lally, John Potter	168

7 ROLEX SPORTS CAR SERIES 250 *driven by* VISITFLORIDA.COM AT ROAD AMERICA

Road America — Elkhart Lake, WI — June 23, 2012 — 4.048-mile, 14-turn natural road course — 2 Hours

Pos.	Sic	No.	Class	Pic	Drivers	Car	Laps
1	1	01	DP	1	Scott Pruett, Memo Rojas	TELMEX BMW/Riley	49
2	2	8	DP	2	Enzo Potolicchio, Ryan Dalziel	Starworks Motorsport Ford/Riley	49
3	5	60	DP	3	John Pew, Oswaldo Negri Jr.	LiveOn Ford/Riley	49
4	3	5	DP	4	Terry Borcheller, David Donohue	Action Express Racing Corvette DP	49
5	10	7	DP	5	Scott Mayer, Colin Braun	Starworks Motorsport Ford/Riley	49
6	7	9	DP	6	Darren Law, Joao Barbosa, JC France	Action Express Racing Corvette DP	47
7	11	69	GT	1	Emil Assentato, Jeff Segal	FXDD Ferrari 458	47
8	15	94	GT	2	Bill Auberlen, Paul Dalla Lana, Billy Johnson	Turner Motorsport BMW M3	47
9	14	70	GT	3	Sylvain Tremblay, Jonathan Bomarito	Mazdaspeed Mazda RX-8	47
10	18	42	GT	4	Dane Cameron, Wayne Nonnamaker	Theracesite.com Mazda RX-8	47
11	17	59	GT	5	Leh Keen, Andrew Davis	The Brumos Companies Porsche GT3	47
12	12	57	GT	6	Robin Liddell, John Edwards	Stevenson Auto Group Camaro GT.R	47
13	25	31	GT	7	Eric Curran, John Heinricy	Whelen Engineering Corvette	47
14	20	41	GT	8	Charles Putman, Charles Espenlaub	Bass2BillFish Mazda RX-8	47
15	16	88	GT	9	Jordan Taylor, Paul Edwards	Autohaus Motorsports Camaro GT.R	47
16	24	73	GT	10	Patrick Lindsey, Eric Foss	Horton Autosport Porsche GT3	47
17	21	40	GT	11	Joe Foster, Patrick Dempsey	Visit Florida Mazda RX-8	47
18	22	51	GT	12	Dion von Moltke, Jim Norman	APR Tuned Audi R8	46
19	23	43	GT	13	Joe Nonnamaker, Will Nonnamaker	Theracesite.com Mazda RX-8	46
20	6	10	DP	7	Max Angelelli, Ricky Taylor	SunTrust Racing Corvette DP	42
21	4	90	DP	8	Antonio Garcia, Richard Westbrook	Spirit of Daytona Corvette DP	41
22	13	44	GT	14	John Potter, Andy Lally	Magnus Racing Porsche GT3	36
23	8	2	DP	9	Alex Popow, Lucas Luhr	Soloson Ford/Riley	31
24	26	15	GT	15	John Ware Jr., Timmy Hill, Kevin O'Connell	Poynt.com Mustang Boss 302R	29
25	9	99	DP	10	Jon Fogarty, Alex Gurney	GAINSCO Auto Insurance Corvette DP	12
26	19	67	GT	16	Steven Bertheau, Spencer Pumpelly	Sargent & Lundy Porsche GT3	1

LENGTH OF RACE: 2:00:02.193 — MARGIN OF VICTORY: 3.747 seconds — CAUTIONS: 2 for 10 laps — AVERAGE SPEED (DP): 99.146 mph — AVERAGE SPEED (GT): 94.278 mph — POLESITTER(DP): Set by points (rain) — POLESITTER(GT): Set by points (rain) — BEST LAP TIME (DP): Richard Westbrook, No. 90 Spirit of Daytona Corvette DP – 2:01.744 (119.700 mph) — BEST LAP TIME (GT): Bill Auberlen, No. 94 Turner Motorsport BMW M3 – 2:11.828 (110.544 mph)

TOP 3 DP POINTS	POINTS	TOP 3 GT POINTS	POINTS
1 – Scott Pruett, Memo Rojas	205	1 – Jeff Segal, Emil Assentato	220
2 – Enzo Potolicchio, Ryan Dalziel	200	2 – Robin Liddell	199
3 – David Donohue	196	3 – Jonathan Bomarito, Sylvain Tremblay	193

8 SAHLEN'S SIX HOURS OF THE GLEN AT WATKINS GLEN

Watkins Glen International (long course) — Watkins Glen, NY — July 1, 2012 — 3.4-mile, 11-turn natural road course — 6 Hours

Pos.	Sic	No.	Class	Pic	Drivers	Car	Laps
1	3	9	DP	1	Darren Law, Joao Barbosa	Action Express Racing Corvette DP	182
2	7	99	DP	2	Jon Fogarty, Alex Gurney	GAINSCO Auto Insurance Corvette DP	182
3	9	8	DP	3	Enzo Potolicchio, Ryan Dalziel, Sebastien Bourdais	Duncan Ford/Riley	182
4	1	01	DP	4	Scott Pruett, Memo Rojas	TELMEX BMW/Riley	182
5	2	90	DP	5	Antonio Garcia, Richard Westbrook, Oliver Gavin	Spirit of Daytona Corvette DP	182
6	8	60	DP	6	John Pew, Oswaldo Negri Jr.	LiveOn Ford/Riley	182
7	6	5	DP	7	Terry Borcheller, David Donohue	Action Express Racing Corvette DP	182
8	5	2	DP	8	Alex Popow, Lucas Luhr	Soloson Ford/Riley	181
9	11	7	DP	9	Scott Mayer, Colin Braun, Mark Wilkins	Starworks Motorsport Ford/Riley	181
10	10	77	DP	10	Jim Lowe, Paul Tracy, Brian Frisselle	COMBOS Ford Dallara	180
11	16	57	GT	1	Robin Liddell, John Edwards	Stevenson Auto Group Camaro GT.R	174
12	20	94	GT	2	Bill Auberlen, Paul Dalla Lana, Billy Johnson	Turner Motorsport BMW M3	174
13	14	69	GT	3	Emil Assentato, Jeff Segal, Anthony Lazzaro	FXDD Ferrari 458	174
14	25	03	GT	4	Guy Cosmo, Johannes van Overbeek, Mike Hedlund	Tequila Patron Ferrari 458	174
15	12	75	GT	5	Jordan Taylor, Matt Bell, Ronnie Bremer	Stevenson Auto Group	174
16	19	59	GT	6	Leh Keen, Andrew Davis	The Brumos Companies Porsche GT3	173
17	15	70	GT	7	Sylvain Tremblay, Jonathan Bomarito	Mazdaspeed Mazda RX-8	173
18	22	41	GT	8	Charles Putman, Charles Espenlaub, Scott Maxwell	Bass2BillFish Mazda RX-8	172
19	23	42	GT	9	Dane Cameron, Wayne Nonnamaker	Theracesite.com Mazda RX-8	171
20	21	73	GT	10	Patrick Lindsey, Eric Foss, Ryan Eversley	Horton Autosport Porsche GT3	171
21	24	56	GT	11	Robert Kauffman, Rui Aguas	RK Motors Ferrari 458	166
22	13	52	GT	12	Frank Stippler, Marc Basseng	APR Tuned Audi R8	164
23	31	64	GT	13	Eduardo Costabal, Eliseo Salazar, Santiago Orjuela	AGUNSA Porsche GT3	164
24	29	43	GT	14	Joe Sahlen, Joe Nonnamaker, Will Nonnamaker	Theracesite.com Mazda RX-8	164
25	28	67	GT	15	Al Carter, Spencer Pumpelly, Wolf Henzler	BePositive Porsche GT3	161
26	30	40	GT	16	Joe Foster, Patrick Dempsey, Tom Long	Visit Florida Mazda RX-8	158
27	18	17	GT	17	Martin Ragginger, Claudio Burtin	Foametix Porsche GT3	140
28	32	51	GT	18	Dion von Moltke, Jim Norman, Ian Baas	APR Tuned Audi R8	139
29	27	66	GT	19	Ben Keating, Damien Faulkner, Bryan Sellers	Forgeline Porsche GT3	137
30	17	31	GT	20	Boris Said, Eric Curran, Lawson Aschenbach	Whelen Engineering	119
31	4	10	DP	11	Max Angelelli, Ricky Taylor	SunTrust Racing Corvette DP	100
32	26	44	GT	21	Andy Lally, John Potter	Magnus Racing Porsche GT3	12

LENGTH OF RACE: 6:01:34.427 — MARGIN OF VICTORY: 0.238 seconds — CAUTIONS: 6 for 25 laps — AVERAGE SPEED (DP): 102.827 mph — AVERAGE SPEED (GT): 98.031 mph — POLESITTER(DP): Scott Pruett, No. 01 TELMEX BMW/Riley – 1:41.309 (120.818 mph) — POLESITTER(GT): Jordan Taylor, No. 75 Stevenson Auto Group Camaro GT.R – 1:50.475 (110.475 mph) — BEST LAP TIME (DP): Alex Gurney, No. 99 GAINSCO Auto Insurance Corvette DP – 1:42.774 (119.096 mph) — BEST LAP TIME (GT): Bill Auberlen, No. 94 Turner Motorsport BMW M3 – 1:51.274 (109.999 mph)

TOP 3 DP POINTS	POINTS	TOP 3 GT POINTS	POINTS
1 – Scott Pruett, Memo Rojas	233	1 – Emil Assentato, Jeff Segal	250
2 – Enzo Potolicchio, Ryan Dalziel	230	2 – Robin Liddell	234
3 – Darren Law	226	3 – Paul Dalla Lana	221

9 BRICKYARD GRAND PRIX AT INDIANAPOLIS

Indianapolis Motor Speedway — Indianapolis, IN — July 27, 2012 — 2.534-mile, 13-turn stadium road course — 3 Hours

Pos.	Sic	No.	Class	Pic	Drivers	Car	Laps
1	5	2	DP	1	Sebastien Bourdais, Alex Popow	Soloson Ford/Riley	91
2	8	01	DP	2	Scott Pruett, Memo Rojas	TELMEX BMW/Riley	91
3	2	10	DP	3	Max Angelelli, Ricky Taylor	SunTrust Racing Corvette DP	91
4	6	02	DP	4	Juan Pablo Montoya, Scott Dixon	Chevron BMW/Riley	91
5	25	44	GT	1	John Potter, Andy Lally	Magnus Racing Porsche GT3	91
6	12	70	GT	2	Sylvain Tremblay, Jonathan Bomarito	Mazdaspeed Mazda RX-8	91
7	15	59	GT	3	Leh Keen, Andrew Davis	The Brumos Companies Porsche GT3	91
8	23	94	GT	4	Bill Auberlen, Paul Dalla Lana, Billy Johnson	Turner Motorsport BMW M3	91
9	18	69	GT	5	Emil Assentato, Jeff Segal	FXDD Ferrari 458	91
10	32	17	GT	6	Claudio Burtin, Martin Ragginger	Foametix Porsche GT3	91
11	13	31	GT	7	Boris Said, Eric Curran	Whelen Engineering Corvette	91
12	21	43	GT	8	Dane Cameron, Wayne Nonnamaker	Theracesite.com Mazda RX-8	91
13	22	41	GT	9	Charles Putman, Charles Espenlaub	Visit Florida Mazda RX-8	91
14	19	88	GT	10	Jordan Taylor, Bill Lester	Autohaus Motorsports Camaro GT.R	91
15	10	9	DP	5	Darren Law, Joao Barbosa	Action Express Racing Corvette DP	90
16	11	77	DP	6	Jim Lowe, Paul Tracy	M&M's Snack Mix Ford Dallara	90
17	7	8	DP	7	Enzo Potolicchio, Ryan Dalziel	Duncan Ford/Riley	90
18	26	66	GT	11	Jorg Bergmeister, Ben Keating	TRG Porsche GT3	90
19	3	5	DP	8	Terry Borcheller, David Donohue	Action Express Racing Corvette DP	88
20	31	15	GT	12	Kevin O'Connell	Poynt.com Mustang Boss 302R	85
21	24	64	GT	13	Eduardo Costabal, Eliseo Salazar	TRG Porsche GT3	84
22	30	56	GT	14	Robert Kauffman, Rui Aguas	RK Motors Ferrari 458	83
23	14	57	GT	15	Robin Liddell, John Edwards	Stevenson Auto Group Camaro GT.R	61
24	34	87	GT	16	Jan Heylen, Tony Ave	Vehicle Technologies Dodge Viper	74
25	4	90	DP	9	Antonio Garcia, Richard Westbrook	Spirit of Daytona Corvette DP	73
26	20	75	GT	17	Matt Bell, Ronnie Bremer	Stevenson Auto Group Camaro GT.R	61
27	1	99	DP	10	Jon Fogarty, Alex Gurney	GAINSCO Auto Insurance Corvette DP	52
28	16	51	GT	18	Dion von Moltke, Jim Norman	APR Tuned Audi R8	51
29	17	73	GT	19	Patrick Lindsey, Eric Foss	Horton Autosport Porsche GT3	48
30	27	42	GT	20	Will Nonnamaker	Theracesite.com Mazda RX-8	47
31	29	40	GT	21	Joe Foster, Patrick Dempsey	Visit Florida Mazda RX-8	45
32	9	60	DP	11	John Pew, Oswaldo Negri Jr.	Liveon.com Ford/Riley	32
33	33	72	GT	22	Milton Grant, Kevin Grant	Grant Racing Porsche GT3	32
34	28	46	GT	23	Sebastian Saavedra	Hub Garage Corvette	23

LENGTH OF RACE: 3:00:55.304 — MARGIN OF VICTORY: 1.271 seconds — CAUTIONS: 9 for 34 laps — AVERAGE SPEED (DP): 76.827 mph — AVERAGE SPEED (GT): 76.427 mph — POLESITTER(DP): Jon Fogarty, No. 99 GAINSCO Auto Insurance Corvette DP – 1:23.035 (109.862 mph) — POLESITTER(GT): Jonathan Bomarito, No. 70 SpeedSource Mazda RX-8 – 1:30.359 (100.957 mph) — BEST LAP TIME (DP): Sebastien Bourdais, No. 2 Soloson Ford/Riley – 1:22.712 (110.291 mph) — BEST LAP TIME (GT): Jorg Bergmeister, No. 66 TRG Porsche GT3 – 1:29.770 (101.620 mph)

TOP 3 DP POINTS	POINTS	TOP 3 GT POINTS	POINTS
1 – Scott Pruett, Memo Rojas	265	1 – Emil Assentato, Jeff Segal	276
2 – Enzo Potolicchio, Ryan Dalziel	254	2 – Robin Liddell	250
3 – Darren Law	252	3 – Paul Dalla Lana; Jonathan Bomarito, Sylvain Tremblay	249

10 CONTINENTAL TIRE 200 AT WATKINS GLEN

Watkins Glen International — Watkins Glen, NY — August 11, 2012 — 2.45-mile, 7-turn natural road course — 2 Hours

Pos.	Sic	No.	Class	Pic	Drivers	Car	Laps
1	4	8	DP	1	Ryan Dalziel, Lucas Luhr	Starworks Motorsport Ford/Riley	91
2	3	2	DP	2	Sebastien Bourdais, Alex Popow	Soloson Ford/Riley	91
3	5	01	DP	3	Scott Pruett, Memo Rojas	TELMEX BMW/Riley	91
4	1	10	DP	4	Max Angelelli, Ricky Taylor	Sun Trust Racing Corvette DP	91
5	8	99	DP	5	Jon Fogarty, Alex Gurney	GAINSCO Auto Insurance Corvette DP	91
6	7	5	DP	6	David Donohue, Jordan Taylor	Action Express Racing Corvette DP	91
7	9	60	DP	7	John Pew, Oswaldo Negri Jr.	Liveon.com Ford/Riley	90
8	17	94	GT	1	Bill Auberlen, Paul Dalla Lana	Turner Motorsport BMW M3	87
9	10	31	GT	2	Boris Said, Eric Curran	Whelen Engineering Corvette	87
10	16	59	GT	3	Leh Keen, Andrew Davis	The Brumos Companies Porsche GT3	87
11	19	44	GT	4	John Potter, Andy Lally	Magnus Racing Porsche GT3	87
12	6	9	DP	8	Darren Law, Joao Barbosa	Action Express Racing Corvette DP	86
13	22	41	GT	5	Charles Putman, Charles Espenlaub	Bass2BillFish Mazda RX-8	86
14	21	42	GT	6	Wayne Nonnamaker, Joe Nonnamaker	Theracesite.com Mazda RX-8	86
15	13	69	GT	7	Emil Assentato, Jeff Segal	FXDD Ferrari 458	84
16	25	46	GT	8	Michael Baughman, James Davison	Vet-U-Caution.com Corvette	83
17	23	49	GT	9	Joe Sahlen, Will Nonnamaker	Western New York Flash Mazda RX-8	83
18	15	43	GT	10	Dane Cameron, Wayne Nonnamaker	Theracesite.com Mazda RX-8	81
19	12	73	GT	11	Patrick Lindsey, Eric Foss	Neo Synthetic Oil Porsche GT3	76
20	14	70	GT	12	Sylvain Tremblay, Jonathan Bomarito	Mazdaspeed Mazda RX-8	73
21	20	51	GT	13	Dion von Moltke, Jim Norman	APR Tuned Audi R8	70
22	11	57	GT	14	Robin Liddell, John Edwards	Stevenson Auto Group Camaro GT.R	66
23	24	56	GT	15	Robert Kauffman	RK Motors Ferrari 458	23
24	18	40	GT	16	Joe Foster, Patrick Dempsey	Visit Florida Mazda RX-8	17
25	2	90	DP	9	Antonio Garcia, Richard Westbrpok	Spirit of Daytona Corvette DP	1

LENGTH OF RACE: 2:00:47.712 — MARGIN OF VICTORY: 0.817 seconds — CAUTIONS: 3 for 14 laps — AVERAGE SPEED (DP): 111.356 mph — AVERAGE SPEED (GT): 105.557 mph — POLESITTER(DP): Ricky Taylor, No. 10 SunTrust Corvette DP – 1:06.039 (133.557 mph) — POLESITTER(GT): Boris Said, No. 31 Whelen Engineering Corvette – 1:12.674 (121.364 mph) — BEST LAP TIME (DP): Ryan Dalziel, No. 8 Starworks Motorsport Ford/Riley – 1:05.645 (134.359 mph) — BEST LAP TIME (GT): Boris Said, No. 31 Whelen Engineering Corvette – 1:12.308 (121.978 mph)

TOP 3 DP POINTS	POINTS	TOP 3 GT POINTS	POINTS
1 – Scott Pruett, Memo Rojas	295	1 – Emil Assentato, Jeff Segal	300
2 – Ryan Dalziel	289	2 – Paul Dalla Lana	284
3 – Darren Law	275	3 – Jonathan Bomarito, Sylvain Tremblay	268

11 MONTREAL 200 AT MONTREAL

Circuit Gilles Villeneuve — Montreal, Quebec, Canada — August 18, 2012 — 2.709-mile, 15-turn road course — 2 Hours

Pos.	Sic	No.	Class	Pic	Drivers	Car	Laps
1	2	01	DP	1	Scott Pruett, Memo Rojas	TELMEX BMW/Riley	66
2	1	99	DP	2	Jon Fogarty, Alex Gurney	GAINSCO Auto Insurance Corvette DP	66
3	7	5	DP	3	David Donohue, Paul Tracy	Action Express Racing Corvette DP	66
4	5	9	DP	4	Darren Law, Joao Barbosa	Action Express Racing Corvette DP	66
5	4	10	DP	5	Max Angelelli, Ricky Taylor	SunTrust Racing Corvette DP	66
6	8	60	DP	6	John Pew, Oswaldo Negri Jr.	Liveon.com Ford/Riley	66
7	9	2	DP	7	Alex Popow, Alex Tagliani	Soloson Ford/Riley	66
8	3	8	DP	8	Ryan Dalziel, Alex Tagliani	Duncan Ford/Riley	66
9	10	57	GT	1	Robin Liddell, John Edwards	Stevenson Auto Group Camaro GT.R	64
10	14	69	GT	2	Emil Assentato, Jeff Segal	FXDD Ferrari 458	64
11	13	43	GT	3	Dane Cameron, Wayne Nonnamaker	Theracesite.com Mazda RX-8	64
12	11	59	GT	4	Leh Keen, Andrew Davis	The Brumos Companies Porsche GT3	64
13	15	70	GT	5	Sylvain Tremblay, Jonathan Bomarito	Mazdaspeed Mazda RX-8	63
14	21	41	GT	6	Charles Putman, Charles Espenlaub	Bass2BillFish Mazda RX-8	63
15	12	31	GT	7	Boris Said, Eric Curran	Whelen Engineering Corvette	63
16	19	40	GT	8	Scott Maxwell, Tom Long	Visit Florida Mazda RX-8	63
17	18	51	GT	9	Dion von Moltke, Jim Norman	APR Tuned Audi R8	63
18	20	42	GT	10	Joe Nonnamaker, Will Nonnamaker	Theracesite.com Mazda RX-8	62
19	16	44	GT	11	John Potter, Andy Lally	Magnus Racing Porsche GT3	58
20	17	94	GT	12	Paul Dalla Lana, Billy Johnson	Turner Motorsport BMW M3	17
21	6	90	DP	9	Richard Westbrook, Michael Valiante	Spirit of Daytona Corvette DP	1

TIME OF RACE: 2:00:16.057 — MARGIN OF VICTORY: 22.902 seconds — CAUTIONS: 2 for 10 laps — AVERAGE SPEED (DP): 89.322 mph — AVERAGE SPEED (GT): 85.917 mph — POLESITTER(DP): Jon Fogarty, No. 99 GAINSCO Auto Insurance Corvette DP – 1:33.135 (104.713 mph) — POLESITTER(GT): John Edwards, No. 57 Stevenson Auto Group Camaro GT.R – 1:39.096 (98.414 mph) — Fastest Race Lap (DP): Alex Tagliani, No. 2 Soloson Ford/Riley – 1:33.035 (104.825 mph) — Fastest Race Lap (GT): Jeff Segal, No. 69 FXDD Ferrari 458 – 1:39.640 (97.876 mph)

TOP 3 DP POINTS	POINTS	TOP 3 GT POINTS	POINTS
1 – Scott Pruett, Memo Rojas	330	1 – Emil Assentato, Jeff Segal	332
2 – Ryan Dalziel	312	2 – Paul Dalla Lana	303
3 – Darren Law	303	3 – Robin Liddell	302

12 CONTINENTAL TIRE SPORTS CAR FESTIVAL *powered by* MAZDA AT LAGUNA SECA

Mazda Raceway Laguna Seca — Monterey, CA — September 9, 2012 — 2.238-mile, 11-turn natural road course — 2 Hours, 45 Minutes

Pos.	Sic	No.	Class	Pic	Drivers	Car	Laps
1	1	90	DP	1	Antonio Garcia, Richard Westbrook	Spirit of Daytona Corvette DP	111
2	2	99	DP	2	Jon Fogarty, Alex Gurney	GAINSCO Auto Insurance Corvette DP	111
3	6	8	DP	3	Ryan Dalziel, Alex Tagliani	Starworks Motorsport Ford/Riley	111
4	9	60	DP	4	John Pew, Oswaldo Negri Jr.	Liveon.com Ford/Riley	111
5	8	9	DP	5	Darren Law, Joao Barbosa	Action Express Racing Corvette DP	111
6	5	01	DP	6	Scott Pruett, Memo Rojas	TELMEX BMW/Riley	111
7	4	10	DP	7	Max Angelelli, Ricky Taylor	SunTrust Racing Corvette DP	111
8	3	2	DP	8	Alex Popow, Alex Tagliani	Starworks Motorsport Ford/Riley	111
9	7	5	DP	9	David Donohue, Paul Tracy	Action Express Racing Corvette DP	110
10	10	7	DP	10	Scott Mayer, Colin Braun	Starworks Motorsport Ford/Riley	110
11	16	43	GT	1	Dane Cameron, Wayne Nonnamaker	Theracesite.com Mazda RX-8	106
12	15	69	GT	2	Emil Assentato, Jeff Segal	FXDD Ferrari 458	106
13	18	44	GT	3	John Potter, Andy Lally	Magnus Racing Porsche GT3	106
14	11	63	GT	4	Olivier Beretta, Alessandro Balzan	Scuderia Corsa Ferrari 458	106
15	27	03	GT	5	Mike Hedlund, Johannes van Overbeek	Tequila Patron Ferrari 458	106
16	13	59	GT	6	Leh Keen, Andrew Davis	The Brumos Companies Porsche GT3	106
17	14	31	GT	7	Boris Said, Eric Curran	Whelen Engineering Corvette	106
18	26	57	GT	8	Robin Liddell, John Edwards	Stevenson Auto Group Camaro GT.R	106
19	17	70	GT	9	Sylvain Tremblay, Jonathan Bomarito	Mazdaspeed Mazda RX-8	105
20	21	94	GT	10	Bill Auberlen, Paul Dalla Lana	Turner Motorsport BMW M3	105
21	20	41	GT	11	Charles Putman, Charles Espenlaub	Bass2BillFish Mazda RX-8	105
22	19	51	GT	12	Dion von Moltke, Jim Norman	APR Tuner Audi R8	104
23	22	40	GT	13	Joe Foster, Patrick Dempsey	Visit Florida Mazda RX-8	103
24	25	49	GT	14	Joe Sahlen, Will Nonnamaker	Western New York Flash Mazda RX-8	103
25	23	42	GT	15	Wayne Nonnamaker, Joe Nonnamaker	Theracesite.com Mazda RX-8	100
26	12	73	GT	16	Patrick Lindsey, Eric Foss	Neo Synthetics Porsche GT3	85
27	24	87	GT	17	Jan Heylen, Tony Ave	3-Dimensional.com Dodge Viper	83

LENGTH OF RACE: 2:45:15.988 — MARGIN OF VICTORY: 3.878 seconds — CAUTIONS: 2 for 8 laps — AVERAGE SPEED (DP): 90.279 mph — AVERAGE SPEED (GT): 86.247 mph — POLESITTER(DP): Richard Westbrook, No. 90 Spirit of Daytona Corvette DP – 1:21.042 (99.415 mph) — POLESITTER(GT): Alessandro Balzan, No. 63 Scuderia Corsa Ferrari 458 – 1:27.594 (91.979 mph) — BEST LAP TIME (DP): Richard Westbrook, No. 90 Spirit of Daytona Corvette DP – 1:22.478 (97.684 mph) — BEST LAP TIME (GT): Alessandro Balzan, No. 63 Scuderia Corsa Ferrari 458 – 1:28.301 (91.242 mph)

TOP 3 DP POINTS	POINTS	TOP 3 GT POINTS	POINTS
1 – Scott Pruett, Memo Rojas	355	1 – Emil Assentato, Jeff Segal	364
2 – Ryan Dalziel	342	2 – Robin Liddell	325
3 – Darren Law	329	3 – Paul Dalla Lana	324

13 CHAMPIONSHIP WEEKEND *presented by* BMW AT LIME ROCK PARK

Lime Rock Park — Lakeville, CT — September 29, 2012 — 1.53-mile, 7-turn natural road course — 2 Hours, 45 Minutes

Pos.	Sic	No.	Class	Pic	Drivers	Car	Laps
1	4	10	DP	1	Max Angelelli, Ricky Taylor	SunTrust Racing Corvette DP	167
2	1	90	DP	2	Antonio Garcia, Richard Westbrook	Spirit of Daytona Corvette DP	167
3	3	99	DP	3	Jon Fogarty, Alex Gurney	GAINSCO Auto Insurance Corvette DP	167
4	6	5	DP	4	David Donohue, Brian Frisselle	Action Express Racing Corvette DP	167
5	7	9	DP	5	Darren Law, Joao Barbosa	Action Express Racing Corvette DP	167
6	5	8	DP	6	Ryan Dalziel, Alex Popow	Starworks Motorsport Ford/Riley	167
7	2	01	DP	7	Scott Pruett, Memo Rojas	TELMEX BMW/Riley	167
8	10	2	DP	8	Jorge Goncalvez, Martin Fuentes	Starworks Motorsport Ford/Riley	165
9	9	7	DP	9	Alex Popow, Billy Johnson	Starworks Motorsport Ford/Riley	164
10	8	60	DP	10	John Pew, Oswaldo Negri Jr.	LiveOn Ford/Riley	163
11	11	57	GT	1	Robin Liddell, John Edwards	Stevenson Auto Group Camaro GT.R	159
12	26	51	GT	2	Dion von Moltke, Jim Norman	APR Tuned Audi R8	159
13	13	63	GT	3	Alessandro Balzan, Johannes van Overbeek	Scuderia Corsa Ferrari 458	159
14	21	41	GT	4	Charles Putman, Charles Espenlaub	Bass2BillFish Mazda RX-8	159
15	25	66	GT	5	Spencer Pumpelly, Bob Doyle	RUFocused.com Porsche GT3	159
16	19	44	GT	6	John Potter, Andy Lally	Magnus Racing Porsche GT3	159
17	17	31	GT	7	Boris Said, Eric Curran	Whelen Engineering Corvette	158
18	23	69	GT	8	Emil Assentato, Jeff Segal	FXDD Ferrari 458	156
19	18	40	GT	9	Joe Foster, Tom Long	Share A Little Sunshine Mazda RX-8	155
20	24	42	GT	10	Joe Nonnamaker, Will Nonnamaker	Theracesite.com Mazda RX-8	110
21	14	70	GT	11	Sylvain Tremblay, Jonathan Bomarito	Mazdaspeed Mazda RX-8	154
22	16	43	GT	12	Dane Cameron, Wayne Nonnamaker	Theracesite.com Mazda RX-8	110
23	22	73	GT	13	Patrick Lindsey, Jason Hart	Neo Synthetic Oil USA Porsche GT3	107
24	20	93	GT	14	Will Turner, Michael Marsal	Turner Motorsport BMW M3	97
25	12	59	GT	15	Andrew Davis, Leh Keen	The Brumos Companies Porsche GT3	35
26	15	94	GT	16	Bill Auberlen, Paul Dalla Lana	Turner Motorsport BMW M3	

LENGTH OF RACE: 2:45:34.285 — MARGIN OF VICTORY: 0.334 seconds — CAUTIONS: 5 for 29 laps — AVERAGE SPEED (DP): 92.873 mph — AVERAGE SPEED (GT): 88.389 mph — POLESITTER(DP): Richard Westbrook, No. 90 Spirit of Daytona Corvette DP – 49.091 (110.000 mph) — POLESITTER(GT): John Edwards, No. 57 Stevenson Auto Group Camaro GT.R – 53.983 (100.031 mph) — BEST LAP TIME (DP): Richard Westbrook, No. 90 Spirit of Daytona Corvette DP – 49.913 (108.188 mph) — BEST LAP TIME (GT): John Edwards, No. 57 Stevenson Auto Group Camaro GT.R – 54.539 (99.012 mph)

TOP 3 DP POINTS	POINTS	TOP 3 GT POINTS	POINTS
1 – Scott Pruett, Memo Rojas	379	1 – Emil Assentato, Jeff Segal	387
2 – Ryan Dalziel	367	2 – Robin Liddell	360
3 – Darren Law	355	3 – Paul Dalla Lana	339

GRAND-AM, AMERICAN LE MANS SERIES SET EYES TO THE FUTURE

It was an announcement few ever expected.

Last September, leaders of GRAND-AM Road Racing and the American Le Mans Series presented by Tequila Patrón met at Daytona International Speedway to announce a landmark merger of the two organizations that will result in a unified series in 2014.

GRAND-AM and the ALMS will continue to run separate schedules for 2013. But next January, both groups will race under one banner, beginning with the 2014 Rolex 24 At Daytona.

Under the terms of the merger, the following entities combined with GRAND-AM: the American Le Mans Series; the International Motor Sports Association, which sanctions ALMS events; the Road Atlanta race track facility in Braselton, GA; the Chateau Elan Hotel and Conference Center in Sebring, FL; and Sebring International Raceway, via a reassignment of the lease agreement with the Sebring Airport Authority to operate the raceway.

"This announcement is transforming sports car racing on this continent, along with having world-wide industry implications," said GRAND-AM President and CEO Ed Bennett. "Aside from the organizations involved, everybody wins: drivers, teams, manufacturers, sponsors, tracks – and most all, the fans."

The potential of the series can be seen immediately when considering the potential of an expanded North American Endurance Championship presented by VISITFLORIDA.com. The competition, which began in 2012, includes the three longest events on the Rolex Series schedule, with the Rolex 24 at Daytona, Sahlen's Six Hours of The Glen at Watkins Glen International and the Brickyard Grand Prix at Indianapolis Motor Speedway. In 2014 sports car fans anticipate the storied Mobil 1 Twelve Hours of Sebring fueled by Fresh From Florida and the Petit Le Mans at Road Atlanta joining the NAEC.

Fans won't have to wait until 2014 to catch a glimpse of the future.

On August 10-11, GRAND-AM and the ALMS race together for the first time when they hold separate races at Road America in Elkhart Lake, Wisconsin. The Rolex Series and Continental Tire Sports Car Challenge will compete at the historic circuit on Saturday, with the ALMS racing on Sunday.

The ALMS began operations in 1999, with GRAND-AM debuting in 2000. Both organizations were created in the aftermath of the late-90's departure of the highly popular IMSA Camel GT circuit in North America. IMSA was founded in 1969 by John Bishop and then-NASCAR President Bill France Sr.

"The merger looks good from a business standpoint but it also 'feels good' from a historical standpoint," Bennett said. "Both GRAND-AM and the ALMS have lineages tied to Daytona Beach, Daytona International Speedway and the France Family. This announcement is a proud moment for all involved, as we now look forward to a bright future for sports car racing."

2013 NASCAR K&N PRO SERIES EAST SCHEDULE

Date	Track (Length)	Location
February 19 *^	Daytona International Speedway (.4-mile)	Daytona Beach, FL
March 16	Bristol Motor Speedway (.533-mile)	Bristol, TN
March 23	Greenville Pickens Speedway (.5-mile)	Greenville, SC
April 13	Five Flags Speedway (.5-mile)	Pensacola, FL
April 25	Richmond International Raceway (.75-mile)	Richmond, VA
June 1	Bowman Gray Stadium (.25-mile)	Winston-Salem, NC
June 7 *	Iowa Speedway (.875-mile)	Newton, IA
June 22	Langley Speedway (.396-mile)	Hampton, VA
July 13	Columbus Motor Speedway (.333-mile)	Columbus, OH
July 20	CNB Bank Raceway Park (.52-mile)	Clearfield, PA
August 2 *	Iowa Speedway (.875-mile)	Newton, IA
September 2	Greenville Pickens Speedway (.5-mile)	Greenville, SC
September 21	New Hampshire Motor Speedway (1.058-mile)	Loudon, NH
September 27	Dover International Speedway (1-mile)	Dover, DE
October 18	Road Atlanta (2.54-mile road course)	Braselton, GA
November 2	Rockingham Speedway (1-mile)	Rockingham, NC

* Combination race with NASCAR K&N Pro Series West
^ Non-points event

2013 NASCAR K&N PRO SERIES WEST SCHEDULE

Date	Track (Length)	Location
February 19	Daytona International Speedway (.4-mile)	Daytona Beach, FL
March 2	Phoenix International Raceway (1-mile)	Avondale, AZ
May 4	Stockton 99 Speedway (.25-mile)	Stockton, CA
May 25	Brainerd International Raceway (2.5–mile road course)	Brainerd, MN
June 7 *	Iowa Speedway (.875-mile)	Newton, IA
June 9	Lebanon I-44 Speedway (.375-mile)	Lebanon, MO
June 22	Sonoma Raceway (1.99-mile road course)	Sonoma, CA
July 27	Colorado National Speedway (.375-mile)	Dacono, CO
August 2 *	Iowa Speedway (.875-mile)	Newton, IA
August 17	Evergreen Speedway (.646-mile)	Monroe, WA
August 24	Spokane County Raceway (.5-mile)	Airway Heights, WA
September 14	Miller Motorsports Park (2.2-mile road course)	Tooele, UT
September 28	NAPA Speedway (.5-mile)	Albuquerque, NM
October 12	All American Speedway (.333-mile)	Roseville, CA
October 26	Kern County Raceway Park (.5-mile)	Bakersfield, CA
November 9	Phoenix International Raceway (1-mile)	Avondale, AZ

* Combination race with NASCAR K&N Pro Series East
^ Non-points event

2013 NASCAR CANADIAN TIRE SERIES SCHEDULE

Date	Track (Length)	Location
May 19	Canadian Tire Motorsport Park (2.459-mile road course)	Bowmanville, ON
June 15	Delaware Speedway (.5-mile)	Delaware, ON
June 22	Speedway at Canadian Tire Motorsport Park (.5-mile)	Bowmanville, ON
July 7	Circuit ICAR (2.113-mile road course)	Mirabel, QC
July 13	Motoplex Speedway (.5-mile)	Vernon, BC
July 17	Auto Clearing Motor Speedway (.333-mile)	Saskatoon, SK
July 27	Autodrome St. Eustache (.4-mile)	St. Eustache, QC
August 11	Circuit de Trois-Rivieres (1.53-mile road course)	Trois-Rivieres, QC
August 17	Riverside International Speedway (.333-mile)	Antigonish, NS
September 1	Canadian Tire Motorsport Park (2.459-mile road course)	Bowmanville, ON
September 7	Barrie Speedway (.333-mile)	Barrie, ON
September 21	Kawartha Speedway (.375-mile)	Peterborough, ON

2013 NASCAR TOYOTA SERIES SCHEDULE

Date	Track (Length)	Location
March 1	Phoenix International Raceway (1-mile)	Avondale, AZ
March 24	Autódromo Potosino (.5-mile)	San Luis Potosí, Mexico
April 6	Autódromo Hermanos Rodríguez (1-mile)	Mexico City, Mexico
April 21	Nuevo Autódromo de Querétaro (.75-mile)	Querétaro, Mexico
May 11	El Dorado Speedway (.625-mile)	Chihuahua, Mexico
May 26	Autódromo Internacional de Aguascalientes (.875-mile)	Aguascalientes, Mexico
June 16	Autódromo Miguel E. Abed (1.25-mile)	Puebla, Mexico
June 30	Autódromo Monterrey (1-mile)	Apodaca, Mexico
July 28	Nuevo Autódromo de Querétaro (.75-mile)	Querétaro, Mexico
August 11	Autódromo Hermanos Rodríguez (1-mile)	Mexico City, Mexico
August 25	Autódromo Potosino (.5-mile) *	San Luis Potosí, Mexico
September 8	Autódromo Miguel E. Abed (1.25-mile) *	Puebla, Mexico
September 29	El Dorado Speedway (.625-mile) *	Chihuahua, Mexico
October 13	Autódromo Internacional de Aguascalientes (.875-mile) *	Aguascalientes, Mexico
November 10	Autódromo Hermanos Rodríguez (1-mile) *	Mexico City, Mexico

* Chase Event

All Schedules Subject To Change

2013 NASCAR WHELEN MODIFIED TOUR SCHEDULE

Date	Track (Length)	Location
February 19 *^	Daytona International Speedway (.4-mile)	Daytona Beach, FL
April 14	Thompson International Speedway (.625-mile)	Thompson, CT
April 28	Stafford Motor Speedway (.5-mile)	Stafford, CT
May 11	Monadnock Speedway (.25-mile)	Winchester, NH
May 24	Stafford Motor Speedway (.5-mile)	Stafford, CT
June 22	Waterford Speedbowl (.375-mile)	Waterford, CT
June 29	Riverhead Raceway (.25-mile)	Riverhead, NY
July 13	New Hampshire Motor Speedway (1.058-mile)	Loudon, NH
August 2	Stafford Motor Speedway (.5-mile)	Stafford, CT
August 15	Thompson International Speedway (.625-mile)	Thompson, CT
August 21 *	Bristol Motor Speedway (.533-mile)	Bristol, TN
September 14	Riverhead Raceway (.25-mile)	Riverhead, NY
September 21	New Hampshire Motor Speedway (1.058-mile)	Loudon, NH
September 29	Stafford Motor Speedway (.5-mile)	Stafford, CT
October 20	Thompson International Speedway (.625-mile)	Thompson, CT

* Combination race with NASCAR Whelen Southern Modified Tour
^ Non-points event

2013 NASCAR WHELEN SOUTHERN MODIFIED TOUR SCHEDULE

Date	Track (Length)	Location
February 18 *^	Daytona International Speedway (.4-mile)	Daytona Beach, FL
March 16	Caraway Speedway (.455-mile)	Asheboro, NC
March 23	Southern National Motorsports Park (.4-mile)	Kenly, NC
April 13	South Boston Speedway (.4-mile)	South Boston, VA
April 20	Caraway Speedway (.455-mile)	Asheboro, NC
July 5	Caraway Speedway (.455-mile)	Asheboro, NC
August 3	Bowman Gray Stadium (.25-mile)	Winston-Salem, NC
August 21 *	Bristol Motor Speedway (.533-mile)	Bristol, TN
August 31	Langley Speedway (.395-mile)	Hampton, VA
September 8	Caraway Speedway (.455-mile)	Asheboro, NC
September 21	Southern National Motorsports Park (.4-mile)	Kenly, NC
September 28	Caraway Speedway (.455-mile)	Asheboro, NC
October 10	Charlotte Motor Speedway (.25-mile)	Concord, NC

* Combination race with NASCAR Whelen Modified Tour
^ Non-points event

2013 EURO RACECAR NASCAR TOURING SERIES SCHEDULE

Date	Track (Length)	Location
March 31	Sprint Circuit Paul Armagnac (2.088-mile)	Nogaro, France
April 1	Endurance Circuit Paul Armagnac (2.088-mile)	Nogaro, France
May 11	Circuit de Dijon-Prenois (2.362-mile)	Prenois, France
May 12	Circuit de Dijon-Prenois (2.362-mile)	Prenois, France
June 8	Brands Hatch Circuit (1.198-mile)	Longfield, UK
June 9	Endurance Brands Hatch Circuit (1.198-mile)	Longfield, UK
July 6	Tours Speedway (.375-mile)	Tours, France
July 7	Tours Speedway (.375-mile)	Tours, France
September 1	MotorLand Aragón (non-points) (3.321-mile)	Alcañiz, Spain
September 28	Autodromo Nazionale di Monza (Semifinals) (3.6-mile)	Monza, Italy
September 29	Autodromo Nazionale di Monza (Semifinals) (3.6-mile)	Monza, Italy
October 12	Circuit Le Mans Bugatti (Finals) (2.655-mile)	LeMans, France
October 13	Circuit Le Mans Bugatti (Finals) (2.655-mile)	LeMans, France

2013 GRAND-AM ROLEX SPORTS CAR SERIES SCHEDULE

Date	Track	Location
January 26-27	Rolex 24 At Daytona/Daytona International Speedway (3.56-mile)	Daytona Beach, FL
March 2	Circuit of the Americas (3.40-mile)	Austin, TX
April 6	Barber Motorsports Park (2.3-mile)	Birmingham, AL
April 20	Road Atlanta (2.54-mile)	Braselton, GA
June 1	Raceway at Belle Isle Park (2.1-mile)	Detroit, MI
June 15	Mid-Ohio Sports Car Course (2.258-mile)	Lexington, OH
June 30	Watkins Glen International (3.4-mile)	Watkins Glen NY
July 26	Indianapolis Motor Speedway (2.534-mile)	Indianapolis, IN
August 10	Road America* (4.048-mile)	Elkhart Lake, WI
August 17	Kansas Speedway (2.37-mile)	Kansas City, KS
September 8	Mazda Raceway Laguna Seca (2.238-mile)	Monterey, CA
September 28	Lime Rock Park (1.53-mile)	Lakeville, CT

* Combination weekend with American Le Mans Series

All Schedules Subject to Change

2013 SCHEDULES

NASCAR CAMPING WORLD TRUCK SERIES **2013 SCHEDULE**

Date	Race #	Event - Location	TV
February 22	1	NextEra Energy Resources 250 - Daytona International Speedway	SPEED
April 6	2	Kroger 250 - Martinsville Speedway	SPEED
April 14	3	NASCAR Camping World Truck Series 200 Presented by Cheerwine - Rockingham Speedway	SPEED
April 20	4	SFP 250 - Kansas Speedway	SPEED
May 17	5	North Carolina Education Lottery 200 - Charlotte Motor Speedway	SPEED
May 31	6	Lucas Oil 200 - Dover International Speedway	SPEED
June 7	7	WinStar World Casino 400 - Texas Motor Speedway	SPEED
June 27	8	UNOH 225 - Kentucky Speedway	SPEED
July 13	9	Iowa 200 - Iowa Speedway	SPEED
July 24	10	TBD - Eldora Speedway	
August 3	11	Pocono Mountains 125 - Pocono Raceway	SPEED
August 17	12	VFW 200 - Michigan International Speedway	SPEED
August 21	13	UNOH 200 - Bristol Motor Speedway	SPEED
September 1	14	TBD - Canadian Tire Motorsports Park	SPEED
September 8	15	Iowa 200 - Iowa Speedway	SPEED
September 13	16	NASCAR Camping World Truck Series 225 - Chicagoland Speedway	SPEED
September 28	17	Las Vegas 350 - Las Vegas Motor Speedway	SPEED
October 19	18	Fred's 250 Powered by Coca-Cola - Talladega Superspeedway	SPEED
October 26	19	Kroger 200 - Martinsville Speedway	SPEED
November 1	20	WinStar World Casino 350 - Texas Motor Speedway	SPEED
November 8	21	Phoenix 150 - Phoenix International Raceway	SPEED
November 15	22	Ford 200 - Homestead-Miami Speedway	SPEED

Schedule Subject to Change

2013 SCHEDULES

NASCAR NATIONWIDE SERIES 2013 SCHEDULE

Date	Race #	Event - Location	TV
February 23	1	DRIVE4COPD 300 - Daytona International Speedway	ESPN
March 2	2	Bashas' Supermarkets - Phoenix International Raceway	ESPN 2
March 9	3	Sam's Town 300 - Las Vegas Motor Speedway	ESPN 2
March 16	4	St. Patrick's Day 300 - Bristol Motor Speedway	ESPN
March 23	5	Royal Purple 300 - Auto Club Speedway	ESPN
April 12	6	O'Reilly Auto Parts 300 - Texas Motor Speedway	ESPN 2
April 26	7	ToyotaCare 250 - Richmond International Raceway	ESPN 2
May 4	8	Aaron's 312 - Talladega Superspeedway	ABC
May 10	9	Darlington 200 - Darlington Raceway	ESPN 2
May 25	10	History 300 - Charlotte Motor Speedway	ABC
June 1	11	5-Hour Energy 200 - Dover International Speedway	ESPN
June 8	12	Iowa 250 - Iowa Speedway	ESPN
June 15	13	Alliance Truck Parts 250 - Michigan International Speedway	ABC
June 22	14	Road America 200 - Road America	ESPN
June 28	15	Feed the Children 300 - Kentucky Speedway	ESPN 2
July 5	16	Subway Jalapeño 250 Powered by Coca-Cola - Daytona International Speedway	ESPN
July 13	17	New England 200 - New Hampshire Motor Speedway	ESPN
July 21	18	STP 300 - Chicagoland Speedway	ESPN
July 27	19	Indiana 250 - Indianapolis Motor Speedway	ESPN
August 3	20	Iowa 250 - Iowa Speedway	ESPN 2
August 10	21	NASCAR Nationwide Series at The Glen - Watkins Glen International	ABC
August 17	22	TBD - Mid-Ohio Sports Car Course	ESPN 2
August 23	23	Food City 250 - Bristol Motor Speedway	ESPN
August 31	24	Atlanta 300 - Atlanta Motor Speedway	ESPN 2
September 6	25	Virginia 529 College Savings 250 - Richmond International Raceway	ESPN 2
September 14	26	Dollar General 300 Powered by Coca-Cola - Chicagoland Speedway	ESPN 2
September 21	27	Kentucky 300 - Kentucky Speedway	ESPN
September 28	28	Dover 200 - Dover International Speedway	ESPN 2
October 5	29	Kansas Lottery 300 - Kansas Speedway	ESPN
October 11	30	Dollar General 300 - Charlotte Motor Speedway	ESPN 2
November 2	31	O'Reilly Auto Parts Challenge - Texas Motor Speedway	ESPN
November 9	32	Great Clips 200 - Phoenix International Raceway	ESPN
November 16	33	Ford 300 - Homestead-Miami Speedway	ESPN 2

Schedule Subject to Change

NASCAR SPRINT CUP SERIES 2013 SCHEDULE

Date	Race #	Event - Location	TV	Radio
February 16	*	Sprint Unlimited - Daytona International Speedway	FOX	MRN, SiriusXM
February 17	*	Daytona 500 Qualifying - Daytona International Speedway	FOX	MRN, SiriusXM
February 21	*	Duels - Daytona International Speedway	SPEED	MRN, SiriusXM
February 24	1	Daytona 500 - Daytona International Speedway	FOX	MRN, SiriusXM
March 3	2	Subway Fresh Fit 500 - Phoenix International Raceway	FOX	MRN, SiriusXM
March 10	3	Kobalt Tools 400 - Las Vegas Motor Speedway	FOX	PRN, SiriusXM
March 17	4	Food City 500 - Bristol Motor Speedway	FOX	PRN, SiriusXM
March 24	5	Auto Club 400 - Auto Club Speedway	FOX	MRN, SiriusXM
April 7	6	Virginia 500 - Martinsville Speedway	FOX	MRN, SiriusXM
April 13	7	Texas 500 - Texas Motor Speedway	FOX	PRN, SiriusXM
April 21	8	STP 400 - Kansas Speedway	FOX	MRN, SiriusXM
April 27	9	Toyota Owners 400 - Richmond International Raceway	FOX	MRN, SiriusXM
May 5	10	Aaron's 499 - Talladega Superspeedway	FOX	MRN, SiriusXM
May 11	11	Bojangles' Southern 500 - Darlington Raceway	FOX	MRN, SiriusXM
May 18	*	NASCAR Sprint All-Star Race - Charlotte Motor Speedway	SPEED	MRN, SiriusXM
May 26	12	Coca-Cola 600 - Charlotte Motor Speedway	FOX	PRN, SiriusXM
June 2	13	Dover 400 - Dover International Speedway	FOX	MRN, SiriusXM
June 9	14	Pocono 400 - Pocono Raceway	TNT	MRN, SiriusXM
June 16	15	Michigan 400 - Michigan International Speedway	TNT	MRN, SiriusXM
June 23	16	Toyota/Save Mart 350 - Sonoma Raceway	TNT	PRN, SiriusXM
June 29	17	Quaker State 400 - Kentucky Speedway	TNT	PRN, SiriusXM
July 6	18	Coke Zero 400 Powered by Coca-Cola - Daytona International Speedway	TNT	MRN, SiriusXM
July 14	19	New Hampshire 300 - New Hampshire Motor Speedway	TNT	PRN, SiriusXM
July 28	20	Crown Royal Presents the "Your Hero's Name Here" 400 at the Brickyard - Indianapolis Motor Speedway	ESPN	IMS, SiriusXM
August 4	21	Pennsylvania 400 - Pocono Raceway	ESPN	MRN, SiriusXM
August 11	22	NASCAR Sprint Cup Series at The Glen - Watkins Glen International	ESPN	MRN, SiriusXM
August 18	23	Pure Michigan 400 - Michigan International Speedway	ESPN	MRN, SiriusXM
August 24	24	IRWIN Tools Night Race - Bristol Motor Speedway	ABC	PRN, SiriusXM
September 1	25	AdvoCare 500 - Atlanta Motor Speedway	ESPN	PRN, SiriusXM
September 7	26	Federated Auto Parts 400 - Richmond International Raceway	ABC	MRN, SiriusXM
September 15	27	GEICO 400 - Chicagoland Speedway	ESPN	MRN, SiriusXM
September 22	28	SYLVANIA 300 - New Hampshire Motor Speedway	ESPN	PRN, SiriusXM
September 29	29	AAA 400 - Dover International Speedway	ESPN	MRN, SiriusXM
October 6	30	Hollywood Casino 400 - Kansas Speedway	ESPN	MRN, SiriusXM
October 12	31	Bank of America 500 - Charlotte Motor Speedway	ABC	PRN, SiriusXM
October 20	32	Camping World 500 - Talladega Superspeedway	ESPN	MRN, SiriusXM
October 27	33	Goody's Relief 500 - Martinsville Speedway	ESPN	MRN, SiriusXM
November 3	34	AAA Texas 500 - Texas Motor Speedway	ESPN	PRN, SiriusXM
November 10	35	Kobalt Tools 500 - Phoenix International Raceway	ESPN	MRN, SiriusXM
November 17	36	Ford 400 - Homestead-Miami Speedway	ESPN	MRN, SiriusXM

Schedule Subject to Change

2013 SCHEDULES